Mel Bay Presents

# Systematic Studies for Flamenco Guitar

## Estúdios sistemáticos para la guitarra flamenca

## by Juan Serrano



### DISC 1

| Track #'s | |
|---|---|
| 1-10 | **Sevillanas:** 10 studies, page 8 [8:16] |
| 11-24 | **Alegrías por arriba:** Variations and 10 studies, page 40 [5:14] |
| 25-38 | **Alegrías por medio:** Variations and 10 studies, page 72 [5:32] |
| 39-52 | **Bulerías:** Variations and 10 studies, page 108 [6:10] |
| 53-65 | **Colombianas:** Variations and 10 studies, page 152 [5:52] |
| 66-79 | **Fandangos:** Variations and 10 studies, page 188 [5:29] |
| 80-92 | **Farrucas:** Variations and 10 studies, page 224 [6:24] |

### DISC 2

| Track #'s | |
|---|---|
| 1-10 | **Granainas:** 10 studies, page 258 [7:04] |
| 11-24 | **Romeras:** Variations and 10 studies, page 298 [5:08] |
| 25-37 | **Siguiriyas:** Variations and 10 studies, page 328 [5:17] |
| 38-51 | **Soleares:** Variations and 10 studies, page 352 [4:25] |
| 52-64 | **Tangos:** Variations and 10 studies, page 380 [4:53] |
| 65-74 | **Tarantas:** 10 studies, page 412 [6:42] |

## A Falseta Anthology

## Antología de falsetas

*Sevillanas*
*Alegrías por arriba*
*Alegrías por medio*
*Bulerías*
*Colombianas*
*Fandangos*
*Farrucas*
*Granainas*
*Romeras*
*Siguiriyas*
*Soleares*
*Tangos*
*Tarantas*

**This book is available either by itself or packaged with a companion audio and/or video recording. If you have purchased the book only, you may wish to purchase the recordings separately. The publisher strongly recommends using a recording along with the text to assure accuracy of interpretation and make learning easier and more enjoyable.**

1 2 3 4 5 6 7 8 9 0





***Visit us on the Web at www.melbay.com — E-mail us at email@melbay.com***

**In memory of**

# MEL BAY

**1913-1997**

**The man that worked**
**all his life to raise**
**guitar music to the level**
**we know today.**
**With love and deep respect**

**Juan Serrano**

---

**A la memoria de**

# MEL BAY

**1913-1997**

**El hombre que trabajó**
**toda su vida para elevar**
**la música de la guitarra**
**al nivel que se conoce**
**en nuestros días.**
**Con cariño y profundo respeto**

**Juan Serrano**

# CONTENTS - ÍNDICE

# INTRODUCTION

All of the flamenco forms are based on one traditional rhythmical phrase of 8 or 12 beats (musically 3/4, 4/4, or 3/4 and 6/8). The rhythmical flamenco phrase is called *compás*. The melodic themes that are played between each compás are called *falsetas*. A falseta can be composed of several flamenco compases. The flamenco selections are composed of its traditional compás with some rhythmical variations and several falsetas. Between falseta and falseta the compás or one of its variations is played. The falsetas melodically are all different and are composed of different techniques, tremolos, picados arpeggios, rasgueados and different chords.

Almost all of the flamenco aficionados know which is the compás of each form and how to play it. Many prefer not to play compositions of other guitarists, but they prefer to learn many new falsetas in order to make their own arrangements.

This book is composed of 10 Sevillanas and 10 falsetas of each one of the most popular and traditional of the flamenco forms:

*Sevillanas, Alegrías por Arriba, Alegrías por Medio, Bulerías, Colombianas, Fandangos, Farrucas, Granainas, Romeras, Siguiriyas, Soleares, Tangos and Tarantas*

All of the falsetas can be used as technical studies. Each falseta is equivalent to one study. It is recommended that each of the falsetas be practiced very slowly, following the fingering marked in each, so that the fingers memorize the order that they must follow. Thus, the synchronization of the two hands can be perfected and the falsetas can be played with more ease.

There are many flamenco guitarists that play the notes very clearly with a good sound. These guitarists are called "clean guitarists" (clear) within the flamenco world. There are others that are good musicians and have a very good sense of rhythm, but do not have a good technique. The notes sound sloppy. These guitarists are called "dirty guitarists" (sloppy) in the flamenco world.

It doesn't matter what type of music is played, jazz, classical or flamenco. All of the notes should sound clear with each one having its musical value.

<u>*Note*</u>

Falsetas are the melodic phrases that are played between compás and compás. Compás is the rhythmical phrase that is played between falseta and falseta.

## SYMBOLS

- The numbers 1 - 2 - 3 - 4, signify the fingers of the left hand.
- The letters P - I - M - A - S signify the fingers of the right hand.
- The Roman numerals designate the position, I - II - III etc.
- A letter C preceding a Roman numeral signifies Barre: CI - CII - CIII etc.
- The numbers in circles designate the strings. For example, a three in a circle ③ means the note played on the third string, a four ④ fourth string etc.

## TRANSLATIONS FOR MUSIC AND TABLATURE

Freestroke ———— Tirando
Reststroke ———— Apoyando
Scale ———— Picado

# INTRODUCCIÓN

Todas las formas flamencas están basadas en una frase rítmica tradicional de ocho o doce tiempo (musicalmente 3/4, 4/4 o 3/4 y 6/8). La frase rítmica flamenca se llama *compás*. Los temas melódicos que se tocan entre compás y compás se llaman *falsetas*. Una falseta se puede componer de varios compases flamencos. Las selecciones flamencas se componen de su compás tradicional, con algunas variaciones rítmicas, y varias falsetas. Entre falseta y falseta se ejecuta el compás o una de sus variaciones. Las falsetas melódicamente son todas diferentes y se componen de diferentes técnicas, trémolos, picados, arpegios, rasgueados y diferentes acordes.

Casi todos los aficionados de flamenco saben cual es el compás de cada forma y como tocarlo. Muchos prefieren el no tocar composiciones de otros guitarristas, pero si les gusta aprender muchas falsetas nuevas para así poder hacer sus propios arreglos.

Este libro esta compuesto de 10 Sevillanas, y 10 falsetas, de cada una de las formas mas populares y tradicionales de la música flamenca.

*Sevillanas, Alegrías Por Arriba, Alegrías Por Medio, Bulerías, Colombianas, Fandangos, Farrucas, Granainas, Romeras, Siguiriyas, Soleares. Tangos Y Tarantas.*

Todas las falsetas se pueden usar como estudios técnicos. Cada falseta es equivalente a un estudio.

Recomiendo que se practique muy despacio y que aprendan de memoria la digitación marcada en cada una de las falsetas. Así, la sincronización de las dos manos se hará más fácil y se podrán ejecutar todas las falsetas con más perfección.

Hay muchos guitarristas flamencos que tocan todas las notas muy claras y todo suena bonito y agradable. A estos guitarristas se les llaman en el mundo flamenco, guitarristas limpios. Hay otros que son muy buenos músicos y que tienen muy buen compás, pero no tienen buena técnica y las notas no suenan claras. A estos guitarristas en el mundo flamenco se les llaman guitarristas sucios.

No importa que clase de música se ejecute en la guitarra, jazz, clásico o flamenco. Todas las notas deben de sonar claras, y darle a cada una de ellas el valor de su anotación musical.

<u>Nota</u>

Falsetas son las frases melódicas que se intercalan entre compás y compás.
Compás es la frase rítmica que se intercala entre falseta y falseta.

## SÍMBOLOS

- Los números 1 - 2 - 3 - 4 designan los dedos de la mano izquierda.
- Las letras P - I - M - A - S designan los dedos de la mano derecha.
- Los números Romanos designan la posición, I - II - III, etc.
- Los números Romanos con la letra C por delante significa Cejilla, CI - CII - CIII, etc.
- Los números dentro de un círculo designan las cuerdas. Por ejemplo, un tres dentro de un círculo ③ quiere decir que esa nota se toca en la tercera cuerda, un cuatro ④ cuarta cuerda etc.

## TRADUCCIÓN PARA LA MÚSICA Y LA TABLATURA

Tirando ———— Freestroke
Apoyando ———— Reststroke
Picado ———— Scale

سڤيلانس

# SEVILLANAS

Sevillanas are one of the most popular forms of the flamenco music. One complete Sevillana set is composed of four *coplas*; that is, four different Sevillanas—called 1st, 2nd, 3rd, and 4th. The reason is that the Sevillanas are danceable and each of them is adapted to the choreography of the dance. The complete dance is divided into four parts. The choreography of the dance is based on the rhythm, not the melody, therefore the order of the 4 Sevillanas that are in the composition can be interchanged.

This section is composed of 10 different Sevillanas in tone and melody. The order is in a progressive form in technical difficulty (advancement).

It is recommended learning all of the 10 Sevillanas; then playing the four that are liked best and interchanging them in any order. It is also recommended that the second not be attempted until the first is mastered and so on.

Although the compás and the musical form of all of the Sevillanas are the same, the techniques and melodies are completely different in each one of them; therefore when the 10 Sevillanas are learned, it will be much easier to master the rest of the falsetas that make up this book.

The Sevillanas are measured in 3/4. A flamenco compás has 6 beats equivalent to 2 measures of 3/4.

# SEVILLANAS

Las Sevillanas son unas de las formas más populares entre la música flamenca. Una composición completa de Sevillanas consiste en cuatro coplas, o sea, cuatro Sevillanas diferentes que se les llama primera, segunda, tercera y cuarta. La razón es porque las Sevillanas son bailables y cada una de ellas está adaptada a la coreografía del baile. La danza completa está dividida en cuatro partes. Las coreografías del baile están basadas en el ritmo y no en la melodía. Por lo tanto, el orden de las cuatro Sevillanas que se estén usando en la composición puede ser cambiado a la conveniencia del guitarrista que las interprete.

Esta sección de Sevillanas se compone de diez Sevillanas diferentes en tonos y melodías. El orden está en una forma progresiva en dificultad técnica.

Recomiendo que los estudiantes aprendan las diez Sevillanas y así podrán tocar las cuatro que más les gusten y podrán cambiar el orden a su conveniencia y gusto. También recomiendo que hasta que no hayan aprendido bien la primera, no empiecen con la segunda y lo mismo con todas las siguientes.

Aunque el compás y la forma musical de todas las Sevillanas es igual, las técnicas y las melodías son completamente diferentes en cada una de ellas. Por lo tanto, cuando hayan aprendido estas diez Sevillanas les será mucho más fácil el aprendizaje de todas las demás formas que componen este libro.

Todas las Sevillanas se miden en tiempo de 3/4. El compás flamenco se compone de seis tiempos equivalente a dos compases musicales de 3/4.

# *Sevillana I*

Juan Serrano

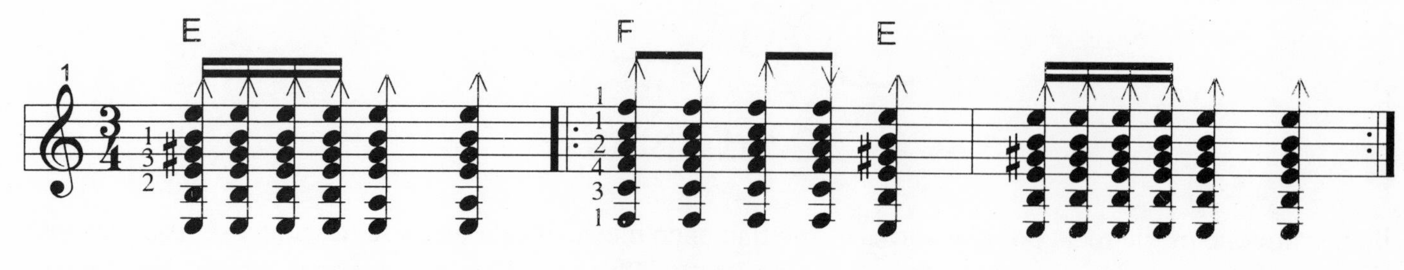


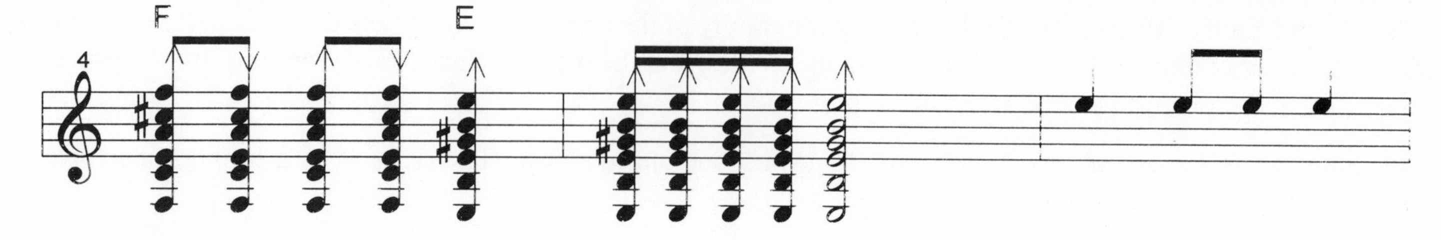

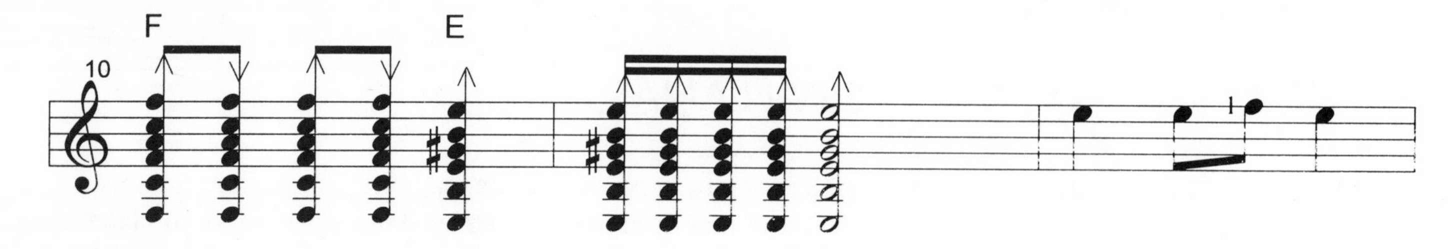

# *Sevillana I*

Juan Serrano

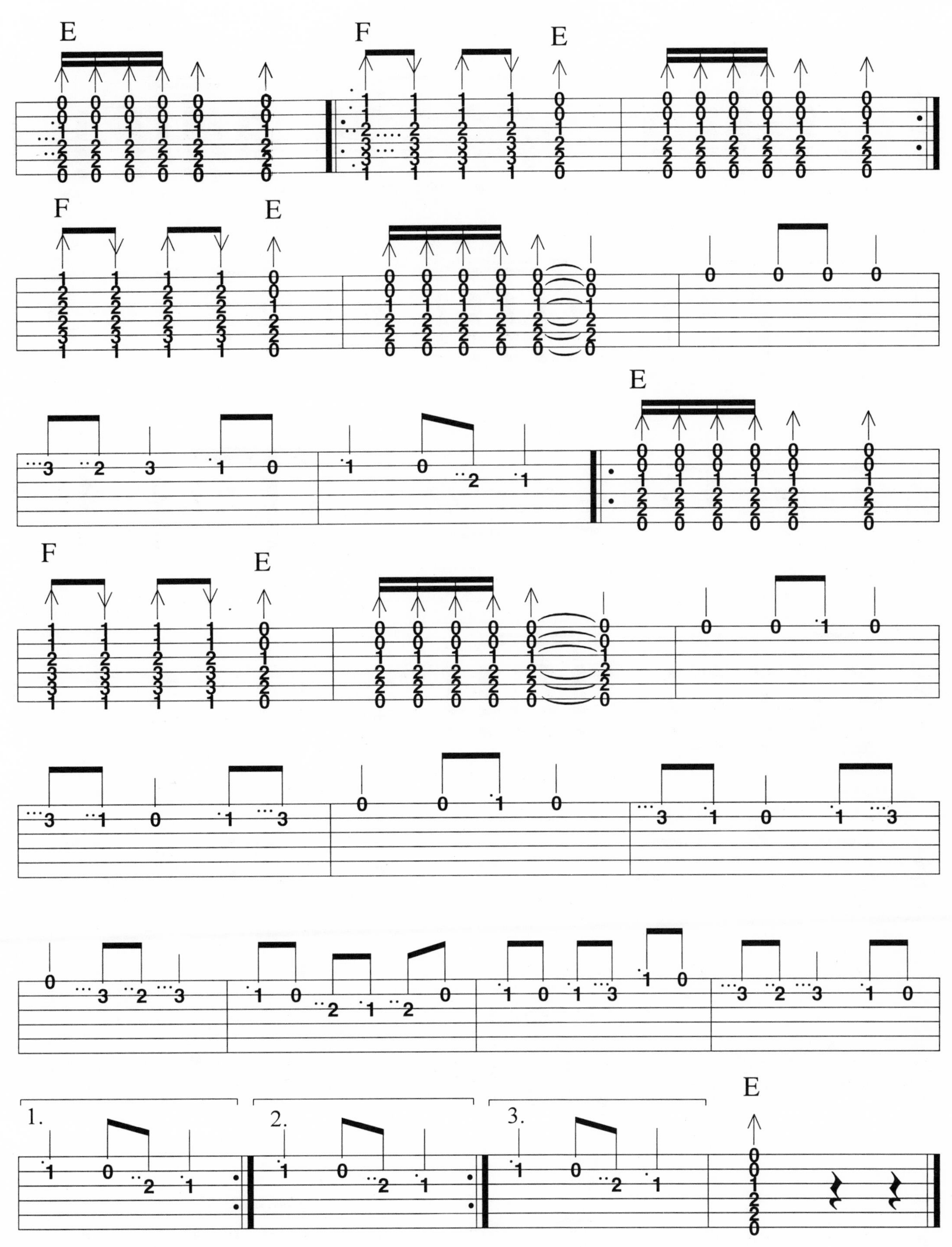

# *Sevillana II*

Juan Serrano

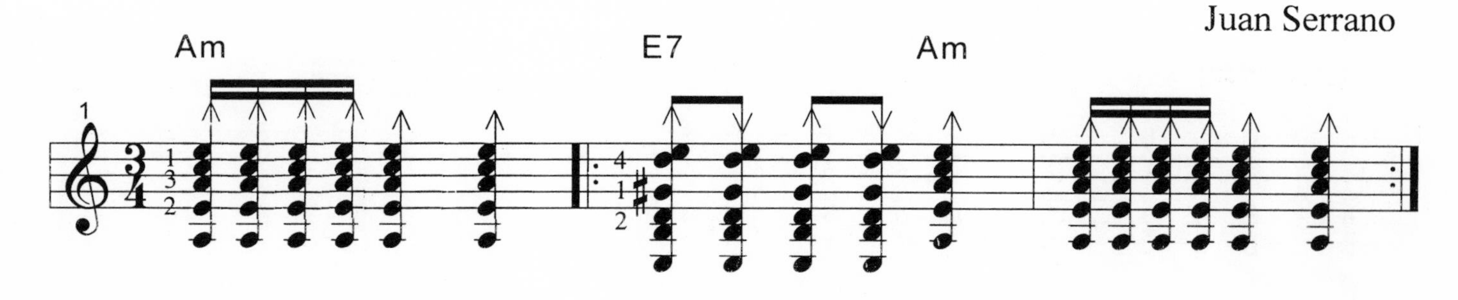


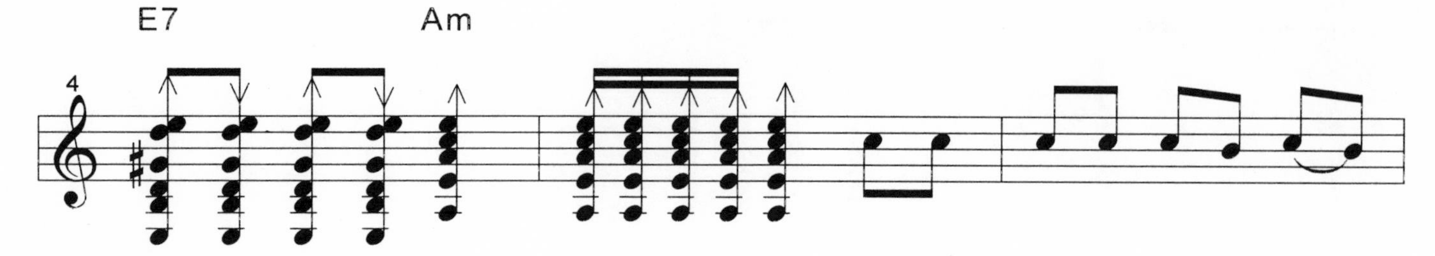

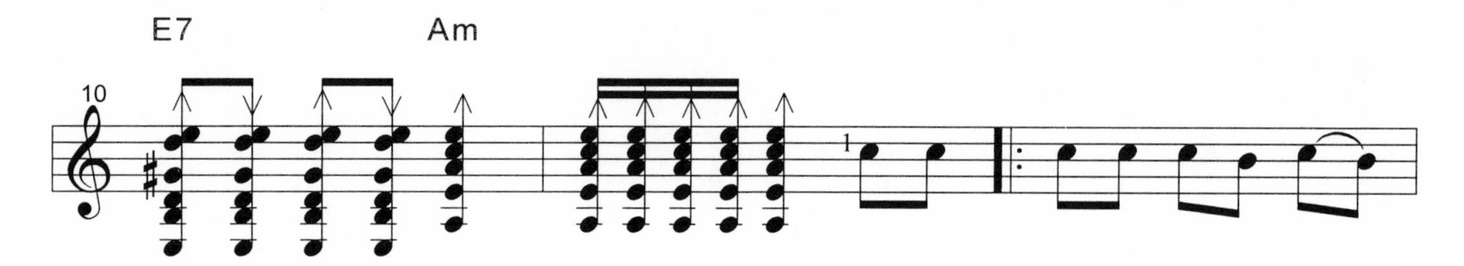

G

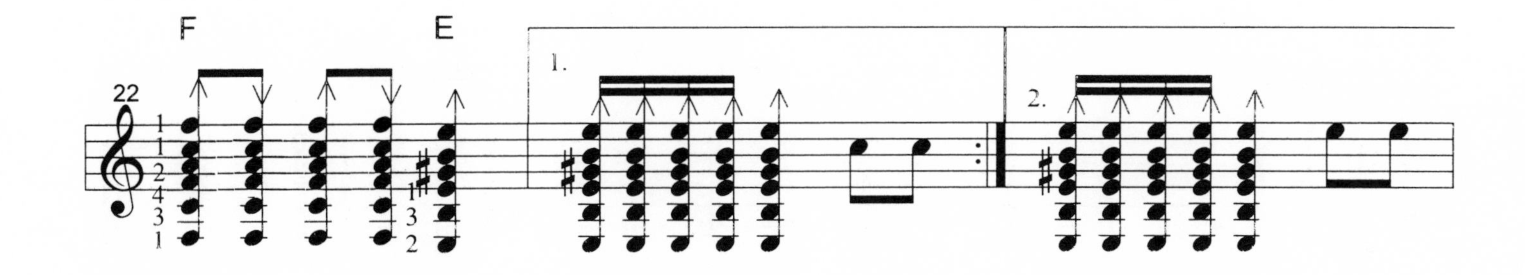
F
E
22
1.
2.

25

Dm
28

Am
31

# *Sevillana II*

Juan Serrano

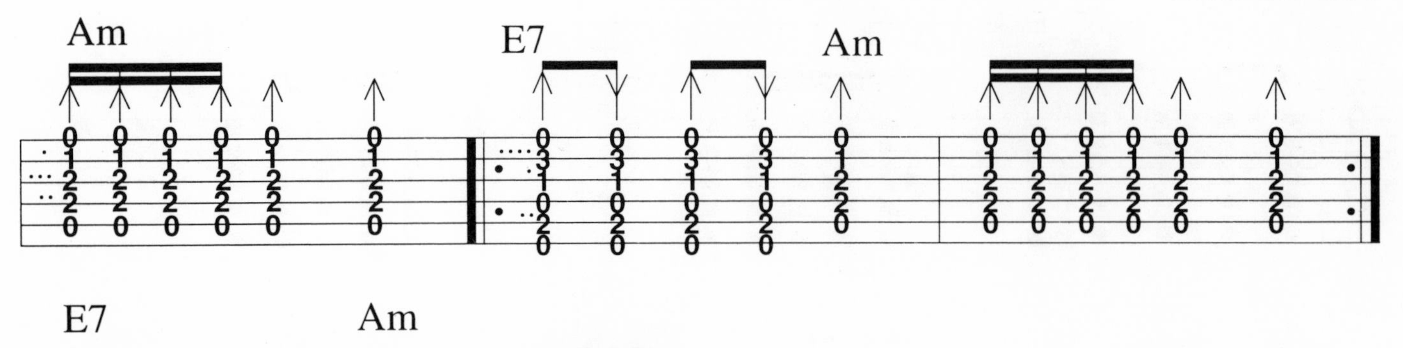


E7 Am

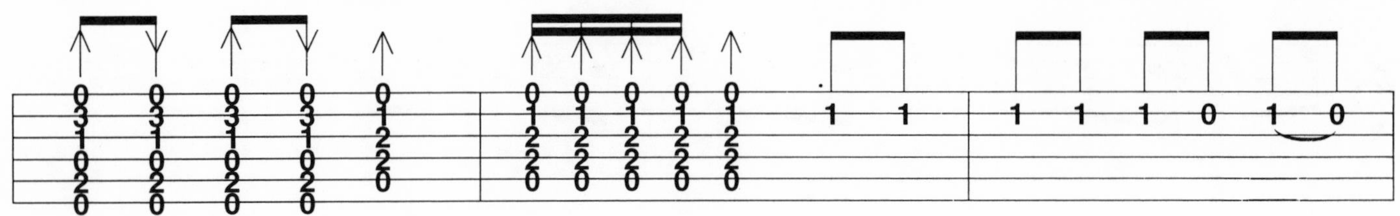

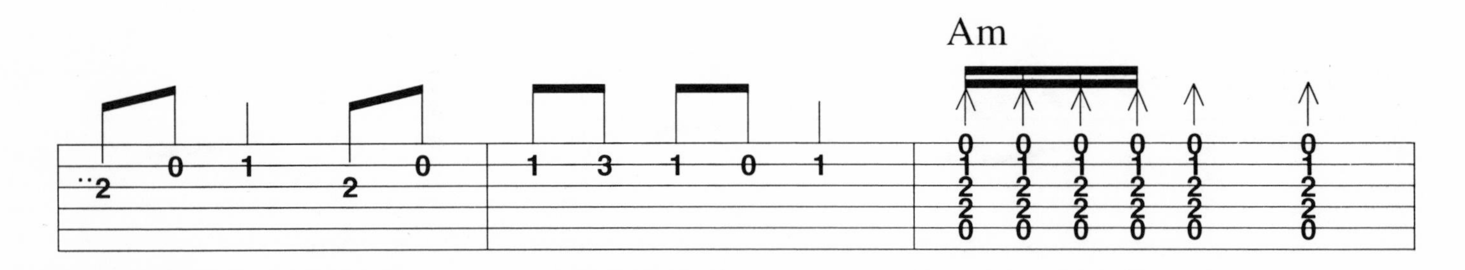


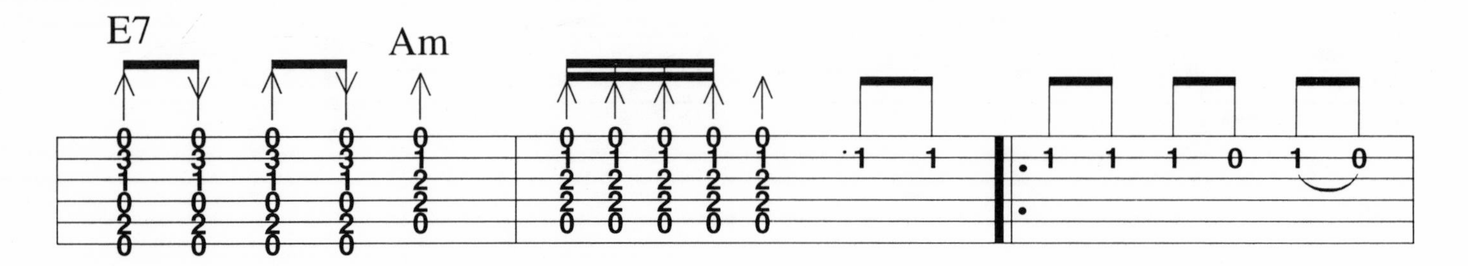


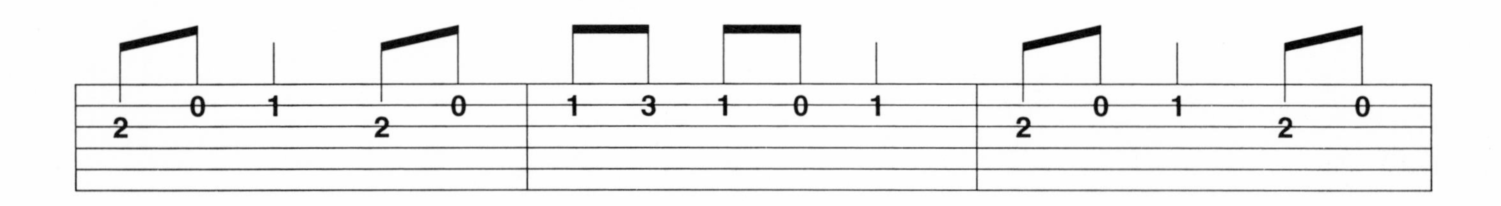

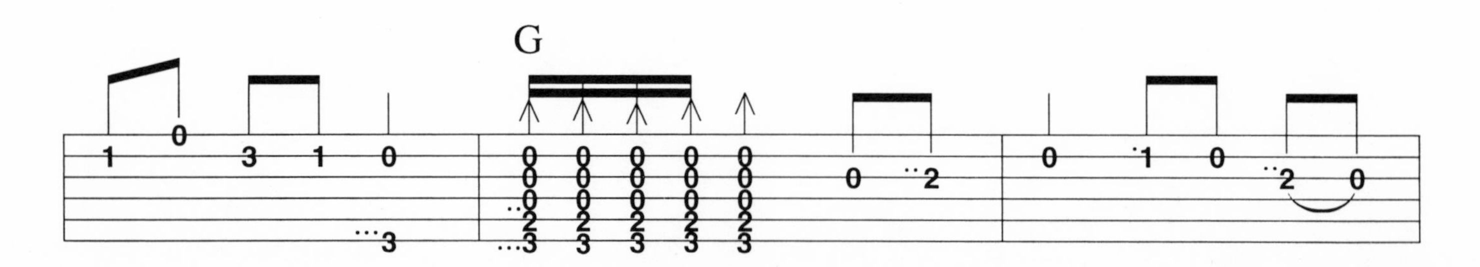

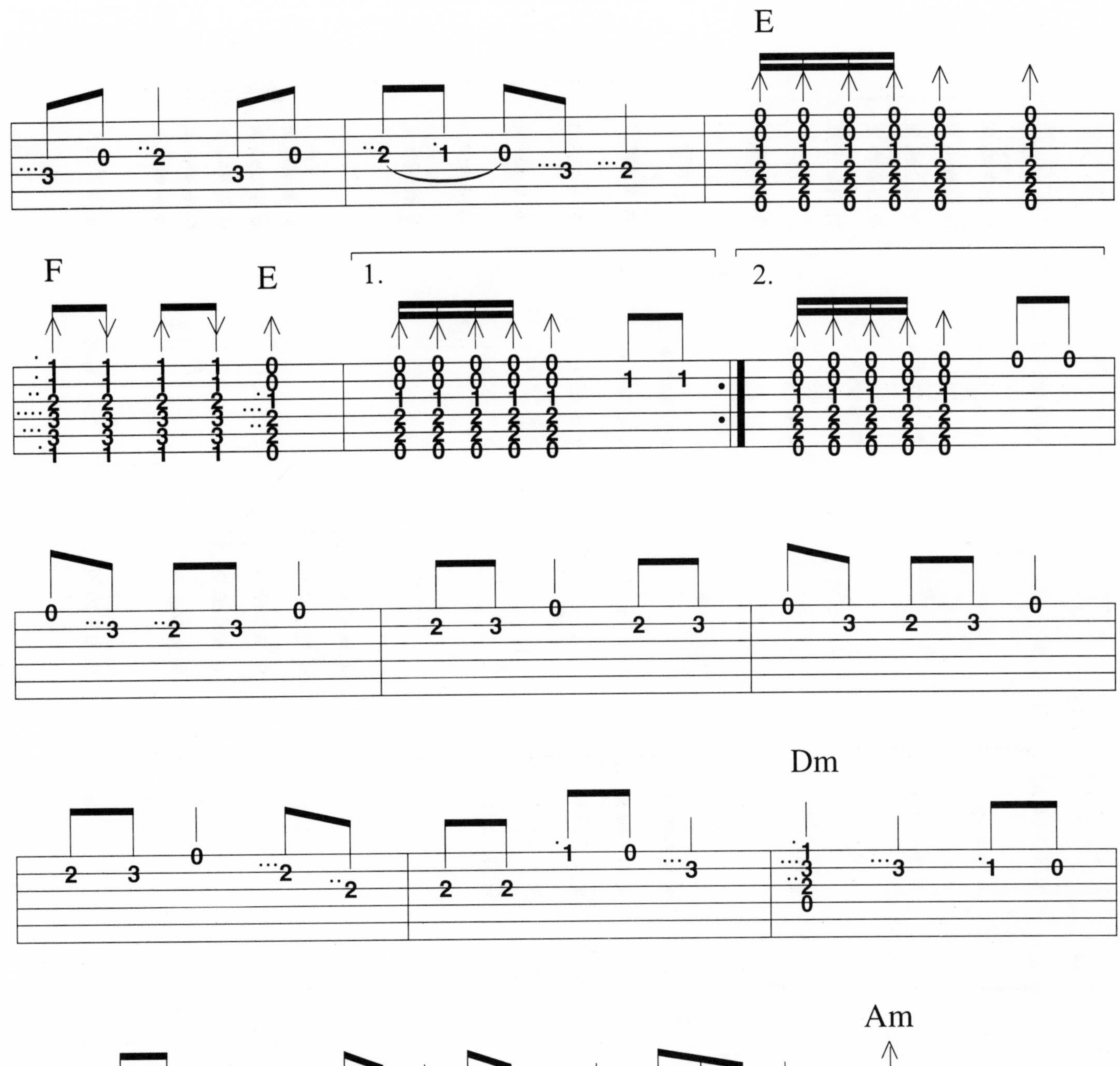
E
F
E
1.
2.
Dm

Am

# *Sevillana III*

Juan Serrano

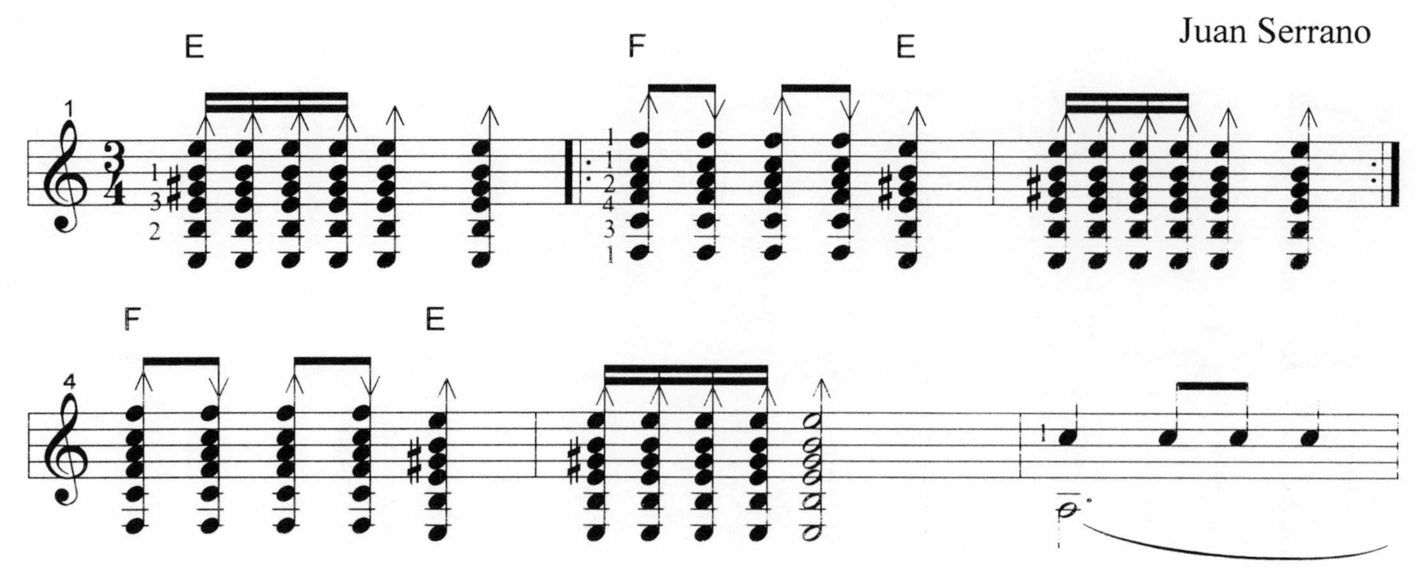

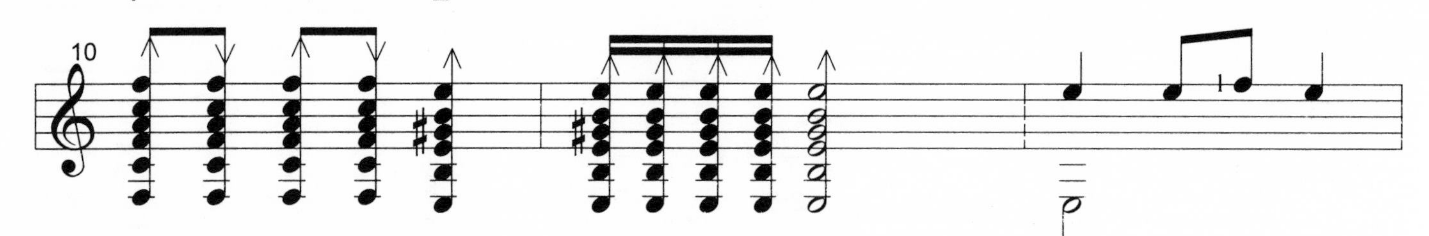


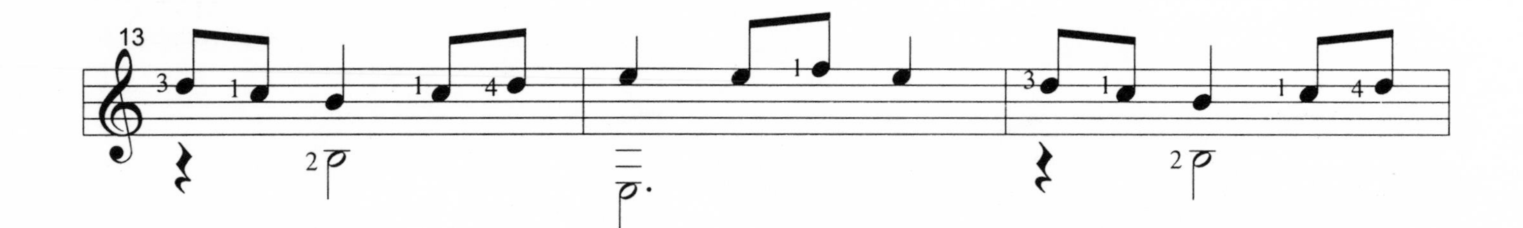

# *Sevillana III*

Juan Serrano

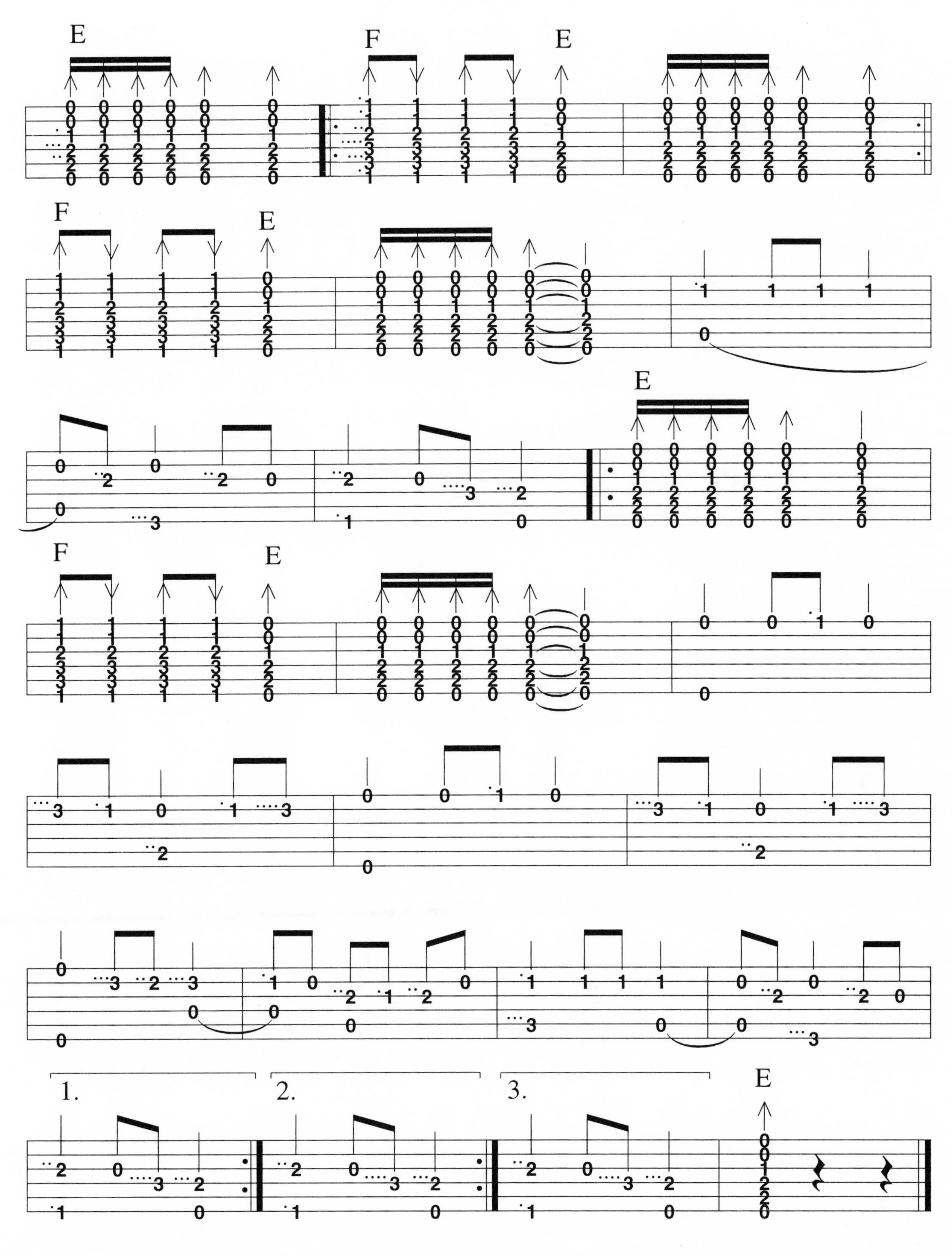

# Sevillana IV

Juan Serrano

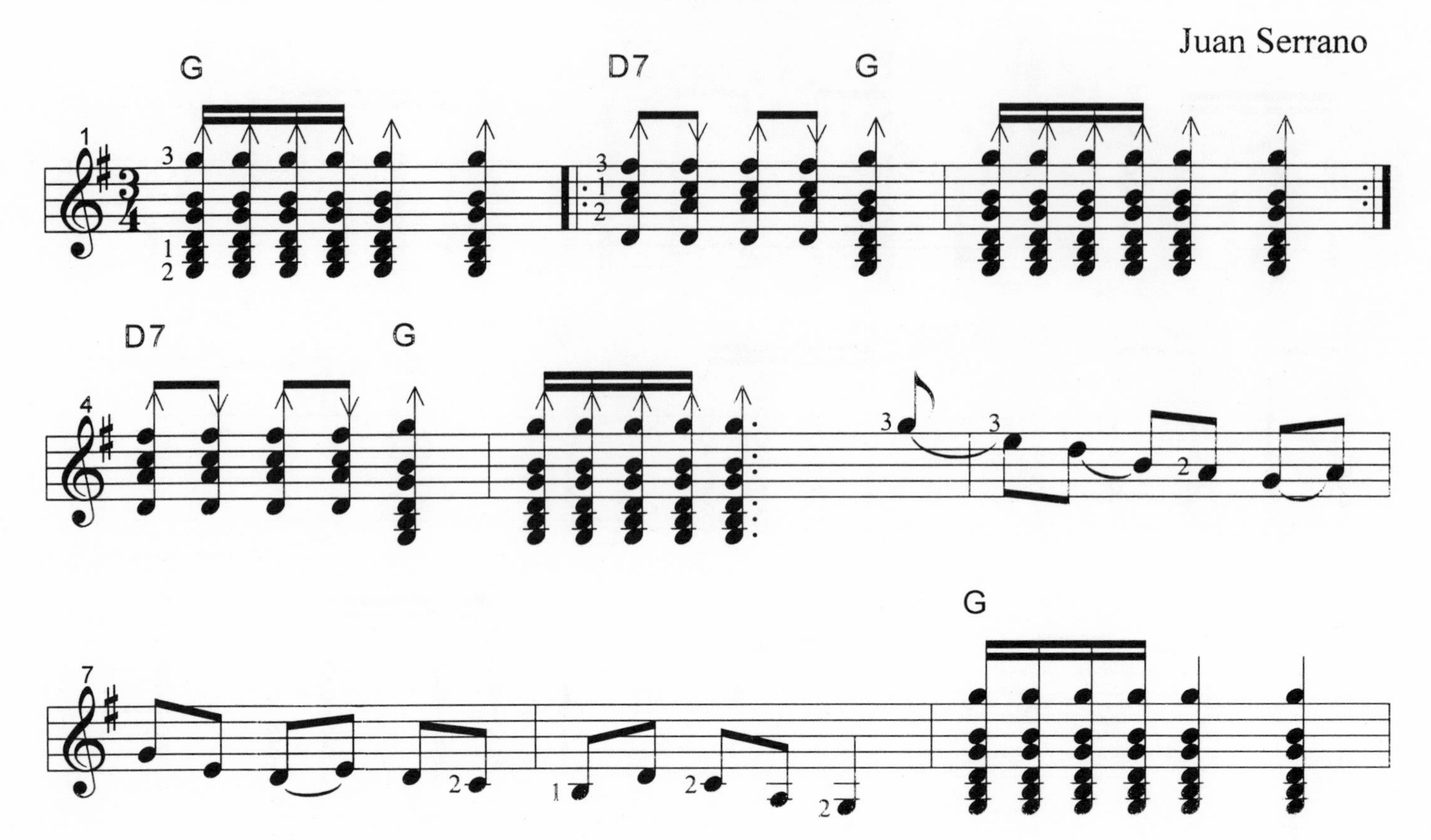


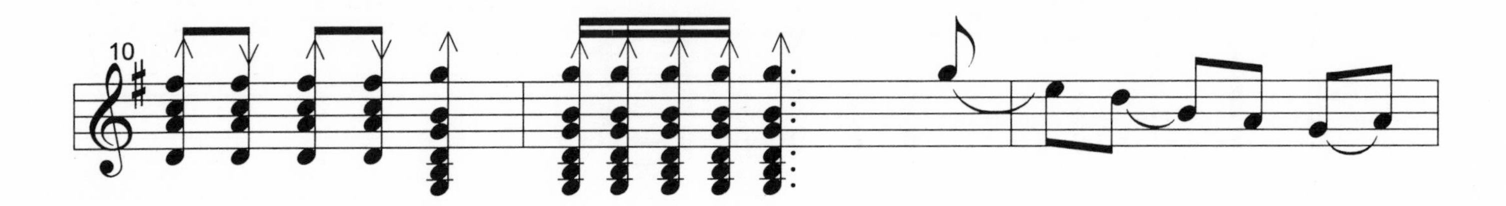


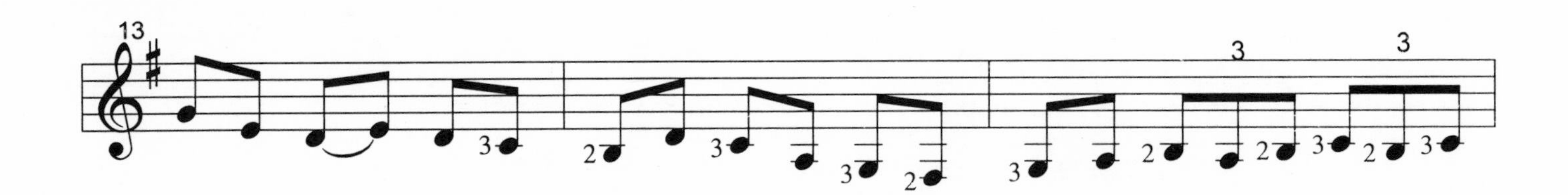

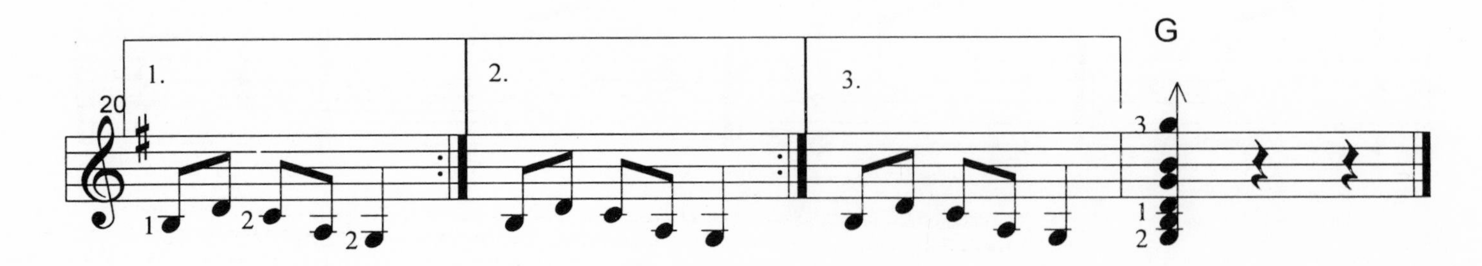

Juan Serrano

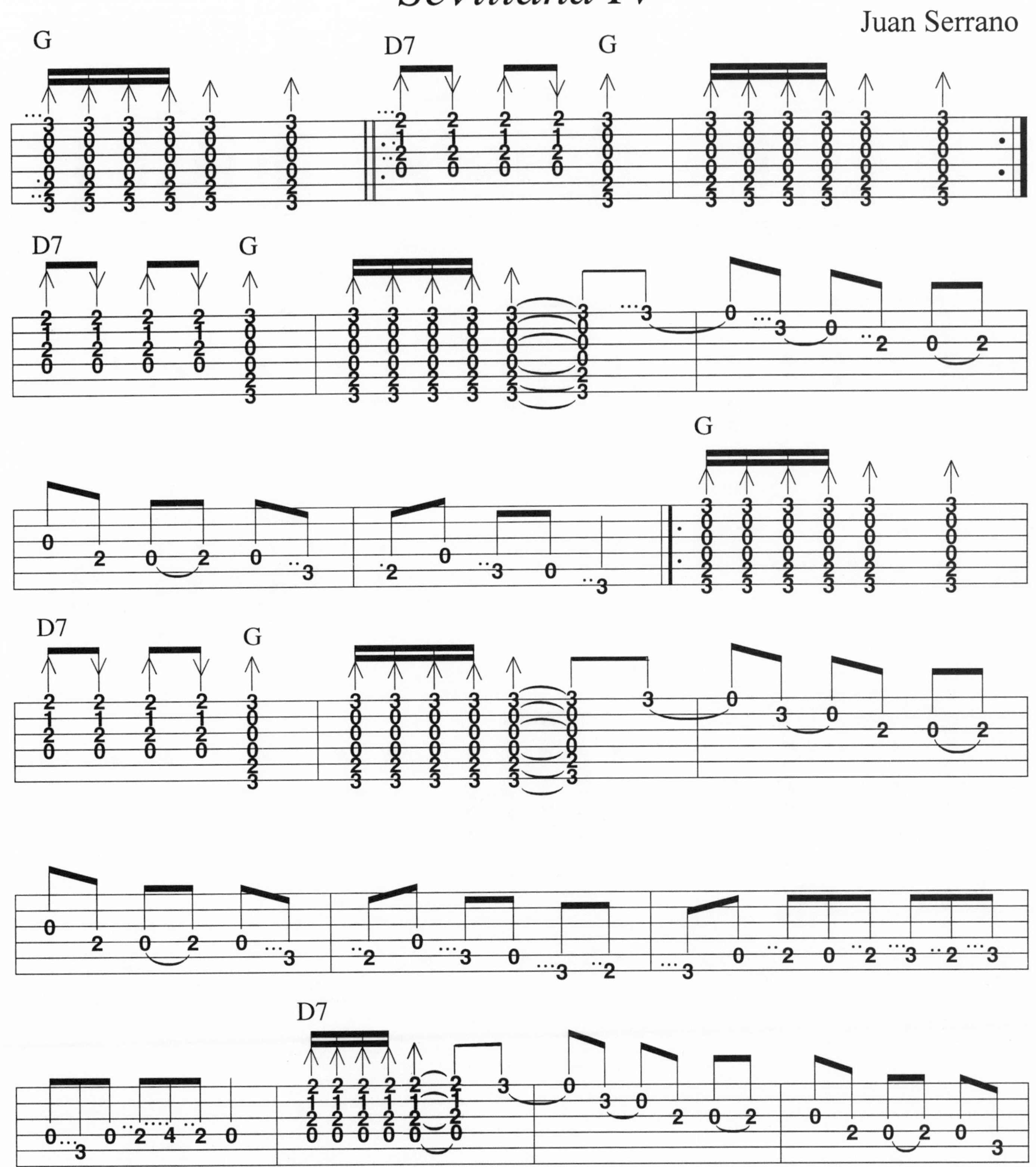


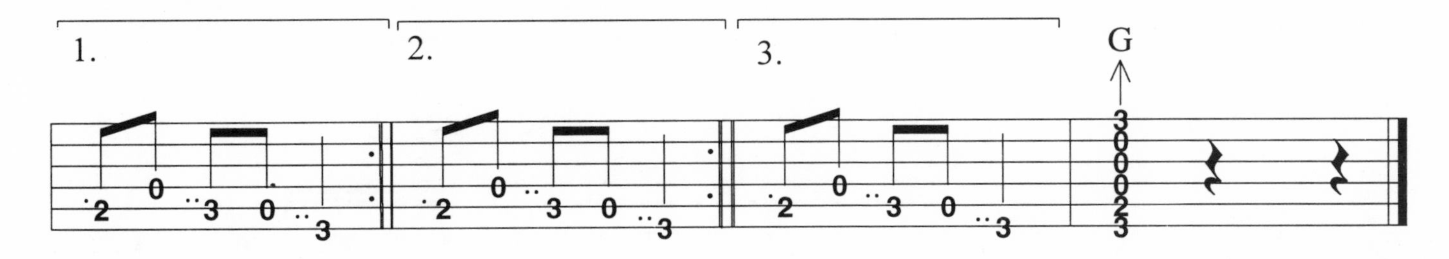

# *Sevillana V*

Juan Serrano

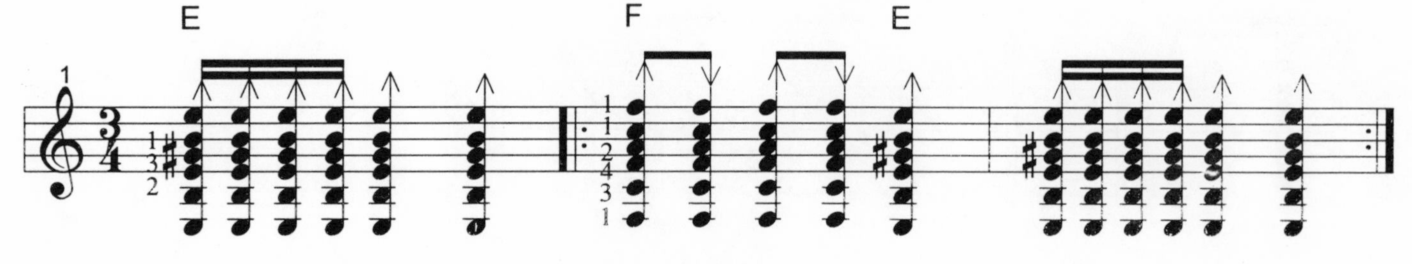


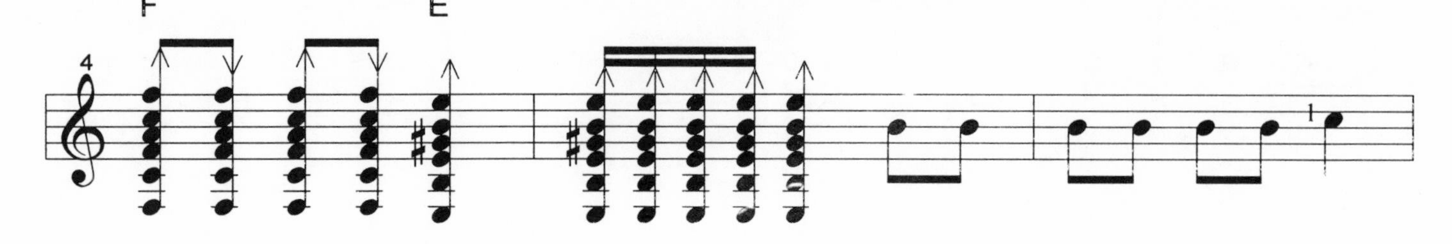


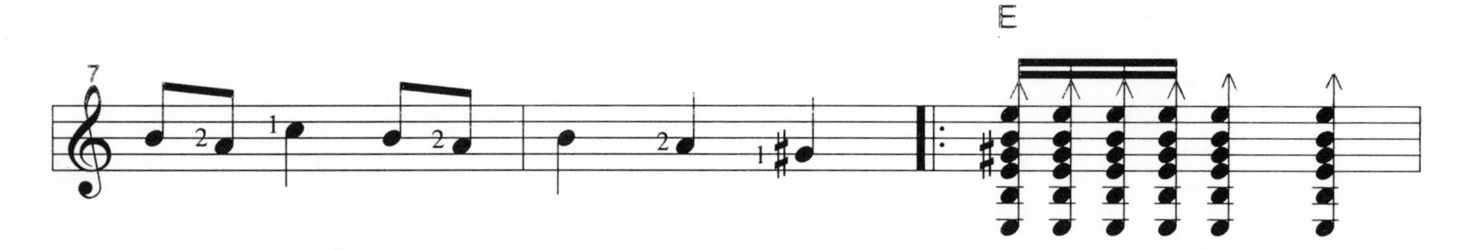


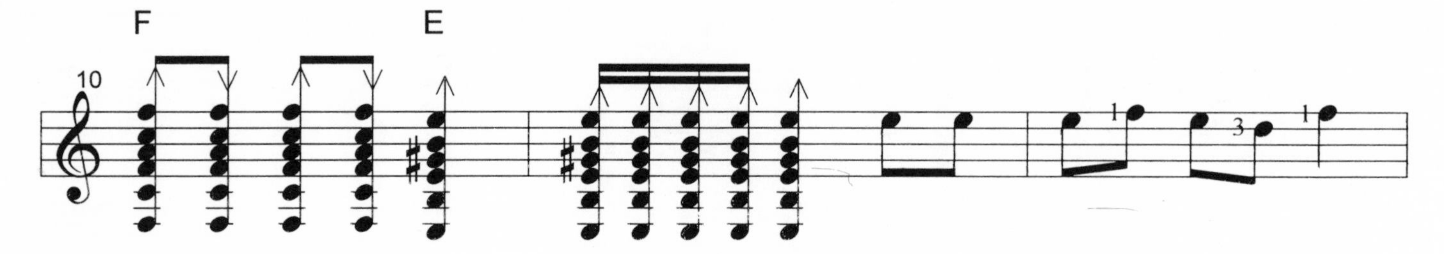

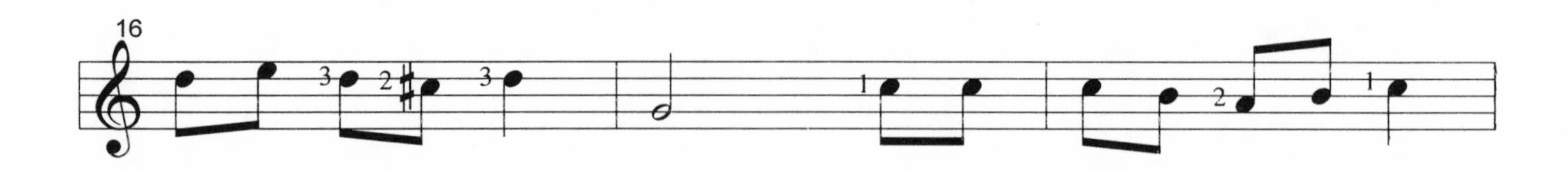

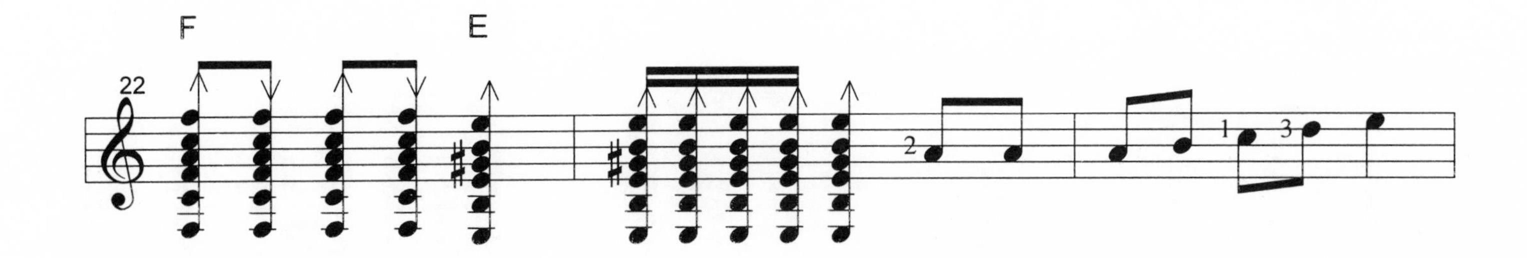


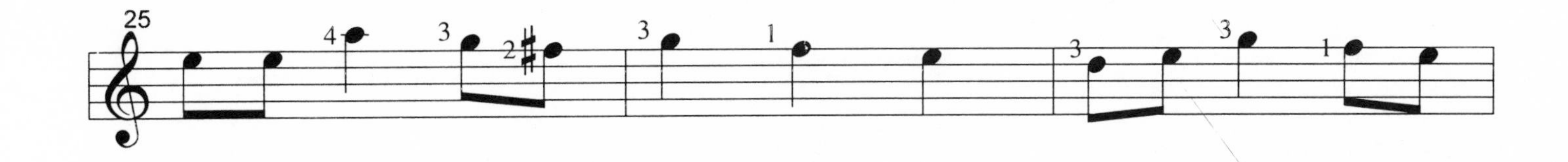

Am

# Sevillana V

Juan Serrano

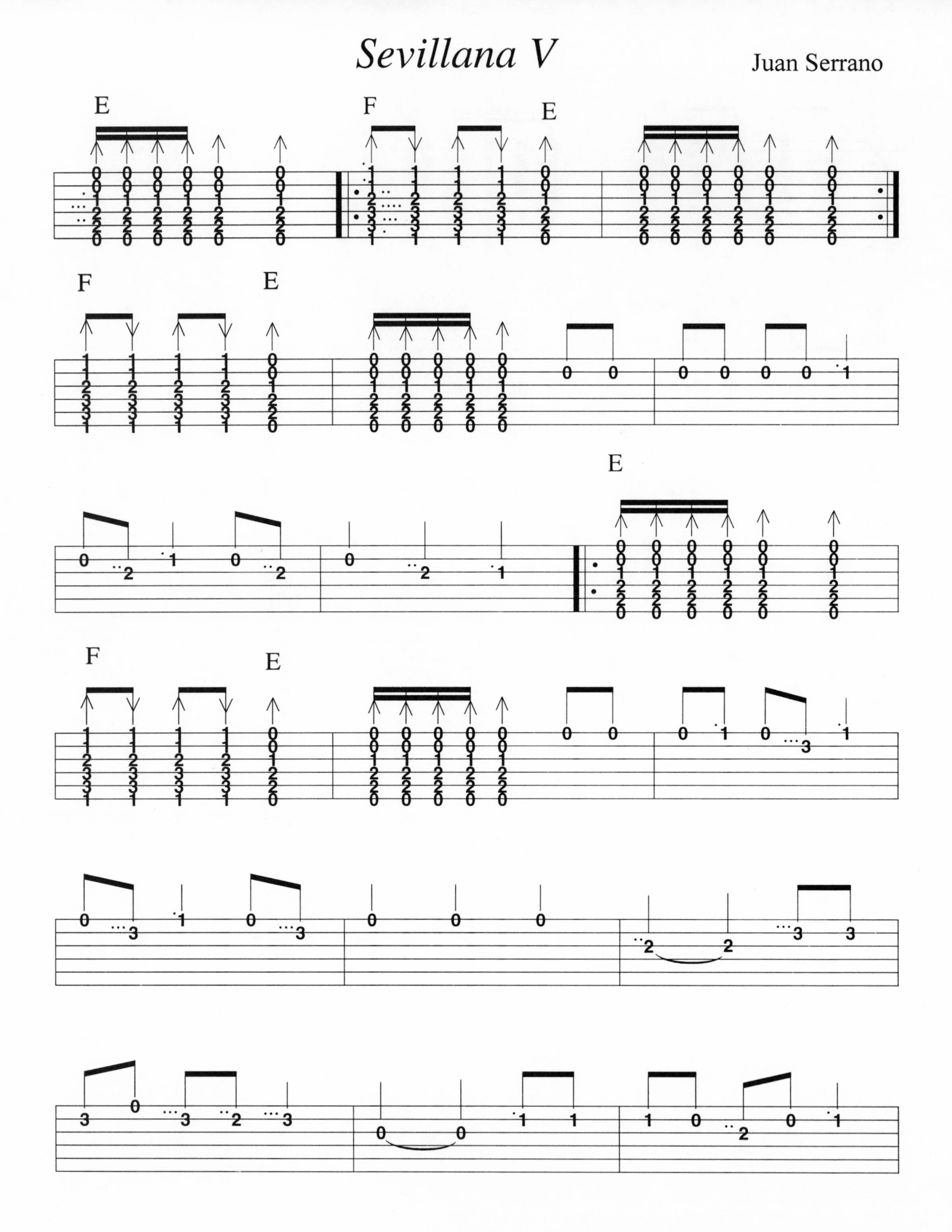

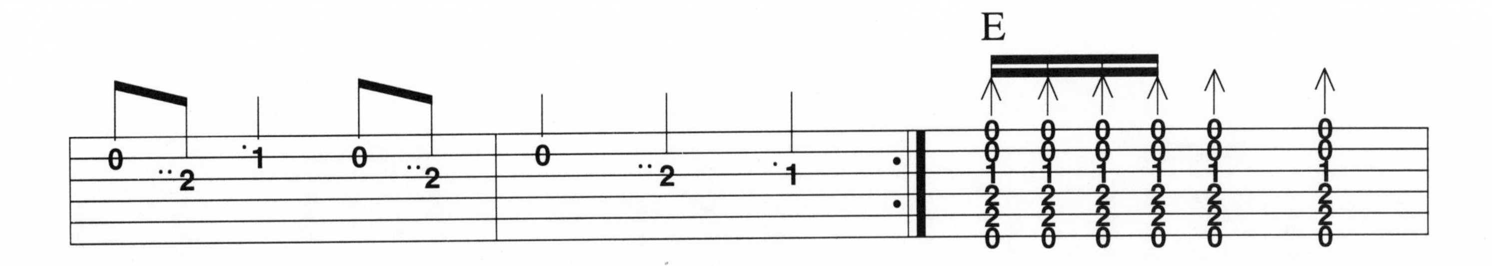
E

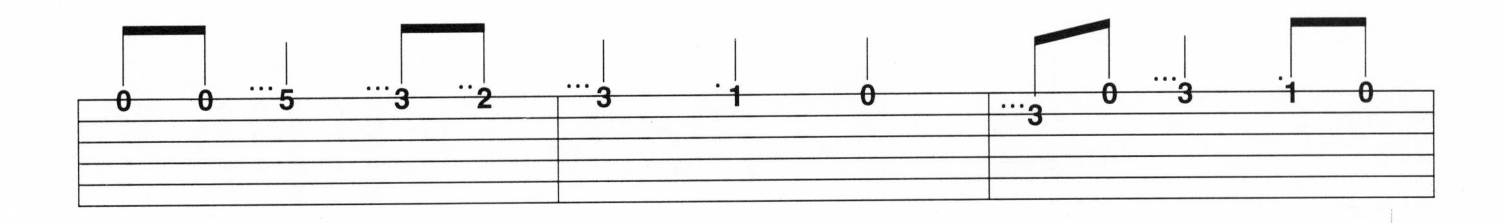
F
E

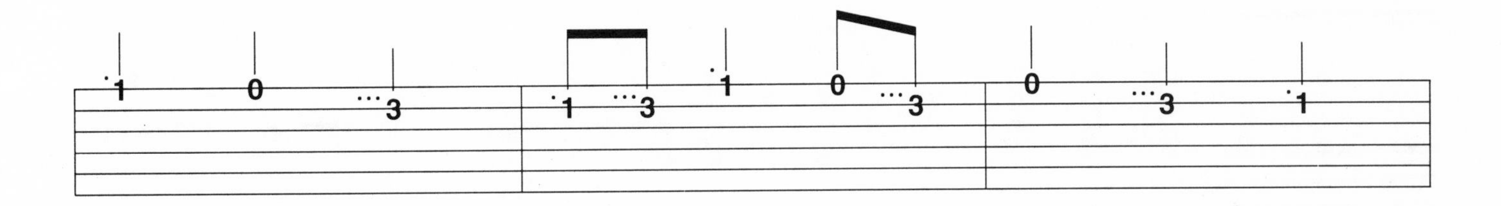

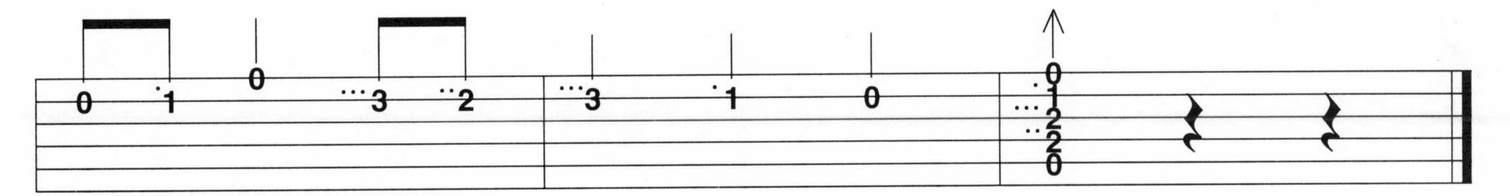

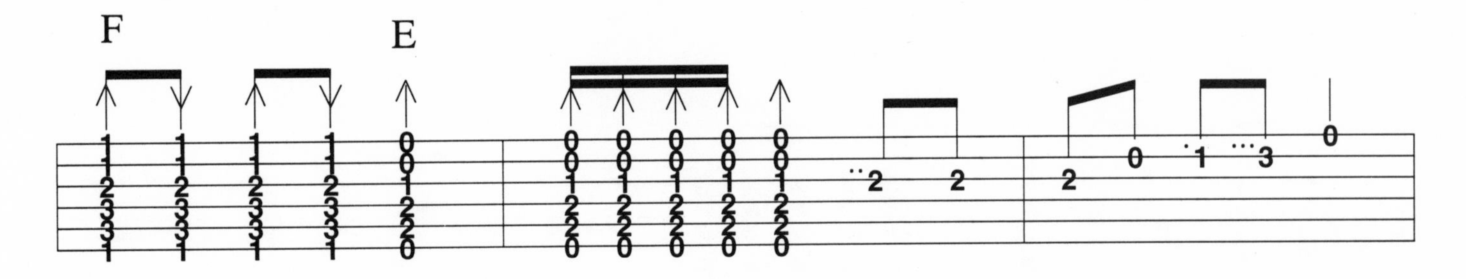
Am

# Sevillana VI

Juan Serrano

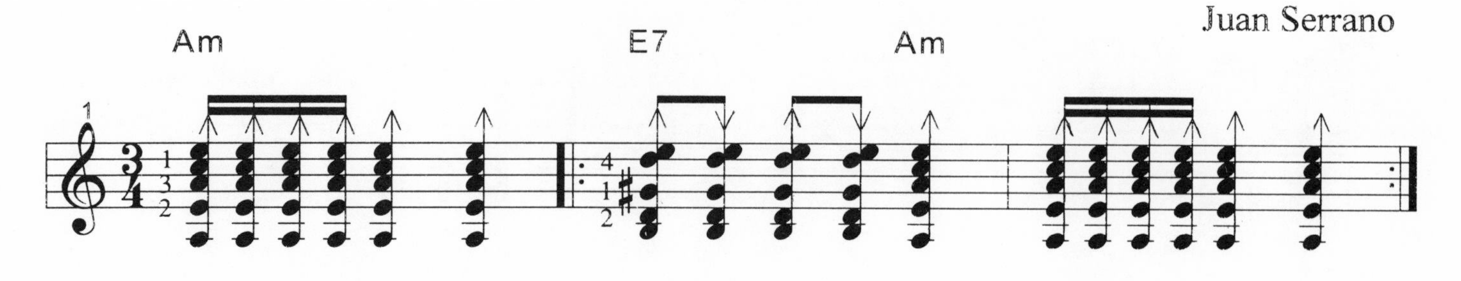


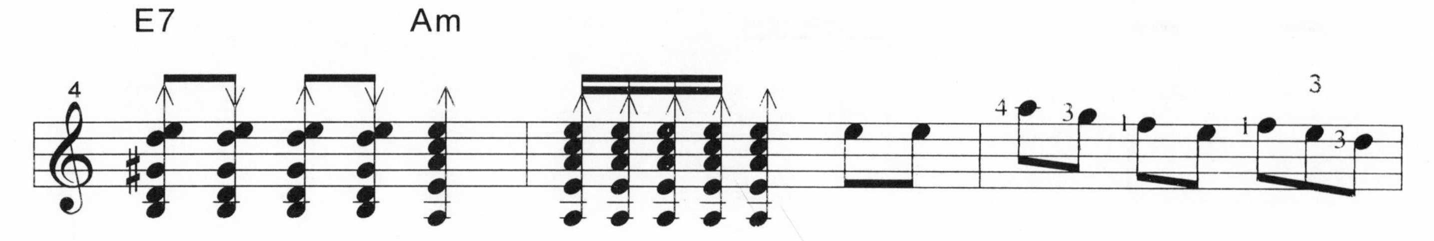

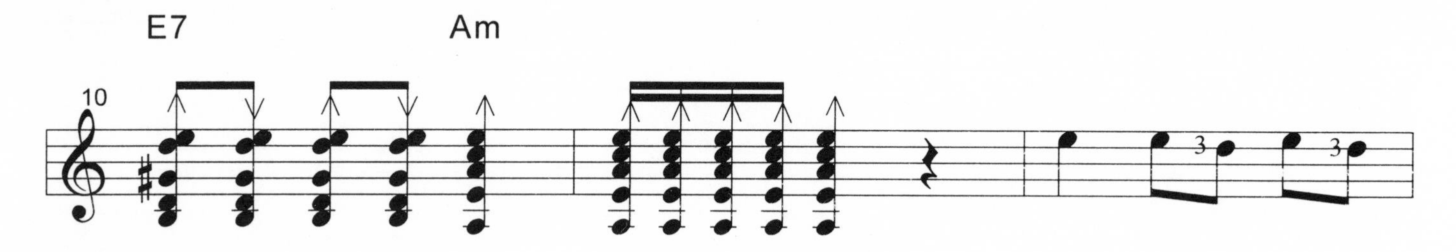

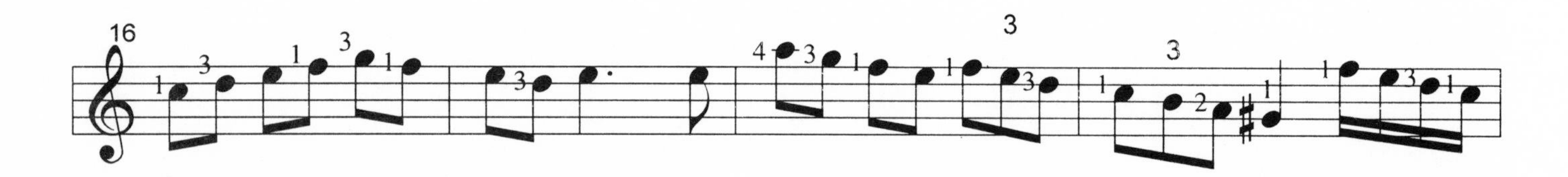

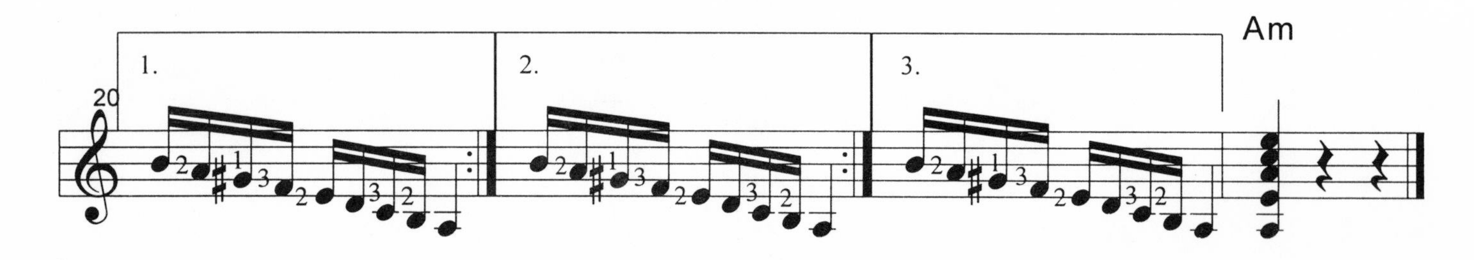

# Sevillana VI

Juan Serrano

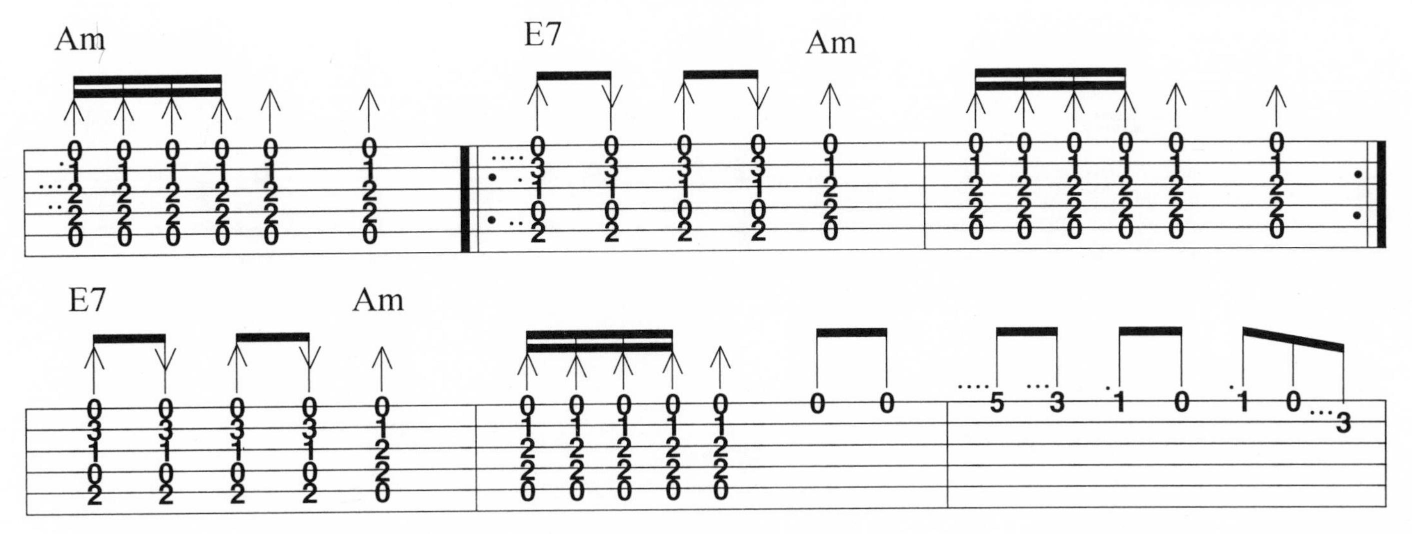


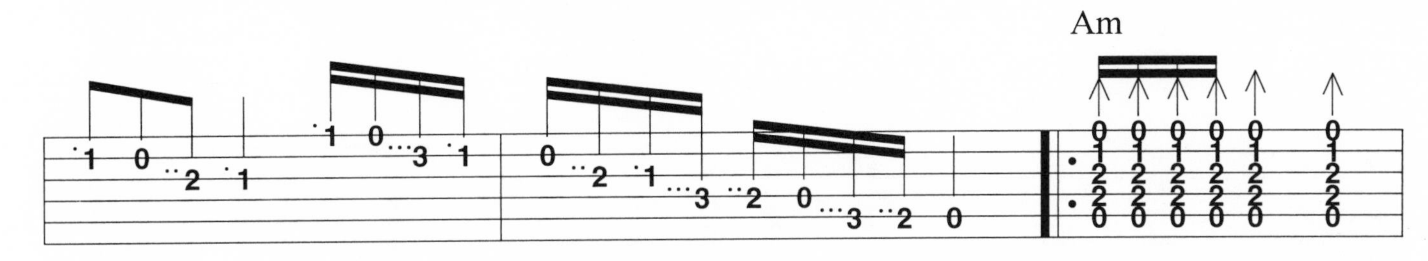


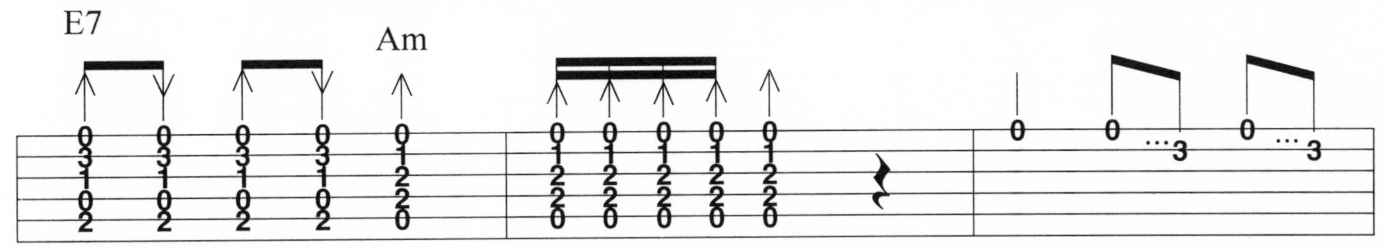


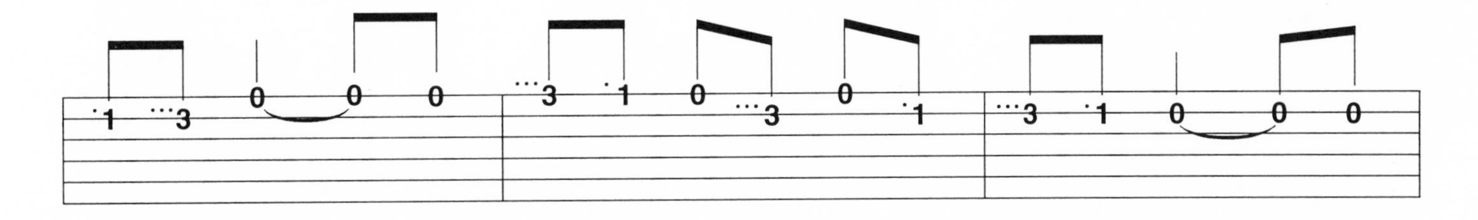

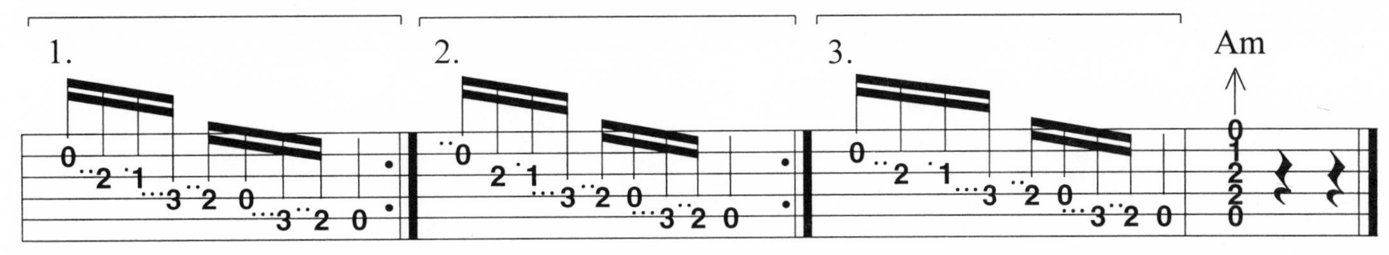

# *Sevillana VII*

Juan Serrano

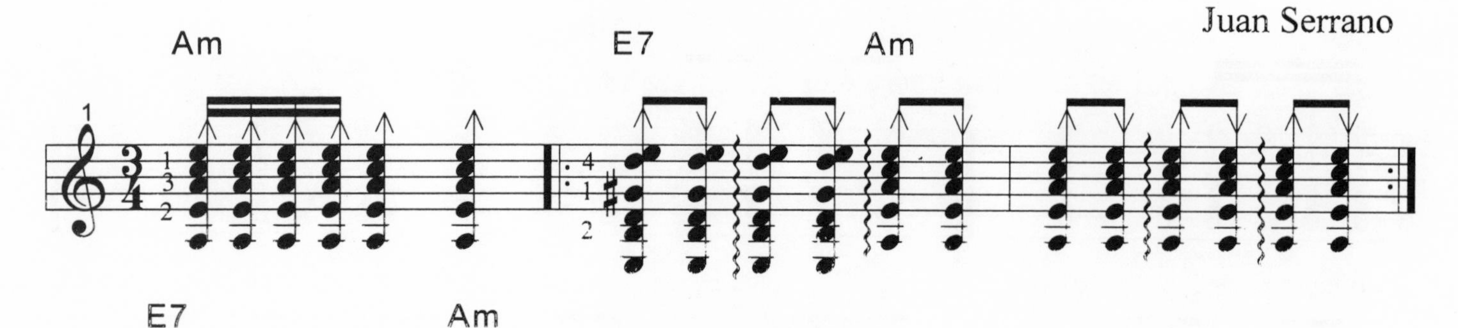


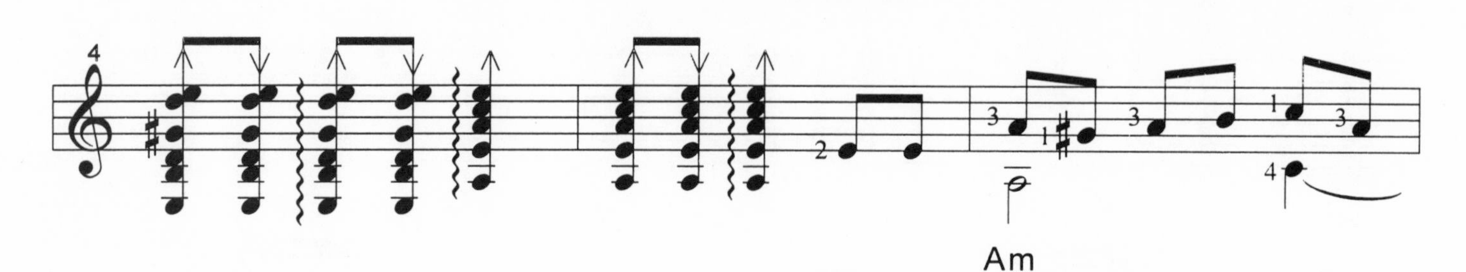

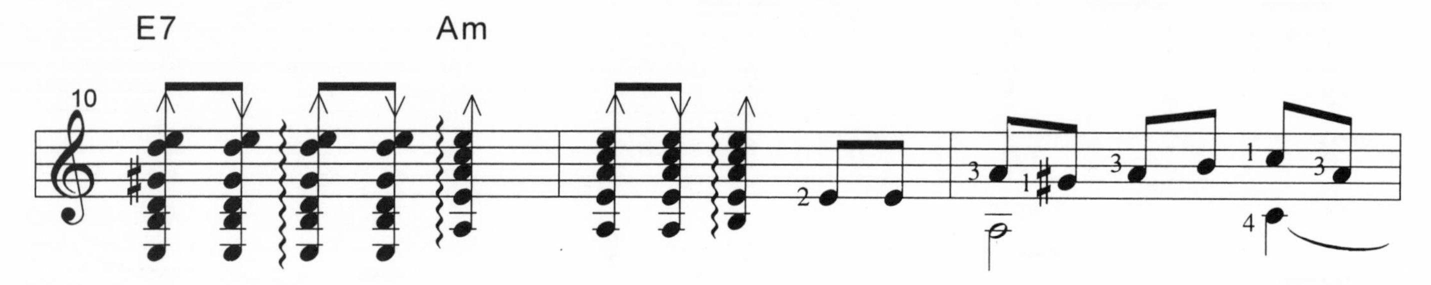


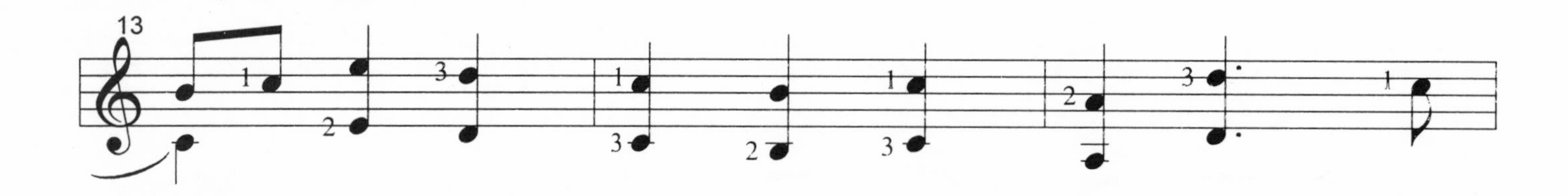

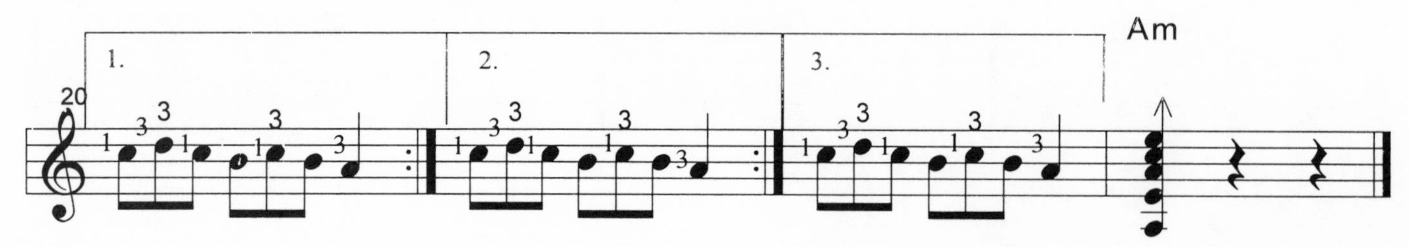

# *Sevillana VII*

Juan Serrano

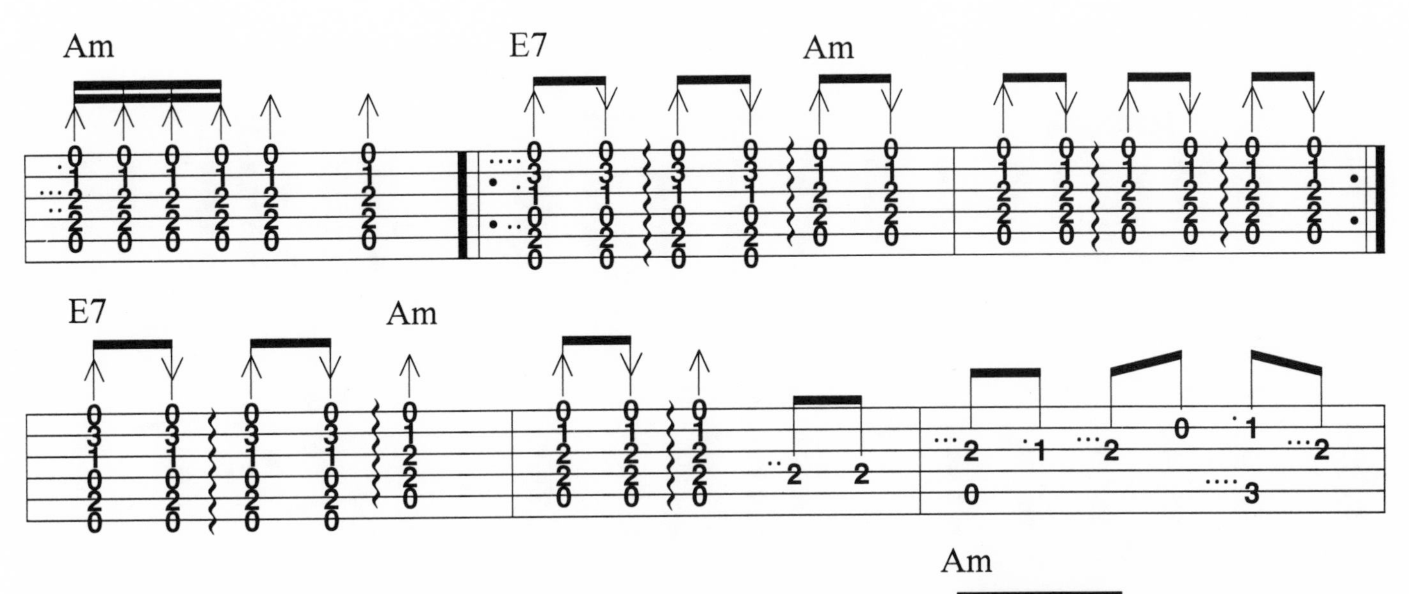


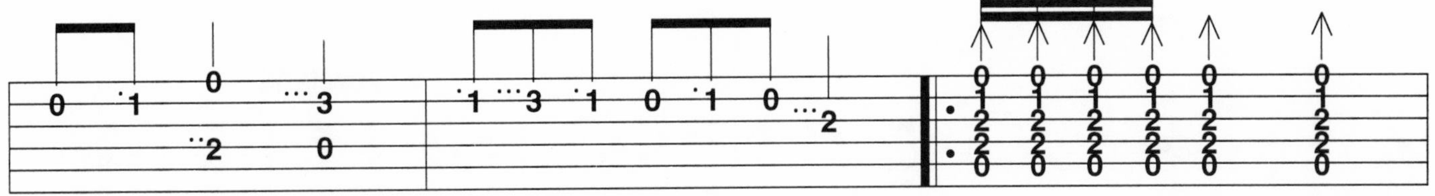

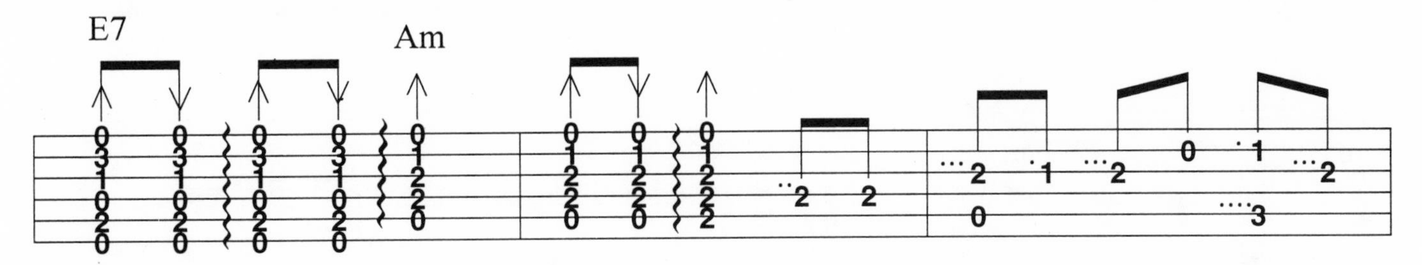


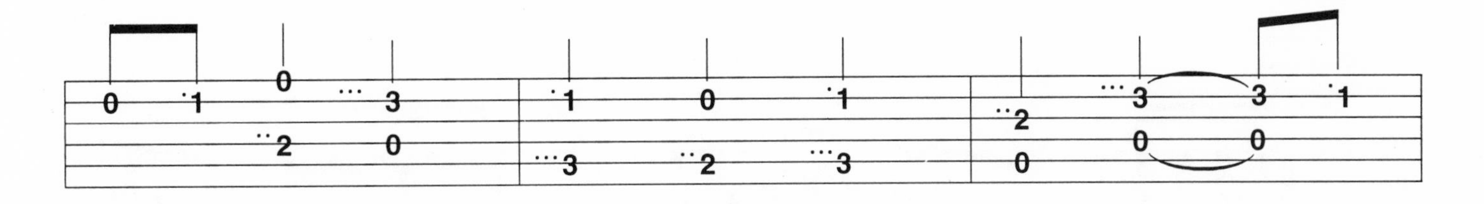

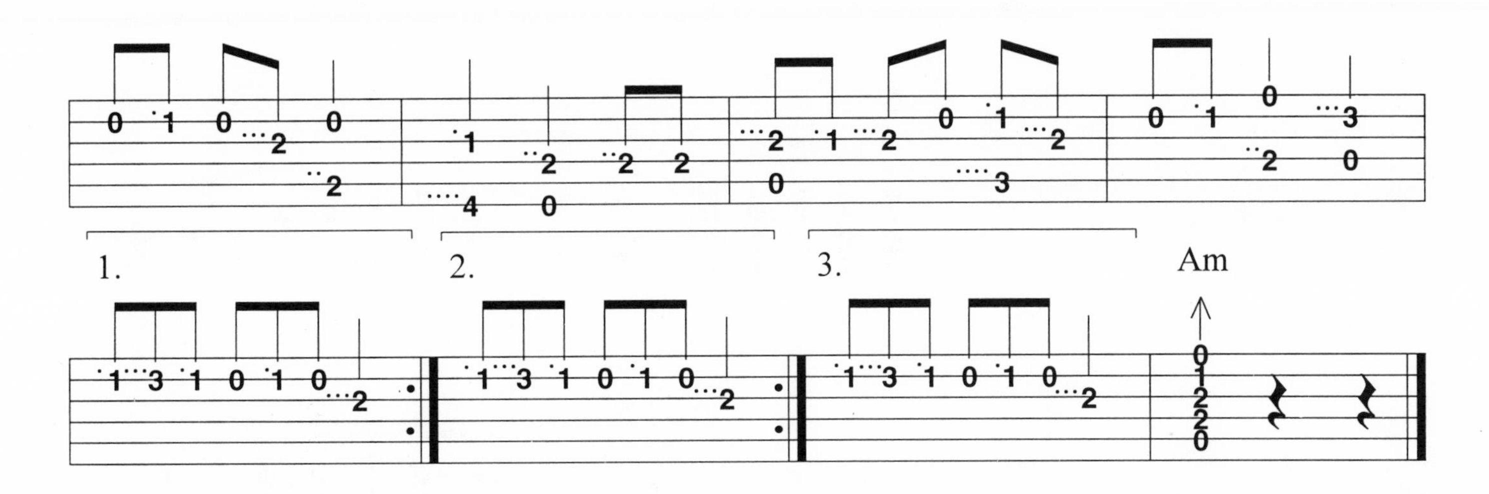

# Sevillana VIII

Juan Serrano

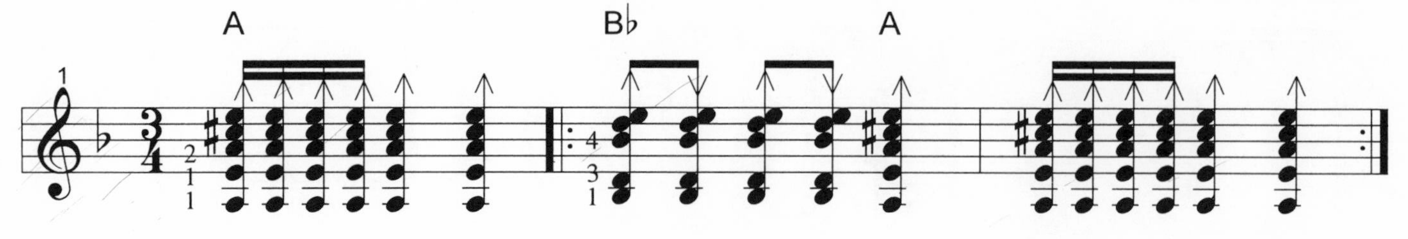


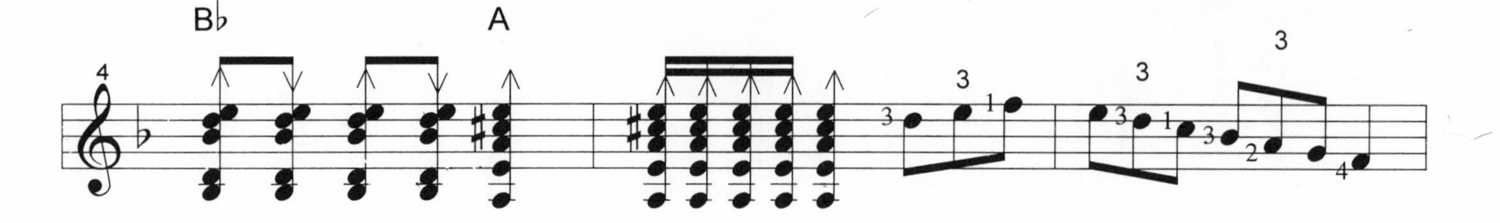

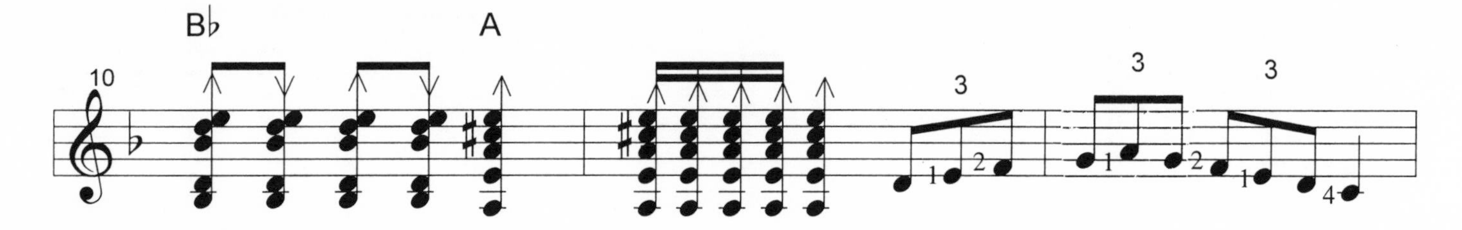


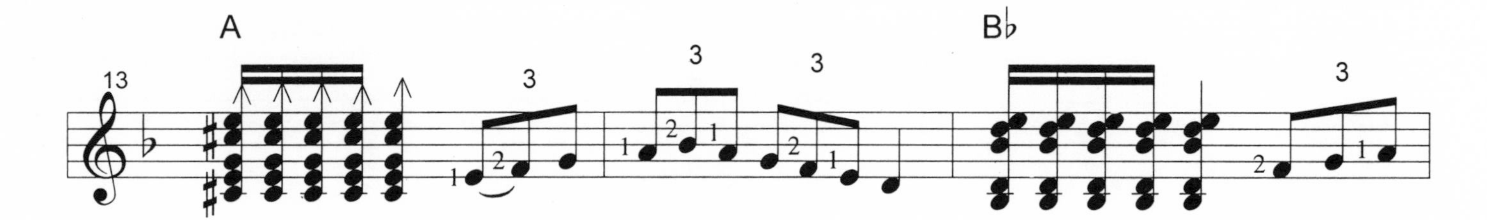


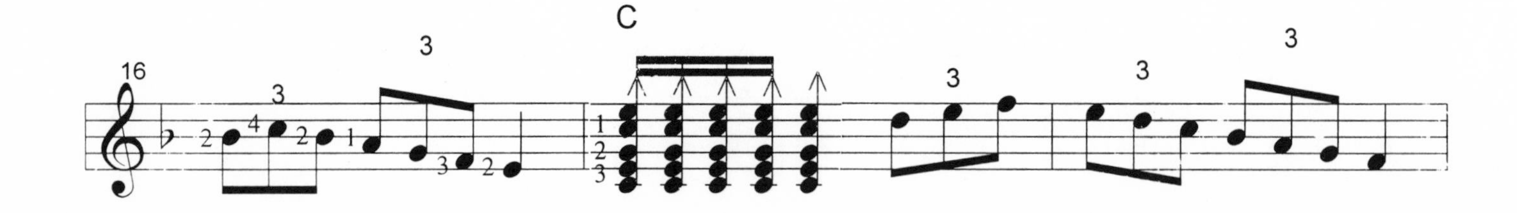

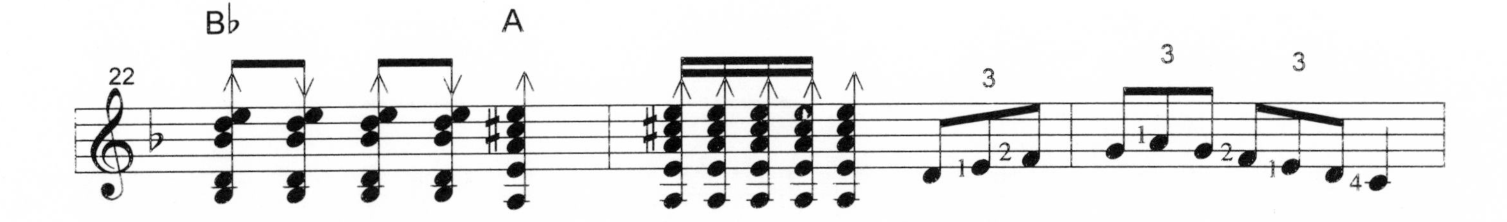
22
B♭
A

25
A
B♭

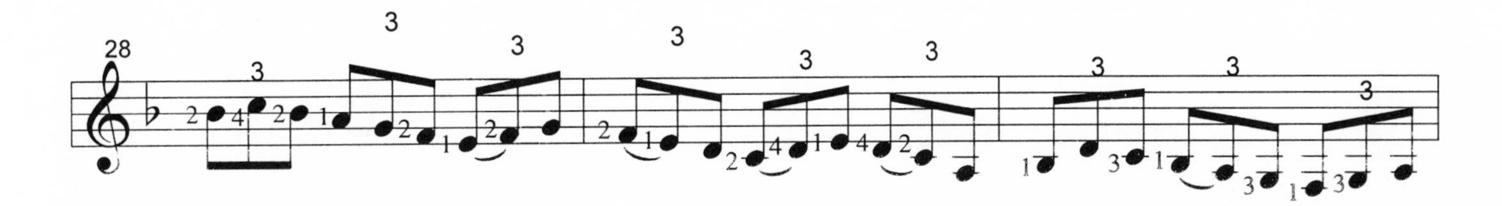
28

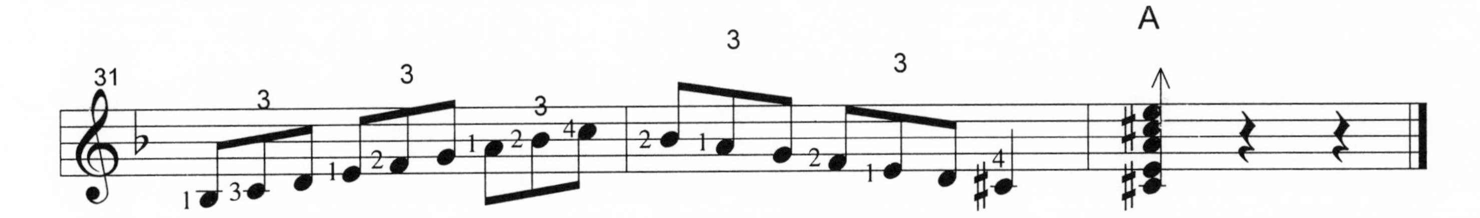
31
A

# *Sevillana VIII*

Juan Serrano

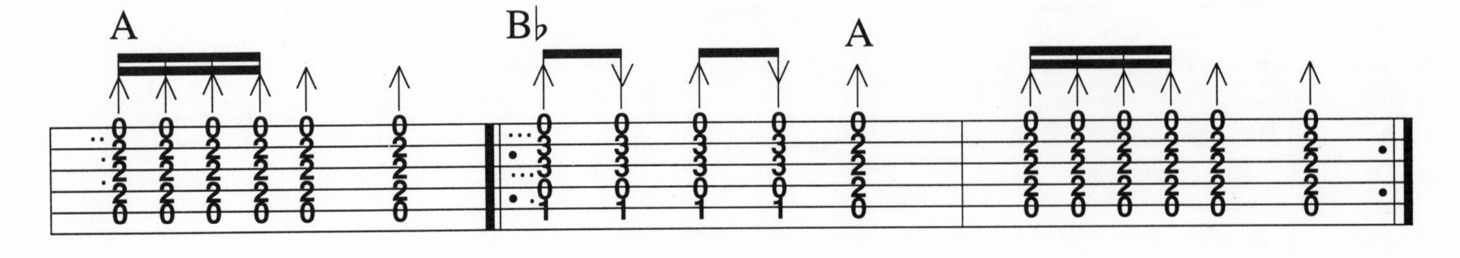


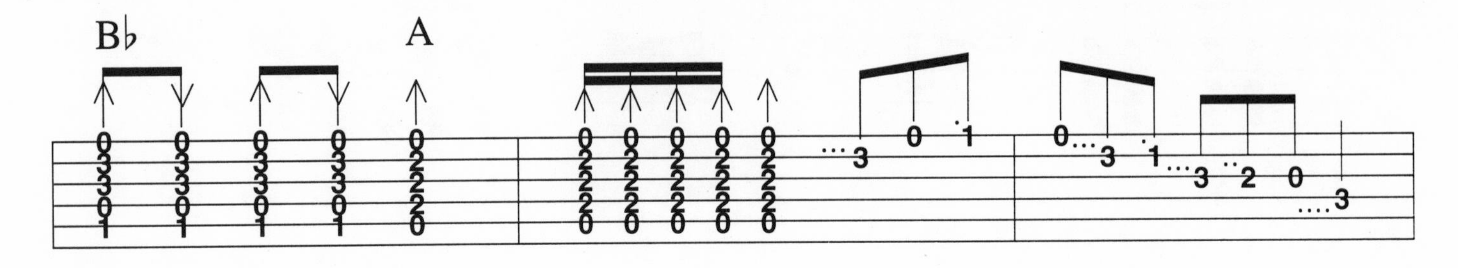


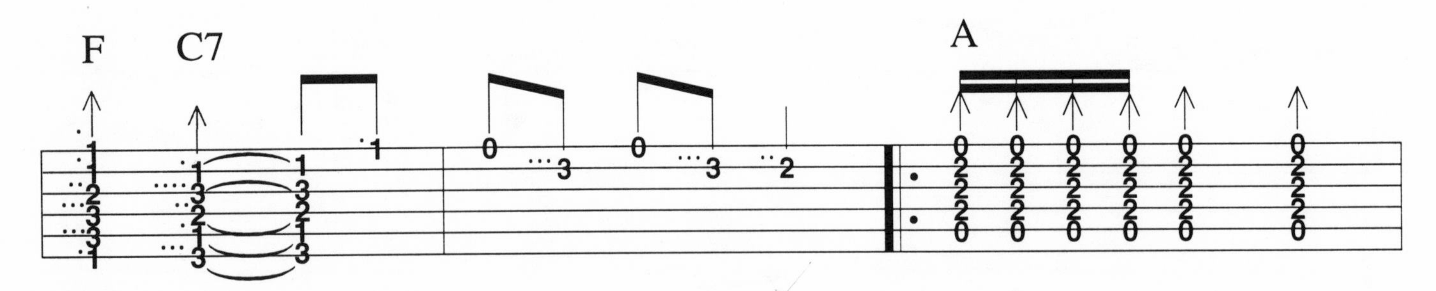


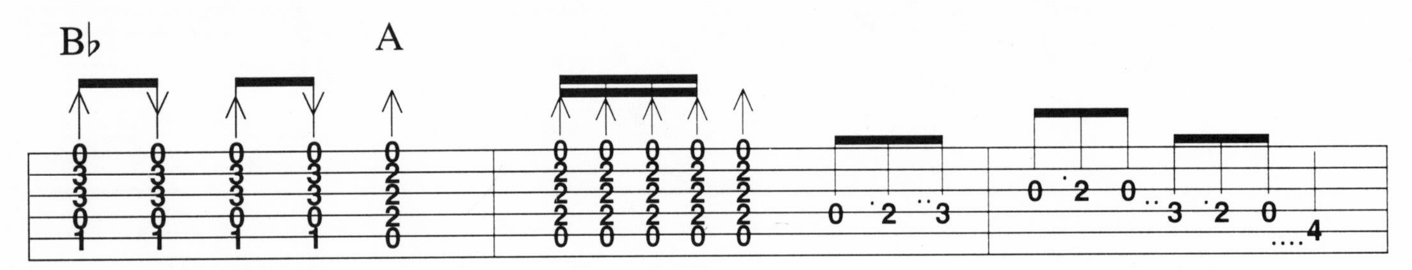


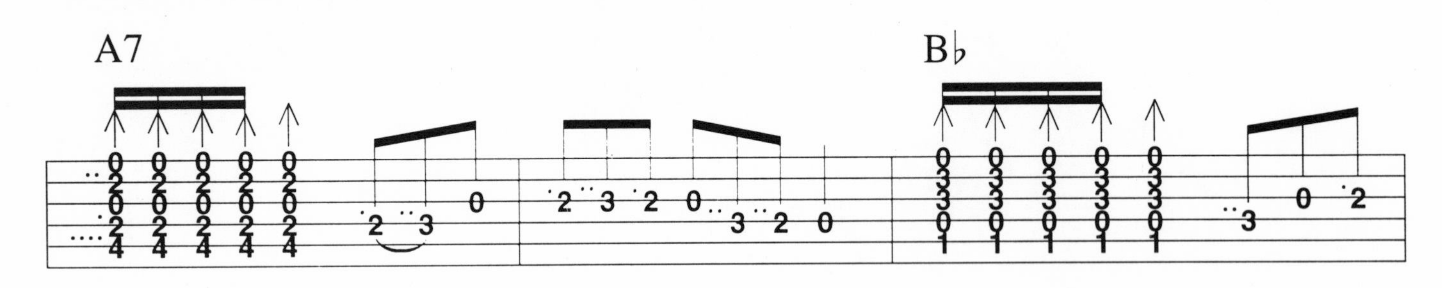


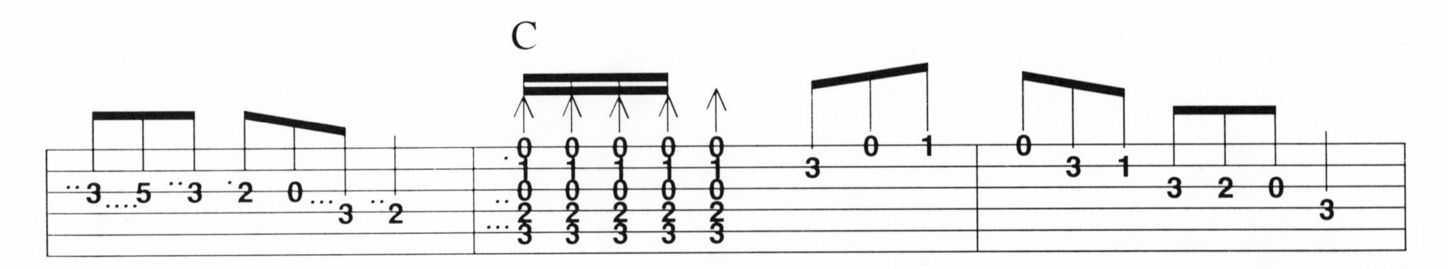

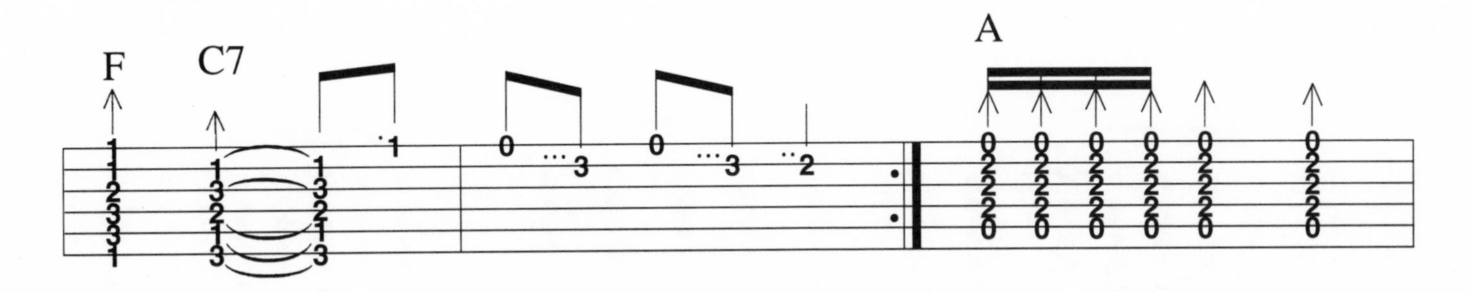
F
C7
A

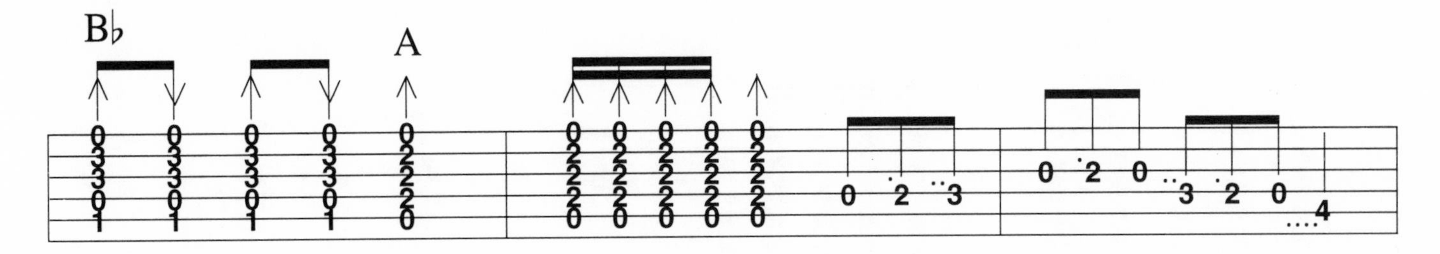
B♭
A

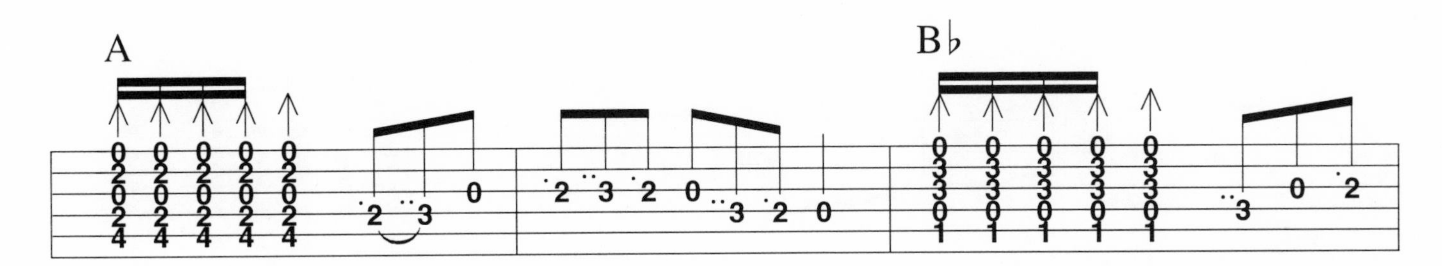
A
B♭

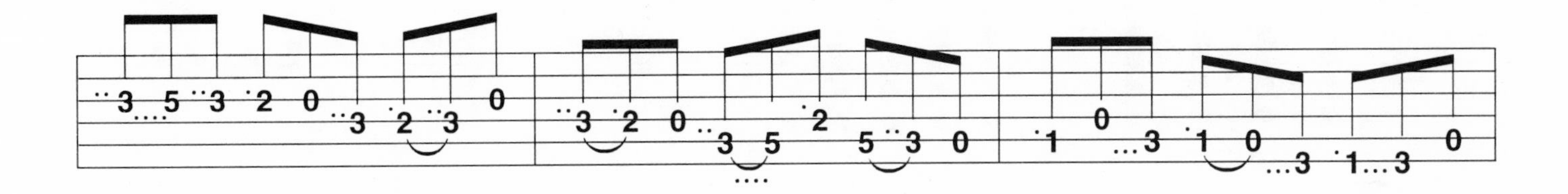

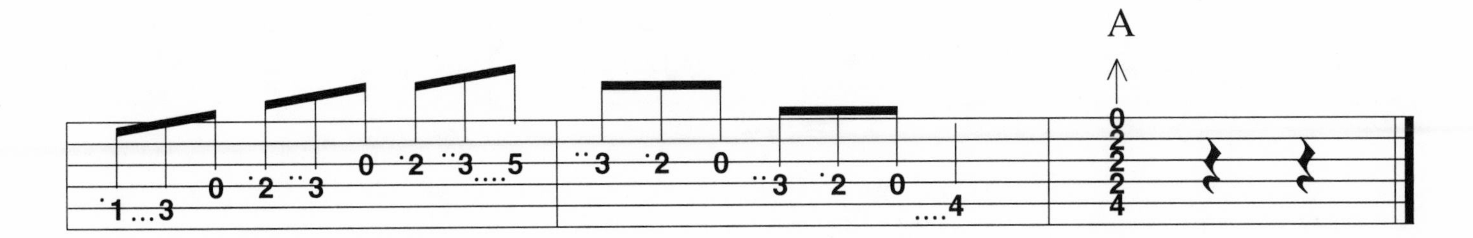
A

# *Sevillana IX*

Juan Serrano

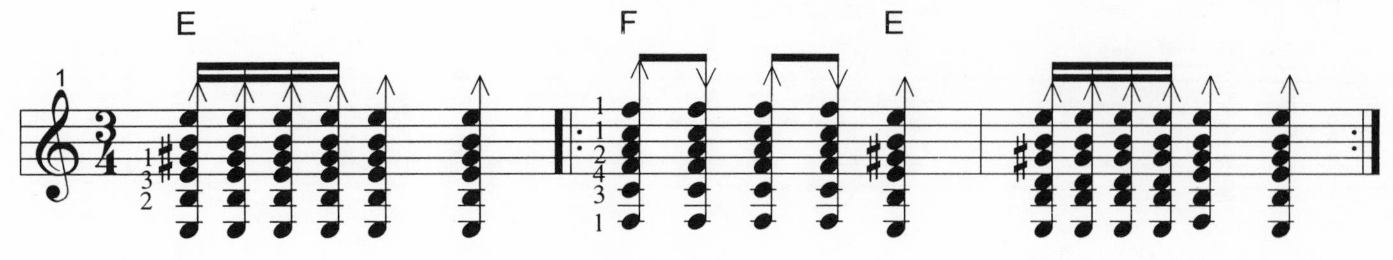


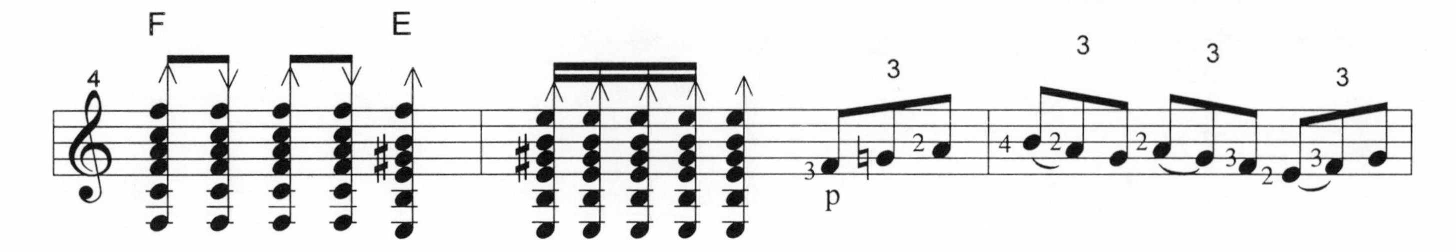


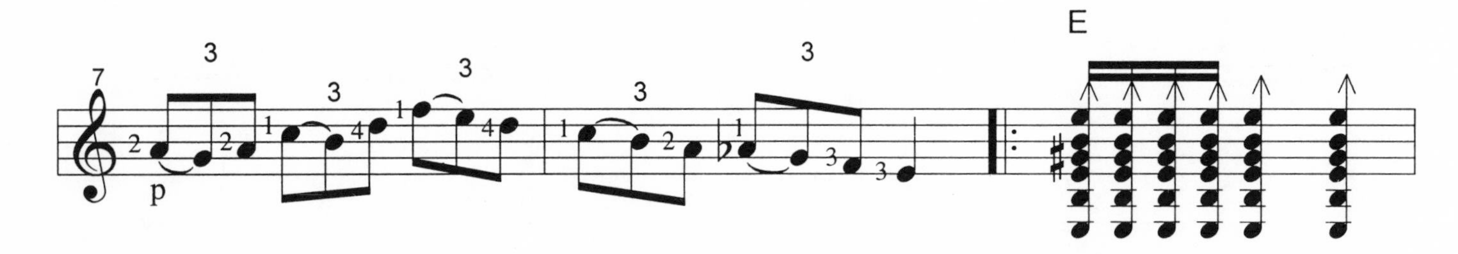


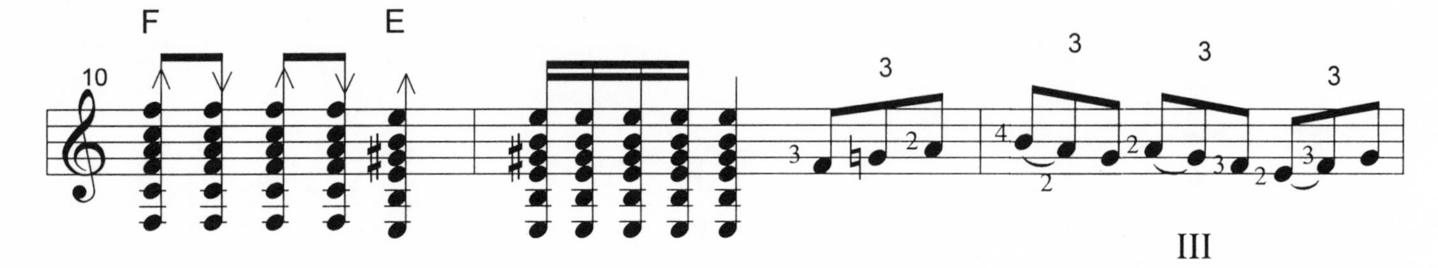

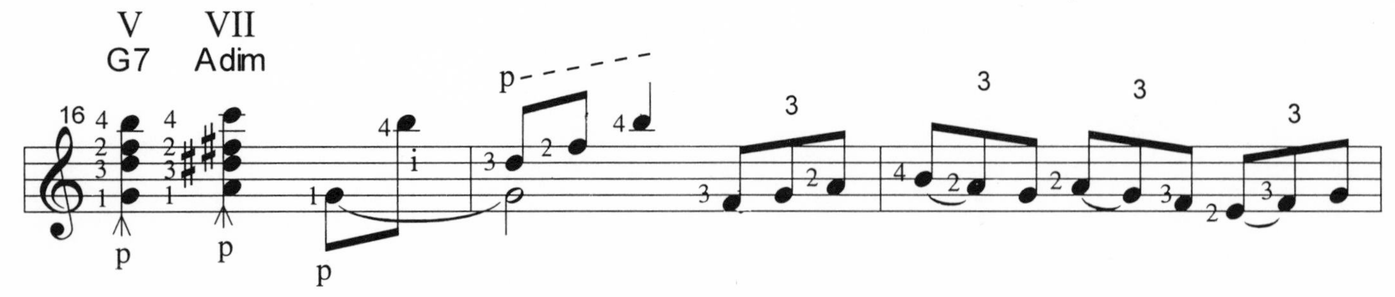


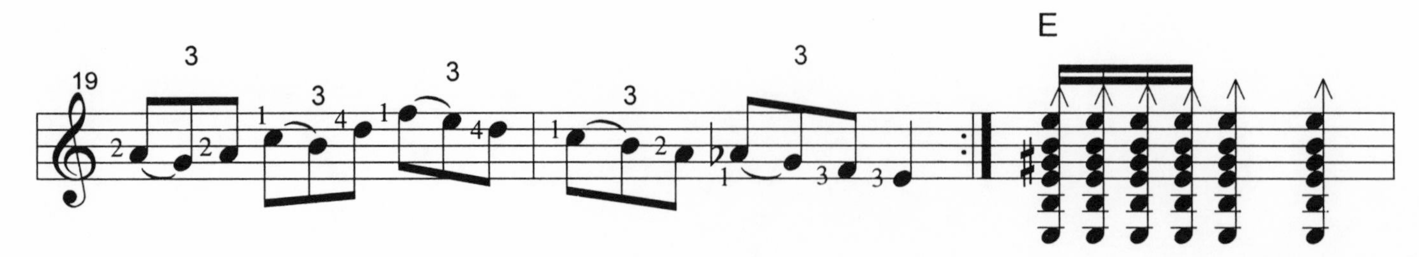

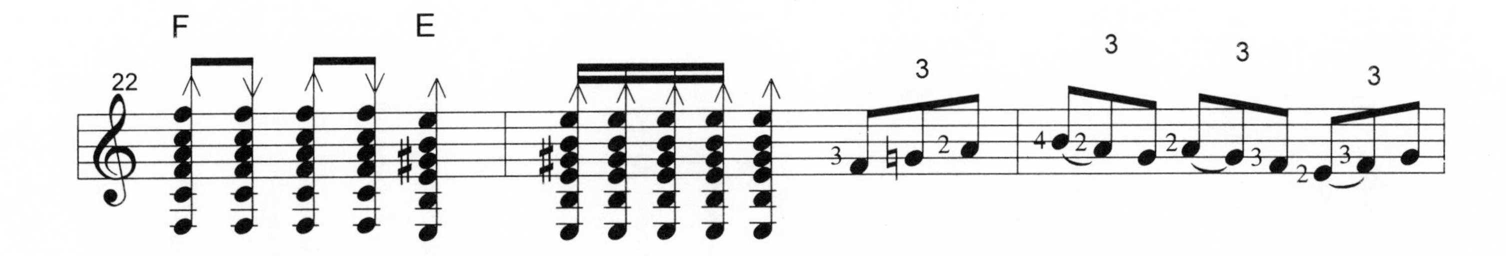
F
E
22

25

28

31
E

# *Sevillana IX*

Juan Serrano

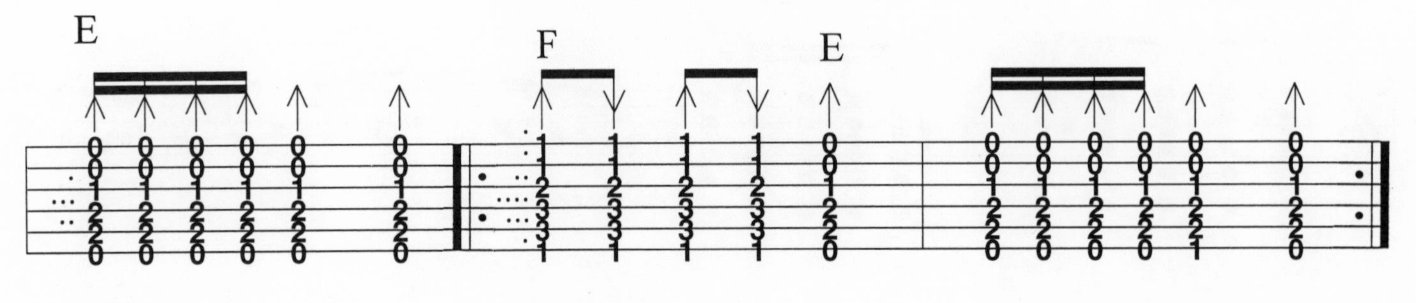


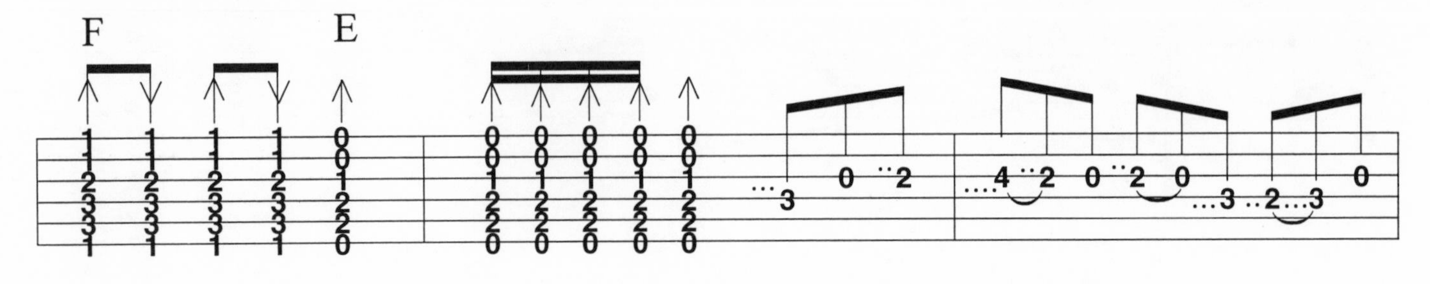


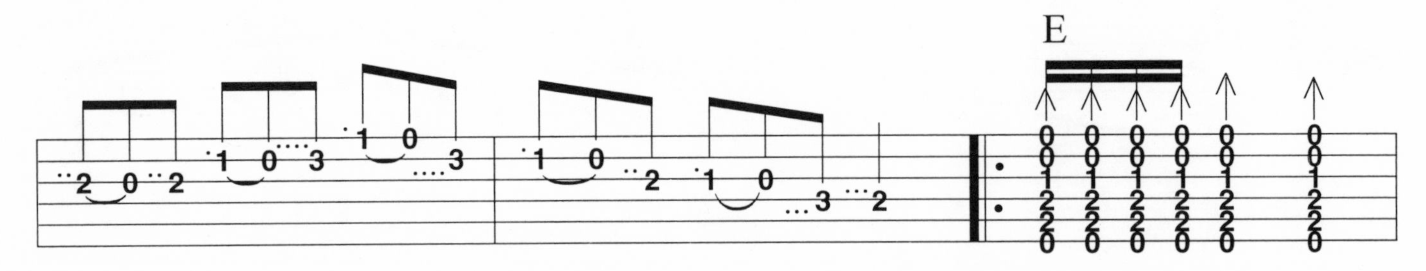


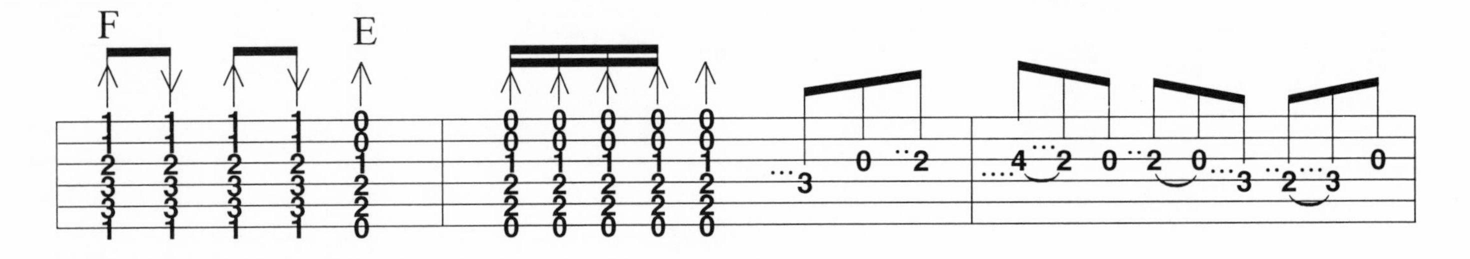


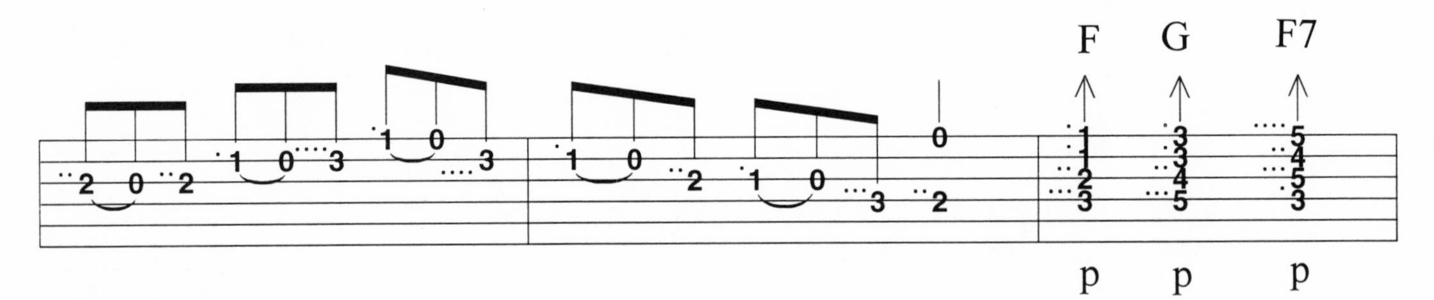


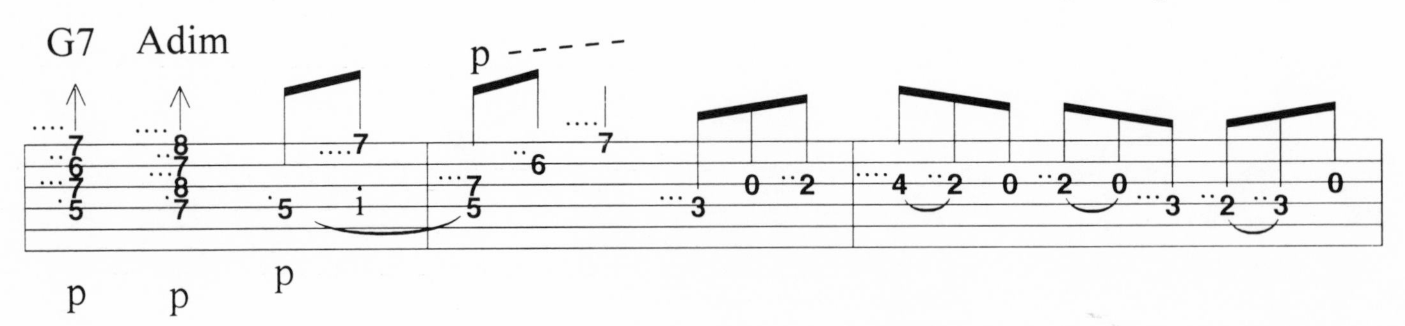

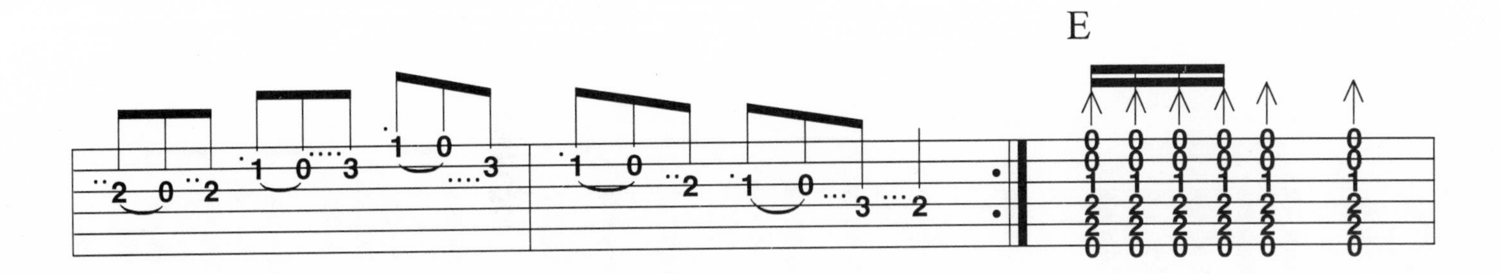
E

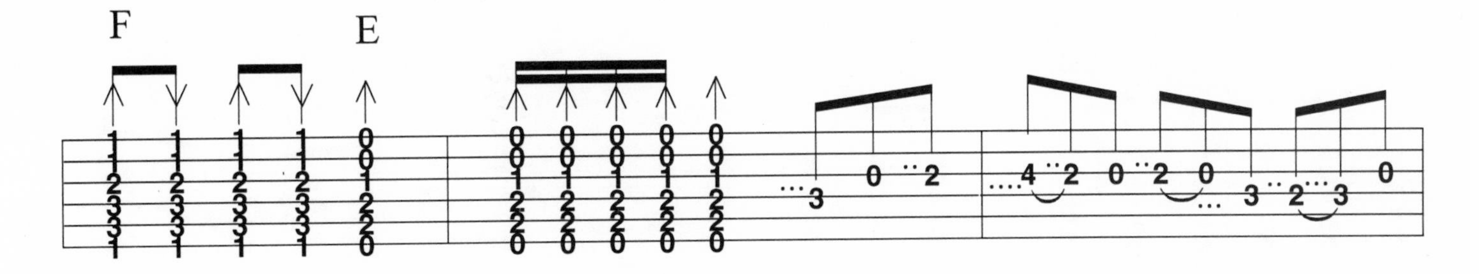
F
E

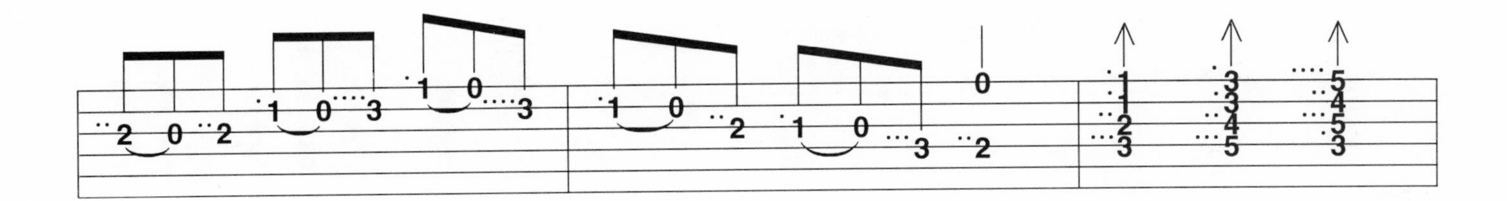

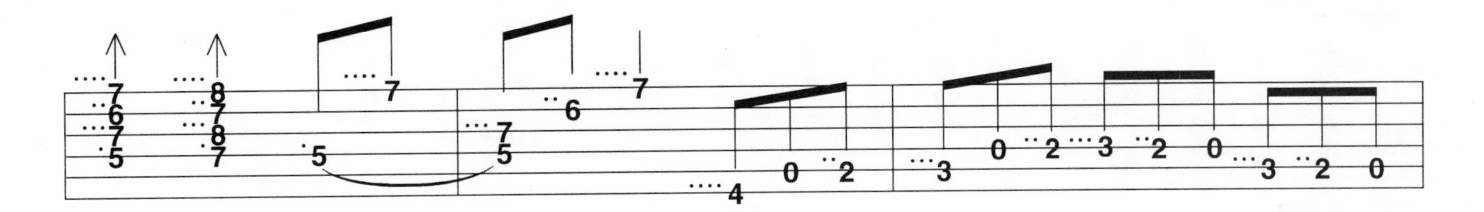

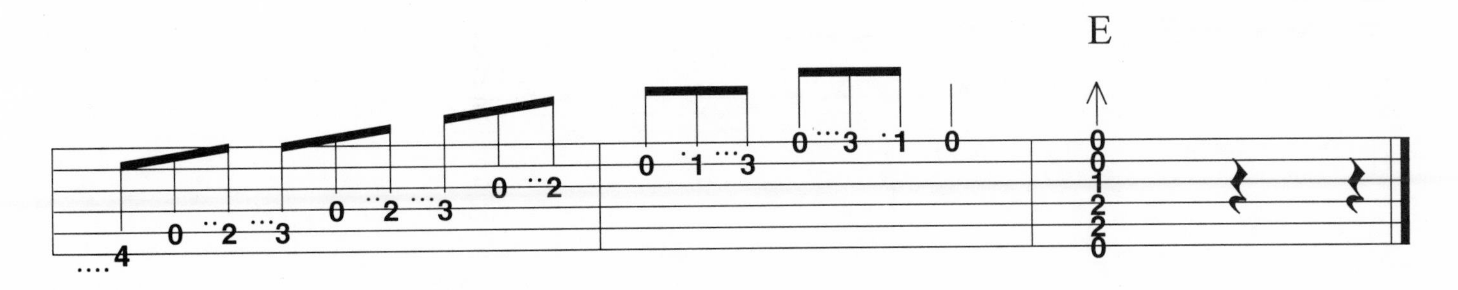
E

# *Sevillana X*

Juan Serrano

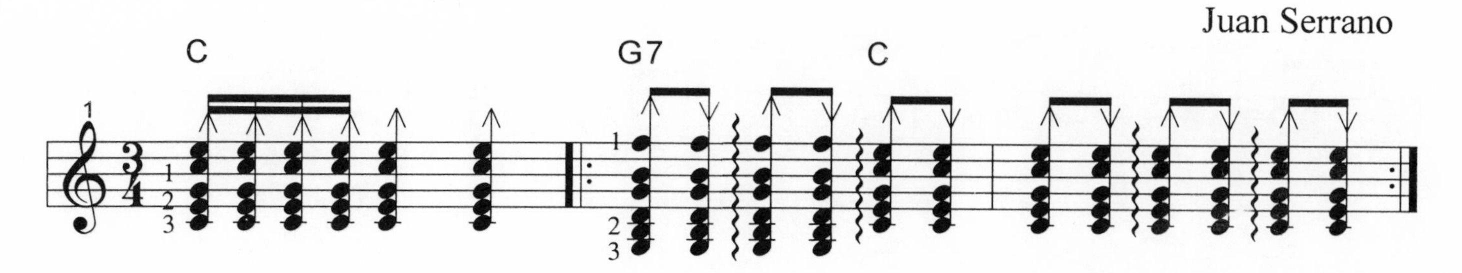


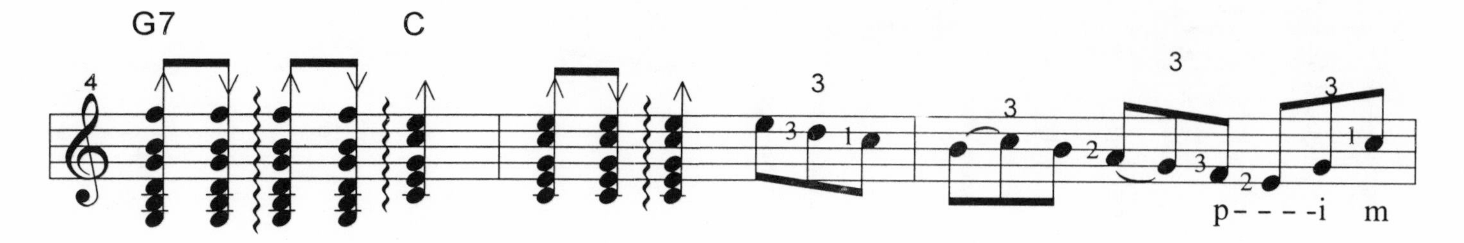

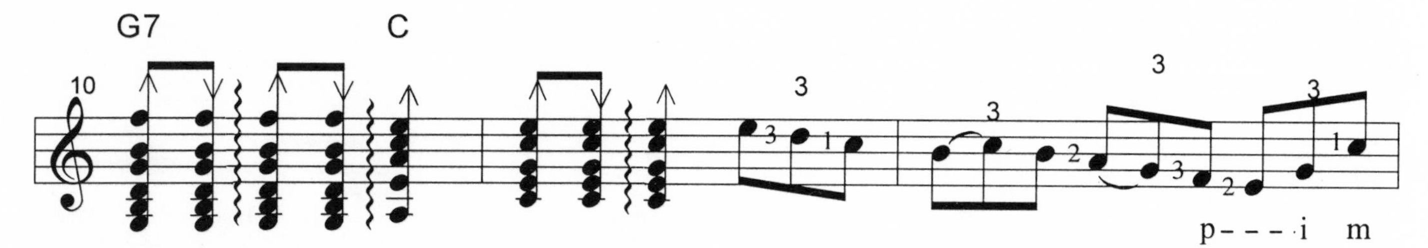

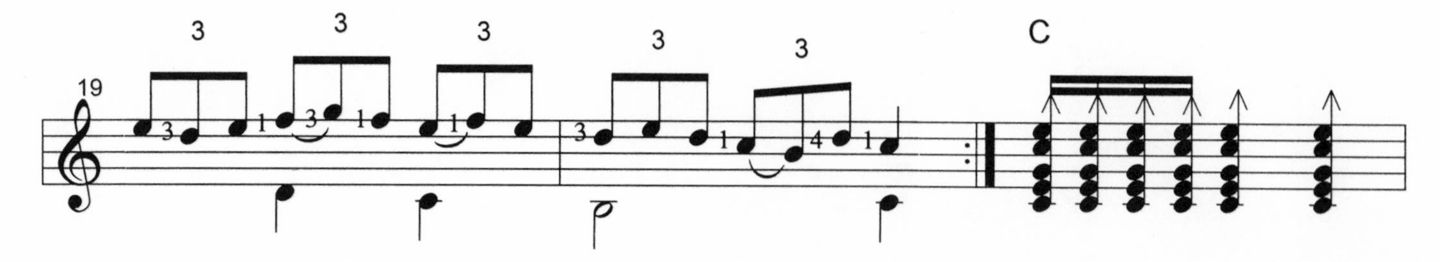

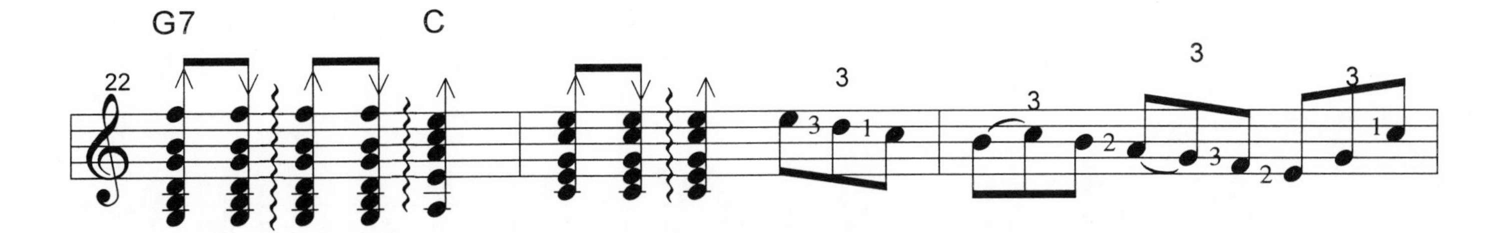
G7
C
22

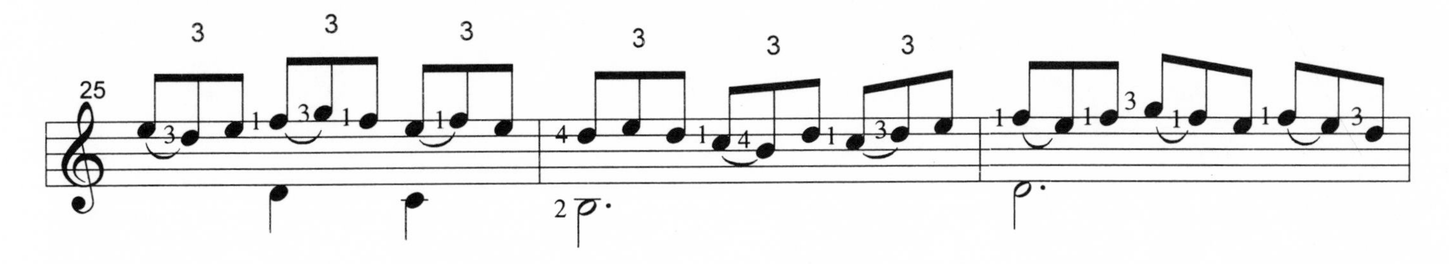
25

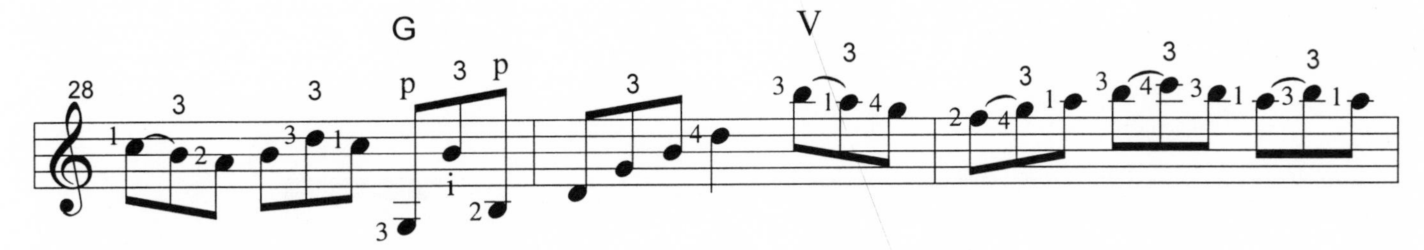
G
V
28

III
C
31

# *Sevillana X*

Juan Serrano

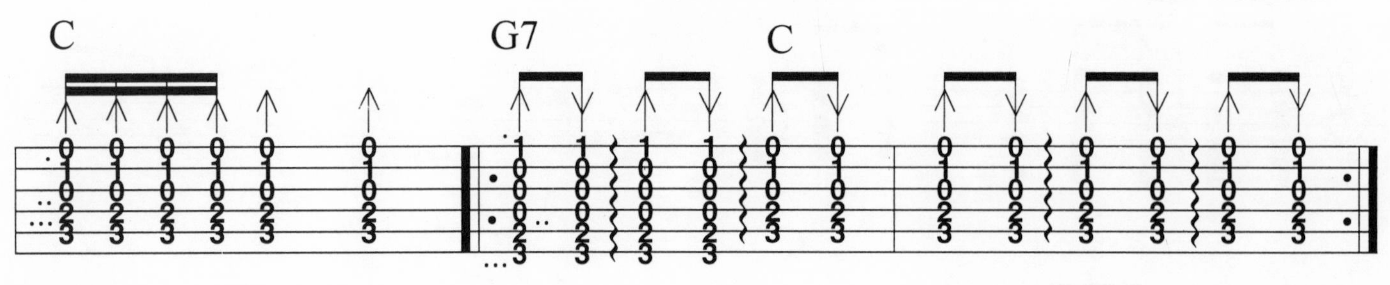


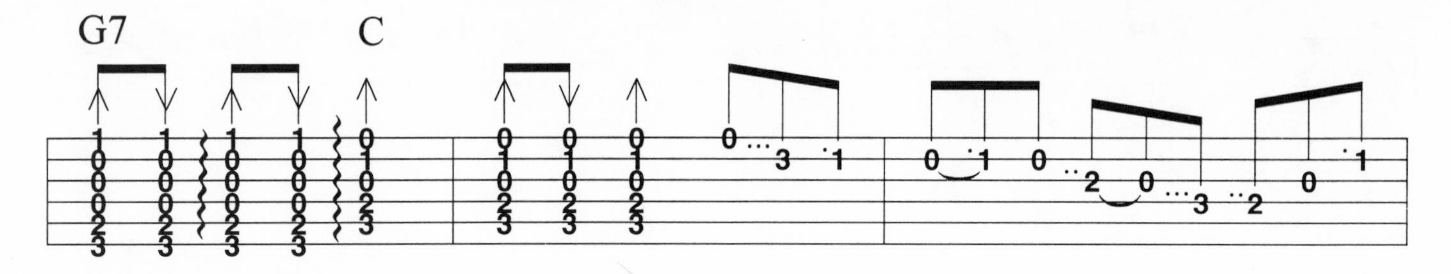


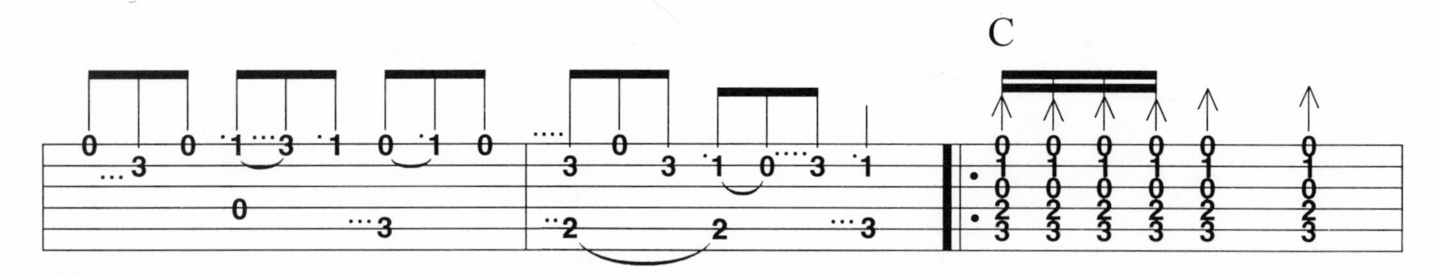


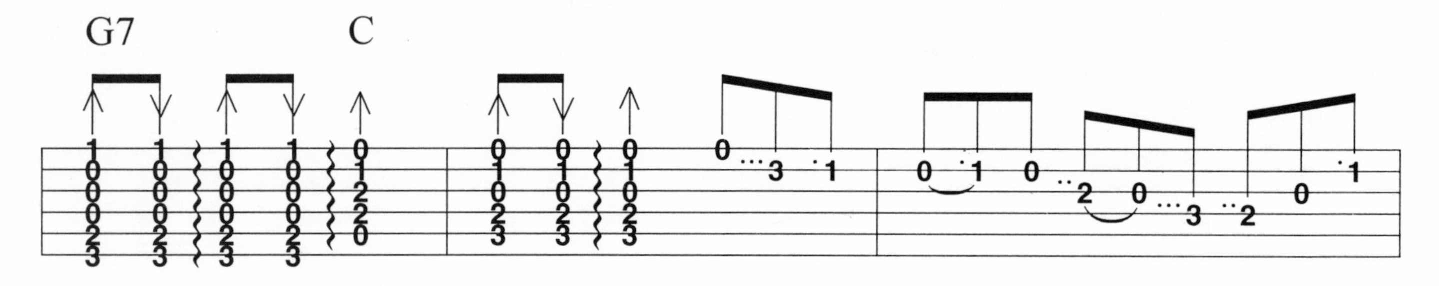


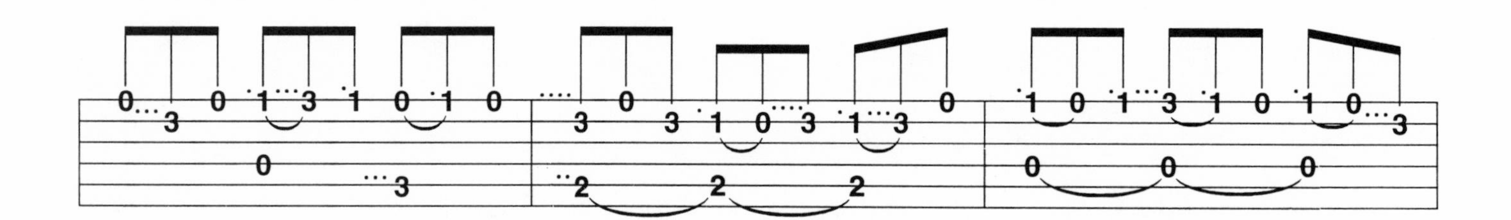

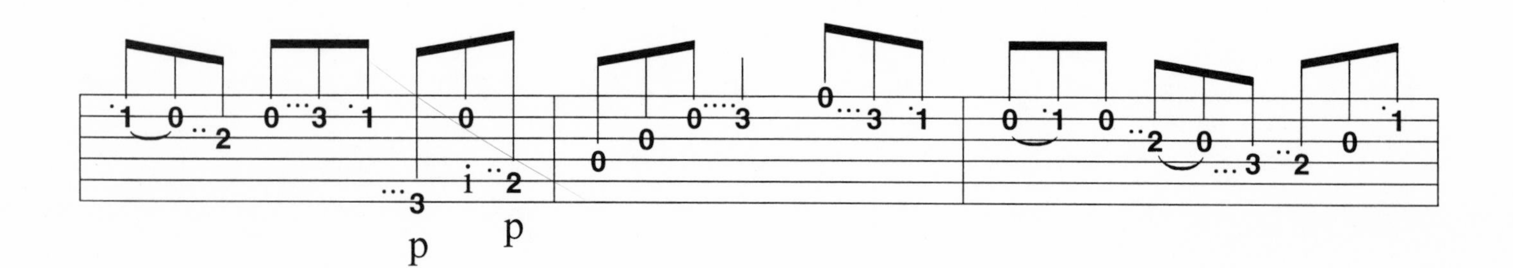

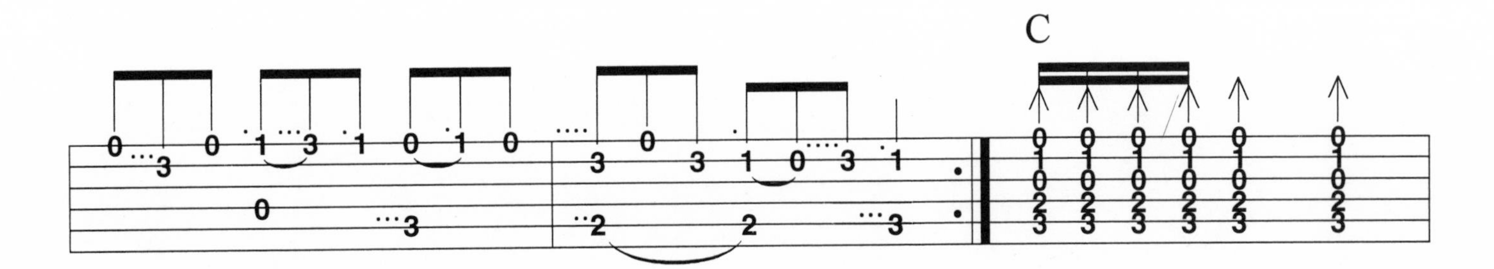
C

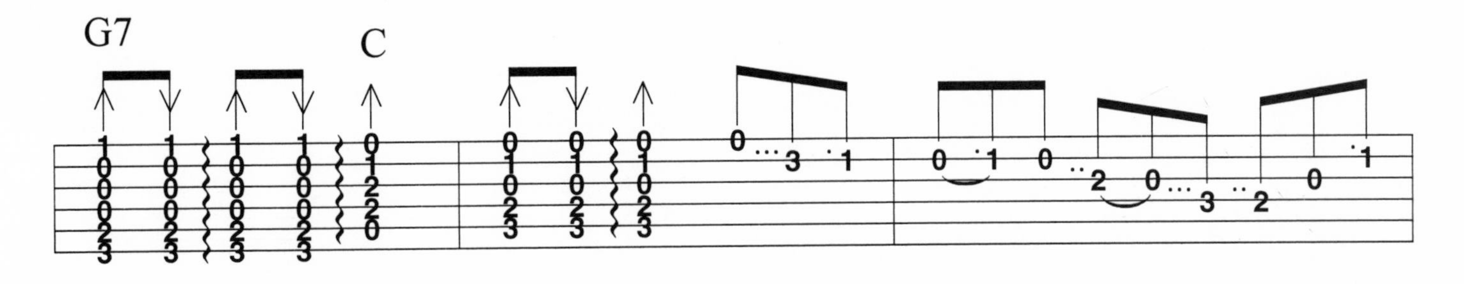
G7
C

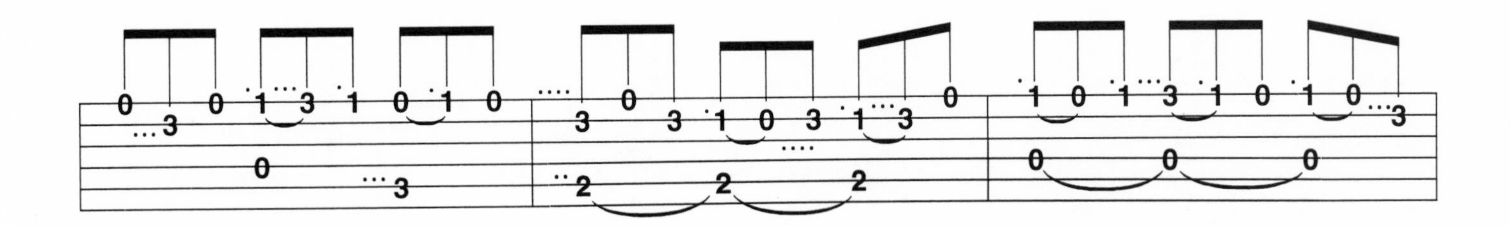

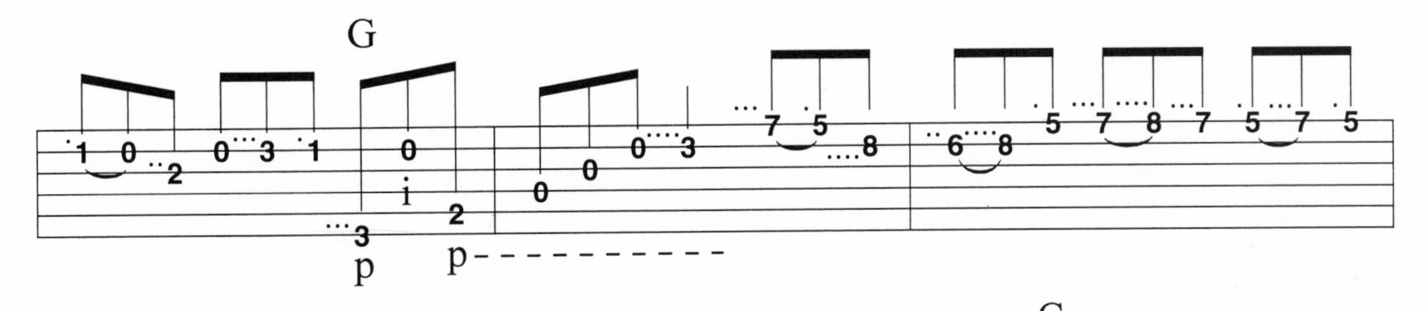
G
i
p
p

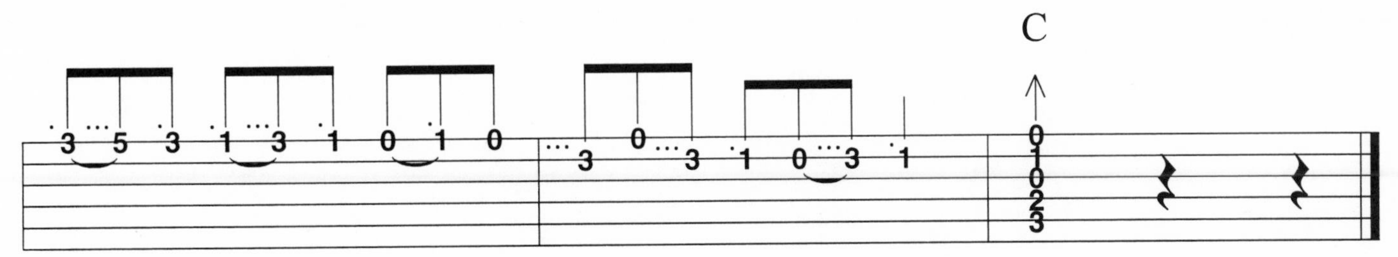
C

أليكرياس بور أرّيبا

# ALEGRÍAS POR ARRIBA

The Alegrías evolved from the light and rhythmic Jota that was sung in Cádiz around 1808. Possibly it is the most popular flamenco form of all the styles originating in Cádiz. The Alegrías are characterized by the richness of their toques and the difficulty of the dance.

Although the Alegrías is one form, many variations exist, for example, Alegrías por Arriba, Alegrías por Medio, Alegrías de Córdoba, Mirabrás, Romeras, Caracoles and Cantiñas. The Alegrías por Arriba and the Mirabrás are played in the key of E major, the Alegrías por Medio played in A major, Alegrías de Córdoba in E minor, and Romeras and Caracoles in C major. Cantiñas can be played in either of the three major keys previously mentioned, depending on the cantaor's preference. Because all forms of Alegrías are sung and danced, the guitar, traditionally only served as accompaniment to the song and dance.

All of the Alegrías por Arriba falsetas are in a technical progressive order. It is recommended that the picados (scales) be executed reststroke, with a strict i, m rotation.

All of the variations of the Alegrías are measured in 3/4 time. A flamenco compás has 12 beats, equivalent to 4 measures of 3/4 time, with accents on the 3rd, 6th, 8th, 10th and 12th beats.

*Example:*

| | | | V | | | V | | V | | V | | V |
|---|---|---|---|---|---|---|---|---|---|---|---|---|
| **3/4** | **1** | **2** | **3** | **4** | **5** | **6** | **7** | **8** | **9** | **10** | **11** | **12** |

# ALEGRÍAS POR ARRIBA

Las Alegrías derivan de una Jota ligera y rítmica que se cantaba en Cádiz hacia el 1808. Posiblemente, es la forma flamenca más popular de todos los estilos procedentes de Cádiz. Las Alegrías se caracterizan por la riqueza de sus toques y lo difícil de su baile. Aunque Alegrías es una sola forma, existen muchas variaciones, por ejemplo, Alegrías por Arriba, Alegrías por Medio, Alegrías de Córdoba, Mirabrás, Romeras, Caracoles y Cantiñas.

Las Alegrías por Arriba y el Mirabrás se tocan en el tono de Mi mayor, Alegrías por Medio en La Mayor, Alegrías de Córdoba en Mi menor, y Romeras y Caracoles en Do mayor. Cantiñas se pueden tocar en cualquiera de los tres tonos mayores mencionados anteriormente, depende de la preferencia del cantaor. Ya que todas las formas de Alegrías son cantables y bailables y tradicionalmente la guitarra solo servía como acompañamiento al cante y al baile.

Todas las falsetas de las Alegrías por arriba están en un orden técnico progresivo.

Recomiendo que todos los picados se ejecuten apoyando, y con una rotación estricta de i, m.

Todas las variaciones de las Alegrías se miden en 3/4. Un compás flamenco se compone de doce tiempos equivalentes a cuatro compases musicales de 3/4 con acentos en los tiempos 3, 6, 8, 10 y 12.

*Ejemplo:*

| | | | V | | | V | | V | | V | | V |
|---|---|---|---|---|---|---|---|---|---|---|---|---|
| **3/4** | **1** | **2** | **3** | **4** | **5** | **6** | **7** | **8** | **9** | **10** | **11** | **12** |

# *Alegrias Por Arriba*

Traditional Compas

Juan Serrano

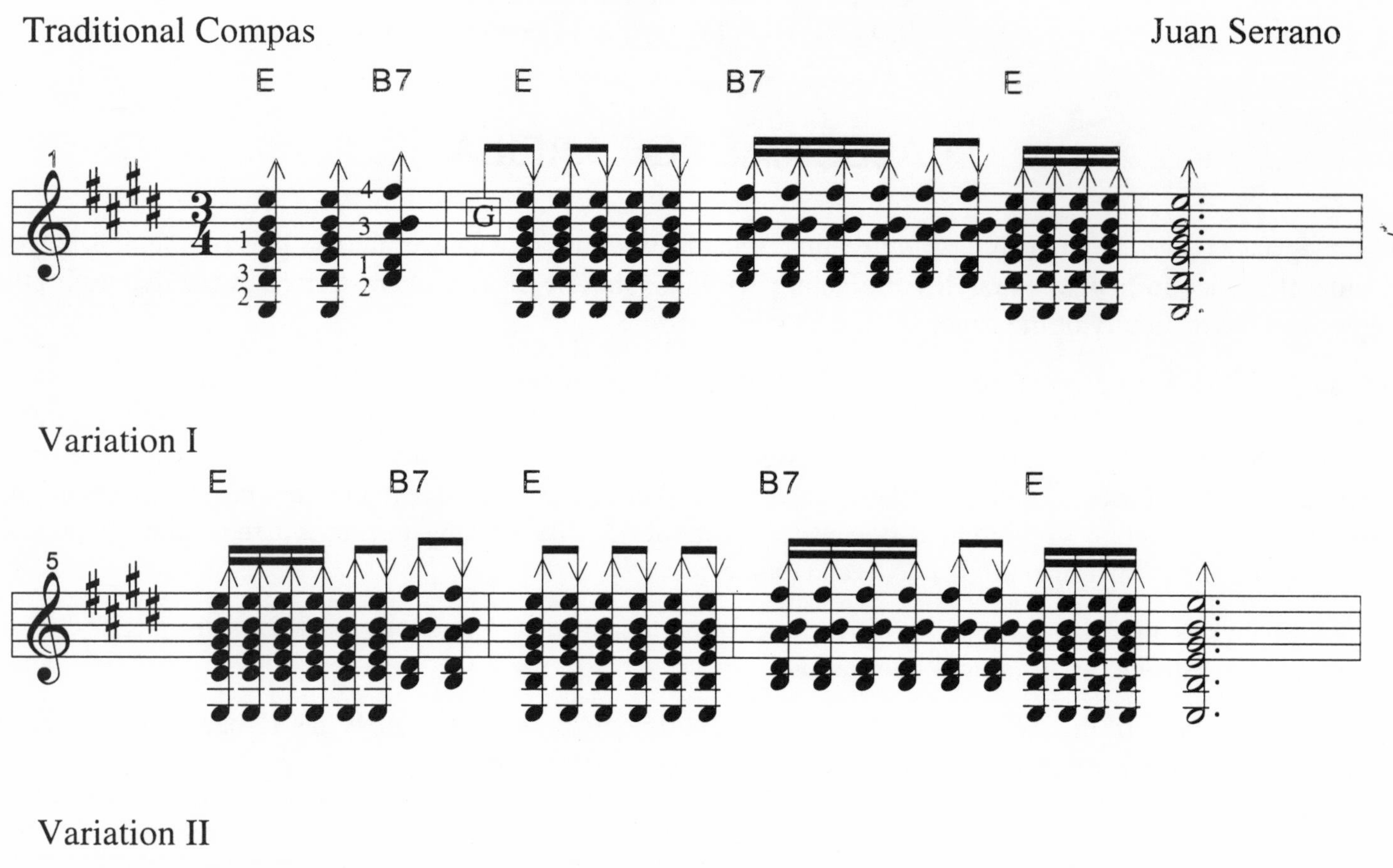


Variation I

Variation II

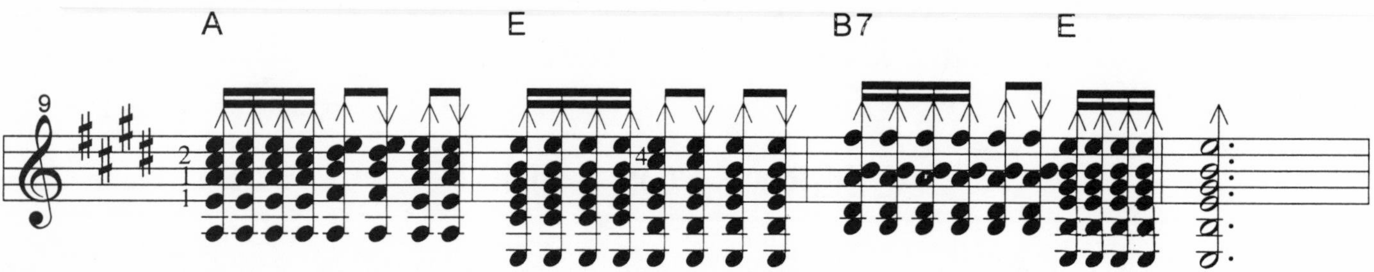


Variation III

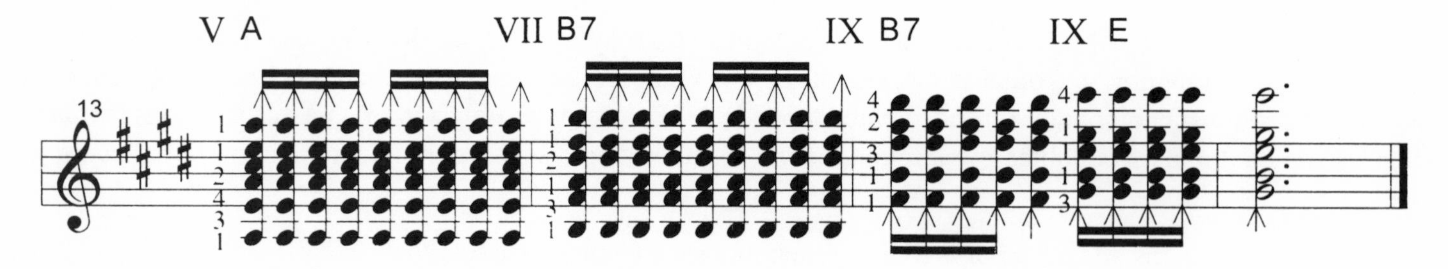

# *Alegrias Por Arriba*

Traditional Compas

Juan Serrano

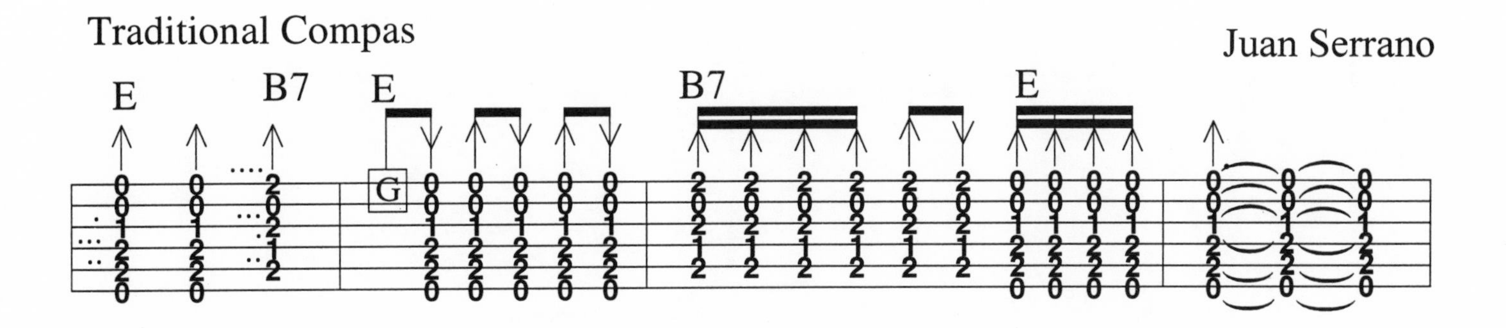


Variation I

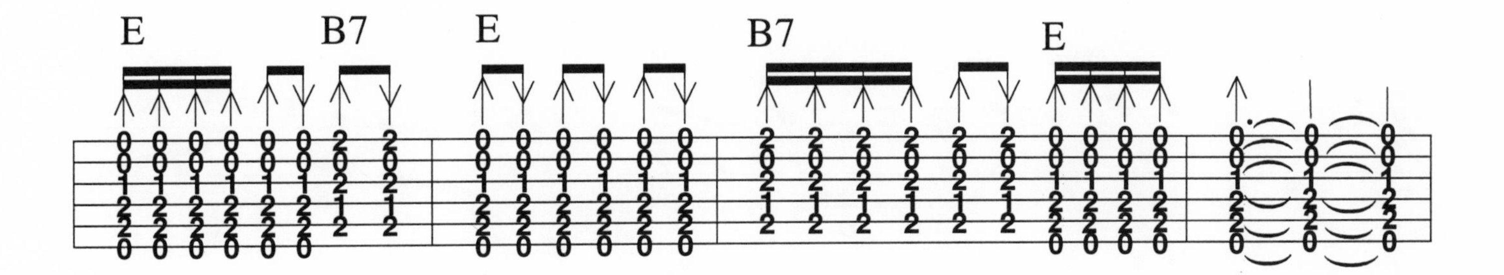


Variation II

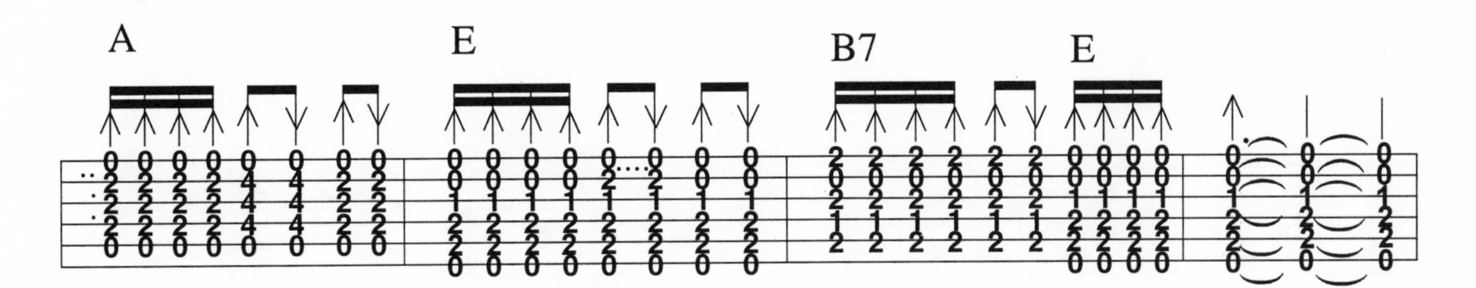


Variation III

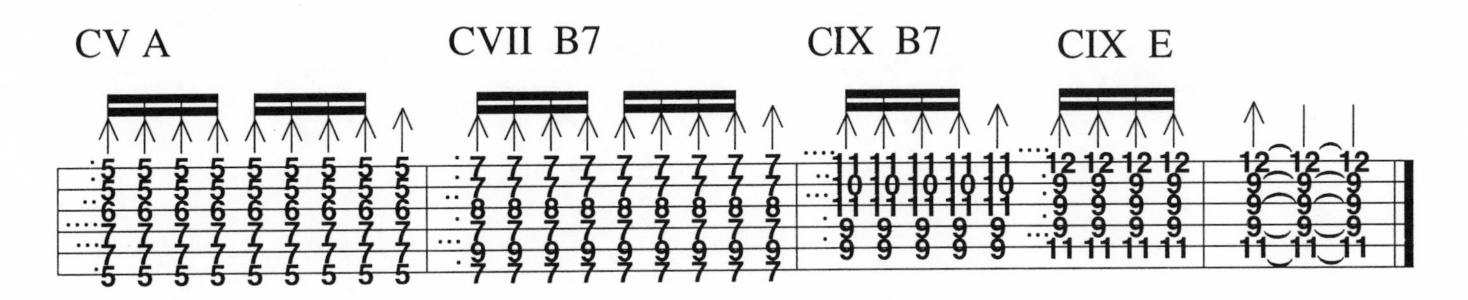

Falseta 1

Juan Serrano

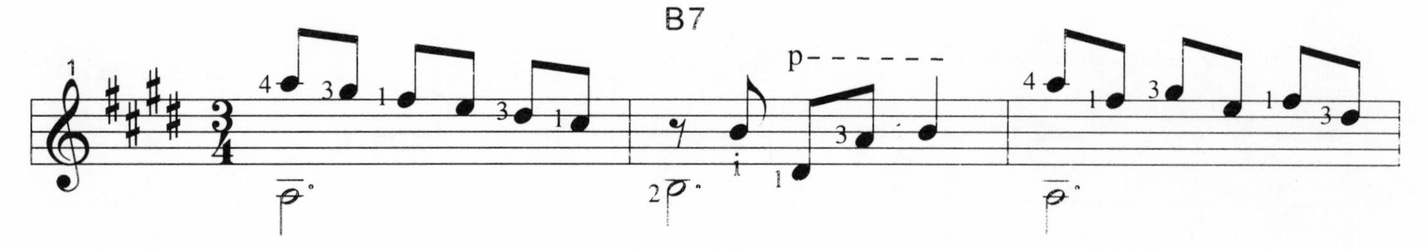


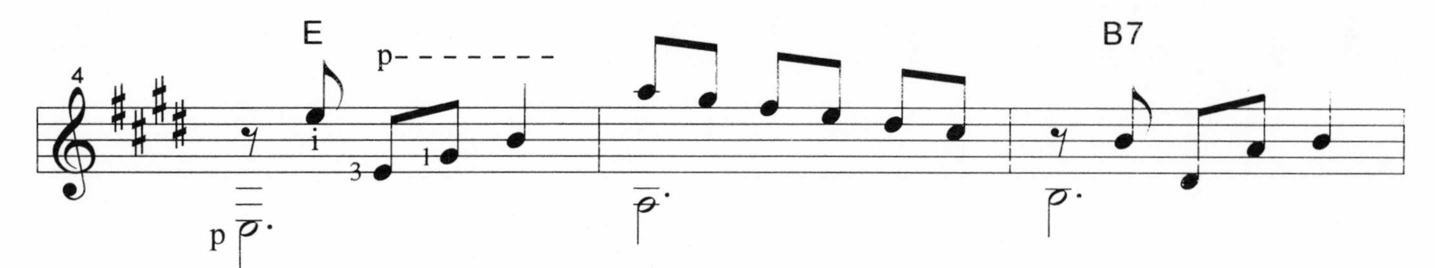

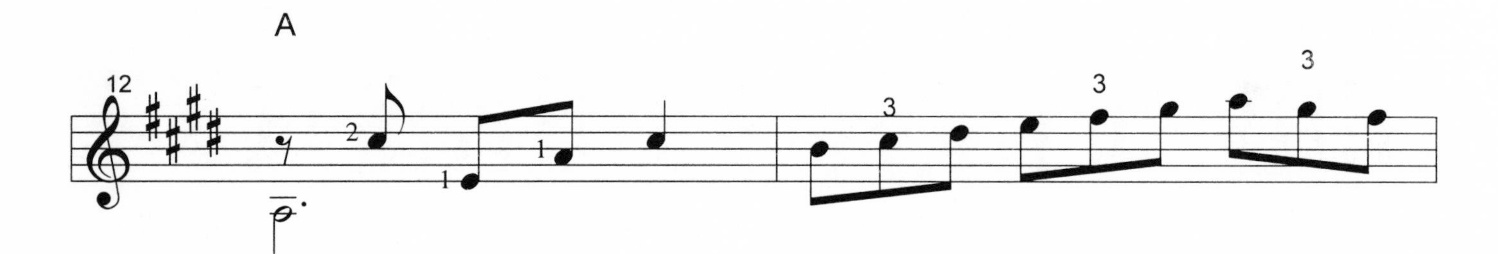


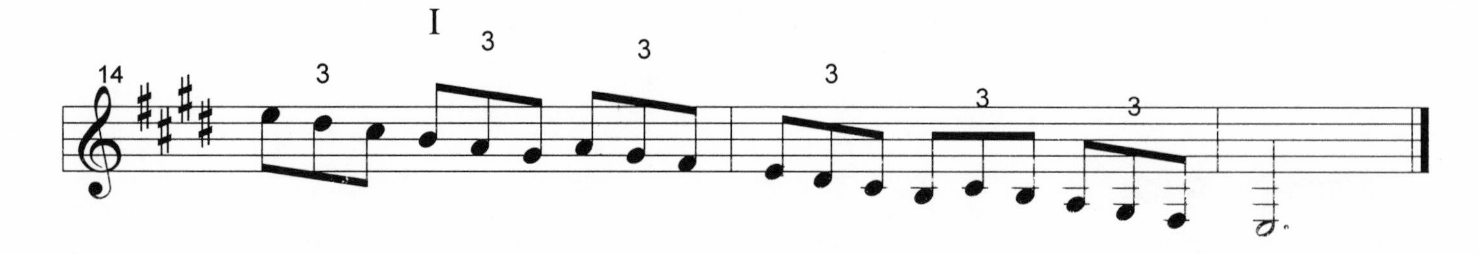

Falseta 1

Juan Serrano

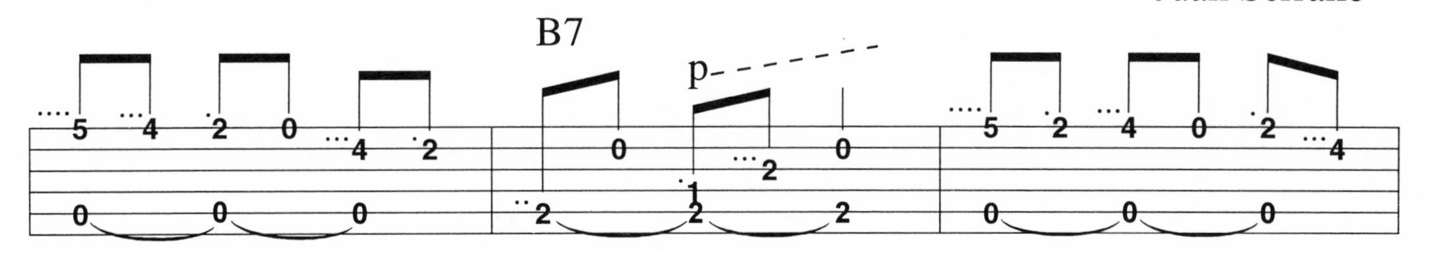


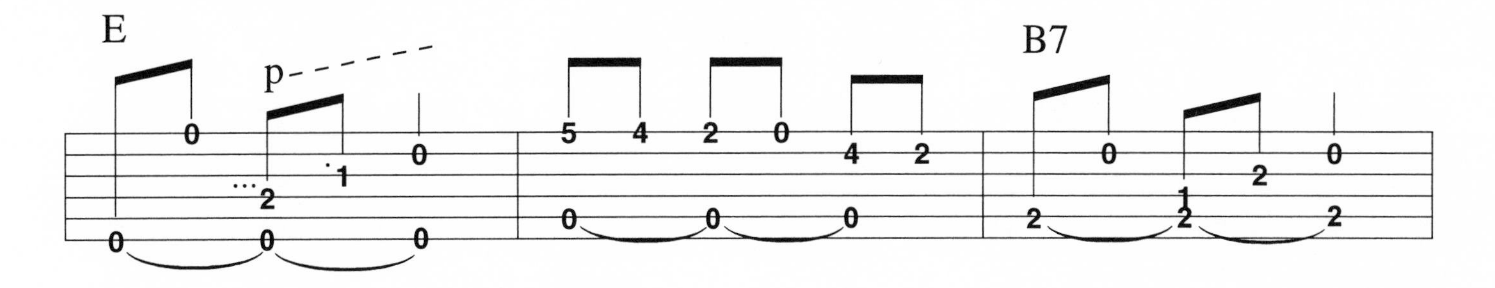


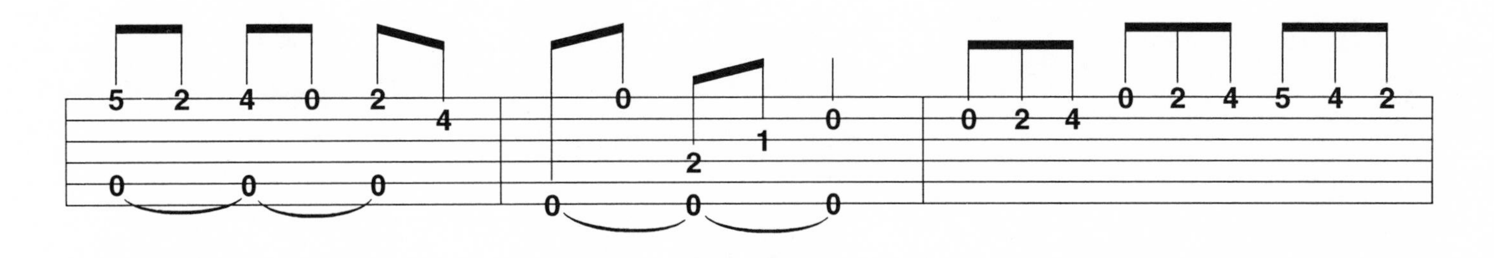

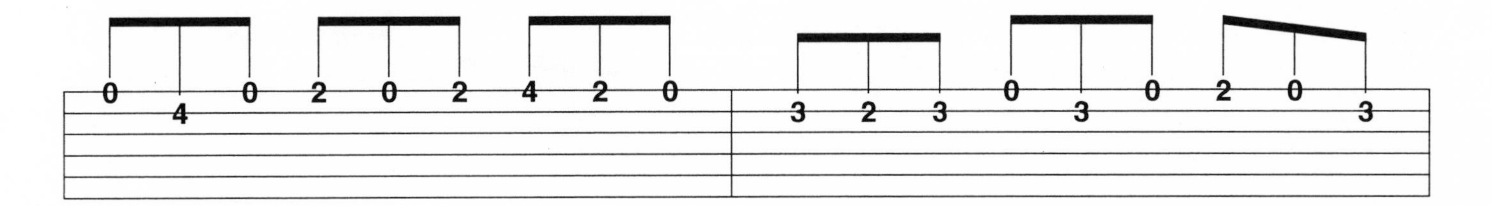

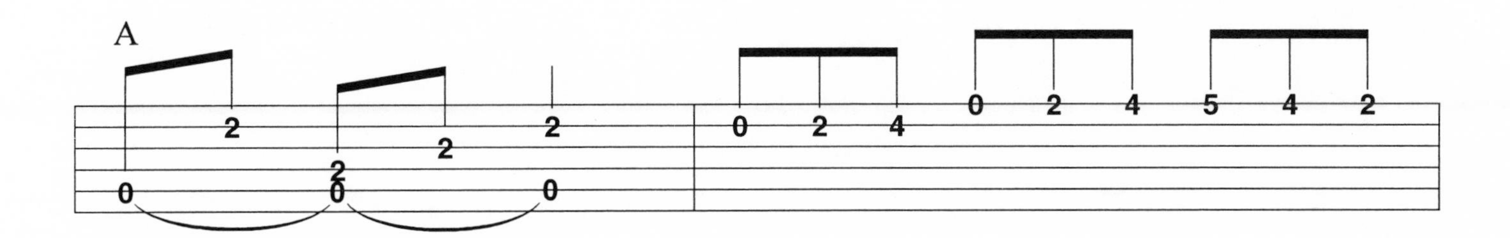


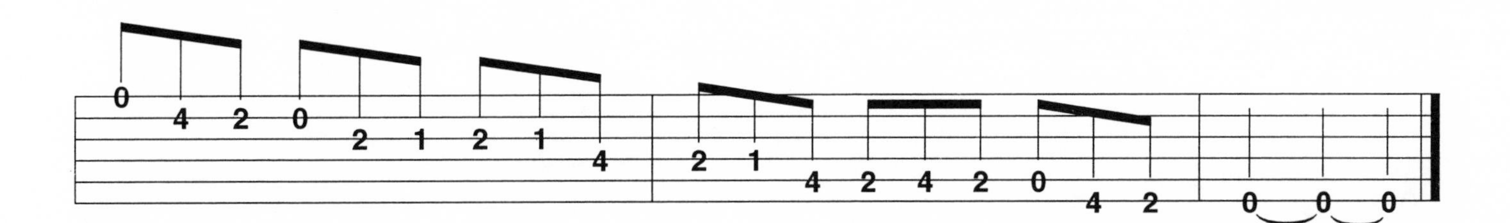

Falseta 2

Juan Serrano

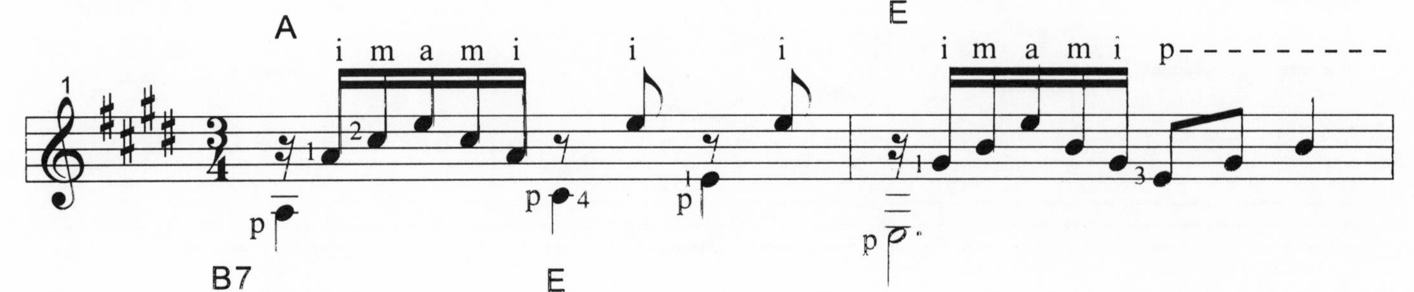

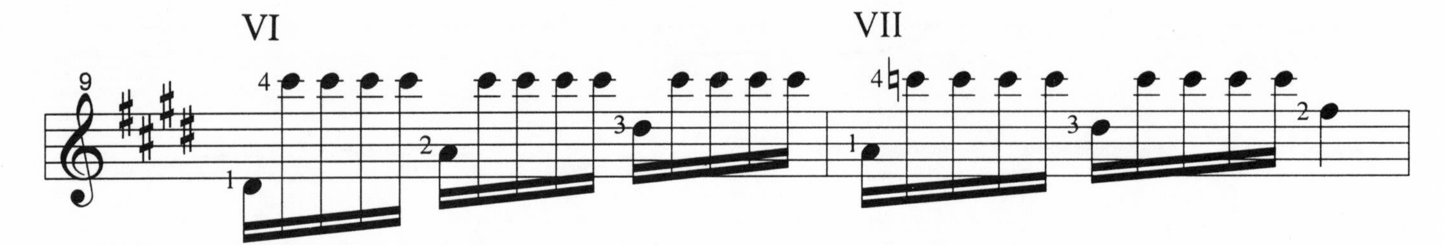

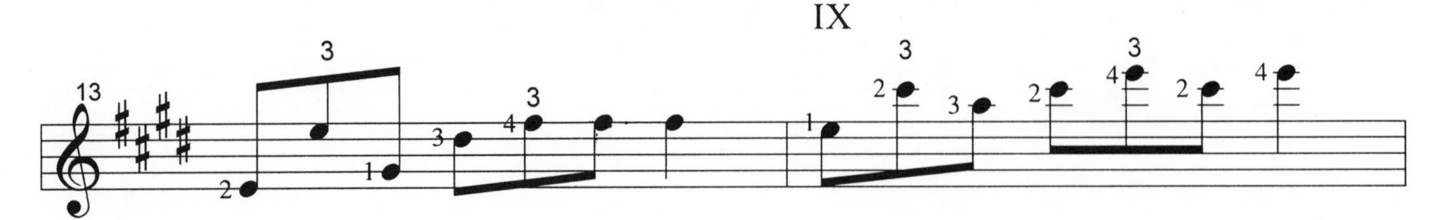


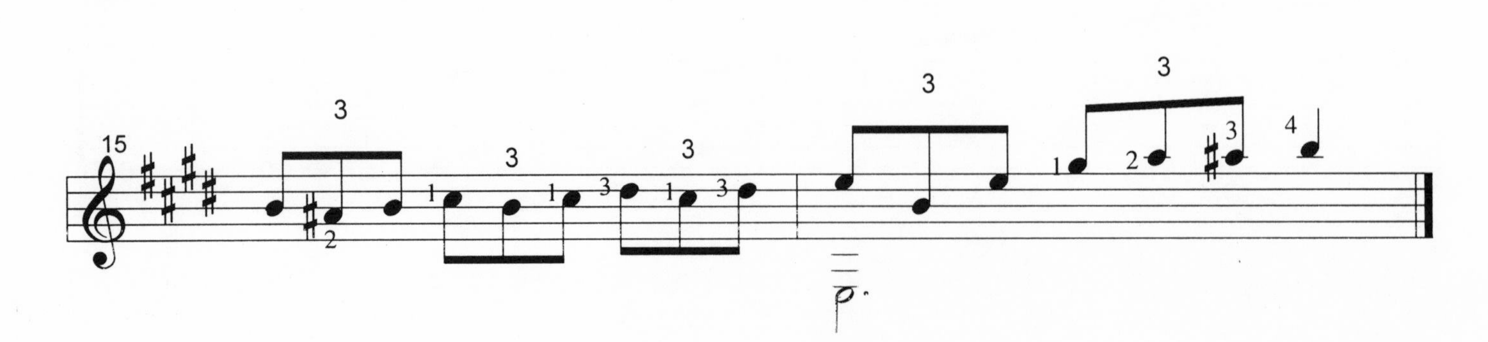

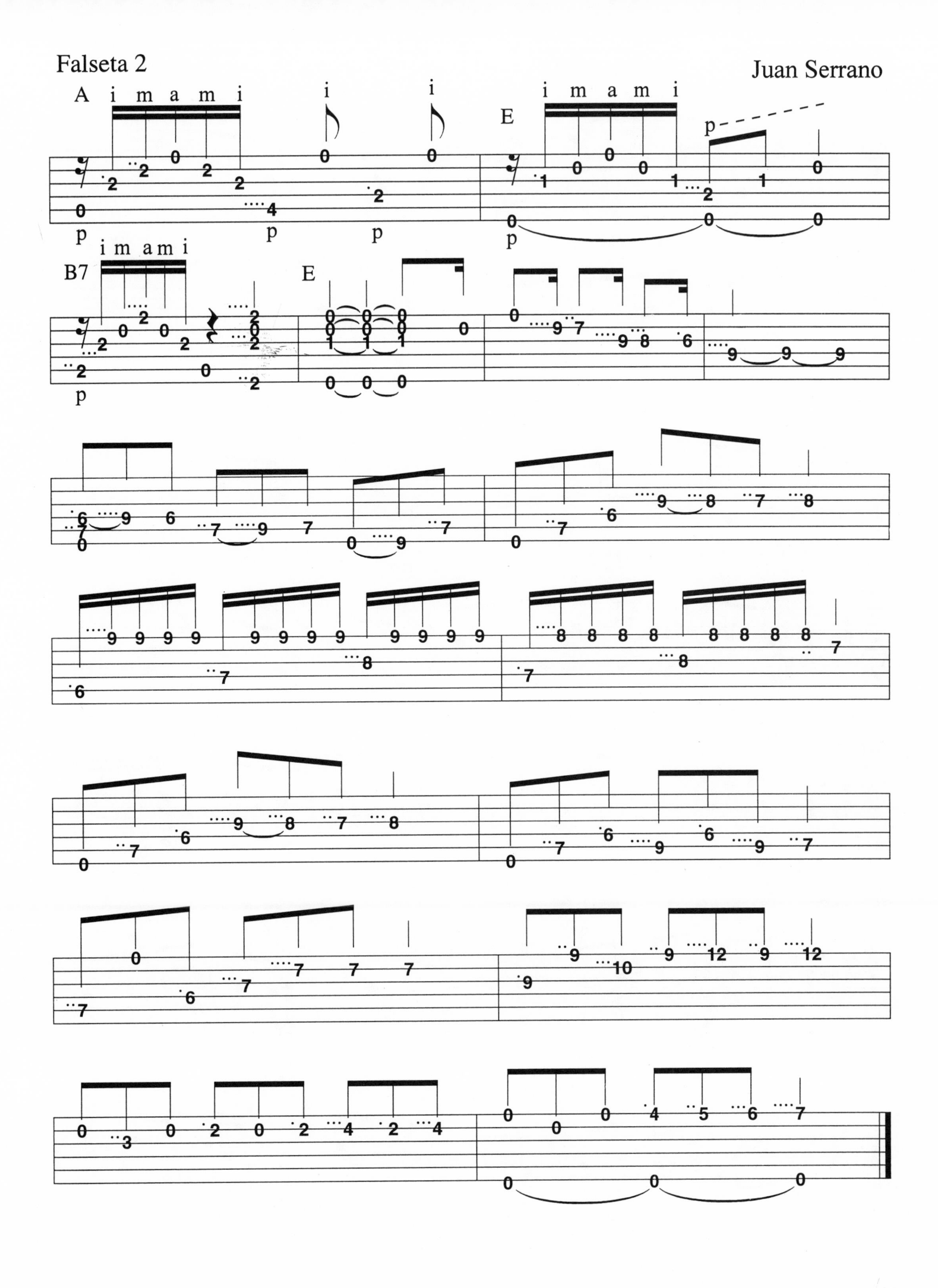
Falseta 2
Juan Serrano
A
i m a m i
i
i
p
p
p
E
i m a m i
p
p
B7
i m a m i
p
E

Falseta 3 Juan Serrano

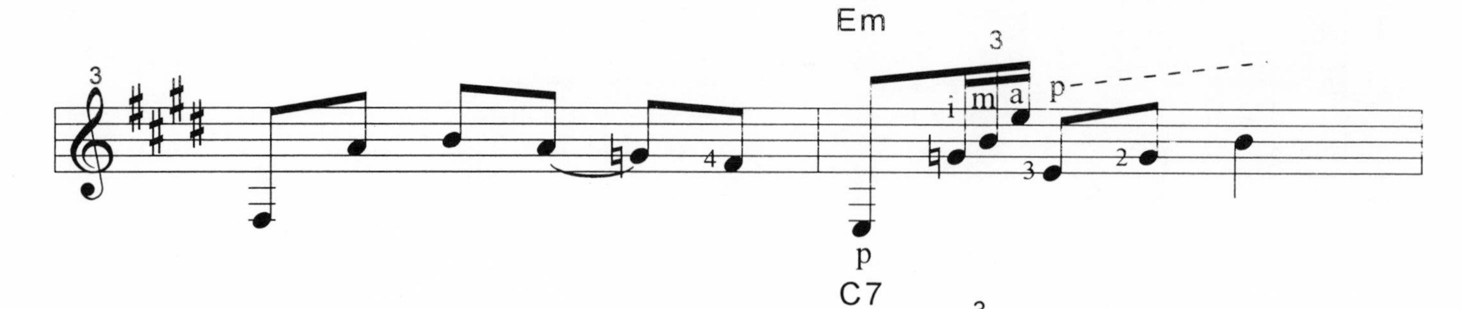


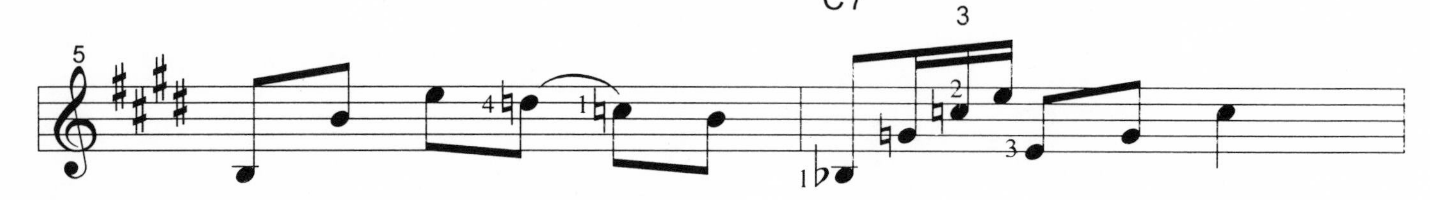


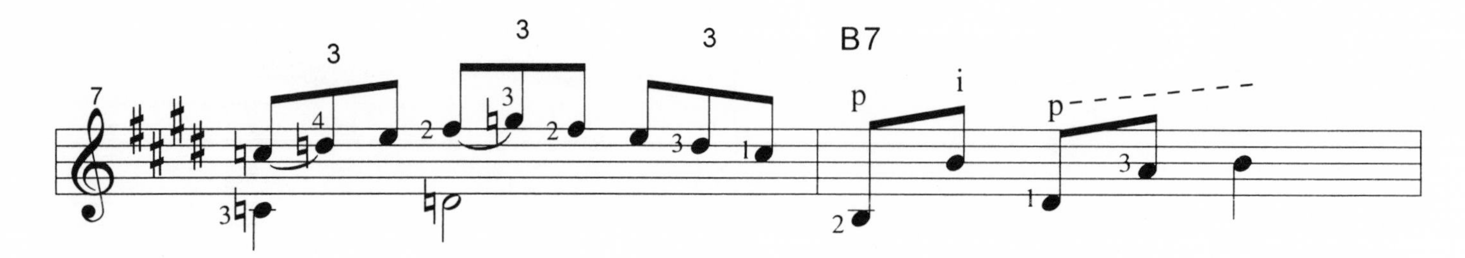


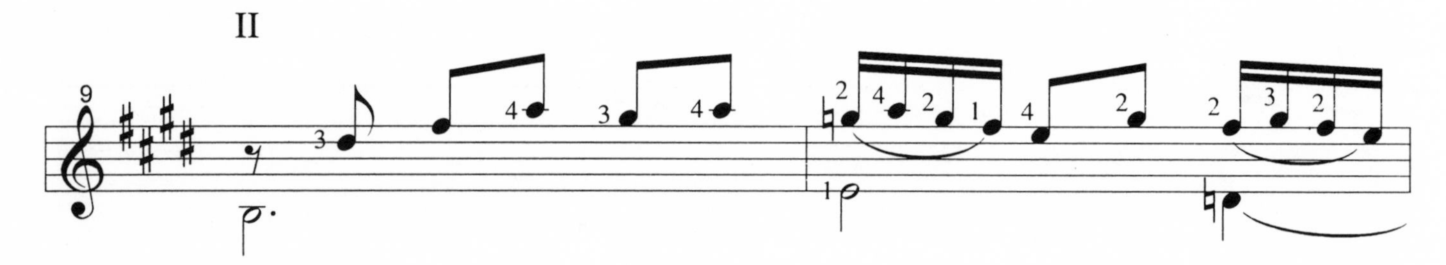


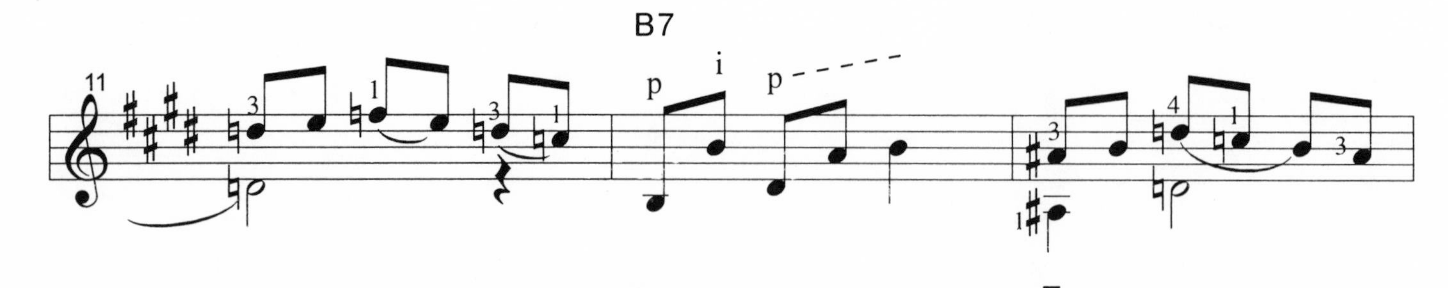

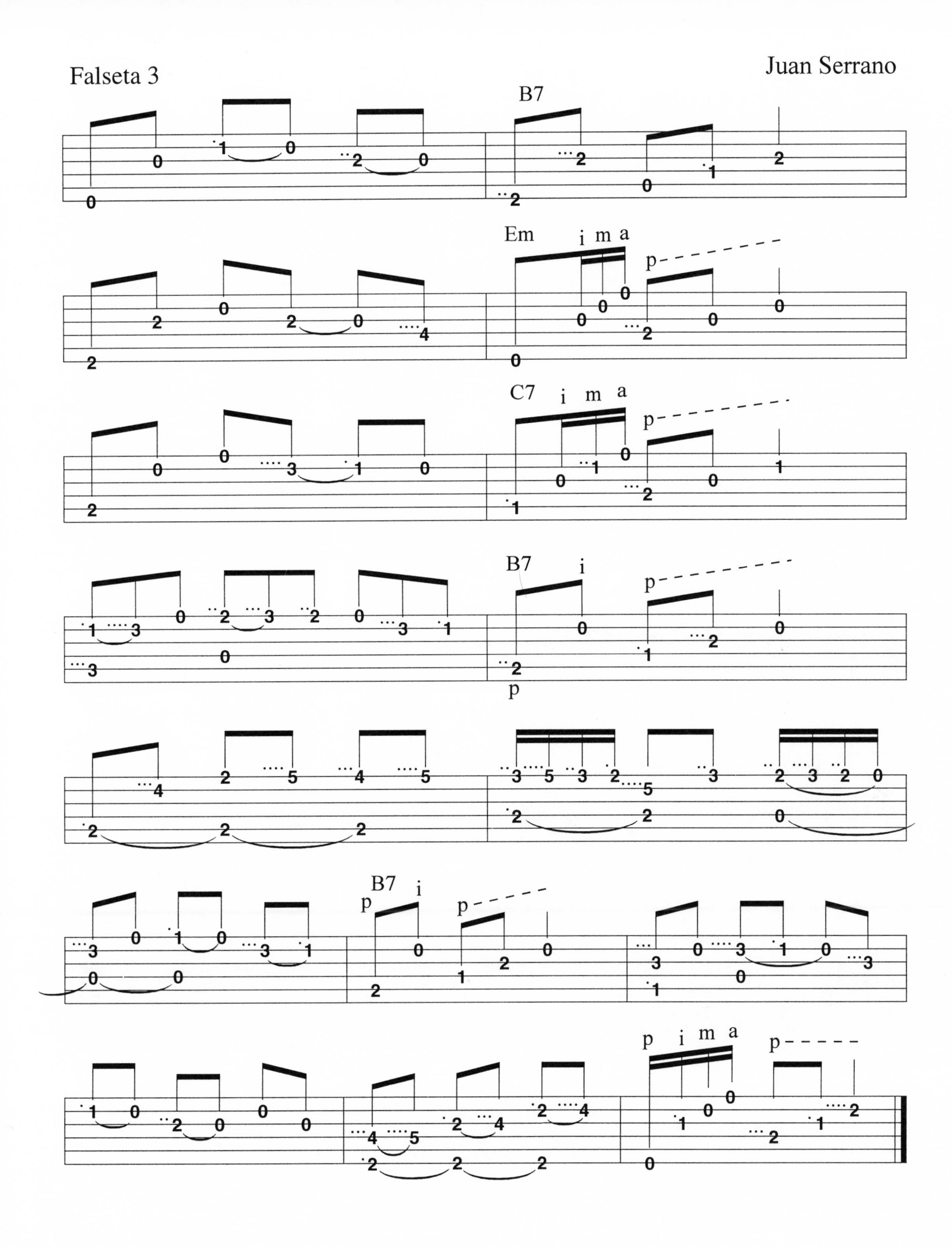
Falseta 3
Juan Serrano
B7
Em
i m a
p
C7
i m a
p
B7
i
p
p
B7
p
i
p
p i m a
p

Falseta 4

Juan Serrano

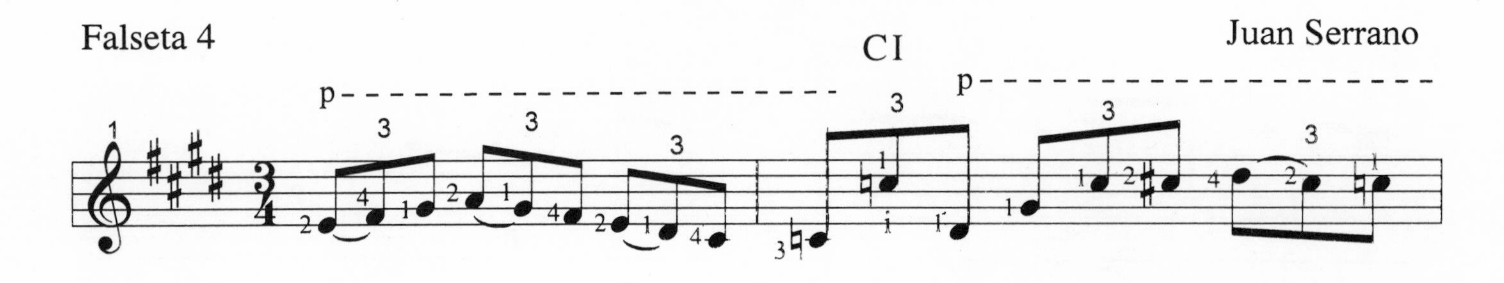

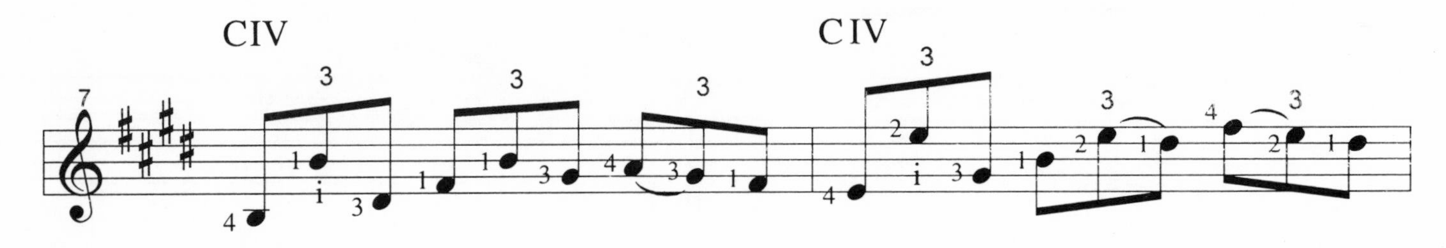

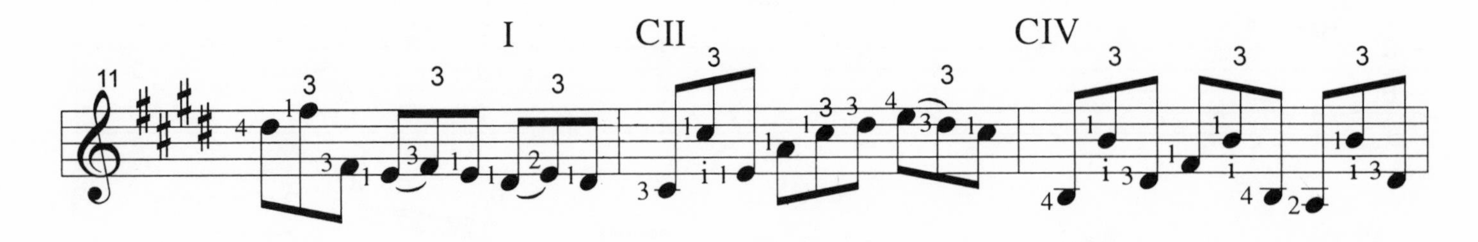


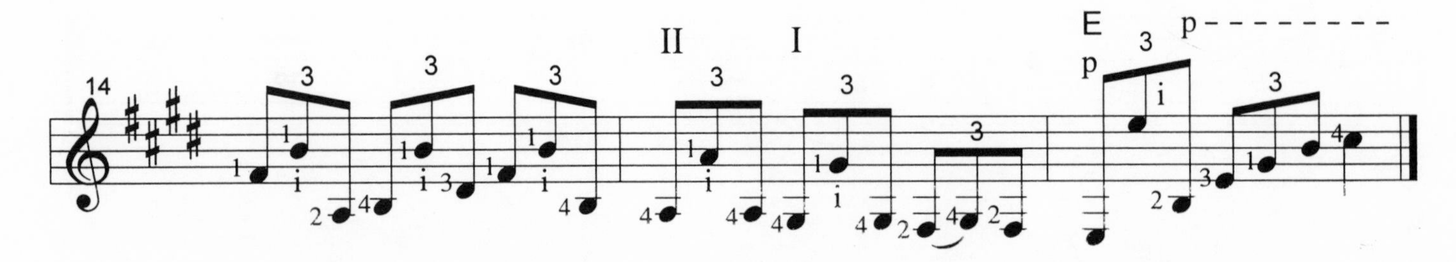

Falseta 4 Juan Serrano

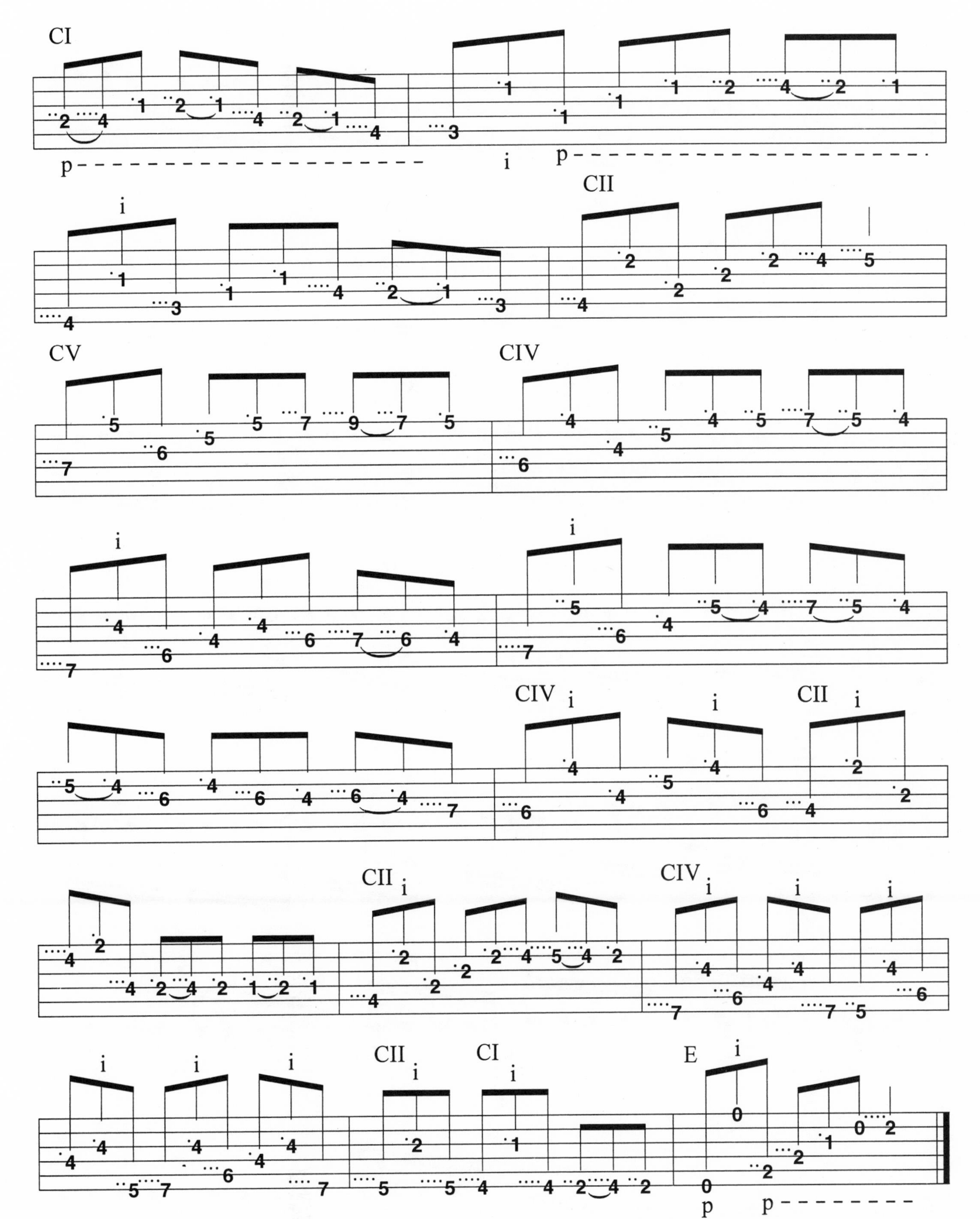

Falseta 5 (Tremolo) Juan Serrano

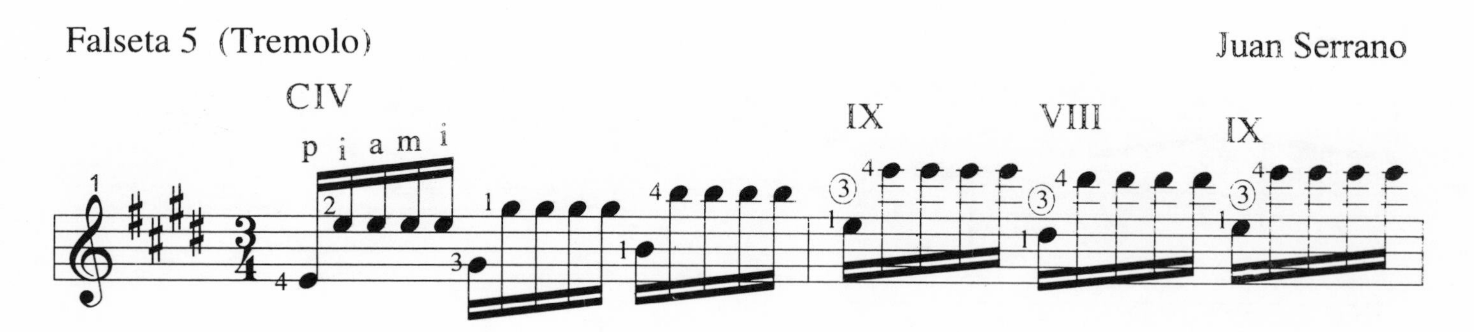


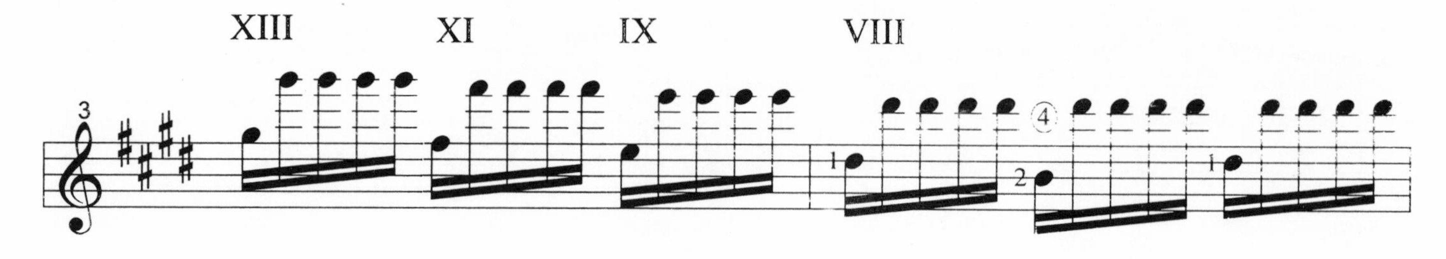

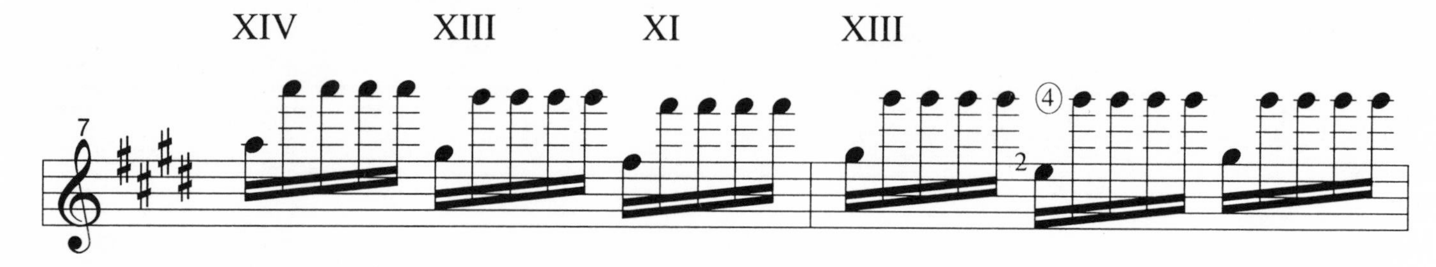


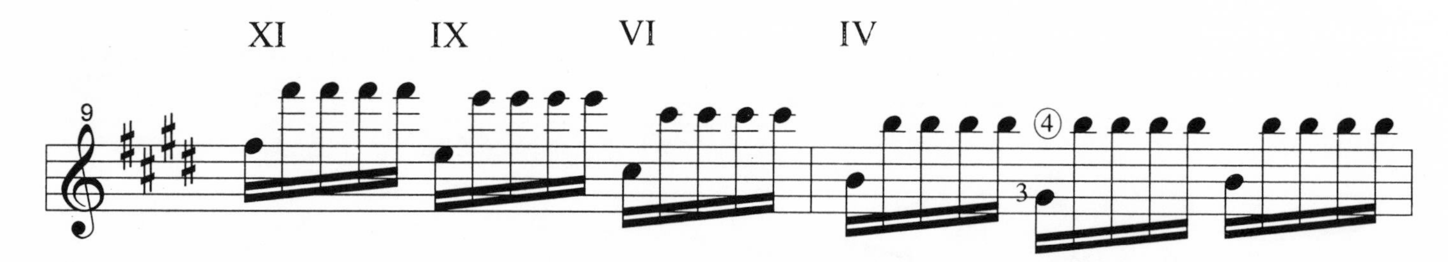


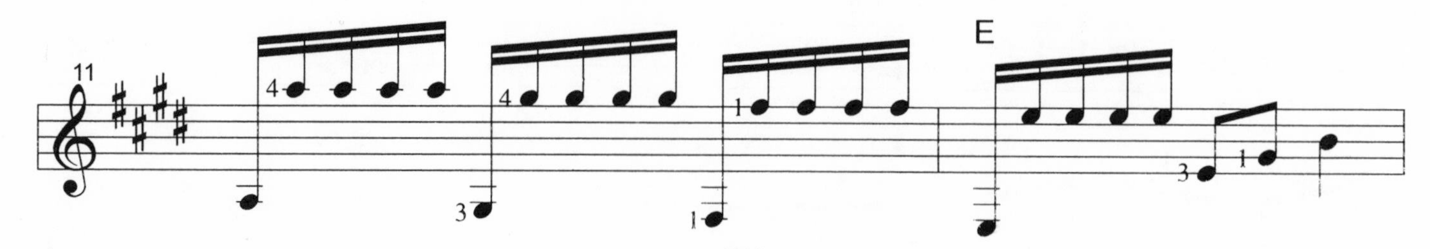


IV

15
IX
XIII
IX
VIII
④

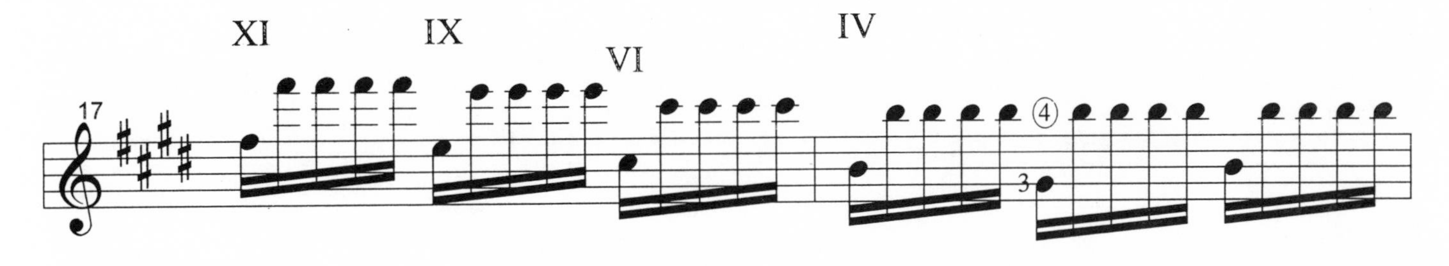
17
XI
IX
VI
IV
④

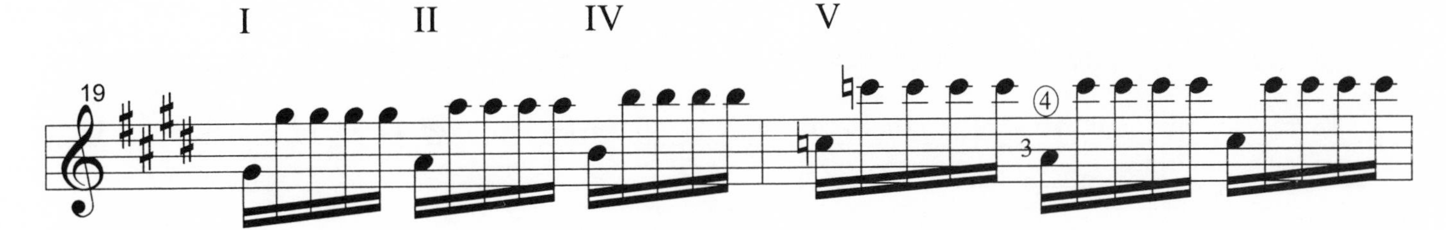
19
I
II
IV
V
④

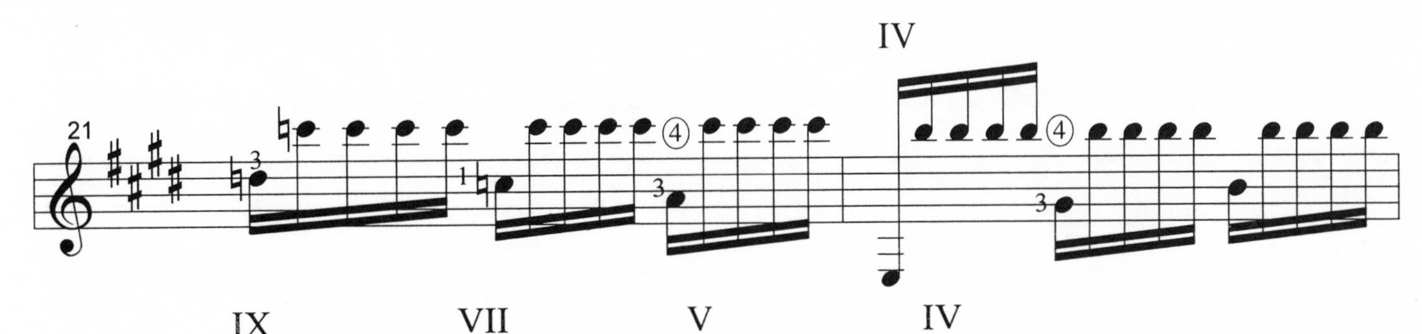
21
IV
④
④

23
IX
VII
V
IV
④

25

27
CII
E

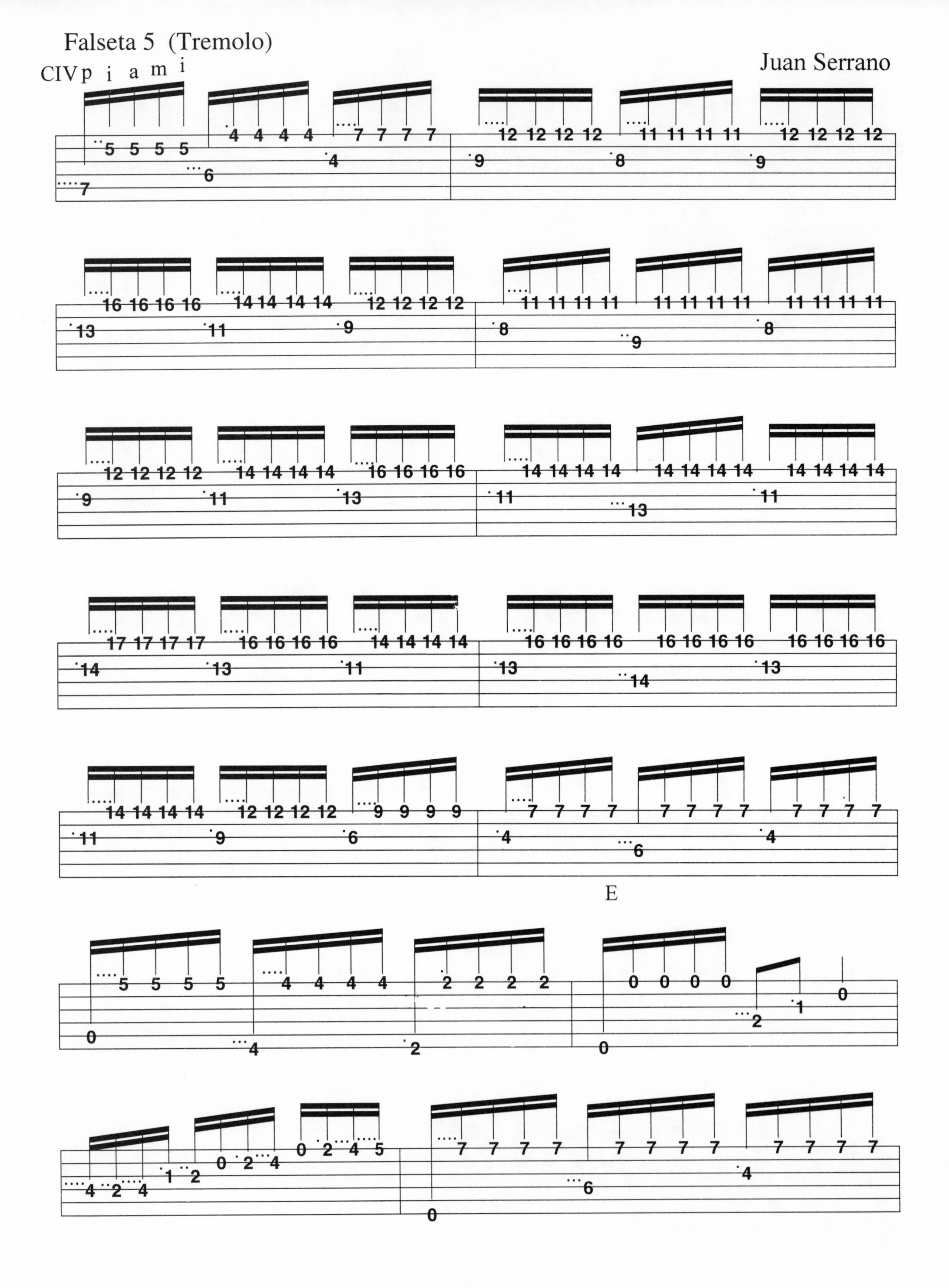
Falseta 5 (Tremolo)
Juan Serrano
CIV p i a m i
E

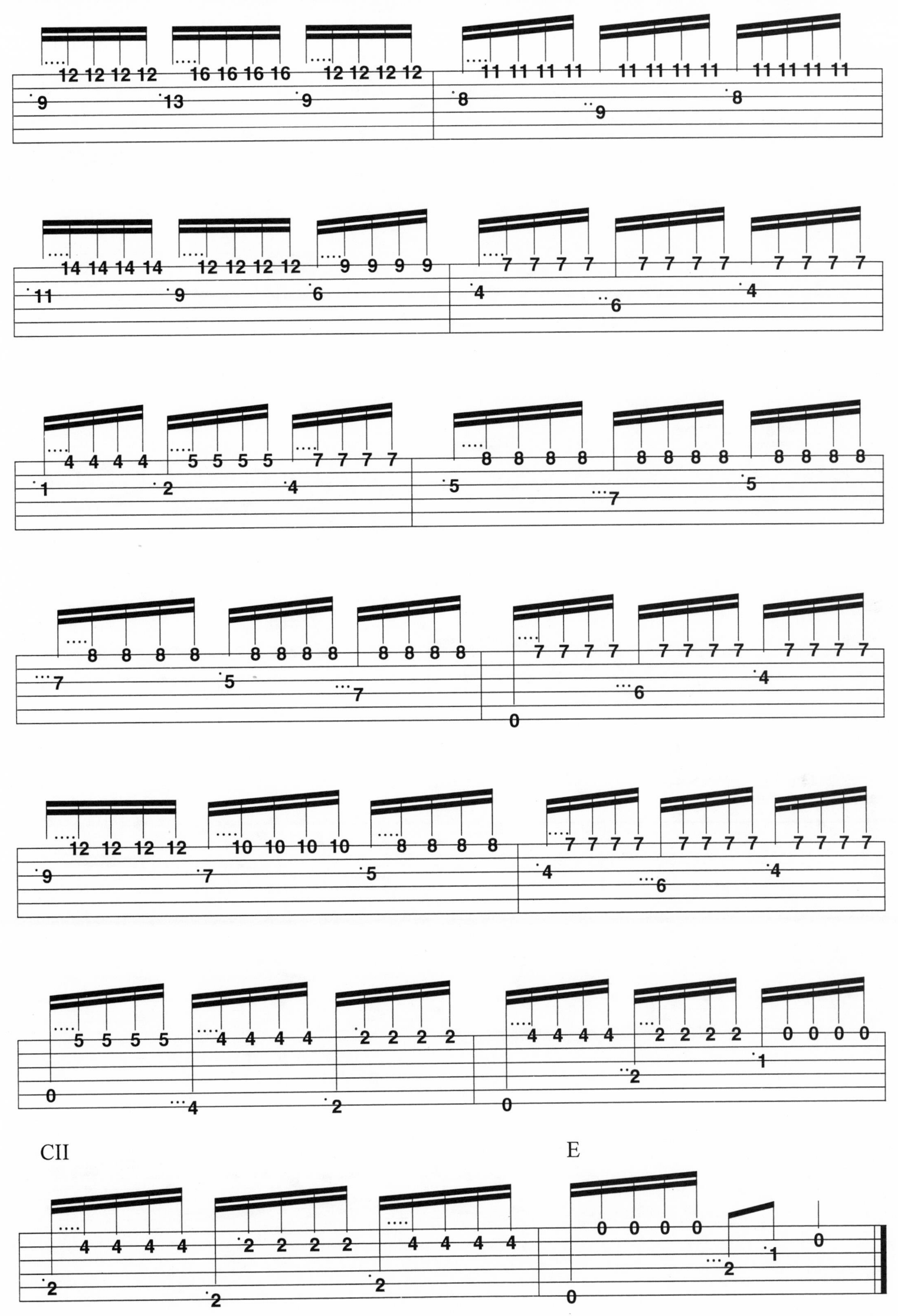
CII
E

## Falseta 6

Juan Serrano

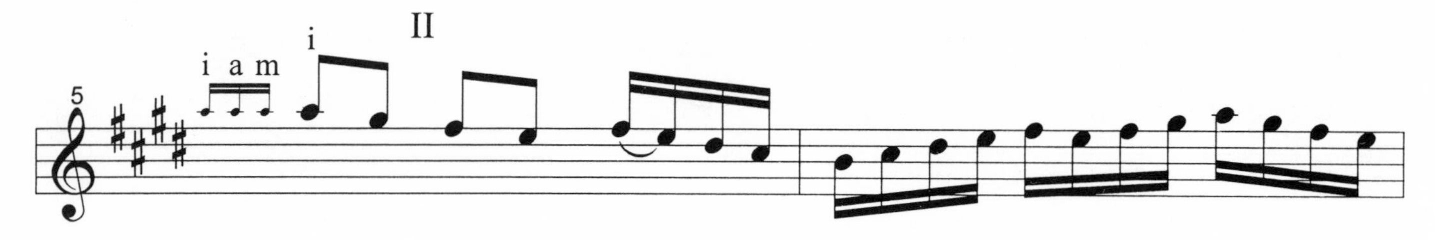

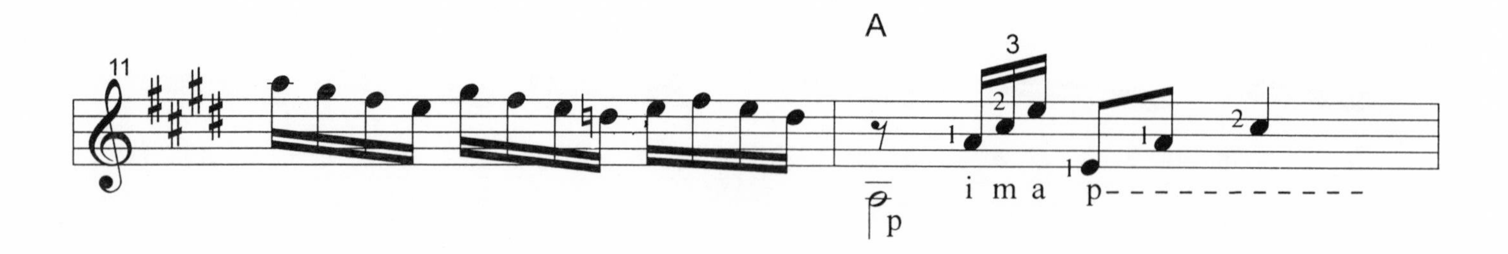

15
I
p
I
II
IV
17
p
p
19
B7
E
i m a p

## Falseta 6

Juan Serrano

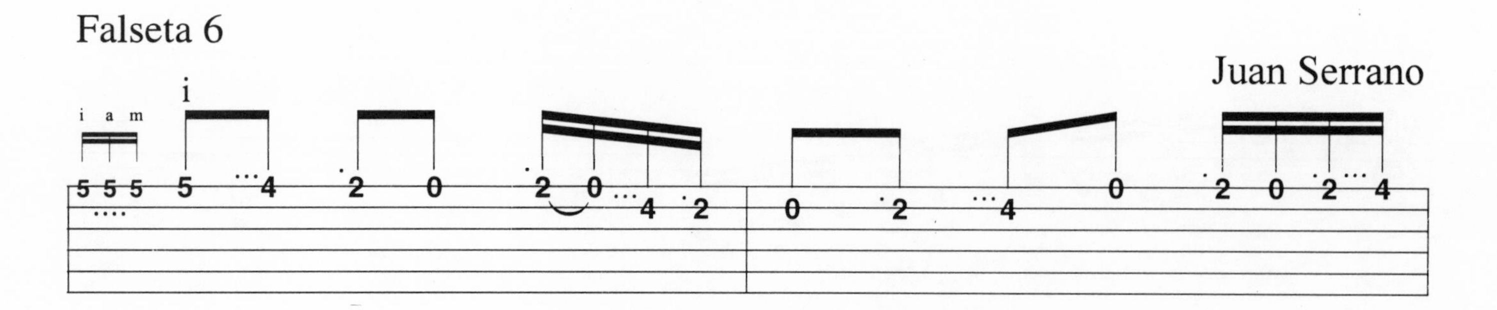


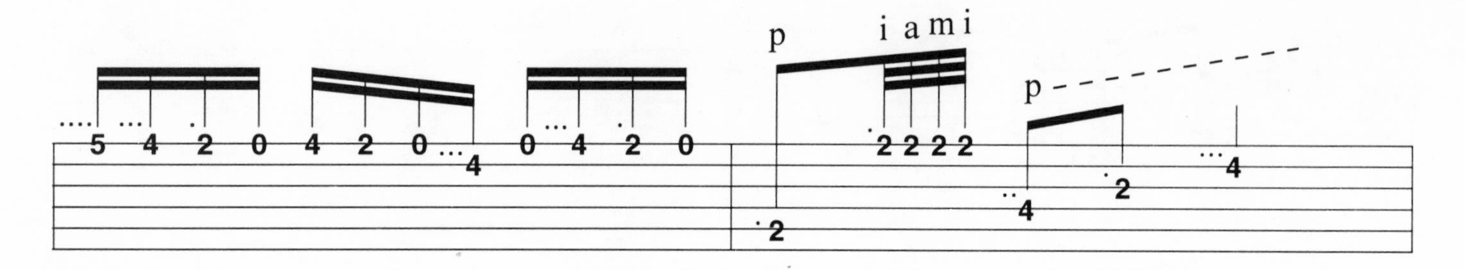


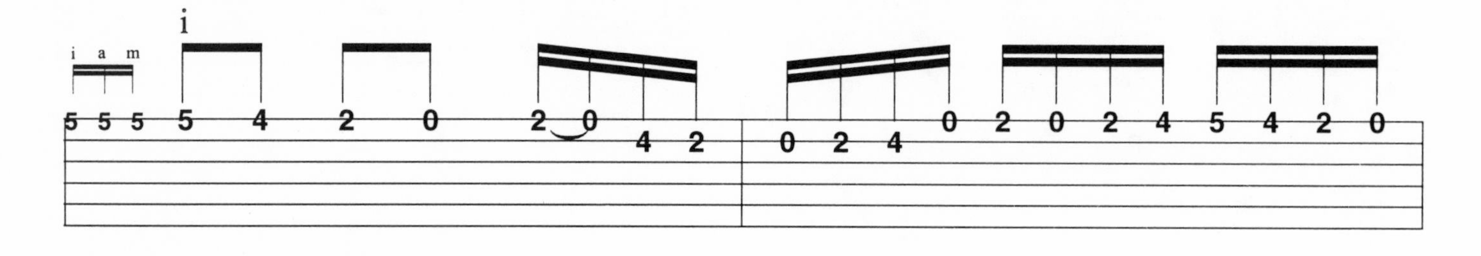


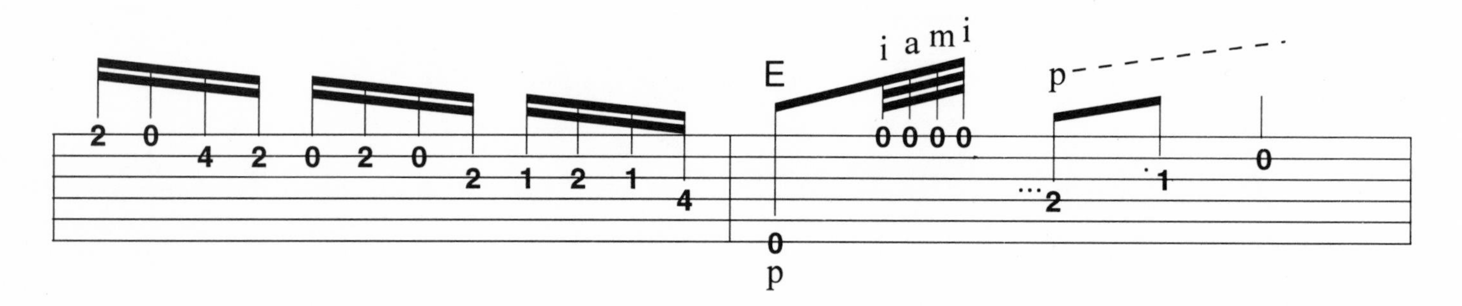


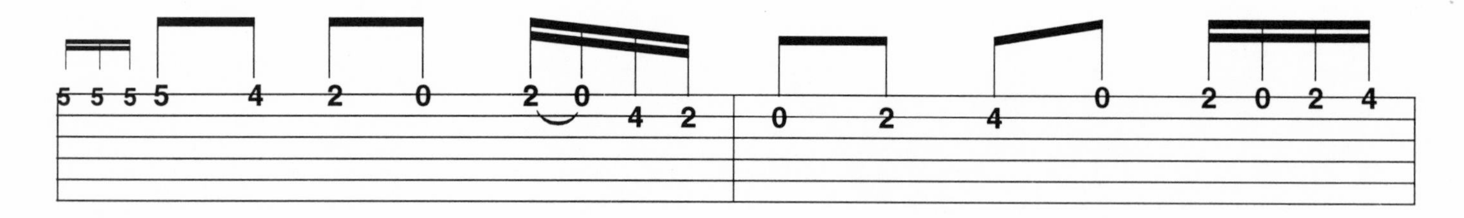

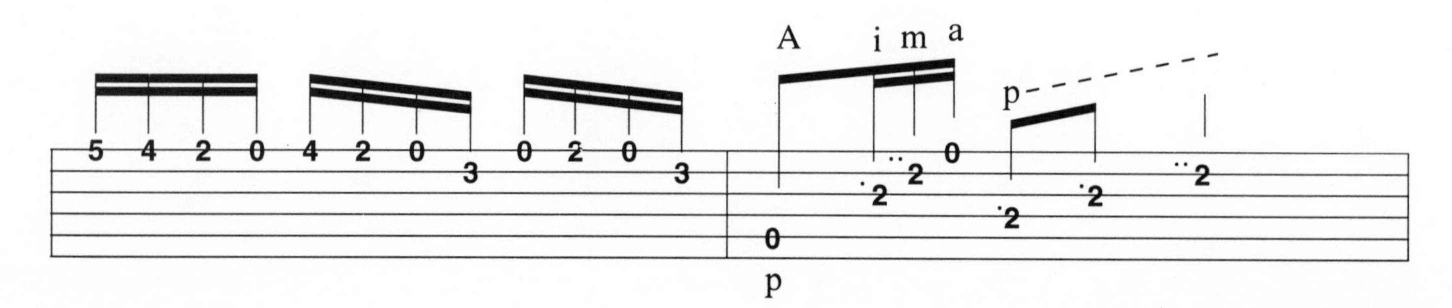

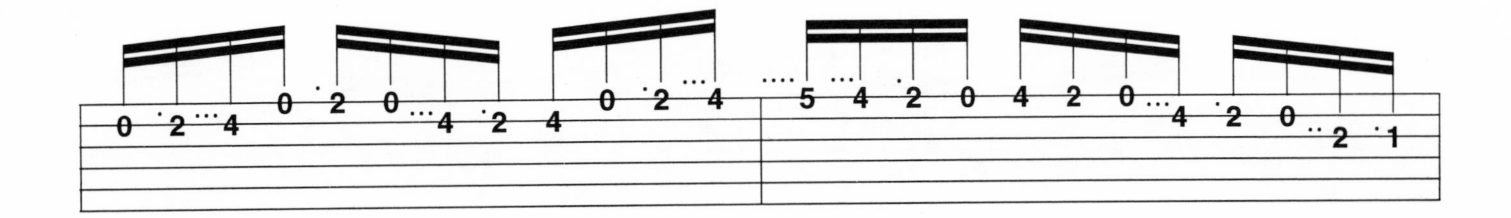

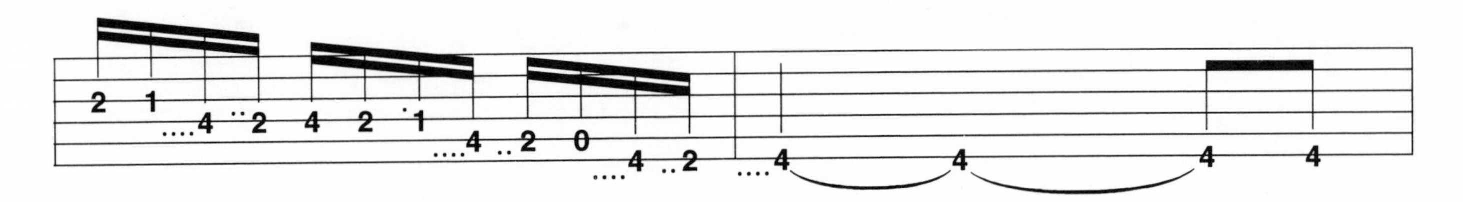

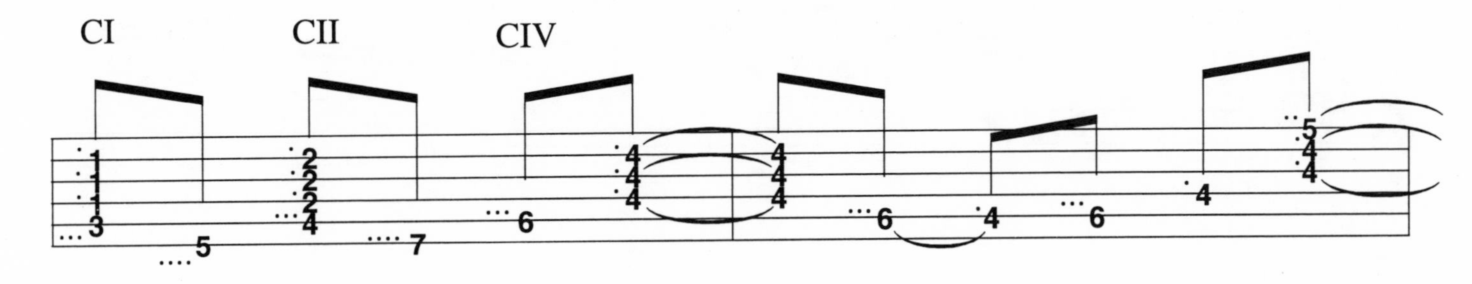
CI
CII
CIV

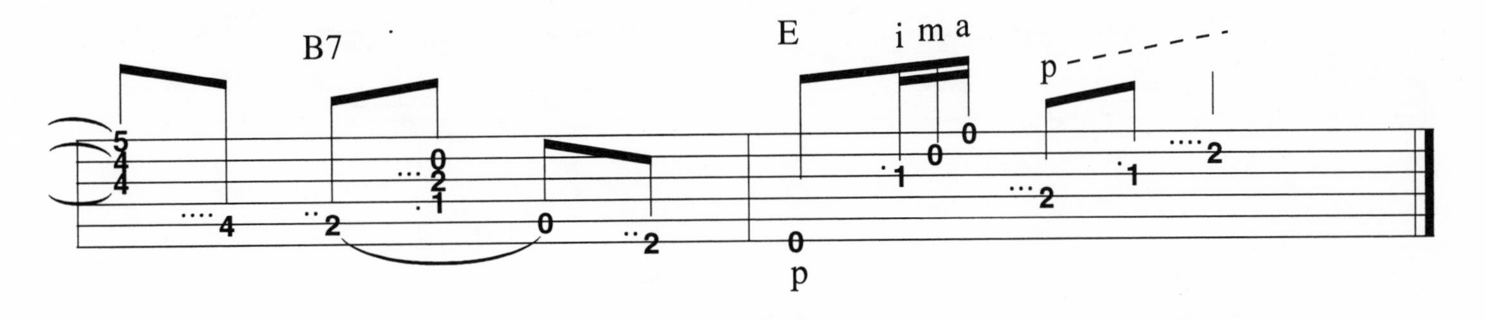
B7
E
i m a
p
p

## Falseta 7

Juan Serrano

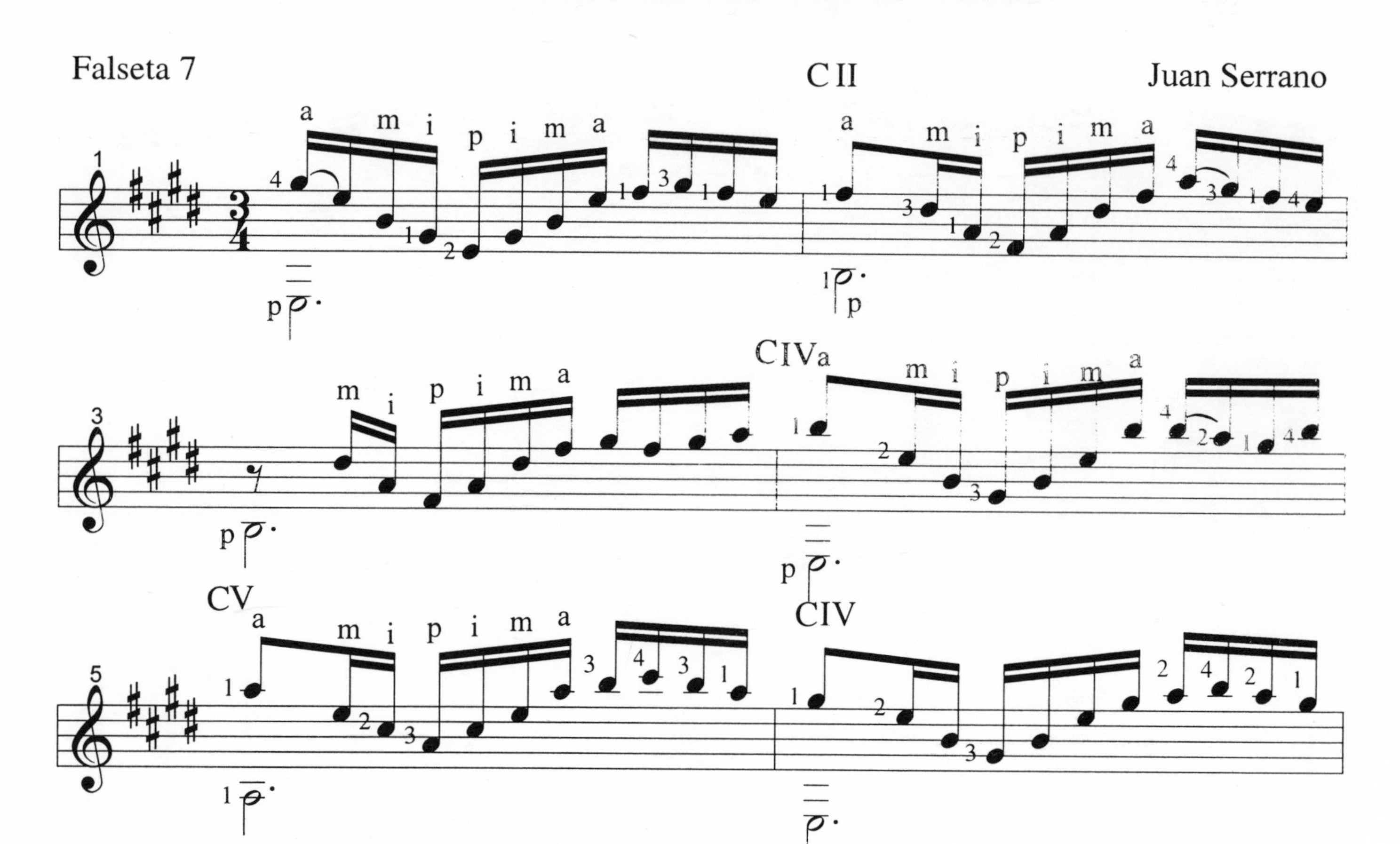


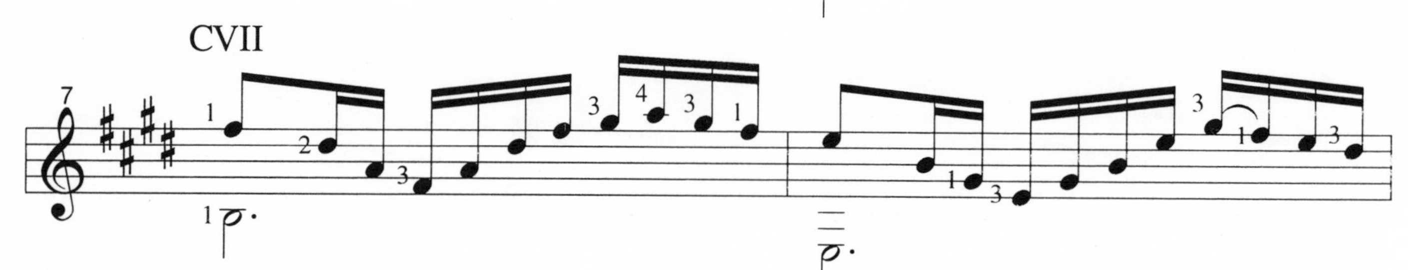

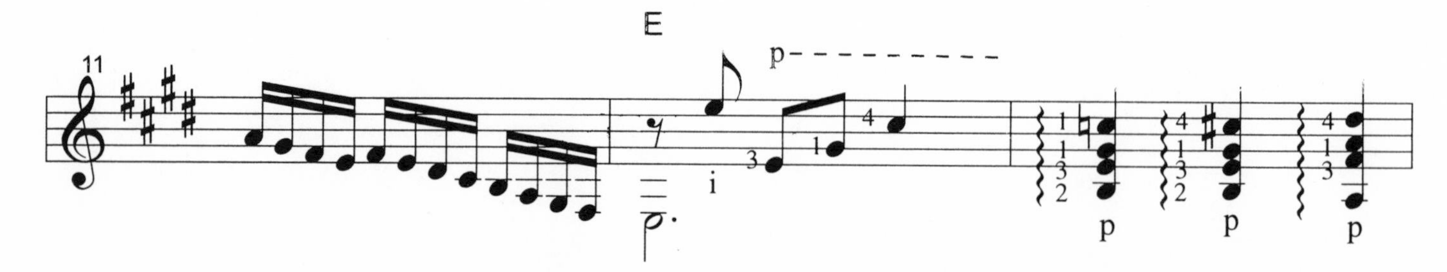


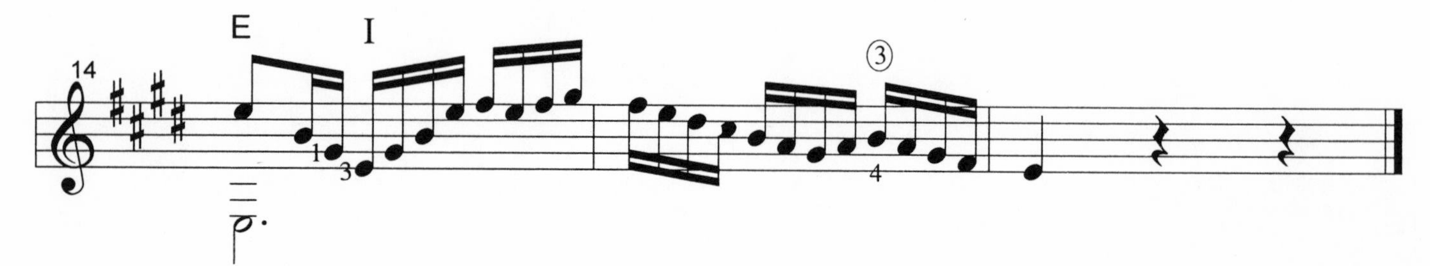

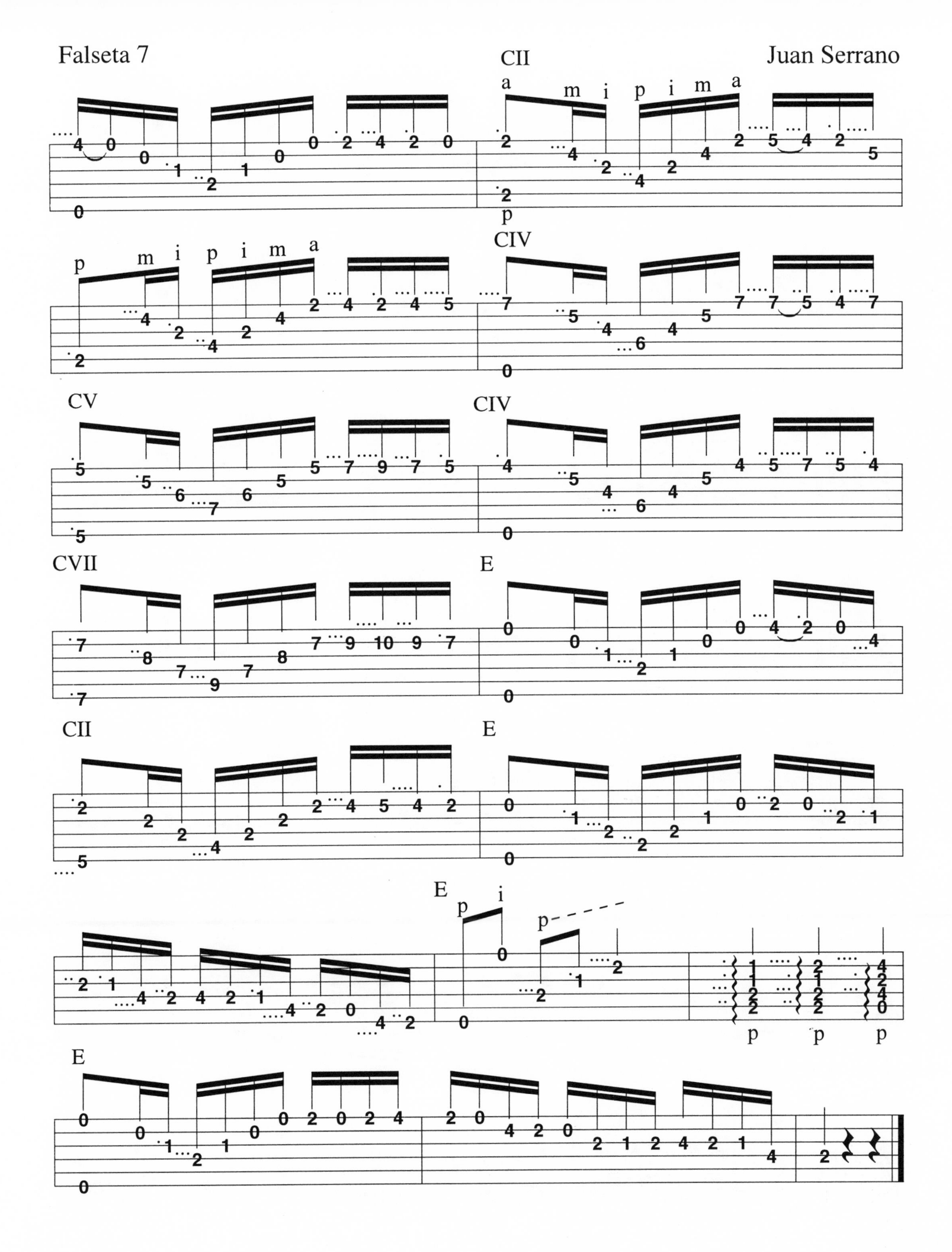
Falseta 7
Juan Serrano
CII
CIV
CV
CIV
CVII
E
CII
E
E
E

## Falseta 8

Juan Serrano

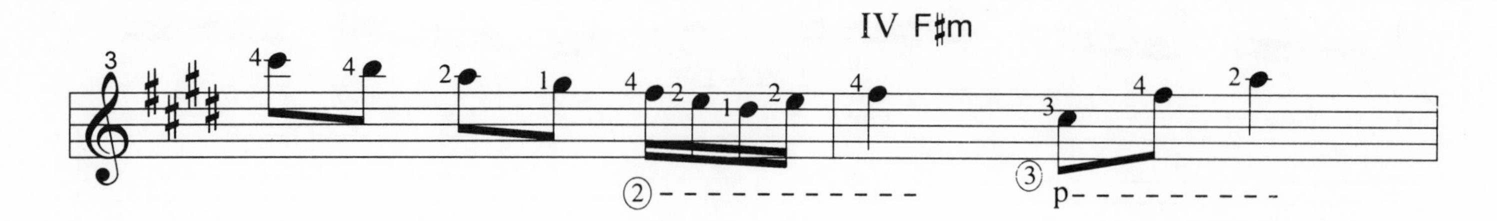


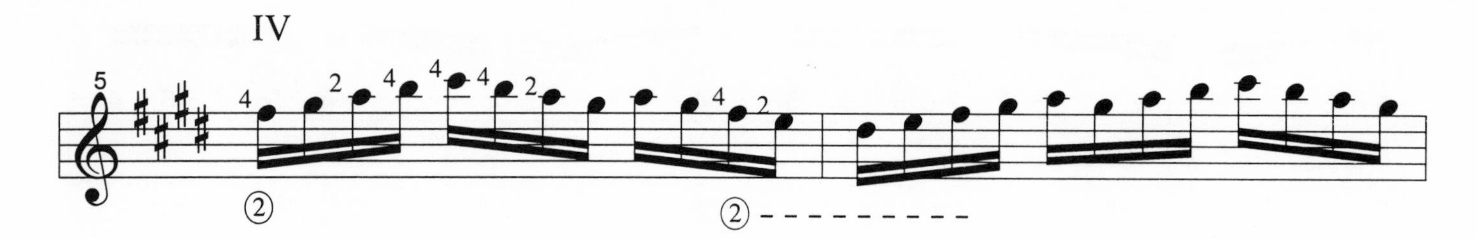

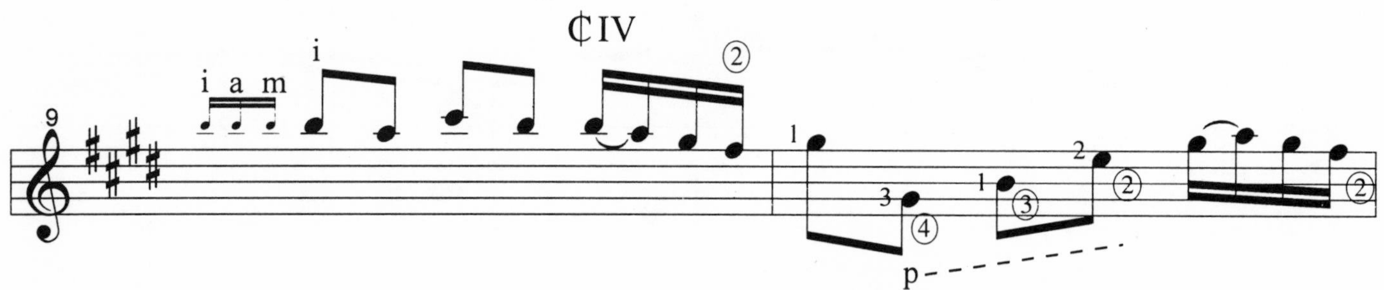

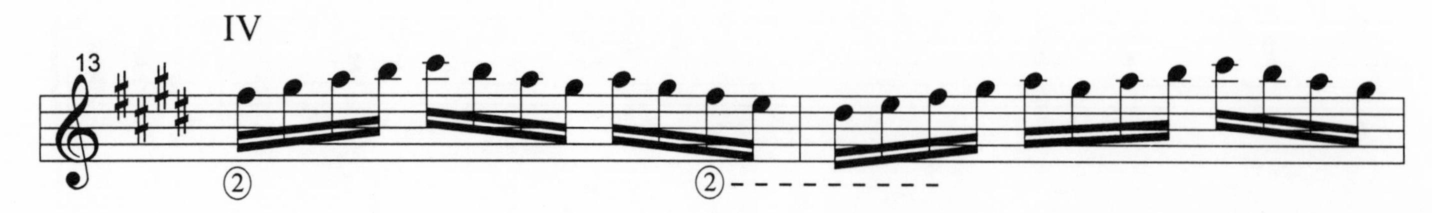

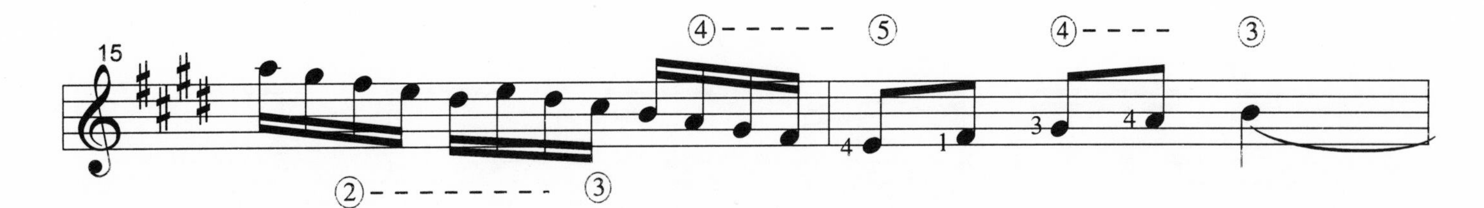
15

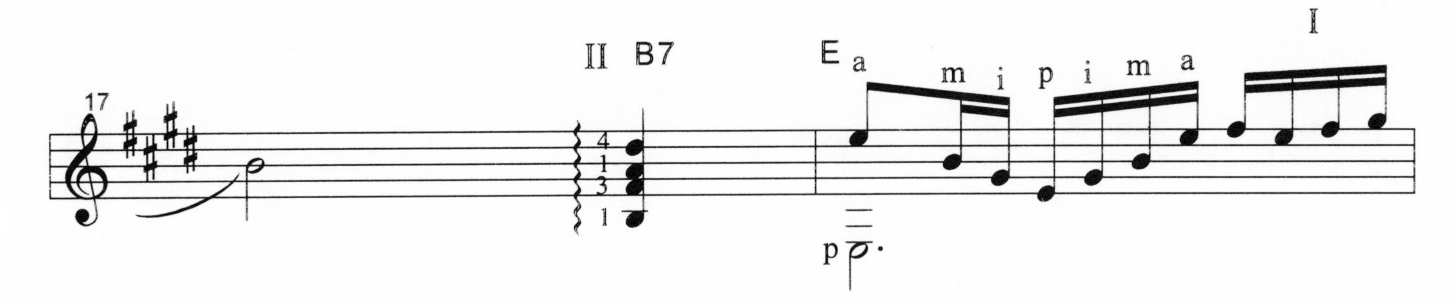
17
II B7
E
a m i p i m a
I
p

19
I

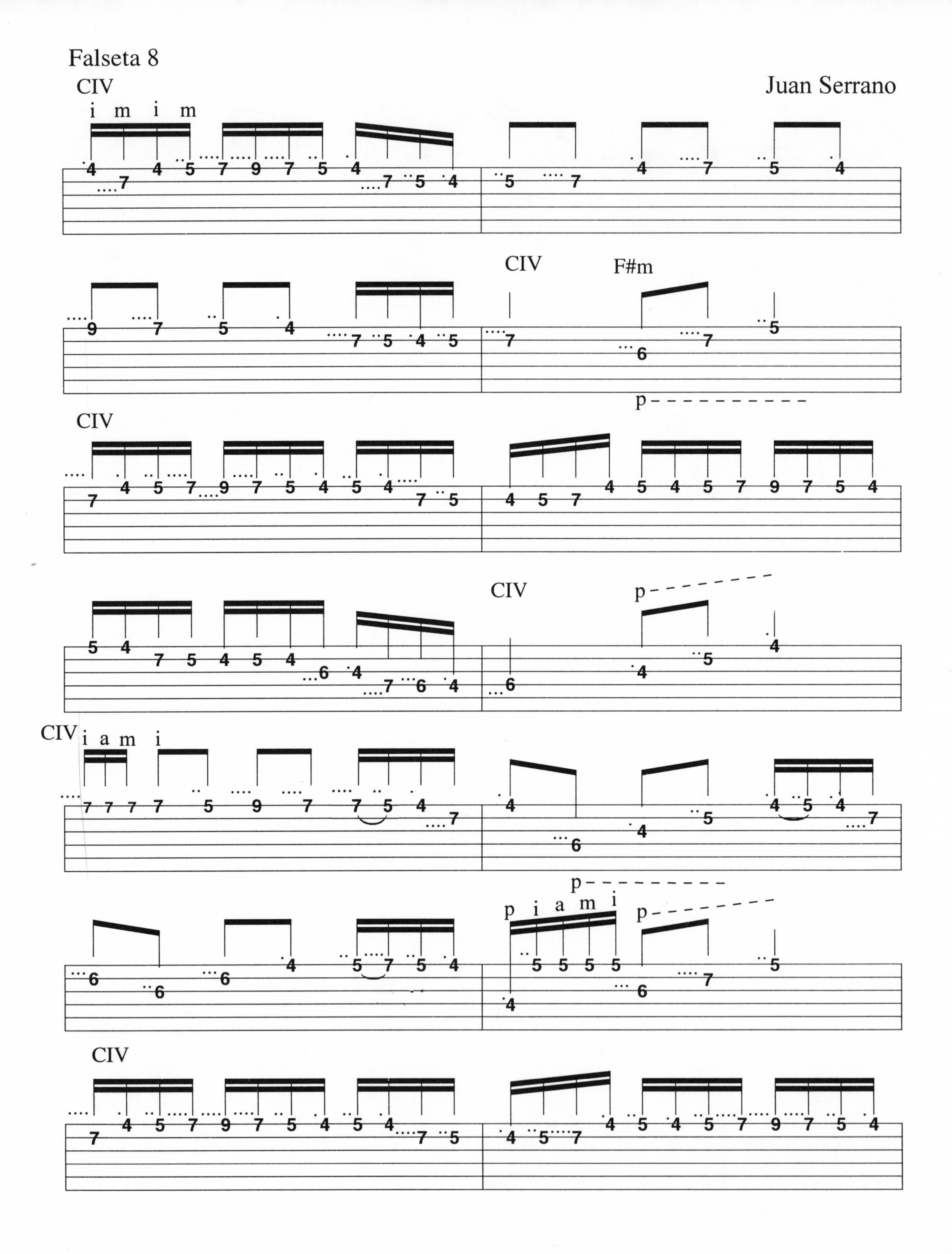
Falseta 8
Juan Serrano
CIV
i m i m
CIV
F#m
CIV
p
CIV
p
CIV
i a m i
p
p i a m i
p
CIV

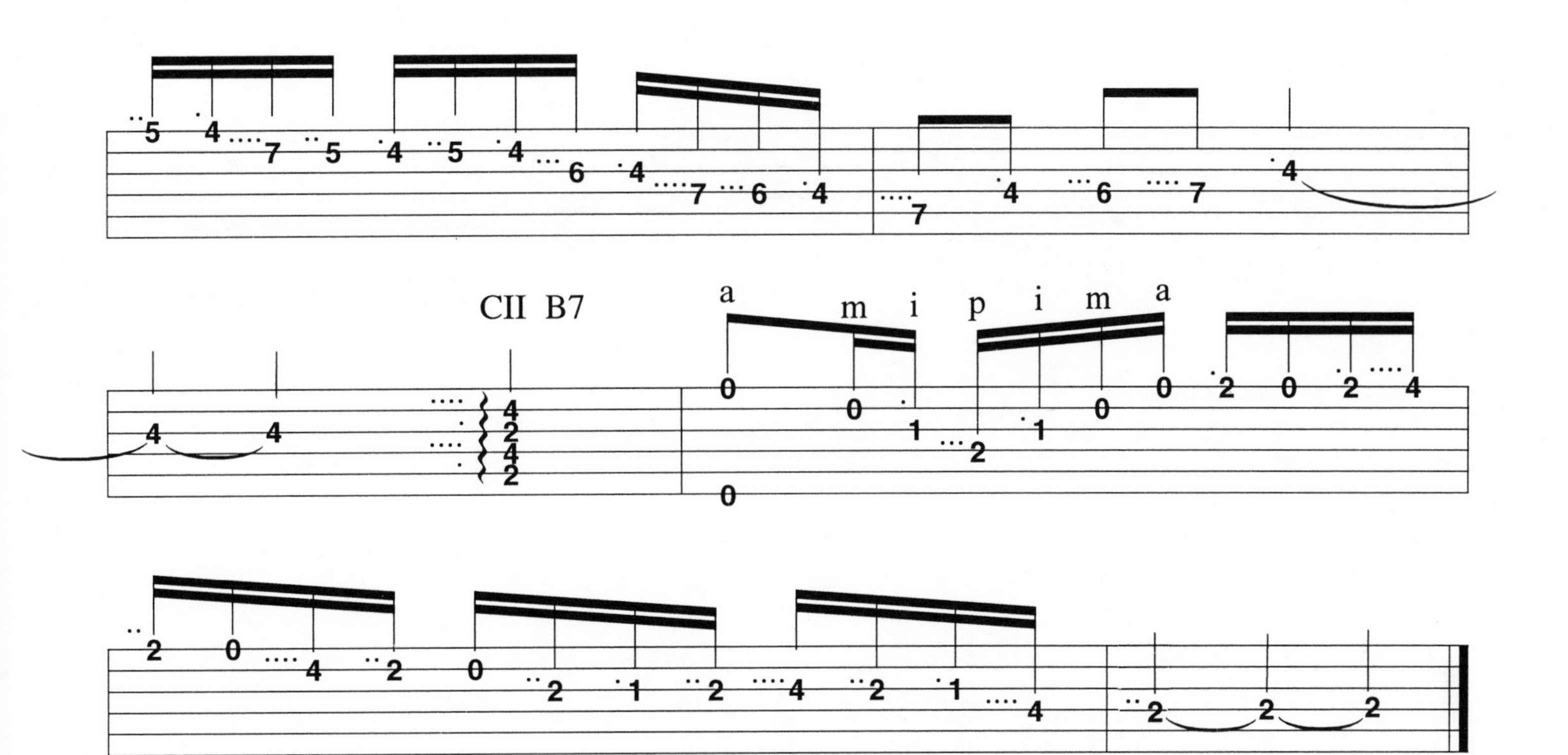
CII B7
a m i p i m a

Falseta 9

Juan Serrano

IV
p- - - - - i m a

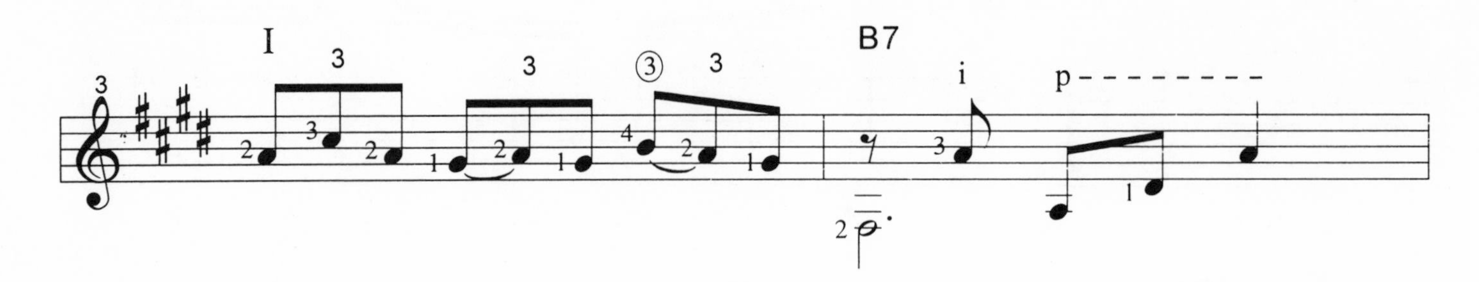


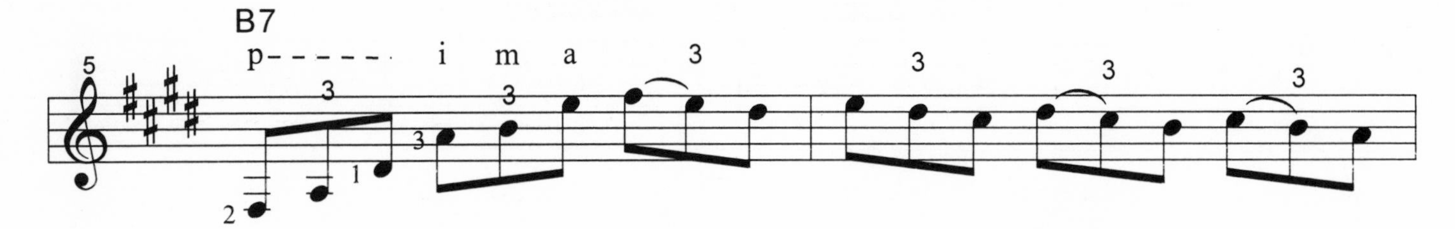

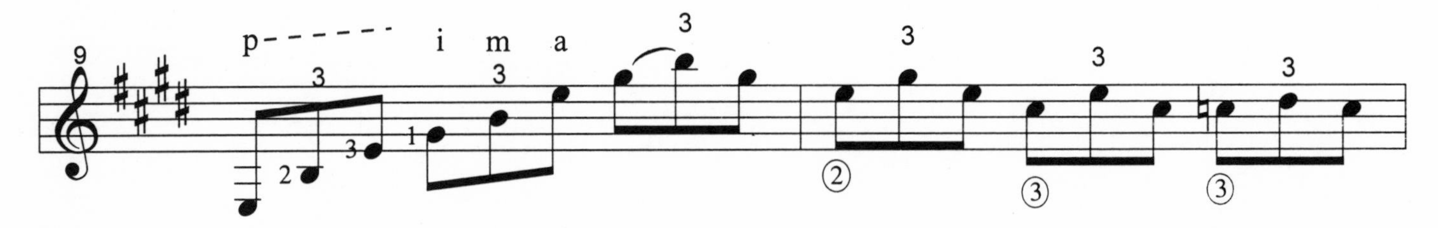


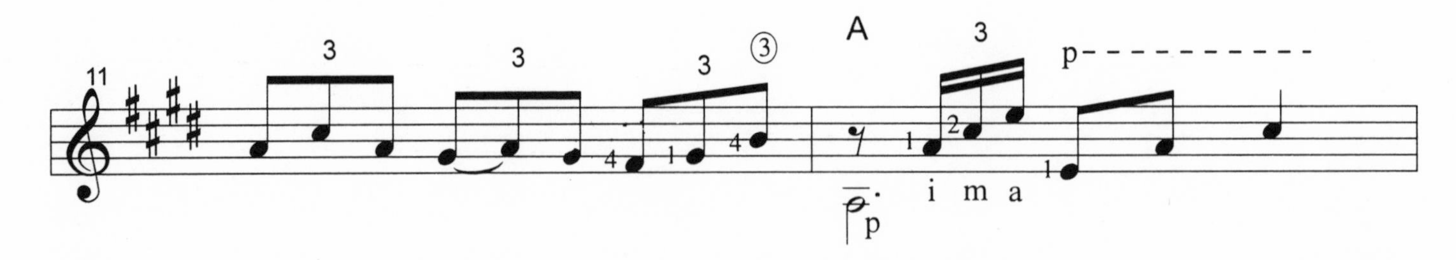

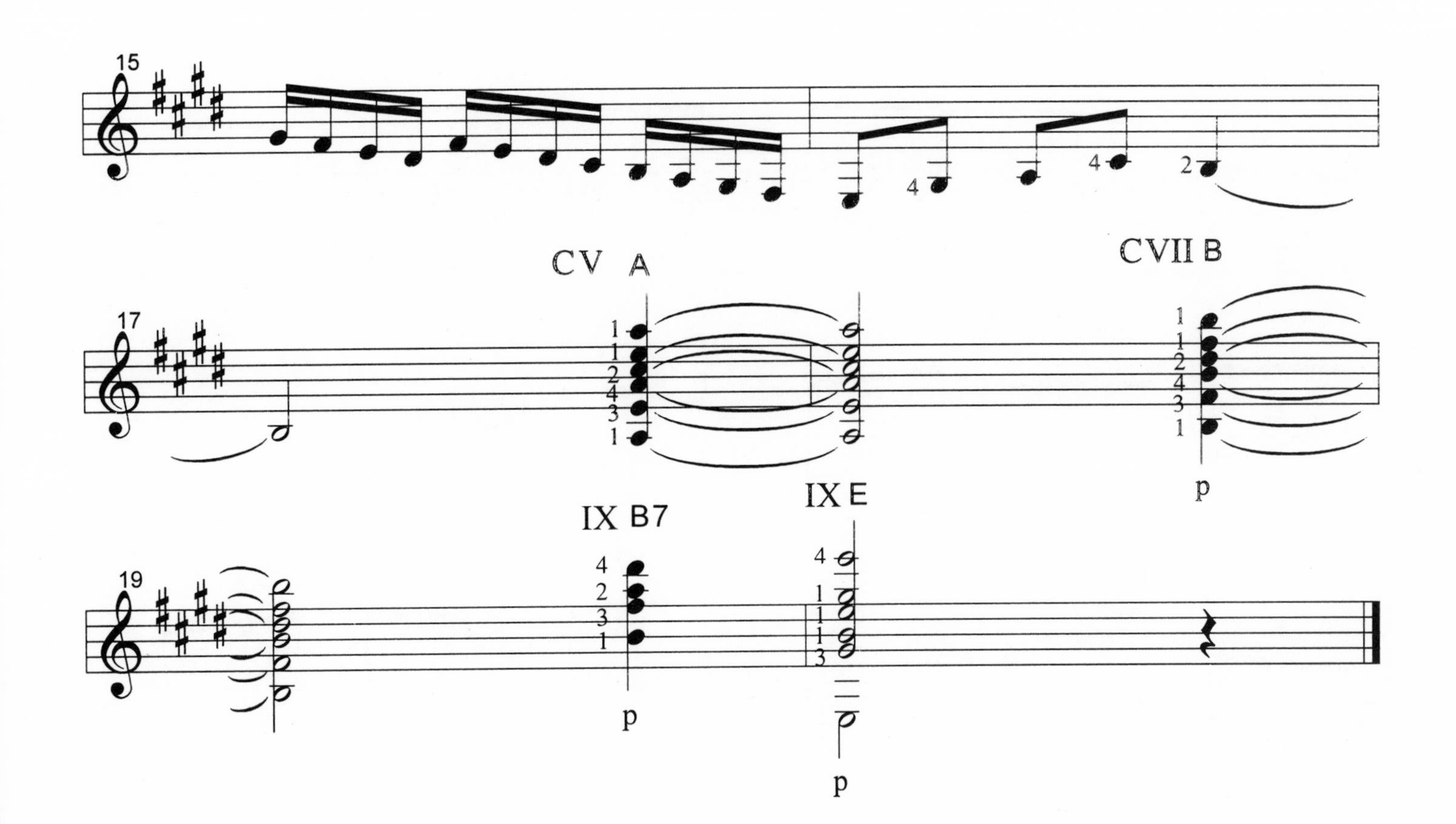
CV A
CVII B
IX B7
IX E
p

E

0 2 2 1 0 0 4 7 4 | 5 4 5 6 5 6 5 4 5

B7 p i p

2 2 2 1 2 1 4 2 1 | 2 2 0 1 2

p i m a

2 0 1 2 0 0 2 0 4 | 0 4 2 4 2 0 2 0 2

E p i m a p

0 2 1 4 2 1 2 1 4 | 0 1 0 0 2 1 0

0 2 2 1 0 0 4 7 4 | 5 4 5 6 5 6 5 4 5

A p i m a p

2 2 2 1 2 1 4 1 4 | 0 2 2 0 2 2 2

A p i m a

0 4 2 2 2 0 2 4 2 0 4 2 | 0 2 4 0 4 2 0 2 1 2 4 2

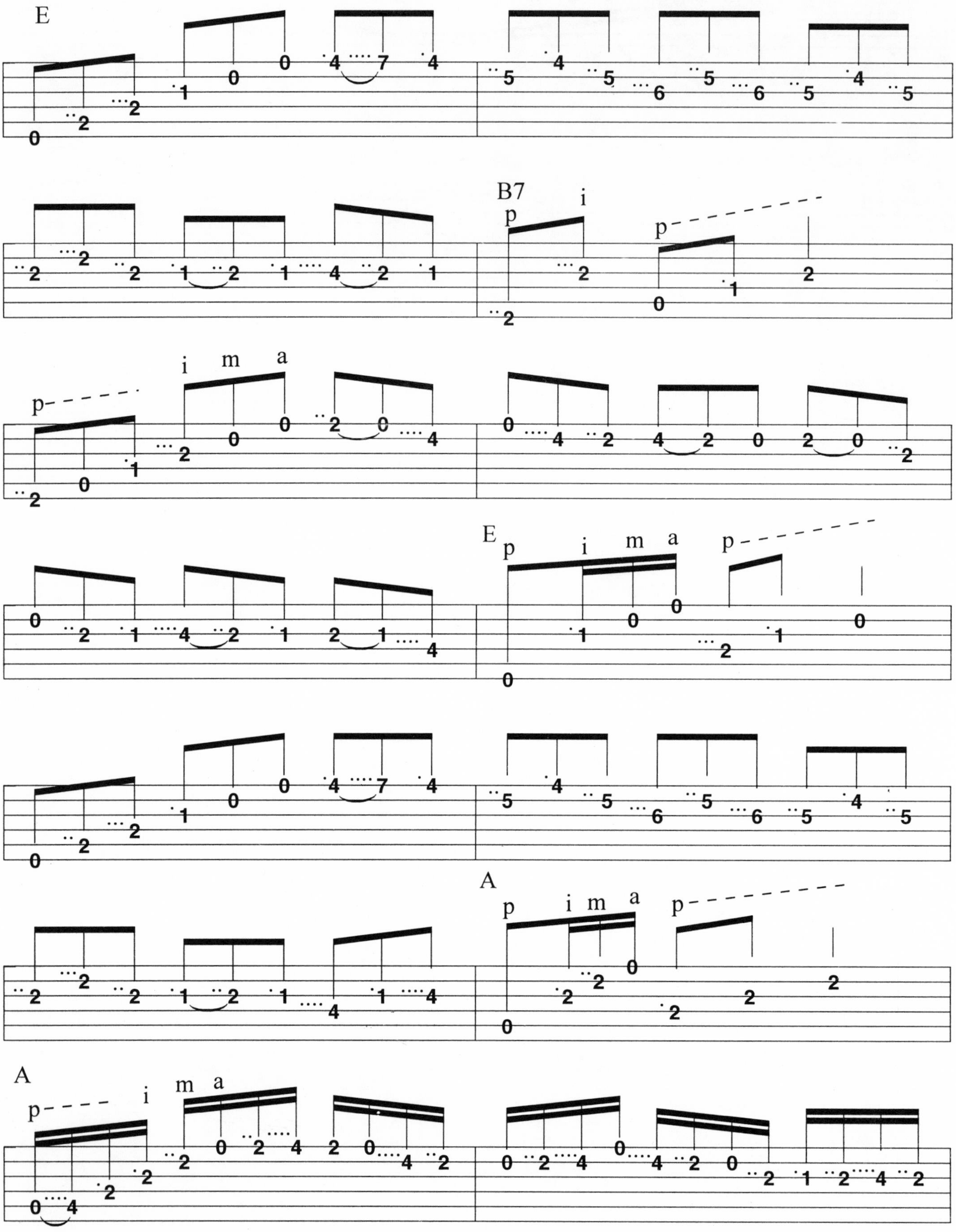

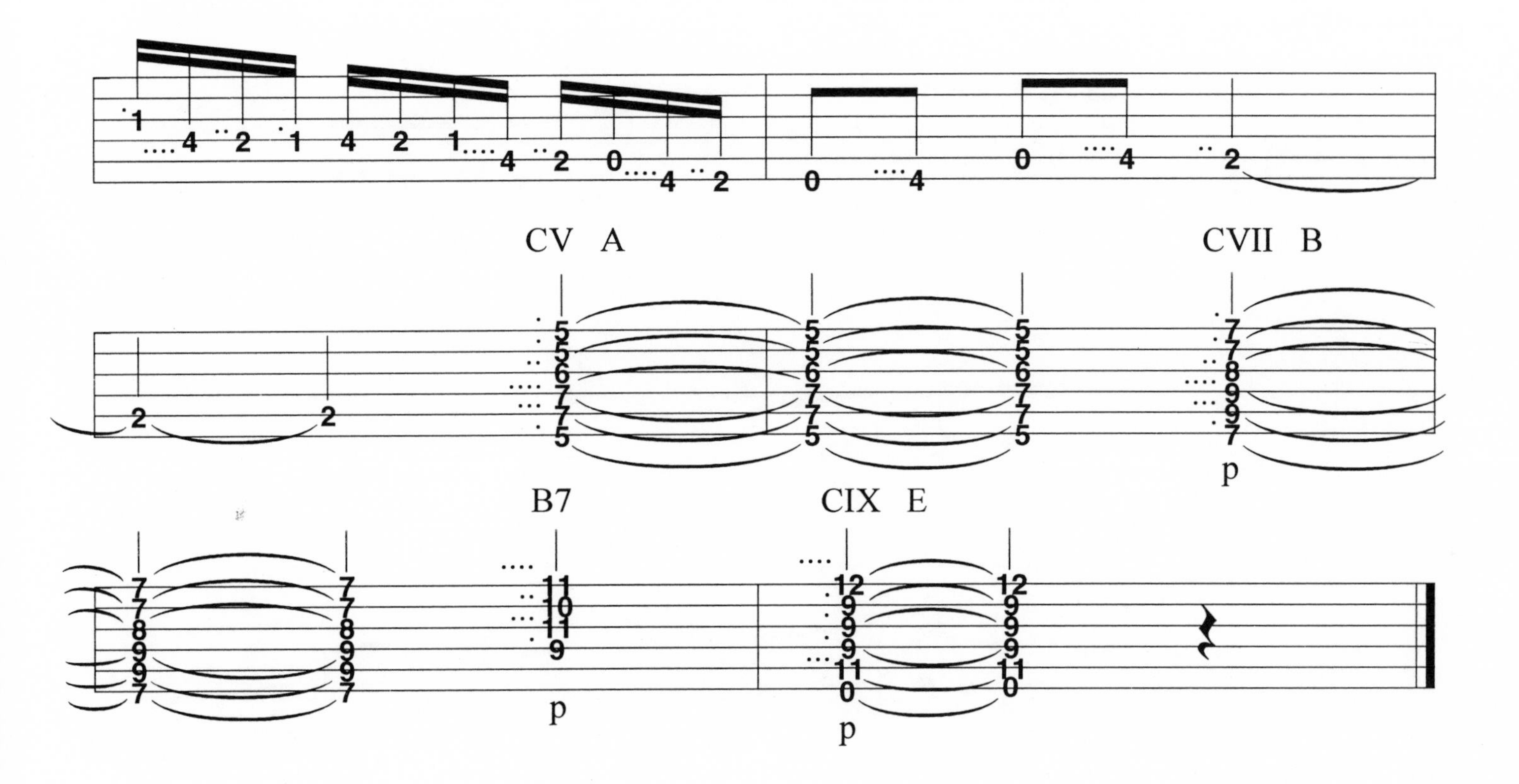
CV A
CVII B
B7
CIX E
p
p
p

## Falseta 10

Juan Serrano

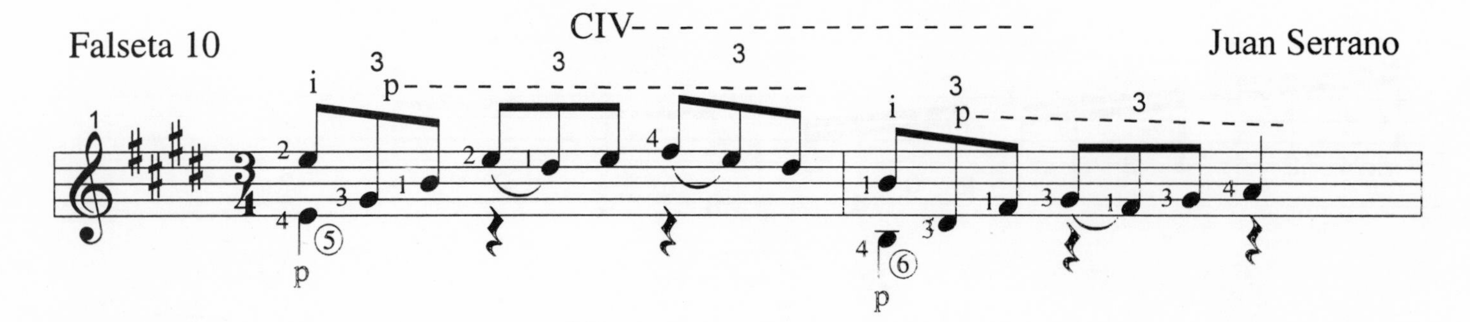

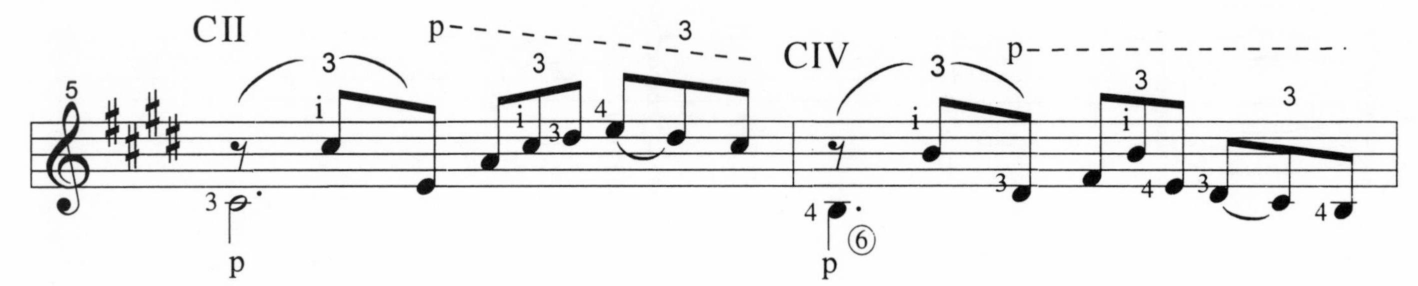

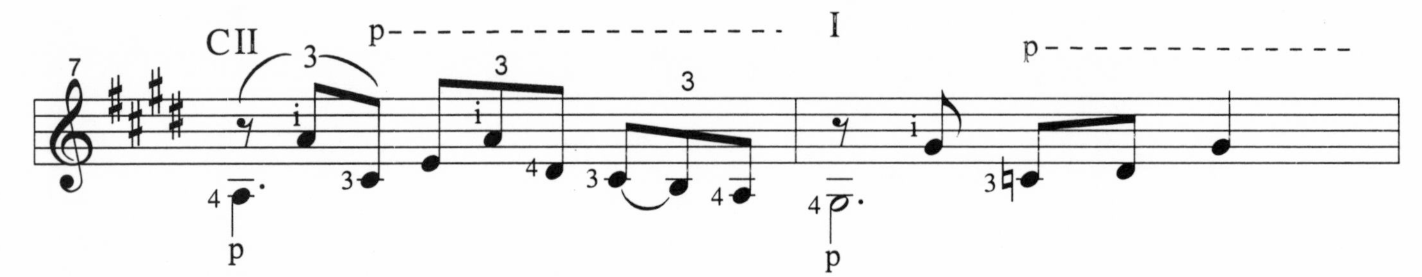

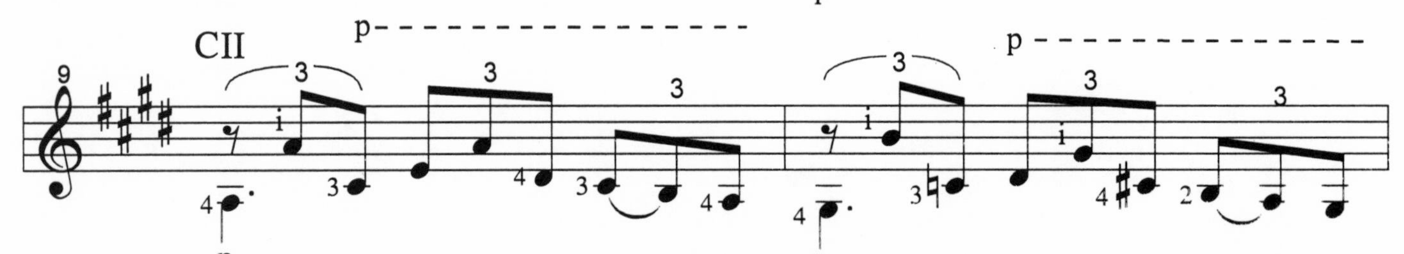

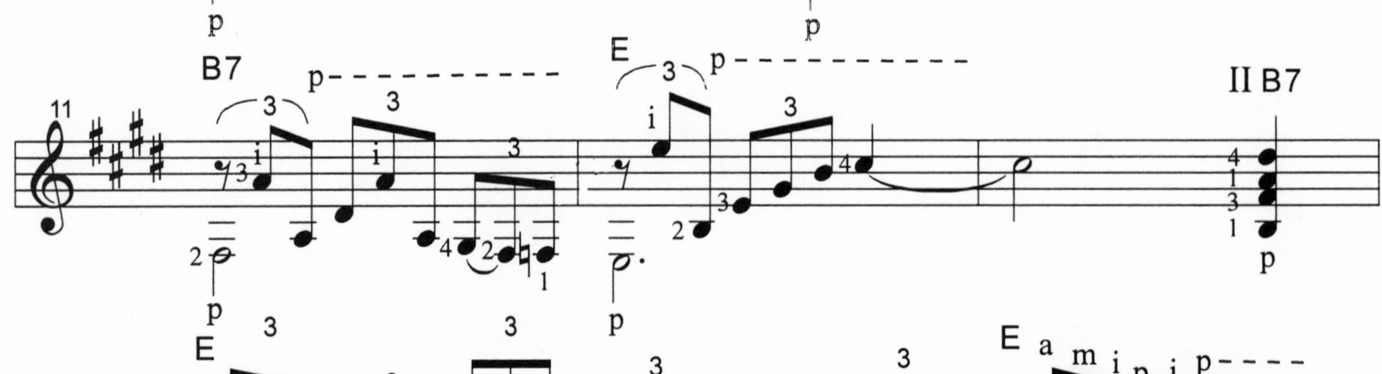

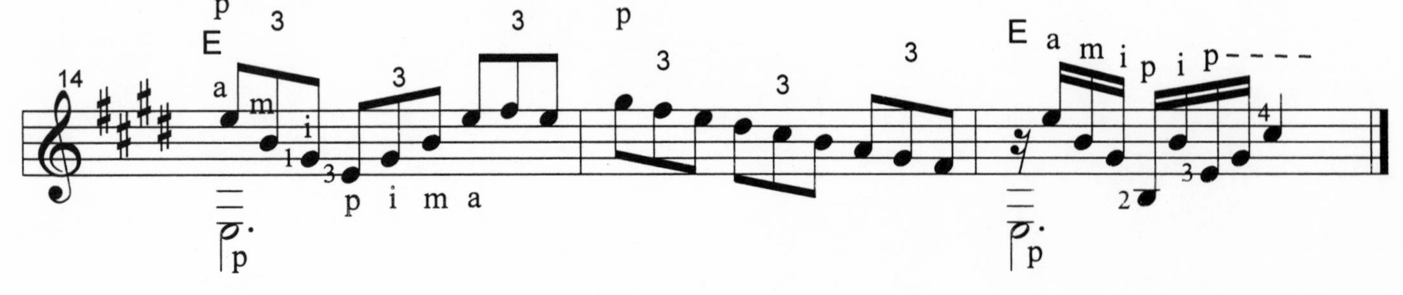

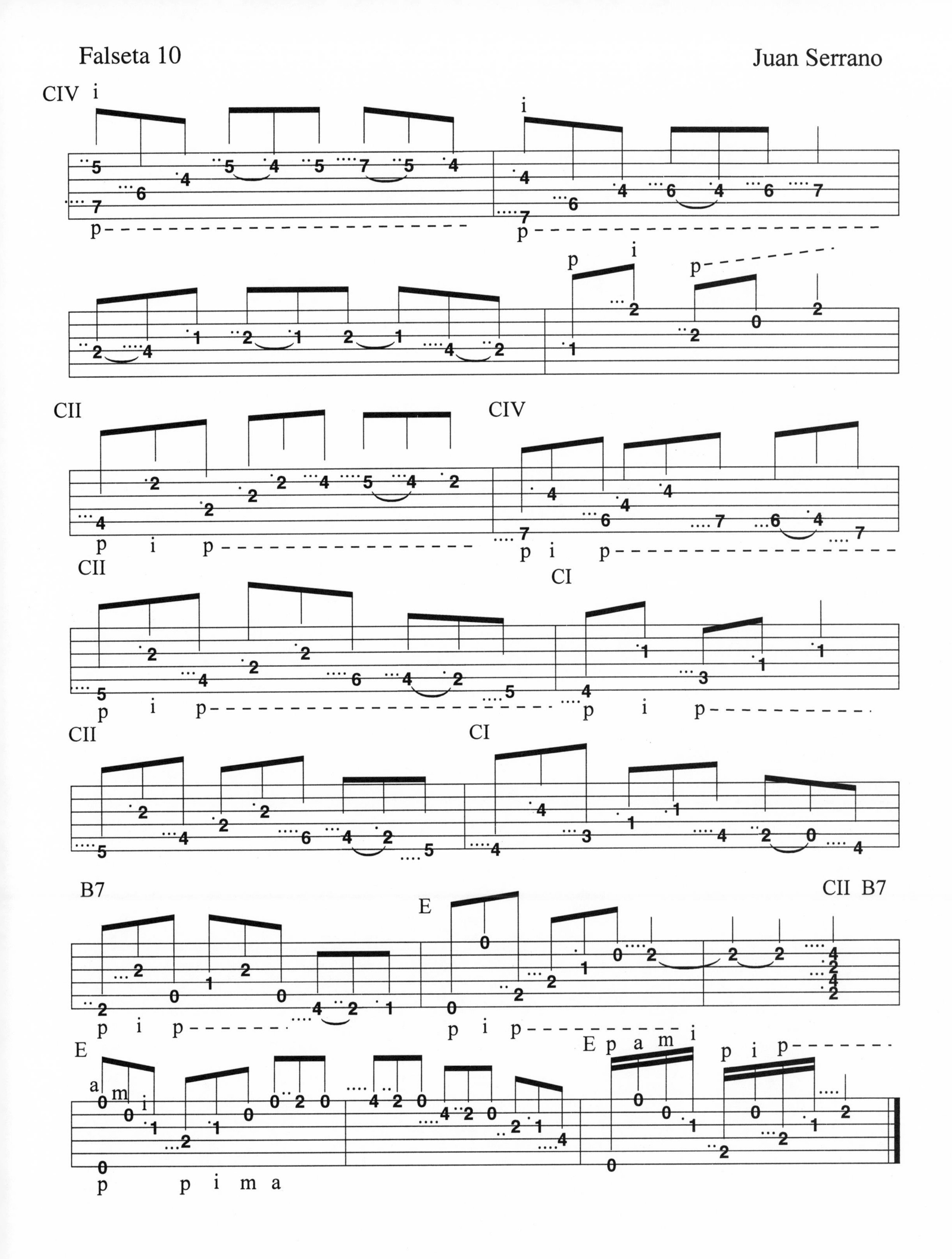
Falseta 10
Juan Serrano
CIV
CII
CIV
CII
CI
CII
CI
B7
E
CII B7
E
E

أليكَريا پورميديو

# ALEGRÍAS POR MEDIO

The rhythmical count and the accents of the Alegrías por Medio are identical to those of the Alegrías por Arriba. The difference is that they are played in the key of A major. Traditionally, the Alegrías por Medio was used only to accompany the dance and the Alegrías por Arriba to accompany the song.

It is recommended that the traditional compás and its three variations be memorized first, so that a sense of the rhythm is attained. The first falseta alternates two notes with the thumb (p) and one with the index (i). The first compás of the first falseta (the first four measures of 3/4) should be practiced repeatedly to become familiar with this technique, before continuing with the rest of the falseta. All the notes of the thumb should be played reststroke.

It is also recommended paying special attention to the syncopation compás in falseta #5. The syncopation begins on beat #12 of the fourth flamenco compás. This compás ends with a picado and should be practiced repeatedly in order to become familiar with the syncopation and to memorize the chords that compose it. The same recommendation is made for the preceding group of falsetas. Until the first is not memorized, the second should not be attempted and so on.

# ALEGRÍAS POR MEDIO

La cuenta rítmica y los acentos de las Alegrías por Medio son idénticos a los de las Alegrías por Arriba. La diferencia es que se tocan en el tono de La mayor. Tradicionalmente, las Alegrías por Medio se usaban sólo para acompañar el baile y las Alegrías por Arriba para acompañar al cante.

Recomiendo que se aprendan de memoria el compás tradicional y las tres variaciones para que se sientan seguros del ritmo. La primera falseta alterna dos notas con el dedo pulgar (p) por una con el dedo índice (i). Practiquen mucho el primer compás de la primera falseta, o sea los cuatro primeros compases de 3/4 para familiarizarse con esa técnica antes de continuar con el resto de la falseta. Todas las notas del pulgar se deben de tocar apoyando.

También, recomiendo atención especial a la falseta #5, donde hay un compás de contratiempo muy difícil de ejecutar. El contratiempo empieza en el tiempo #12 del cuarto compás flamenco. Este compás termina con un picado. Practiquen solamente este compás muchas veces para que se familiaricen con el contratiempo y traten de aprender de memoria los acordes que lo componen.

Hago la misma recomendación que en los grupos de falsetas anteriores. Hasta que no hayan aprendido bien la primera falseta, no empiecen con la segunda y lo mismo con todas las demás.

# *Alegrias Por Medio*

Juan Serrano

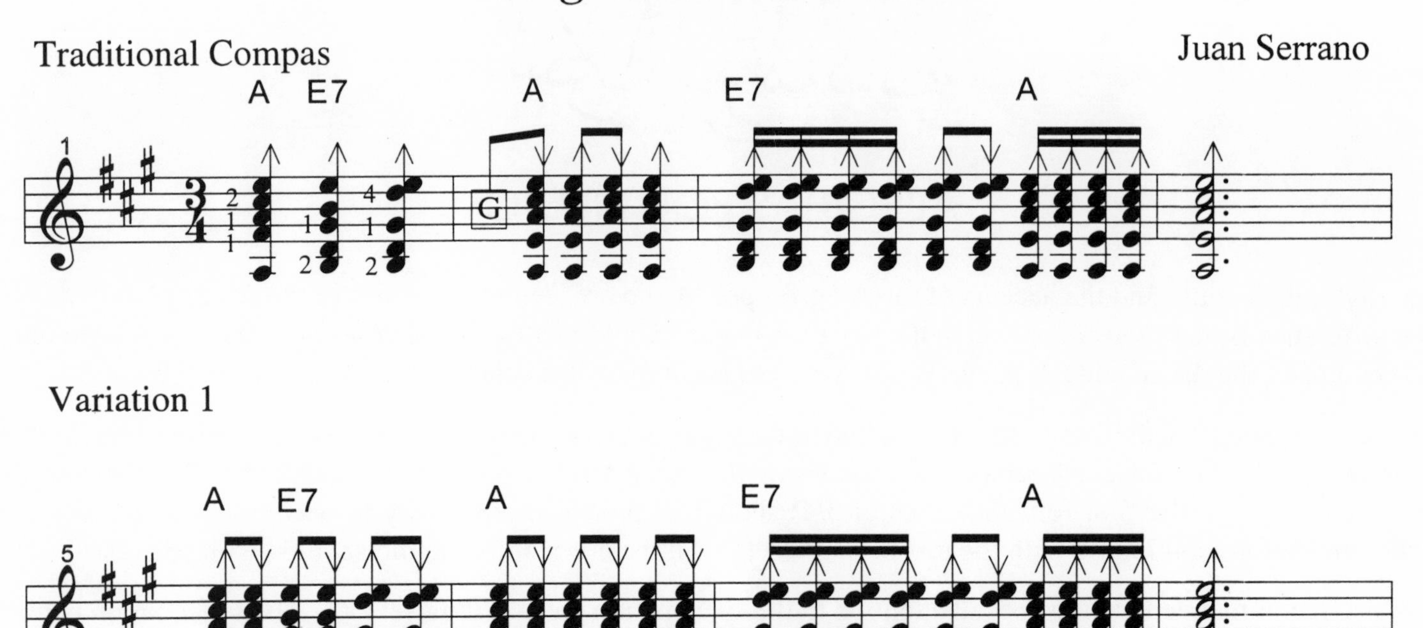


Variation 2

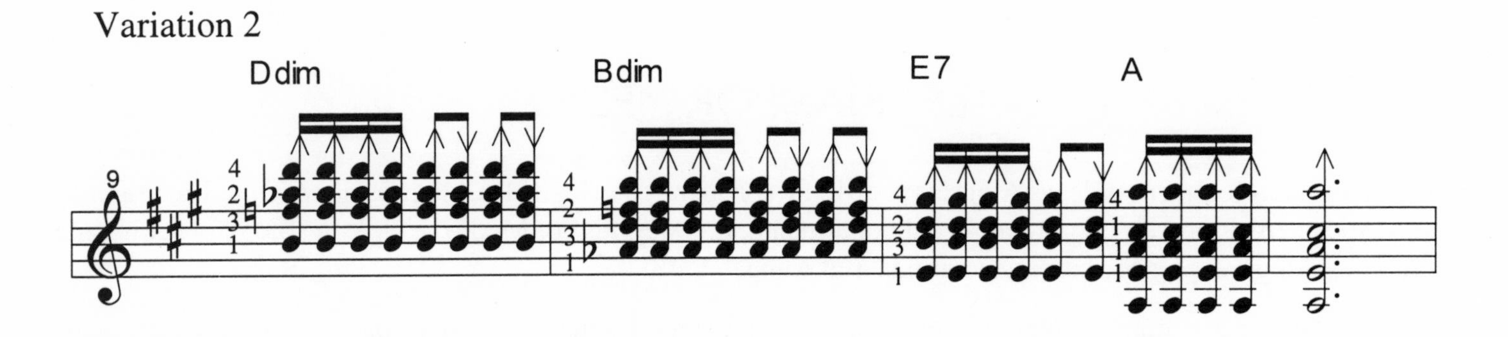


Variation 3

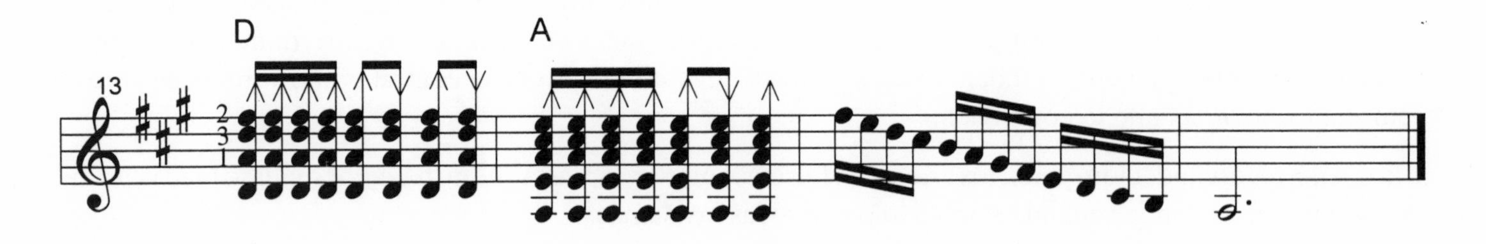

# *Alegrias Por Medio*

## Traditional Compas

Juan Serrano

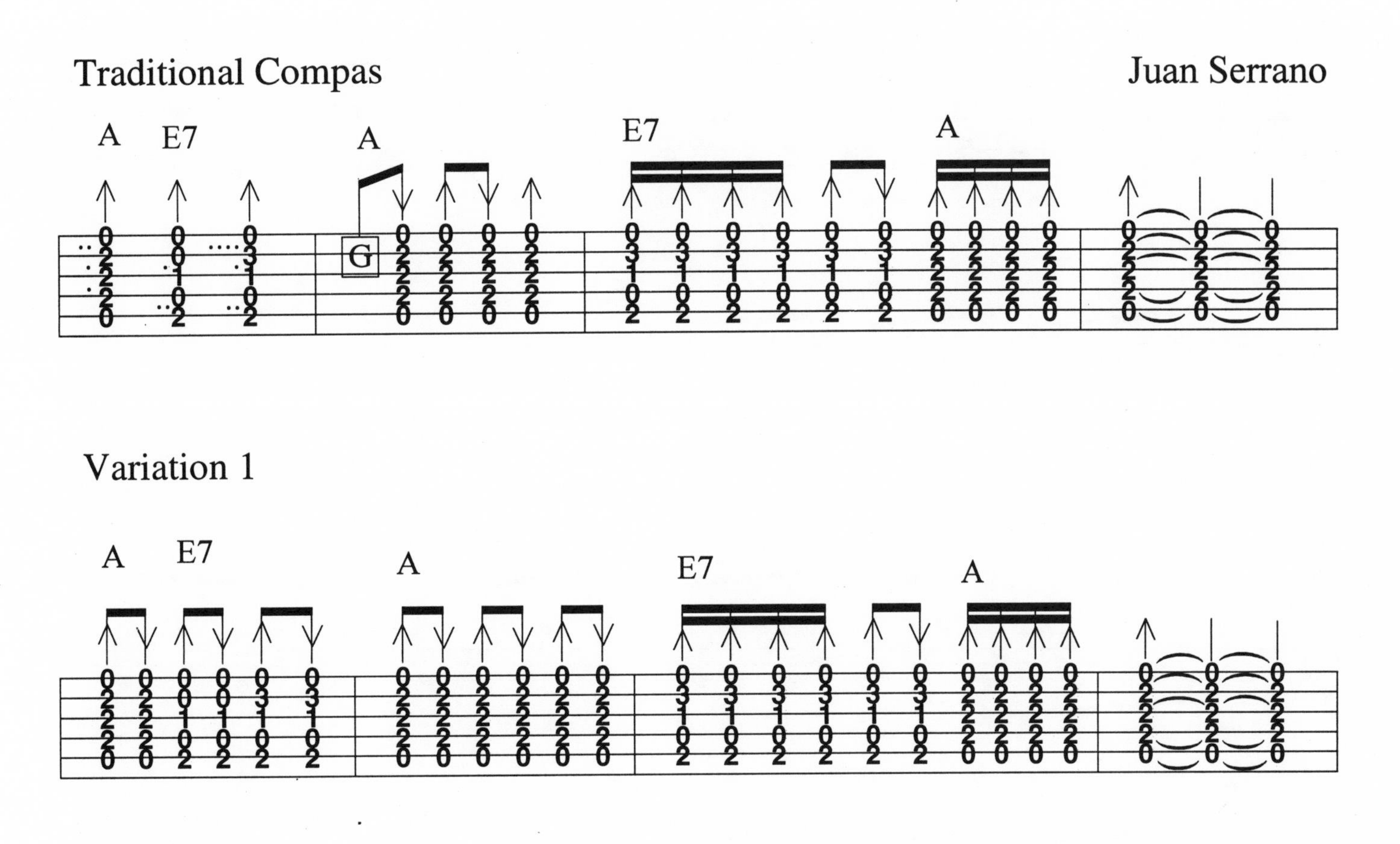


## Variation 2

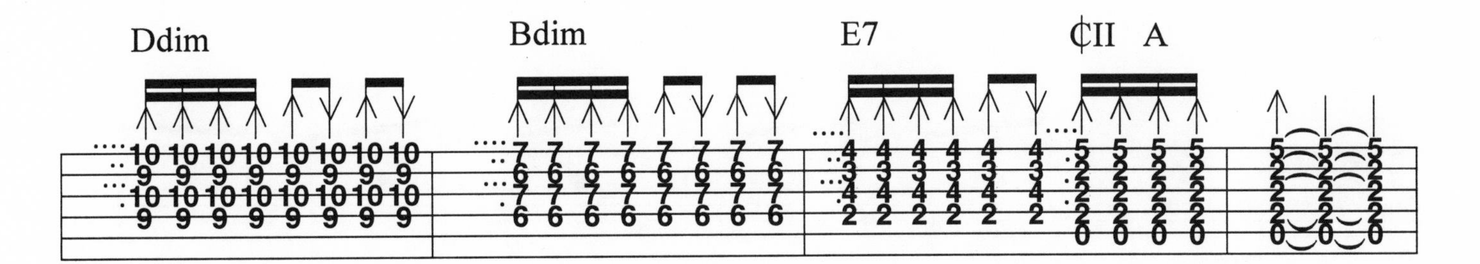


## Variation 3

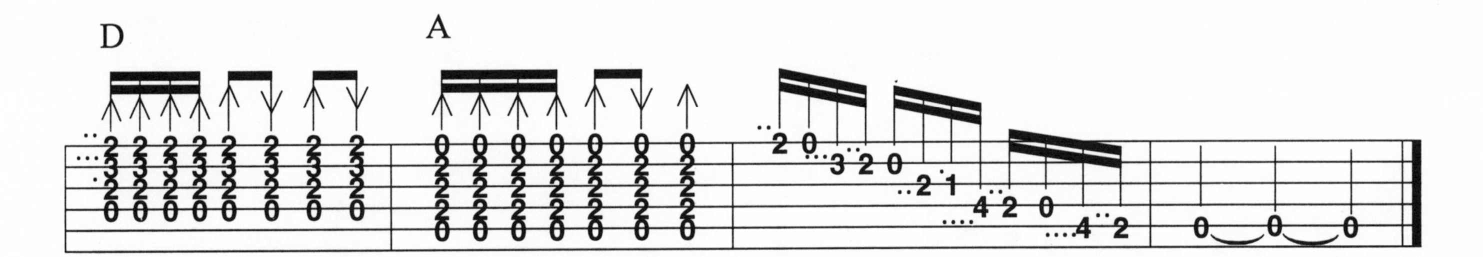

Falseta 1

Juan Serrano

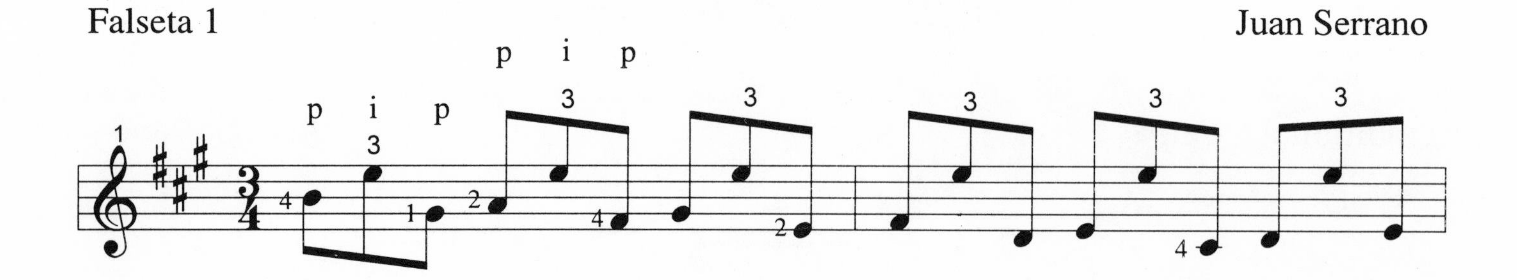


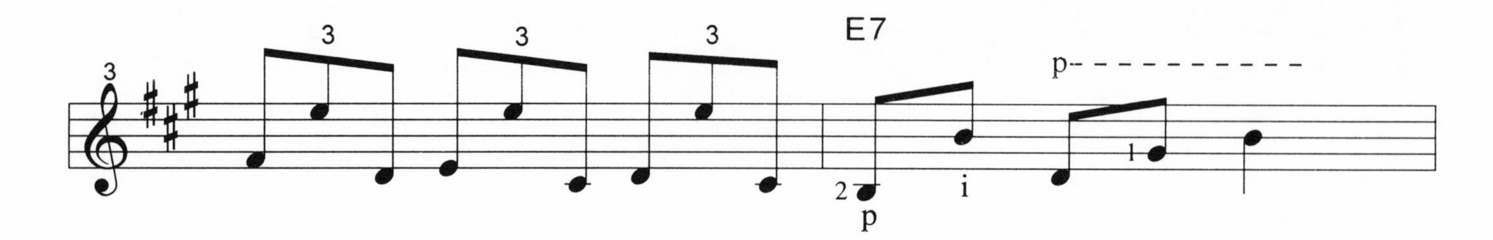


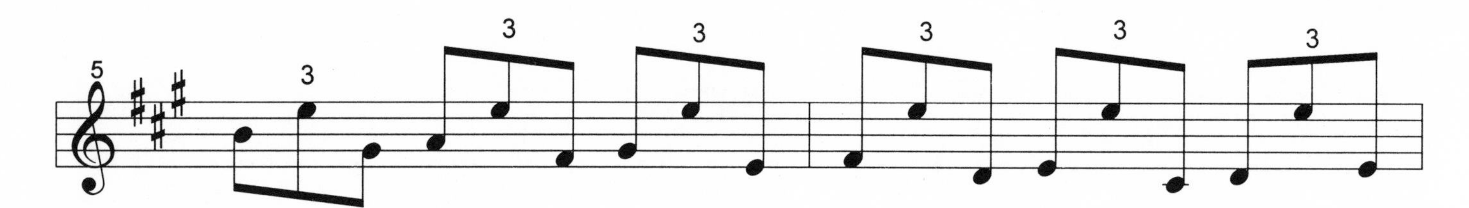

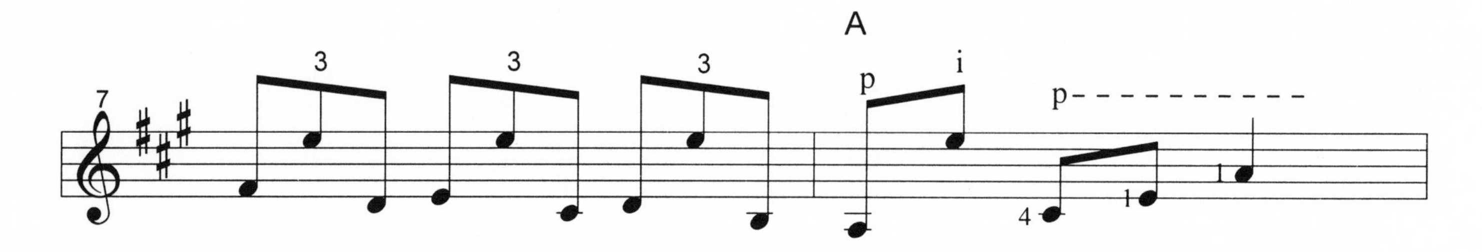


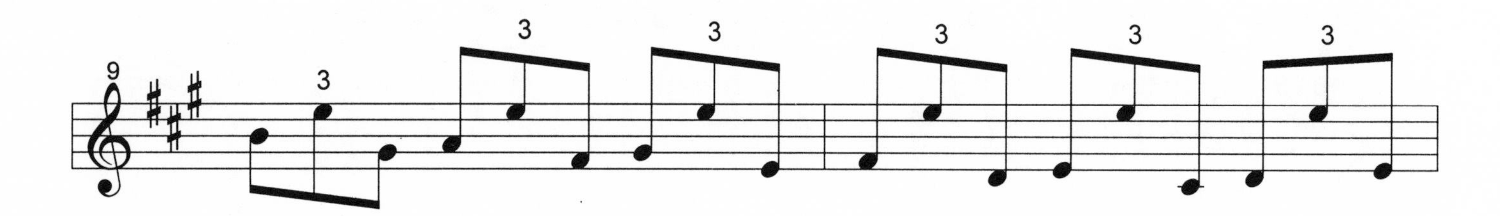

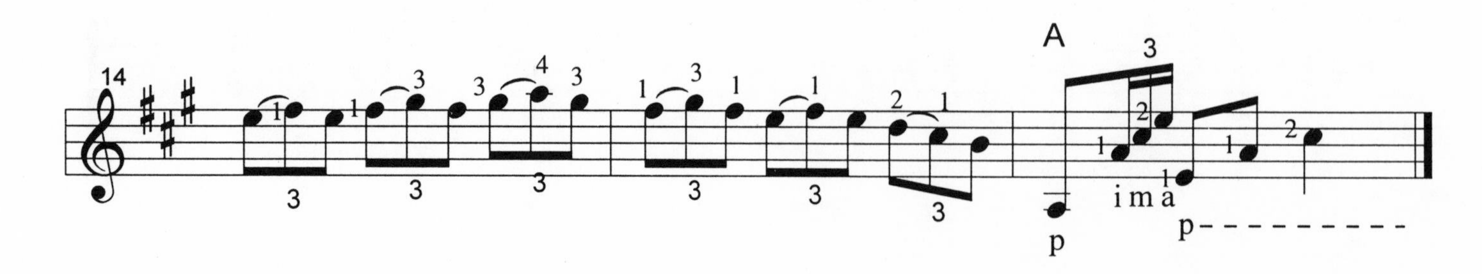

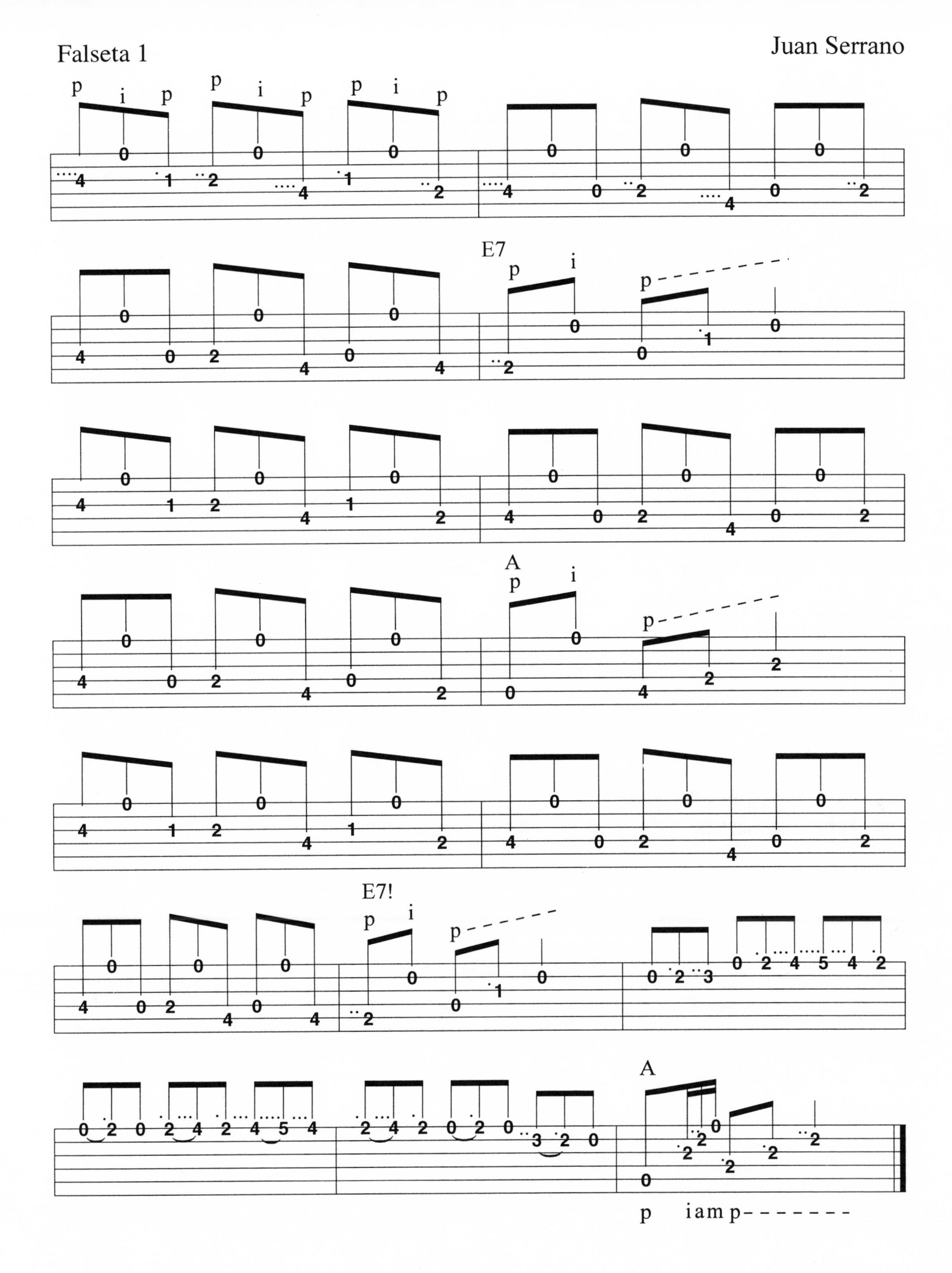
Falseta 1
Juan Serrano
p i p p i p p i p
E7
p i
p
A
p i
p
E7!
p i
p
A
p i a m p

## Falseta 2

Juan Serrano

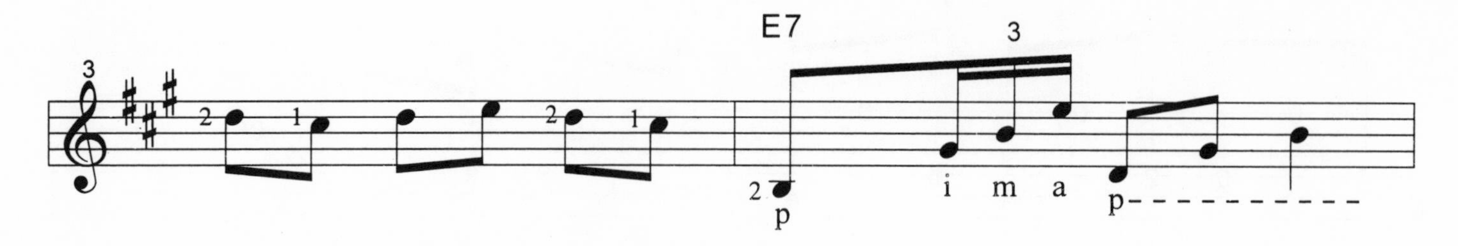

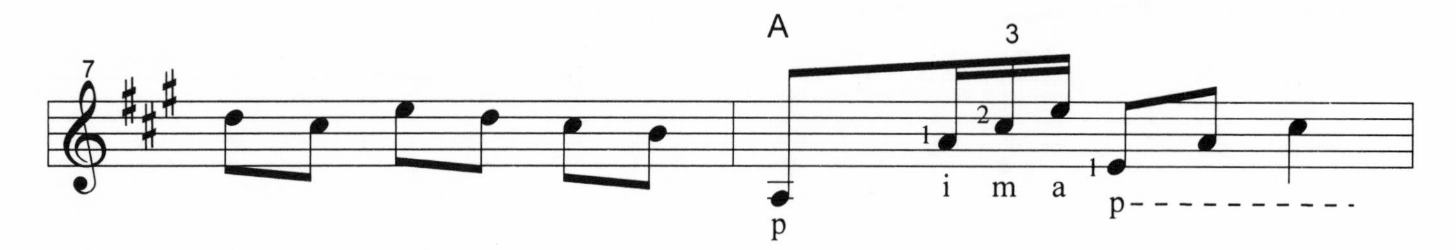

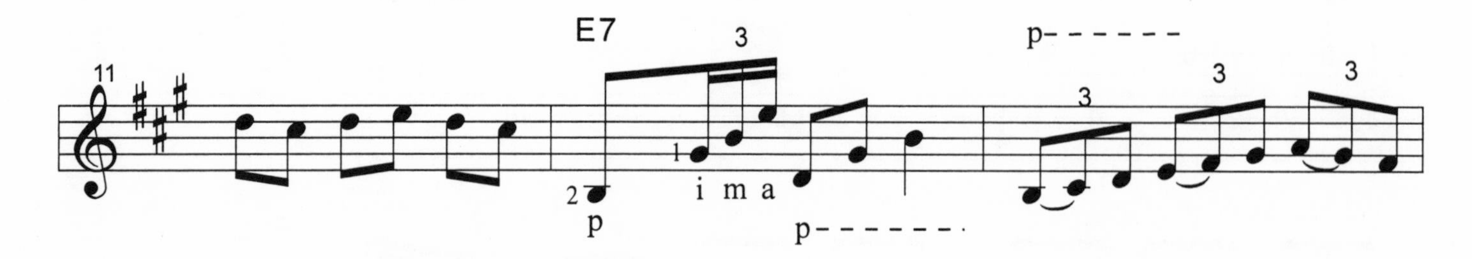


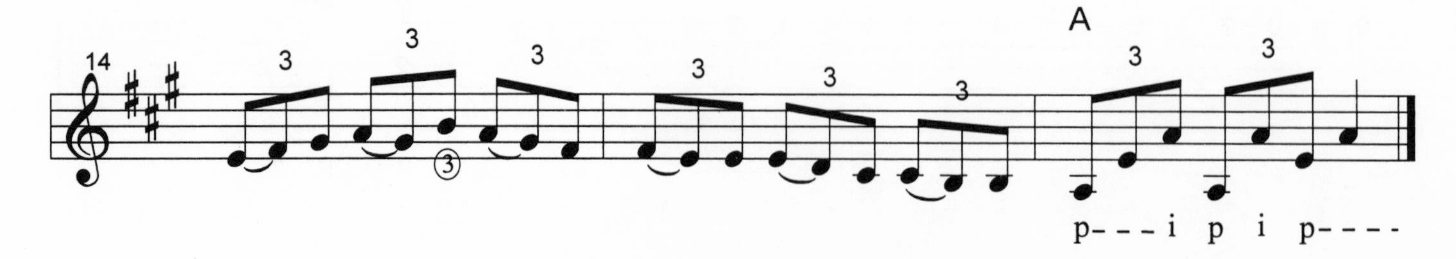

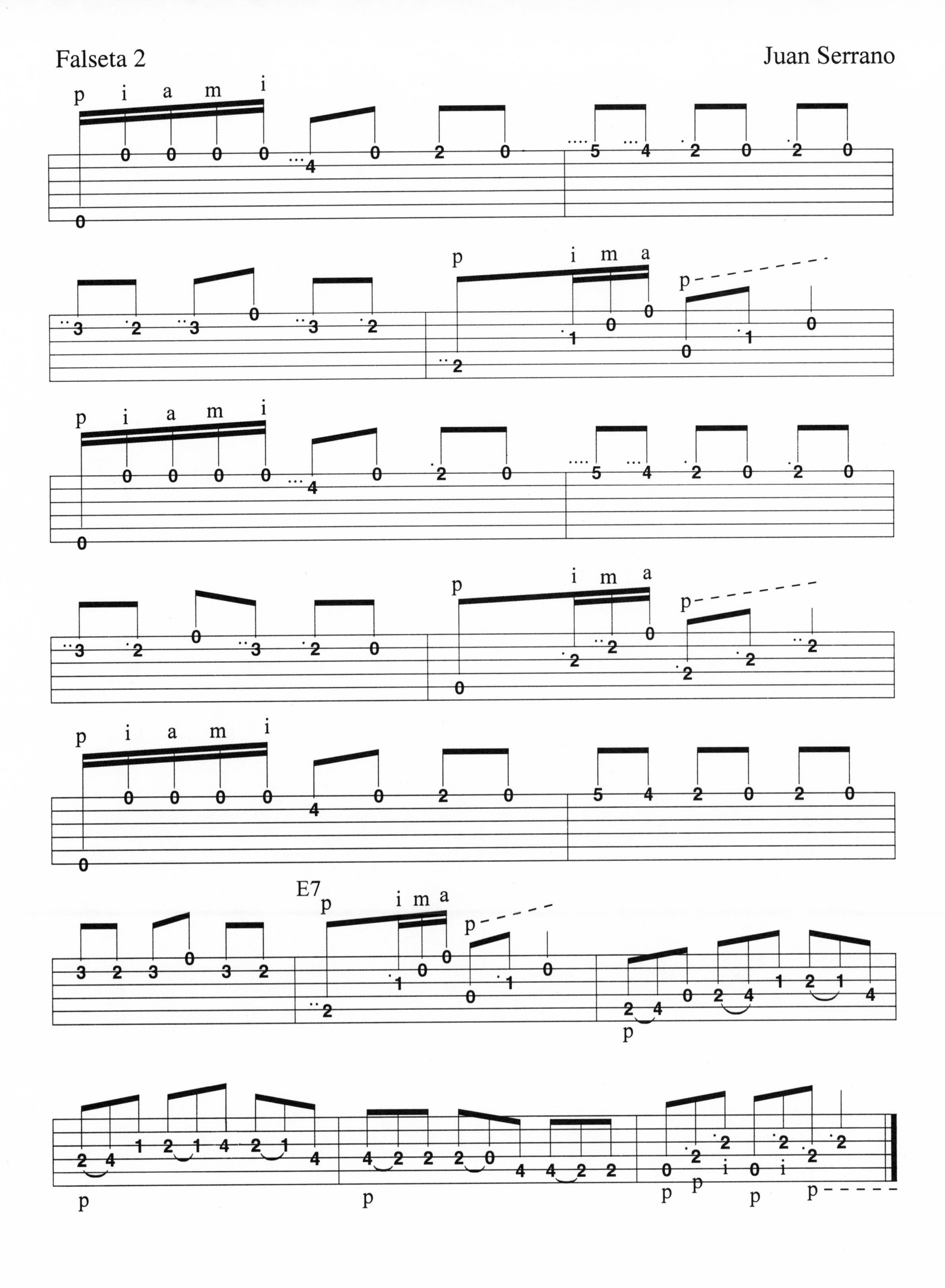
Falseta 2
Juan Serrano
E7

*This page has been left blank to avoid awkward page turns*

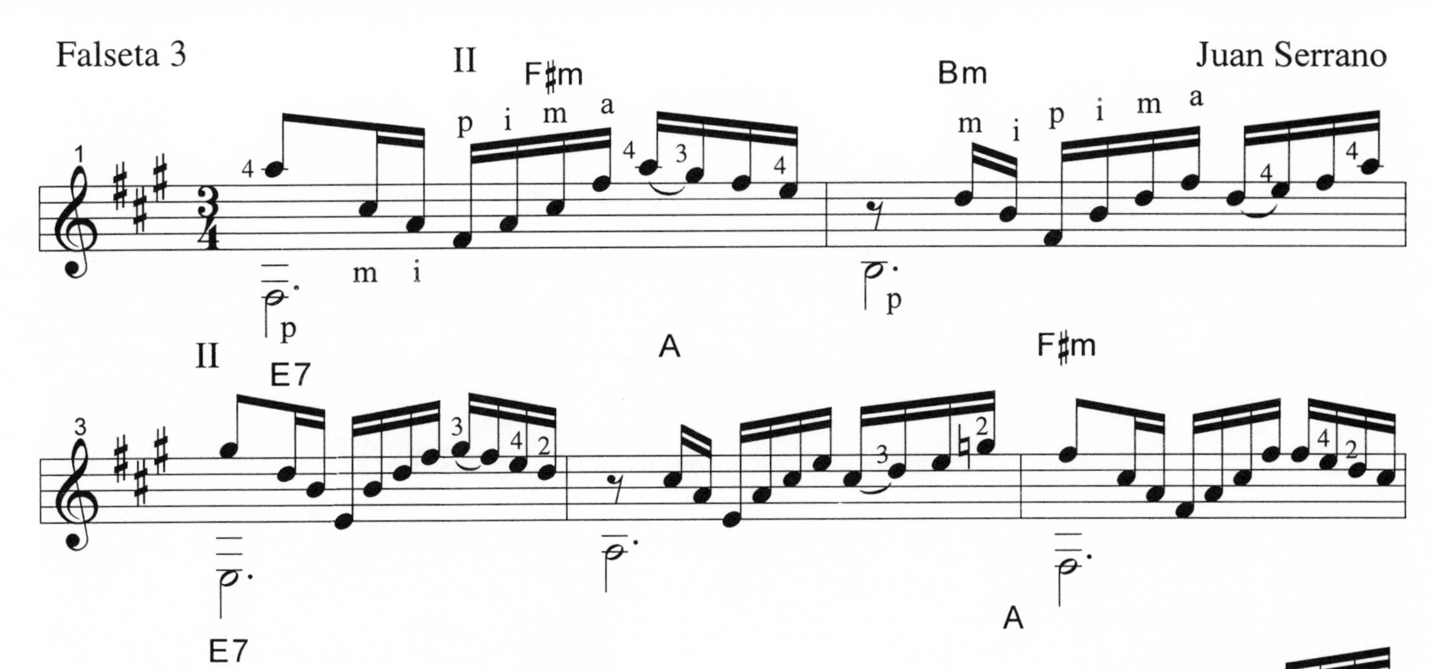
Falseta 3
Juan Serrano
II
F♯m
p i m a
Bm
m i p i m a
m i
p
p
II
E7
A
F♯m

E7
A

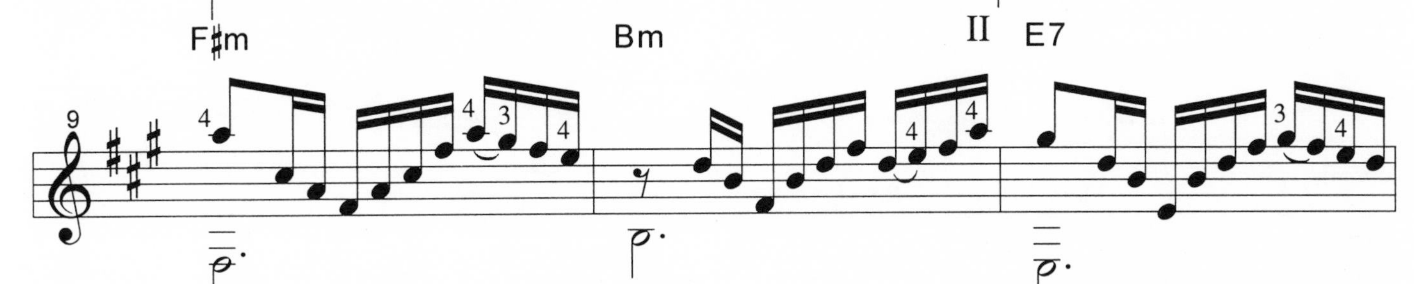
F♯m
Bm
II
E7

A
F♯m
VII
E7

IX
A

I

Falseta 3

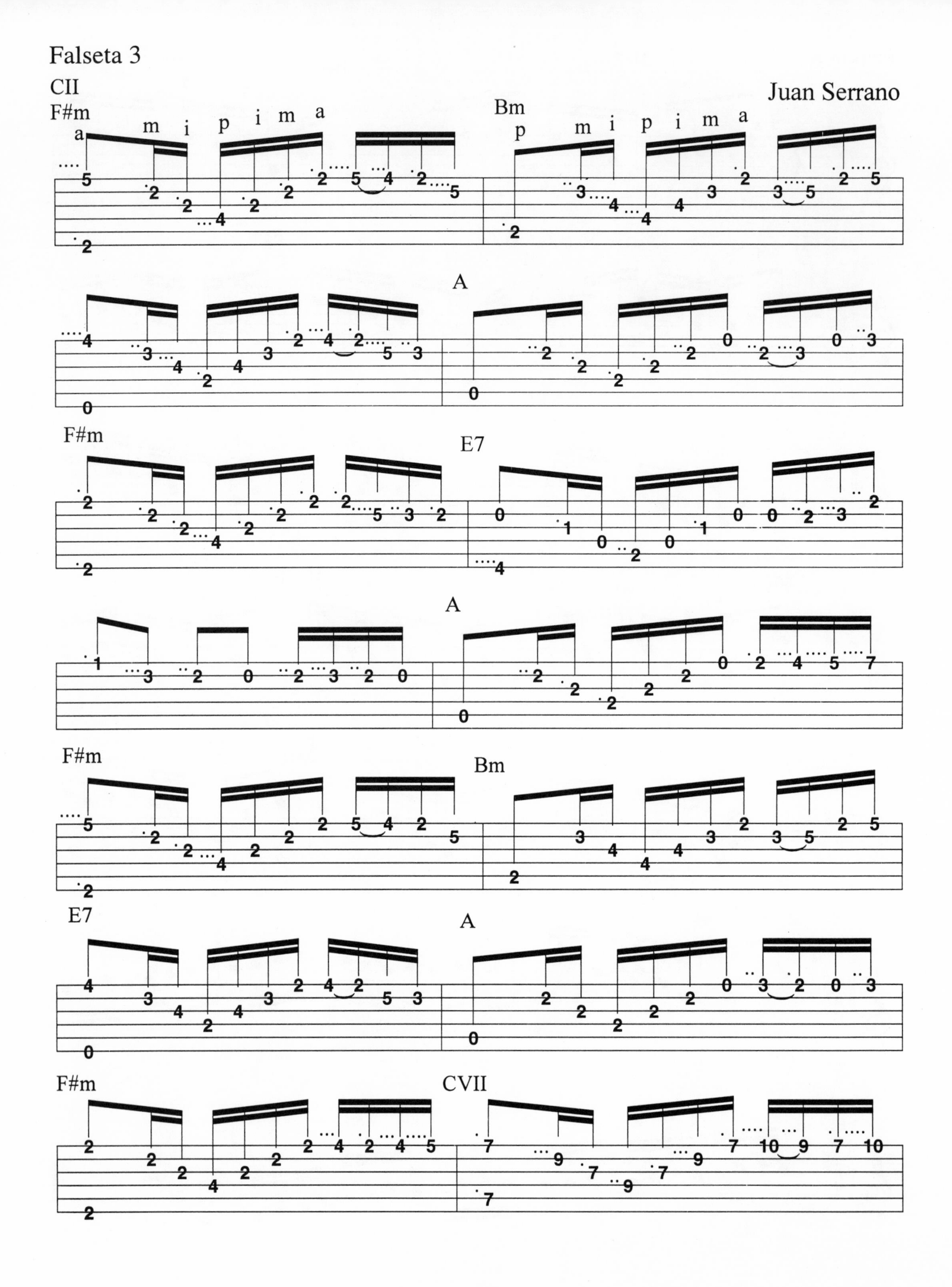
CII
F#m
Juan Serrano
a m i p i m a
Bm
p m i p i m a
A
F#m
E7
A
F#m
Bm
E7
A
F#m
CVII

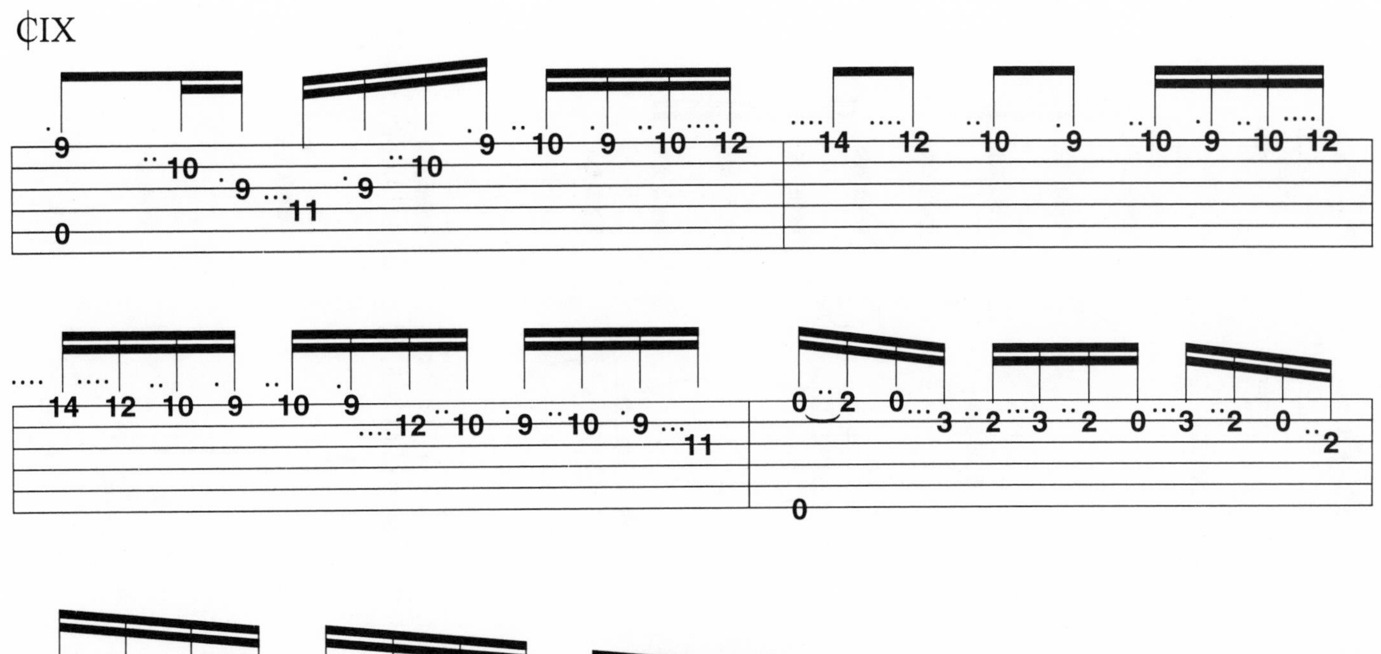
¢IX

## Falseta 4

Juan Serrano

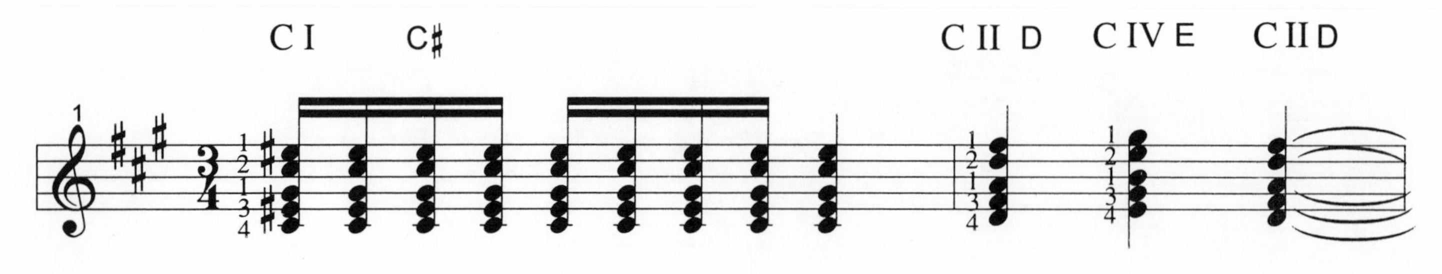


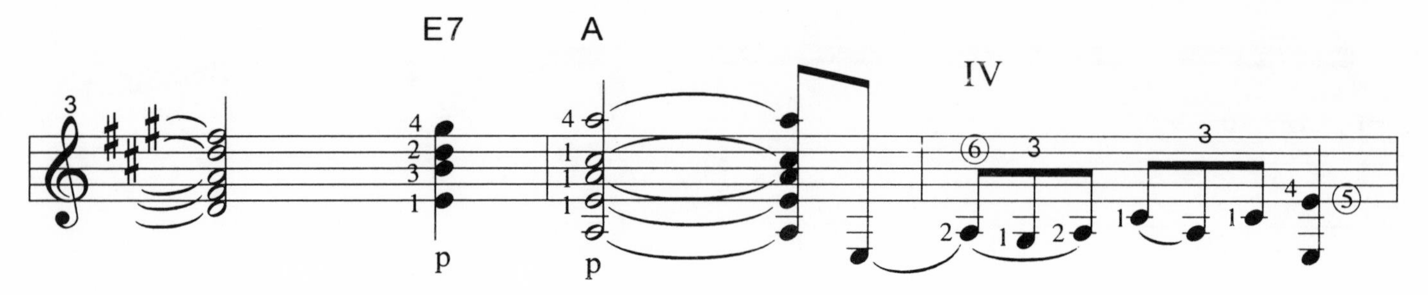


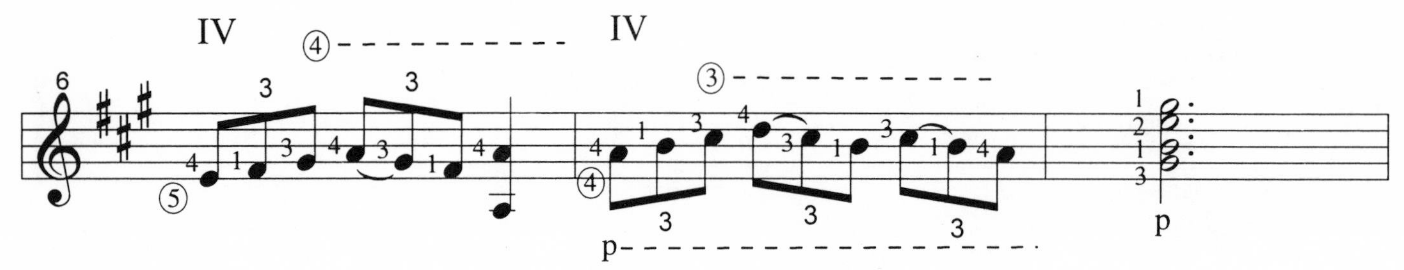


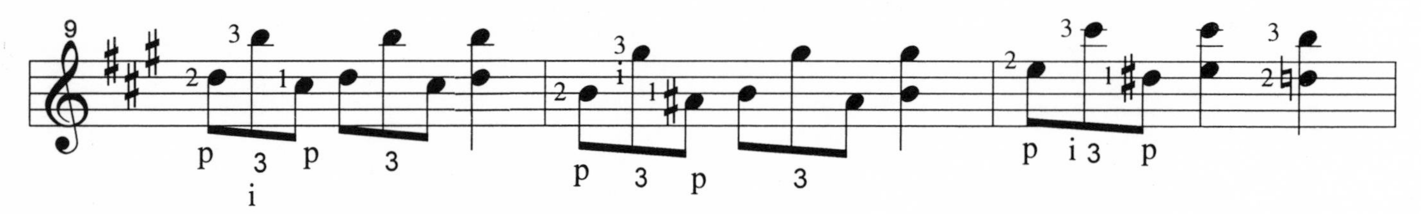

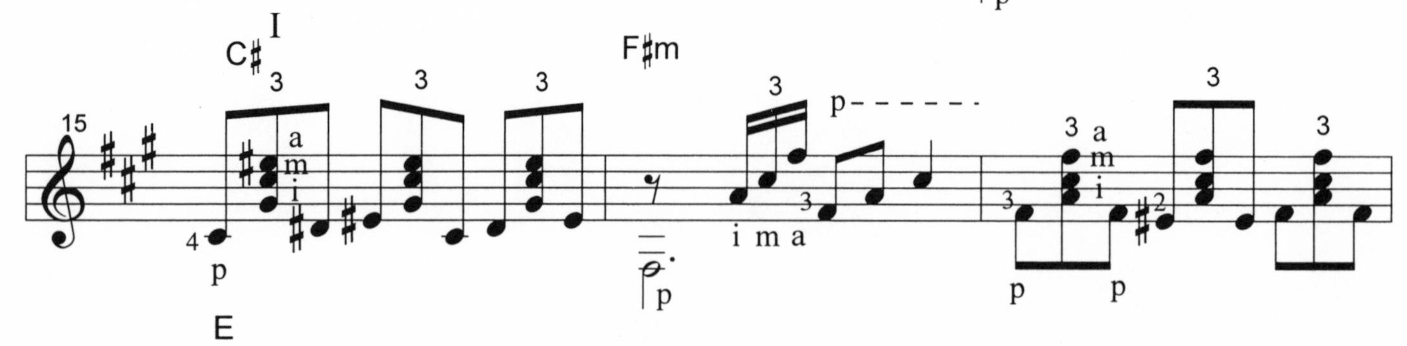


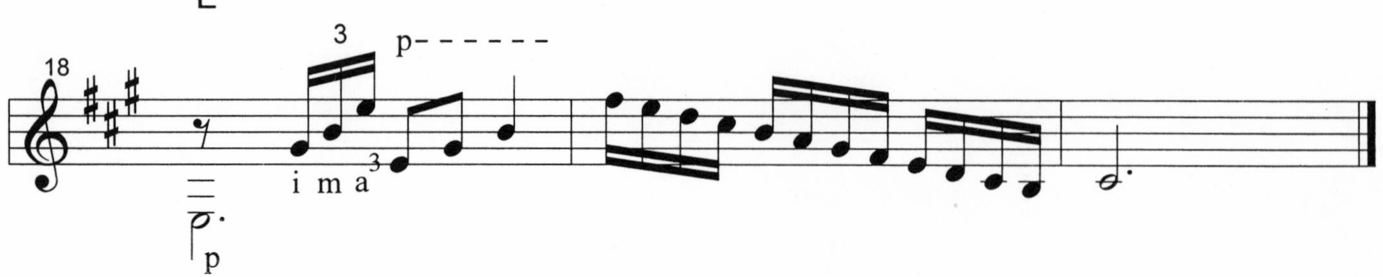

Falseta 4

Juan Serrano

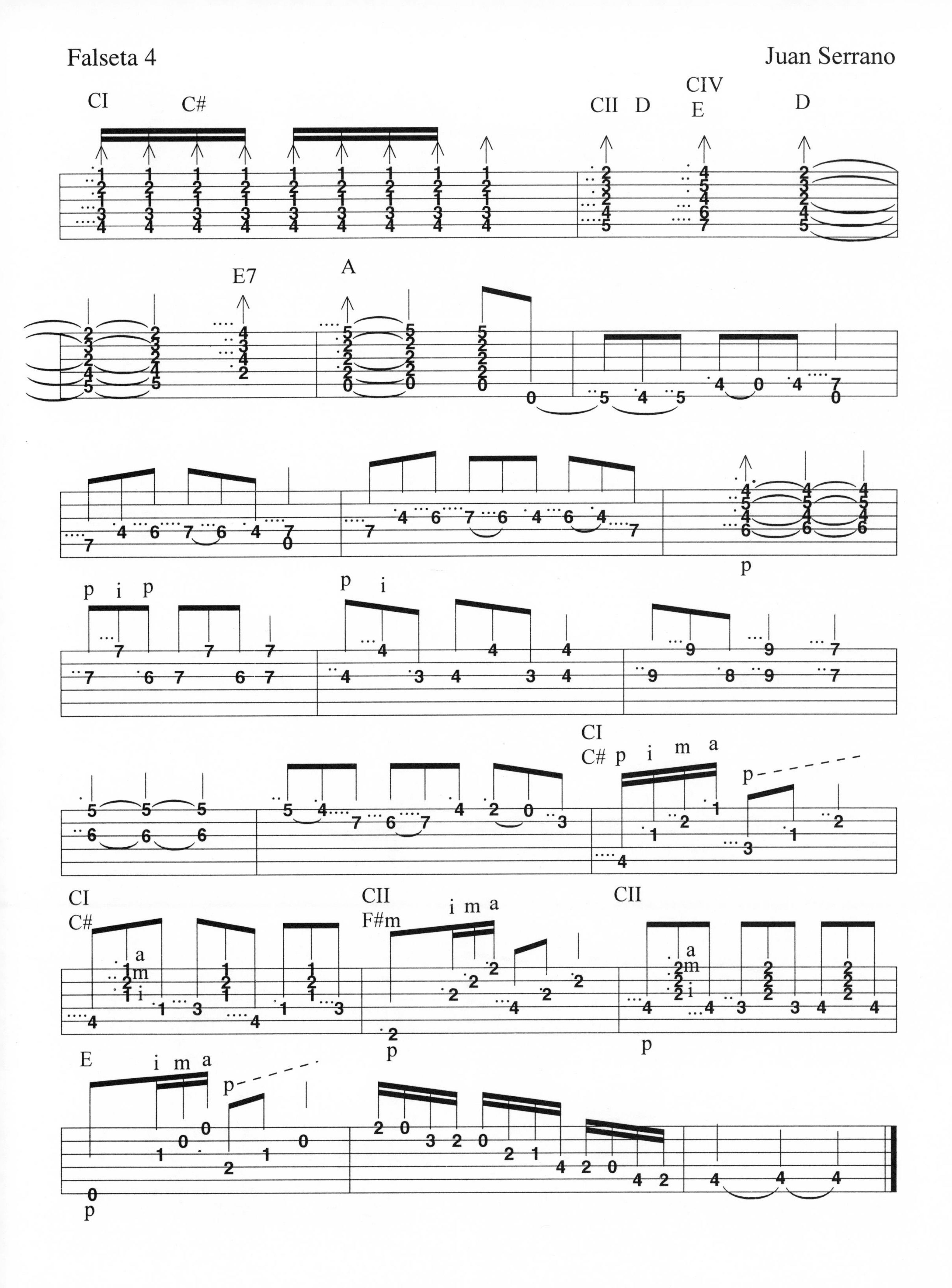

Falseta 5

Juan Serrano

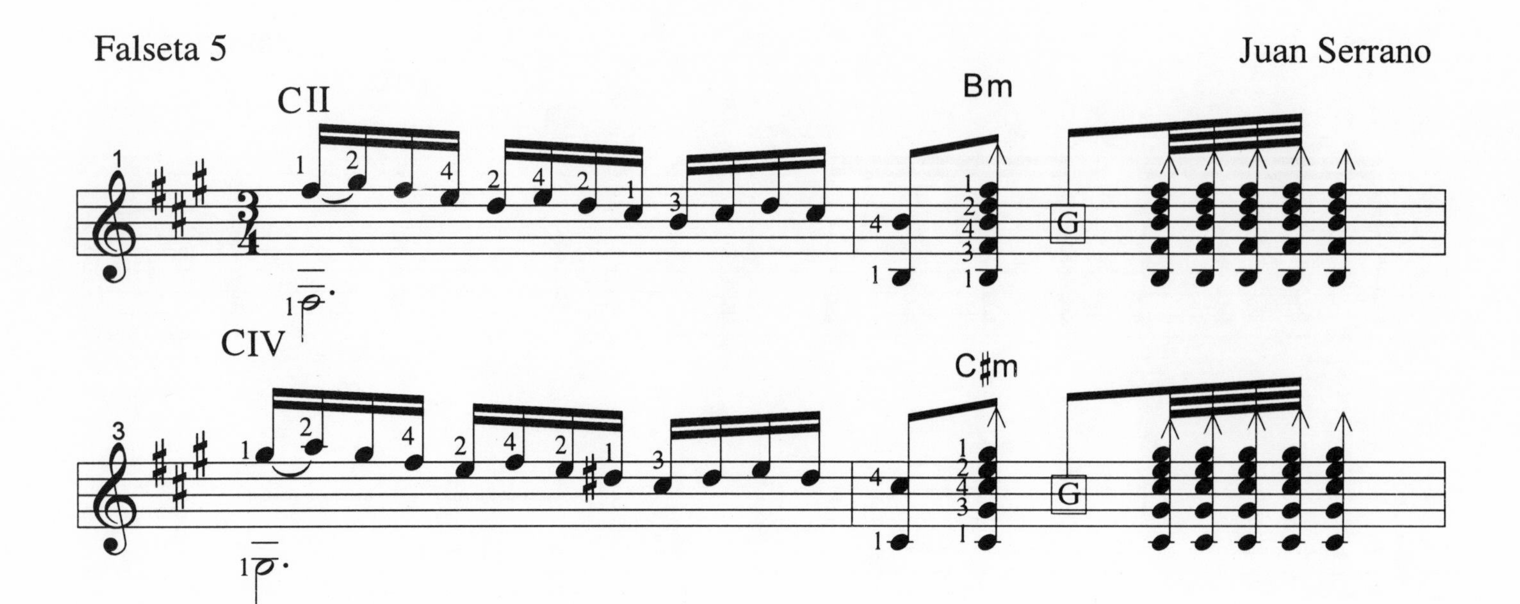

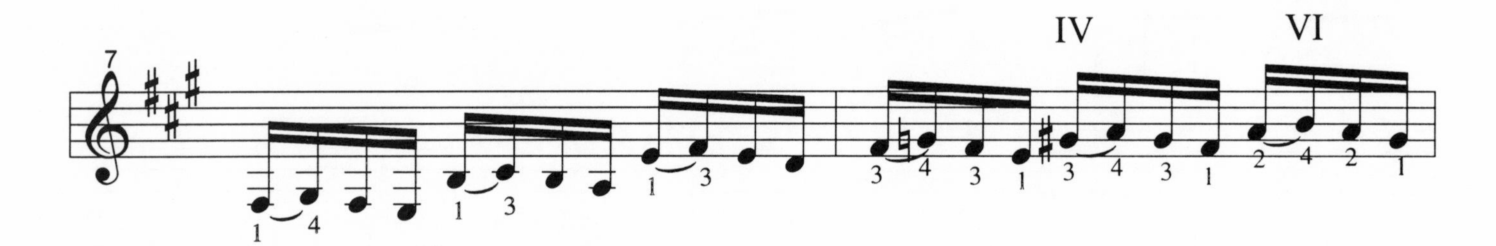


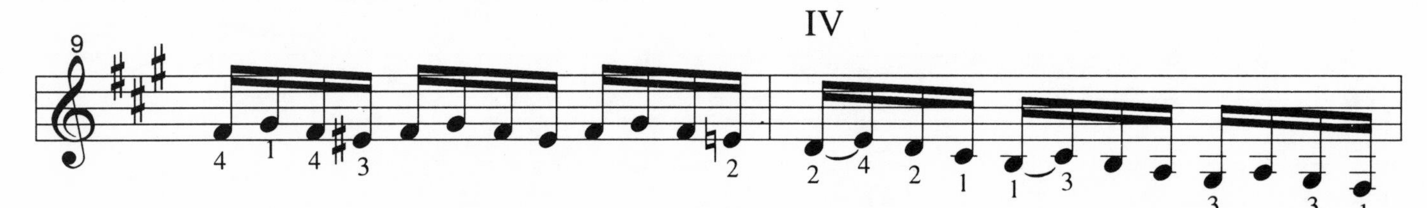


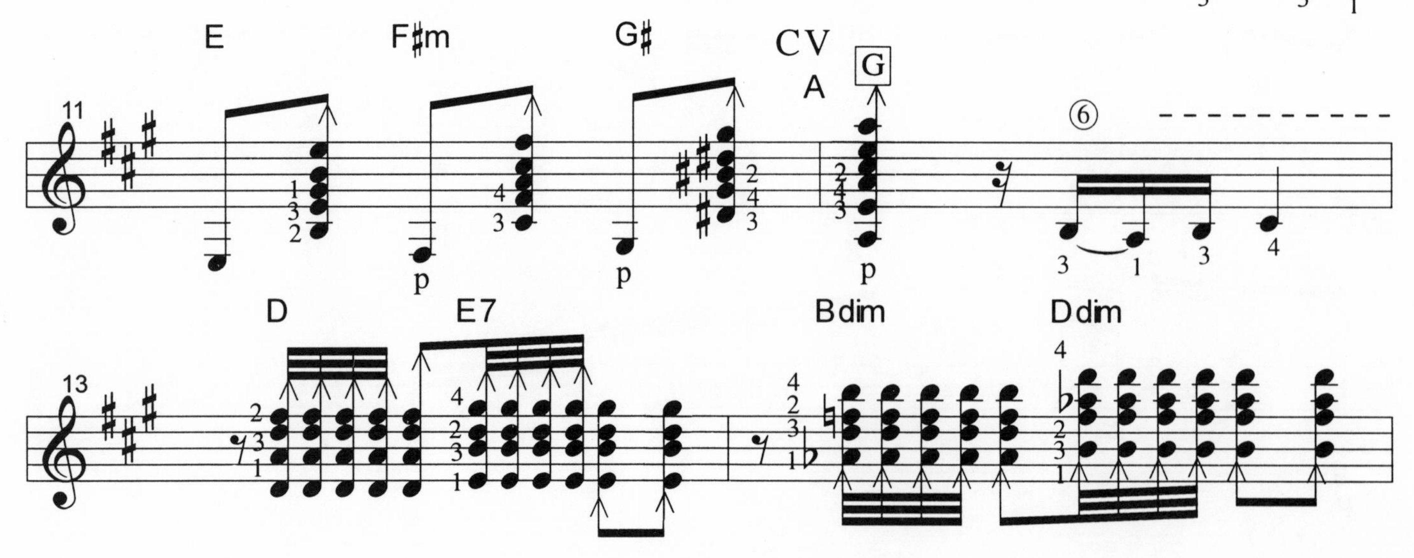

15

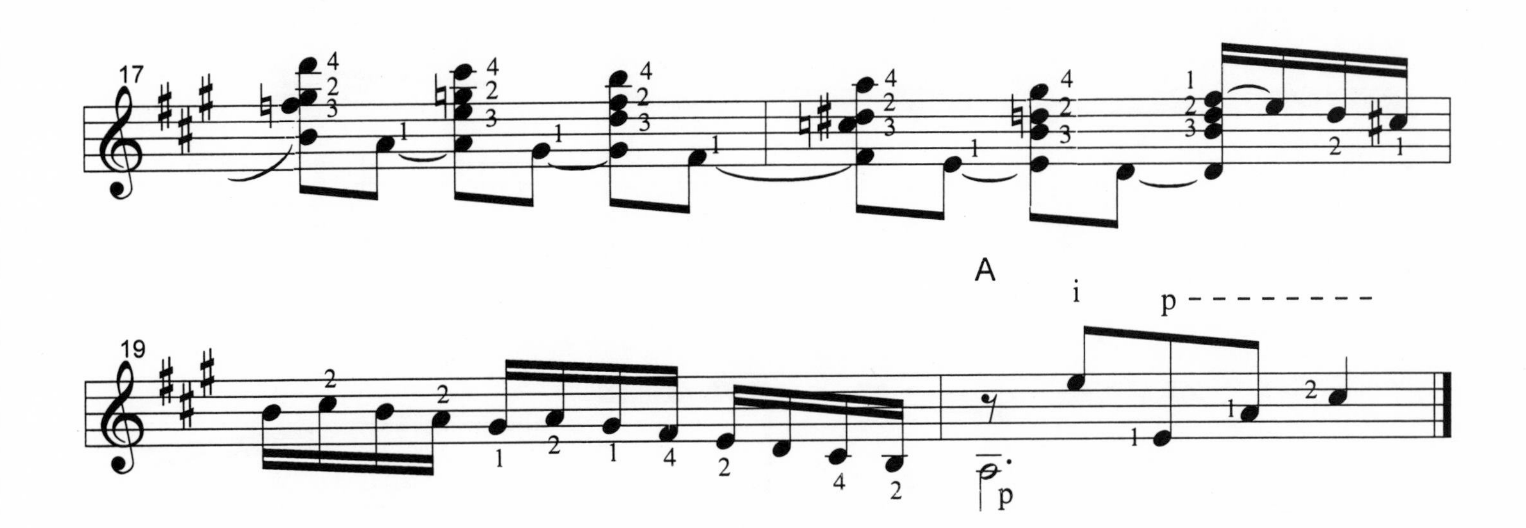
17
19
A
i
p
p

Juan Serrano

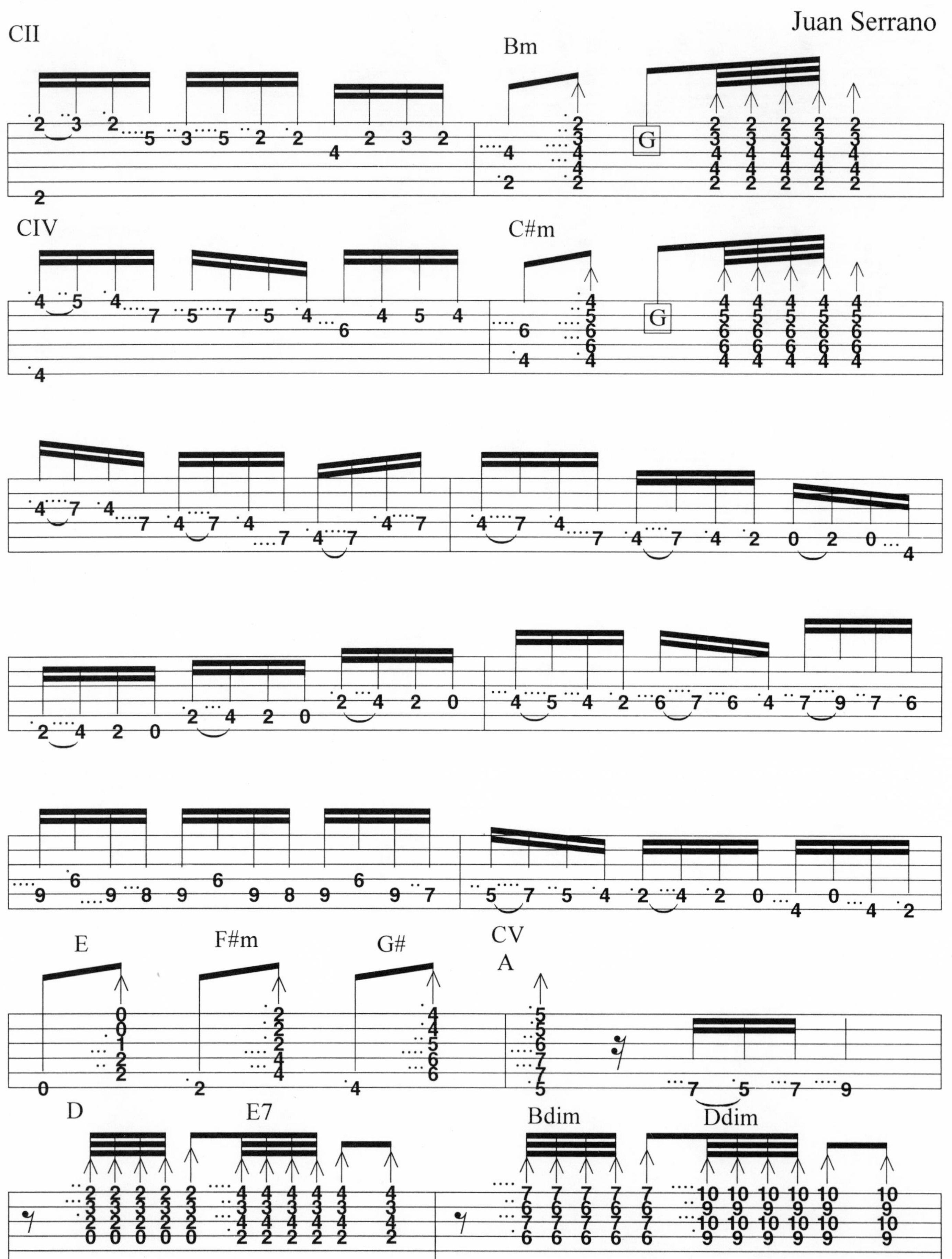

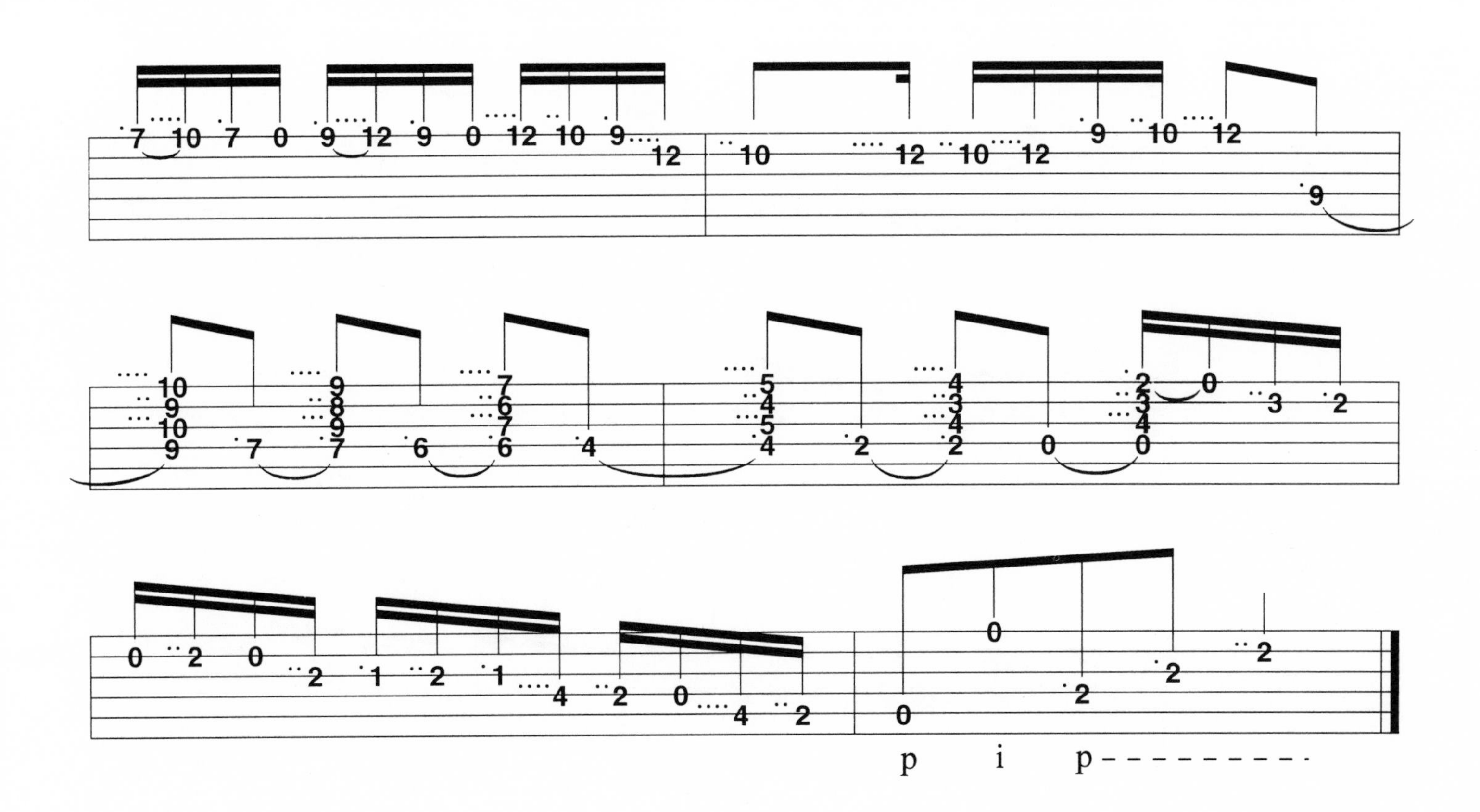
p i p

Falseta 6 (Tremolo)

Juan Serrano

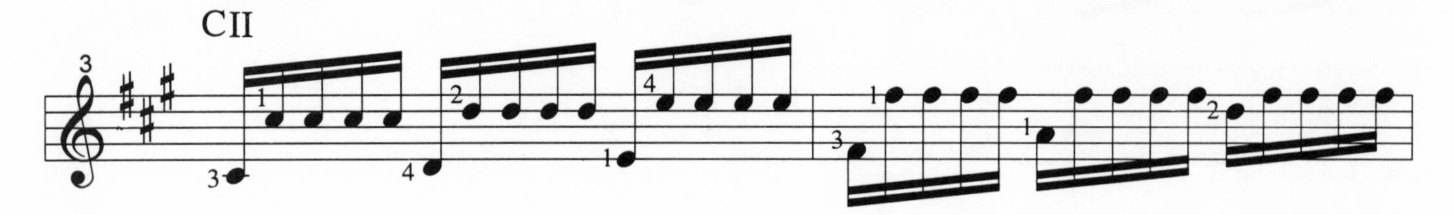


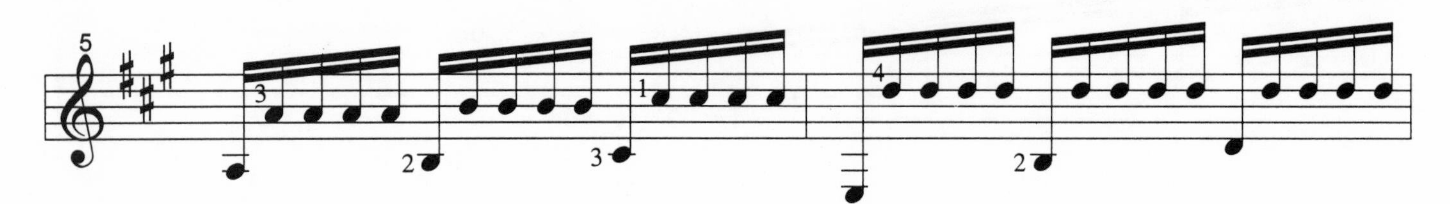

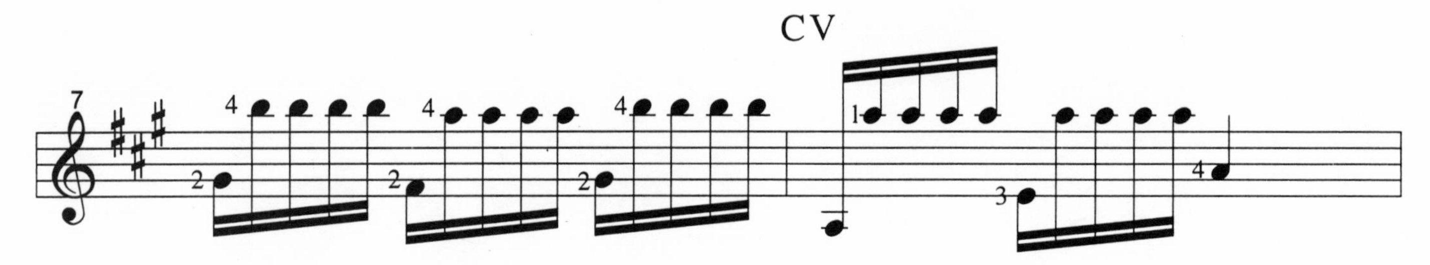


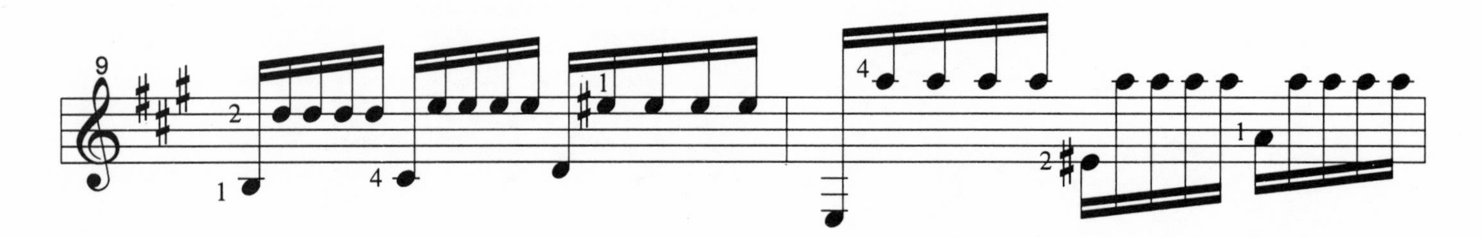

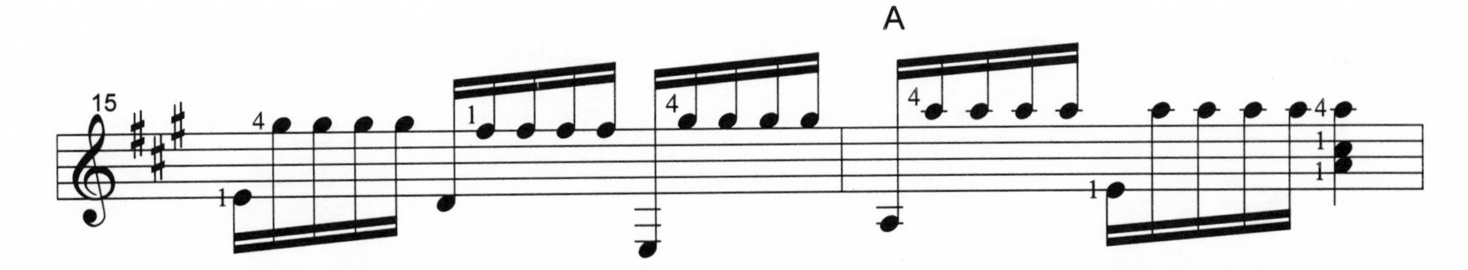
15
A

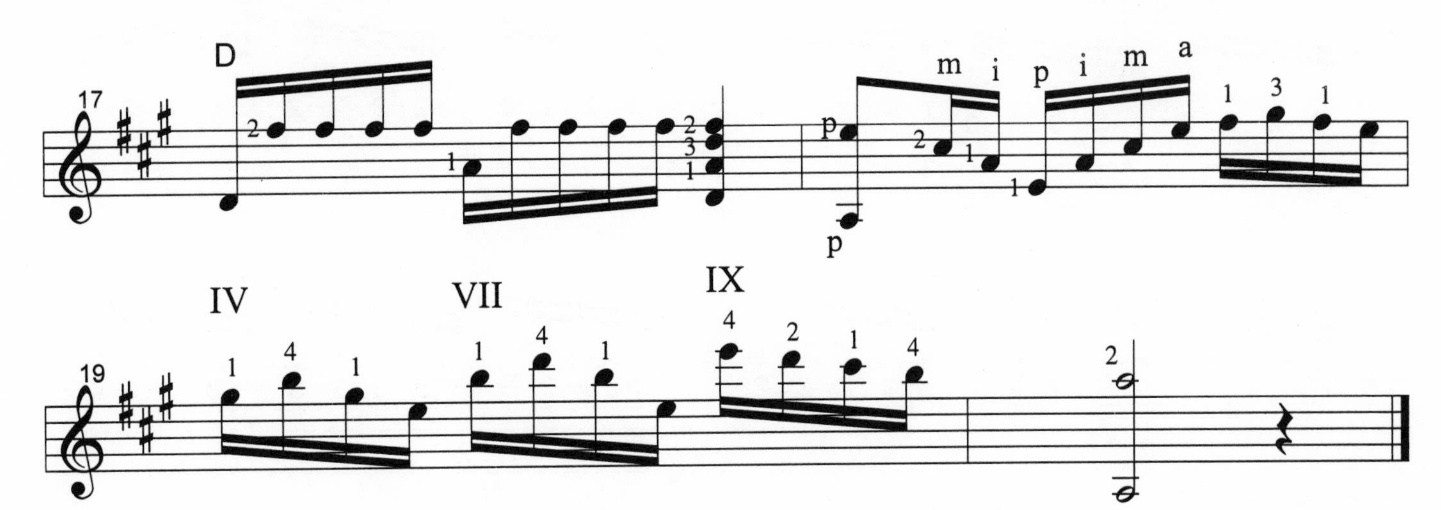
17
D
m i p i m a
p
p
19
IV
VII
IX

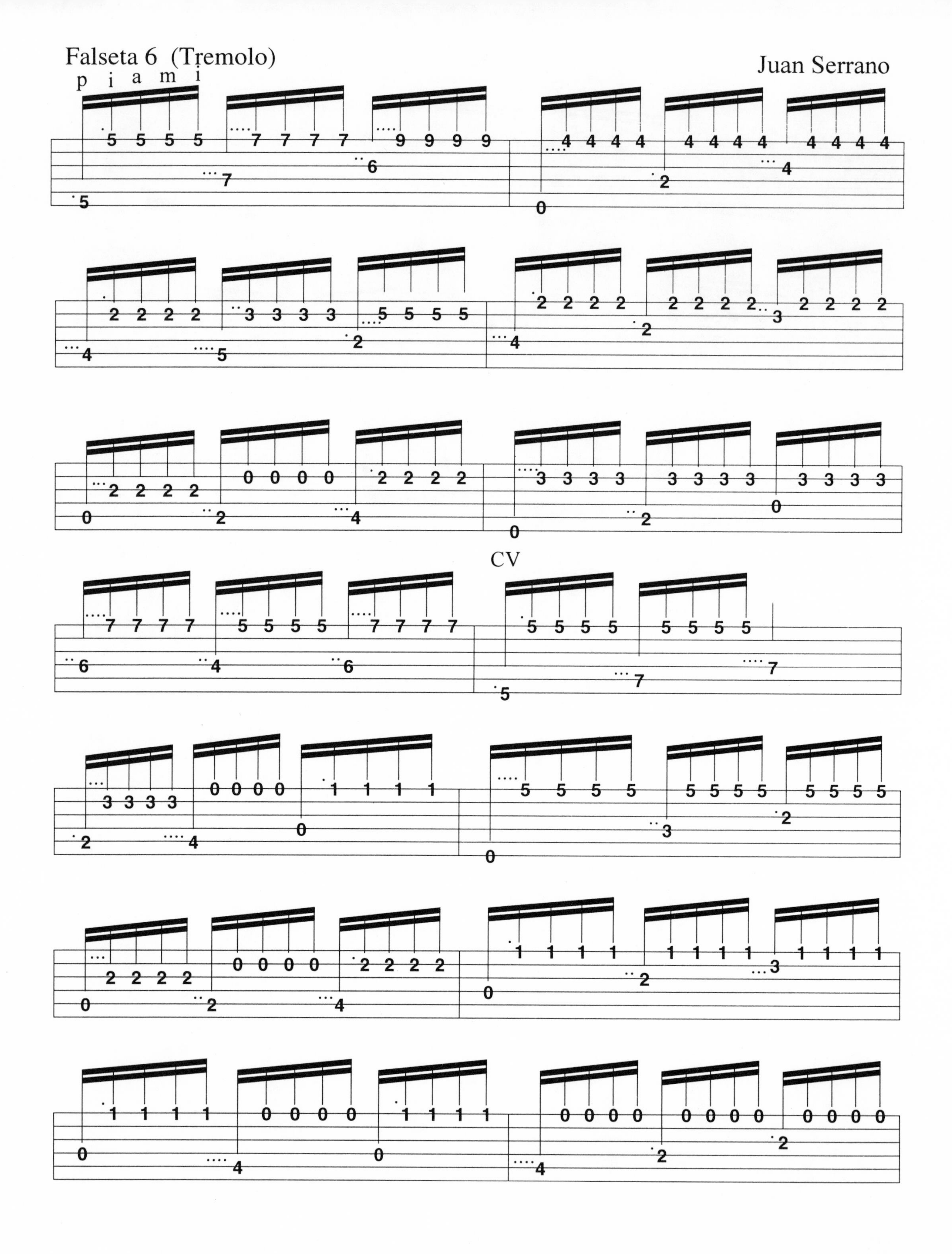
Falseta 6 (Tremolo)
Juan Serrano
p i a m i
CV

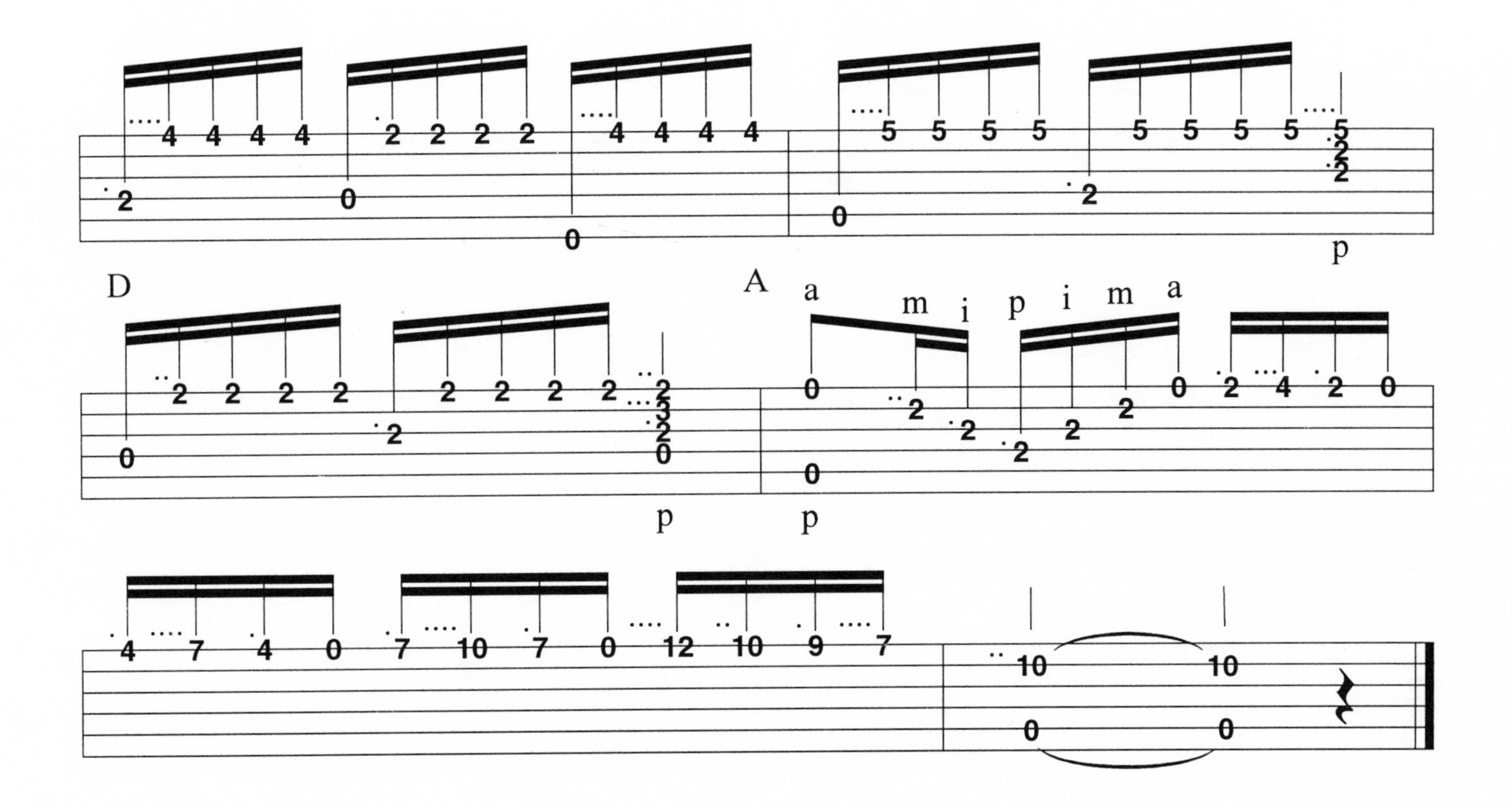
p
D
A
a m i p i m a
p
p

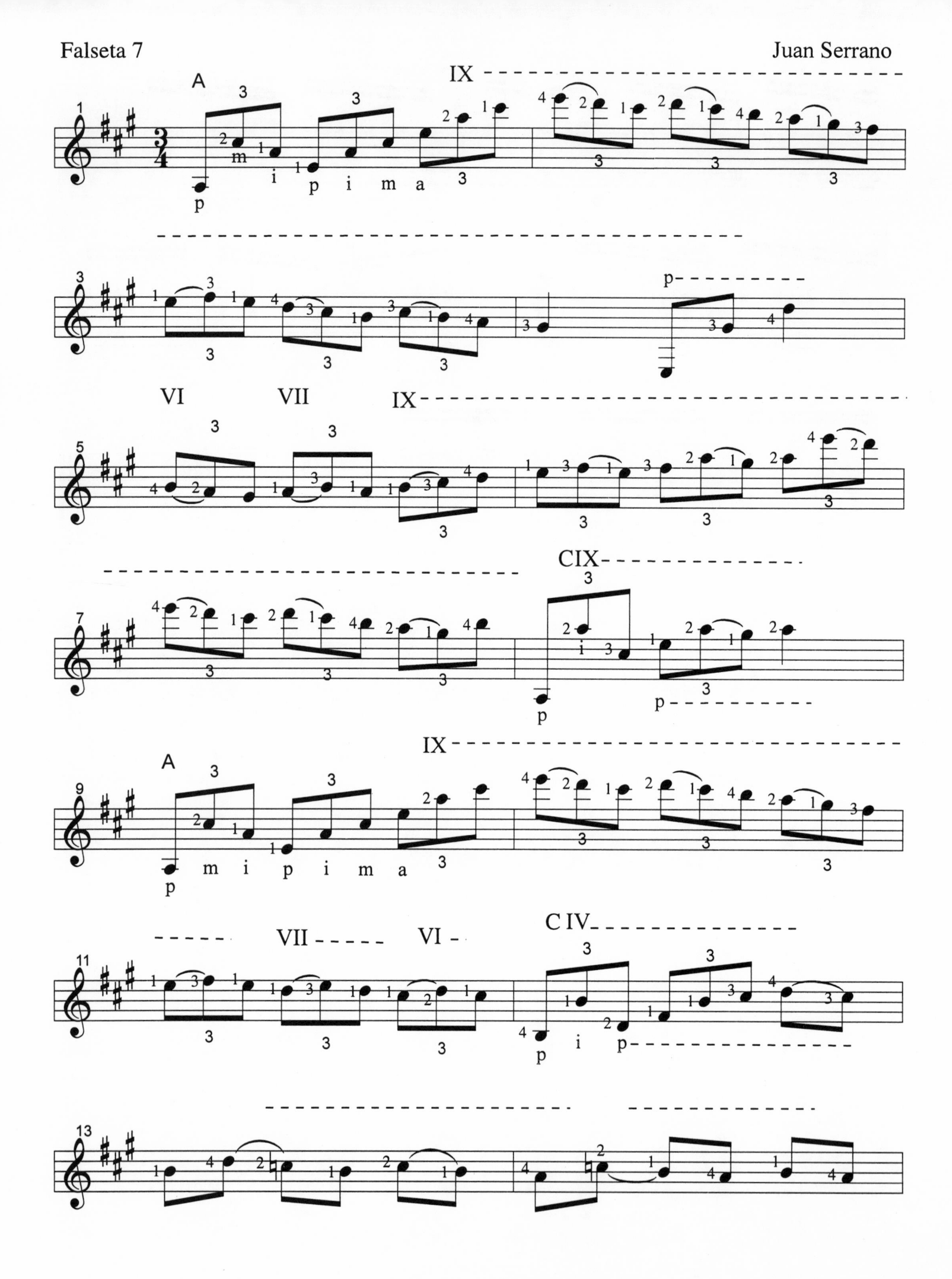
Falseta 7
Juan Serrano
A
IX
VI
VII
IX
CIX
A
IX
VII
VI
C IV

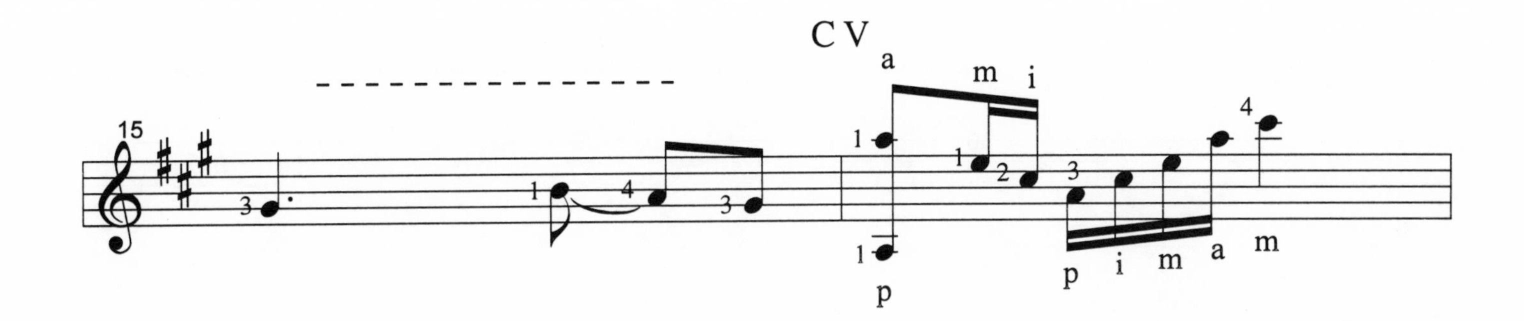
C V
a m i
p i m a m
p

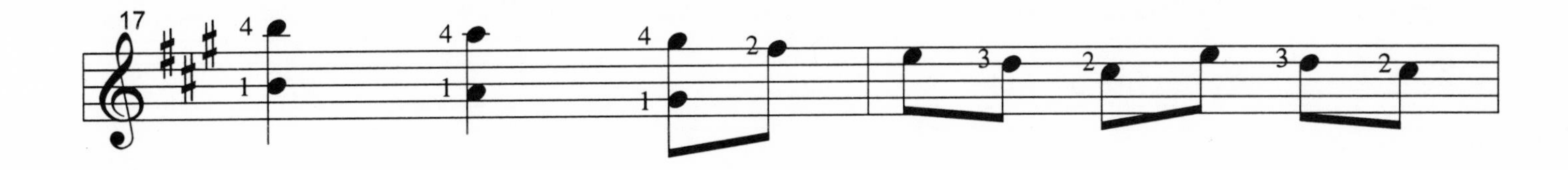

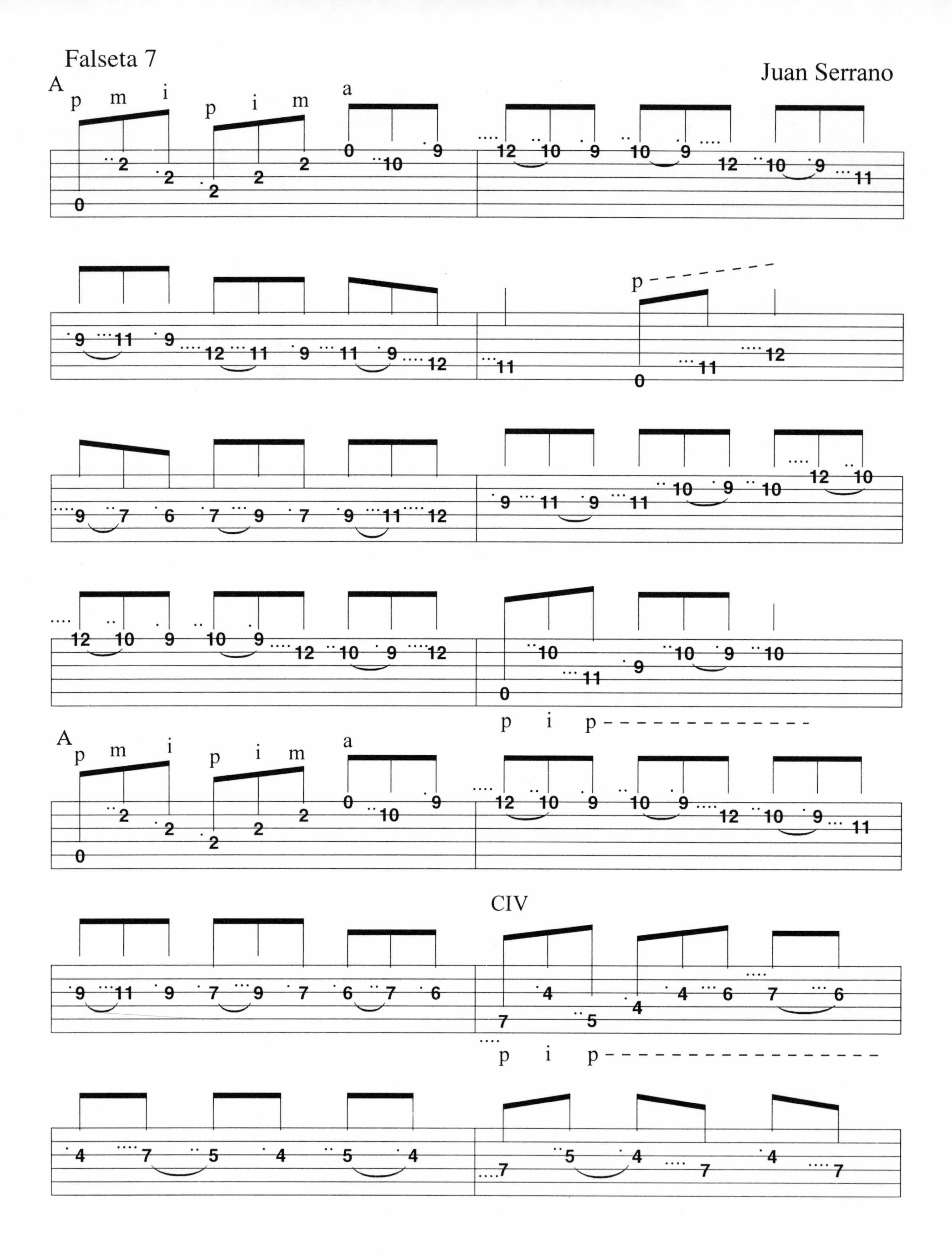
Falseta 7
Juan Serrano
A
p m i p i m a
p
p i p
A
p m i p i m a
CIV
p i p

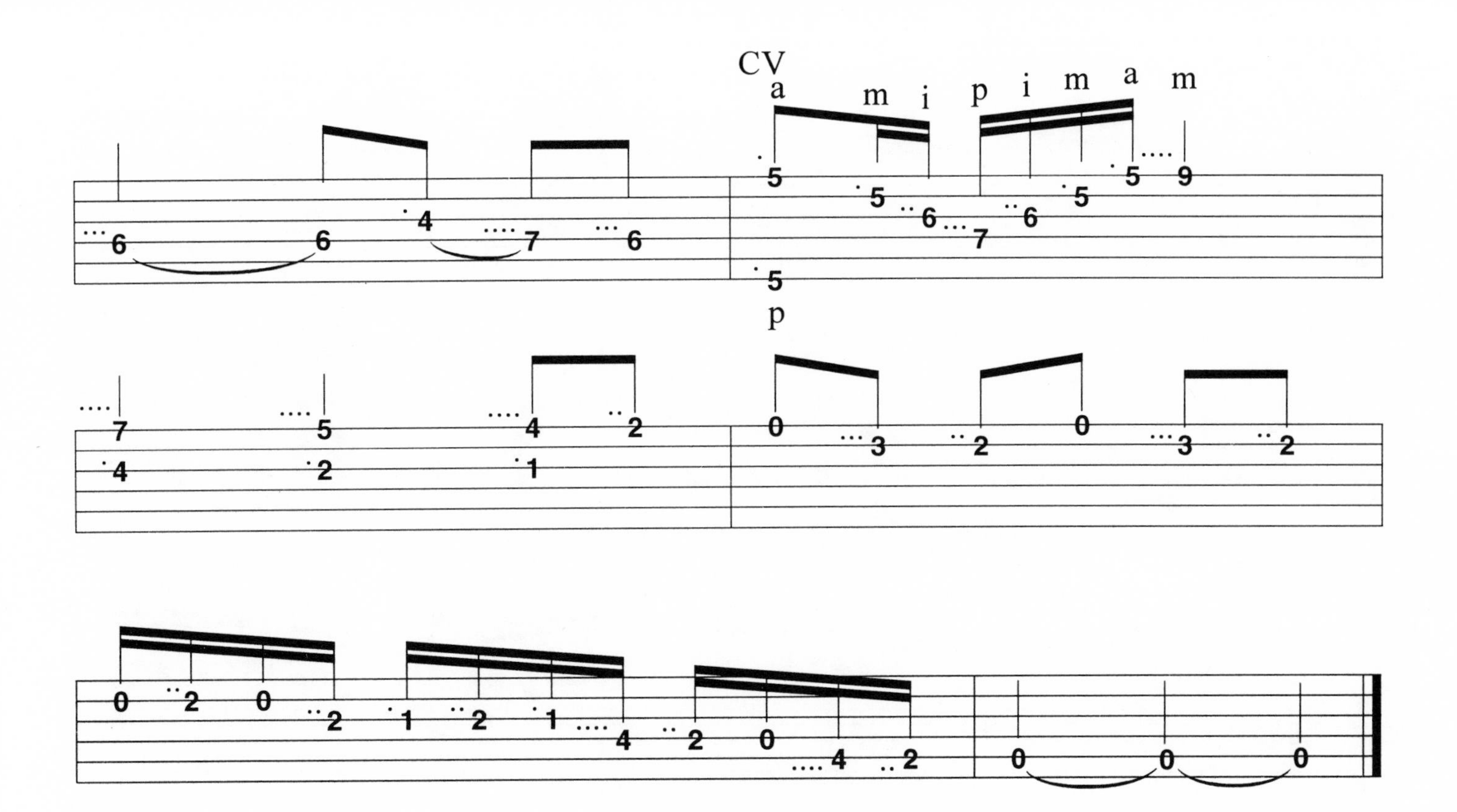
CV
a m i p i m a m
p

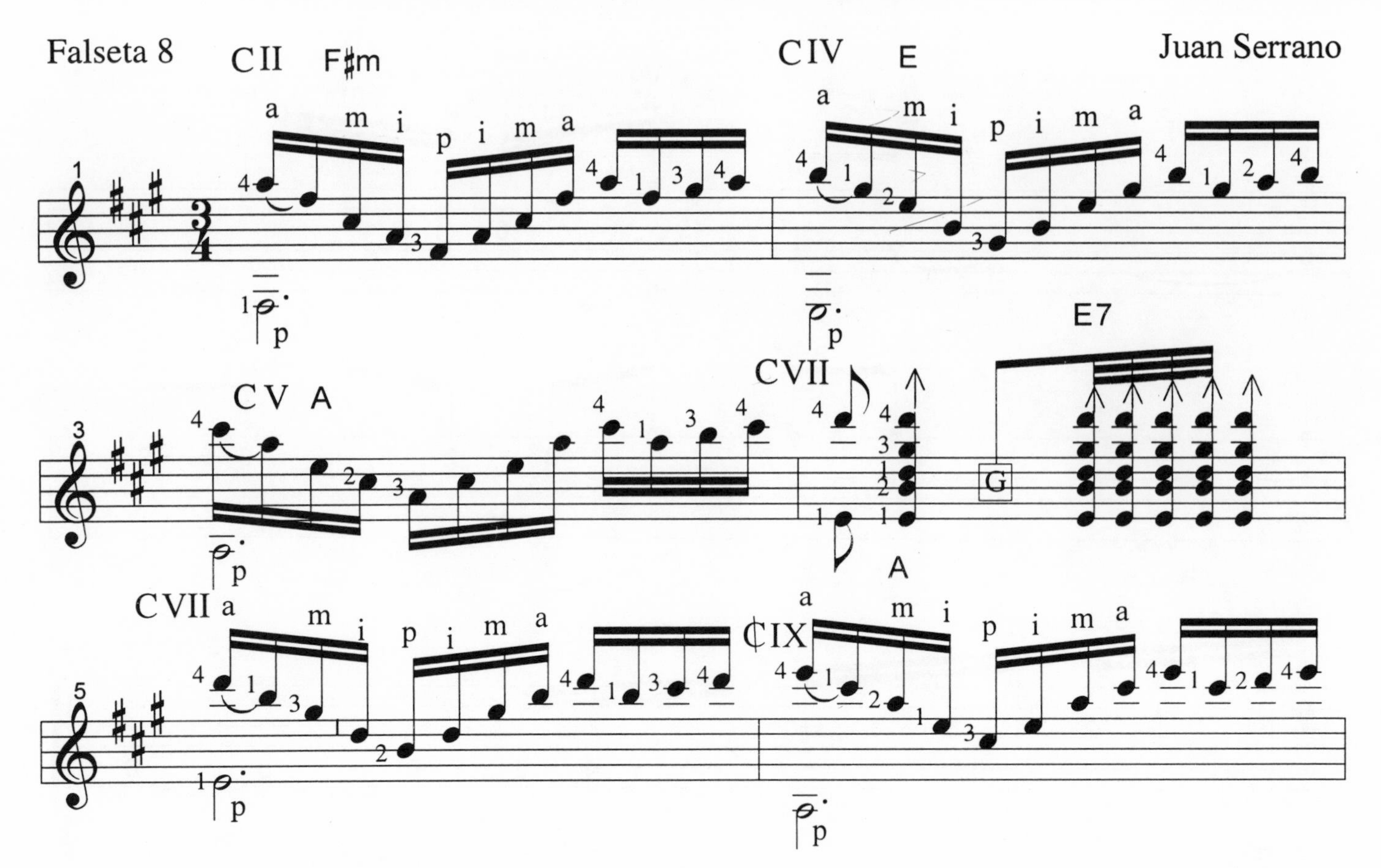
Falseta 8
Juan Serrano
CII F♯m
CIV E
CV A
CVII
E7
A
CVII
CIX

V

IX
VI
IV
II
I
II
IV
CV A

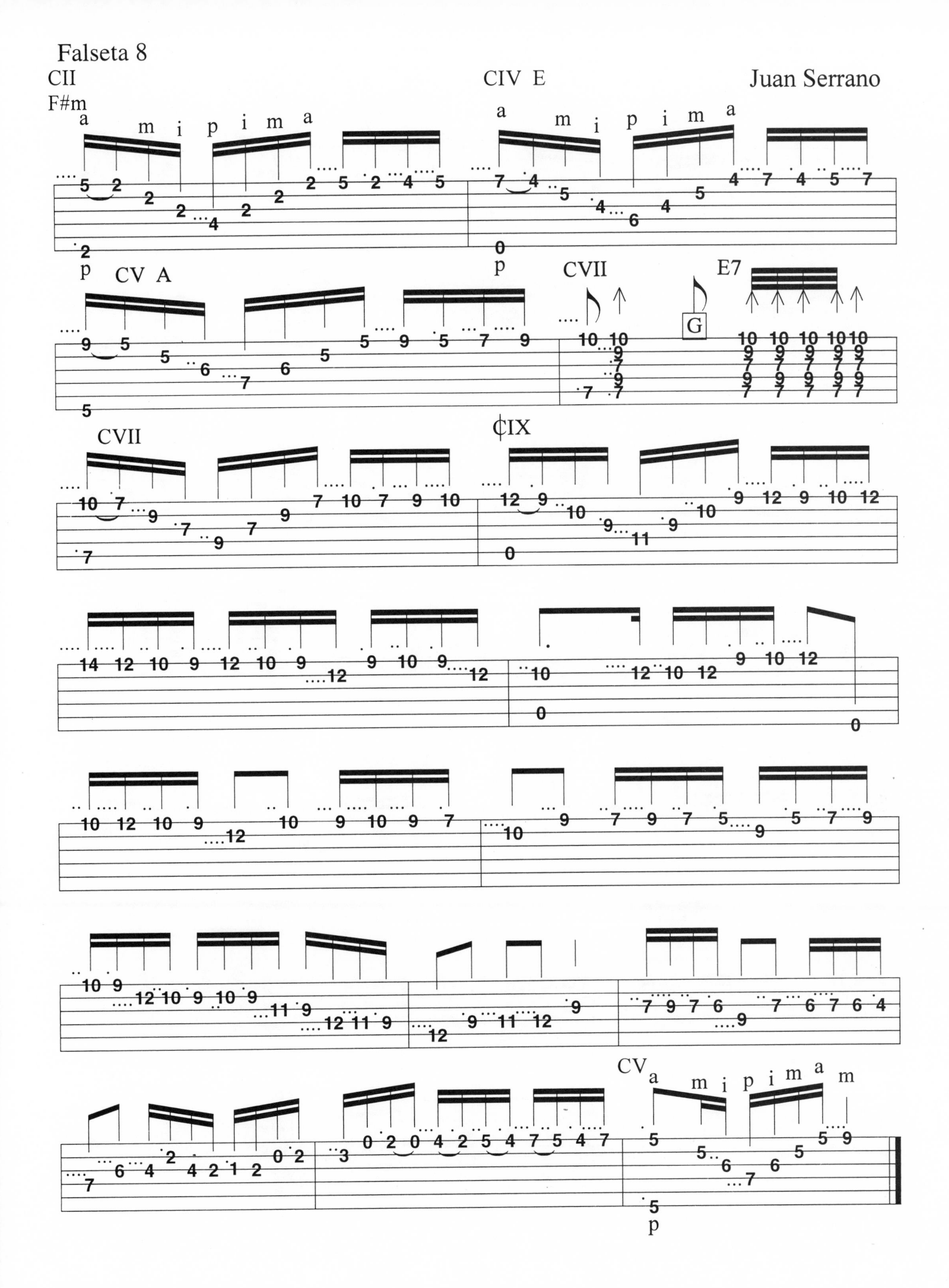
Falseta 8
Juan Serrano
CII
F#m
CIV E
CV A
CVII
E7
G
CVII
¢IX
CV

Falseta 9 Juan Serrano

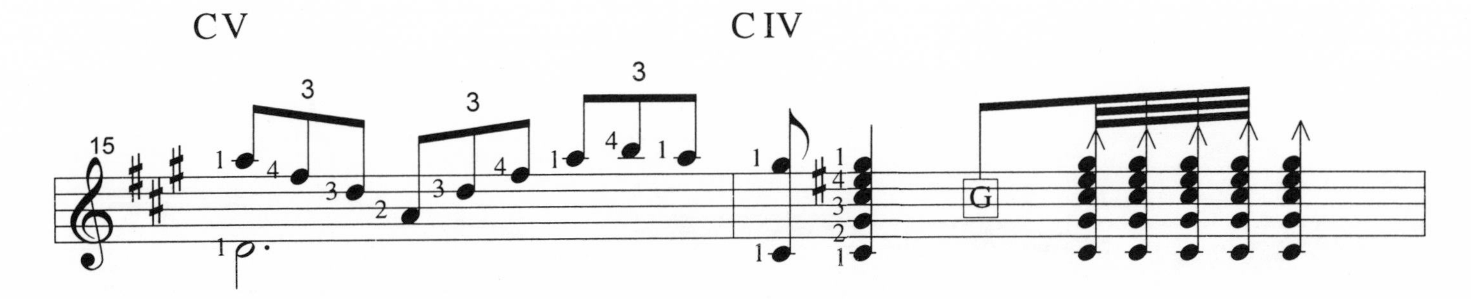
CV
CIV
15
G

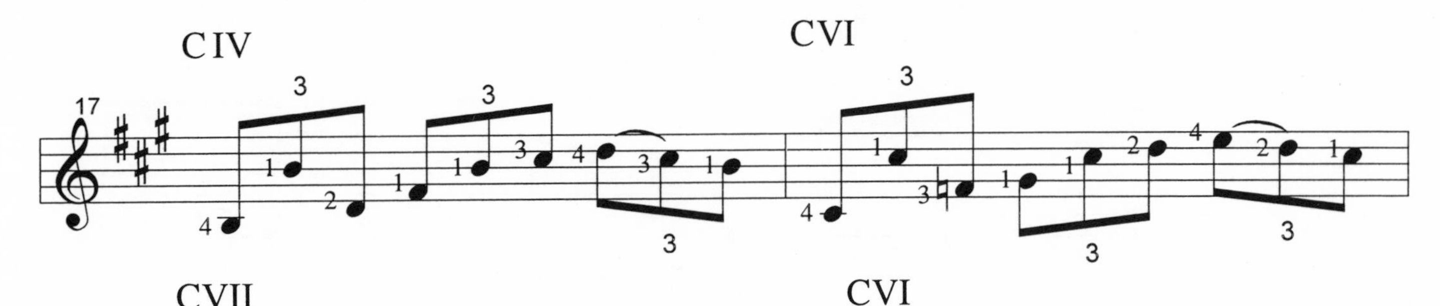
CIV
CVI
17

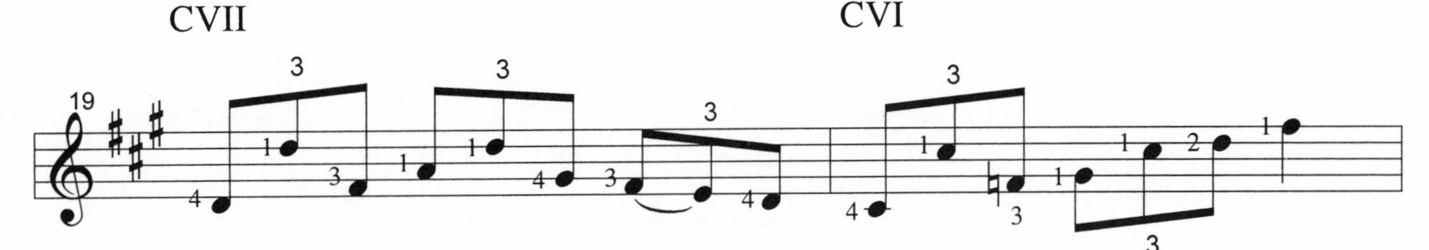
CVII
CVI
19

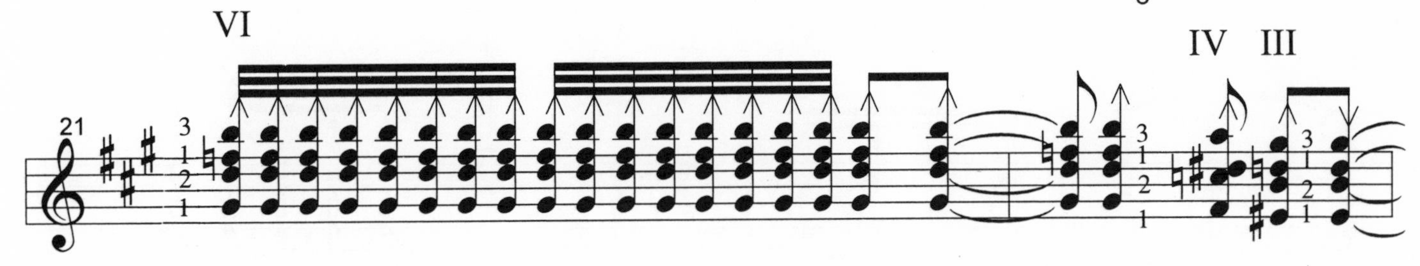
VI
IV III
21

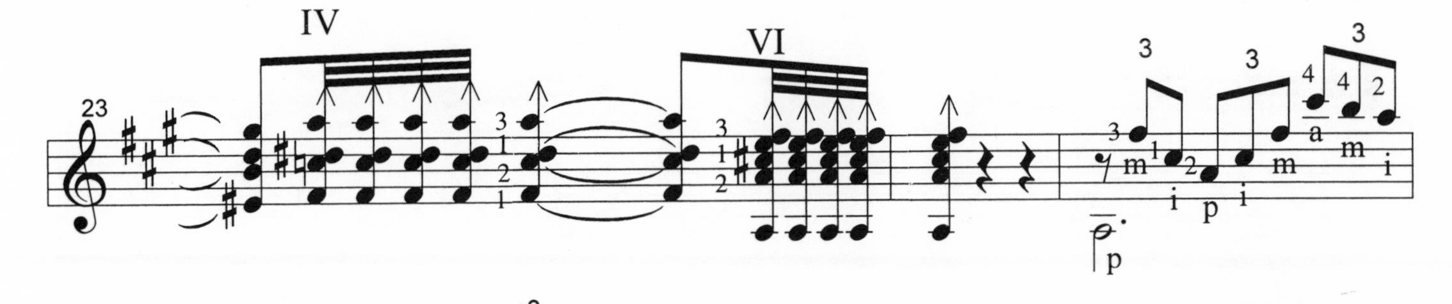
IV
VI
23

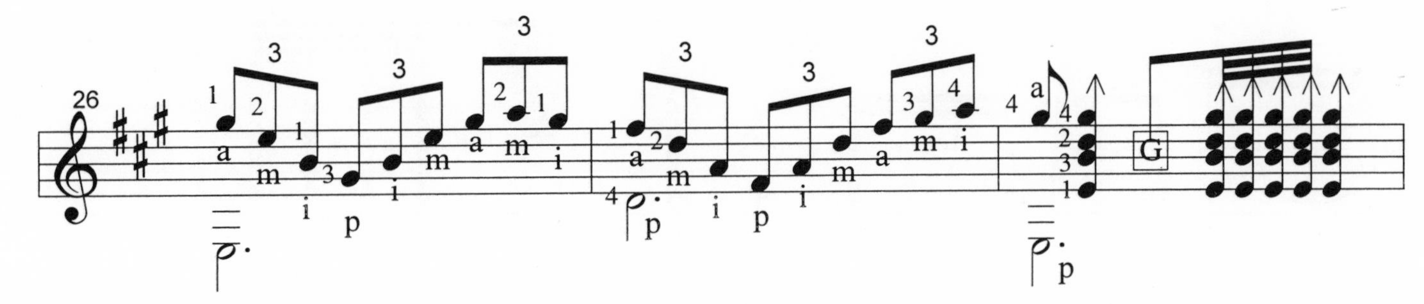
26
G

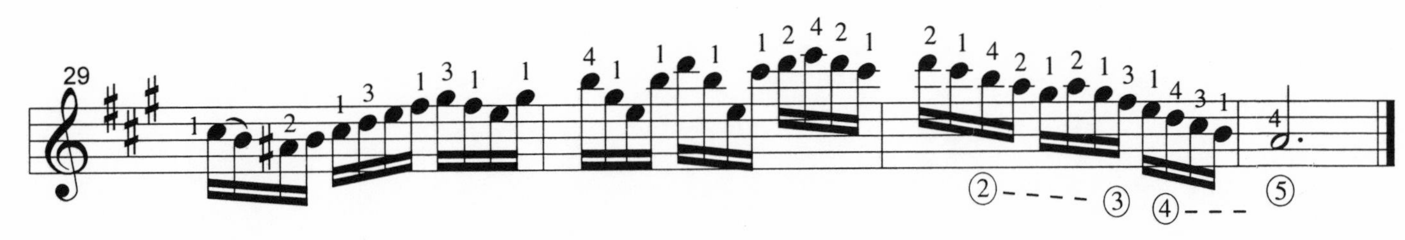
29

## Falseta 9

Juan Serrano

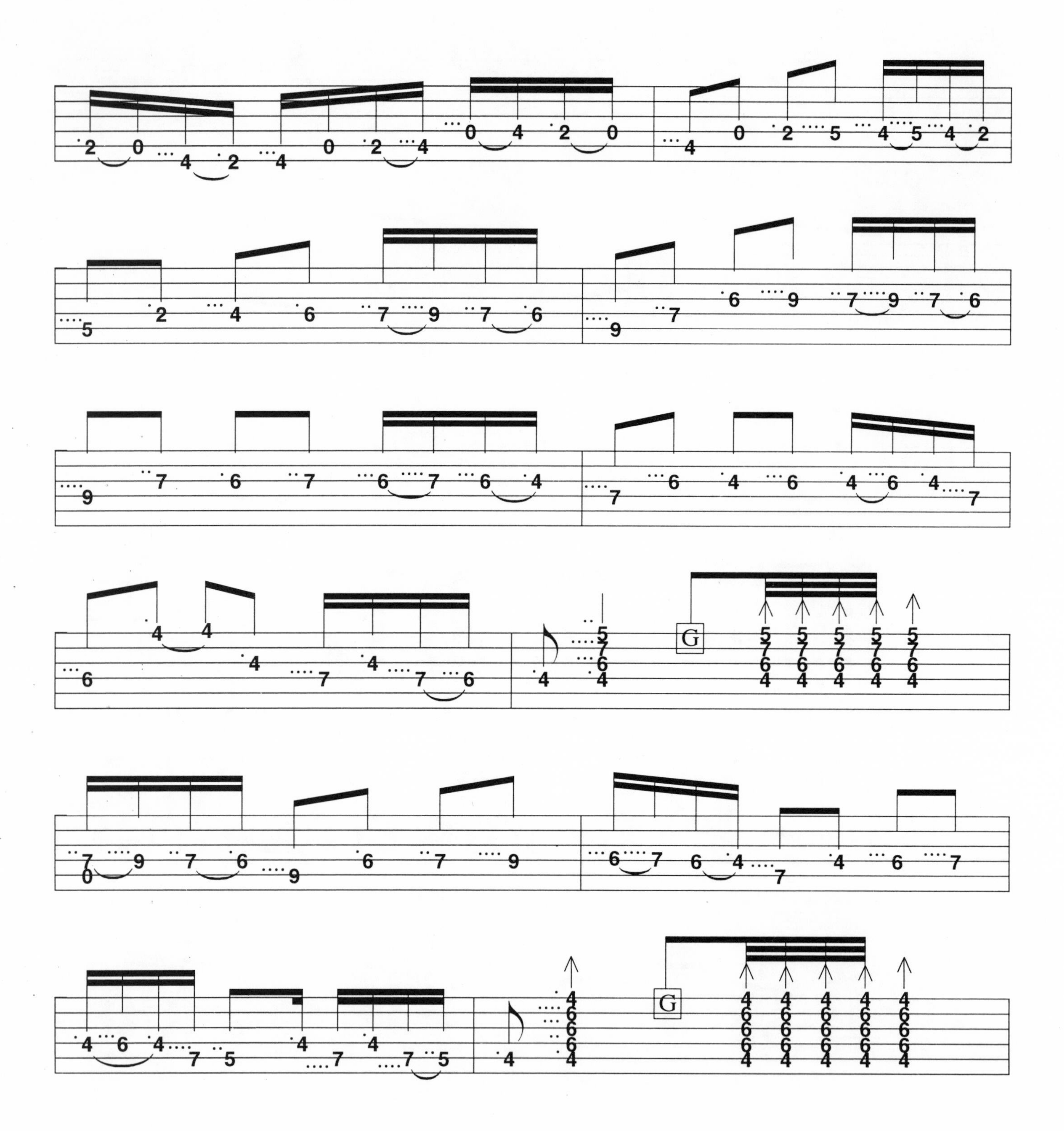

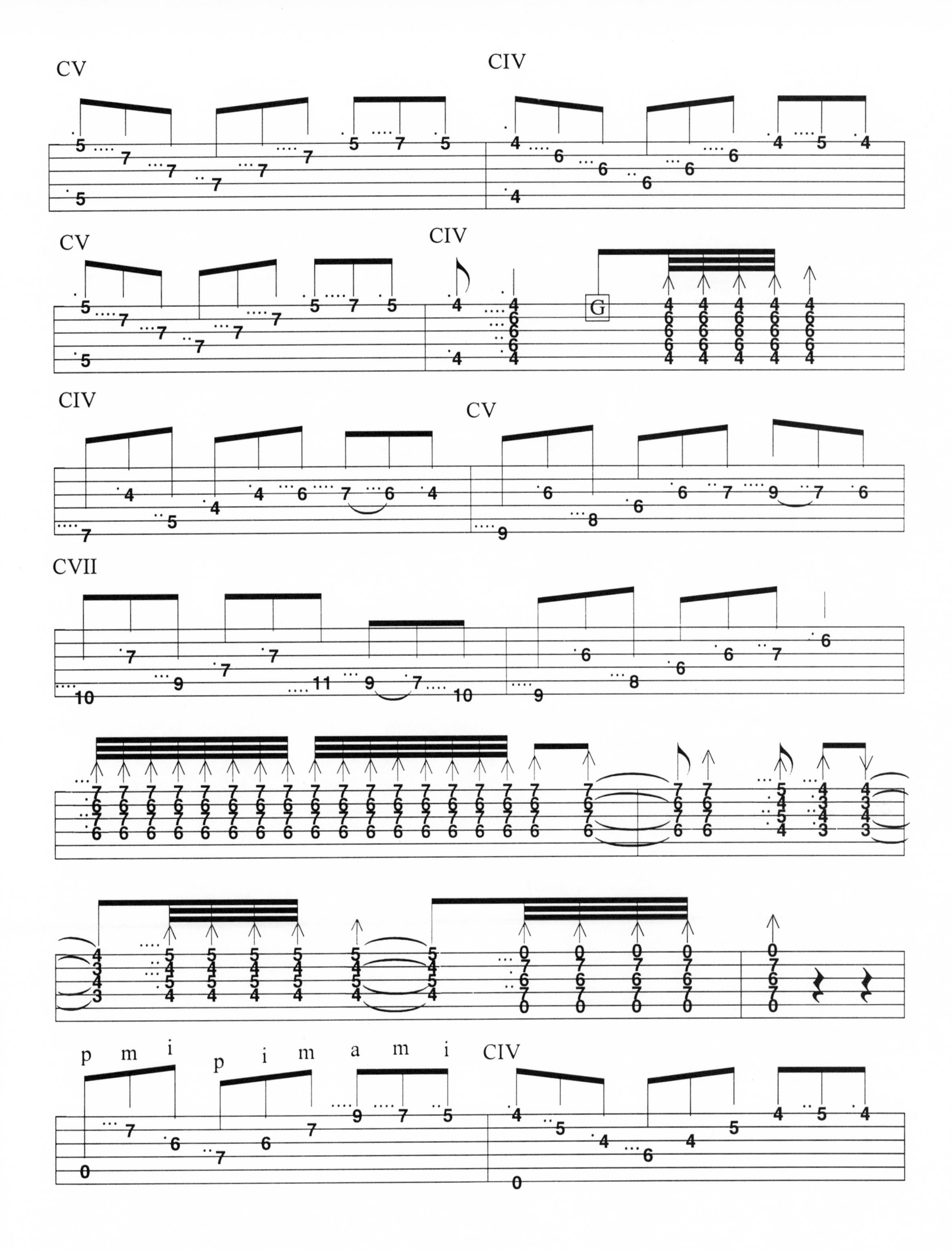
CV
CIV
CV
CIV
G
CIV
CV
CVII
p m i p i m a m i
CIV

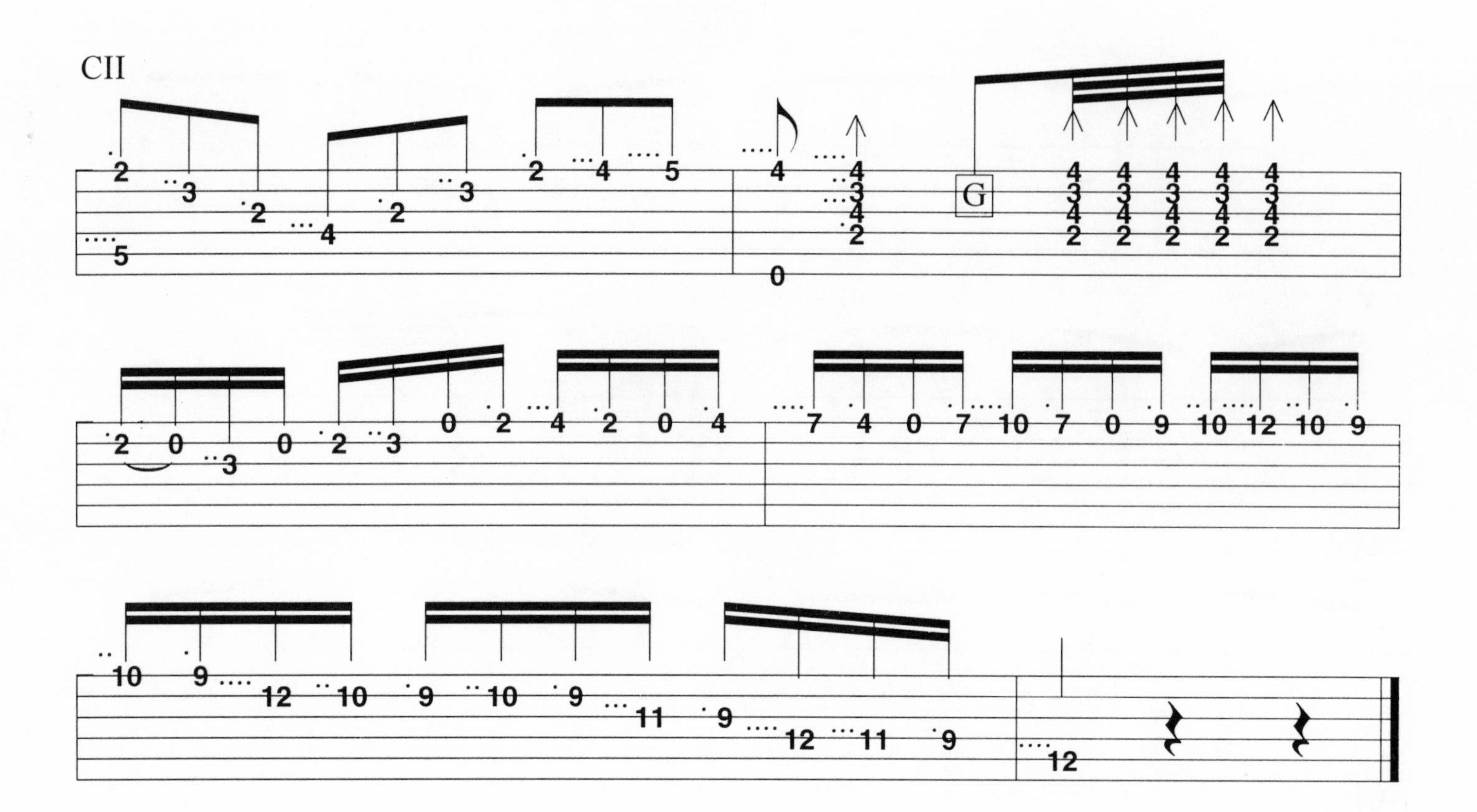
CII
G

*This page has been left blank to avoid awkward page turns*

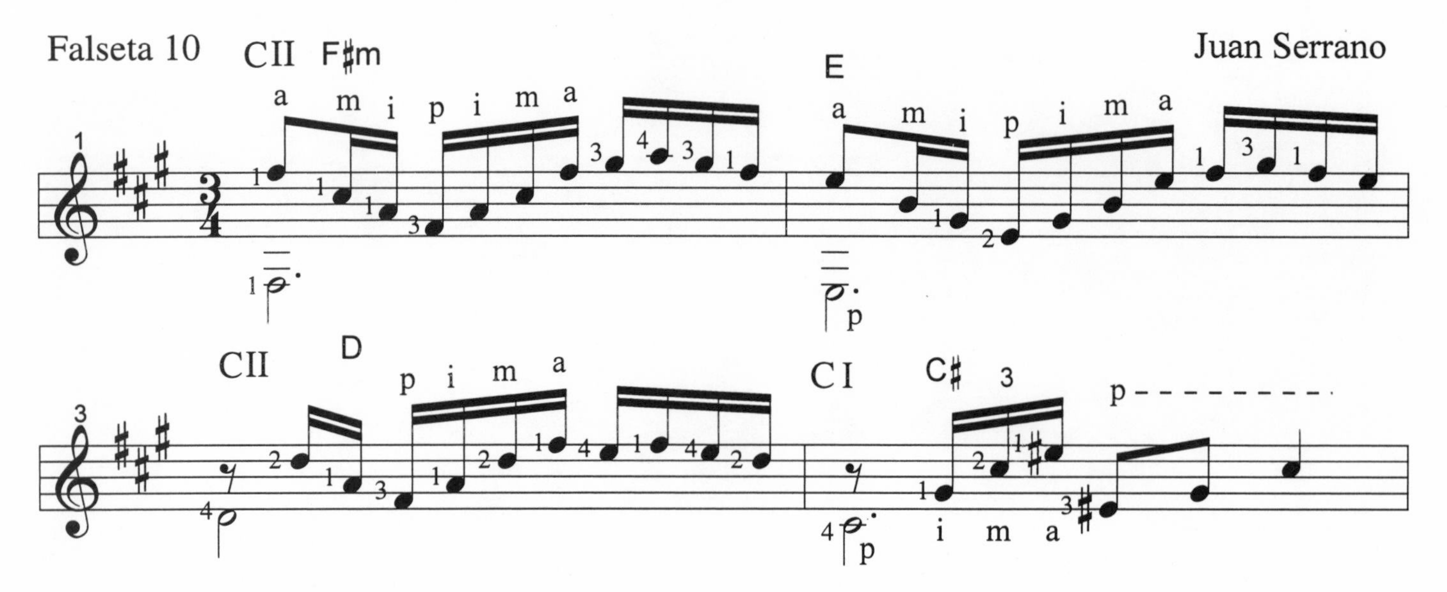
Falseta 10
Juan Serrano
CII F♯m
E
a m i p i m a
a m i p i m a
CII
D
p i m a
C I
C♯
p
i m a

CII F♯m
CIV
E

CV
A
CVII
E7
G

CVII
CV

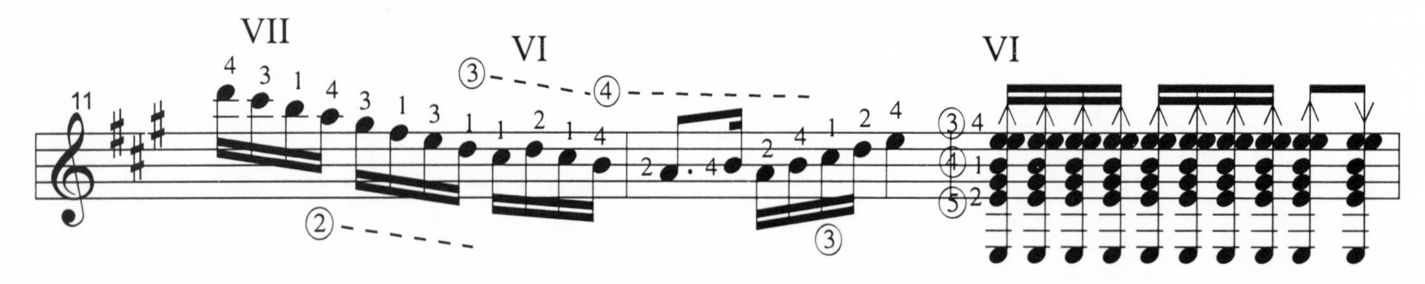
VII
VI
VI

IV
III
A
¢II
E7
G
¢II A

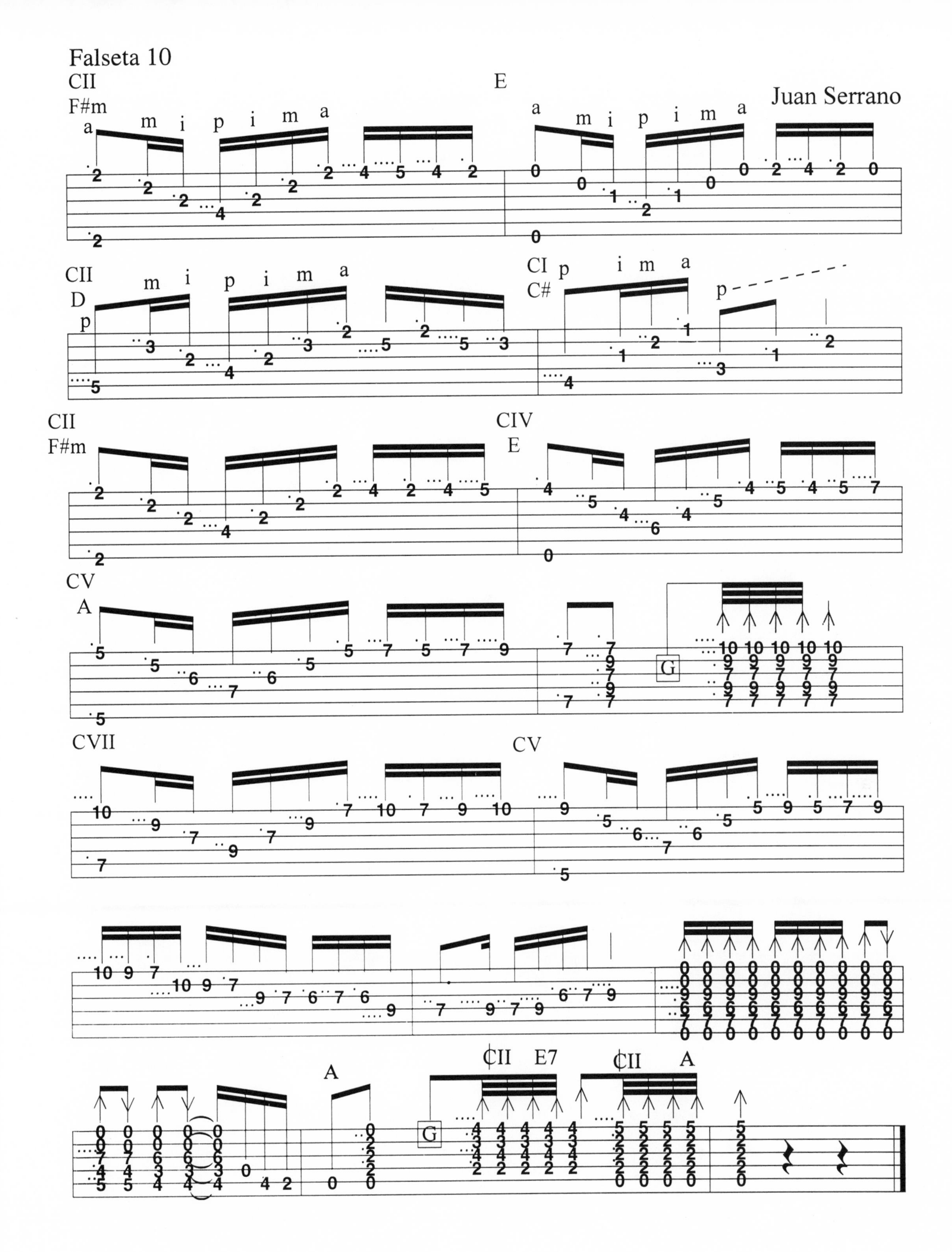
Falseta 10
Juan Serrano
CII
F#m
E
a m i p i m a
CII
D
CI
C#
p i m a
CIV
CV
A
G
CVII
E7

# BULERÍAS

The Bulerías might possibly be the most difficult flamenco form to interpret due to its complexity of syncopation and rhythmical accents. They are measured in 3/8 time. A flamenco compás has 12 beats, equivalent to four measures of 3/8.

The Bulerías falseta traditionally began on the first beat of the flamenco compás or beat #12. Those that begin on the first beat end on the 10th beat, keeping a rest on beats 11 and 12 in order to repeat the compás. Those that begin on the 12th beat end on the 6th beat, completing the beats 7, 8, 9, and 10 with two rasgueados of 2 beats each, or 1 rasgueado of 4 beats, keeping a rest on beats 11 and 12 in order to begin the compás again.

This was traditionally, now with the modern flamenco it can begin with any beat of the flamenco compás although the most common are beats 1, 4, 6, 9 and 12.

The numbers at the beginning of each falseta indicate on what beat the falseta begins. Falsetas #6 and 7 are played with the alzapúa technique. In falseta #6, the first note is marked with a #11. This is the pick up note to begin the alzapúa, although the falseta begins on the 12th beat. Falseta #7 is composed only of the first two compases. The rest are two variations of the same theme.

# BULERÍAS

Las Bulerías posiblemente sean las forma flamenca mas difícil de interpretar por la complicación de los contratiempos y los acentos rítmicos.

Las Bulerías se miden en 3/8. Un compás flamenco se compone de doce tiempos, equivalentes a cuatro compases musicales de 3/8.

Las falsetas de las Bulerías tradicionalmente empezaban en el primer tiempo del compás flamenco o en el tiempo #12. Las que empiezan en el primer tiempo terminan en el tiempo #10, guardando silencio en los tiempos 11 y 12 para empezar otra vez el compás rítmico. Las que empiezan en el tiempo #12 terminan en el tiempo #6, completando los tiempos, 7, 8, 9 y 10, con dos rasgueados de dos tiempos cada uno, o un rasgueado de cuatro tiempos, guardando silencio en los tiempos 11 y 12 para empezar otra vez el compás rítmico.

Eso era tradicionalmente. Hoy, con el flamenco moderno, se empiezan en cualquier tiempo del compás flamenco, aunque los más comunes son los tiempos 1, 4, 6, 9 y 12.

Al principio de cada falseta, he marcado el número del tiempo que empiezan.
Las falsetas 6 y 7, se ejecutan con la técnica de alzapúa. En la falseta # 6, he marcado la primera nota con el #11. Esta nota es solamente la nota de preparación para iniciar el alzapúa. La falseta empieza en el tiempo #12.
La falseta #7 se compone solamente de los dos primeros compases flamencos. El resto son dos variaciones sobre el mismo tema.

# *Bulerias*

Traditional Compas

Juan Serrano

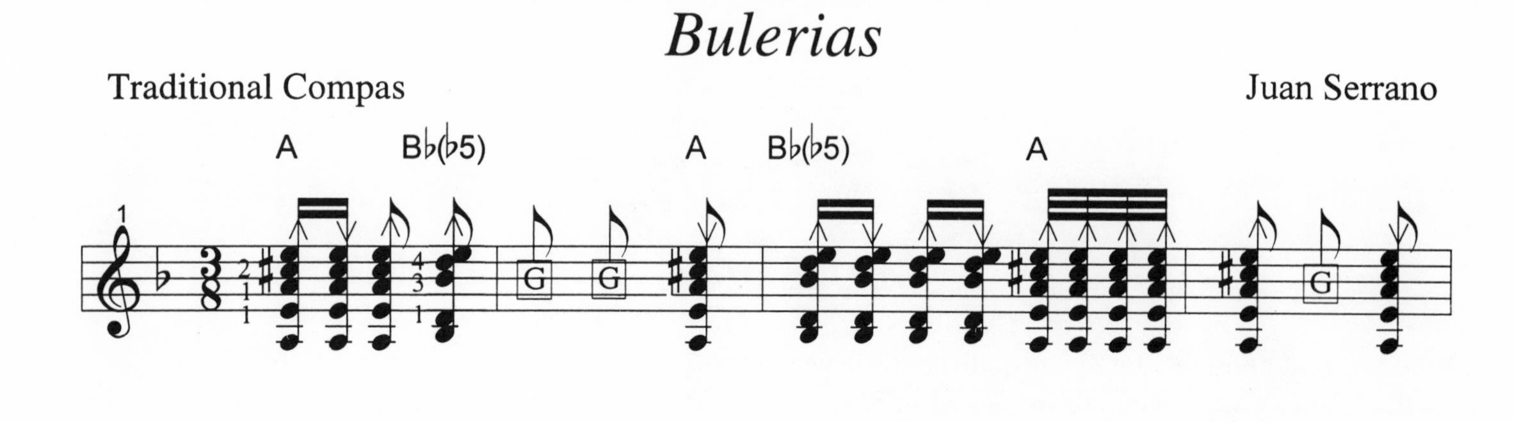


Variation 1

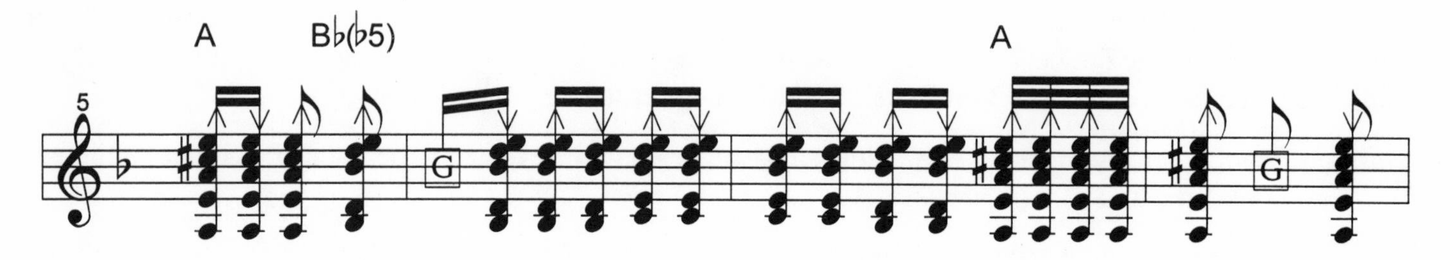


Variation 2

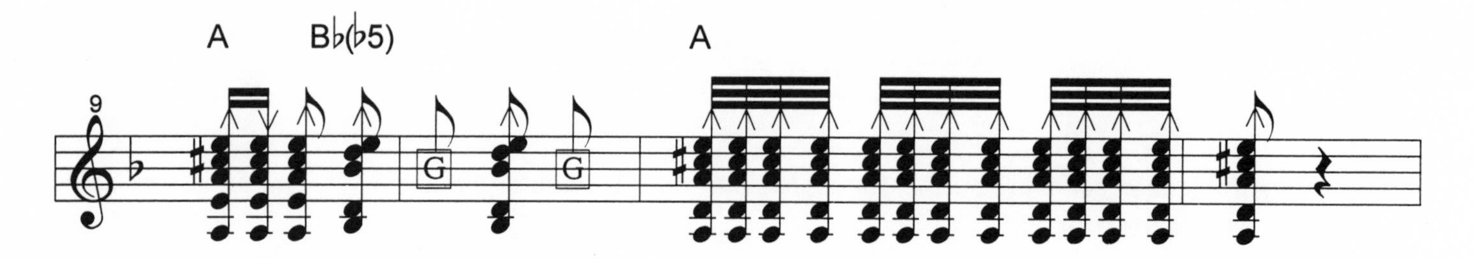


Variation 3

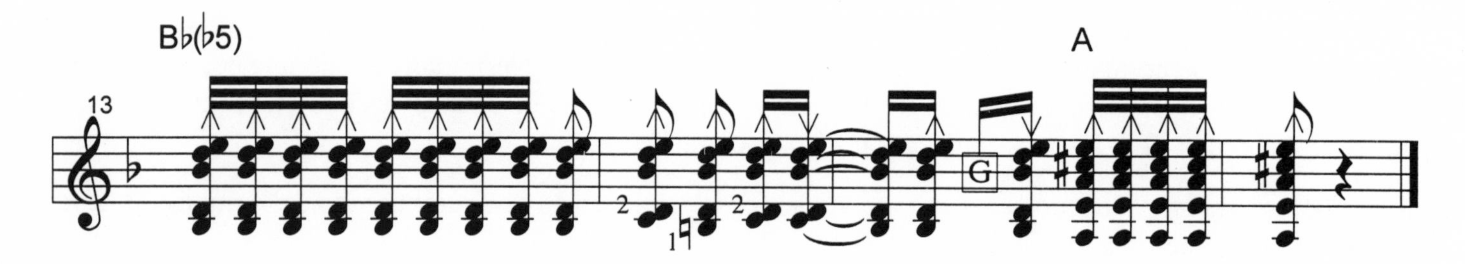

# *Bulerias*

## Traditional Compas

Juan Serrano

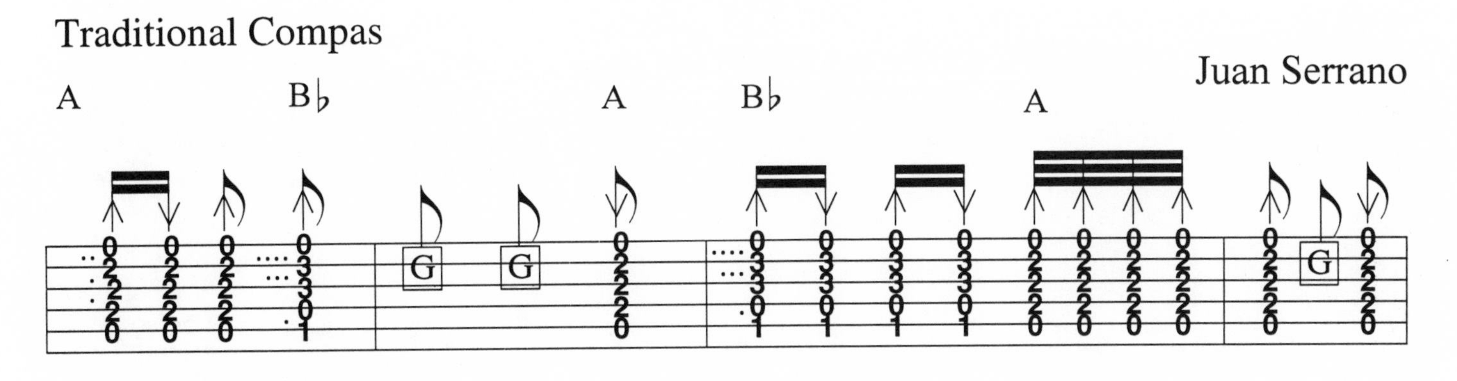


## Variation 1

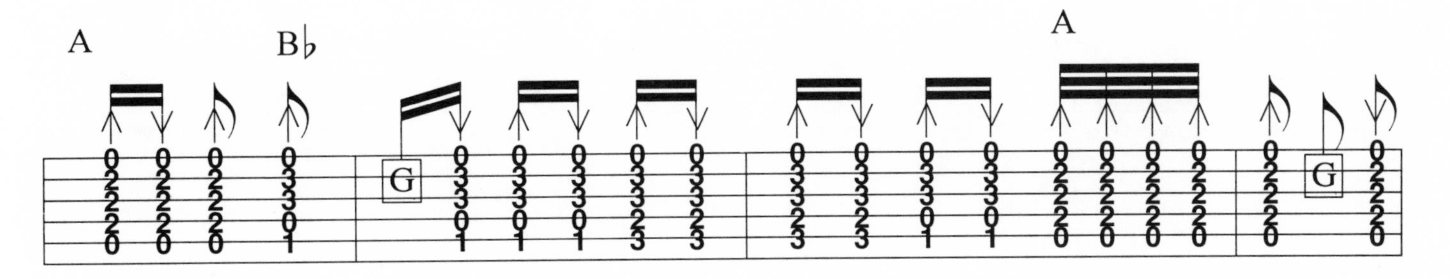


## Variation 2

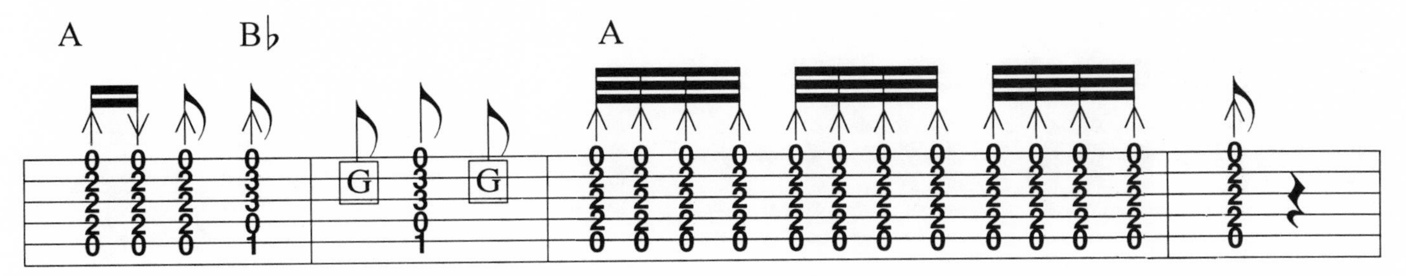


## Variation 3

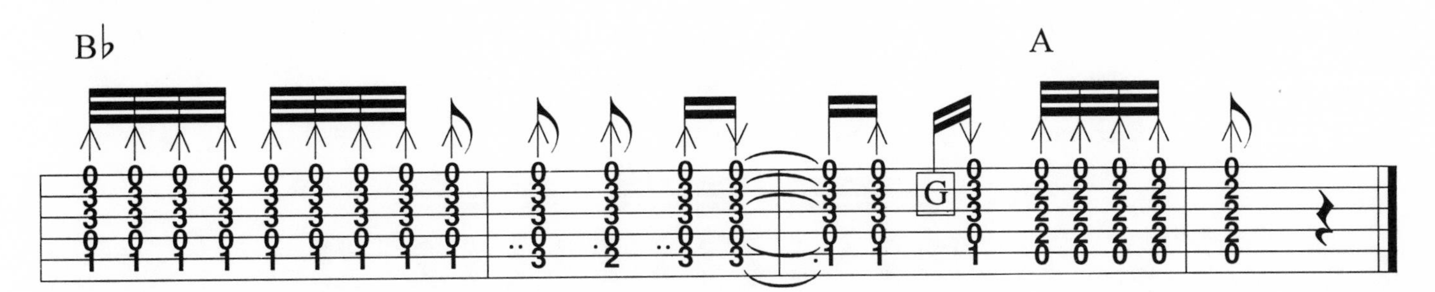

Falseta 1

Juan Serrano

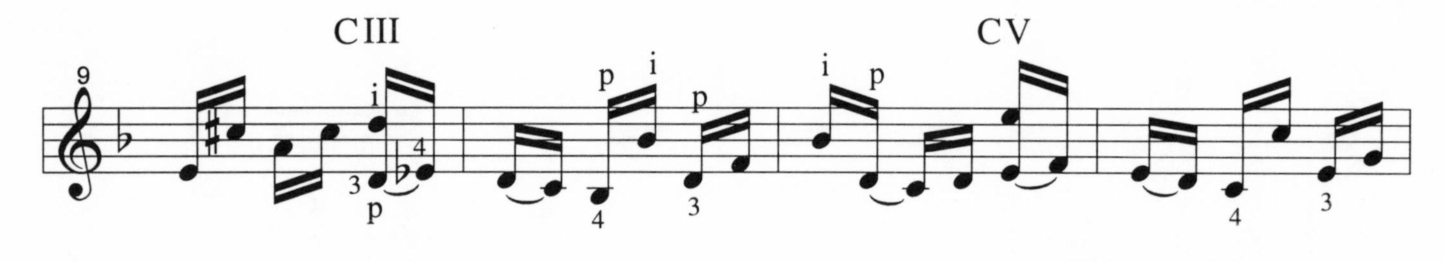


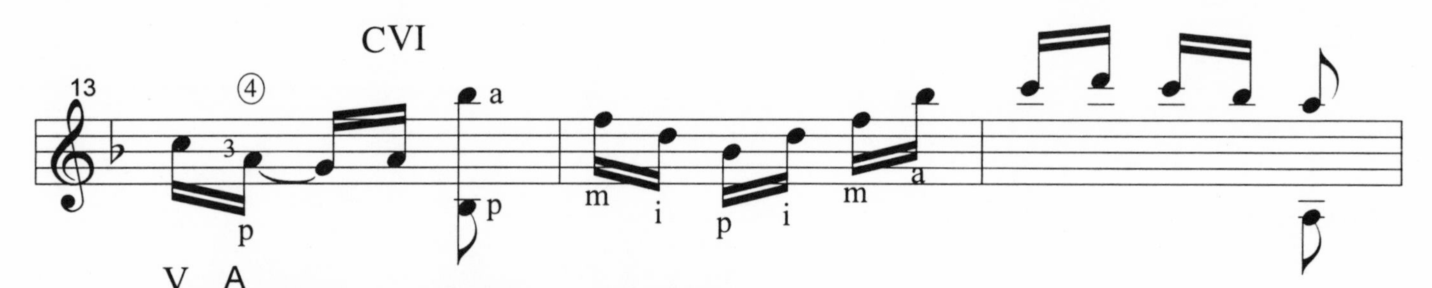


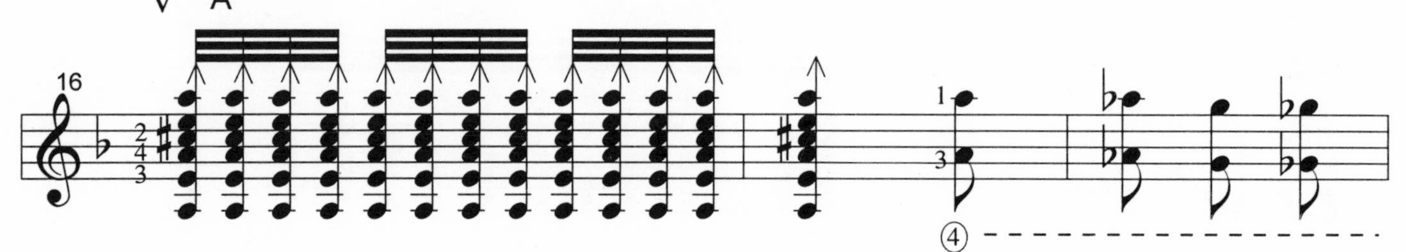

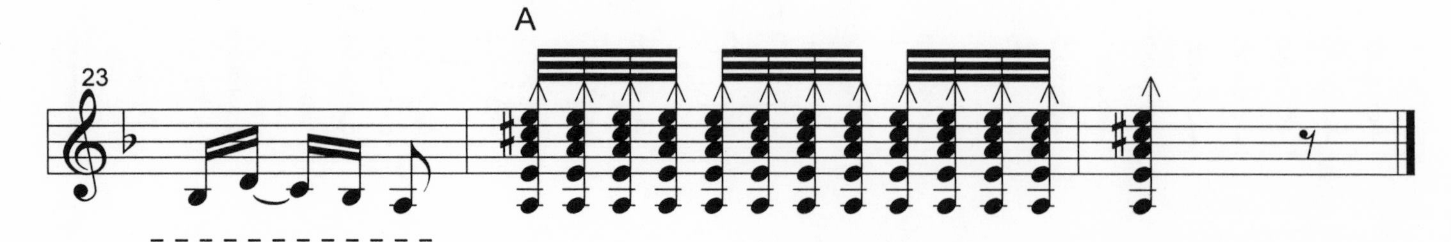

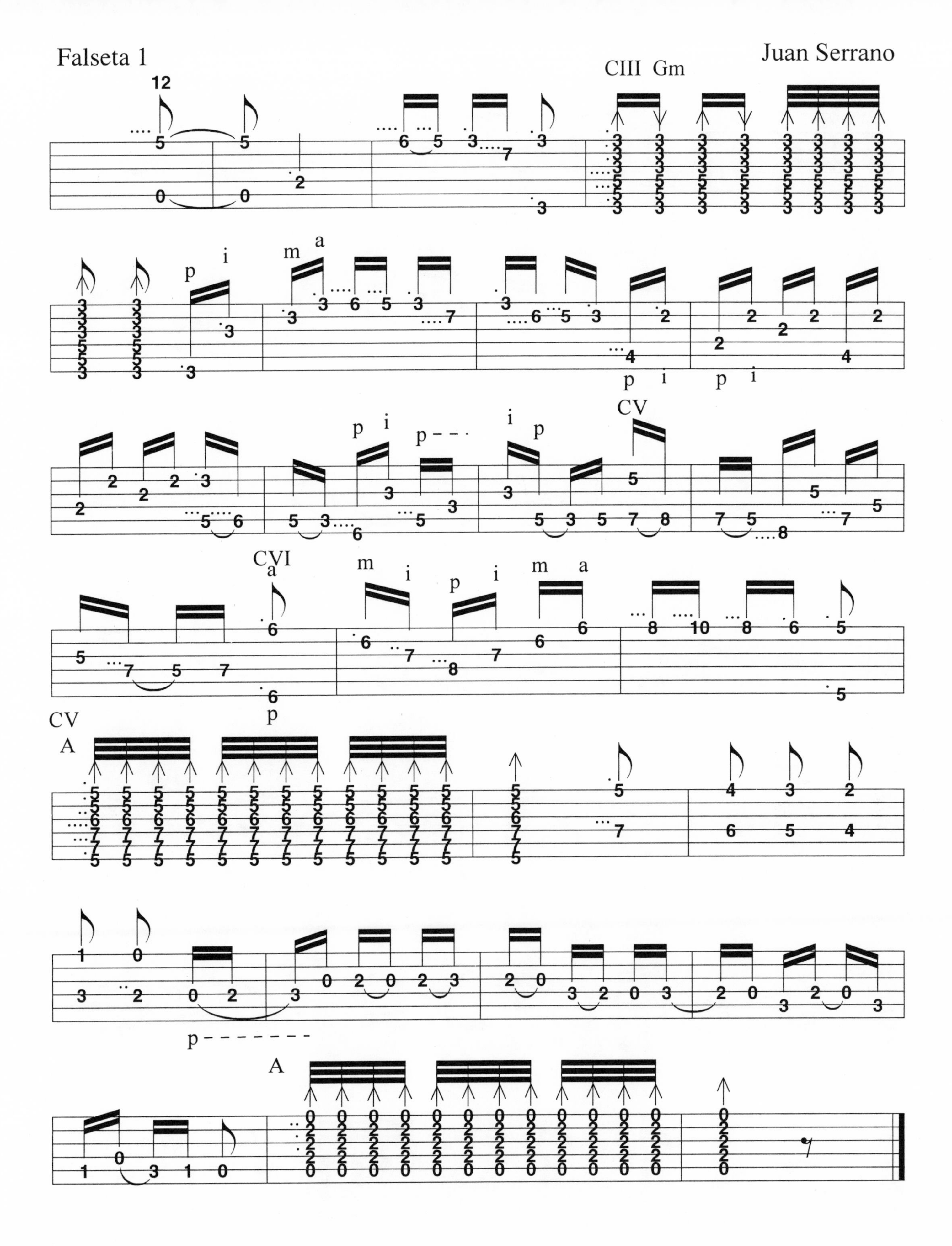
Falseta 1
Juan Serrano
CIII Gm
CV
CVI
A

Falseta 2

Juan Serrano

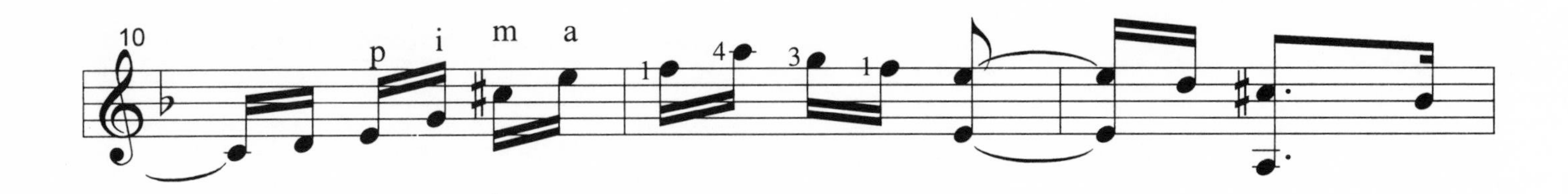

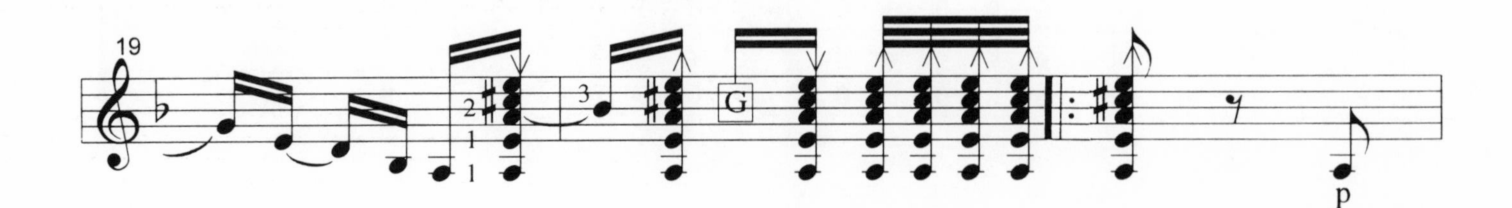

22
1
p
2
1
i
p
i

25
i
i

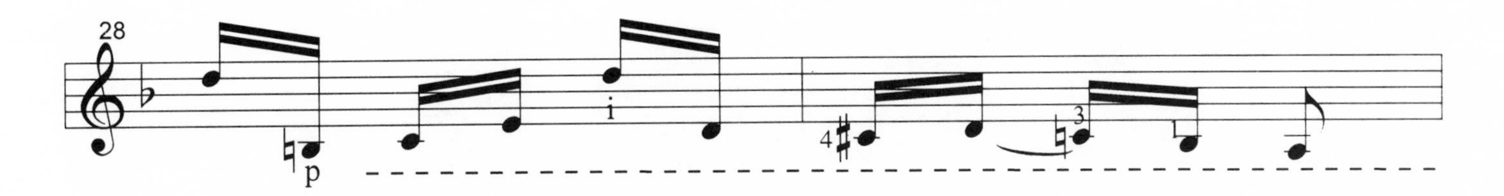
28
p
i
4
3
1

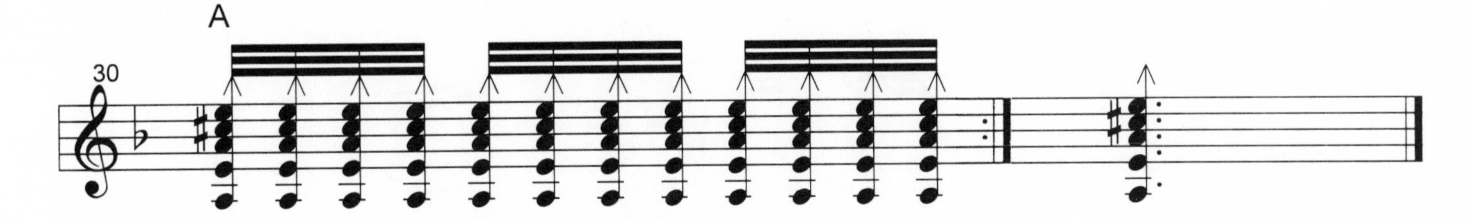
A
30

Falseta 2

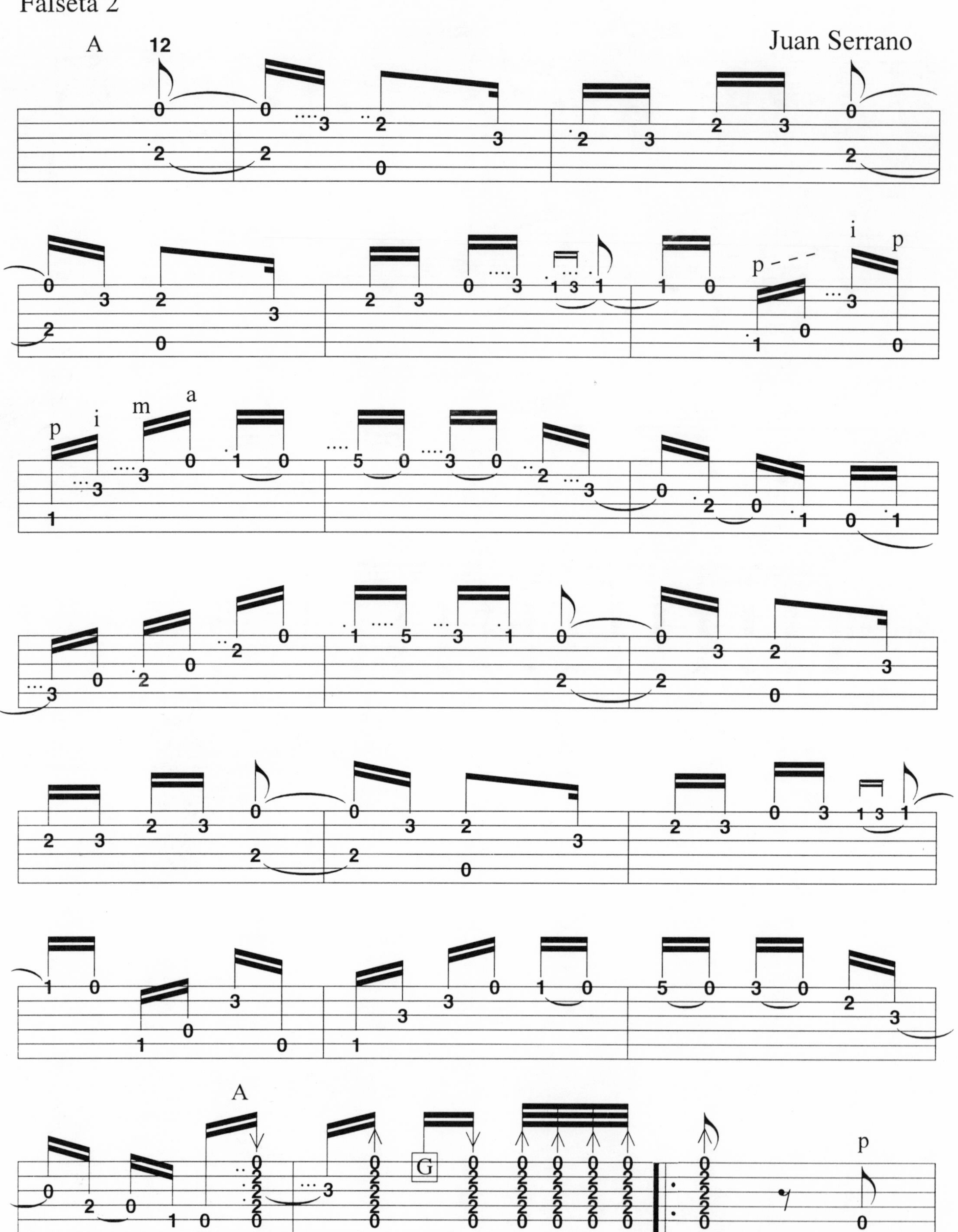
Juan Serrano
A
12
p
i
m
a
G

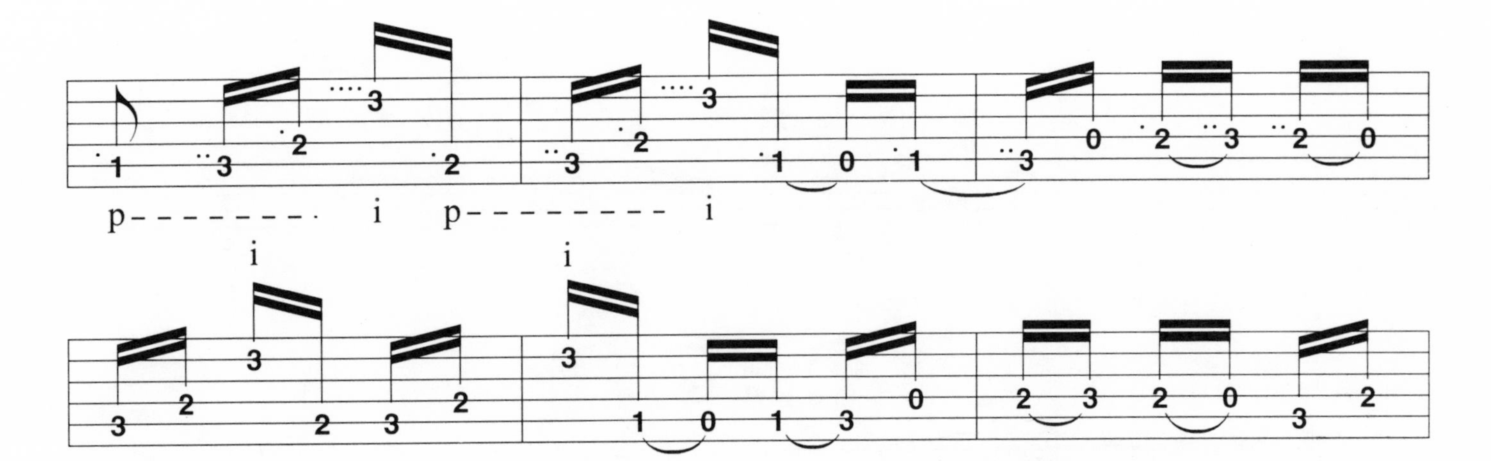
p i p i
i i

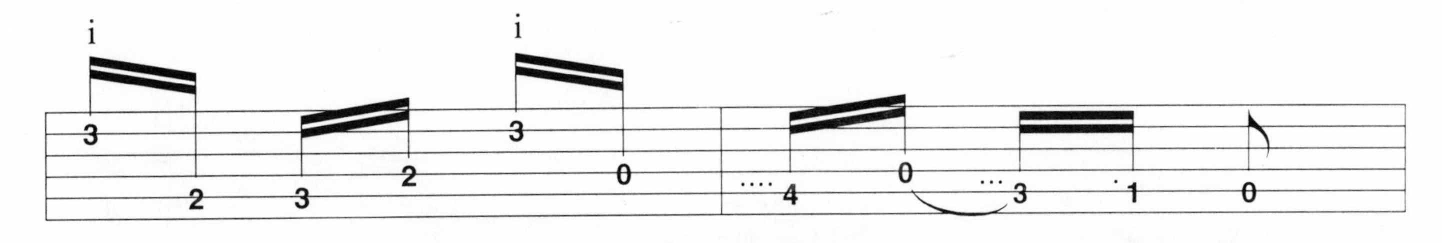
i i

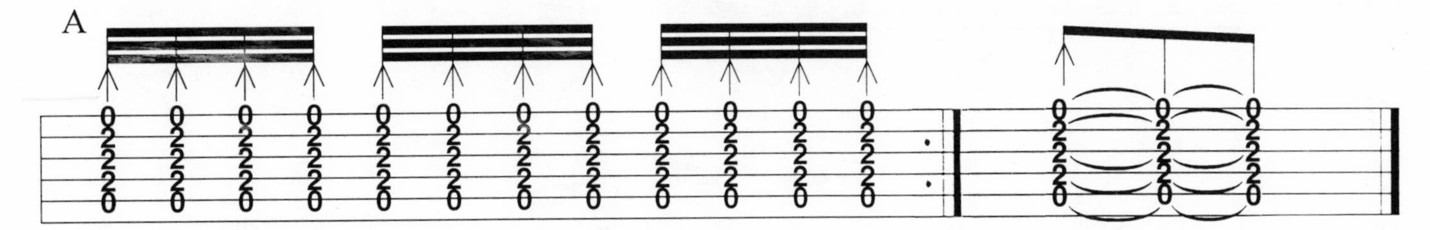
A

Falseta 3

Juan Serrano

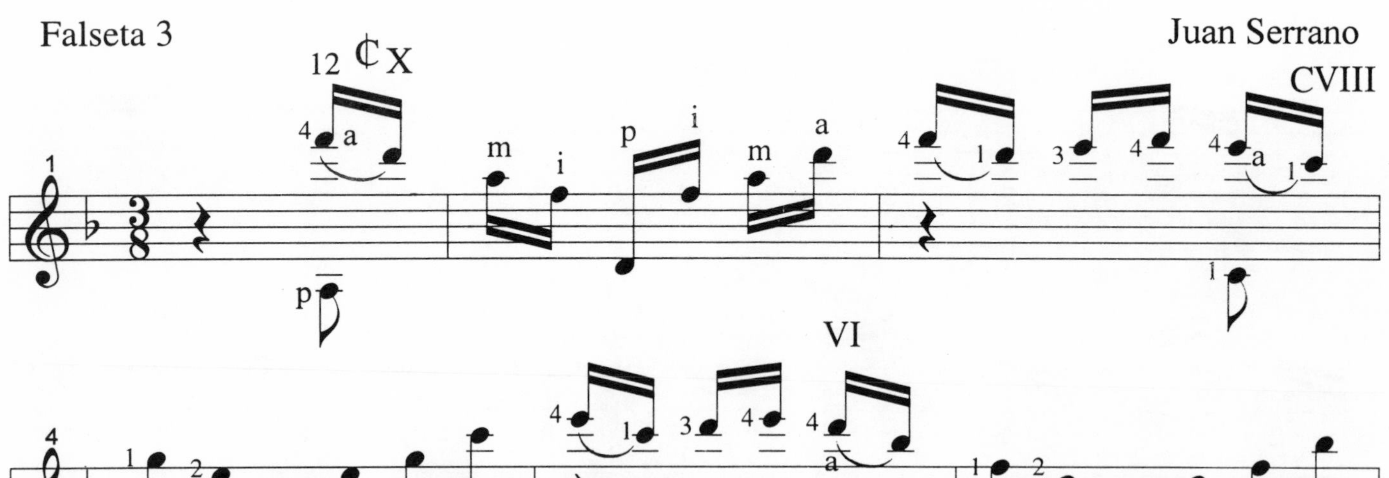


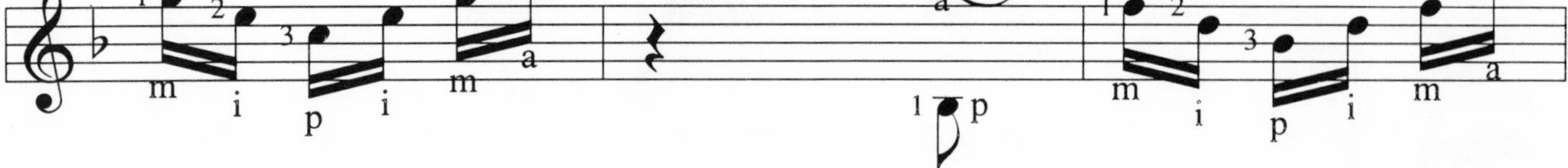

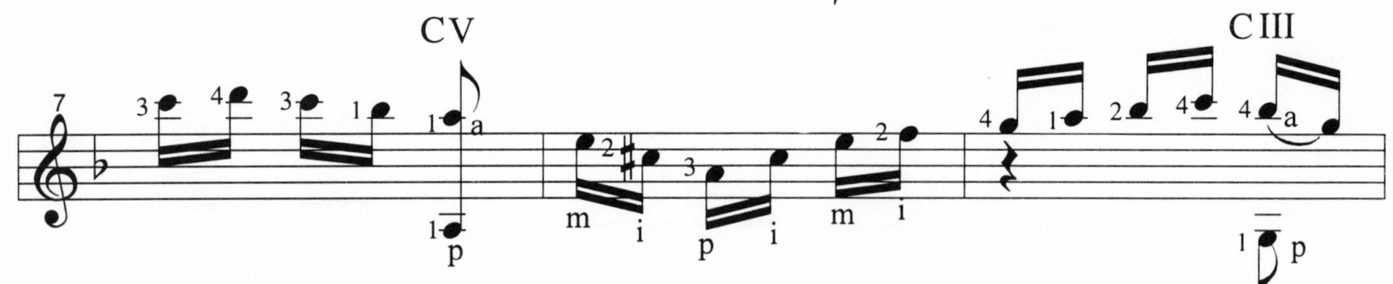


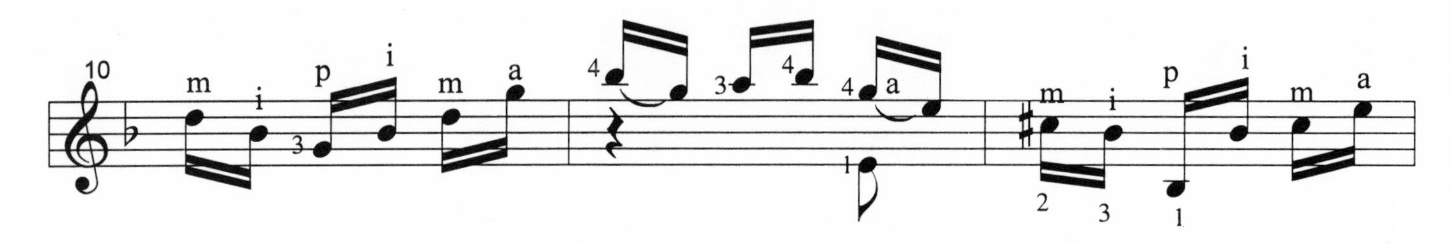


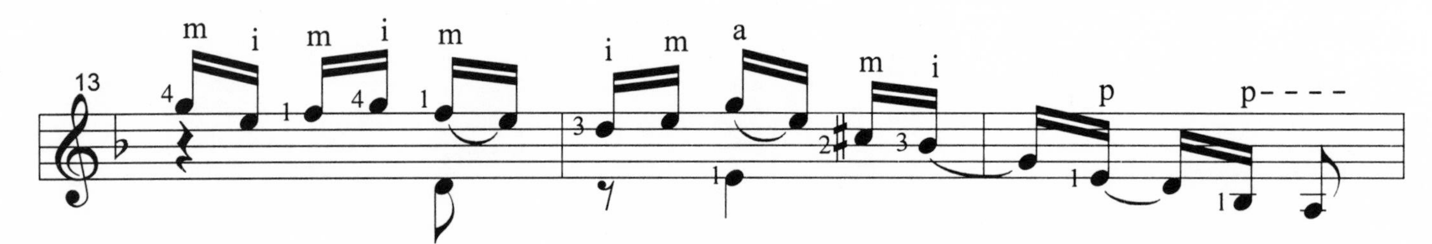

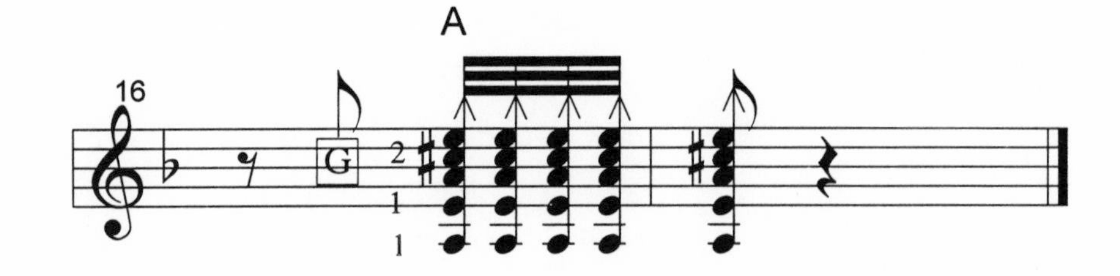

Falseta 3

Juan Serrano

Falseta 4 Juan Serrano

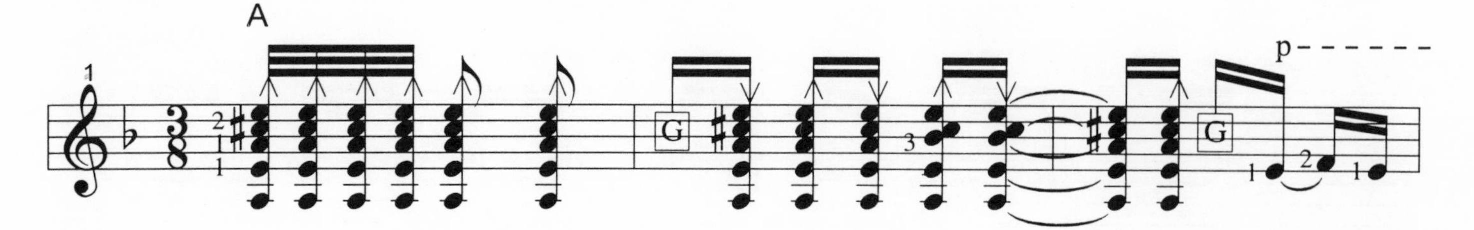

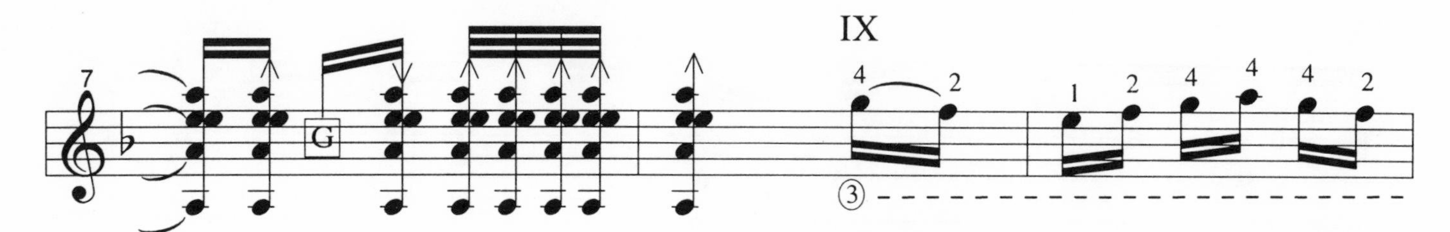


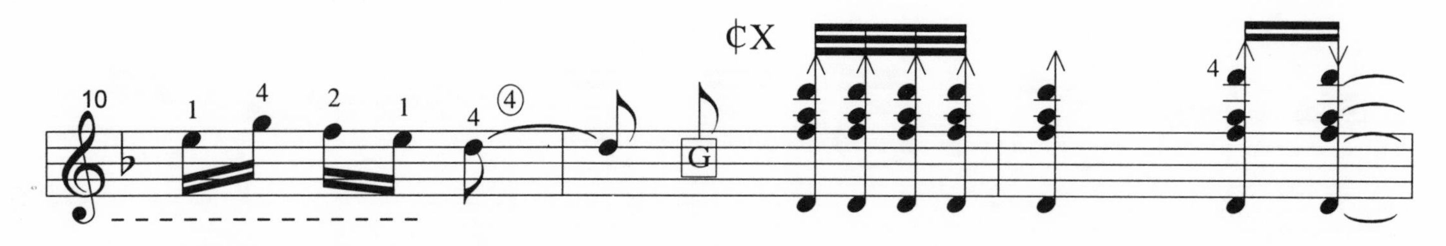


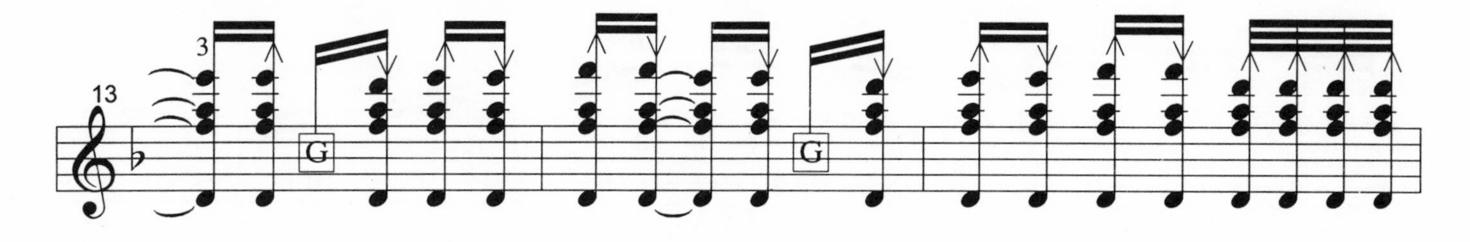

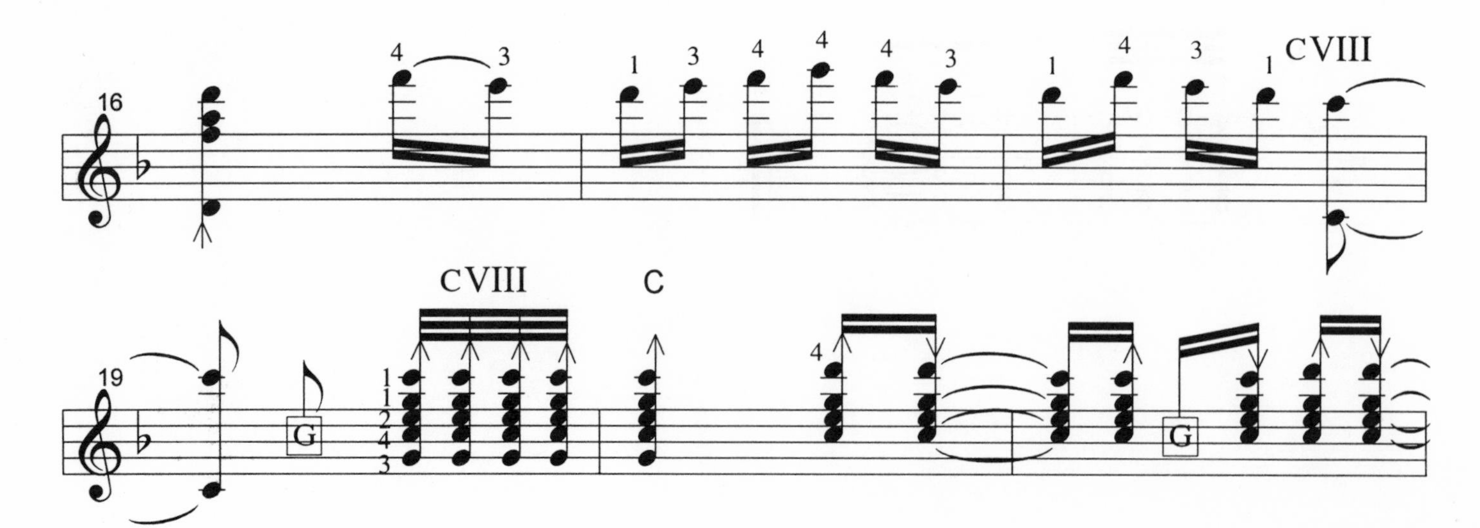

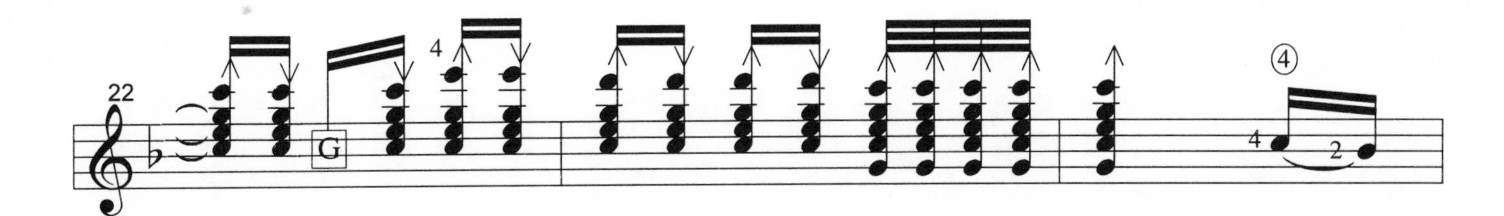
22
G

25
VII
G
VII

28
p

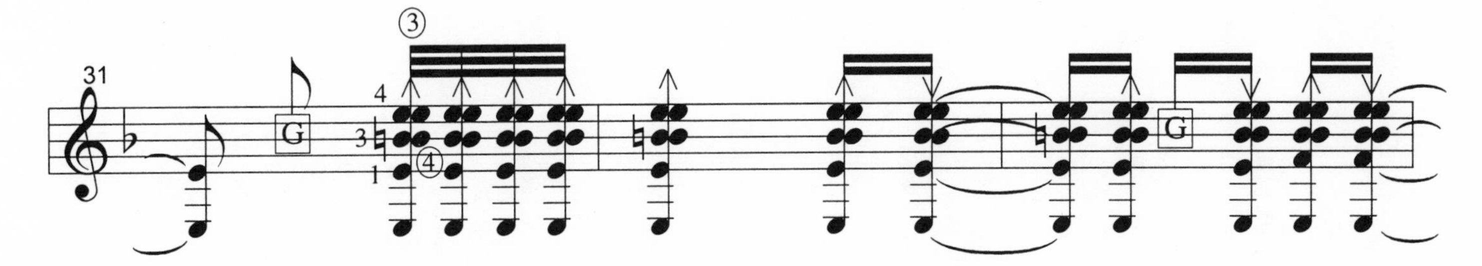
31
G
G

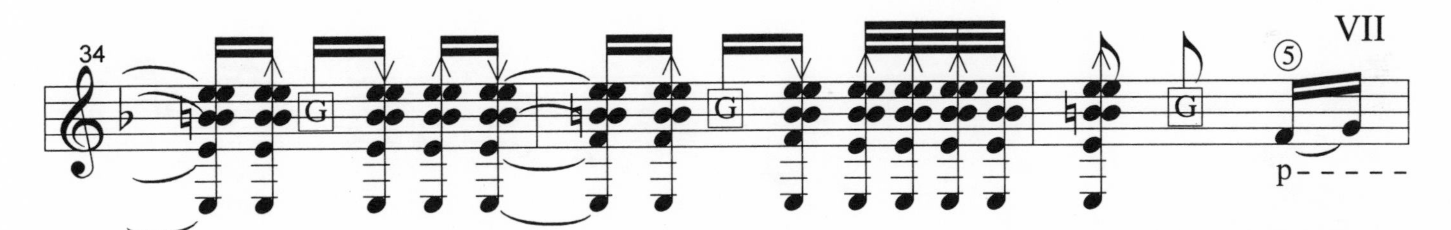
34
G
G
G
VII
p

37
CV
G

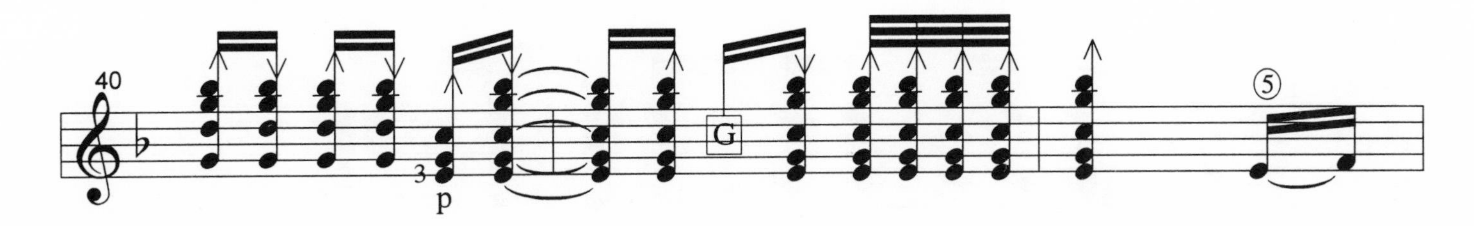
40
p
G

43
④
V
III
G

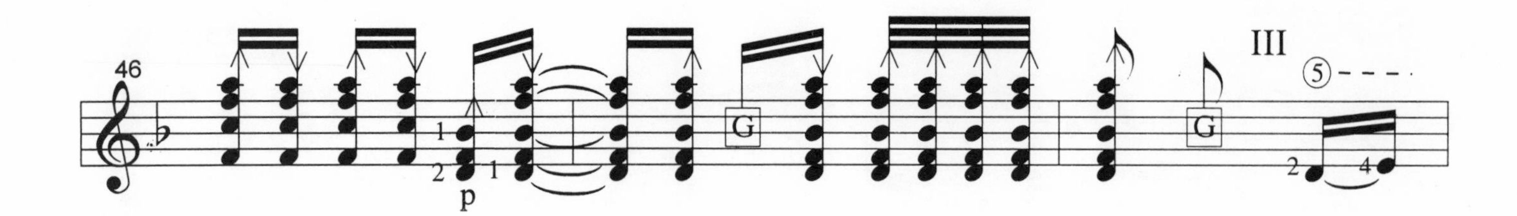
46
p
G
G
III
⑤

49
④
⑤
p

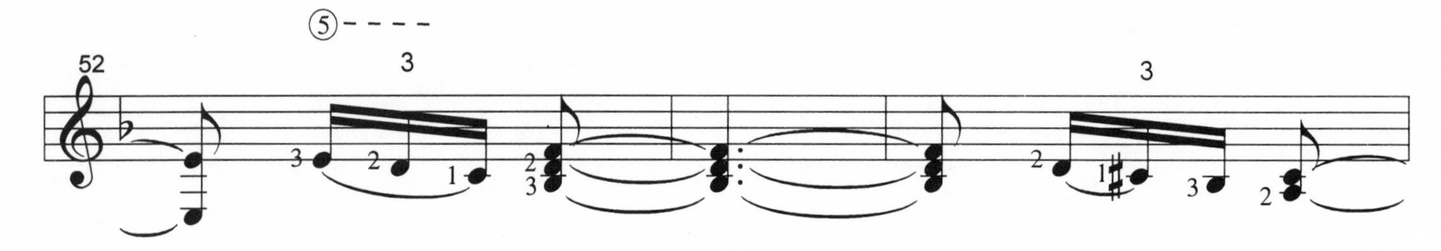
52
⑤
3
3

55

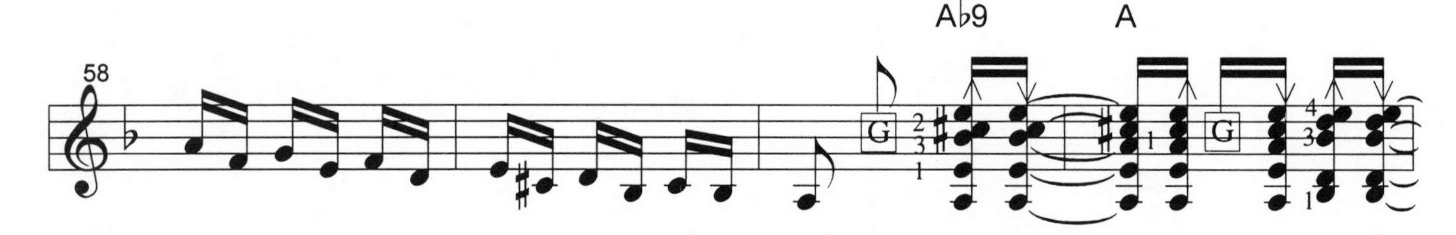
58
A♭9
A
G
G

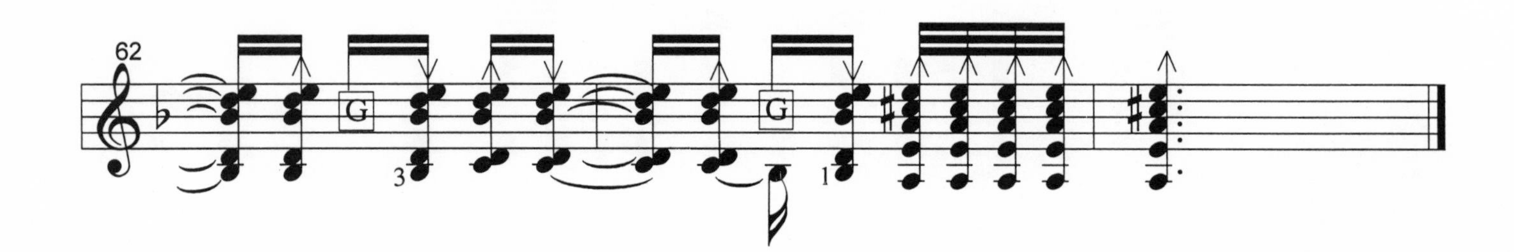
62
G
G

## Falseta 4

A

Juan Serrano

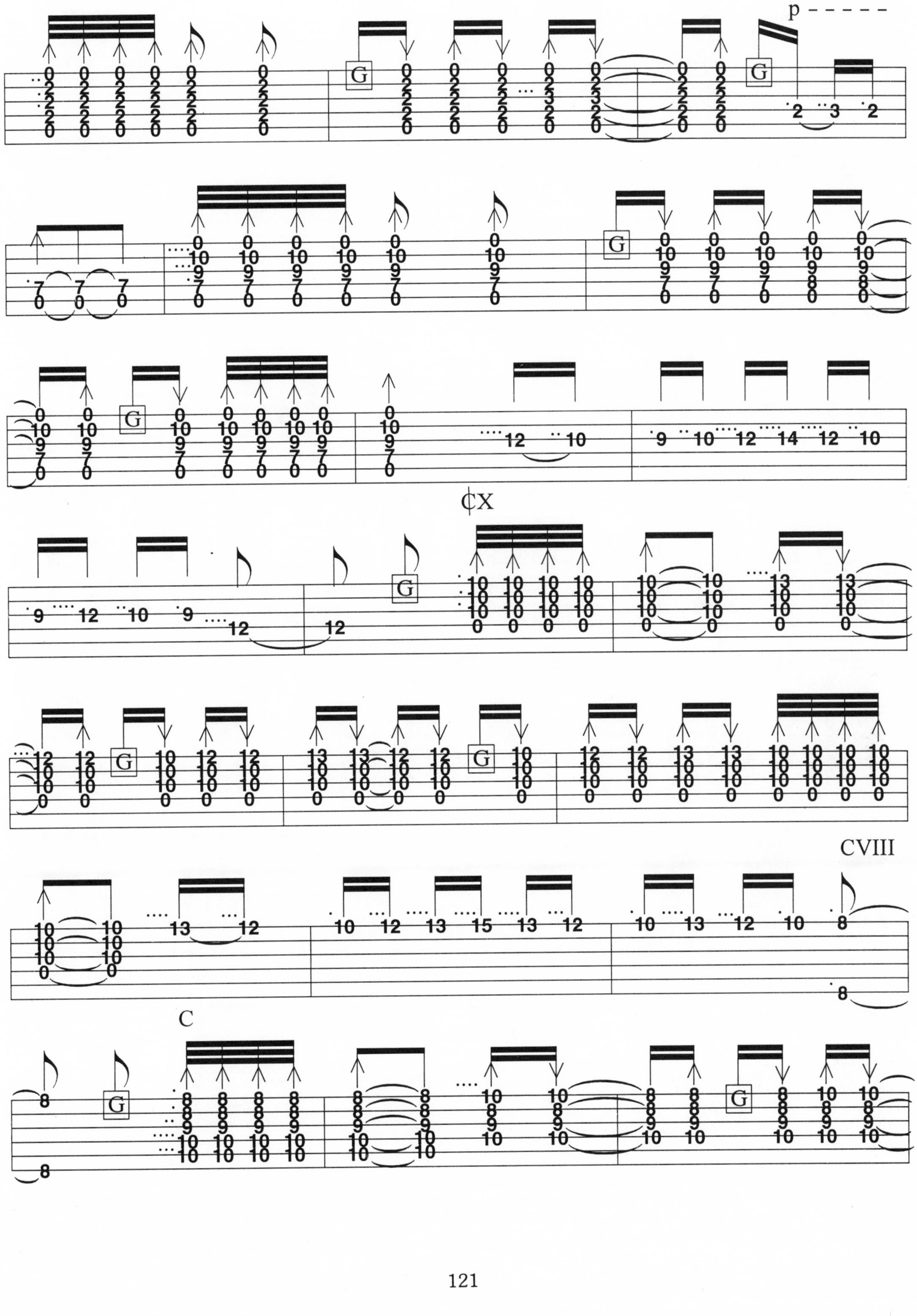

p - - - - -

```
| 0-2-2-2-2-0  0-2-2-2-2-0  0-2-2-2-2-0  0-2-2-2-2-0  0-2-2-2-2-0  0-2-2-2-2-0
| G  0-2-2-2-2-0  0-2-2-2-2-0  0-2-2-2-2-0  0-2-2-3-2-0  0-2-2-3-2-0 | 0-2-2-2-2-0  0-2-2-2-2-0  G  2  3  2

| 7-0  7-0  7-0
| 0-10-9-7-0  0-10-9-7-0  0-10-9-7-0  0-10-9-7-0  0-10-9-7-0  0-10-9-7-0
| G  0-10-9-7-0  0-10-9-7-0  0-10-9-7-0  0-10-9-8-0  0-10-9-8-0

| 0-10-9-7-0  0-10-9-7-0  G  0-10-9-7-0  0-10-9-7-0  0-10-9-7-0  0-10-9-7-0  0-10-9-7-0
| 0-10-9-7-0  12  10
| 9  10  12  14  12  10

| 9  12  10  9  12
| 12  G  CX  10-10-10-10-0  10-10-10-10-0  10-10-10-10-0  10-10-10-10-0
| 10-10-10-0  10-10-10-0  13-10-10-0  13-10-10-0

| 12-10-10-0  12-10-10-0  G  10-10-10-0  12-10-10-0  12-10-10-0
| 13-10-10-0  13-10-10-0  12-10-10-0  12-10-10-0  G  10-10-10-0
| 12-10-10-0  12-10-10-0  13-10-10-0  13-10-10-0  10-10-10-10-0  10-10-10-10-0  10-10-10-10-0  10-10-10-10-0

| 10-10-10-0  10-10-10-0  13  12
| 10  12  13  15  13  12
| 10  13  12  10  CVIII 8-8

| 8-8  G  C  8-8-8-9-10-10  8-8-8-9-10-10  8-8-8-9-10-10  8-8-8-9-10-10
| 8-8-9-10  8-8-9-10  10-8-9-10  10-8-9-10
| 8-8-9-10  8-8-9-10  G  8-8-9-10  10-8-9-10  10-8-9-10
```

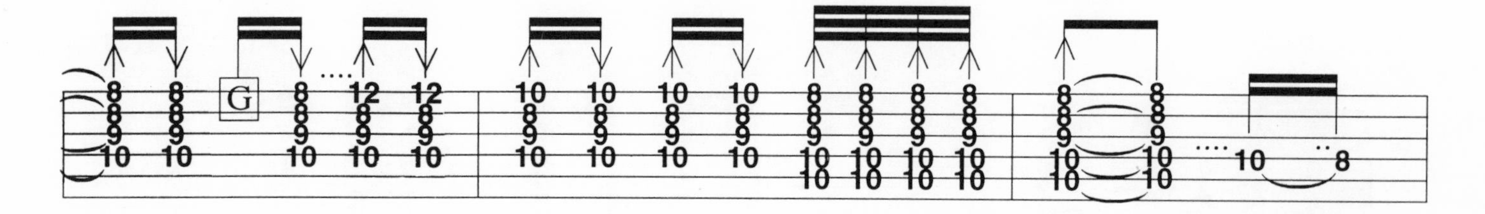

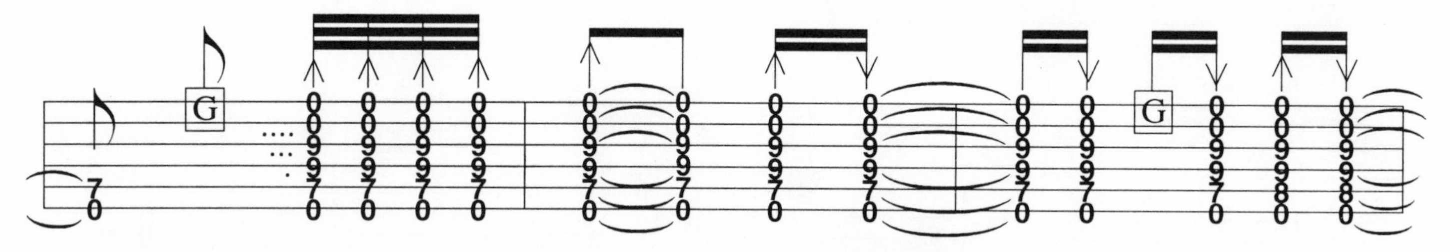

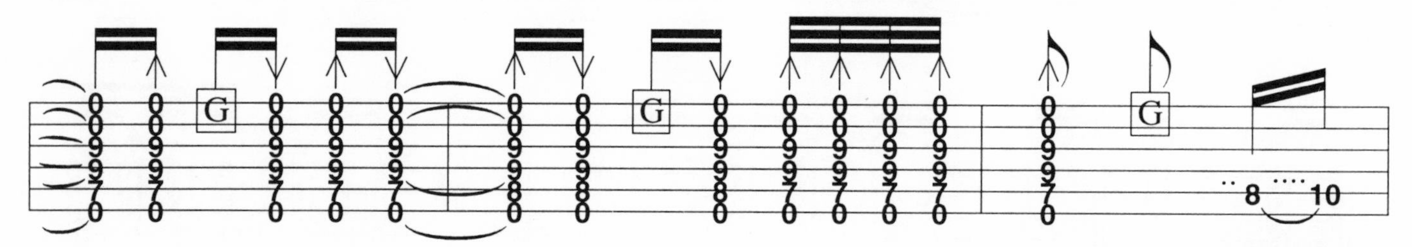

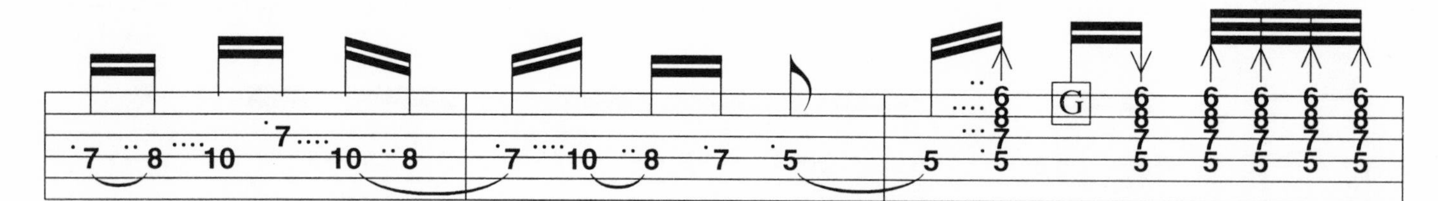

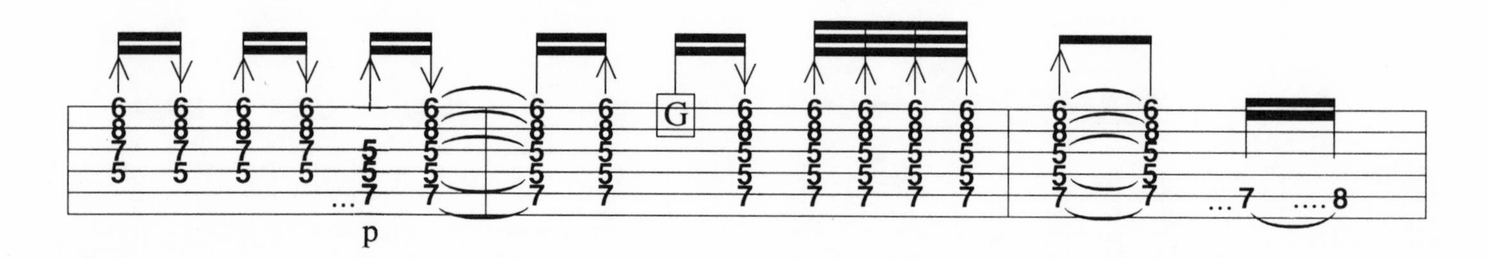

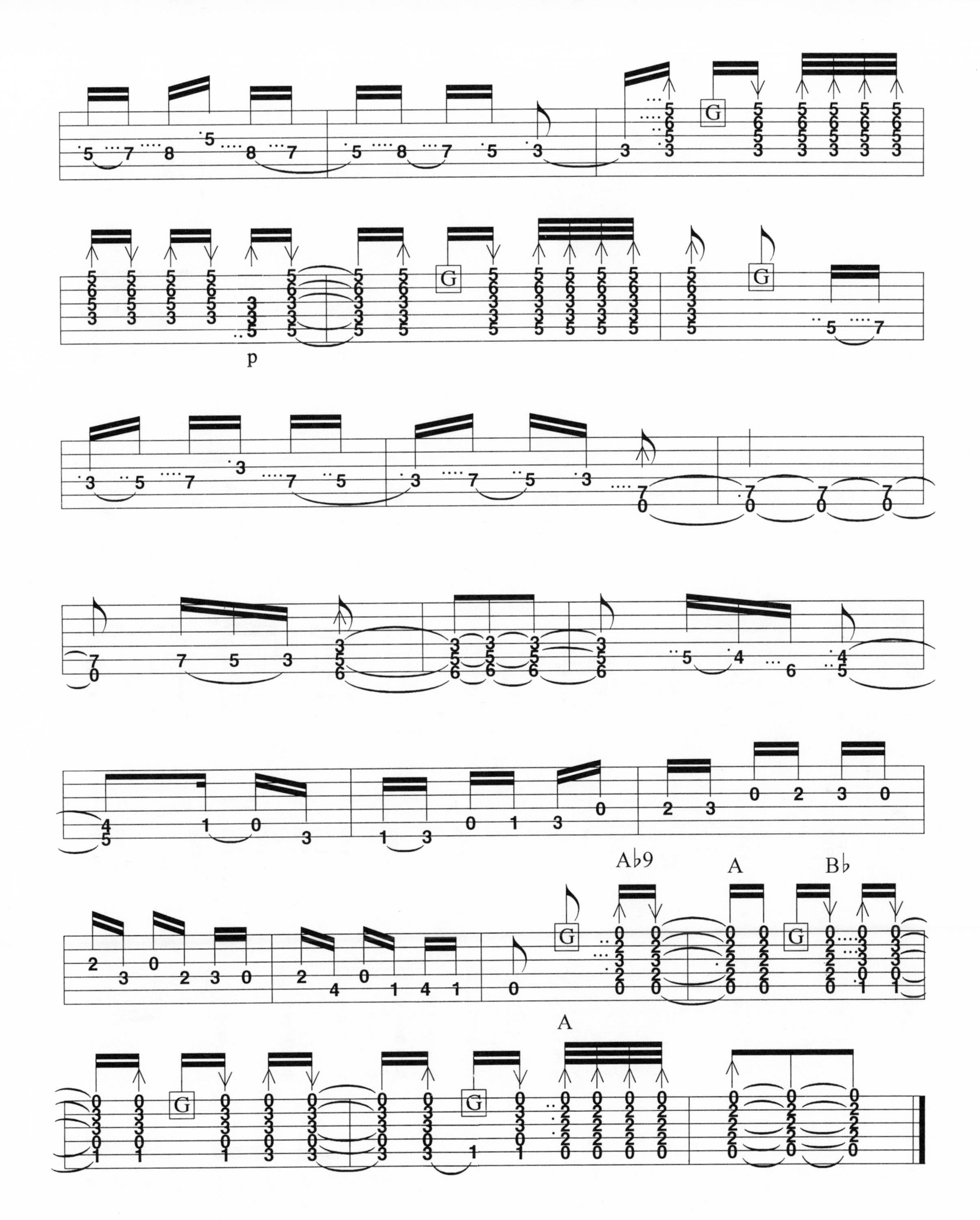
G
p
A♭9
A
B♭
A

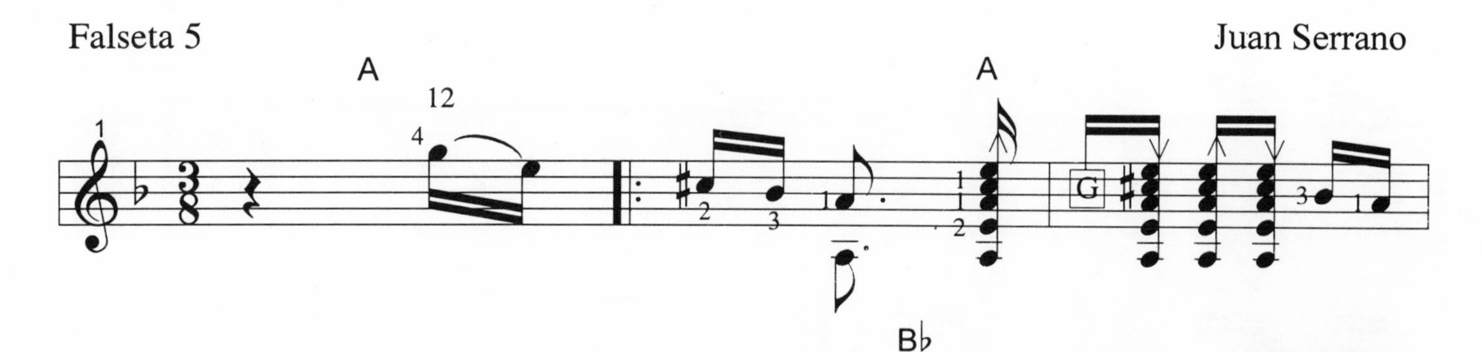
Falseta 5
Juan Serrano
A
A
G

B♭
G

p
G
p

p
A
G

1.
2.
G
p

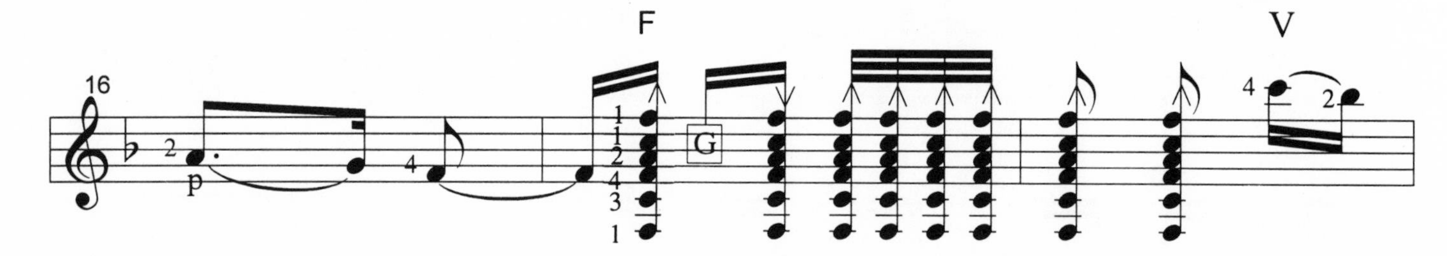
F
G
V

I
C
G

22

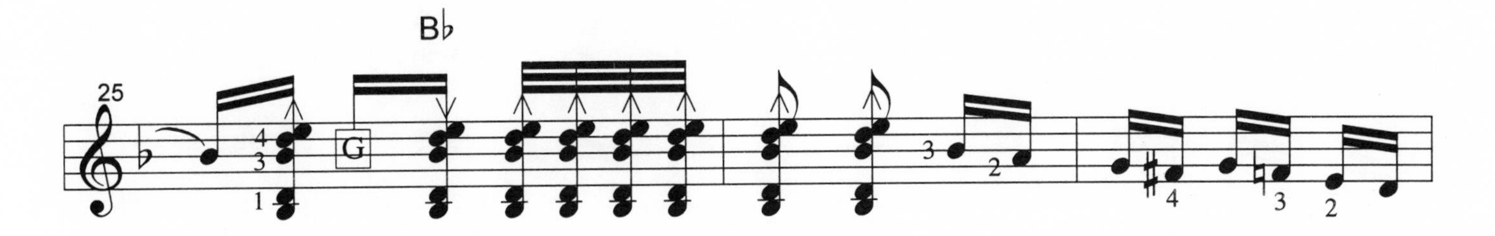
B♭
25
G

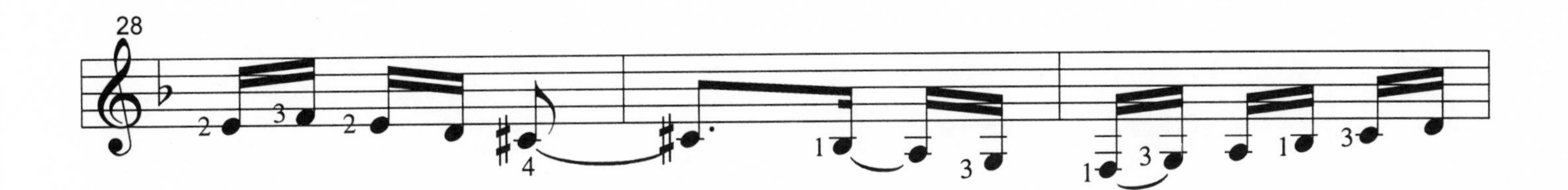
28

31

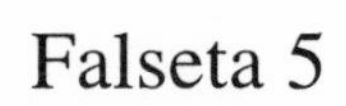

# Falseta 5

Juan Serrano

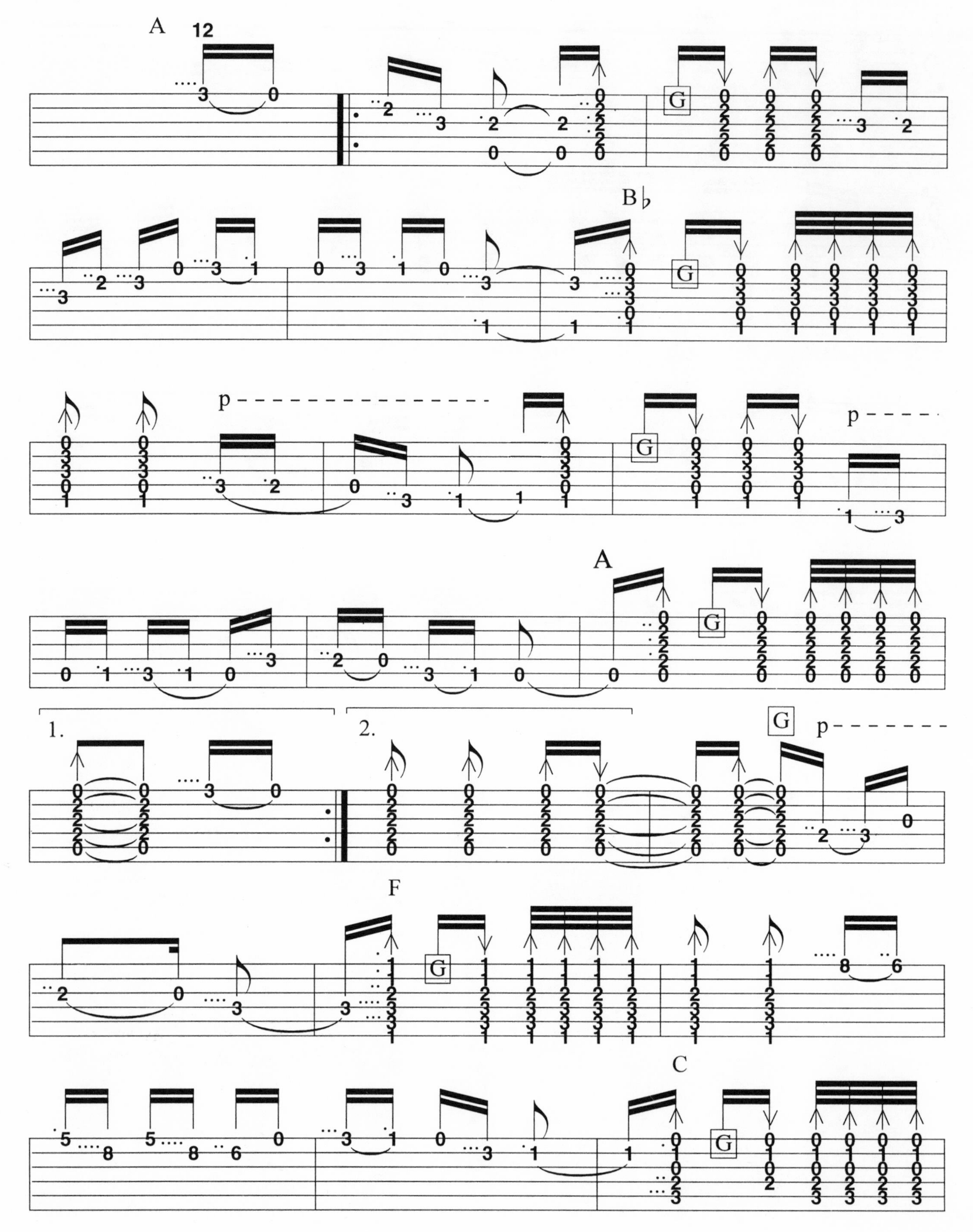

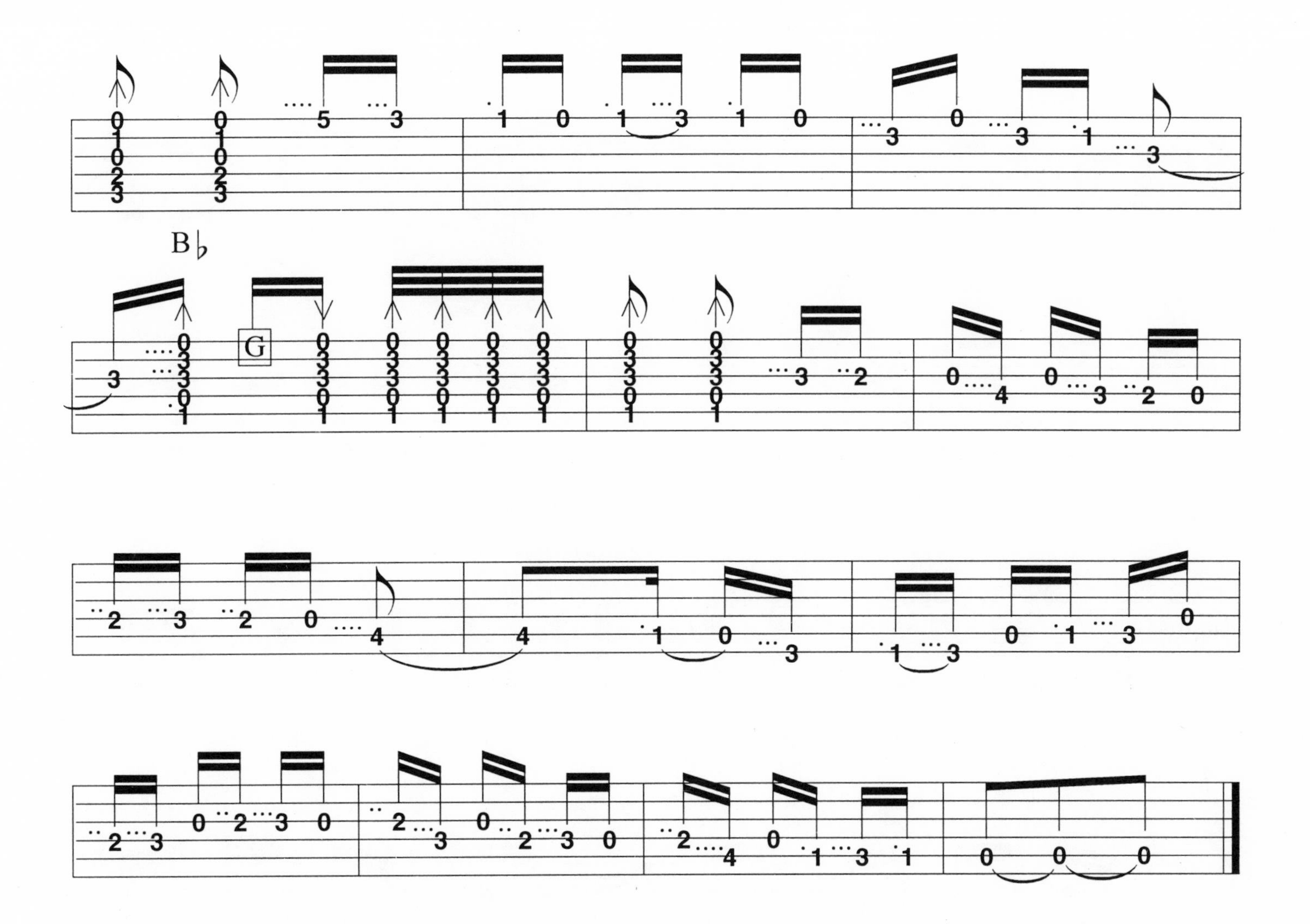
B♭
G

Falseta 6 (Alzapua)

Juan Serrano

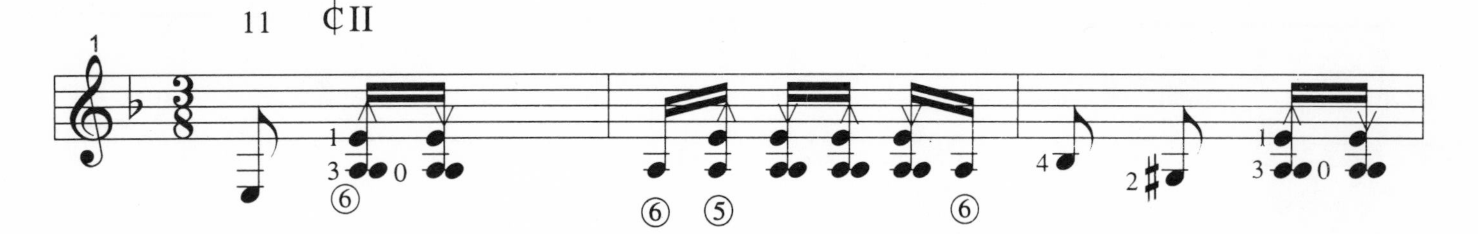

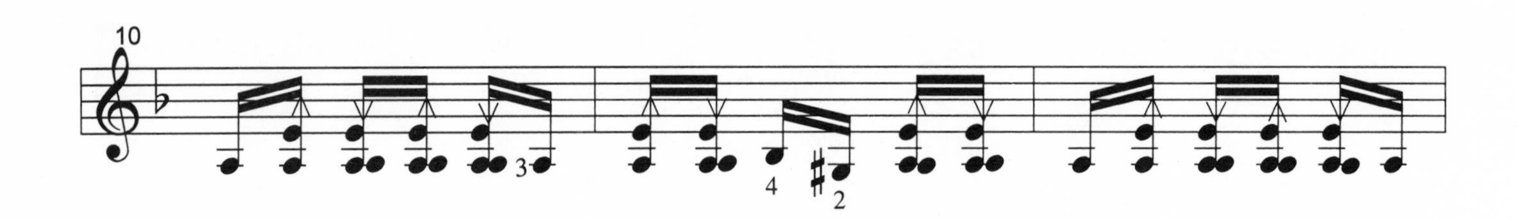

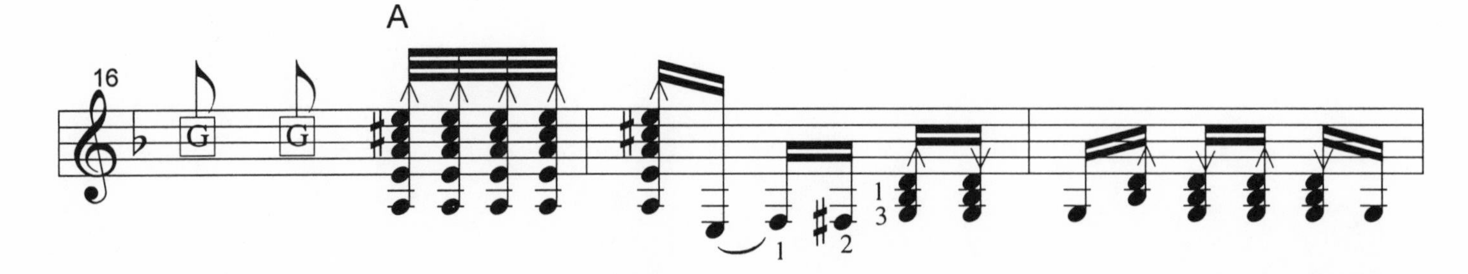

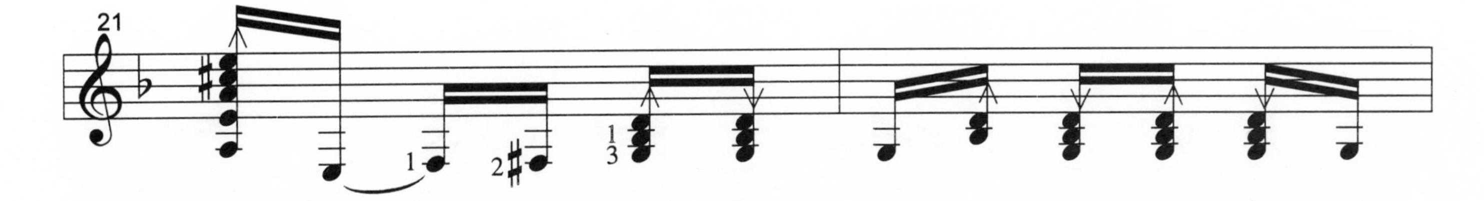
21

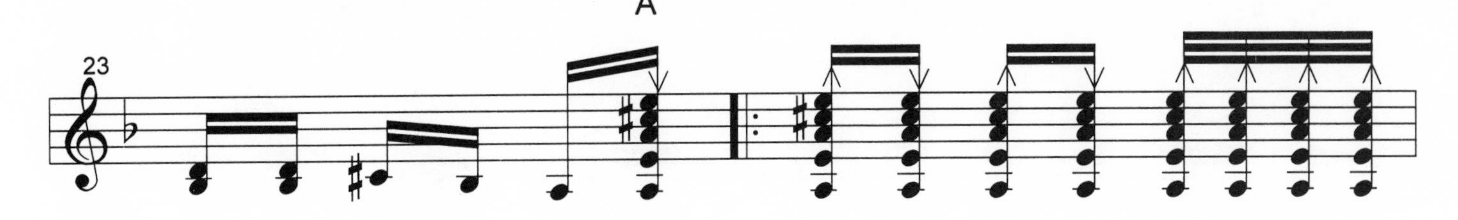
A
23

25
G

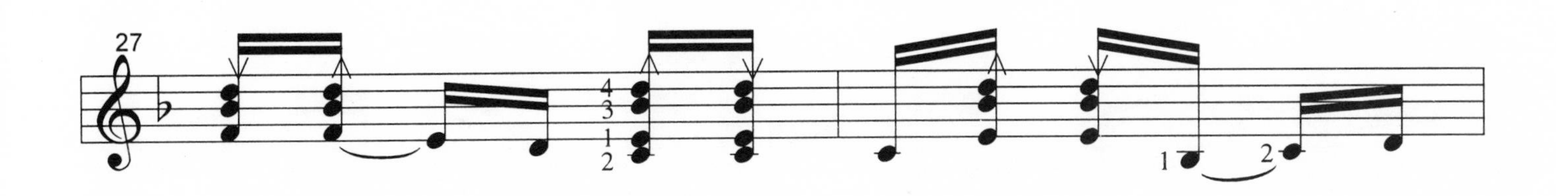
27

29

31

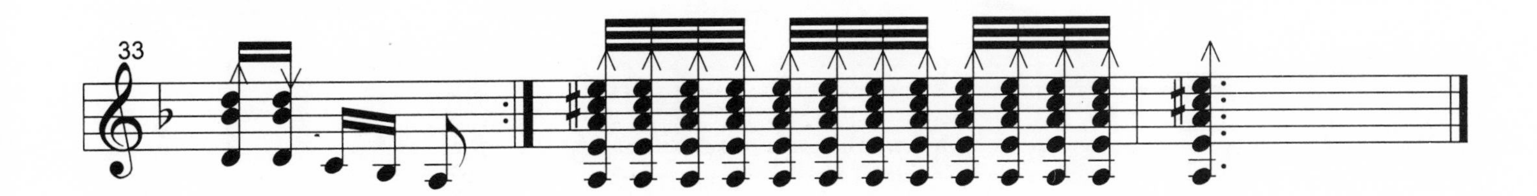
33

Falseta 6 (Alzapua)

Juan Serrano

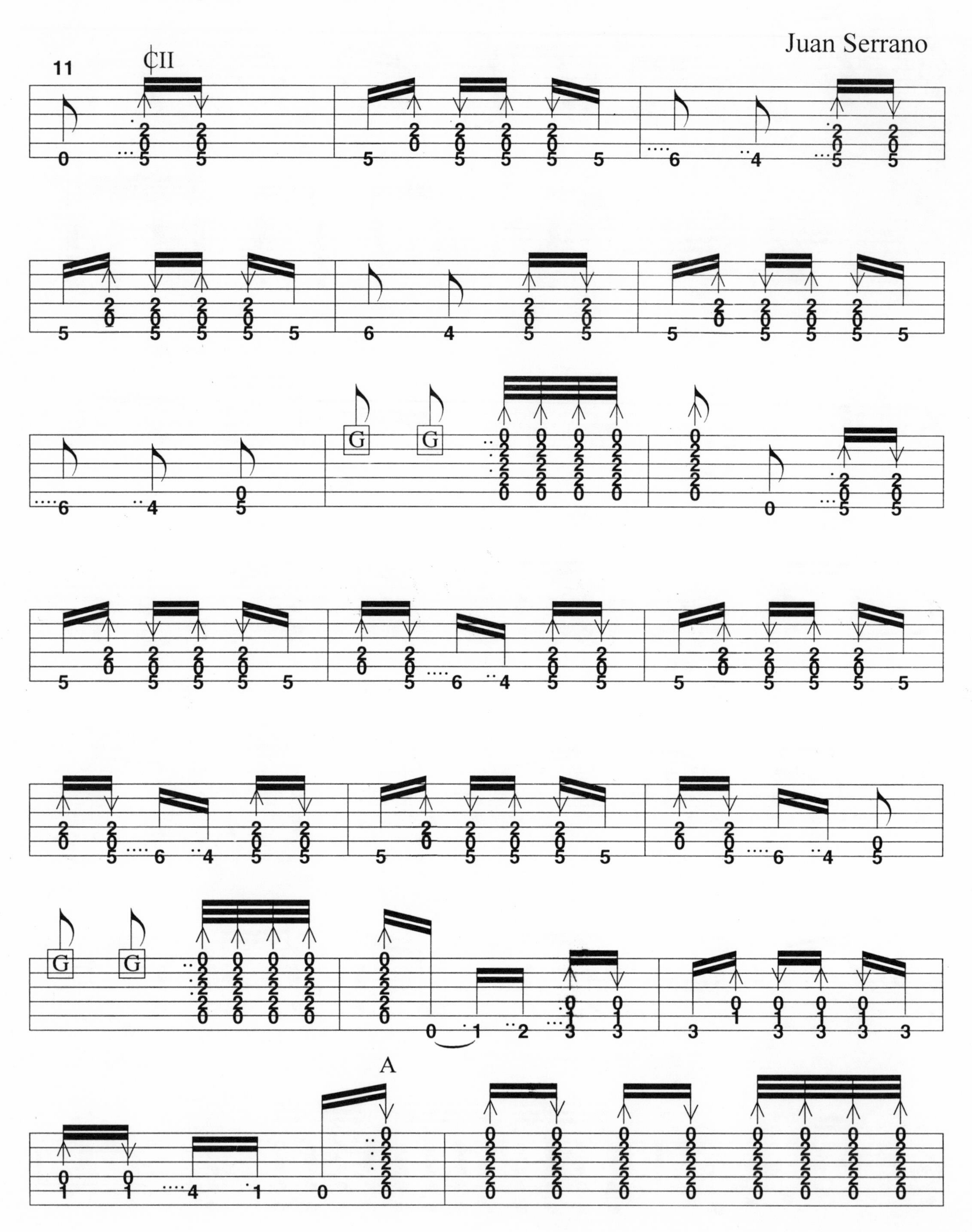

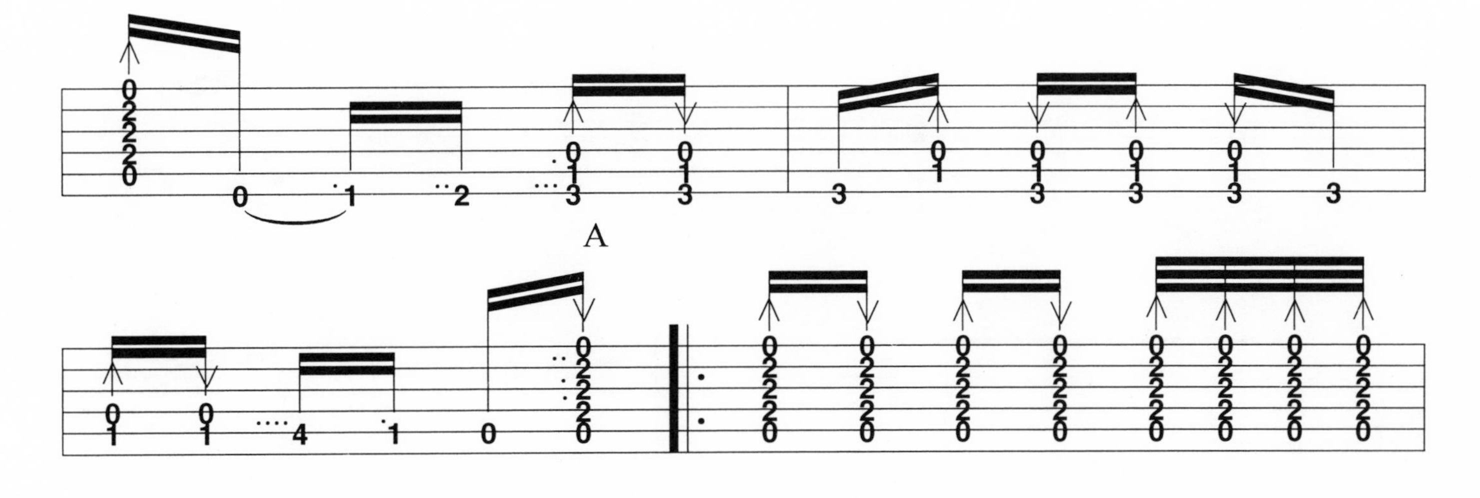
A

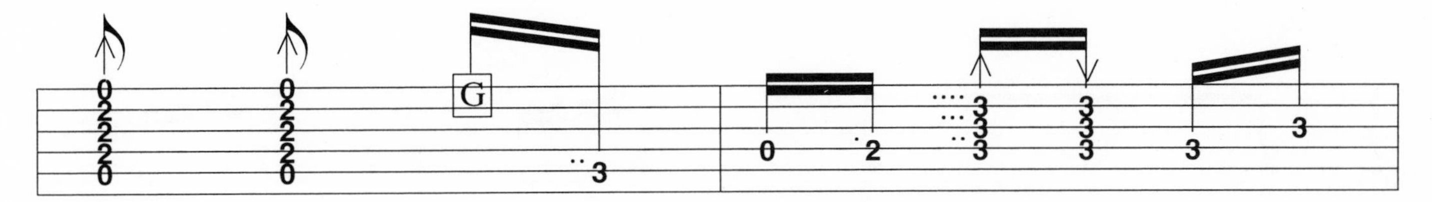
G

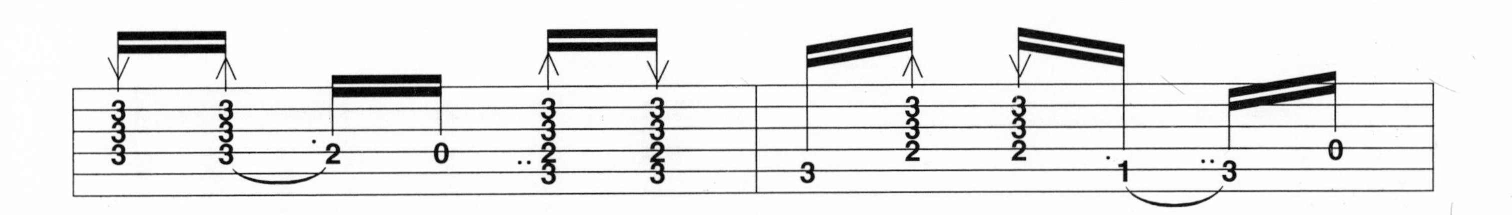

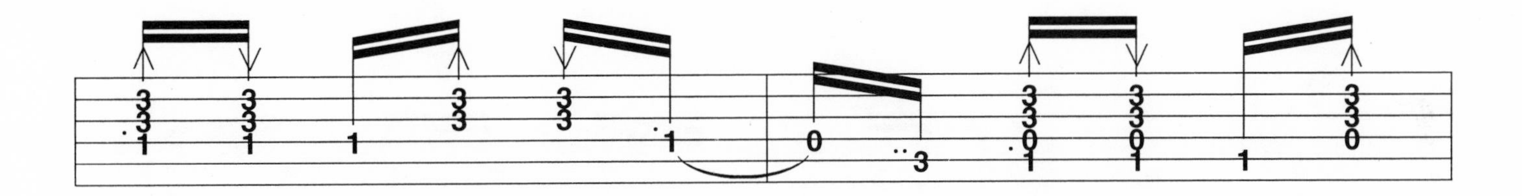

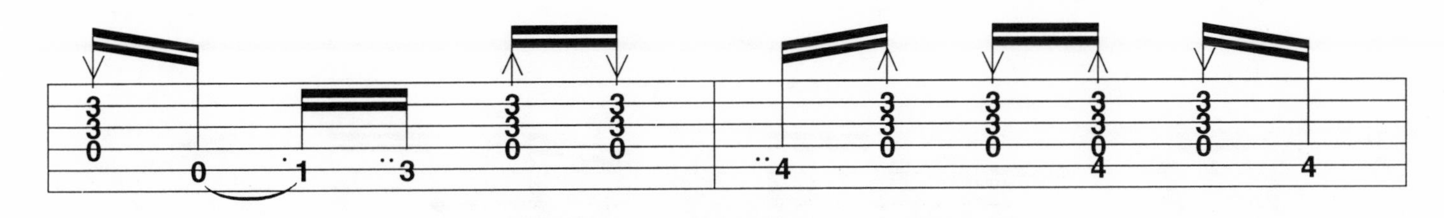

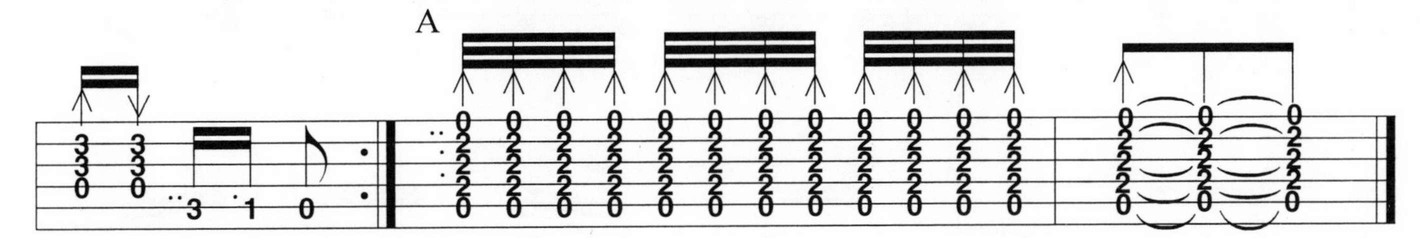
A

Falseta 7 (Alzapua)

Juan Serrano

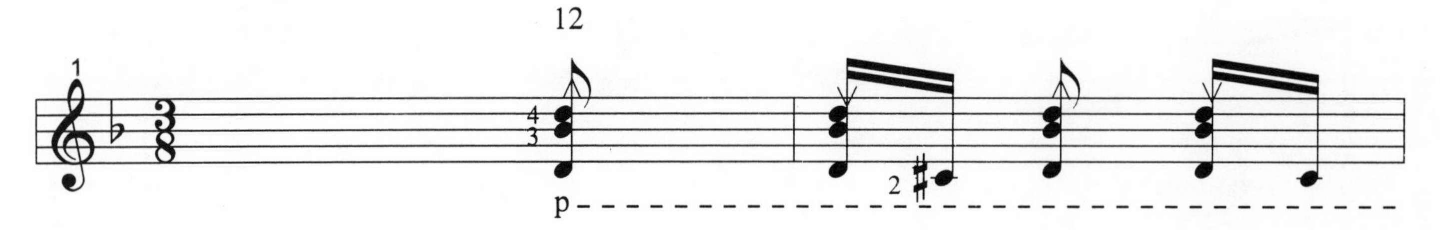


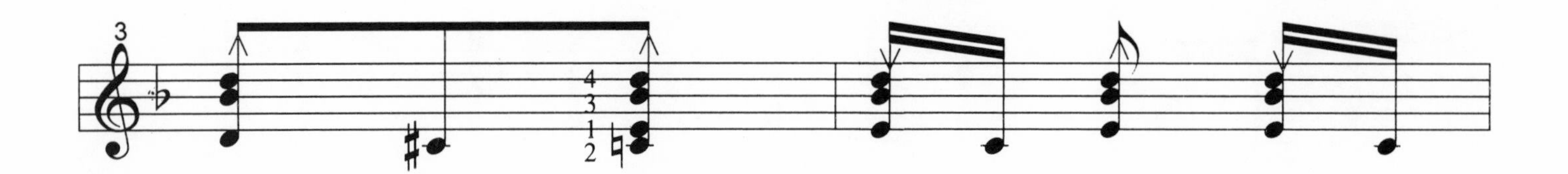

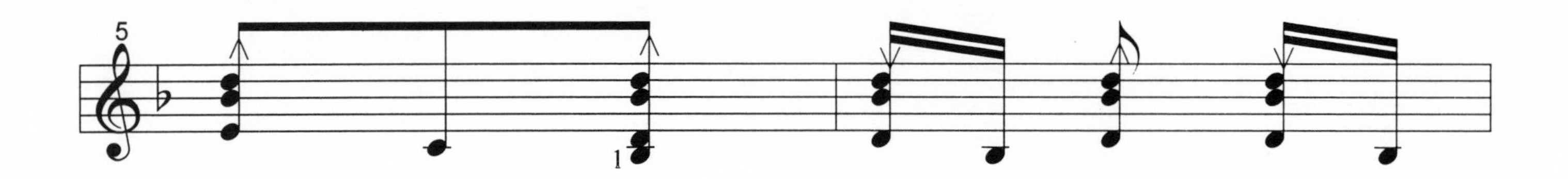

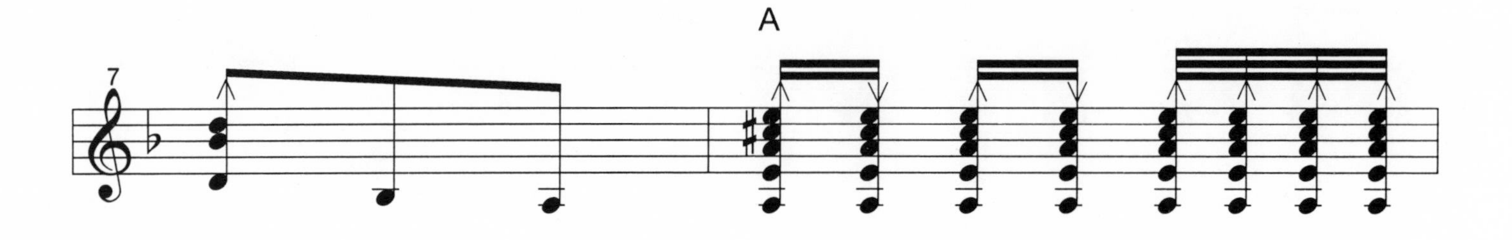


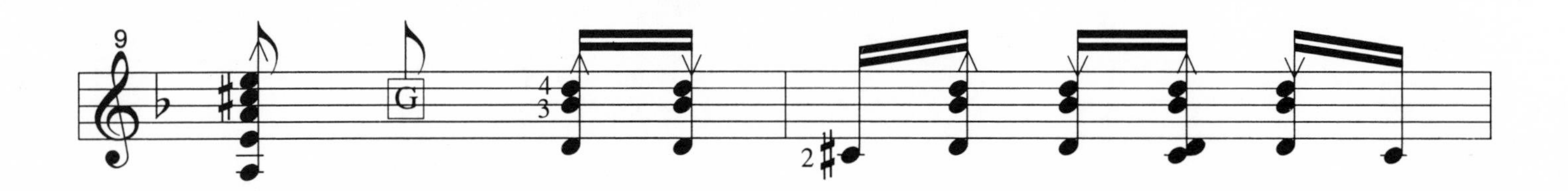

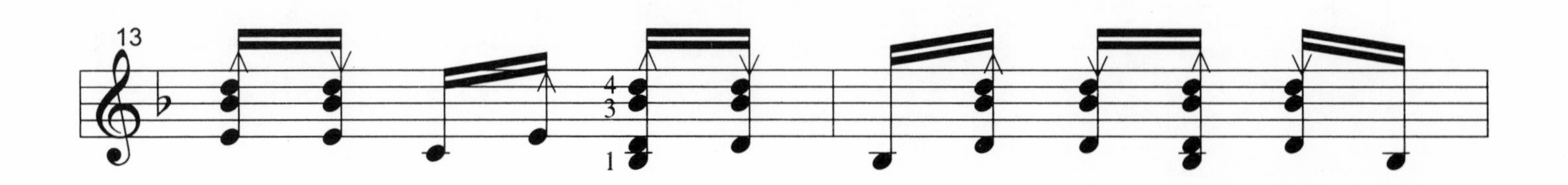

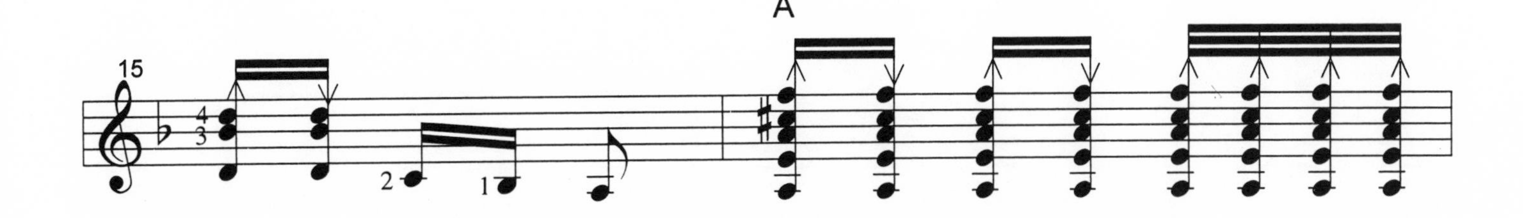
A
15
4
3
2
1

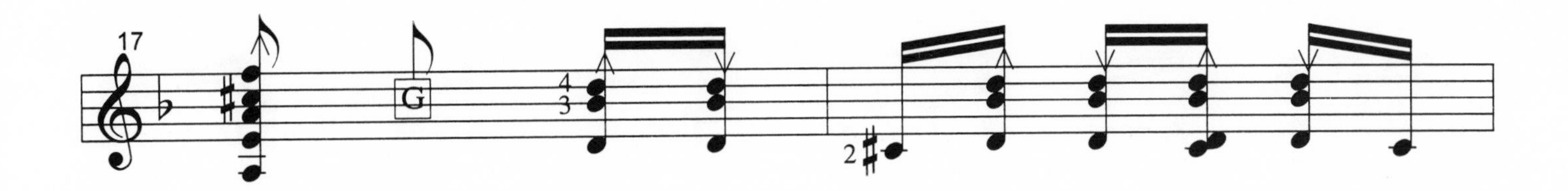
17
G
4
3
2

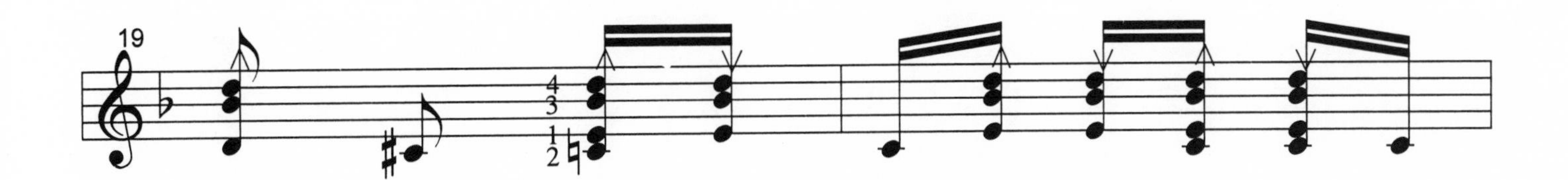
19
4
3
1
2

21
4
3
1

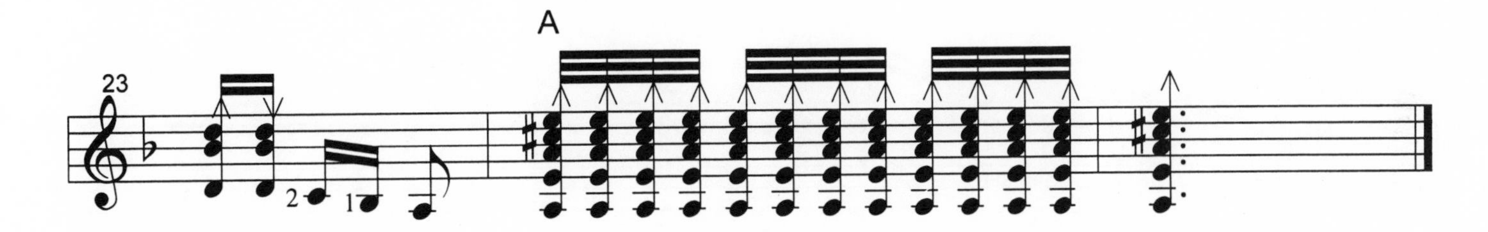
A
23
2
1

Falseta 7 Alzapua

Juan Serrano

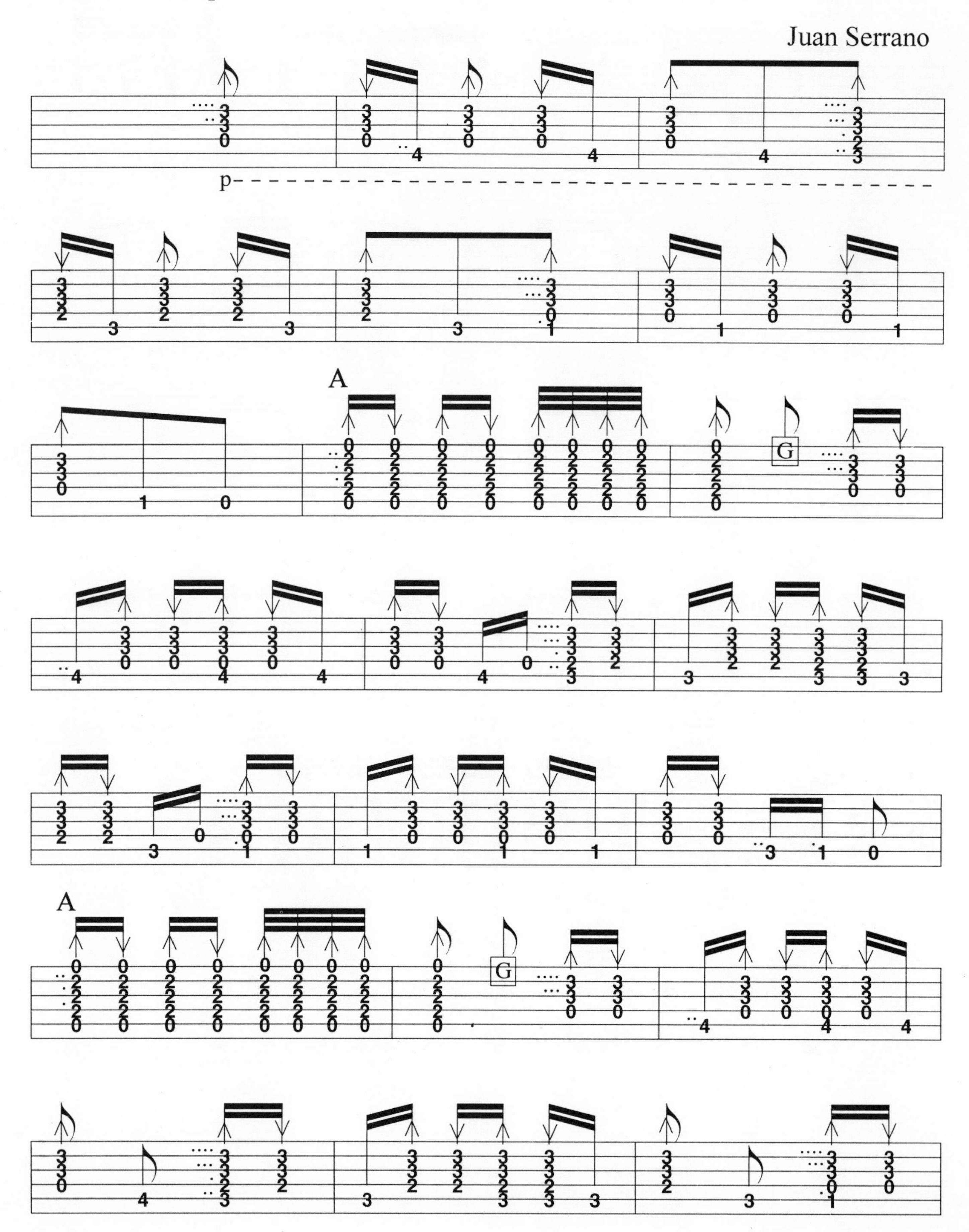

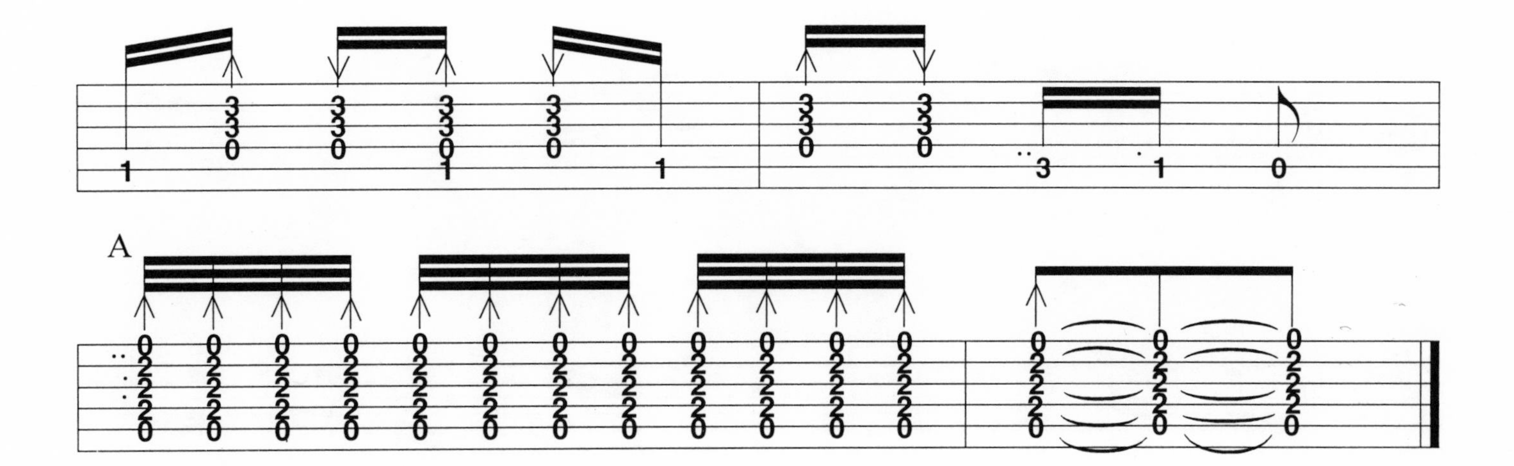
A

## Falseta 8

Juan Serrano

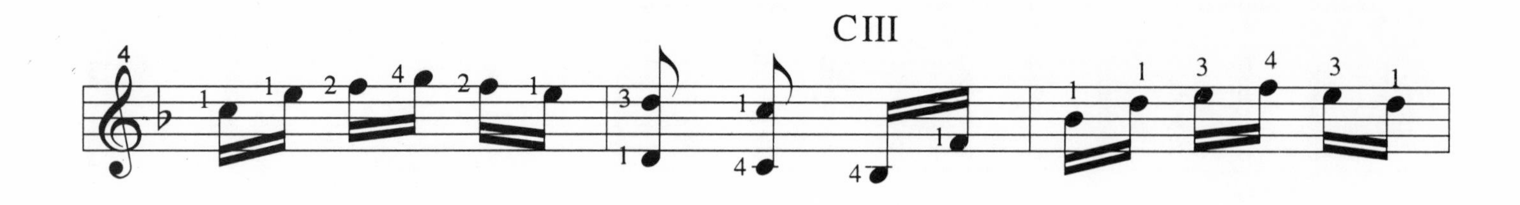

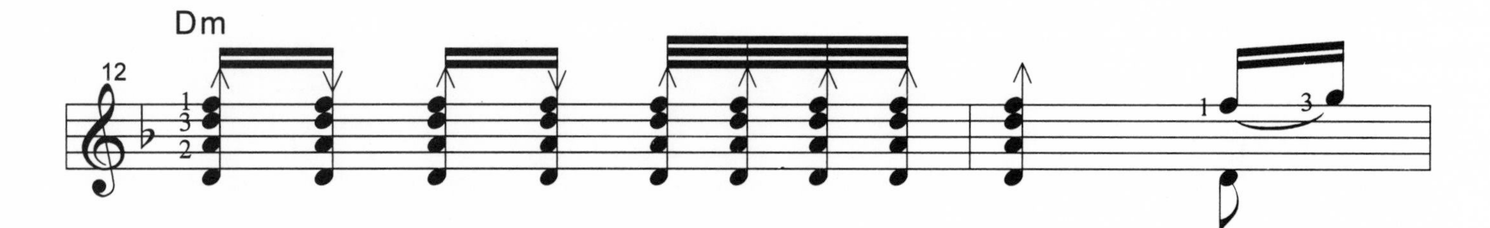

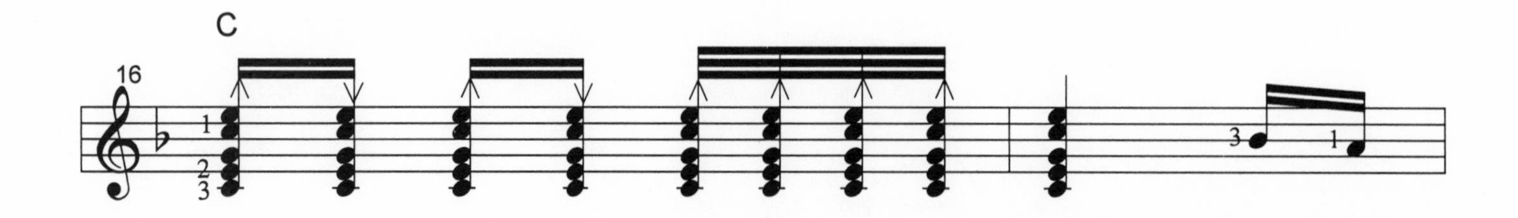

18
B♭

21

24

27

30

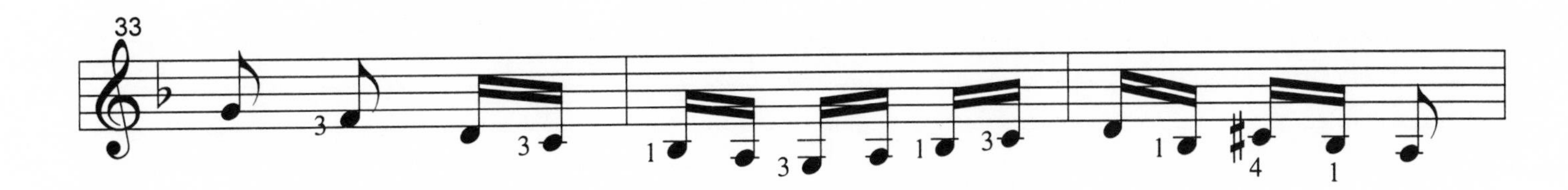
33

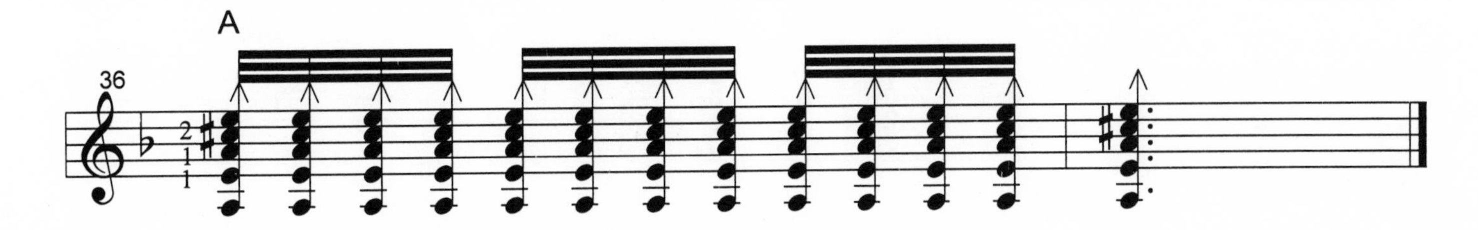
A
36

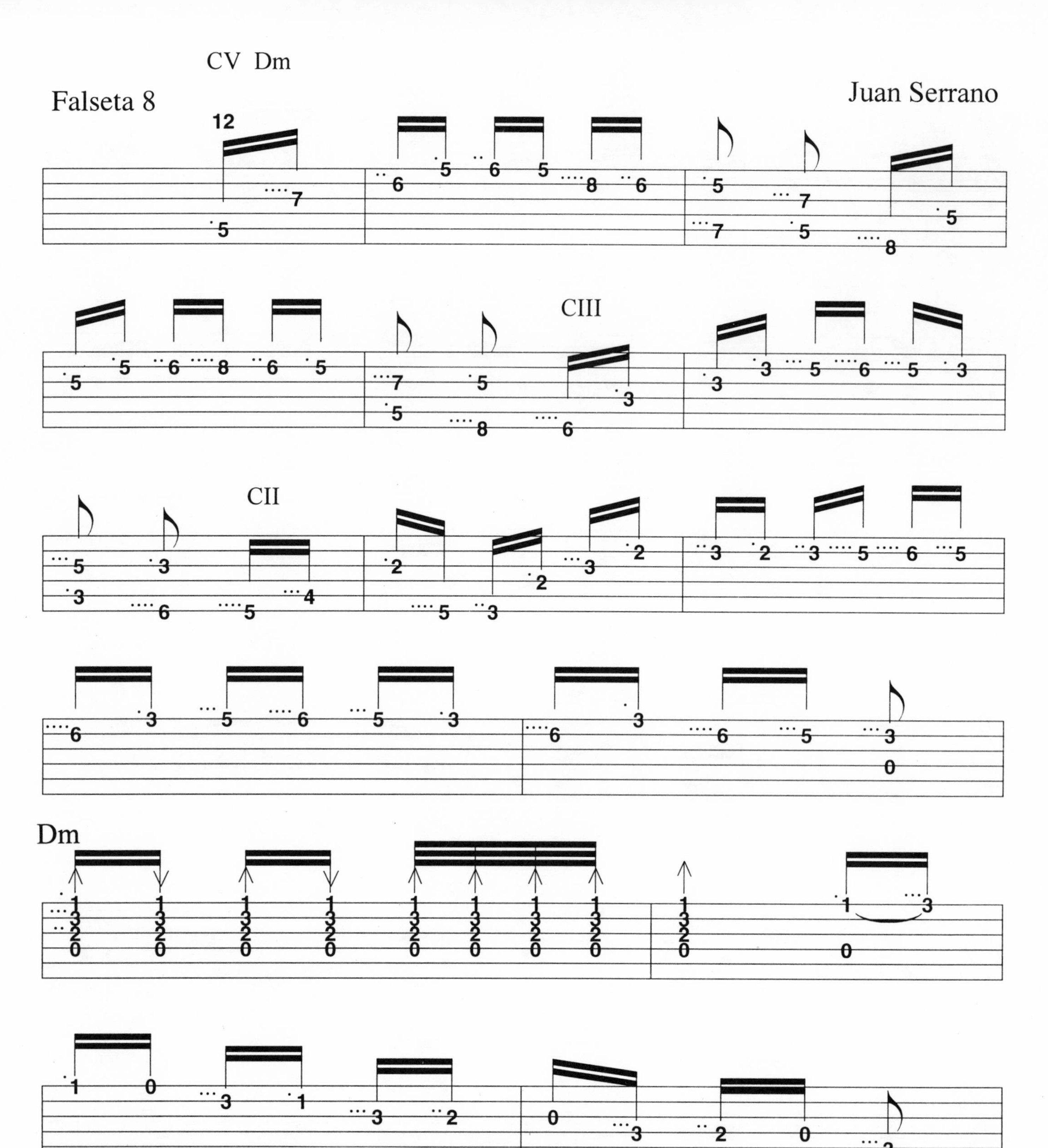
CV Dm
Falseta 8
Juan Serrano
CIII
CII
Dm

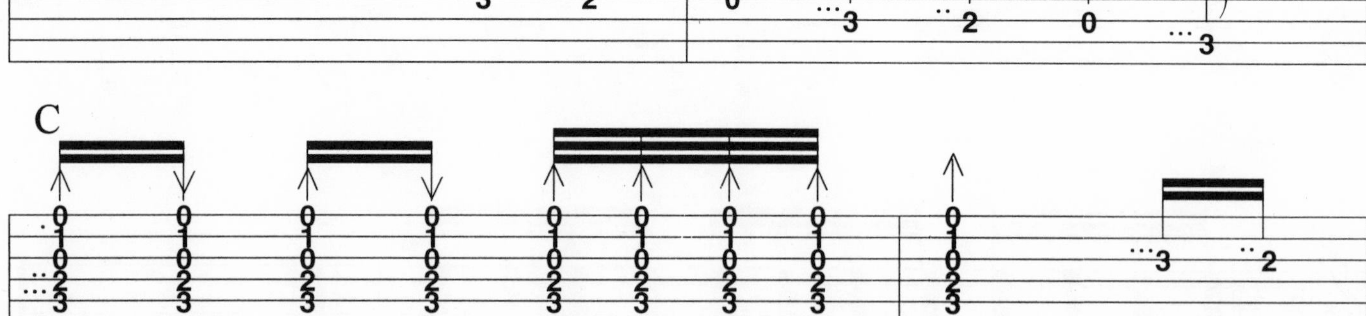
C

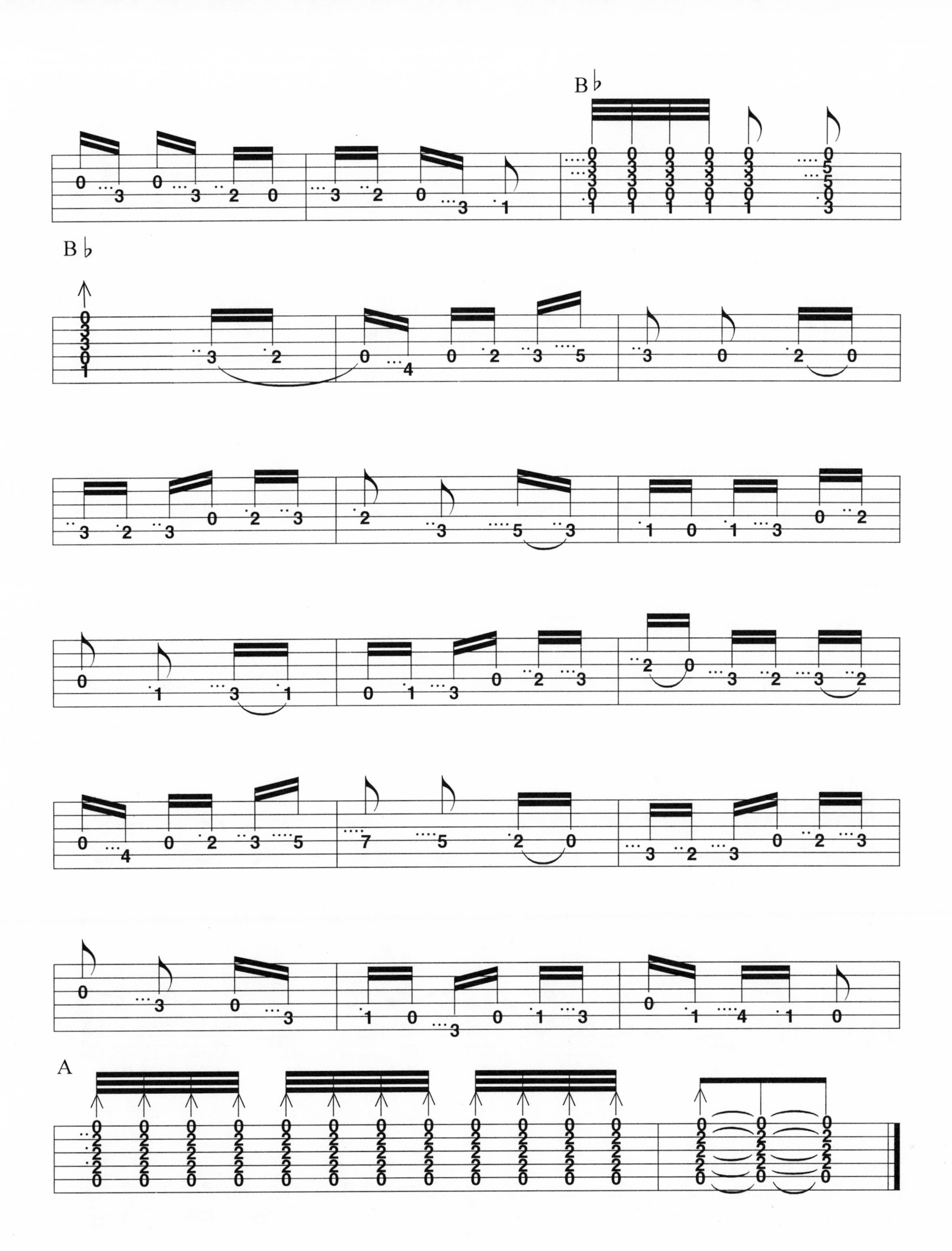
B♭
B♭
A

12
¢III
p

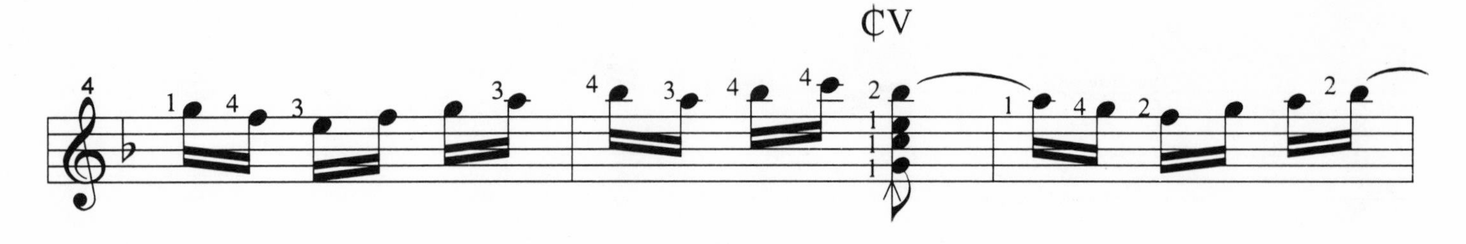
¢V

VI
VIII
X
IX

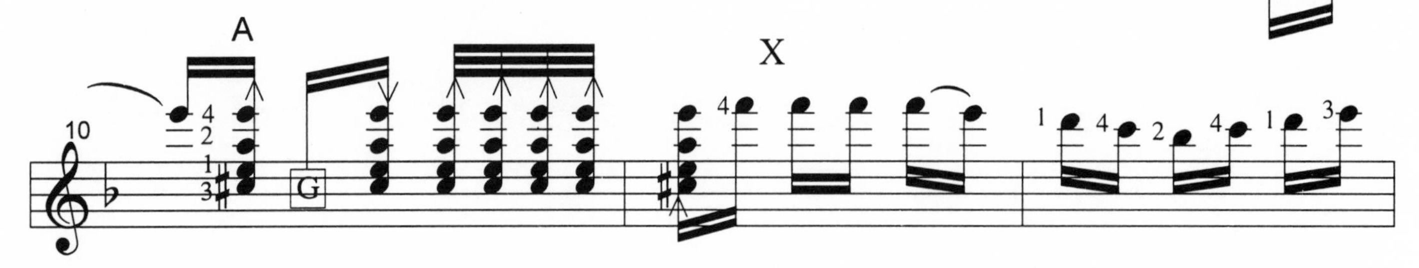
A
G
X

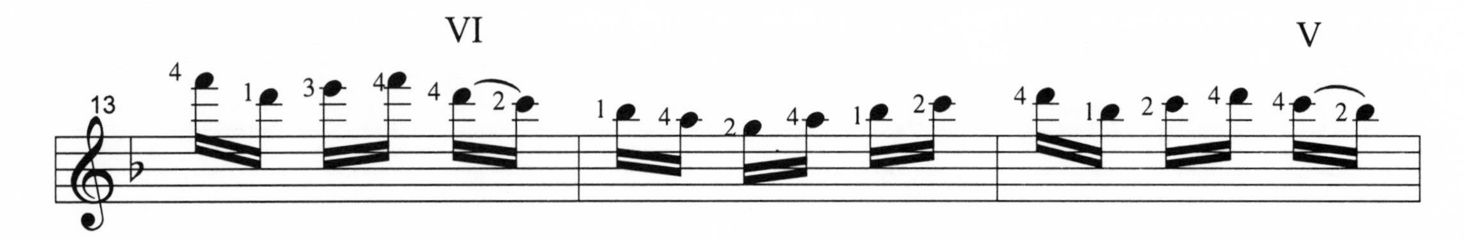
VI
V

V

G
III

22
I

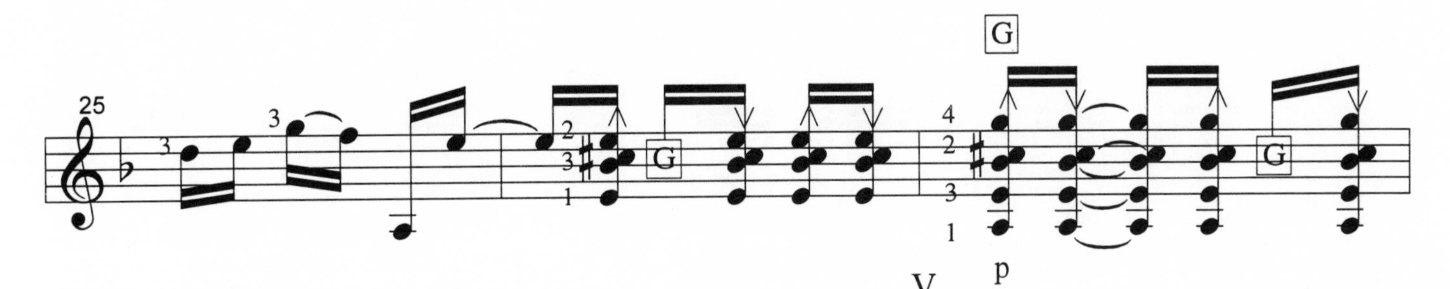
25
G
p

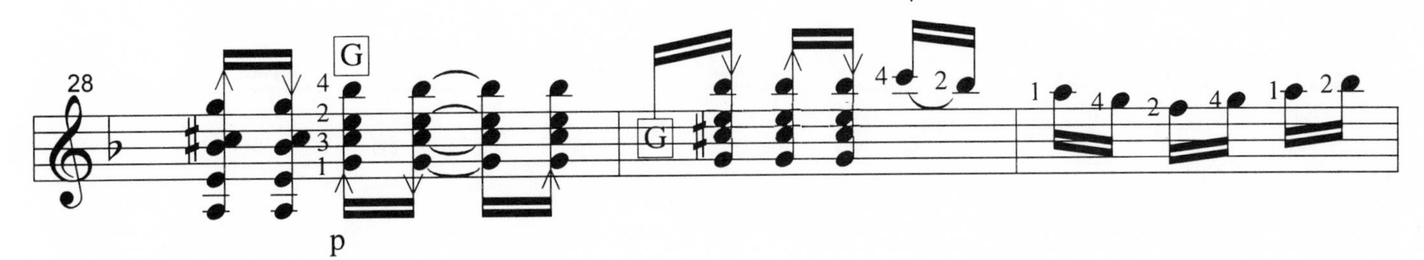
28
G
V
p

31
III

34

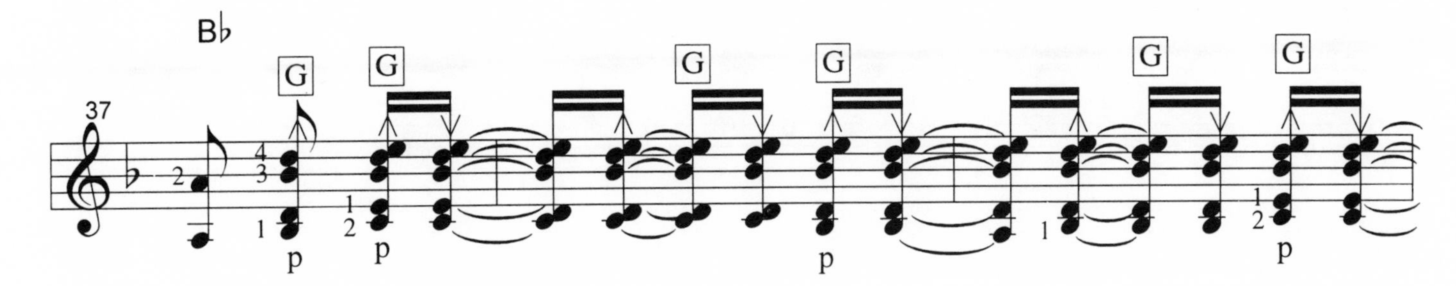
B♭
37
G
p

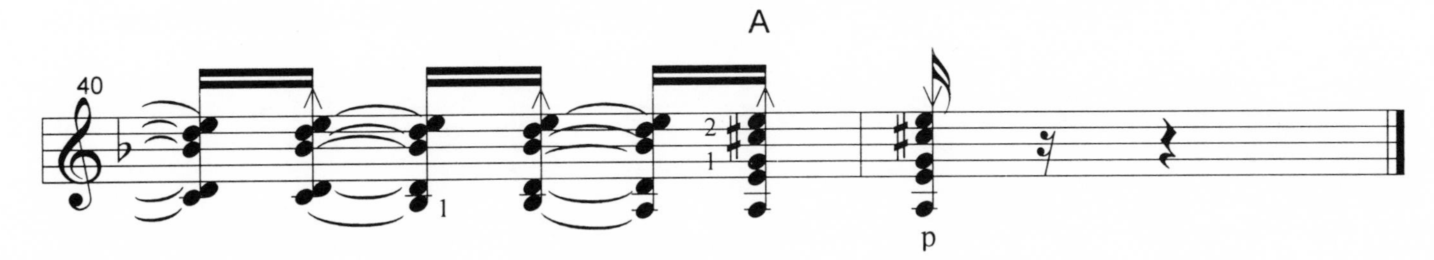
40
A
p

Falseta 9

Juan Serrano

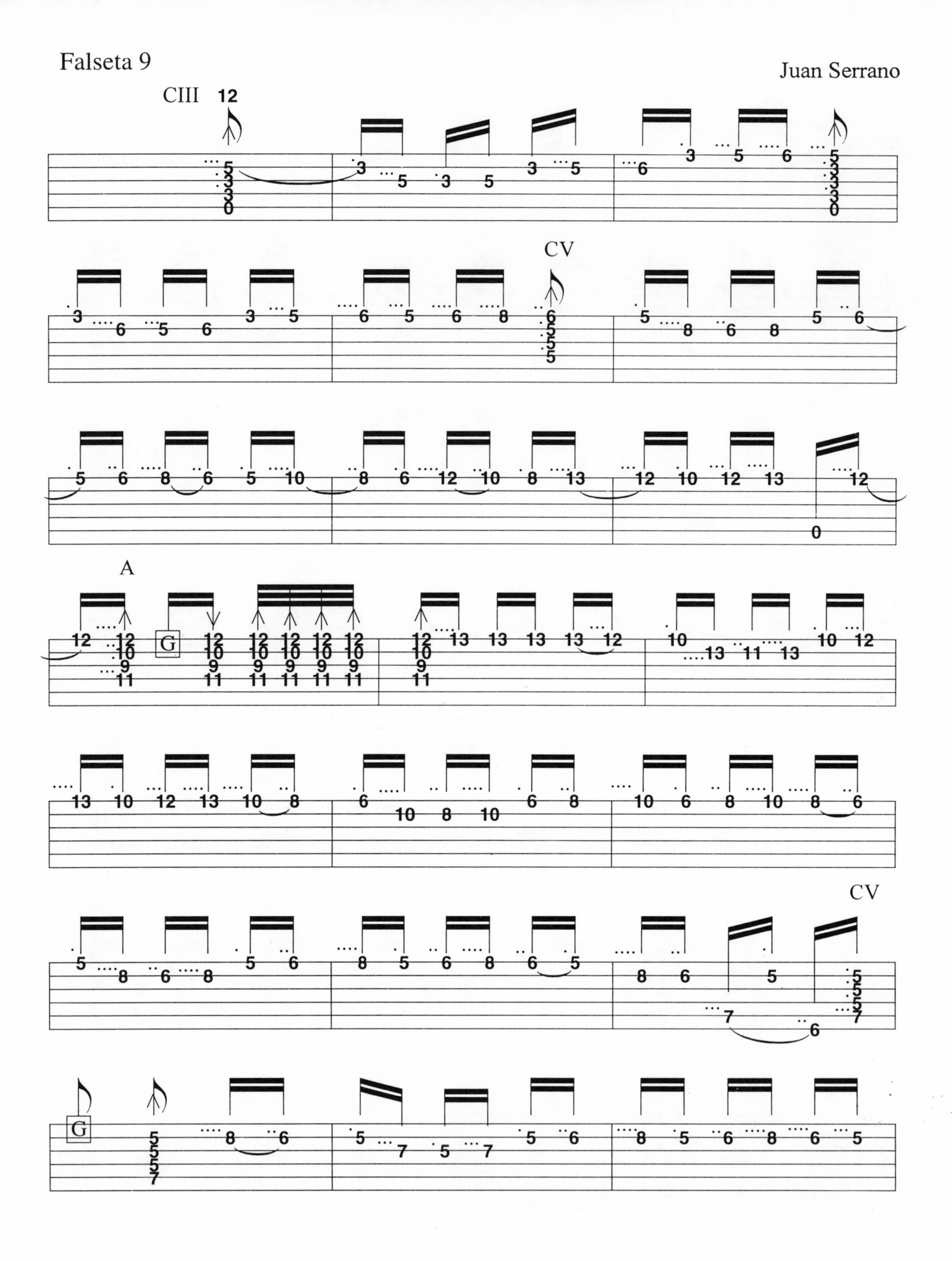

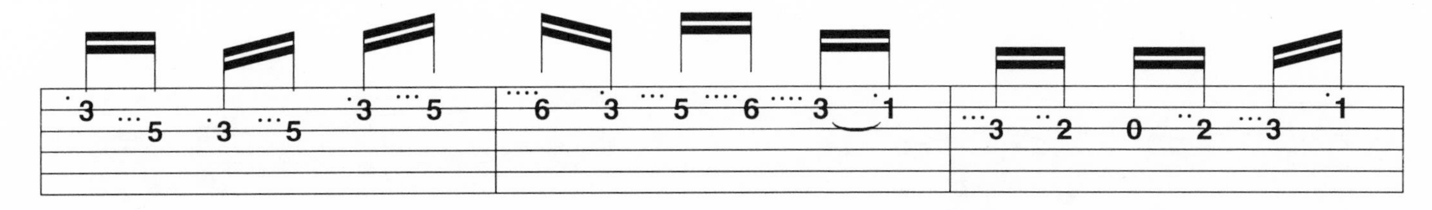

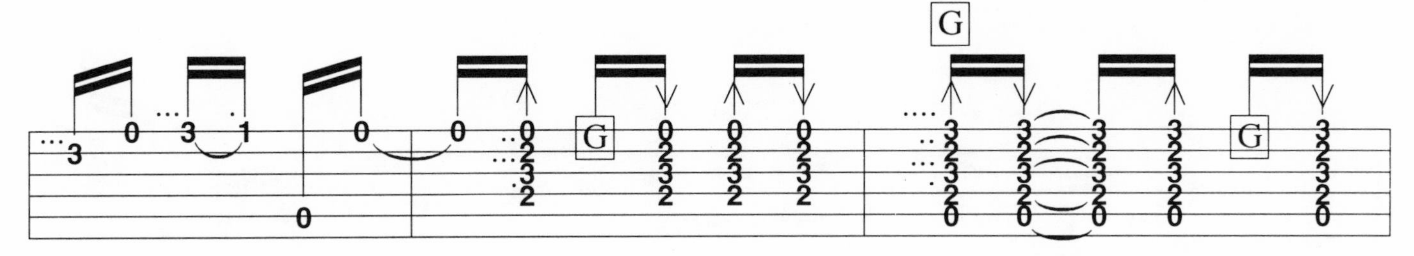
G
G
G

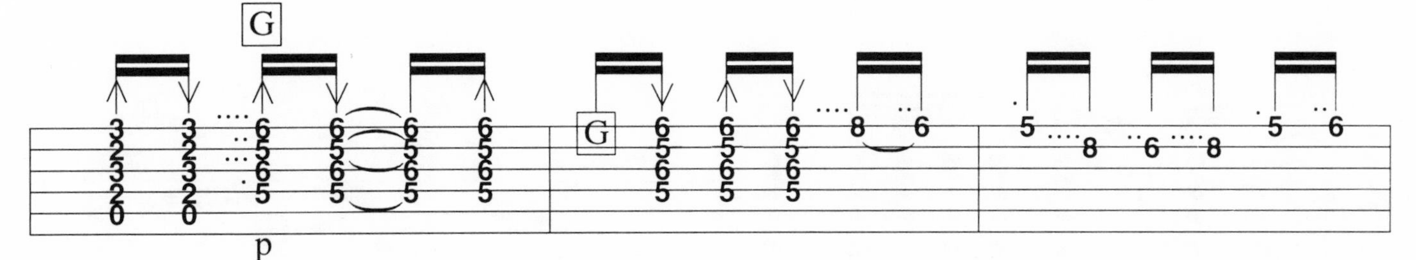
G
G
p

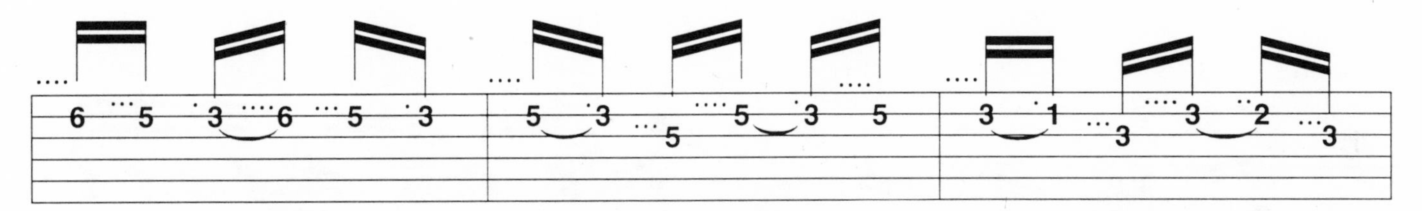

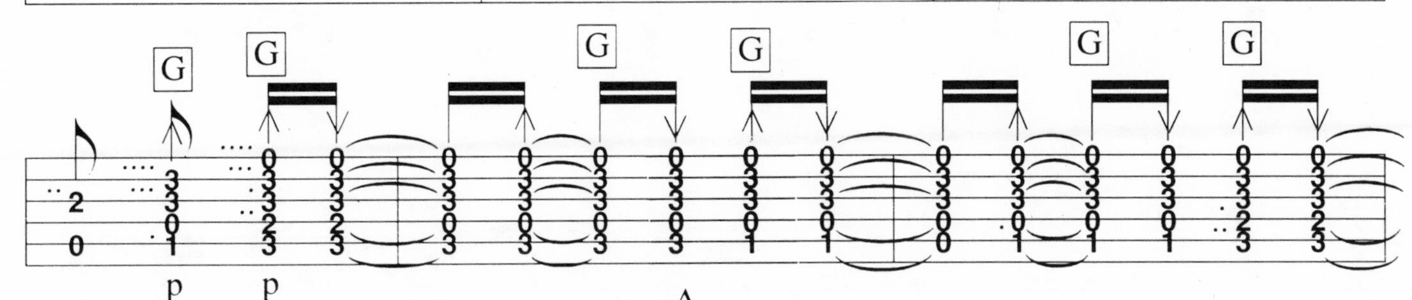
G
G
G
G
G
G
p
p
A

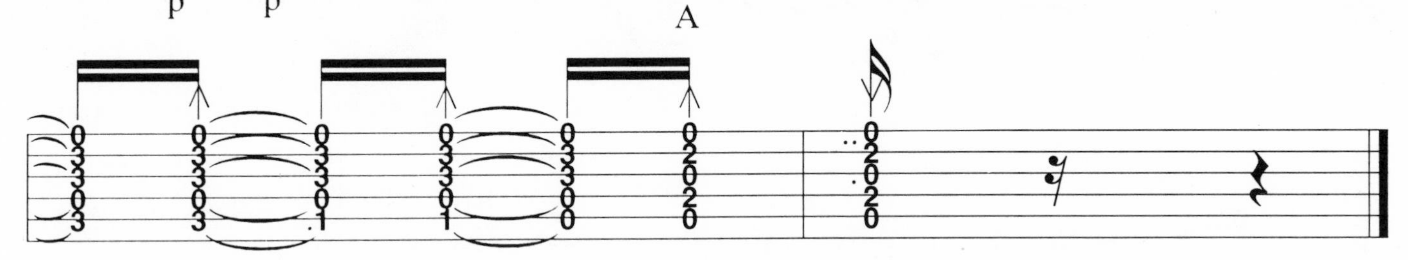

Falseta 10

Juan Serrano

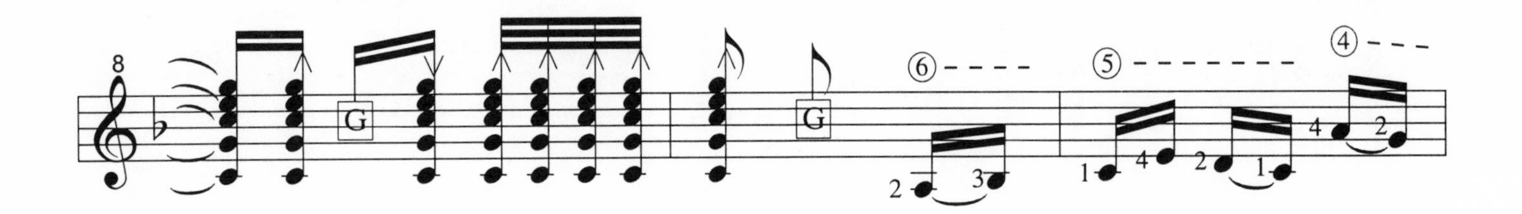

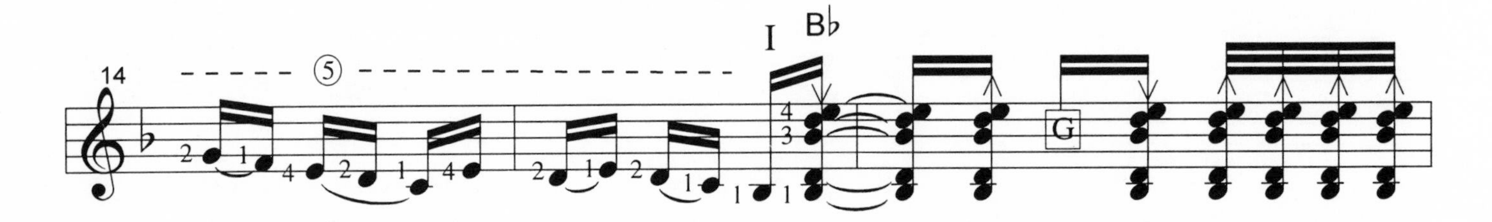

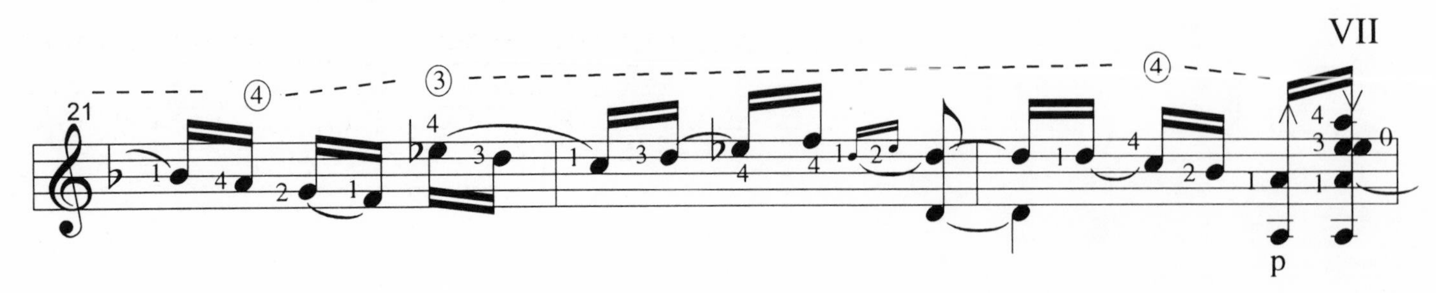

24
V
G

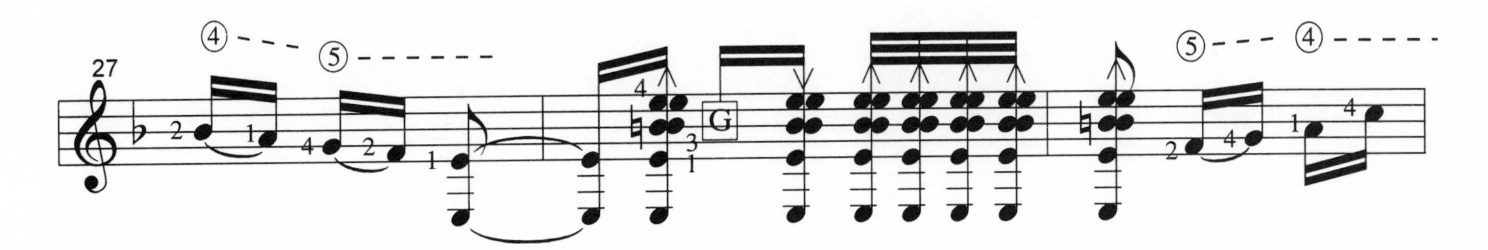
27
G

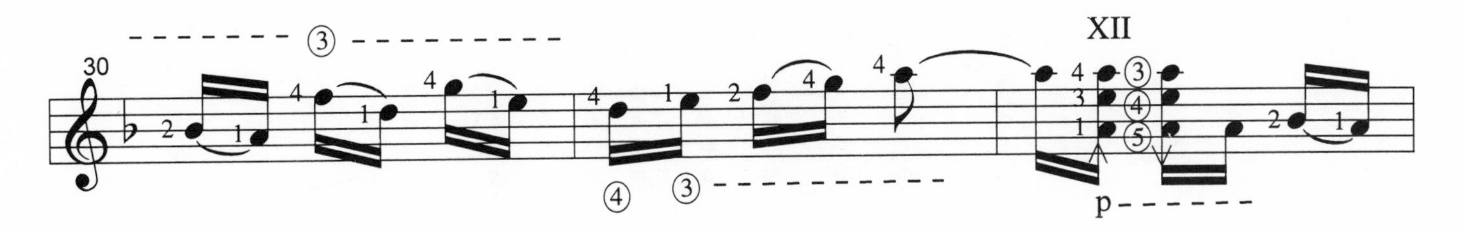
30
XII
p

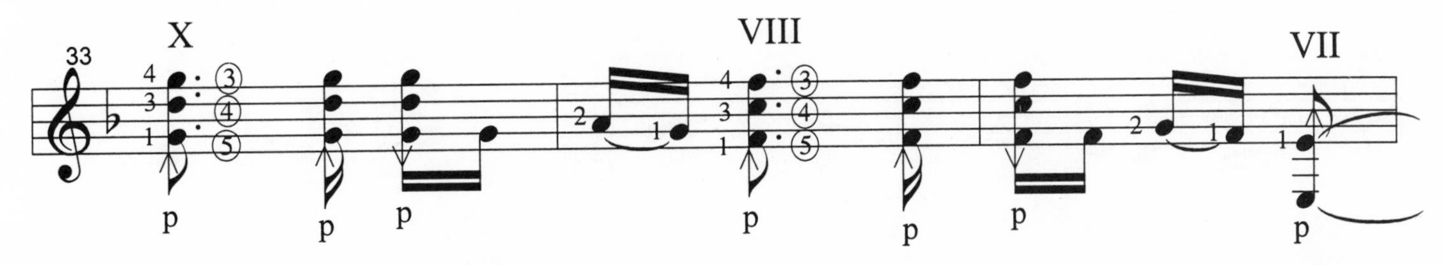
33
X
VIII
VII
p

36
VIII
G

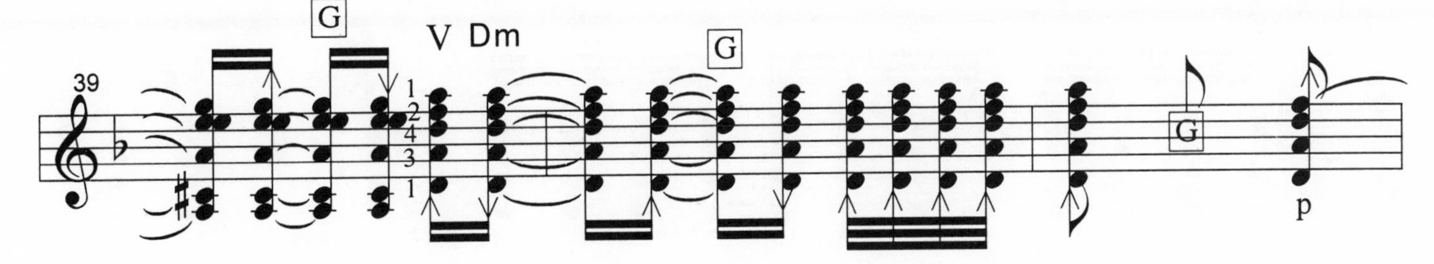
39
G
V Dm
p

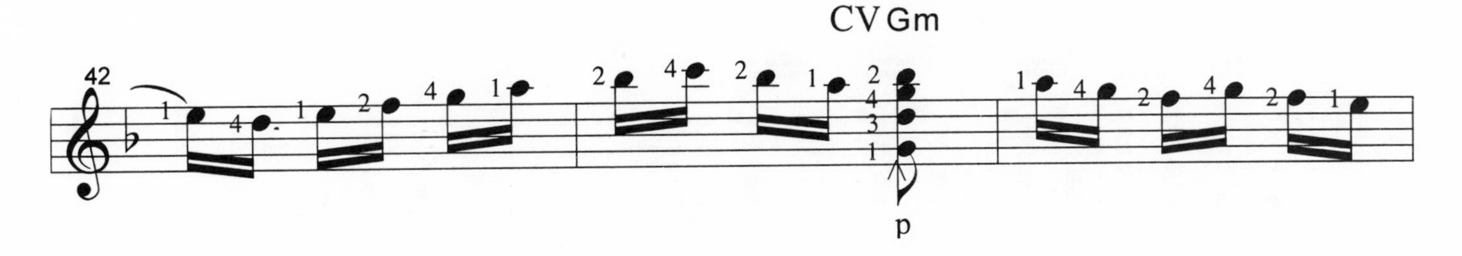
42
CV Gm
p

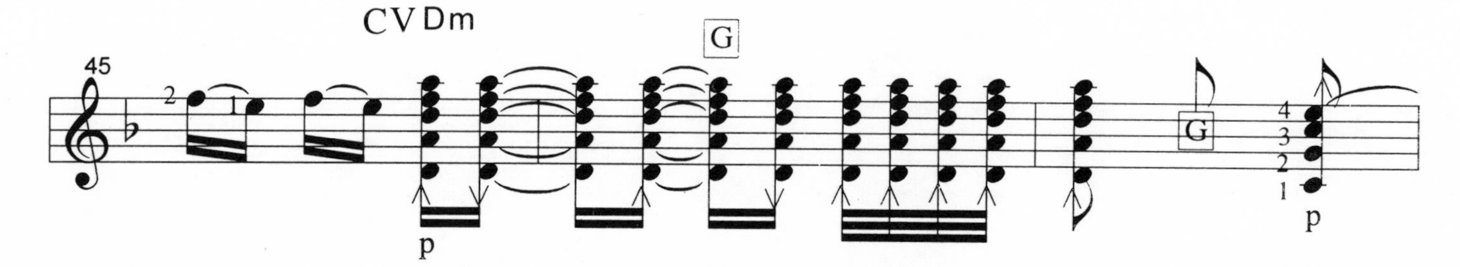
45
CV Dm
G
G

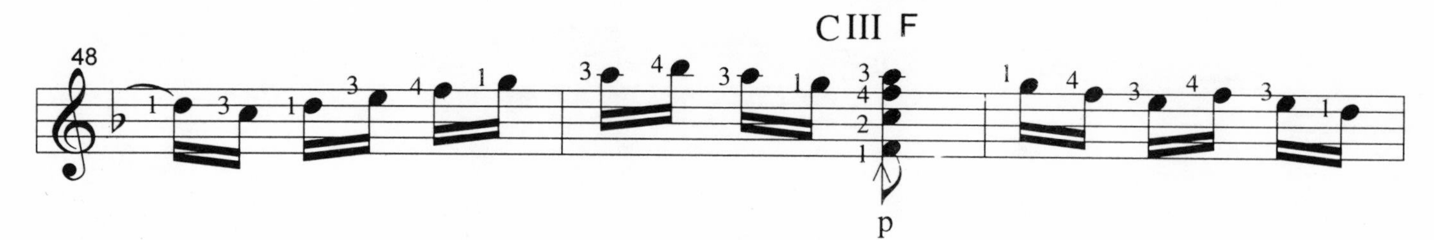
48
CIII F

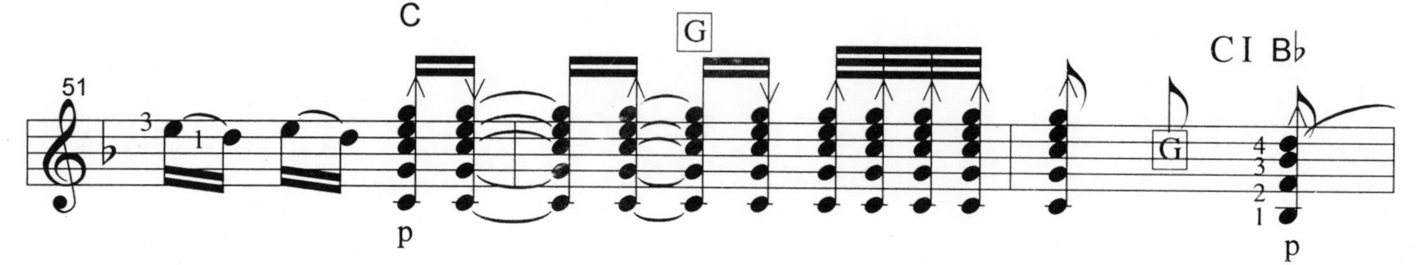
51
C
G
G
CI B♭

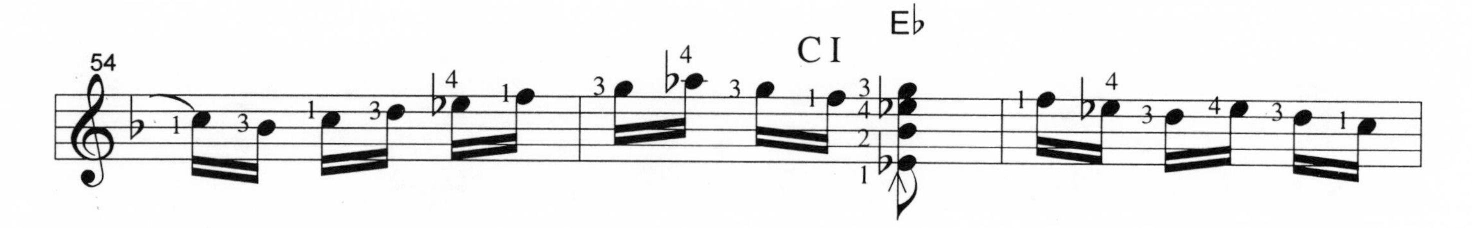
54
CI
E♭

57

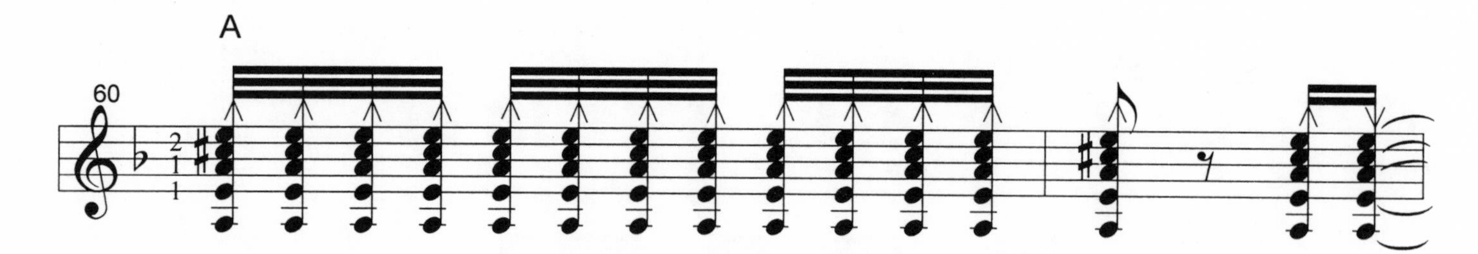
60
A

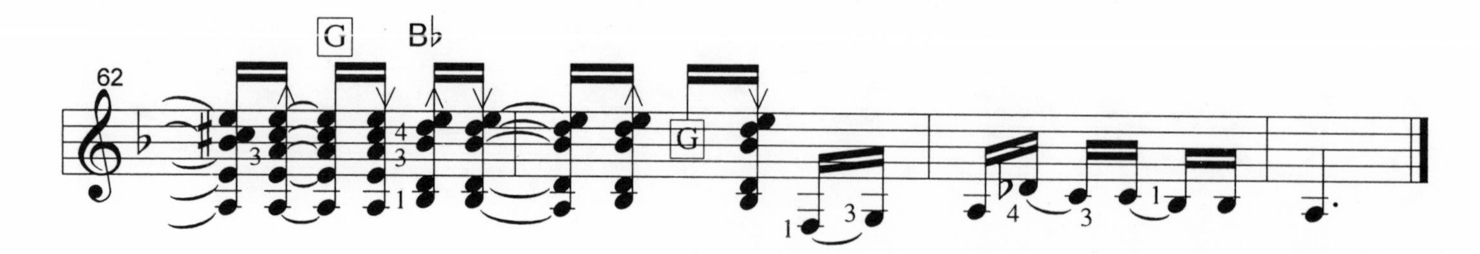
62
G
B♭
G

Falseta 10 Juan Serrano

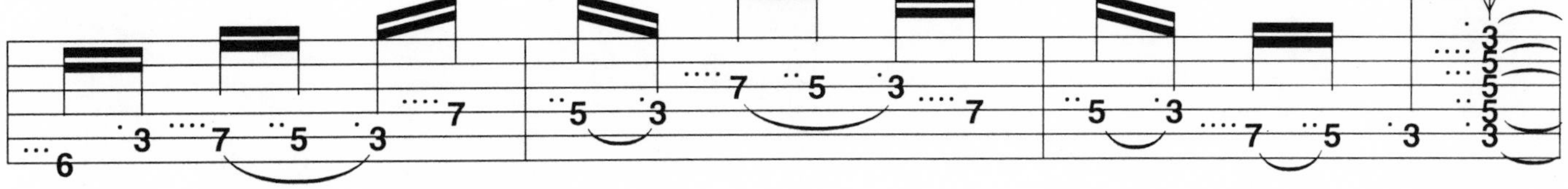


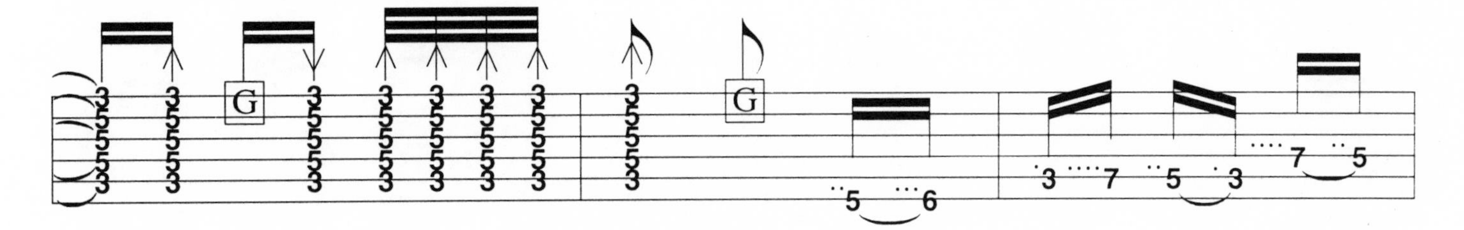

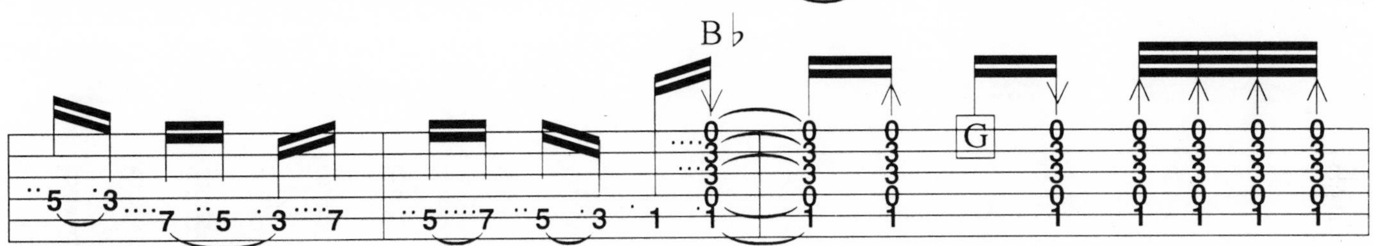


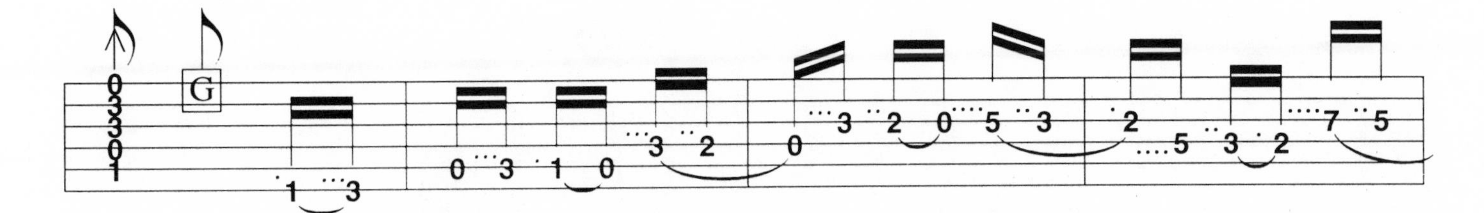


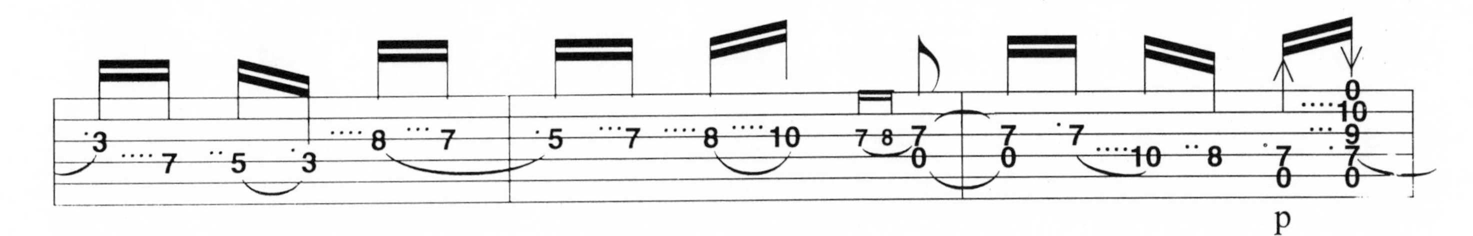

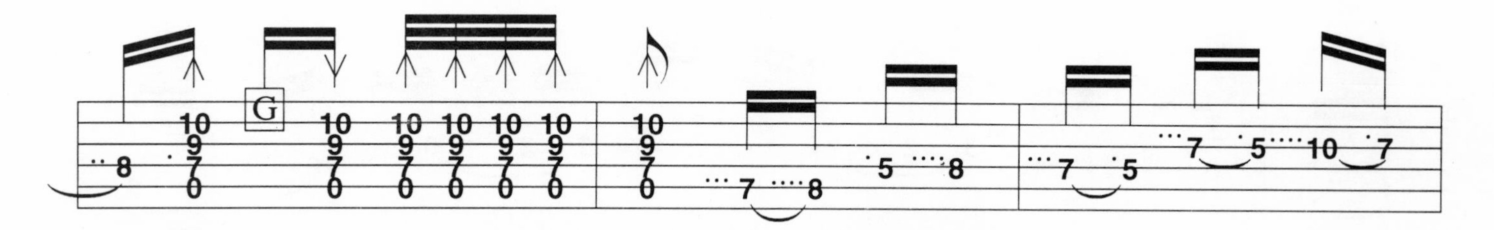
G
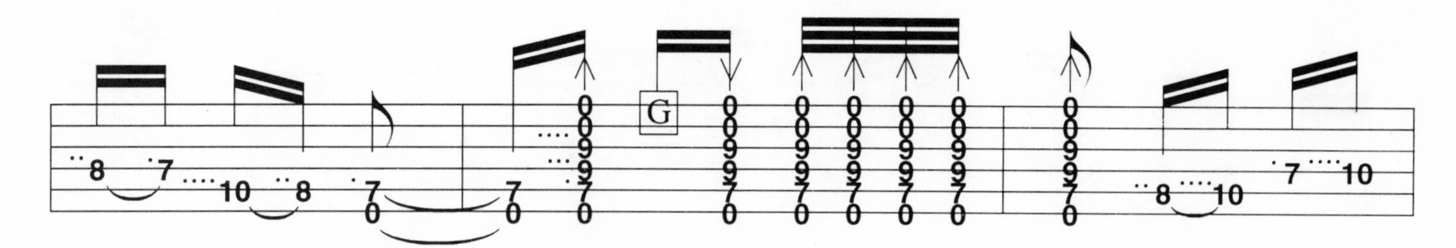
G
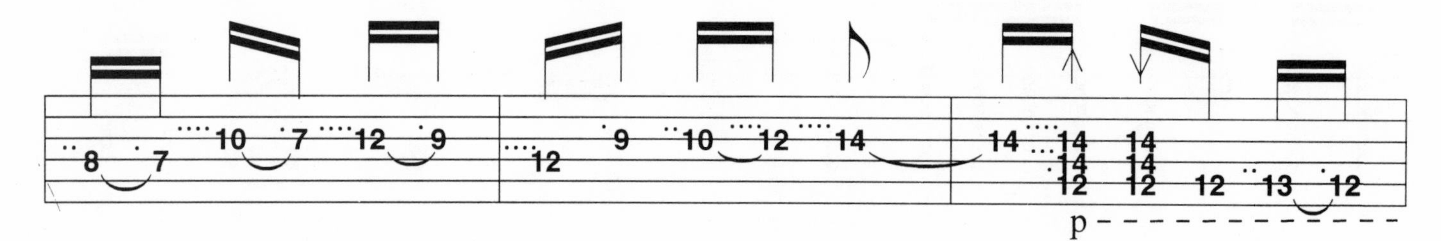
p
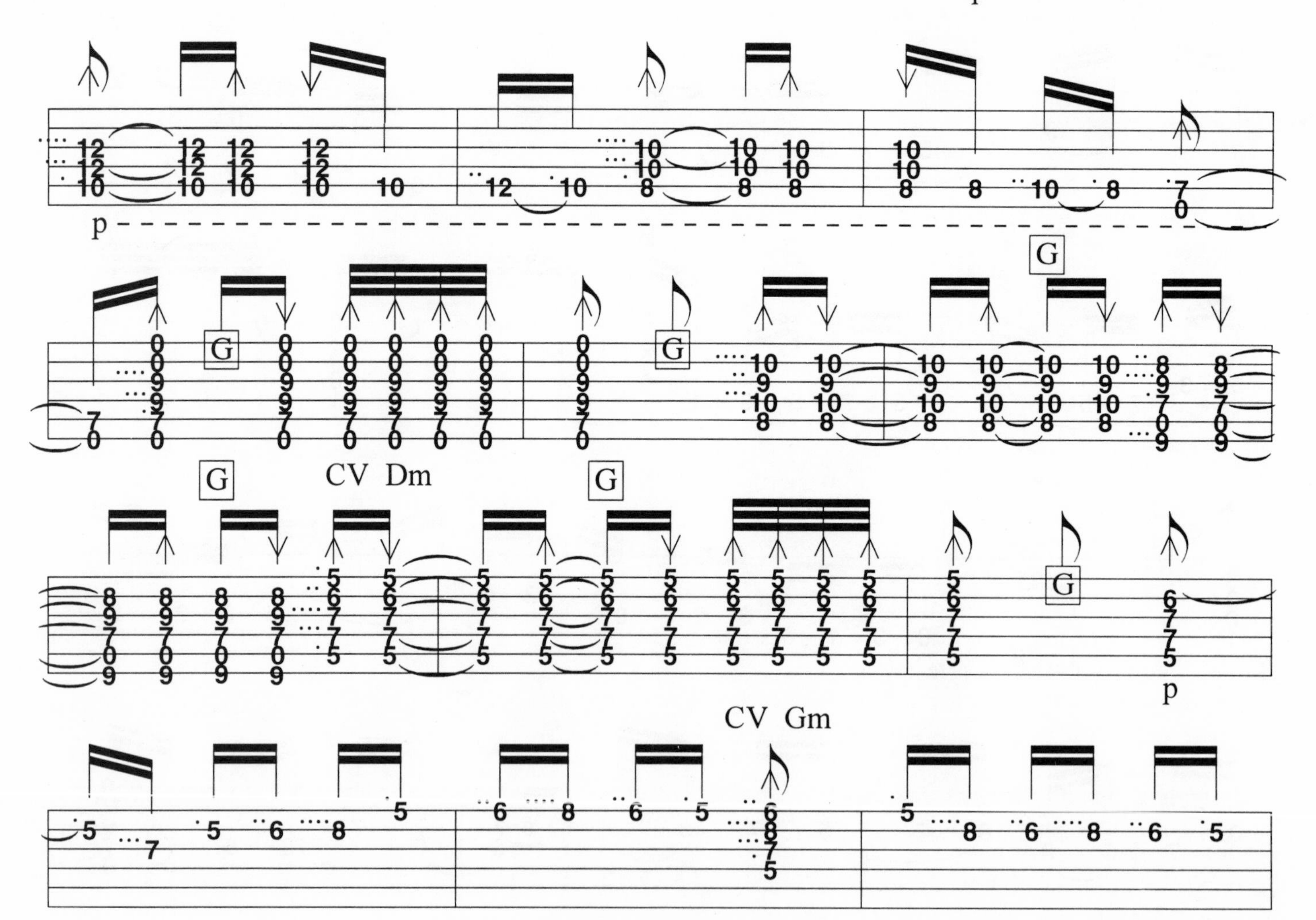
p
G
G
G
G
CV Dm
G
G
p
CV Gm

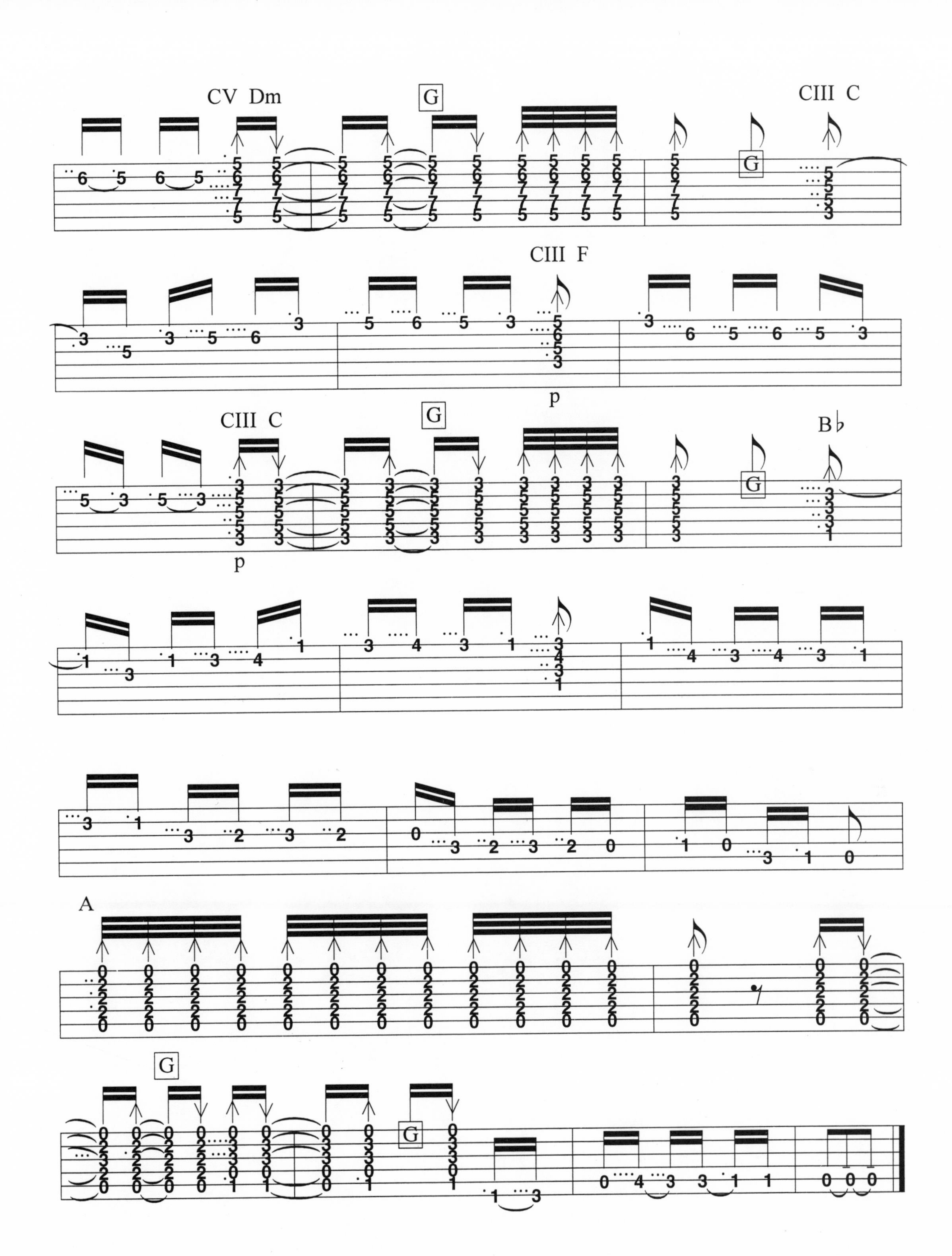
CV Dm
G
CIII C
G
CIII F
p
CIII C
G
B♭
G
p
A
G
G

كولومبيانس

# COLOMBIANAS

The Colombianas are known as styles of "coming and going" in the flamenco world. This name is derived from the fact that some flamenco forms were brought to Latin America and returned with some changes and alterations influenced by the rhythms and melodies of Latin America.

The Colombianas are played in the key of A major and its time is 4/4. A flamenco compás has 8 beats equivalent to 2 measures of 4/4 time.

The traditional compás should be practiced at the beginning and the 3 variations in order to feel sure of the rhythm. It will take time. It is advisable to work on one falseta during each practice session to gain confidence before attempting the next. It is also not a good idea to try to memorize all of the falsetas in a single day.

In some of the Colombianas falsetas, the arpeggio and picado techniques are alternated. This technique is extremely difficult to perfect. The arpeggio is played freestroke and the picado reststroke. It can be found in falsetas # 6, 7, 8 and at the end of #10.

# COLOMBIANAS

Las Colombianas son conocidas entre los flamencos como estilos de ida y vuelta. El nombre de ida y vuelta es derivado de que algunas formas flamencas fueron llevadas a Latino América y a su regreso volvieron con algunos cambios y alteraciones influenciadas por los ritmos y melodías Latino Americanas.

Las Colombianas se tocan en el tono de La mayor y su medida es de 4/4. Un compás flamenco tiene ocho tiempos, equivalentes a dos compases musicales de 4/4.

Practiquen primero el compás tradicional y las tres variaciones para sentirse bien seguros del ritmo.
Tomen su tiempo. Es mejor trabajar en una sola falseta en cada sesión de práctica y sentirse cómodo y seguro antes de tratar la siguiente. No es obligación, ni buena idea, el tratar de aprenderlas todas en un solo día.

En las falsetas # 6 ,7, 8 y final de la #10 de las Colombianas se alternan las técnicas de arpegio y picado al mismo tiempo. Esta técnica es muy difícil de perfeccionarla. El arpegio se toca tirando y el picado apoyando.

# *Colombianas*

Traditional Compas

Juan Serrano

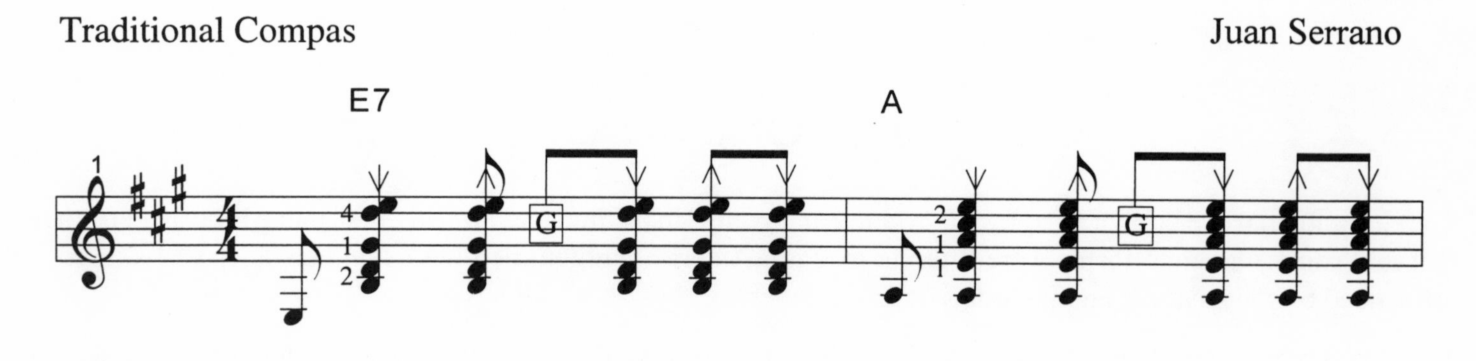


Variation 1

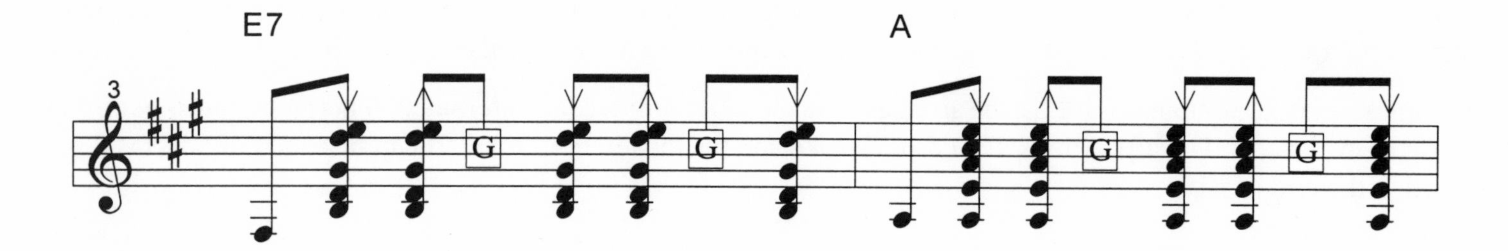


Variation 2 & 3

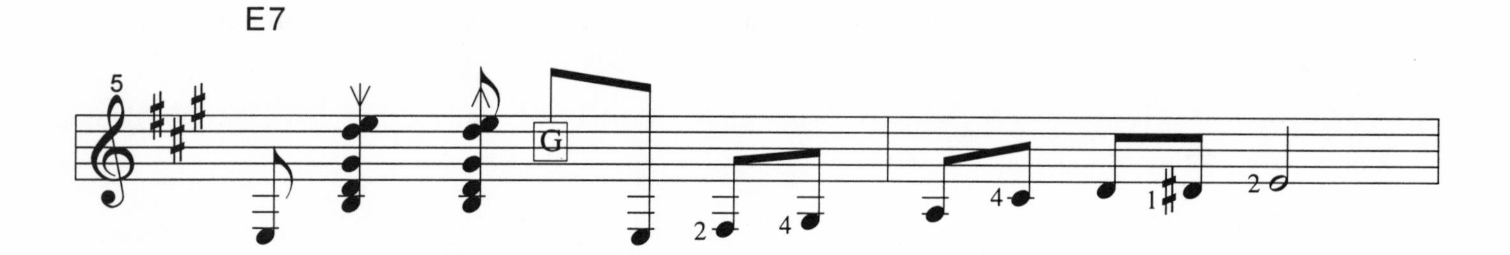


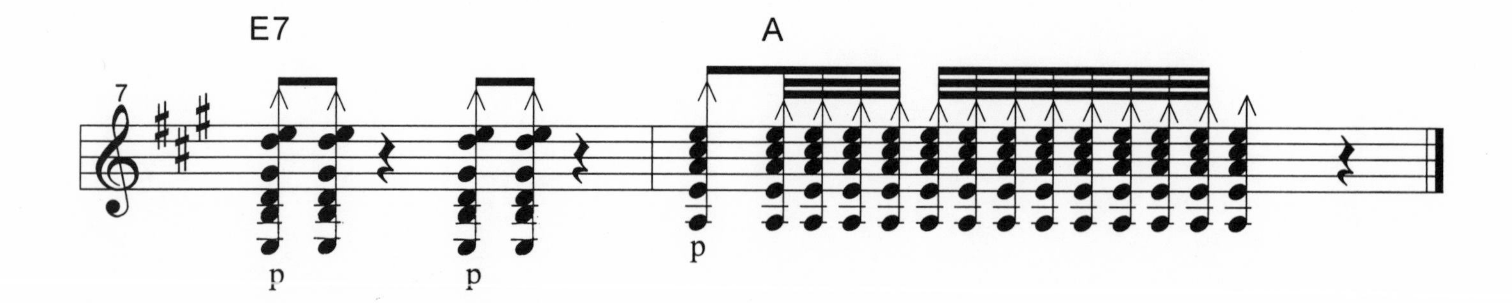

# Colombianas

## Traditional Compas

Juan Serrano

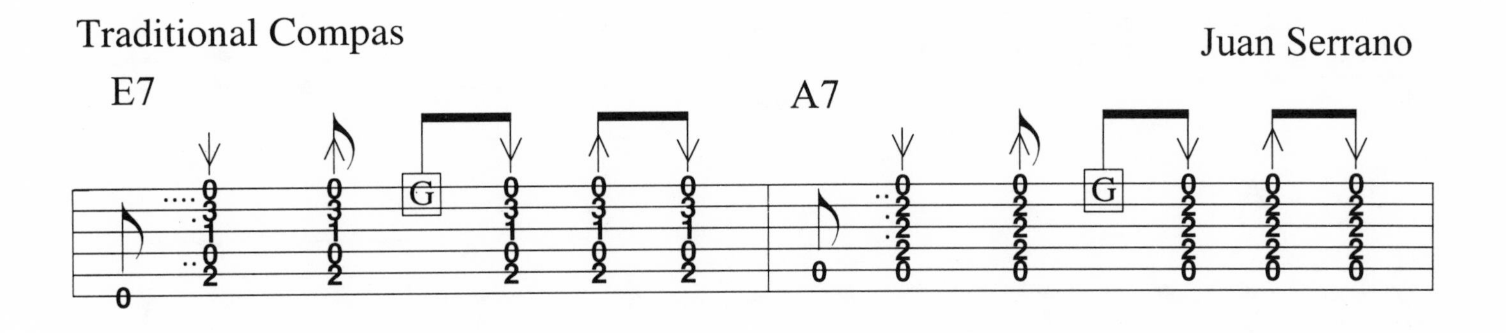


## Variation 1

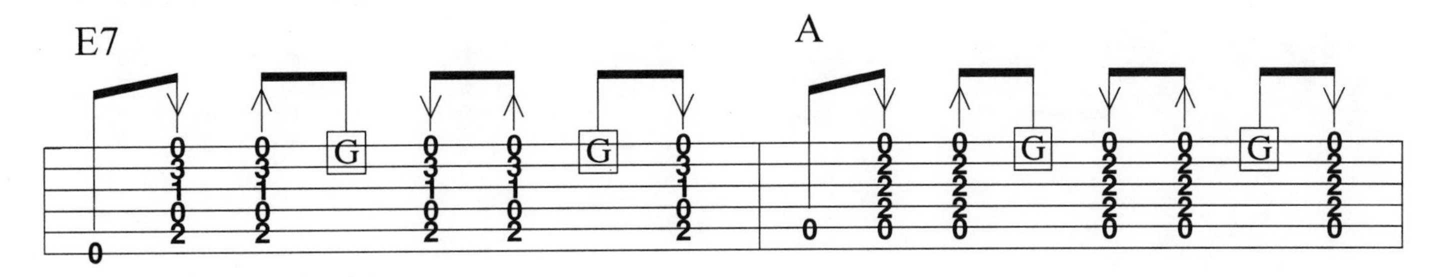


## Variation 2 & 3

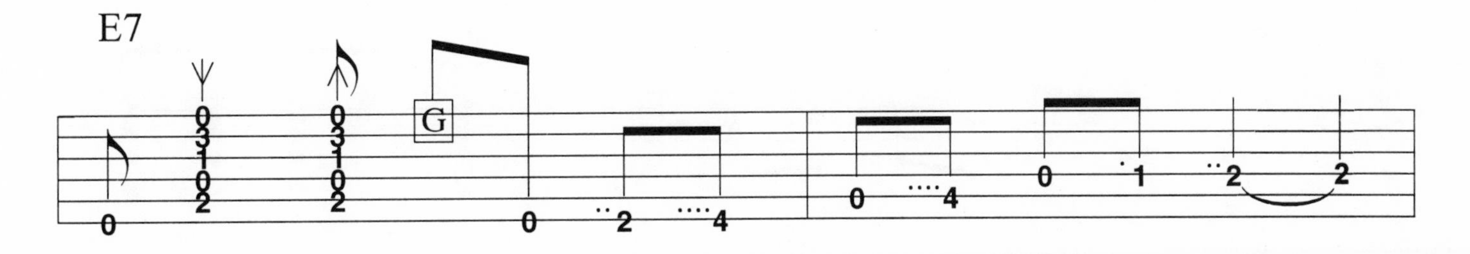


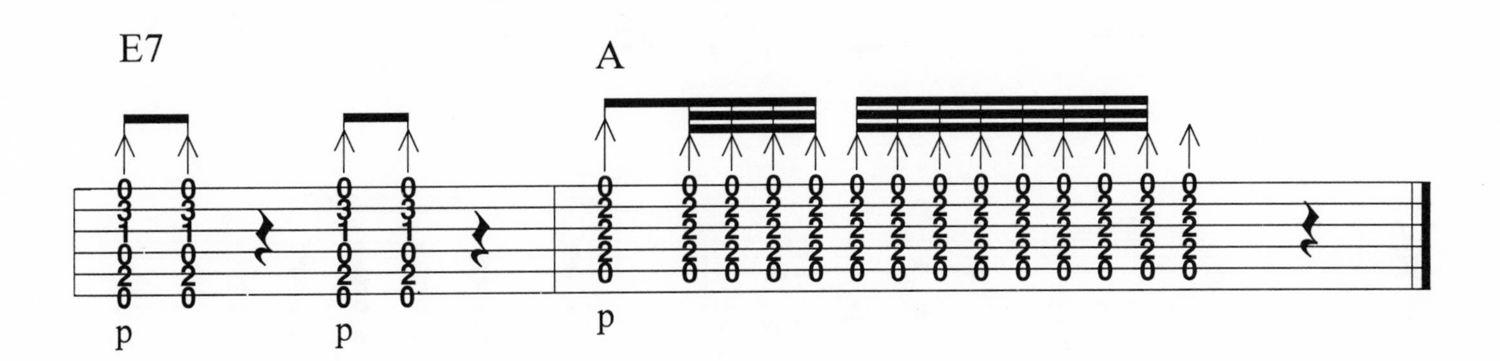

Falseta 1

Juan Serrano

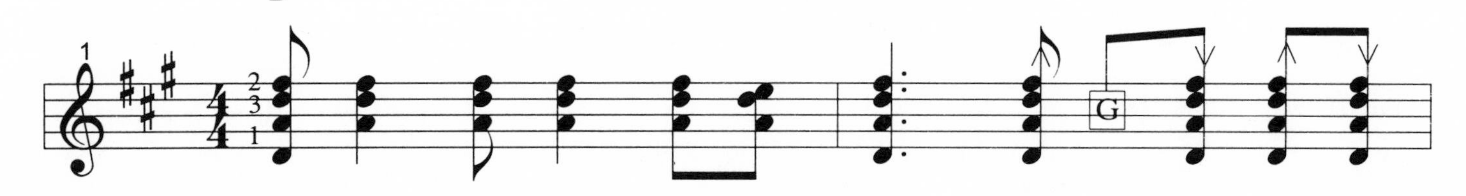


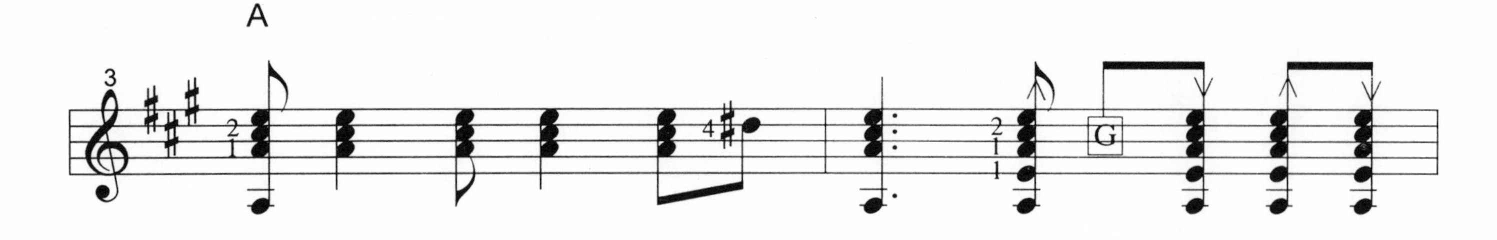

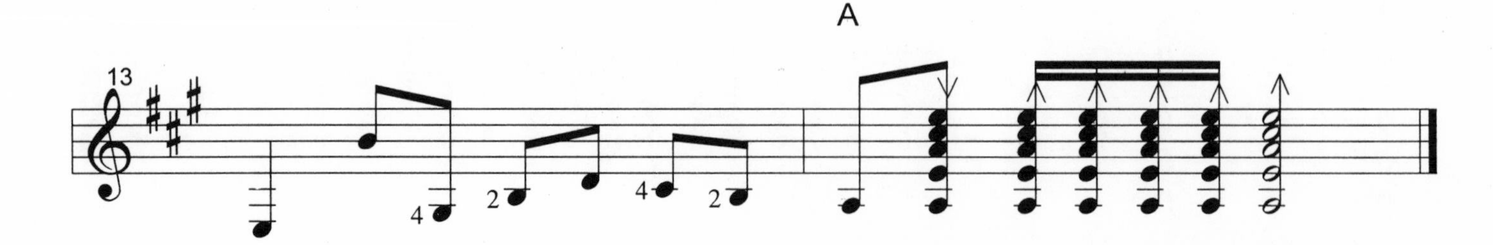

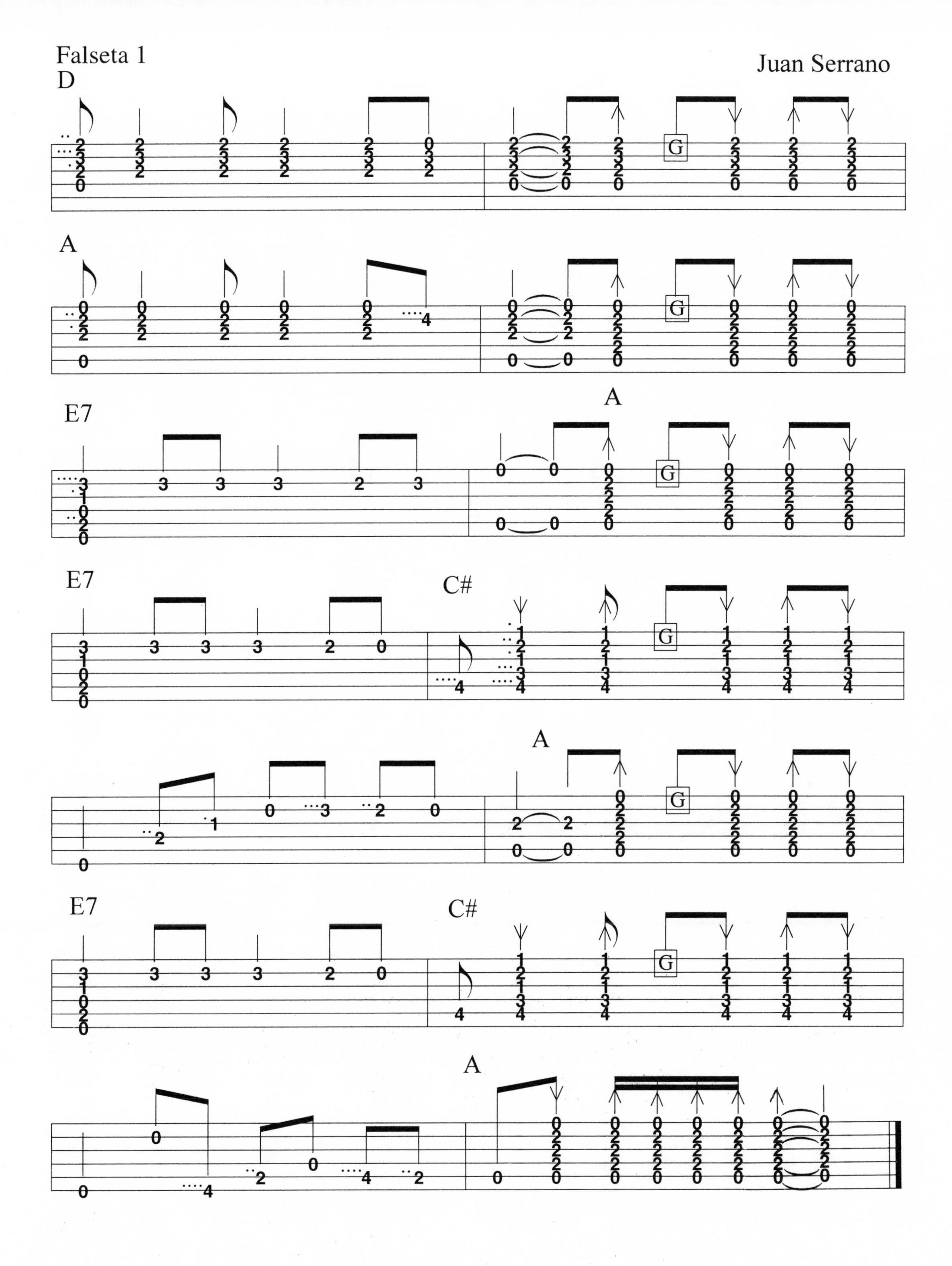

Falseta 1
Juan Serrano
D
G
A
G
E7
A
G
E7
C#
G
A
G
E7
C#
G
A

Falseta 2

Juan Serrano

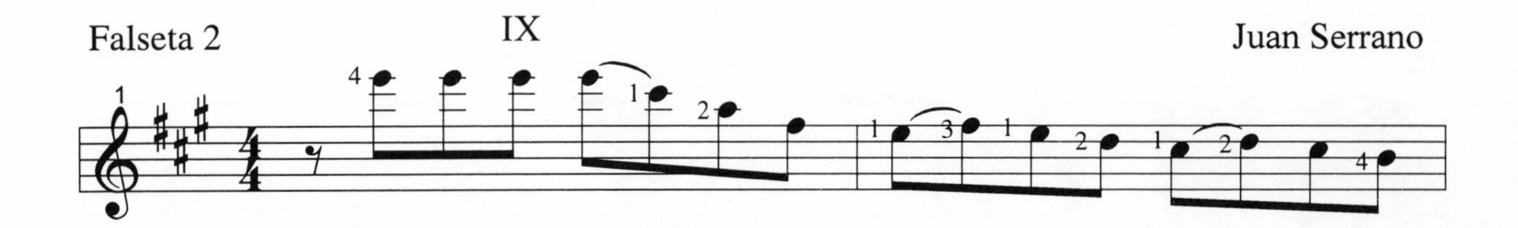

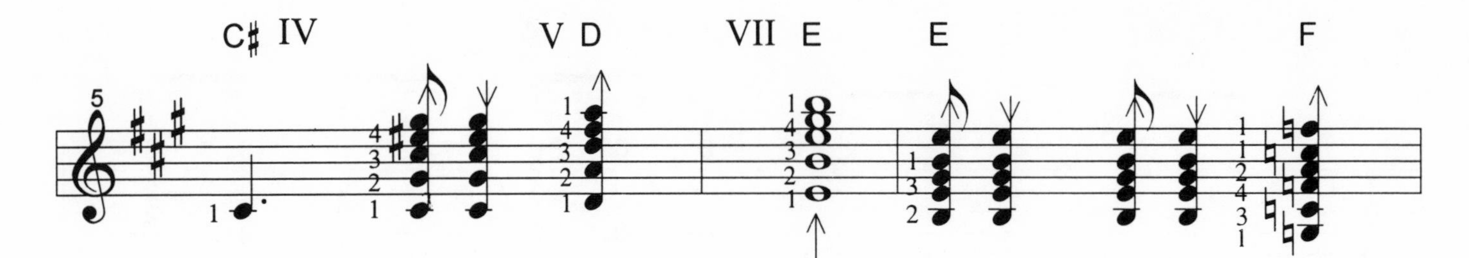

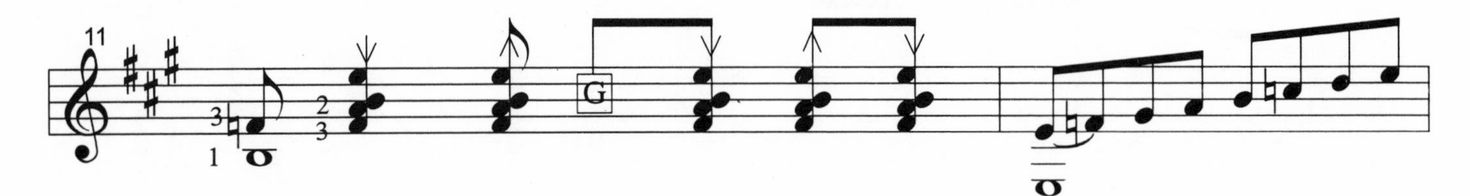


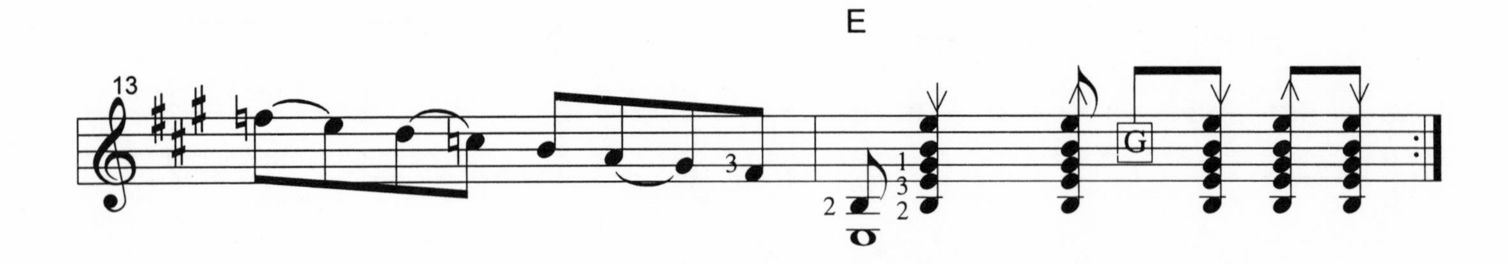


A

IVG♯m

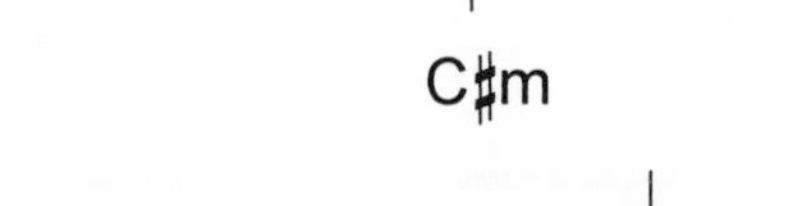
IV
C♯m

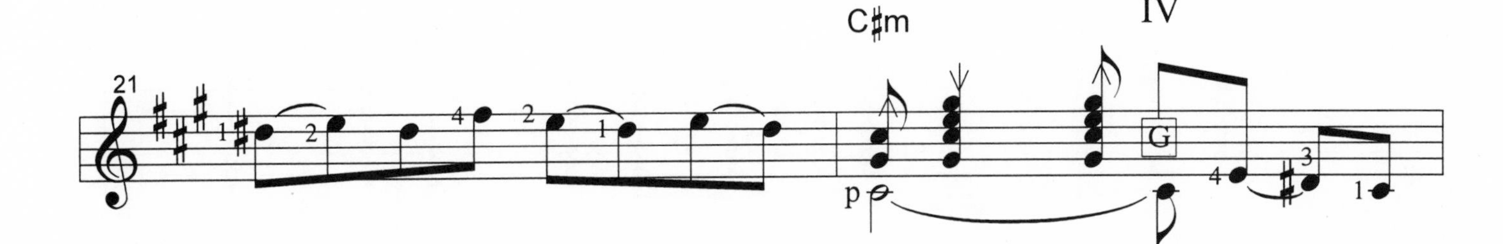
C♯m
IV

G♯m

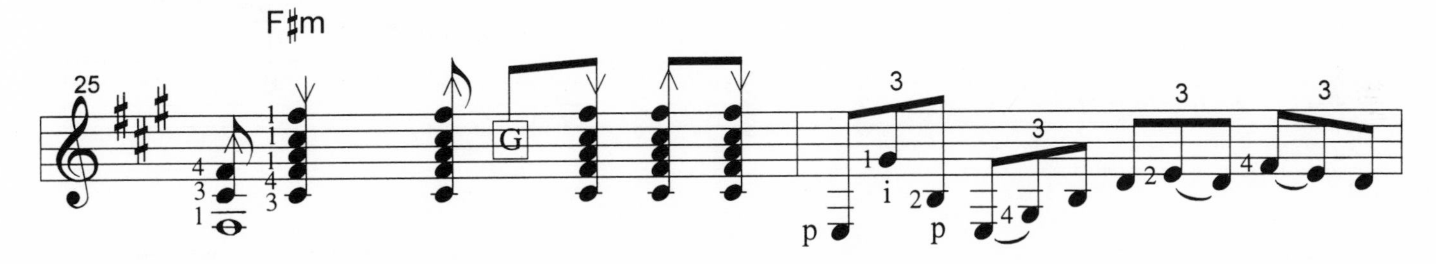
F♯m

A

E7
A

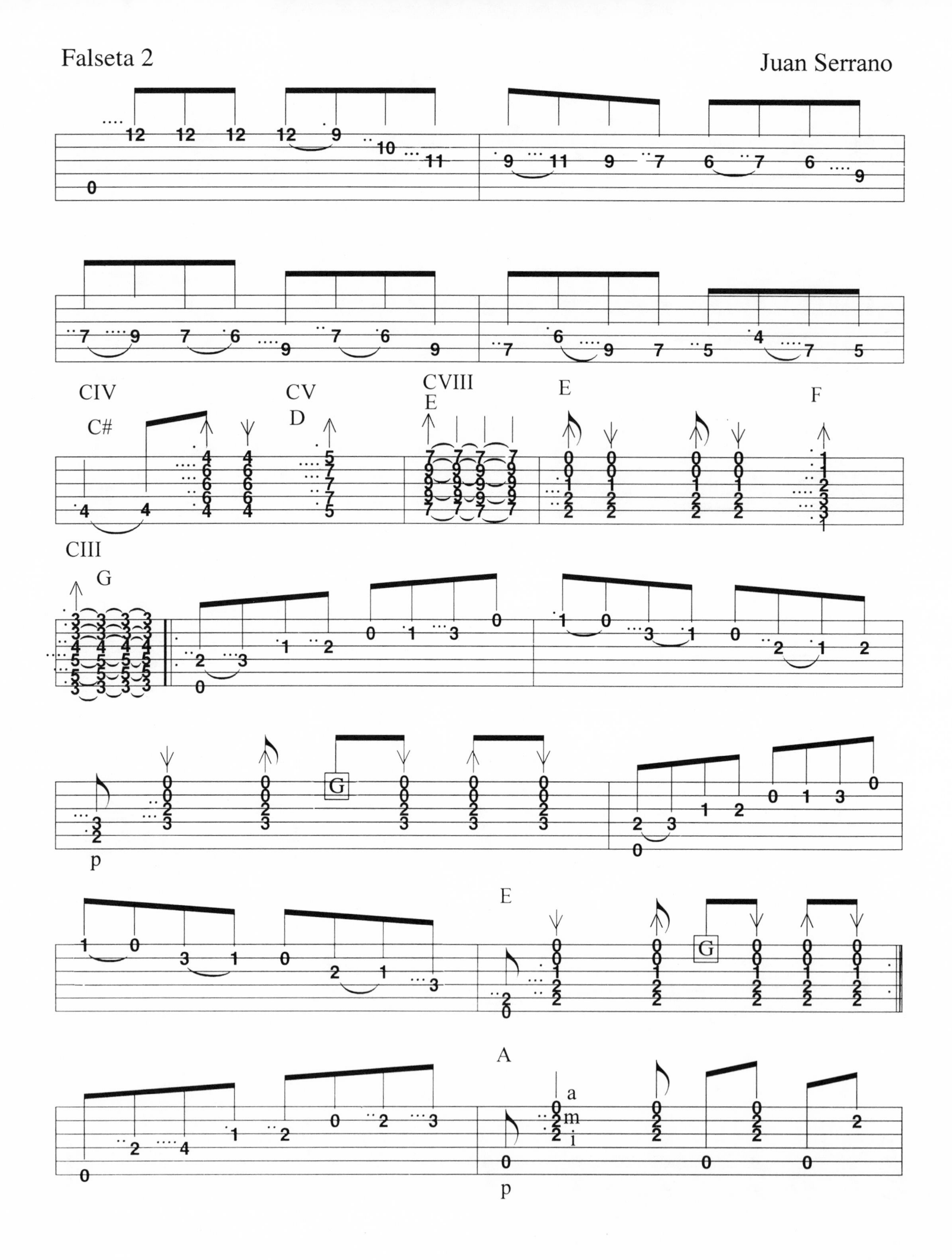
Falseta 2
Juan Serrano
CIV
C#
CV
D
CVIII
E
E
F
CIII
G
p
G
E
G
A
a
m
i
p

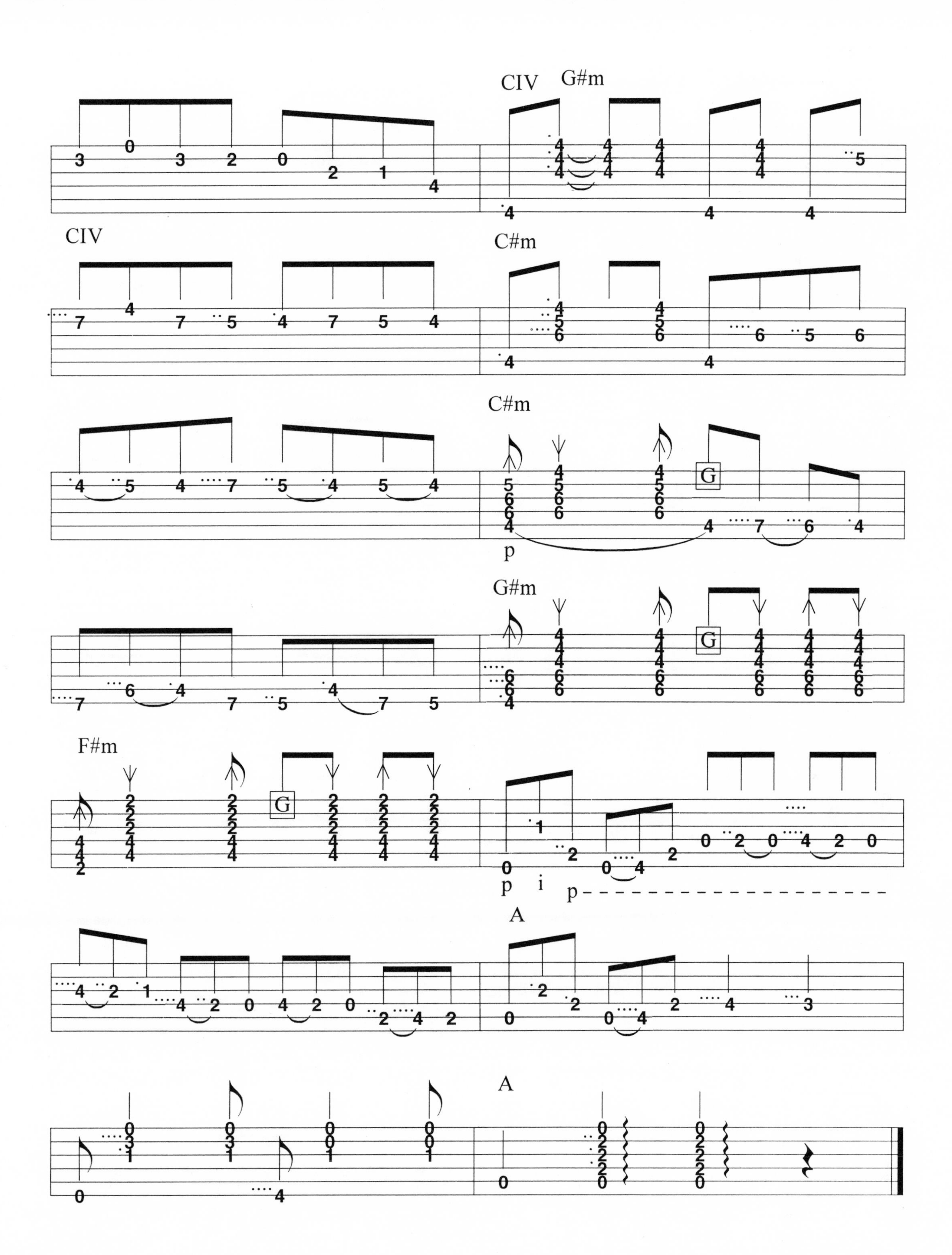
CIV
G#m
CIV
C#m
C#m
p
G
G#m
G
F#m
G
p
i
p
A
A

Falseta 3

Juan Serrano

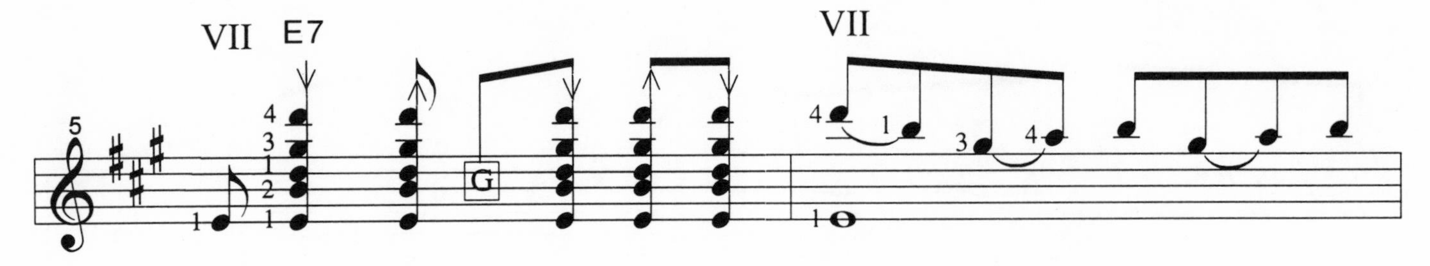

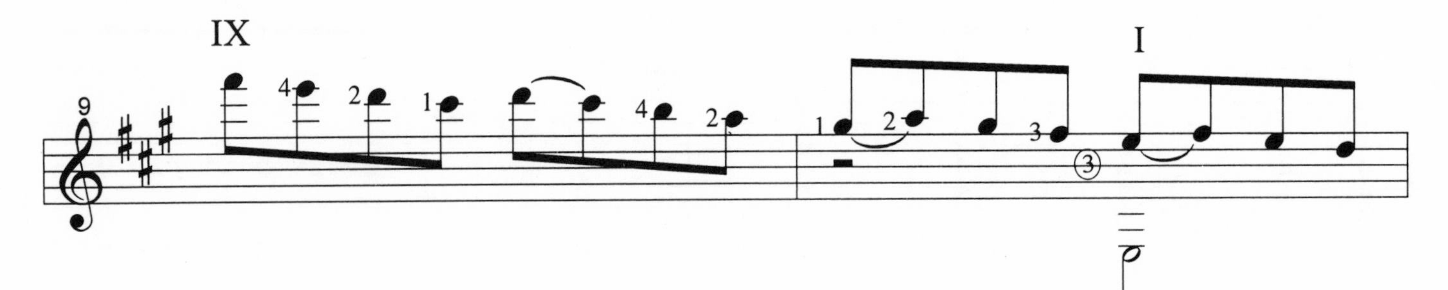

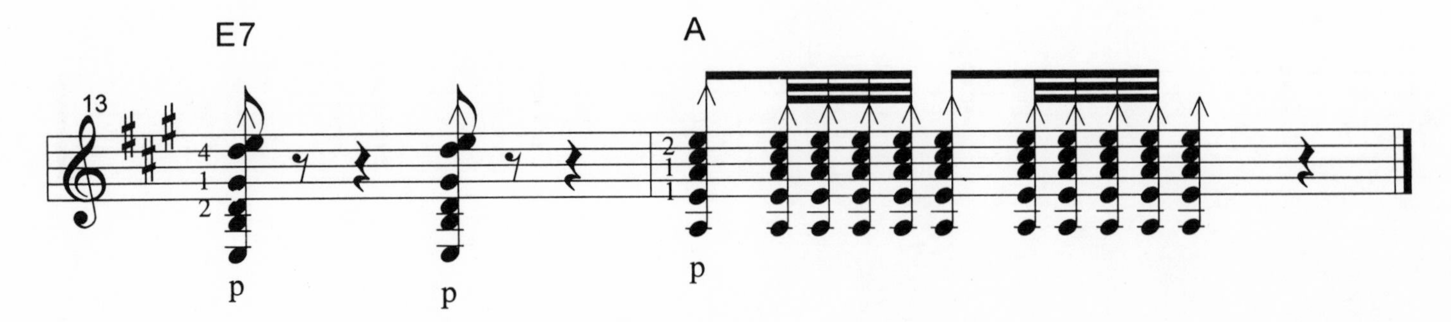

Juan Serrano

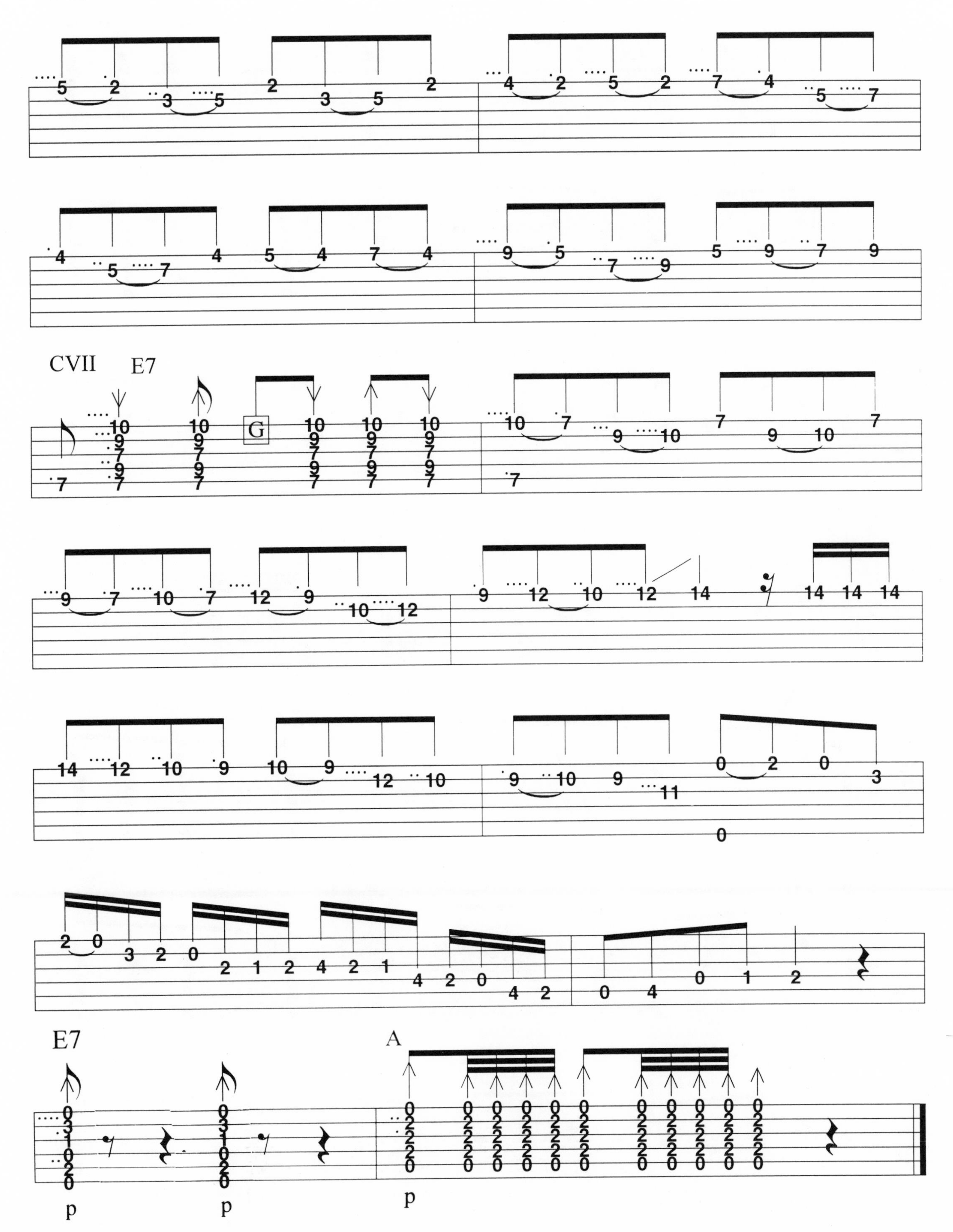

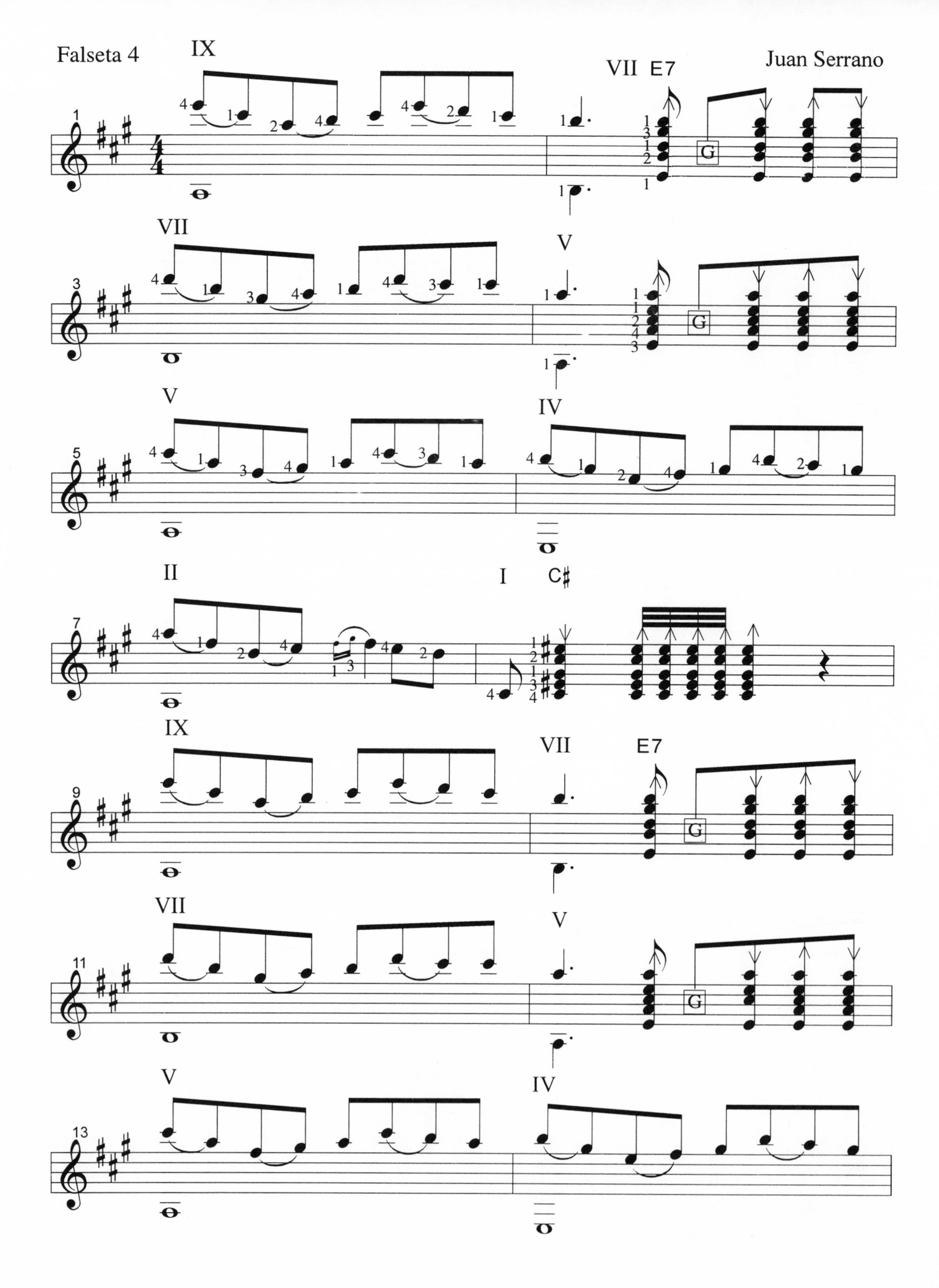
Falseta 4
Juan Serrano
IX
VII E7
G
VII
V
G
V
IV
II
I C♯
IX
VII
E7
G
VII
V
G
V
IV

II
I C♯
15
G
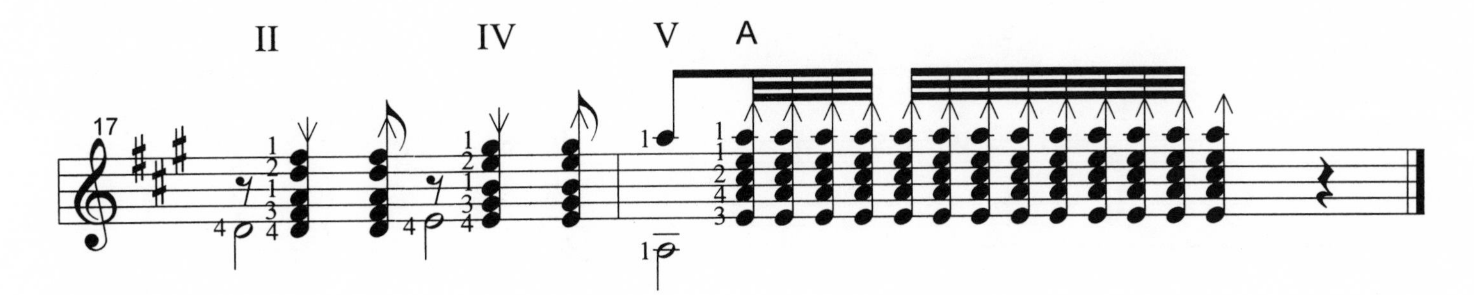
II
IV
V
A
17

Falseta 4

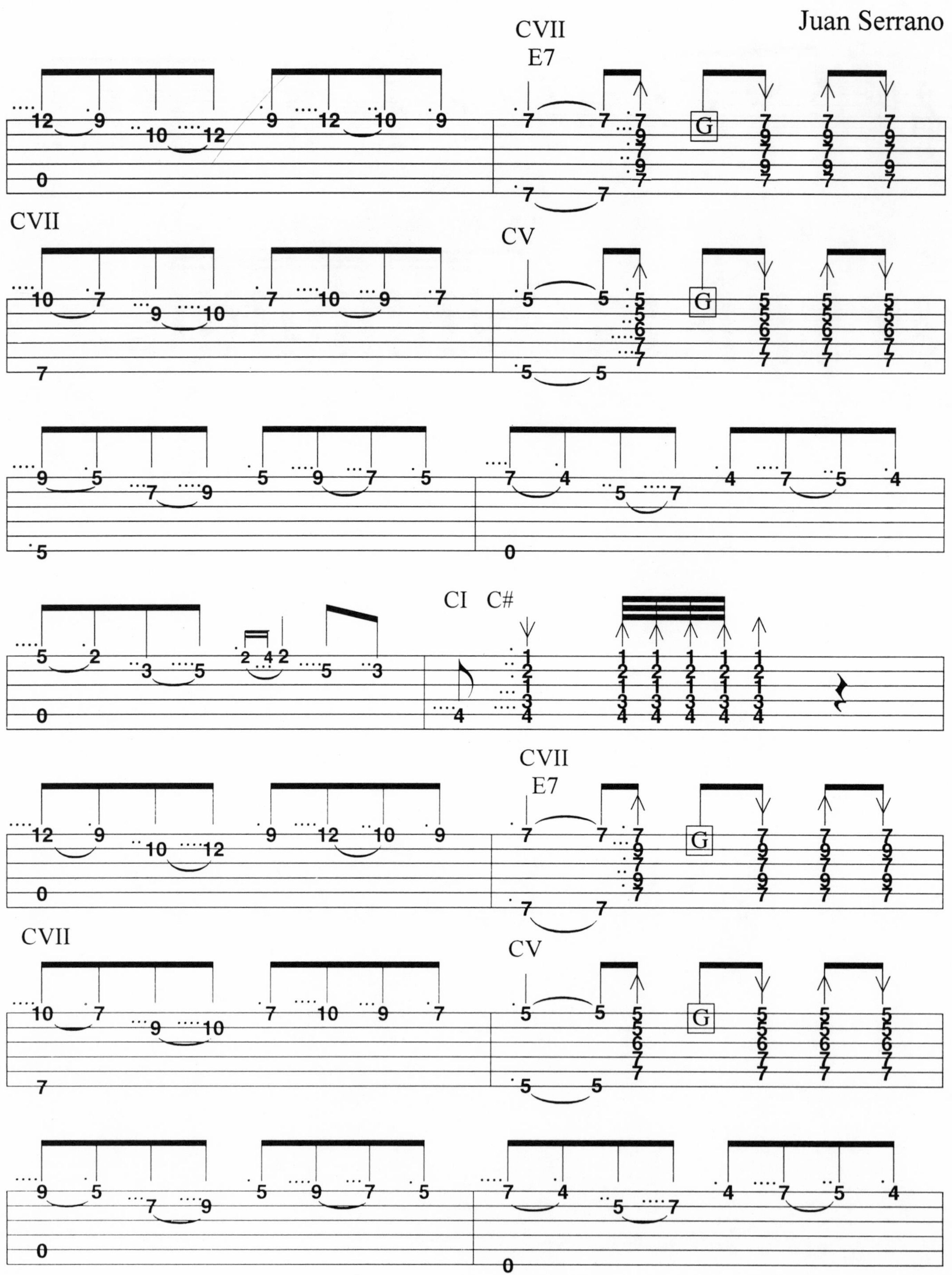
Juan Serrano
CVII
E7
G
CVII
CV
G
CI C#
CVII
E7
G
CVII
CV
G

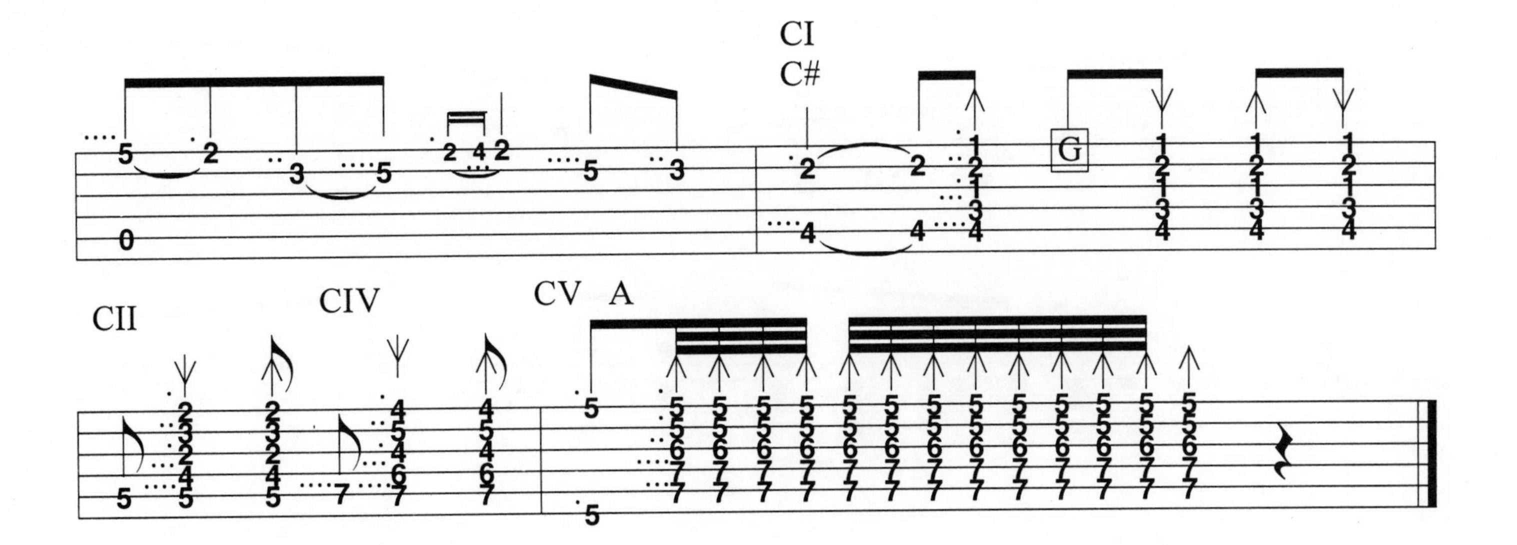
CI
C#
G
CII
CIV
CV
A

Falseta 5

Juan Serrano

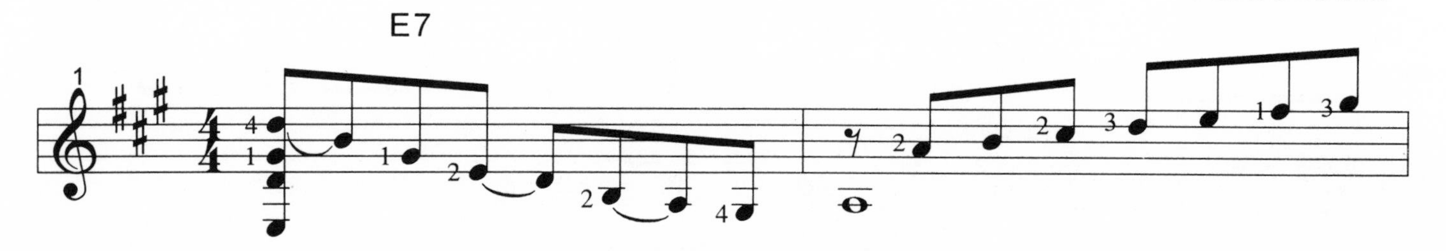


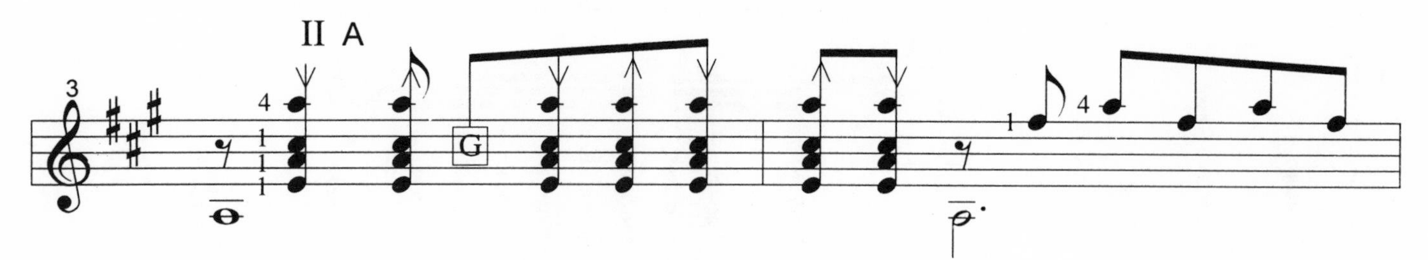


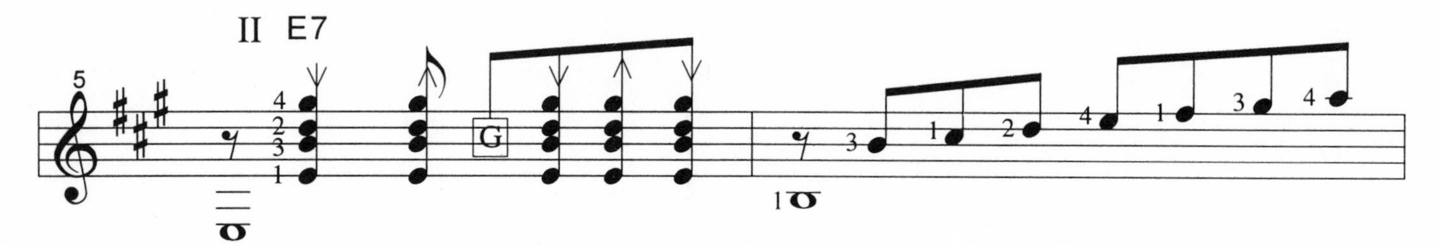


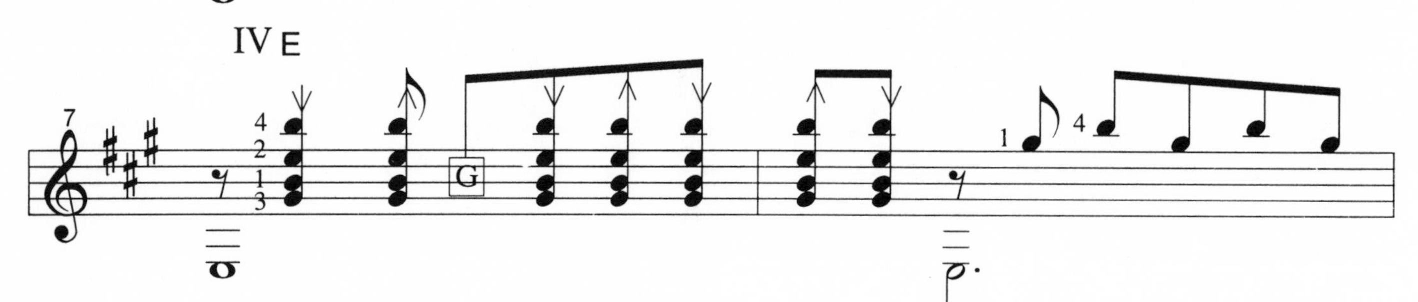


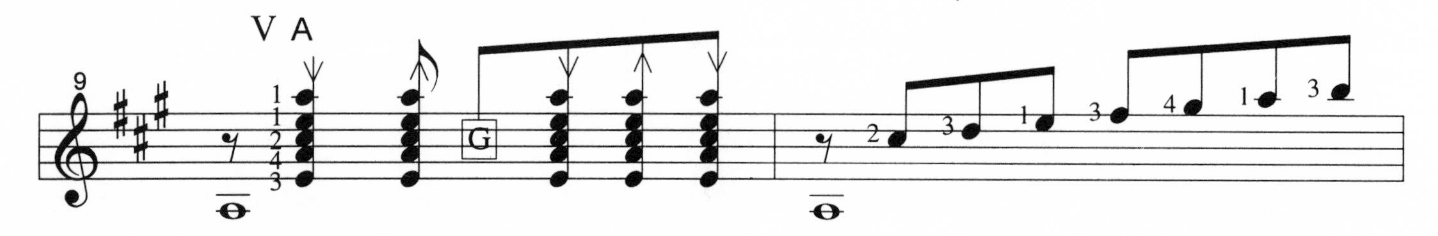


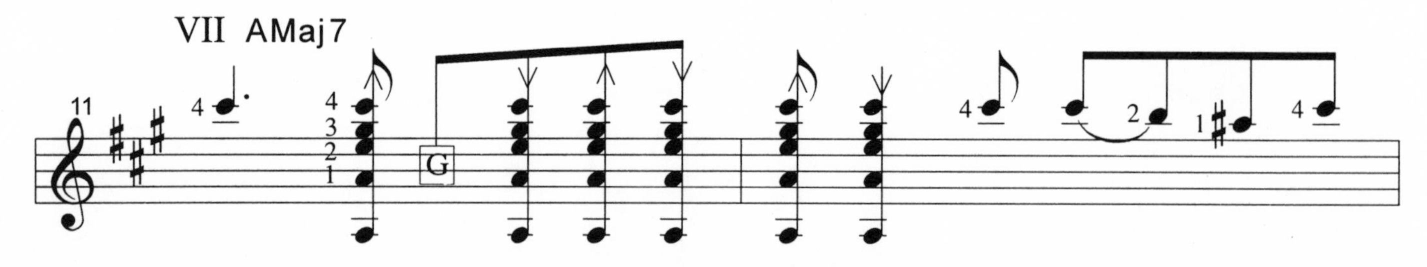


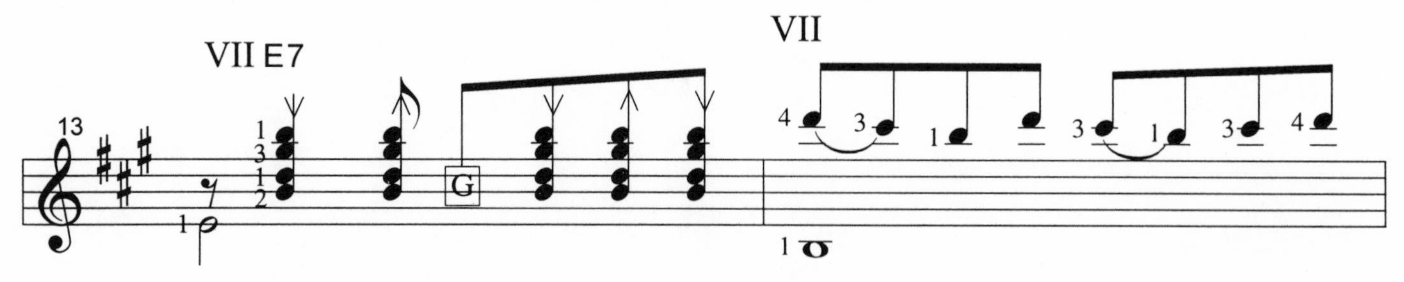

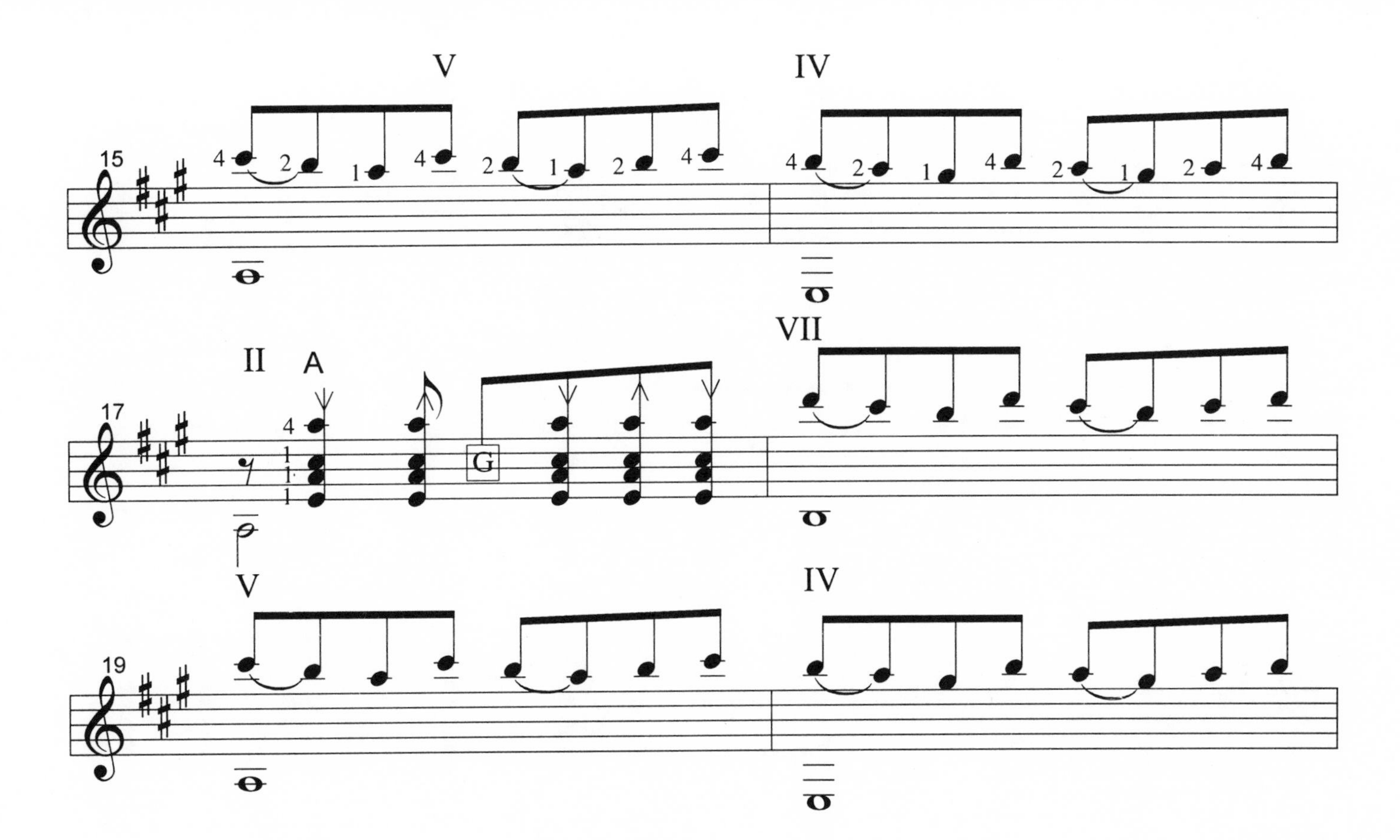
V
IV
15
II
A
G
VII
17
V
IV
19

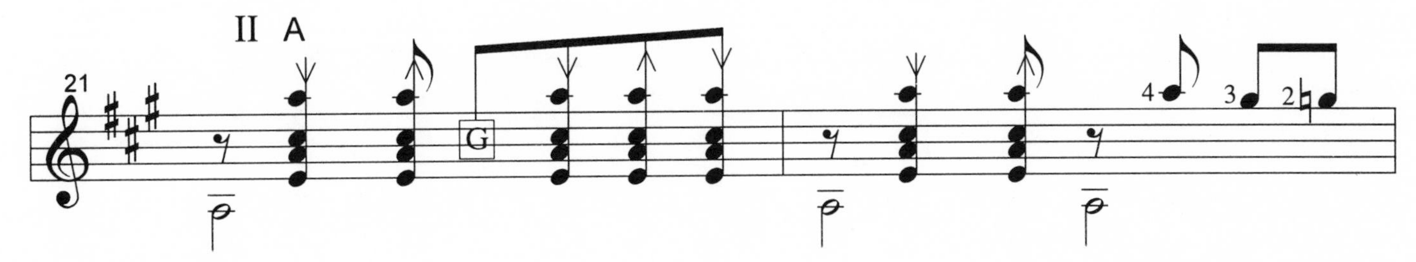
II
A
21
G

D
23
G

A
25
G

E7
27
A
G

E7
I C♯
G

A
G

E7
I C♯
G

A

Falseta 5

Juan Serrano

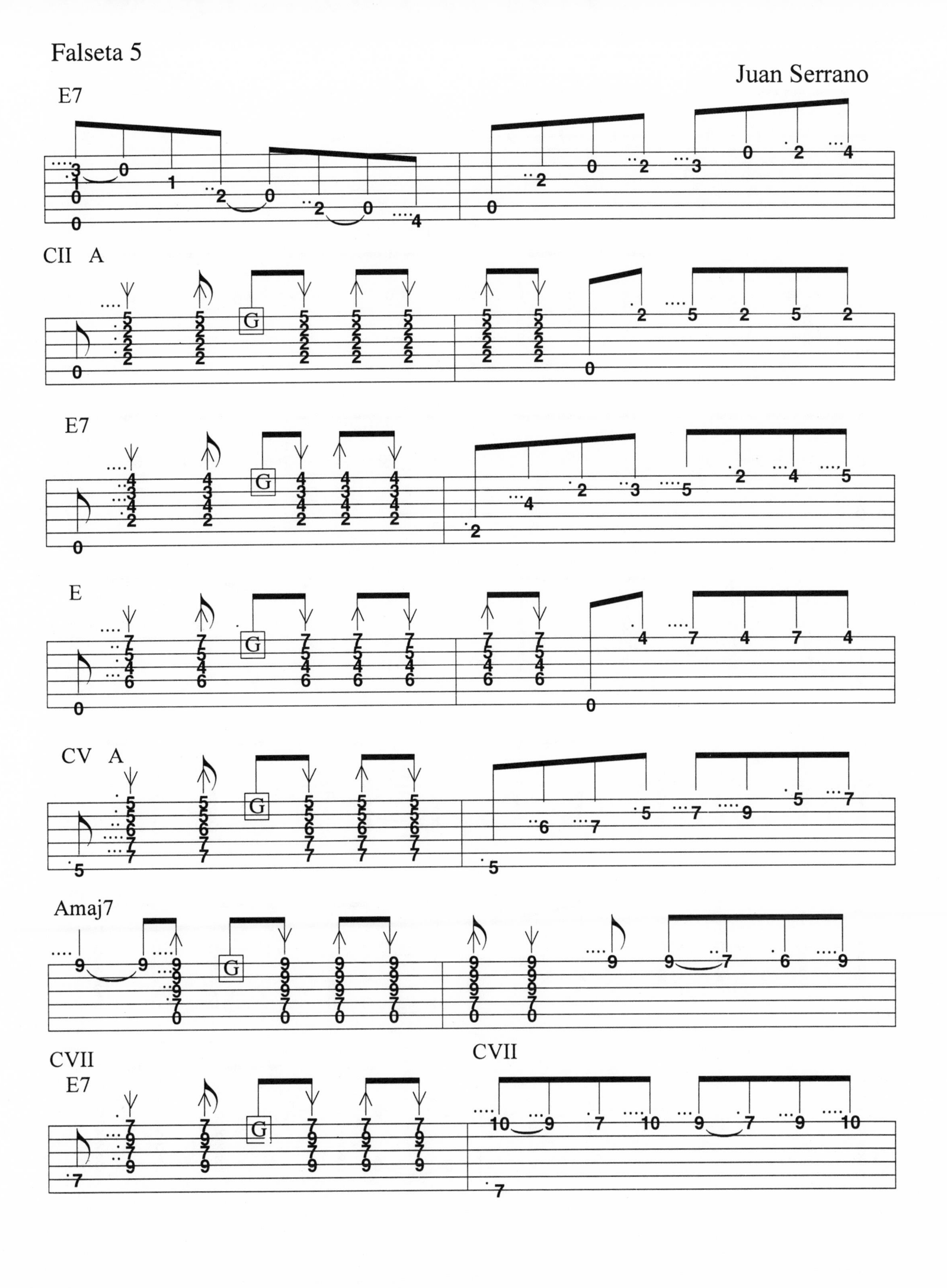

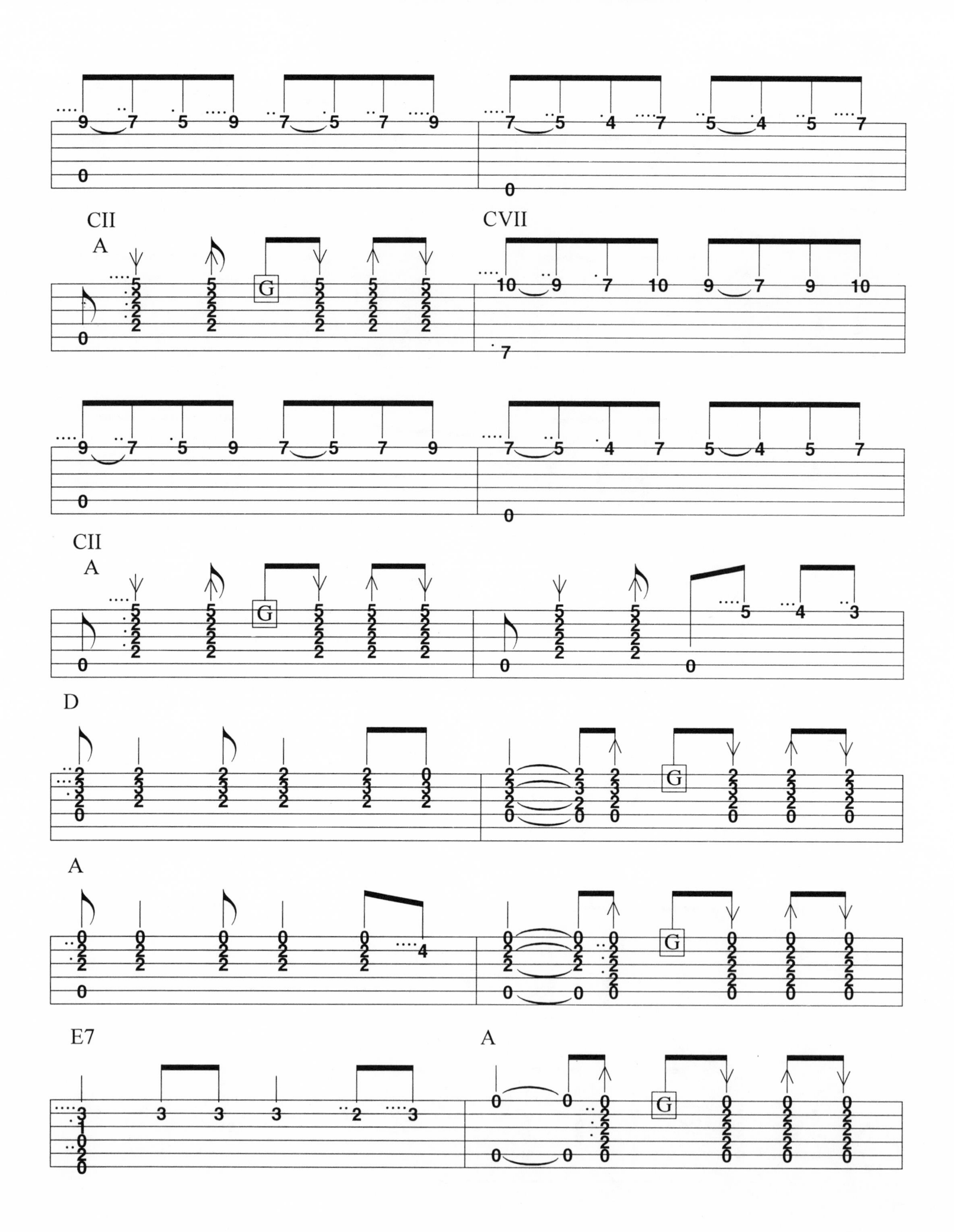
CII
A
G
CVII
CII
A
G
D
G
A
G
E7
A
G

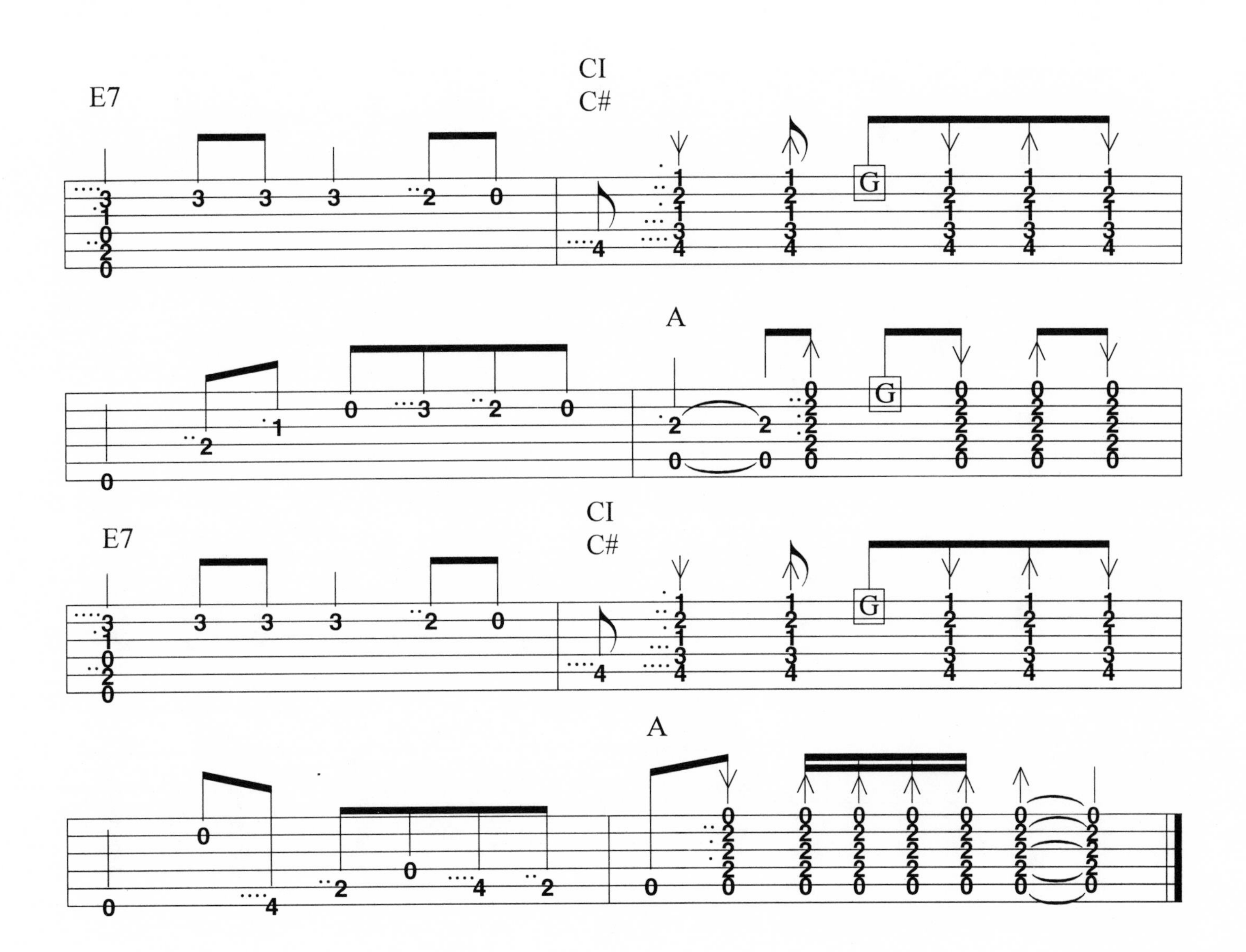
E7
CI
C#
G
A
E7
CI
C#
G
A

Falseta 6

Juan Serrano

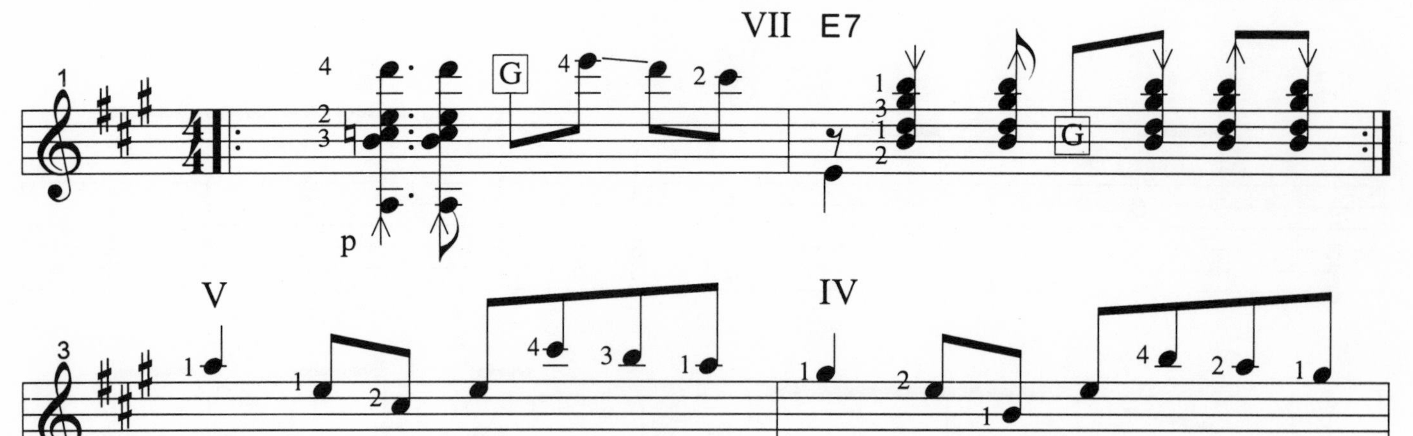


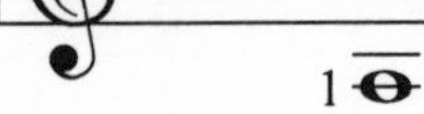

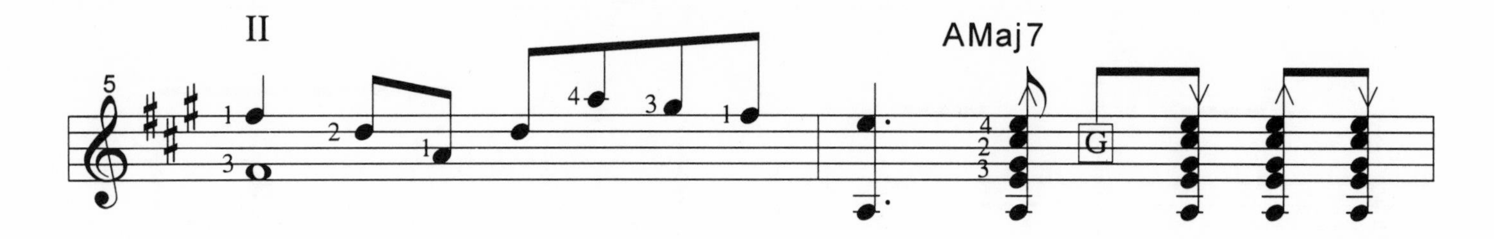


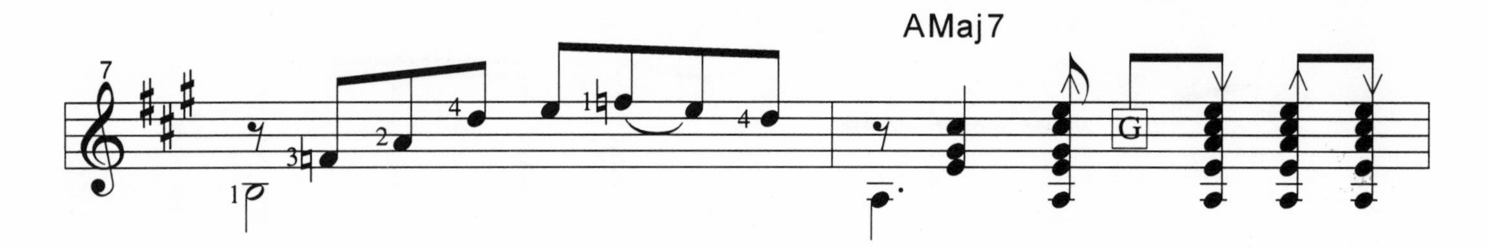


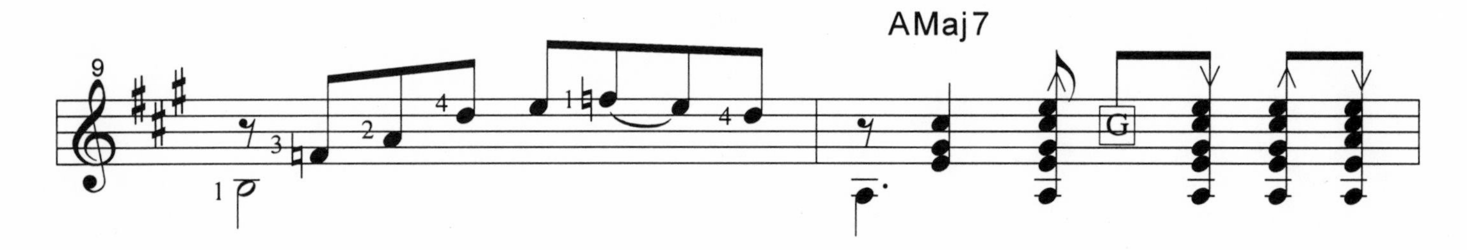

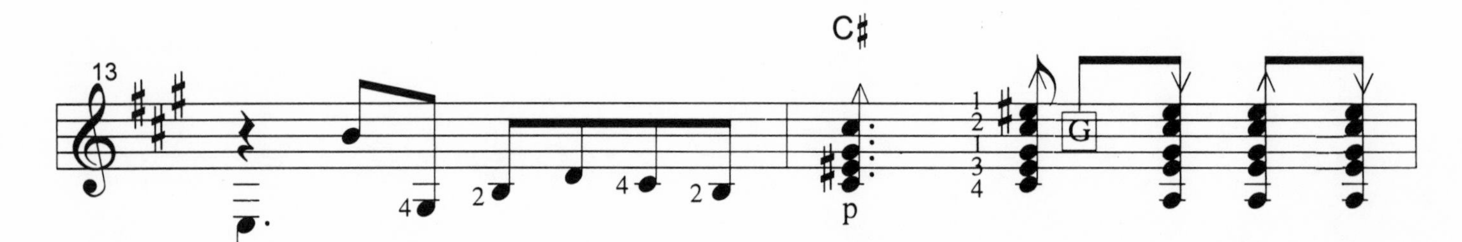

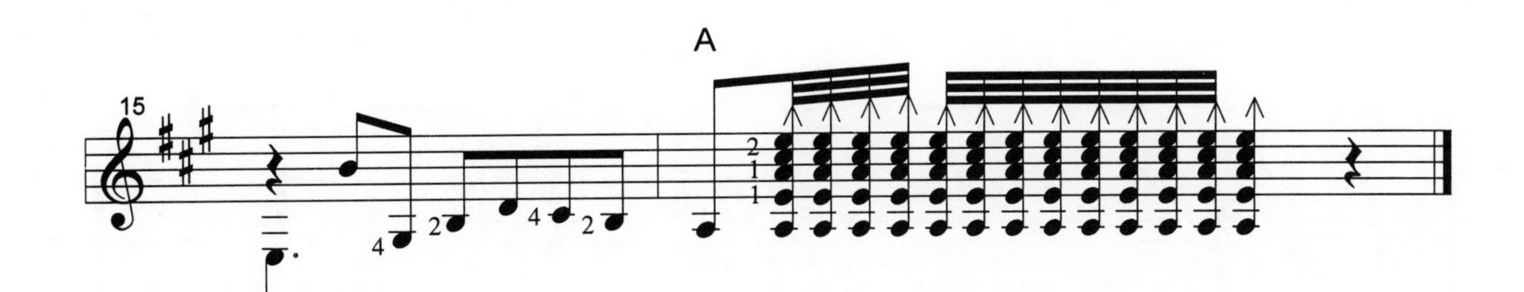
A
15
4
2
4
2
2
1
1

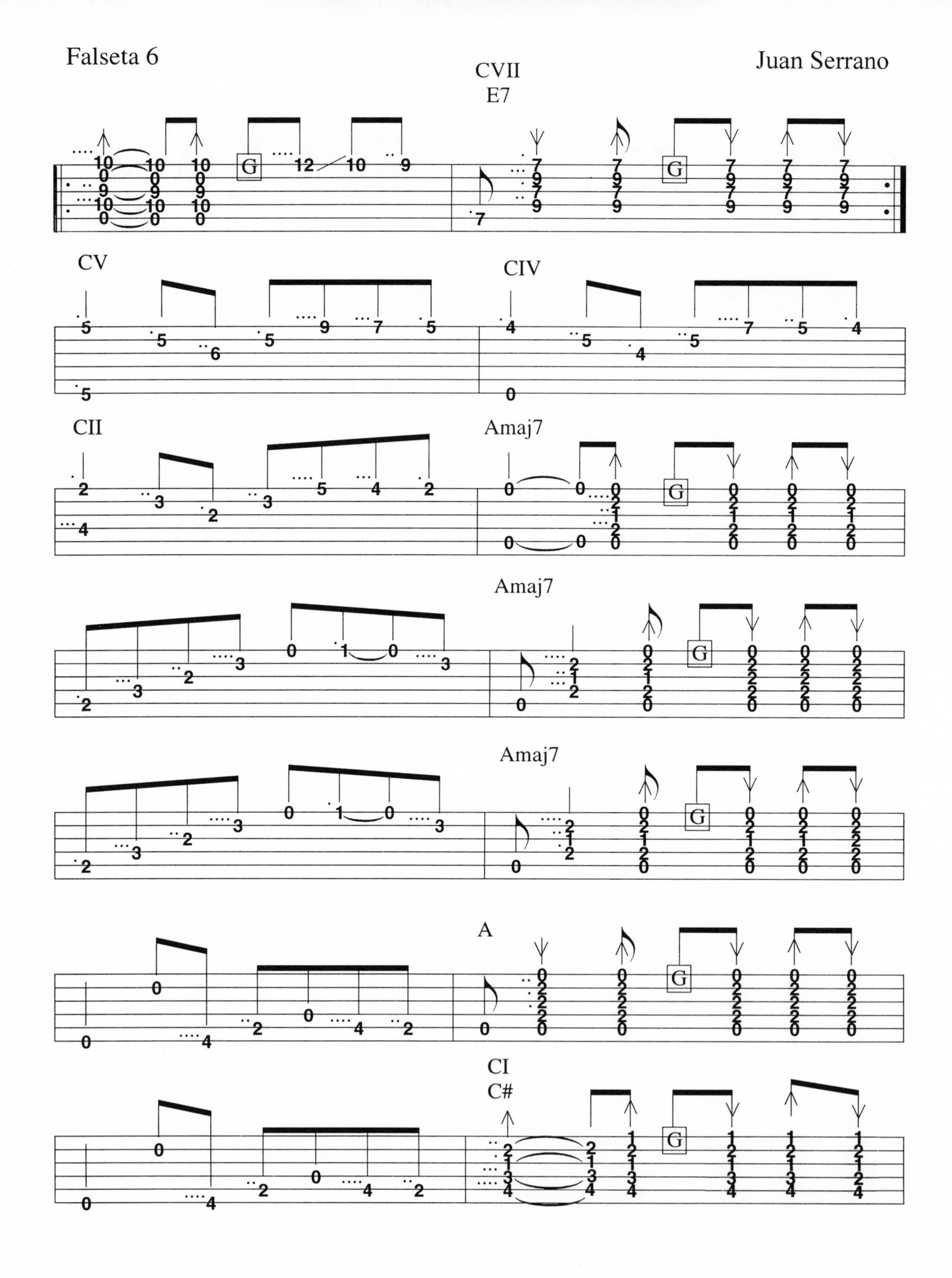
Falseta 6
Juan Serrano
CVII
E7
G
CV
CIV
CII
Amaj7
Amaj7
Amaj7
A
CI
C#

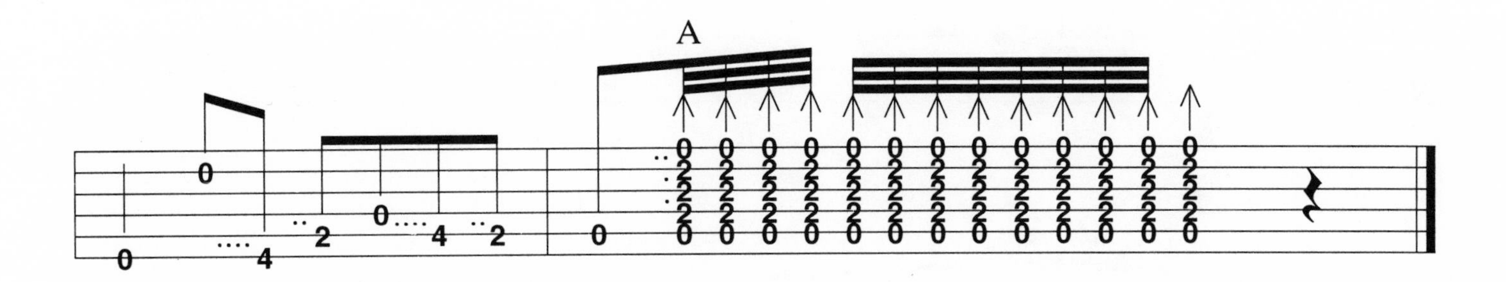
A

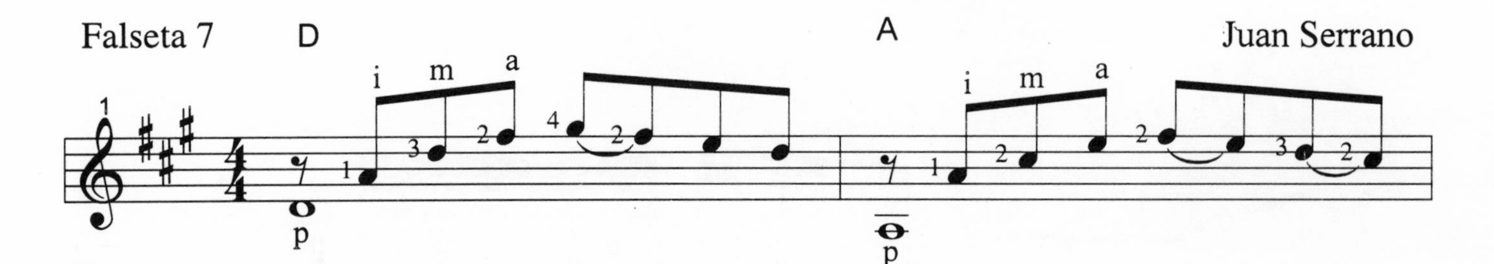
Falseta 7
Juan Serrano
D
A

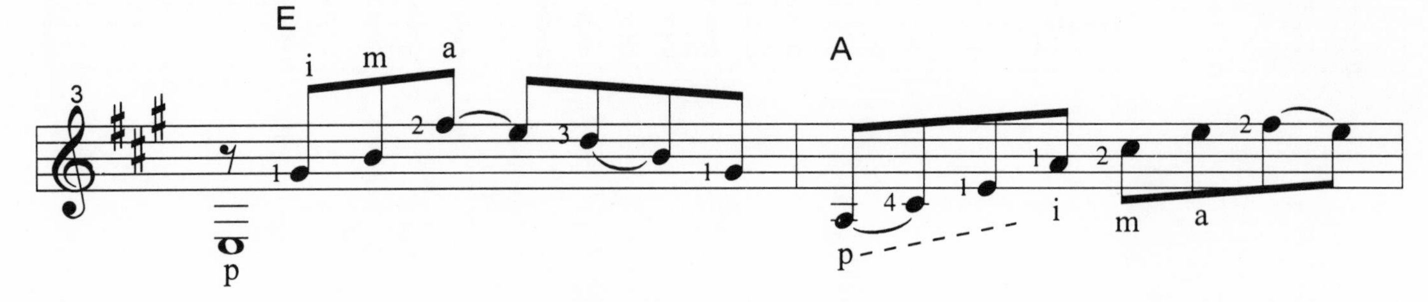
E
A

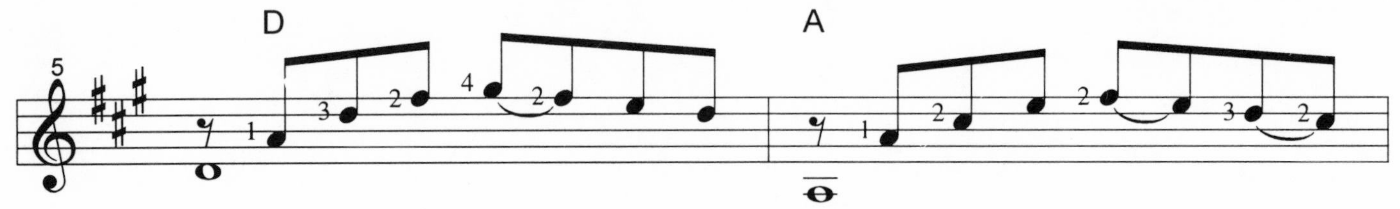
D
A

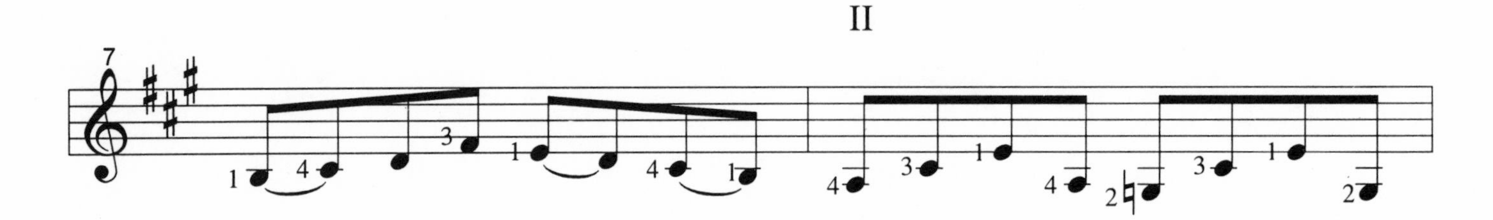
II

II
I

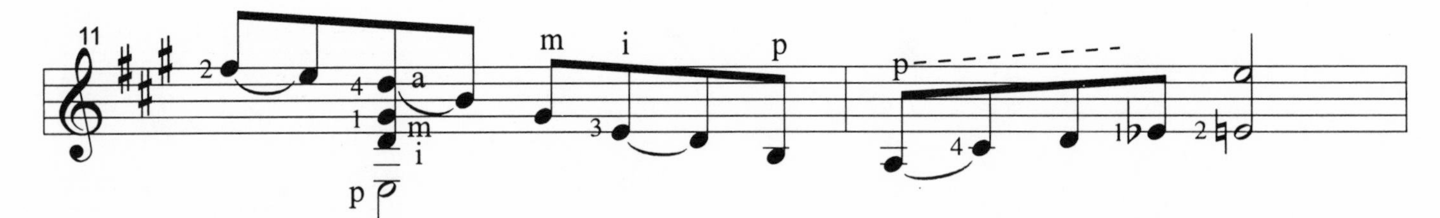

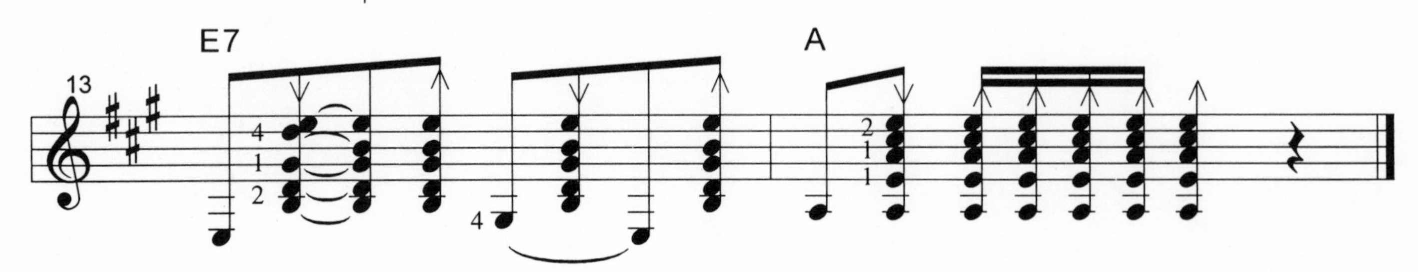
E7
A

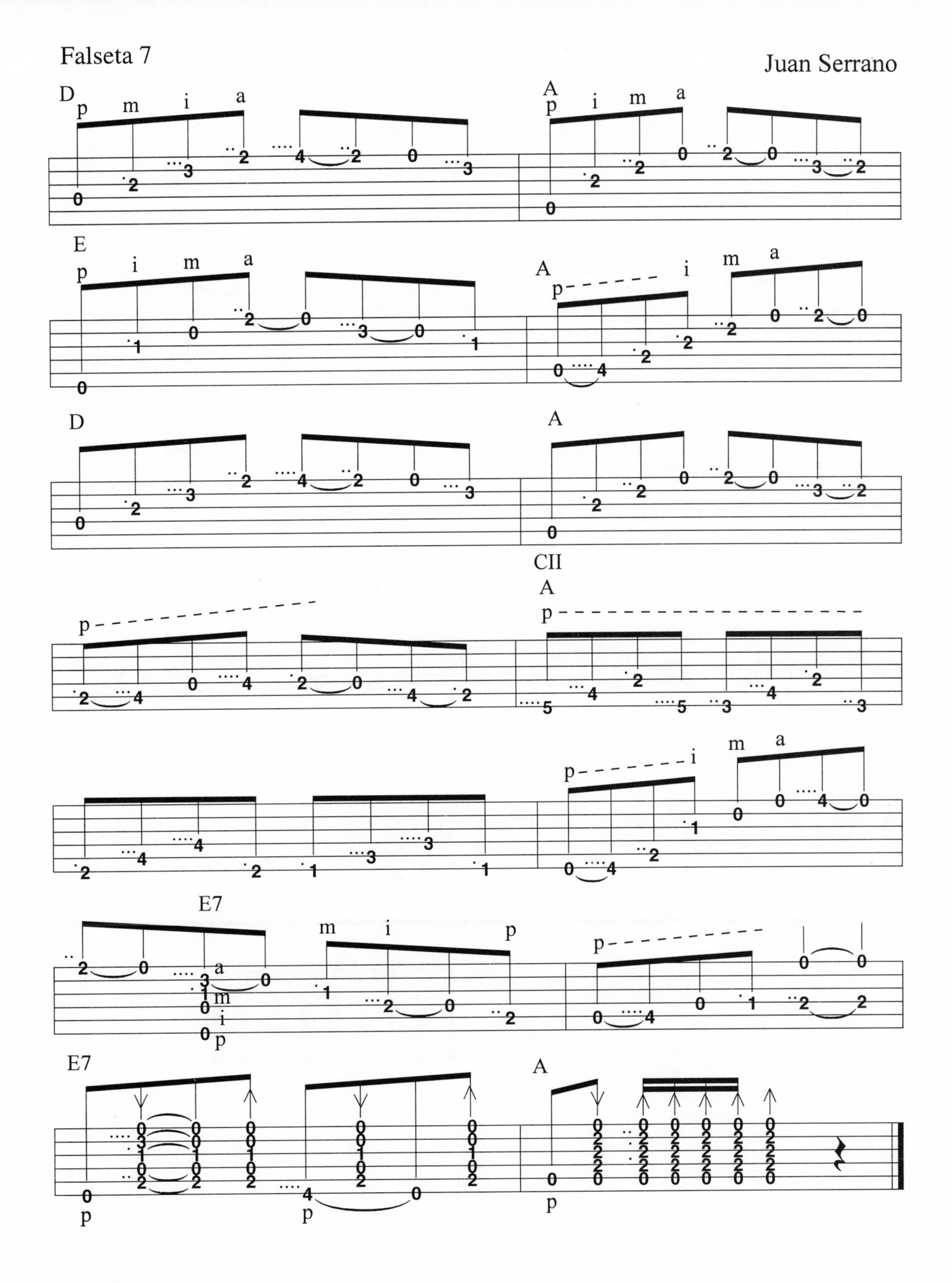
Falseta 7
Juan Serrano
D
A
E
A
D
A
CII
A
E7
E7
A

Falseta 8

Juan Serrano

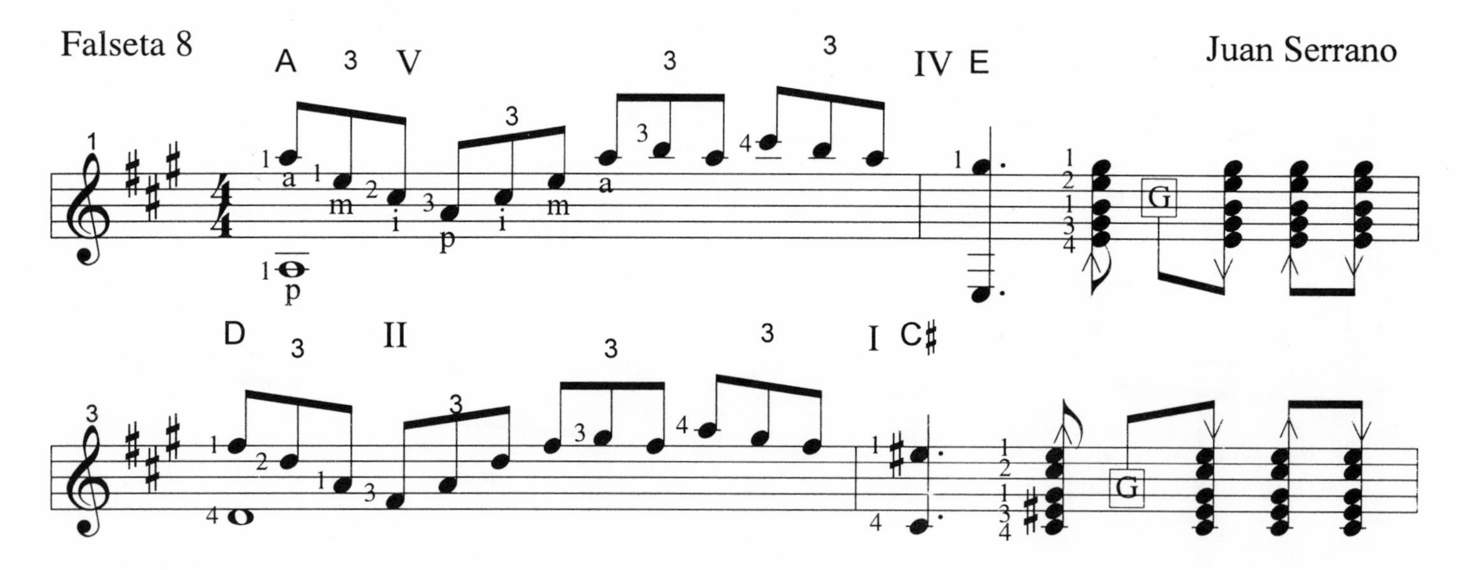


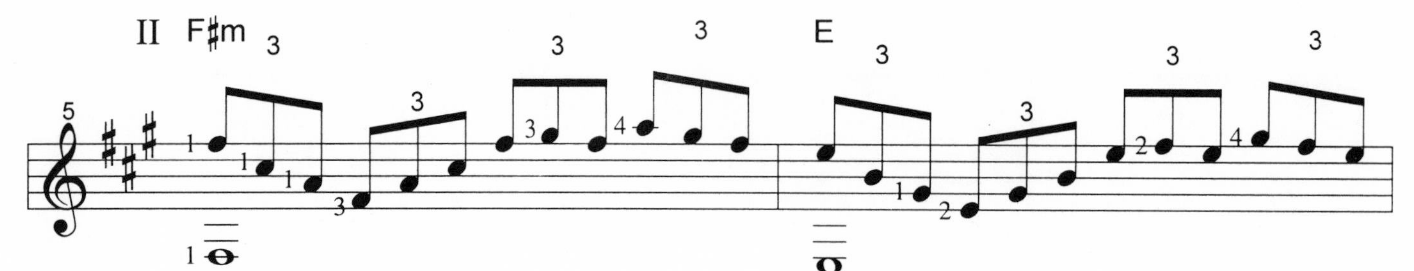


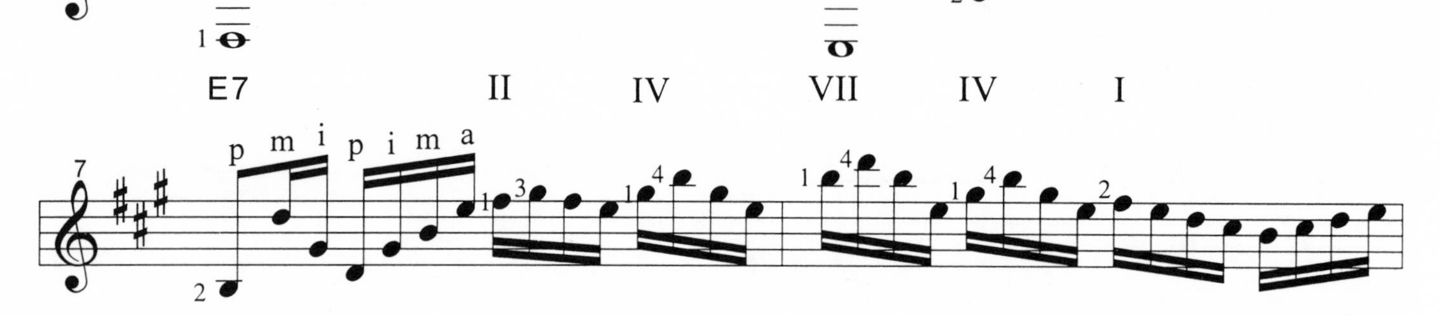

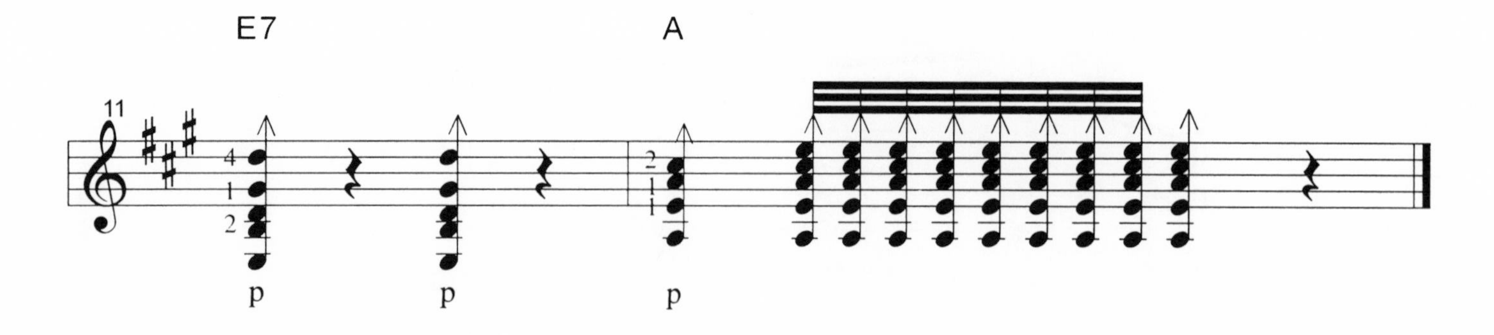

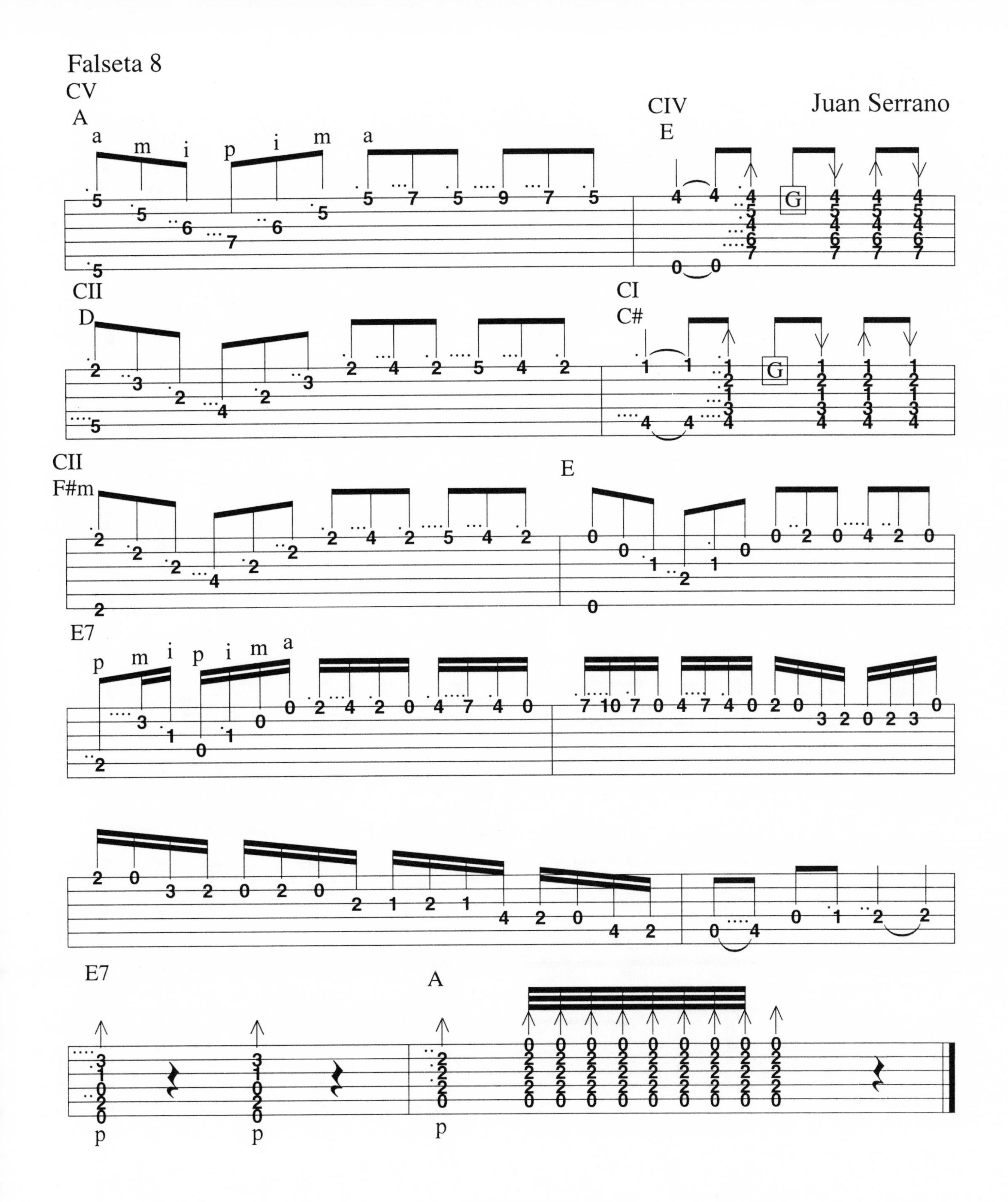
Falseta 8
Juan Serrano
CV
A
a m i p i m a
CIV
E
G
CII
D
CI
C#
G
CII
F#m
E
E7
p m i p i m a
E7
p
p
A
p

Falseta 9

Juan Serrano

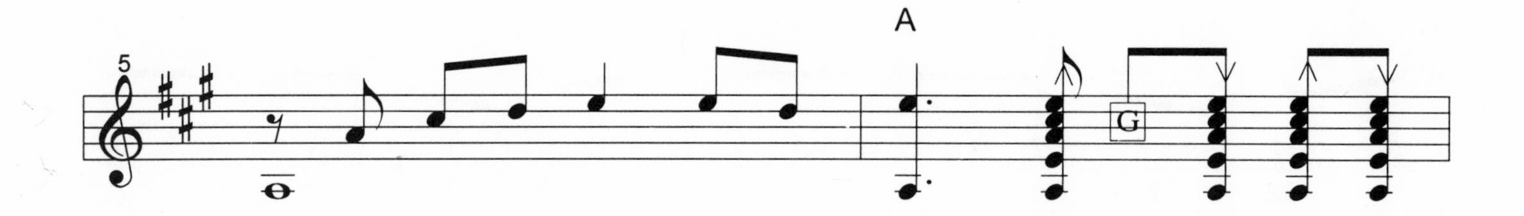

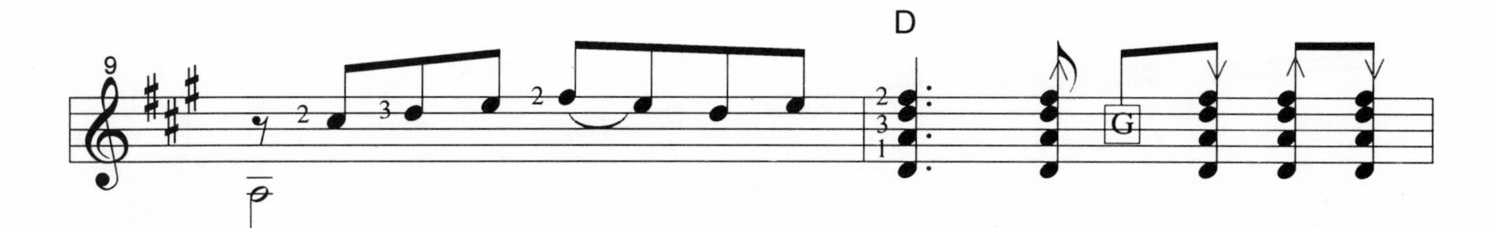

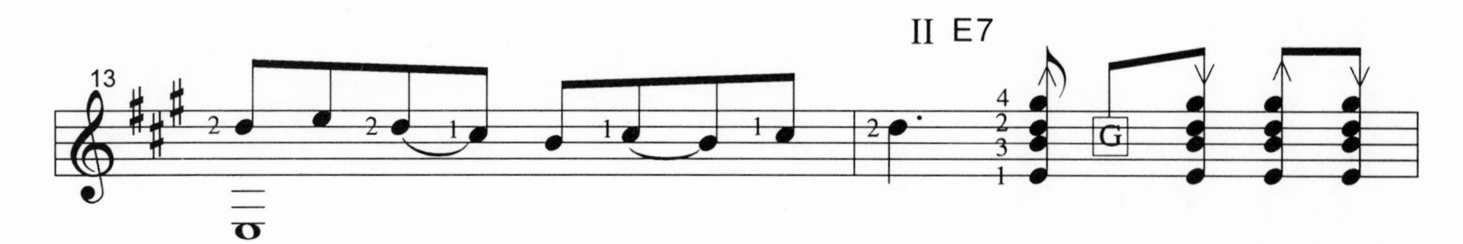

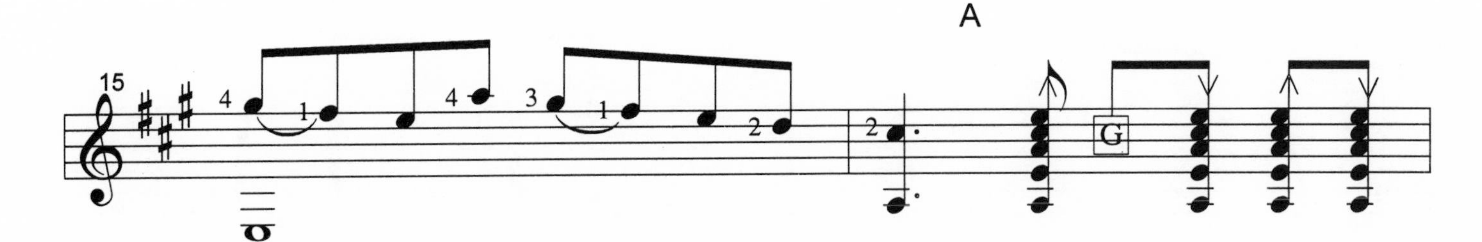
15
A
G

17
D
G

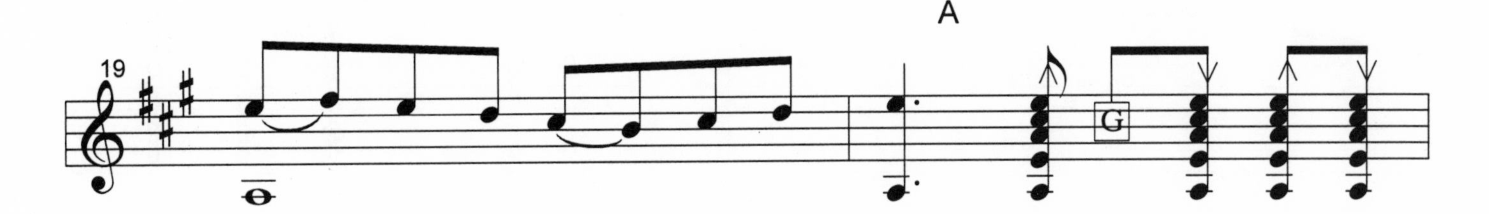
19
A
G

21

23
A

Falseta 9

Juan Serrano

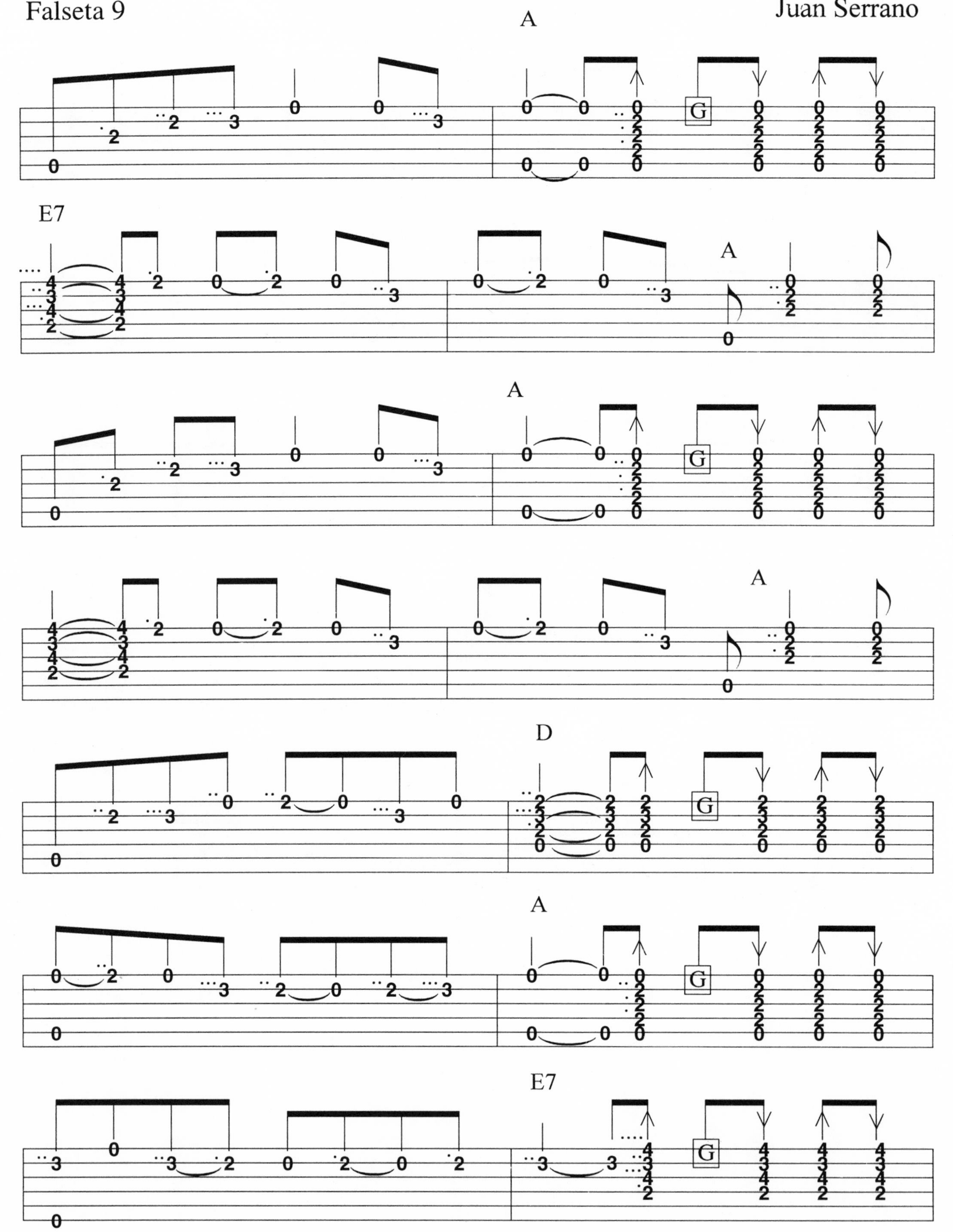

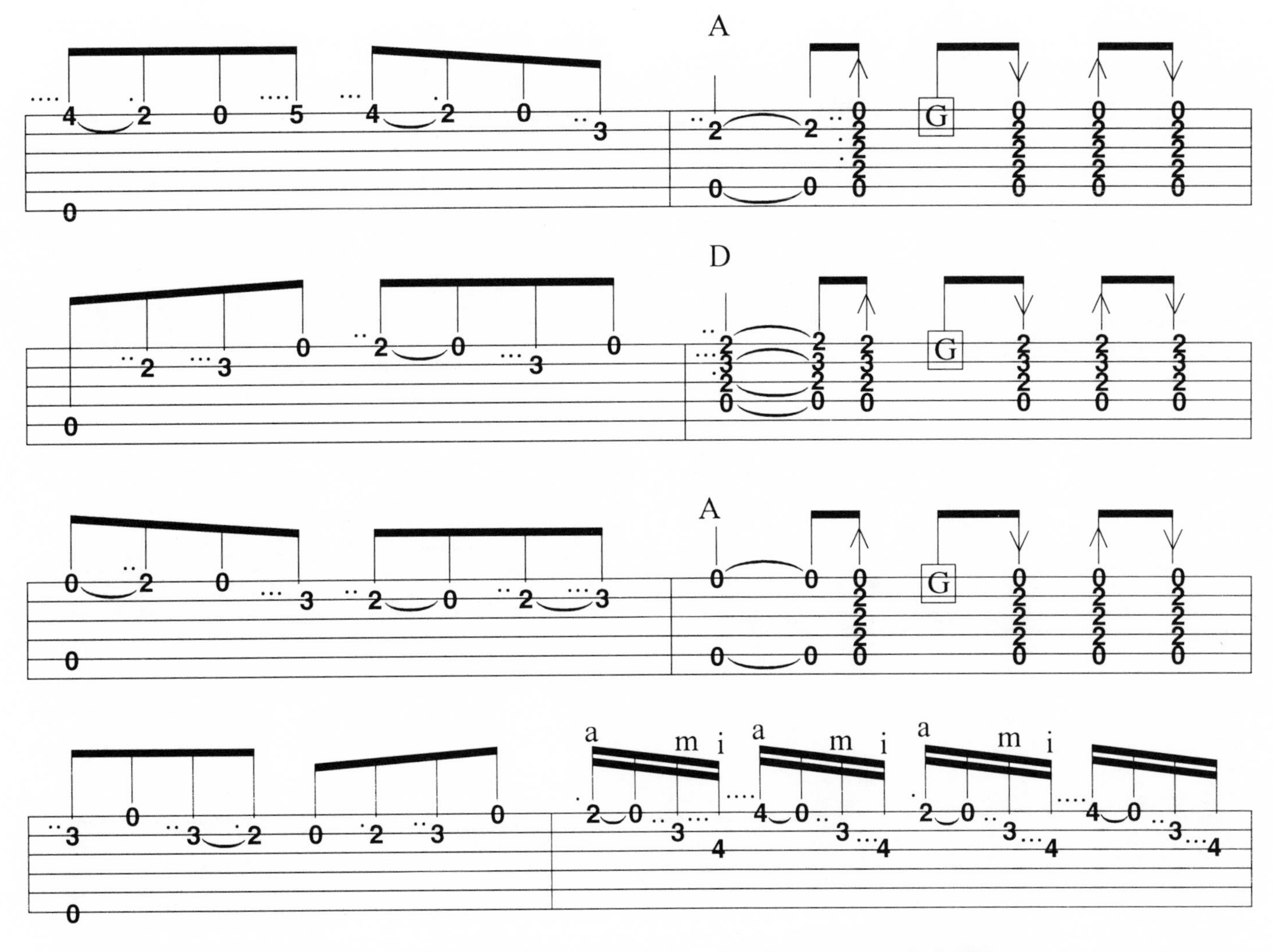
A
G
D
G
A
G
a m i a m i a m i

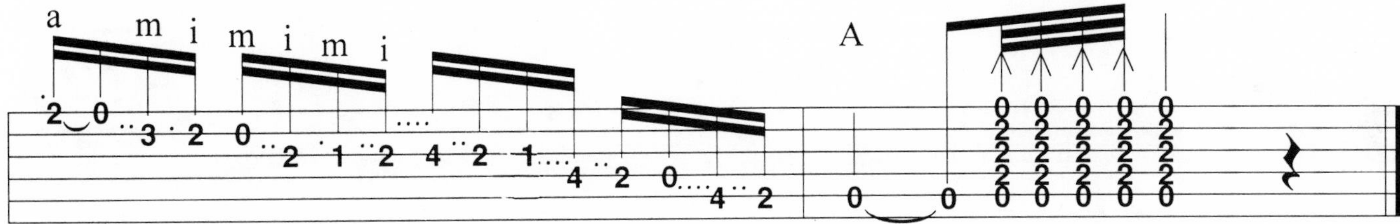
a m i m i m i
A

Falseta 10

Juan Serrano

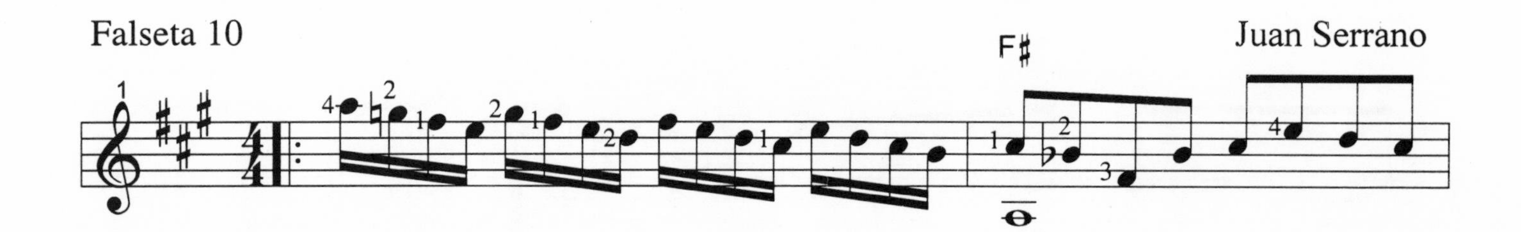

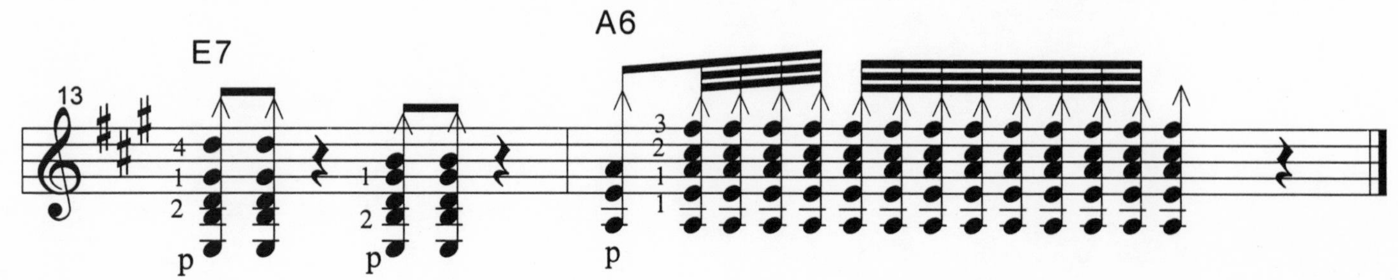

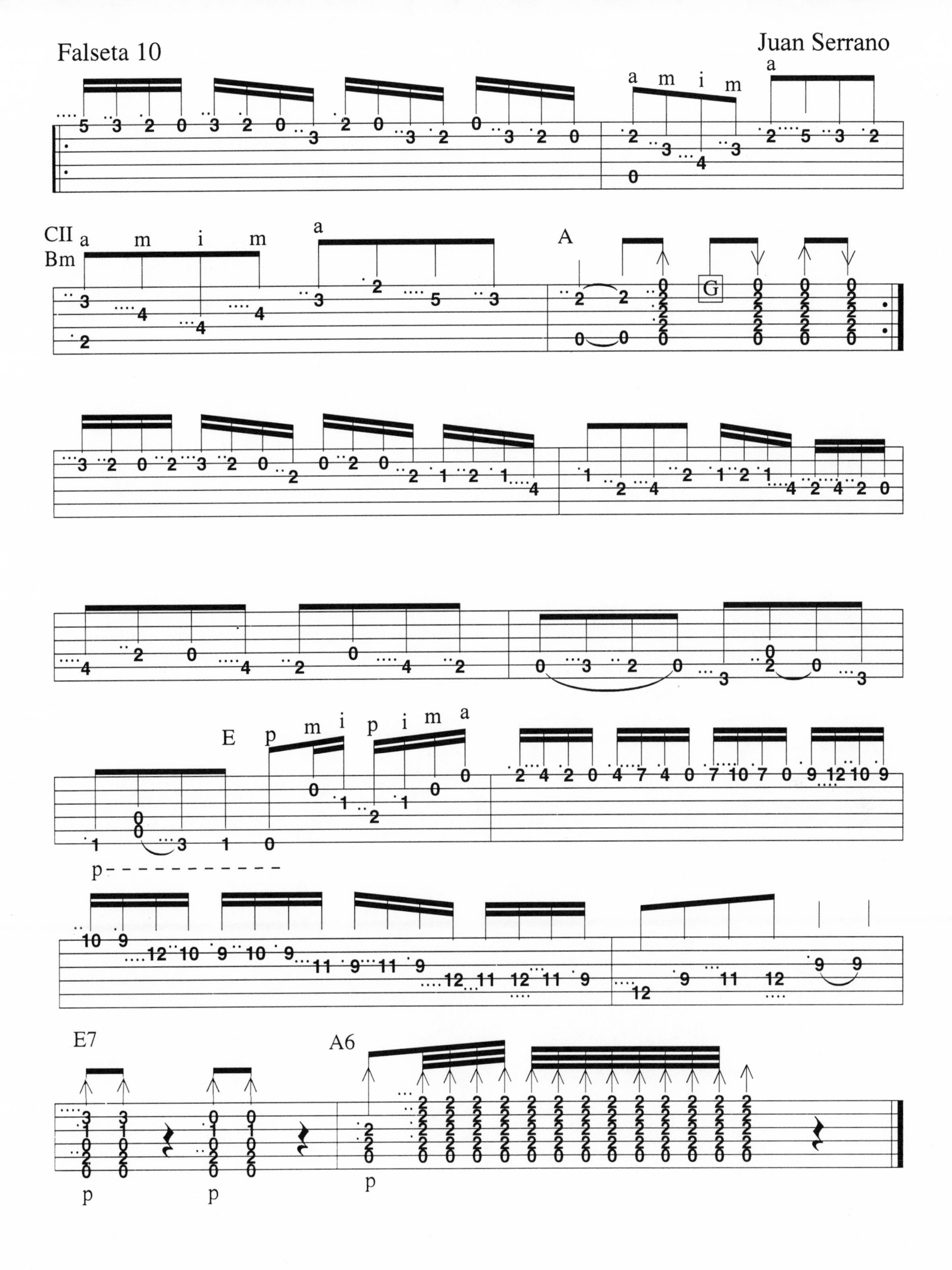
Falseta 10
Juan Serrano
a m i m
a
CII
Bm
a m i m
a
A
G
E
p m i p i m a
p
E7
p
p
A6
p

# FANDANGOS

With certain elements of the Spanish classical dance Andalucia gave birth to an unlimited number of popular coplas (songs) where the Andalucian Fandango emerged. The Fandango became so popular that all of the Andalucian towns created their own Fandango. For this reason, it is one of the largest flamenco families; for example, Fandango de Huelva, del Alonno, de Valverde, de Santa Eulalia, de Lucena, de Almería, besides all of the personal Fandangos created by their own interpreters, such as Fandangos Caracoleros, del Sevillano, del Gordito de Triana, de Pepe Pinto etc.

From the Fandangos all of the free forms such as Malagueñas, Granainas, Tarantas, Murcianas, Mineras, Cartageneras, Rondeñas etc. are derived.

The ten following falsetas are based on the Fandango de Huelva that is a danceable form and has a measure of 12 beats.

It is recommended that each falseta be practiced separately; strictly following the fingering until each one is perfected.

# FANDANGOS

Con ciertos elementos del baile clásico Español, Andalucía dio forma a una inagotable cantera de coplas populares de donde surgió posteriormente el Fandango Andaluz.

El Fandango se hizo tan popular que todos los Pueblos Andaluces crearon su propio Fandango. Por eso, es una de las familias más largas de la música flamenca. Por ejemplo, Fandango de Huelva, del Alonno, de Valverde, de Santa Eulalia, de Lucena, y de Almería. Además de todos los Fandangos personales, creados por sus propios intérpretes, como los Fandangos Caracoleros, del Sevillano, del Gordito de Triana, de Pepe Pinto, etc.

De los Fandangos derivan todas las formas libres, como las Malagueñas, Granainas, Tarantas, Murcianas, Mineras, Cartageneras, Rondeñas, etc.

Las diez falsetas de Fandangos que siguen, están basadas en los Fandangos de Huelva, que son bailables y que tienen un compás flamenco de doce tiempos.

Recomiendo que se practique cada una de las falsetas por separado hasta perfeccionarlas todas y que se sigan estrictamente todas las digitaciones marcadas.

# *Fandangos*

Traditional Compas

Juan Serrano

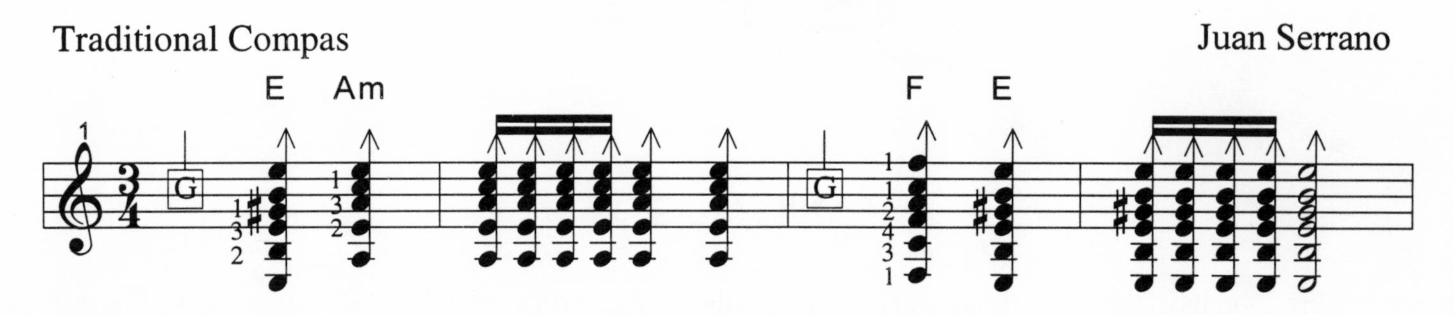


Variation 1

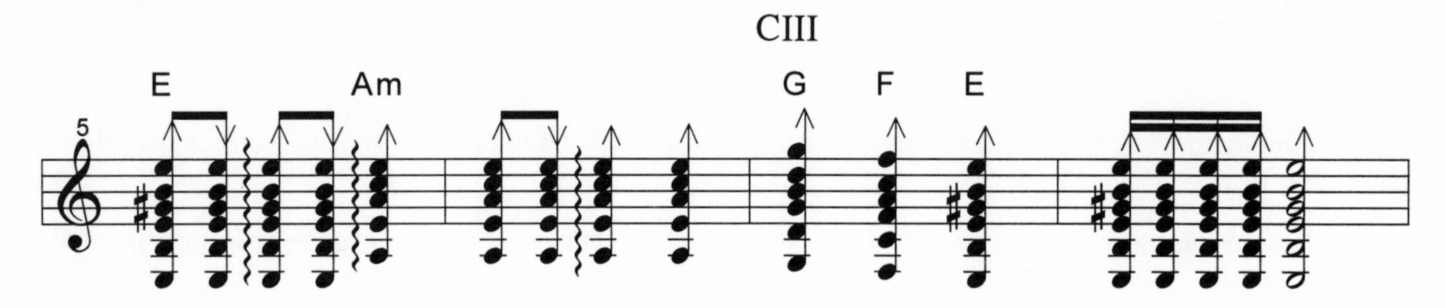


Variation 2

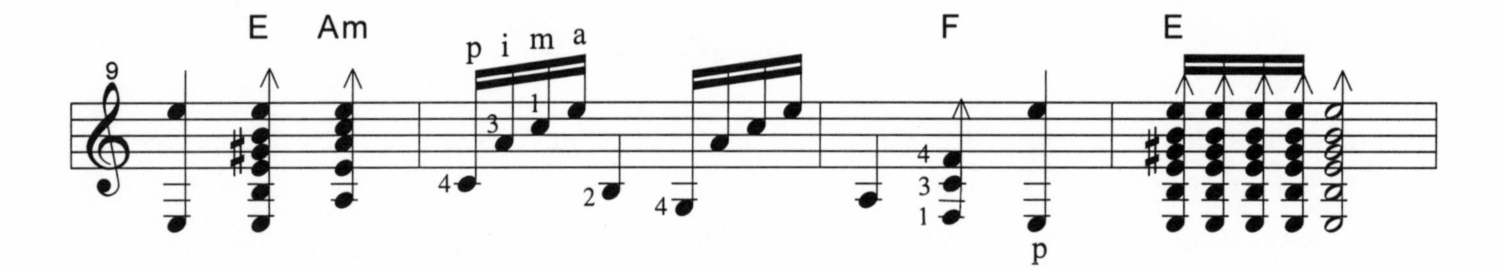


Variation 3

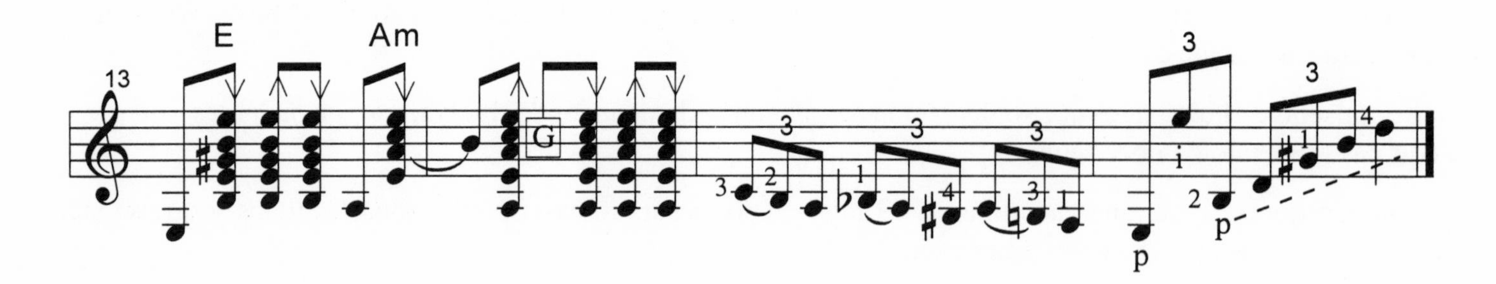

# *Fandangos*

Juan Serrano

## Traditional Compas

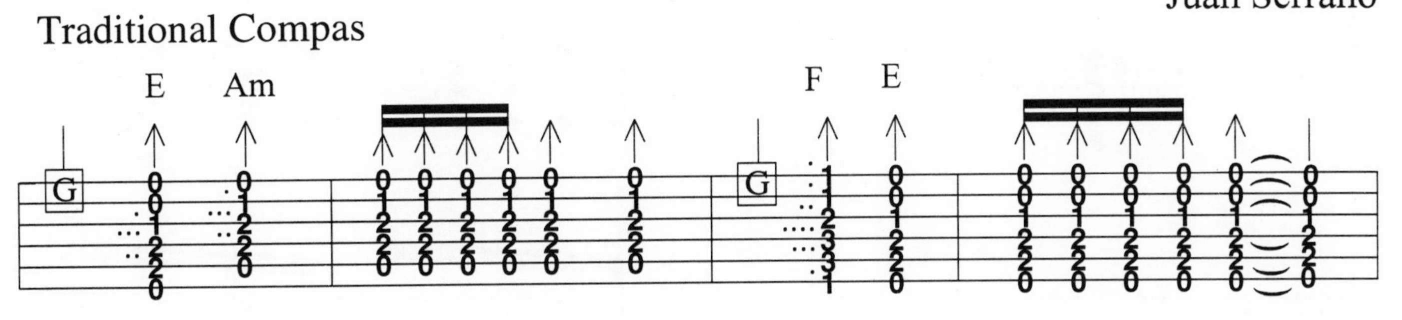


## Variation 1

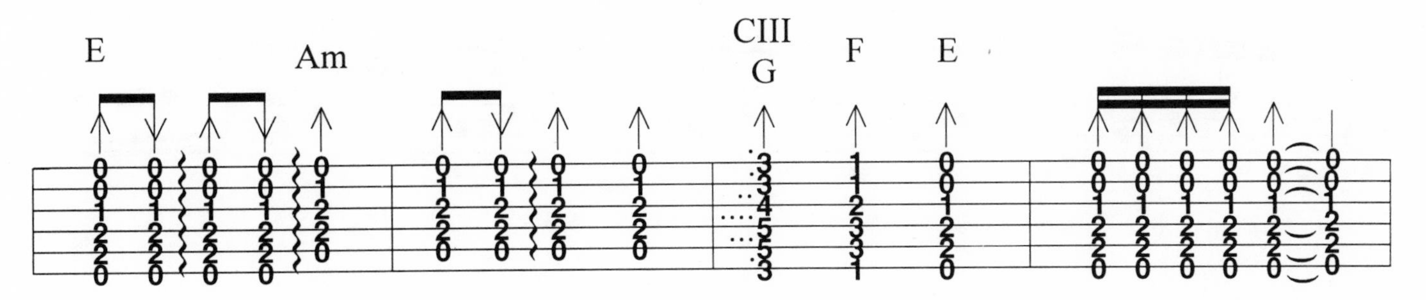


## Variation 2

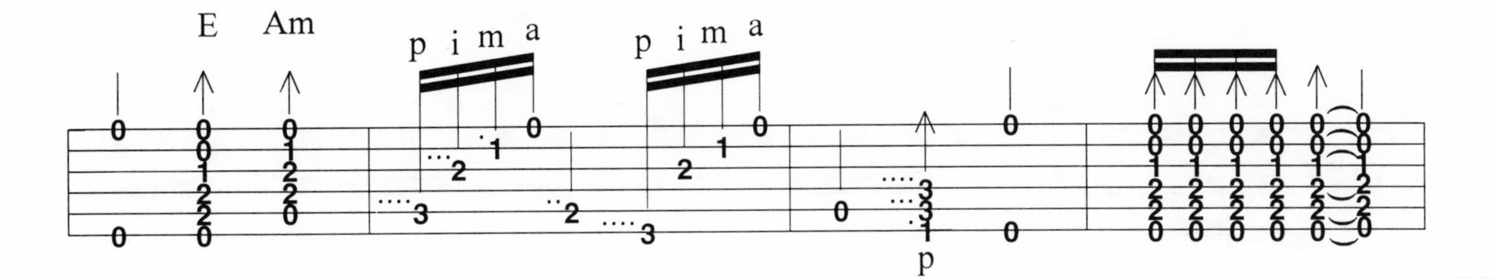


## Variation 3

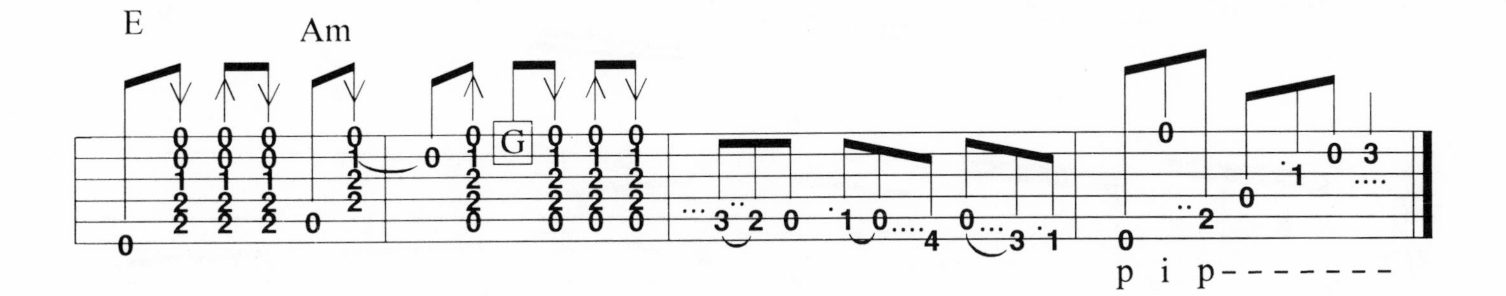

Falseta 1

Juan Serrano

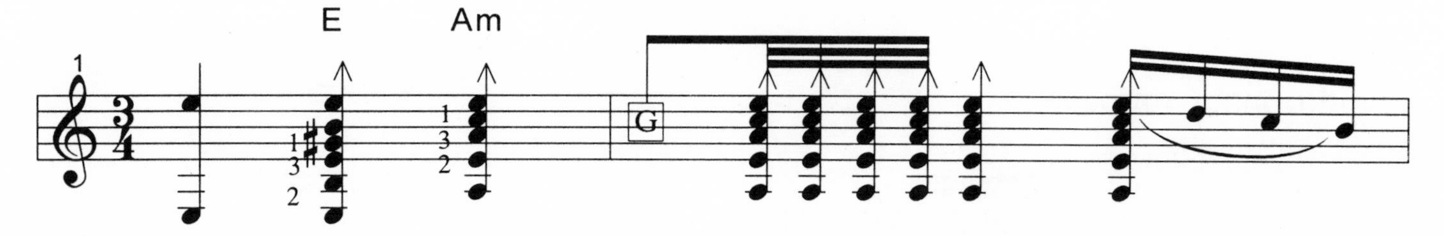


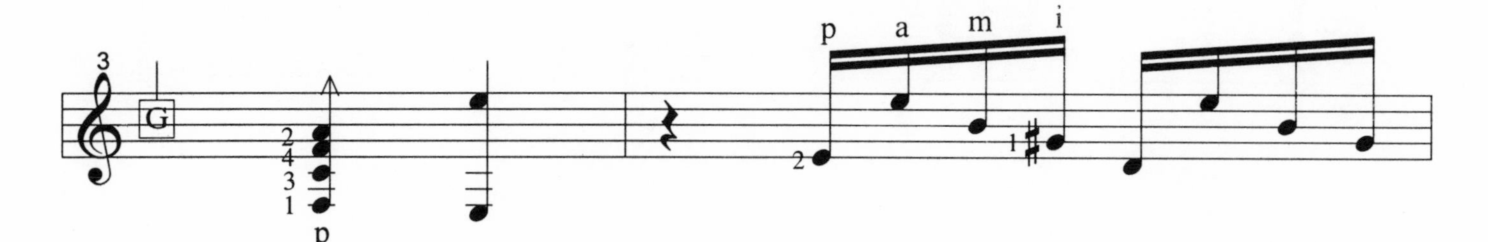

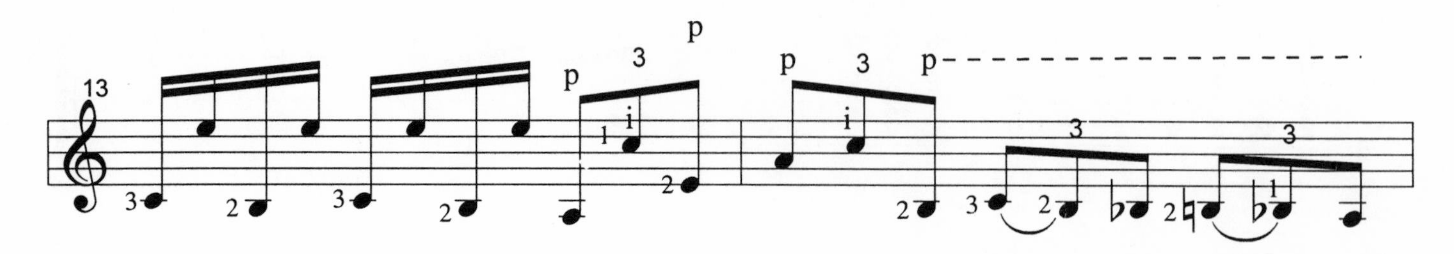

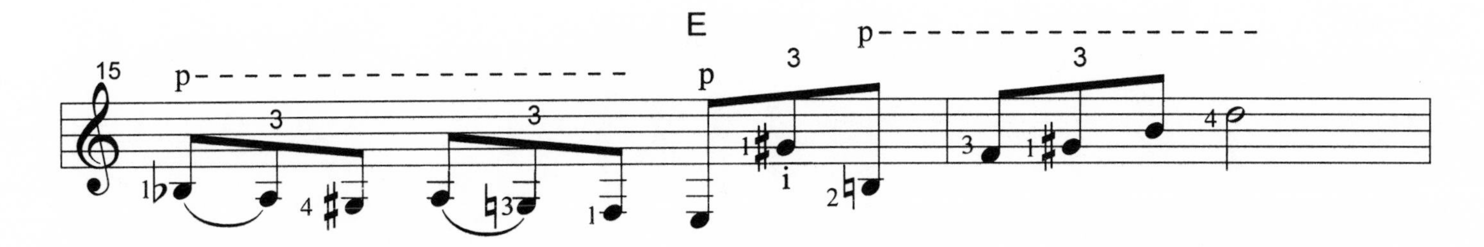
15
E
p
i

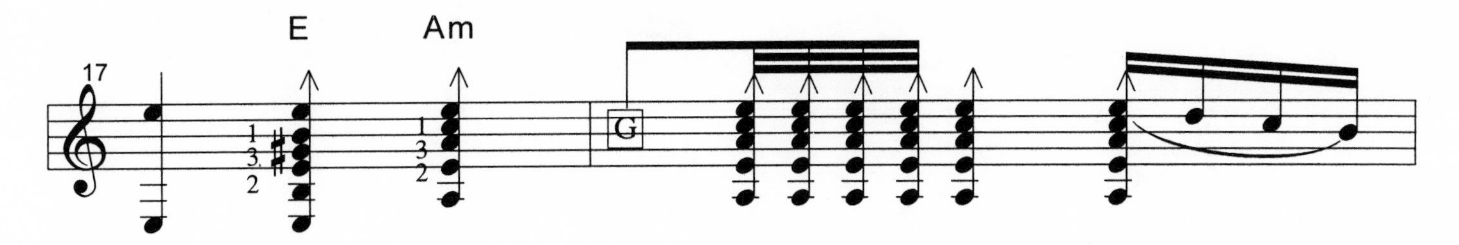
17
E
Am
G

19
G
F
p
i a m i

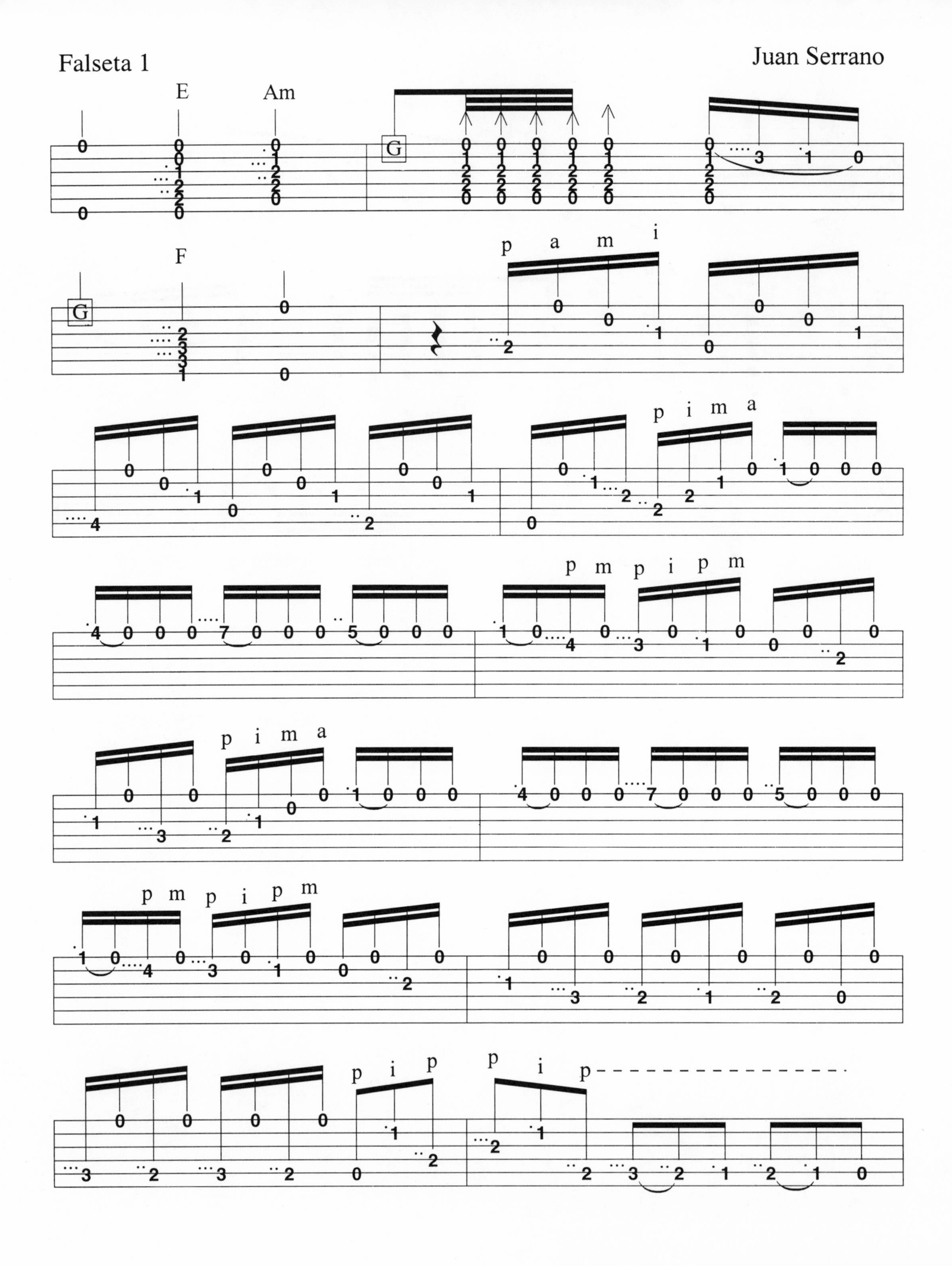

Falseta 1
Juan Serrano
E
Am
G
F
p a m i
p i m a
p m p i p m

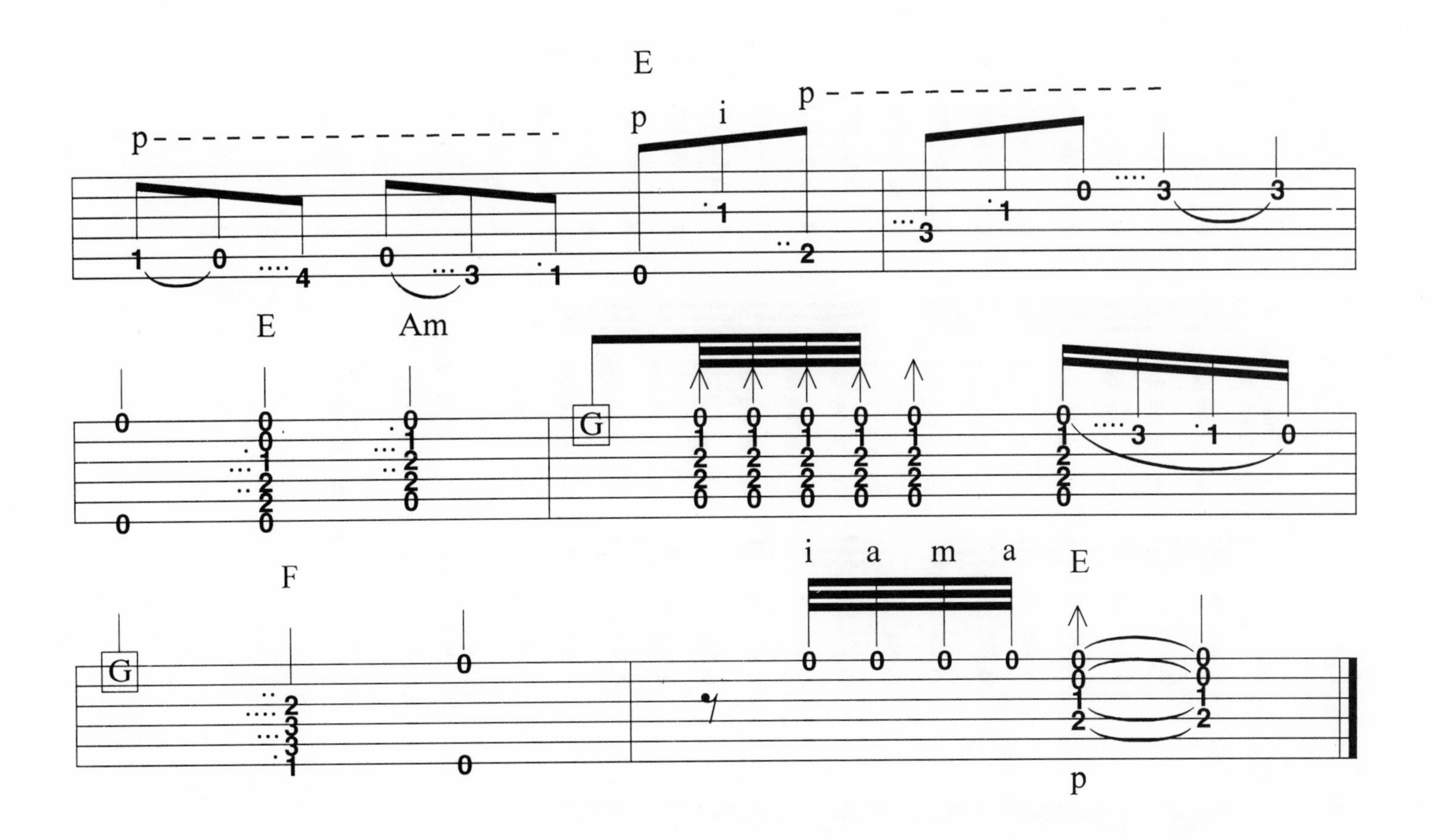
E
p i p
p
E Am
G
F
i a m a
E
G
p

Falseta 2

Juan Serrano

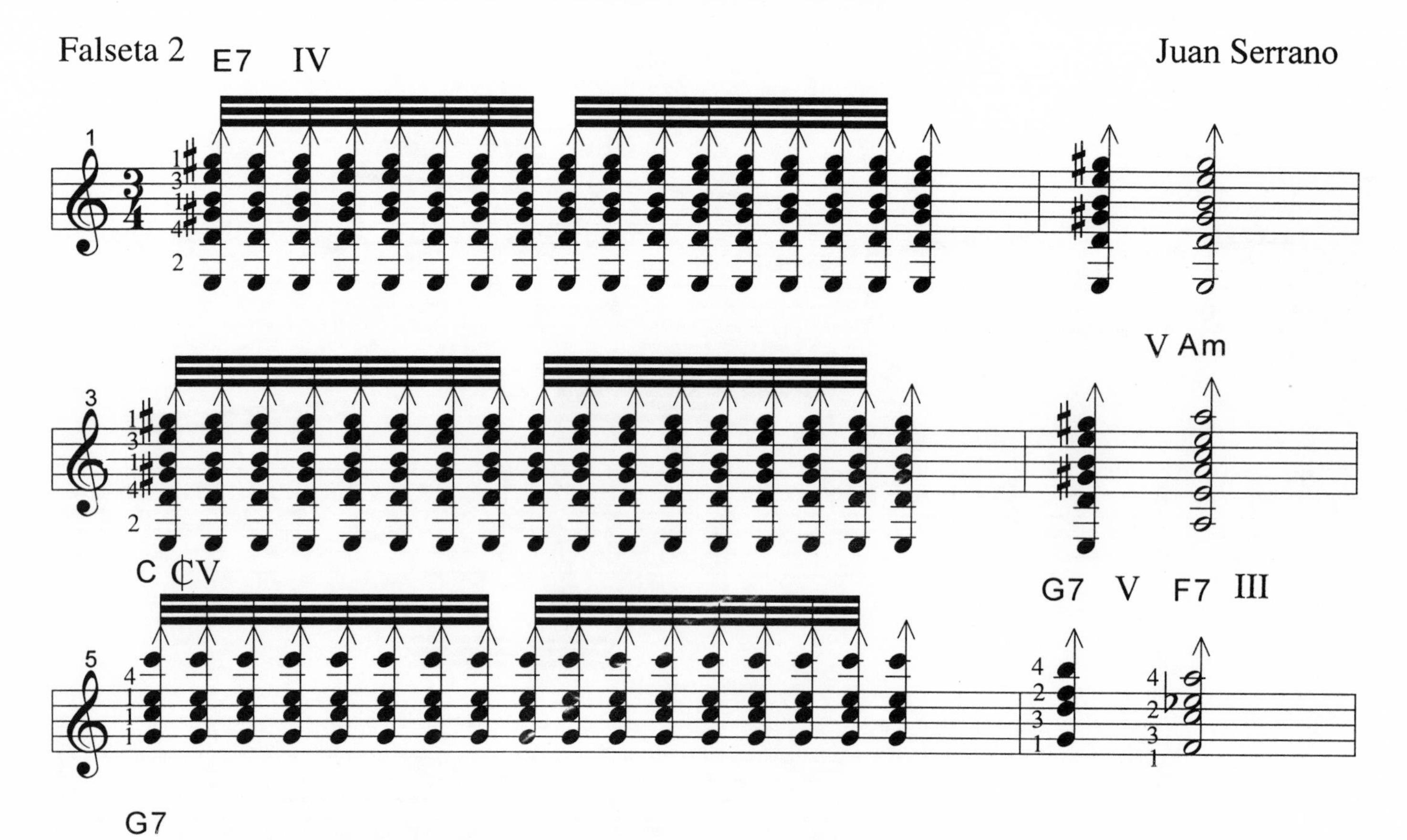


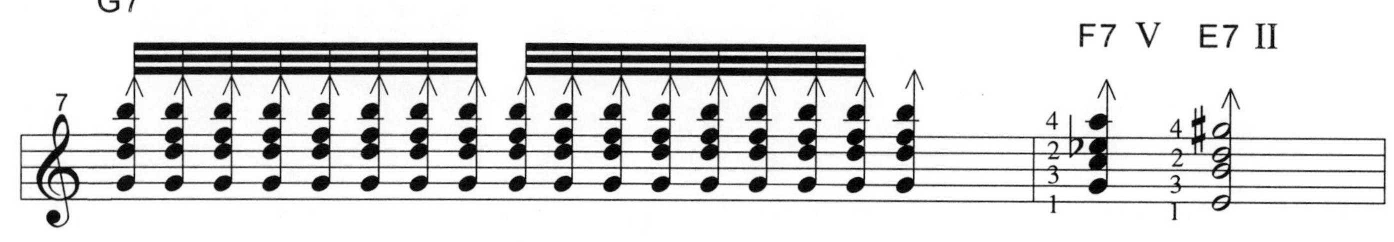

CV

C III

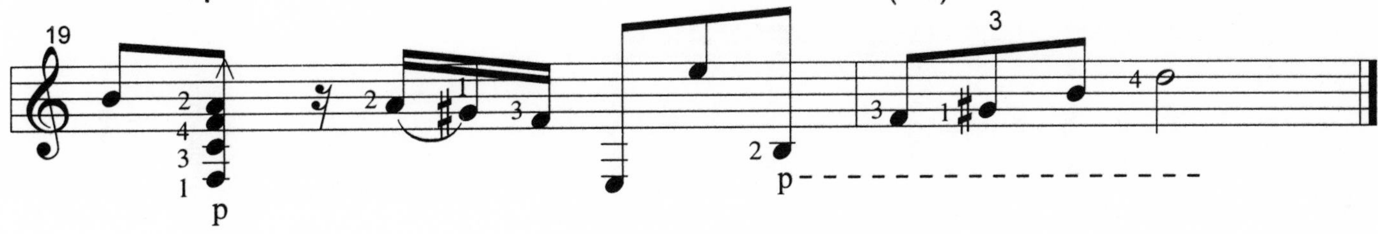
F
E7(♭9)

Falseta 2

Juan Serrano

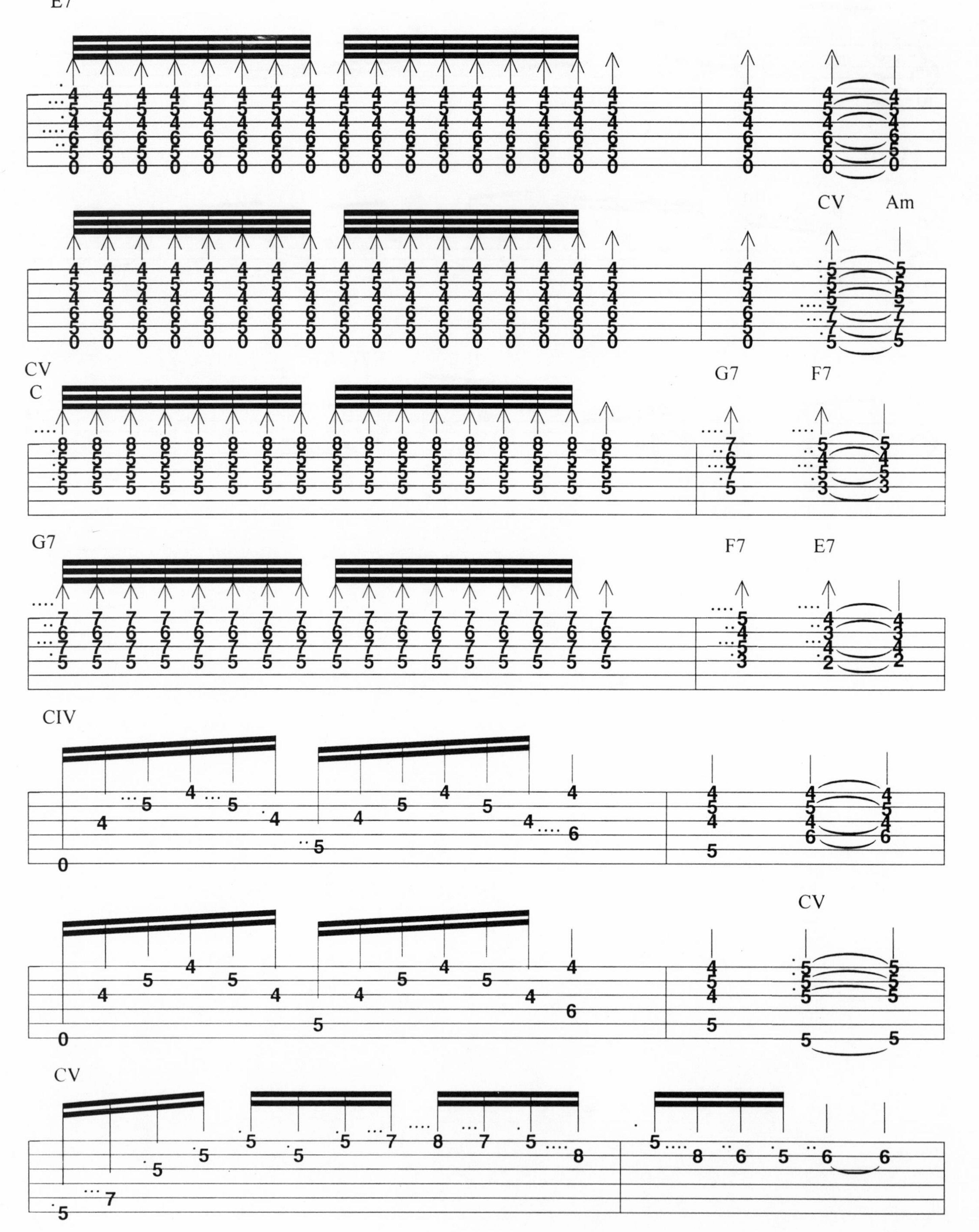

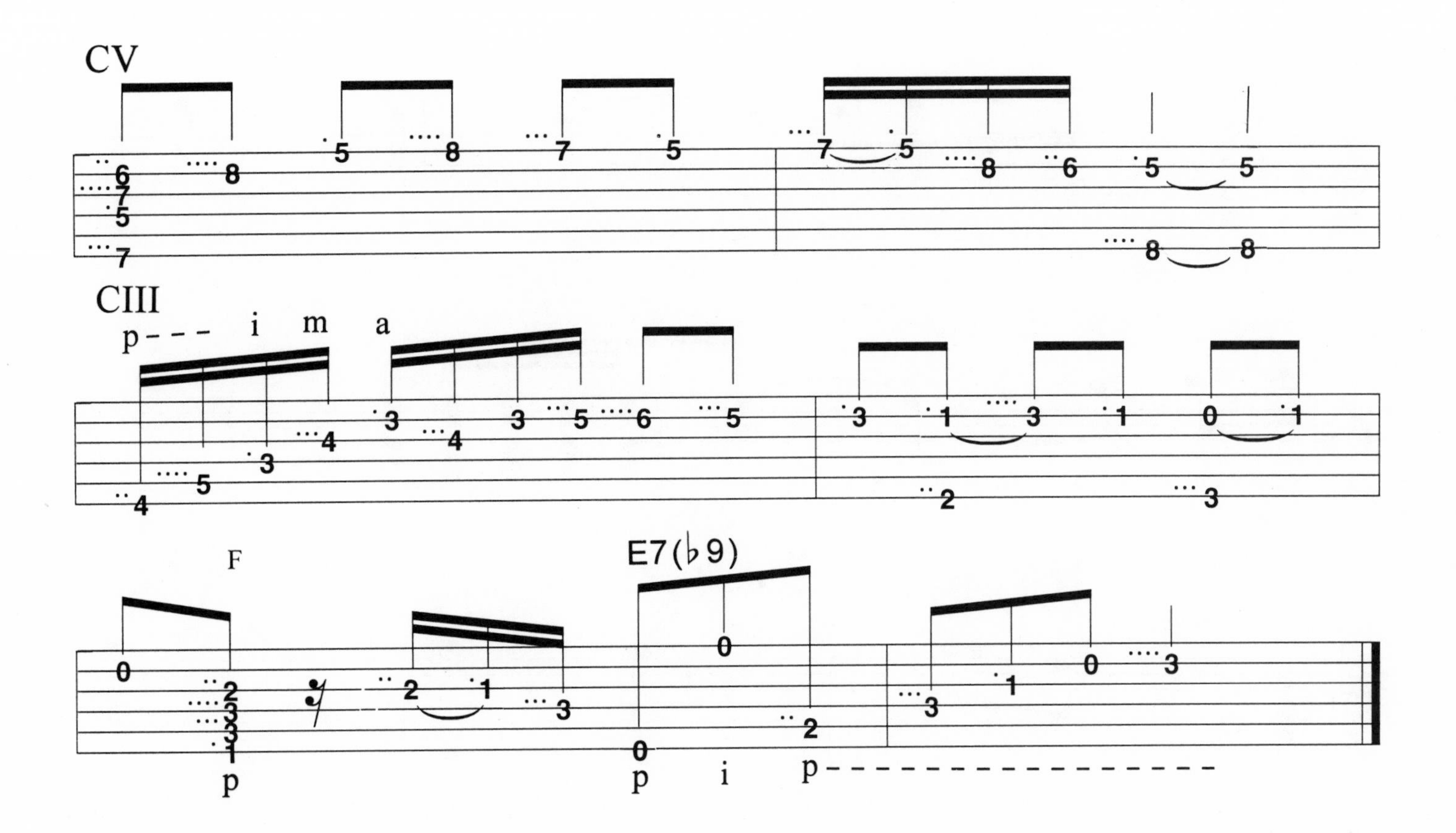
CV
CIII
p - - - i m a
F
E7(♭9)
p
p i p

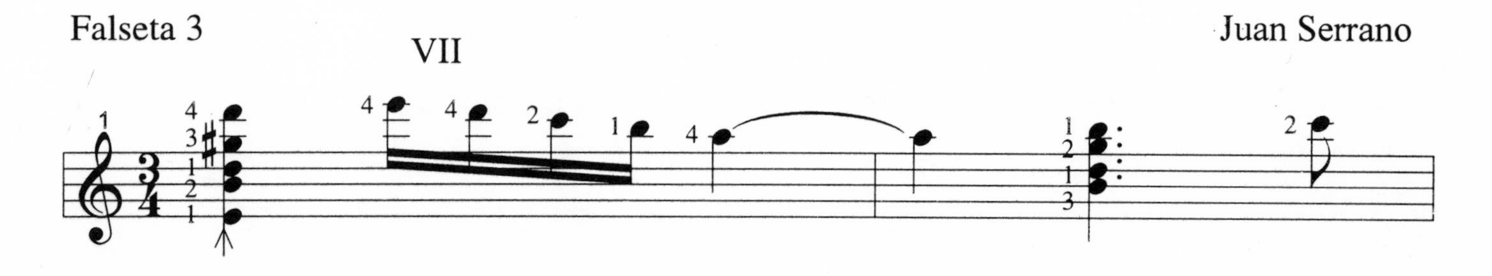
Falseta 3
Juan Serrano
VII

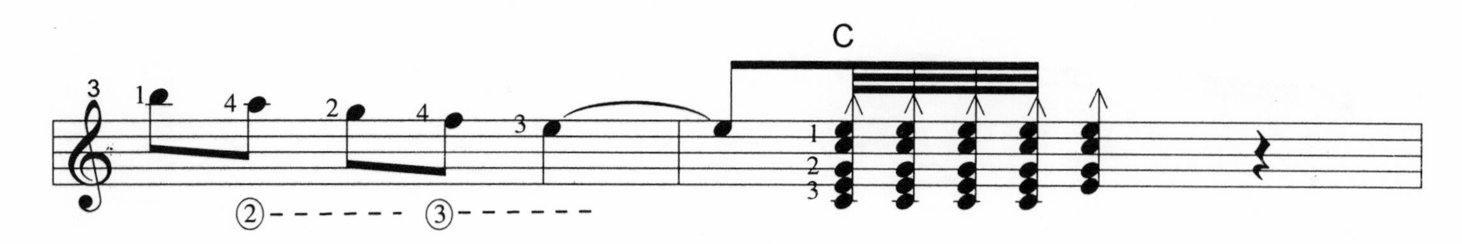
C

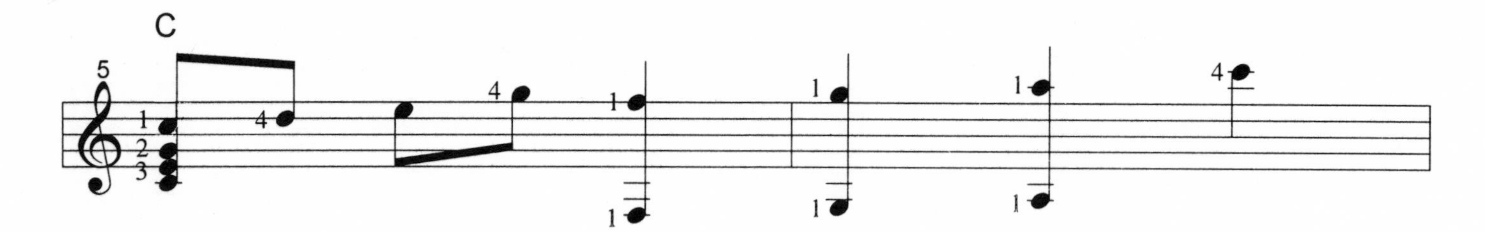
C

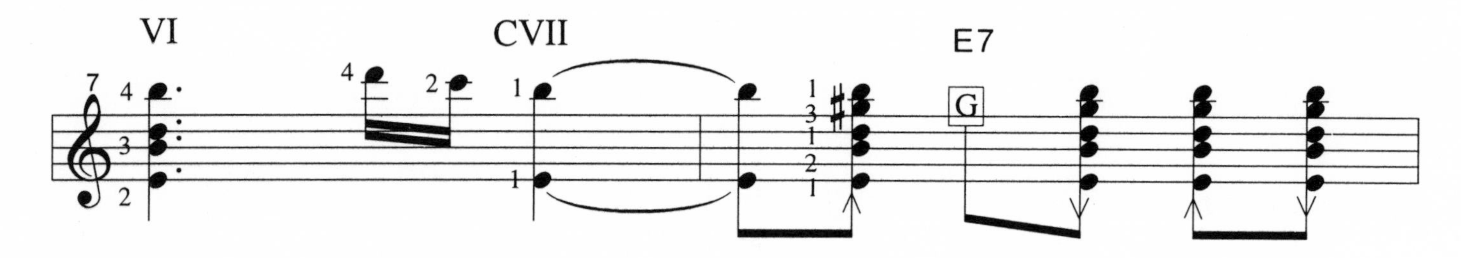
VI
CVII
E7
G

p

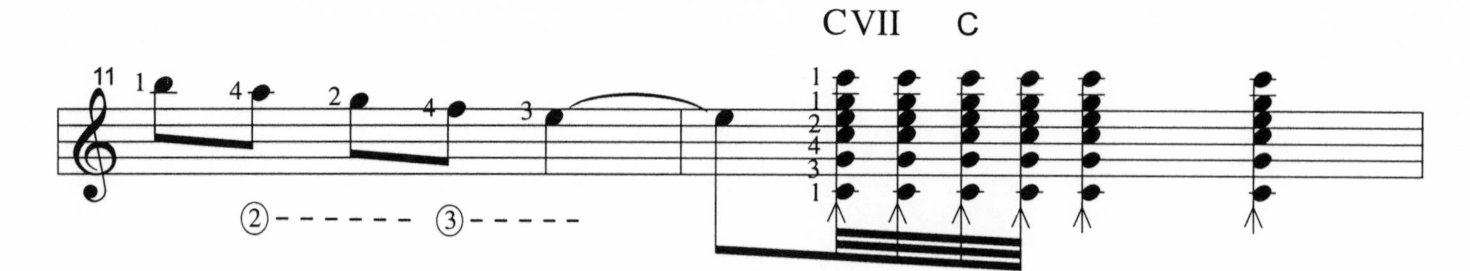
CVII
C

15
CVII
G
G

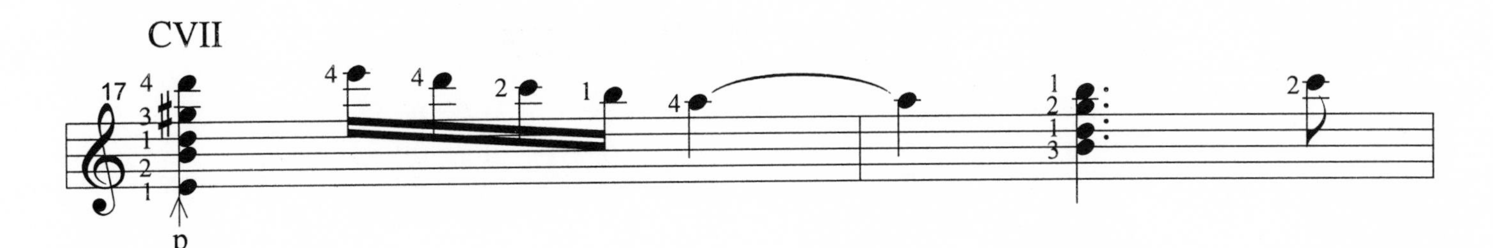
CVII
17
p

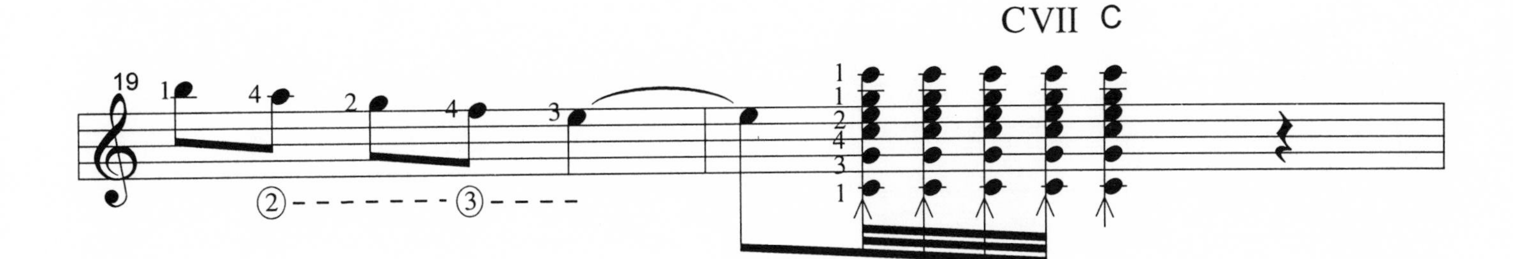
19
CVII
C

21

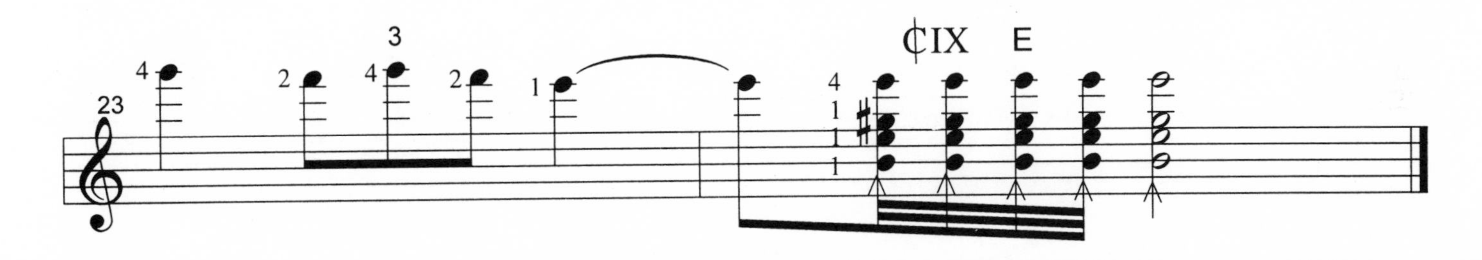
23
CIX
E

## Falseta 3

Juan Serrano

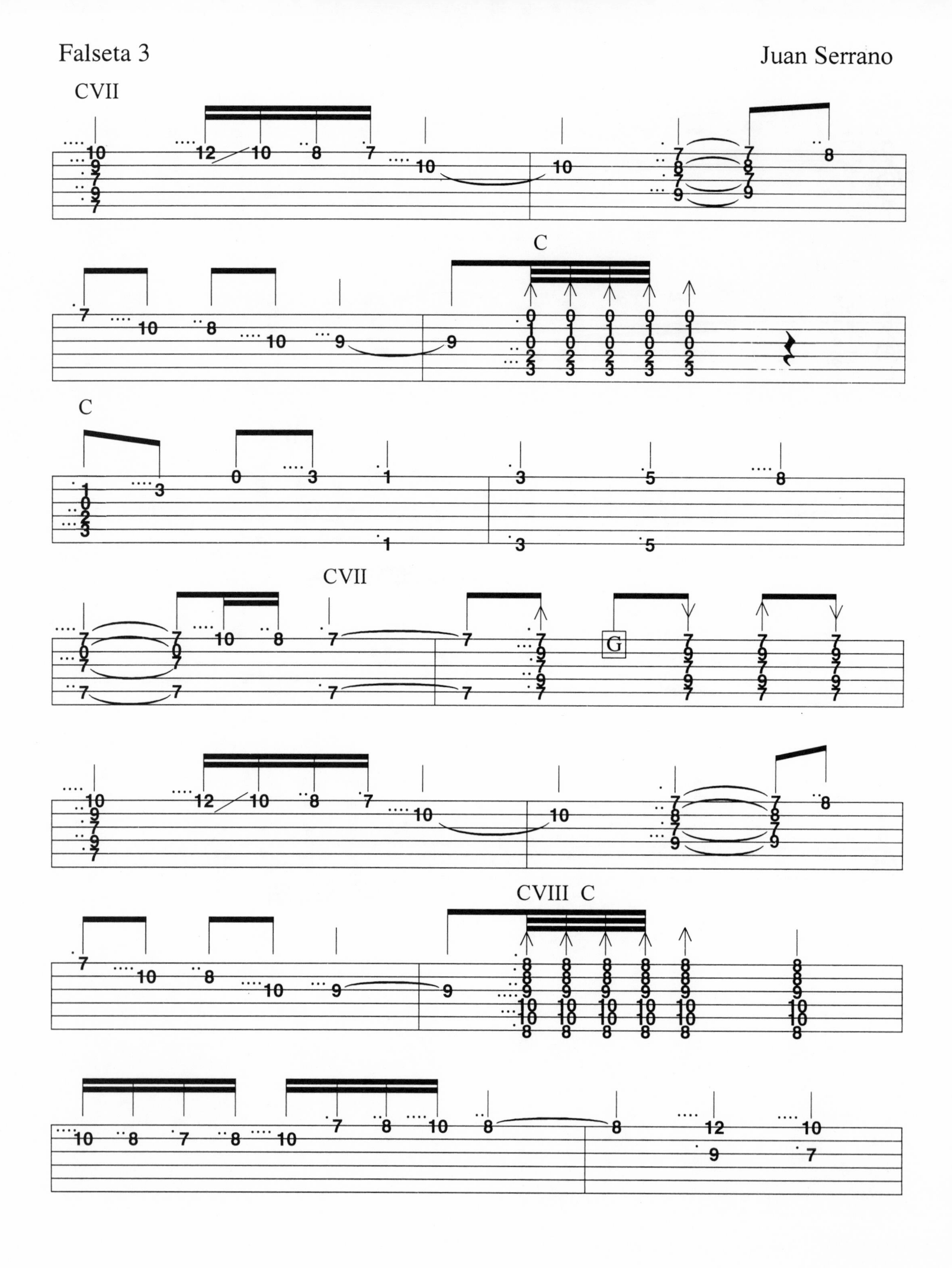

CVII G

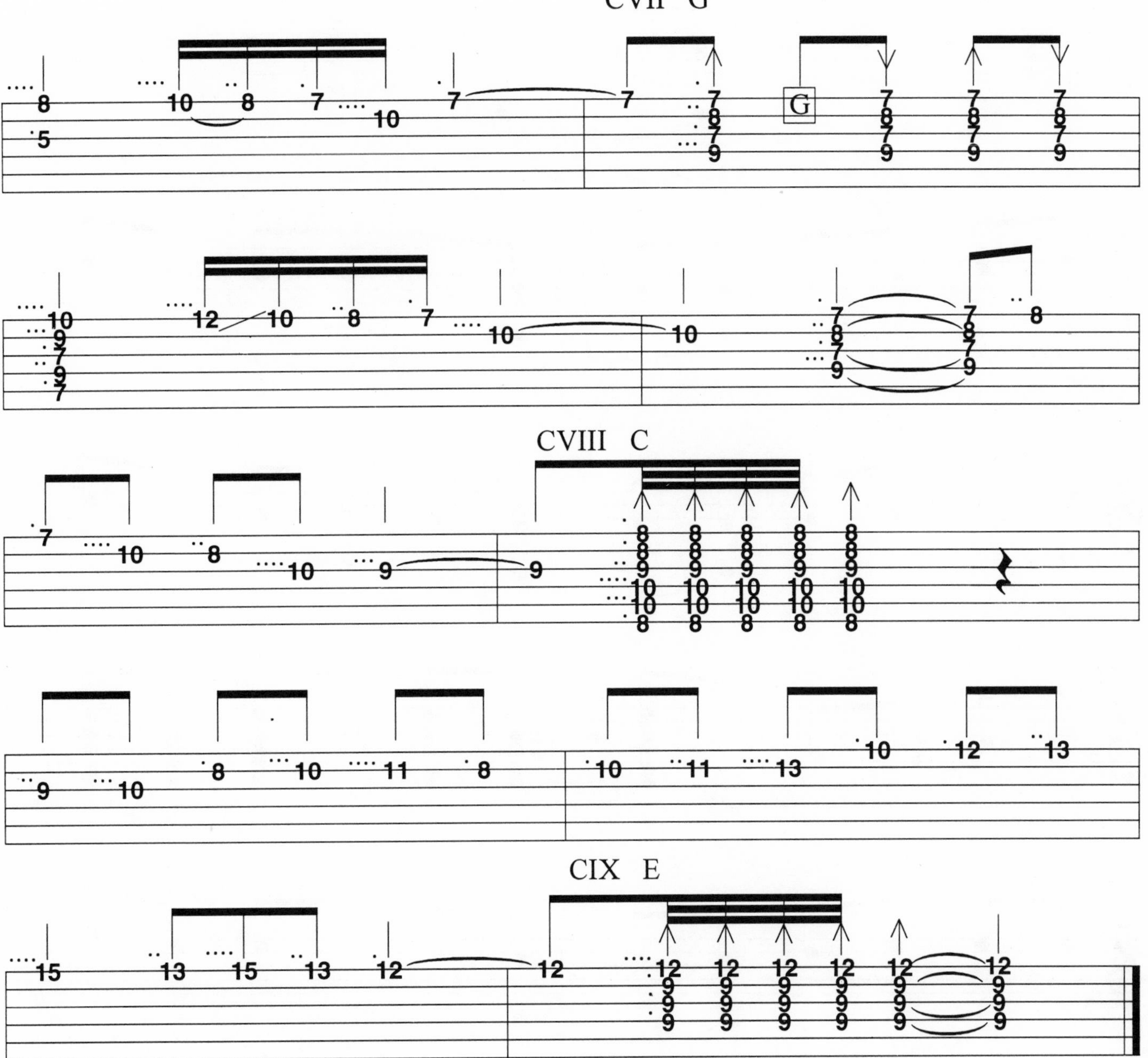
G
CVIII C
CIX E

Falseta 4

Juan Serrano

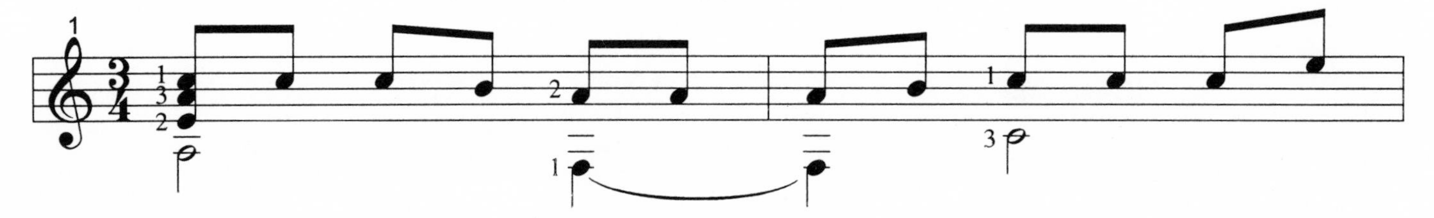

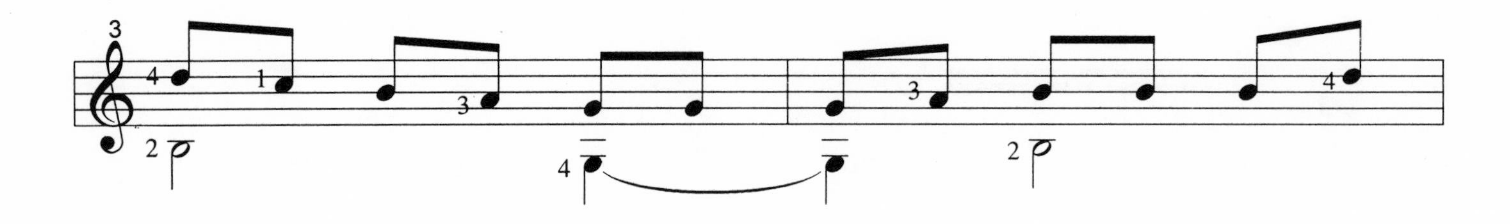

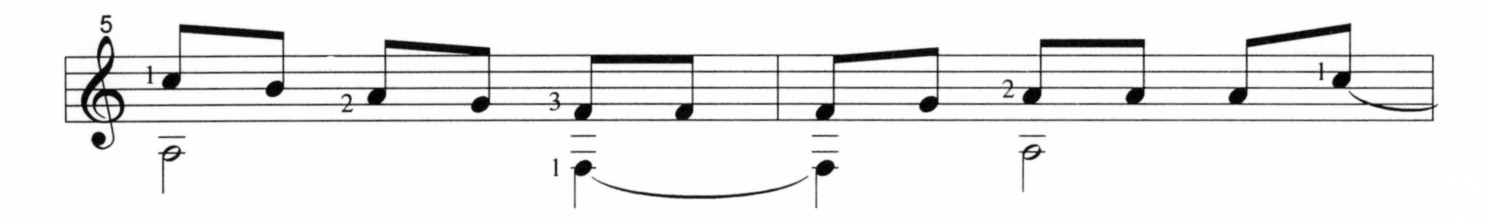

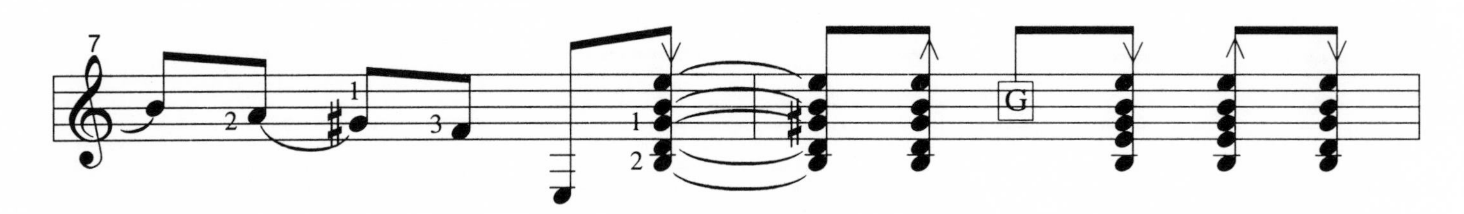


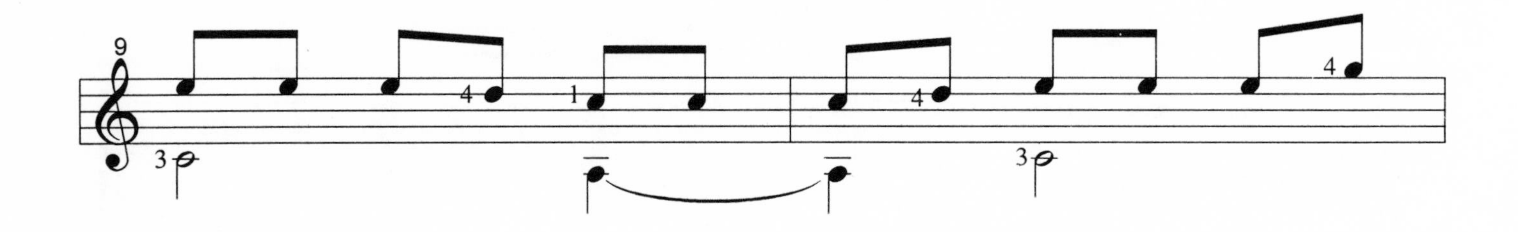

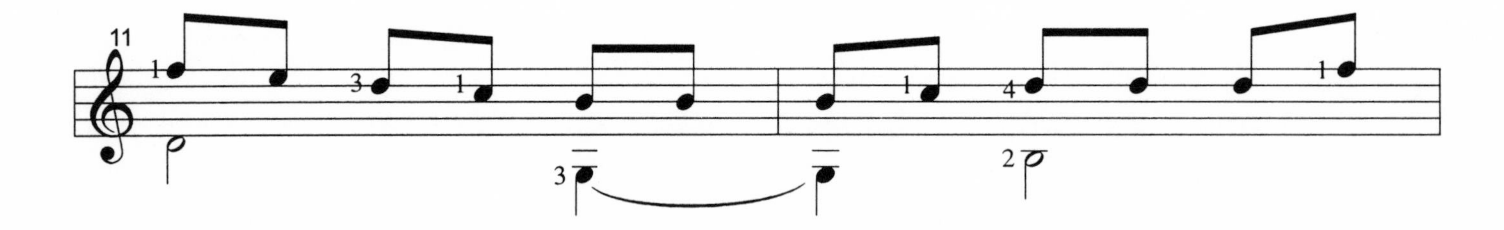

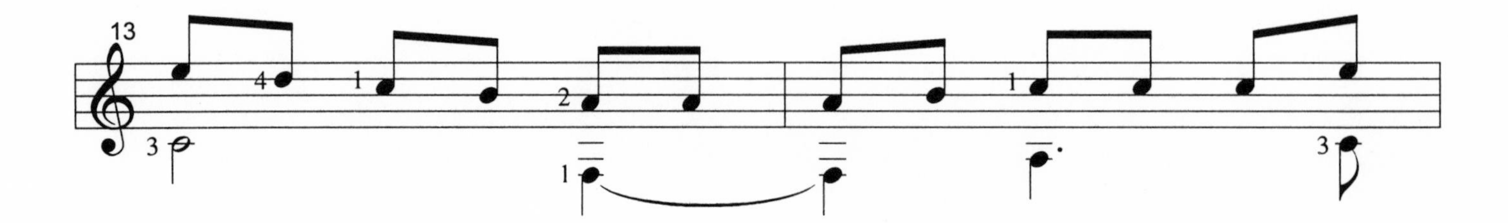

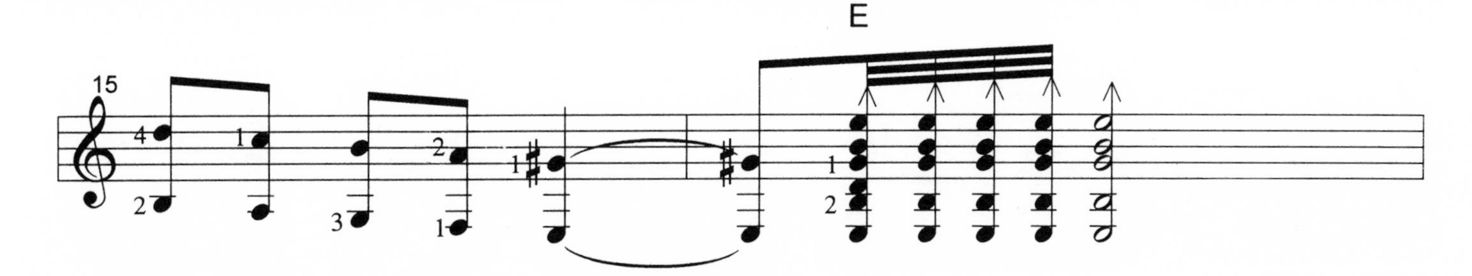
15
E

Am
17

19

21

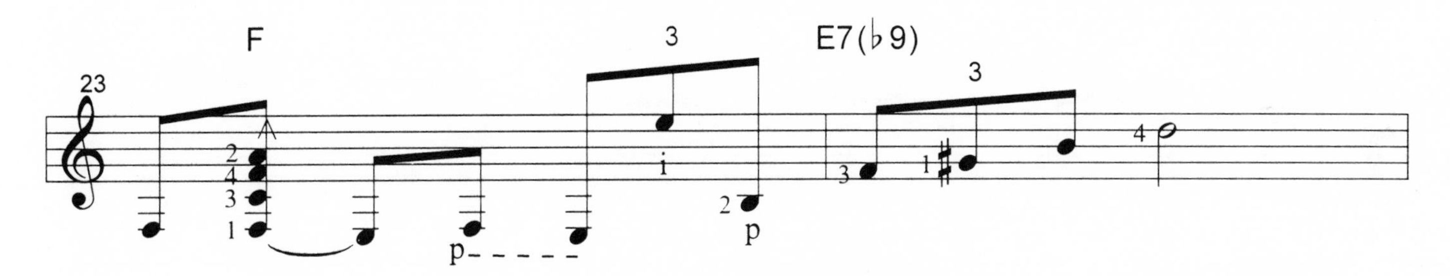
F
E7(♭9)
23
i
p
p

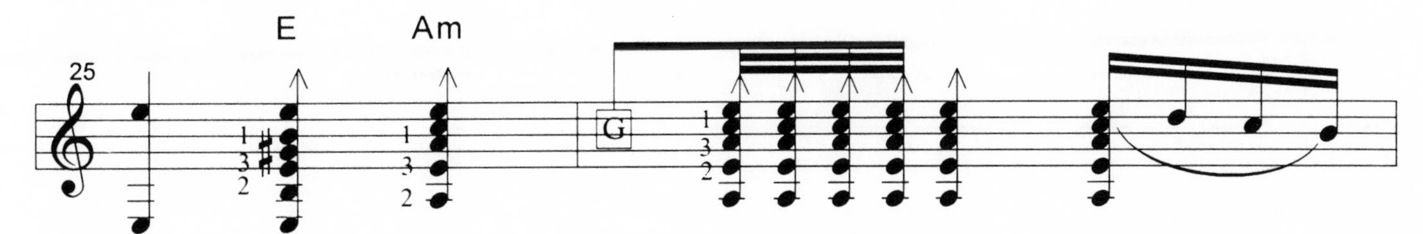
E
Am
25
G

F
E
27
G
i a m i
p
p

Falseta 4

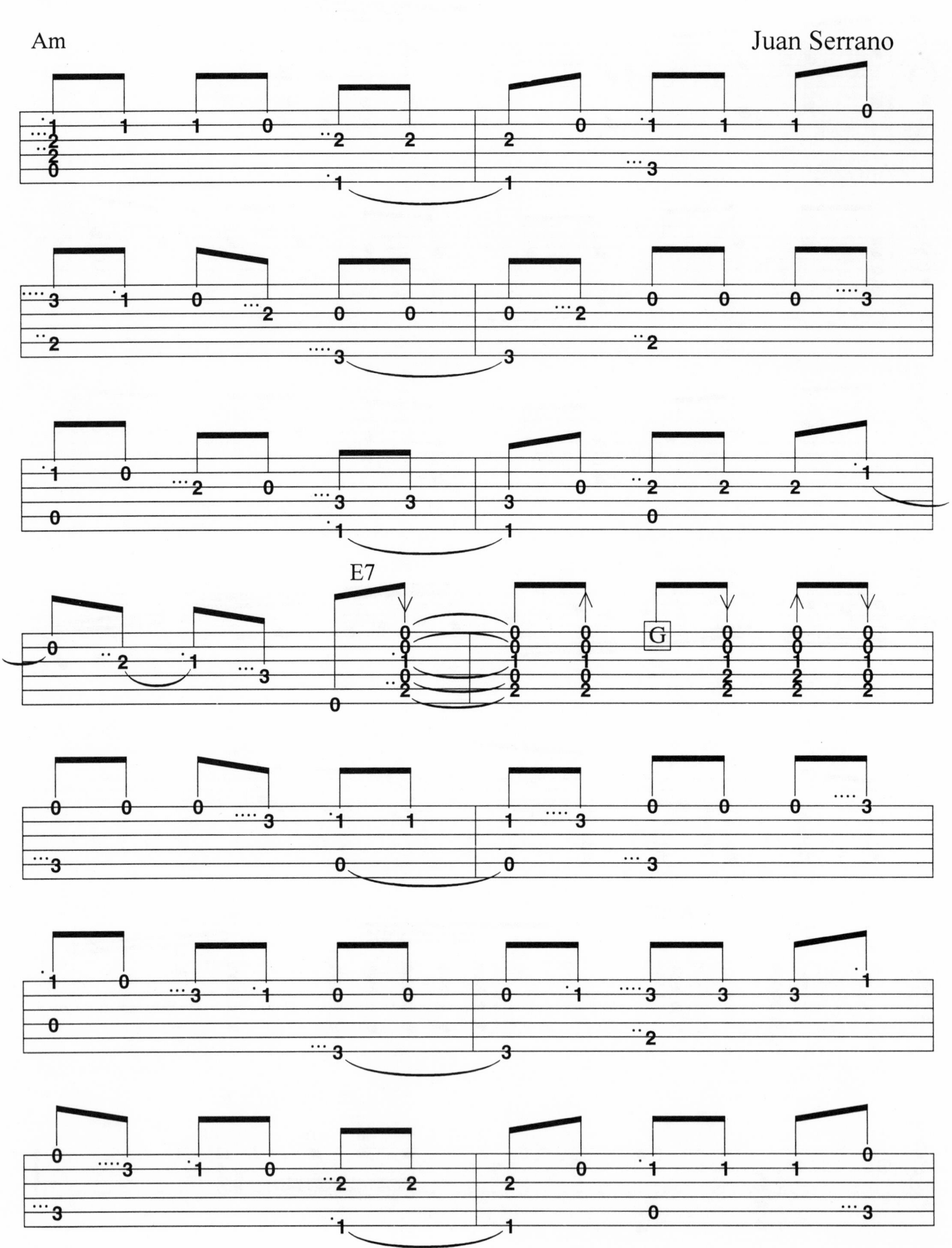

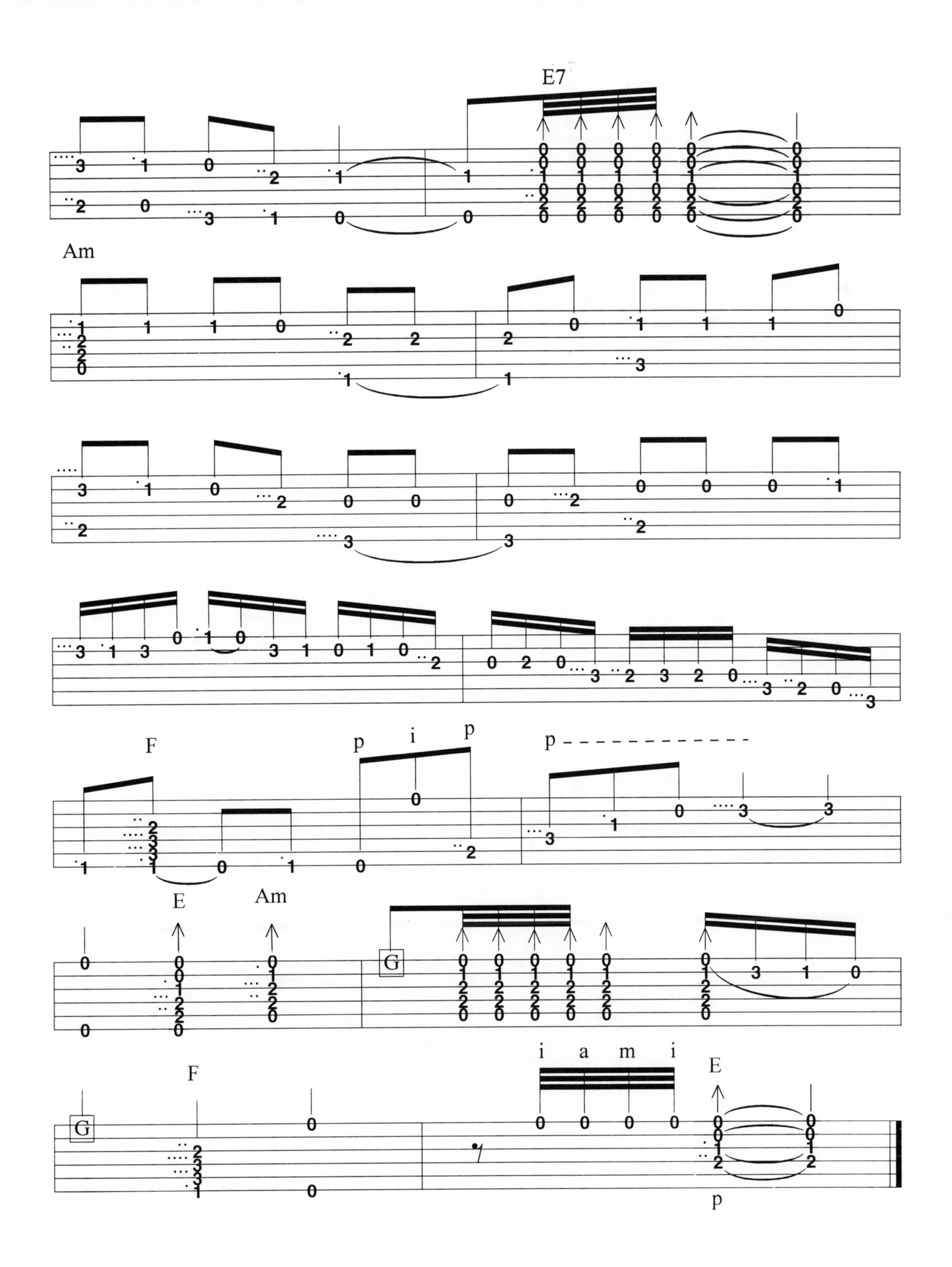
E7
Am
F
p i p
p
E
Am
G
G
F
i a m i
E
p

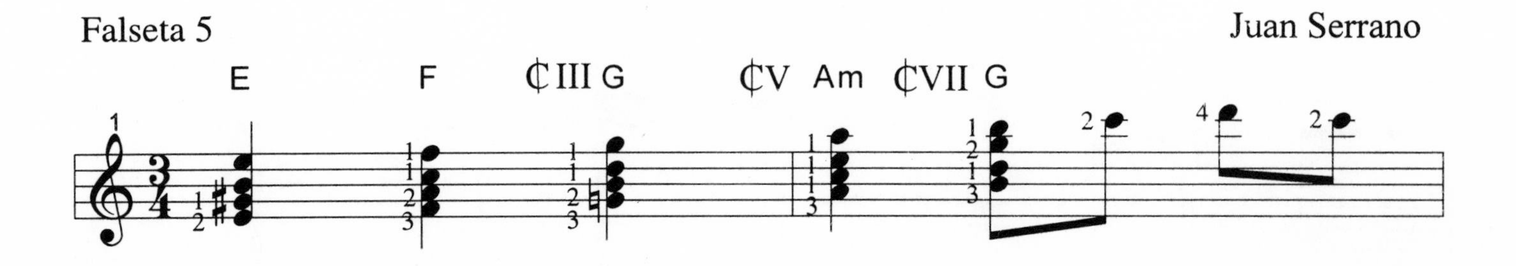
Falseta 5
Juan Serrano
E
F
₵III G
₵V Am
₵VII G

VII

VII

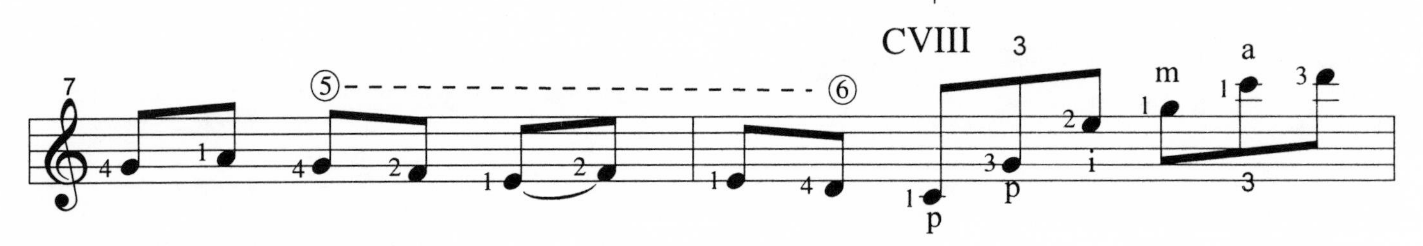
CVIII
m
a

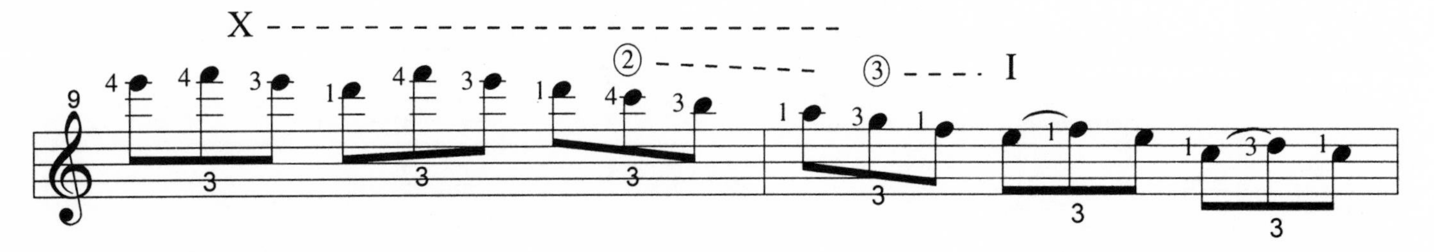
X
I

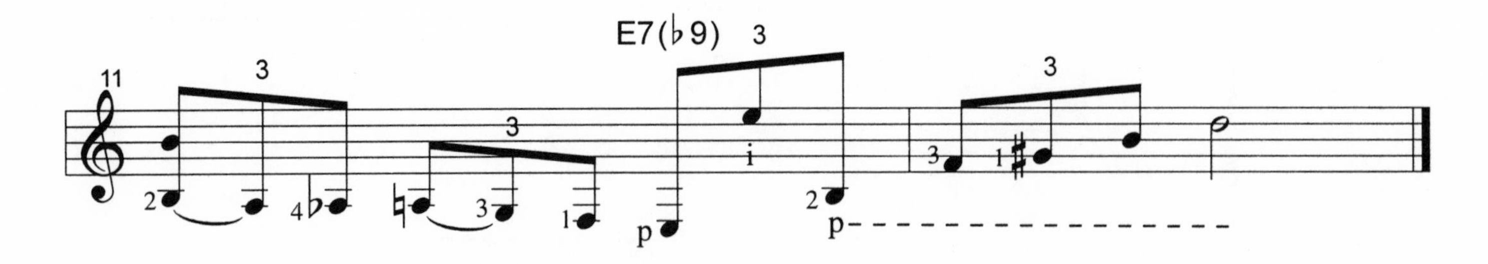
E7(♭9)

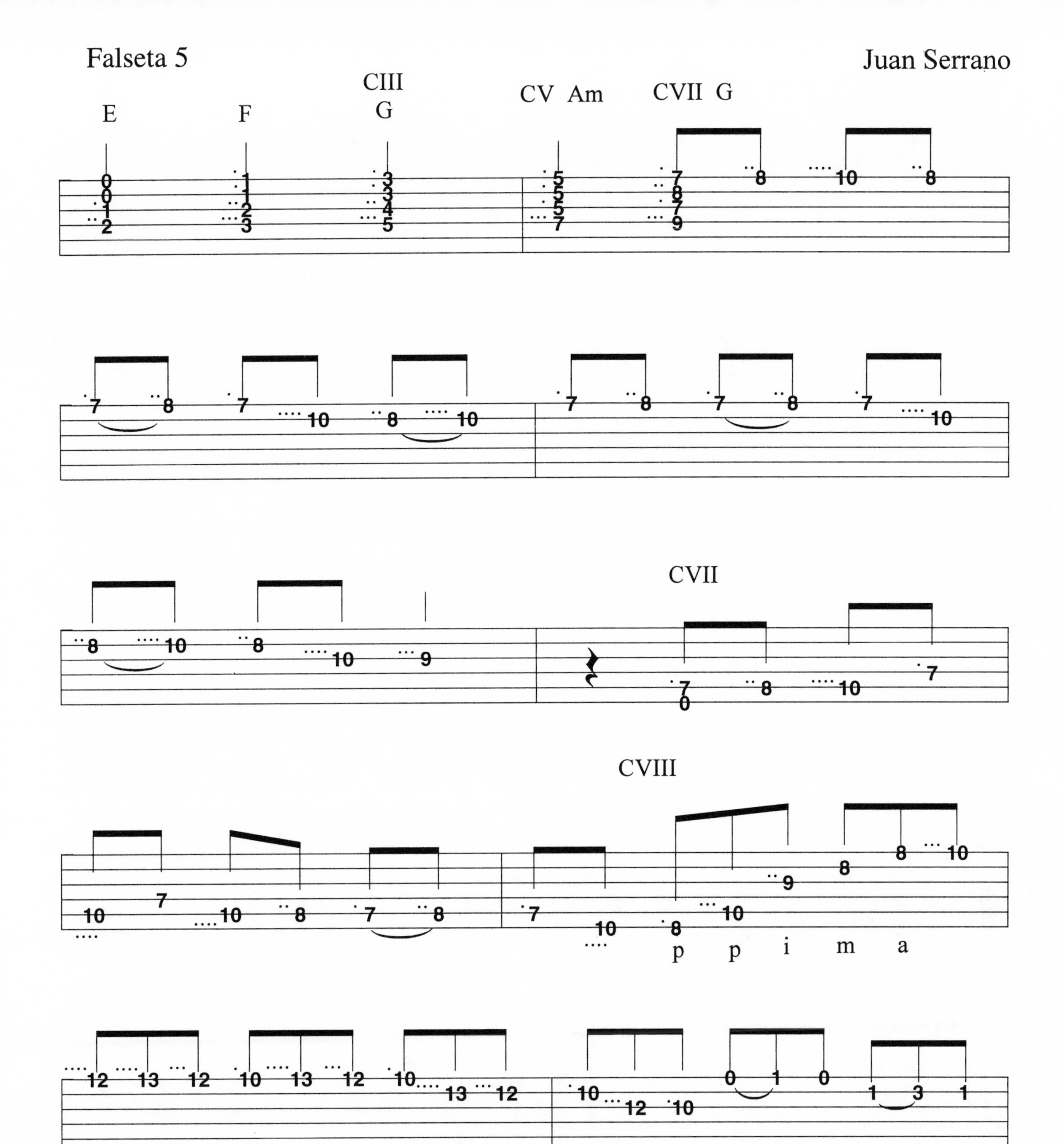
Falseta 5
Juan Serrano
E
F
CIII
G
CV Am
CVII G
CVII
CVIII
p p i m a

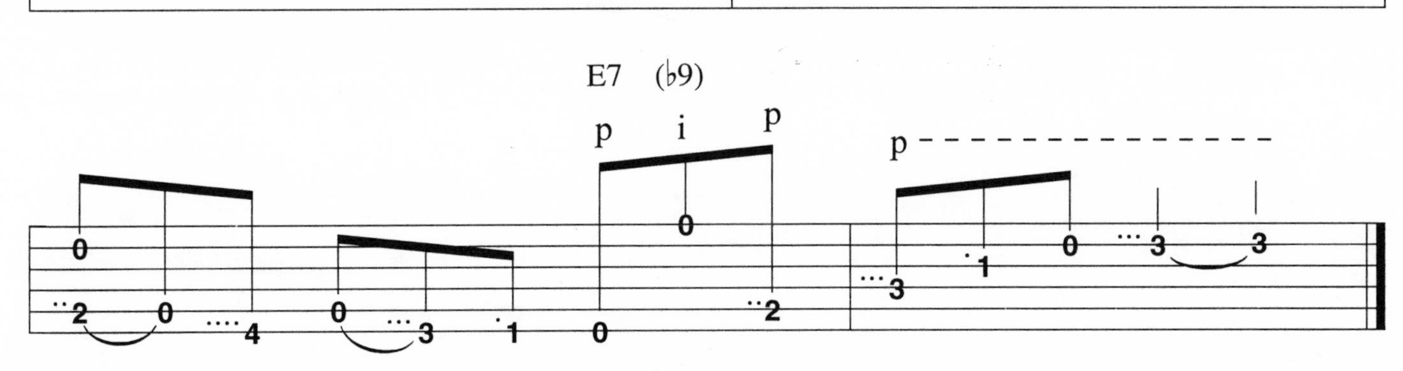
E7 (♭9)
p i p
p

Falseta 6

Juan Serrano

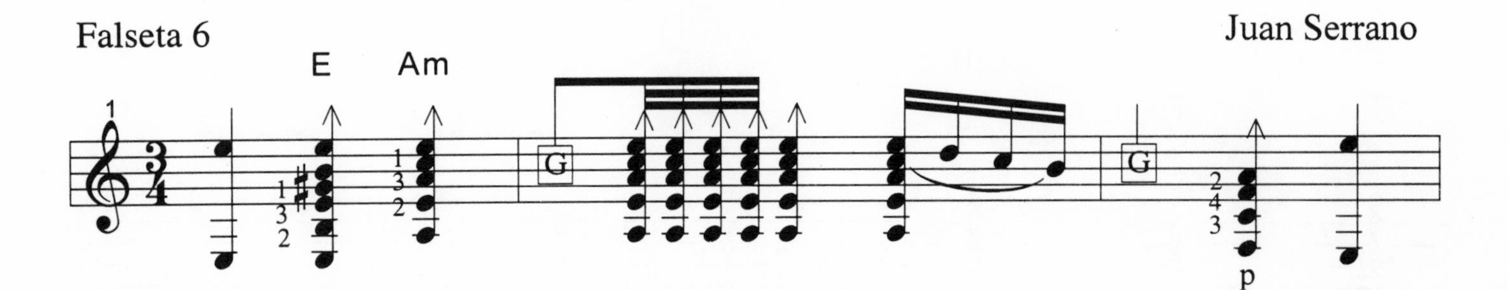

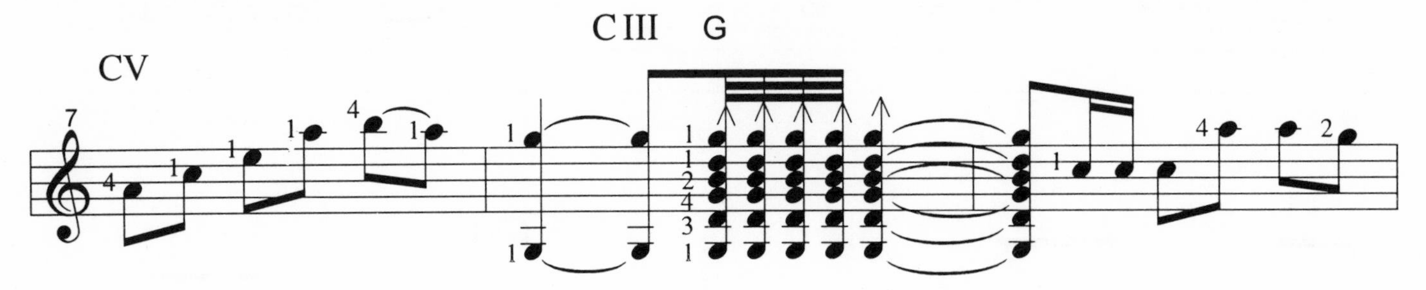

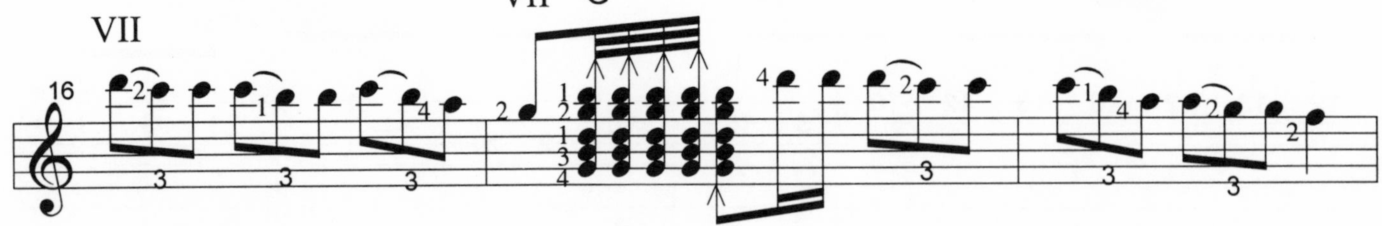


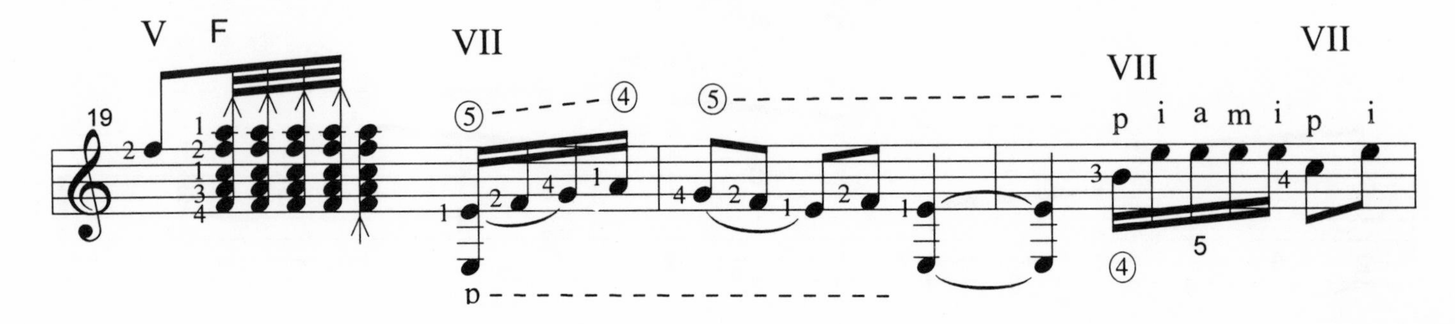

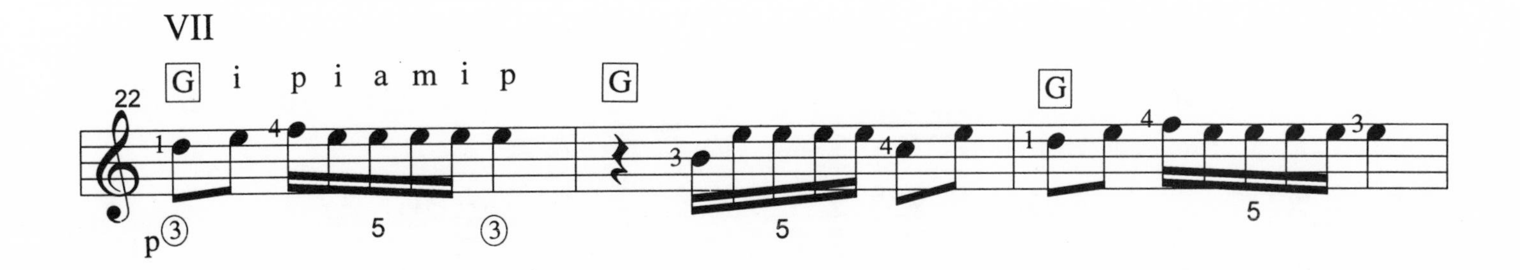
VII
G i p i a m i p
G
G

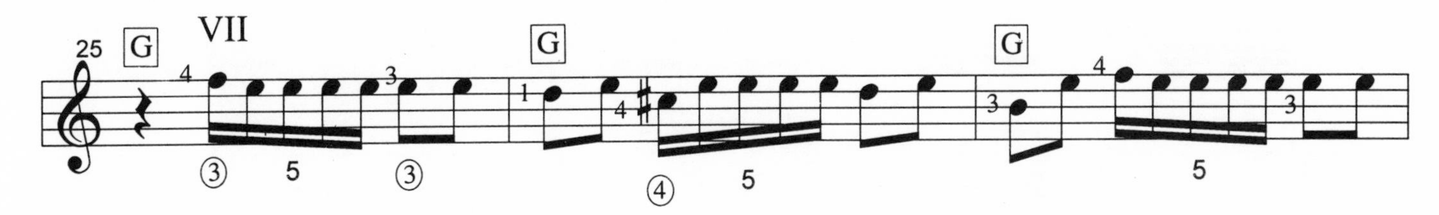
G
VII
G
G

VII
G
VII

CVII G
CV
V F

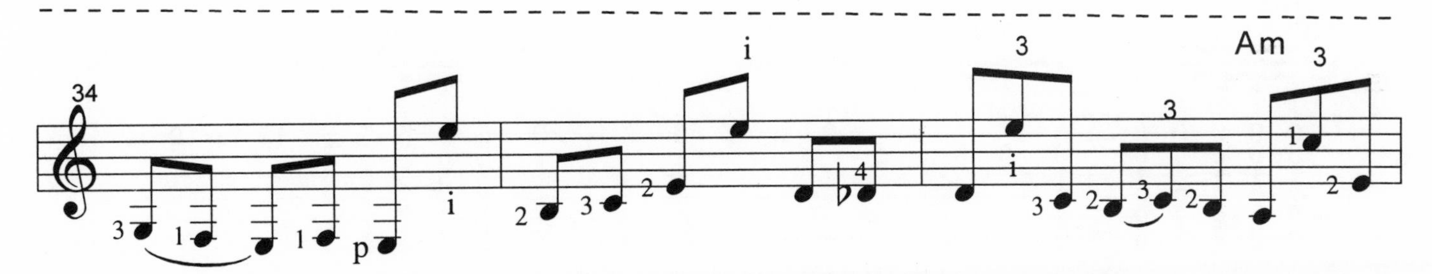
Am

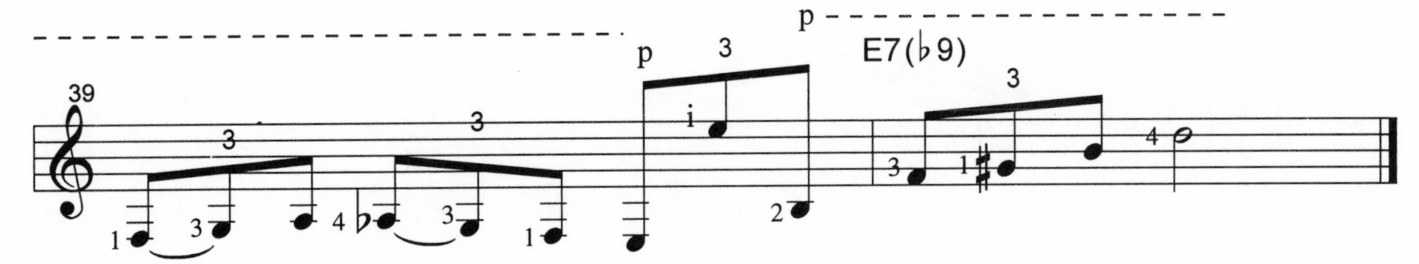
E7(♭9)

Falseta 6

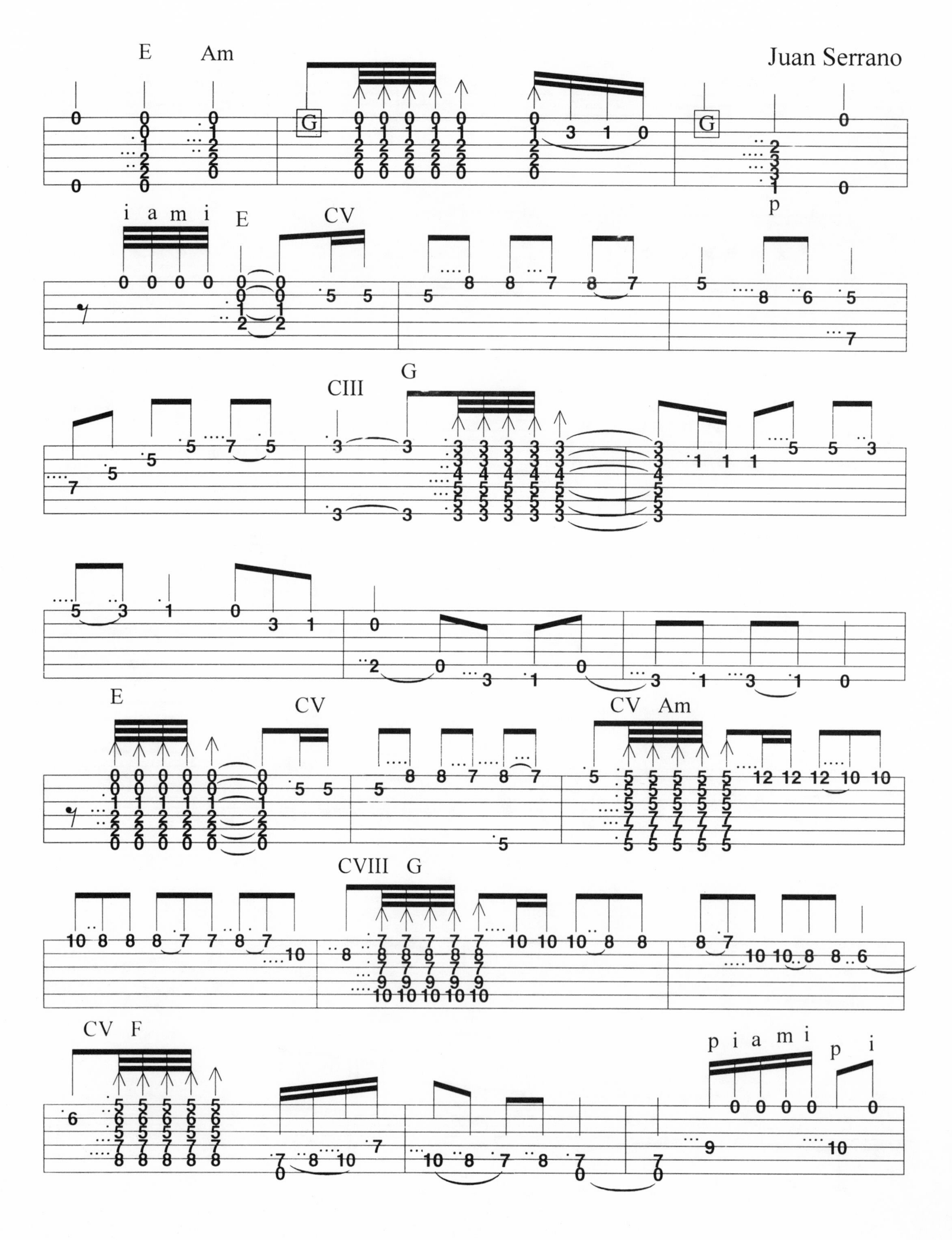

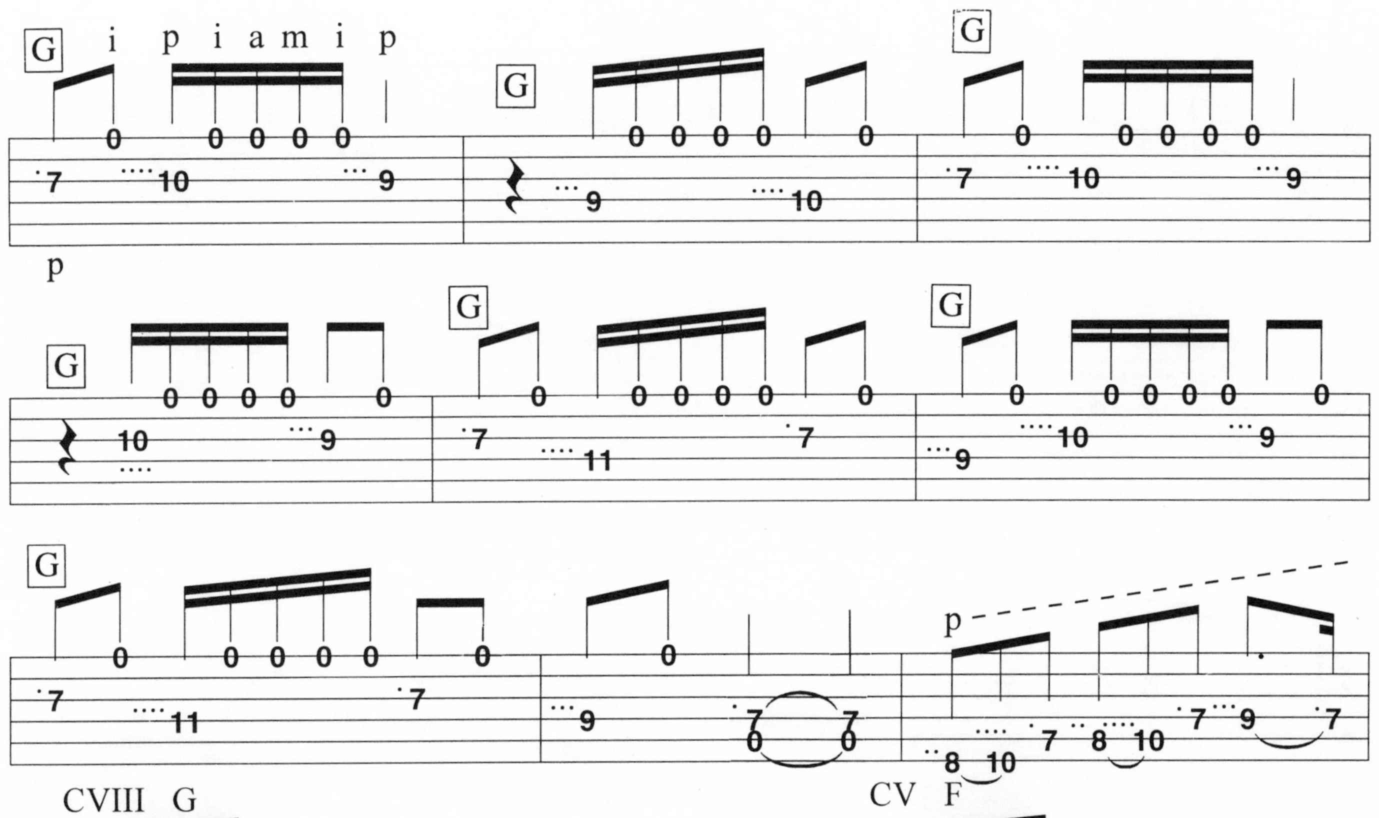
G i p i a m i p
G
G
p
G
G
G
G
p

CVIII G
CV F
p
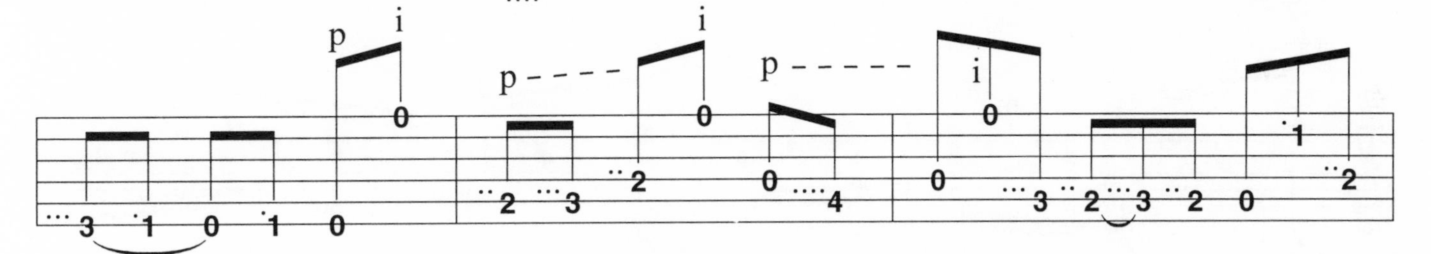
p i
p i
p i
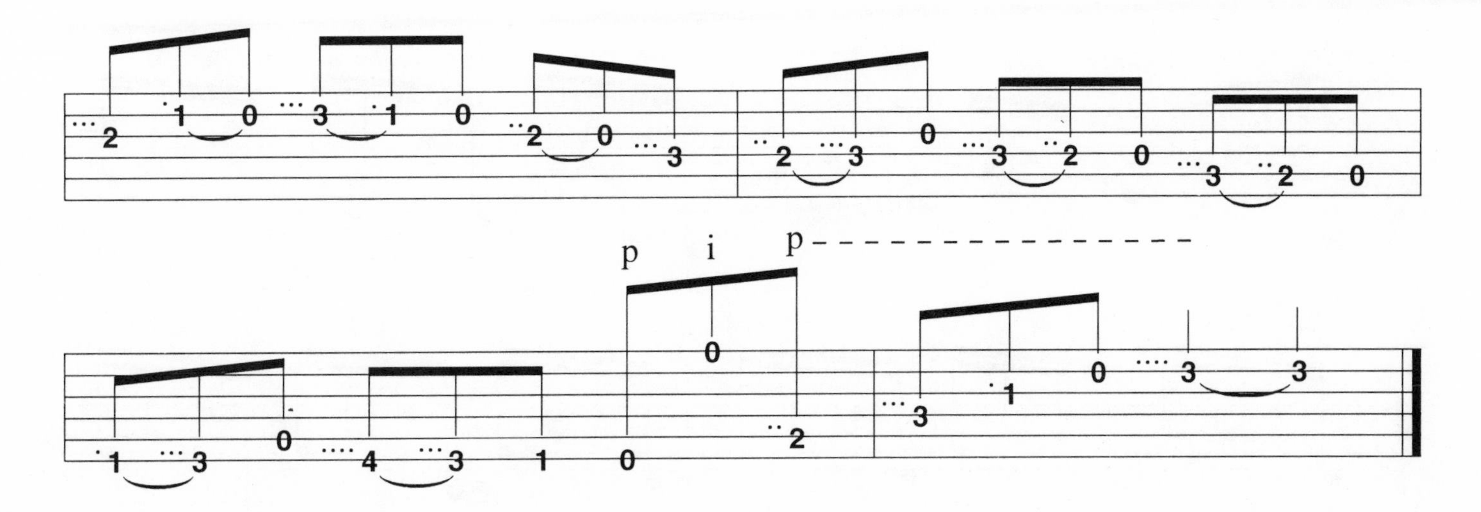
p i p

## Falseta 7

Juan Serrano

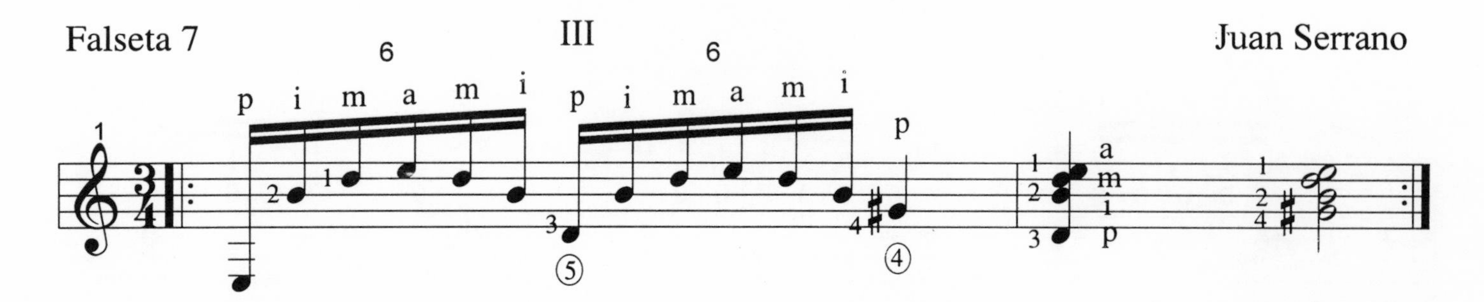

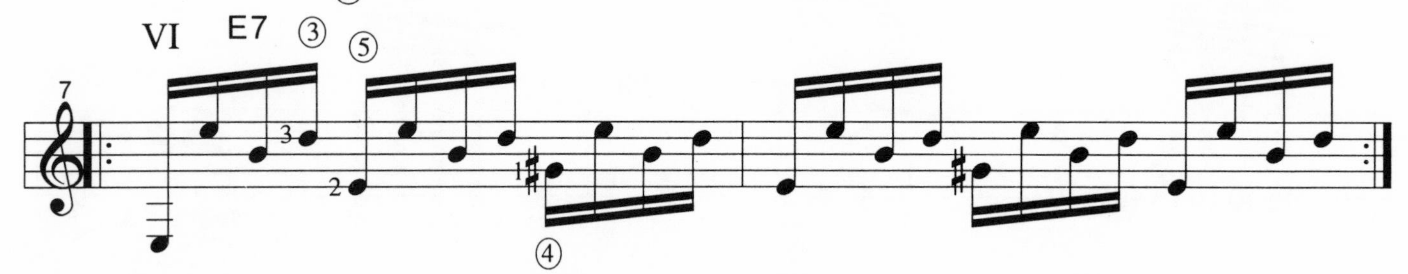


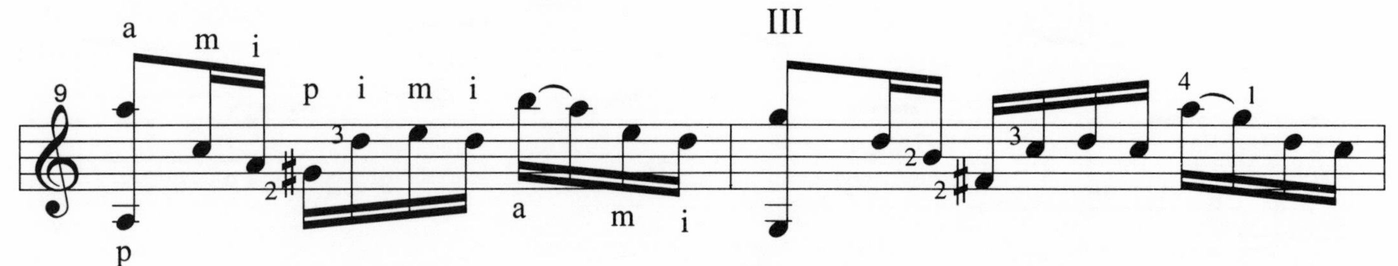


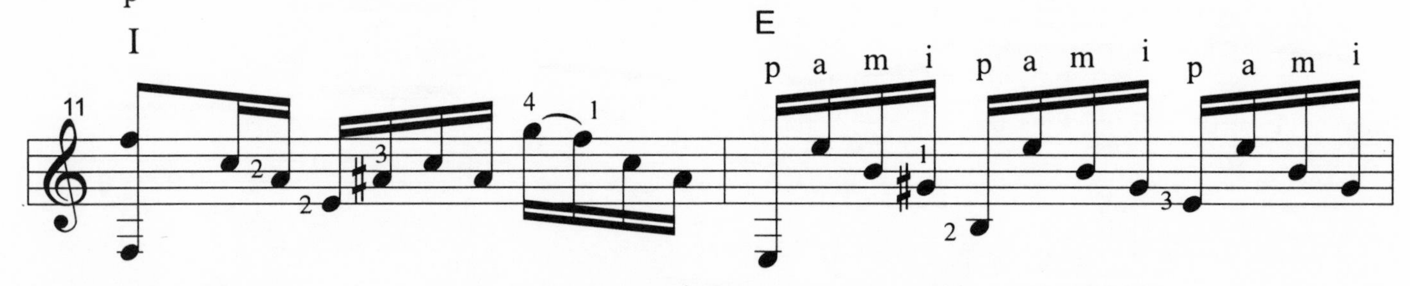

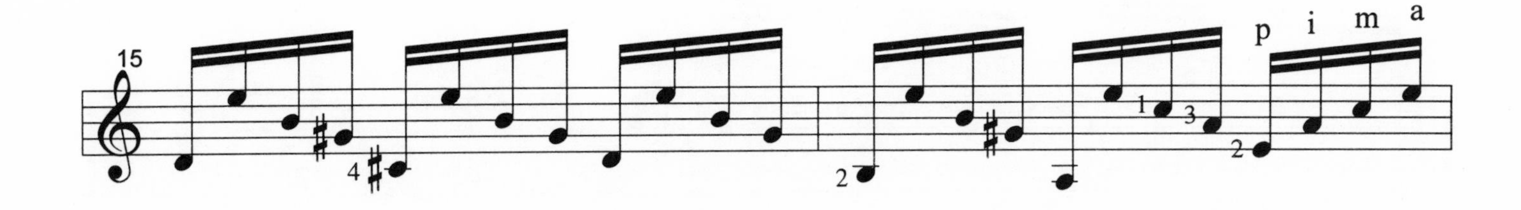
15
p i m a
4
2
1 3
2

17
③
4
4

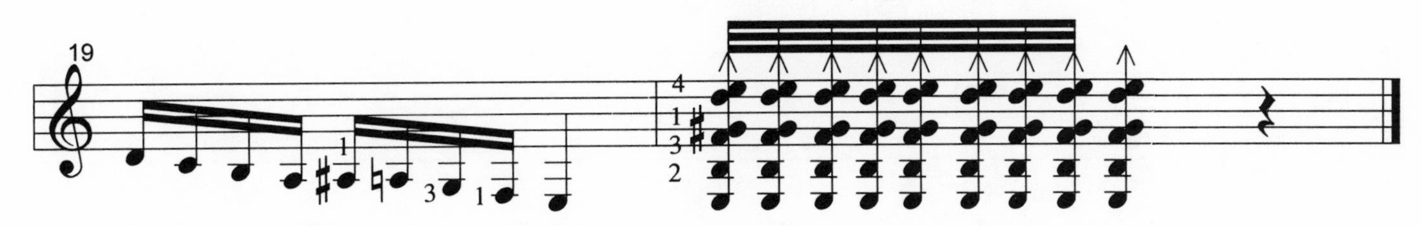
E7(♭9)
19
1
3 1
4
1
3
2

Falseta 7

Juan Serrano

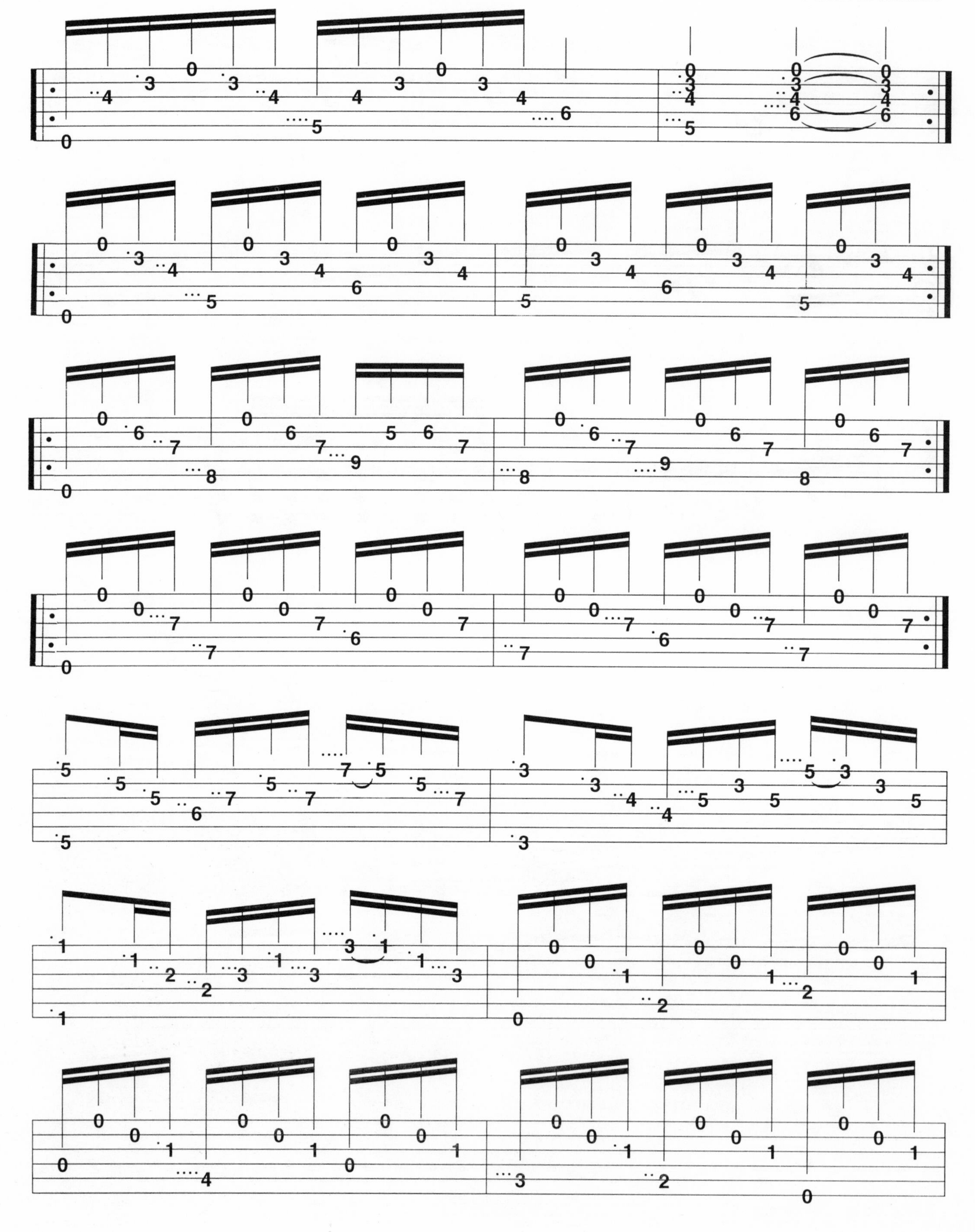

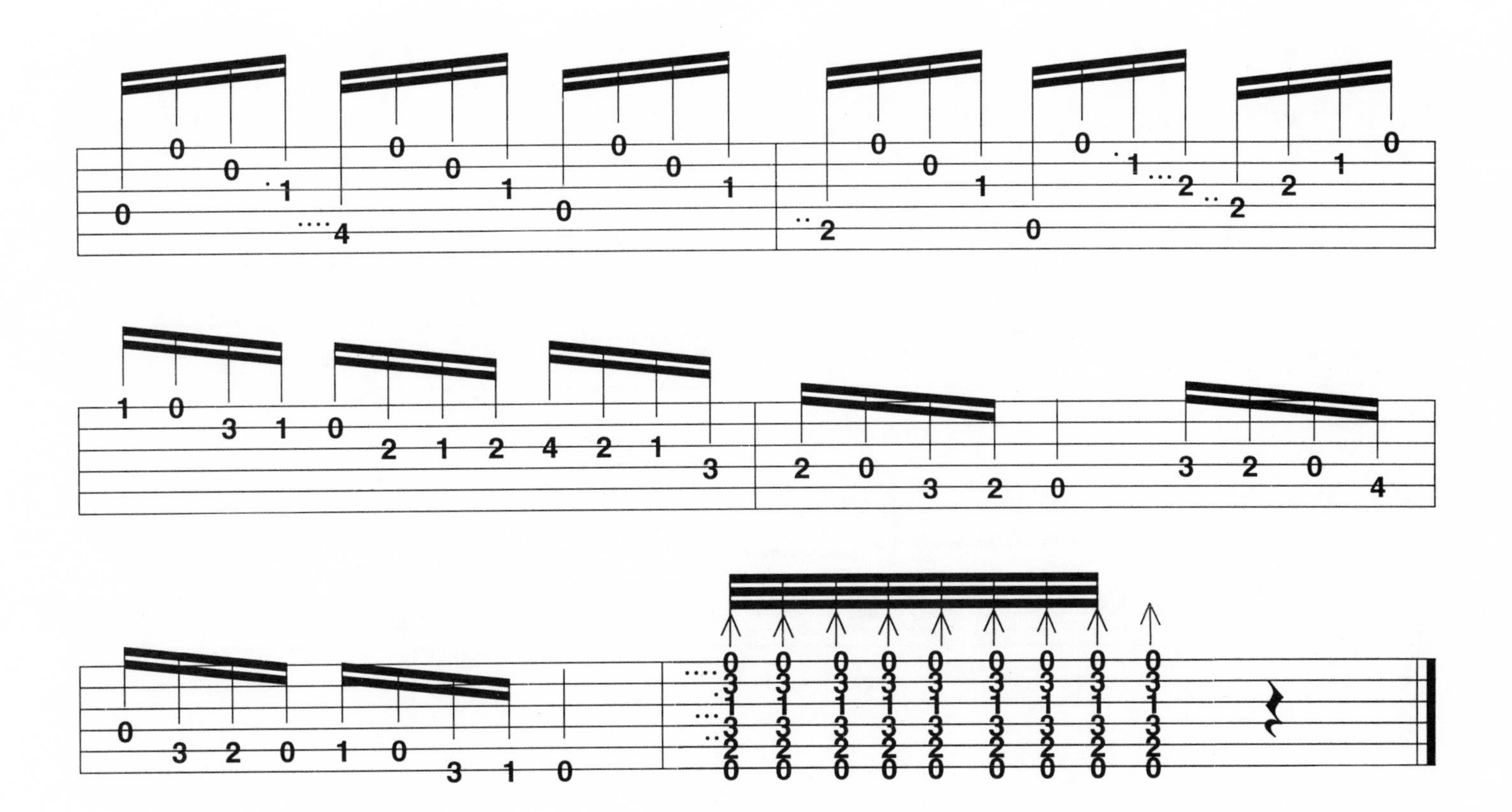

Falseta 8

Juan Serrano

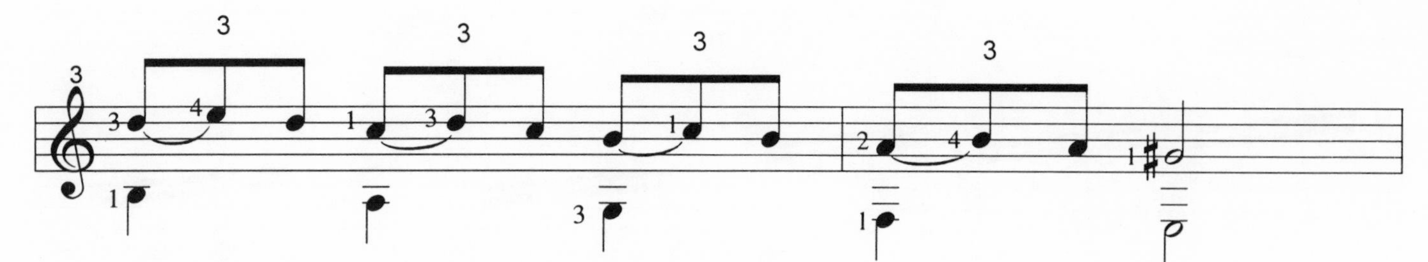
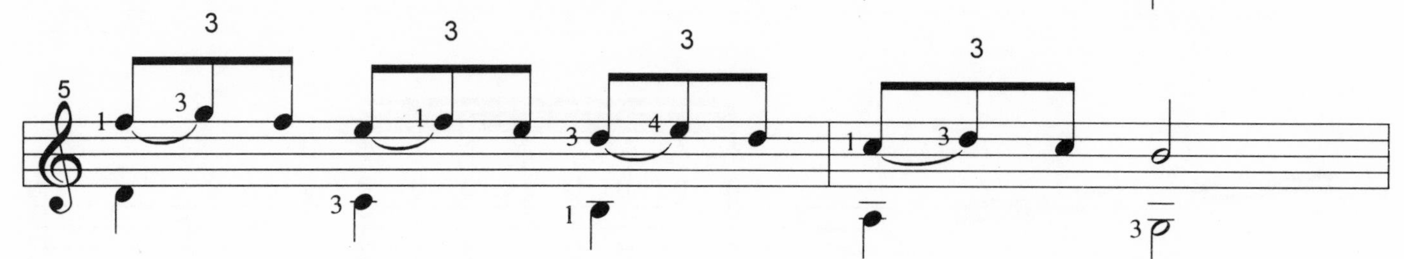

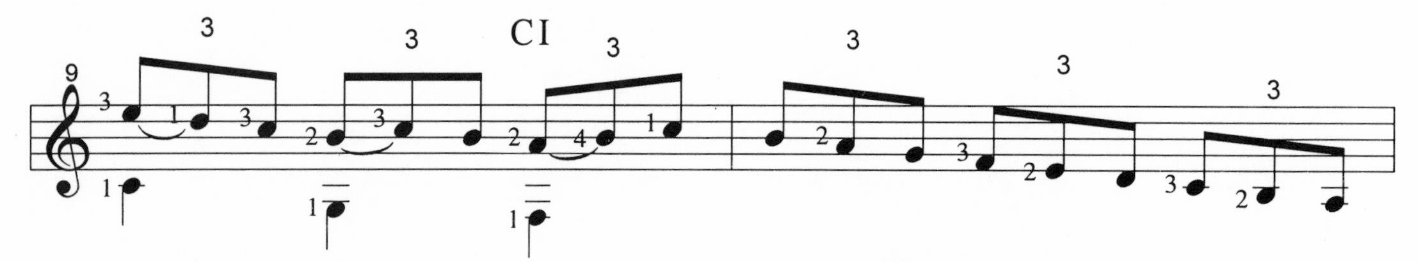

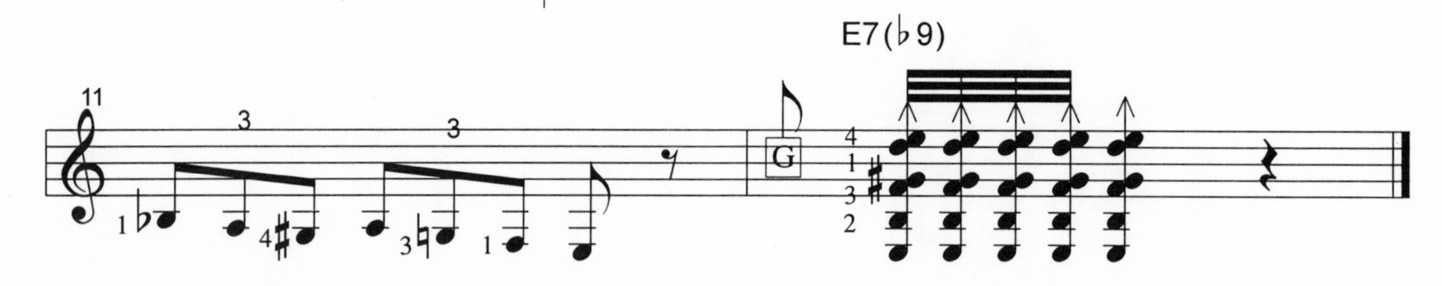

Falseta 8

Juan Serrano

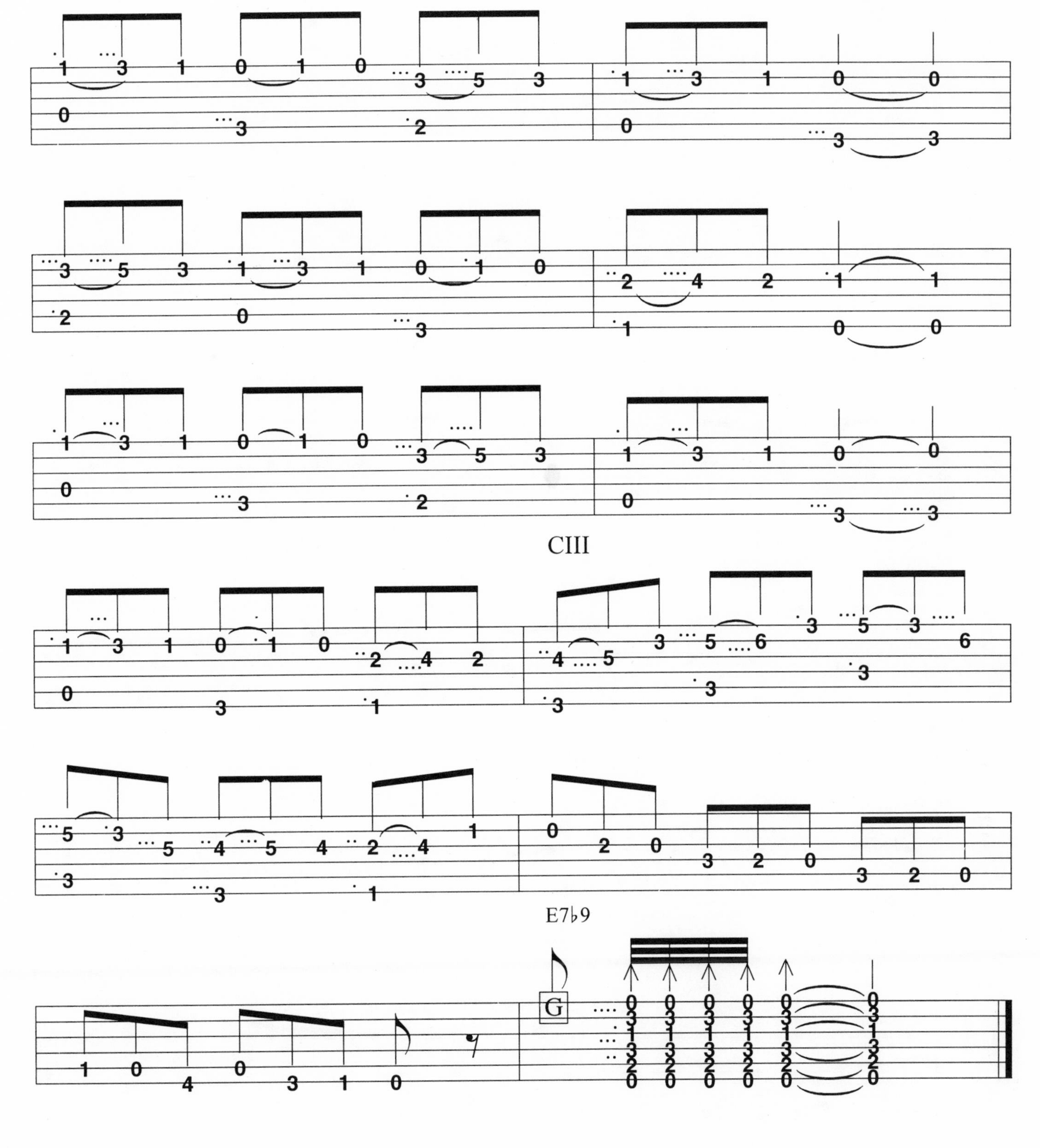

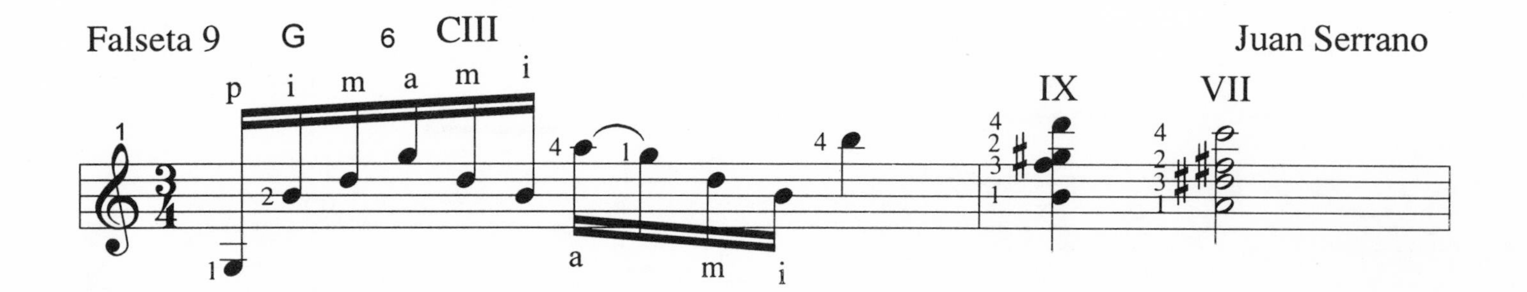
Falseta 9
G 6 CIII
Juan Serrano
p i m a m i
IX
VII
a m i

III

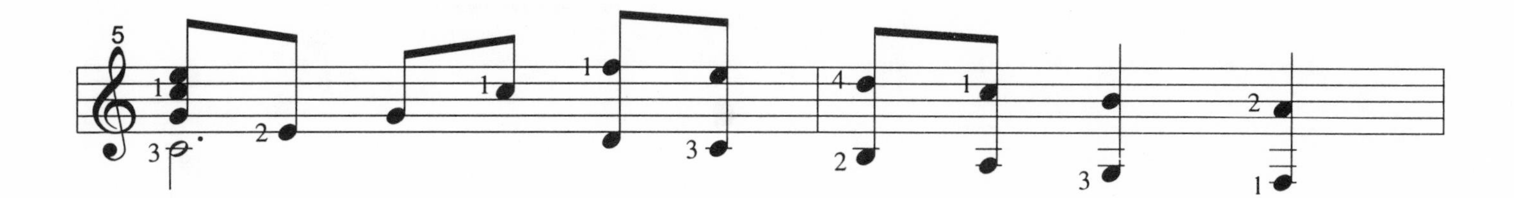

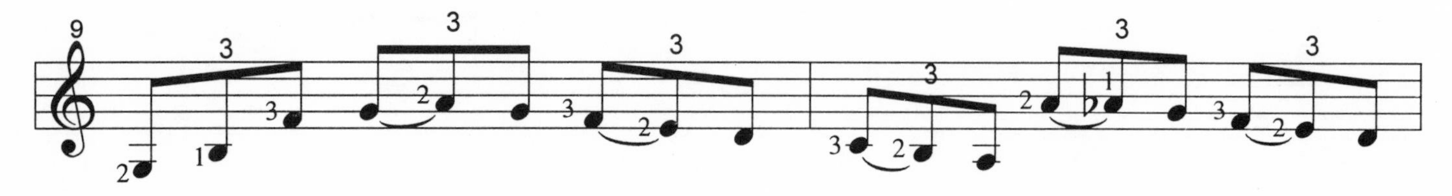

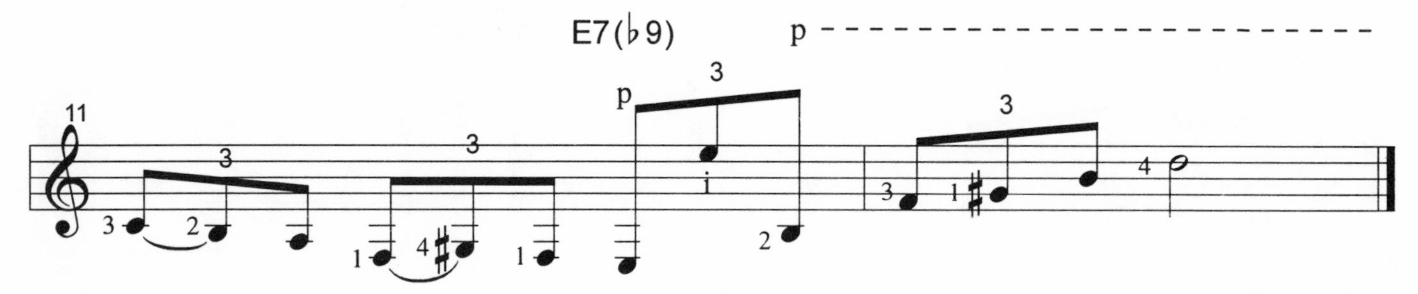
E7(♭9)
p
p
i

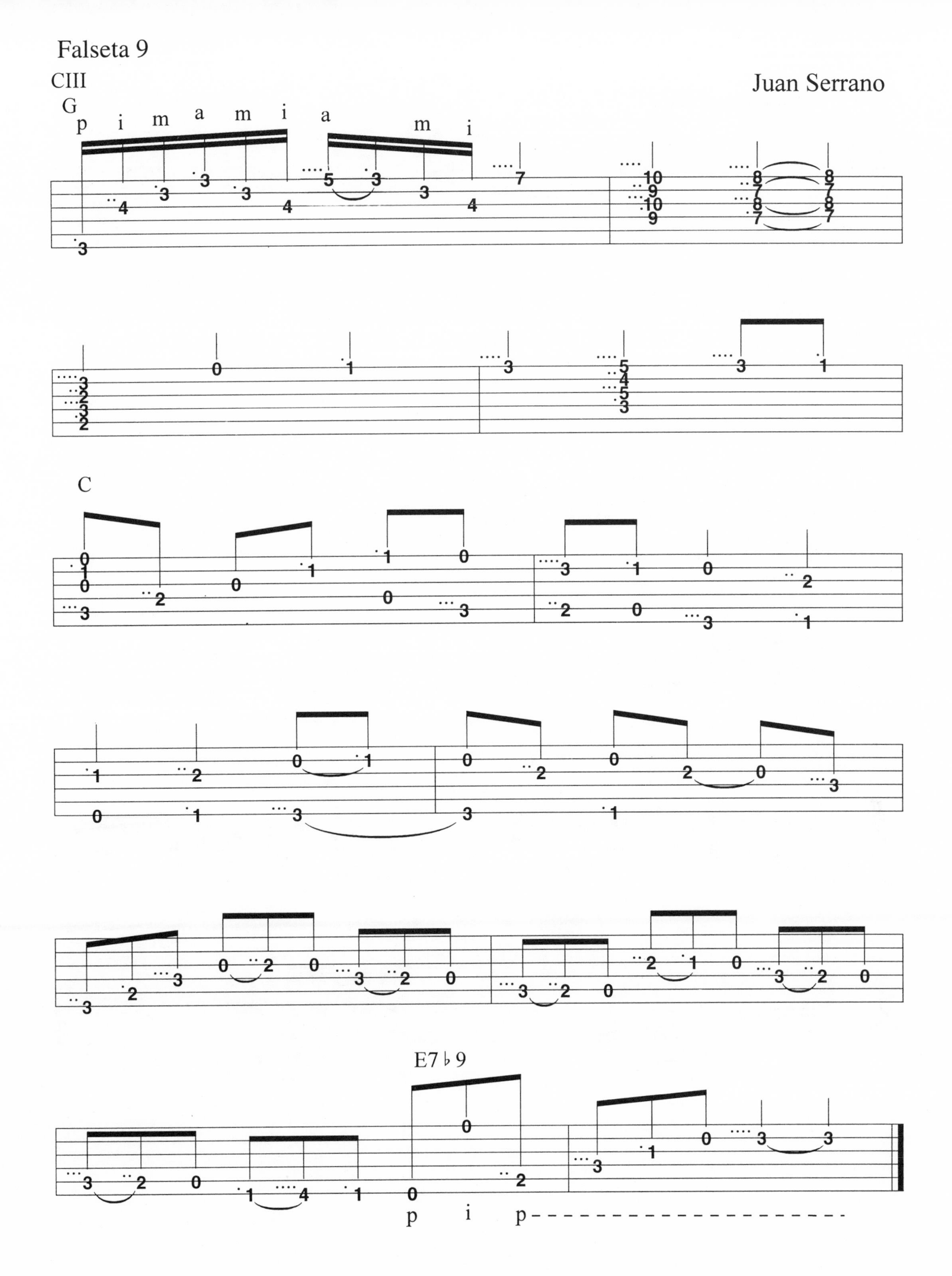
Falseta 9
CIII
Juan Serrano
G
p i m a m i a m i
C
E7♭9
p i p

Falseta 10 | Juan Serrano

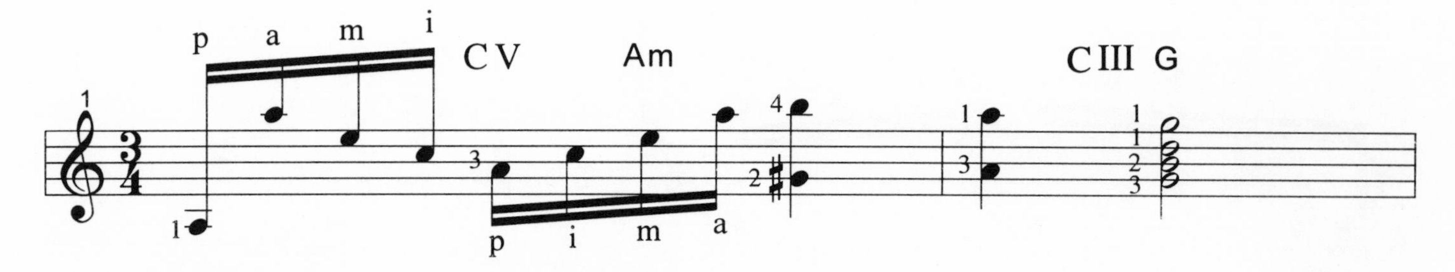

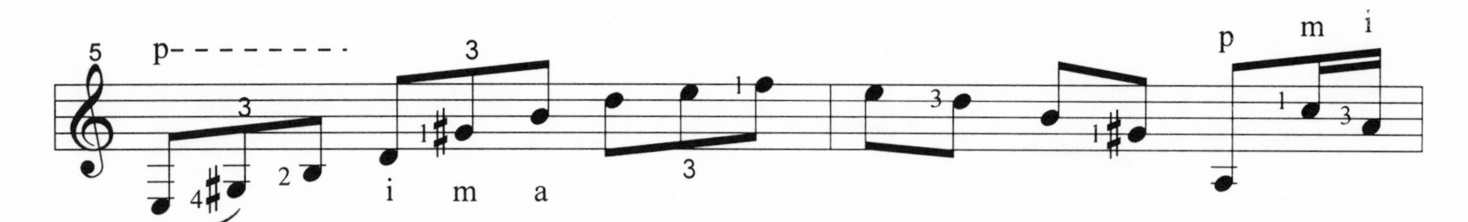

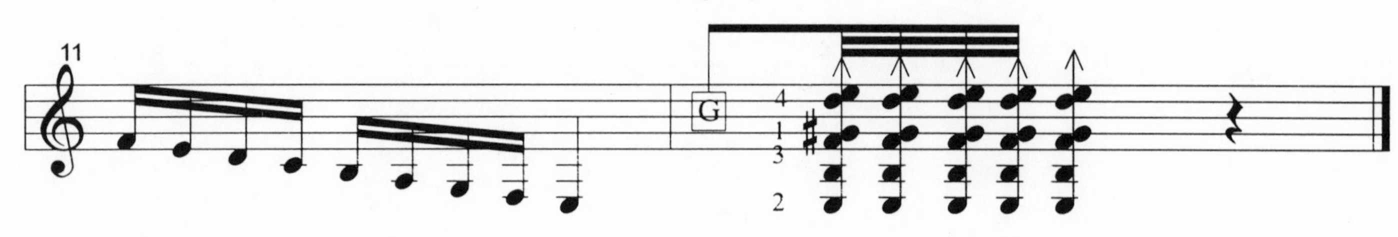

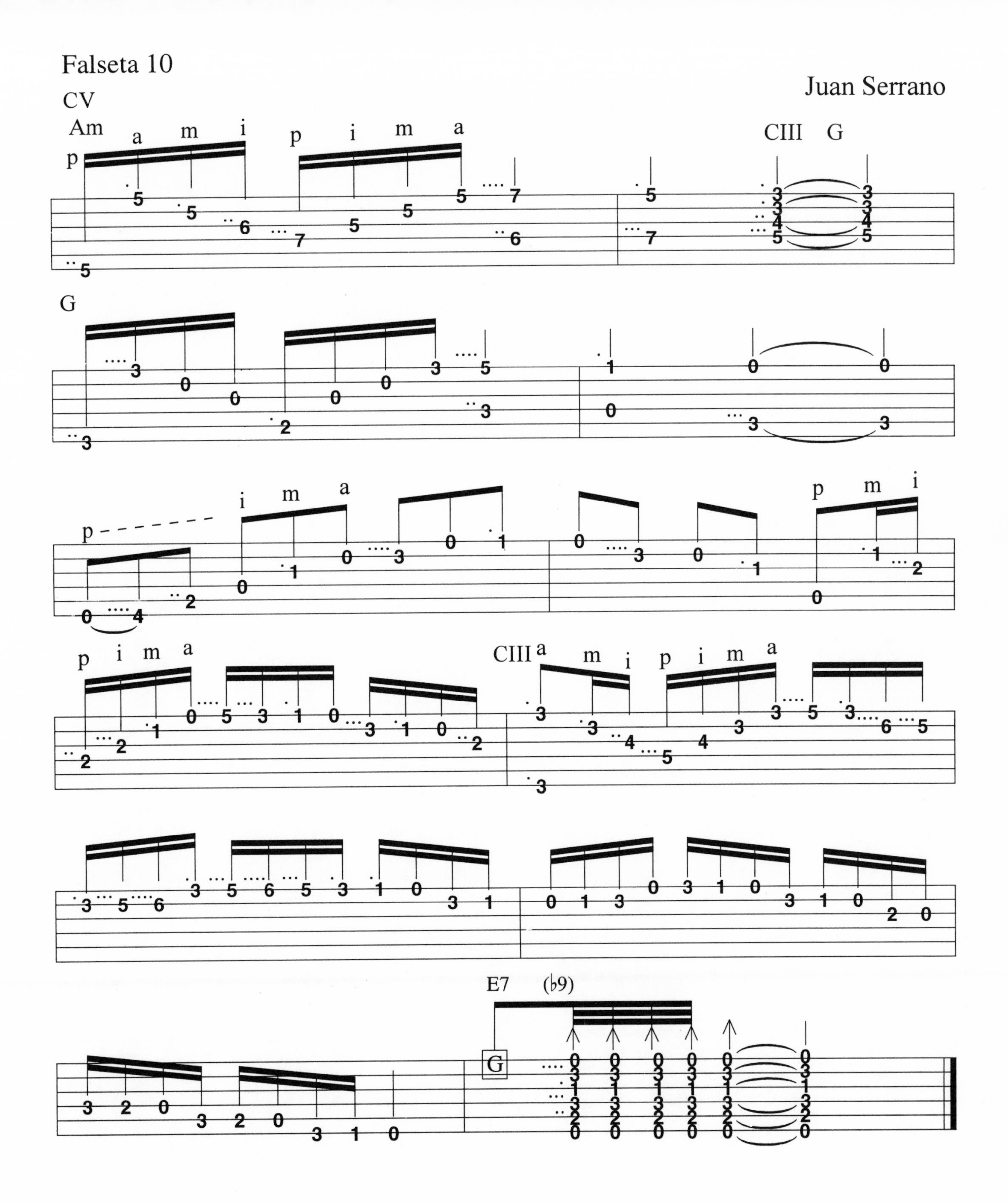
Falseta 10
Juan Serrano
CV
Am
CIII G
G
CIII
E7 (♭9)
G

# FARRUCAS

The Farrucas originated in Galicia. They adapted the Andalucian customs and added the flamenco form. The Farruca falsetas are written in a progressive form, in technique and difficulty, to help in learning them. Once they are mastered, the order can be interchanged.

The Farrucas are played in the key of A minor and are measured in 4/4 time. A flamenco compás consists of 8 beats equivalent to 2 musical measures of 4/4 time. Traditionally, for each 2 or 3 compases that were played, one falseta was inserted. This was due to the form of accompanying the dance and it always predominated the rhythm.

Today, the manner of arranging the flamenco compositions has changed. The modern way of arranging consists of playing several falsetas without rhythmical interruption. The compás is played only at the end of the falsetas group, to add more emotion and to make it more spectacular. In this way, the melody dominates the composition.

Falseta #1 is not difficult and it is easy to memorize the melody. It is recommended that measure #5 be practiced separately until it is perfected. Once the bases of the melody are included, it will be technically more difficult.

In falseta #2, all of the notes of the arpeggios are played freestroke, with the exception of the notes that are played with the anular (a) finger. These are played reststroke. Also, the picado that ends the falseta is played reststroke. It begins measure #11.

Falseta #3 included the tremolo technique. The entire falseta should be played freestroke with the exception of the last two measures #14 and 15 where the notes of the melody (i,m) should be played reststroke and the notes of the bases (p) are freestroke.

Falseta #4 alternates the melody with the rasgueado. This technique is extremely difficult to perfect. Thus, it is recommended that it be practiced slowly, until it is mastered. It is also recommended that special attention be paid to the syncopation of measure #13.

The recommendations for the remaining Farruca falsetas are to follow the fingering of both hands.

# FARRUCAS

Las Farrucas son de procedencia Gallega. Se adaptaron a las costumbres Andaluzas y se agregaron a las formas flamencas. El orden de todas las falsetas está escrito en una forma progresiva, de técnica y dificultad, para facilitar el aprendizaje. Una vez que se aprenden todas las falsetas, el orden puede ser cambiado a capricho del intérprete.

Las Farrucas se tocan en el tono de La menor y se miden en 4/4. Un compás flamenco consiste en ocho tiempos equivalentes a dos compases musicales de 4/4. Tradicionalmente, por cada dos o tres compases rítmicos que se tocaban, se intercalaba una falseta, porque esa era la forma de acompañar al baile y siempre tenía que predominar el ritmo.

En nuestros días ha cambiado la forma de preparar las composiciones flamencas. La forma moderna de preparar las composiciones flamencas consiste en tocar varias falsetas, sin interrupción del compás rítmico. Los compases rítmicos se tocan solamente al final de la composición, para darle más emoción y más espectacularidad. Así, lo que predomina durante las composiciones son las melodías.

La falseta #1 no es difícil, pero sin embargo, es muy bonita y fácil de aprender de memoria la melodía. Recomiendo que el compás musical #5 se practique por separado hasta que lo perfeccionen. Ya que al agregarle los bajos a la melodía se hace bastante más difícil la técnica.

En la falseta #2 todas las notas de los arpegios se tocan tirando, excepto las notas que se tocan con el dedo anular (a) que son todas apoyando. También, se toca apoyando el picado que finaliza la falseta que empieza en el compás musical #11.

La falseta #3 incluye la técnica del tremolo. Toda la falseta se debe de ejecutar tirando, excepto los dos últimos compases musicales, 14 y 15 que las notas de la melodía (i, m) se deben de tocar apoyando y las notas de los bajos, (p) se deben de tocar tirando.

La falseta #4 alterna la melodía con el rasgueado. Esta técnica es bastante difícil de perfeccionar. Por eso, recomiendo que se practique despacio hasta que se perfeccione. También recomiendo que se preste atención especial al contratiempo del compás musical #13.

La recomendación para el resto de las falsetas de las Farrucas es que sigan estrictamente las digitaciones de ambas manos.

# Farrucas

Traditional Compas

Juan Serrano

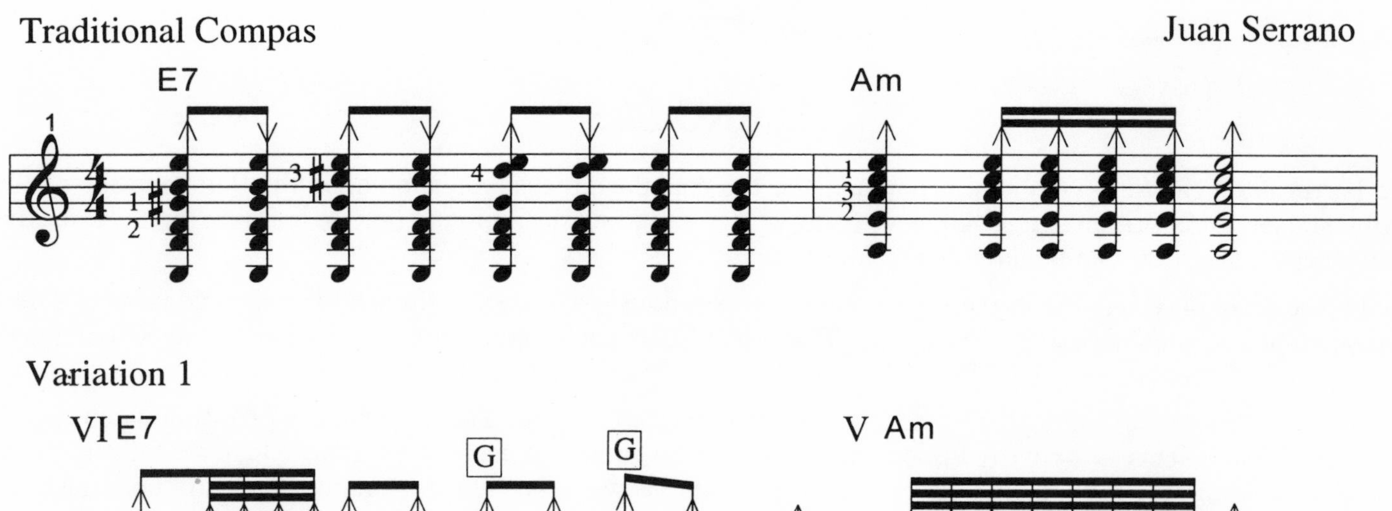


Variation 1

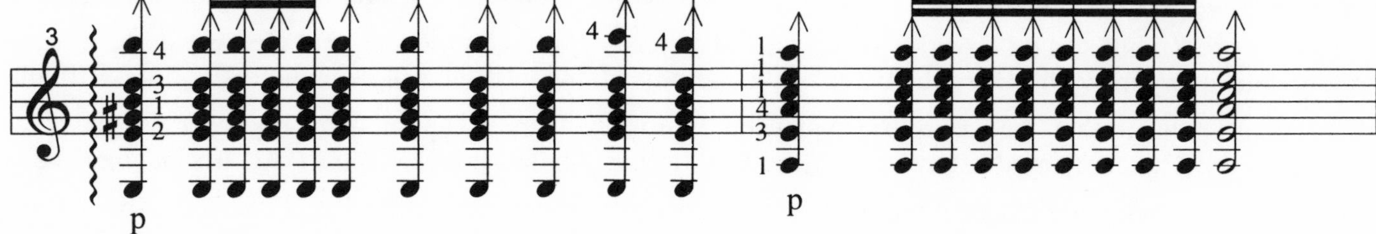


Variation 2 & 3

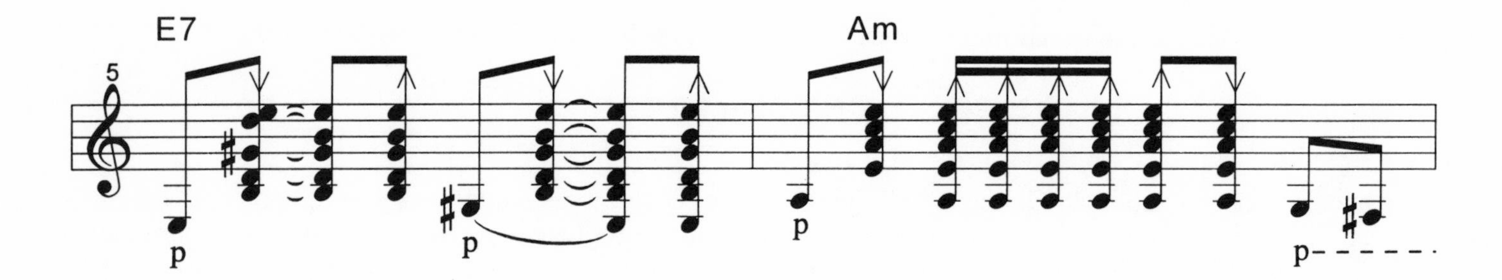


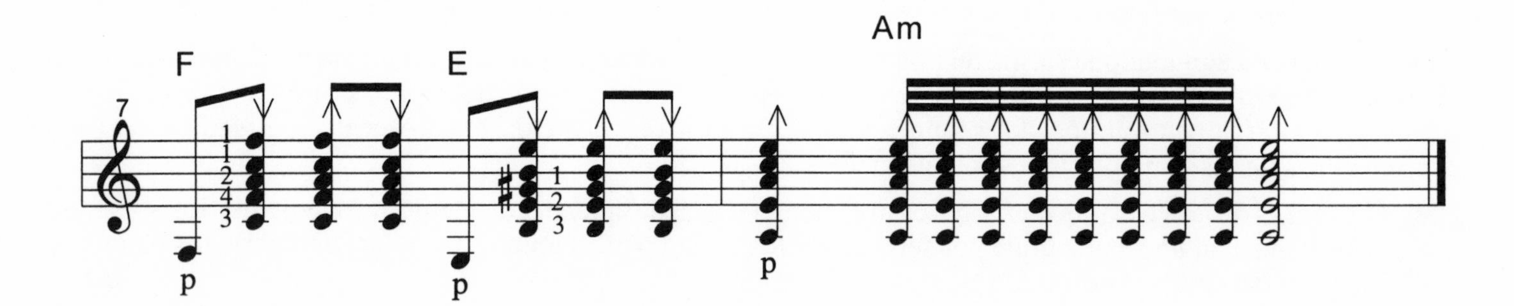

# Farrucas

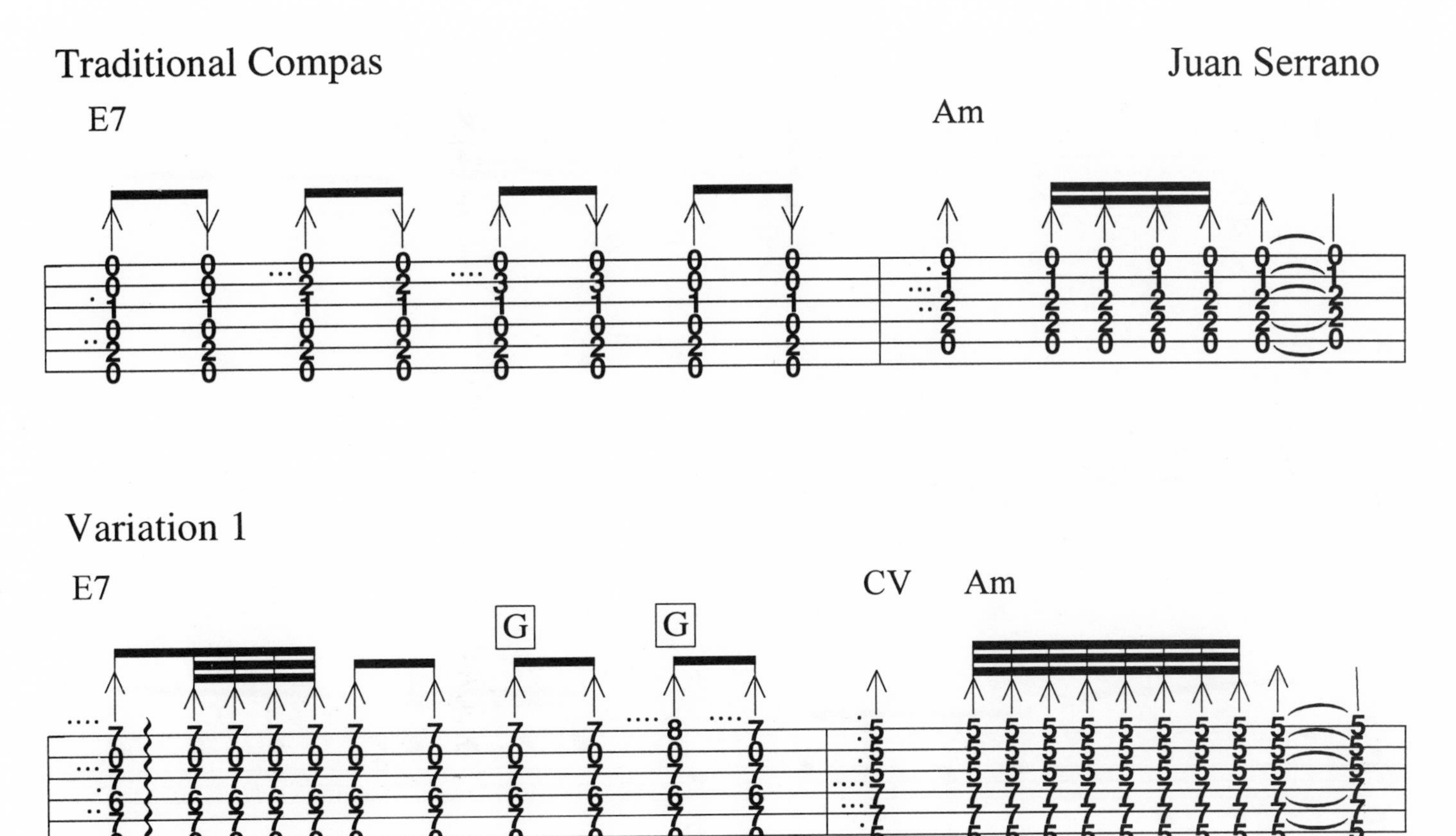


Variation 2 & 3

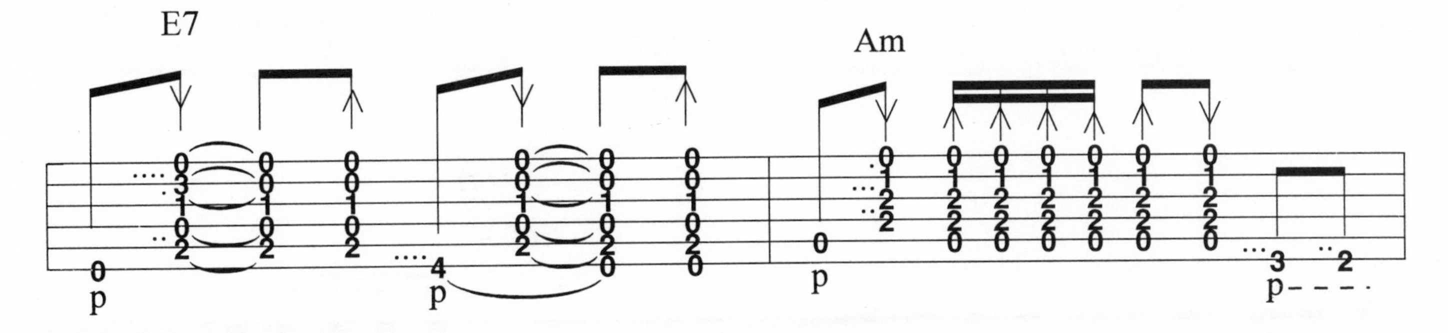


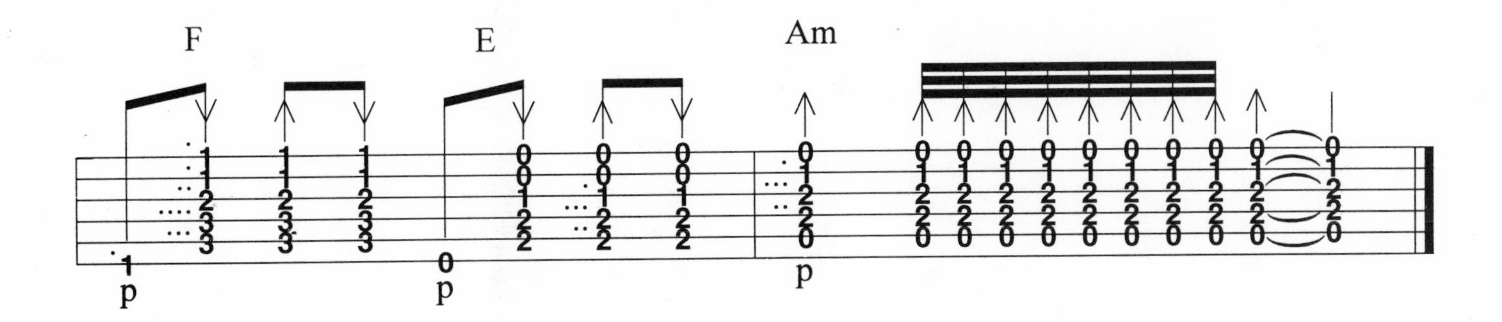

Falseta 1

Juan Serrano

E7 E7 Am

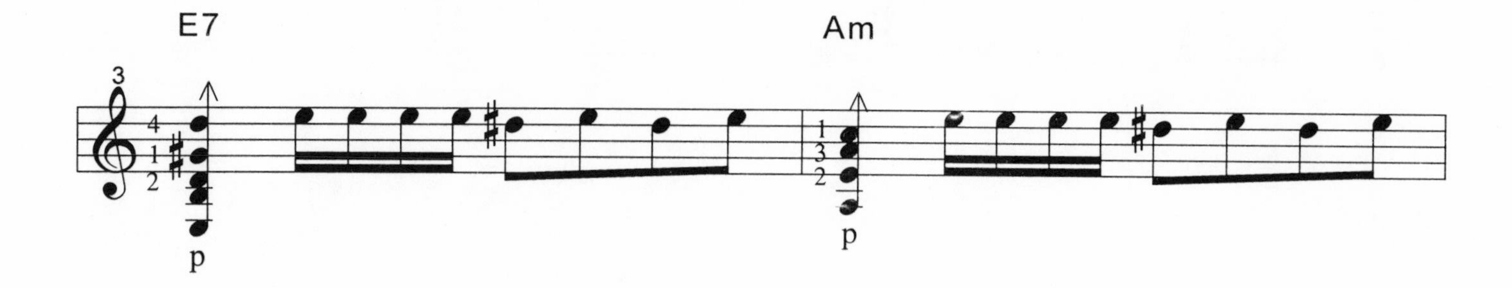


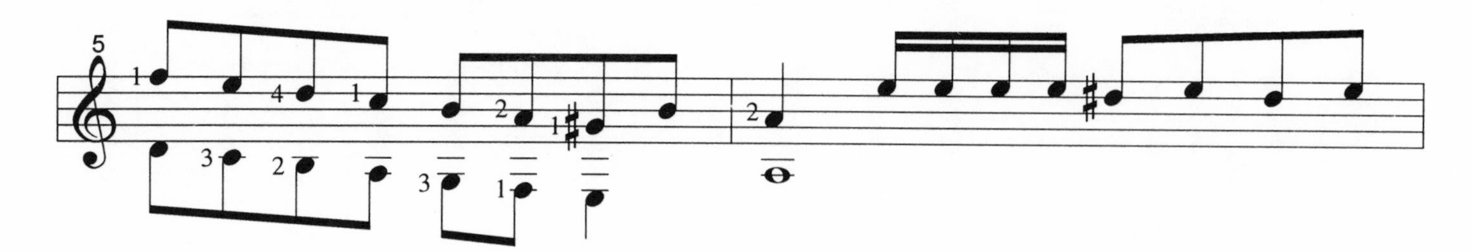

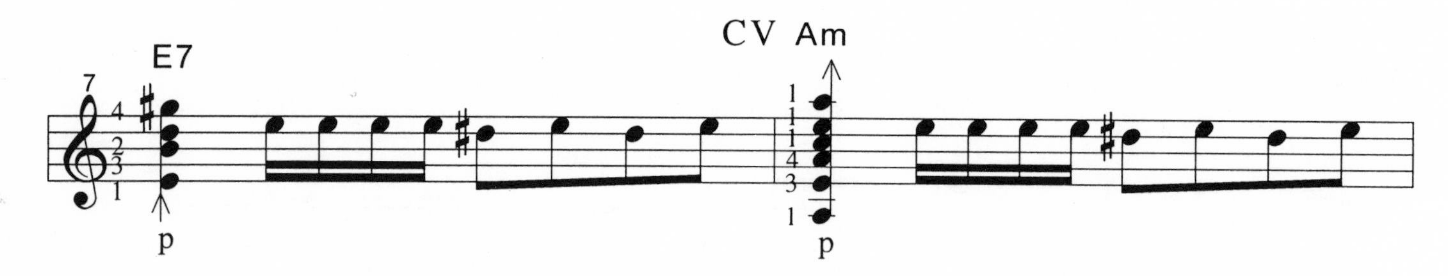

Falseta 1

Juan Serrano

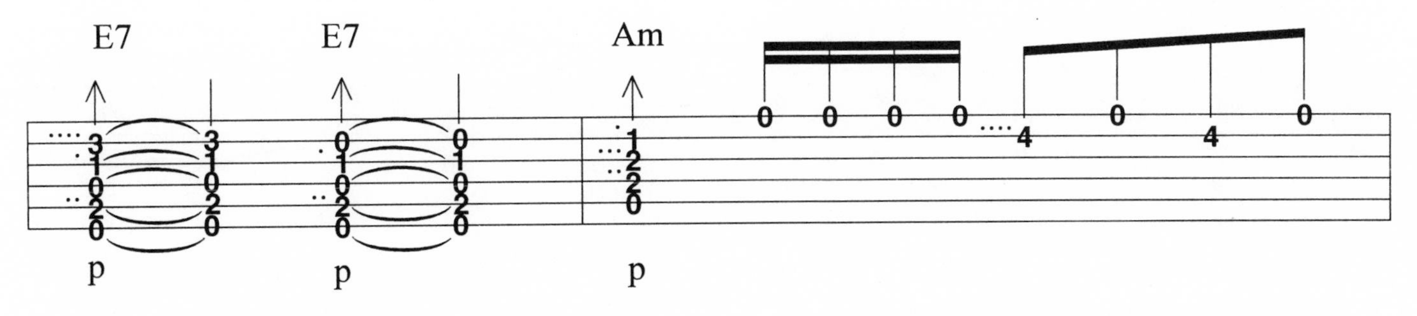


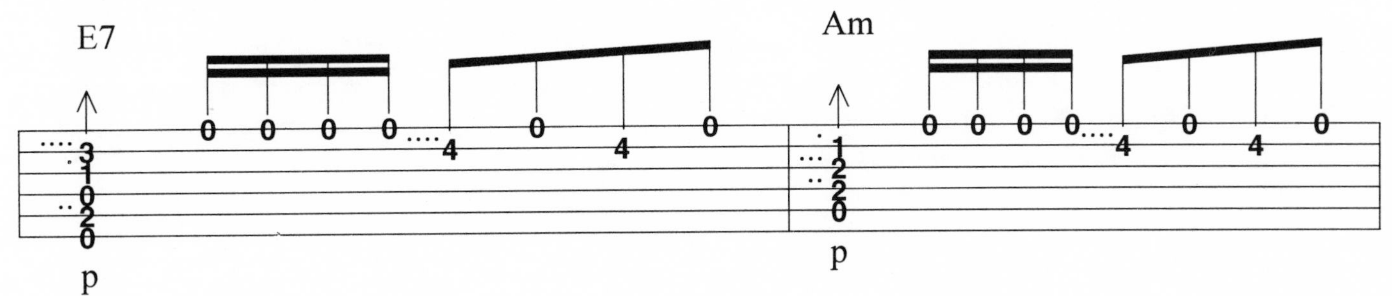


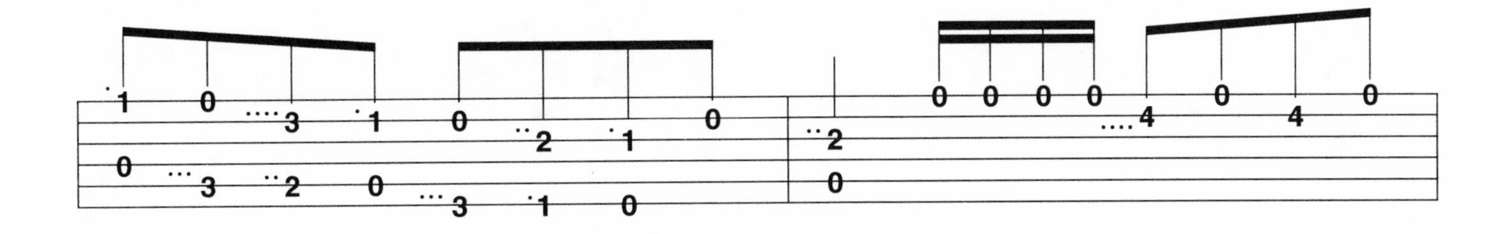

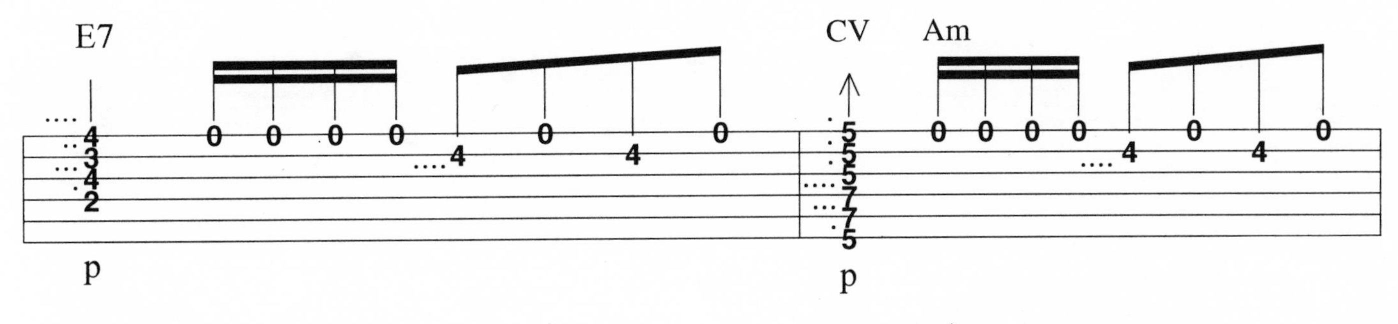


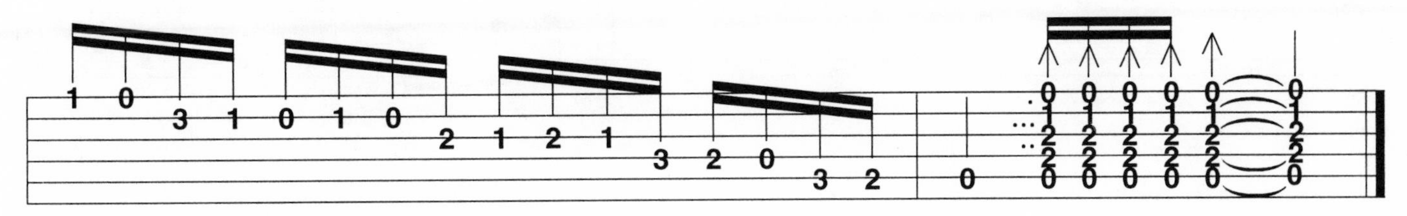

## Falseta 2

Juan Serrano

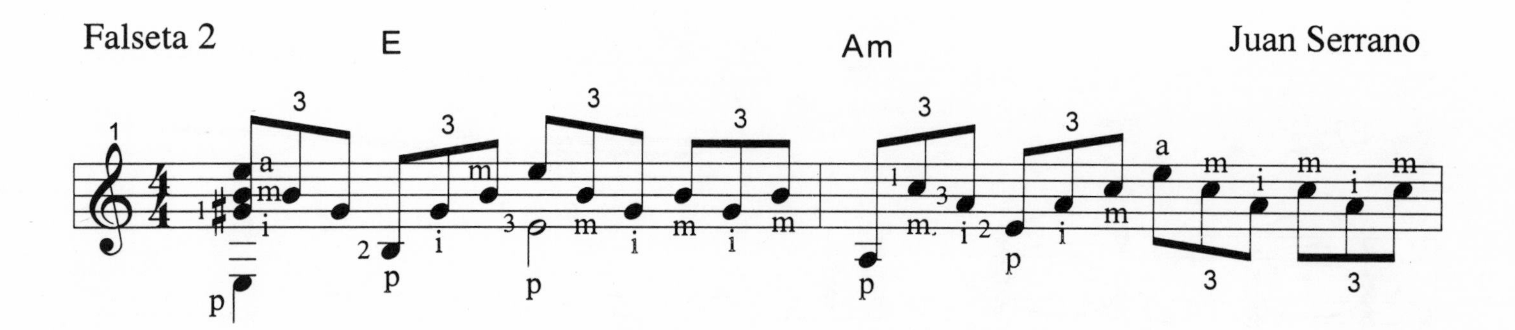


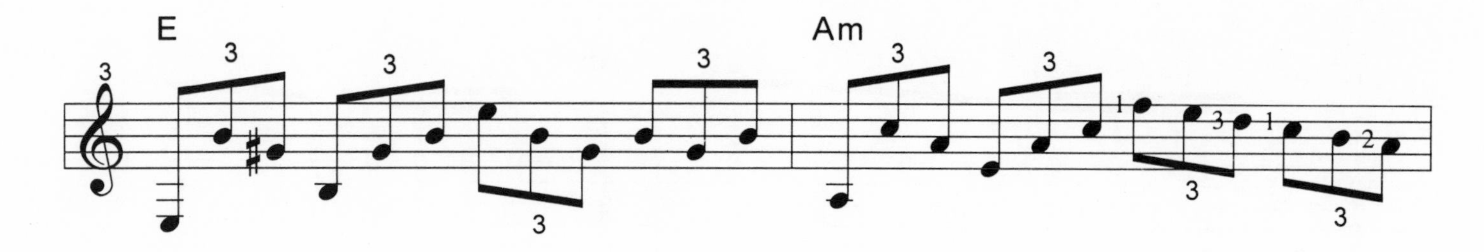


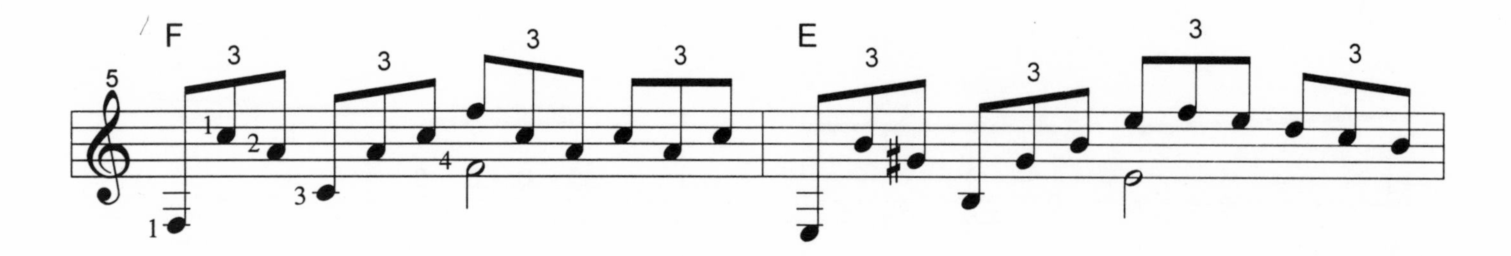


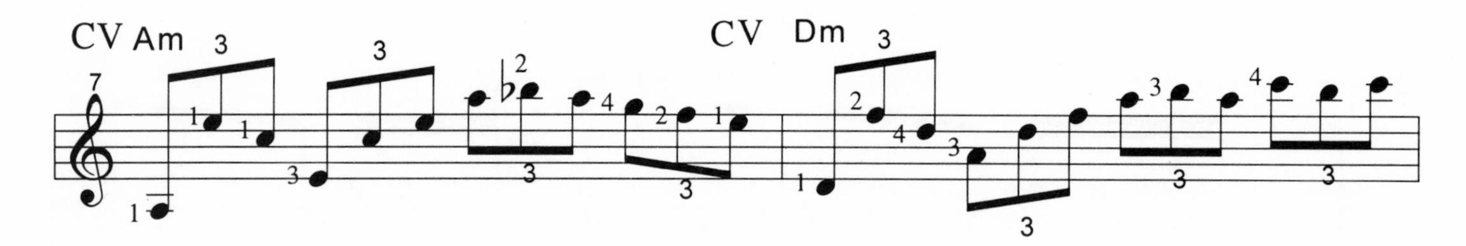


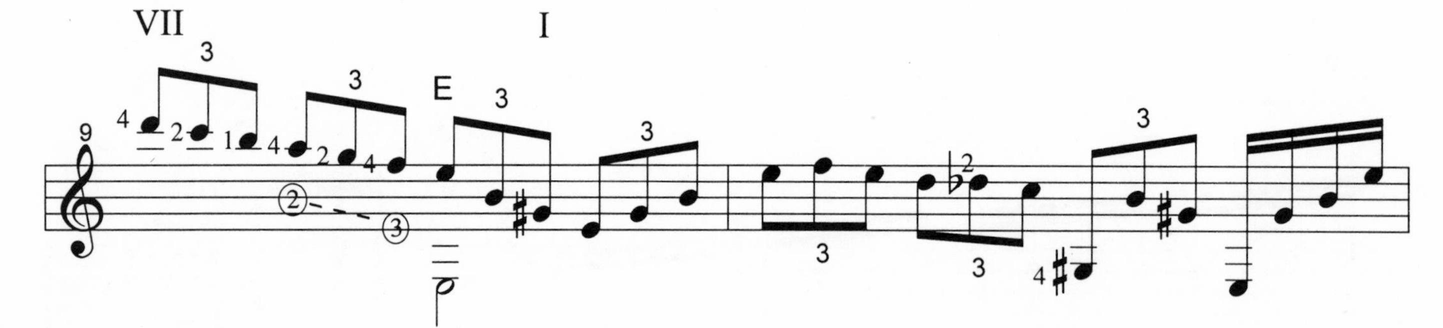

Falseta 2

Juan Serrano

E

a m i p i m a m i m i m

m i

p p

Am

p m i p i m a m i m i m

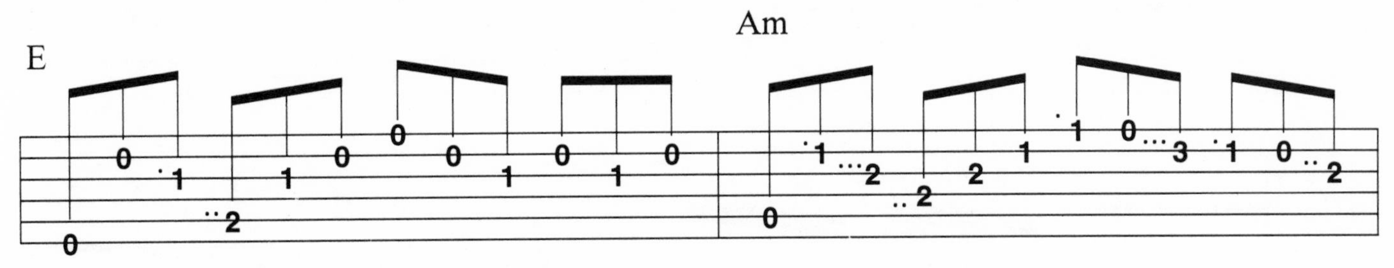


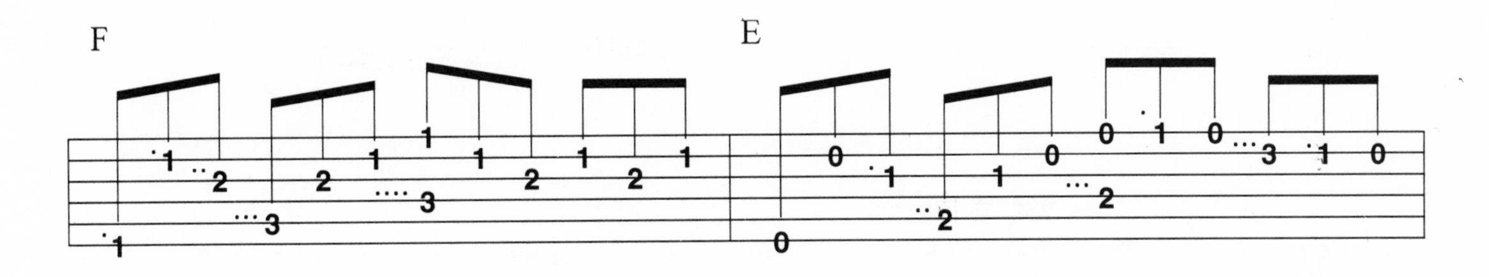


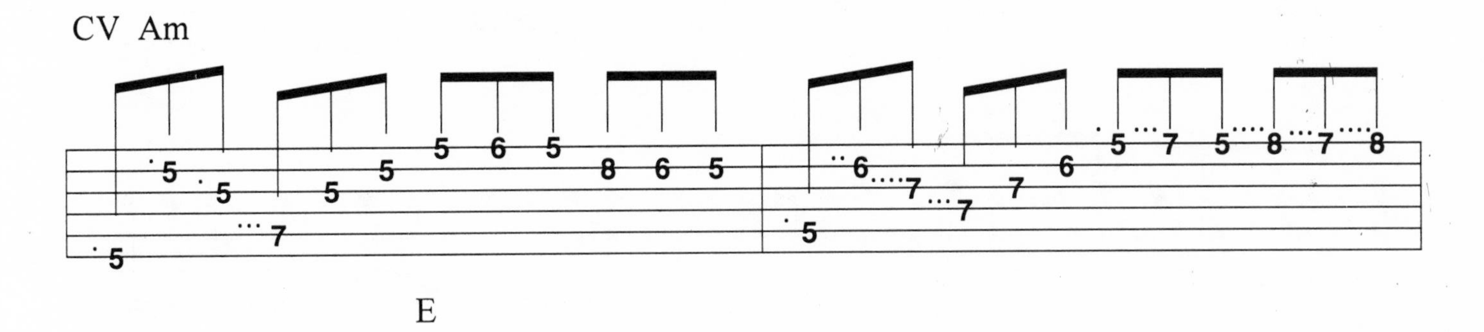


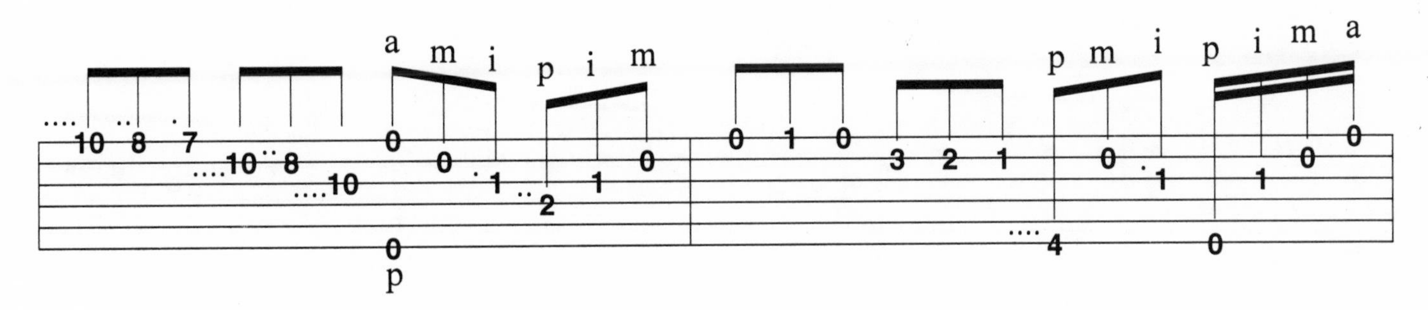


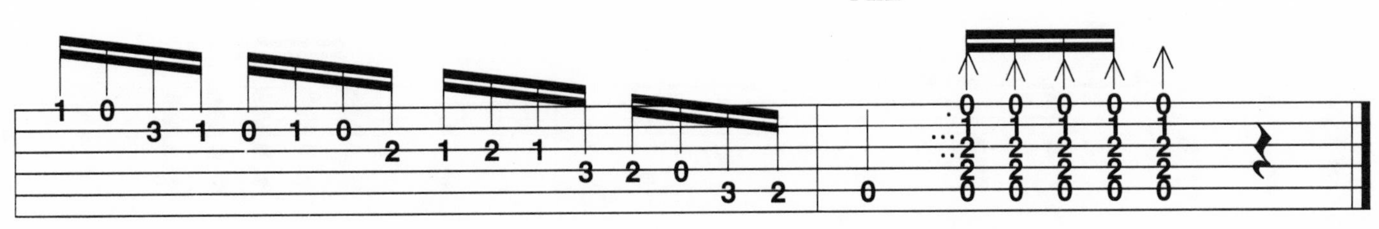

Falseta 3

Juan Serrano

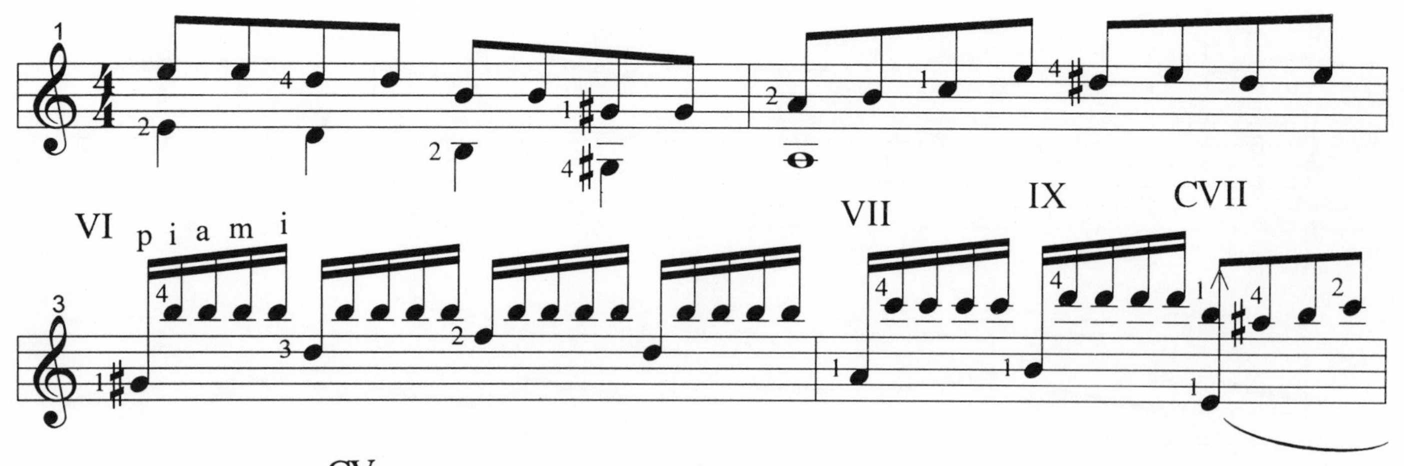


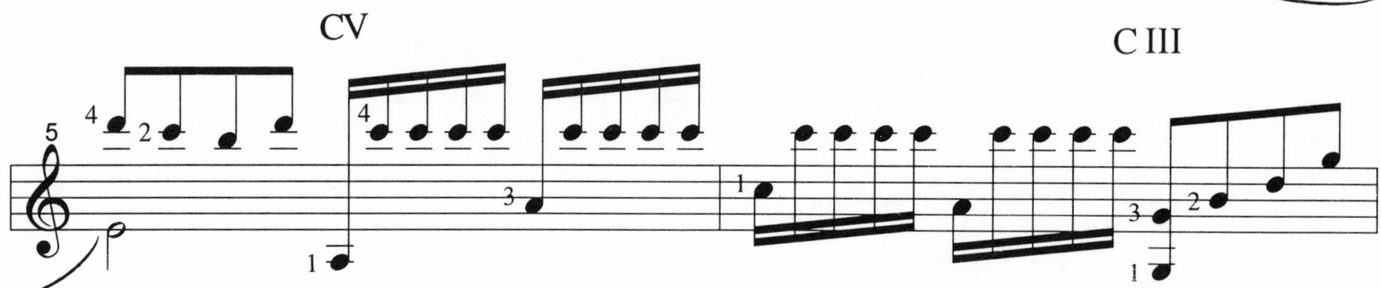


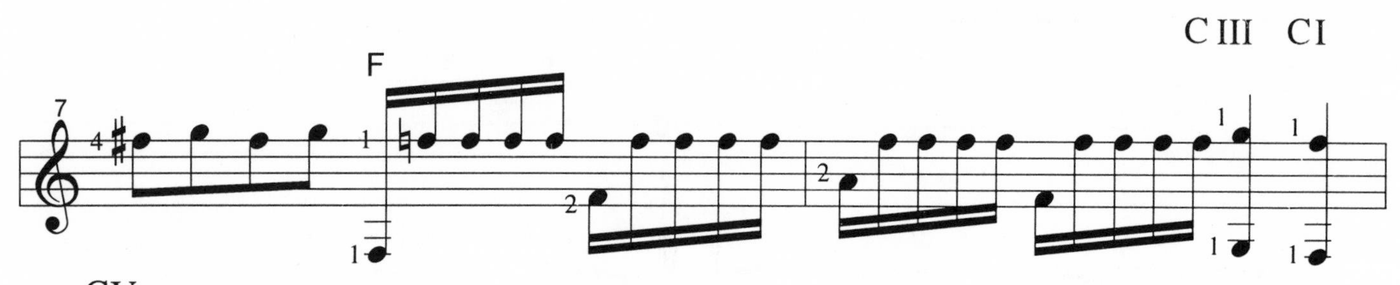

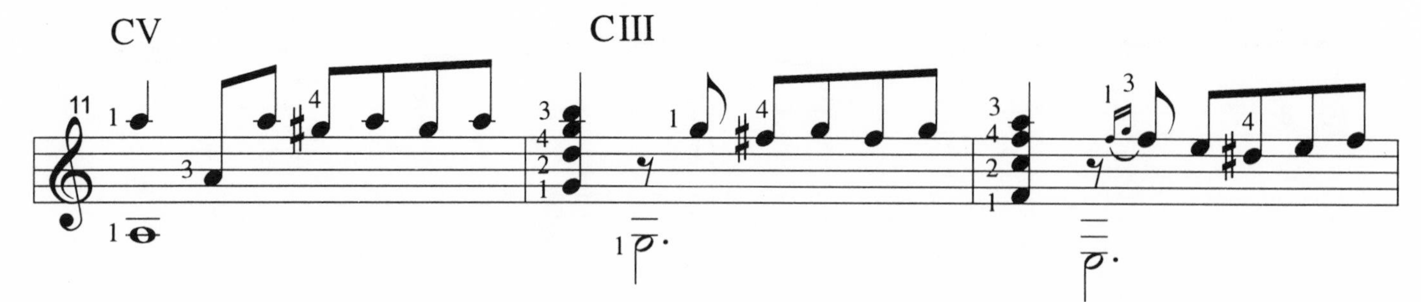

Falseta 3

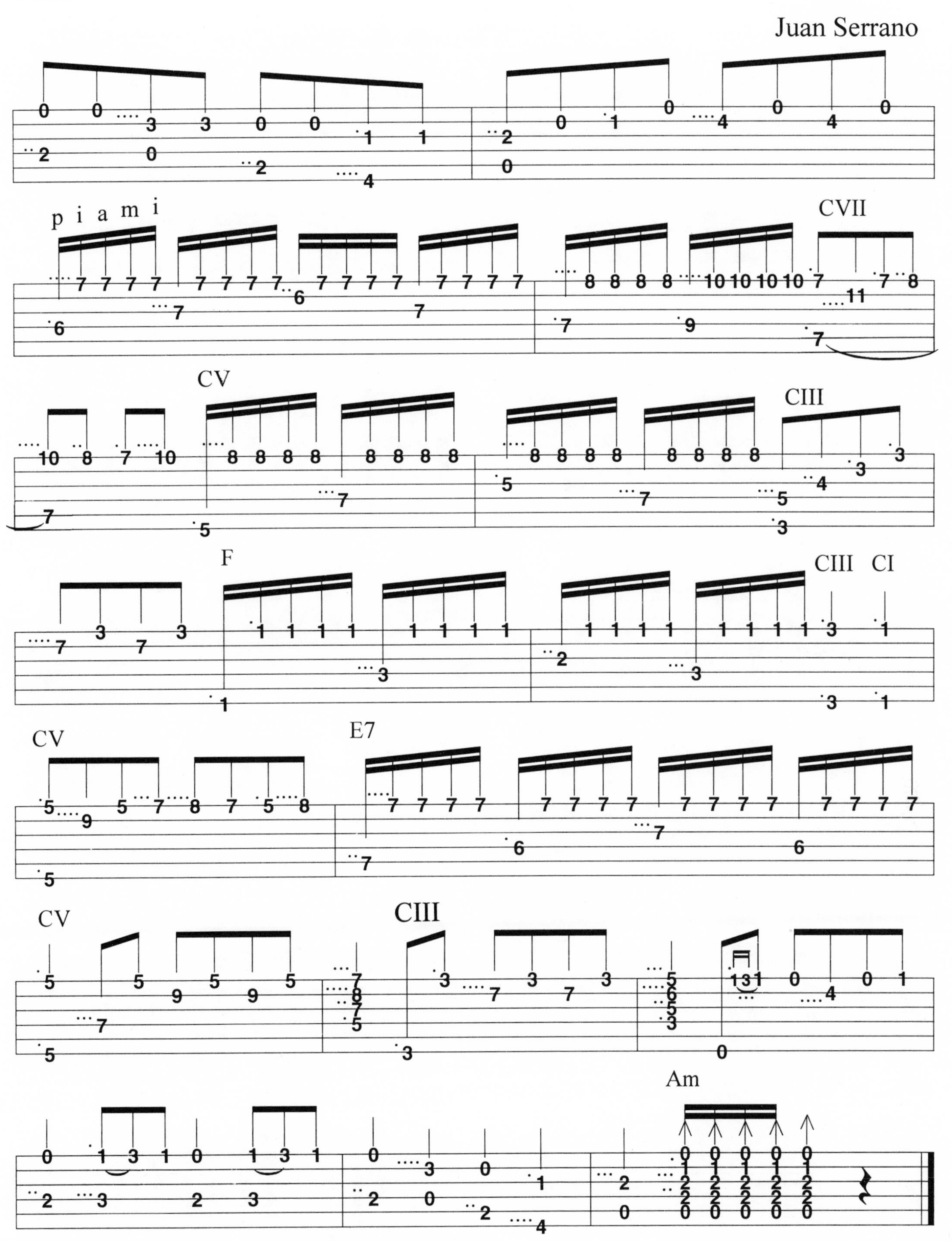

Falseta 4

Juan Serrano

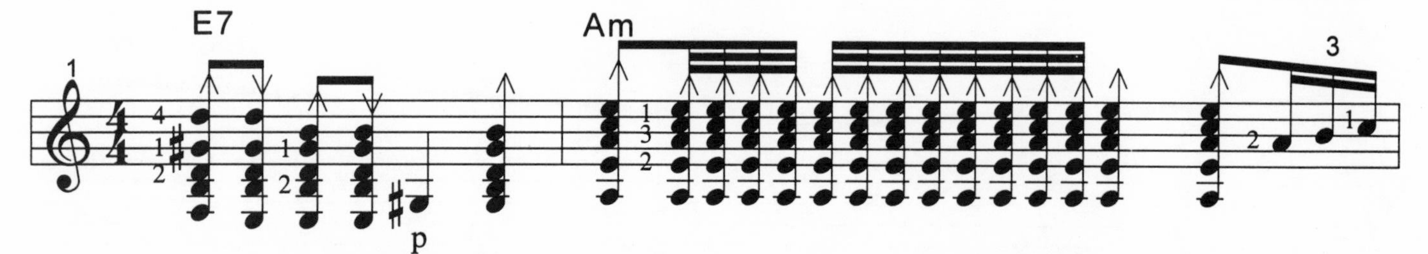

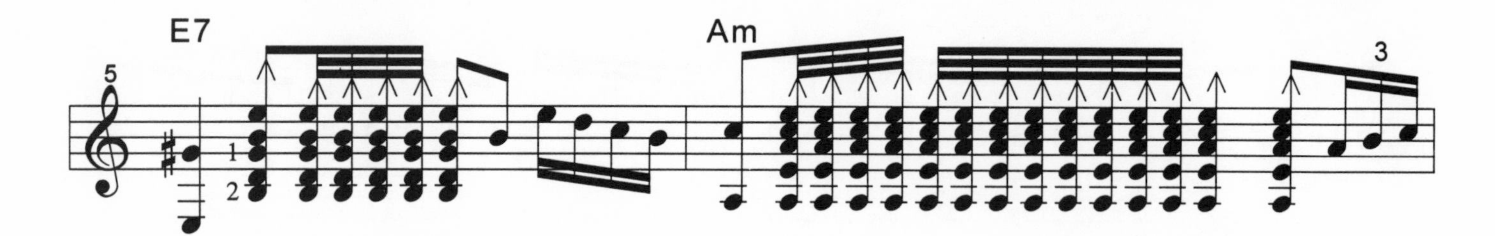

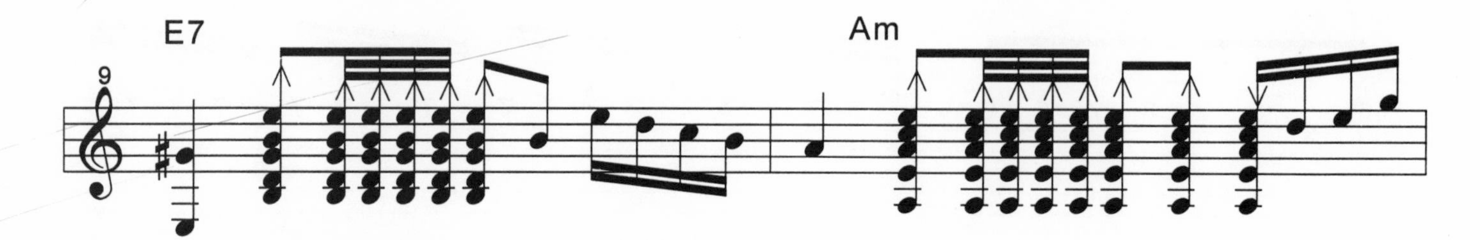


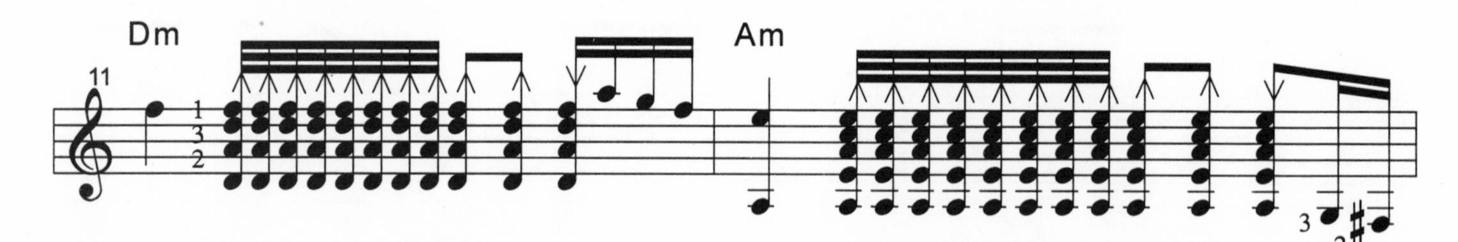

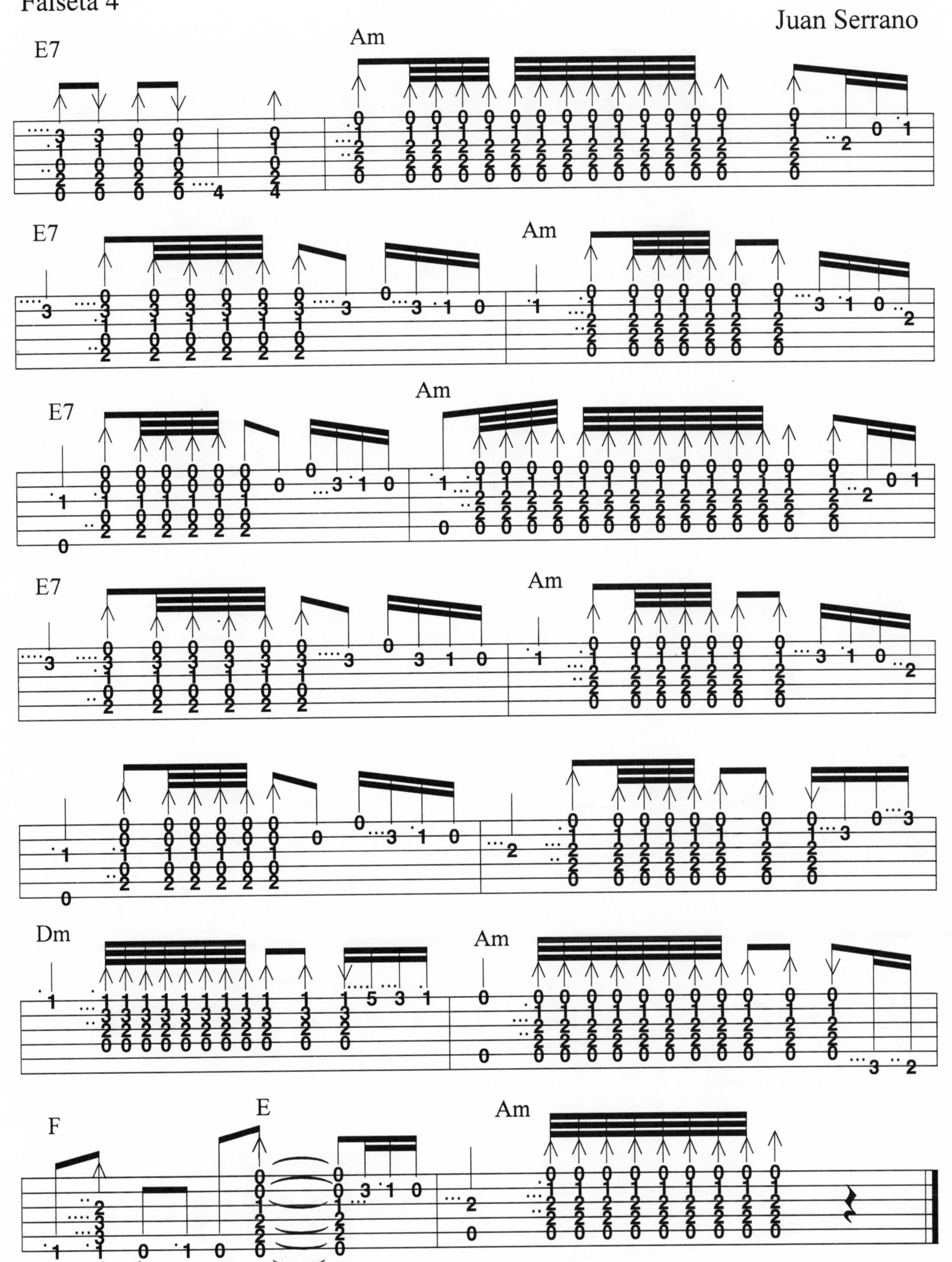
Falseta 4
Juan Serrano
E7
Am
E7
Am
E7
Am
E7
Am
Dm
Am
F
E
Am

Falseta 5

Juan Serrano

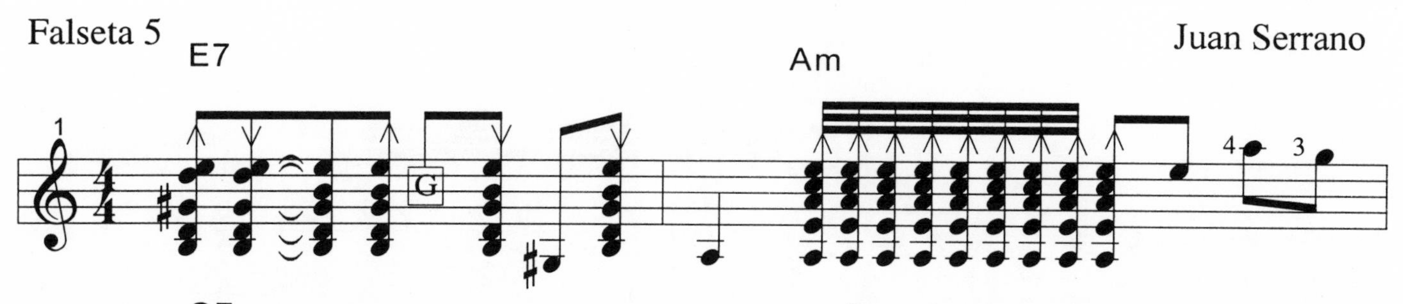


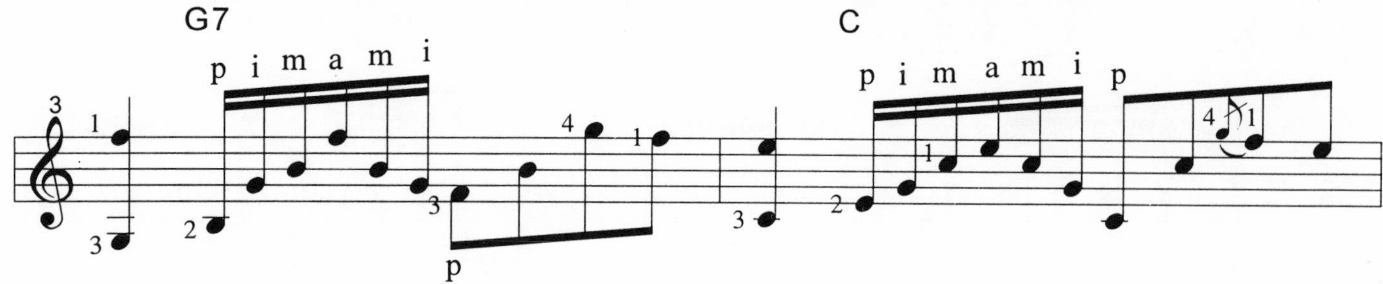


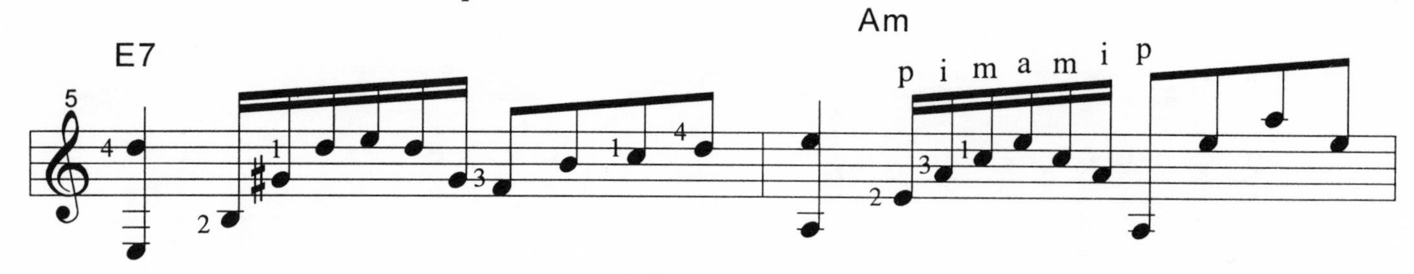

Falseta 5

Juan Serrano

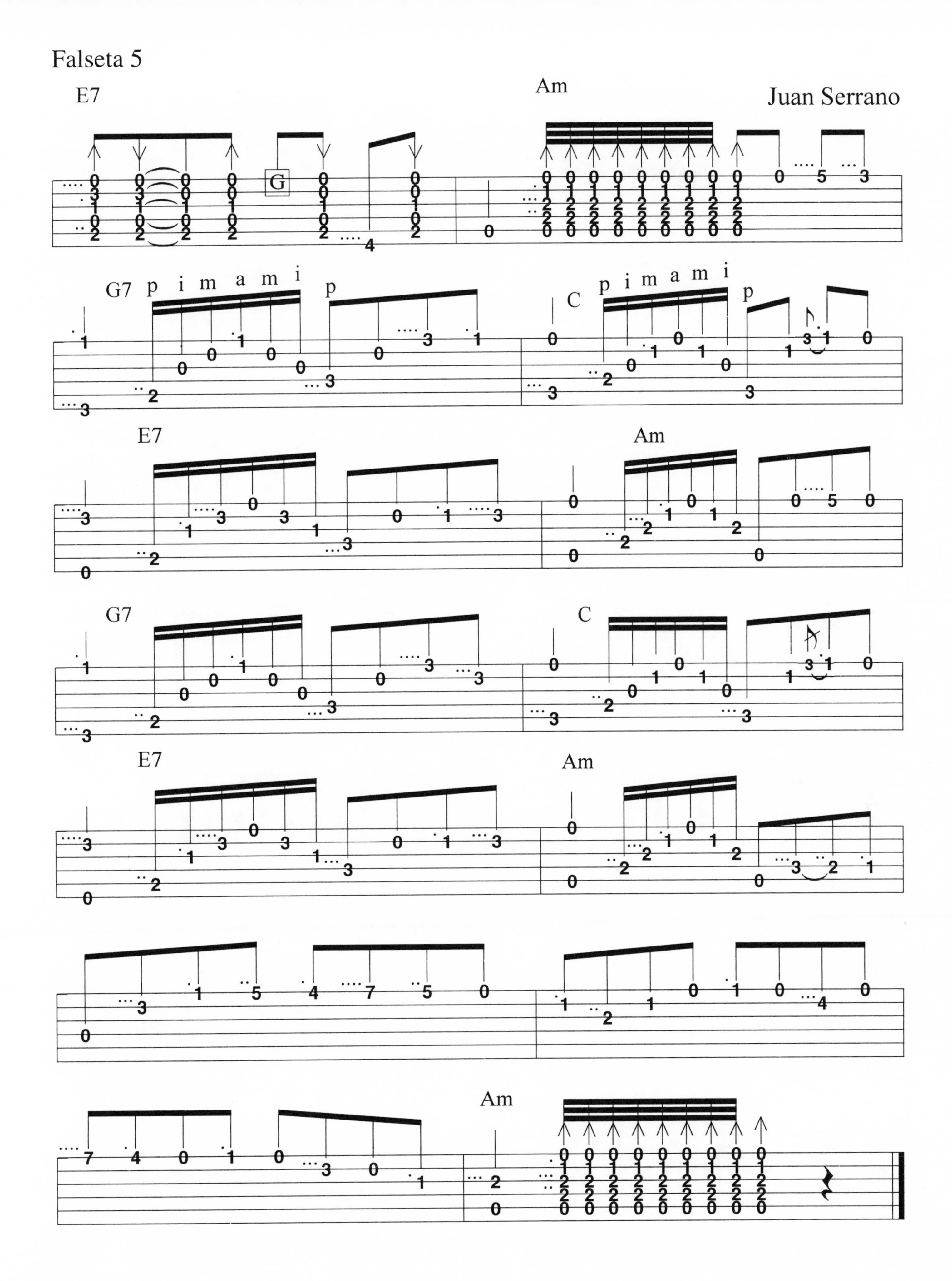

## Falseta 6

Juan Serrano

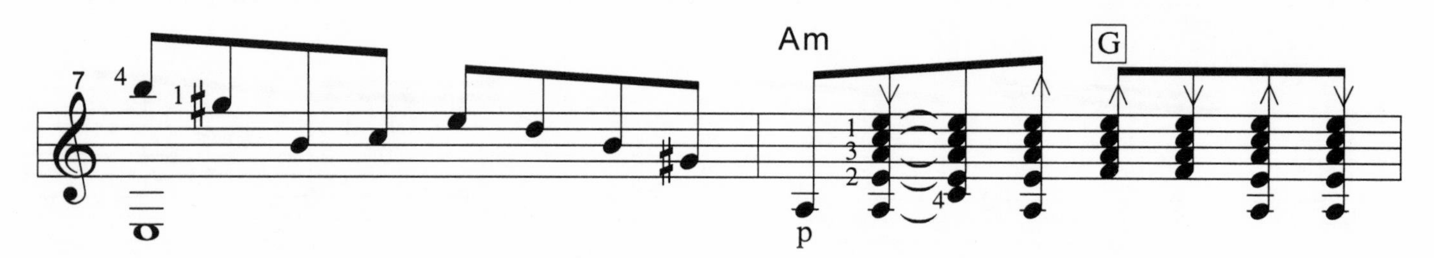


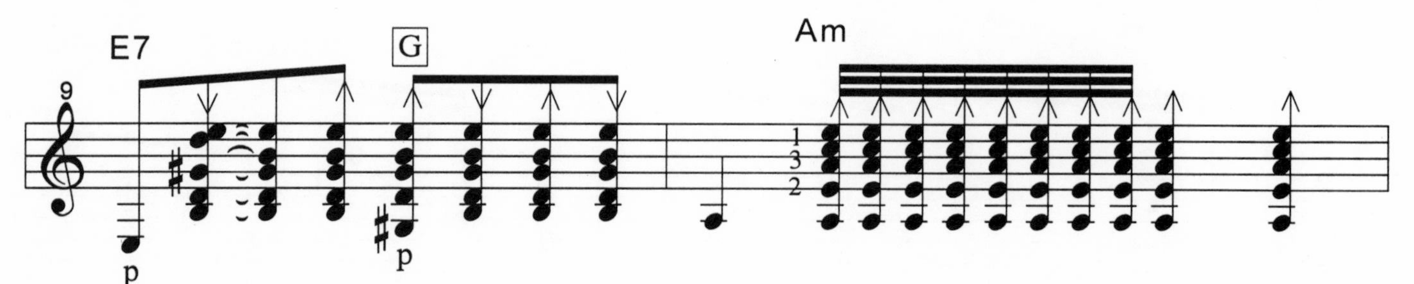

19
E7 VI
p

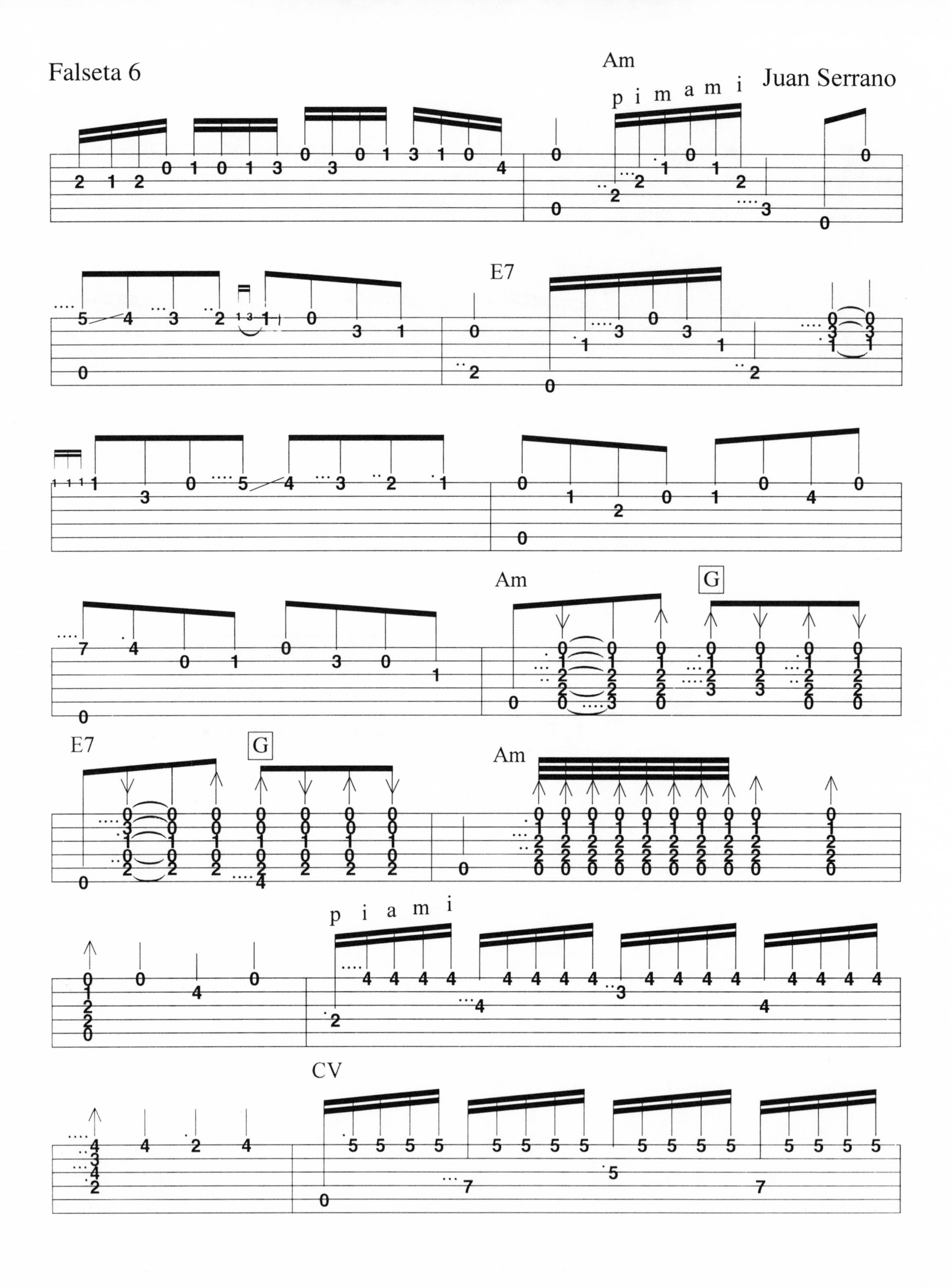
Falseta 6
Juan Serrano
Am
p i m a m i
E7
Am
G
E7
G
Am
p i a m i
CV

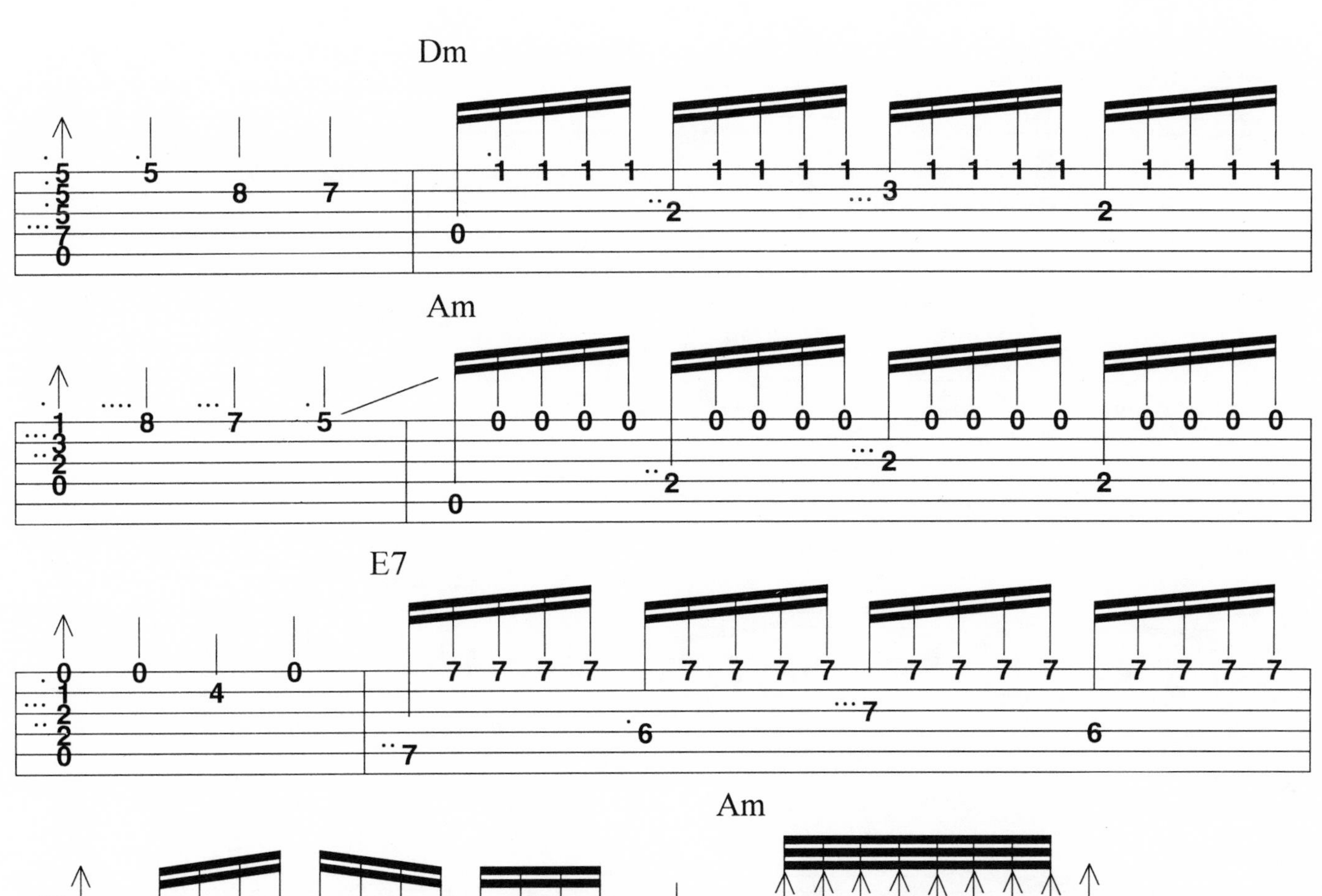
Dm
Am
E7

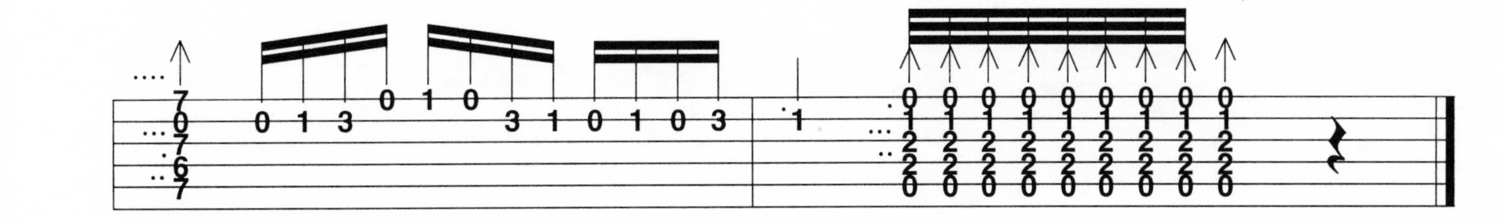
Am

Falseta 7

Juan Serrano

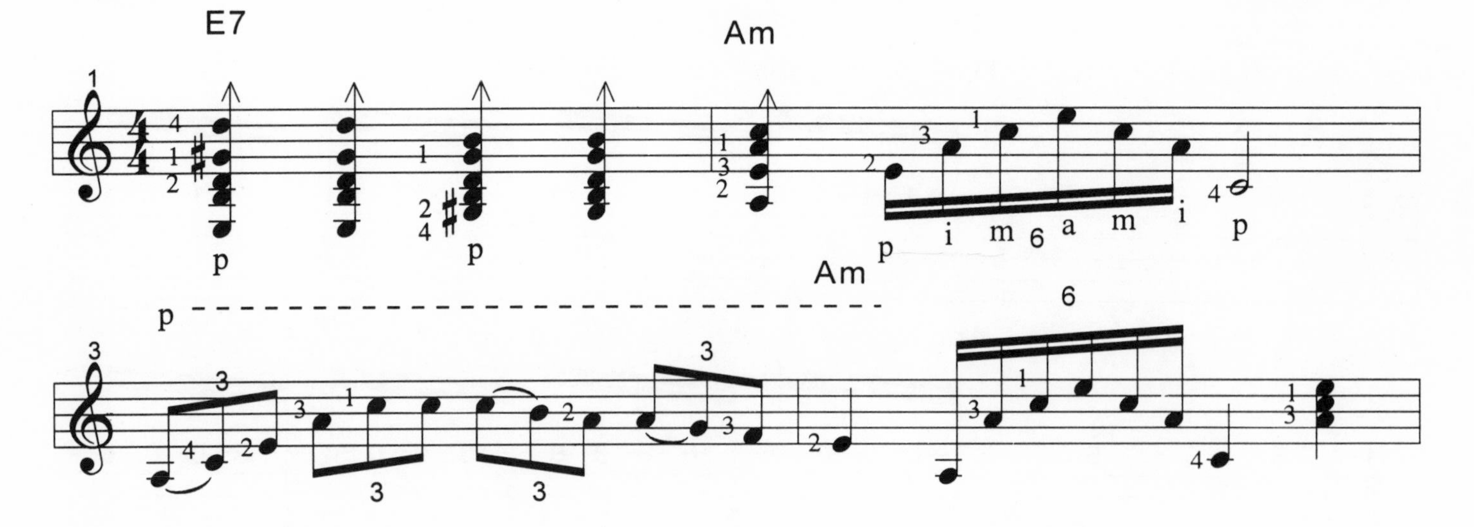


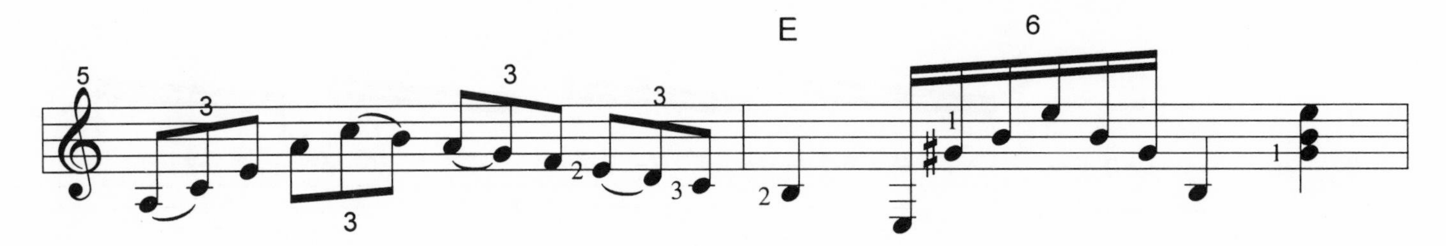

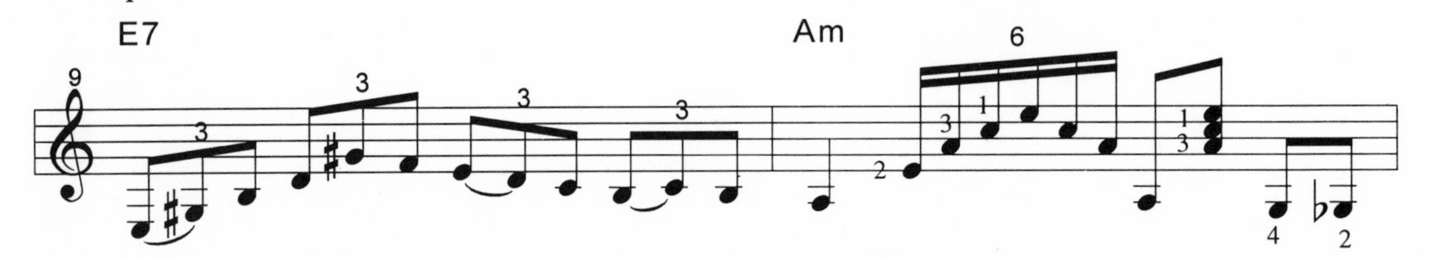

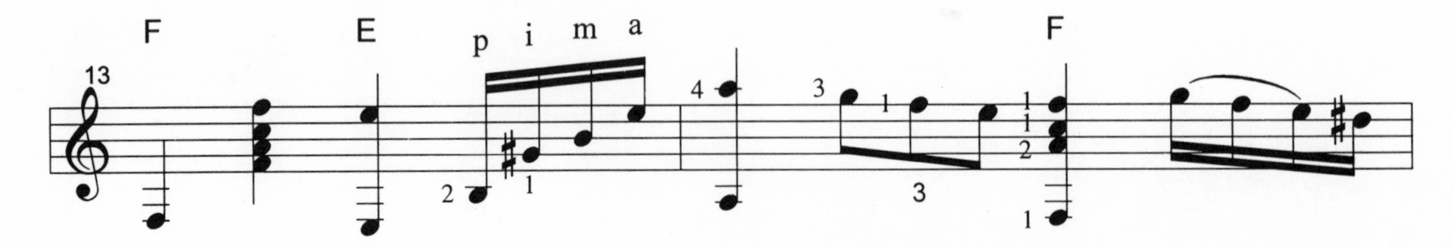

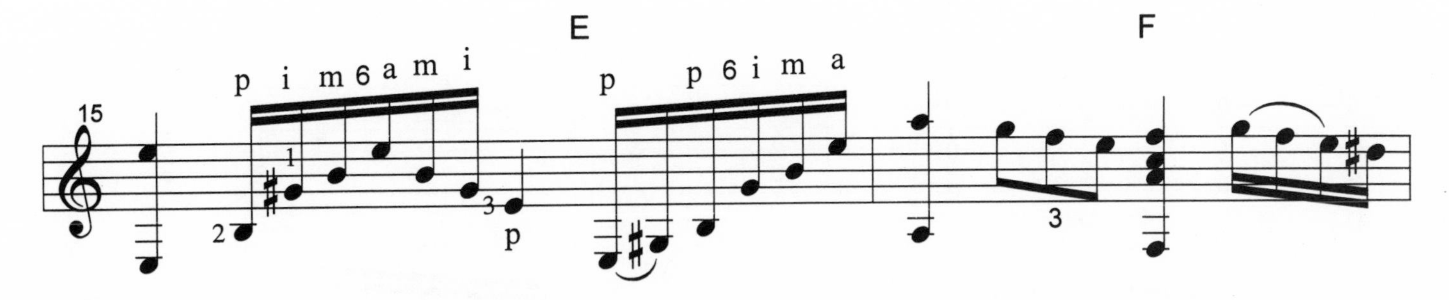
15
E
F
p i m 6 a m i
p p 6 i m a

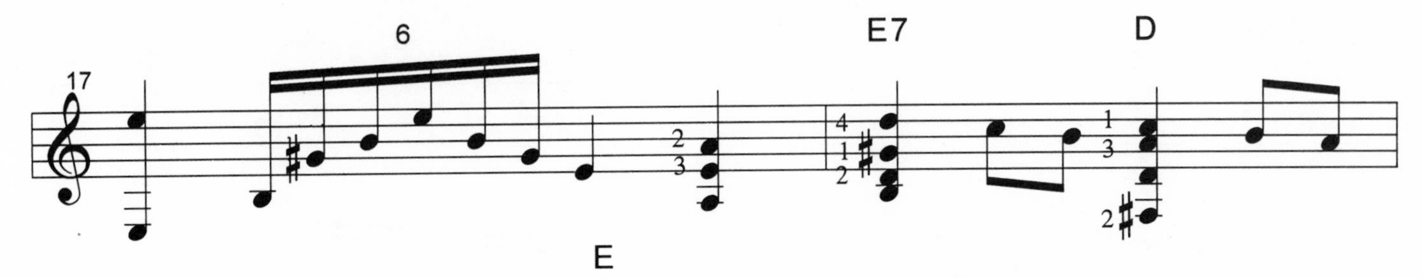
17
6
E7
D

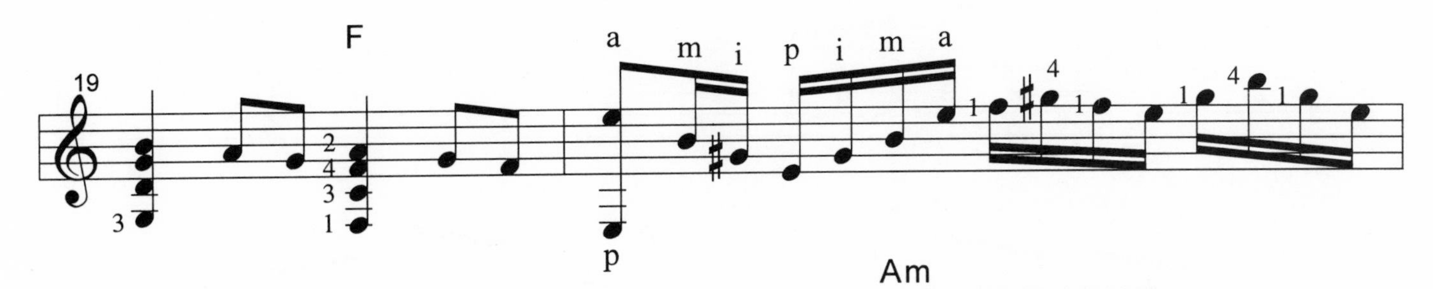
19
F
E
a m i p i m a
p

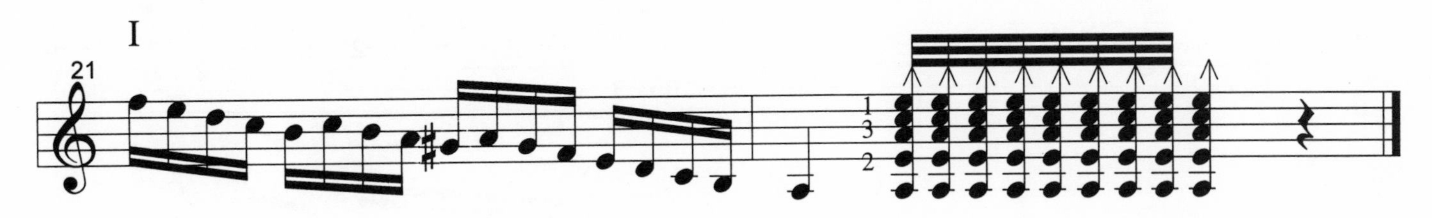
21
I
Am

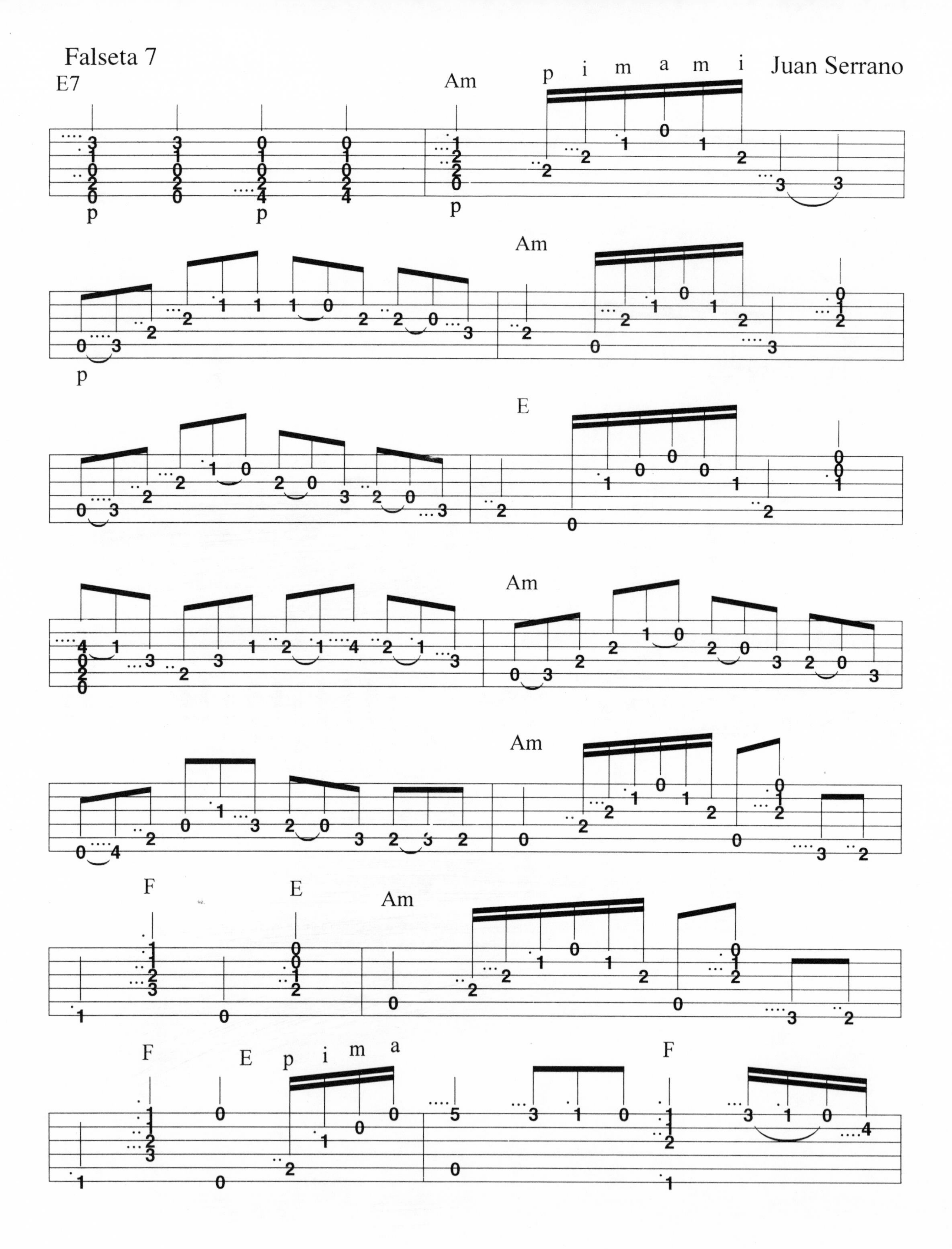
Falseta 7
Juan Serrano
E7
Am
p i m a m i
p
E
F
E p i m a

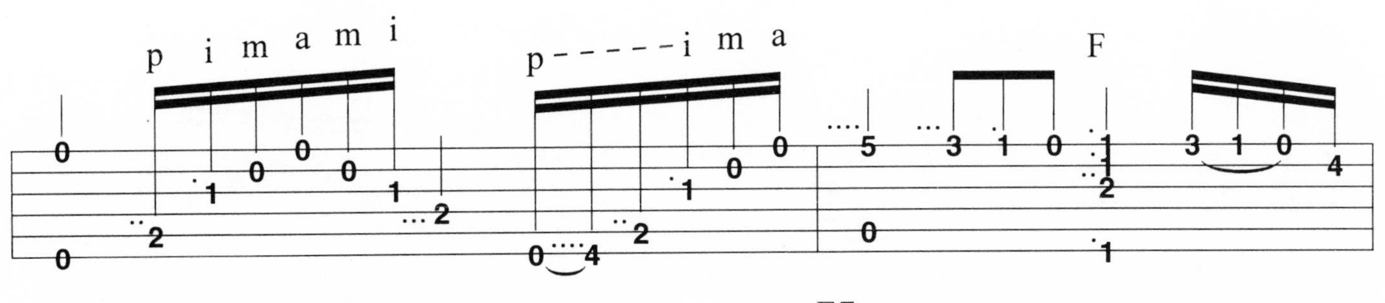
p i m a m i
p i m a
F

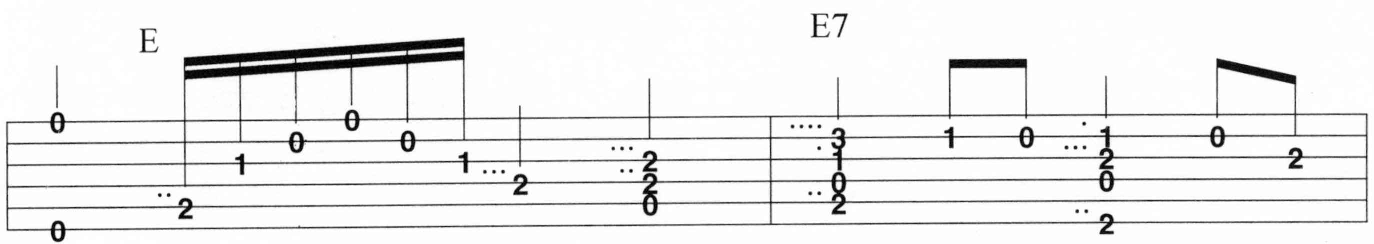
E
E7

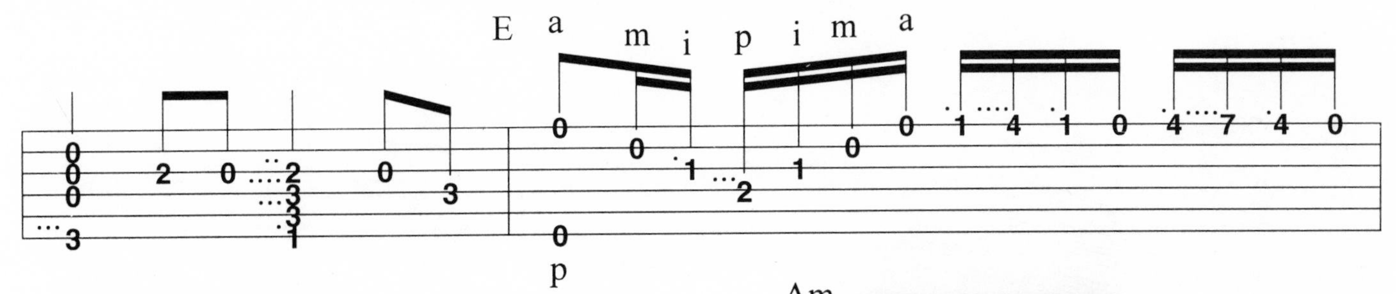
E
a m i p i m a
p

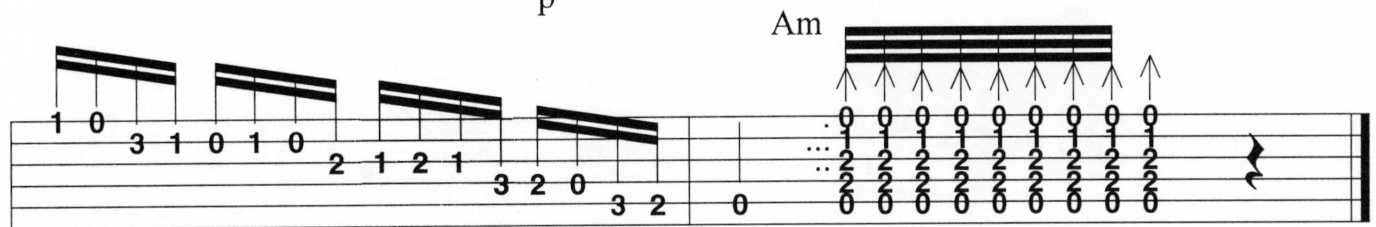
Am

Falseta 8

Juan Serrano

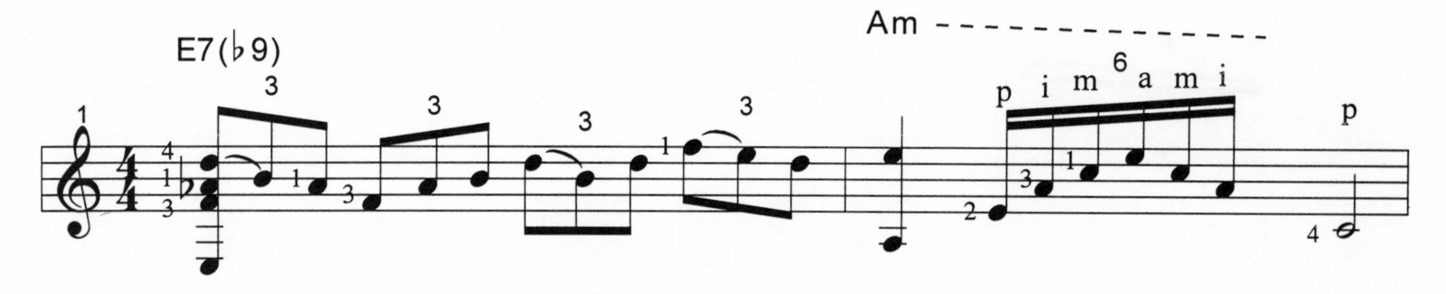


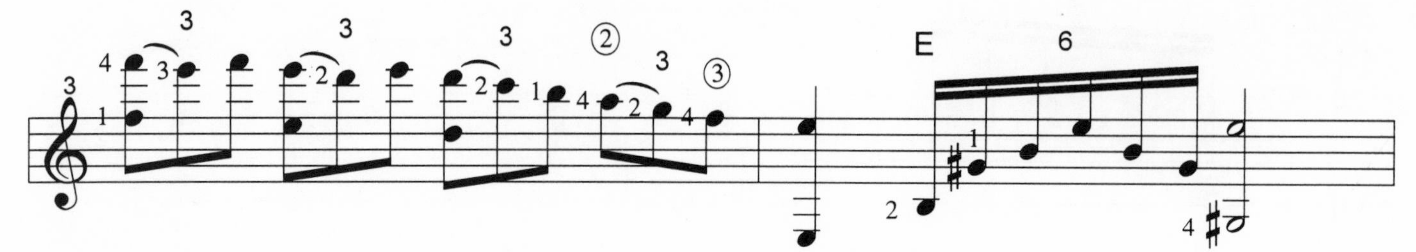

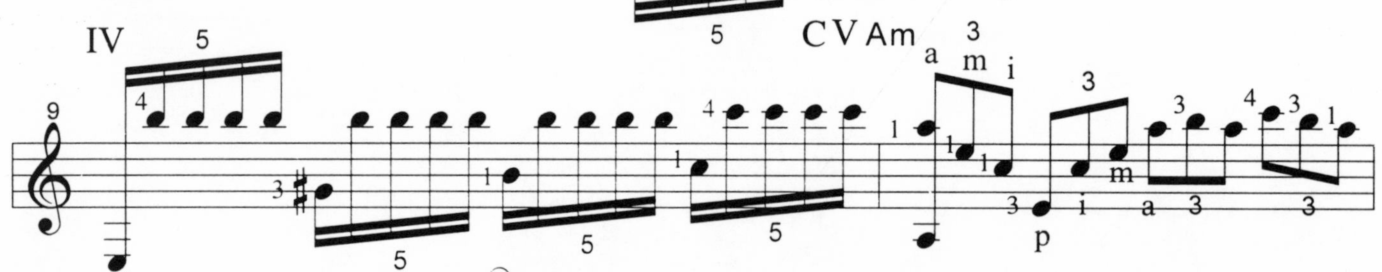


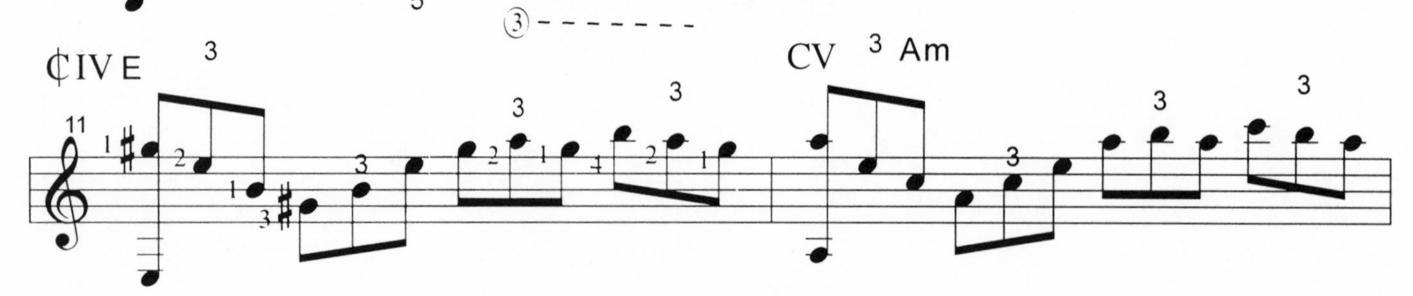


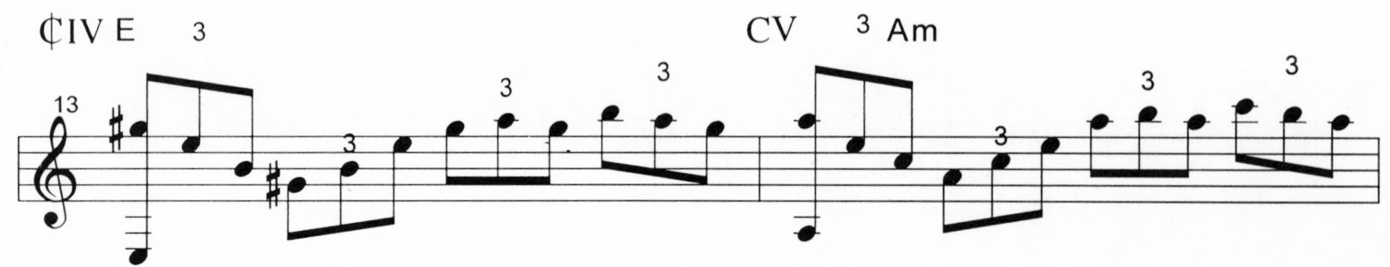

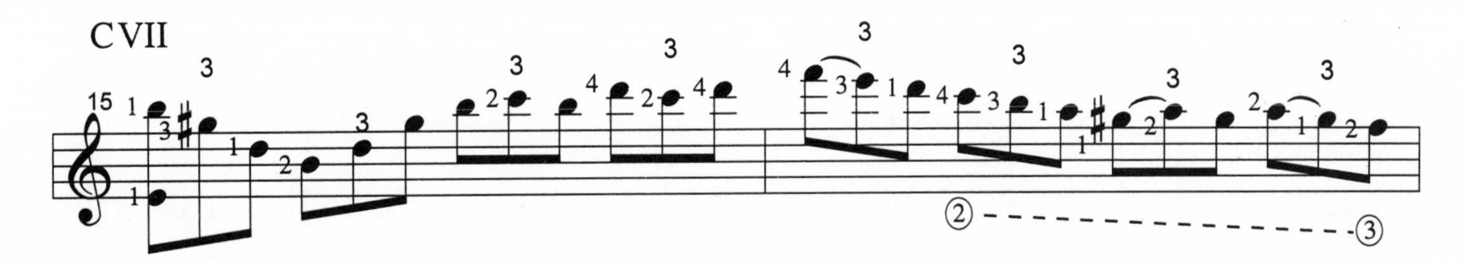
CVII

CIII

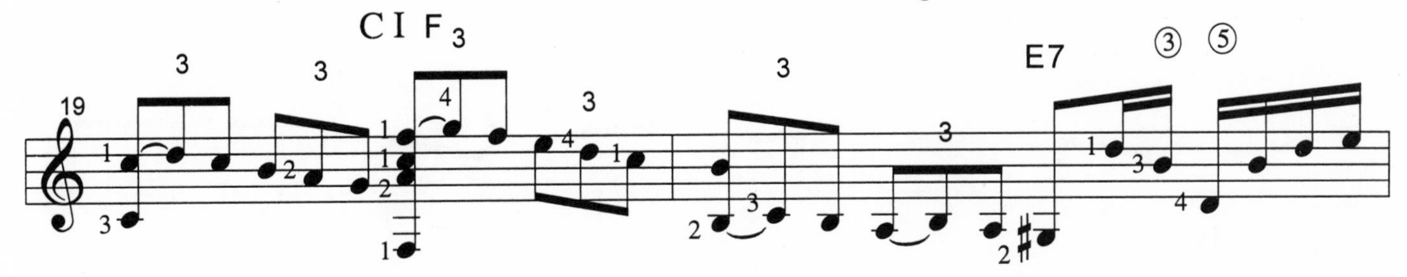
CI F3
E7

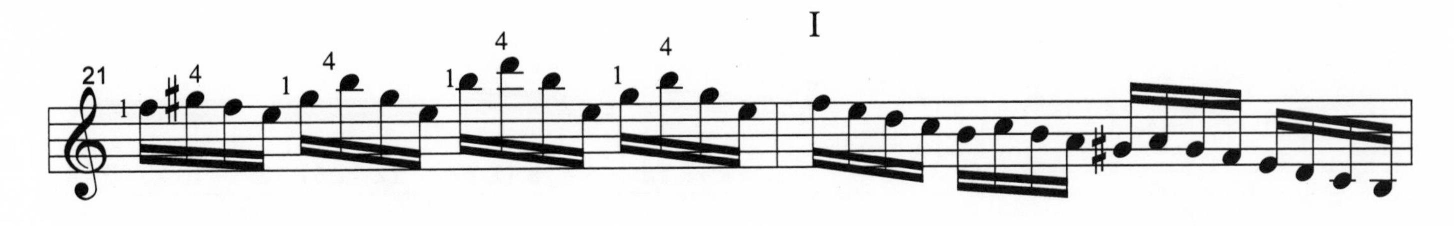
I

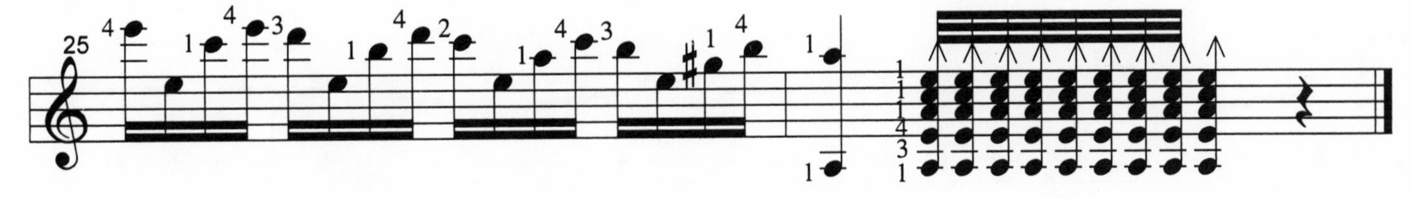
CV Am

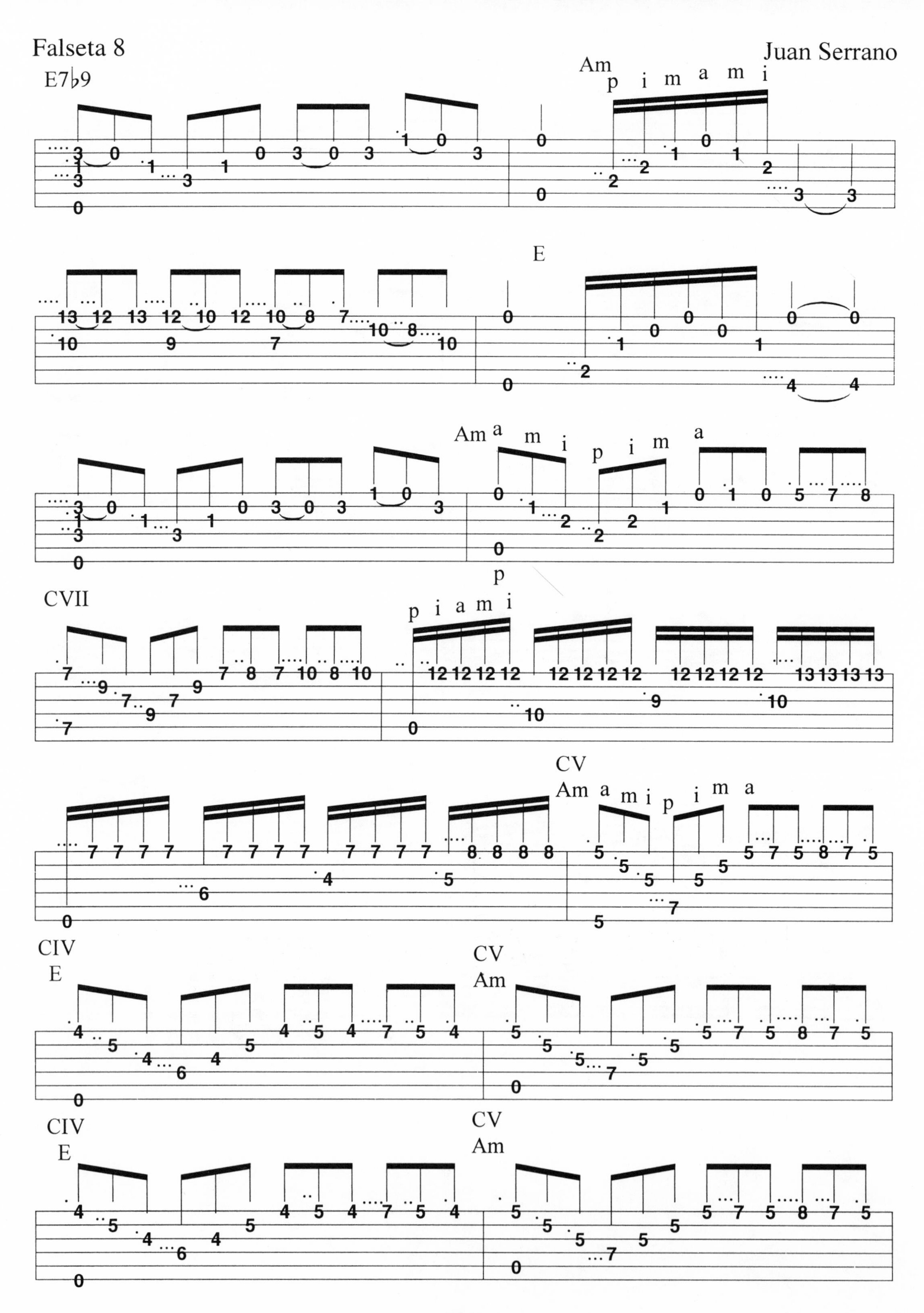
Falseta 8
Juan Serrano
E7♭9
Am
E
Am
CVII
CV
Am
CIV
E
CV
Am
CIV
E
CV
Am

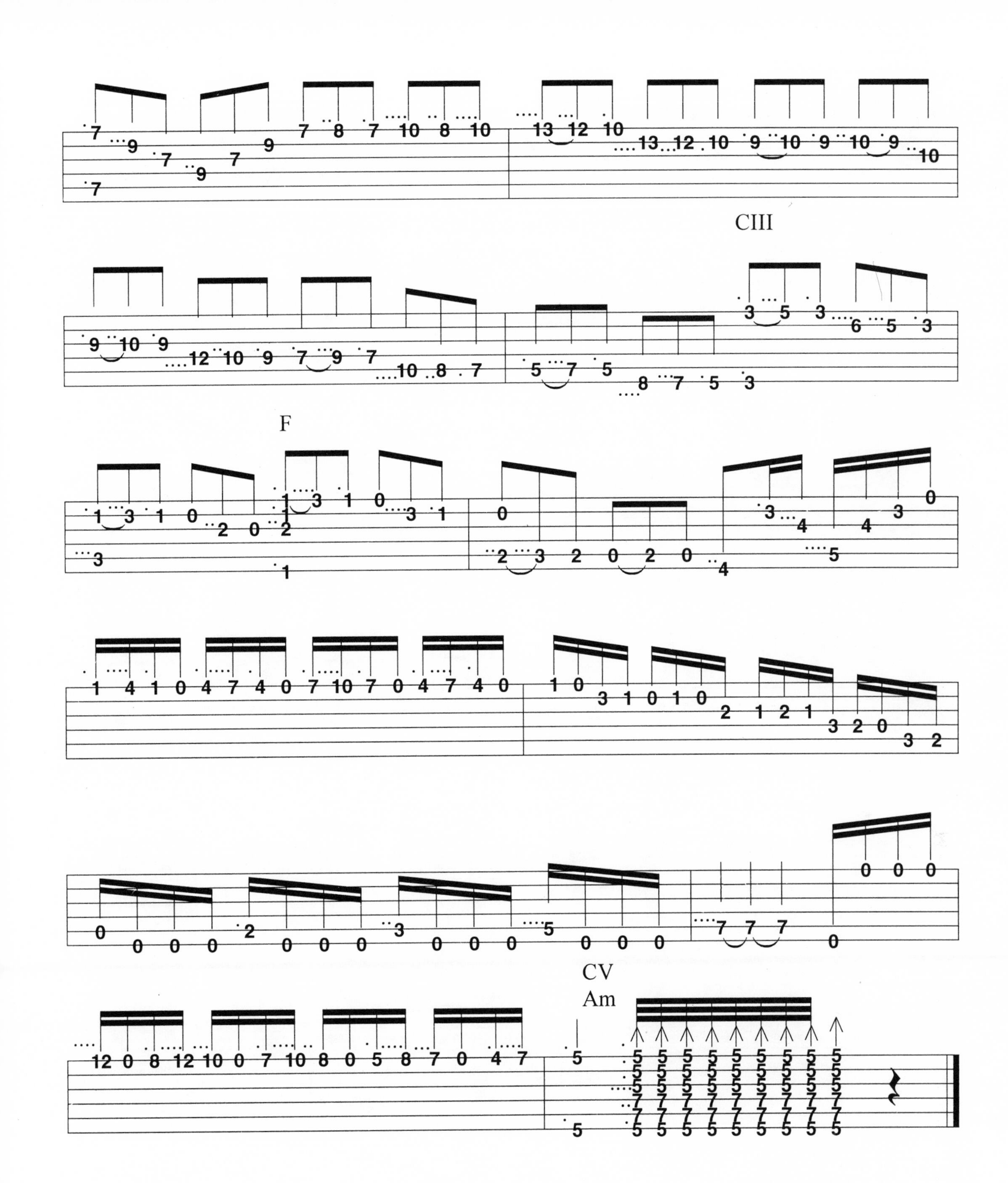
CIII
F
CV
Am

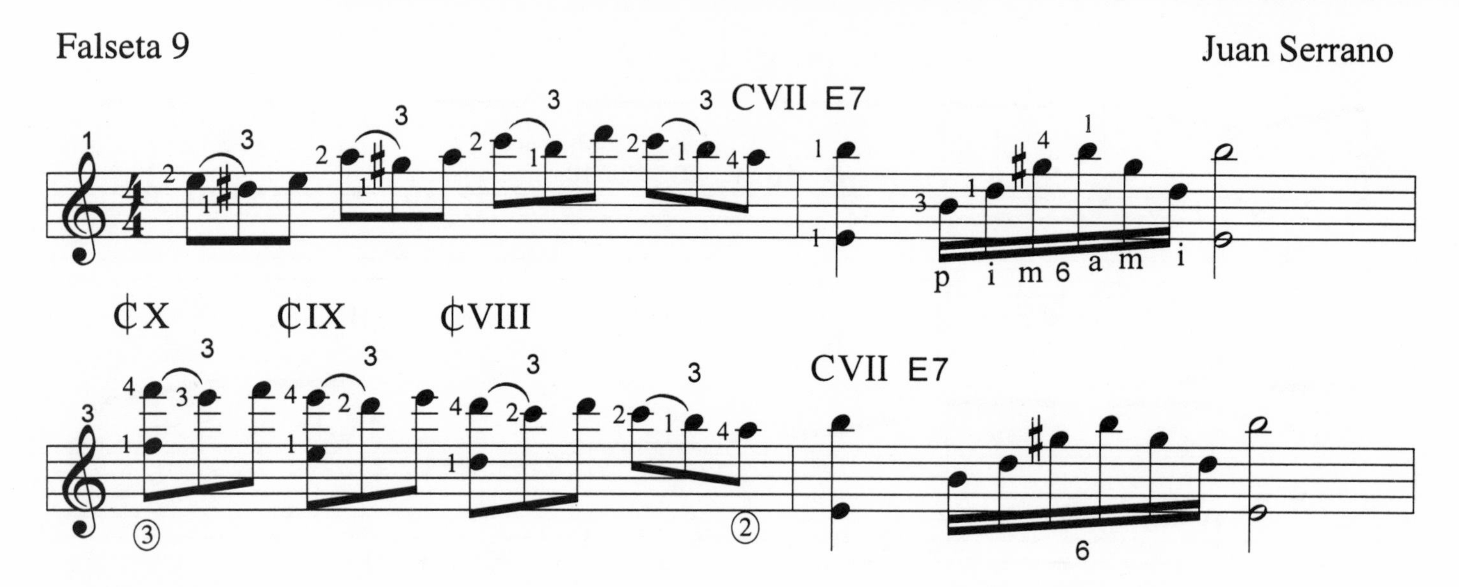
CVII E7
¢X
¢IX
¢VIII
CVII E7

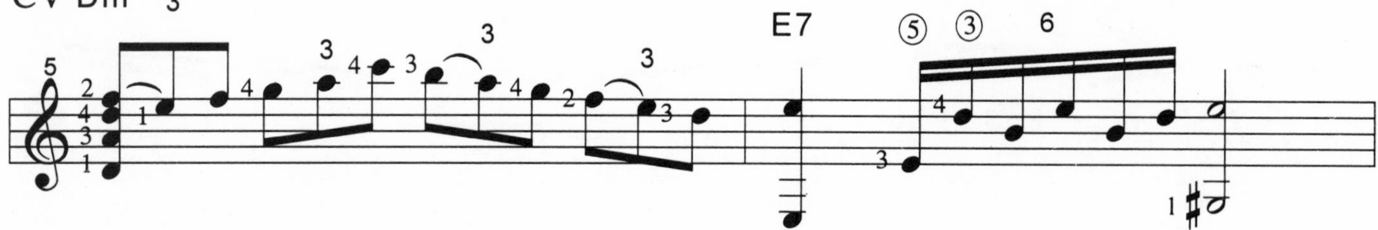
CV Dm
E7

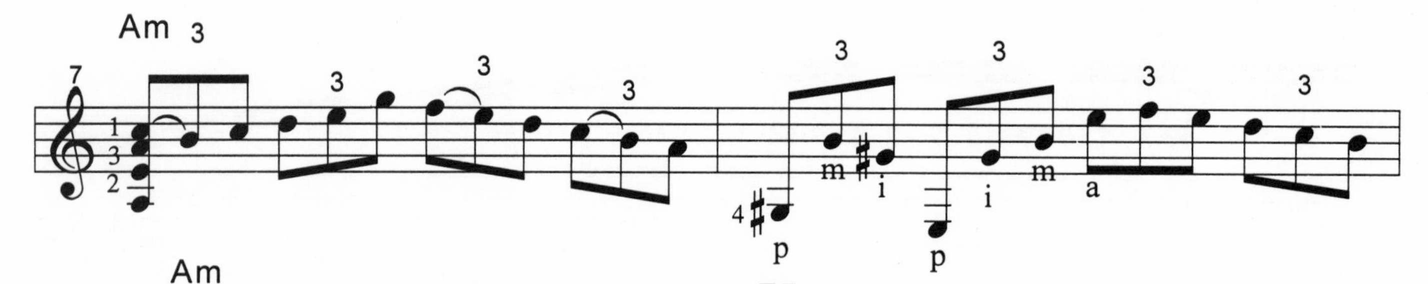
Am

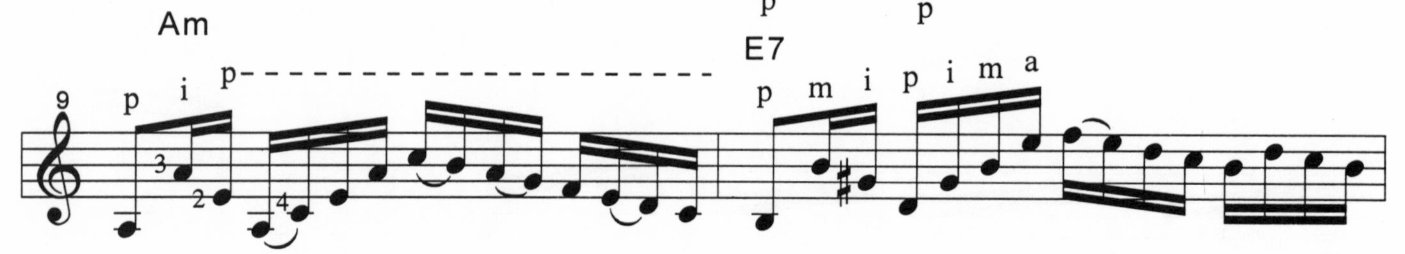
Am
E7

Am
CIII G

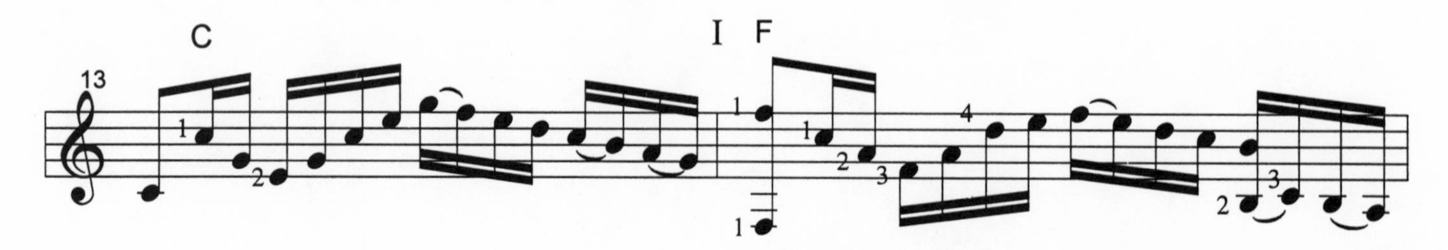
C
I F

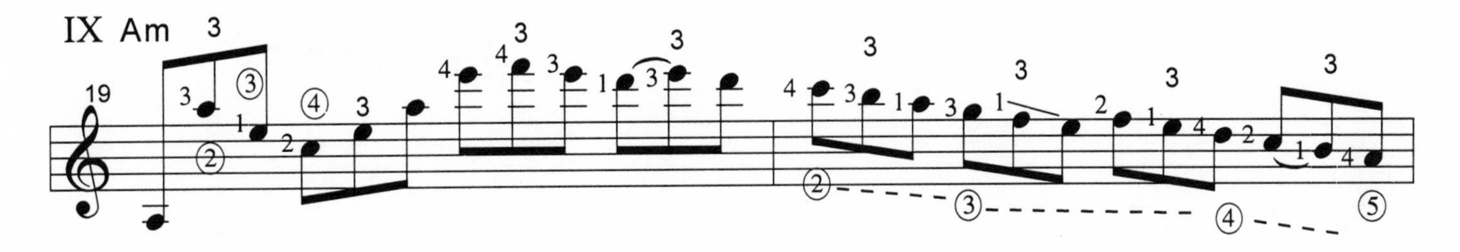
IX Am

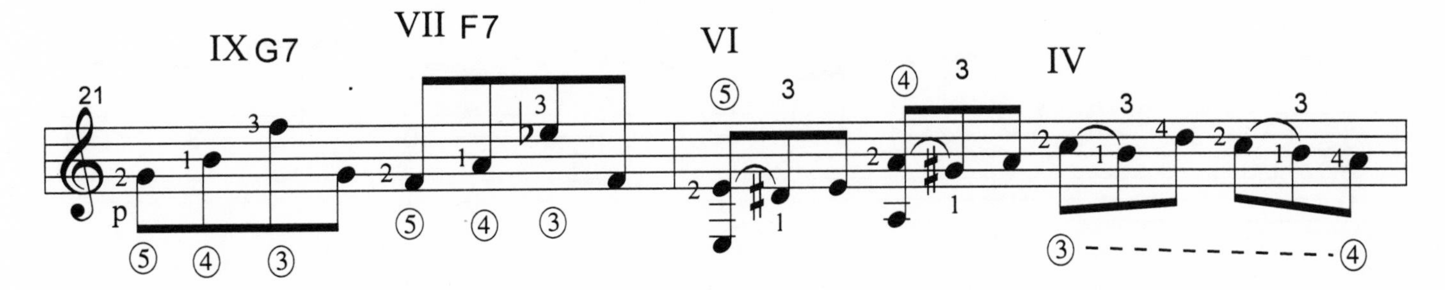
IX G7
VII F7
VI
IV

III
I
E
a m i p i m a

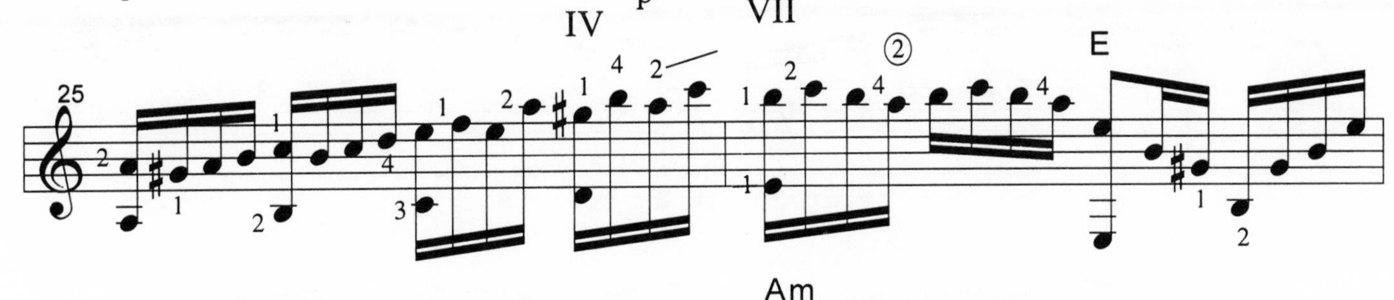
IV
VII
E

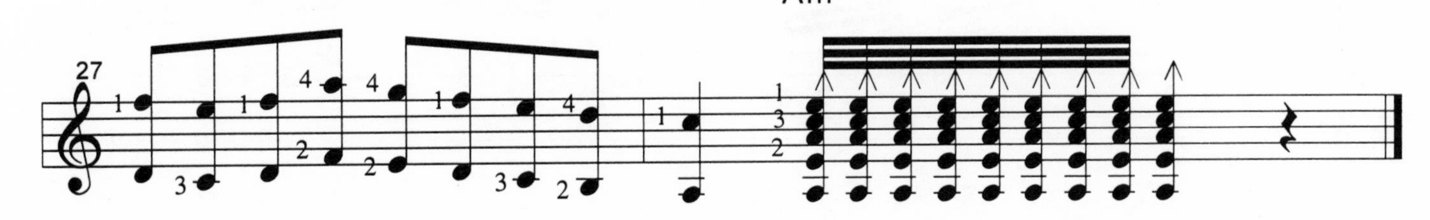
Am

Falseta 9

Juan Serrano

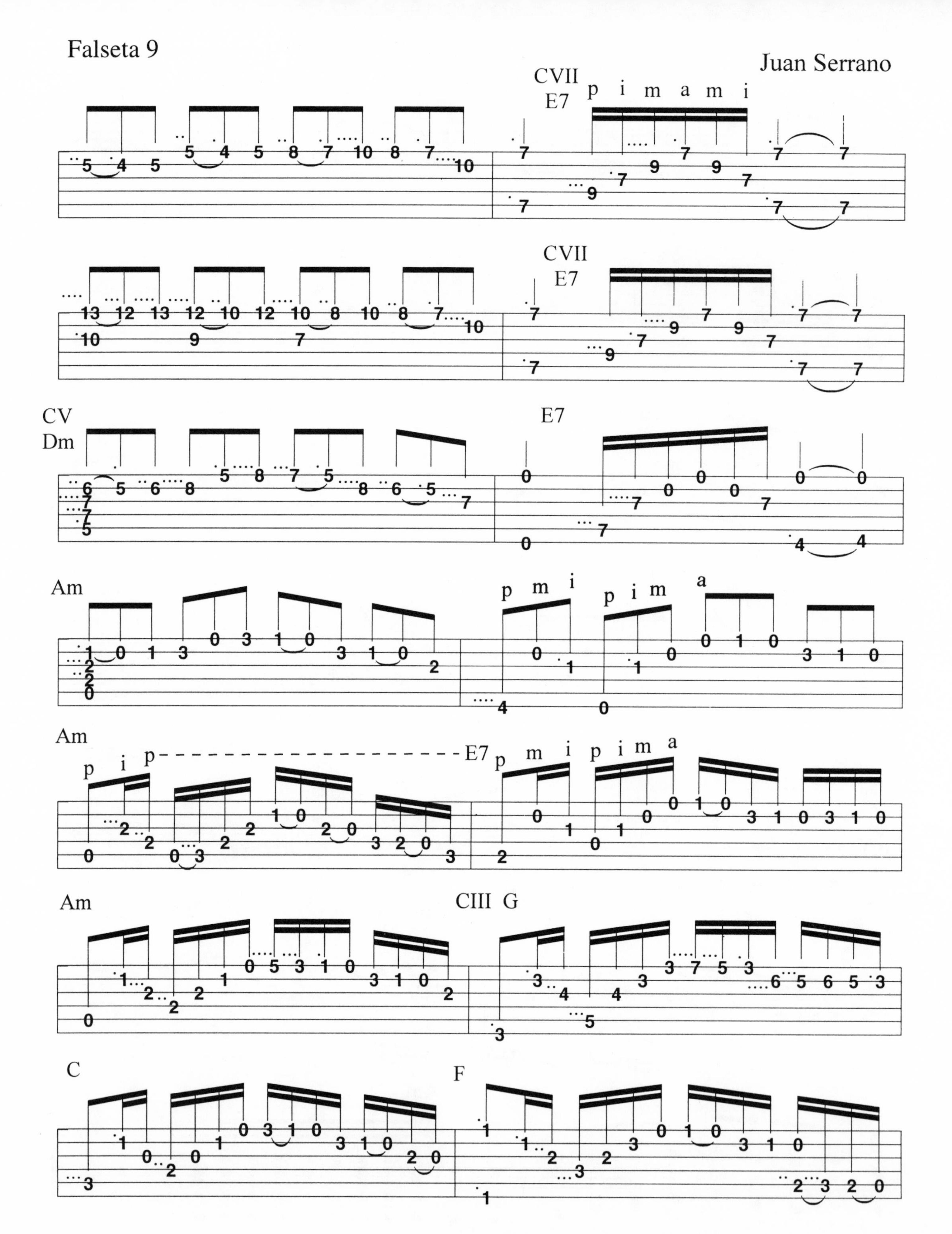

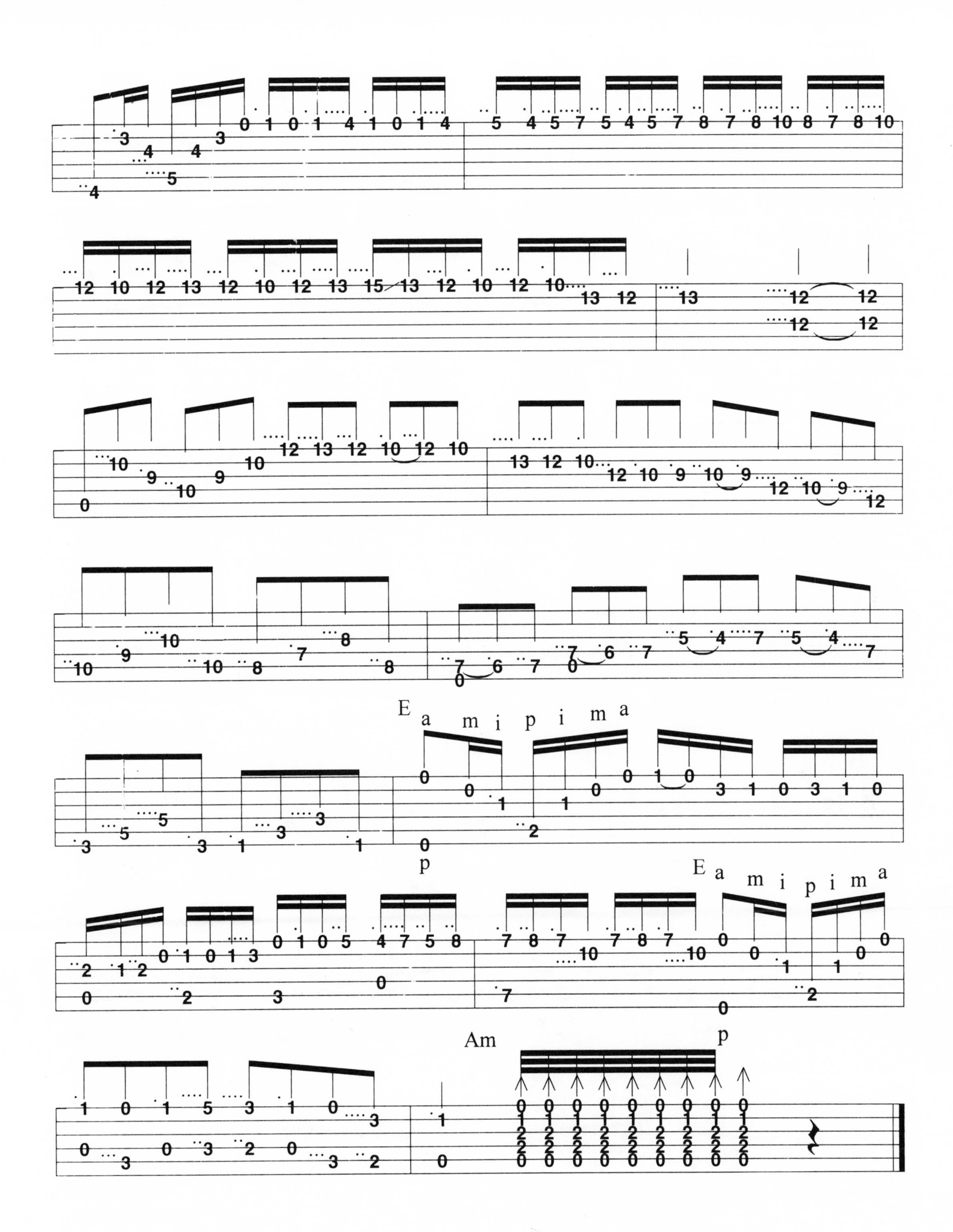
E
a m i p i m a
p
E
a m i p i m a
p
Am

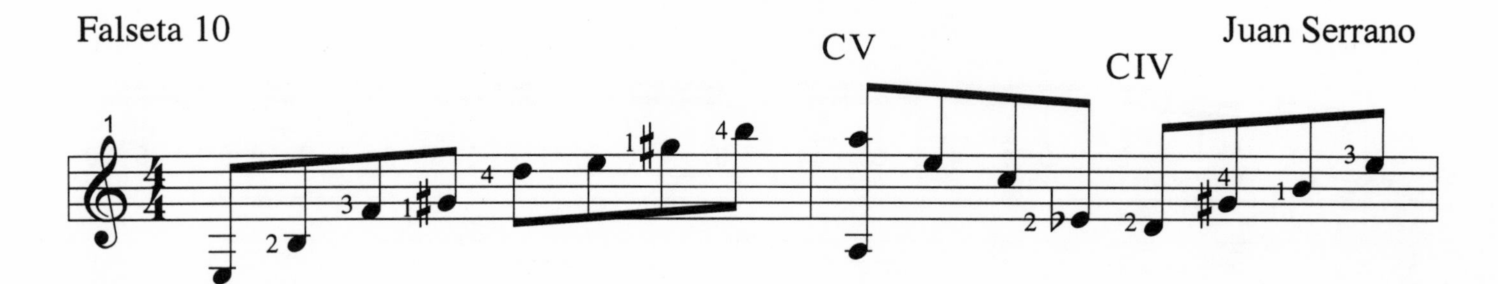
Falseta 10
Juan Serrano
CV
CIV

CVII E7
IX Am

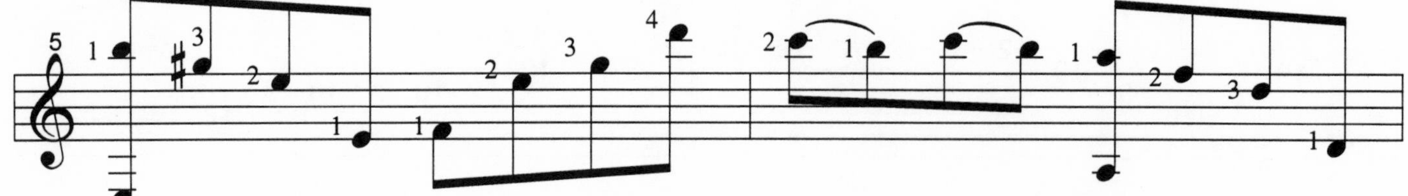
VII
V Dm

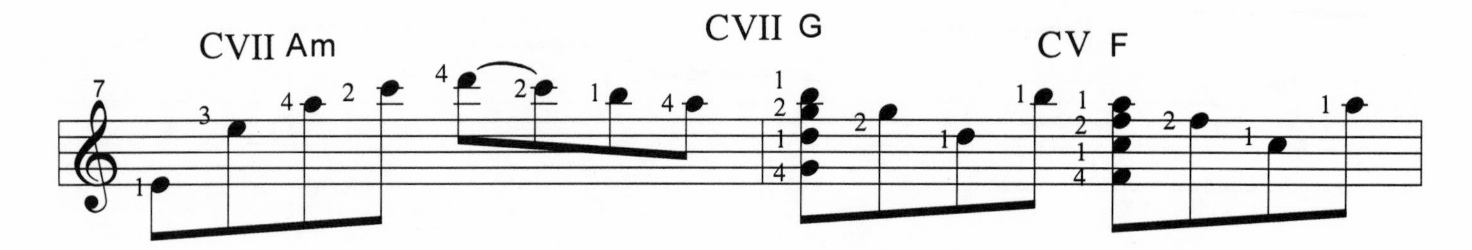
CVII Am
CVII G
CV F

CIV E
Am

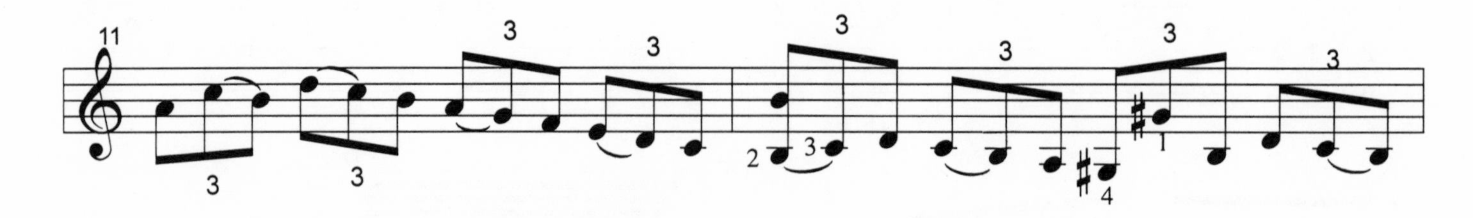

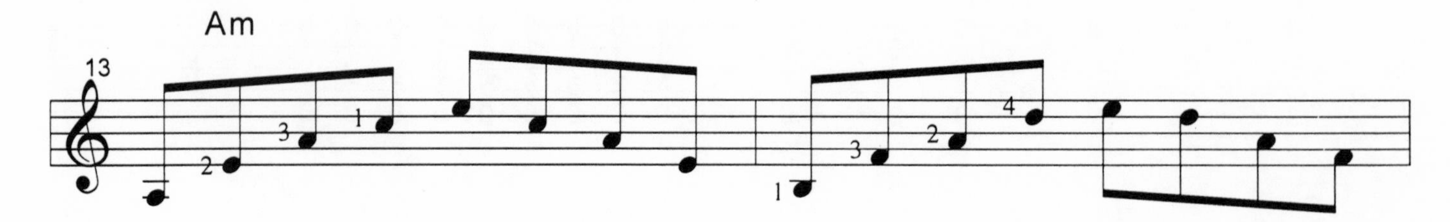
Am

CV Am

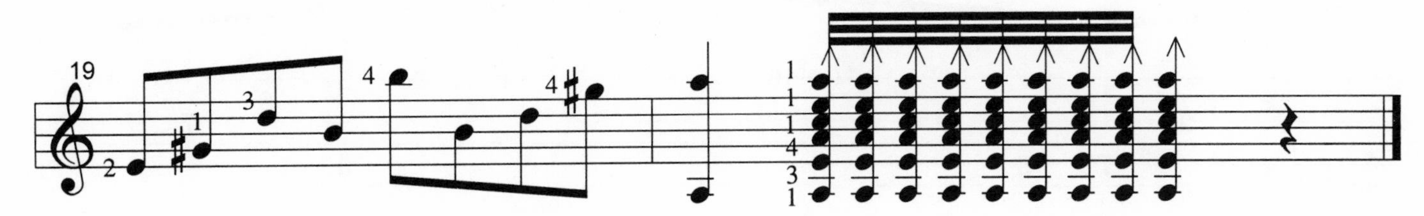

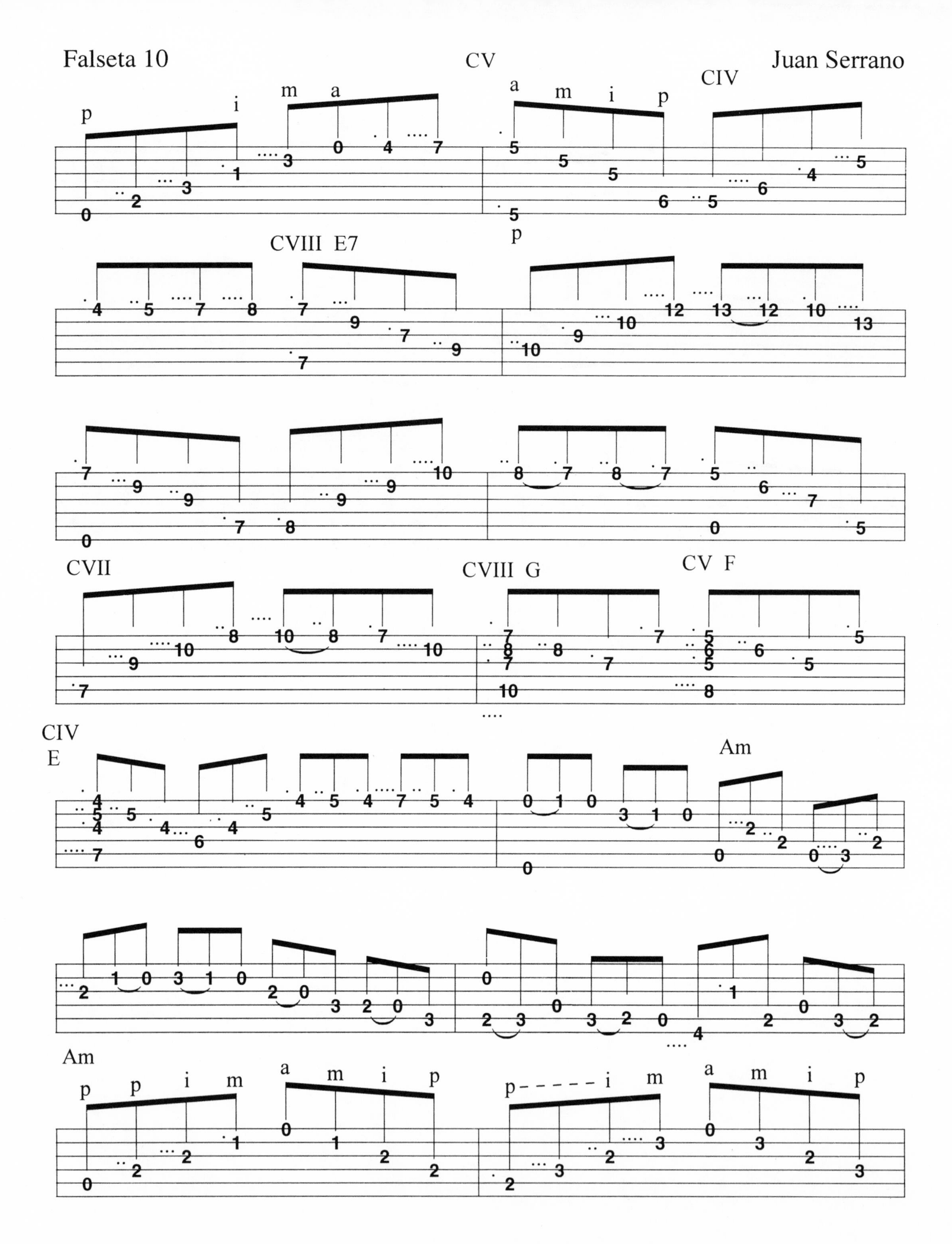
Falseta 10
Juan Serrano
CV
CIV
CVIII E7
CVII
CVIII G
CV F
CIV
E
Am
Am

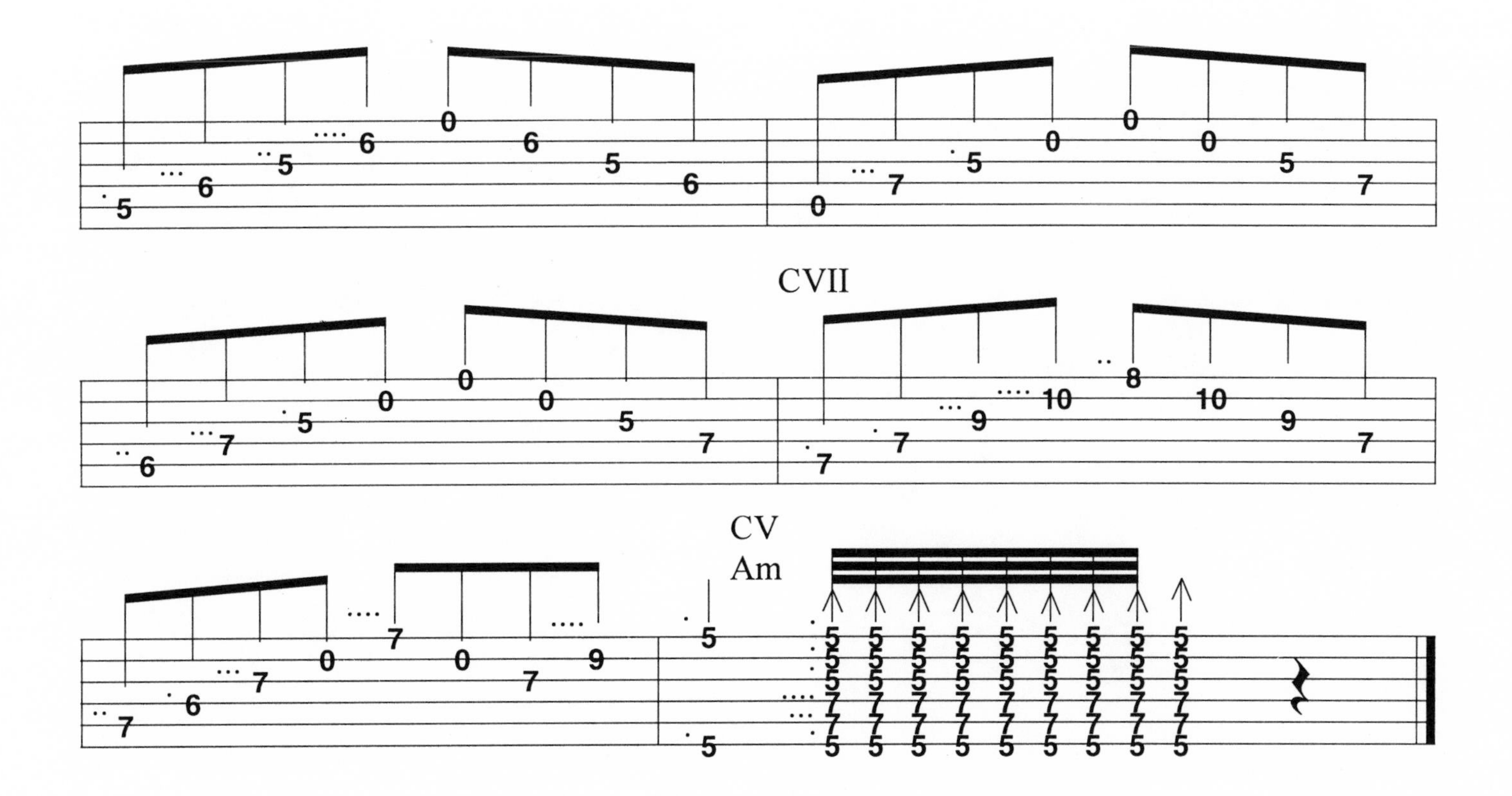
CVII
CV
Am

# GRANAINAS

The Granainas are one of the free flamenco forms. They are called free forms because they do not have a specific compás that identifies them like the majority of the flamenco forms. The melody dominates instead of the rhythm, as in all of the danceable forms.

In the free forms there is more freedom of interpretation because a strict compás must not be adhered to. All of the free forms are derived from the traditional Andalucian Fandango. The Granainas special characteristics are their slides.

The majority of the Granainas falsetas end with a slide on the 6th string that is played by sliding the index finger of the left hand from the first to the 7th fret. Although it is not too difficult to play, it is recommended that this particular technique be practiced repeatedly to obtain a clear sound upon execution. The two notes appearing at the end of the slides have the same sound, but on different strings. The B of the 4th string on the 9th fret and the B of the 2nd string open should both be played at the same time.

In the arpeggios of falseta #2, all the notes must be played freestroke, except the notes played with the ring finger (a) that are played reststroke. The arpeggio of the next to the last measure of falseta #3 ends by dragging only the ring finger of the right hand from the first until the sixth string. Falsetas #6 and #10 end with the same technique. Falseta #7 ends with a picado that connects with the final slide. This picado should be increased in speed when played.

All of the Granainas falsetas can be played more or less fast depending on the interpreter's taste.

# GRANAINAS

Las Granainas son una de las formas flamencas llamadas libres. Se les llaman formas libres porque no tienen un compás específico que las identifica, como la mayoría de las formas flamencas.
En las Granainas predomina la melodía y no el ritmo como en todas las formas bailables.

En las formas libres, se tiene mas libertad de interpretación, ya que no hay que ajustarse a un compás estricto.
Todas las formas libres derivan del Fandango tradicional Andaluz.
La característica especial de las Granainas son los arrastres.

La mayoría de las falsetas de las Granainas finalizan con un arrastre en la sexta cuerda, que se ejecuta deslizando el dedo índice de la mano izquierda, desde el primero al séptimo traste. Aunque no es difícil la ejecución, recomiendo que se practique bastante, para conseguir que todas las notas suenen claras. Las dos notas que aparecen al final de los arrastres tienen el mismo sonido, pero en dos cuerdas diferentes. El Si de la cuarta cuerda en el noveno traste, y el Si de la segunda cuerda al aire. Las dos deben de ser ejecutadas al mismo tiempo.

En los arpegios de la falseta #2 todas las notas se deben de tocar tirando, excepto las notas que se tocan con el dedo anular (a) que se deben de tocar apoyando. El final del arpegio del penúltimo compás musical de la falseta #3, se ejecuta arrastrando el dedo anular de la mano derecha (a) desde la prima hasta la sexta cuerda. Las falsetas #6 y #10 finalizan con la misma técnica. La falseta #7 finaliza con un picado que conecta con el arrastre final. Este picado debe de ir aumentando la velocidad durante su ejecucion.

Todas las falsetas de las Granainas se pueden tocar más o menos rápidas, depende del gusto del intérprete.

# Granainas

Falseta 1

Juan Serrano

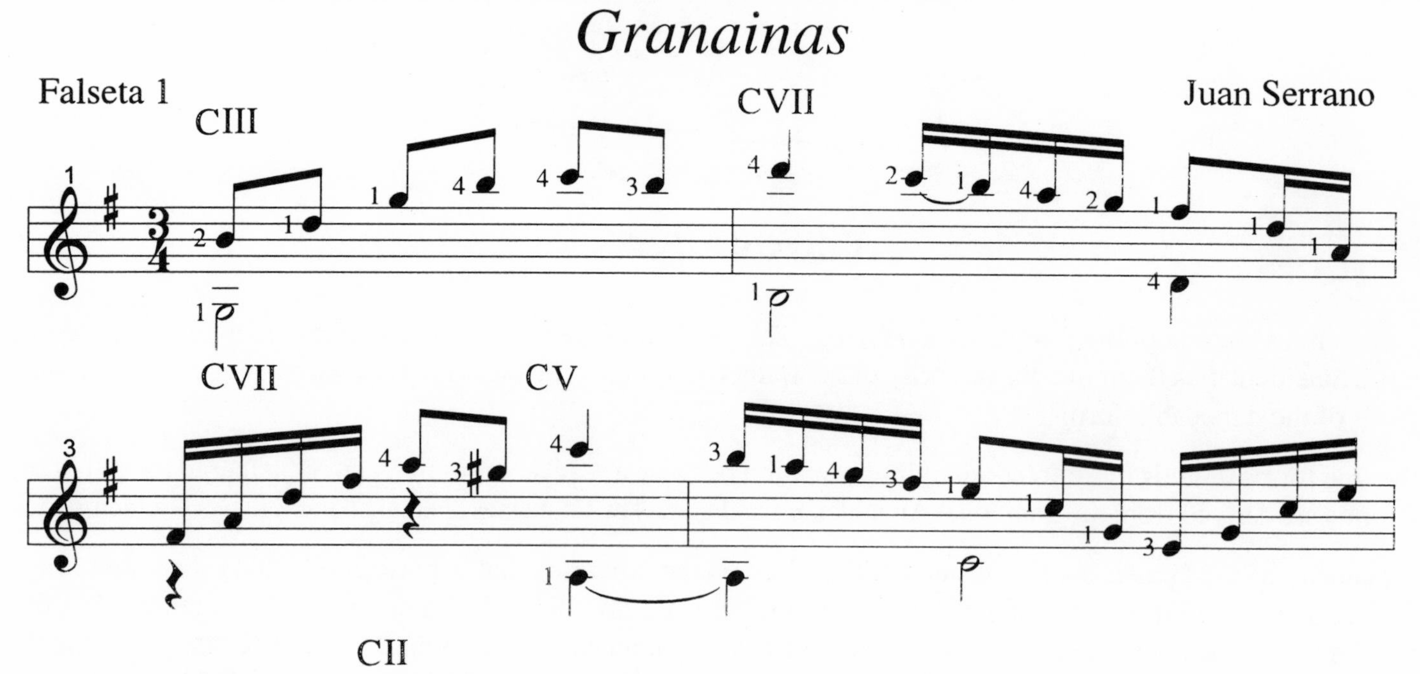

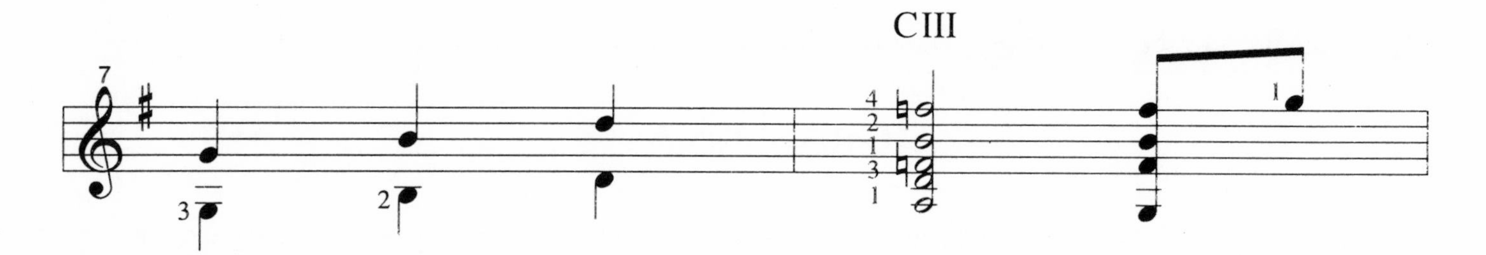

CV

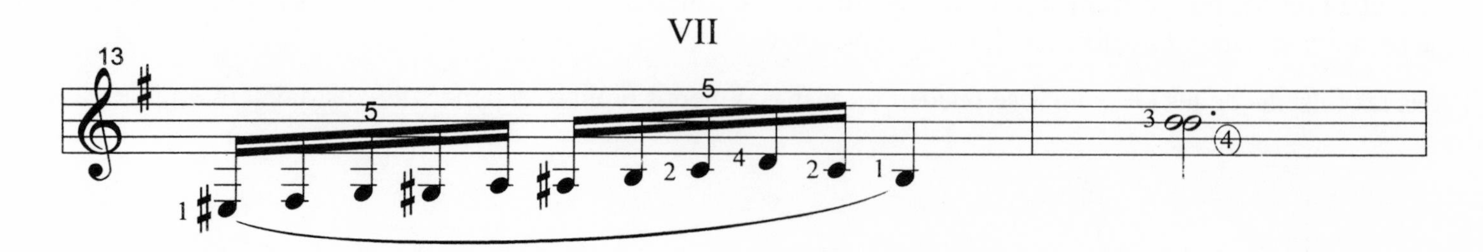

# *Granainas*

Falseta 1

Juan Serrano

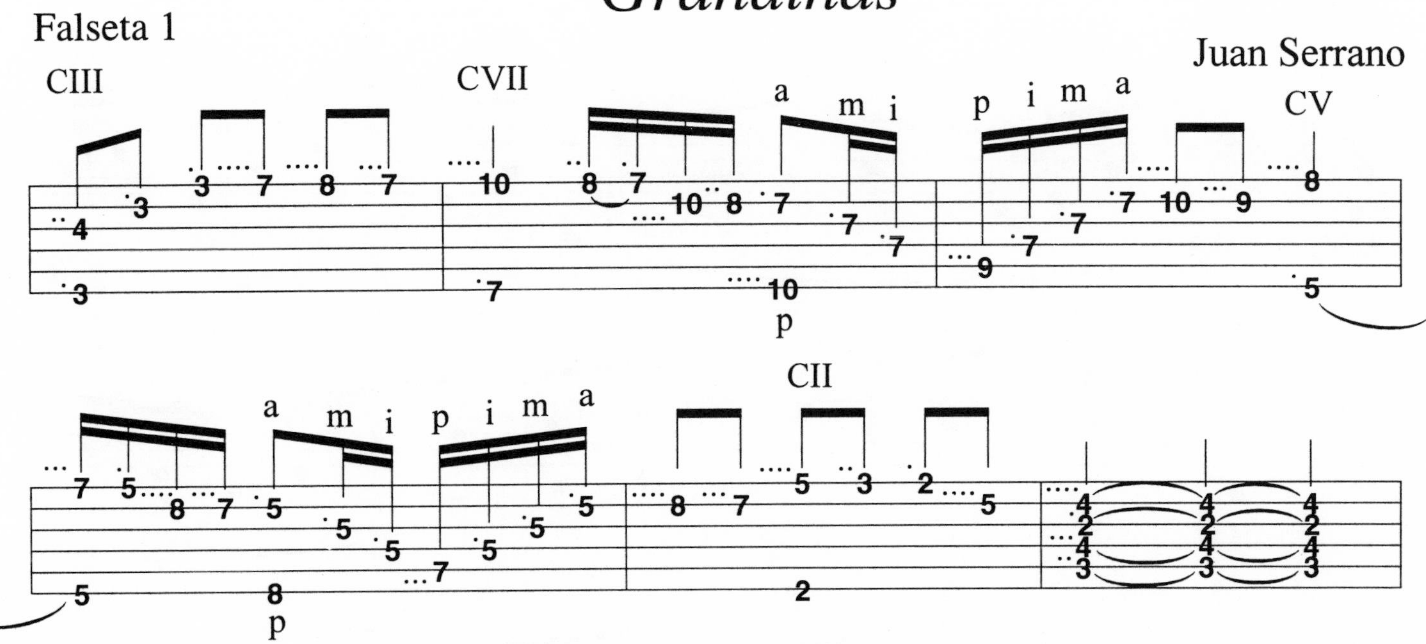


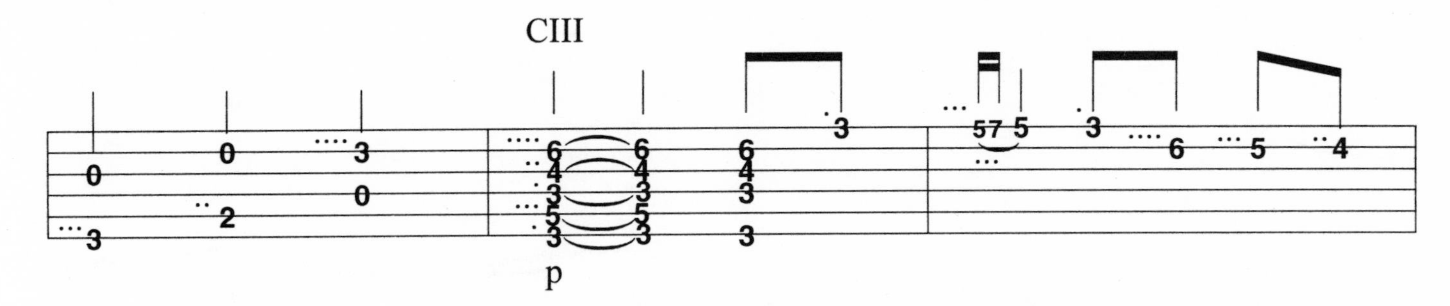


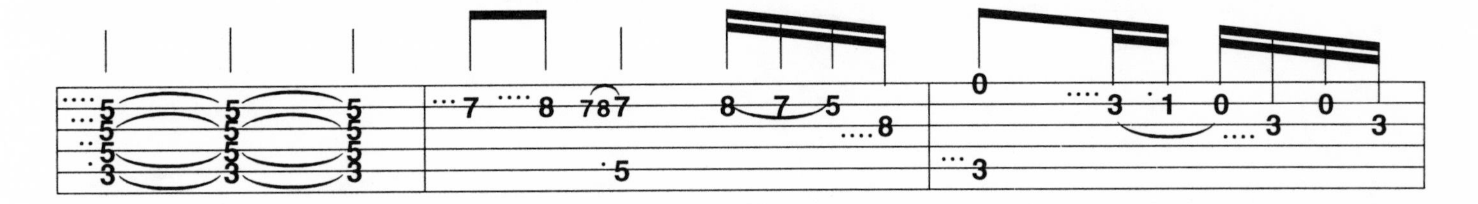


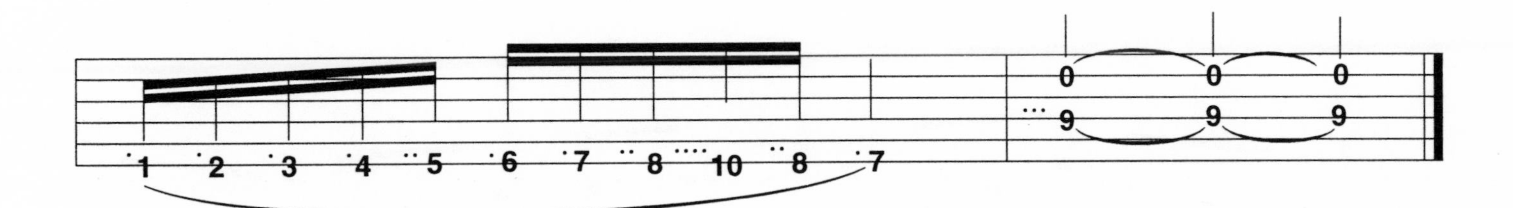

Falseta 2

Juan Serrano

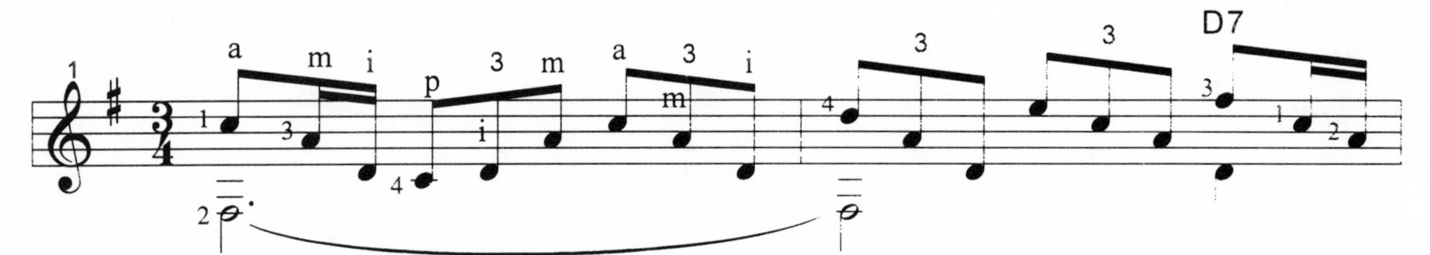

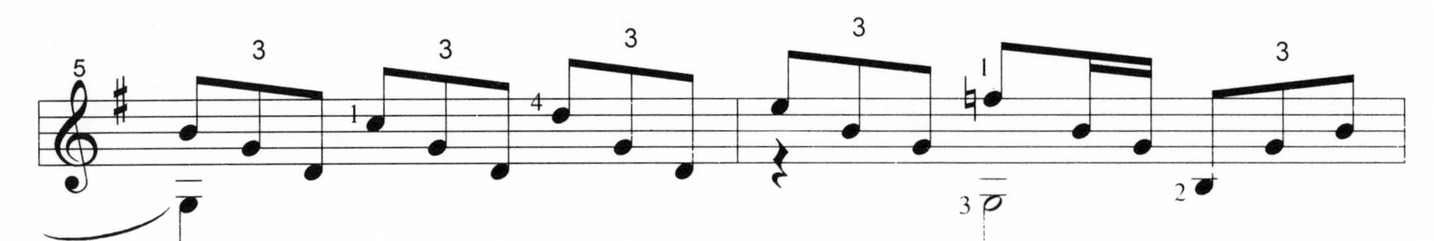

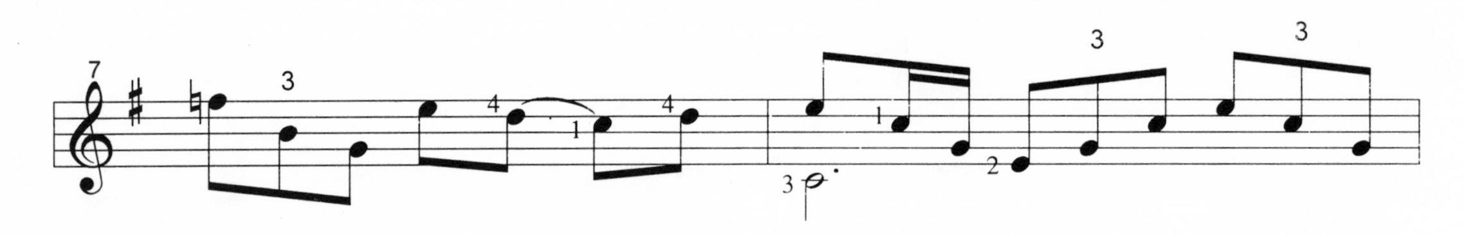

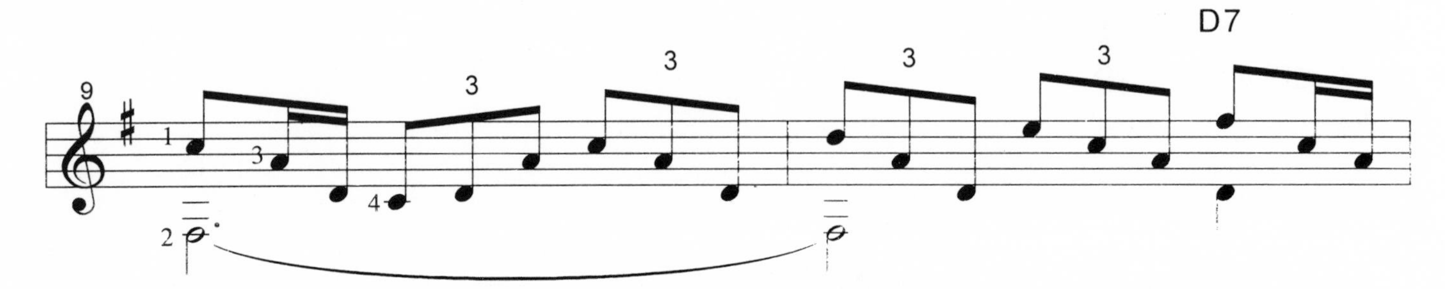

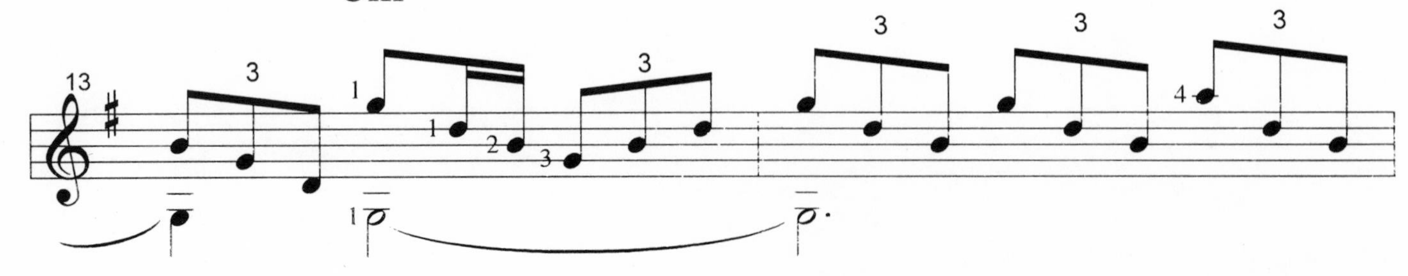

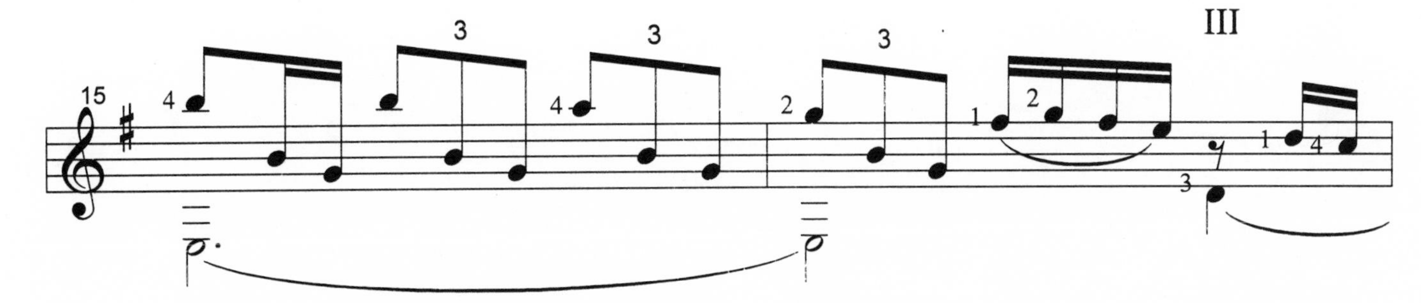
III

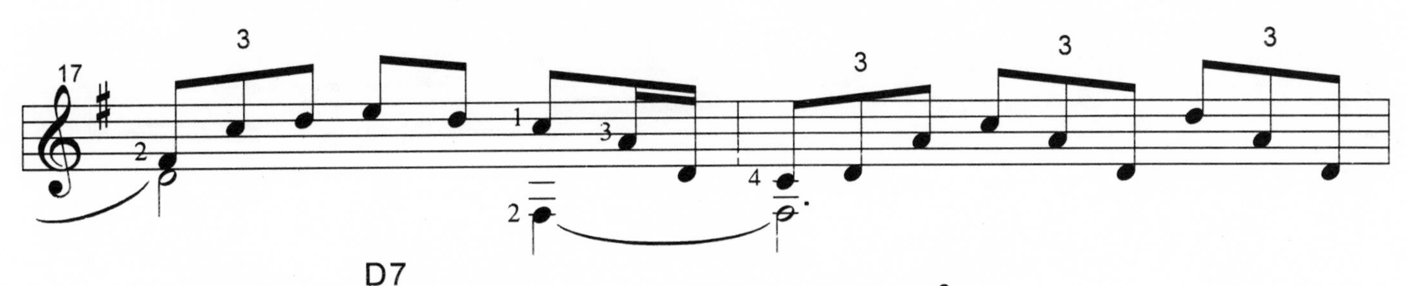

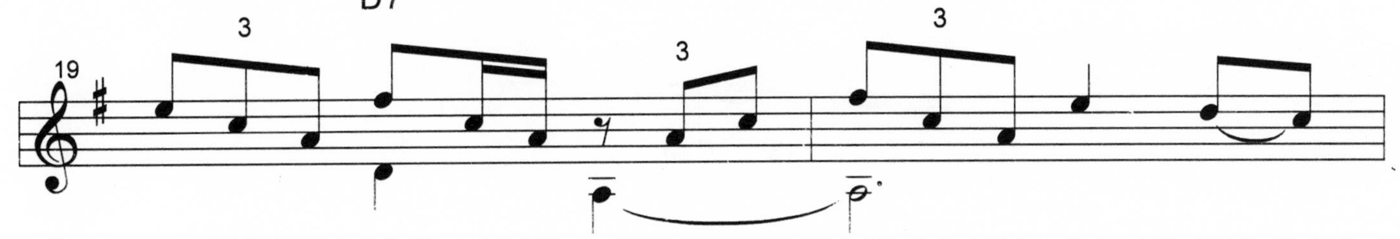
D7

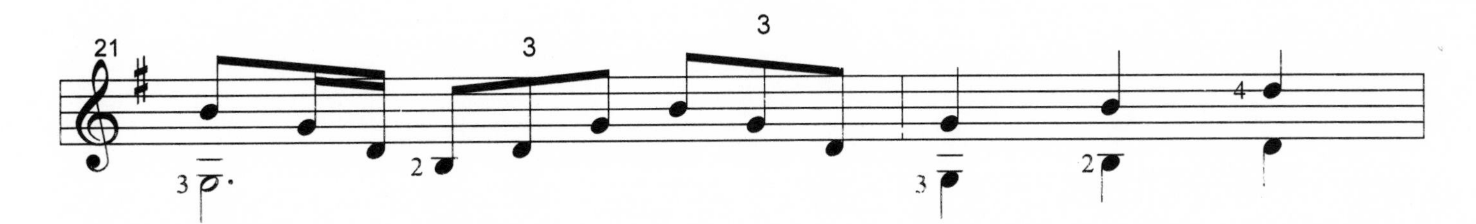

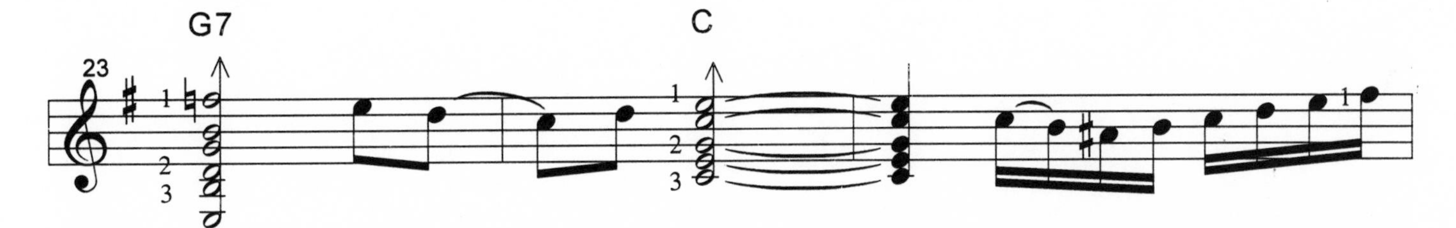
G7
C

II

II
I

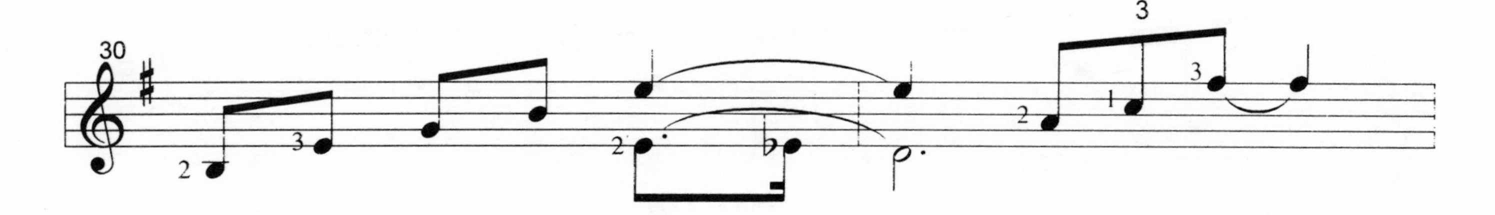
30
3

32

34
6

Falseta 2

Juan Serrano

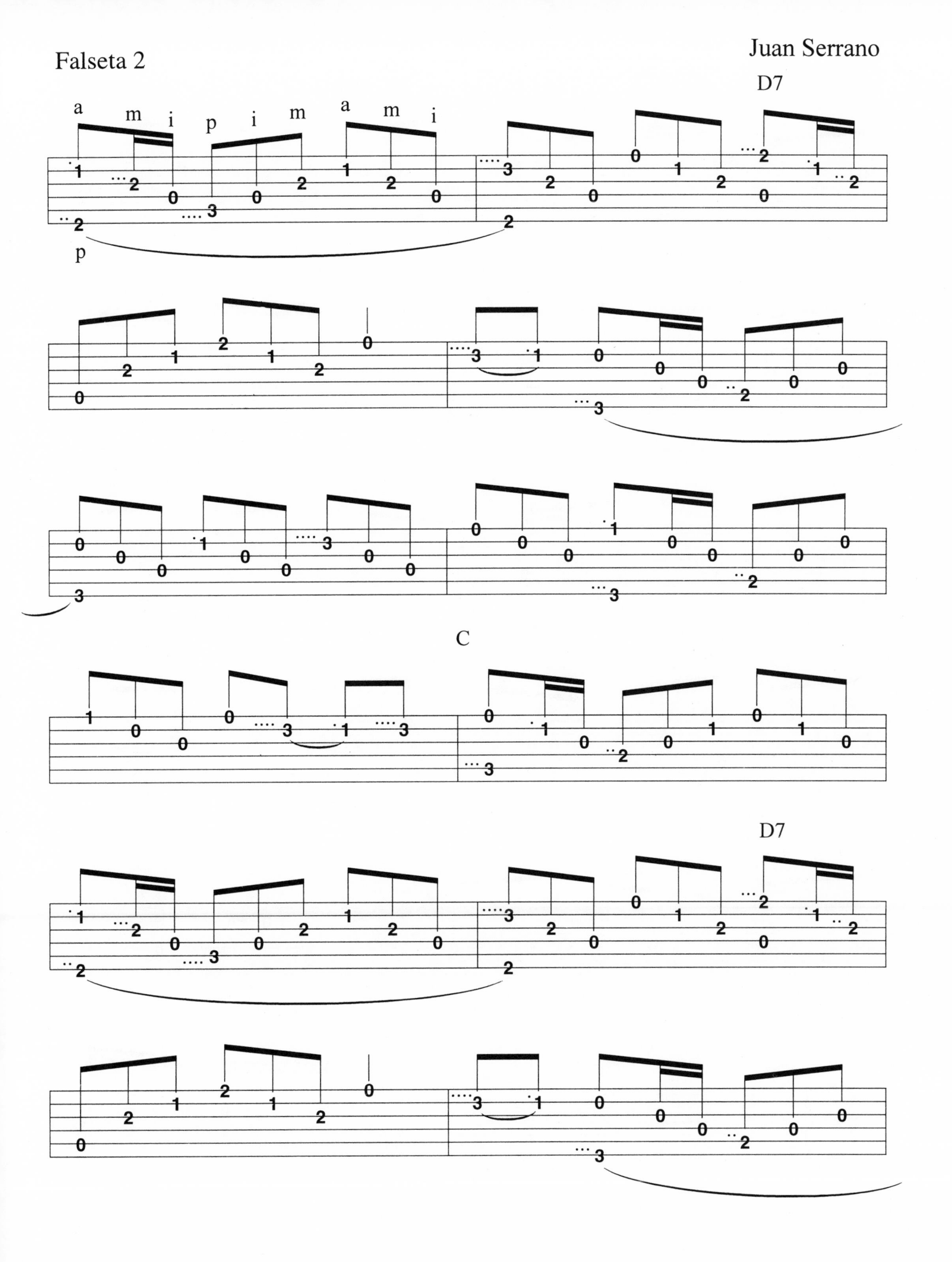

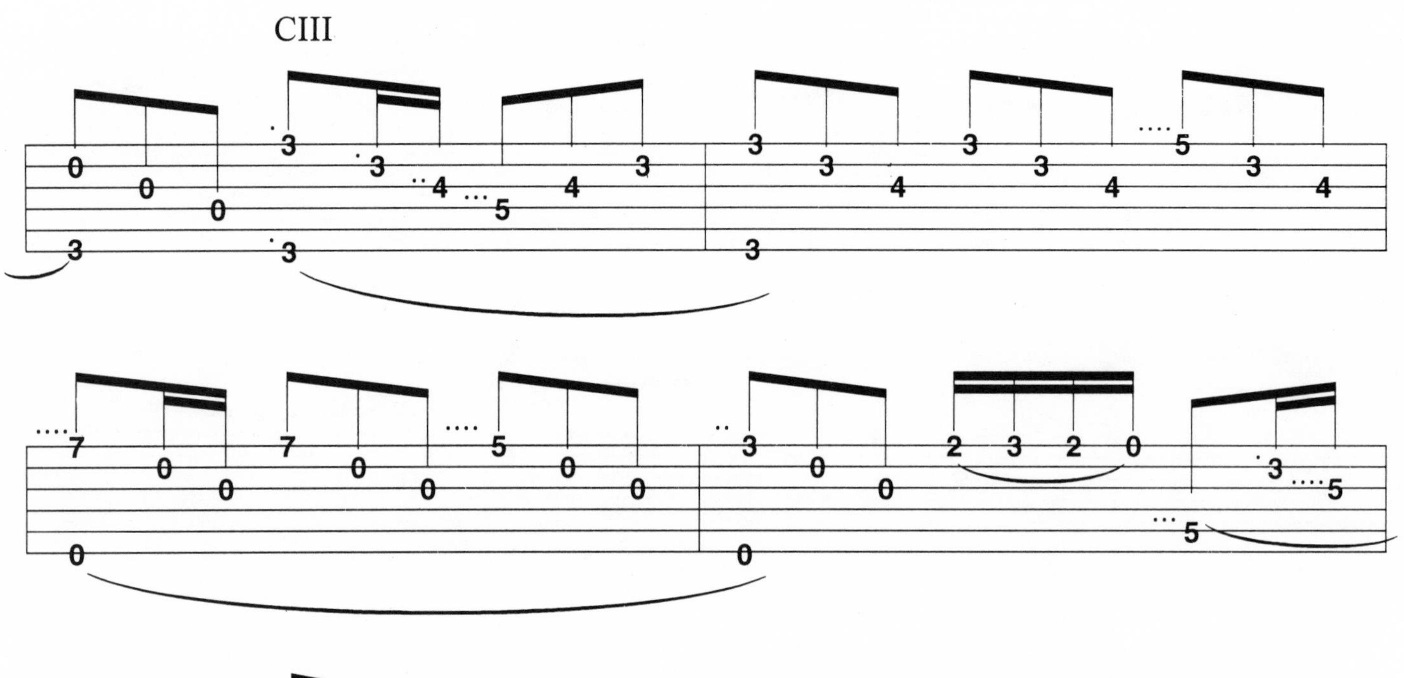


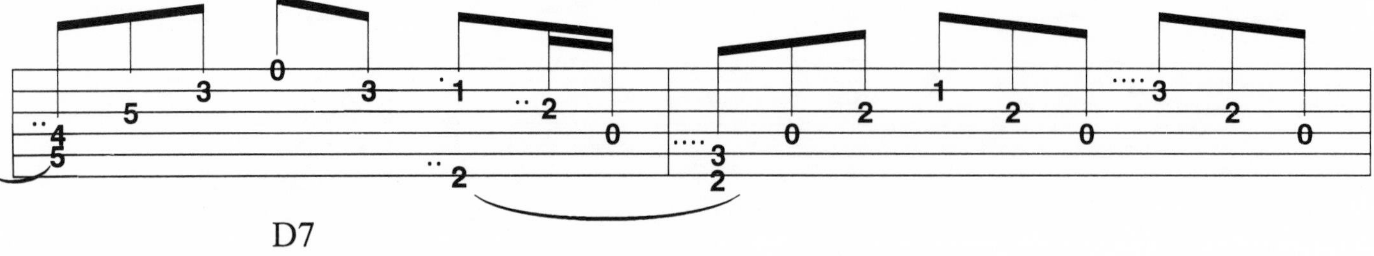

D7

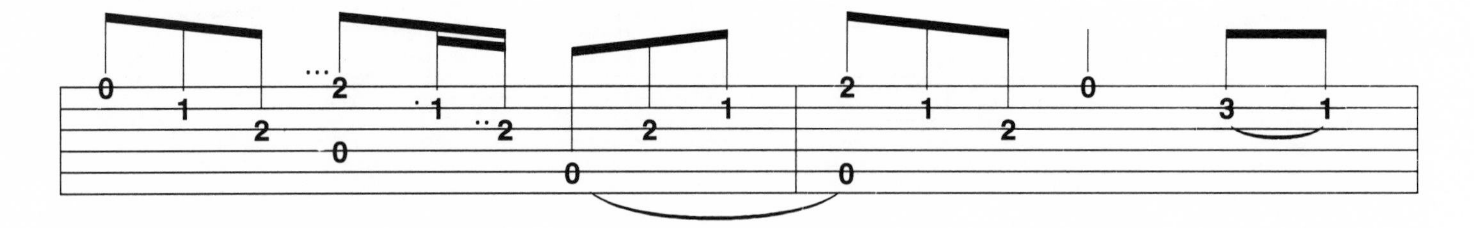

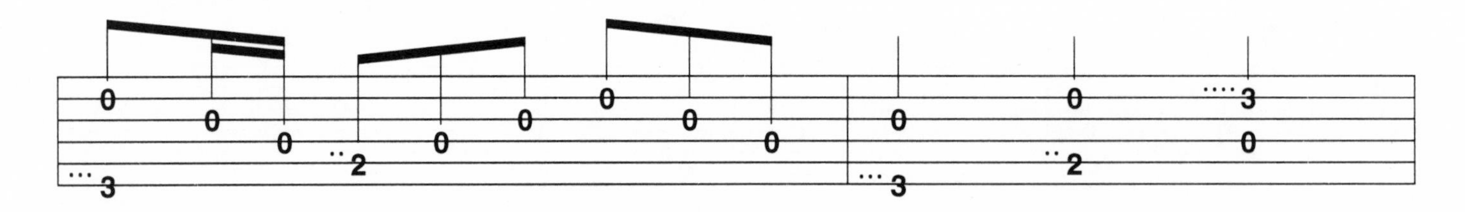

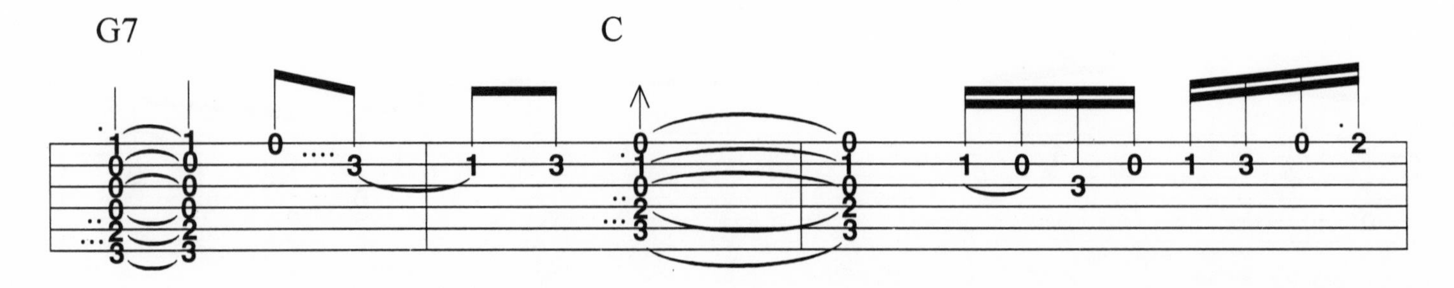

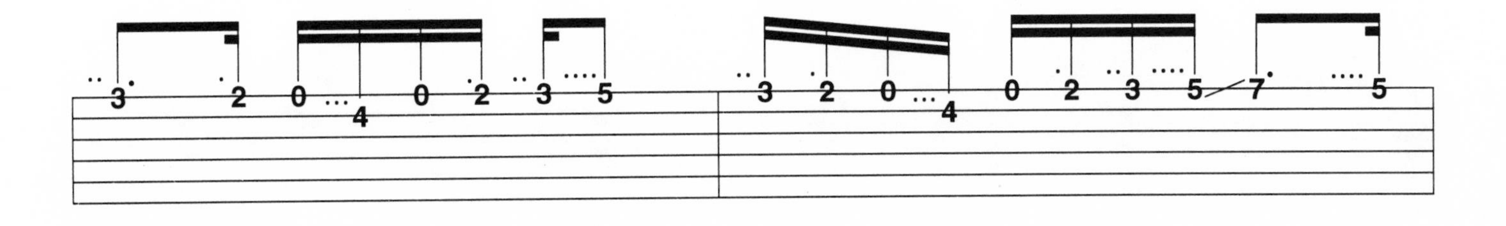

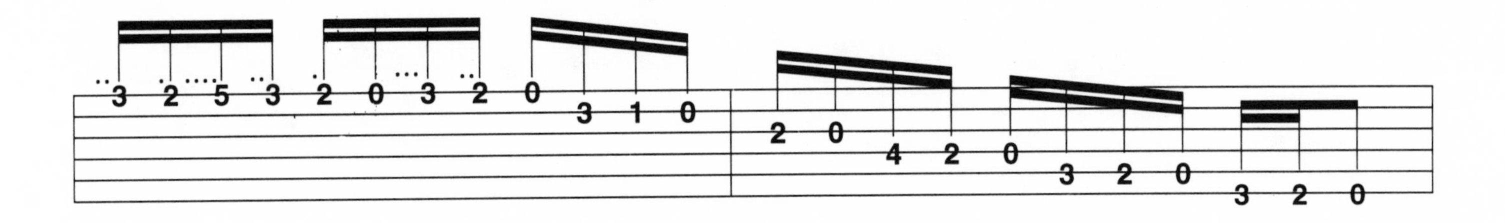

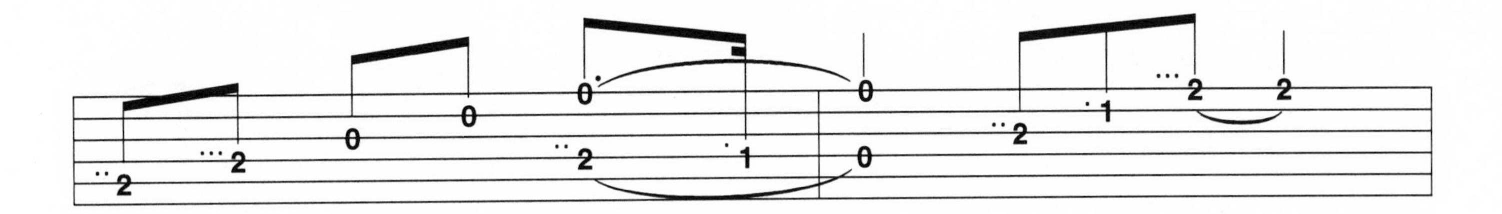

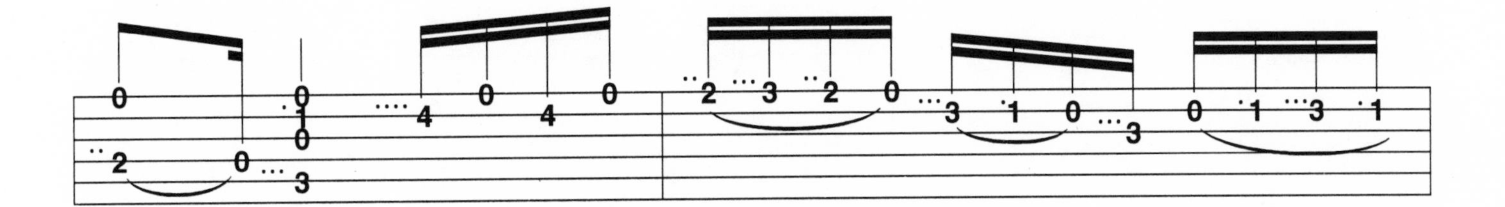

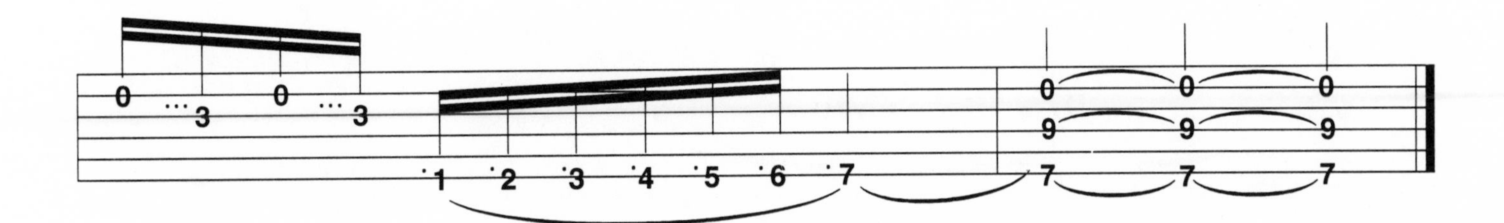

Falseta 3 Juan Serrano

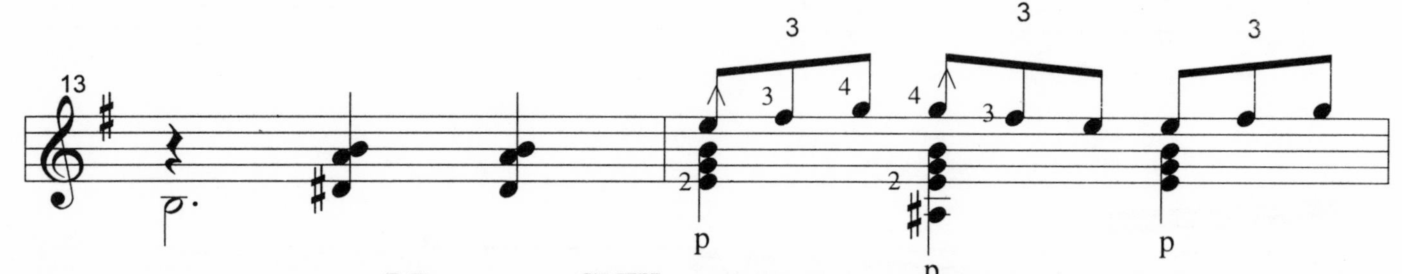

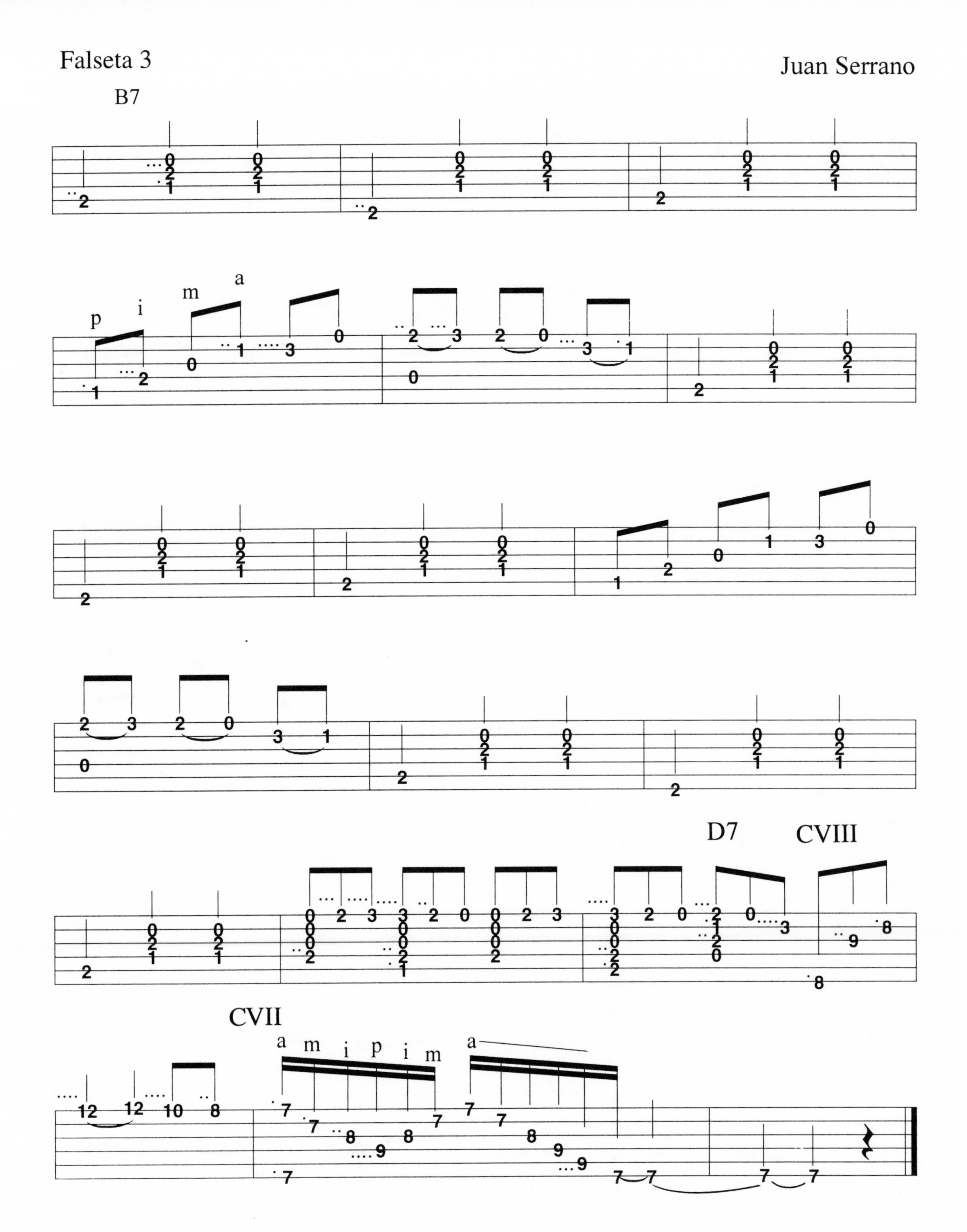
Falseta 3
Juan Serrano
B7
p i m a
D7
CVIII
CVII
a m i p i m
a

## Falseta 4

Juan Serrano

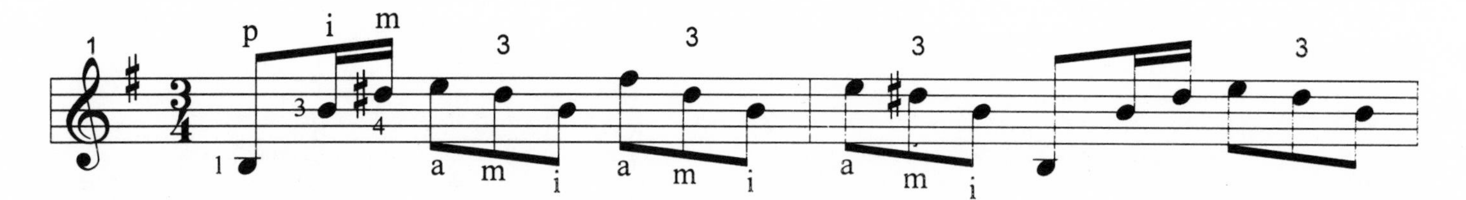

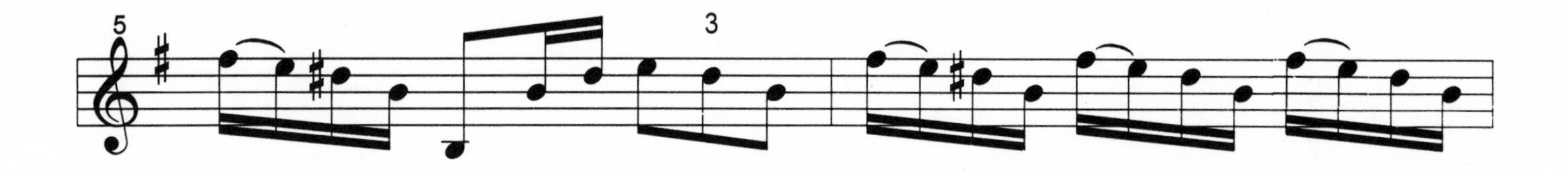

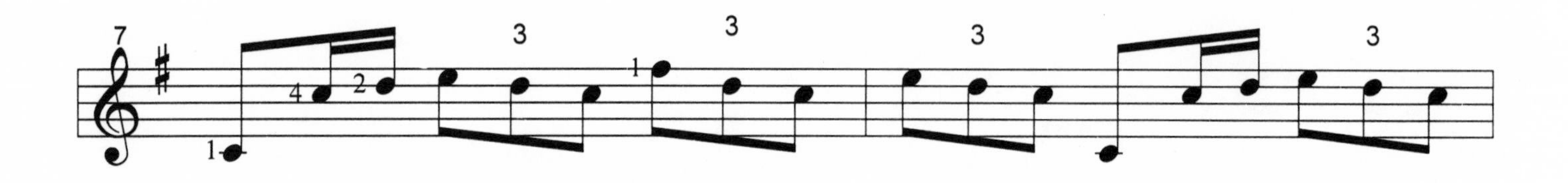

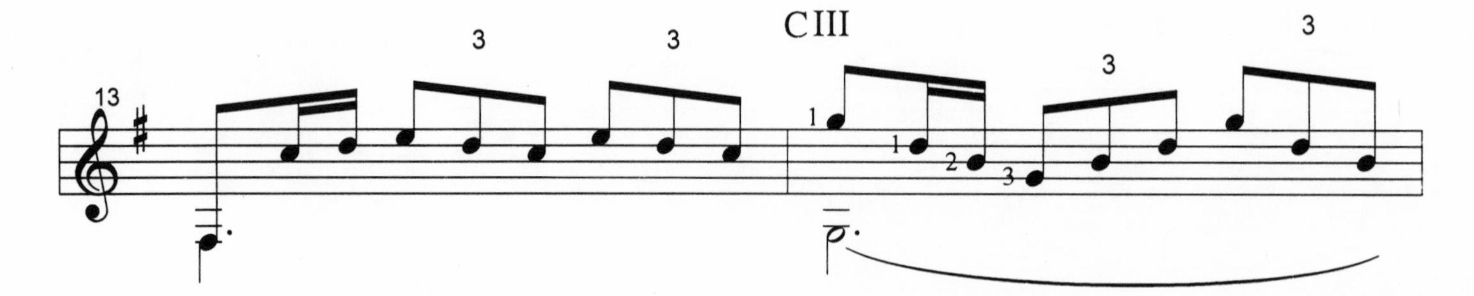

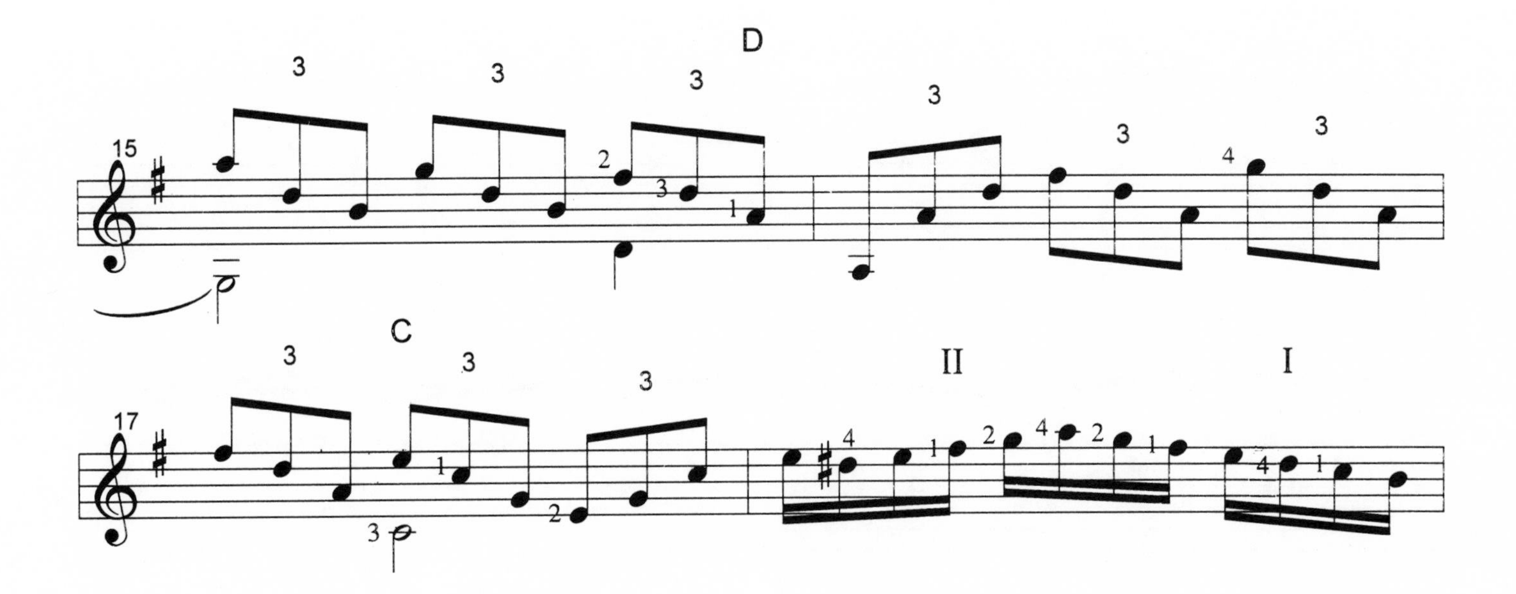
D
C
II
I
VII

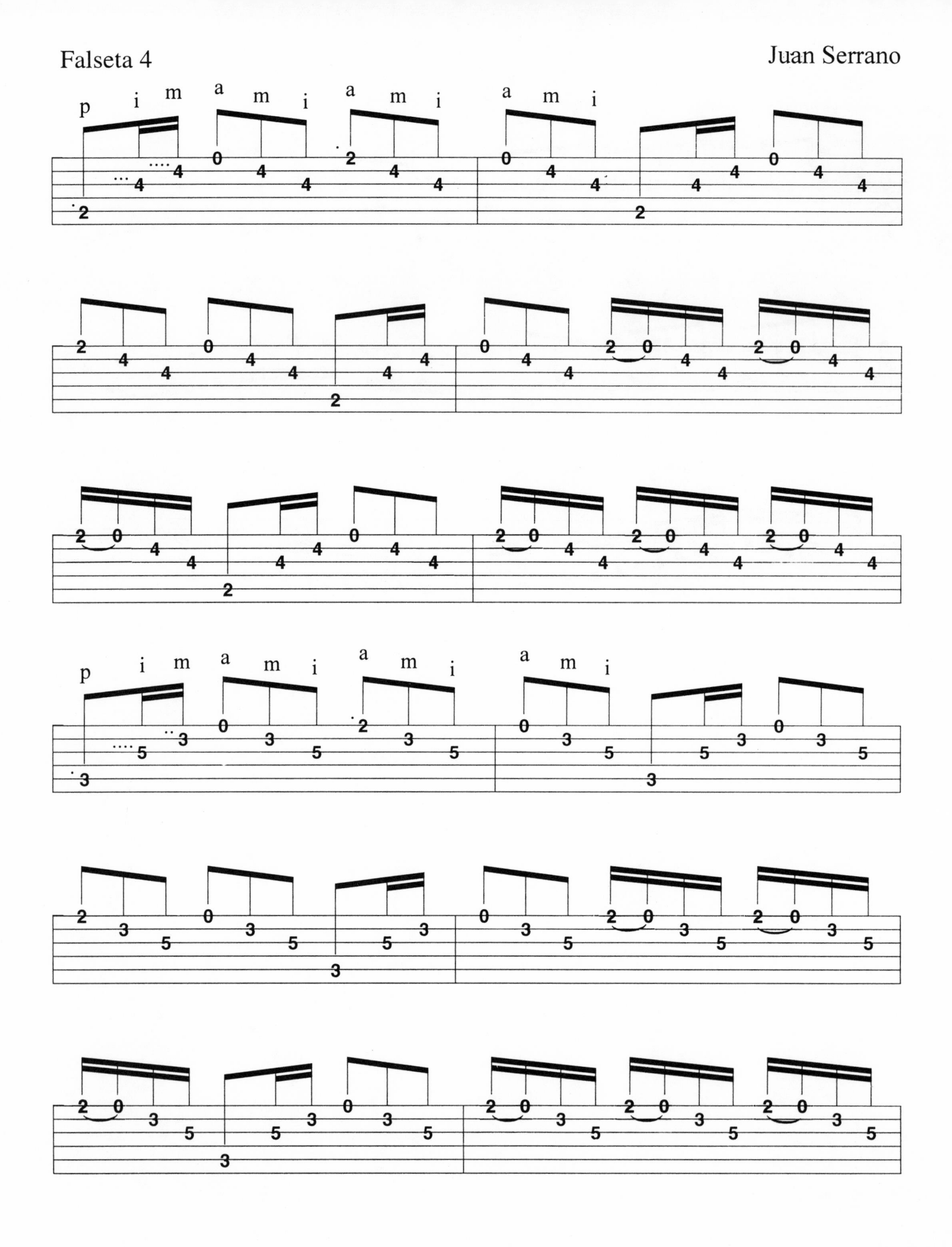
Falseta 4
Juan Serrano

## CIII

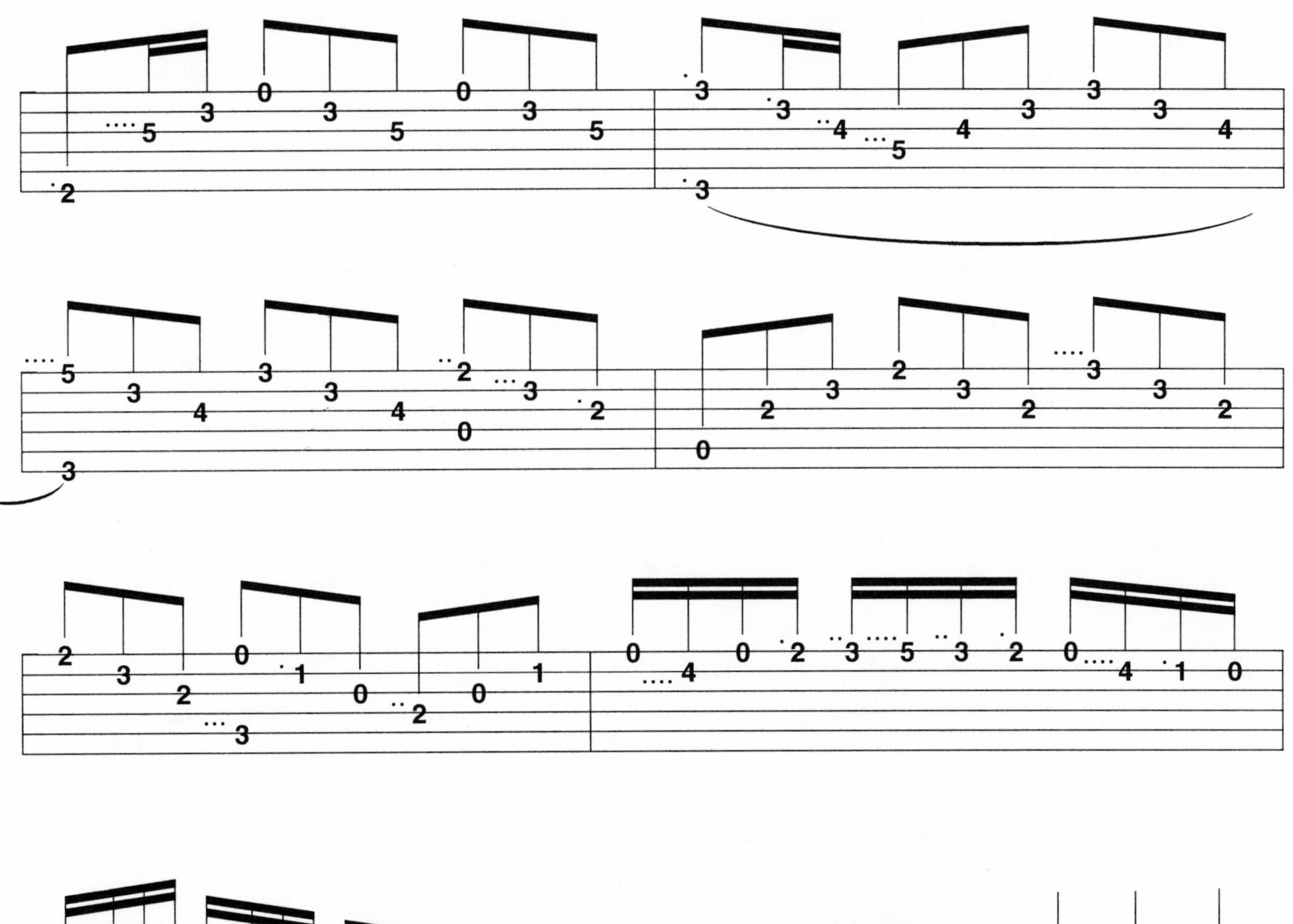

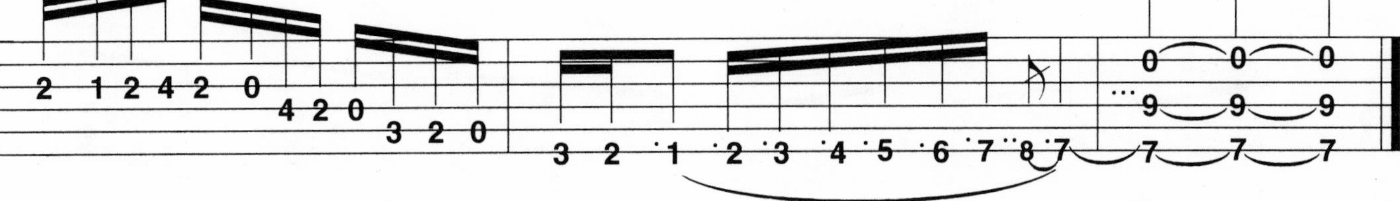

Falseta 5 IV Juan Serrano

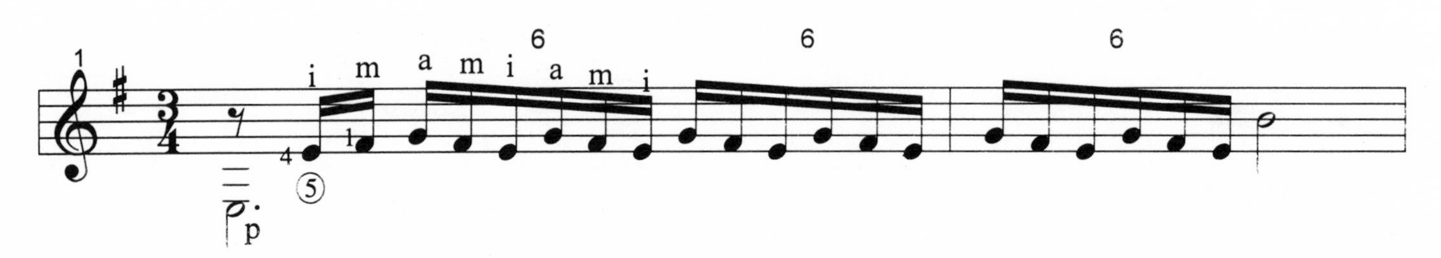


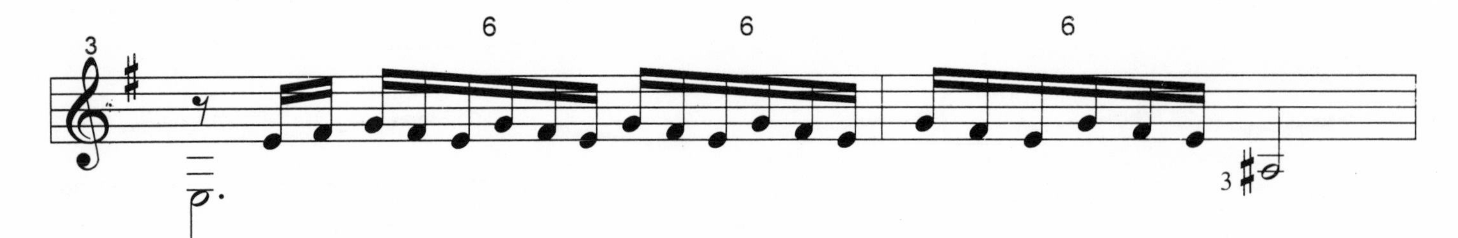

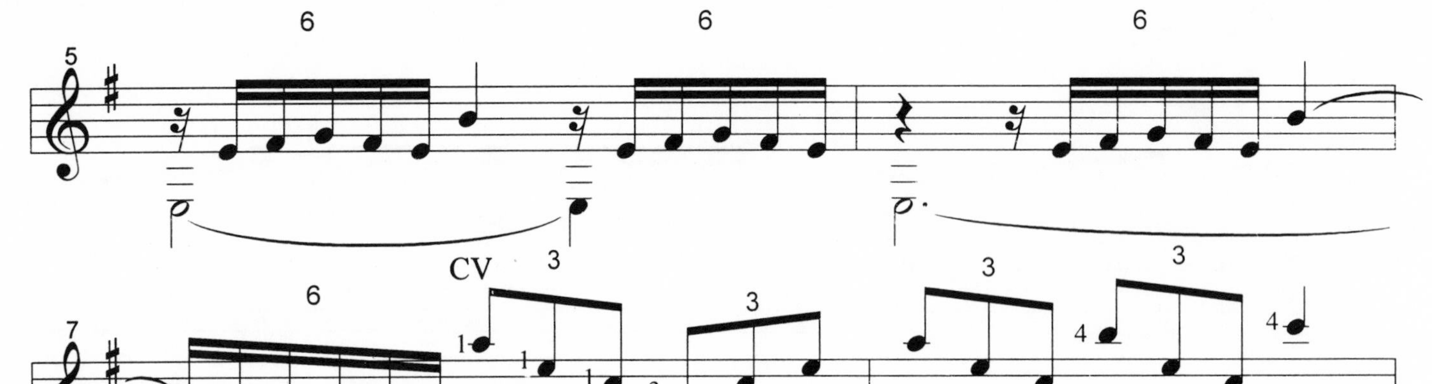

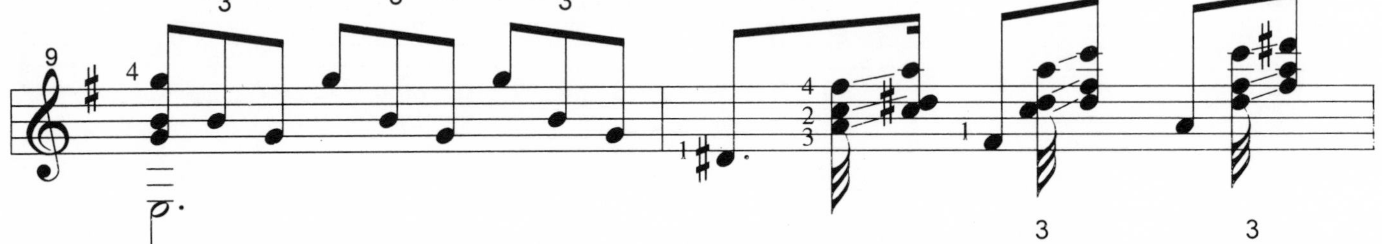

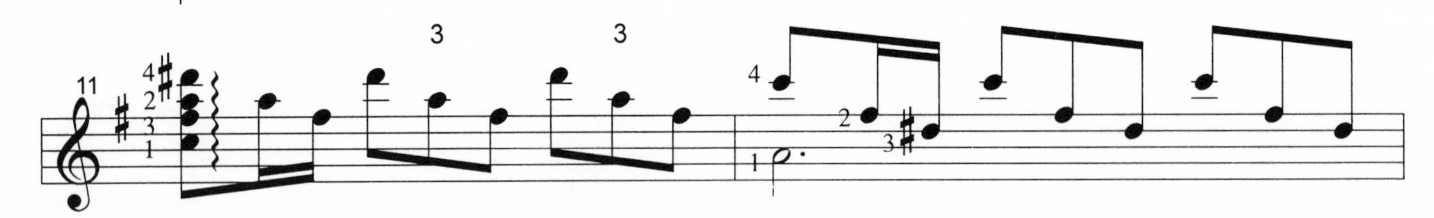

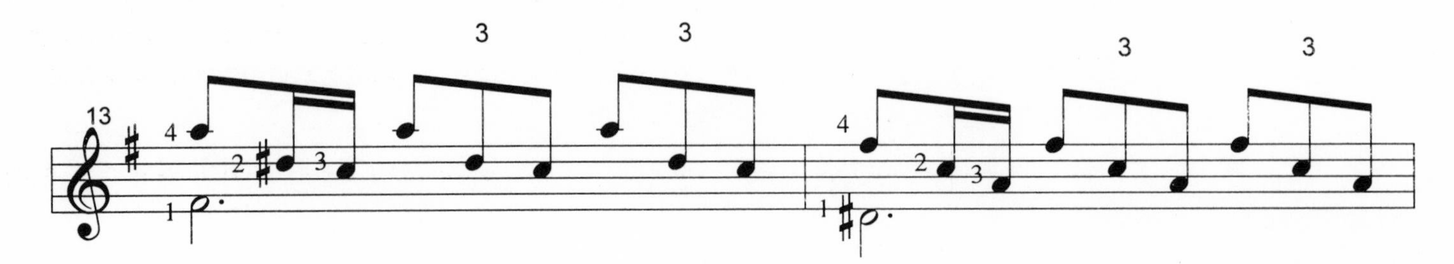

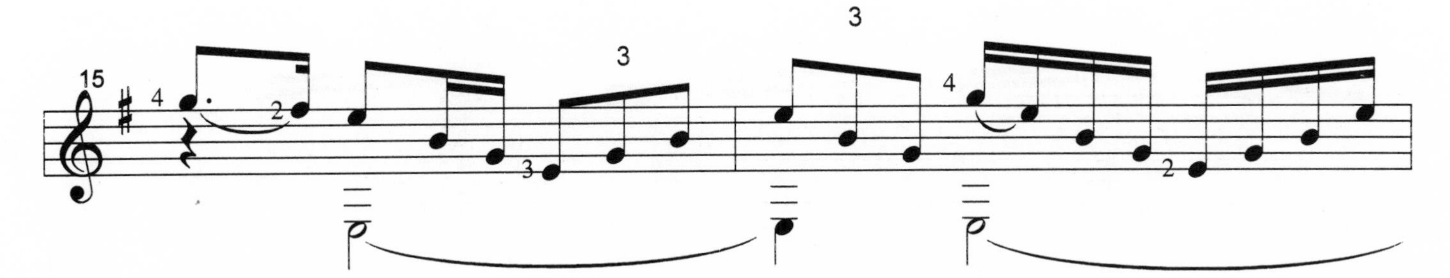
15
3
3

17

19
5
5

Falseta 5

Juan Serrano

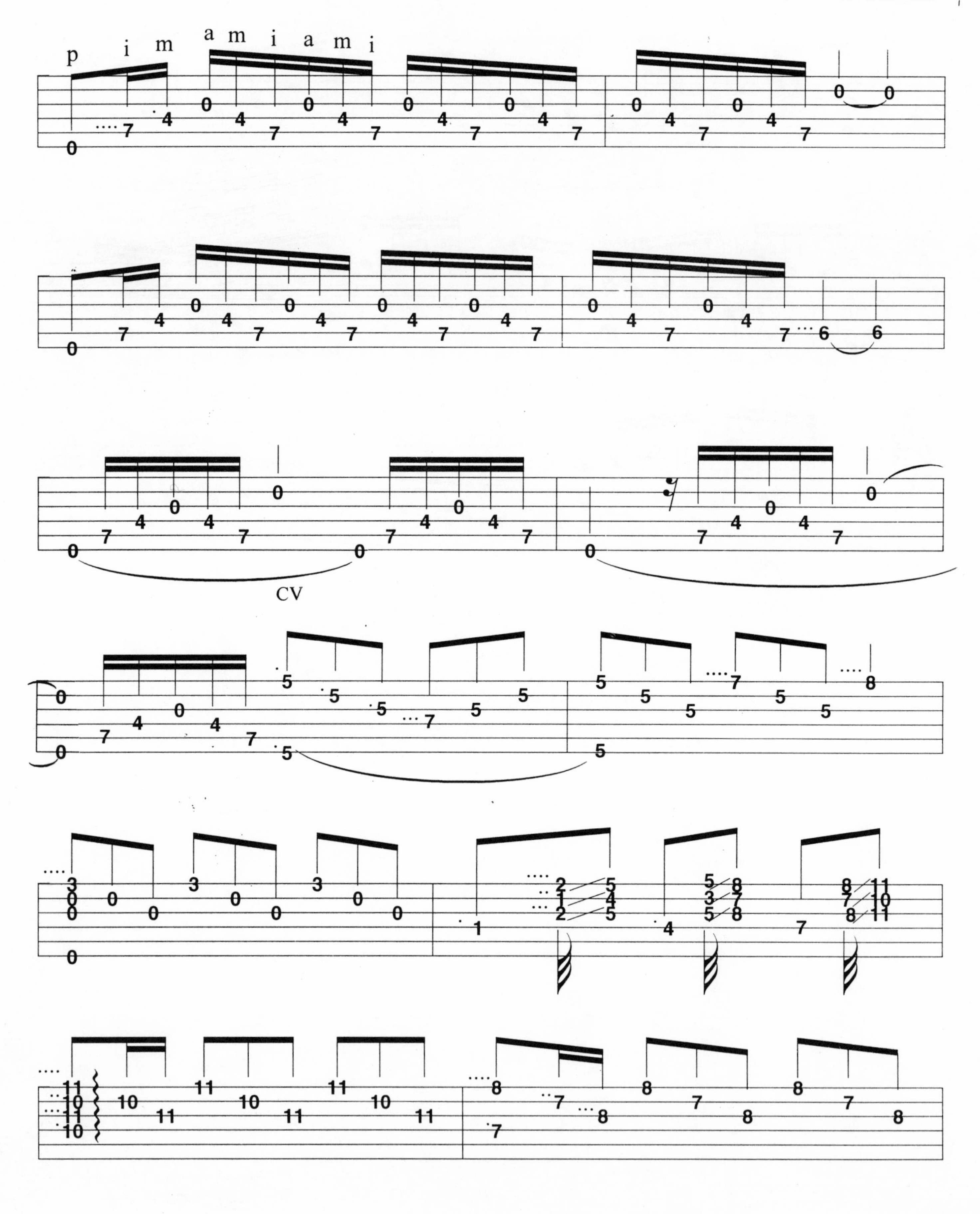

Falseta 6

Juan Serrano

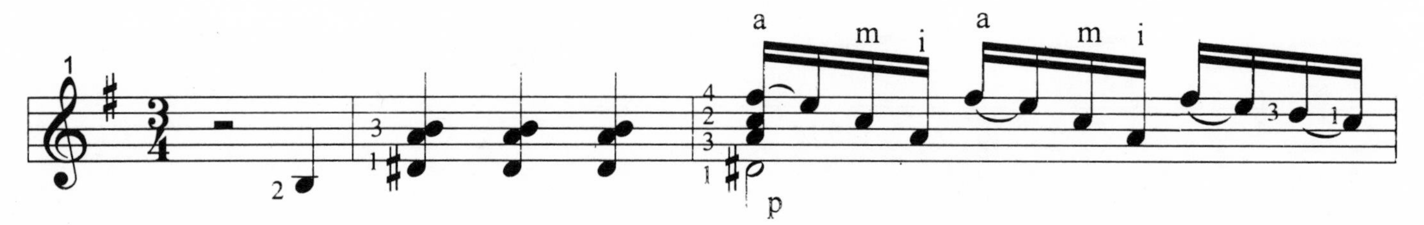


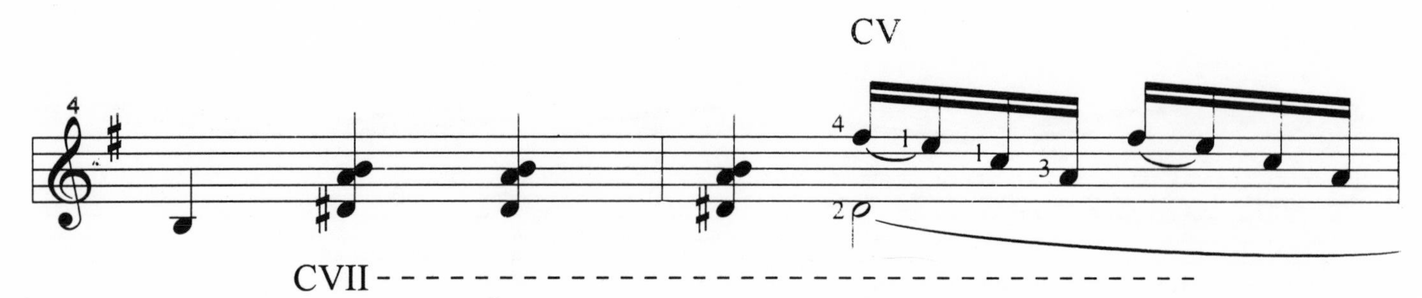


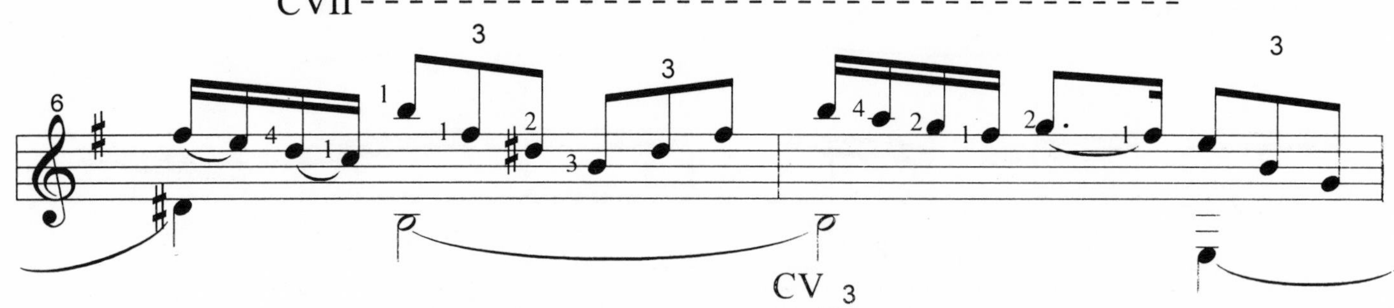

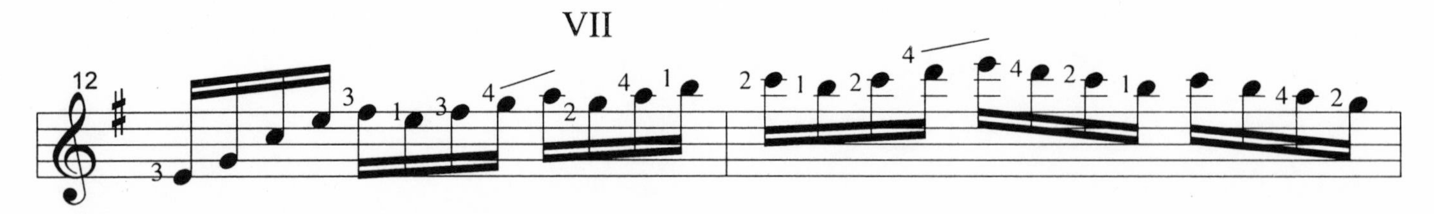


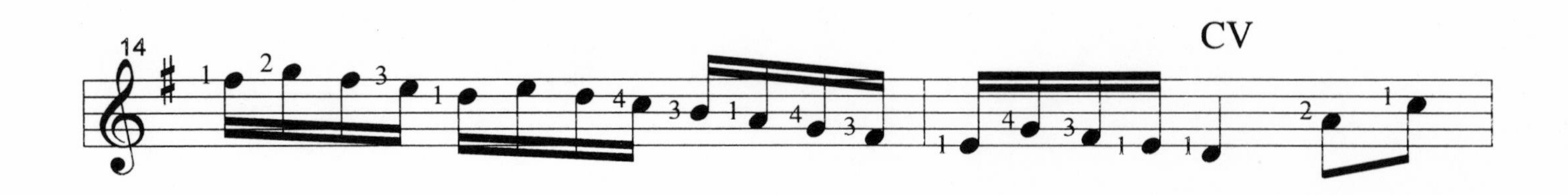

CV

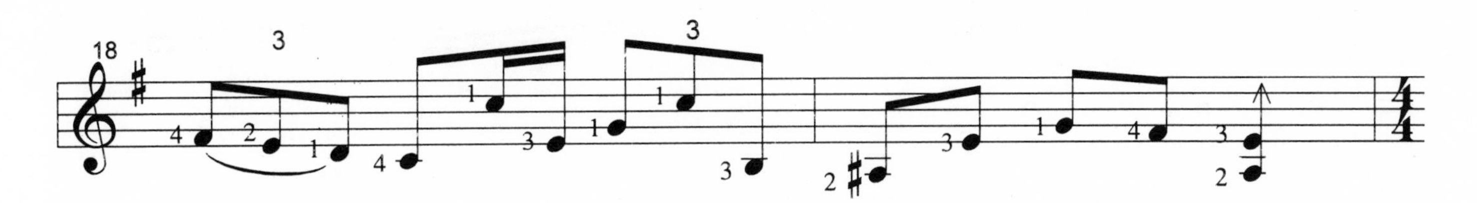

VII
p m i
p- - -i m a

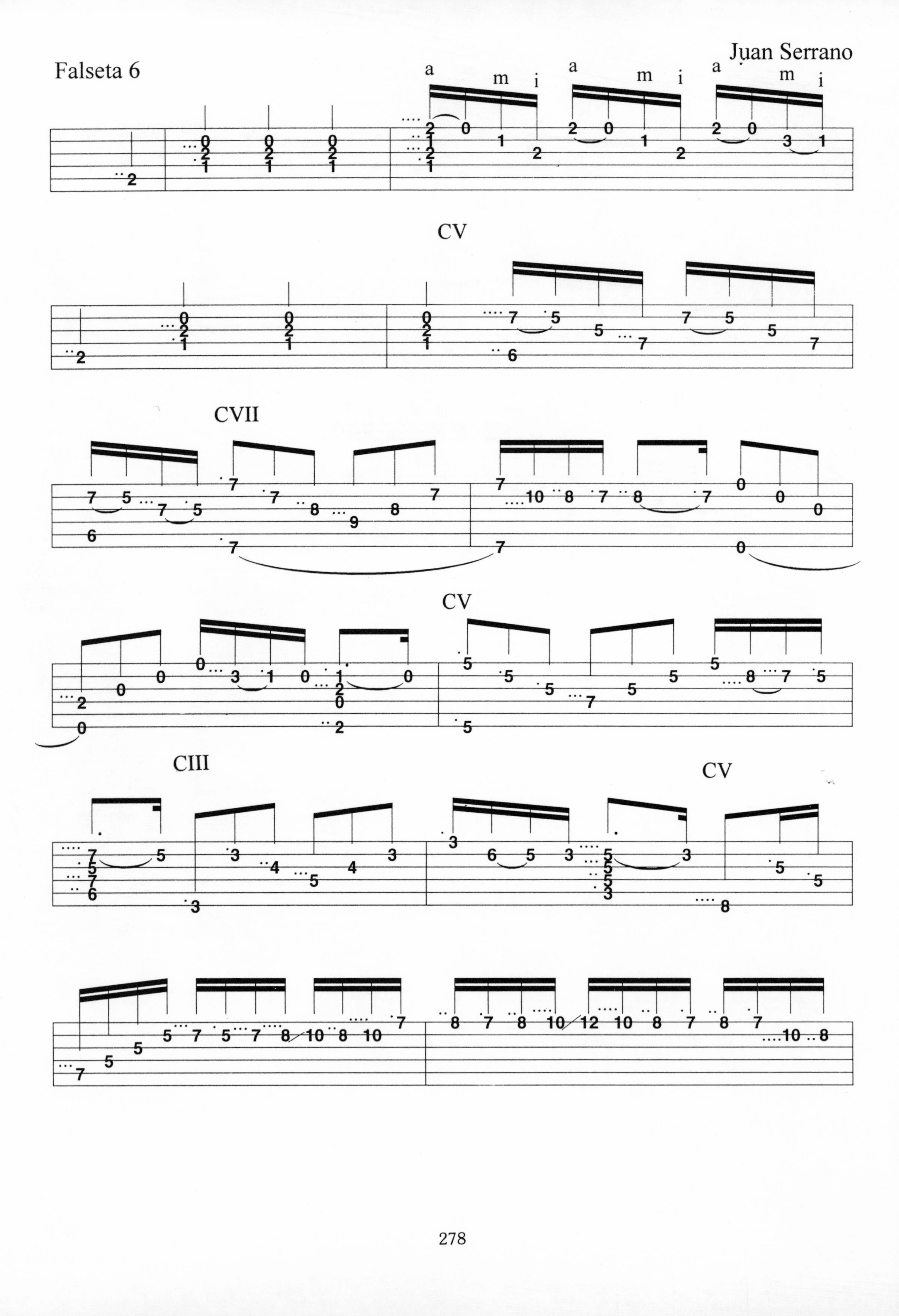

Falseta 6
Juan Serrano
a m i a m i a m i
CV
CVII
CV
CIII
CV

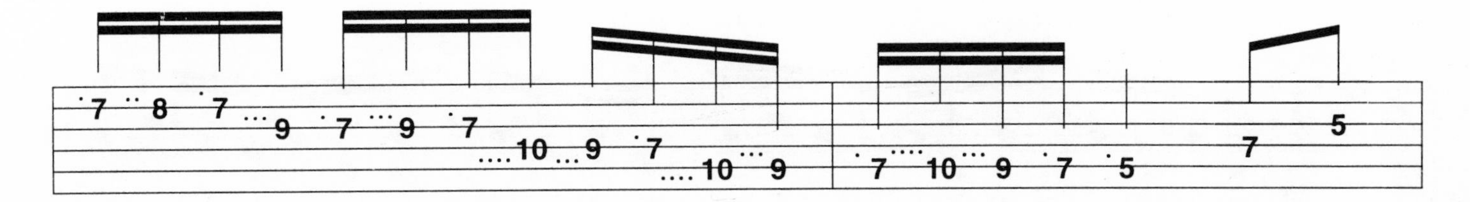

CV

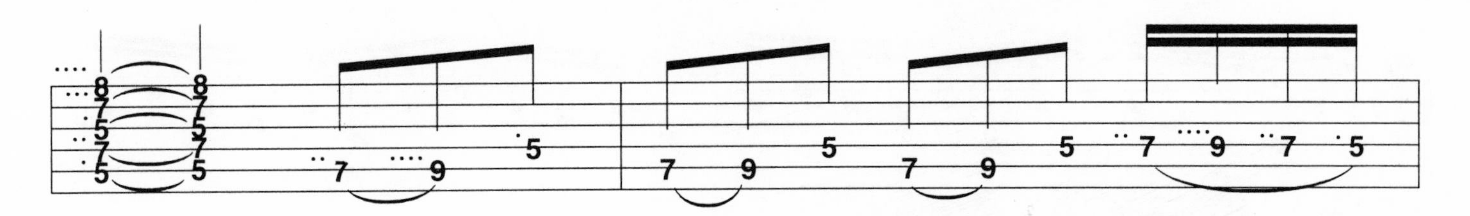

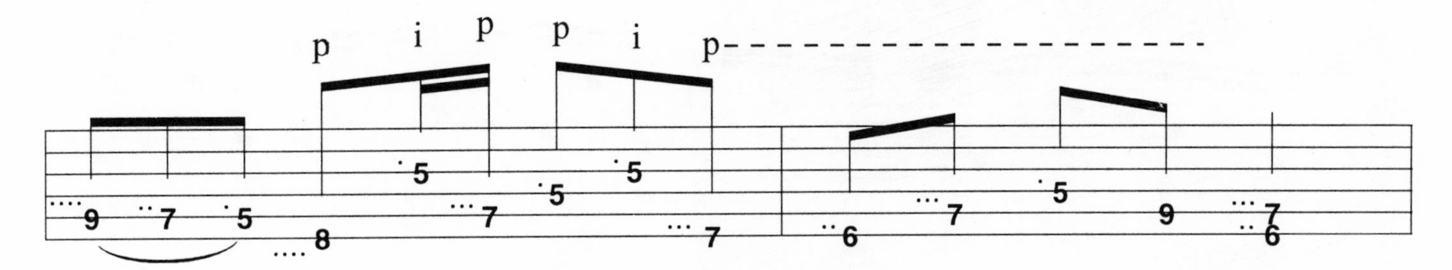


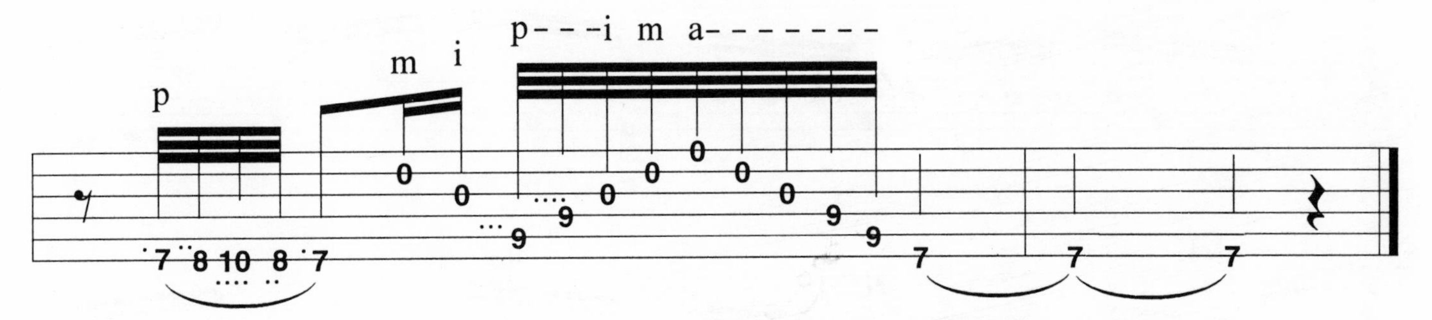

Falseta 7

Juan Serrano

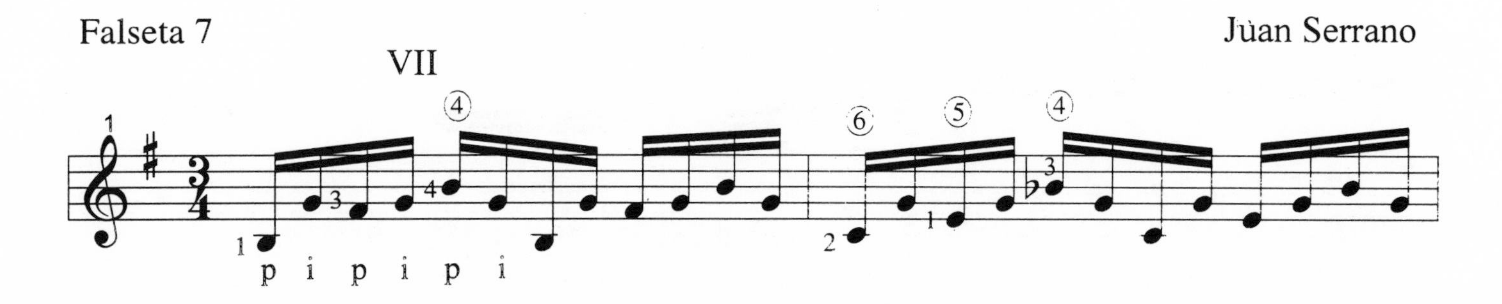

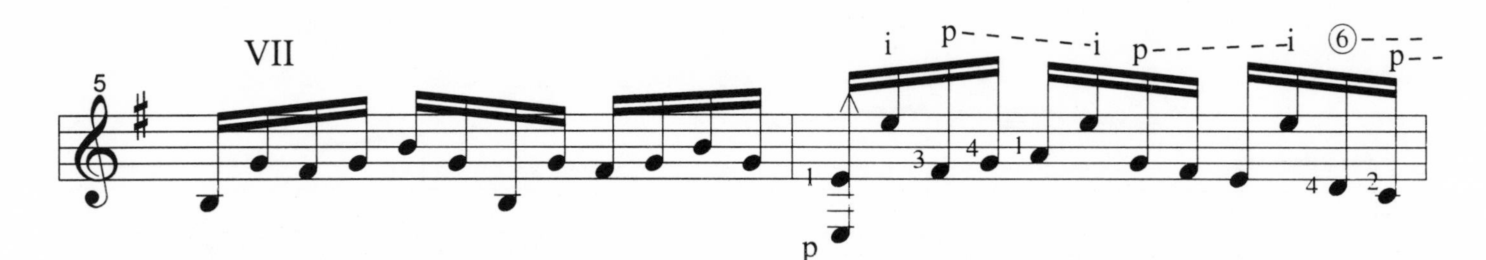

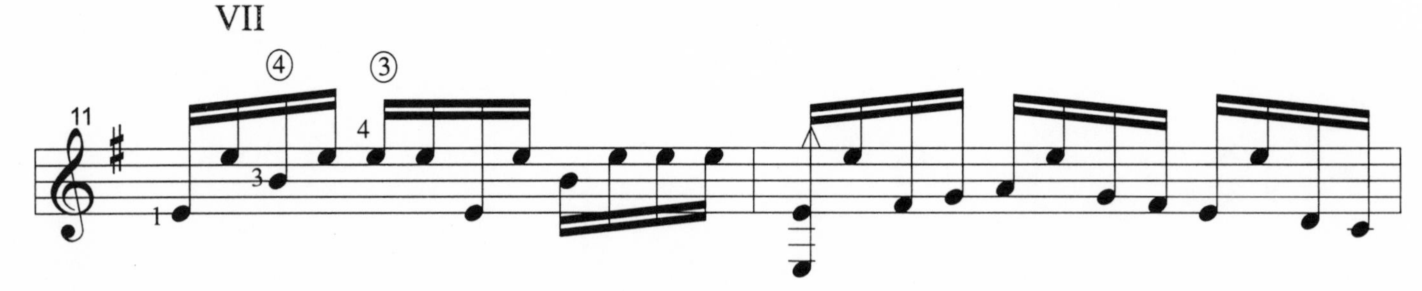

V
CIII G7

III C
II

II - - - - - - - - - - - - - - - - - - - - - - - I
Em
p - - - - i m a

rit.

Juan Serrano

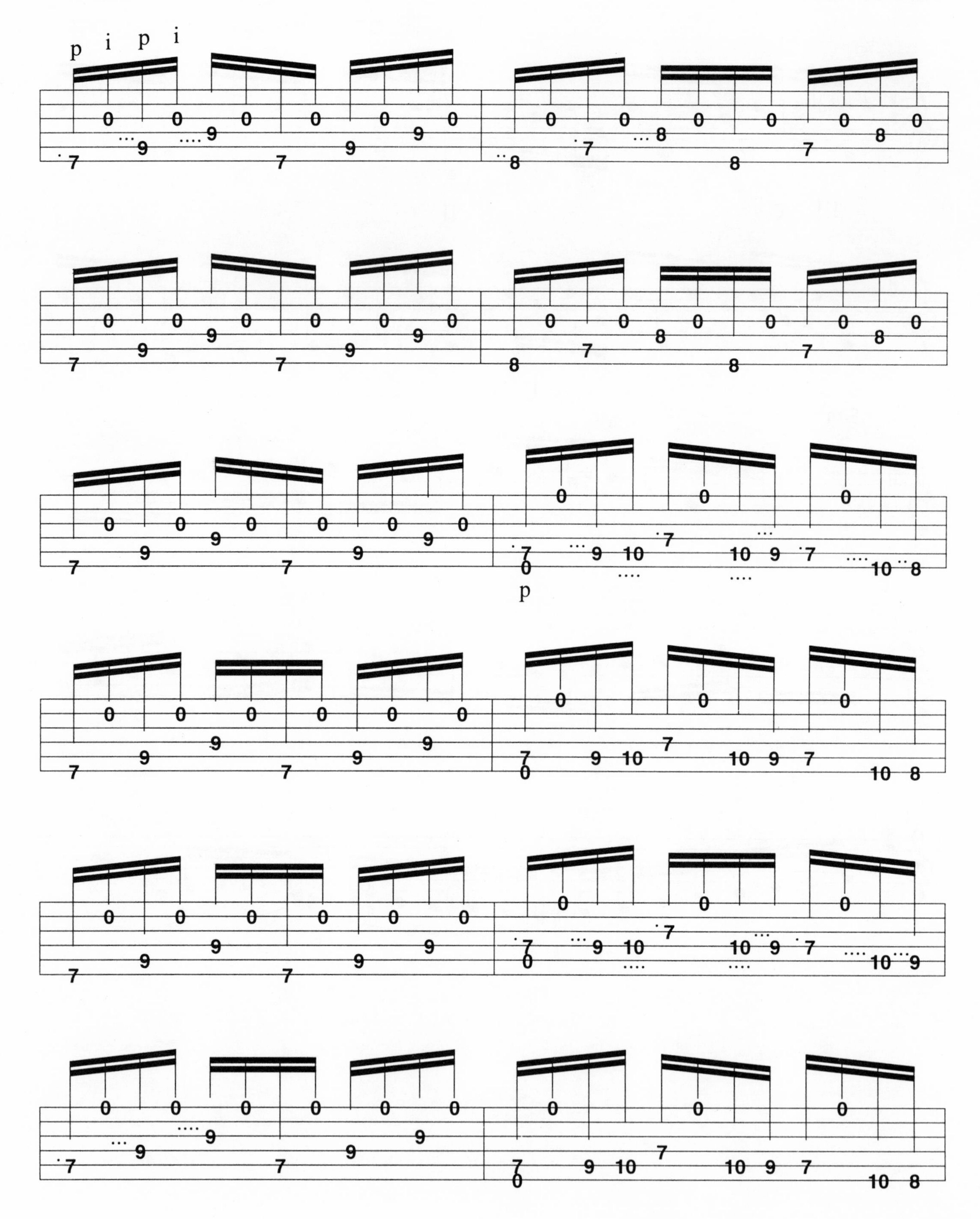

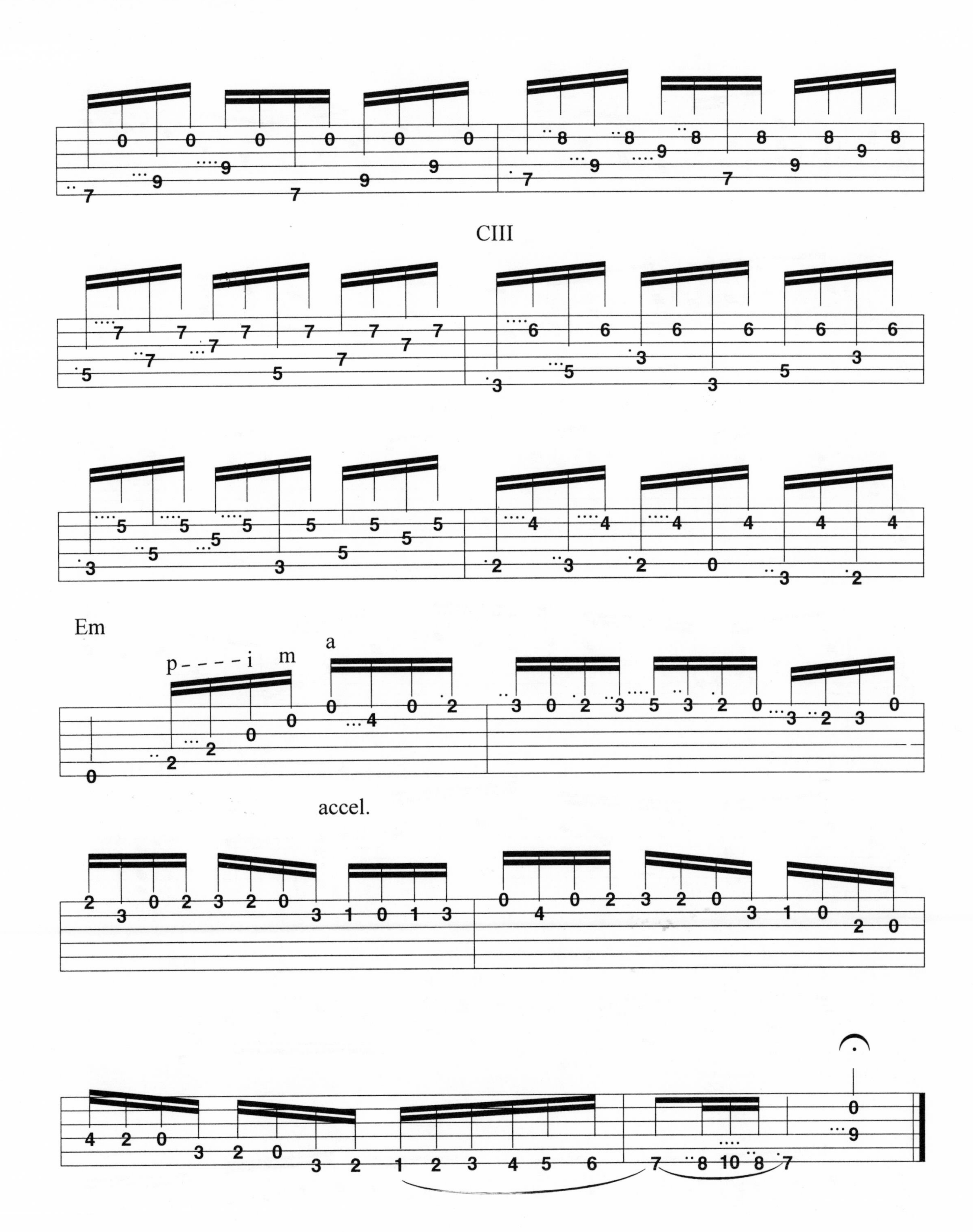
CIII
Em
p - - - - i
m
a
accel.

Falseta 8

Juan Serrano

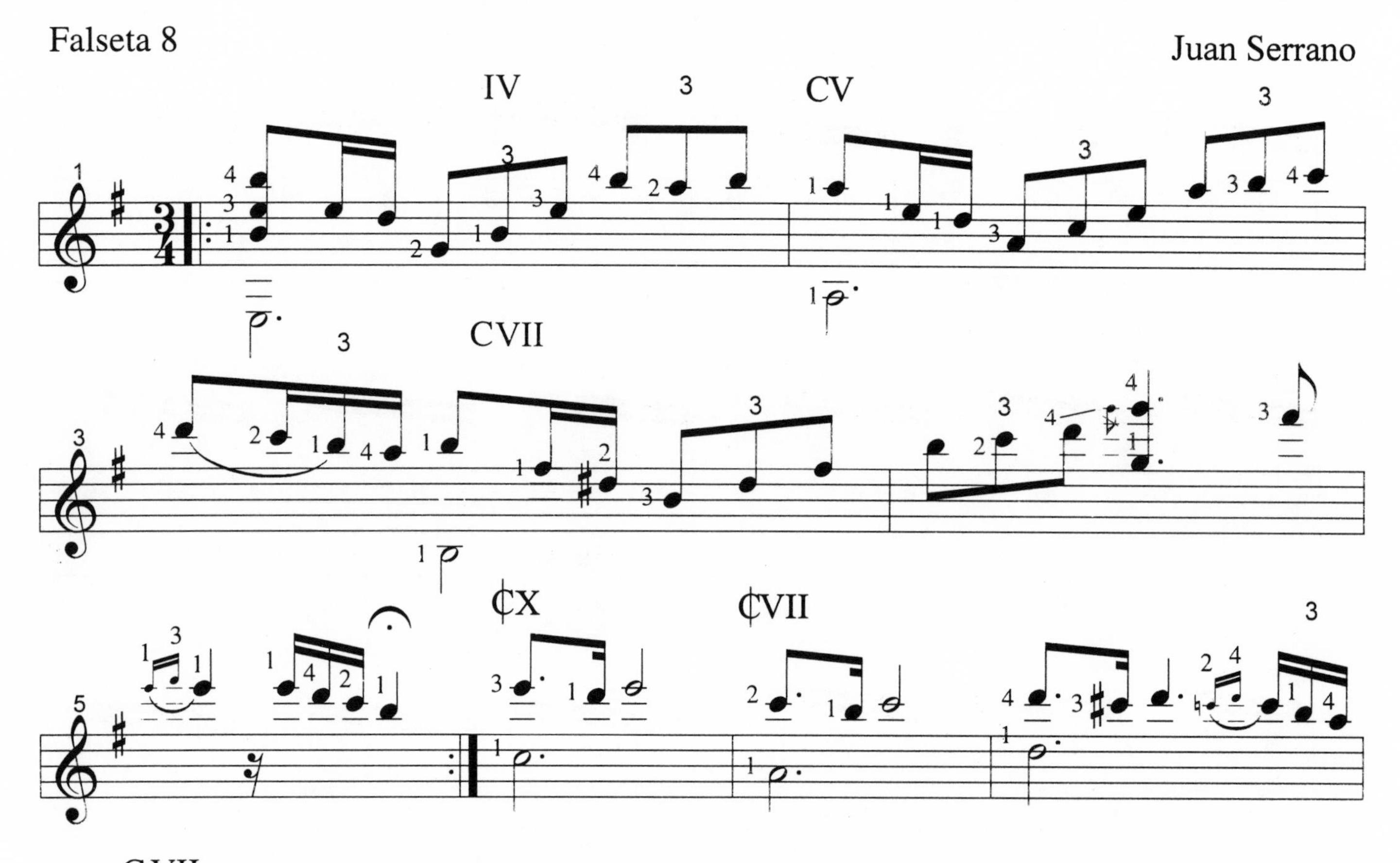


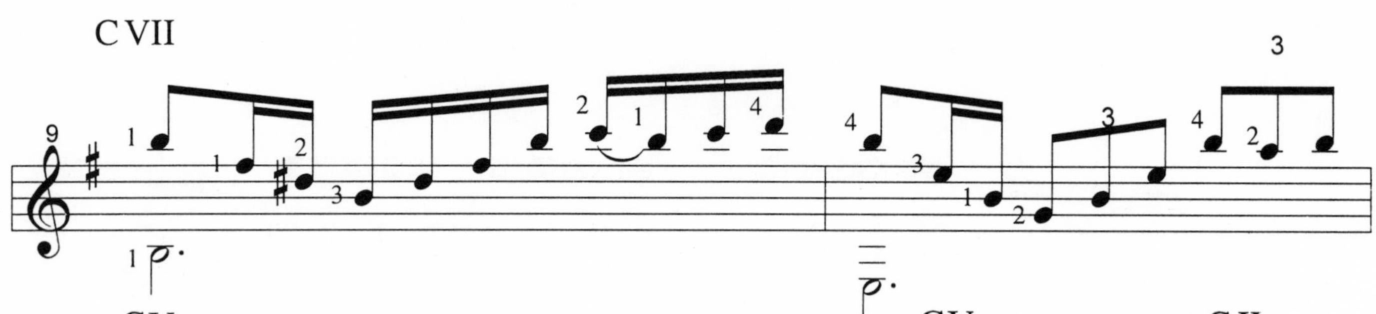


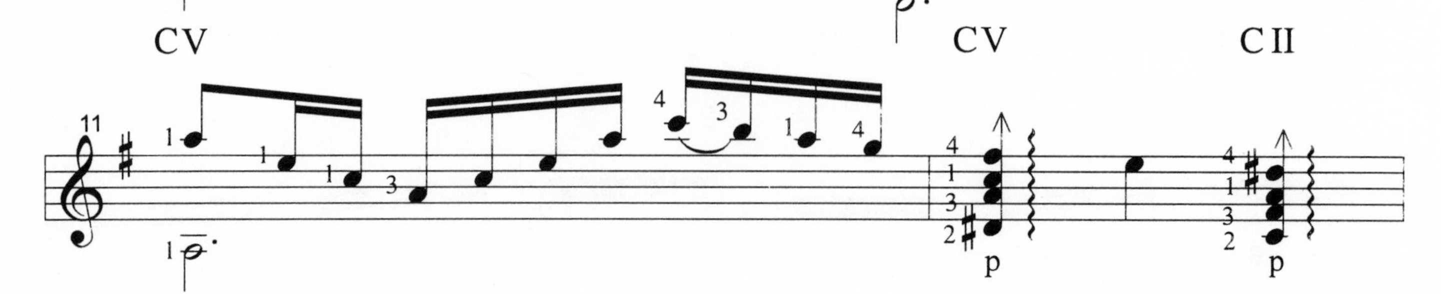


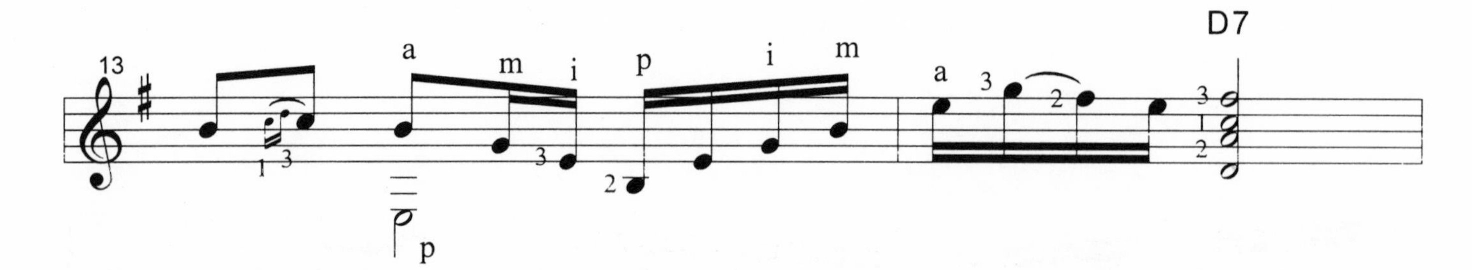

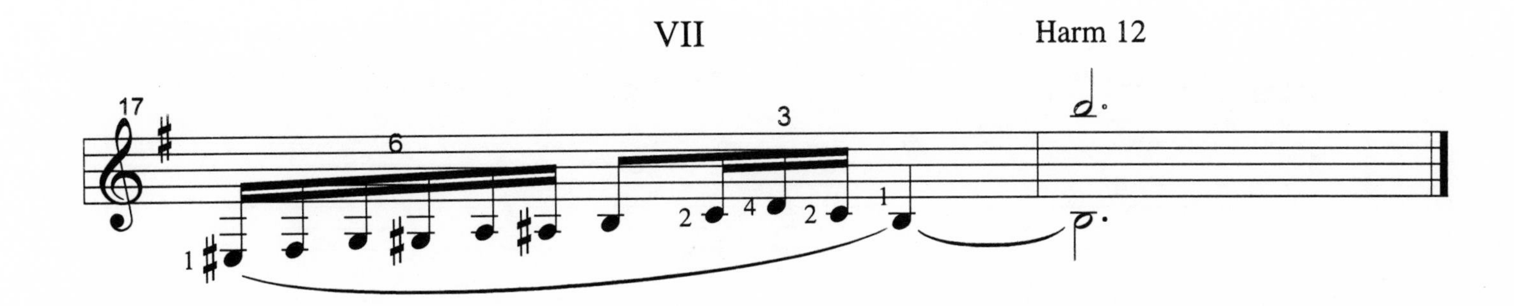
VII
Harm 12
17
6
3

Falseta 8

Juan Serrano

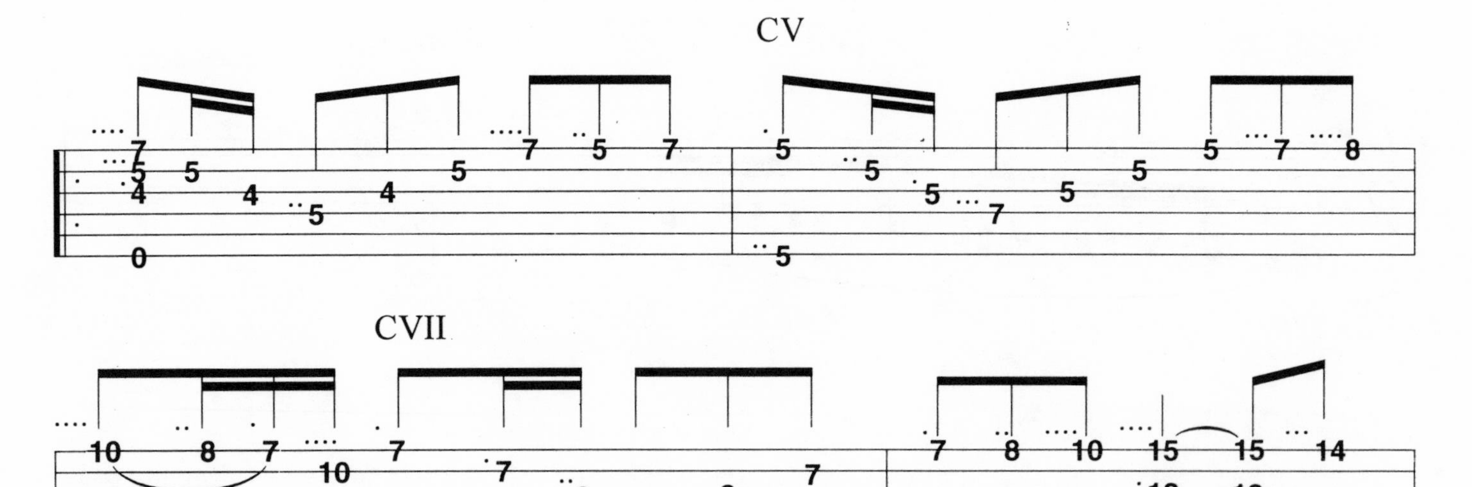


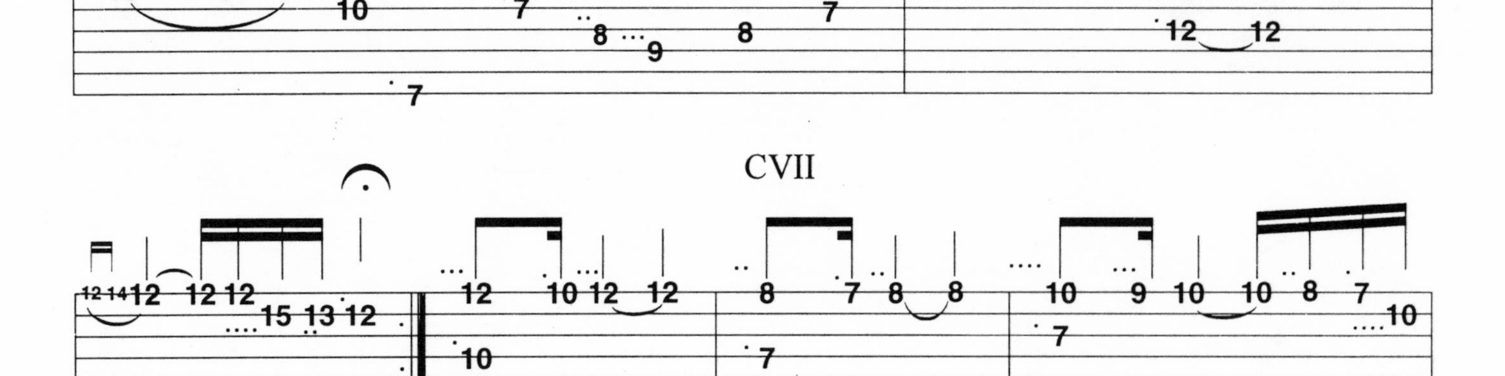


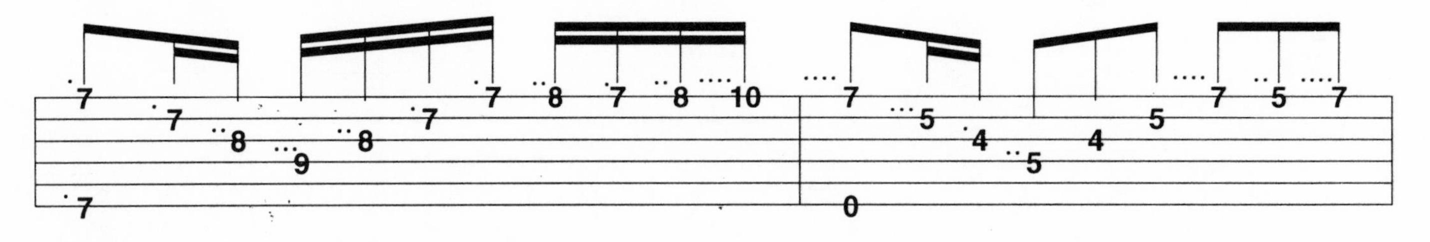

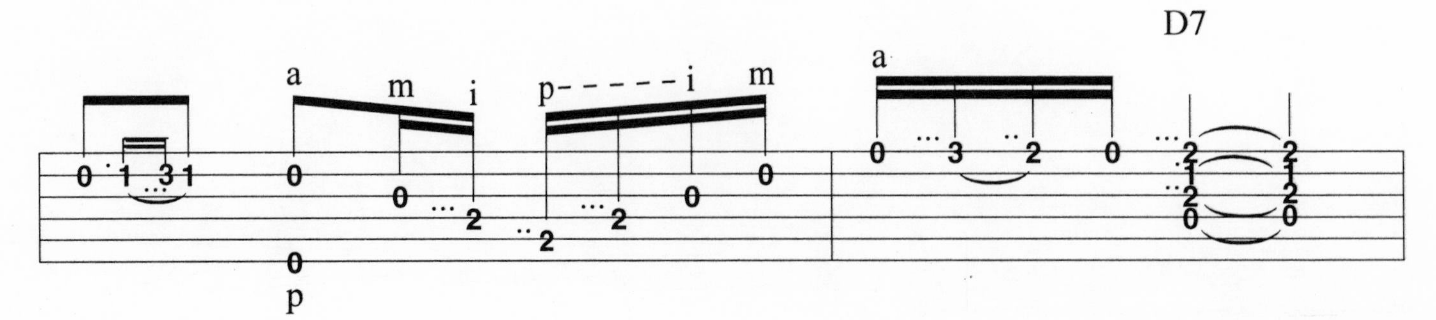

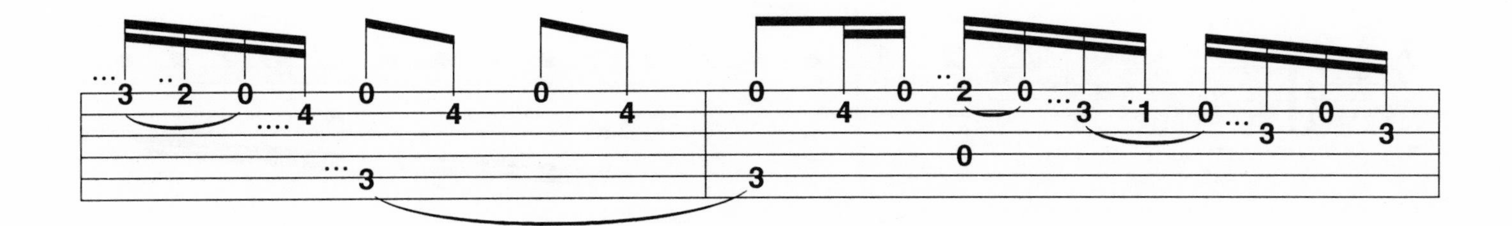

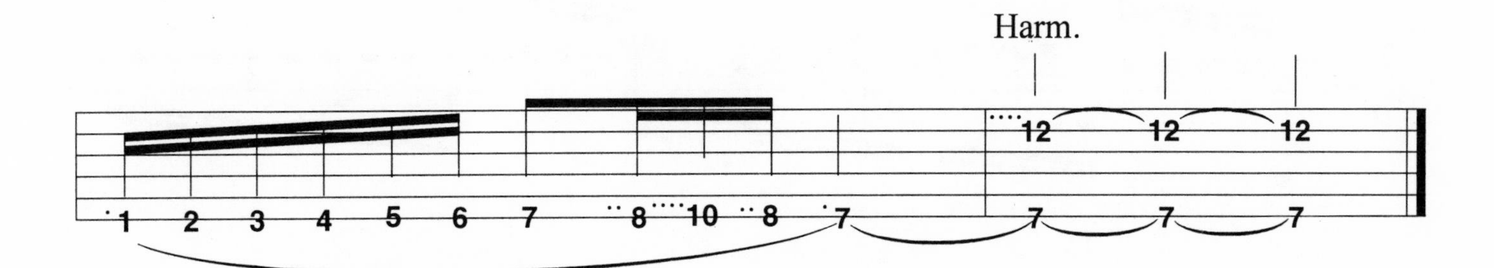
Harm.

Falseta 9

Juan Serrano

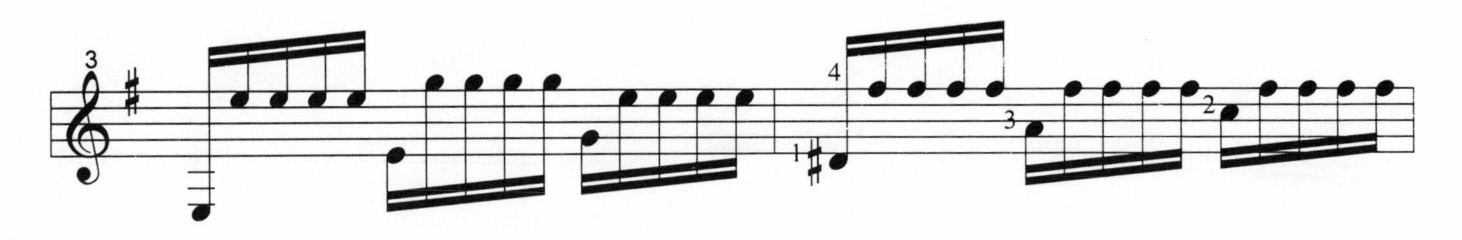

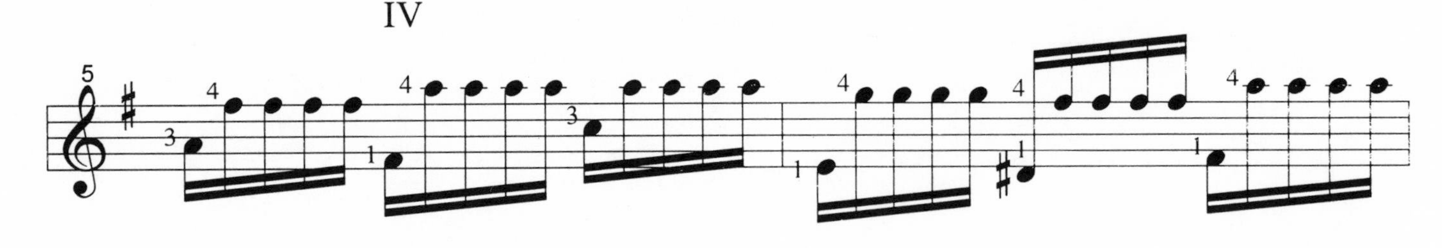

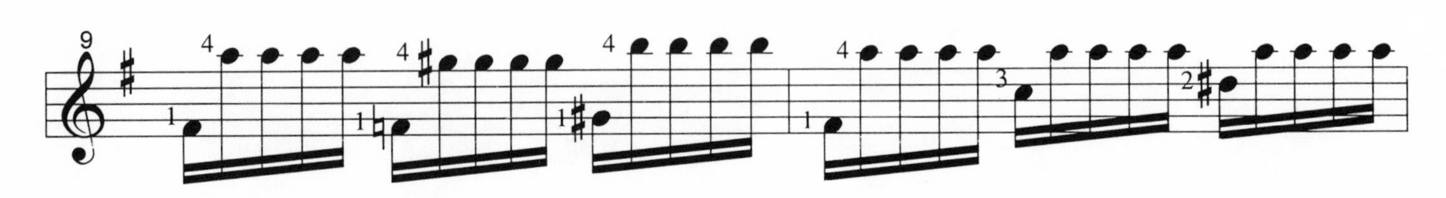


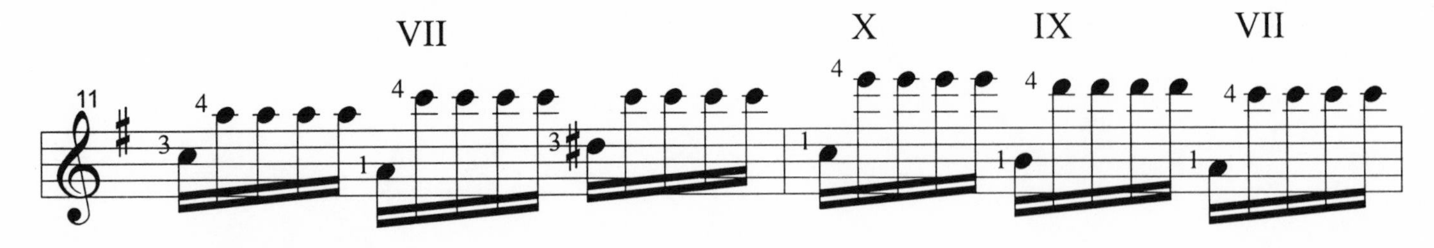


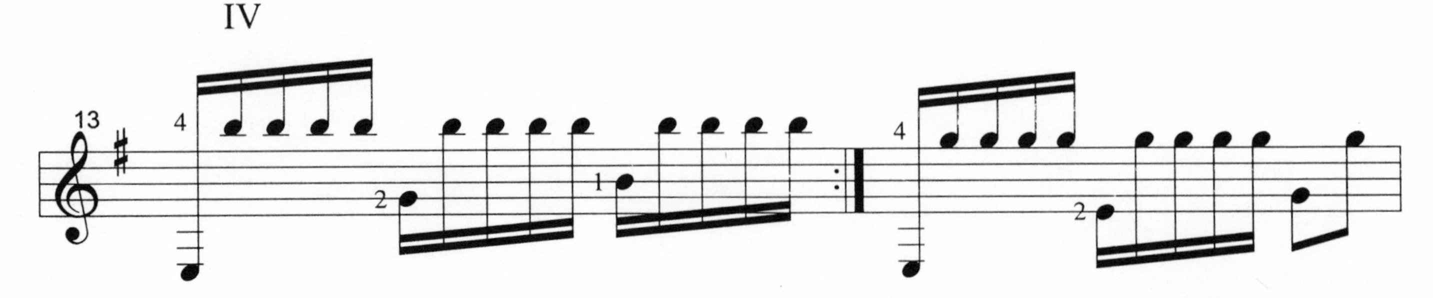

15

17

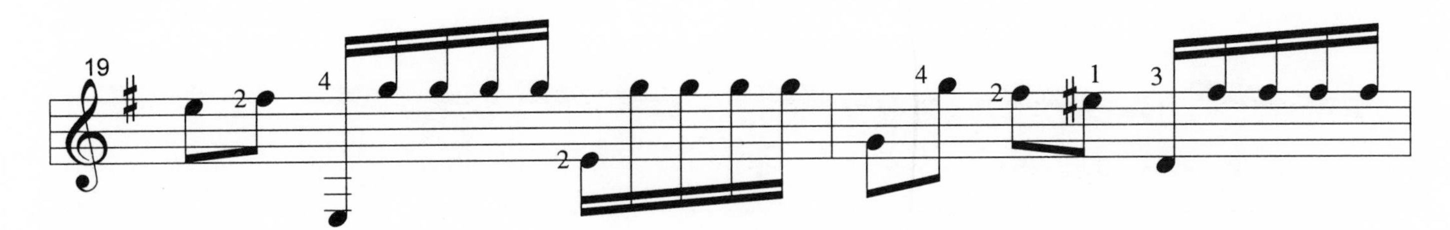
19

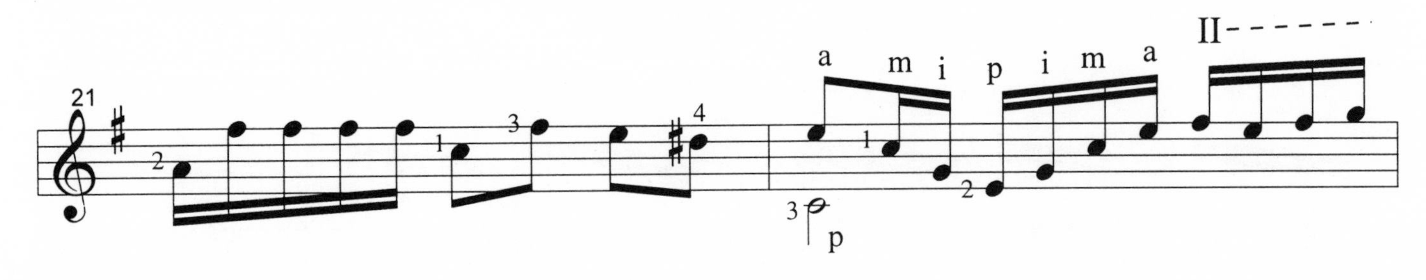
21
a m i p i m a
II
p

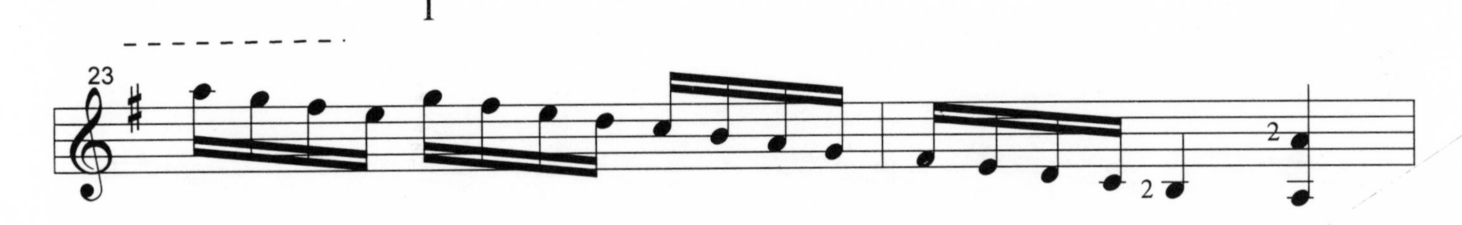
I
23

VII
25

Falseta 9

Juan Serrano

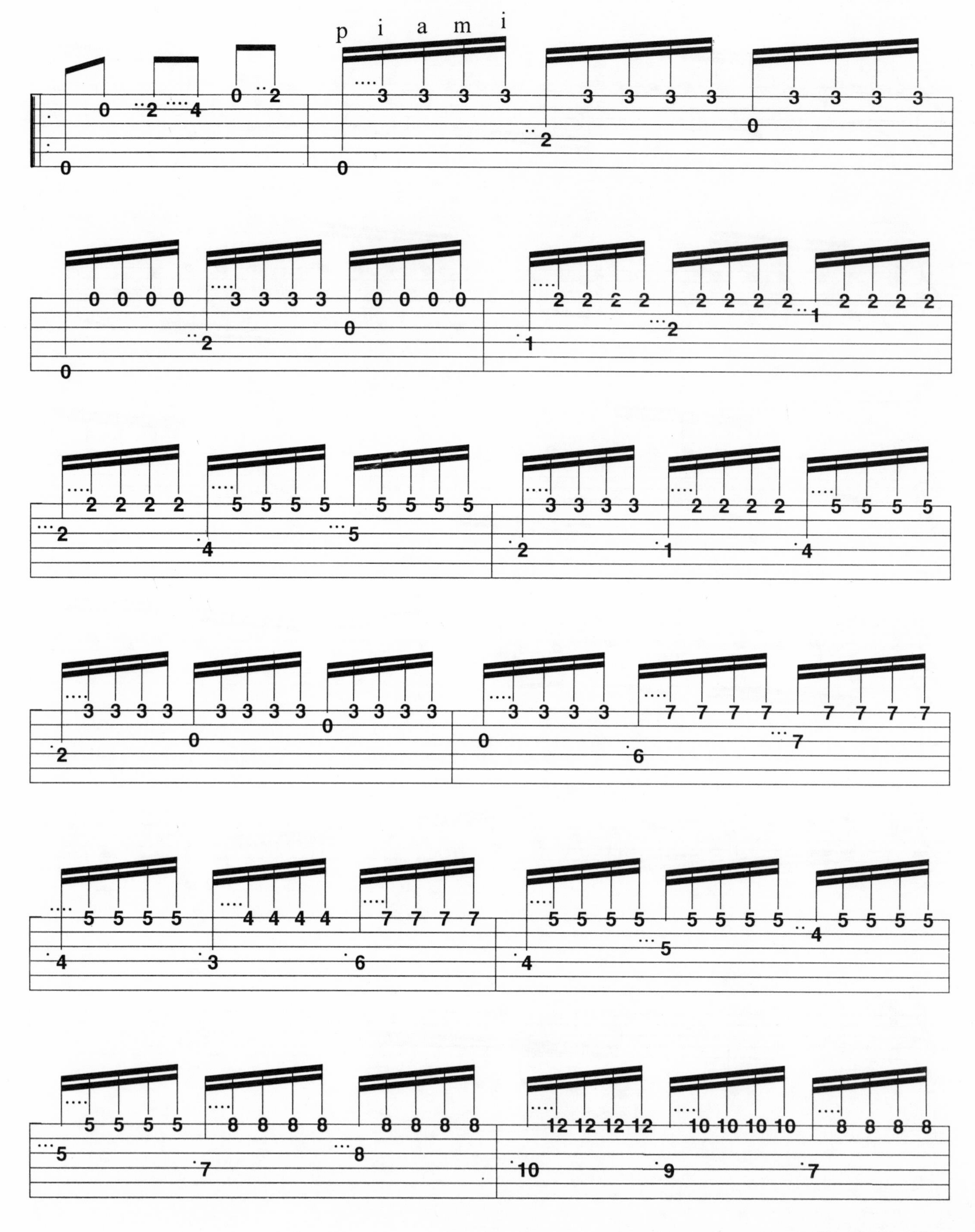

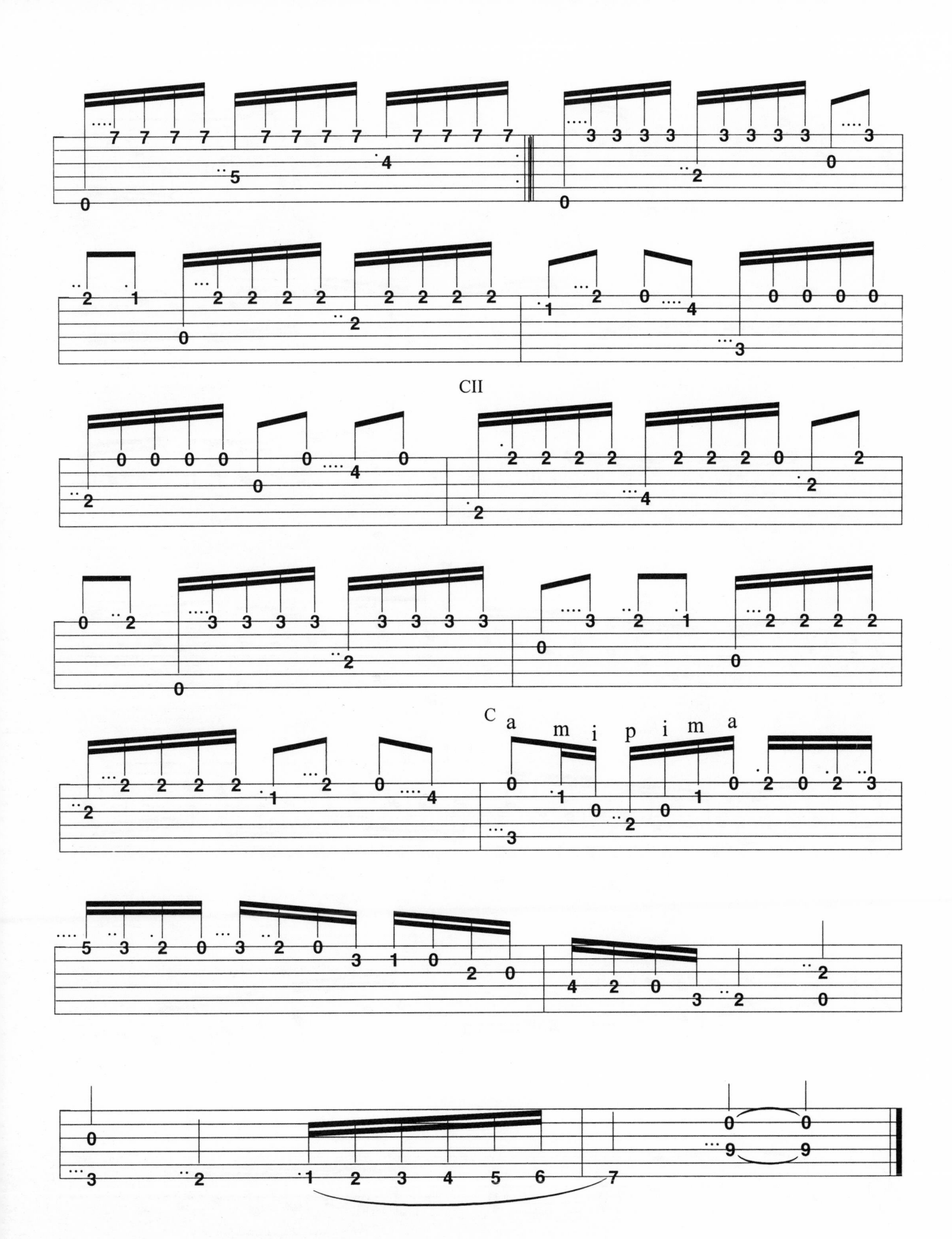
CII
C
a m i p i m a

Falseta 10

Juan Serrano

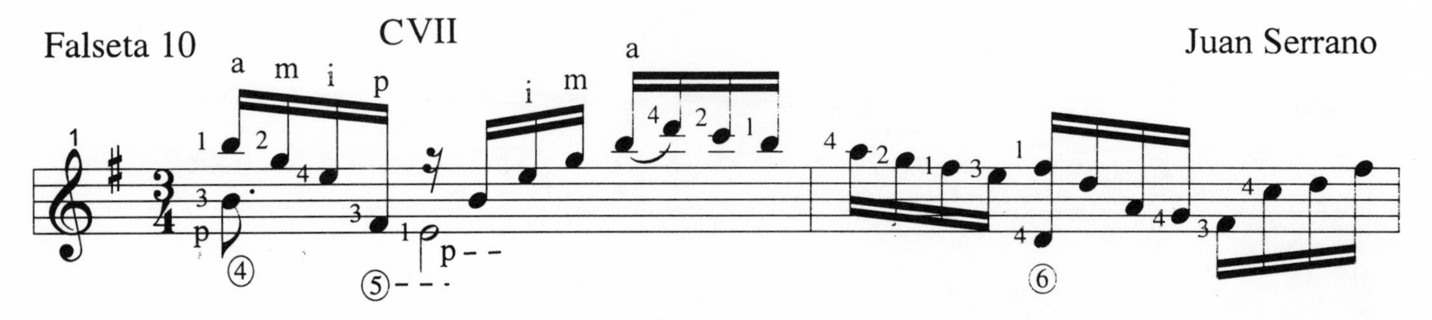

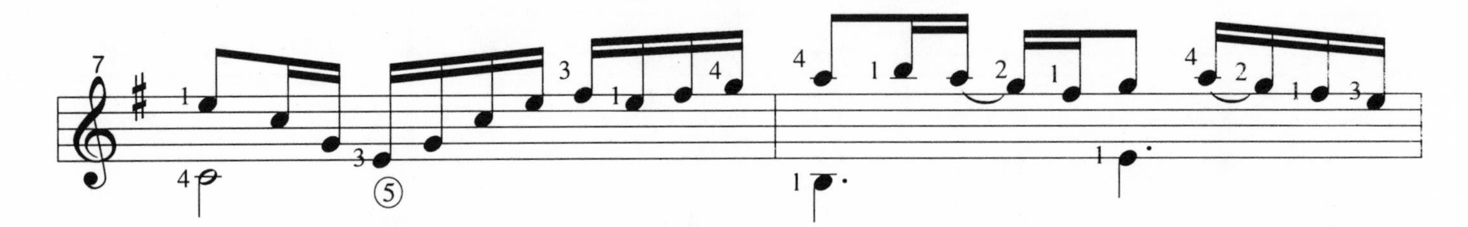

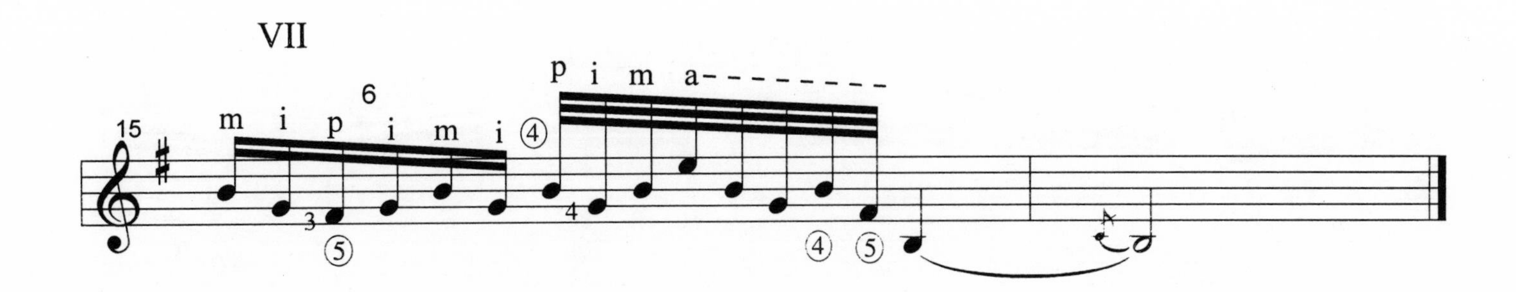
VII
15
m i p i m i
6
p i m a
3
4
⑤
④
④ ⑤

## Falseta 10

Juan Serrano

CVII

m i p p- - - -i m a

p

CV

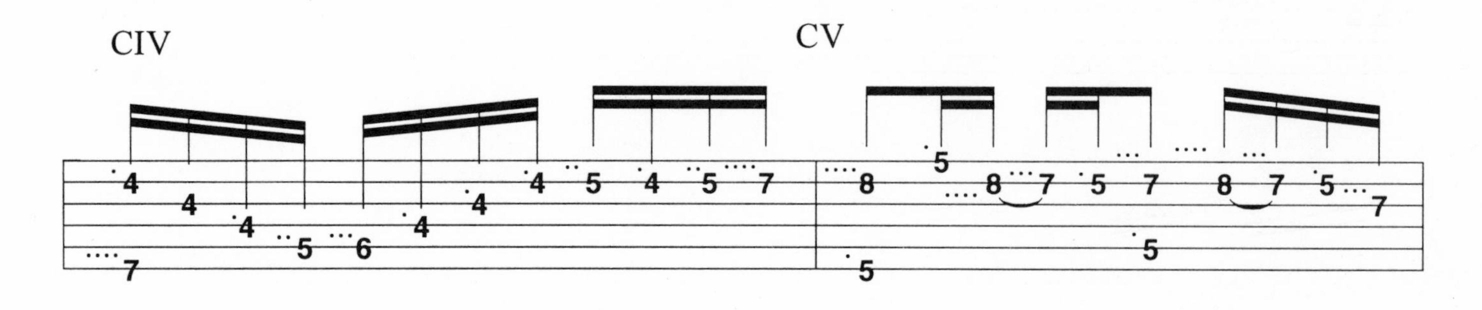


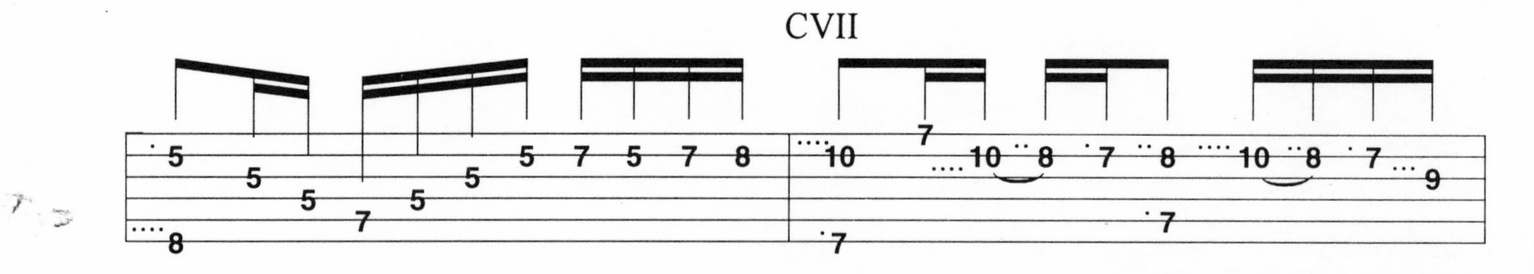


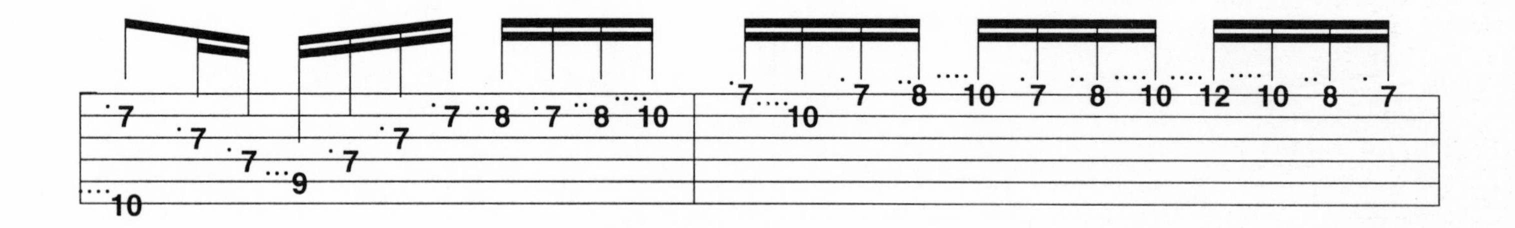

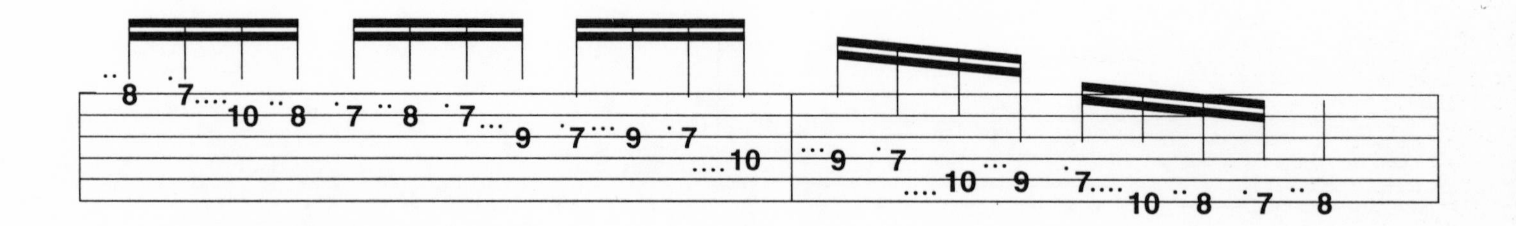

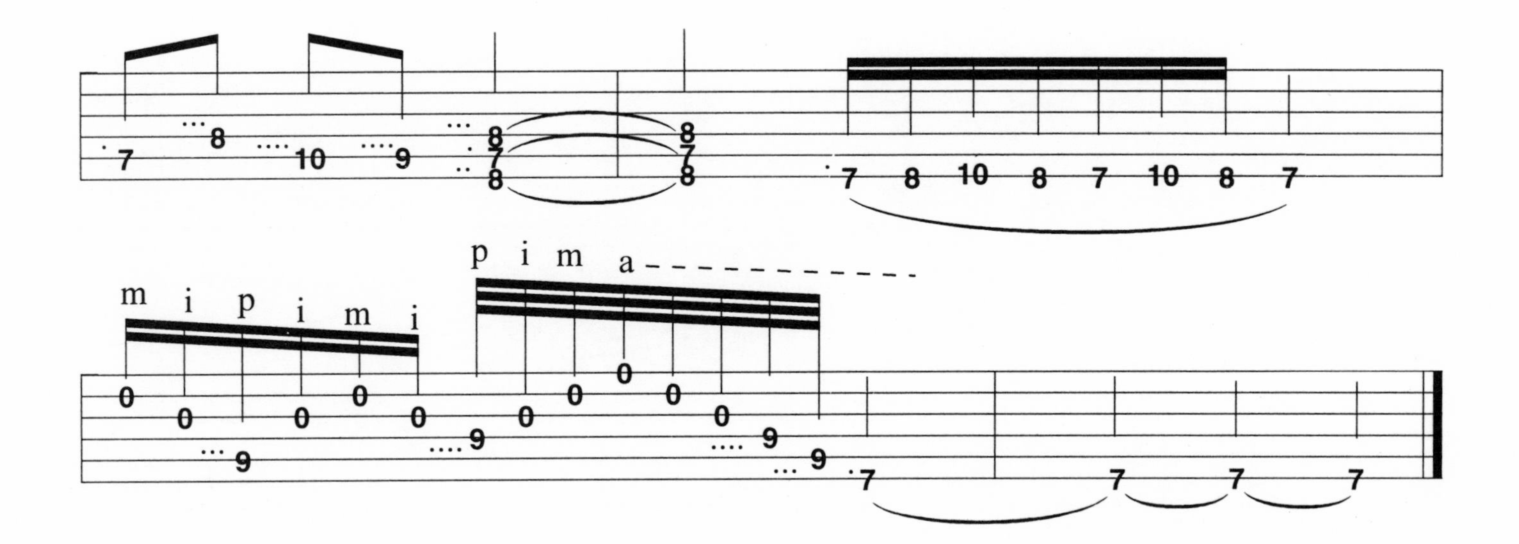
m i p i m i
p i m a

# ROMERAS

The Romeras originate in Cádiz and are from the Alegrías family. Their time and accents are exactly the same. They are measured in 3/4 and a flamenco compás has 12 beats equivalent to 4 measures of 3/4 time. The difference is that the Romeras are played in the key of C major.

The second compás of falseta #1 is an arpeggio that ends with 3 notes played with the thumb (p), reststroke and with force. The same is done in compases #4, 10, 12 and 16. This same technique will be found continually in the Romeras falsetas.

Falseta #2 includes 2 picados that should be played reststroke and very rapidly. The syncopation of the last 4 measures of the same falseta should be practiced frequently.

Falseta #3 is composed of rhythmical phrases, adding a short picado, but very rapidly at the end of each compás. #4 is with arpeggios. All of the notes should be played freestroke with the exception of the notes that are played with the ring finger (a) and the last picado should be played reststroke.

In #5 the tremolo technique is applied. This technique requires much practice to be able to play all of the notes with equal balance of sound and clarity.

For the remaining falsetas, it is recommended that the indicated fingerings be followed.

# ROMERAS

Las Romeras son procedentes de Cádiz y familia de las Alegrías. Por lo tanto, la medida y los acentos son exactamente iguales. Se miden en 3/4 y un compás flamenco se compone de doce tiempos equivalentes a cuatro compases musicales de 3/4. La diferencia es que las Romeras se tocan en el tono de Do mayor.

El segundo compás de la falseta #1 es un arpegio que termina con tres notas que se ejecutan con el dedo pulgar (p) apoyando y con mucha fuerza. Lo mismo ocurre en los compases #4, 10, 12 y 16. Esta misma técnica la encontrarán continuamente en las falsetas de las Romeras.

La falseta #2 incluye dos picados, que se deben de ejecutar apoyando y muy rápidos. Practiquen bastante el contratiempo de los cuatro últimos compases musicales de la misma falseta.

La falseta #3, se compone de frases rítmicas agregándole un picado corto, pero muy rápido al final de cada compás flamenco. La #4, es de arpegios. Todas las notas se deben de tocar tirando, excepto las notas que se tocan con el dedo anular (a) y el último picado que se deben de tocar apoyando.

En la falseta #5 se usa la técnica del tremolo. Esta técnica requiere mucha práctica para poder tocar todas las notas con el mismo balance de sonoridad y claridad.

Para todas las demás, recomiendo que se sigan las digitaciones marcadas.

# *Romeras*

Traditional Compas

Juan Serrano

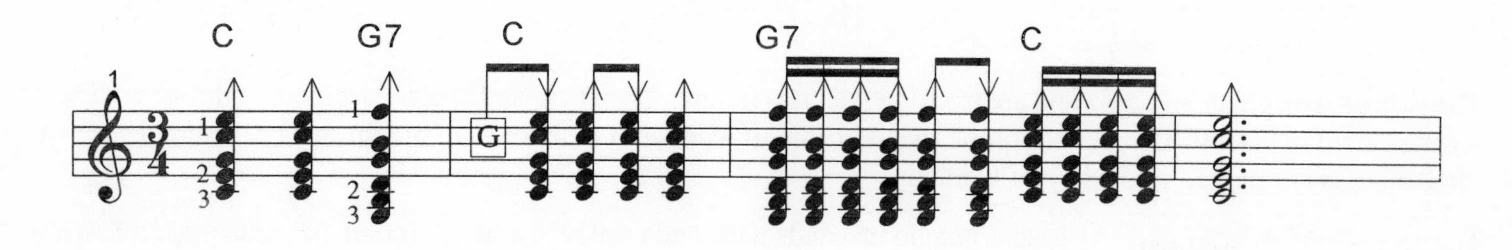


Variation 1

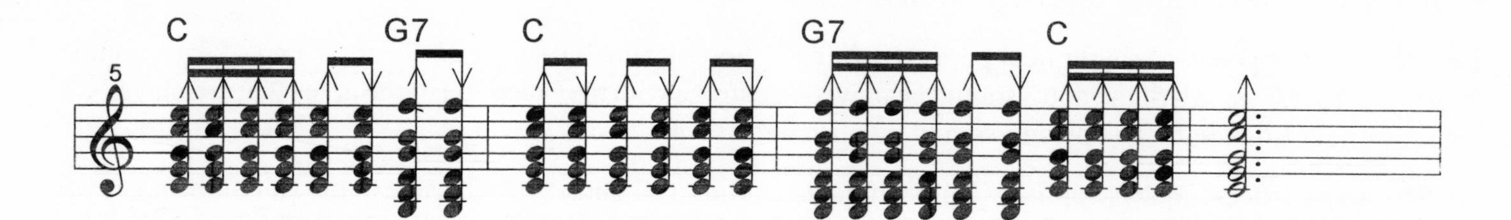


Variation 2

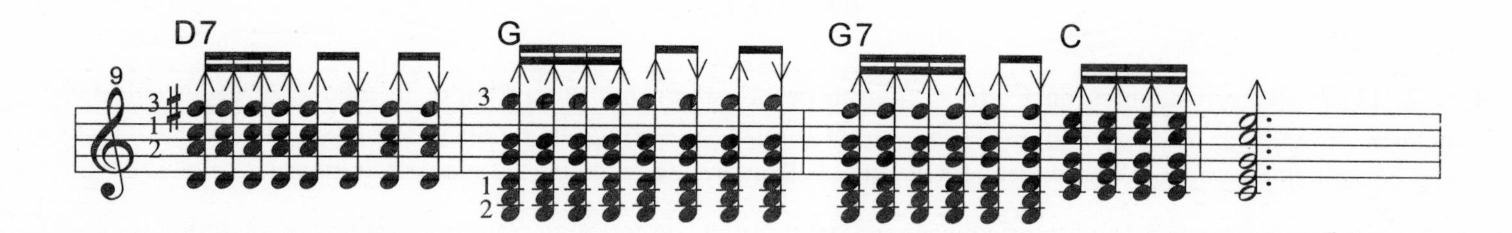


Variation 3

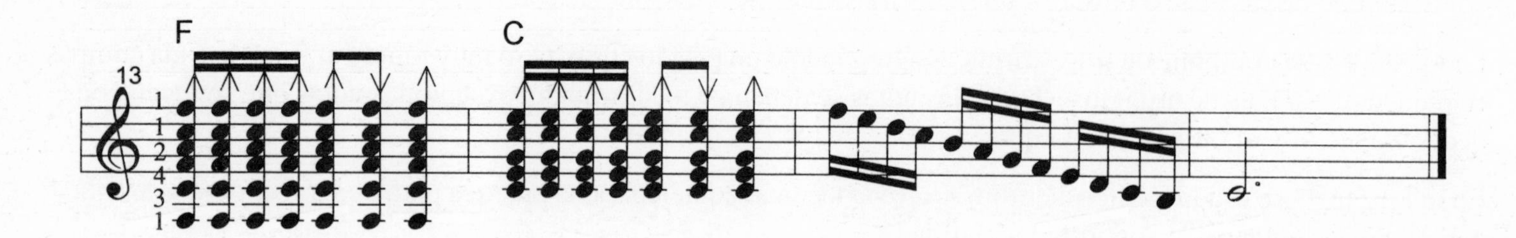

# *Romeras*

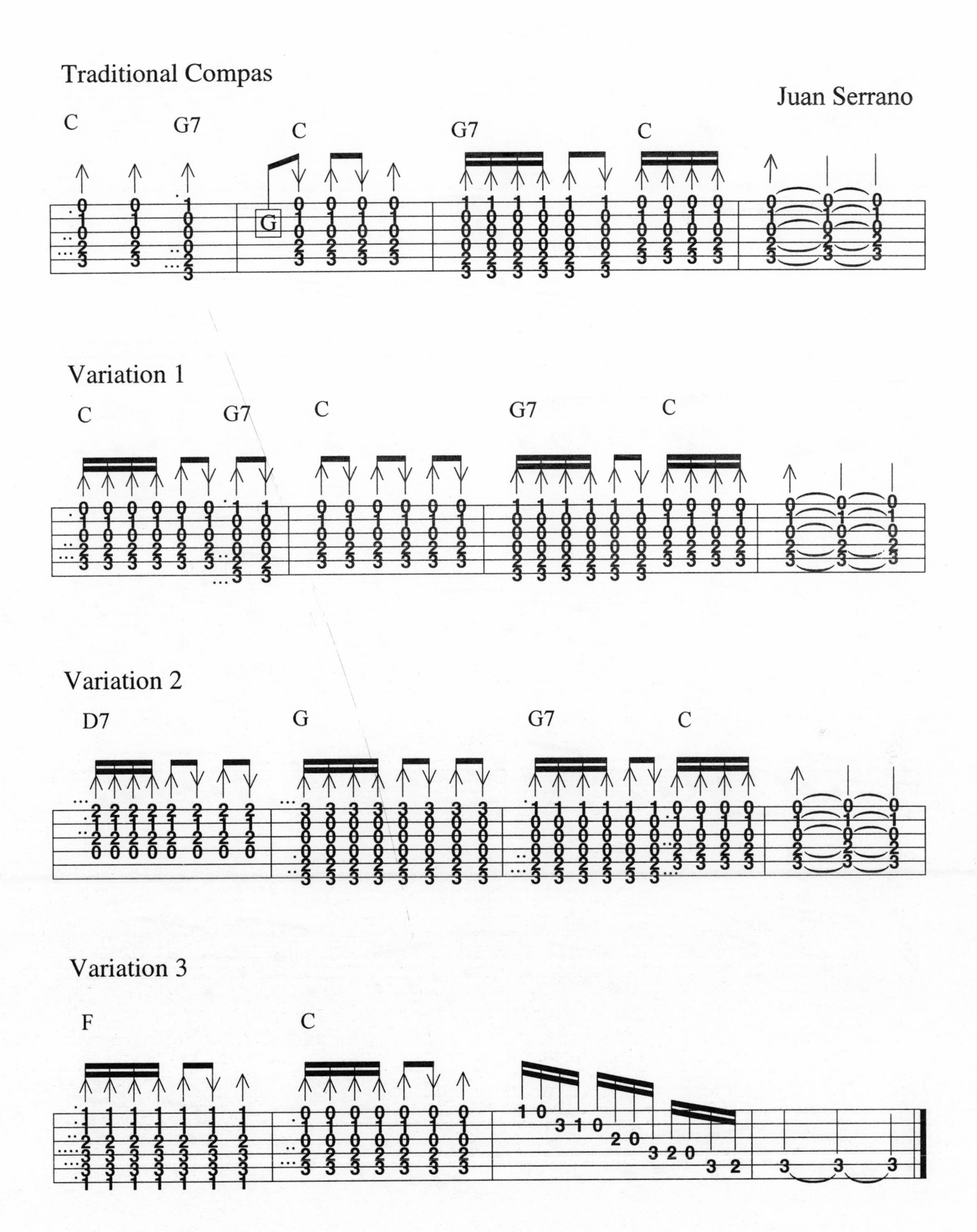

Traditional Compas
Juan Serrano
C
G7
C
G7
C
G
Variation 1
C
G7
C
G7
C
Variation 2
D7
G
G7
C
Variation 3
F
C

Falseta 1

Juan Serrano

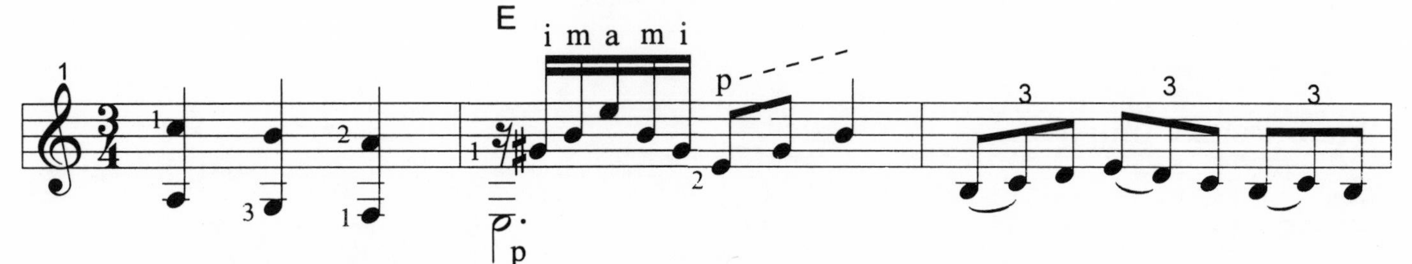


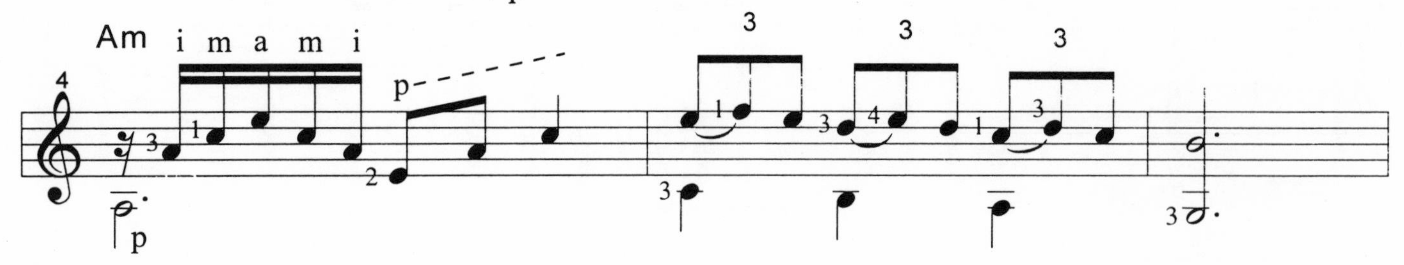

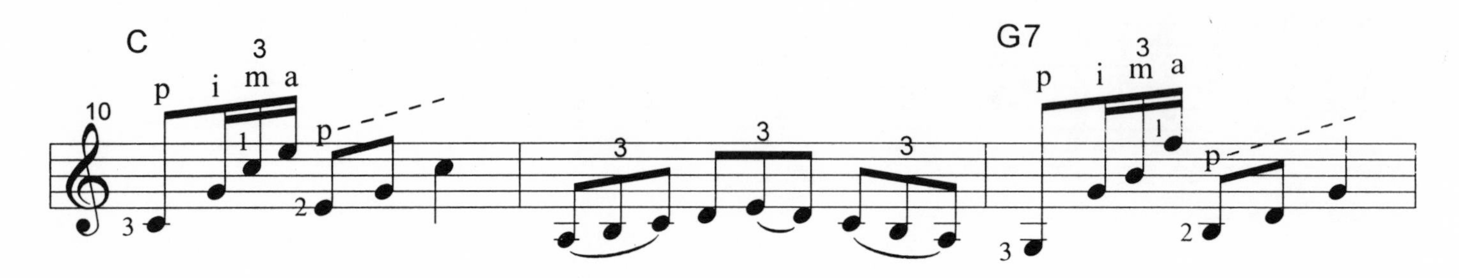

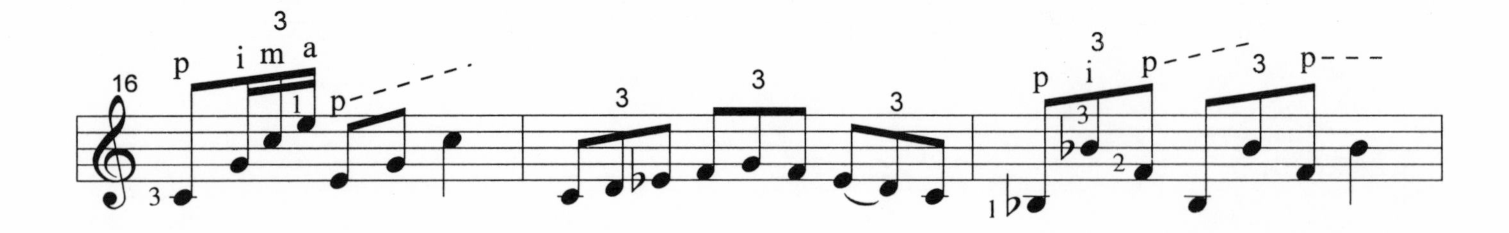


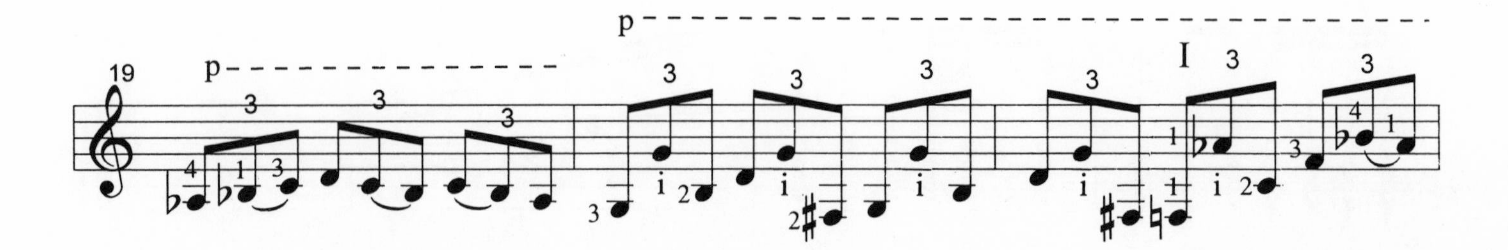

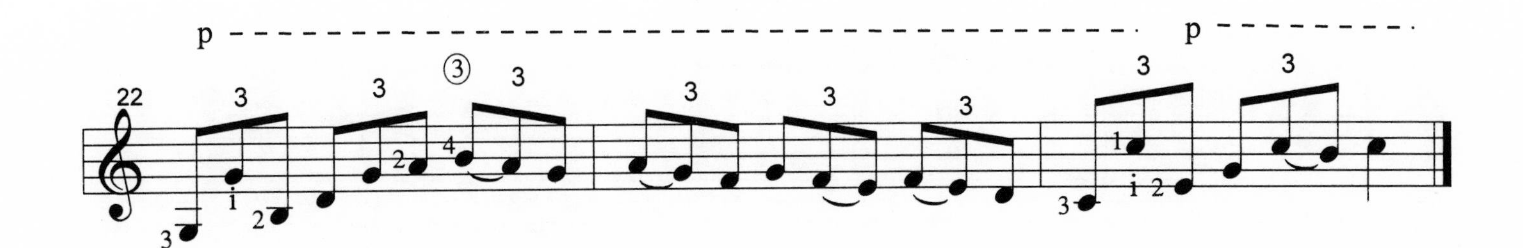

Falseta 1

Juan Serrano

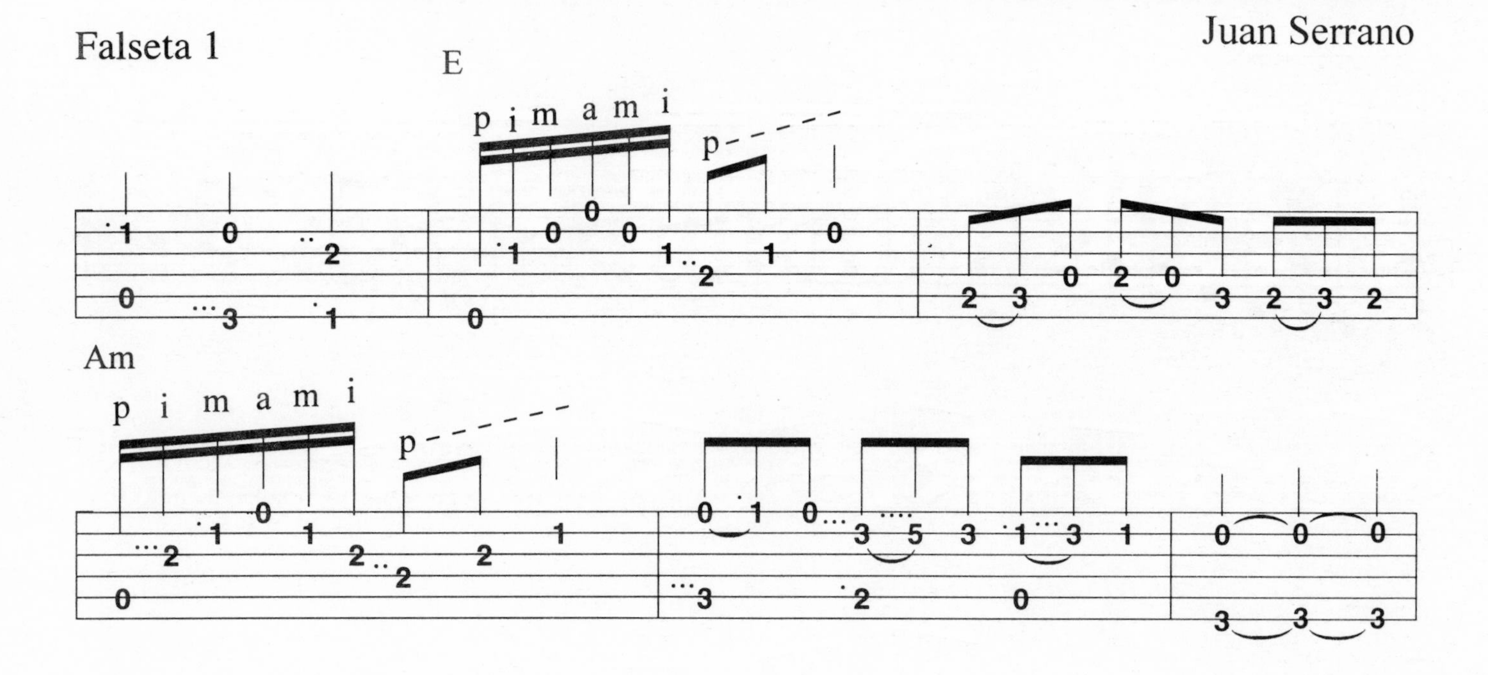

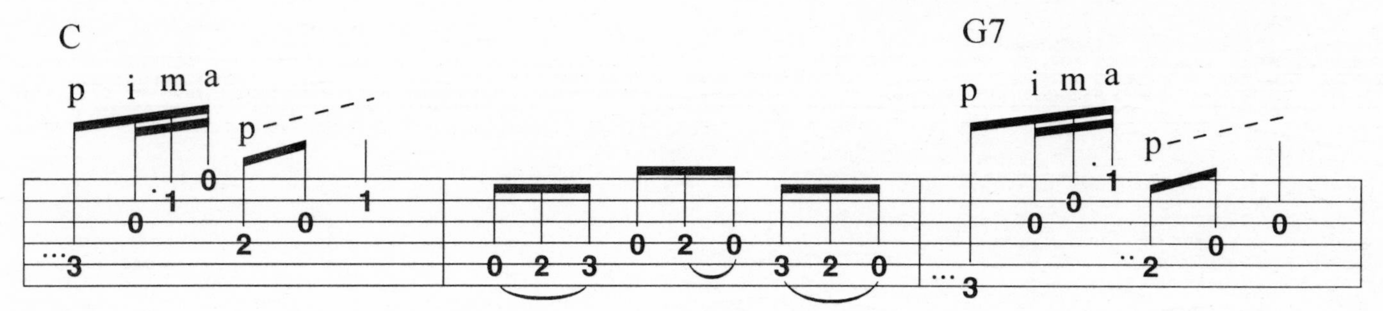


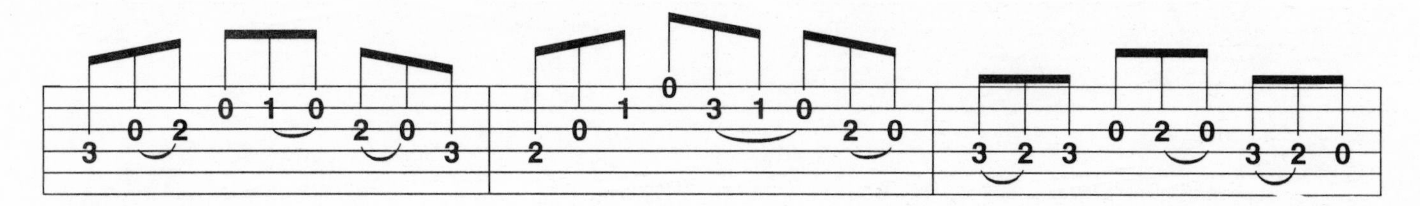

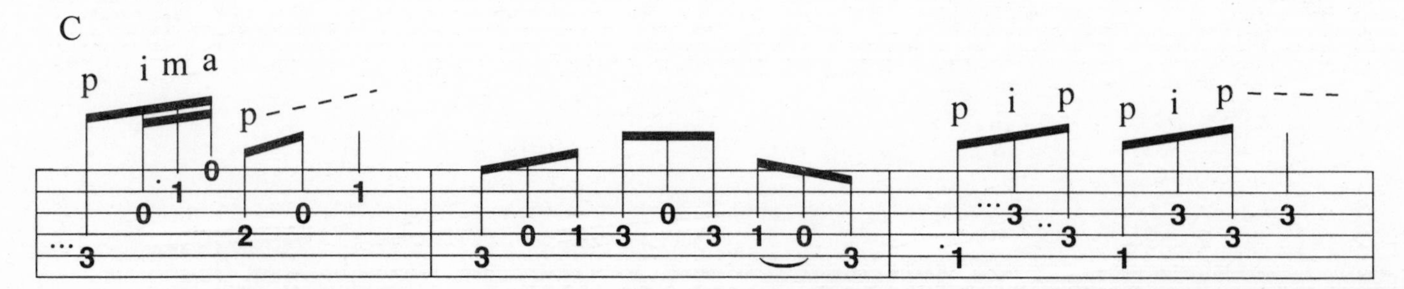

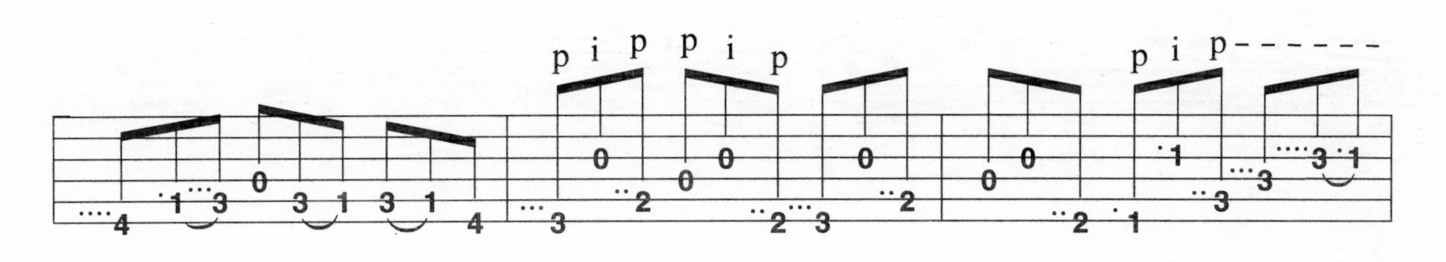
CI
p i p p i p
p i p

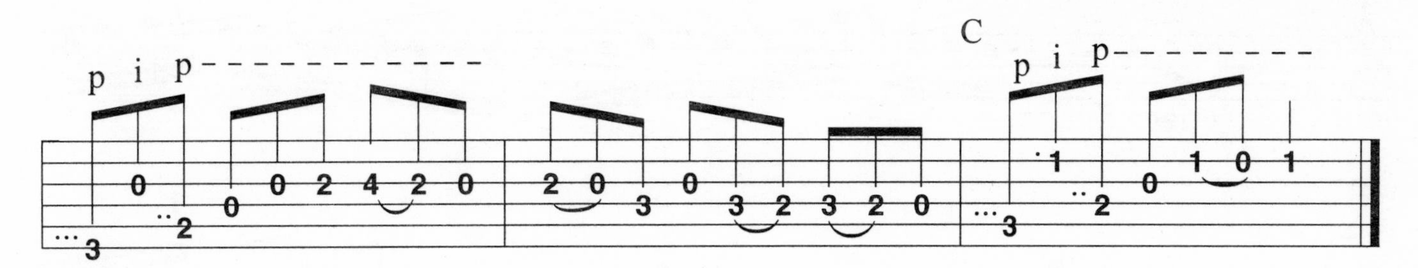
C
p i p
p i p

Falseta 2

Juan Serrano

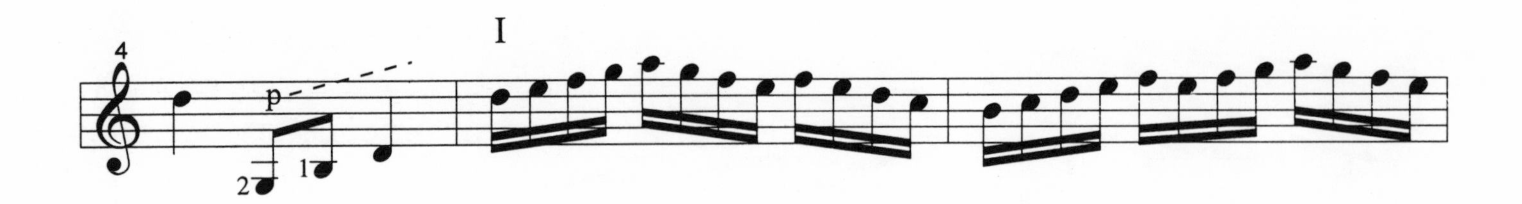

Falseta 2

Juan Serrano

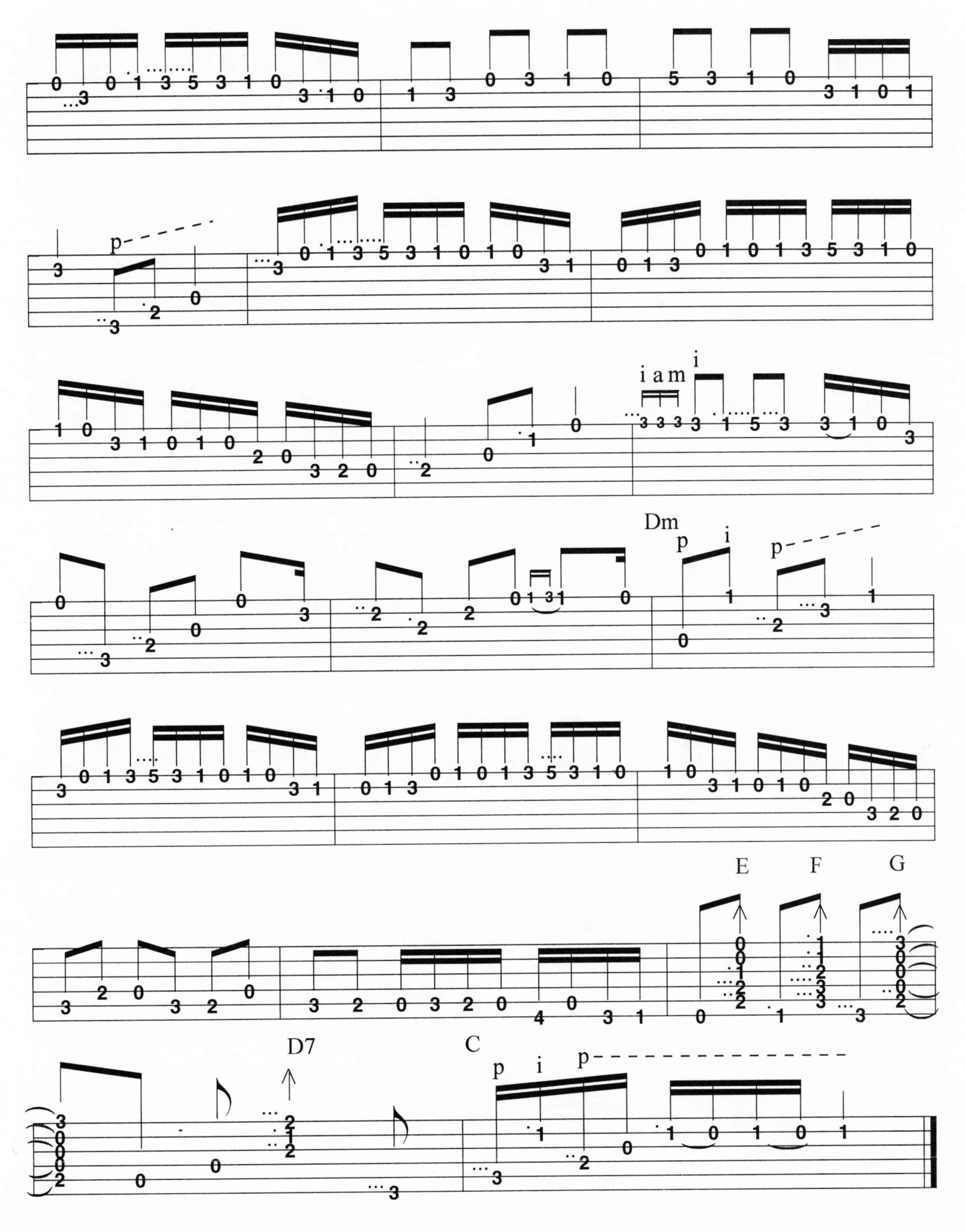

Falseta 3

Juan Serrano

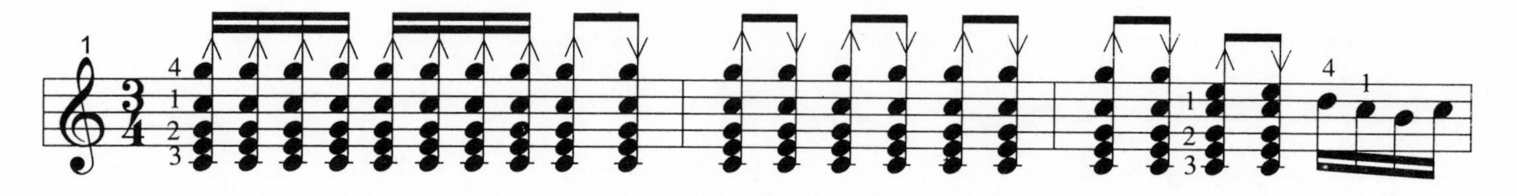


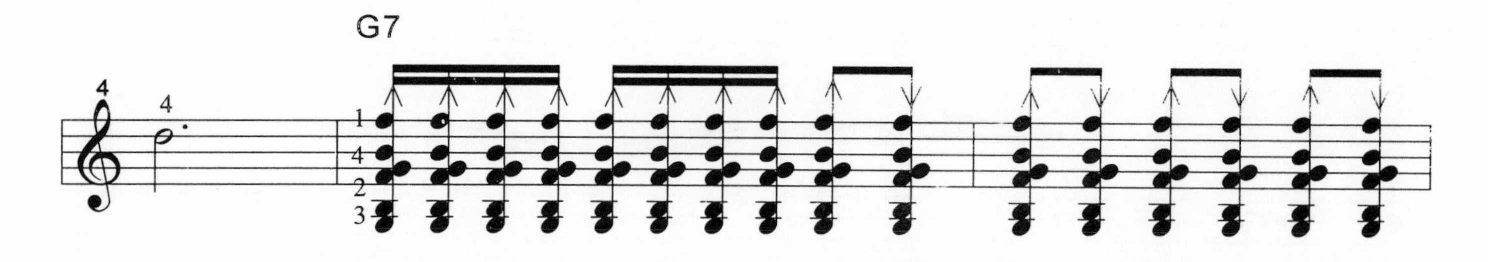


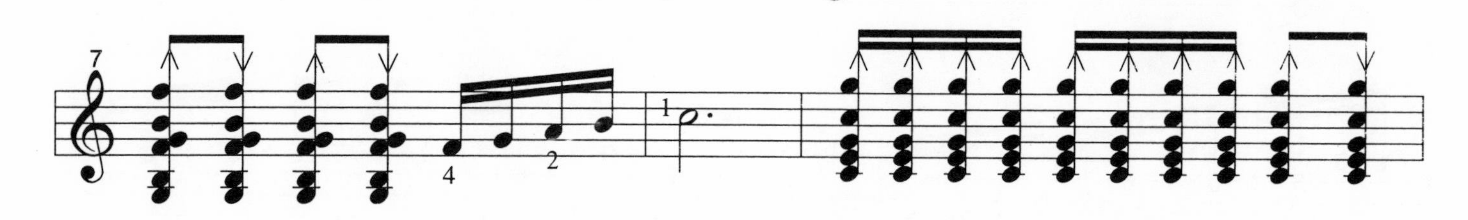


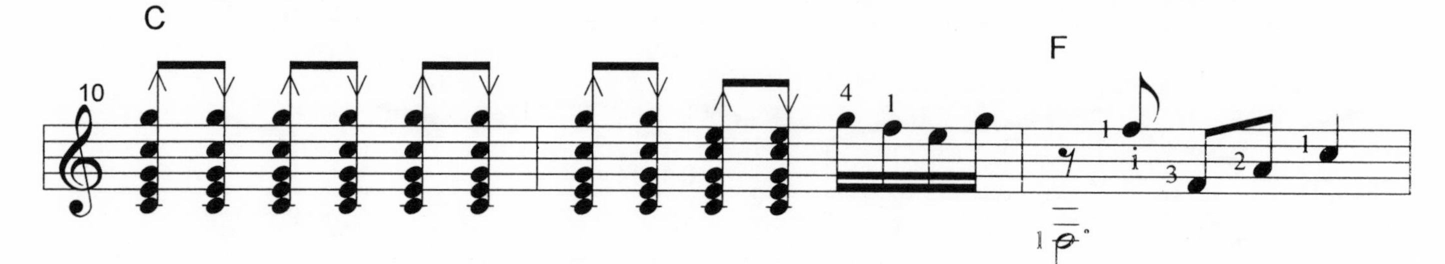


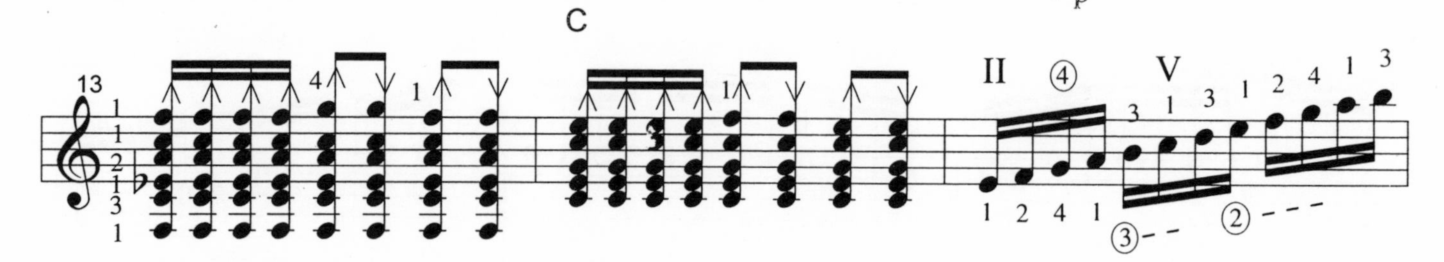


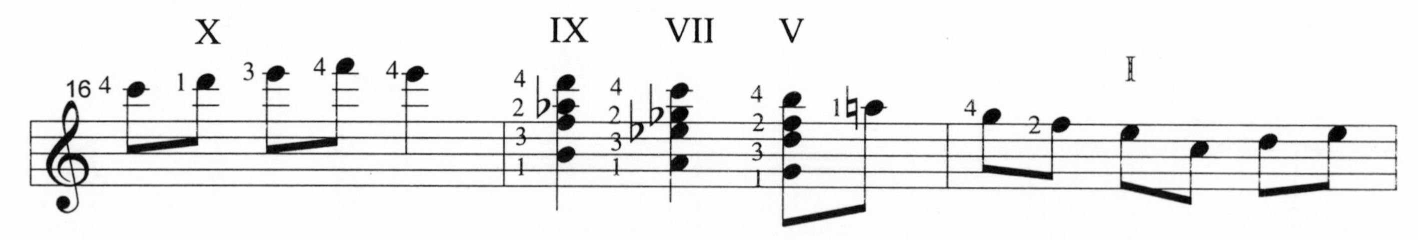

Falseta 3

Juan Serrano

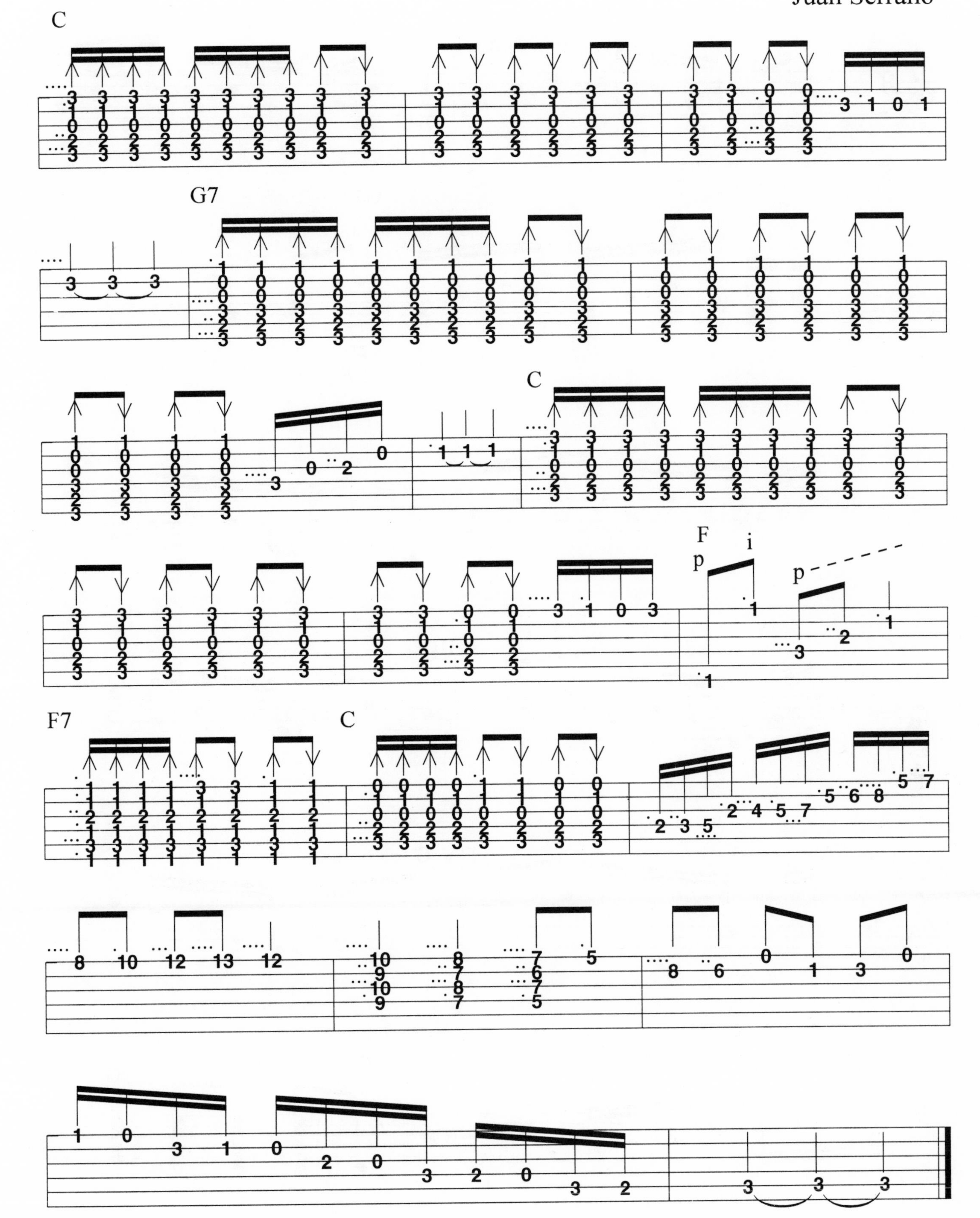

Falseta 4

Juan Serrano

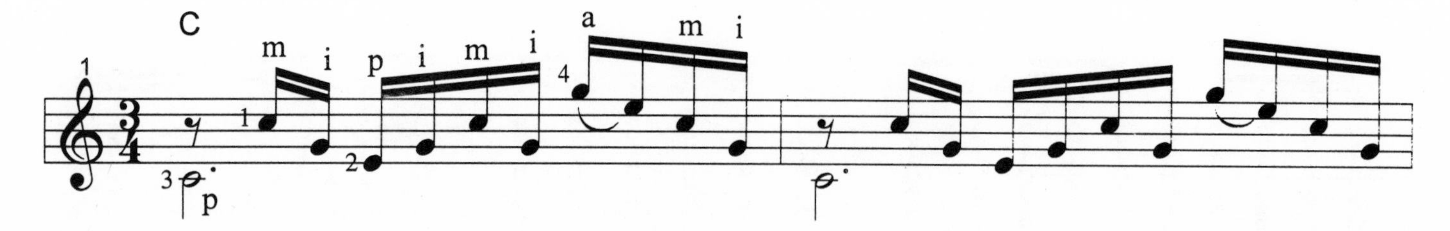

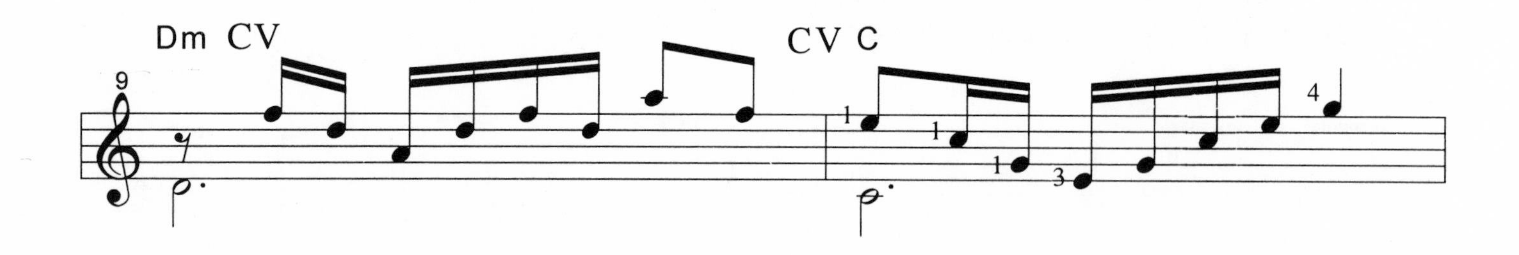

Juan Serrano

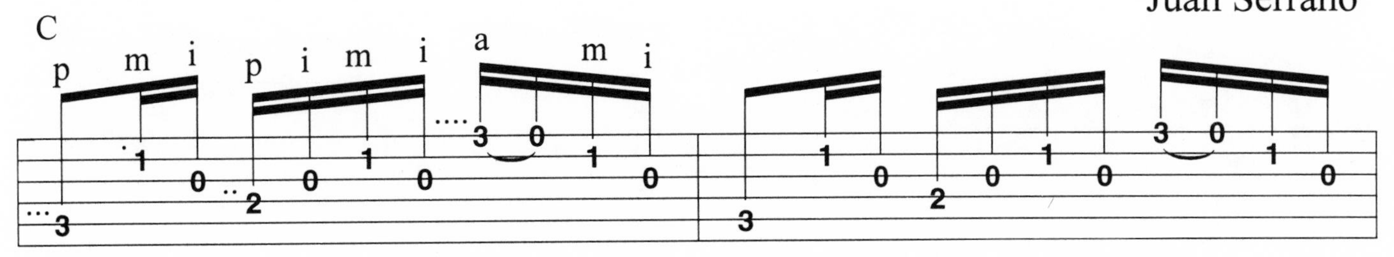


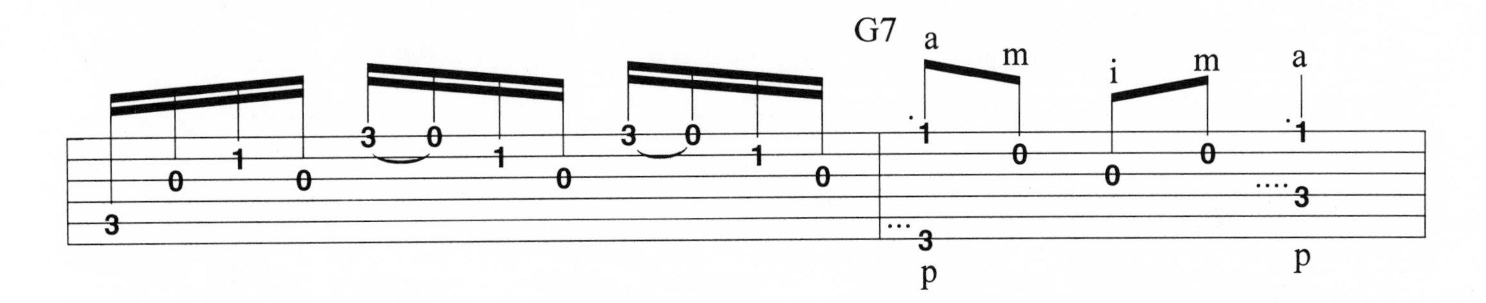


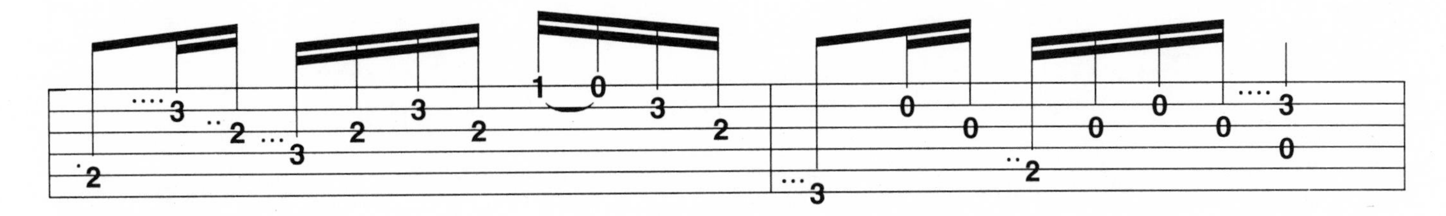

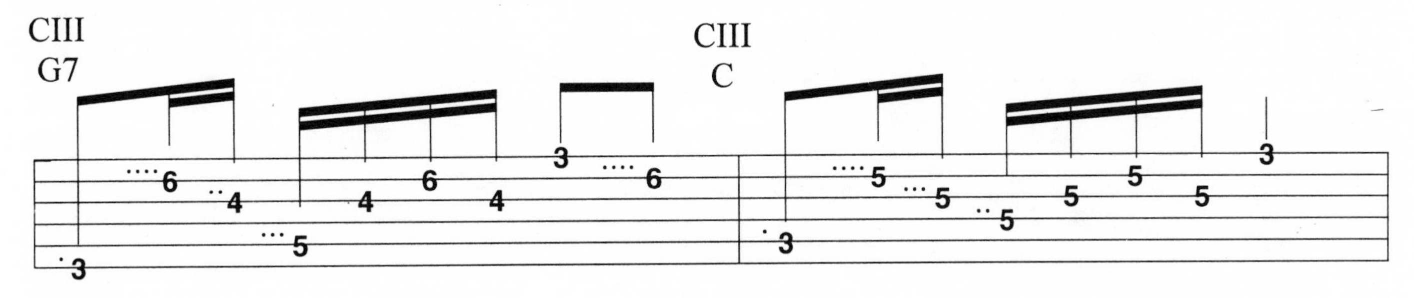


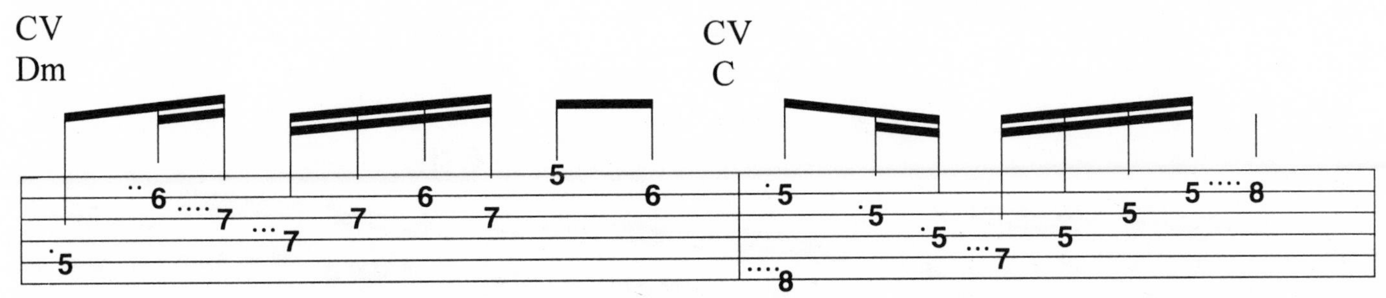


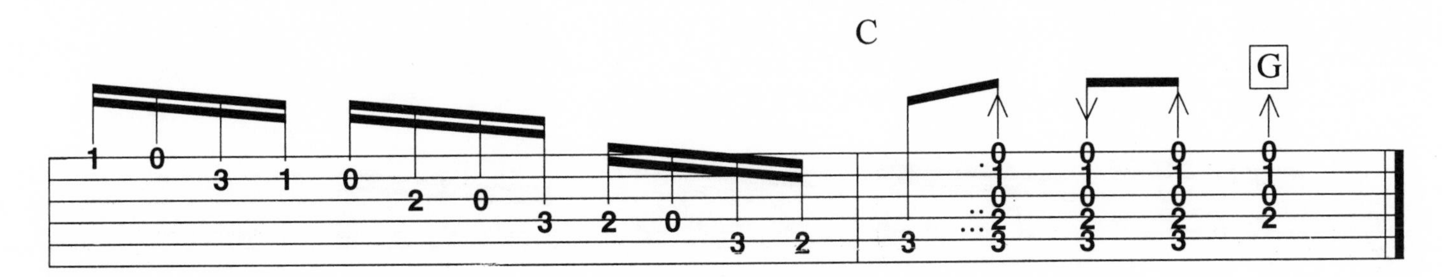

Falseta 5

Juan Serrano

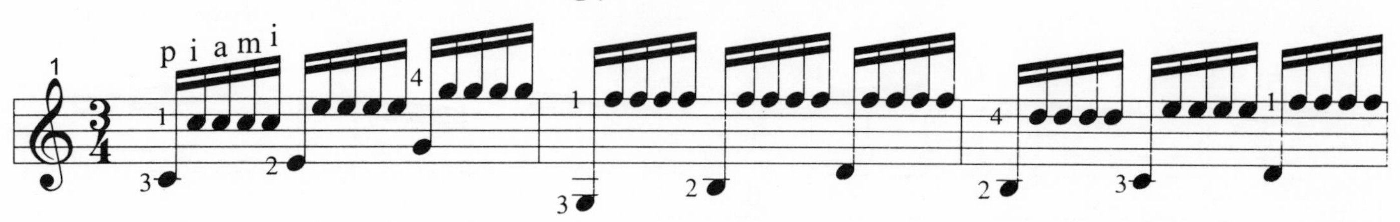

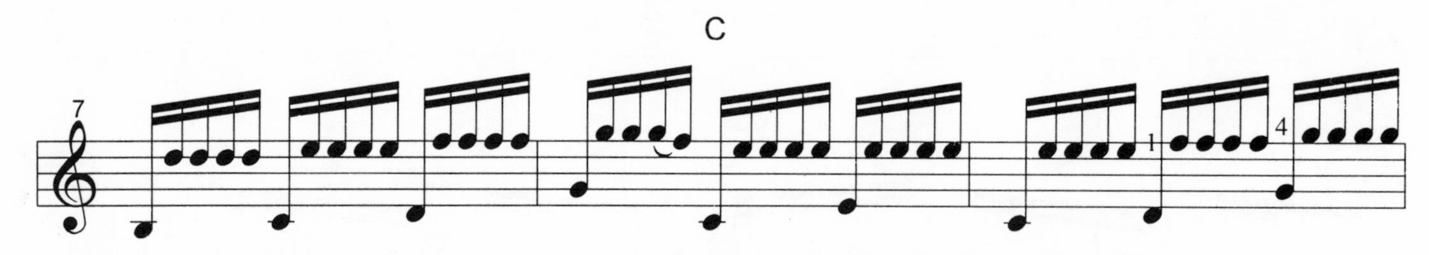


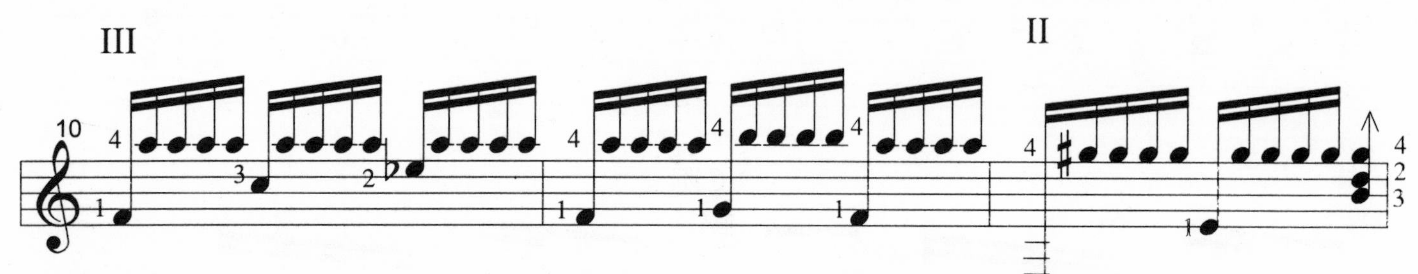


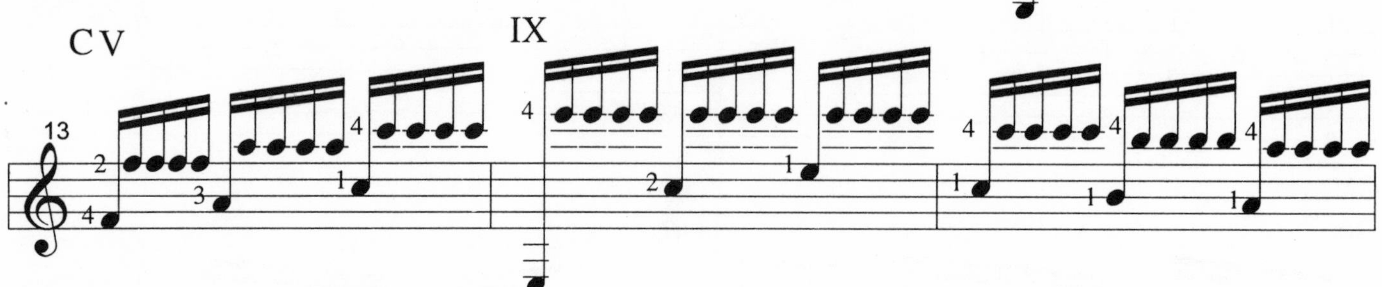


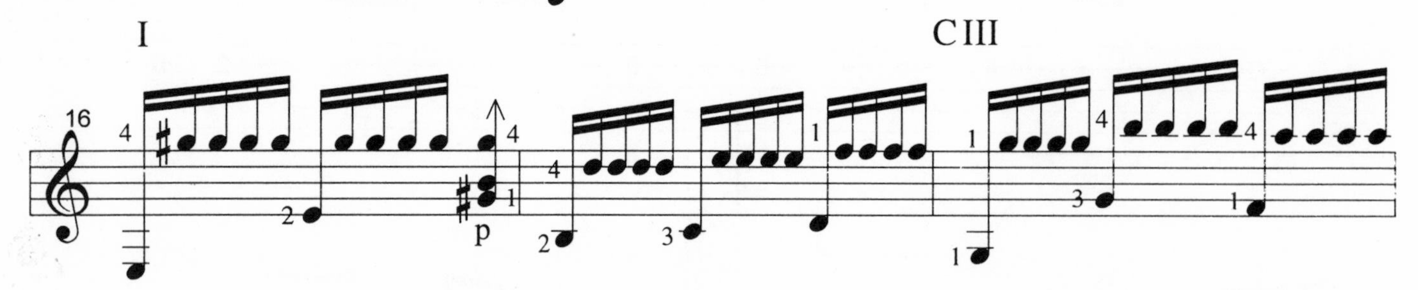

## Falseta 5 (Tremolo)

Juan Serrano

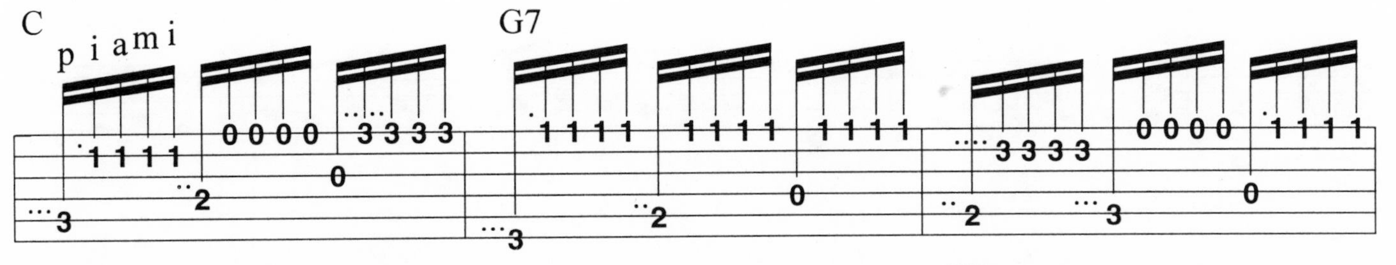


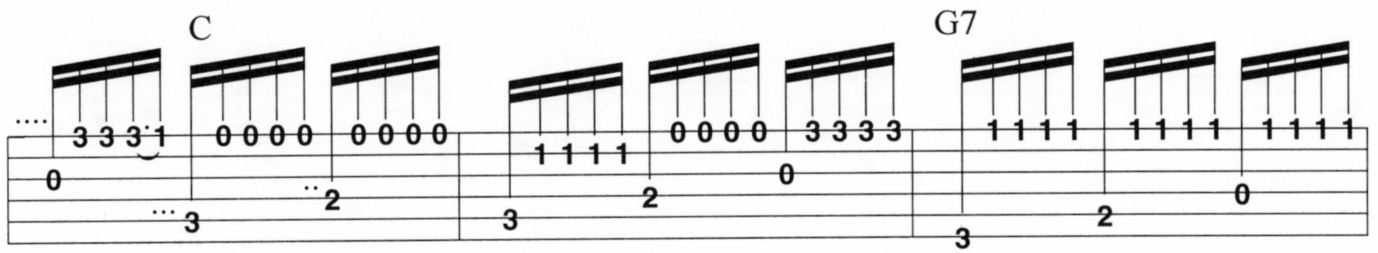


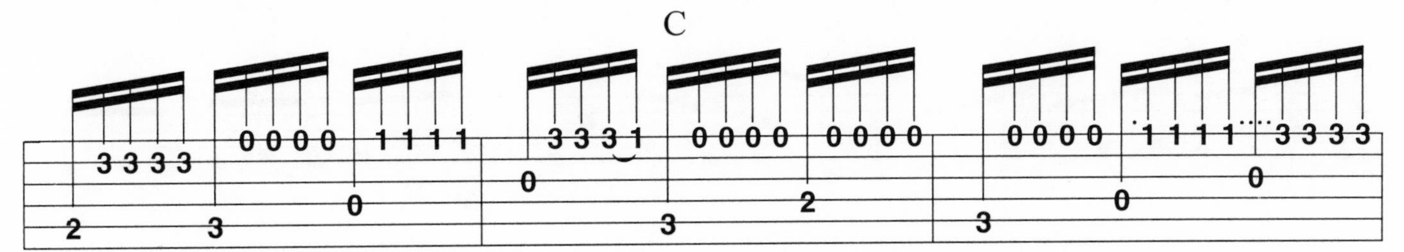


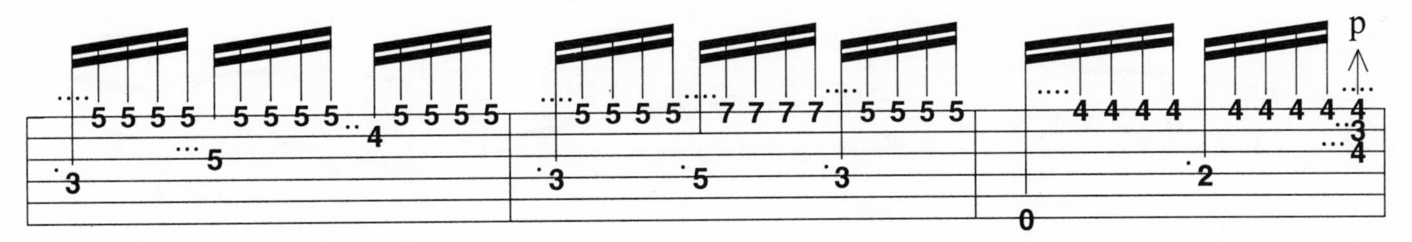


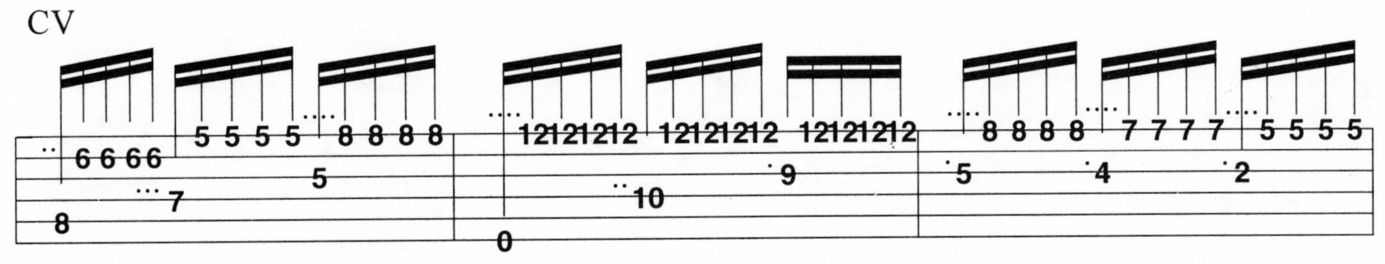


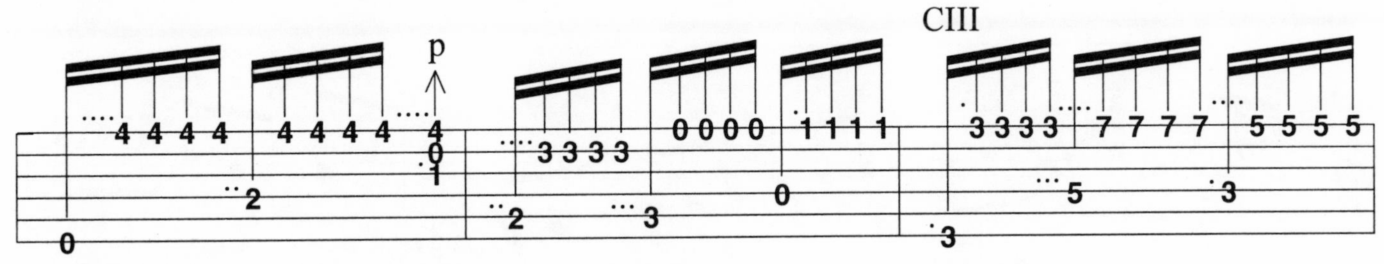


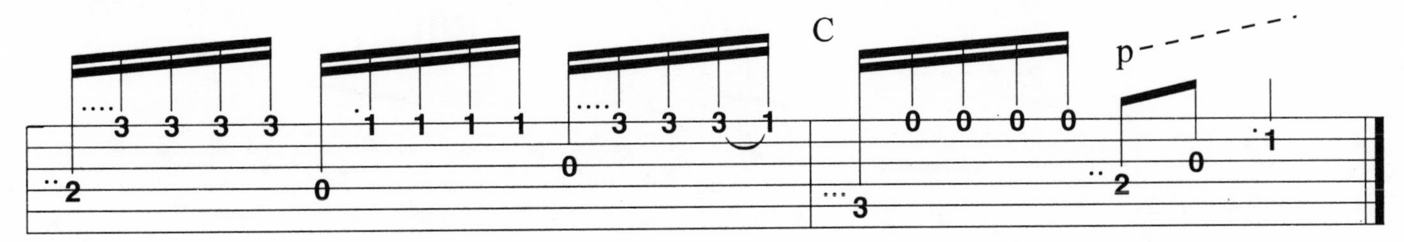

Falseta 6

Juan Serrano

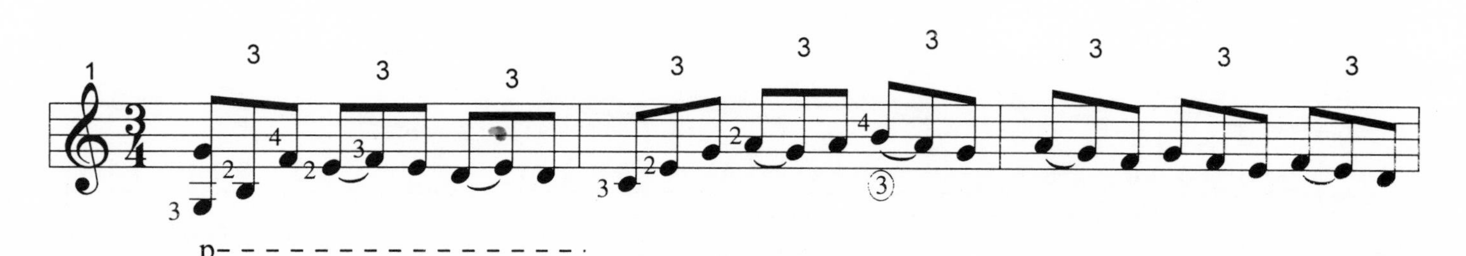

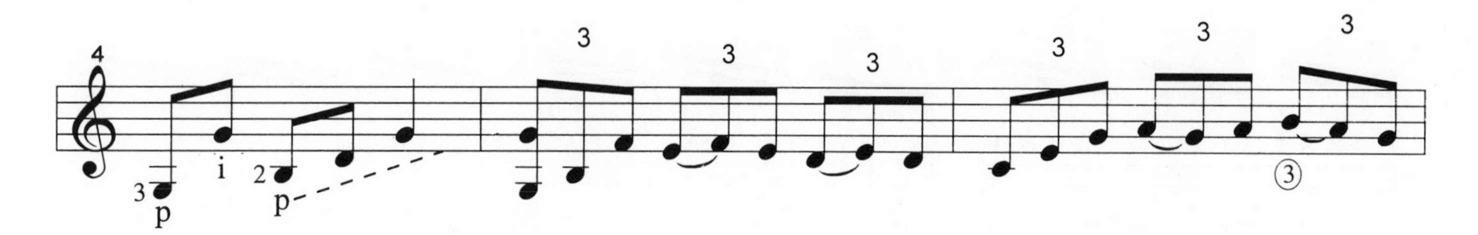

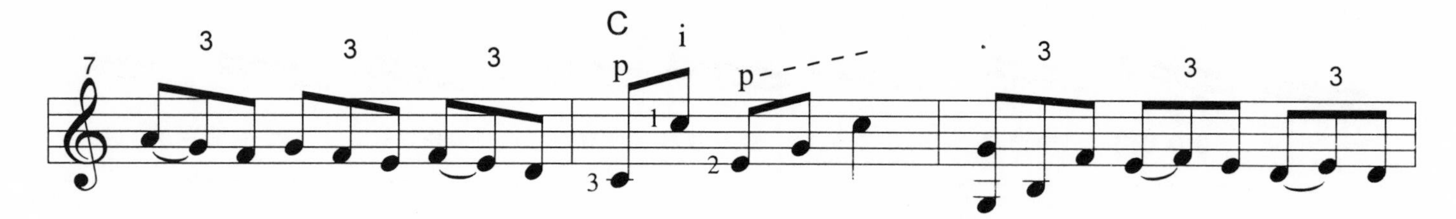

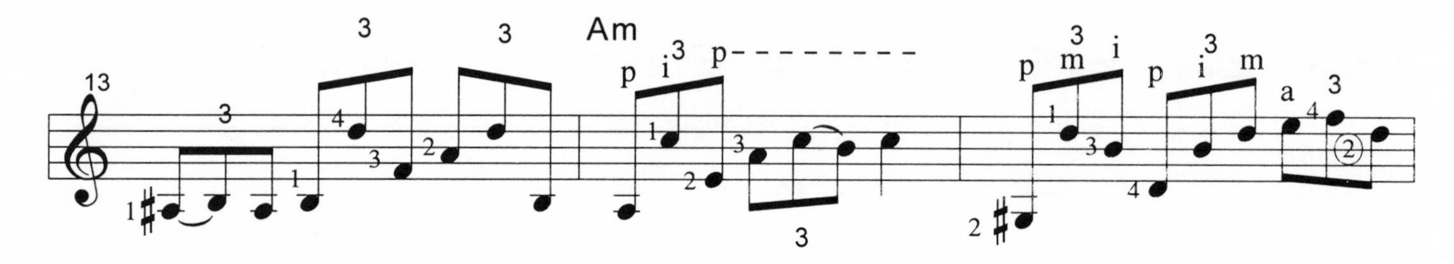


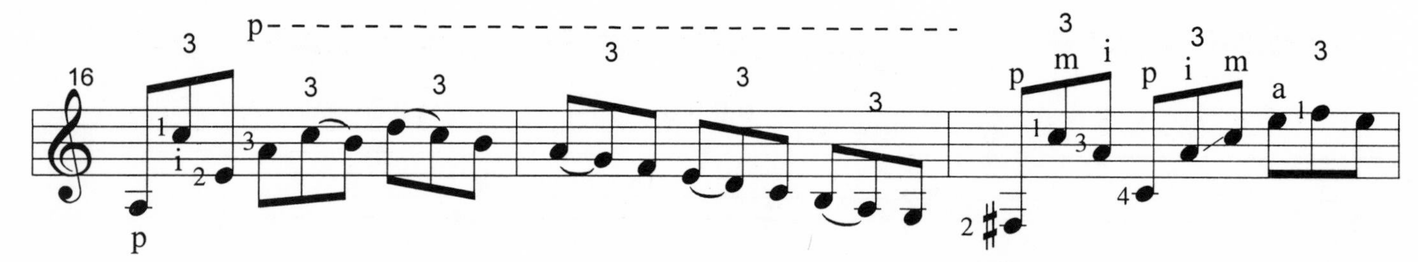

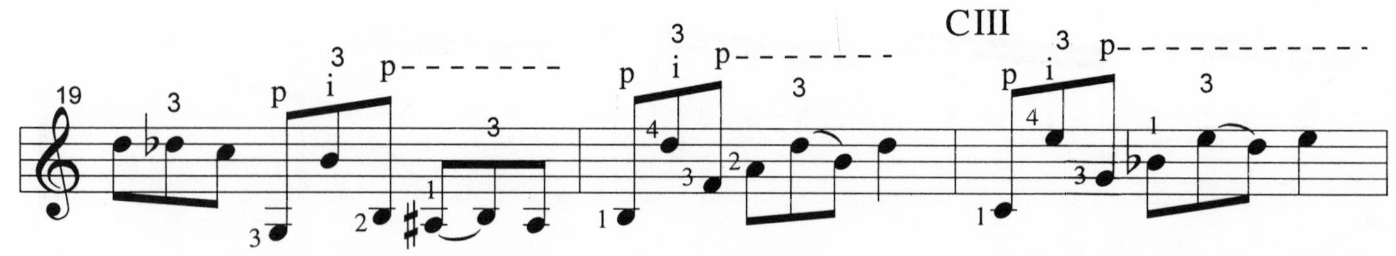

I
22

Falseta 6

Juan Serrano

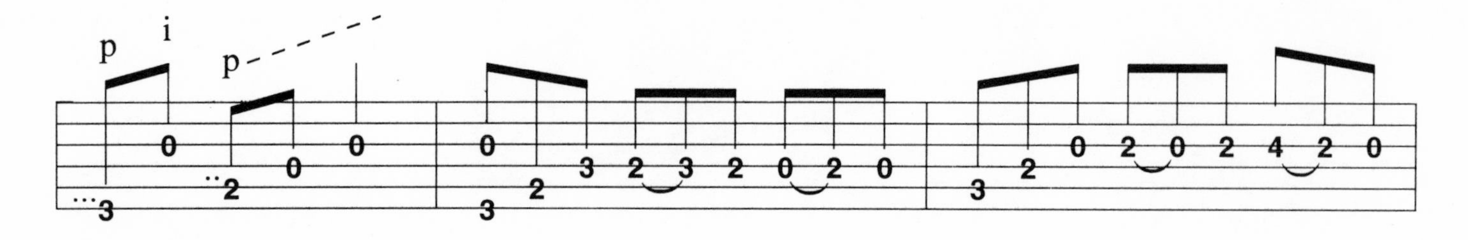


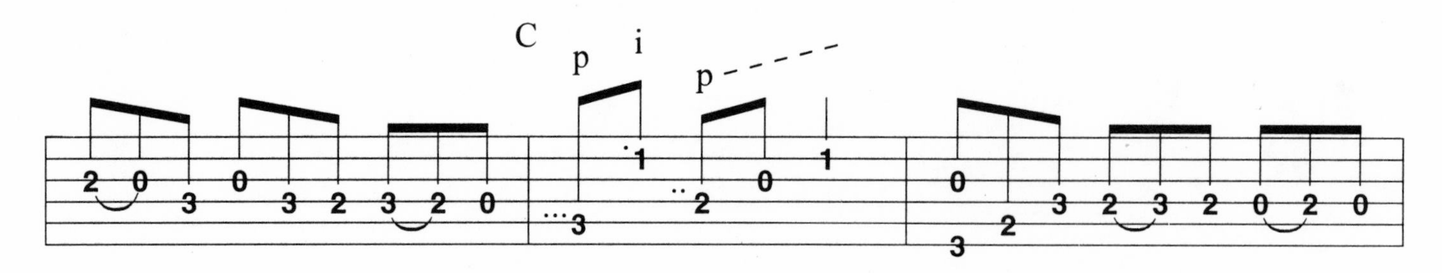


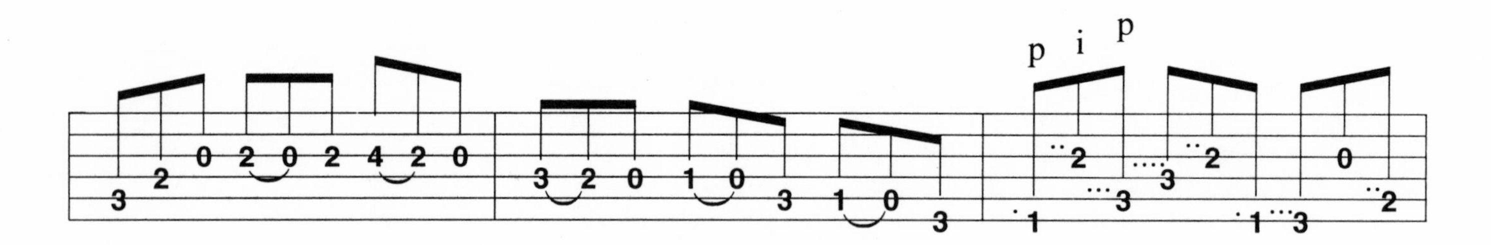


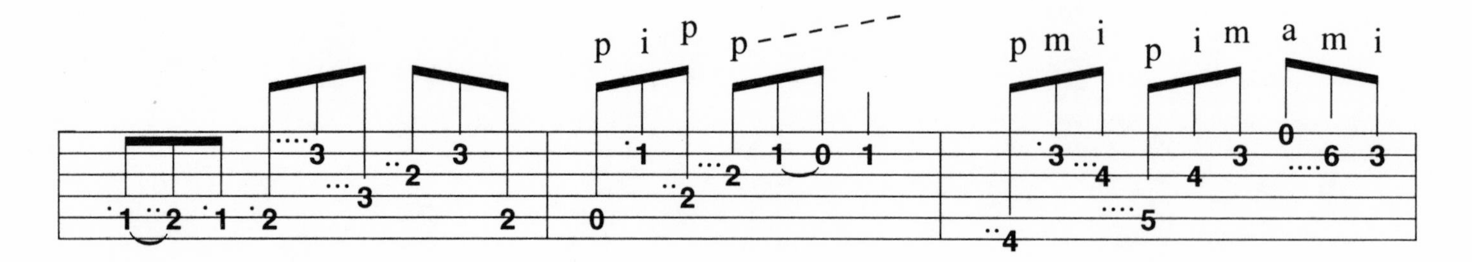


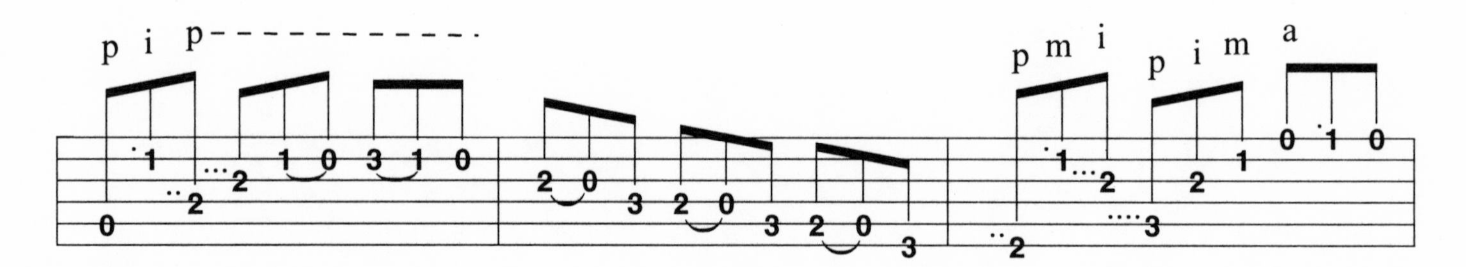

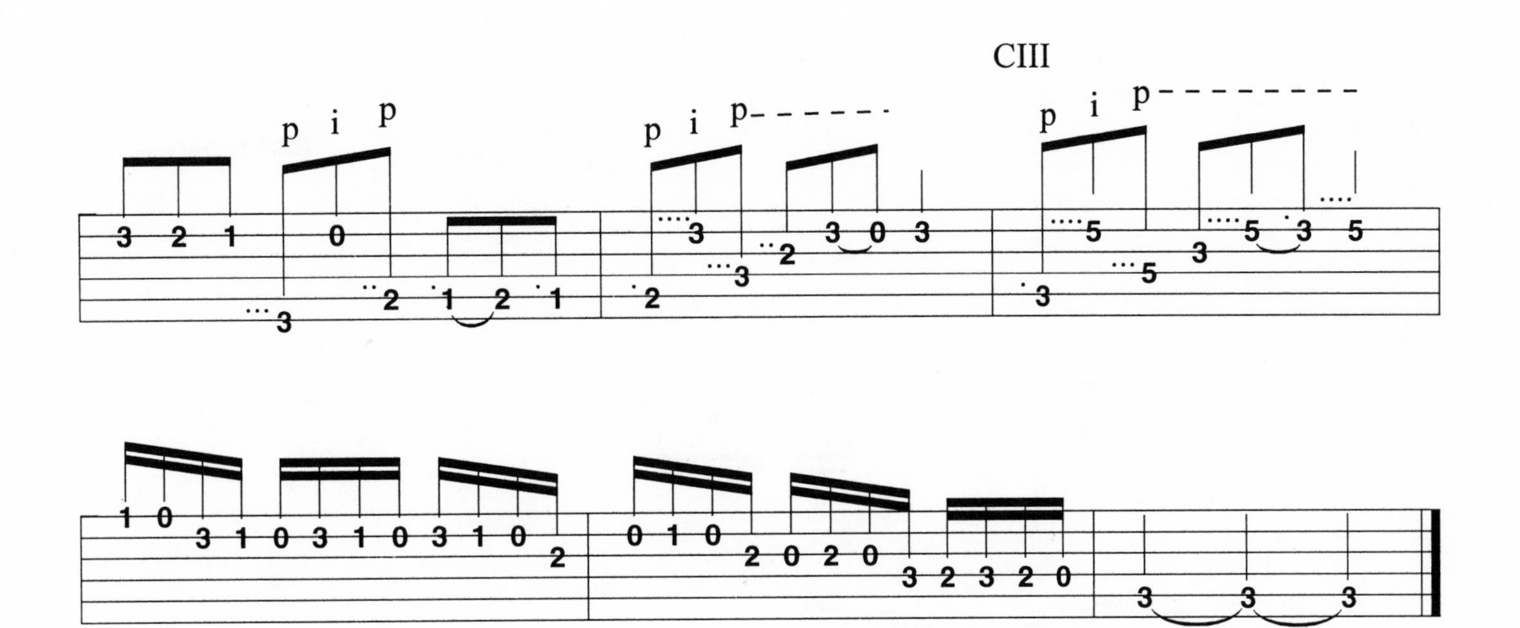
CIII
p i p
p i p
p i p

Falseta 7

Juan Serrano

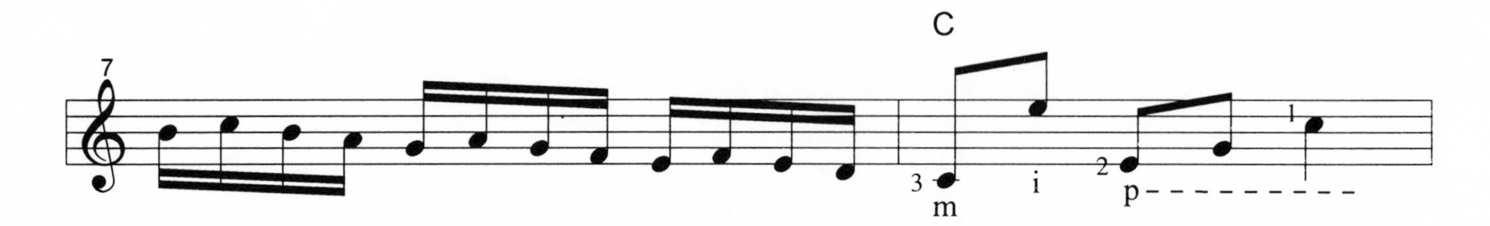


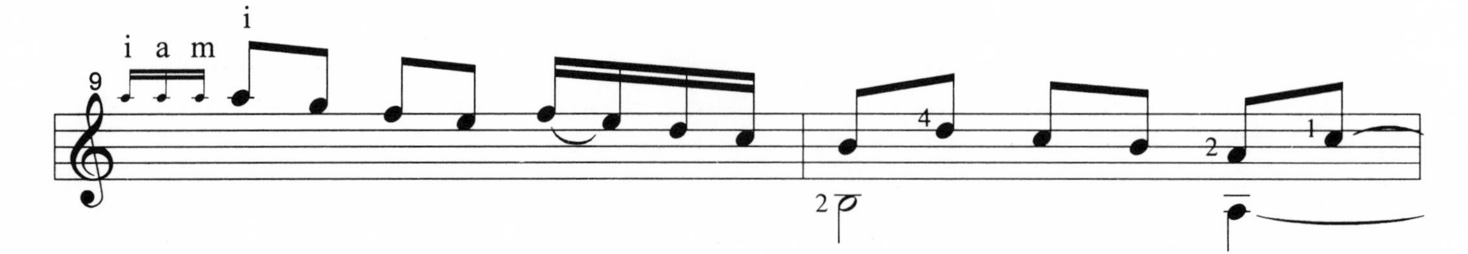


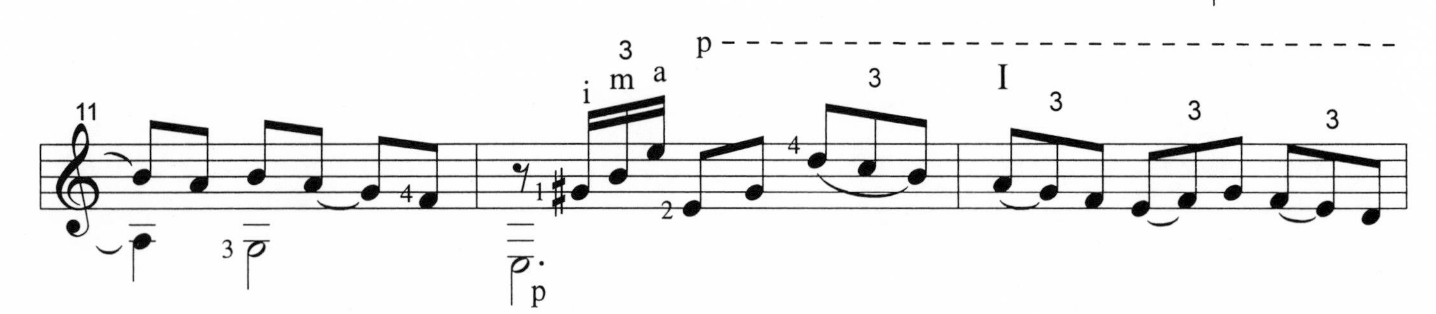


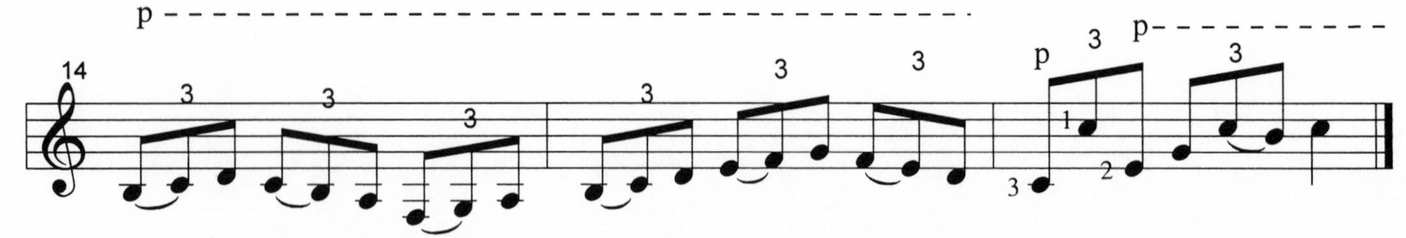

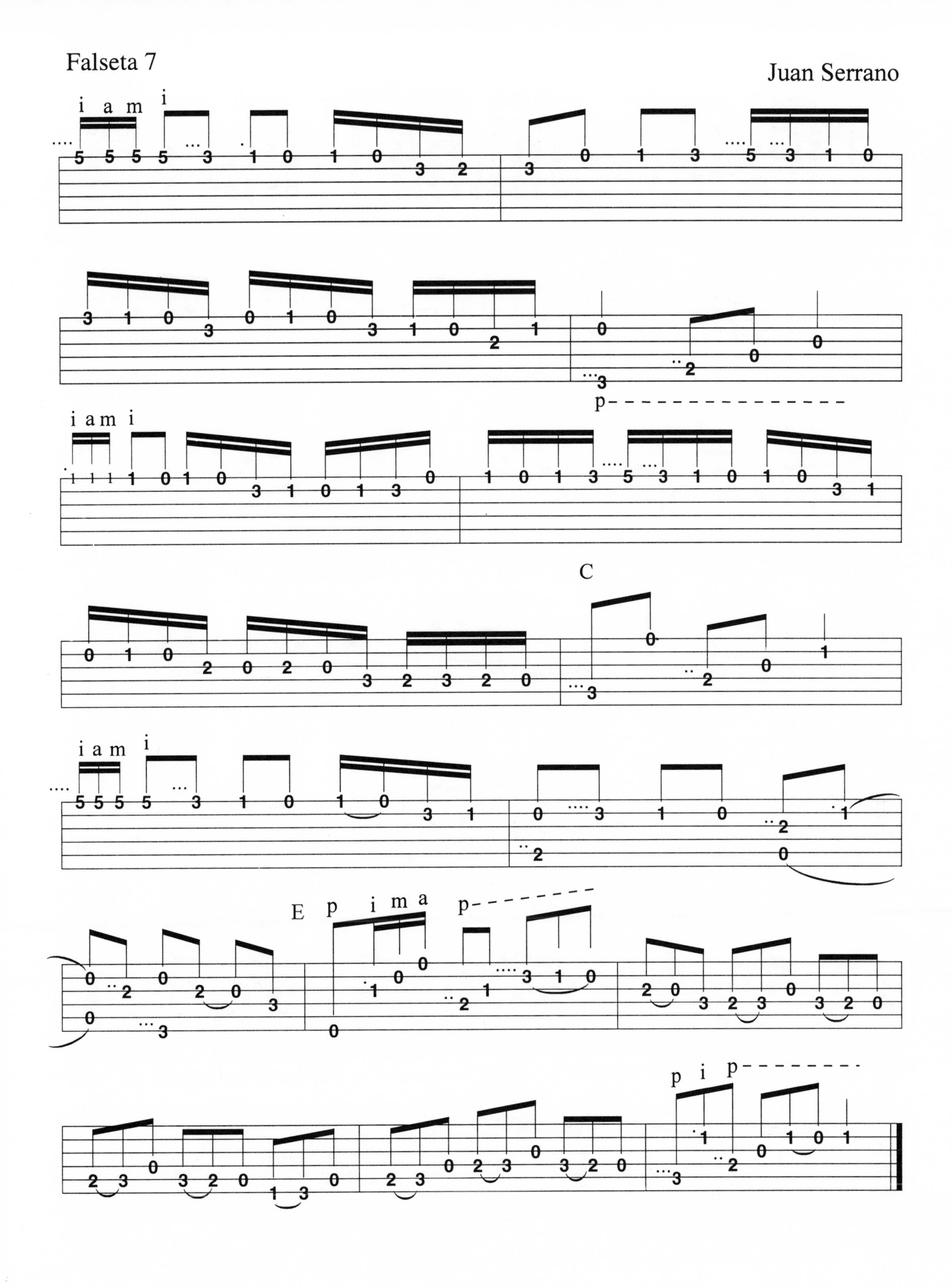
Falseta 7
Juan Serrano
C
E

Falseta 8

Juan Serrano

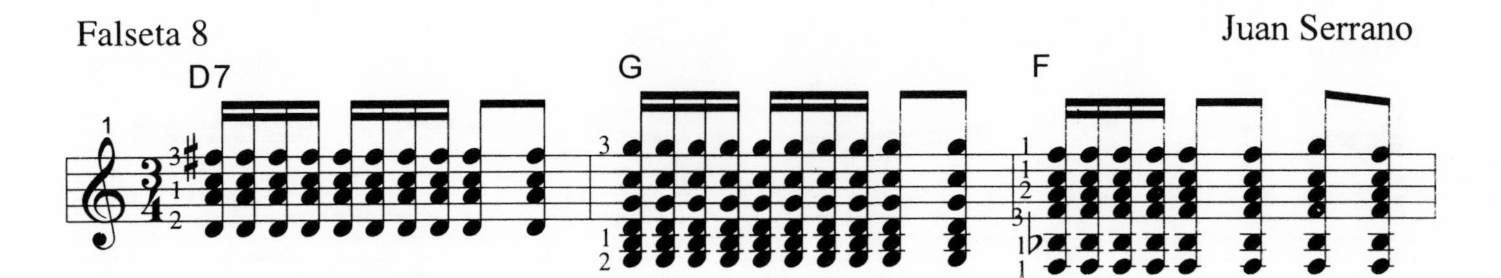


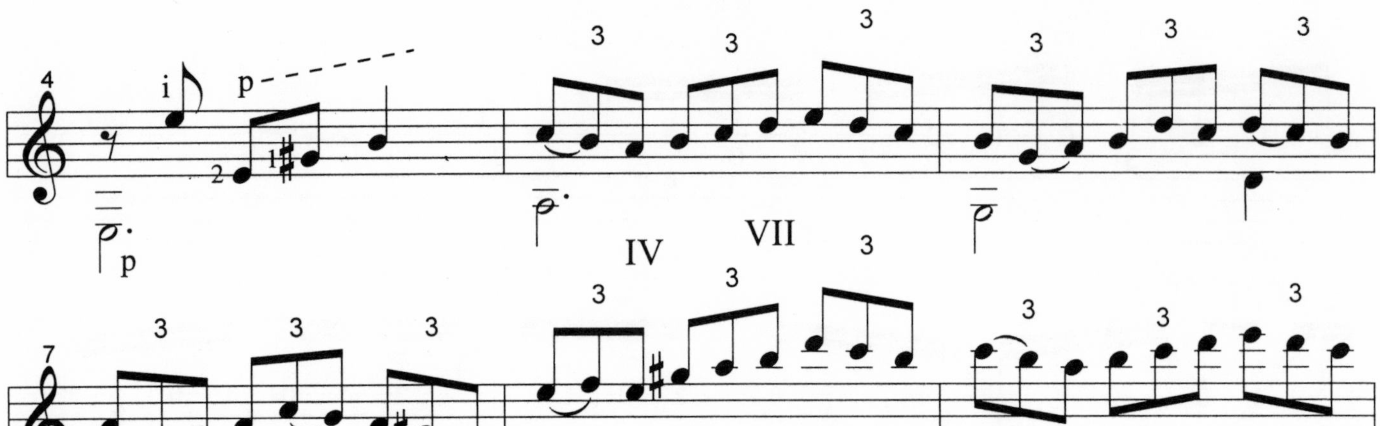


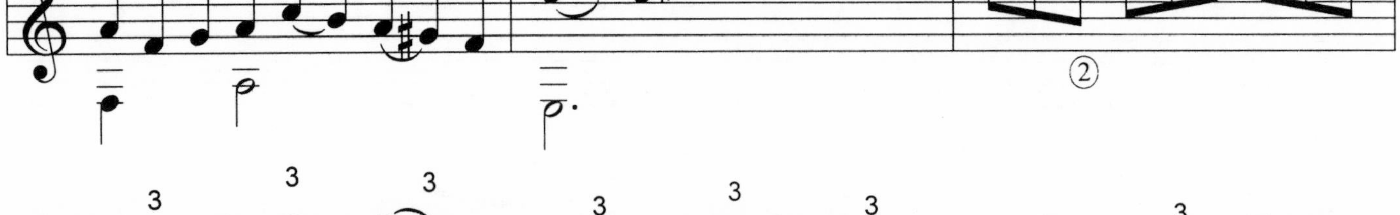

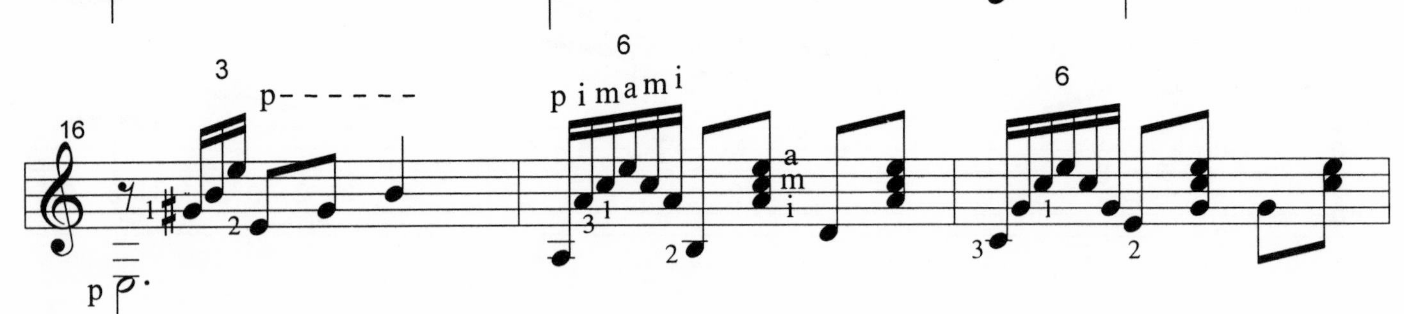


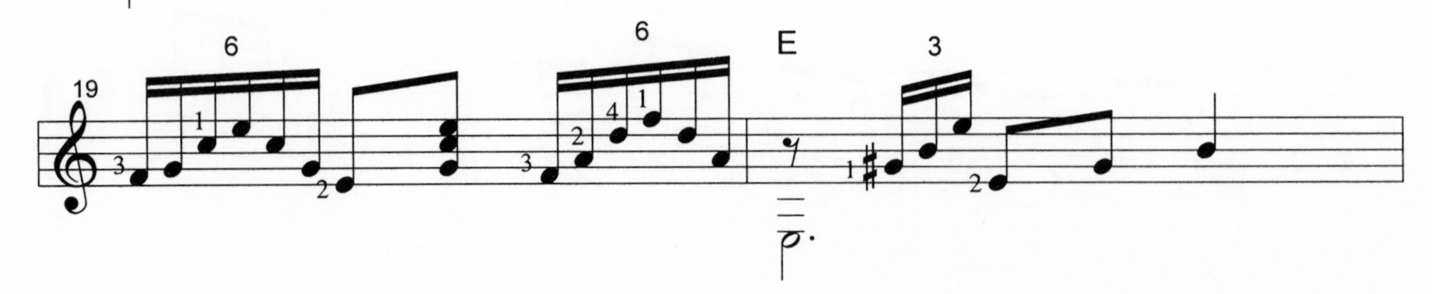

21
p i m a
p

23
C
i m a
p

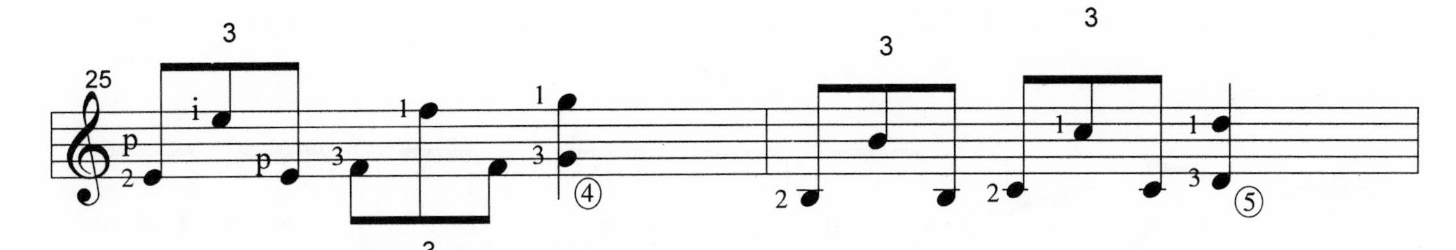
25

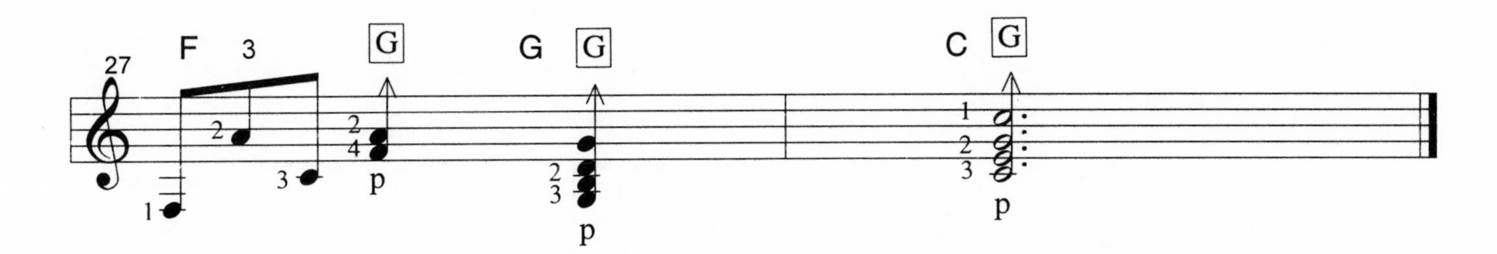
27
F
G
G
G
C
G

## Falseta 8

Juan Serrano

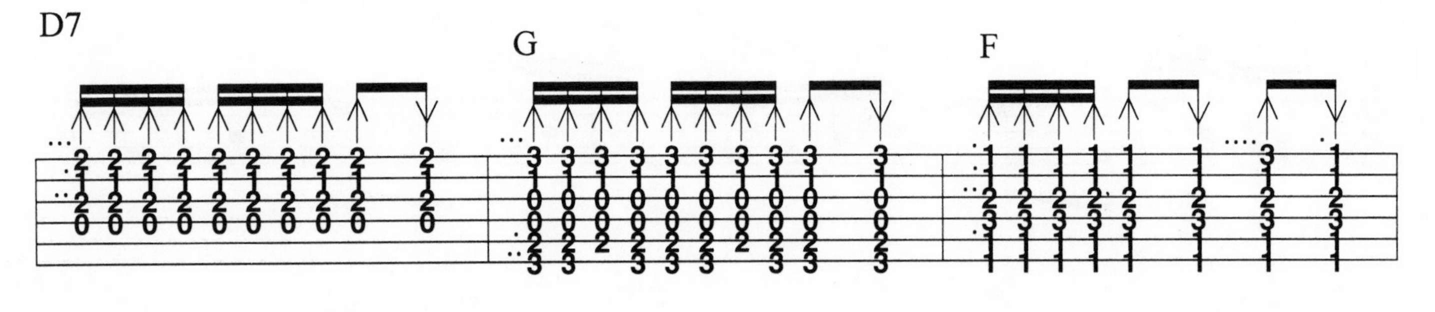


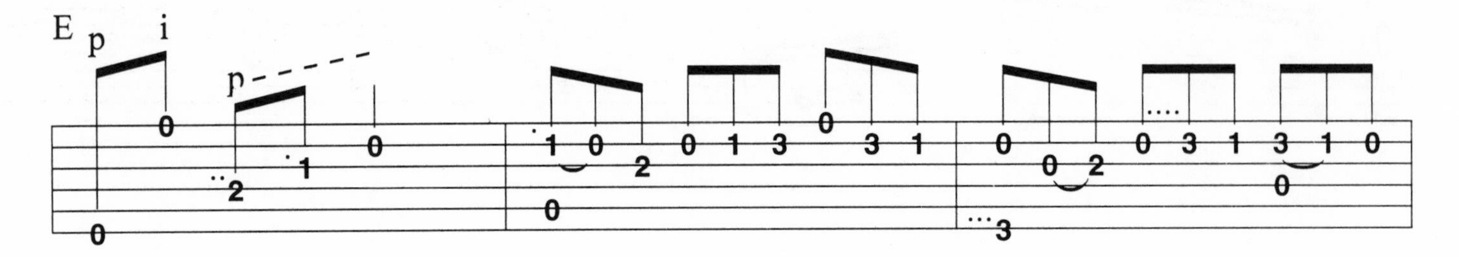


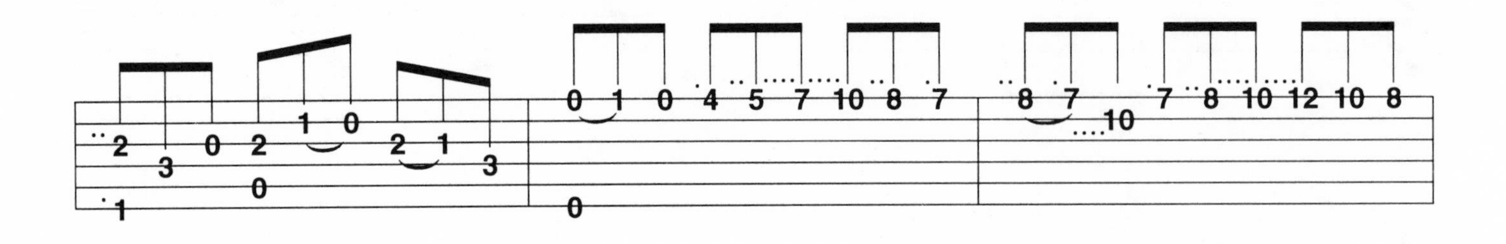

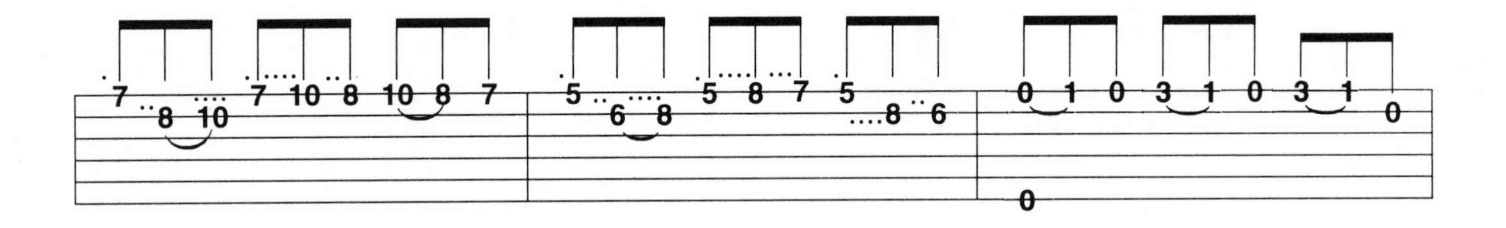

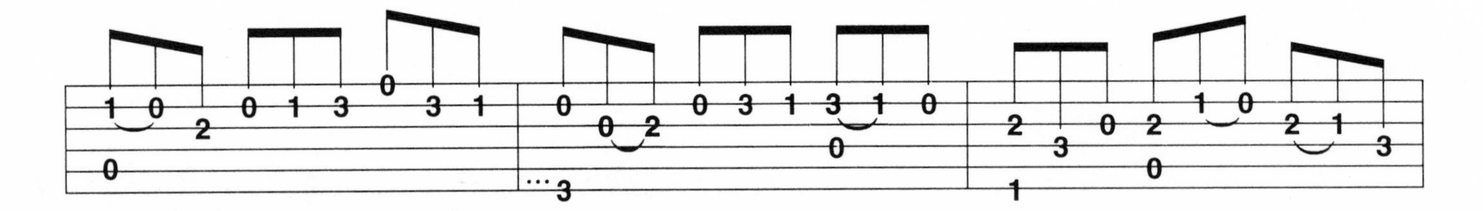

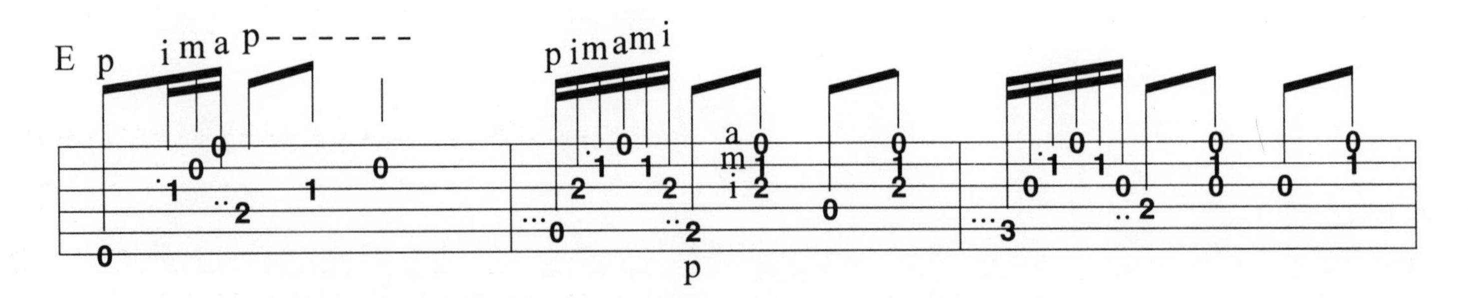

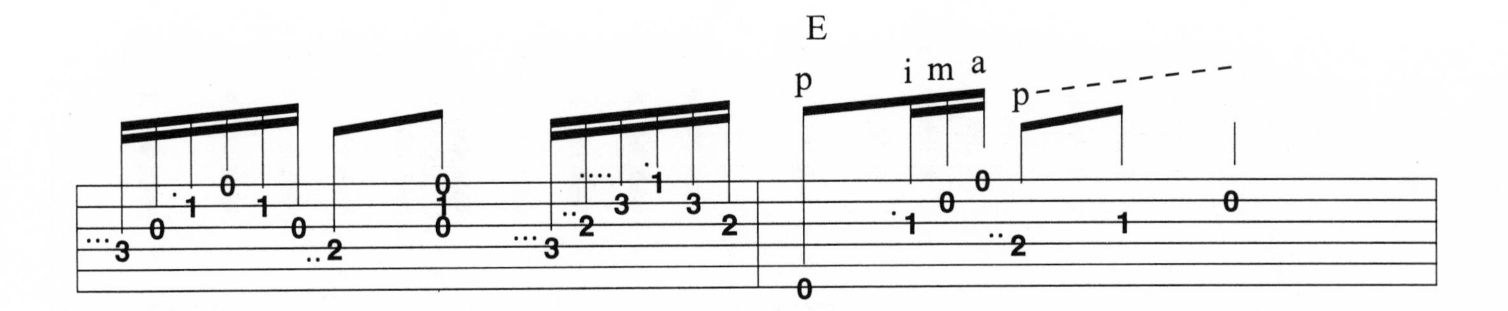
E
p i m a p

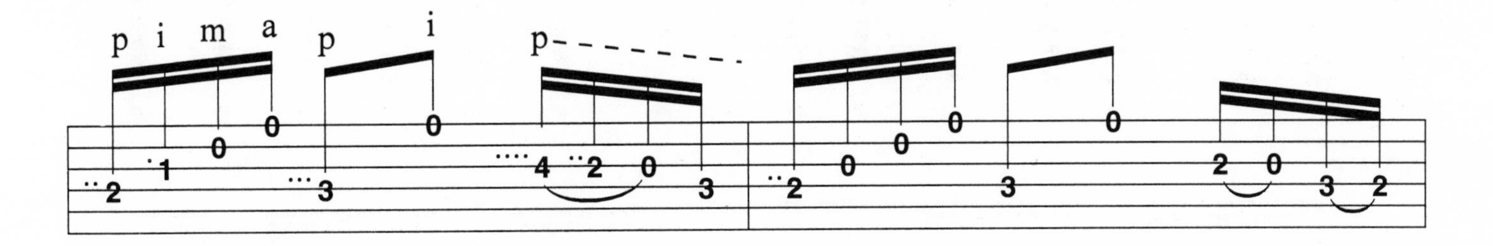
p i m a p i p

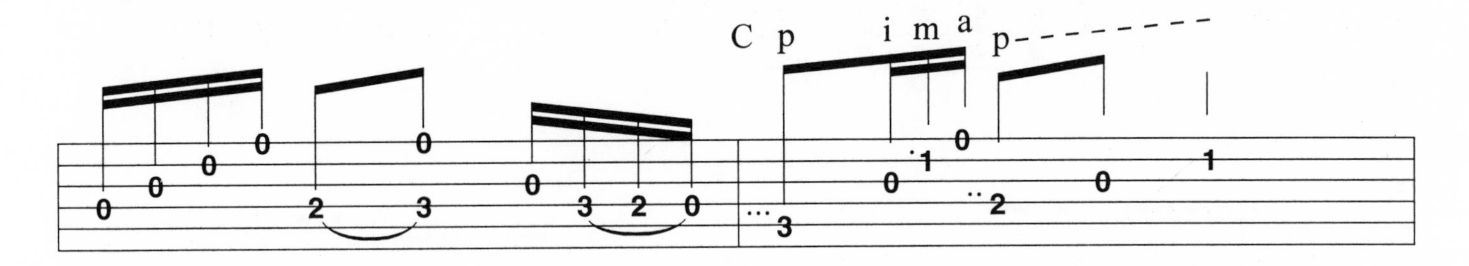
C p i m a p

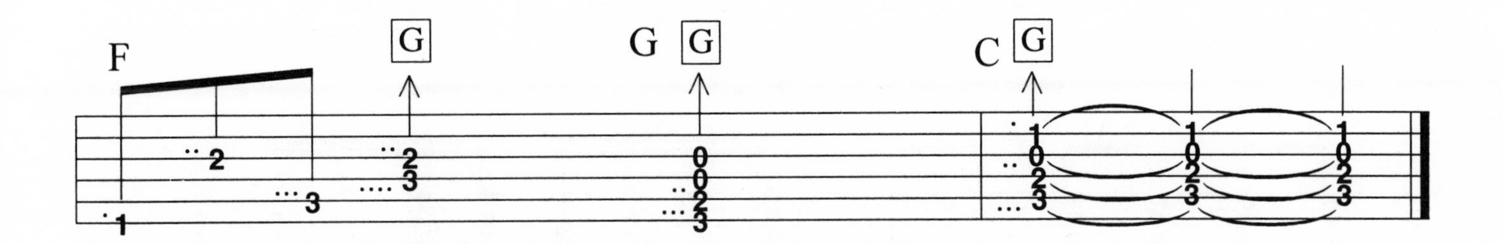
F
G
G G
C G

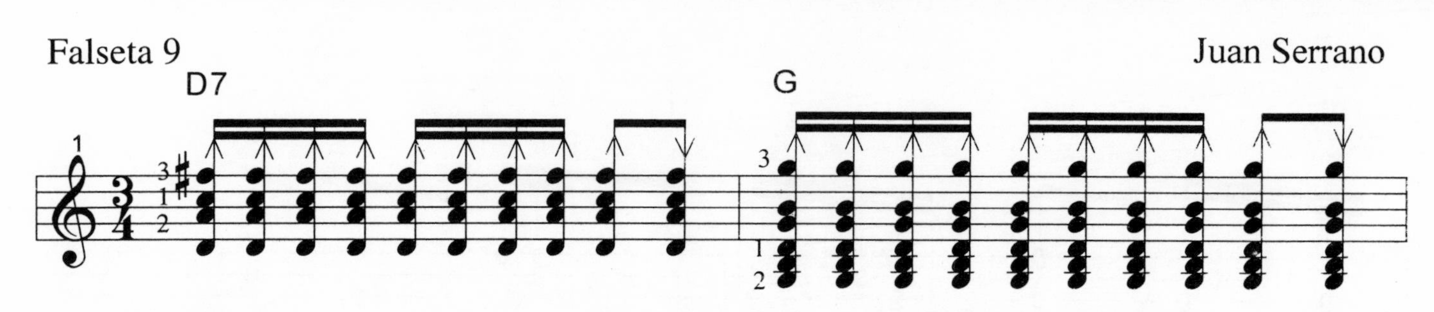
Falseta 9
Juan Serrano
D7
G

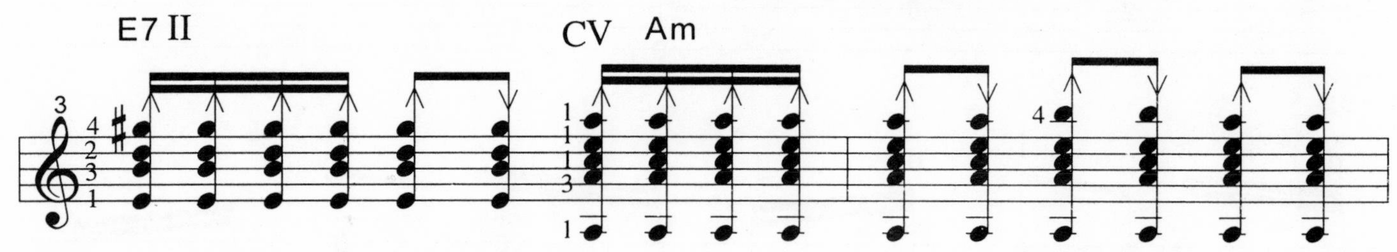
E7 II
CV Am

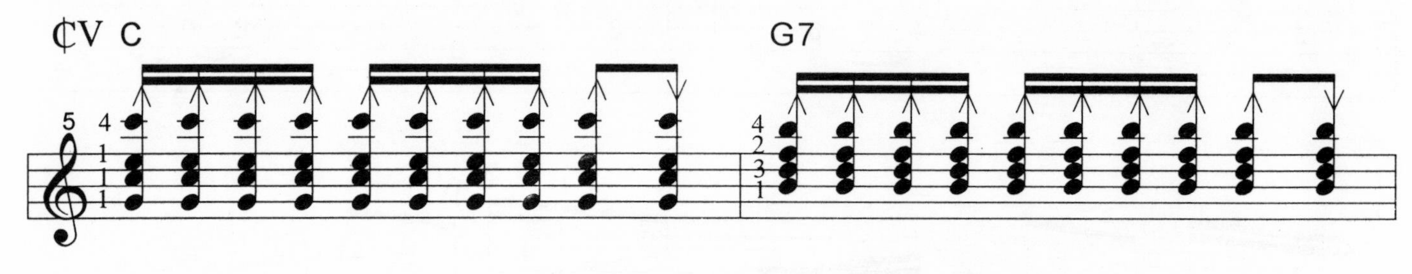
CV C
G7

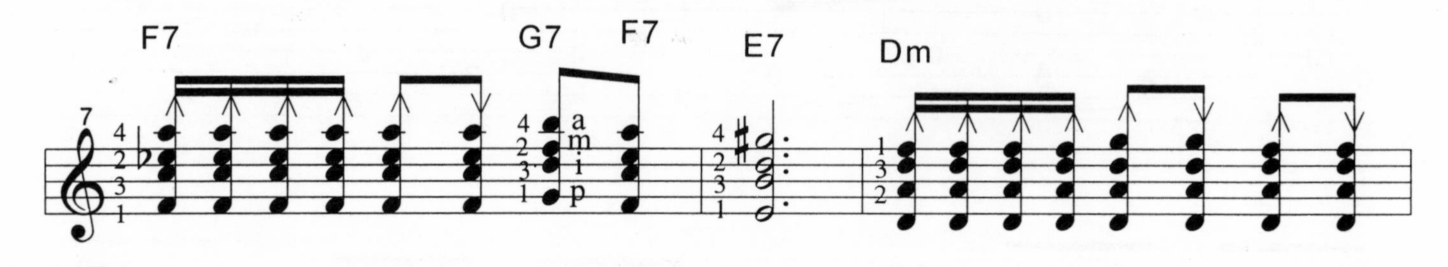
F7
G7
F7
E7
Dm

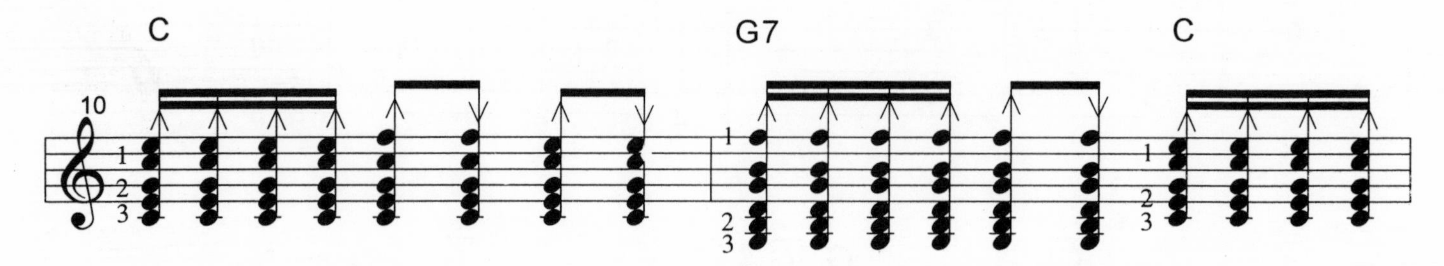
C
G7
C

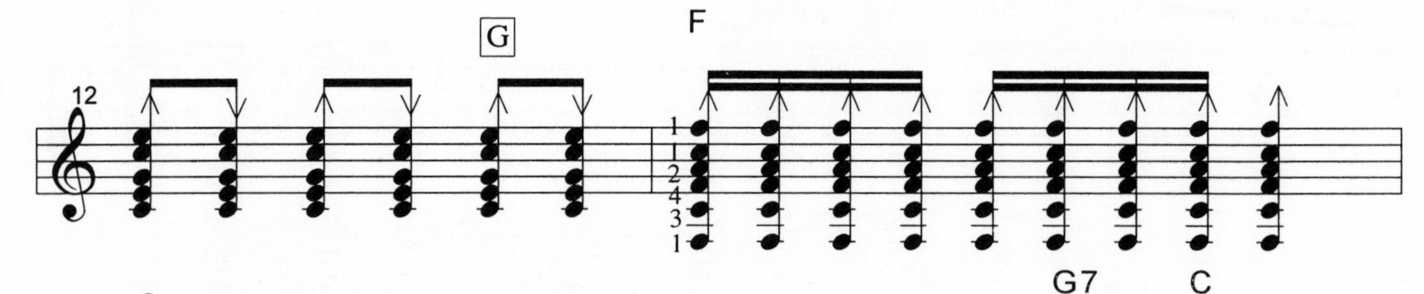
G
F

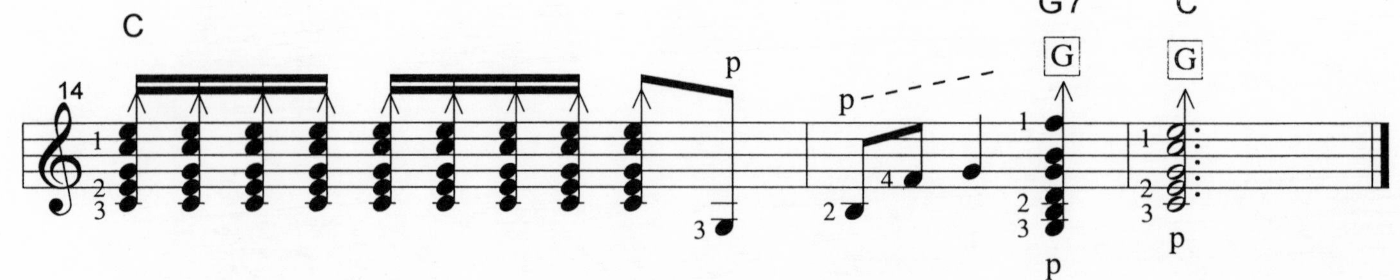
C
G7
C
G
G

# Falseta 9

Juan Serrano

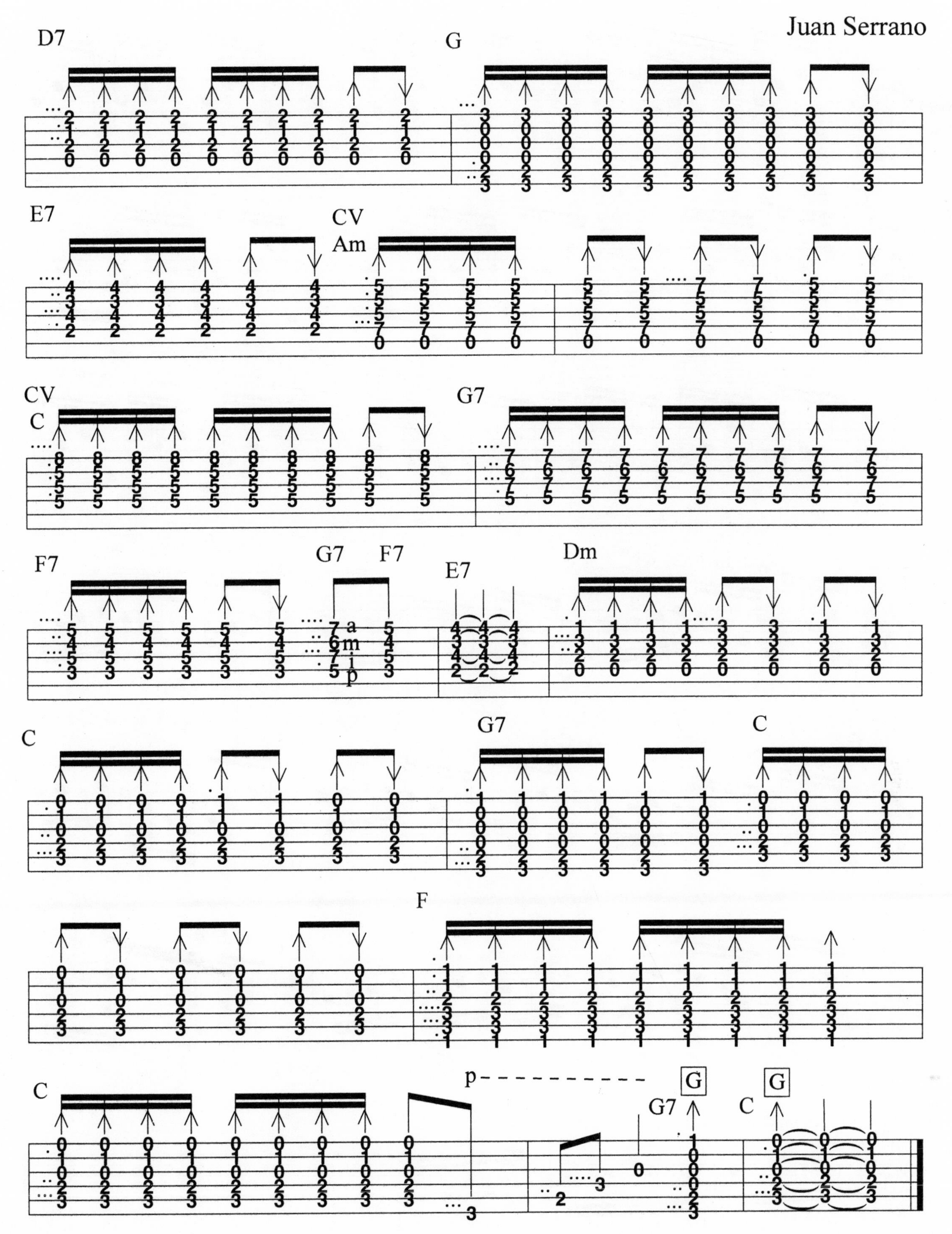

Falseta 10 Juan Serrano

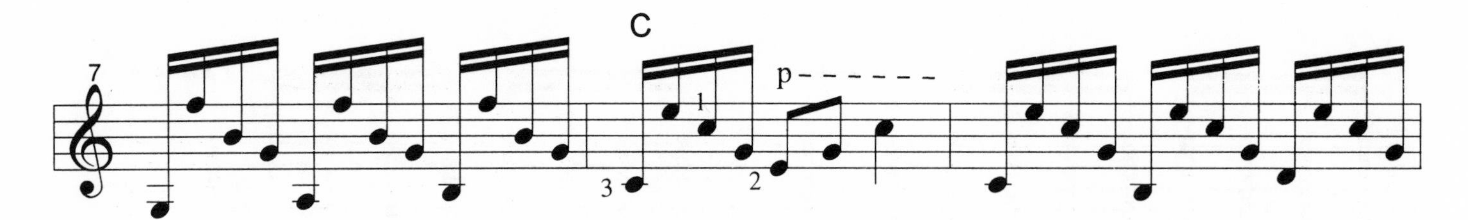


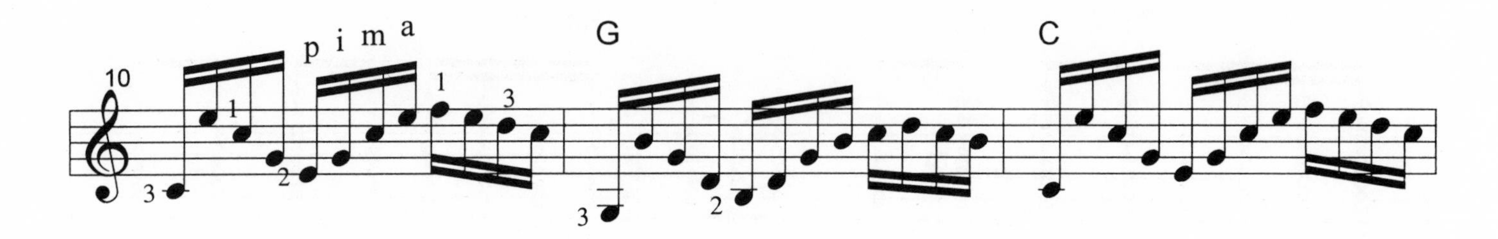

## Falseta 10

Juan Serrano

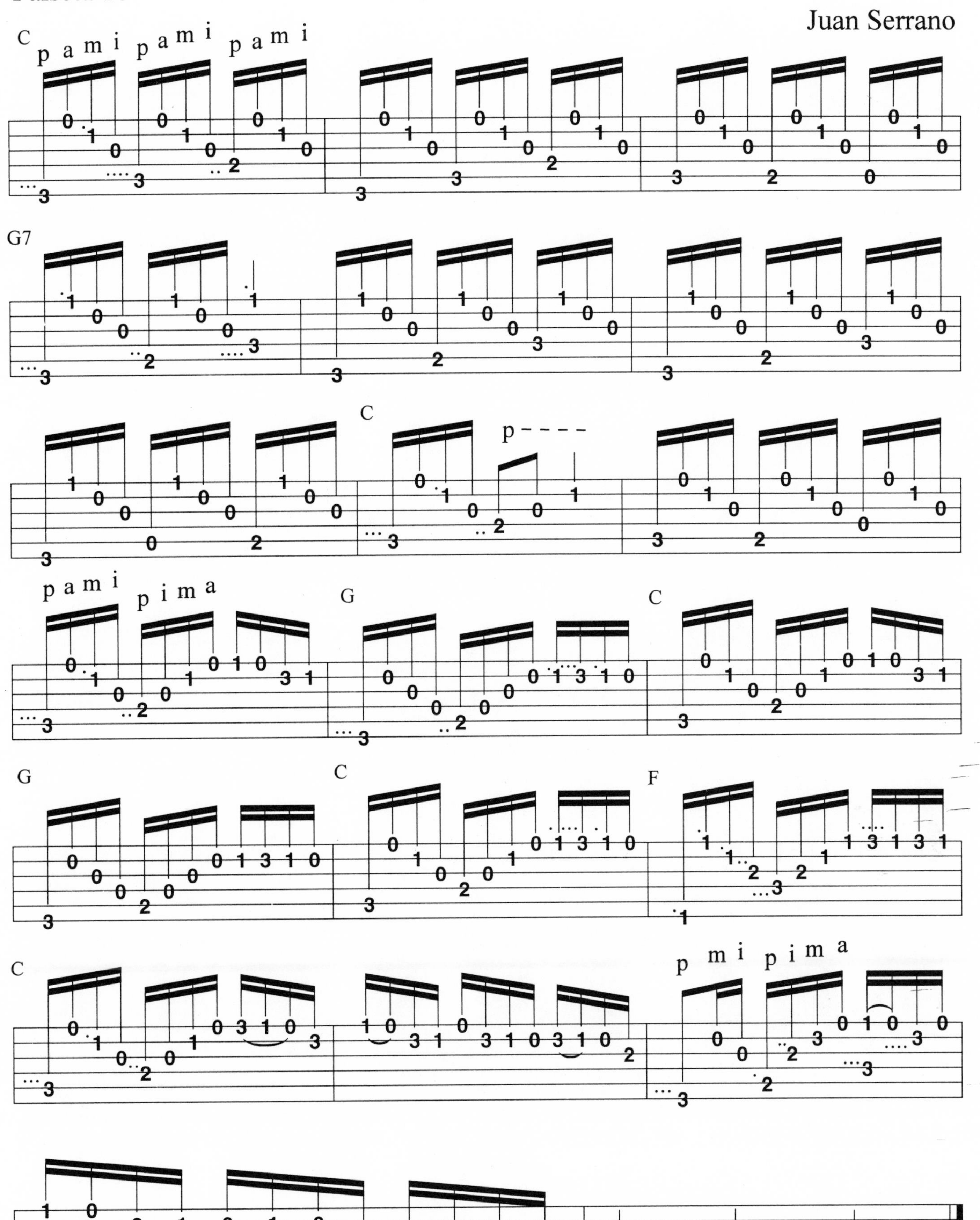


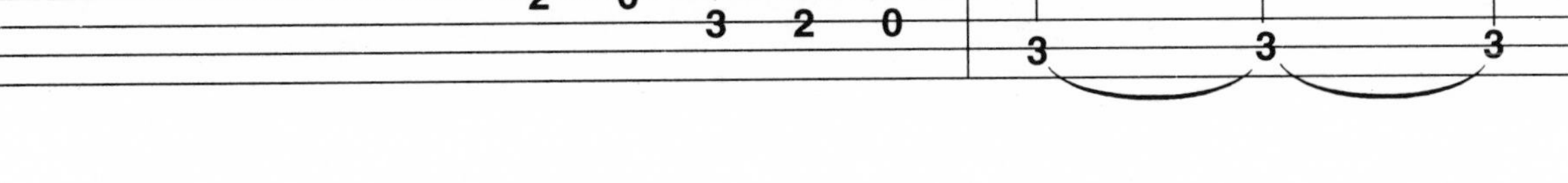

# SIGUIRIYAS

The Siguiriyas are quite possibly the most complicated and difficult flamenco form to understand. A flamenco compás is composed of two different measures—one of 3/4 and the other of 6/8. The complication is because the compás begins on the second beat of 3/4 and ends on the first beat of 3/4. This has caused a great deal of confusion and controversy, even among the professional flamenco guitarists.

It is recommended that these two exercises be practiced at the same time. The accents should be marked with the foot and, at the same time the compás played on the guitar. In the beginning, it will be extremely difficult, but with patience and practice, it can be perfected. The traditional compás should be practiced and the three variations of the same form, keeping the accents with the foot.

The first falseta is played with the thumb (p), with the exception of the indicated notes with the index (i). In the following falseta much care should be taken with the legatos. They should be practiced by themselves until they are perfected. Thus, the falseta will sound good and be easier to interpret.

All of the notations marked should be strictly followed in each measure, the fingering of both hands, as well as the symbols.

**Example of the Siguiriyas compás accent/Ejemplo de los acentos del compás de Siguiriyas**

**Example of the basic compás/Ejemplo del compás básico.**

# SIGUIRIYAS

Las Siguiriyas, posiblemente sean la forma flamenca más complicada y más difícil de entender. Un compás flamenco se compone de dos diferentes compases musicales—uno de 3/4 y otro de 6/8. La complicación es porque el compás flamenco empieza en el segundo tiempo del compás musical de 3/4 y termina en el primer tiempo de 3/4. Esto da lugar a mucha confusión y muchas controversias, inclusive entre los guitarristas flamencos profesionales.

Mi recomendación es que se practiquen los dos ejemplos al mismo tiempo. Los acentos marcándolos con el pie y al mismo tiempo tocar el compás con la guitarra. Al principio, les será dificilísimo. Pero, con paciencia y práctica se puede conseguir. Practiquen mucho el compás tradicional y las tres variaciones de la misma forma marcando los acentos con el pie.

La primera falseta se toca toda con el pulgar (p) excepto las notas marcadas con el índice (i). En la siguiente falseta tengan mucho cuidado con los ligados. Practíquenlos por separado hasta que los perfeccionen. Así, la falseta sonará más bonita y les será más fácil interpretarla.

Sigan estrictamente todas las anotaciones marcadas en cada compás musical, tanto la digitación de ambas manos, como los símbolos.

# *Siguiriyas*

Traditional Compas

Juan Serrano

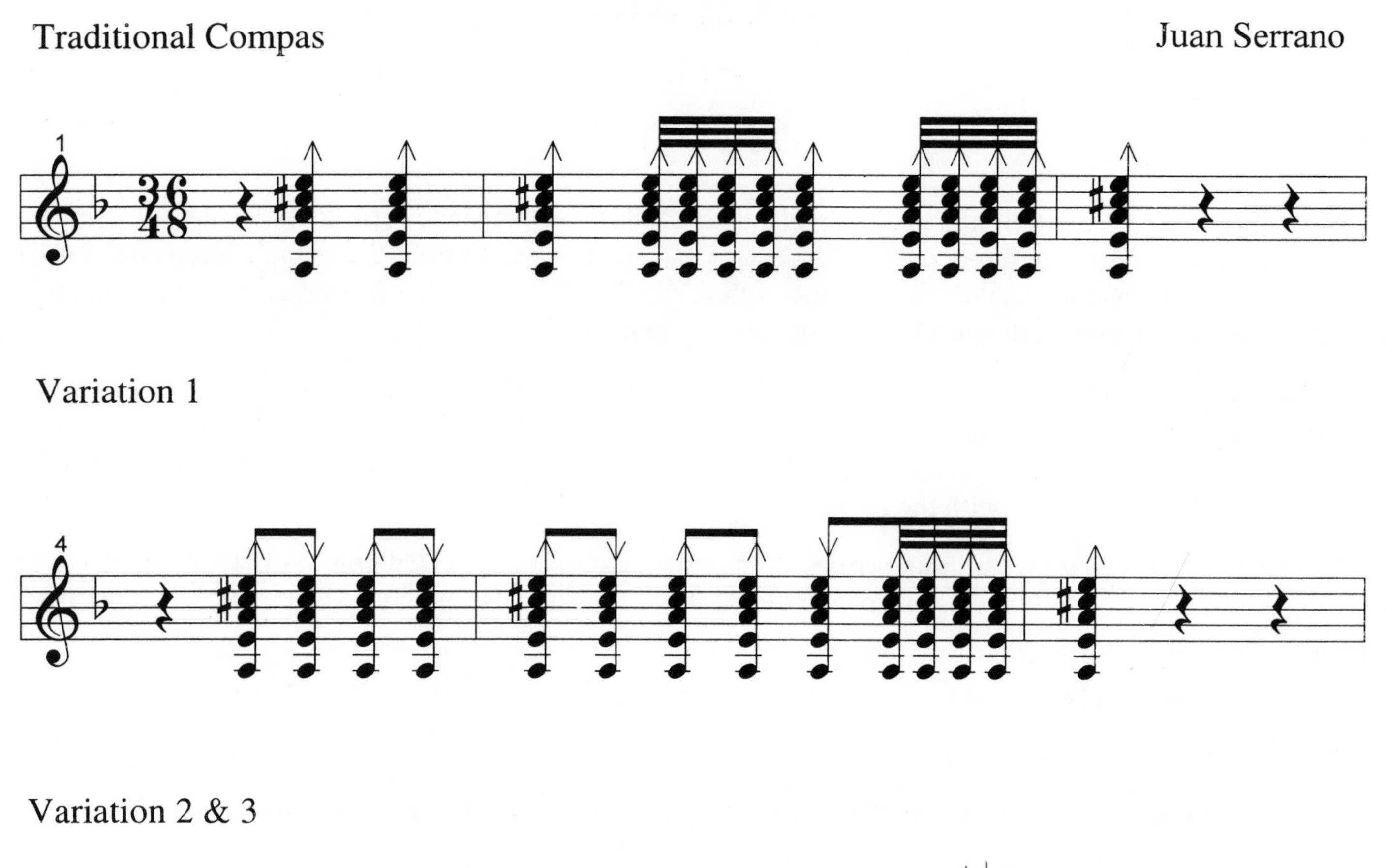


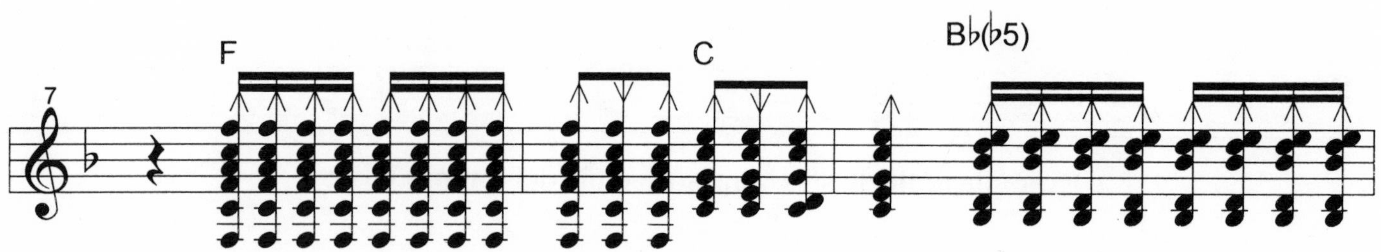

# *Siguiriyas*

## Traditional Compas

Juan Serrano

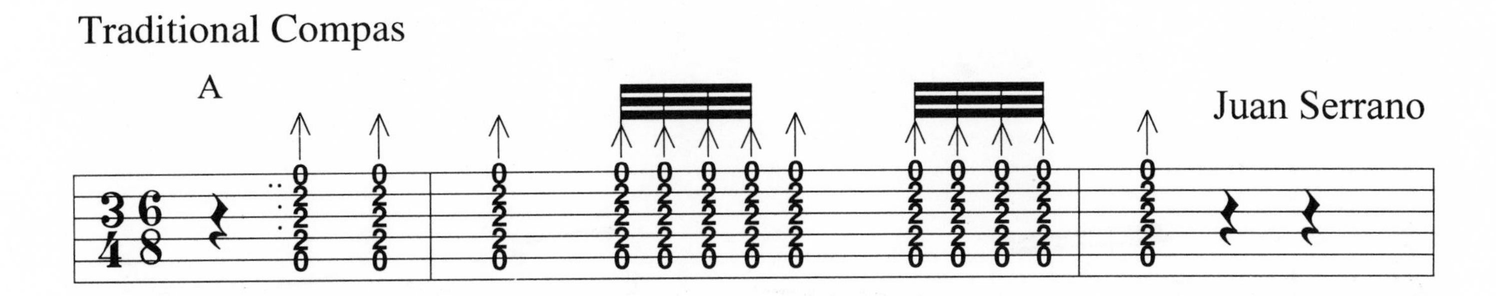


## Variation 1

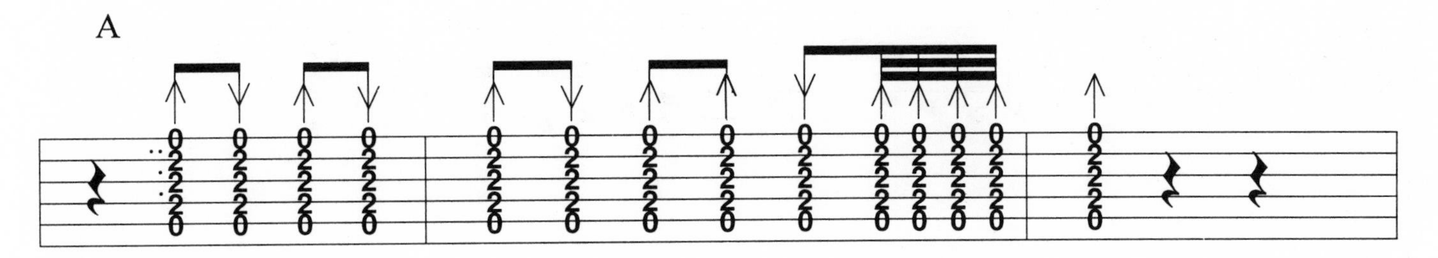


## Variation 2 & 3

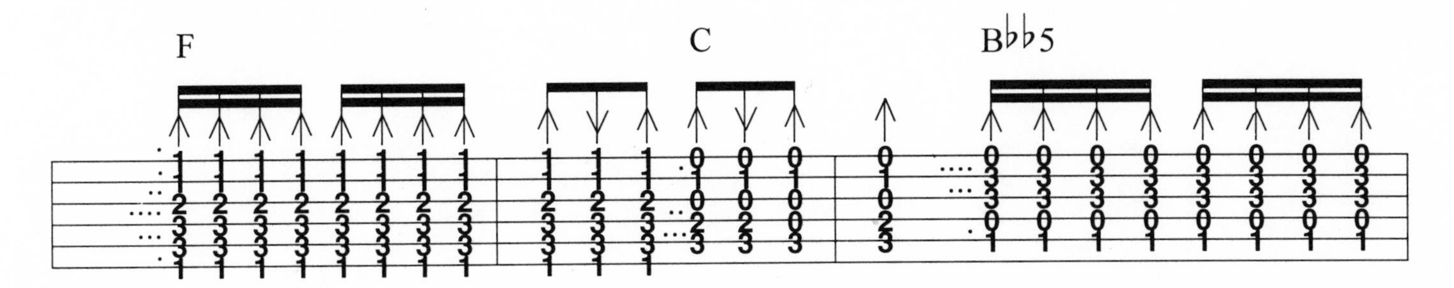


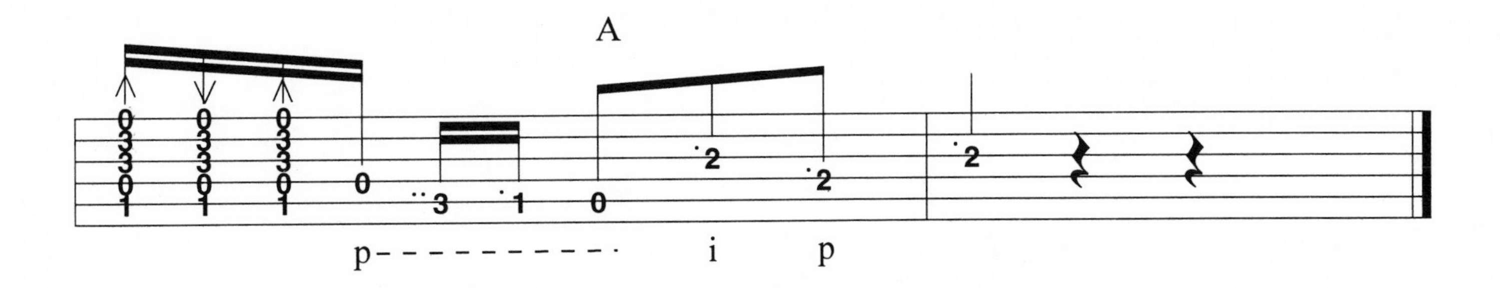

Falseta 1

Juan Serrano

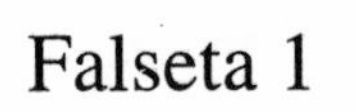


Juan Serrano

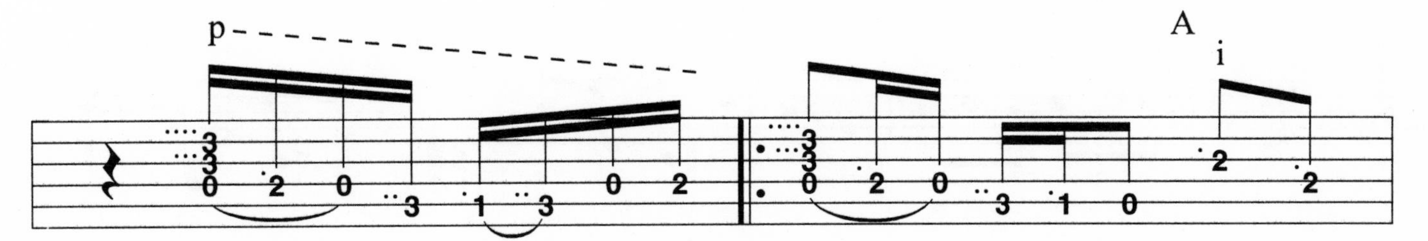


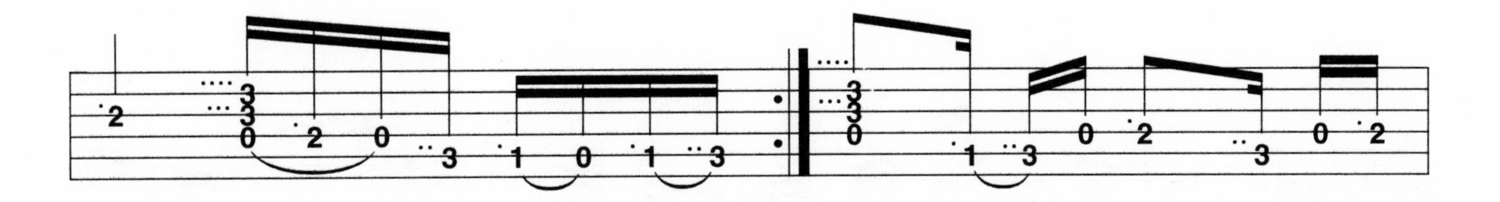

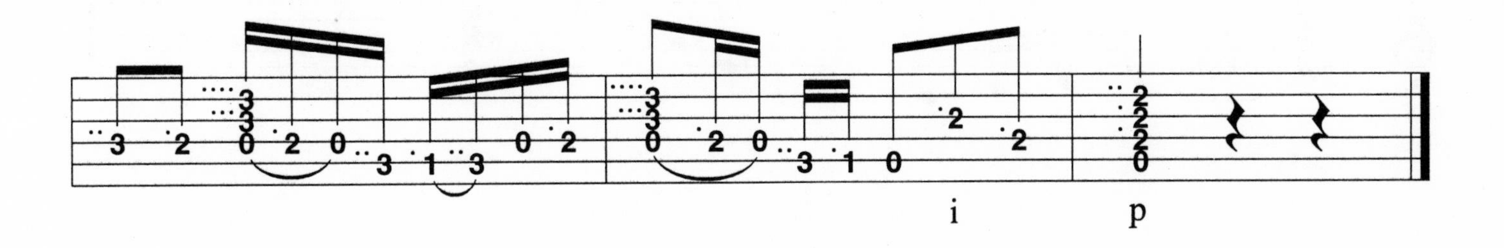

Falseta 2

Juan Serrano

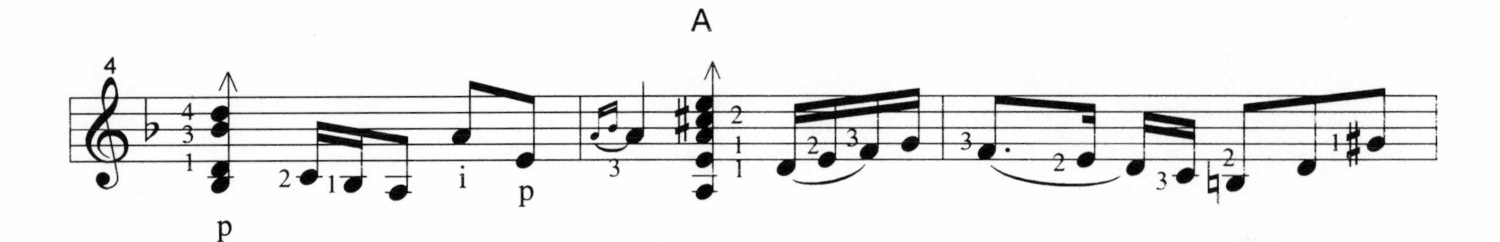

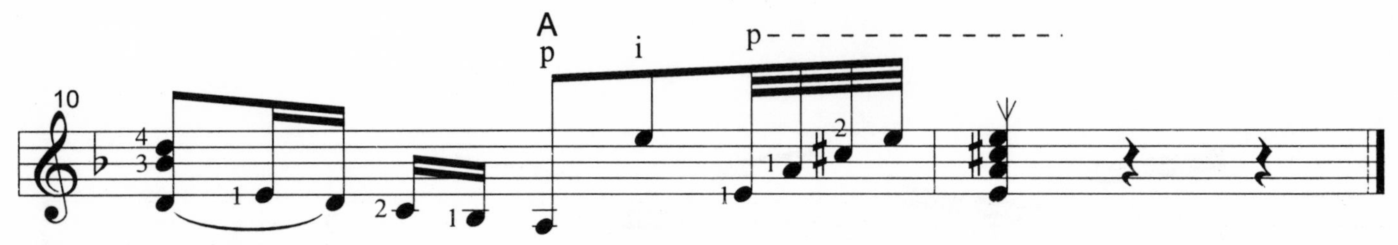

Falseta 2

Juan Serrano

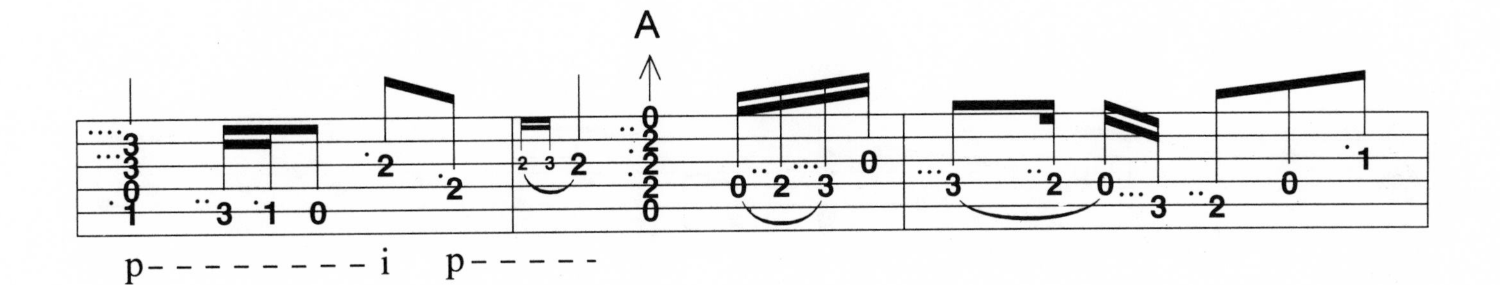

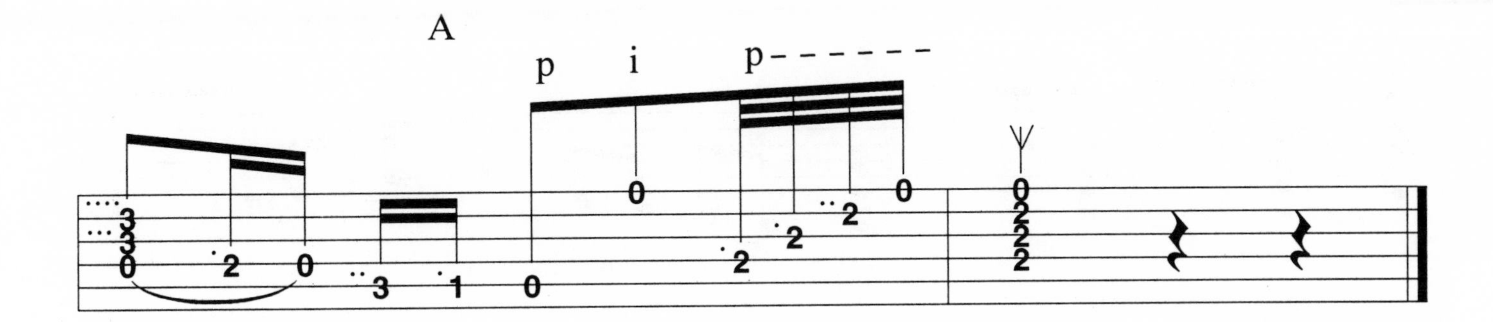

Falseta 3
Juan Serrano
CII

B♭
Dm

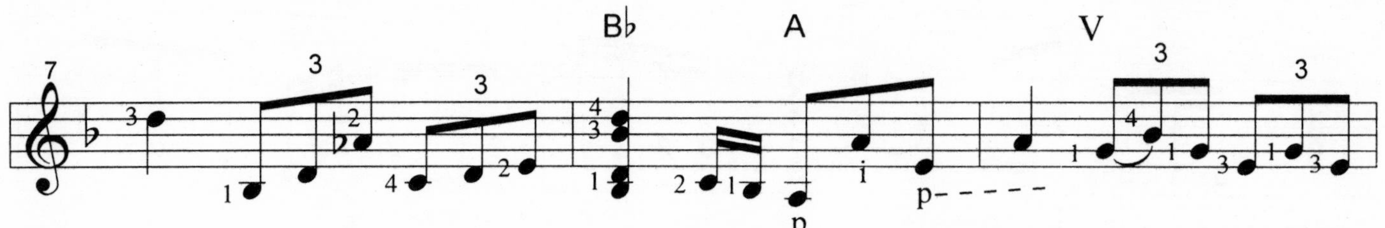
B♭
A
V

III
A

II
V

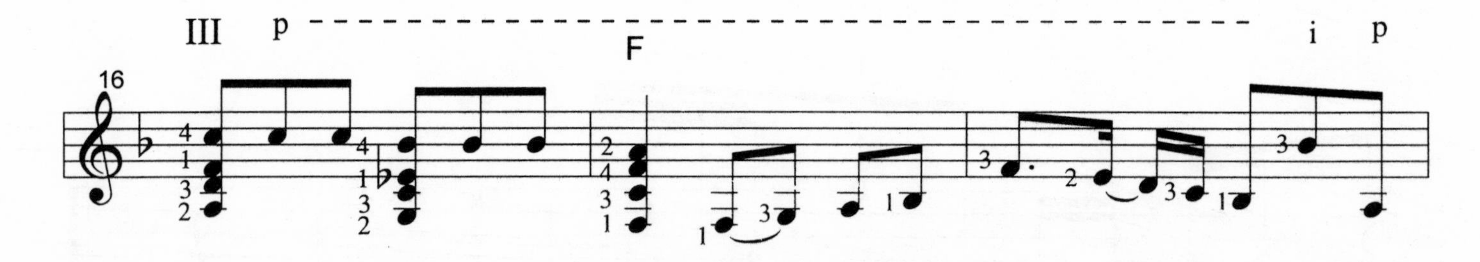
III
F

A

Falseta 3

Juan Serrano

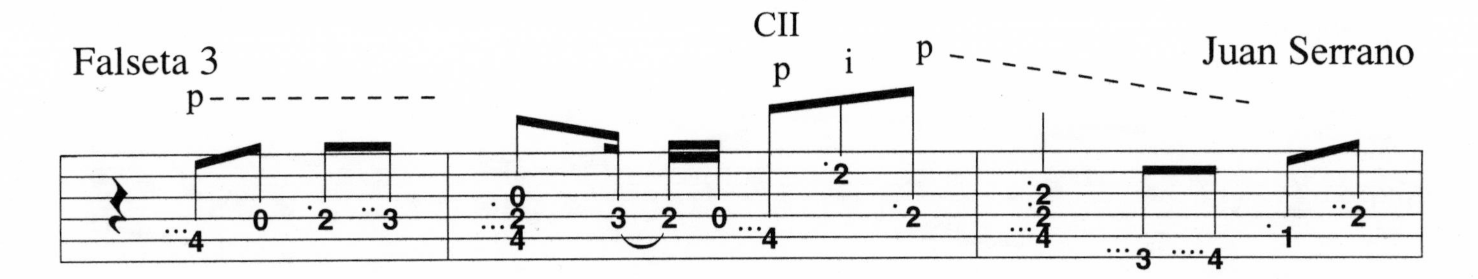


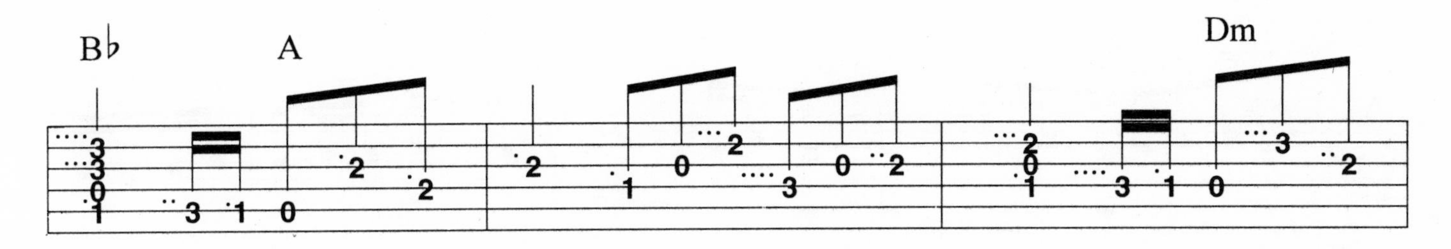


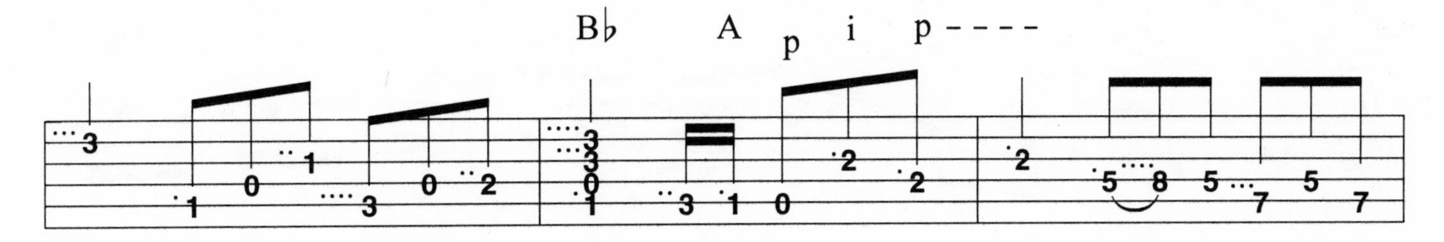


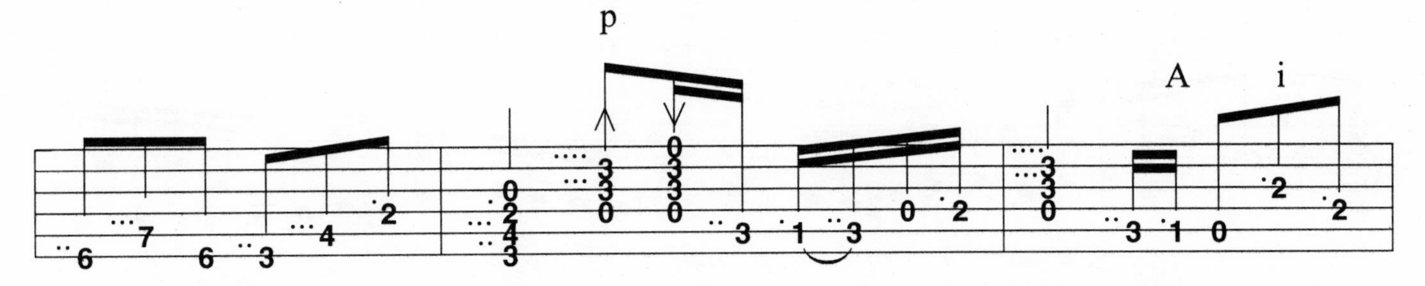


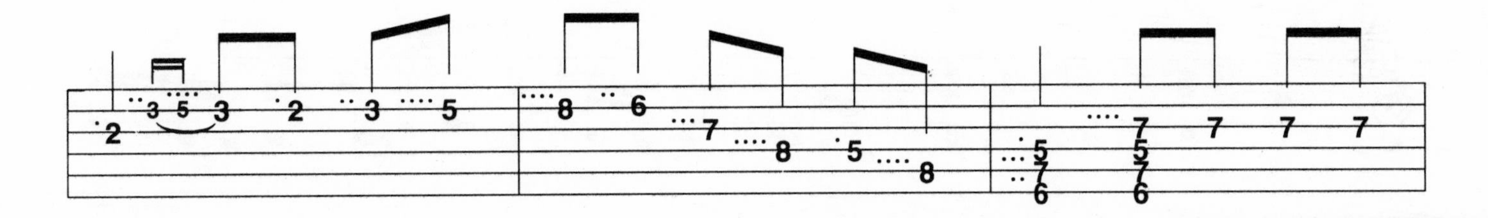

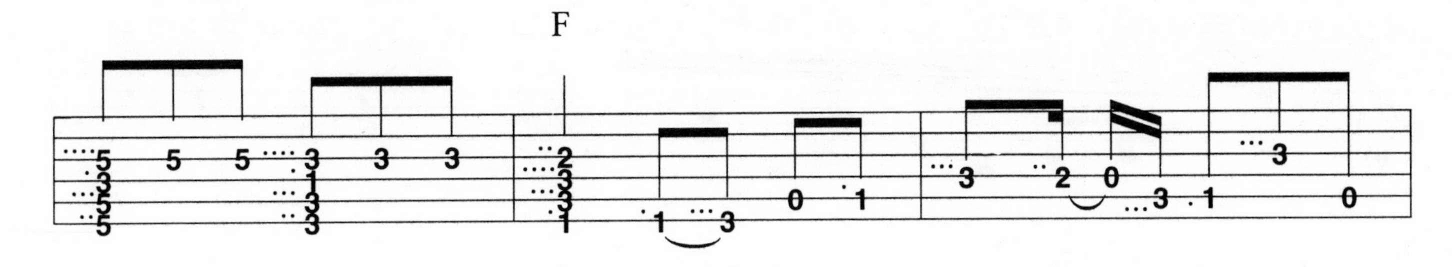


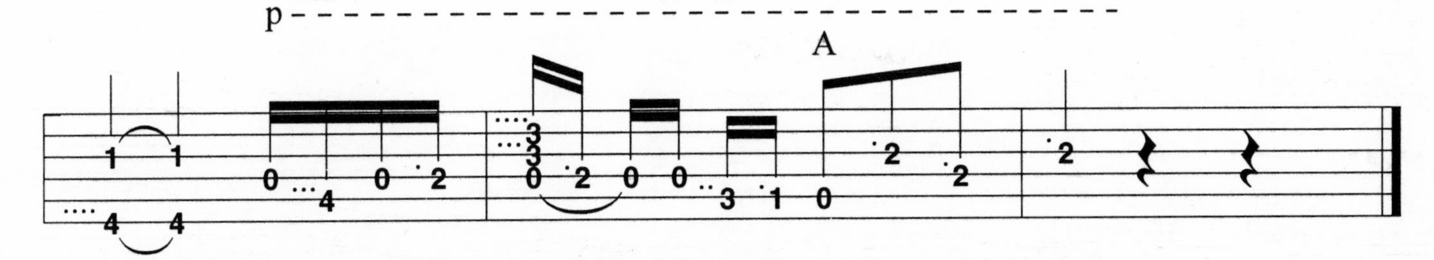

Falseta 4

Juan Serrano

Falseta 4

Juan Serrano

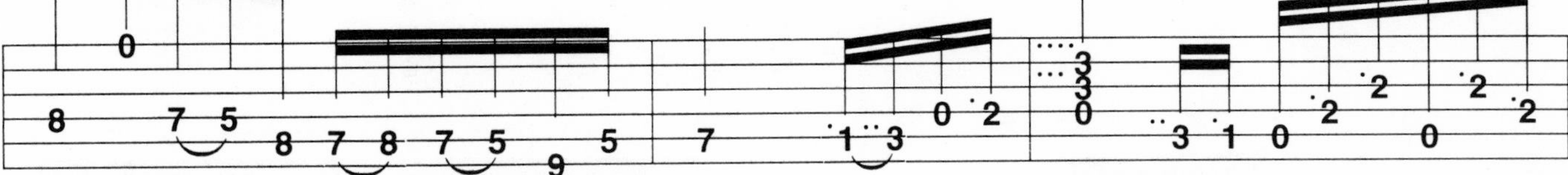

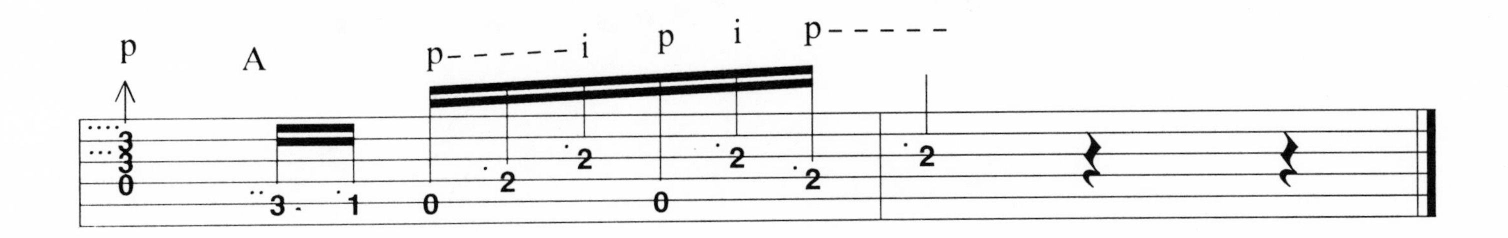

## Falseta 5

Juan Serrano

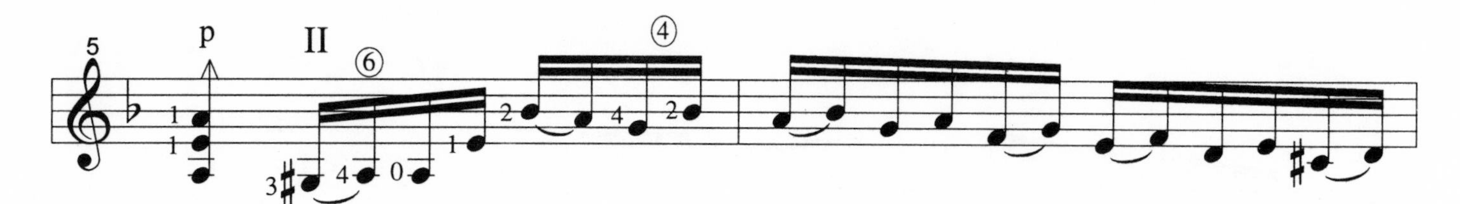


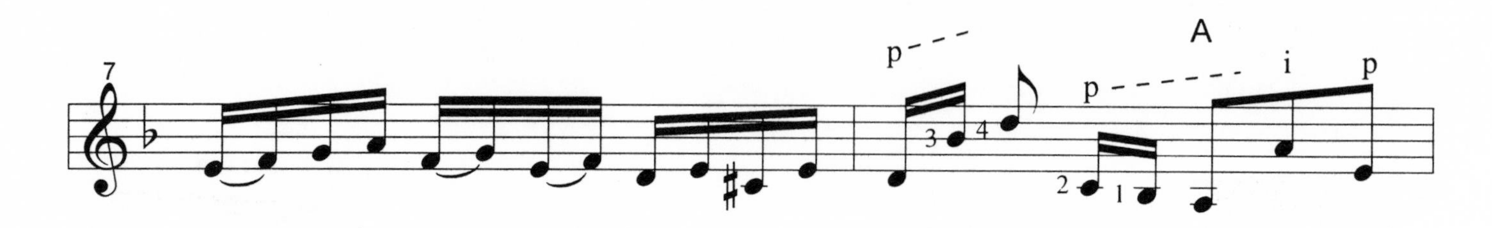


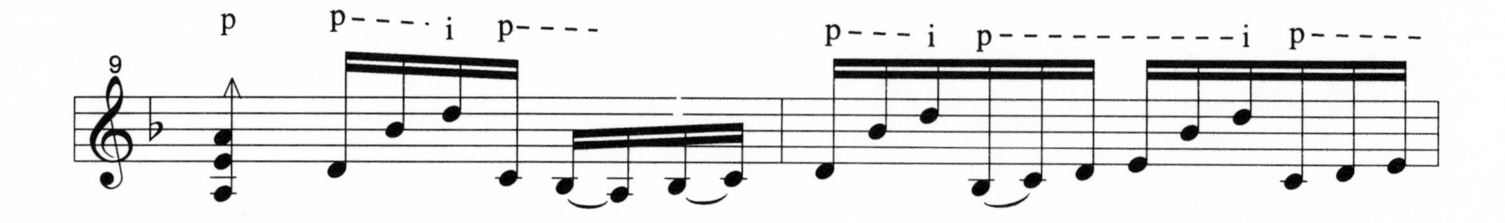


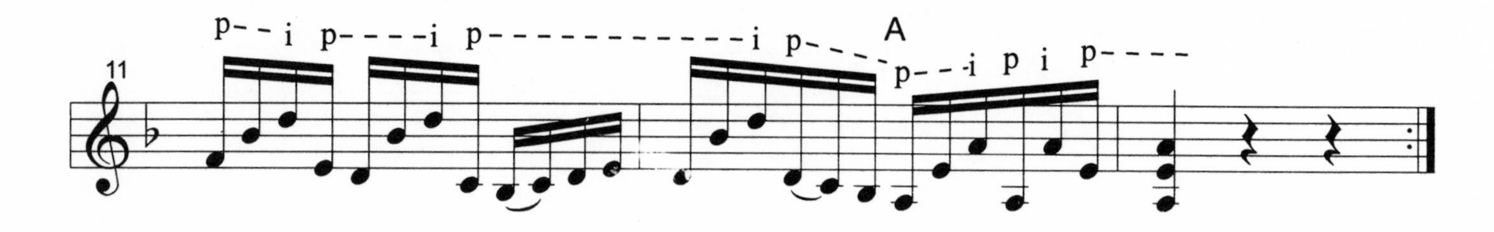

## Falseta 5

Juan Serrano

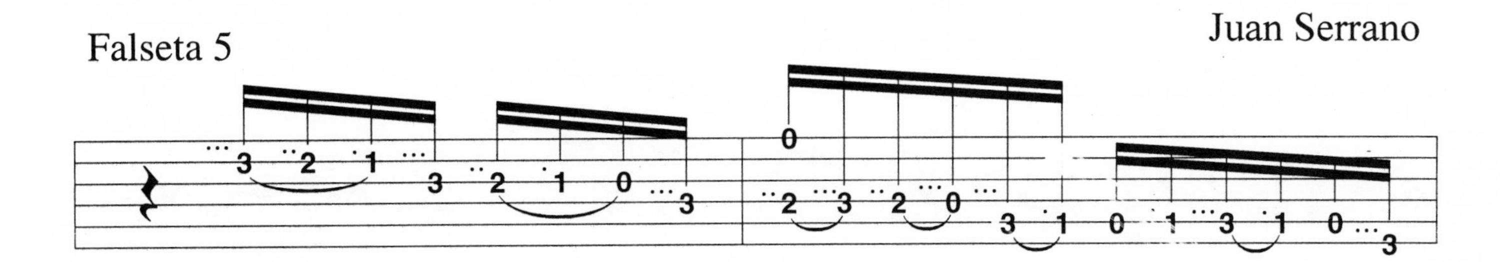

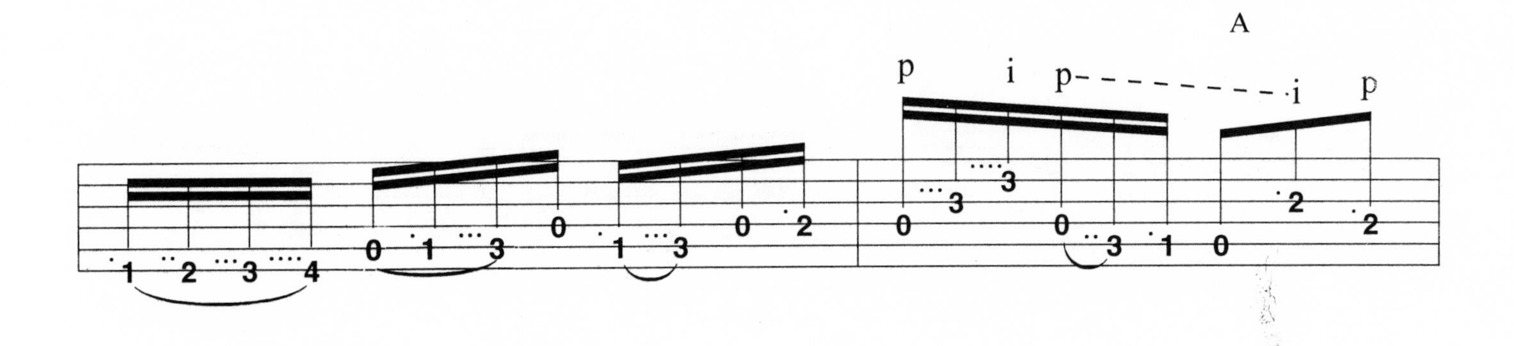

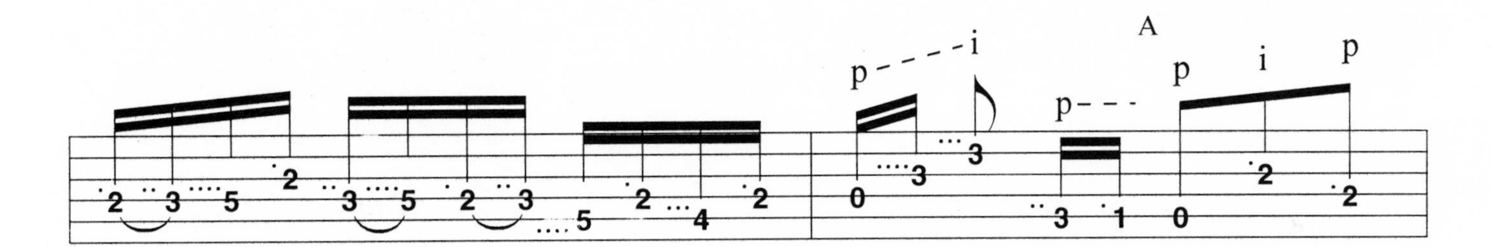

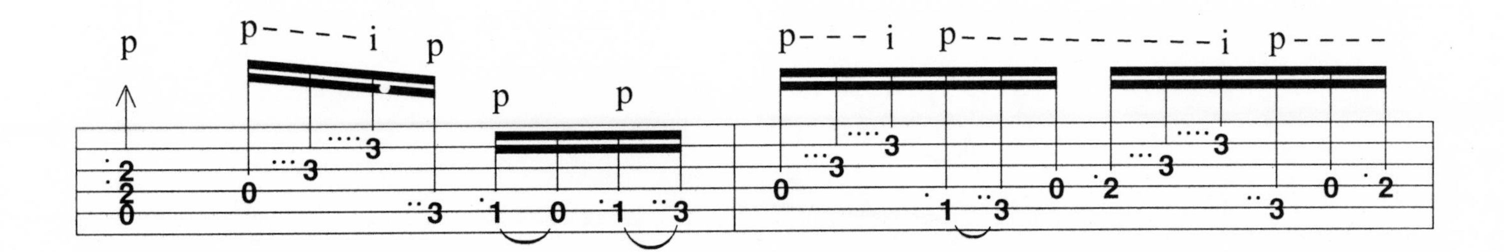

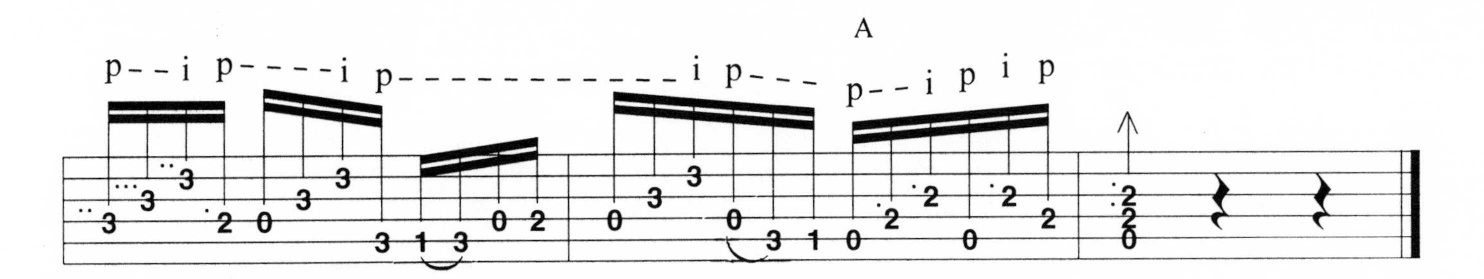

Falseta 6 Juan Serrano

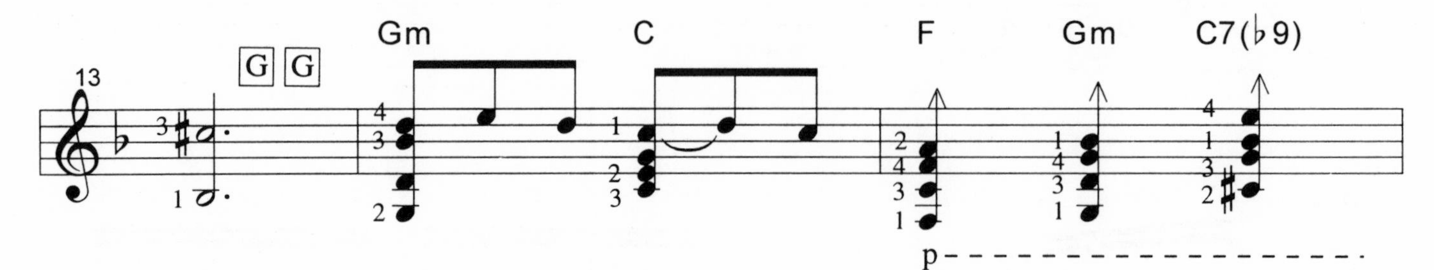

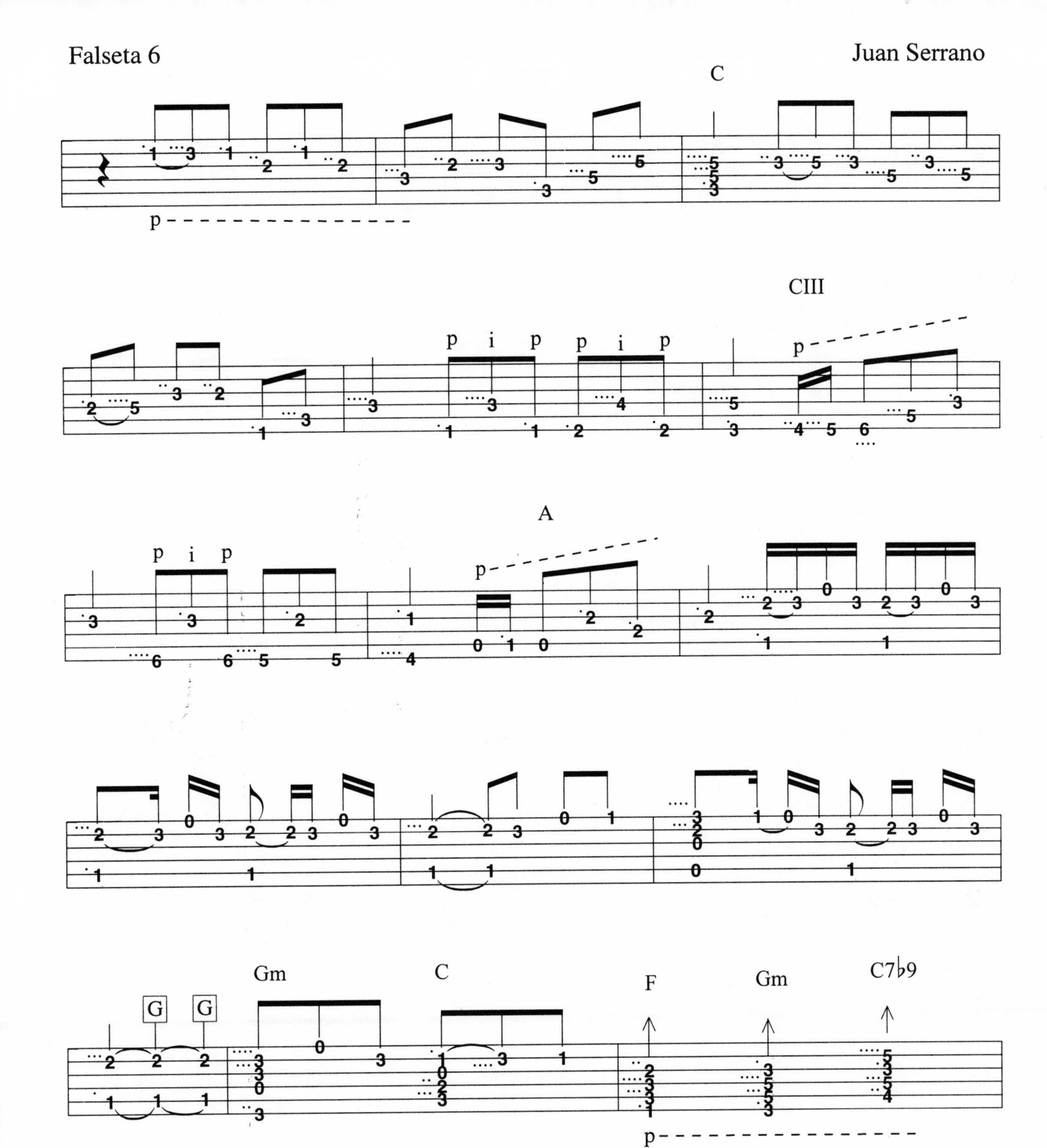
Falseta 6
Juan Serrano
C
p
CIII
p i p p i p
p
A
p i p
p
G G
Gm
C
F
Gm
C7♭9
p

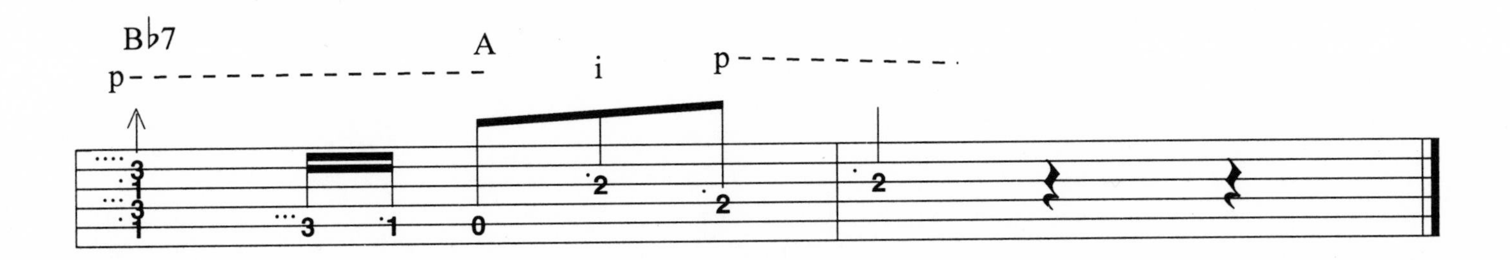
B♭7
p
A
i
p

Falseta 7

Juan Serrano

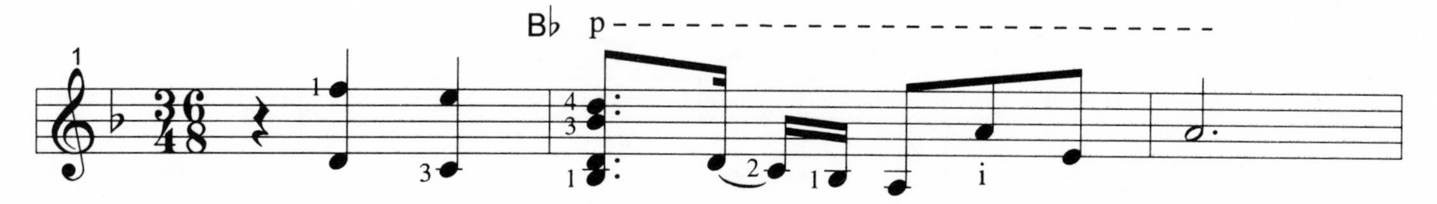


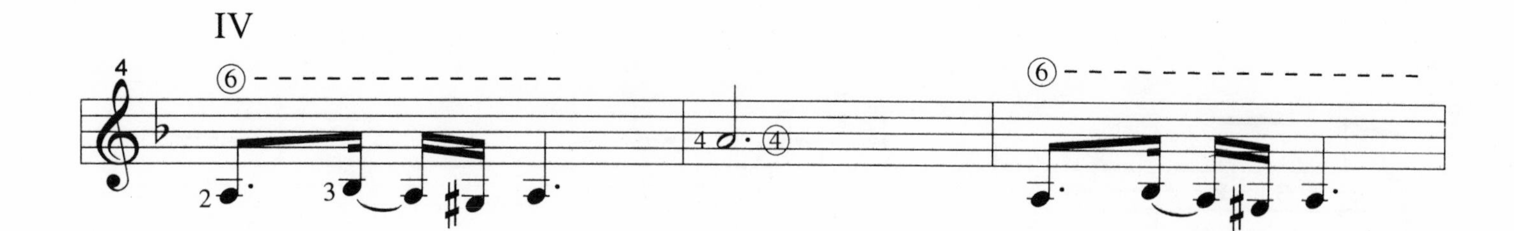

Falseta 7

Juan Serrano

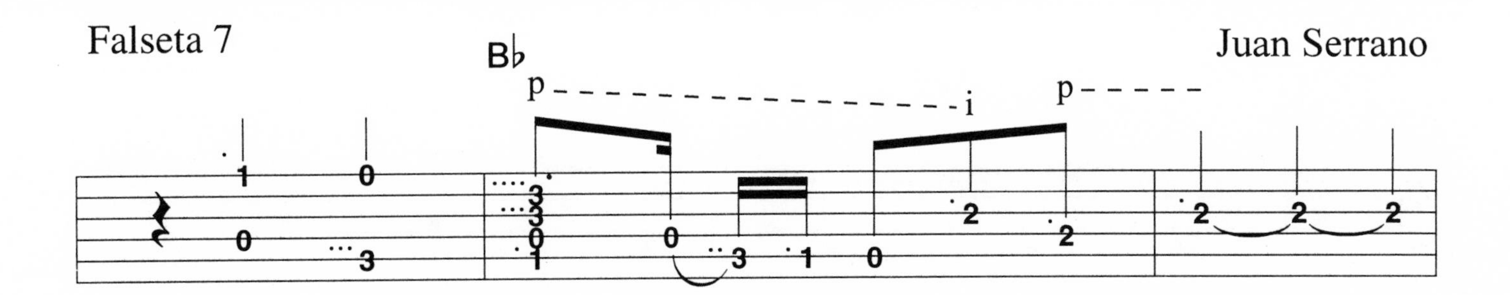


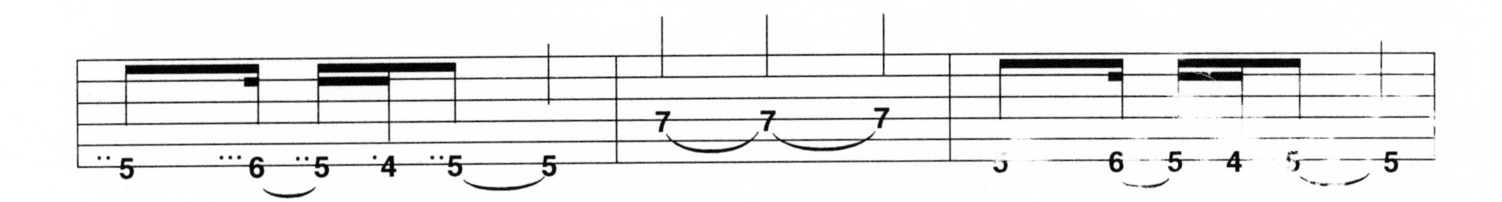

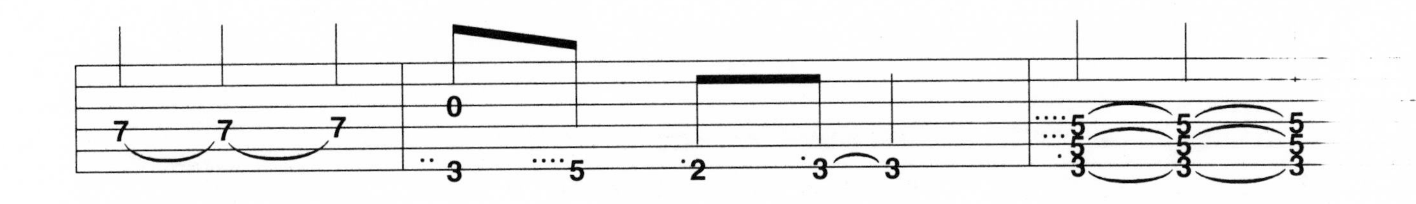

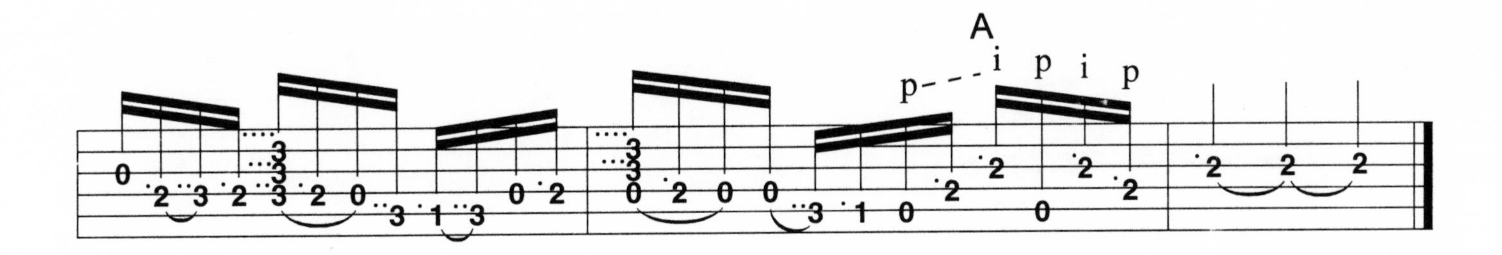

Falseta 8
Juan Serrano
II
II
p

p

IV

III

II

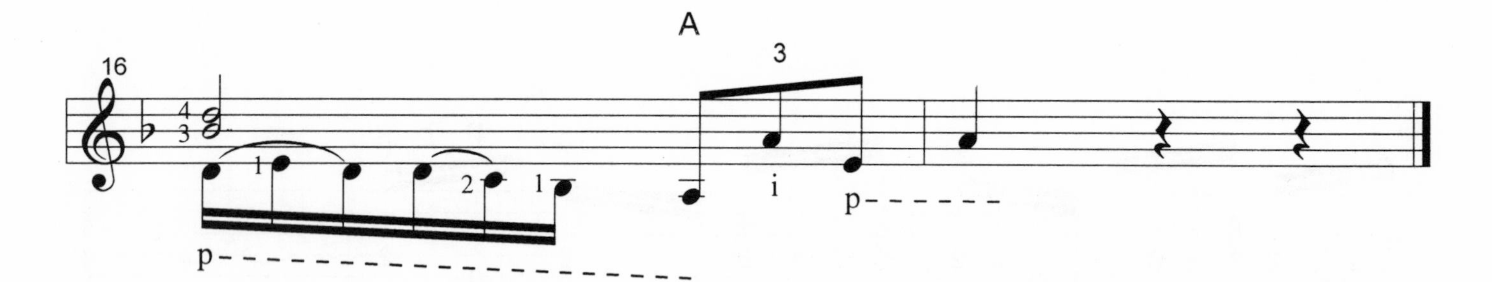
A
i
p
p

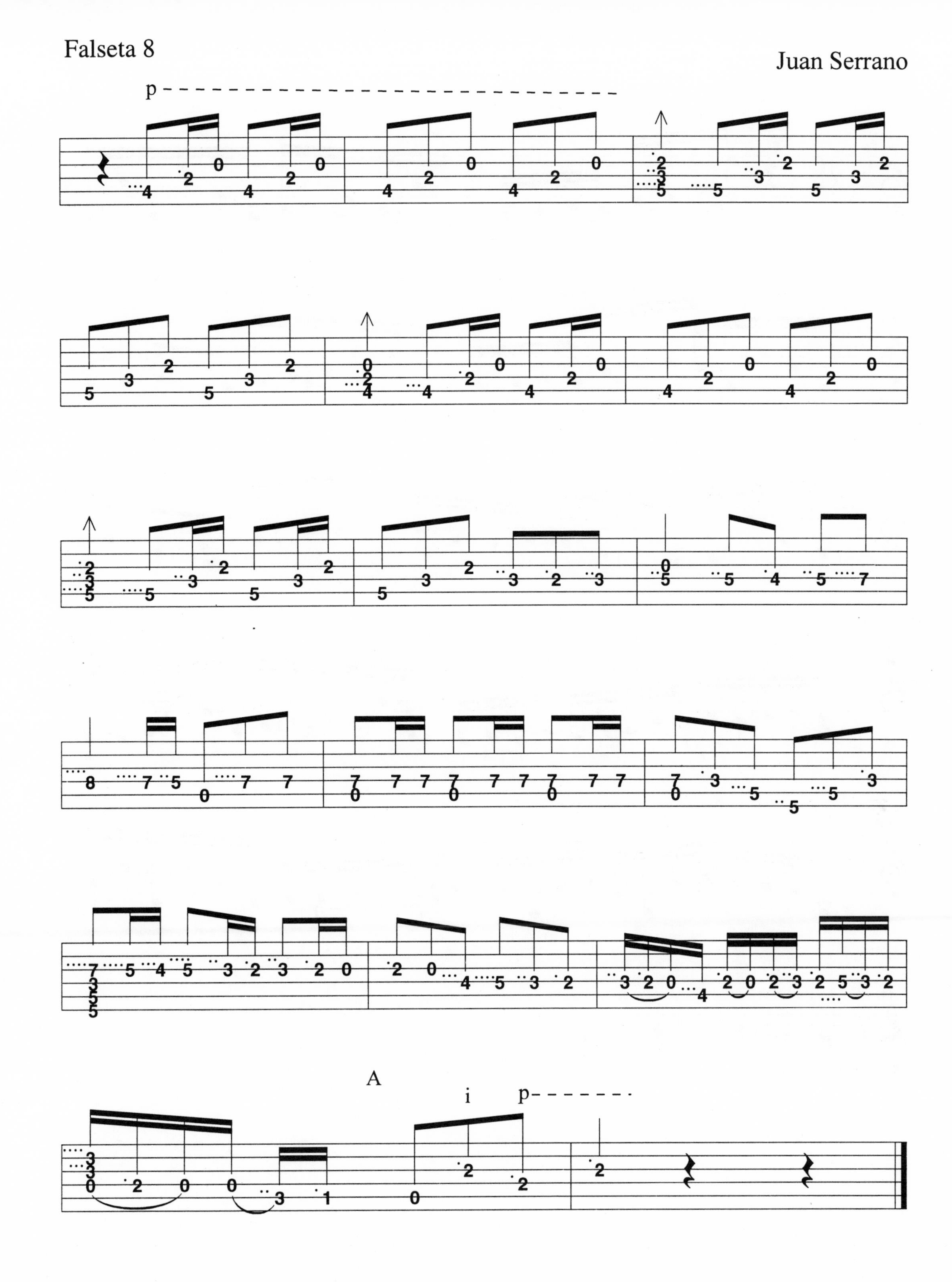
Falseta 8
Juan Serrano
p
A
i
p

## Falseta 9

Juan Serrano

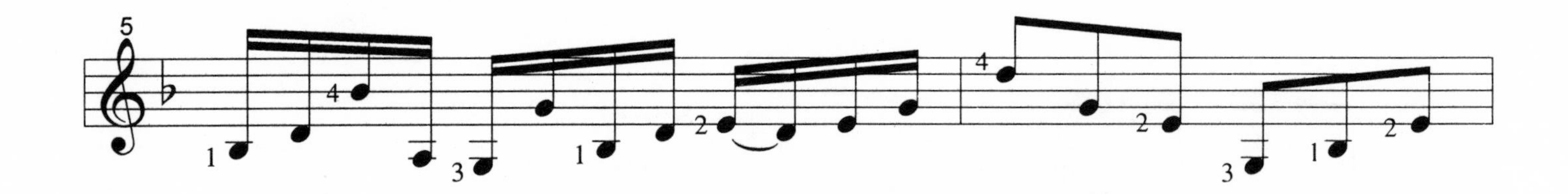

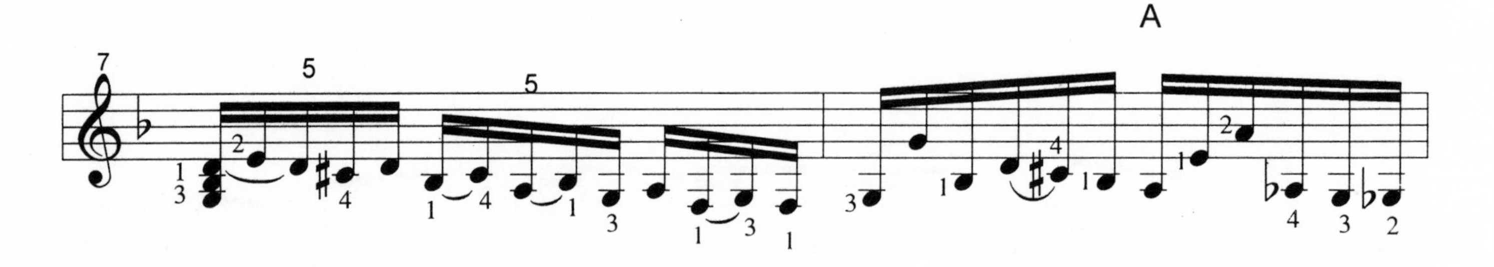


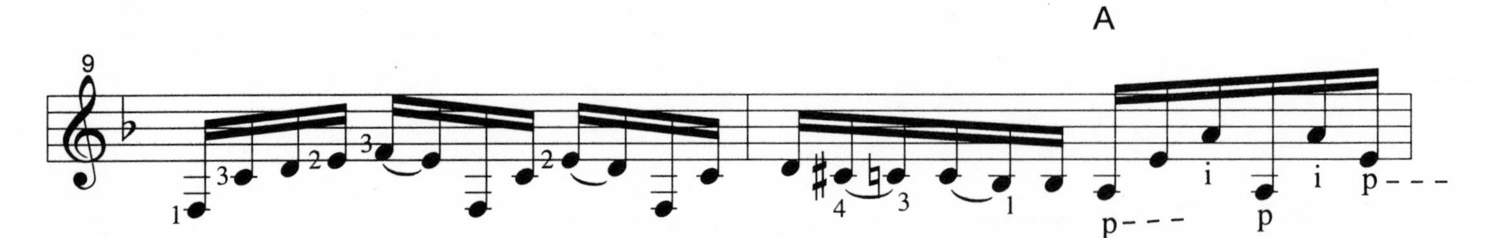


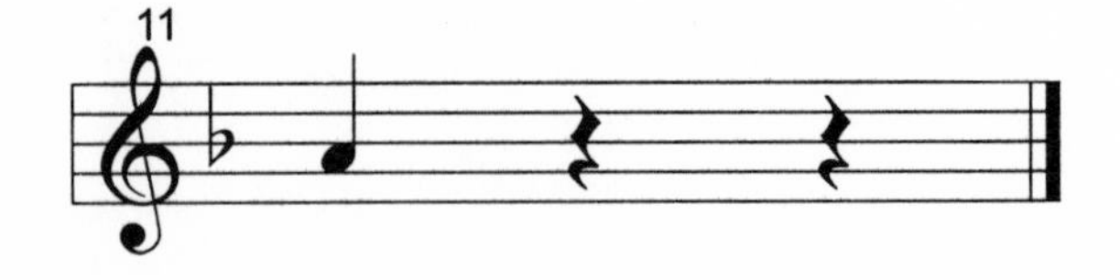

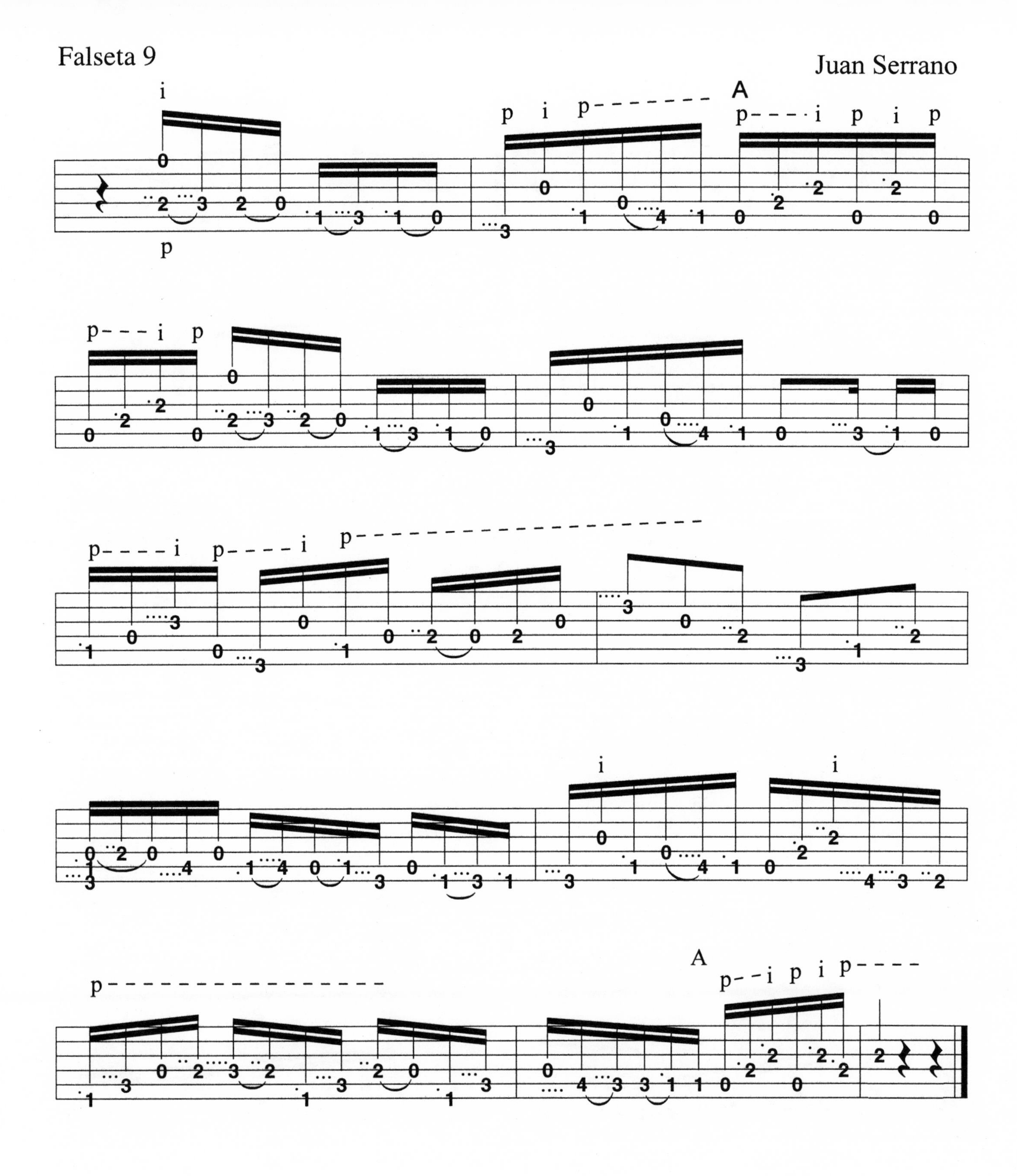
Falseta 9
Juan Serrano
A
A

## Falseta 10

Juan Serrano

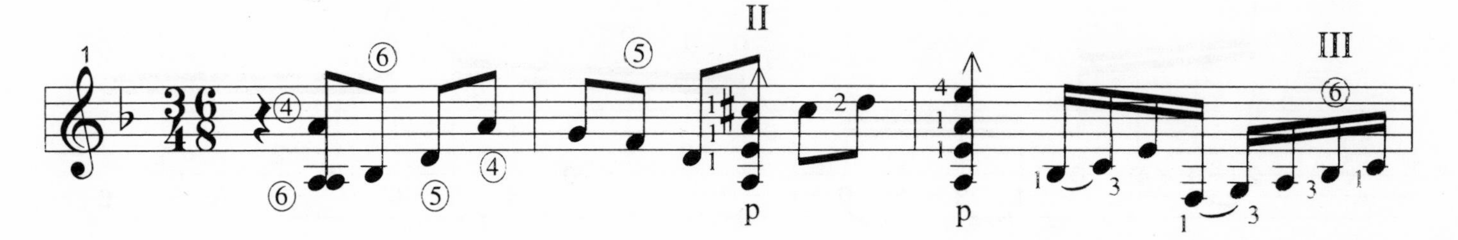

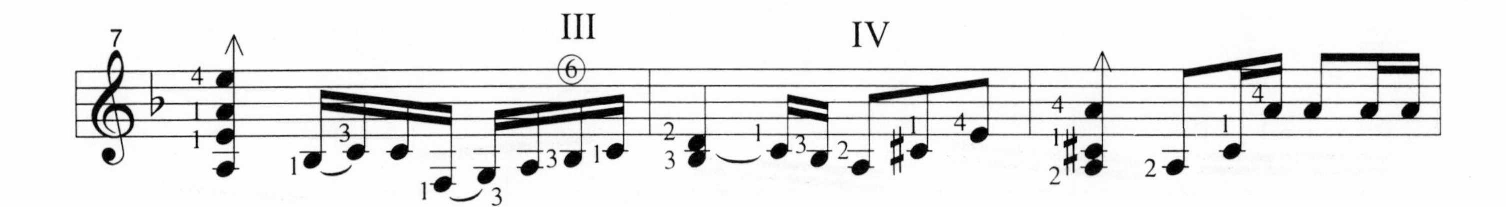


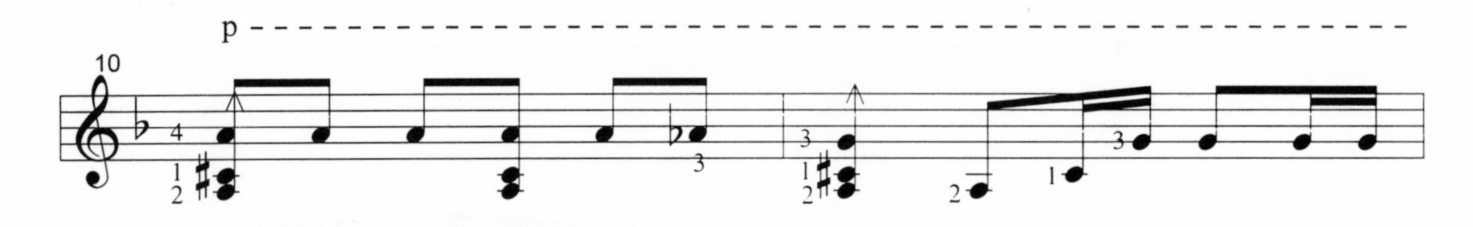

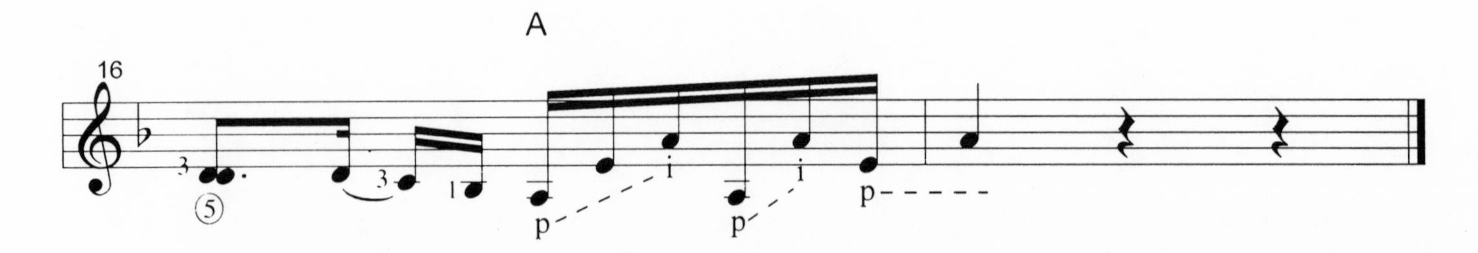

Falseta 10

Juan Serrano

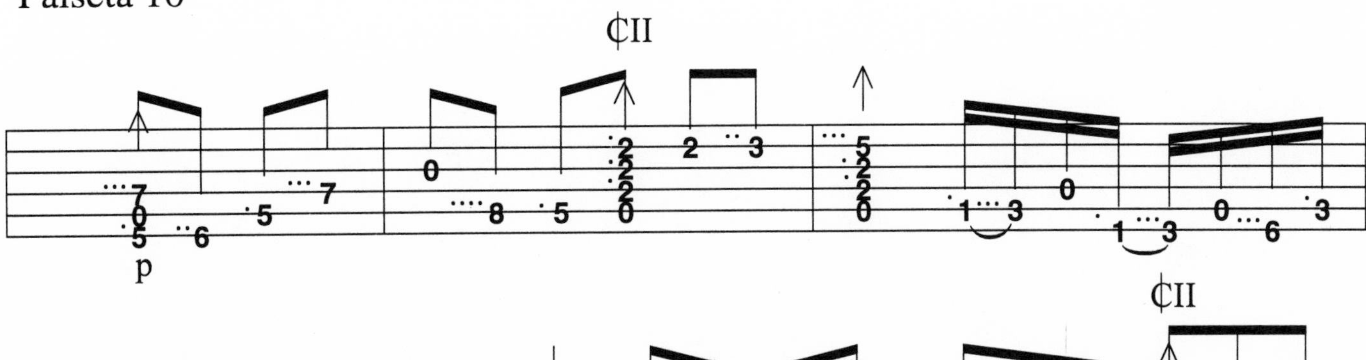

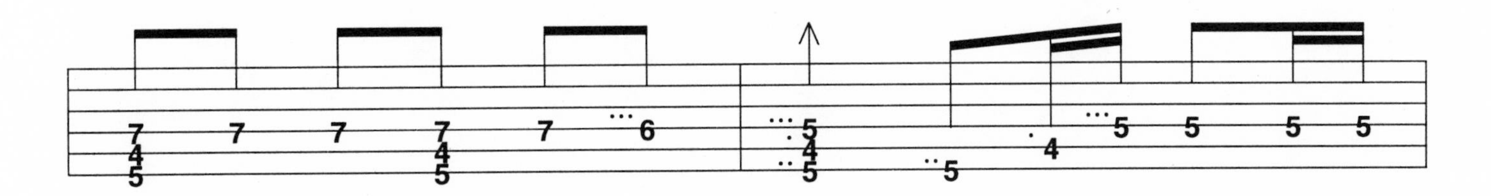

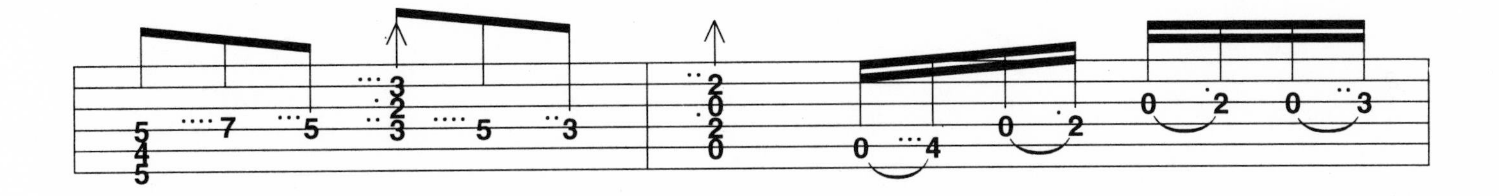

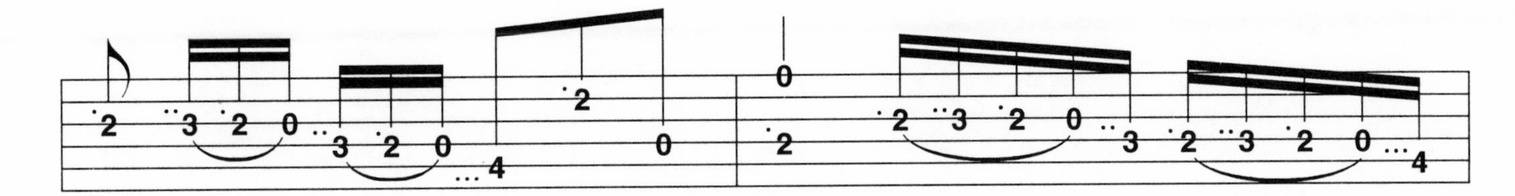

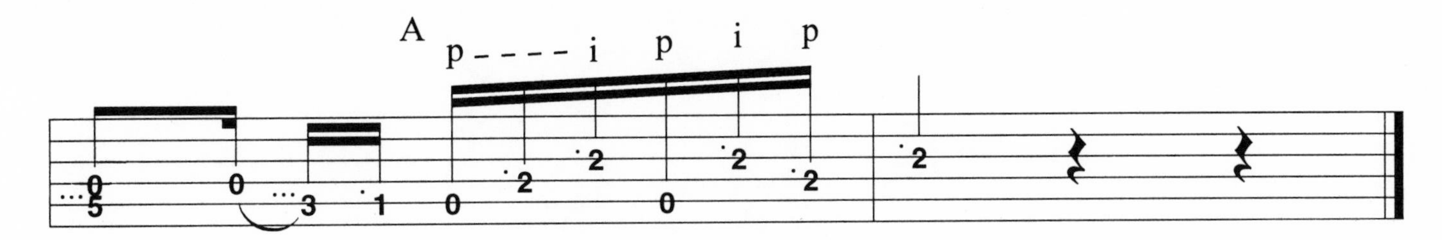

صوليارس

# SOLEARES

The Soleares are one of the basic forms of flamenco known among the aficionados and experts as the "Mother of Flamenco" because from it is derived many other forms.

The Soleares are measured in 3/4 time and one compás consists of 12 beats, equivalent to 4 measures of 3/4. In Soleares, as in other flamenco forms, many of the falsetas are played only with the thumb (p). It is recommended that these falsetas be played very slowly at the beginning, applying strength so that the thumb acquires its own individual independence and little by little will gain speed and confidence.

All of the falsetas played with the thumb (p) should be played reststroke. In the beginning, it is very difficult. But, once the technique is mastered, everything will seem easier, allowing for more liberty in the interpretation. The thumb should have speed so that it can be used as necessary.

There are many rapid passages in which flamenco guitarists prefer to use the thumb instead of the picado.

Falsetas #3 and 8 are played with the thumb reststroke. In # 7 the thumb is freestroke and the notes of the melody are played reststroke, alternating fingers index and middle (i, m).

# SOLEARES

Las Soleares son una de las formas básicas del flamenco, conocidas entre los aficionados y expertos como la "Madre del Flamenco." Porque de ellas derivan muchas otras formas.

Las Soleares se miden en 3/4 y un compás flamenco consiste en 12 tiempos equivalente a cuatro compases musicales de 3/4. En Soleares, como en otras formas flamencas, muchas de las falsetas se ejecutan solamente con el dedo pulgar (p). Estas falsetas se deben de practicar al principio muy despacio y aplicando mucha fuerza para que el dedo pulgar adquiera independencia individual y poco a poco gane velocidad y seguridad.

Todas las falsetas de pulgar deben de ser ejecutadas apoyando. Al principio, es más difícil, pero cuando se desarrolla bien la técnica, todo se hace mas fácil y se puede tener mas libertad en la interpretación. Con el pulgar se debe de tener bastante velocidad para poderla usar cuando sea necesario.

Son muchos los pasajes rápidos donde los guitarristas flamencos prefieren usar el pulgar en lugar de un picado.

Las falsetas #3 y 8 se tocan solamente con el pulgar (p) apoyando. En la falseta #7 el pulgar se usa tirando. Y las notas de la melodía, apoyando y alternando los dedos (i m).

# *Soleares*

Traditional Compas

Juan Serrano

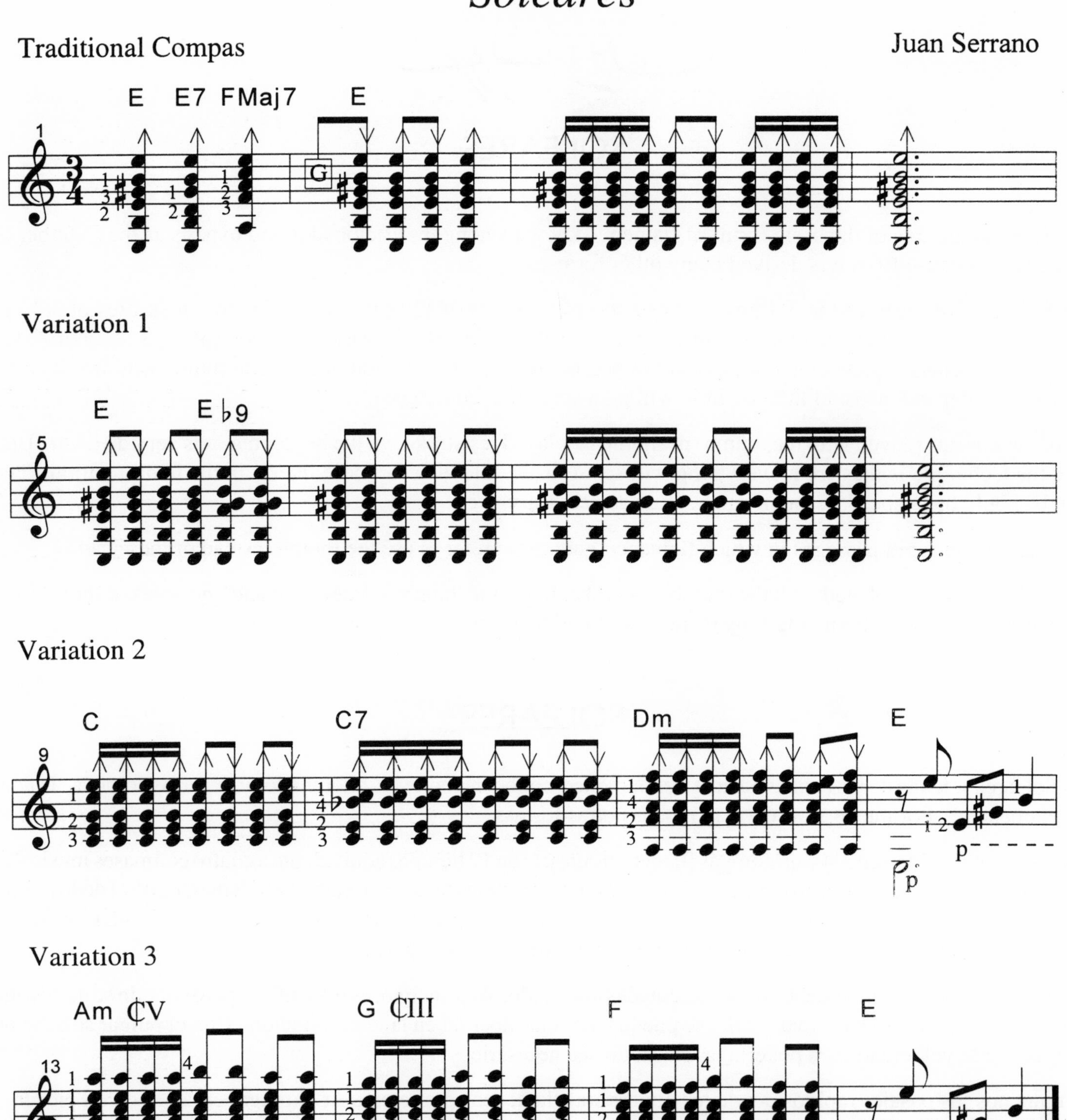

# *Soleares*

Juan Serrano

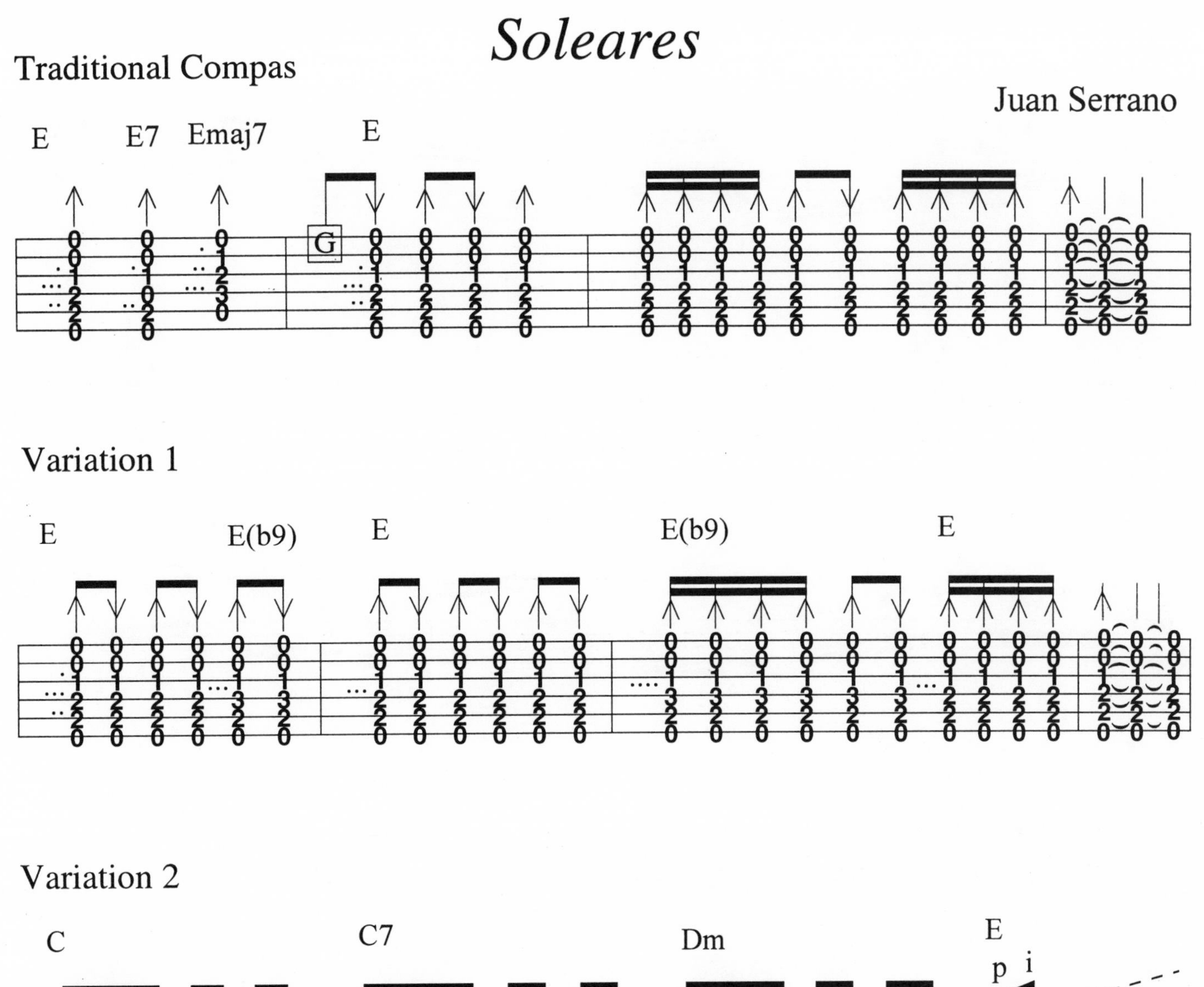


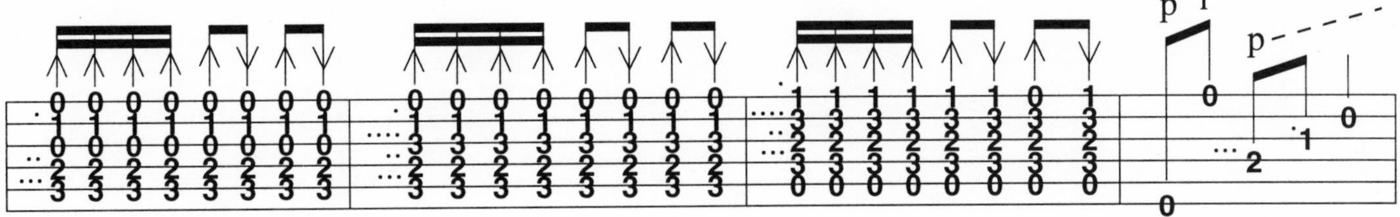


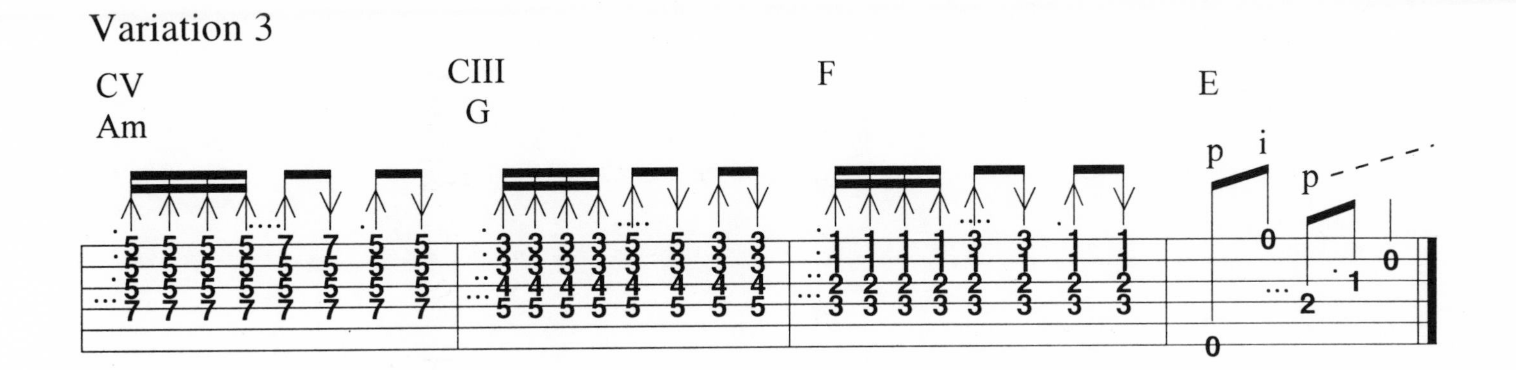

## Falseta 1

Juan Serrano

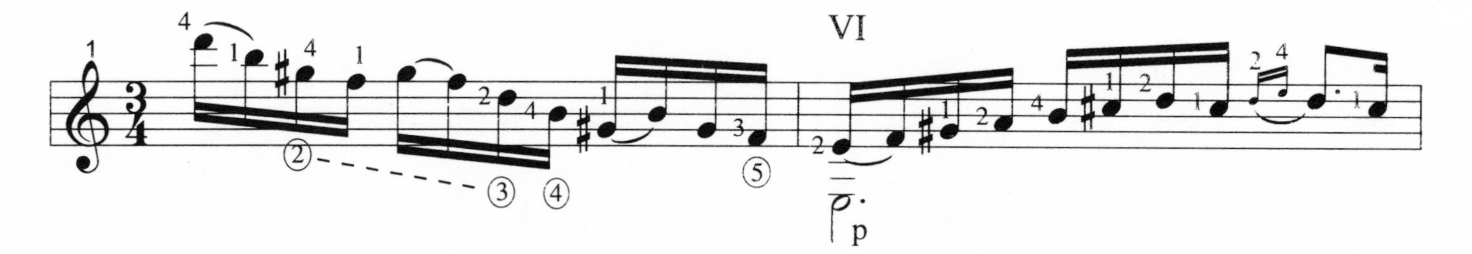

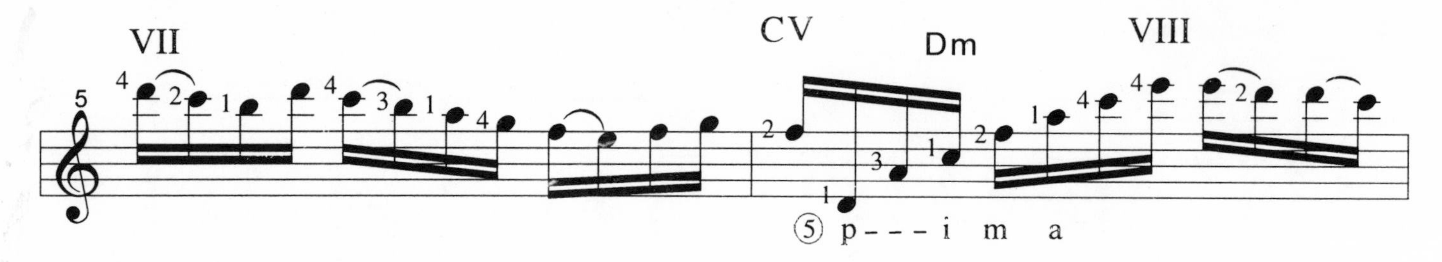


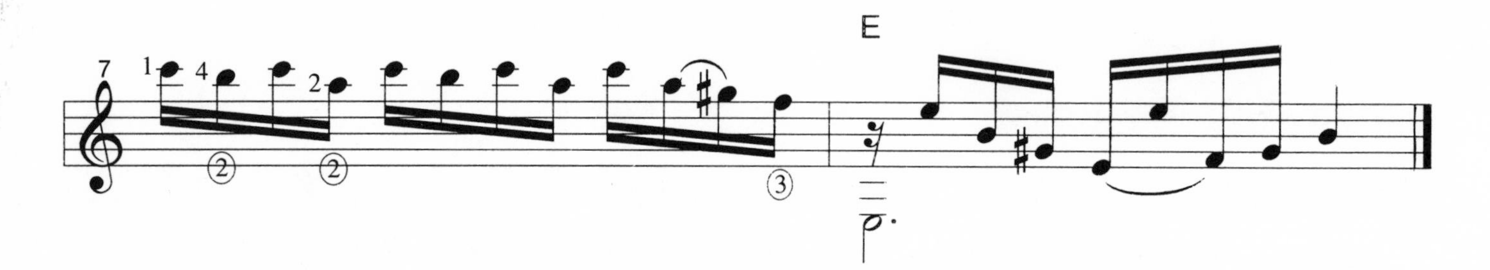

Falseta 1

Juan Serrano

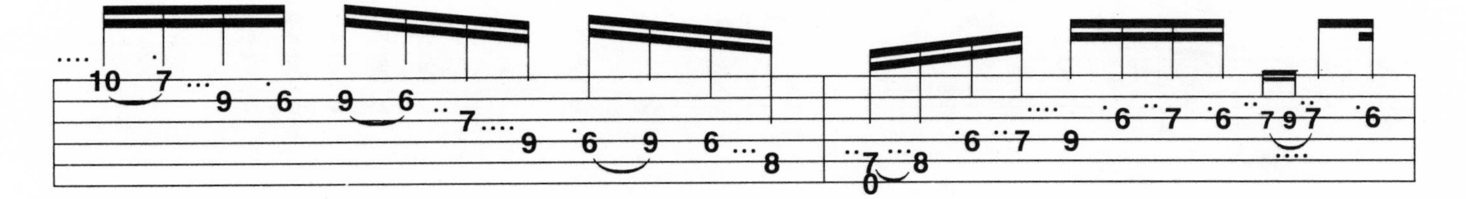

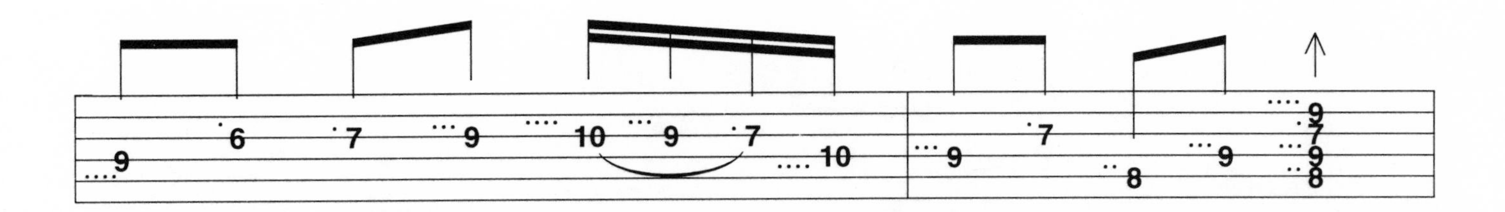

CV
Dm

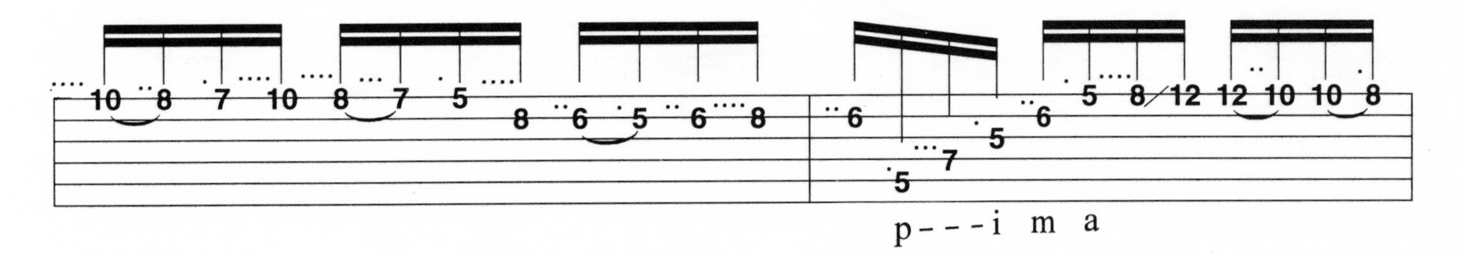


E

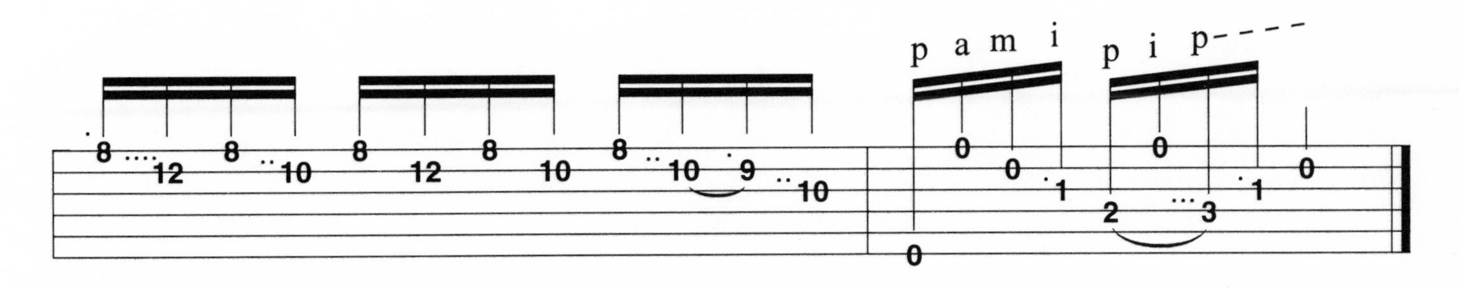

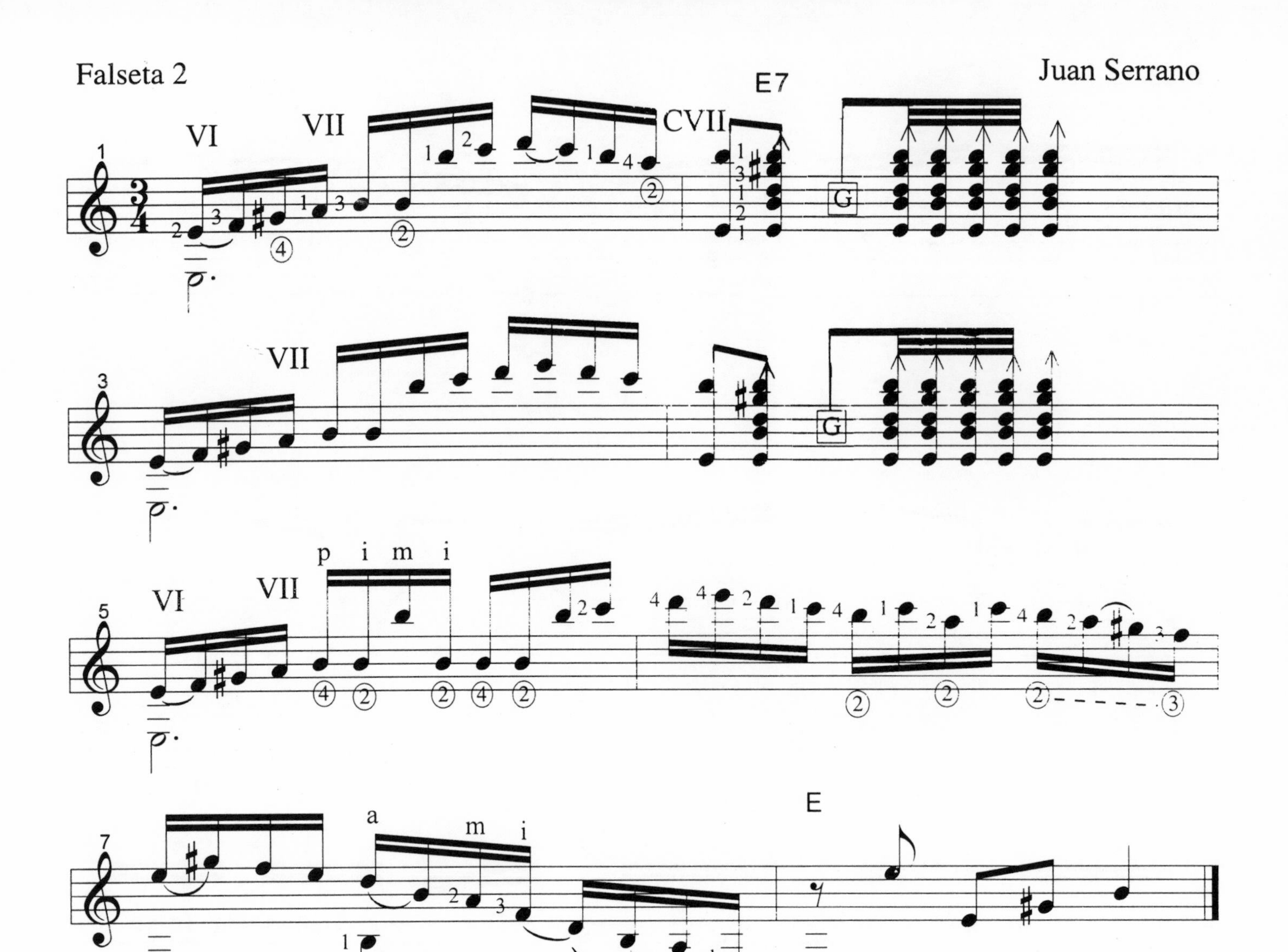
Falseta 2
Juan Serrano
VI
VII
E7
CVII
G
p i m i
a m i
p
E

Falseta 2

Juan Serrano

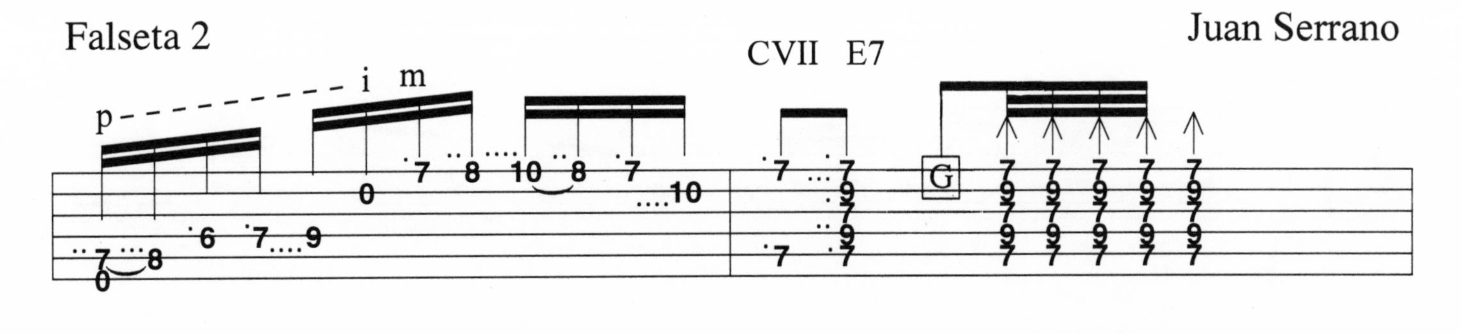


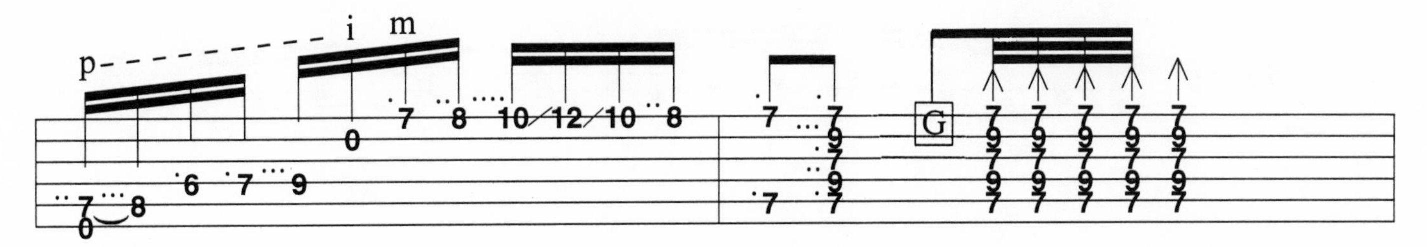

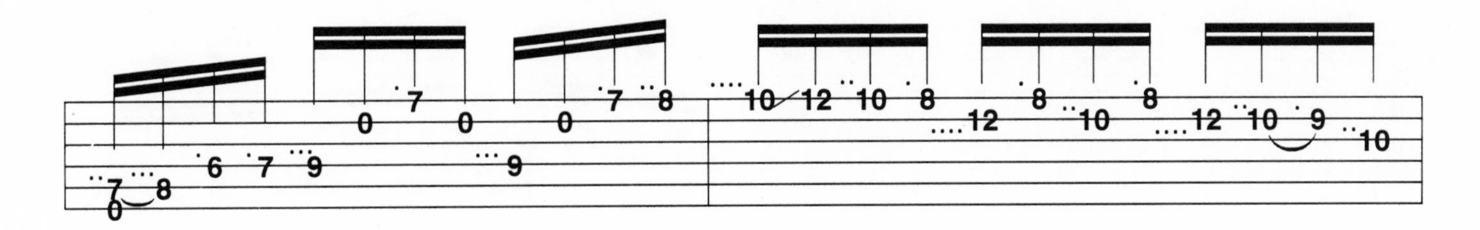

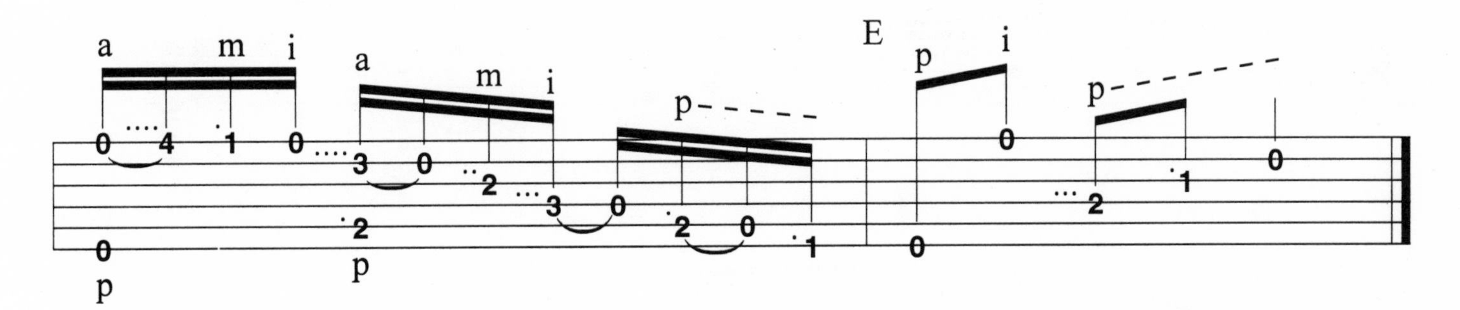

Falseta 3

Juan Serrano

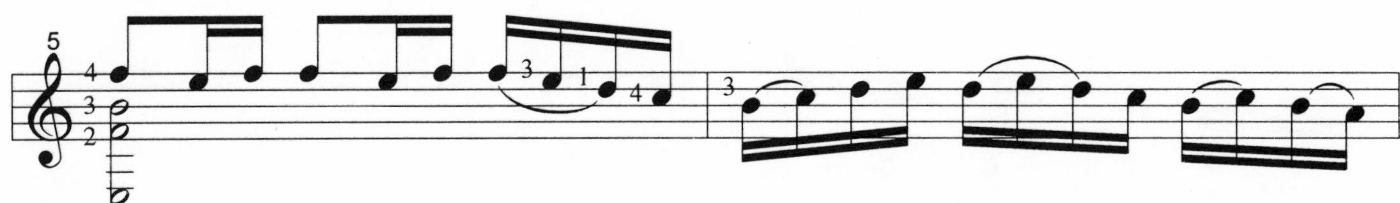

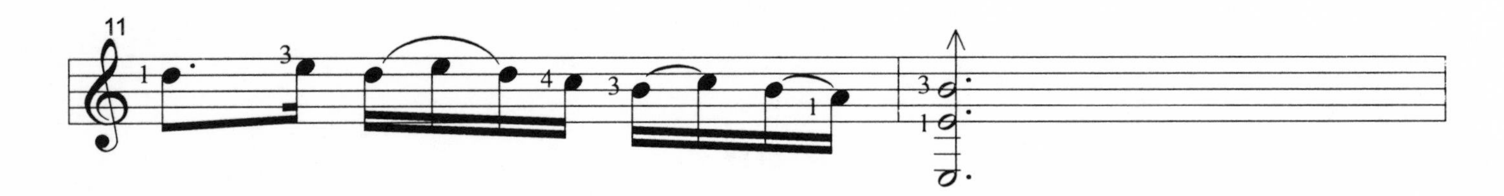

15
E
p
i m a
p

I
17
③
V

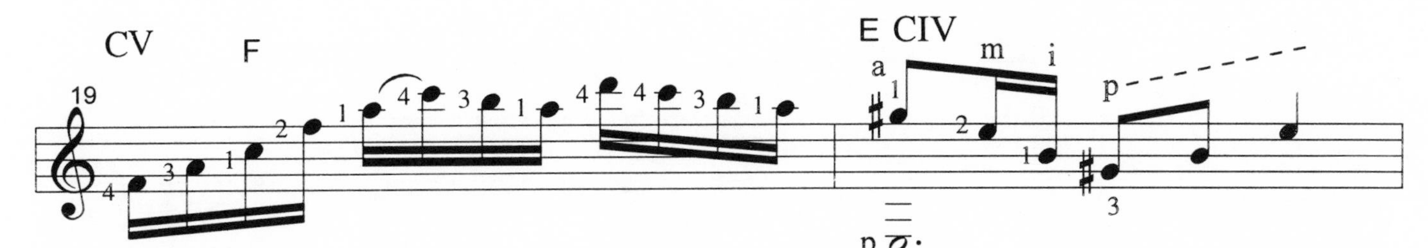
CV
F
19
E CIV
a
m i
p
p

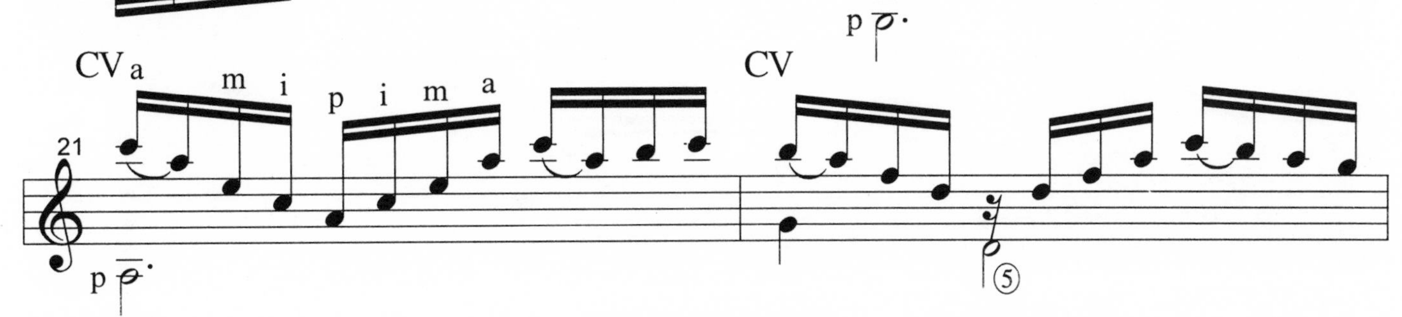
CV a
m i
p i m a
21
p
CV
⑤

CV
23
p
E IV
p
i m a
p
⑤

I
a
m i
p i m a
25
p

27

Falseta 3

Juan Serrano

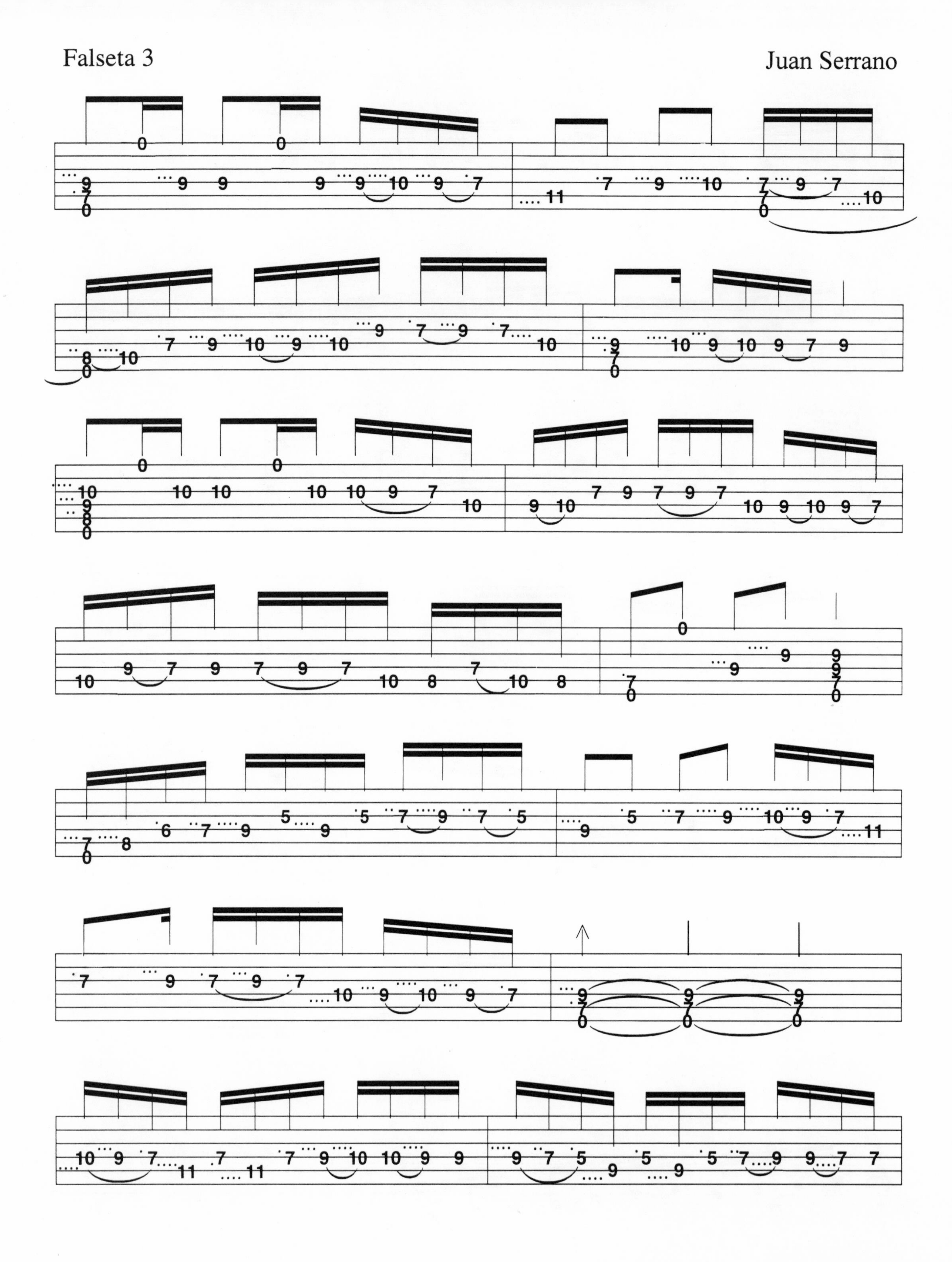

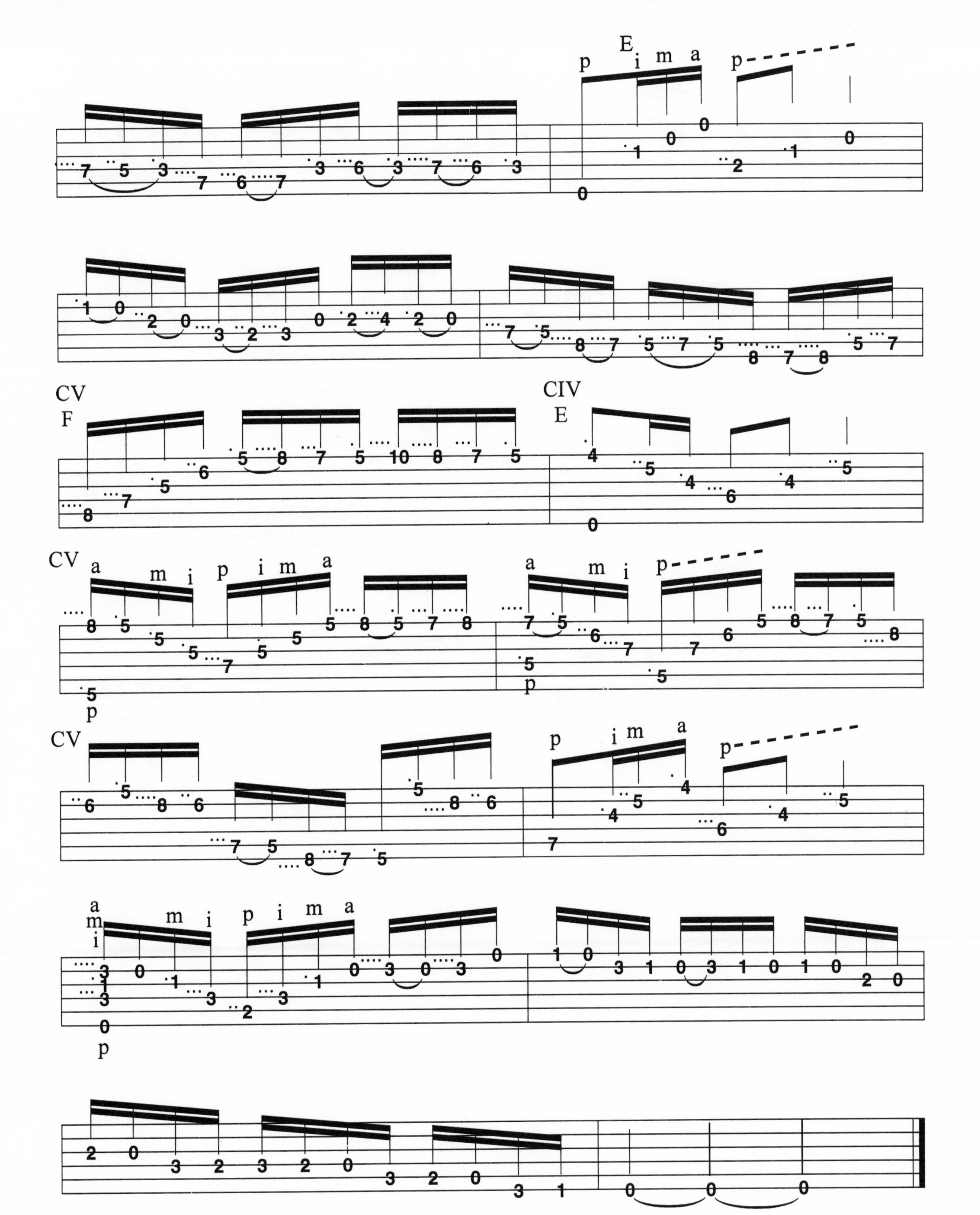
E
p i m a p
CV
F
CIV
E
CV
a m i p i m a
a m i p
p
p
CV
p i m a p
a
m
i
m i p i m a
p

## Falseta 4

Juan Serrano

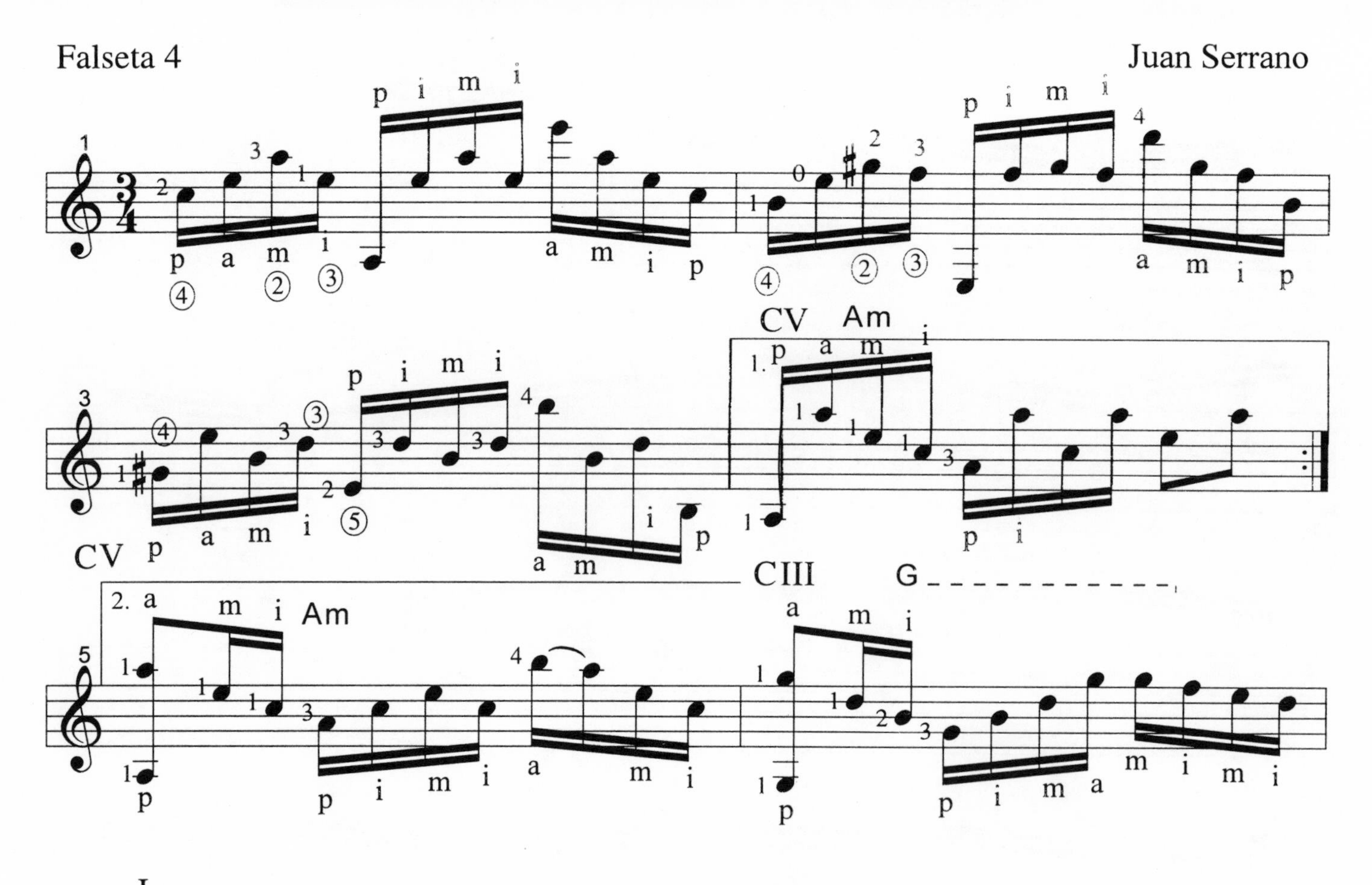

## Falseta 4

Juan Serrano

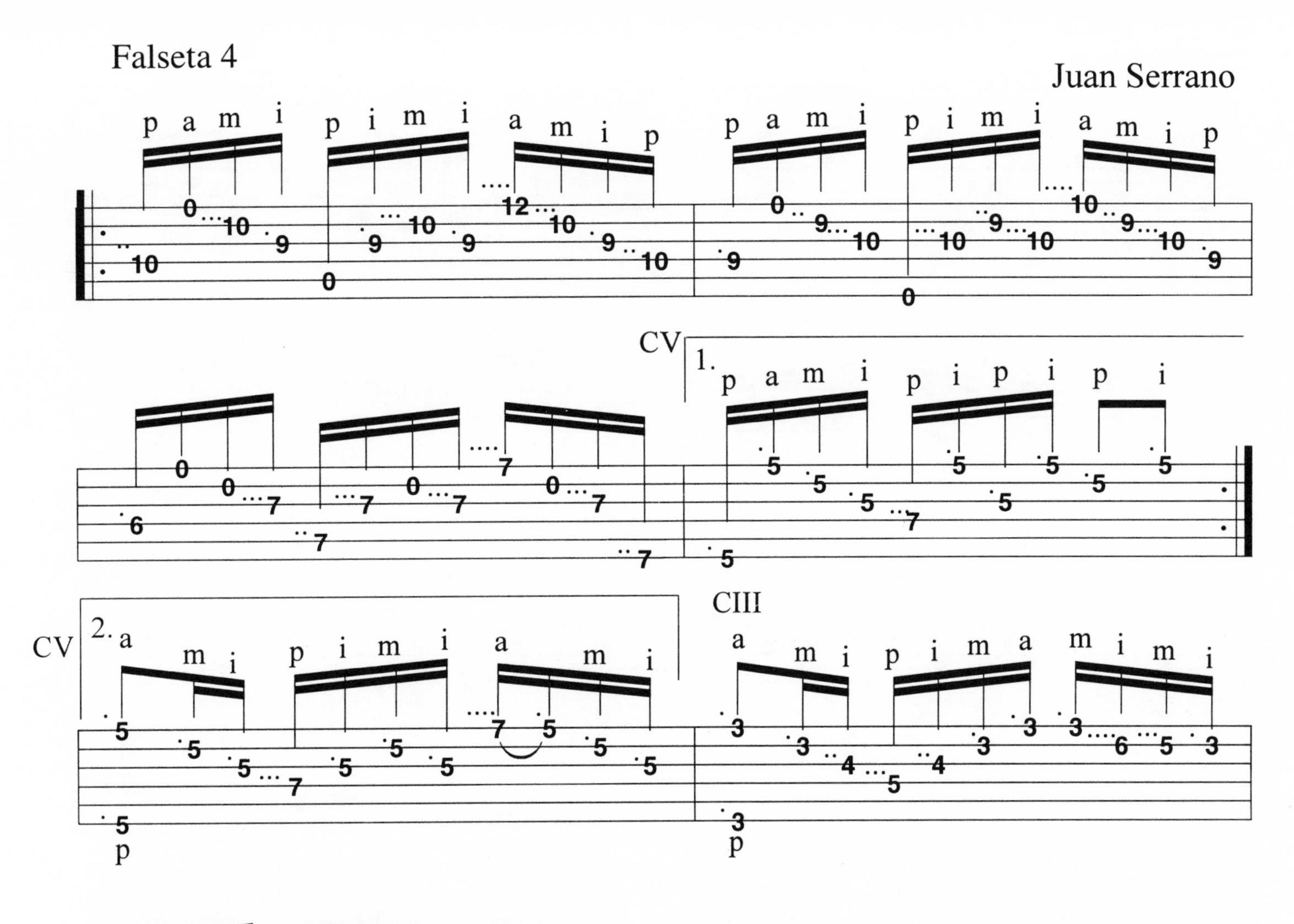


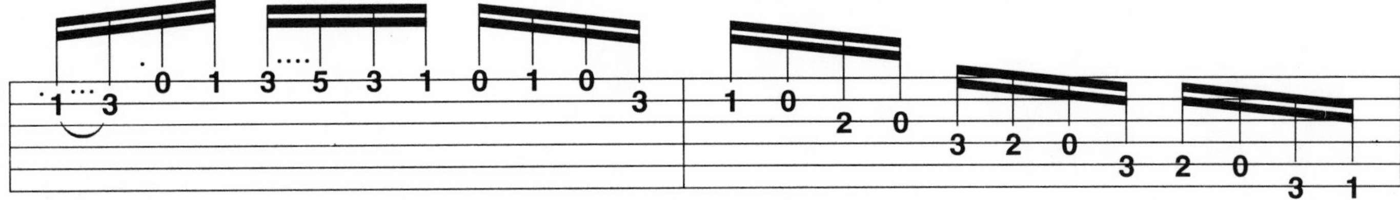

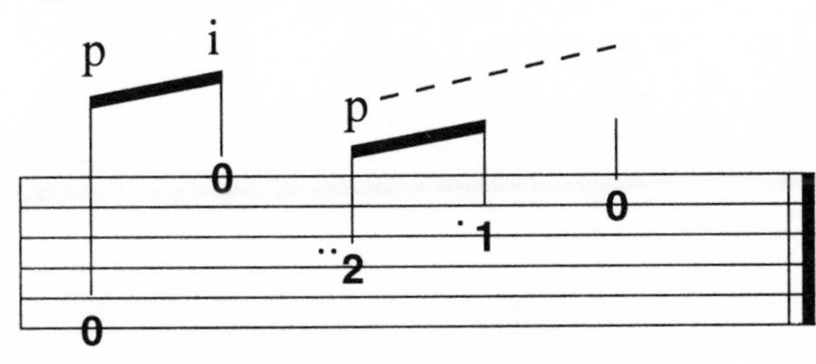

Falseta 5

Juan Serrano

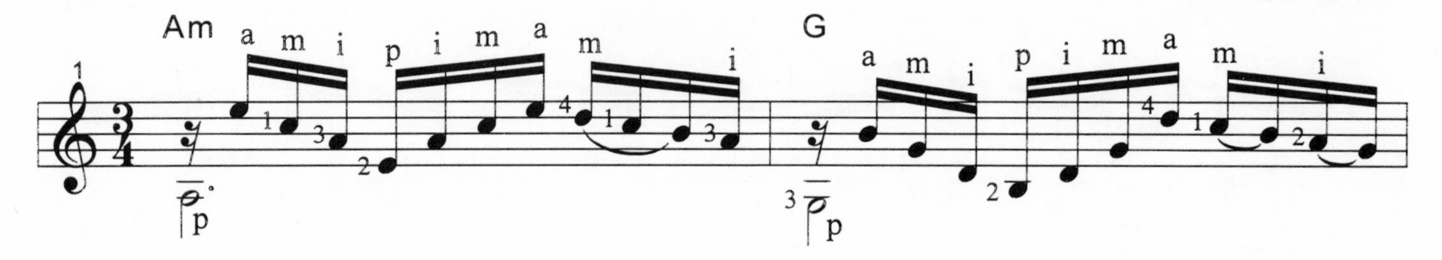


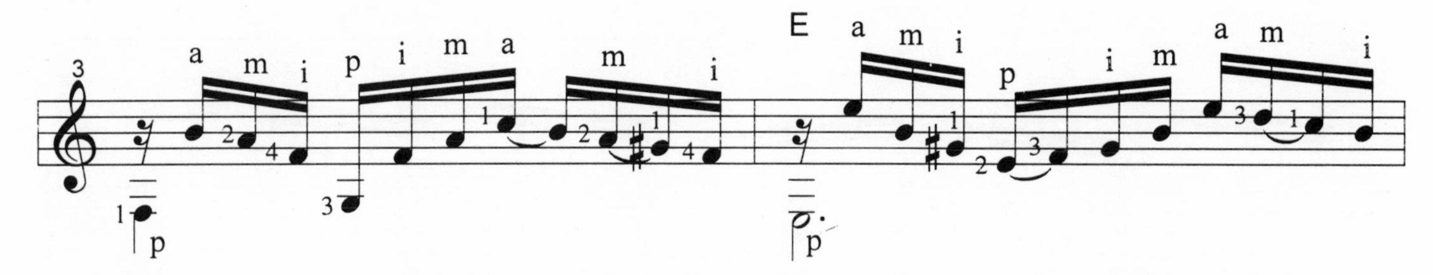


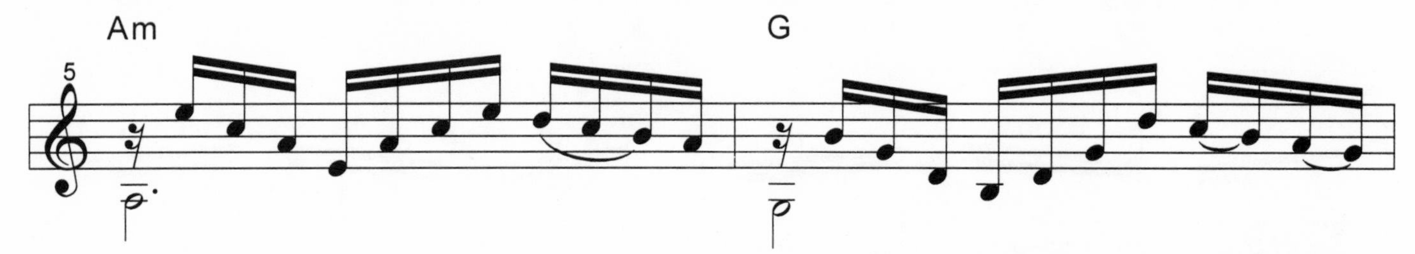

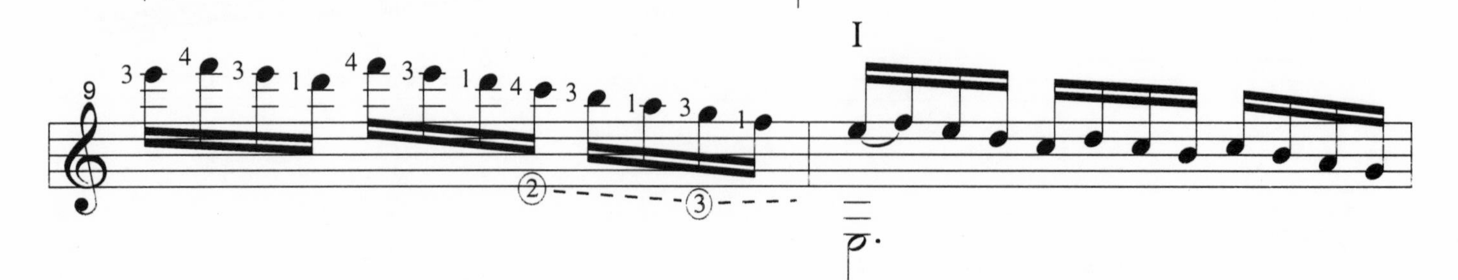


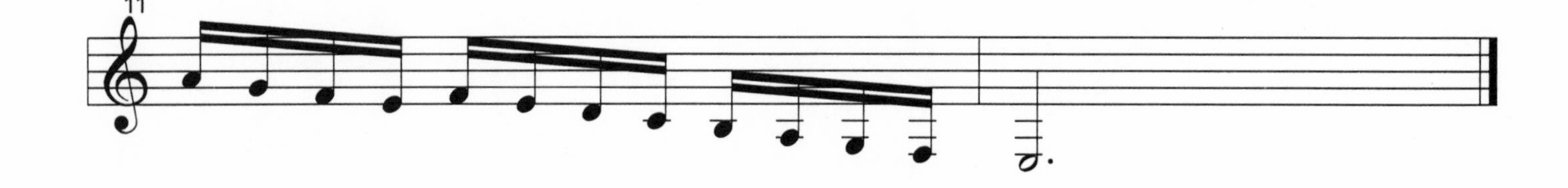

Falseta 5

Juan Serrano

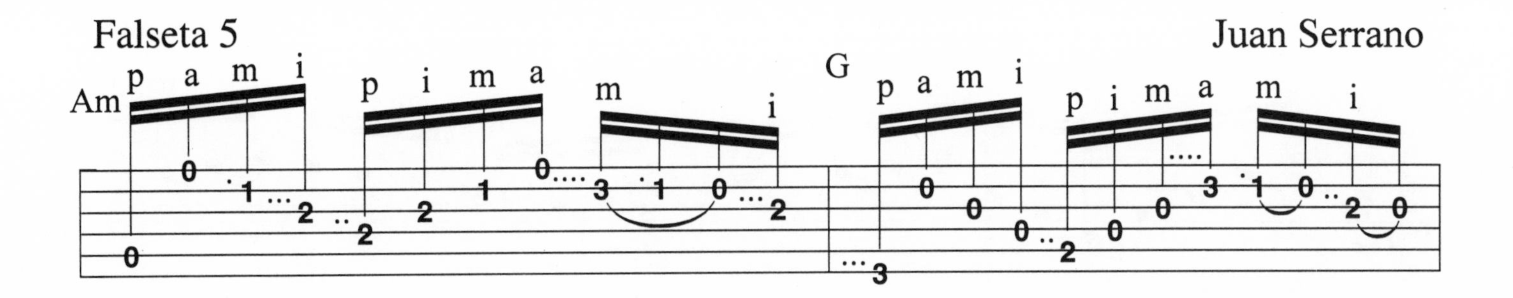


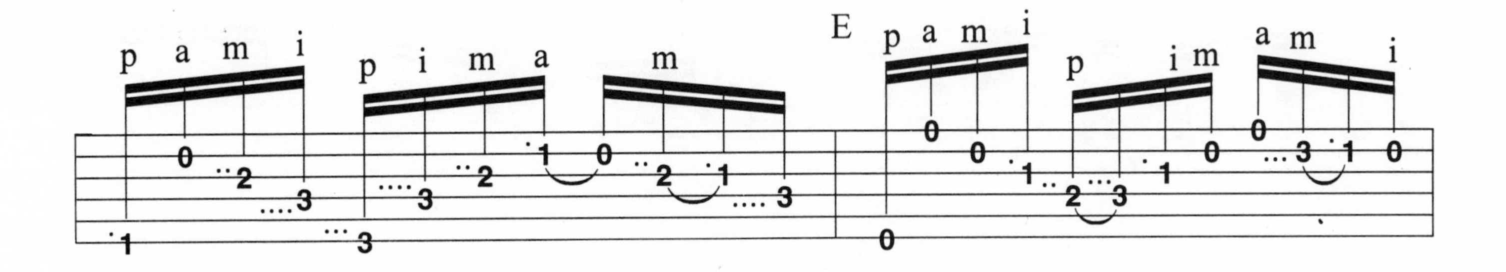


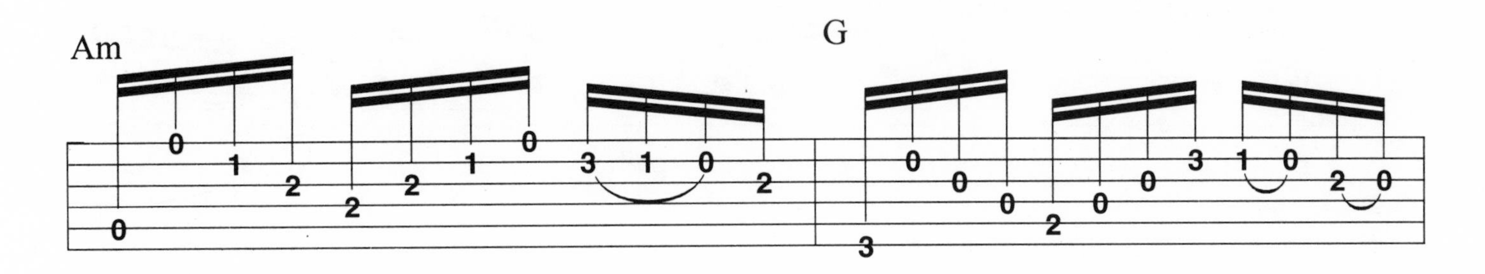


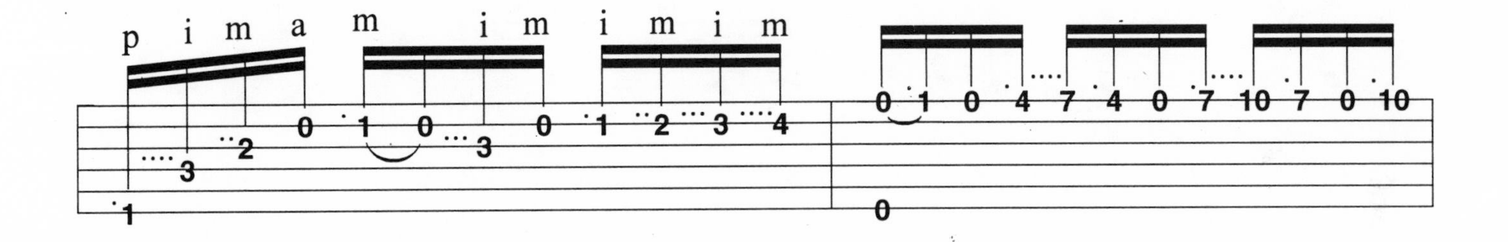


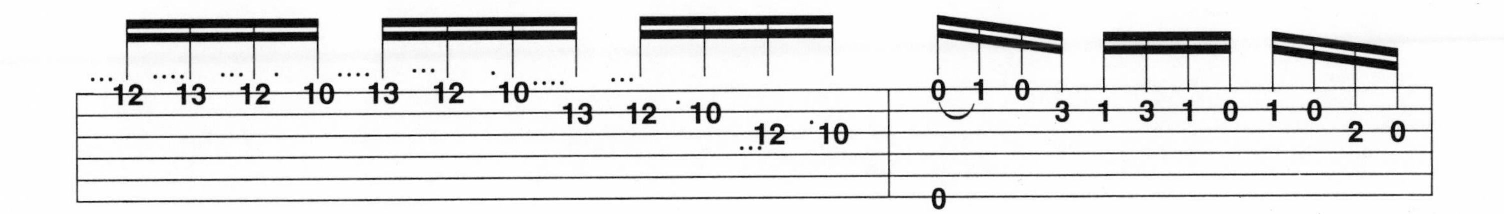

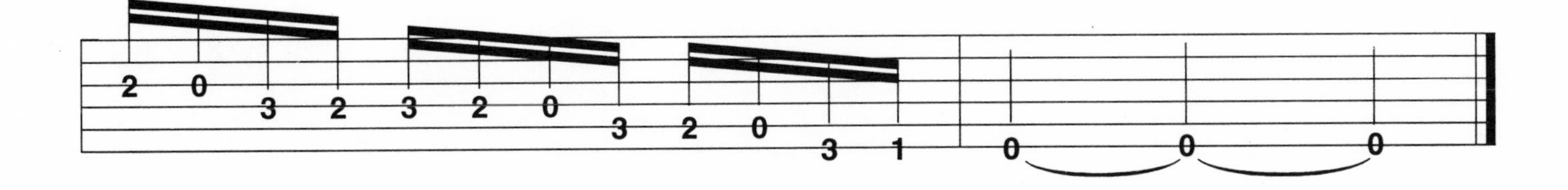

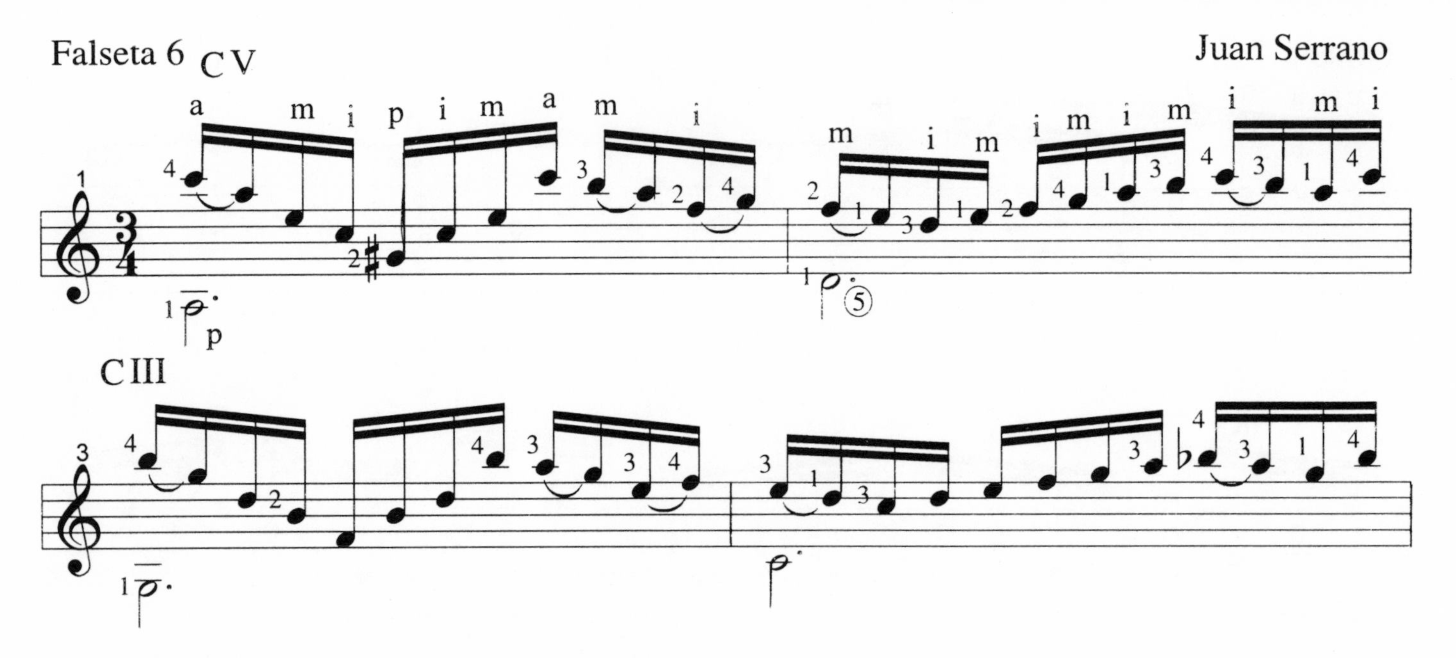
Falseta 6
C V
Juan Serrano

CIII

E

Falseta 6

Juan Serrano

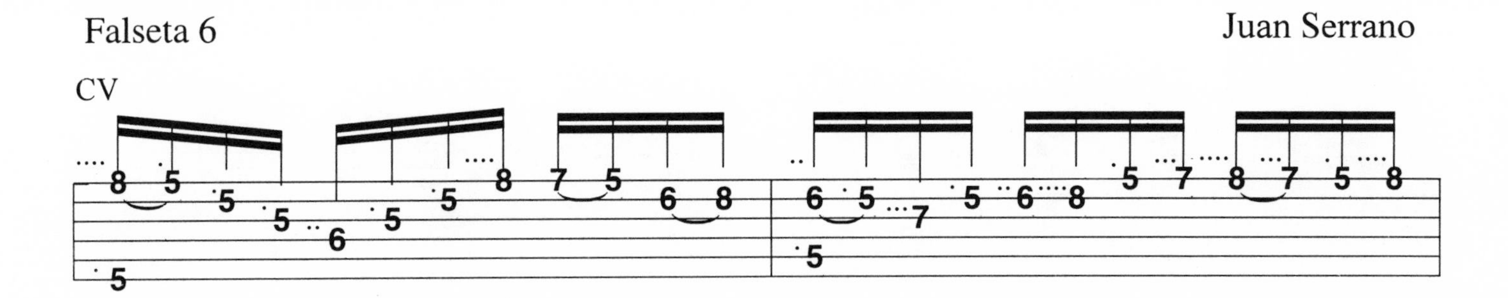


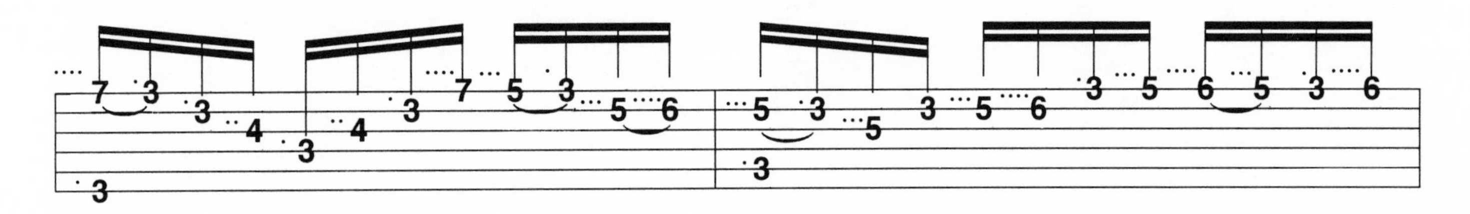


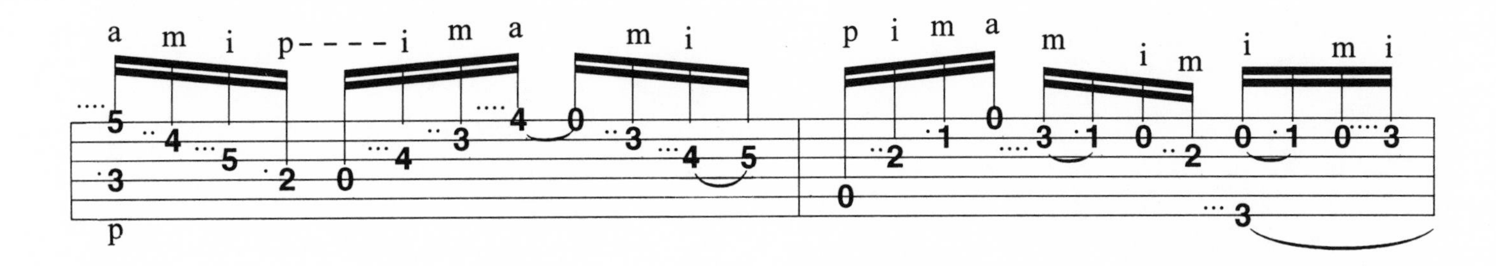


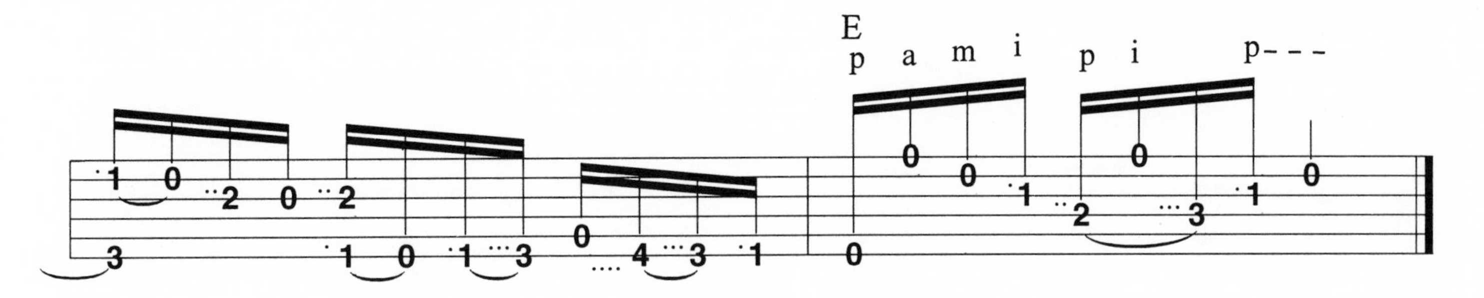

Falseta 7

Juan Serrano

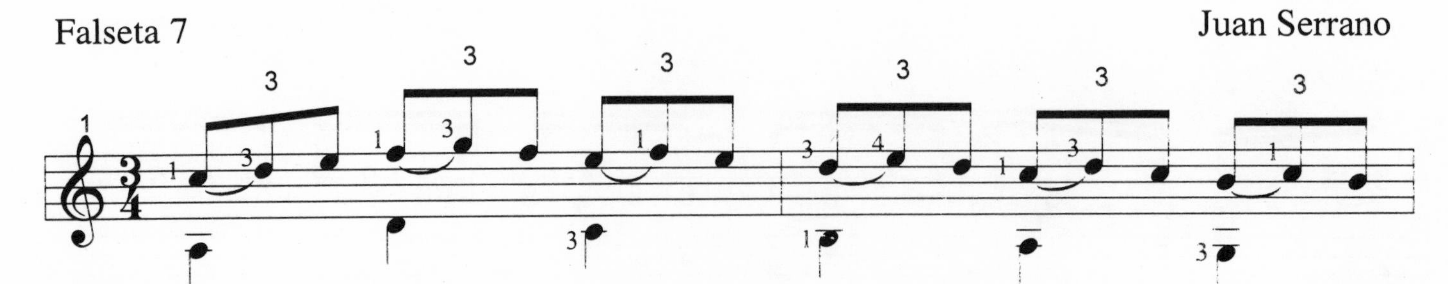

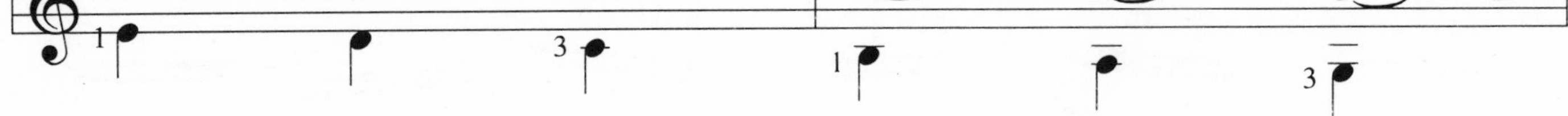

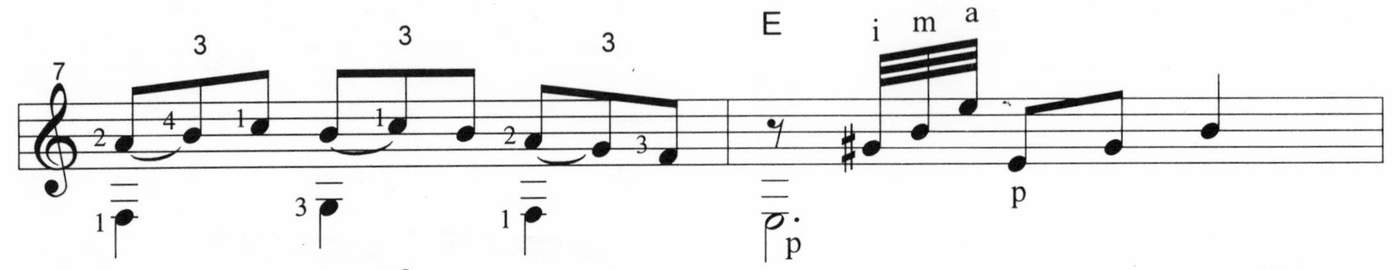


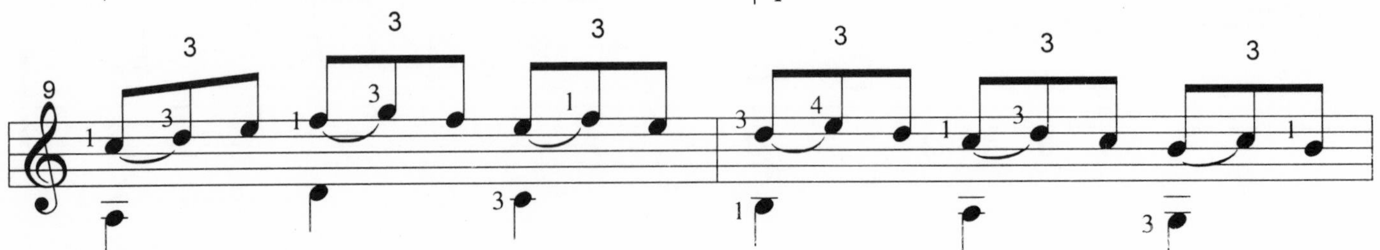

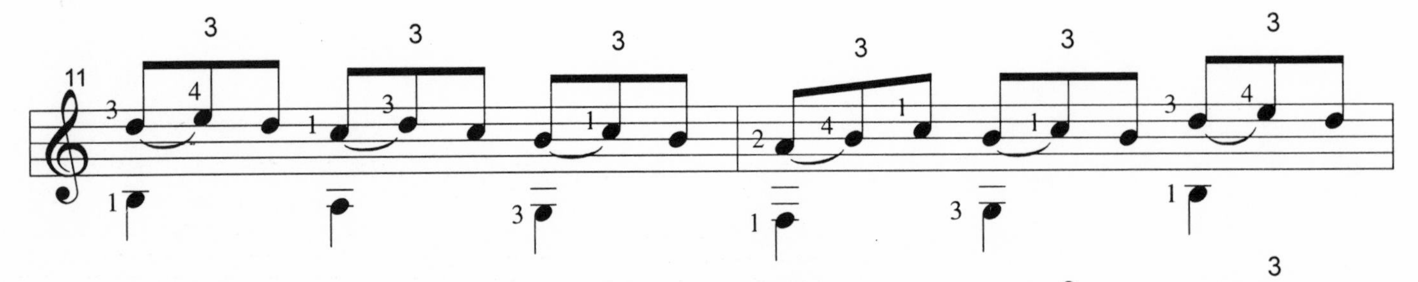

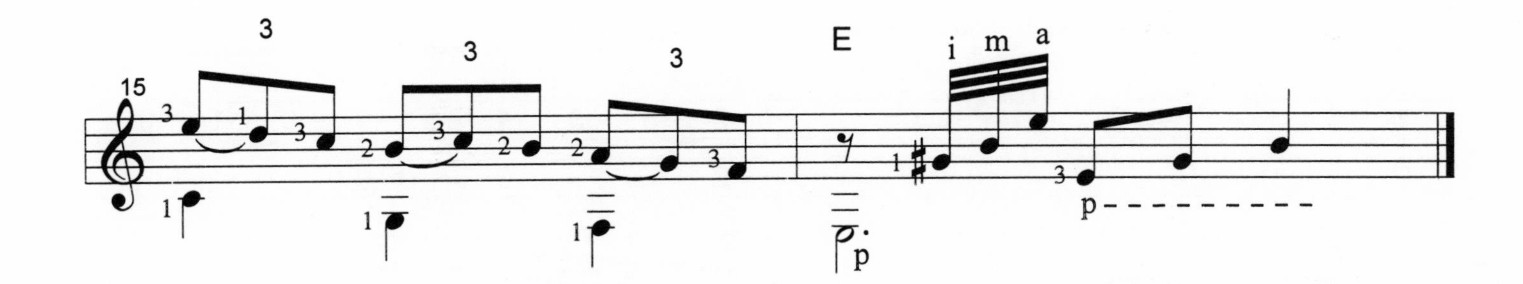
E
i m a
p

Falseta 7

Juan Serrano

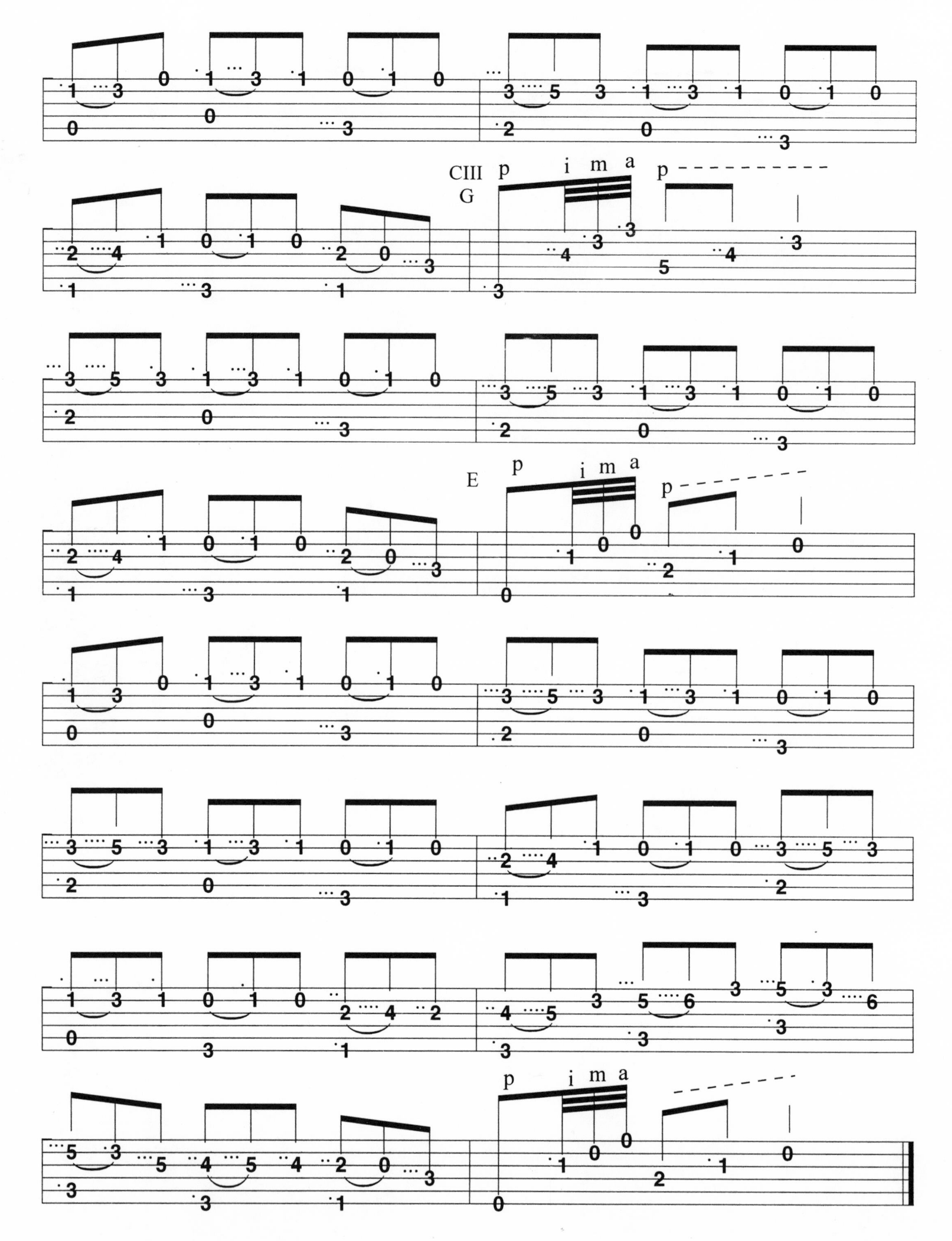

*This page has been left blank to avoid awkward page turns*

Falseta 8

Juan Serrano

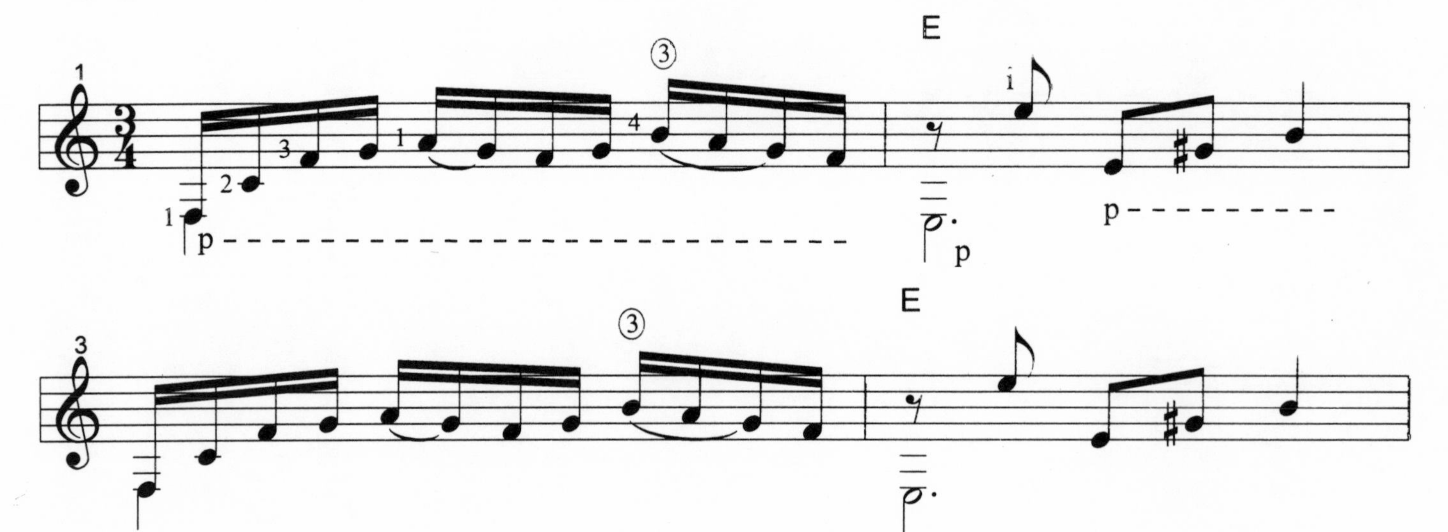

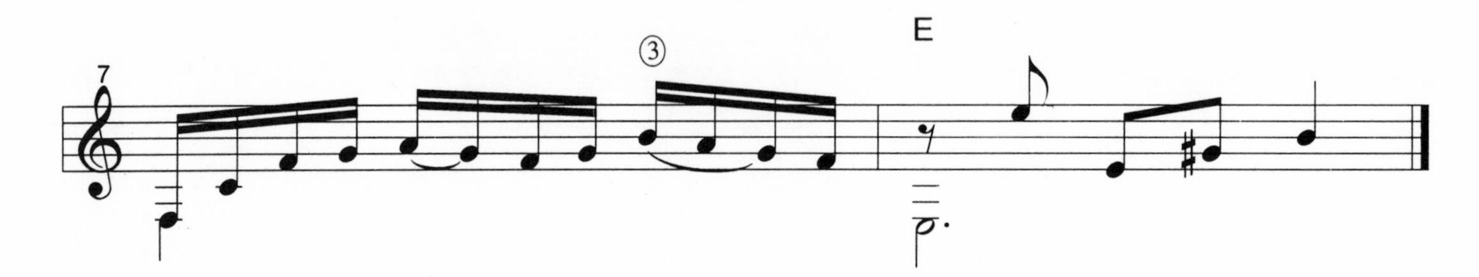


7

3

E

## Falseta 8

Juan Serrano

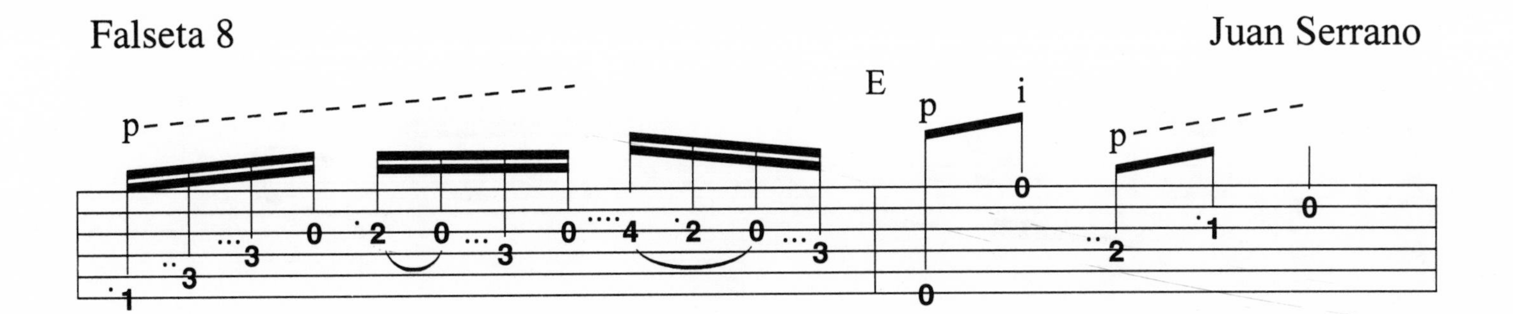


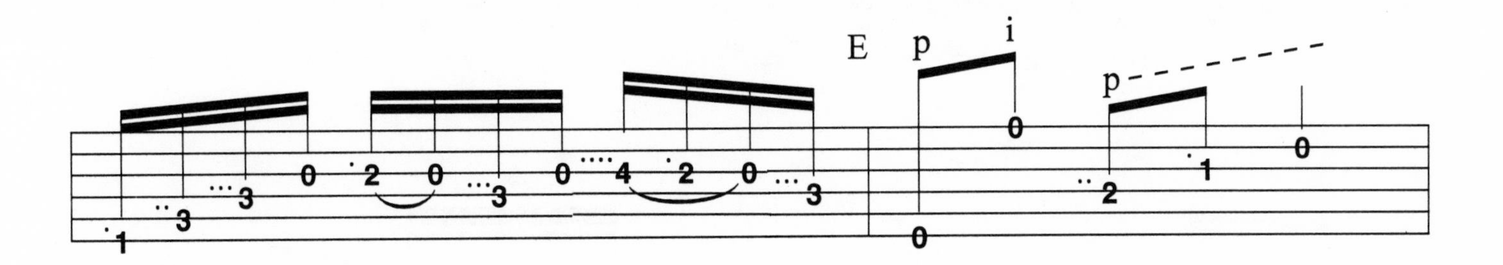


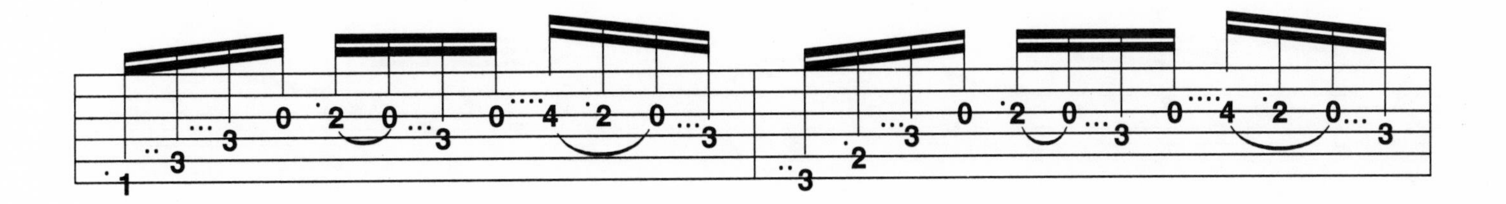

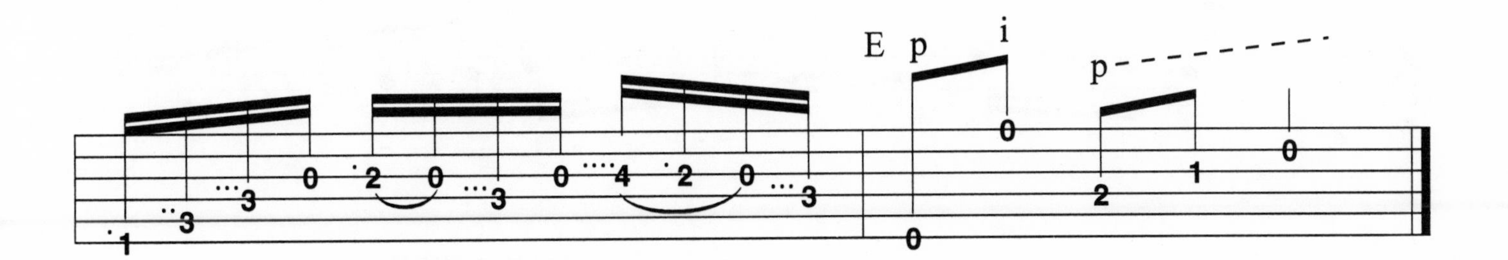

## Falseta 9

Juan Serrano

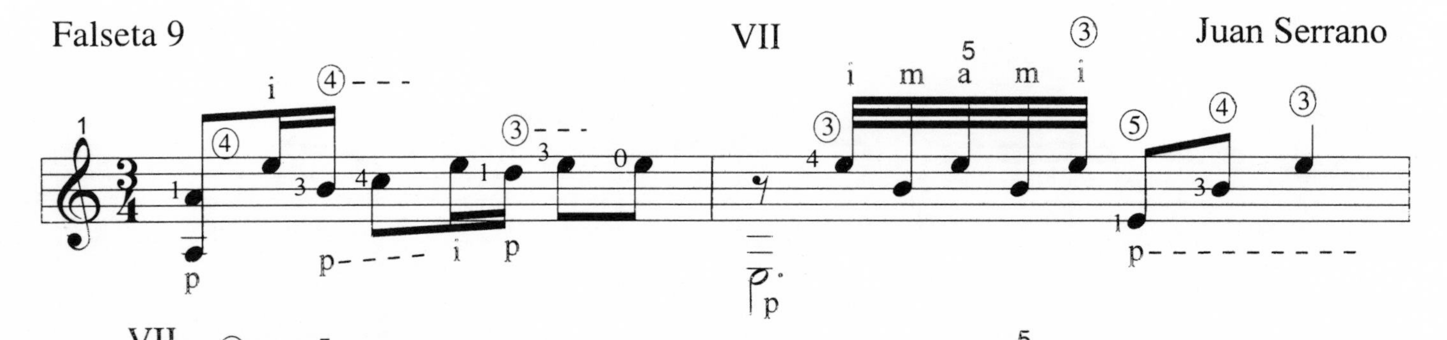

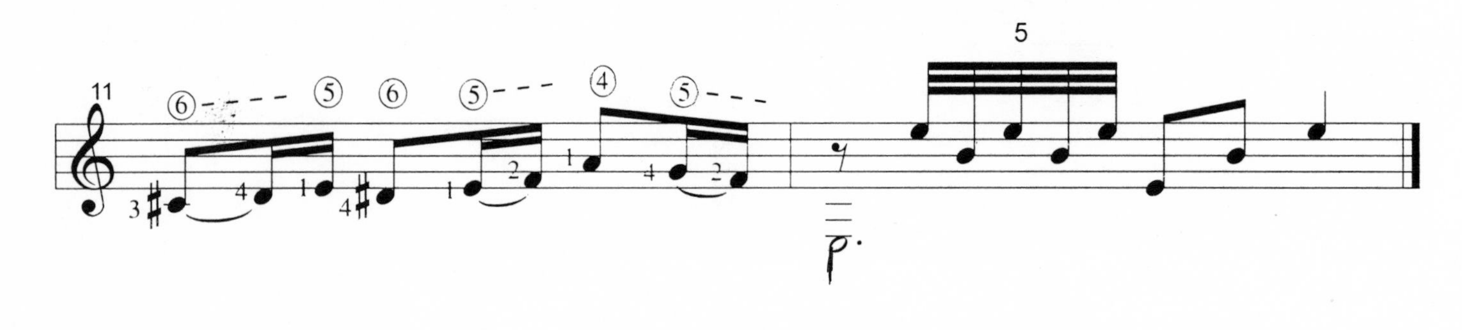

## Falseta 9

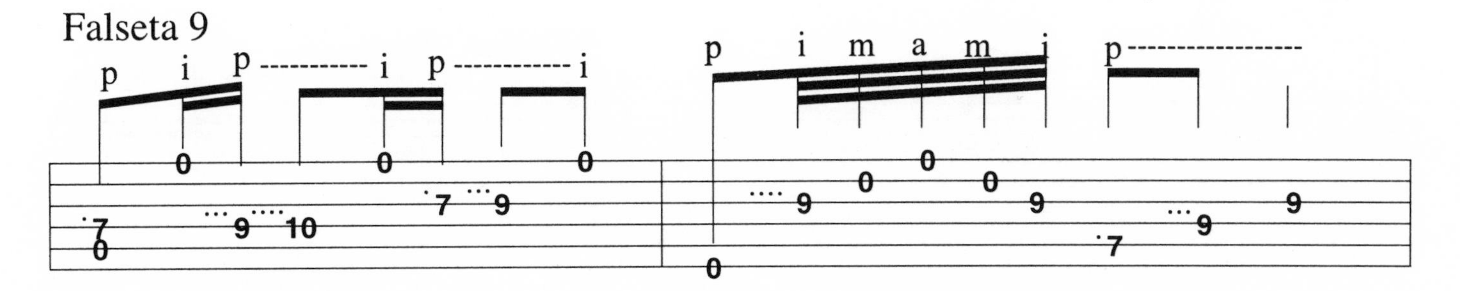


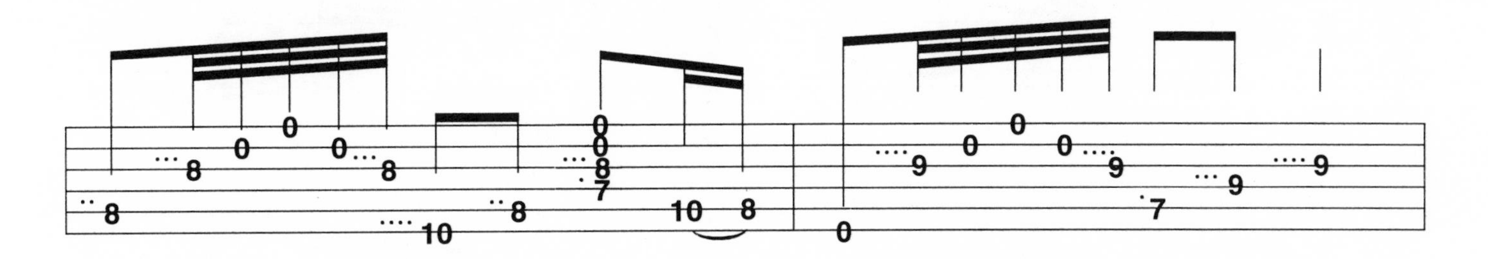

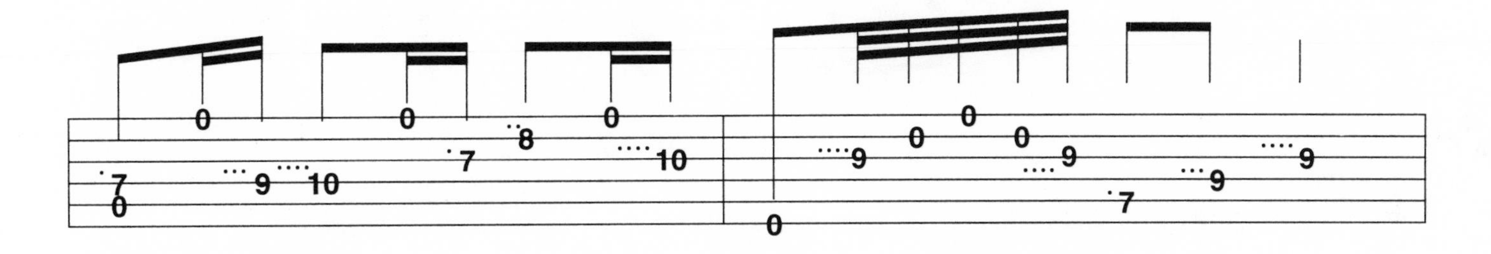

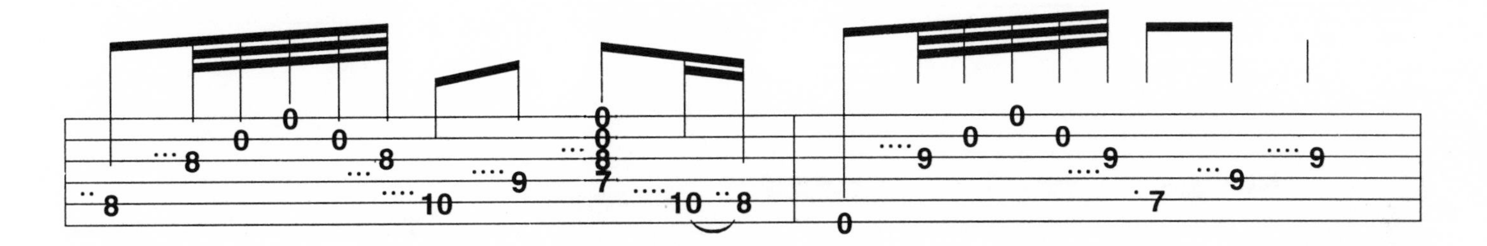

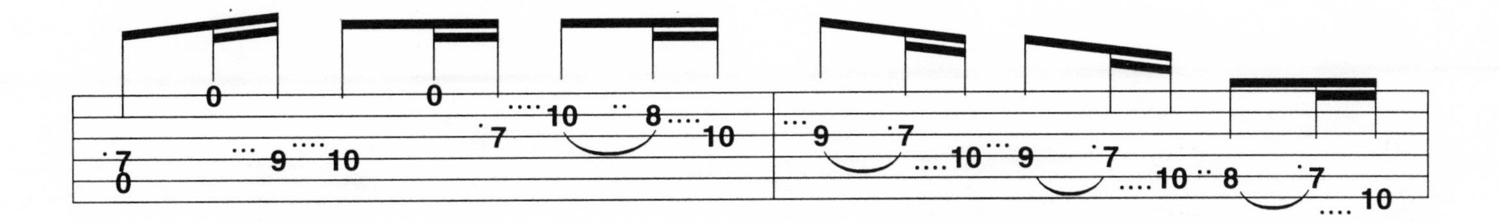

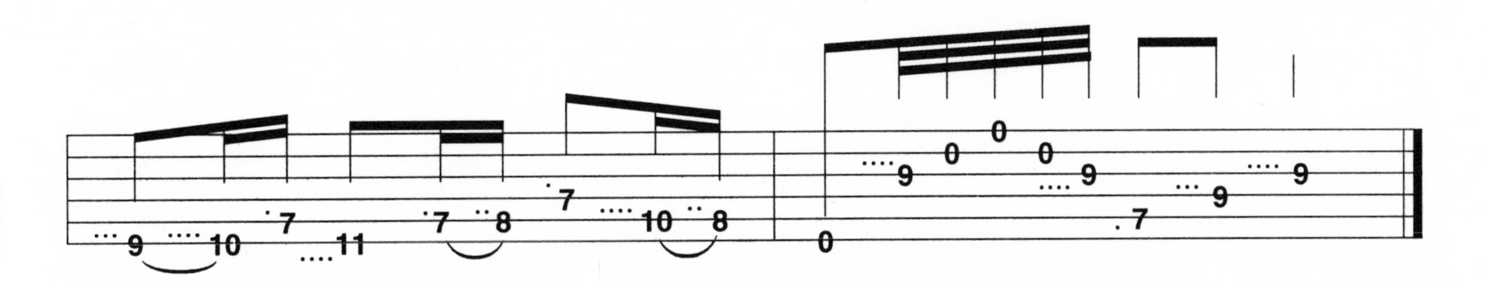

## Falseta 10

Juan Serrano

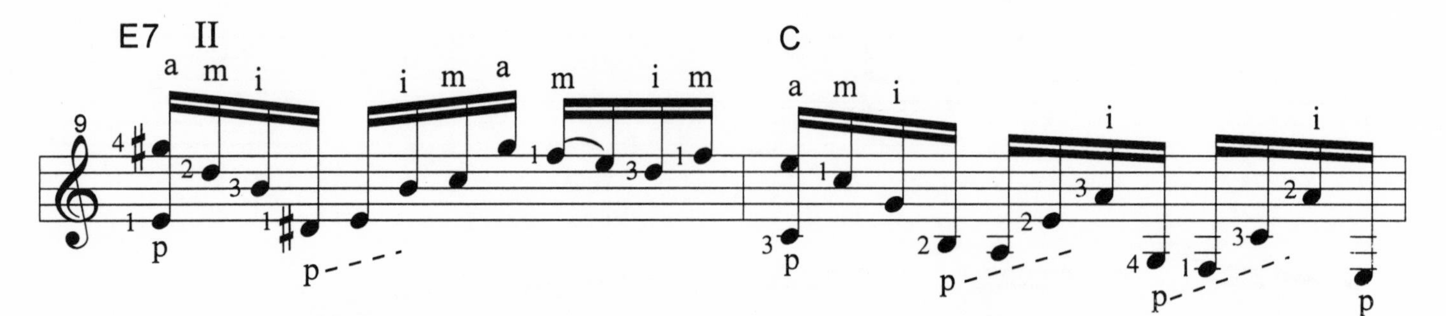


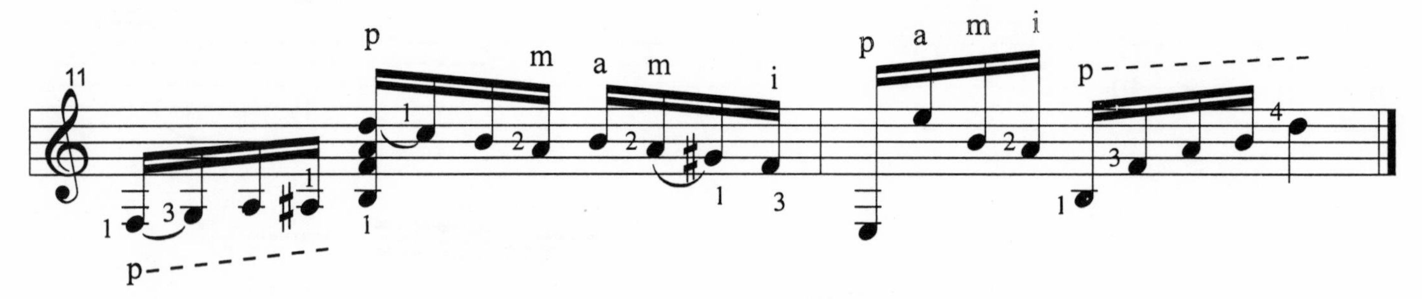

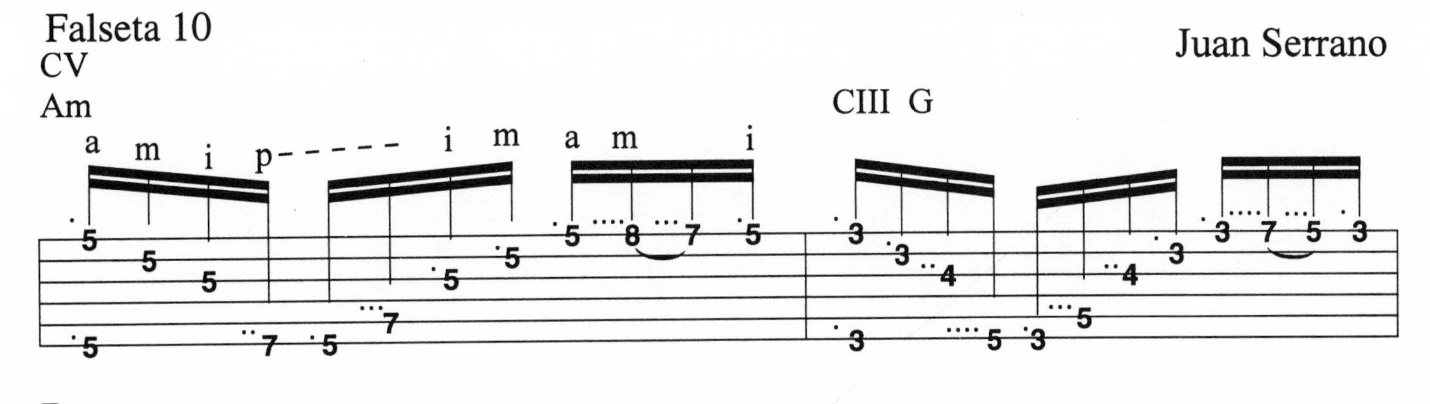
Falseta 10
Juan Serrano
CV
Am
a m i p i m a m i
CIII G

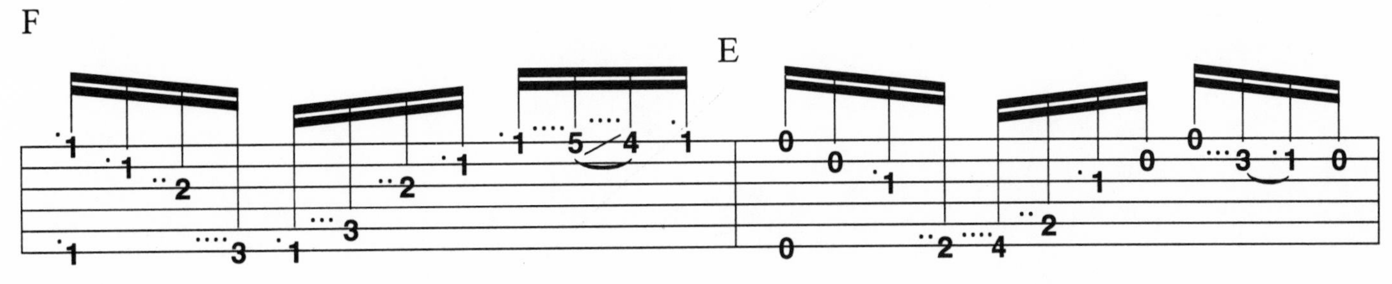
F
E

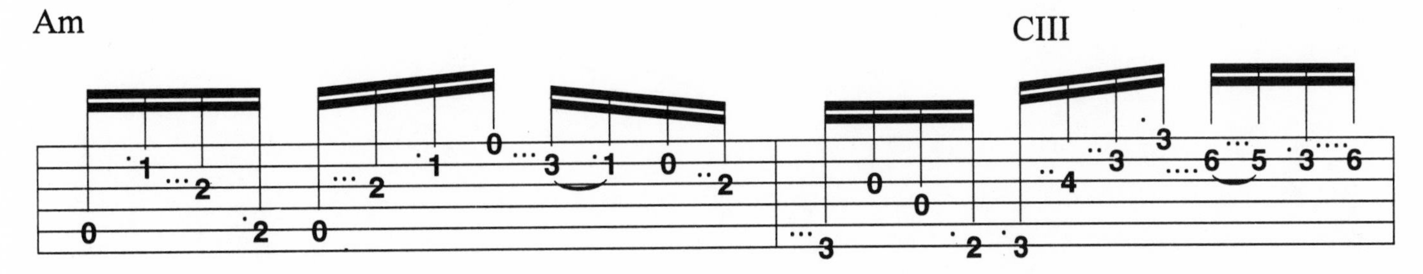
Am
CIII

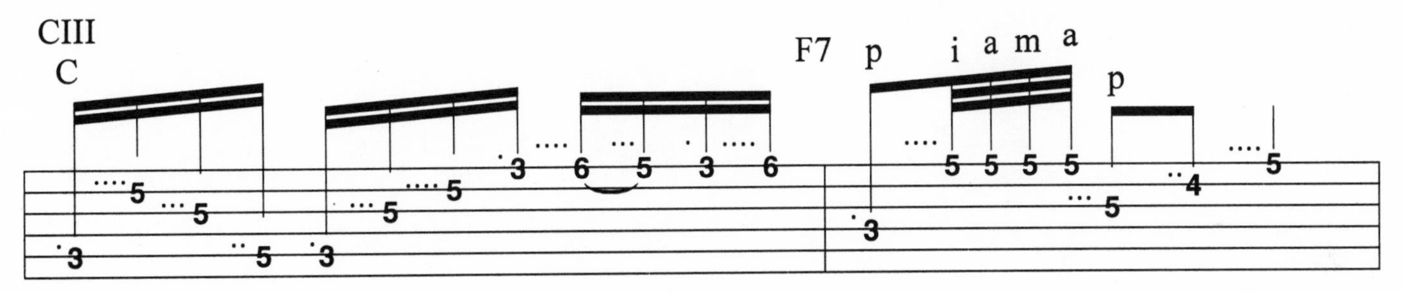
CIII
C
F7
p i a m a
p

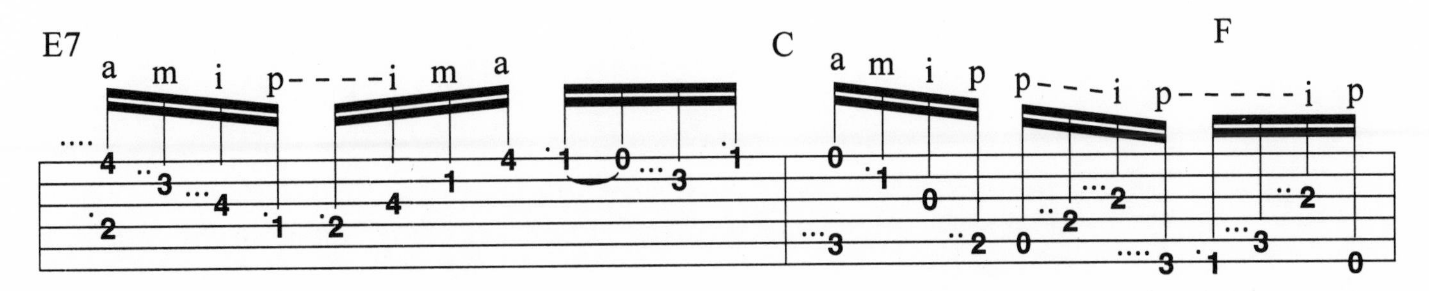
E7
a m i p i m a
C
a m i p p i p i p
F

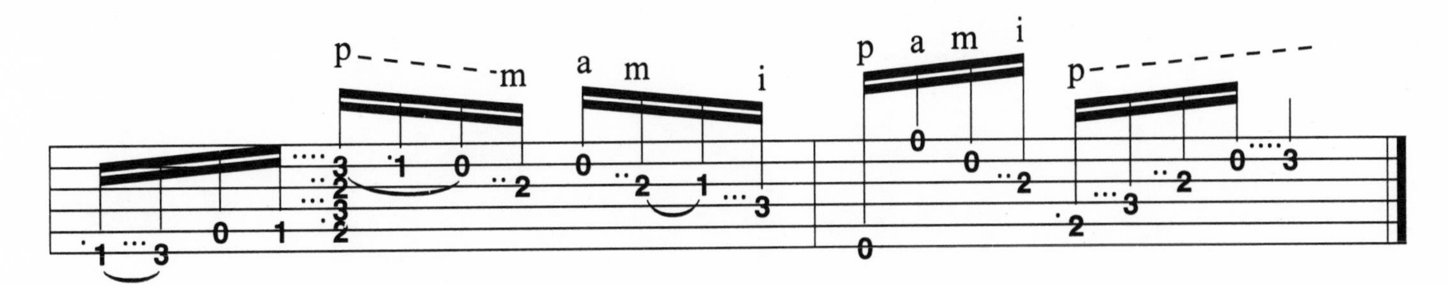
p m a m i
p a m i
p

# TANGOS

The Tangos are one of the basic forms, like the Soleares, Siguiriyas and Fandangos. It is measured in 4/4 and a compás consists of 8 beats, equivalent to 2 measures of 4/4. They are played in the key of D minor, although the flamenco guitarists said that Tangos, Tientos, Siguiriyas and Bulerías por Medio are played in A. This is because all the falsetas and rhythmical compases in these toques always ended in the chord of A, but their musical notation is in D minor, as will be seen in the following ten falsetas.

The falseta #1 is very easy because it is played in 1st position. In #6 the technique of alzapúa is applied. It is recommended that the first two measures be practiced repeatedly, to become familiar with this type of alzapúa where the last two notes of each beat are tied by ascending and descending legatos. The first three notes of each beat are played with the thumb of the right hand, but the sound of the last note is produced by the 2nd finger of the left hand.

All the marked fingerings of the remaining falsetas should be followed.

# TANGOS

Los Tangos son una de las formas básicas, como las Soleares, las Siguiriyas y los Fandangos. Se miden en 4/4 y un compás flamenco se compone de ocho tiempos equivalentes a dos compases musicales de 4/4.

Se tocan en el tono de Re menor, aunque los guitarristas flamencos decían que los Tangos, los Tientos, las Siguiriyas y las Bulerías por Medio se tocaban en el tono de La. Esto es debido a que todas las falsetas y los compases rítmicos de estos toques siempre resuelven en el acorde de La, pero su anotación musical es en Re menor como lo podrán comprobar en las diez próximas falsetas.

La falseta #1 es muy fácil porque se toca toda en primera posición. En la falseta #6 se emplea la técnica de alzapúa. Recomiendo que se practiquen una y otra vez los dos primeros compases musicales para familiarizarse bien con este tipo de alzapúa, donde las dos ultimas notas de cada tiempo están unidas por ligados, ascendentes o descendentes. Las tres primeras notas de cada tiempo se tocan con el dedo pulgar (p) de la mano derecha, pero el sonido de la última nota lo produce el dedo 2 de la mano izquierda.

Para todas las demás falsetas recomiendo que se sigan todas las digitaciones marcadas.

# *Tangos*

Traditional Compas

Juan Serrano

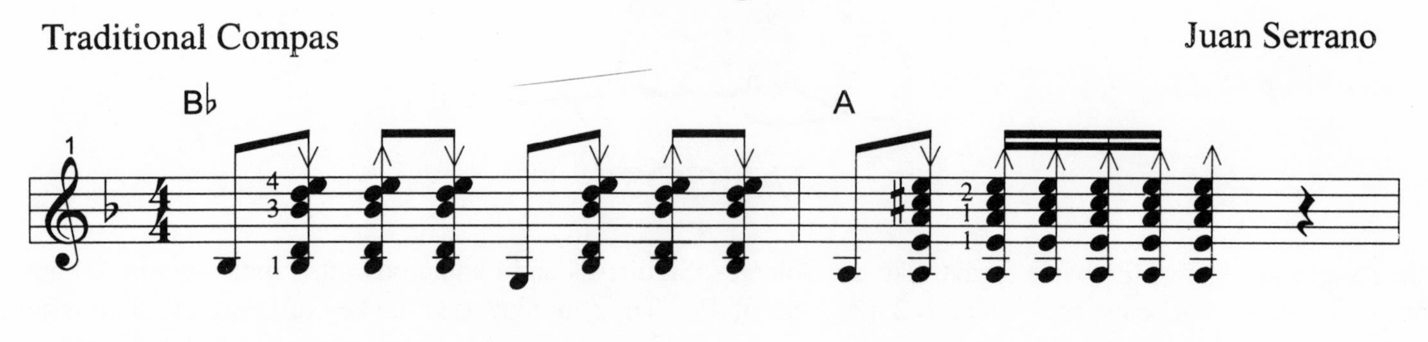


Variation 1

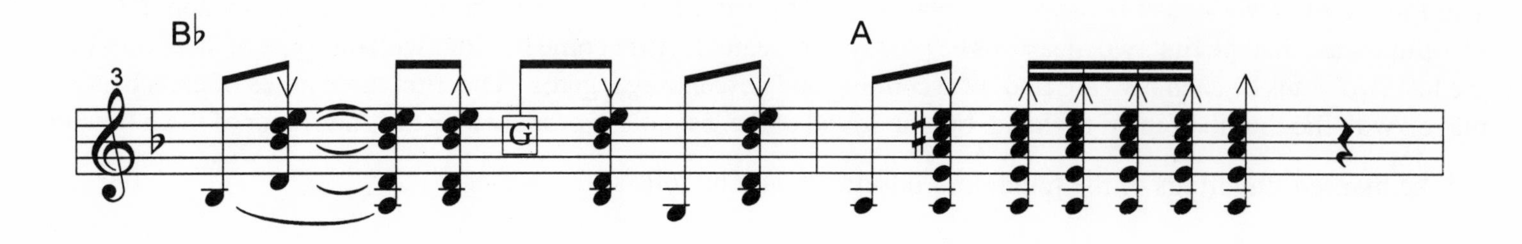


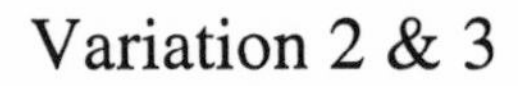

Variation 2 & 3

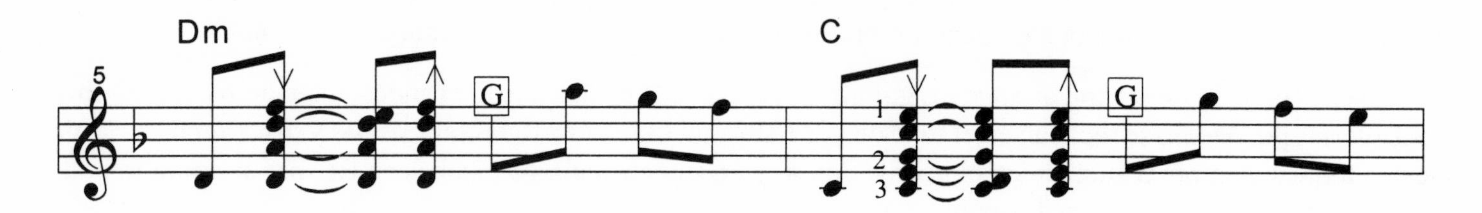

# *Tangos*

## Traditional Compas

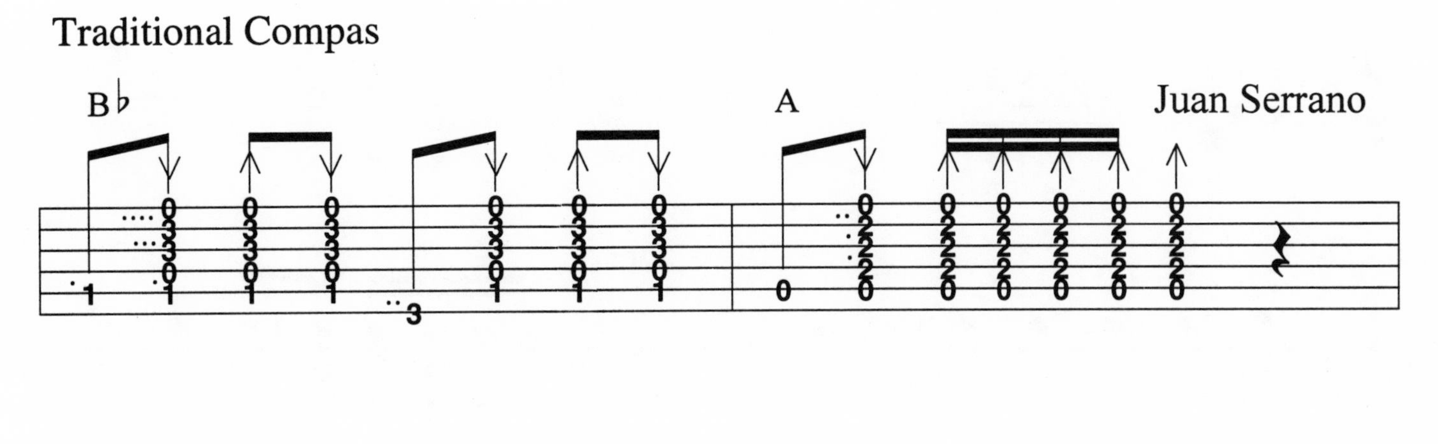


## Variation 1

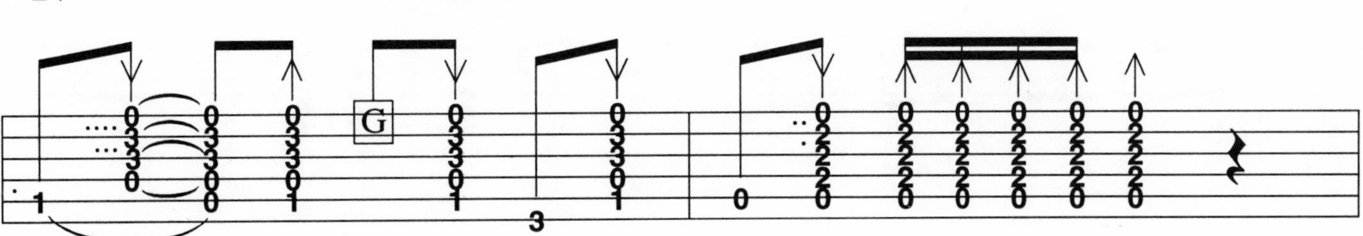


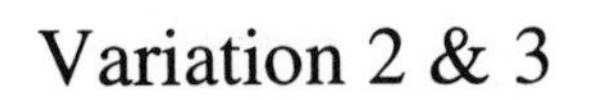

## Variation 2 & 3

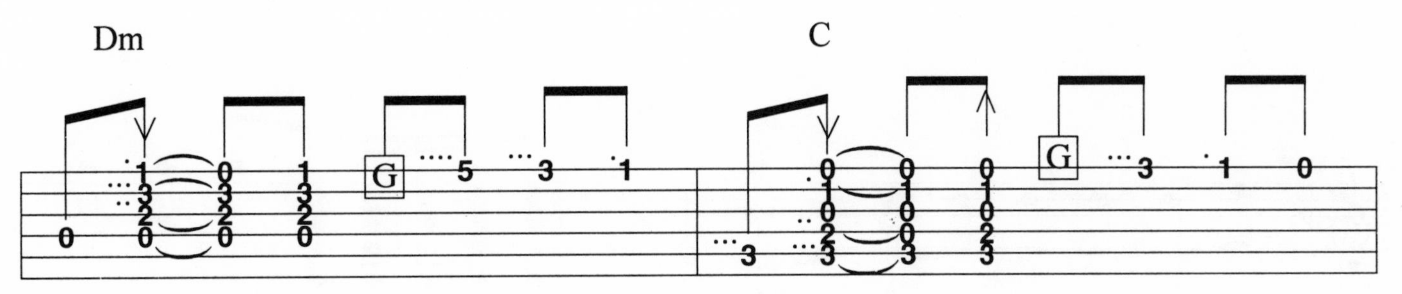


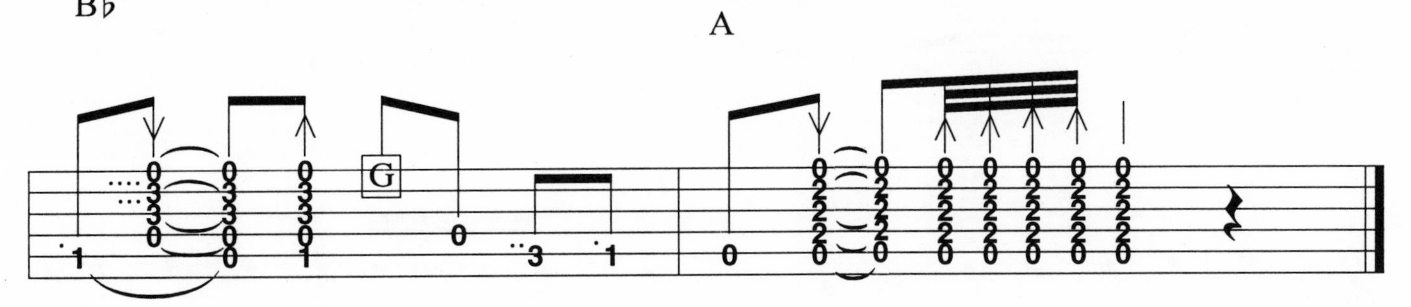

Falseta 1

Juan Serrano

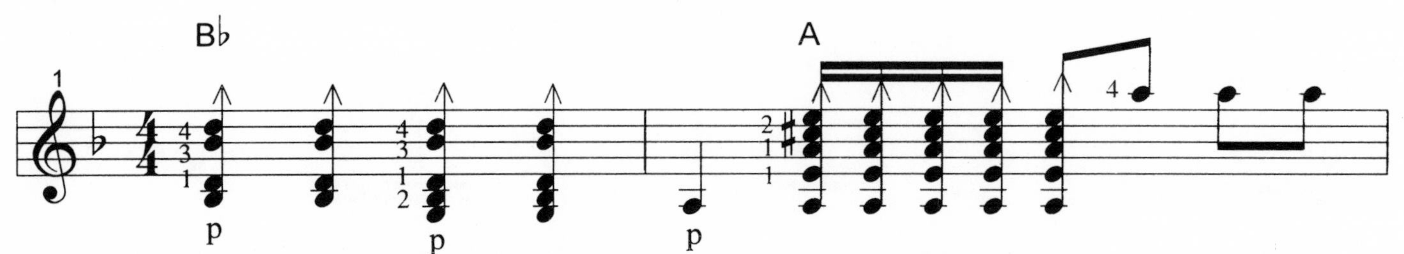

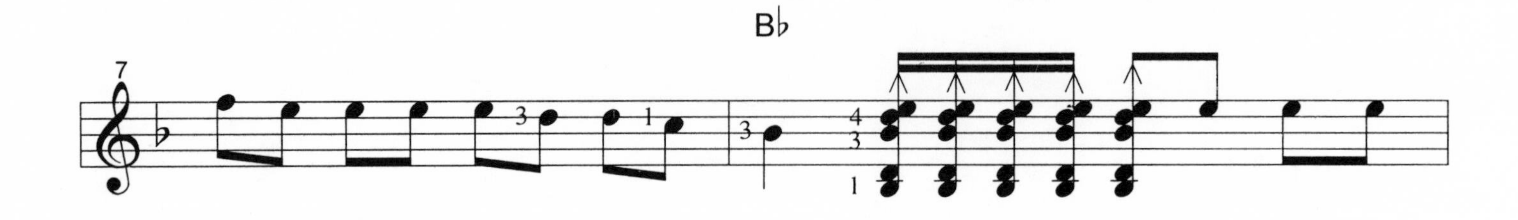


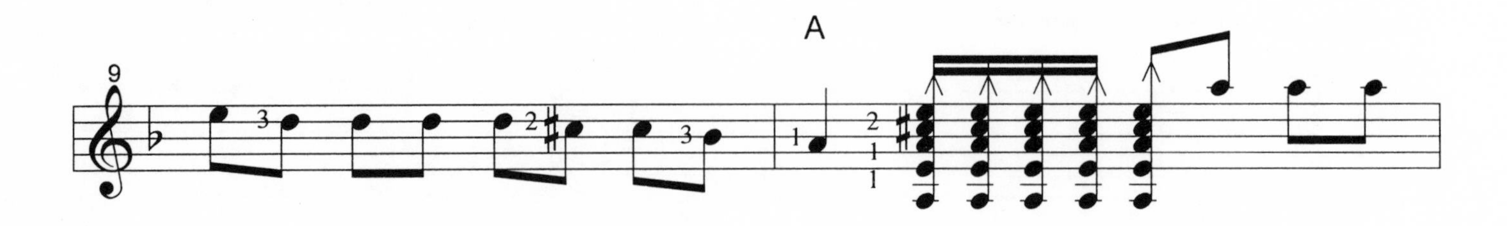

C

13

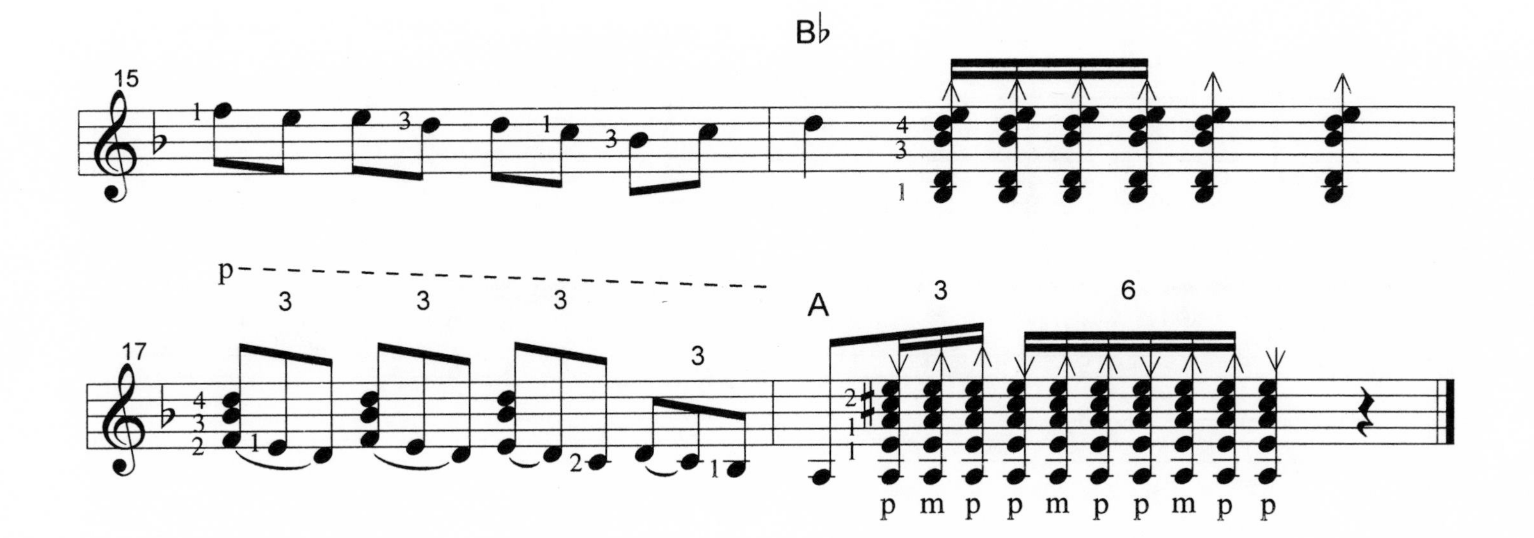
B♭
p
A
p m p p m p p m p p

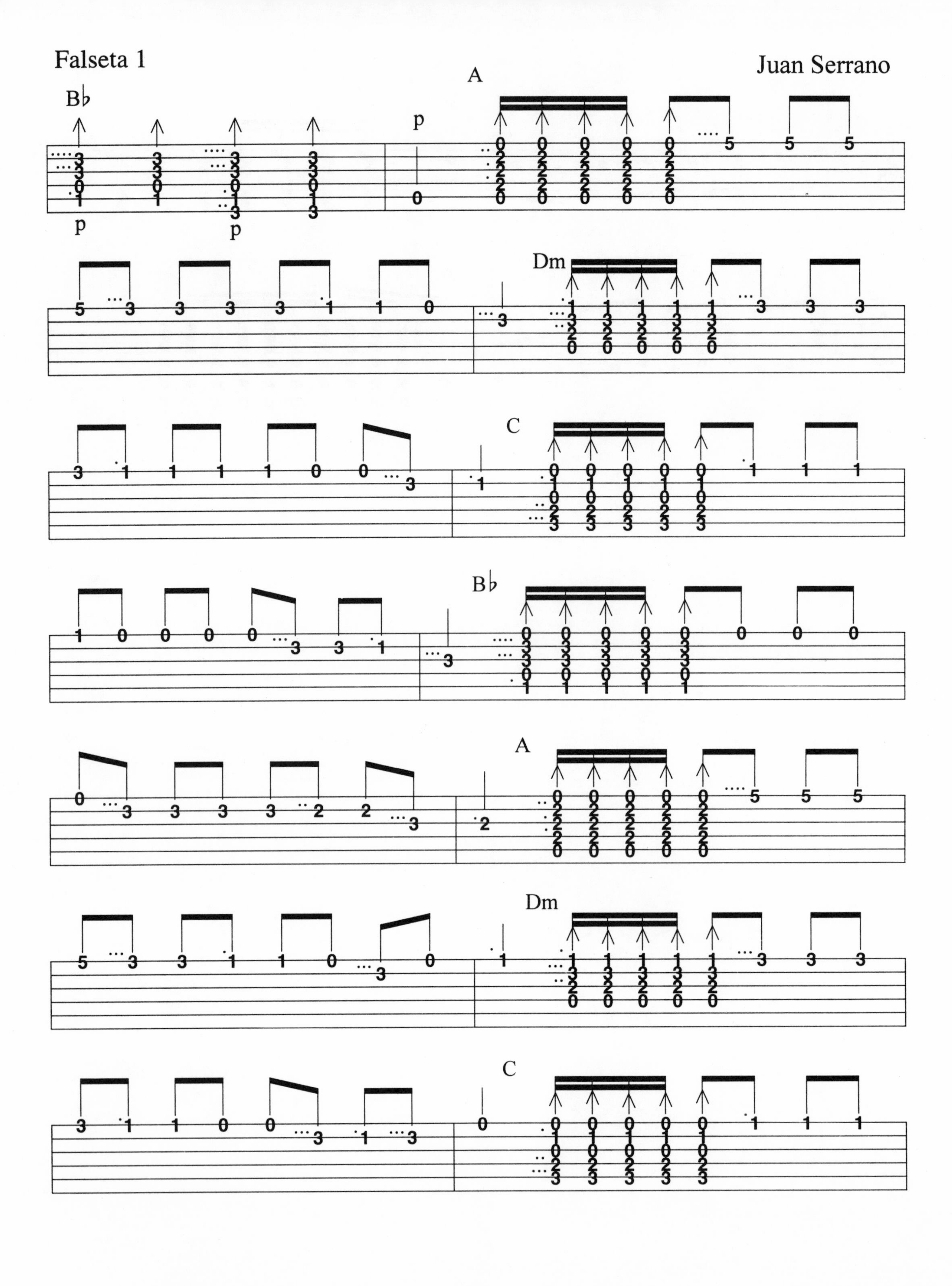
Falseta 1
Juan Serrano
B♭
A
p
p
p
Dm
C
B♭
A
Dm
C

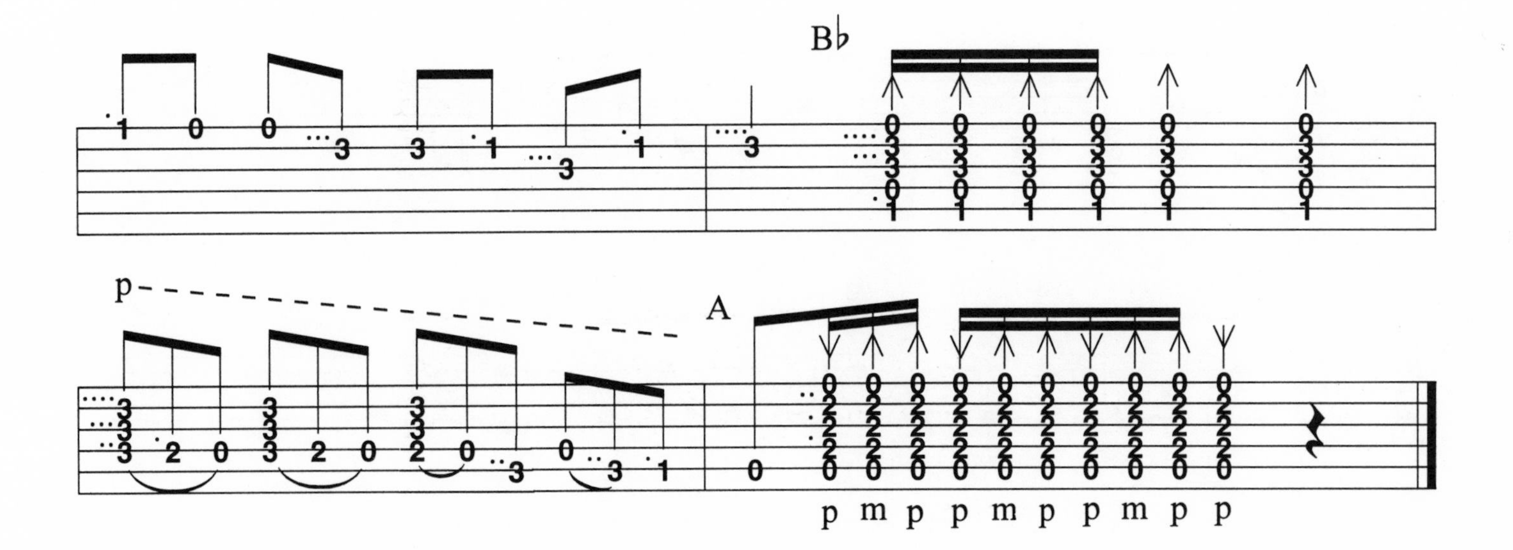
B♭
p
A
p m p p m p p m p p

Falseta 2 — Juan Serrano

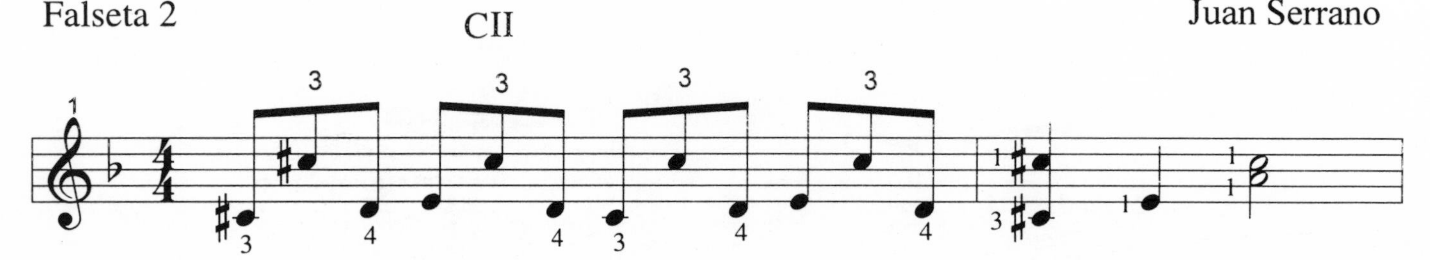


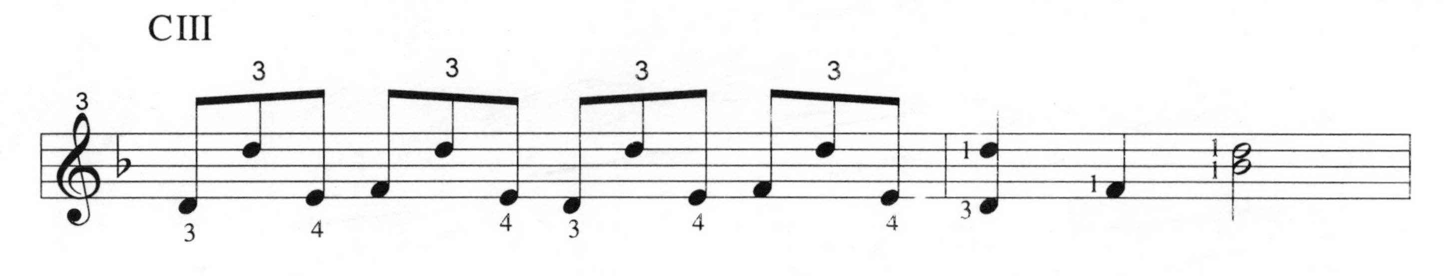

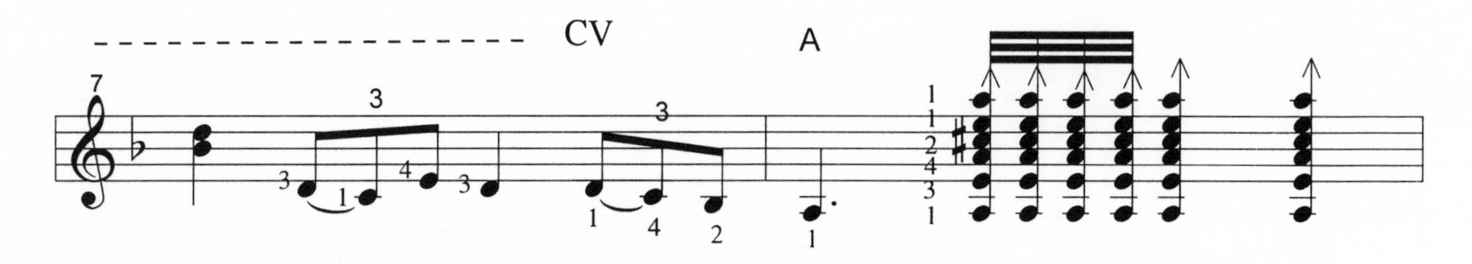

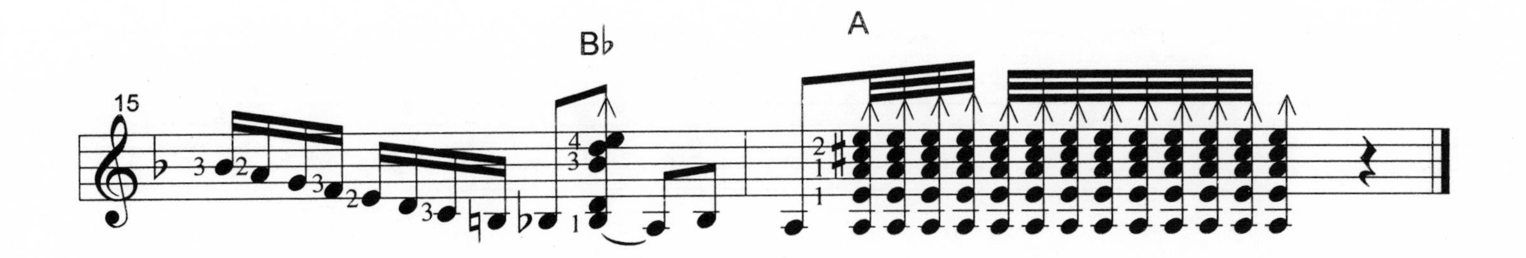
B♭
A

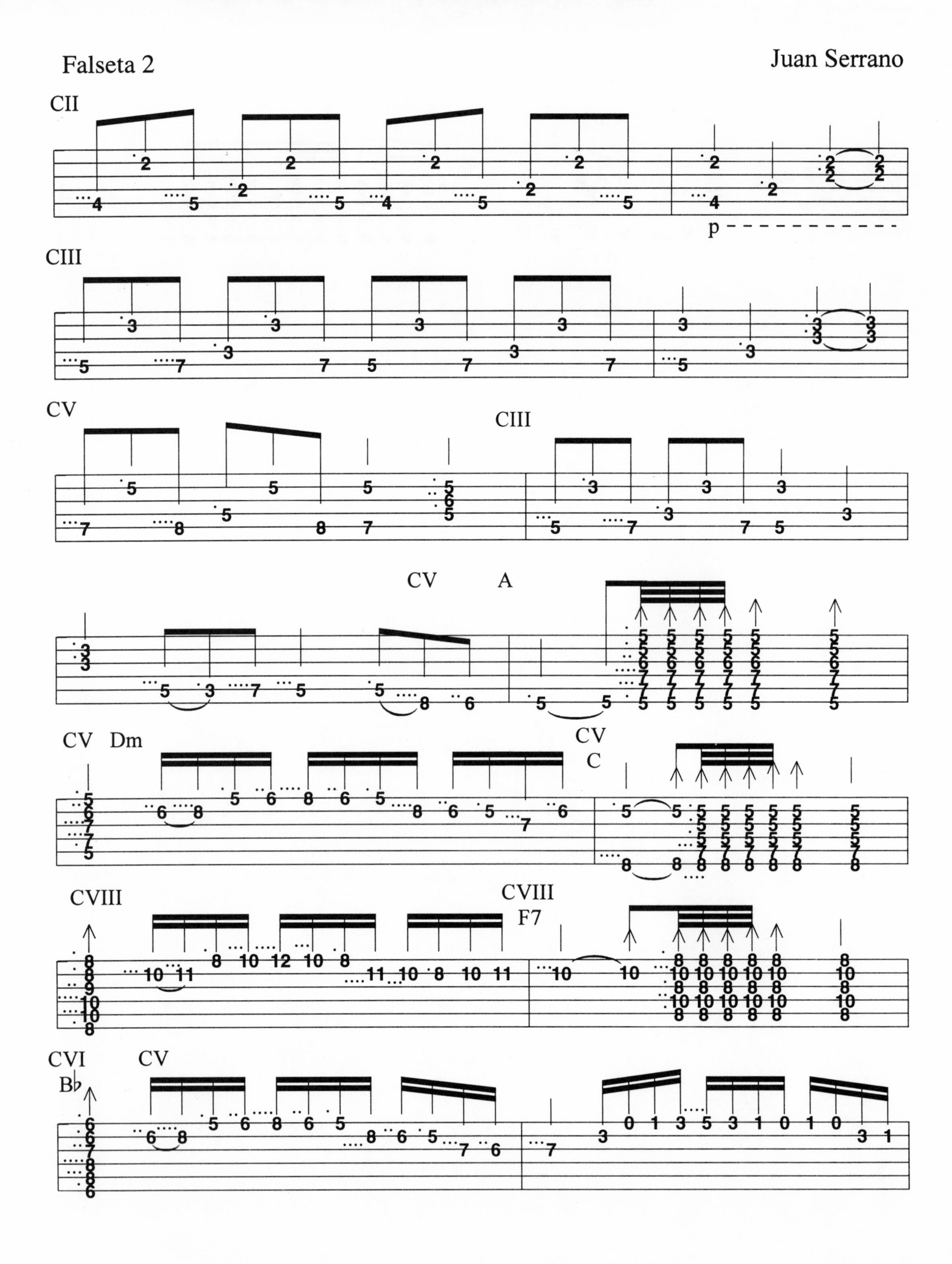
Falseta 2
Juan Serrano
CII
p
CIII
CV
CIII
CV
A
CV
Dm
CV
C
CVIII
CVIII
F7
CVI
B♭
CV

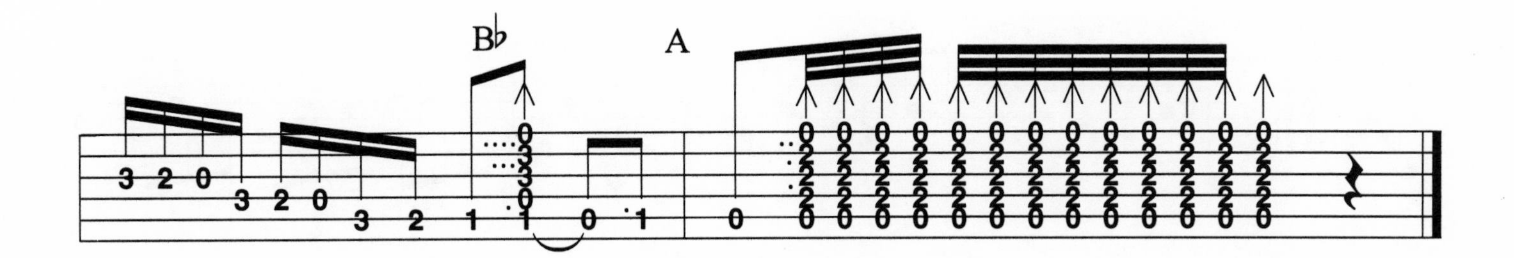
B♭
A

Falseta 3

Juan Serrano

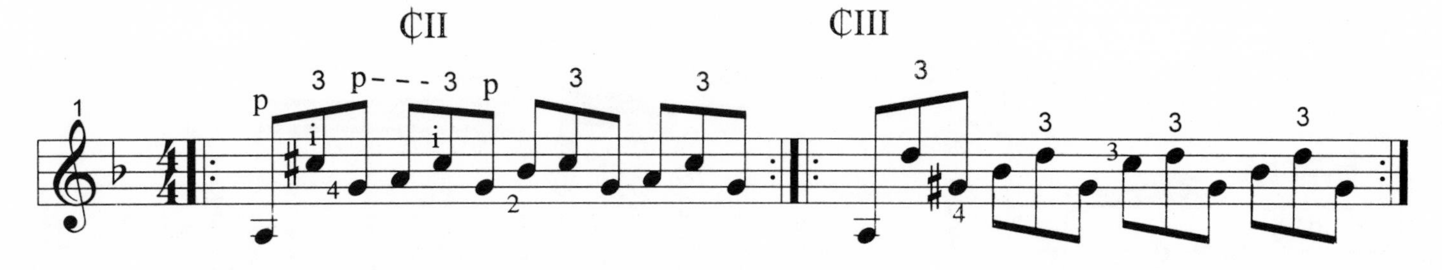


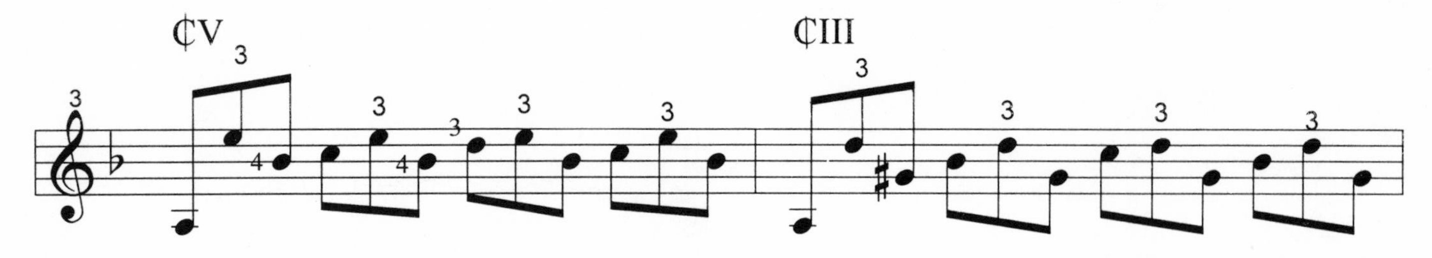


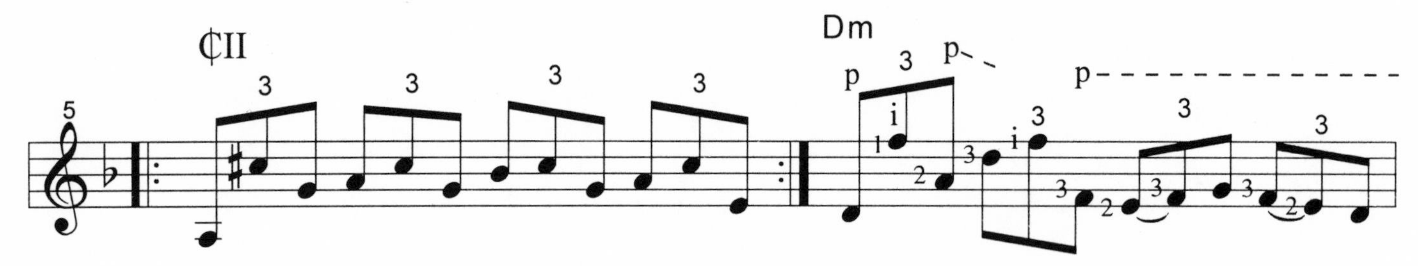


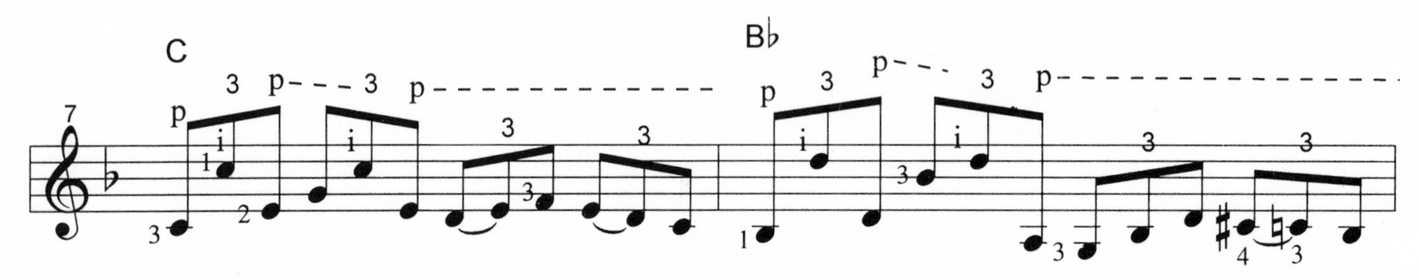


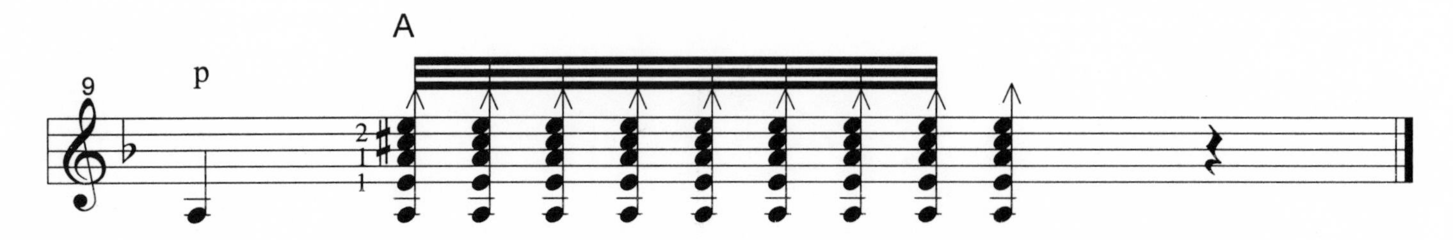

Falseta 3

Juan Serrano

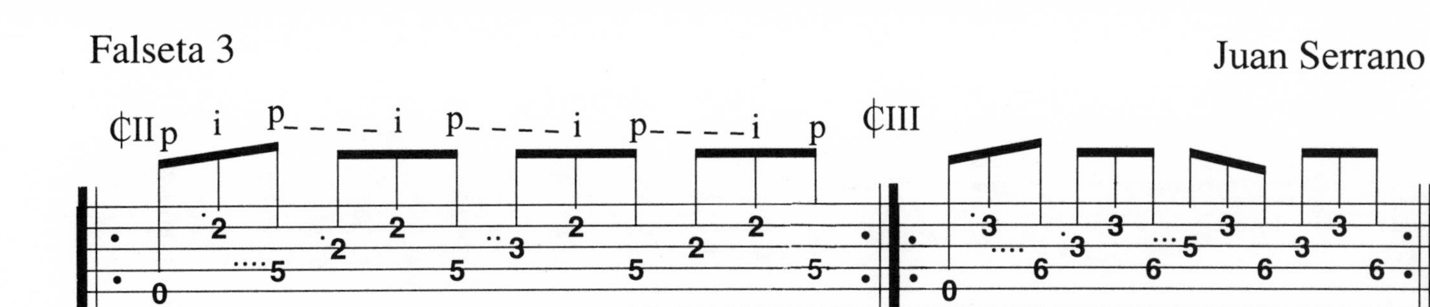


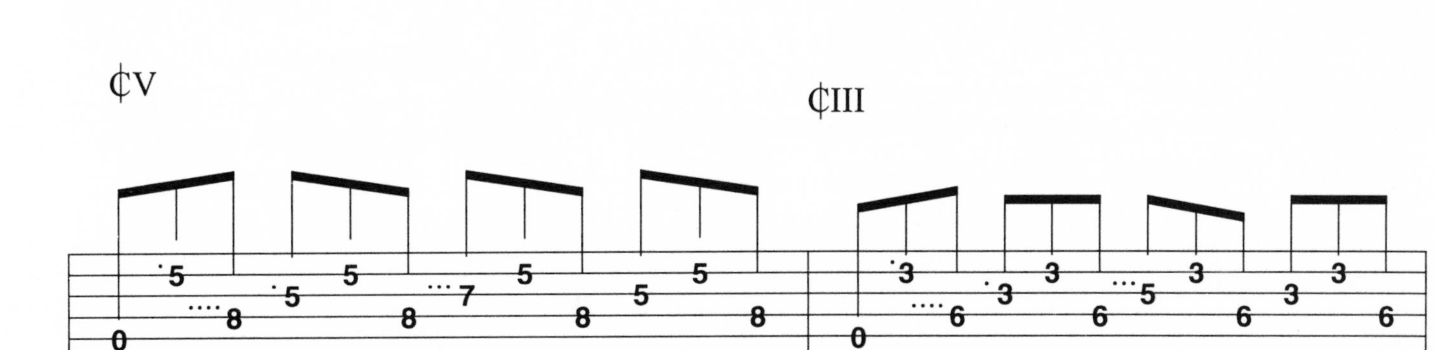


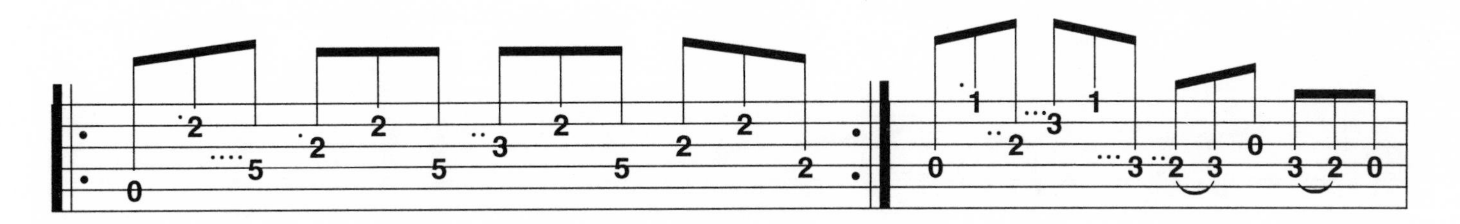


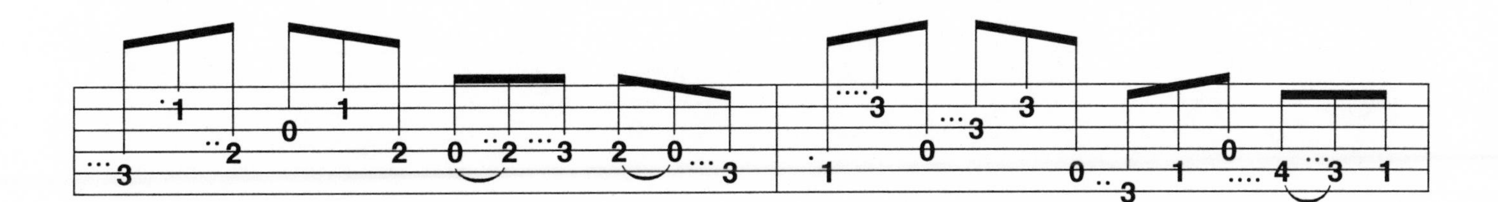


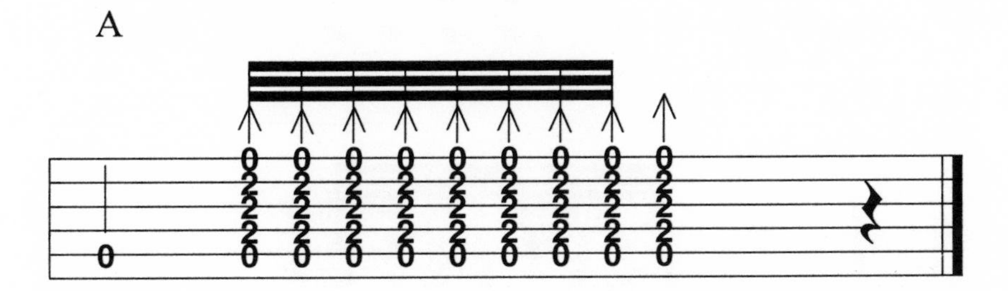

A7

A

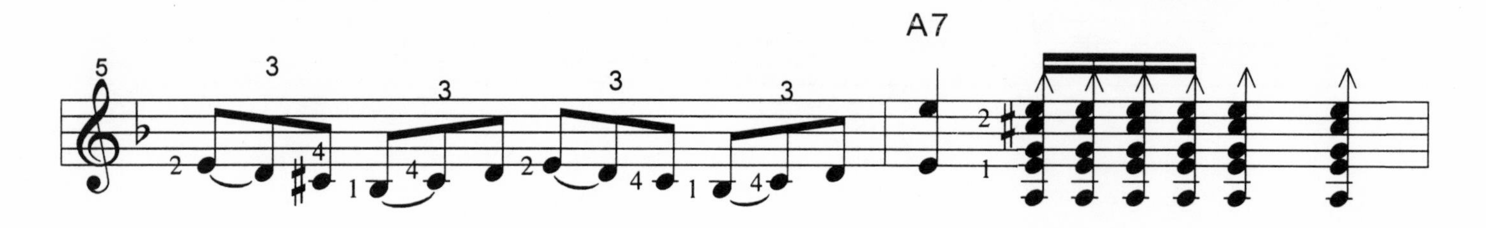
A7

A

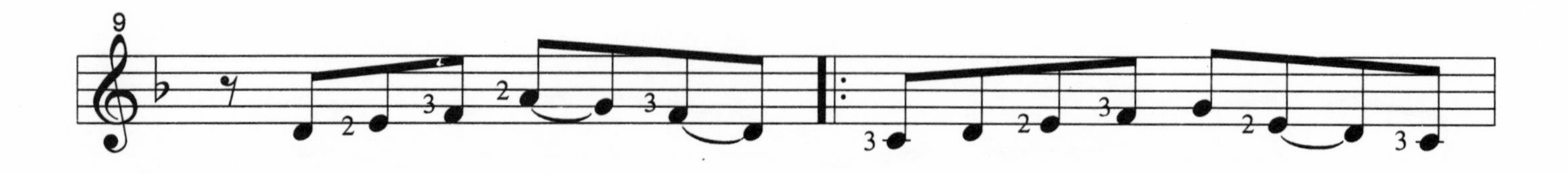

1. A

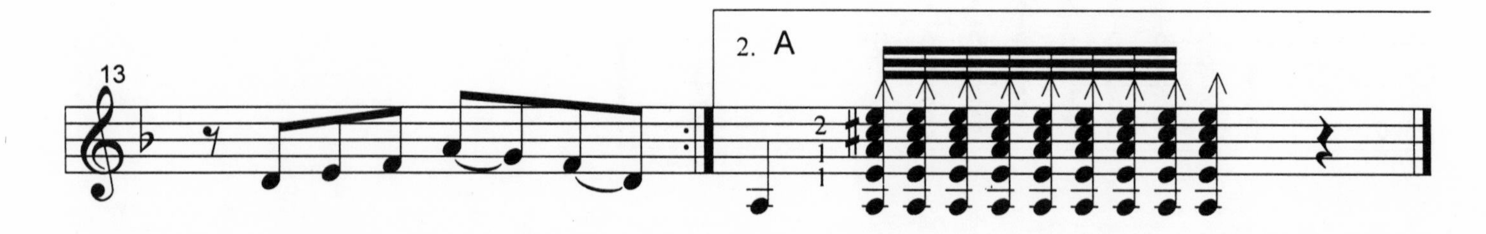
2. A

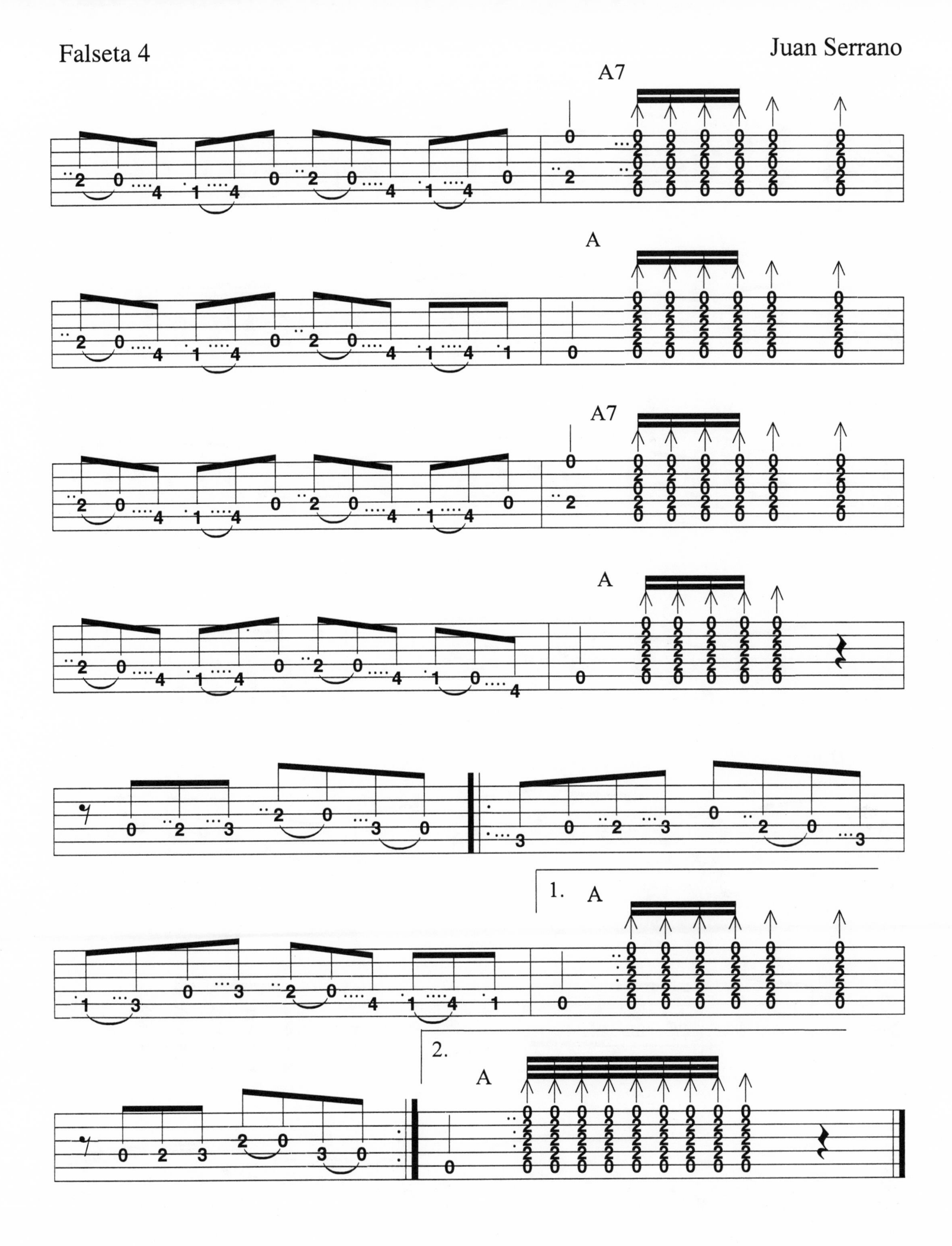
Falseta 4
Juan Serrano
A7
A
A7
A
1.
A
2.
A

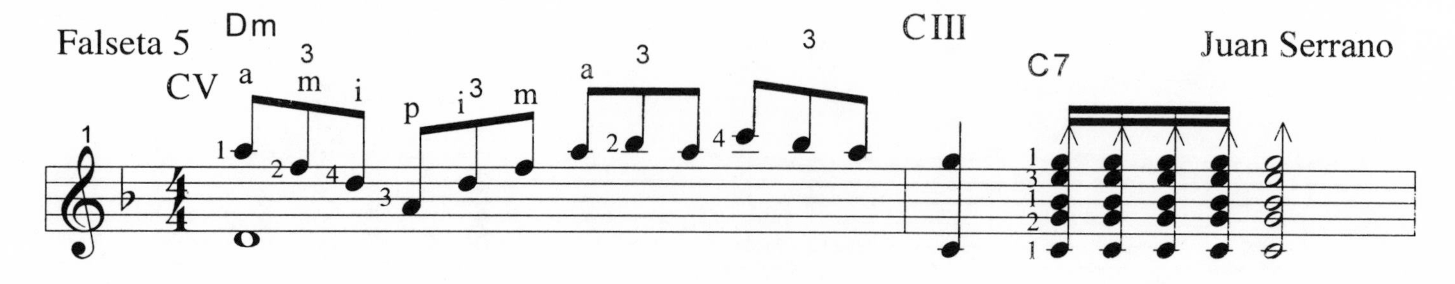
Falseta 5
Juan Serrano
CV
Dm
CIII
C7

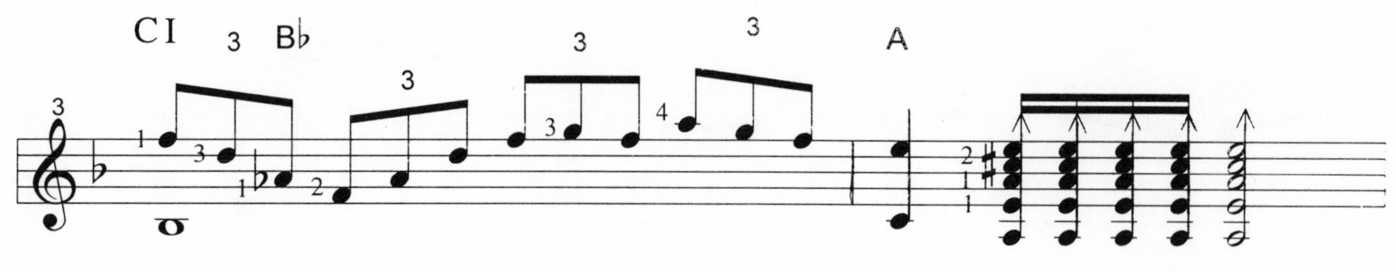
CI
B♭
A

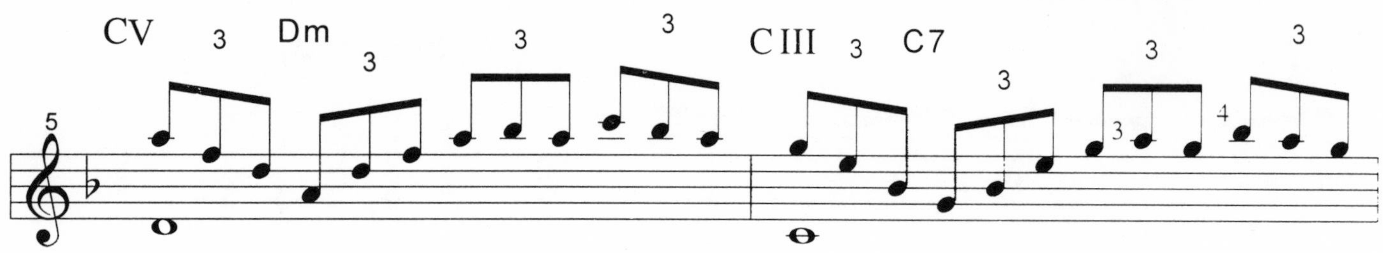
CV
Dm
CIII
C7

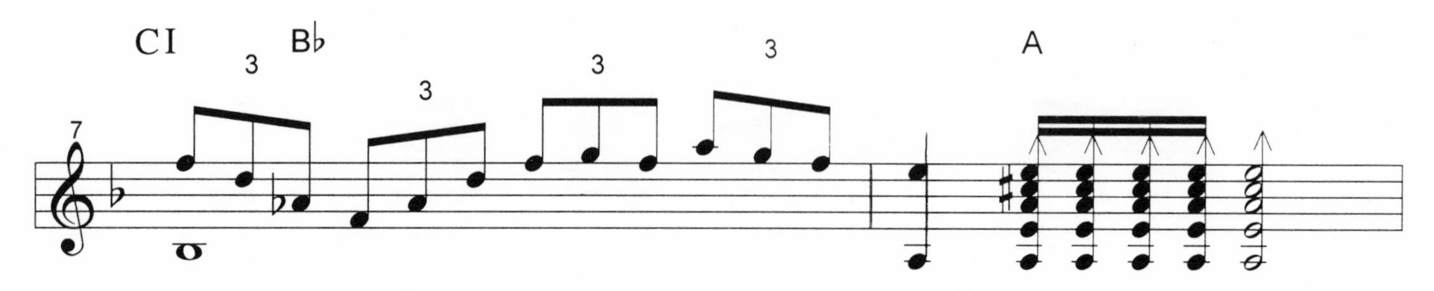
CI
B♭
A

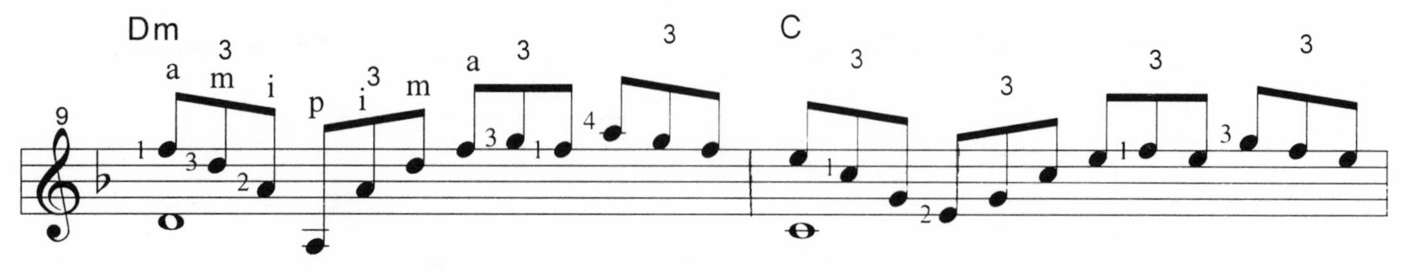
Dm
C

A

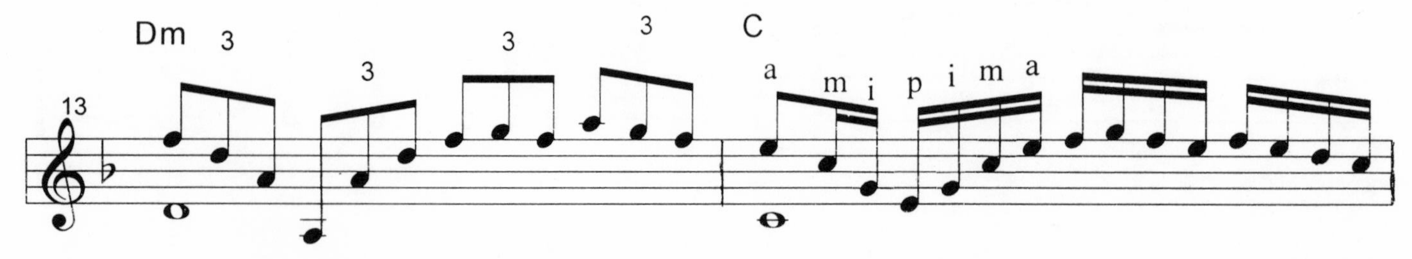
Dm
C

15
A

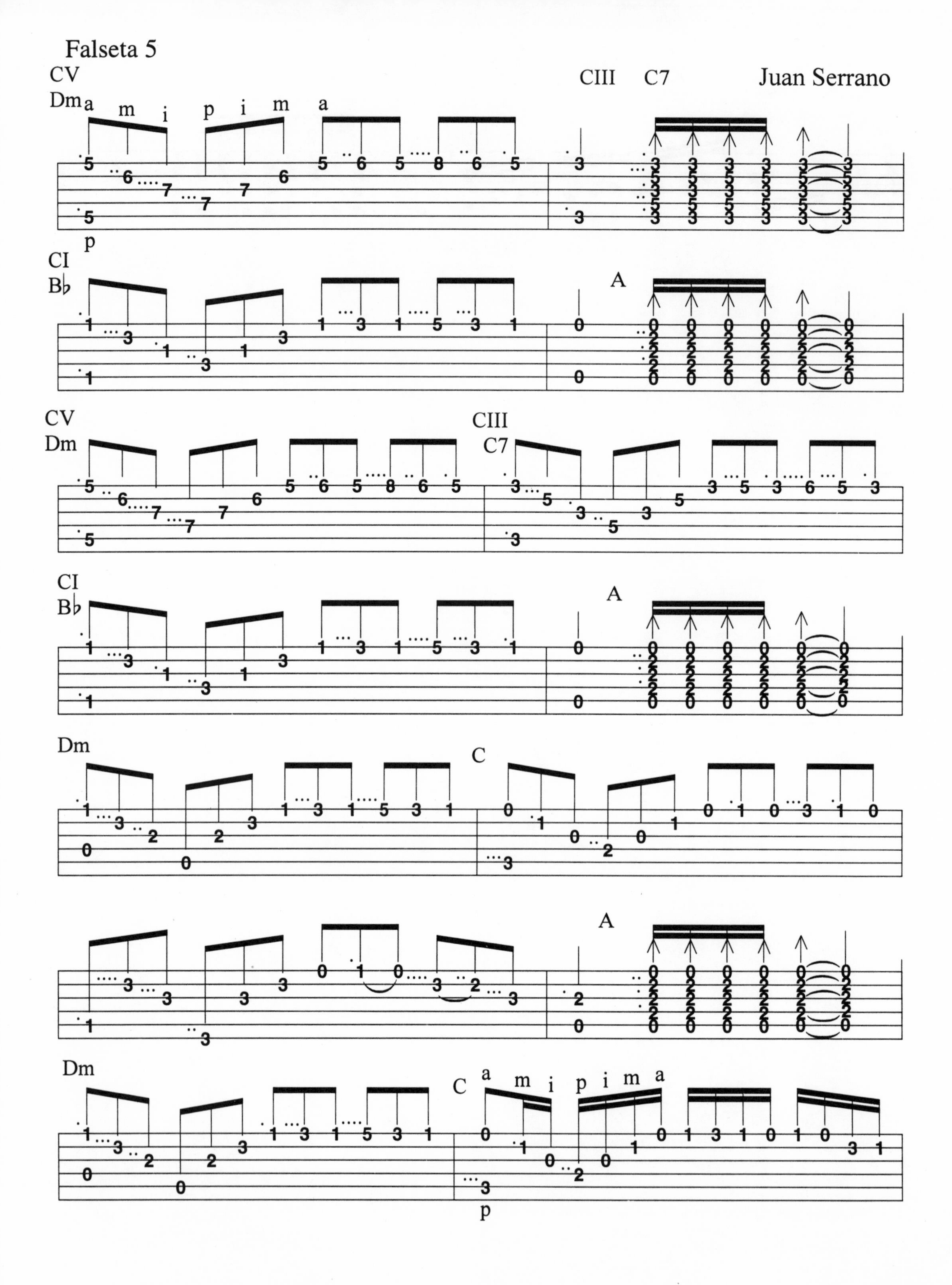
Falseta 5
Juan Serrano
CV
Dm
a m i p i m a
p
CIII
C7
CI
B♭
A
CV
Dm
CIII
C7
CI
B♭
A
Dm
C
A
Dm
C
a m i p i m a
p

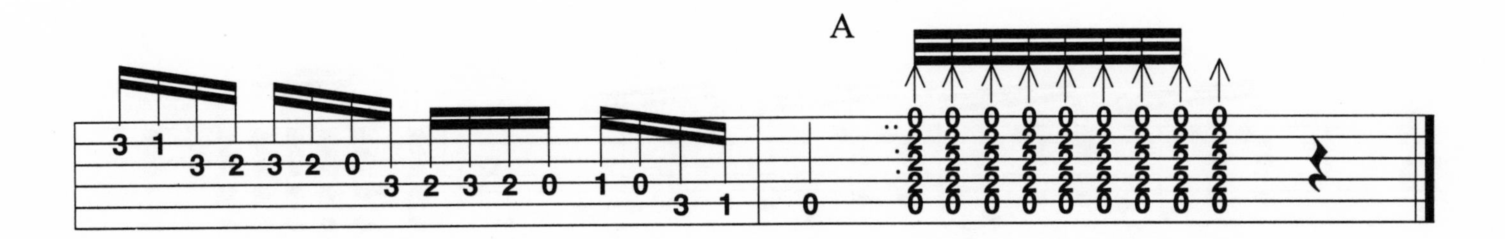
A

Falseta 6 (Alzapua) Juan Serrano

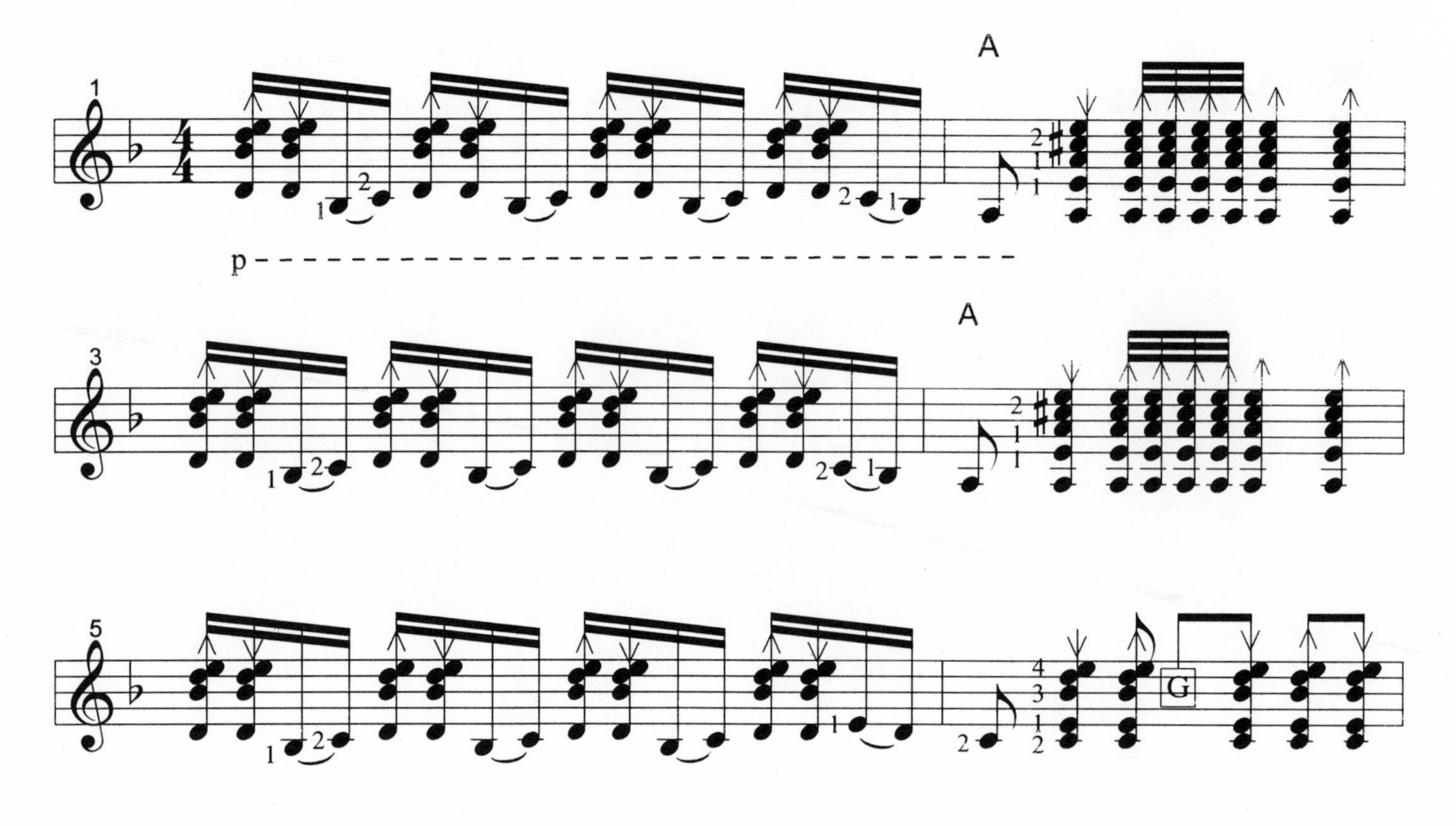

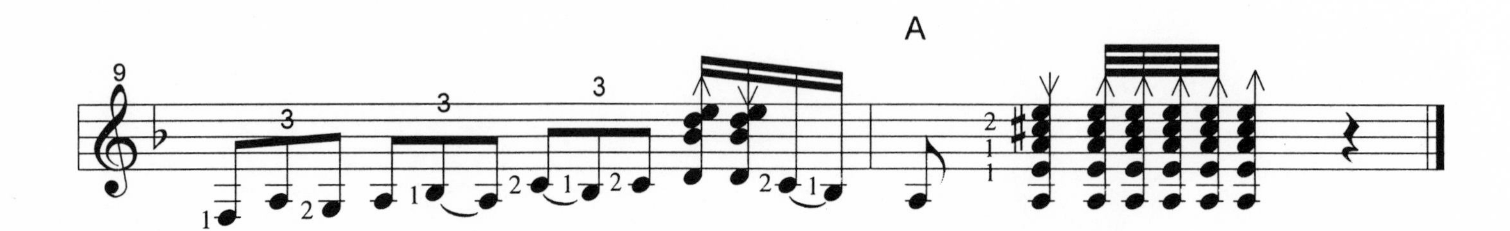

Falseta 6 (Alzapua)

Juan Serrano

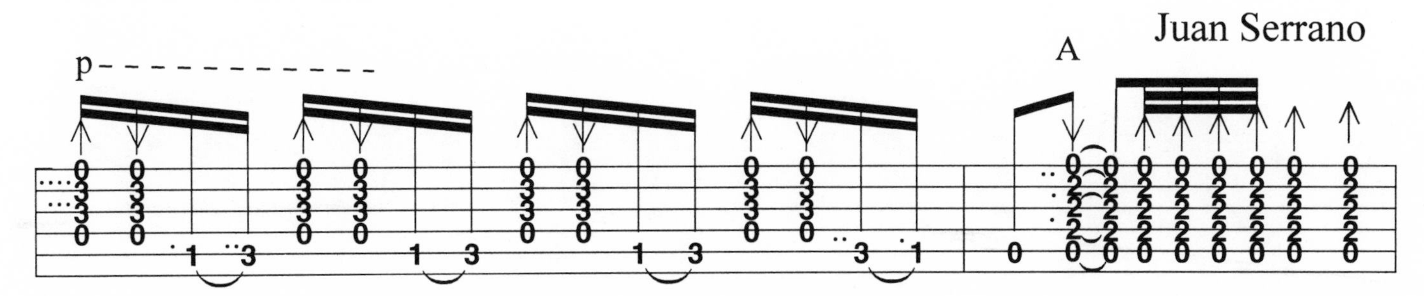


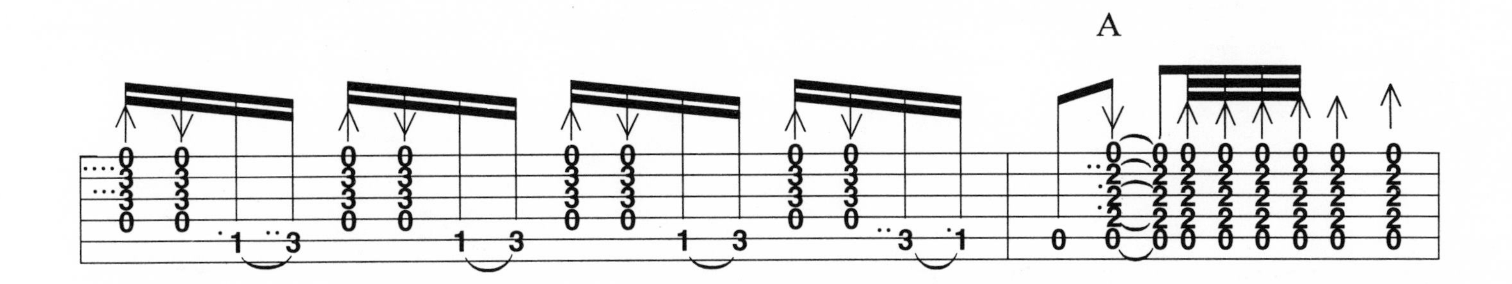


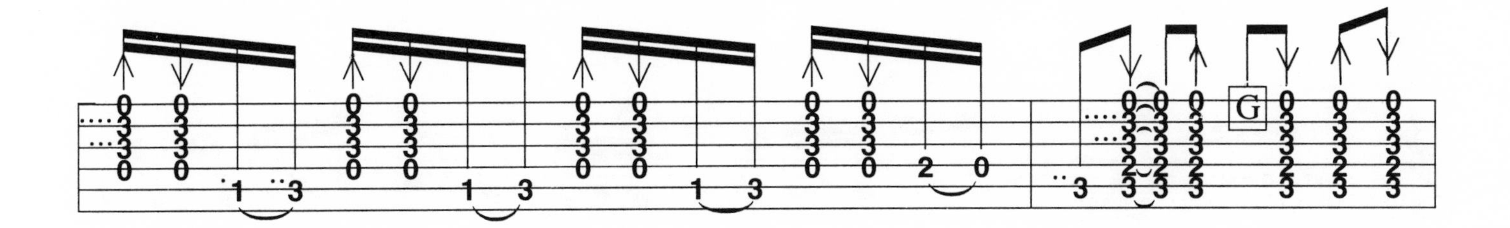


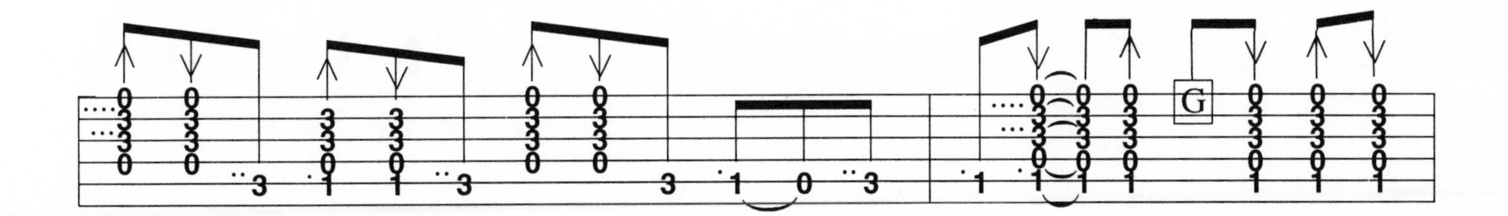


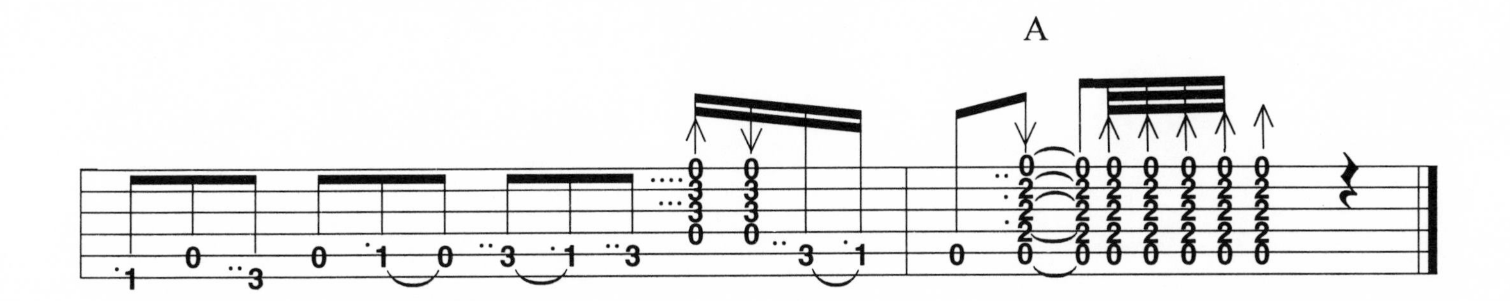

## Falseta 7

Juan Serrano

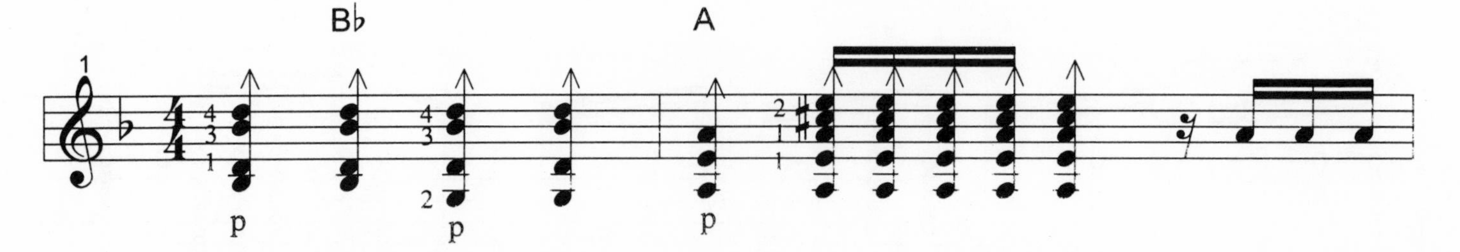

Falseta 7

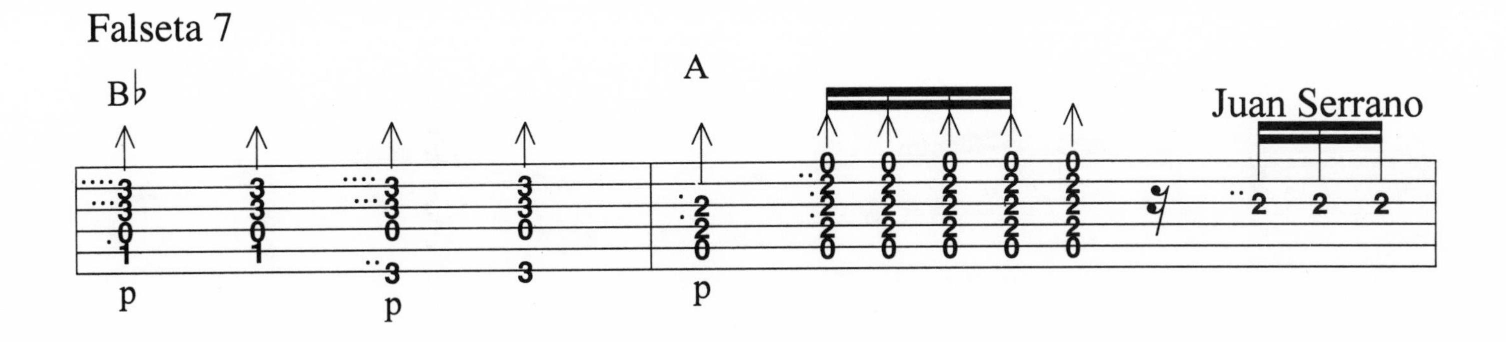

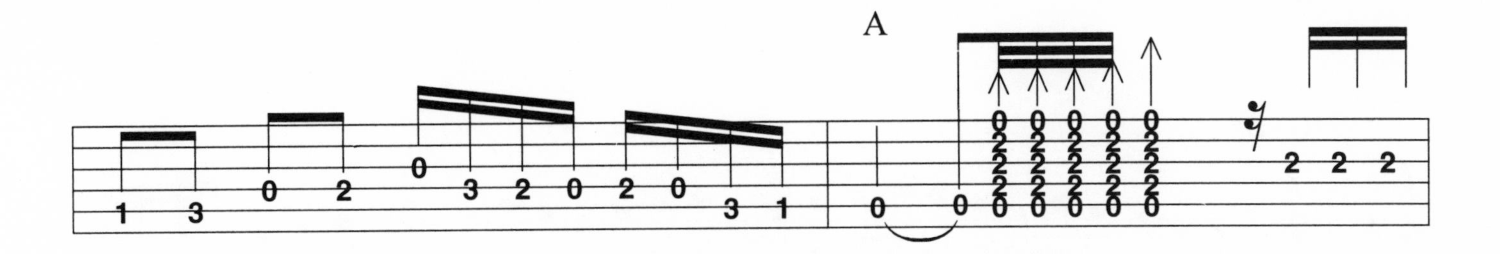


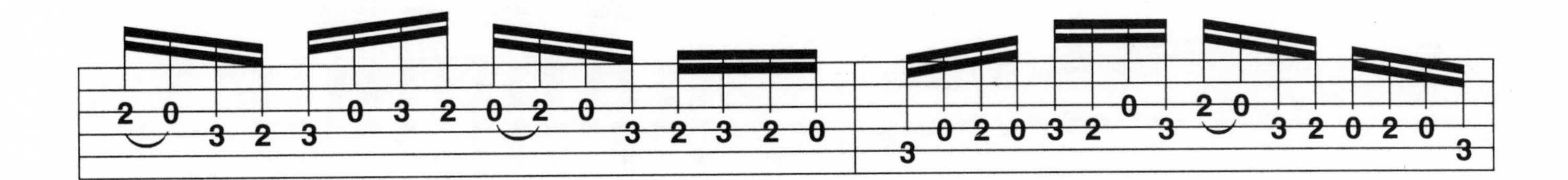

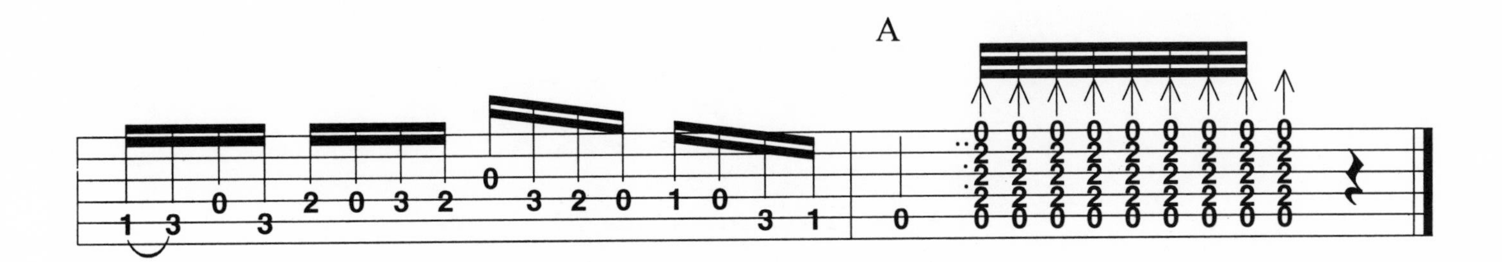

Falseta 8

Juan Serrano

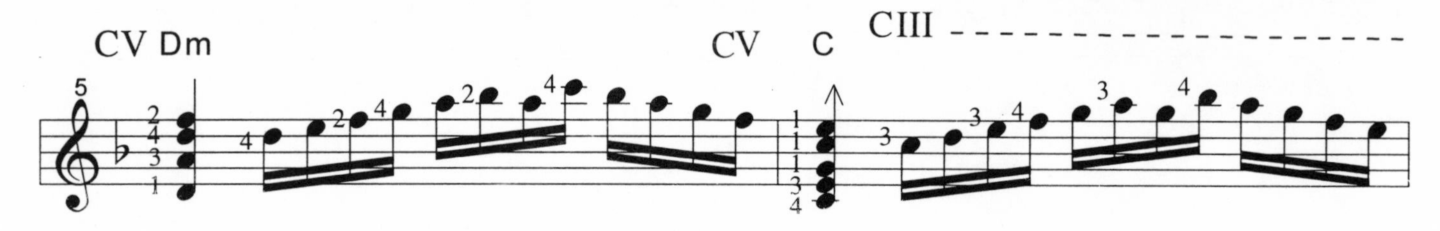


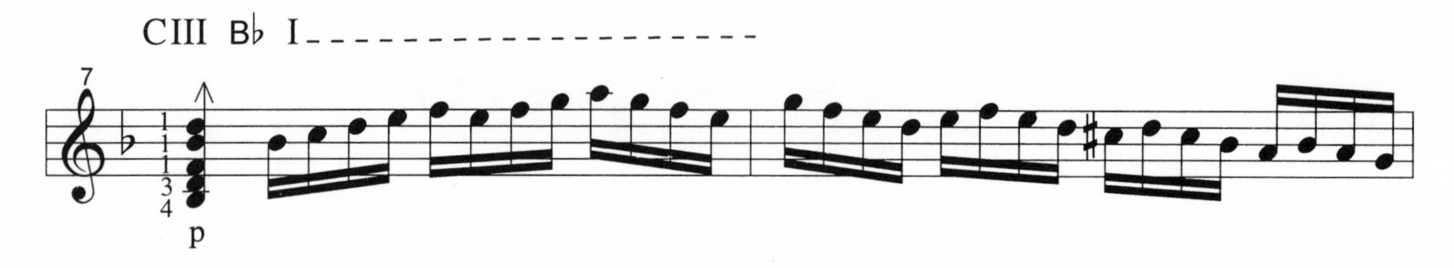


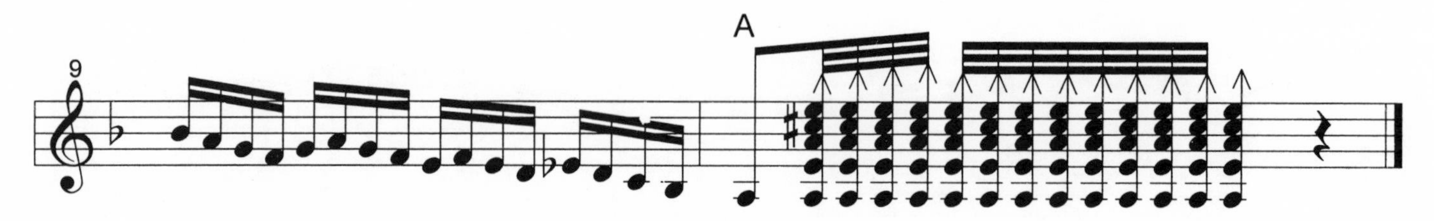

# Falseta 8

Juan Serrano

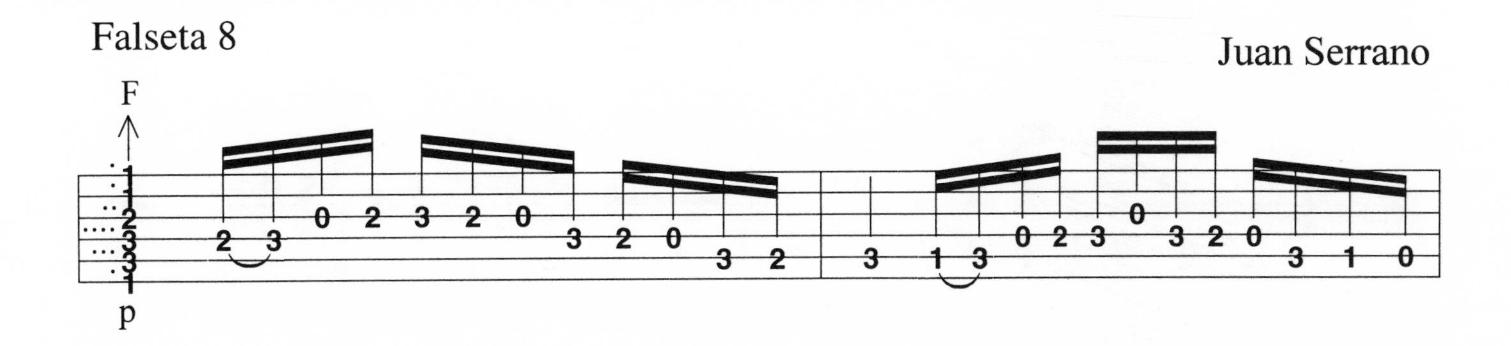


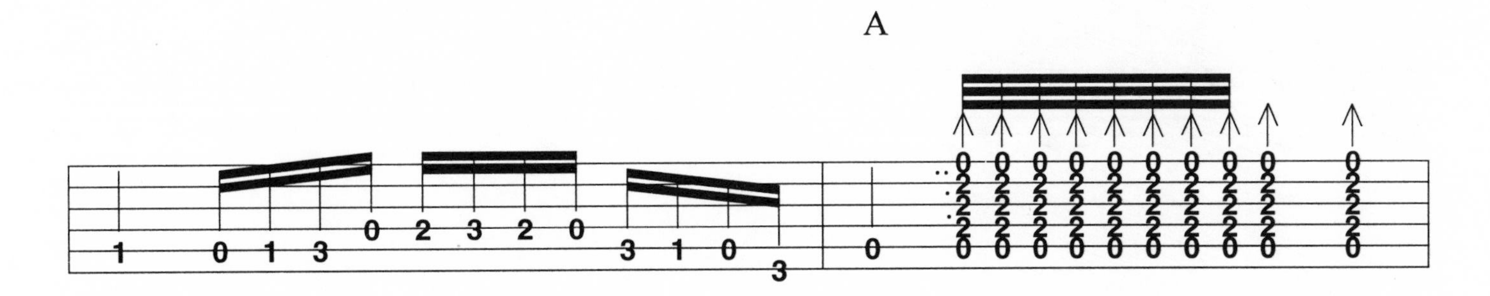


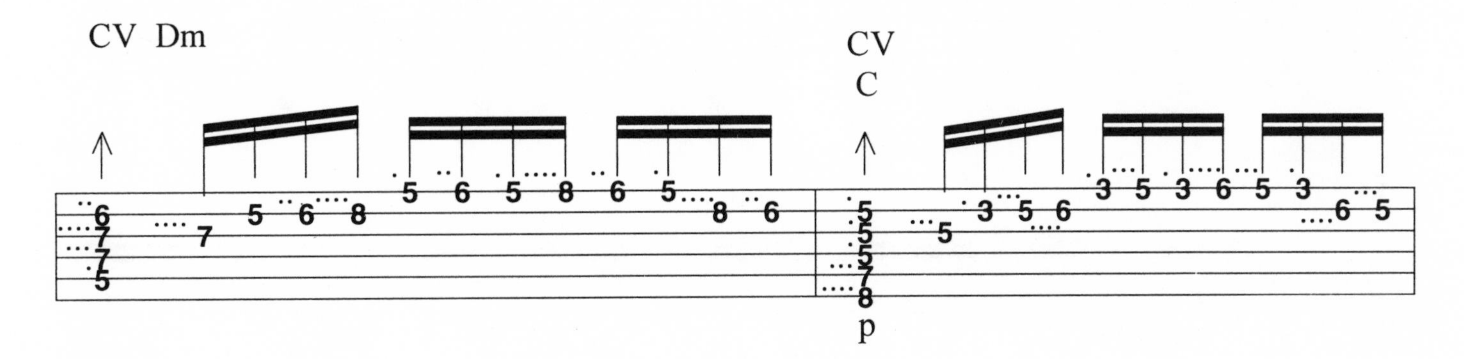

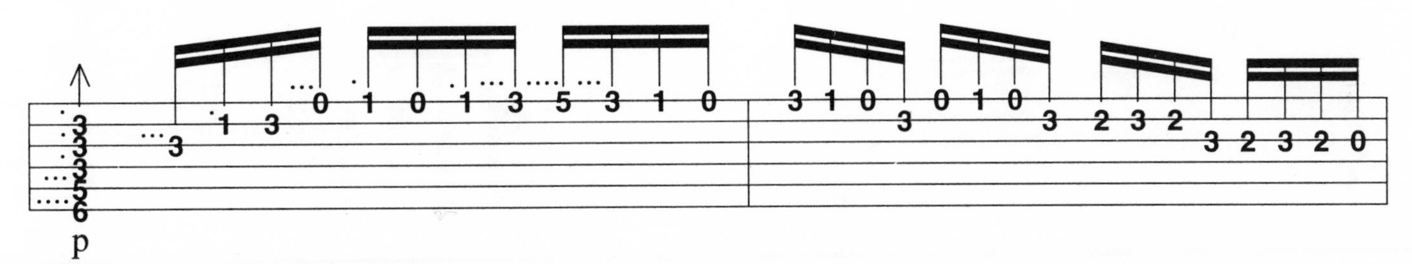


A

## Falseta 9

Juan Serrano

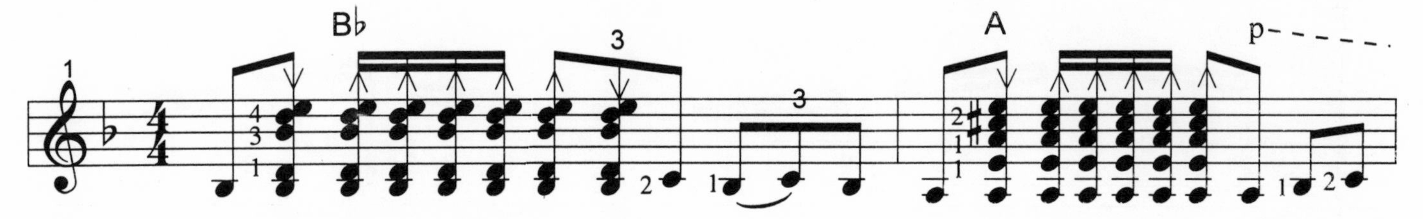

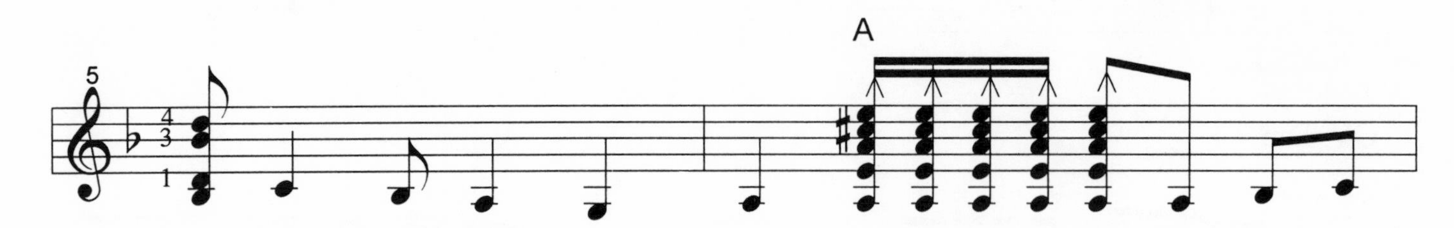

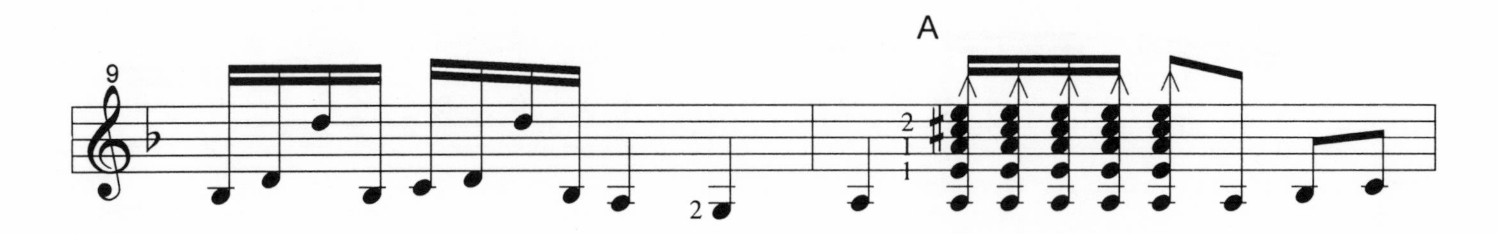

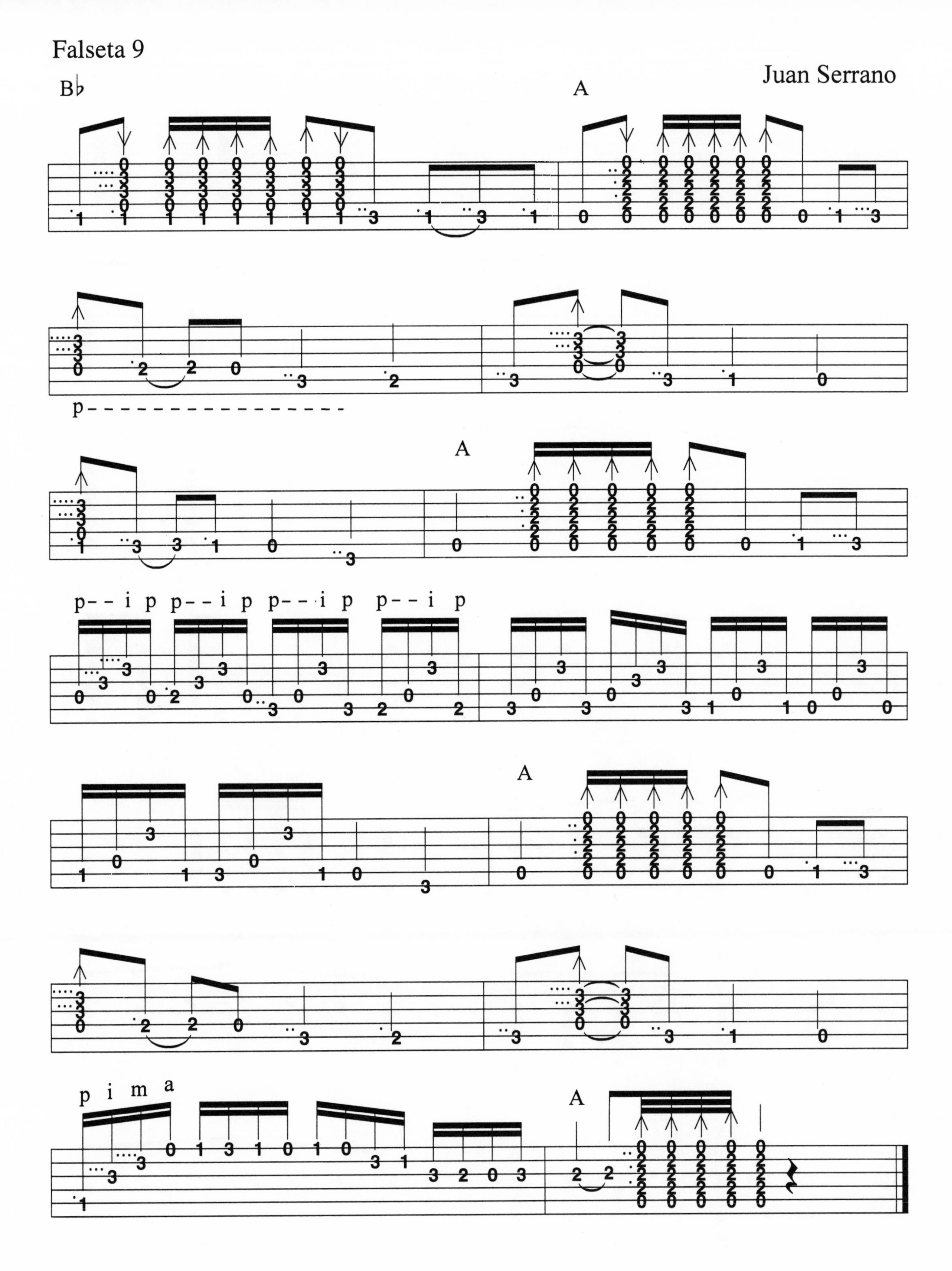
Falseta 9
Juan Serrano
B♭
A
p- - - - - - - - - - - - - - - - -
A
p- - i p p- - i p p- - i p p- - i p
A
p i m a
A

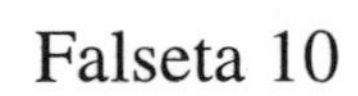


Juan Serrano

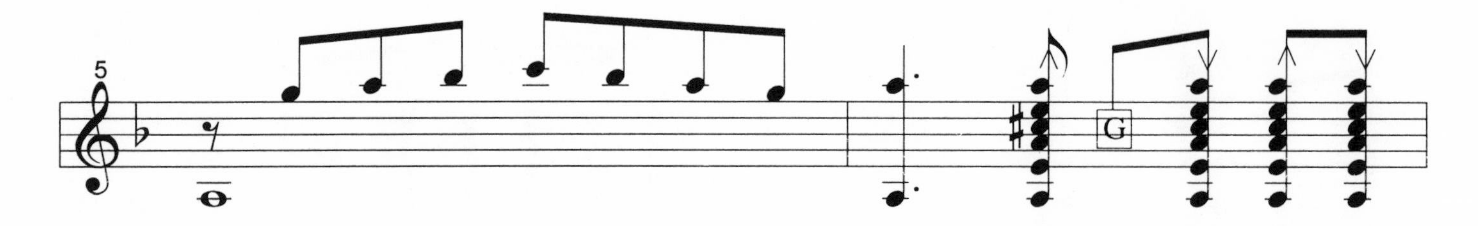

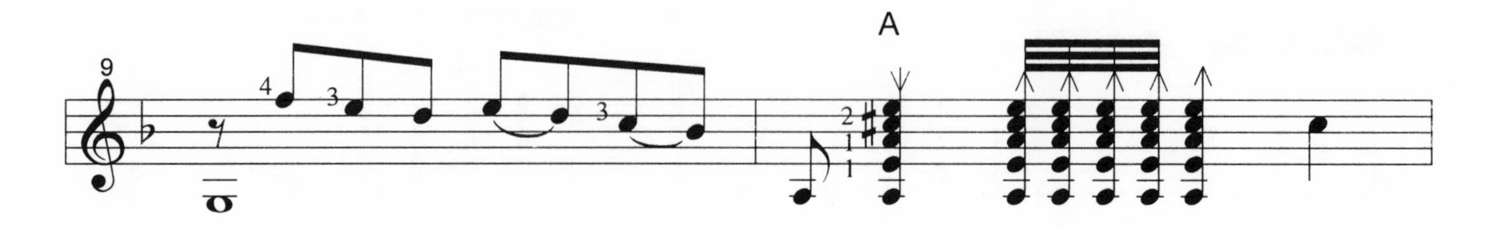


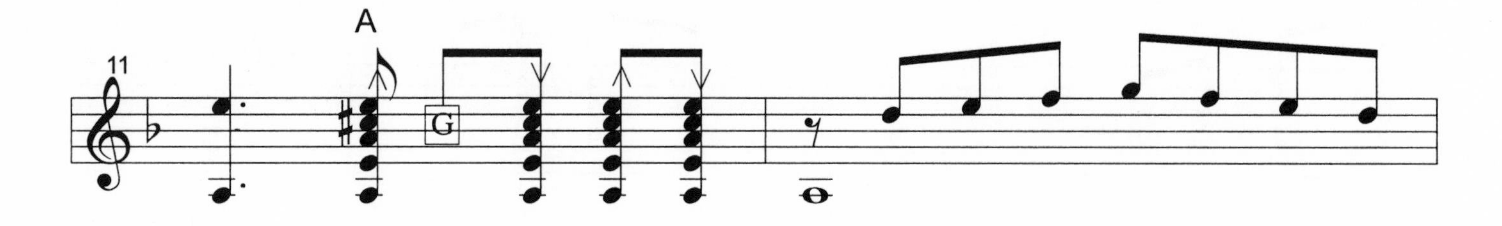


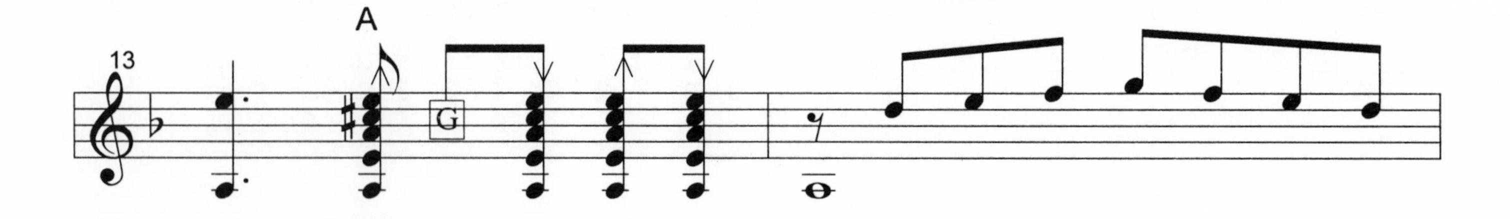

A
15
2
1
1
G

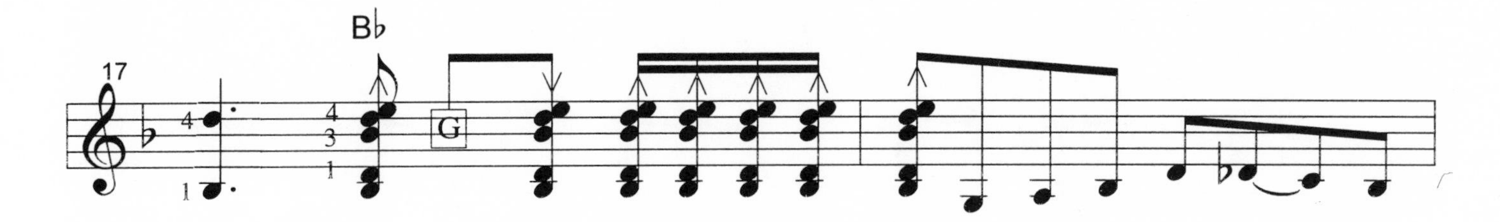
B♭
17
4
1
4
3
1
G

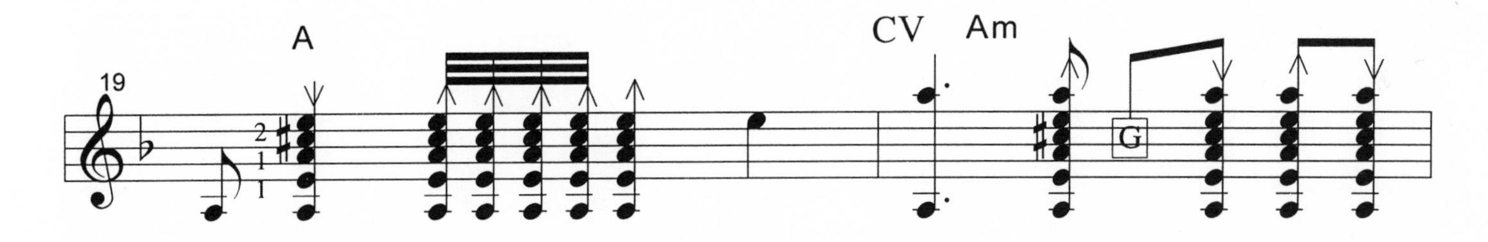
A
19
2
1
1
CV Am
G

CV
21
G

CV
23
G

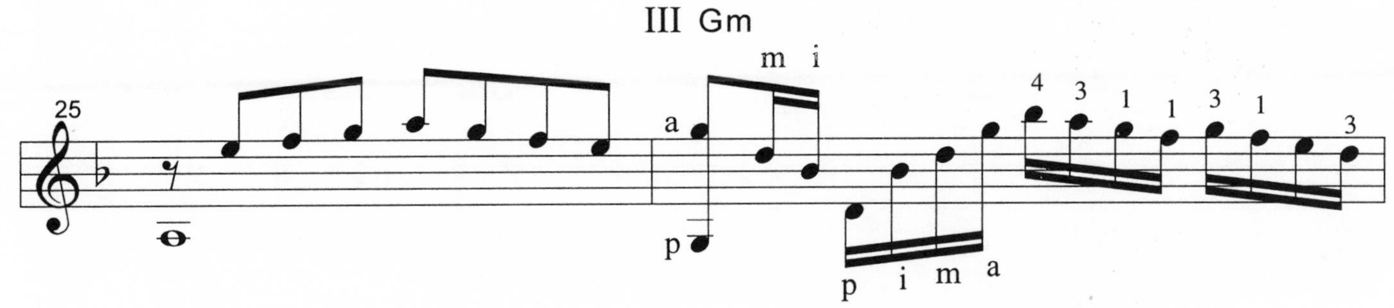
III Gm
25
m i
a
p
4 3 1 1 3 1 3
p i m a

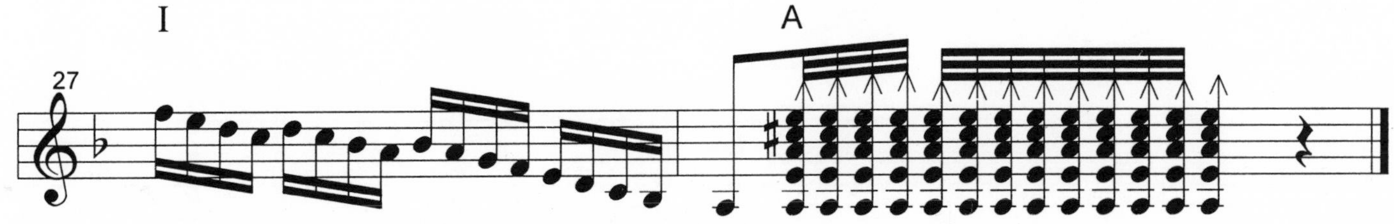
I
27
A

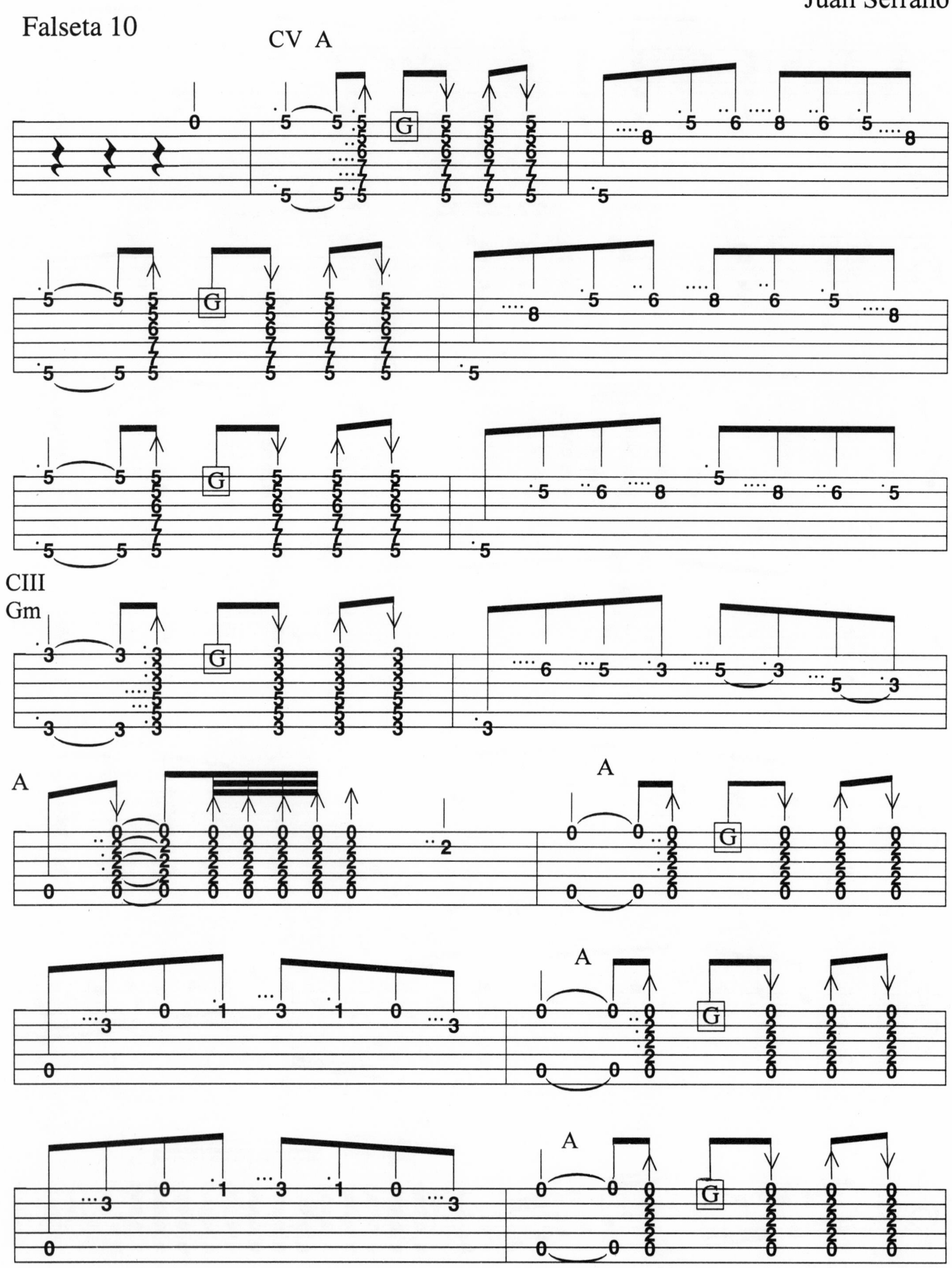
Juan Serrano
Falseta 10
CV A
G
CIII
Gm
A

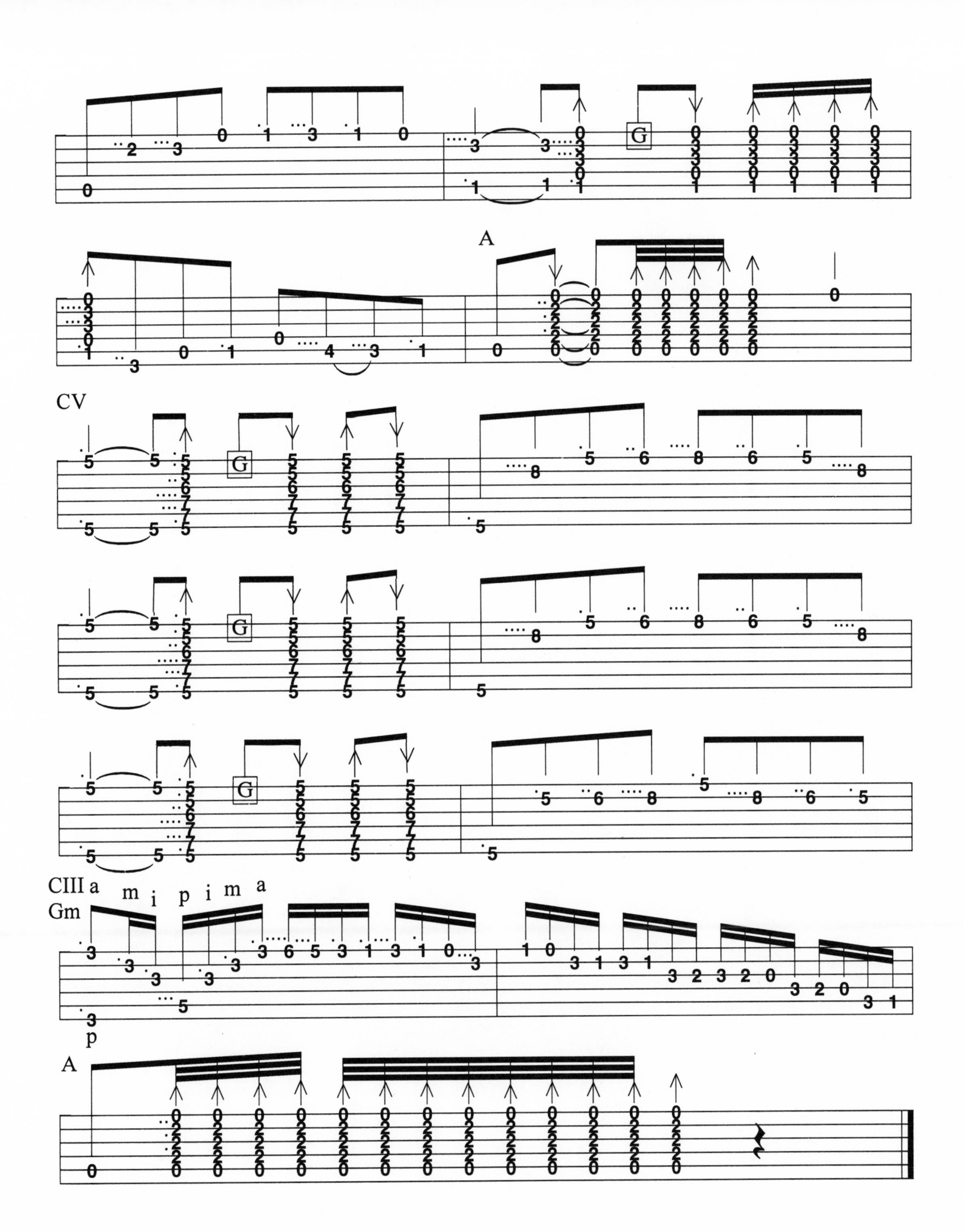
G
A
CV
G
G
G
CIII
Gm
a m i p i m a
p
A

طرانطس

# TARANTAS

Tarantas, like Granainas are a free flamenco form derived from the fandango. They are played in the key of B minor and are one of the most melodic forms among the flamenco music. Their origin is from an Andalucian town called Linares.

It is recommended that the last five measures of the first falseta be practiced repeatedly because all of the Tarantas falsetas have the same or very similar endings. The end of the arpeggio of measure 8 is executed by dragging the ring finger of the right hand from the second to the sixth string; and connecting with the legatos of the left hand played with fingers 1 and 2.

The union of the five measures of the first falseta form the phrase that identifies the Tarantas. For this reason it is very important to memorize it in order to make it easier to connect at the end of the other falsetas.

Once again, it is recommended to strictly follow the marked symbols in each of the falsetas, the position of the left hand, the numbers that represent the strings and the fingering of both hands.

# TARANTAS

Las Tarantas, como las Granainas son formas libres derivadas de los Fandangos. Las Tarantas se tocan en el tono de Si menor y son unas de las formas mas melódicas entre la música flamenca. El lugar de origen de las Tarantas fue un pueblo de Andalucía, llamado Linares, por eso se conocen con el nombre de Tarantas de Linares.

Recomiendo que practiquen mucho los cinco últimos compases de la primera falseta, ya que todas las falsetas de las Tarantas tienen un final igual o muy parecido. El arpegio del compás #8 termina deslizando el dedo anular (a) de la mano derecha desde la segunda hasta la sexta cuerda, conectando con los ligados de la mano izquierda, que se ejecutan con los dedos 1 y 2.

El conjunto de los cinco compases de la primera falseta forman la frase que identifica a las Tarantas. Por eso es muy importante aprenderla de memoria, para que así sea mas fácil el conectarla en los finales de las otras falsetas.

Una vez mas, recomiendo que sigan estrictamente todos los símbolos marcados en cada una de las falsetas, posicion de la mano izquierda, los números que representan las cuerdas y la digitacion de ambas manos.

# *Tarantas*

Falseta 1

Juan Serrano

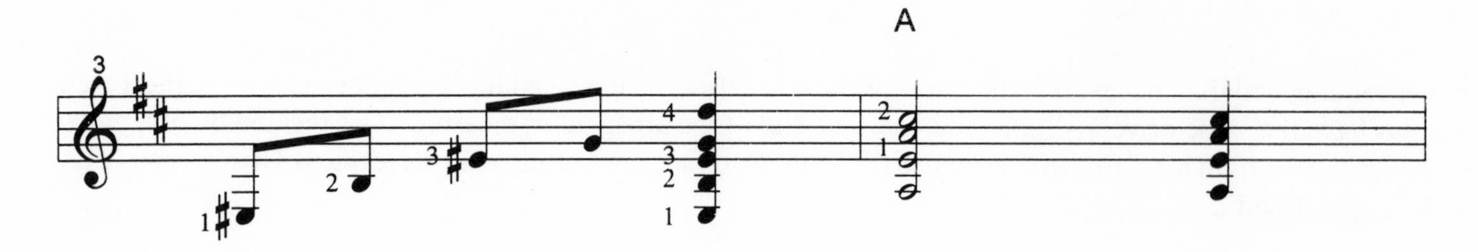

# *Tarantas*

Falseta 1

Juan Serrano

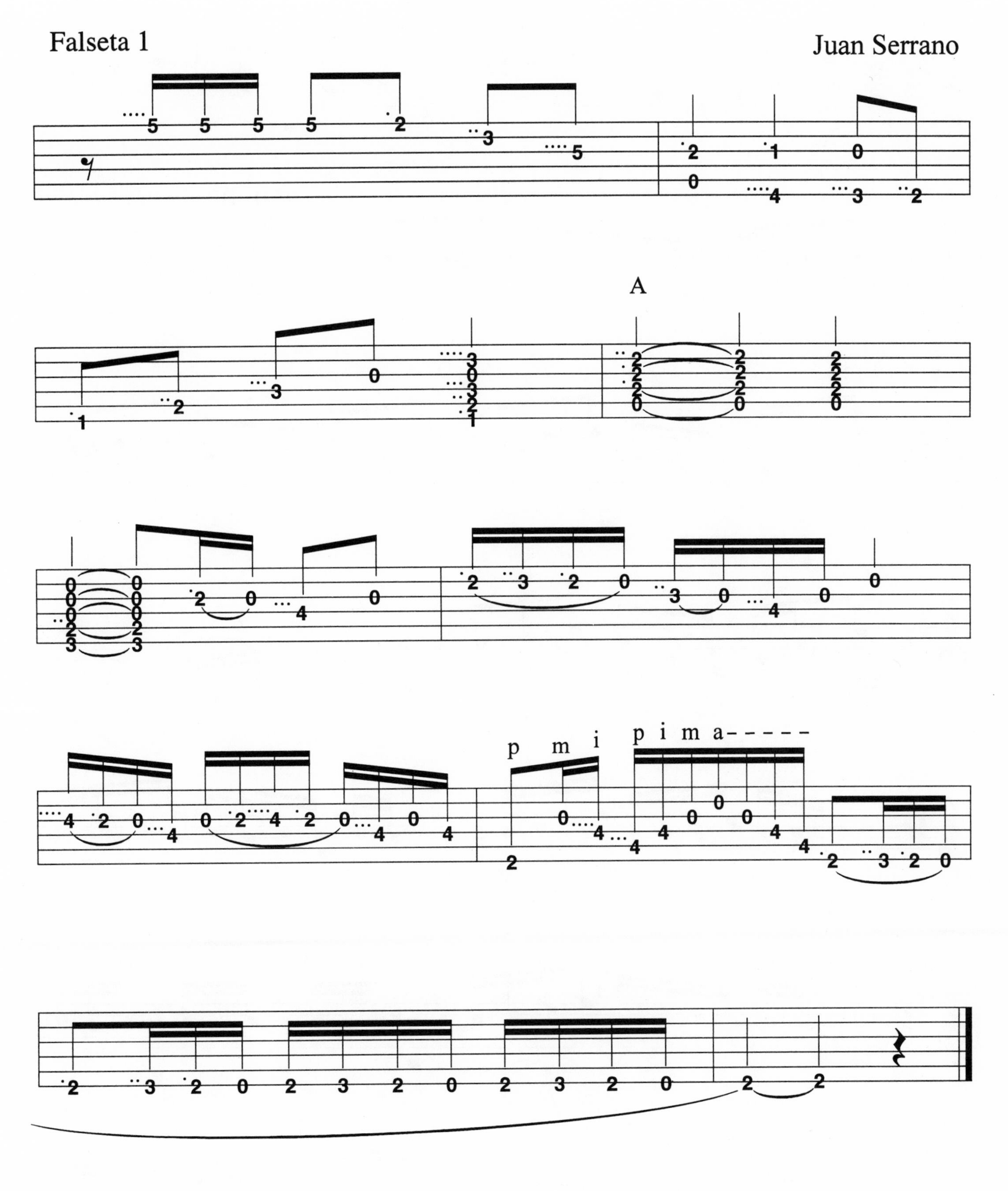

Falseta 2

Juan Serrano

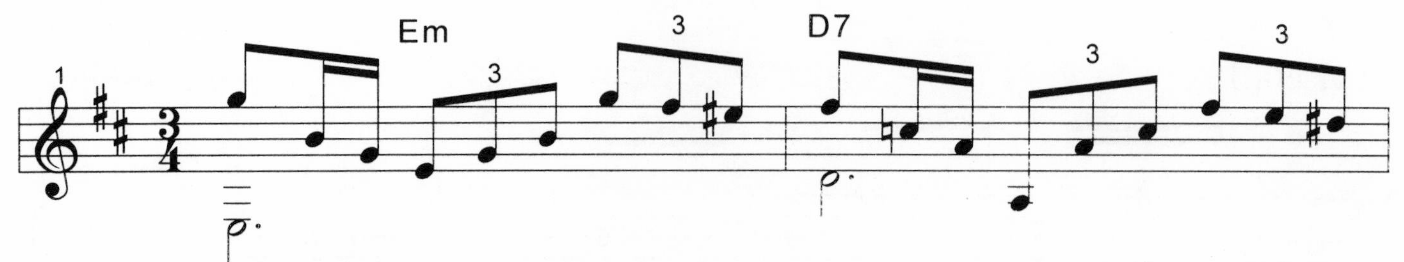

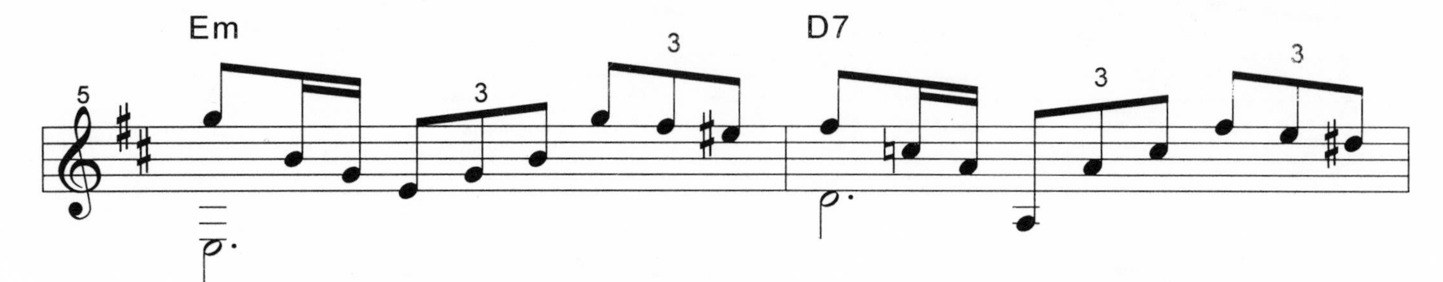


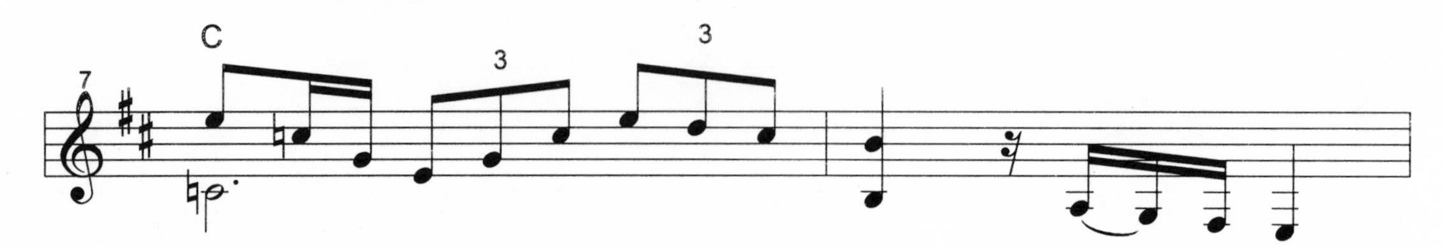

I
C III G
C III C
15
3 1
2

C II
Bm
17

A
G
19
4 2
3 1
3 2
1

II
21

22
1

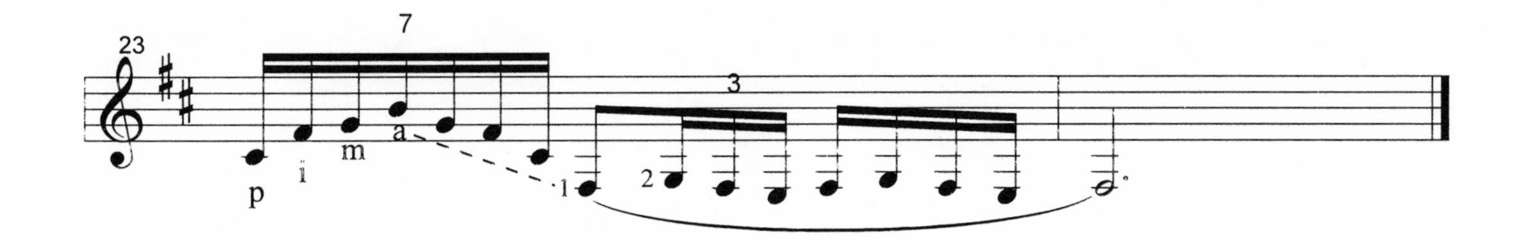
7
3
23
p i m a
1 2

Falseta 2

Juan Serrano

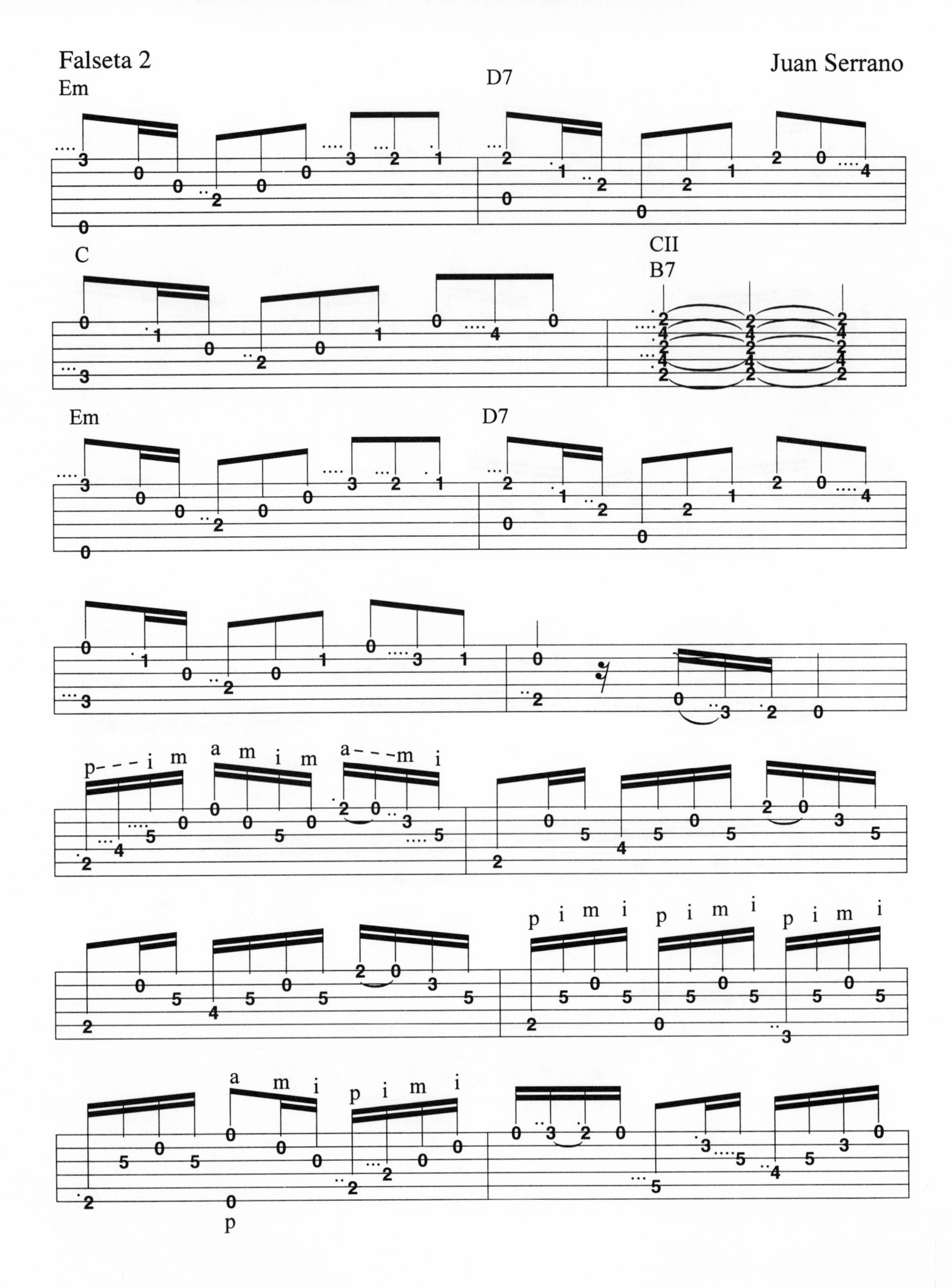

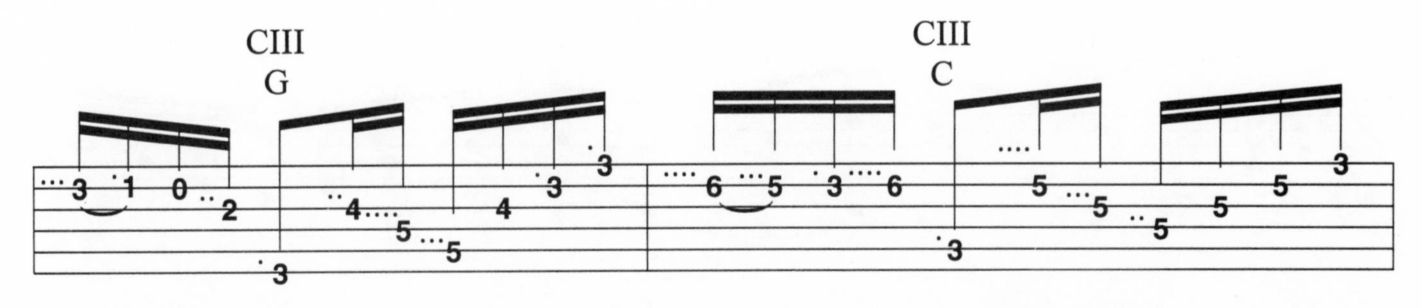
CIII
G
CIII
C

Bm

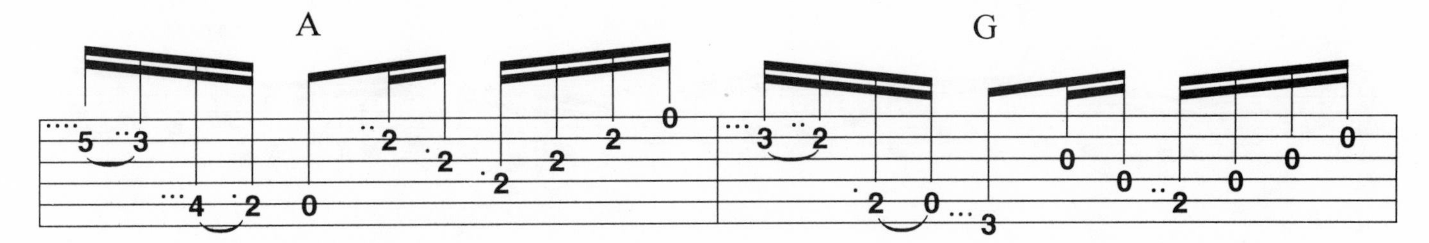
A
G

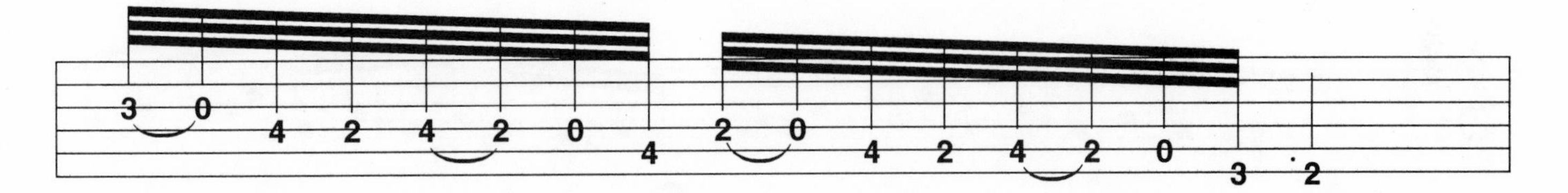

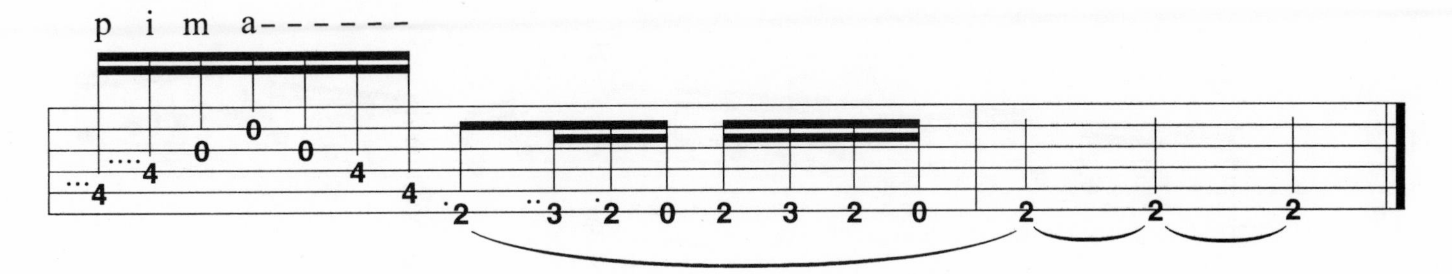
p i m a

Falseta 3

Juan Serrano

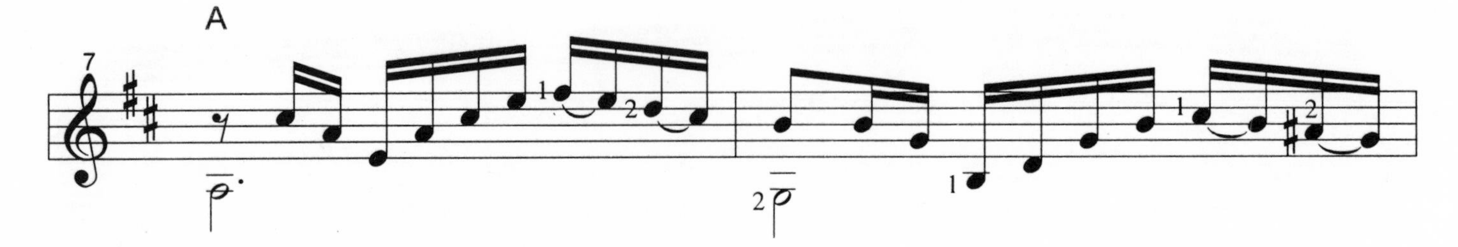

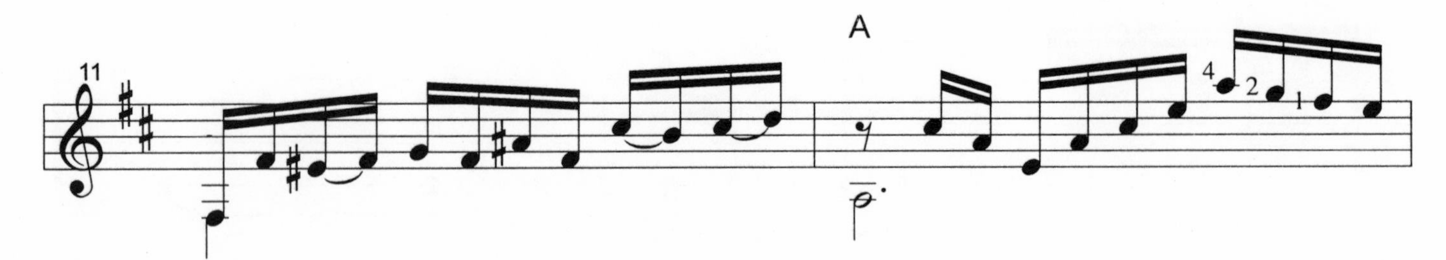


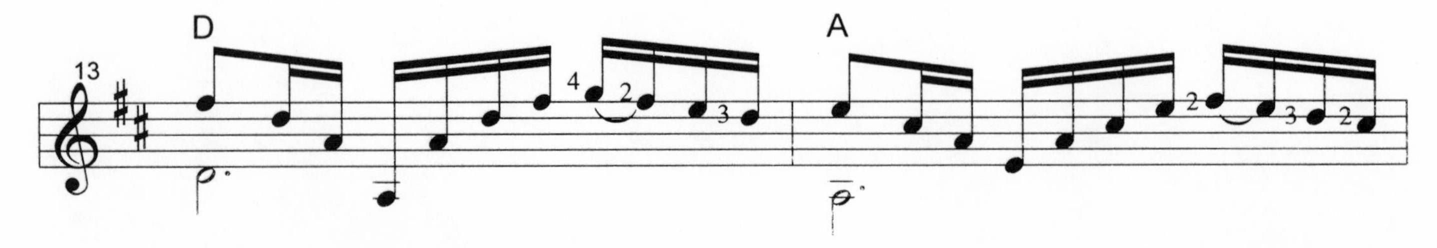

G
D7

G

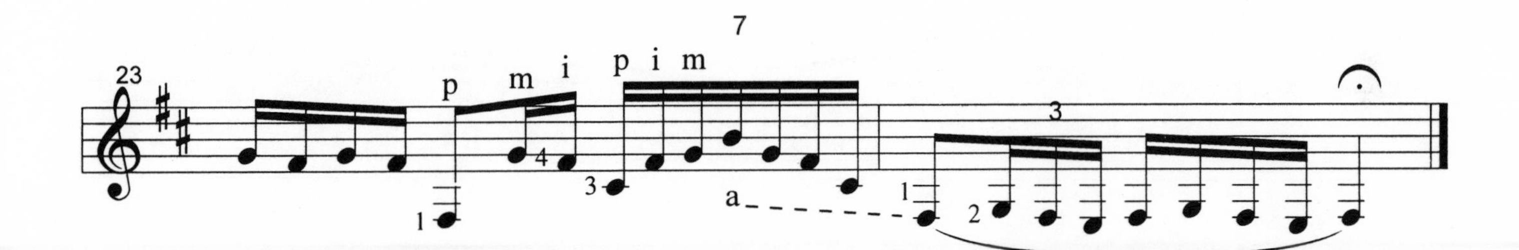
p m i p i m
a

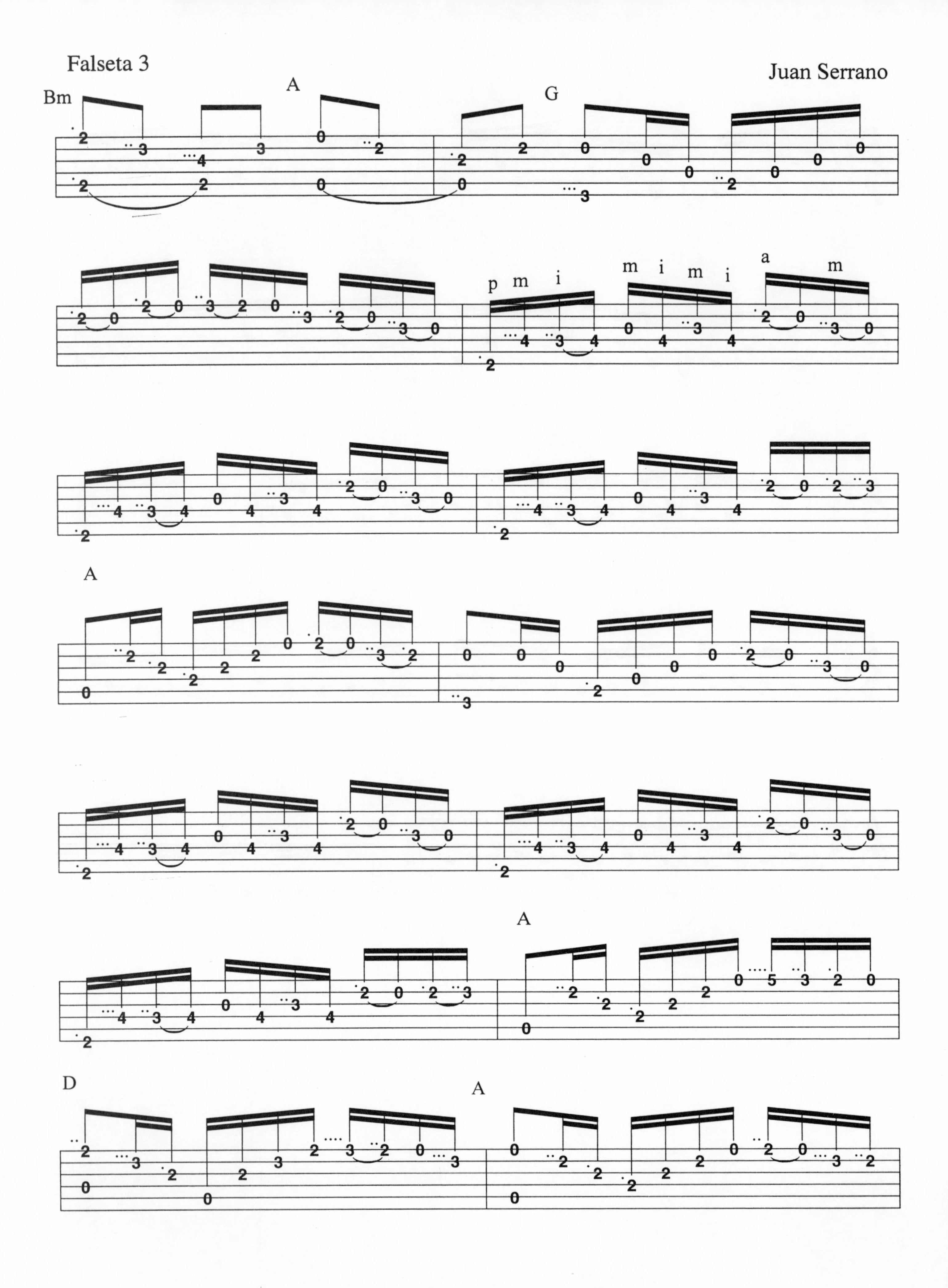
Falseta 3
Juan Serrano
Bm
A
G
p m i
m i m i
a m
A
A
D
A

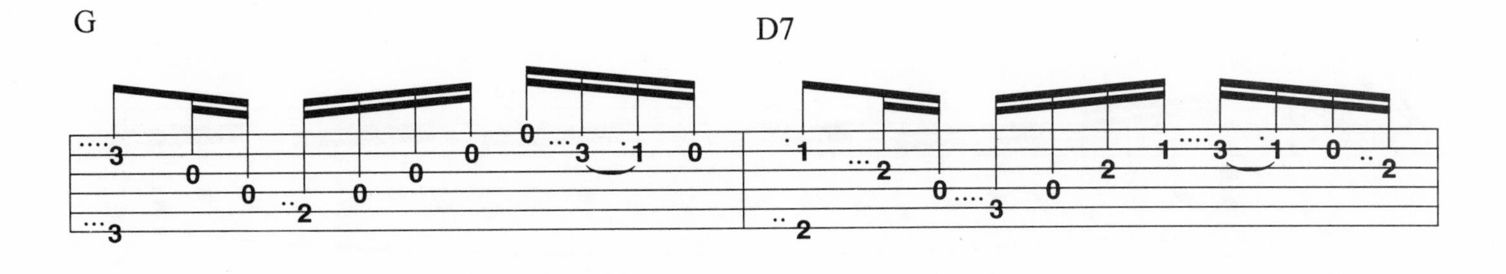
G
D7

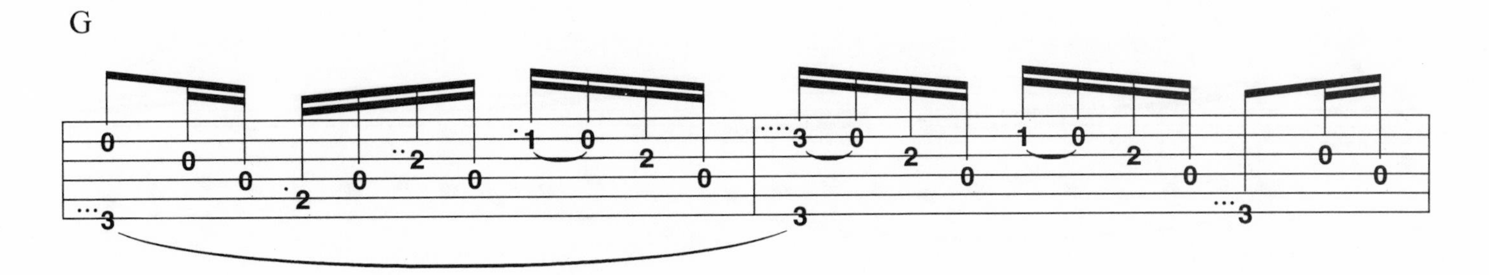
G

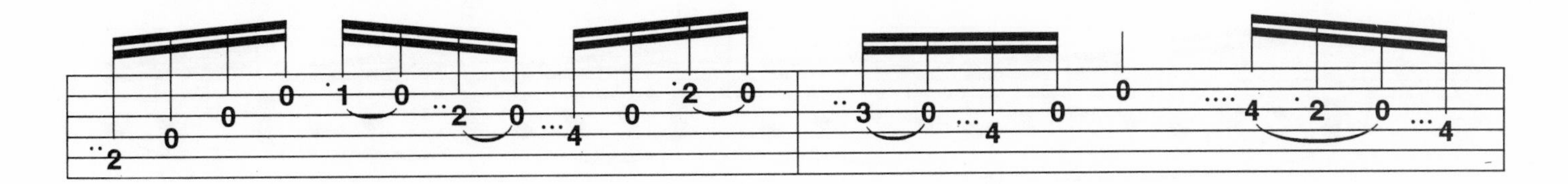

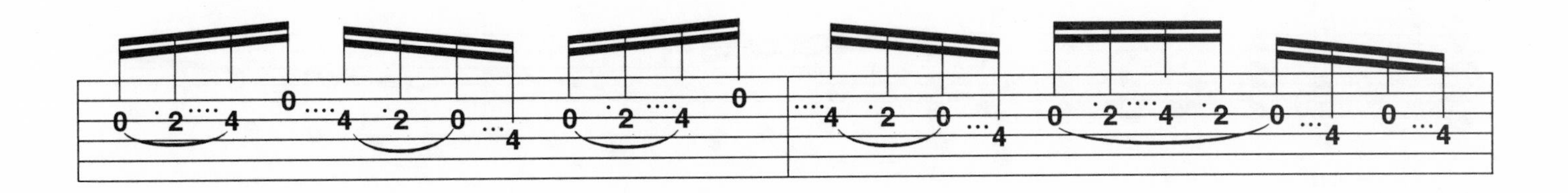

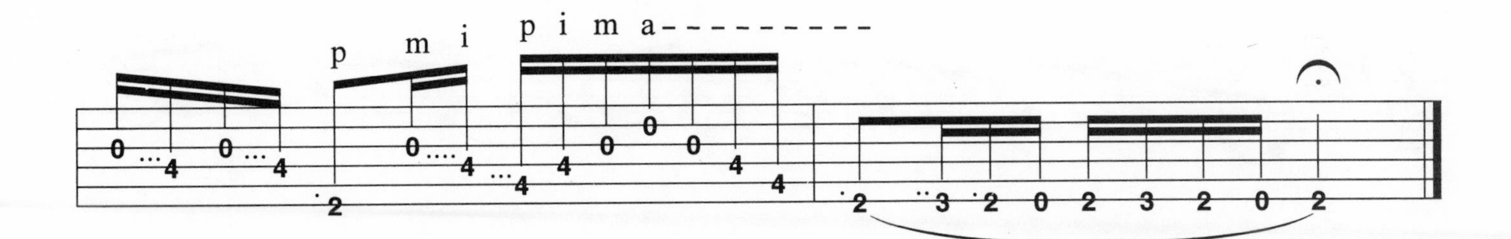
p m i p i m a

Falseta 4

Juan Serrano

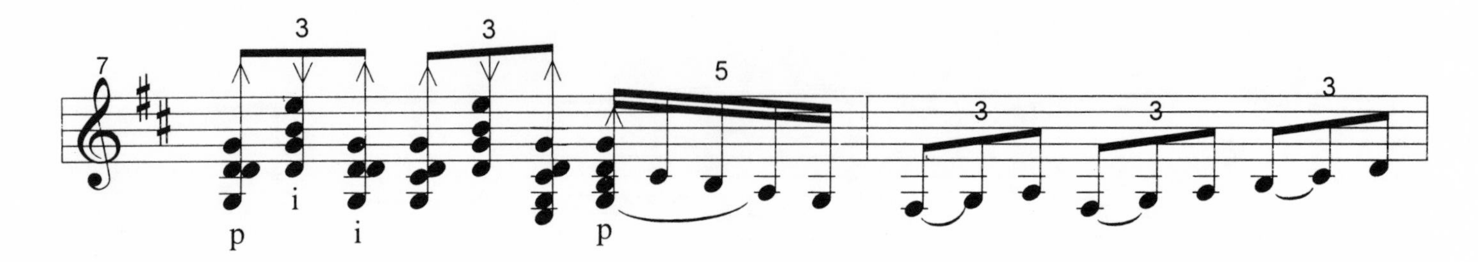


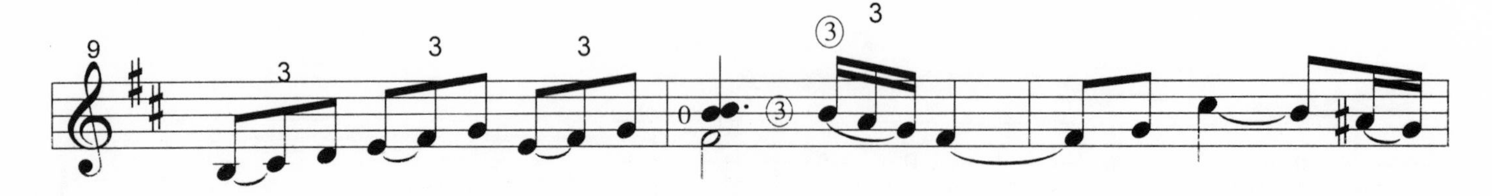

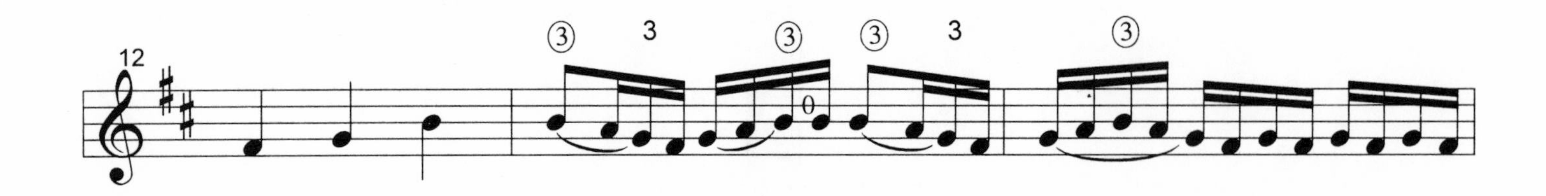

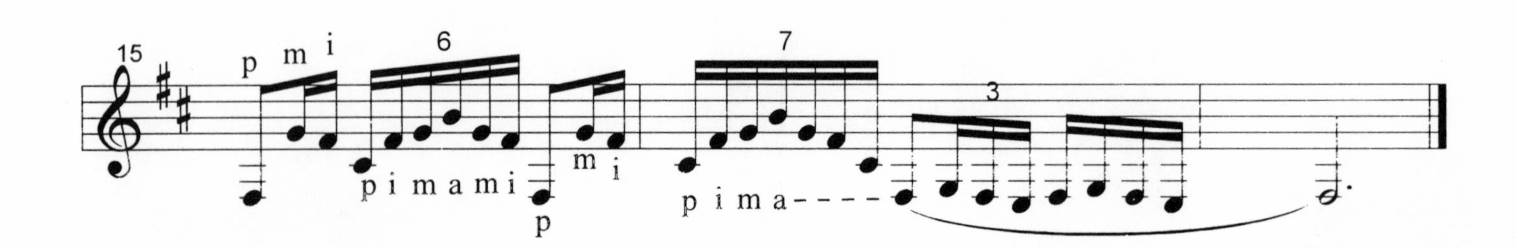

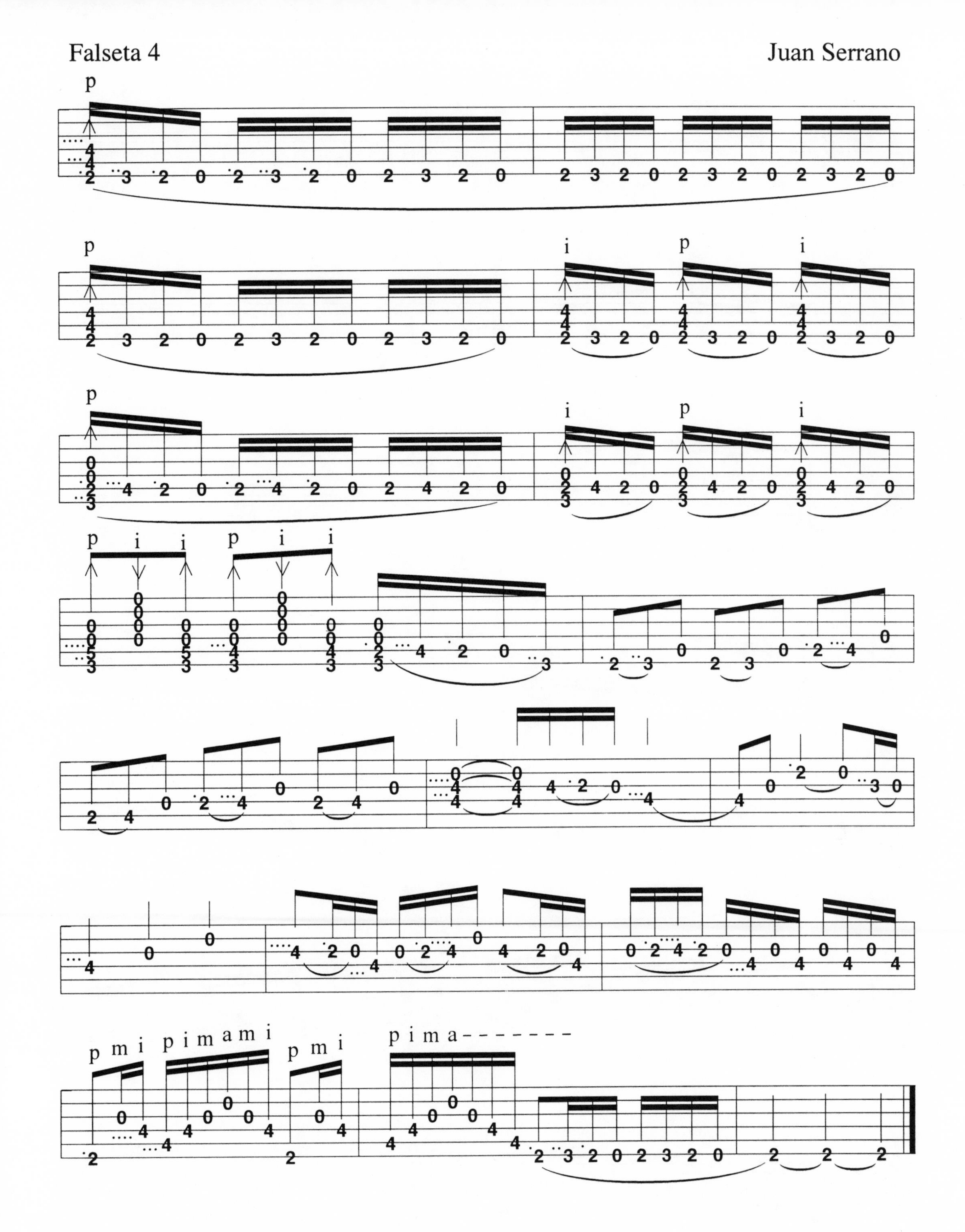
Falseta 4
Juan Serrano

## Falseta 5

Juan Serrano

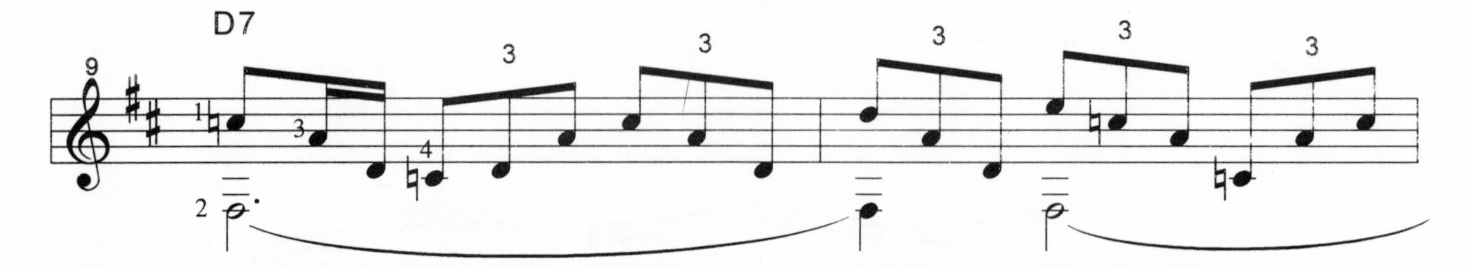

15
3
3
3
3

17
③
③
③
4
1
3
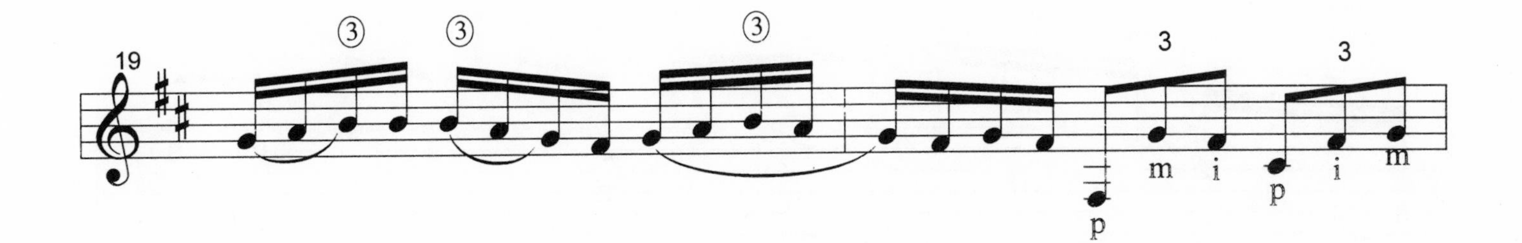
19
③
③
③
3
3
m i
p i m
p
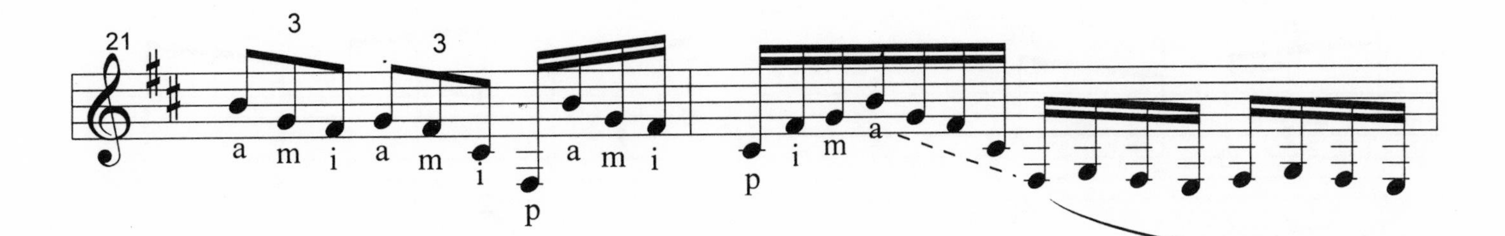
21
3
3
a m i a m i
a m i
p
p i m a

23

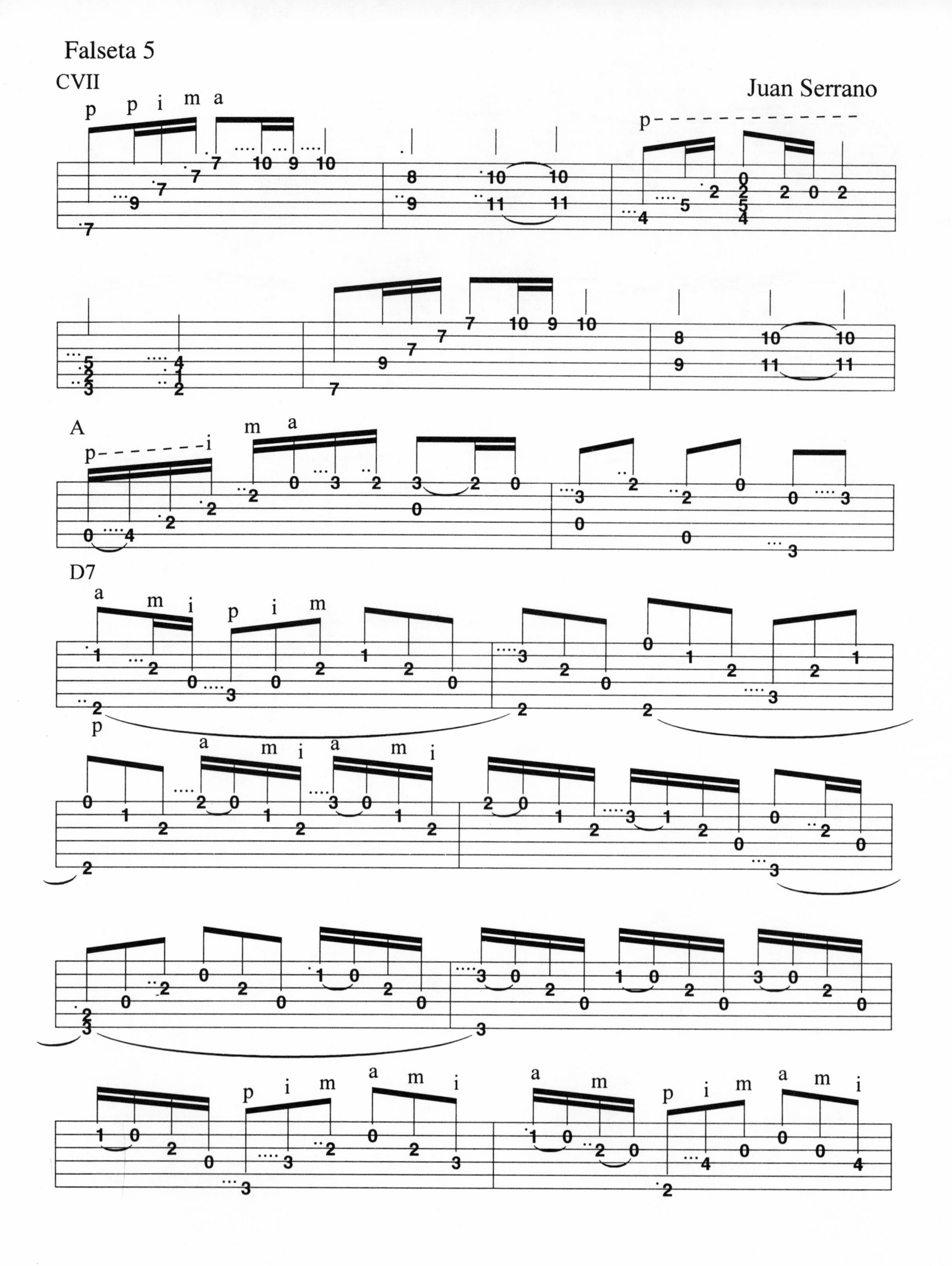
Falseta 5
CVII
Juan Serrano
A
D7

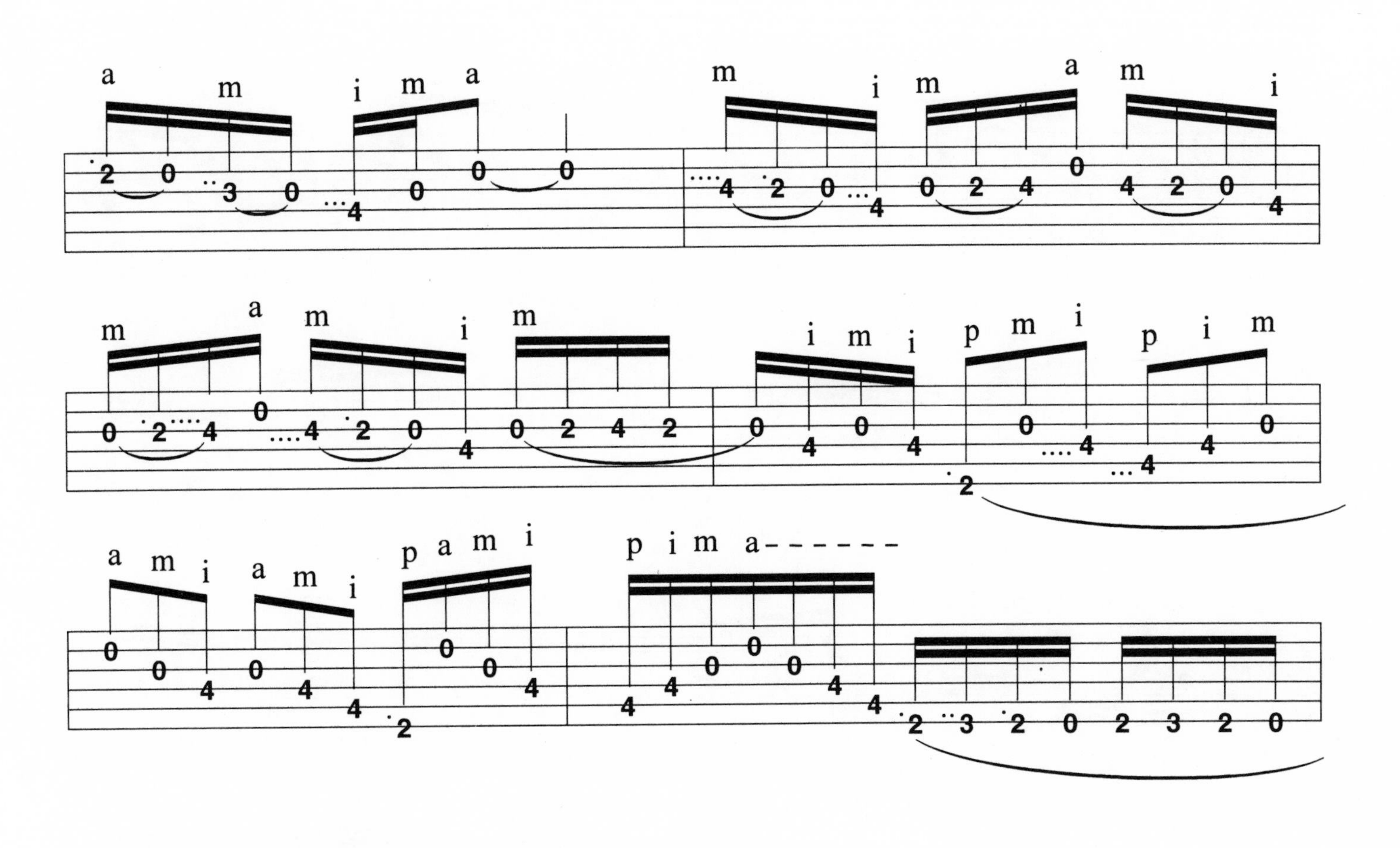

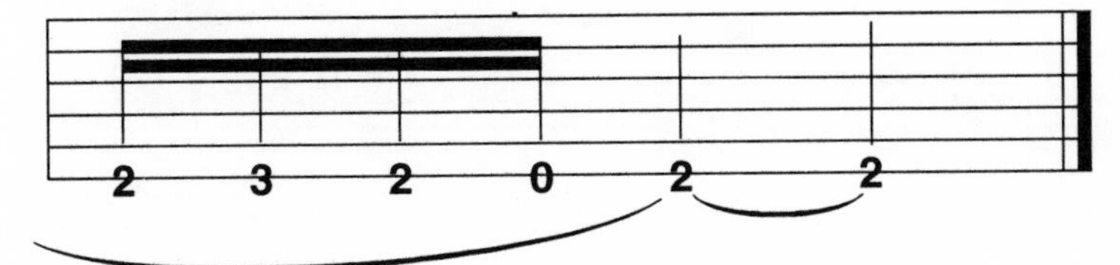

Falseta 6

Juan Serrano

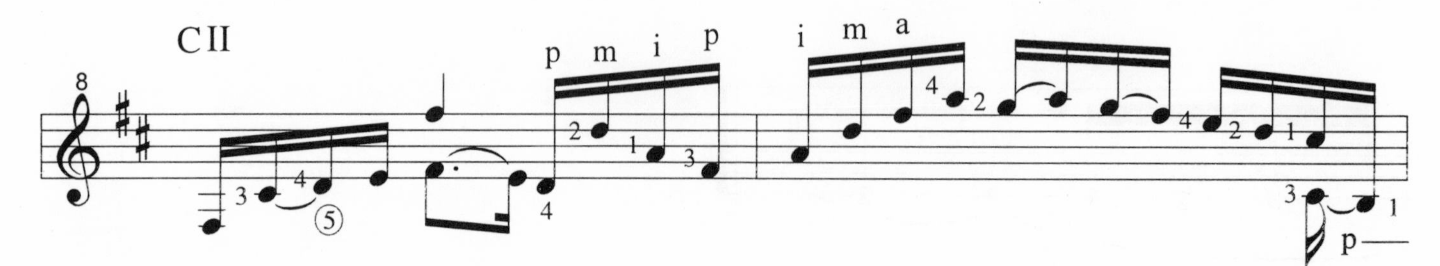

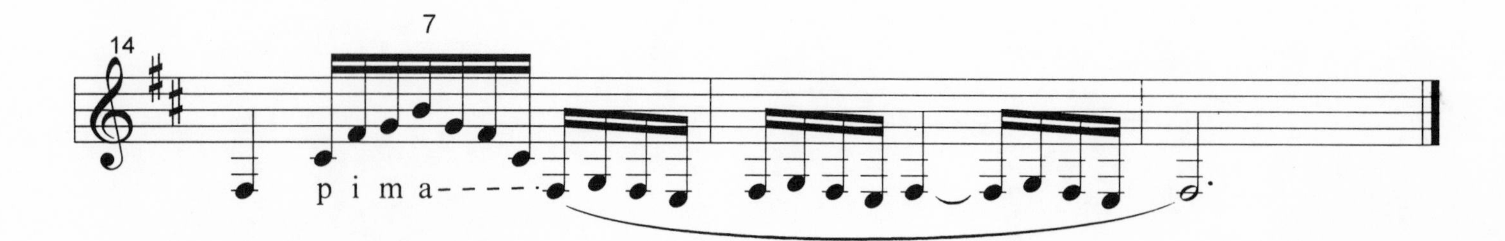

## Falseta 6

Juan Serrano

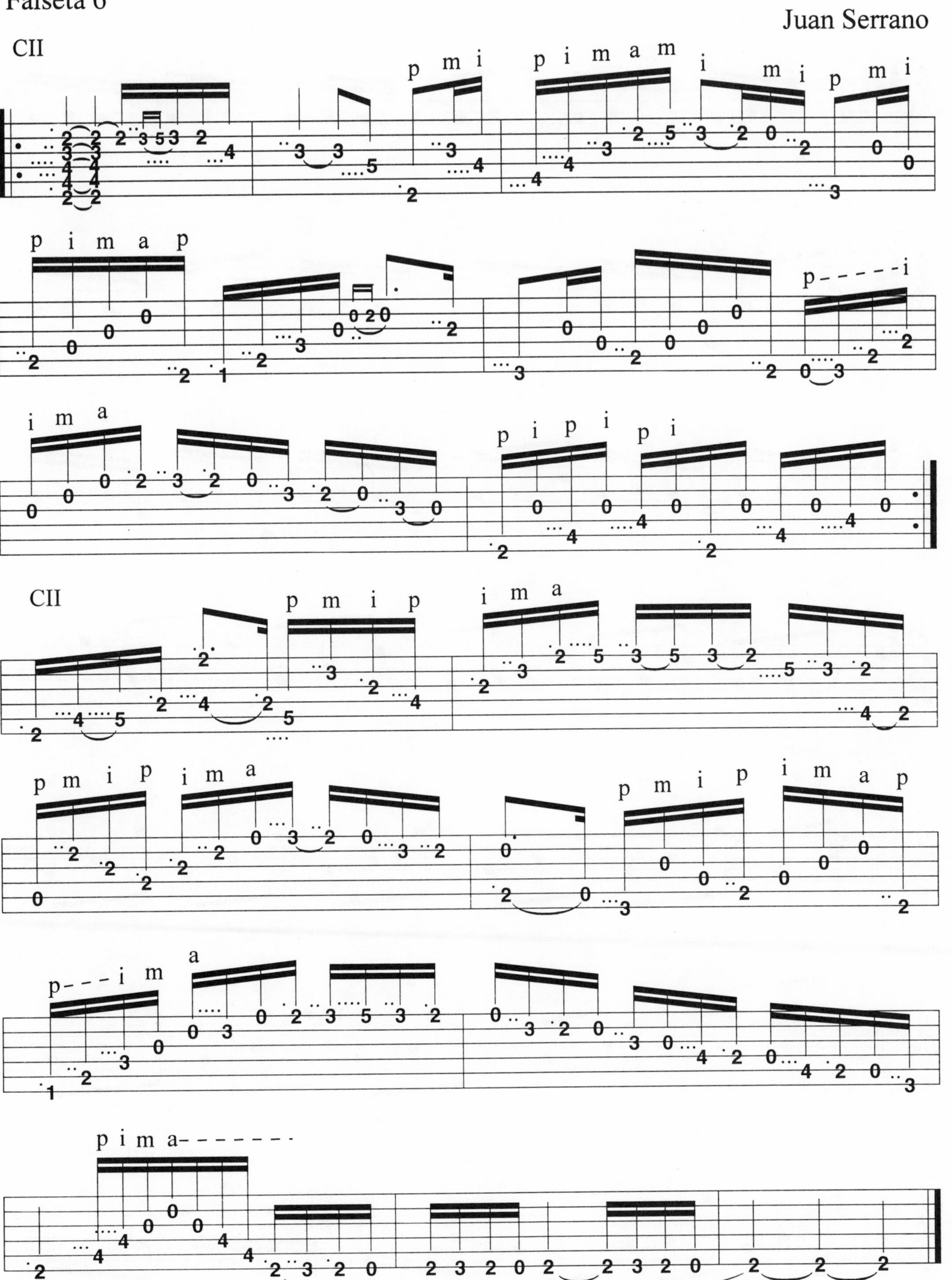

Falseta 7

Juan Serrano

II

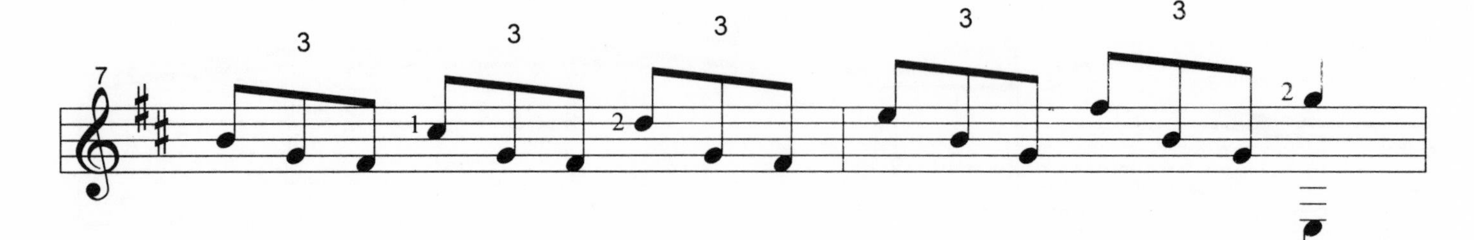

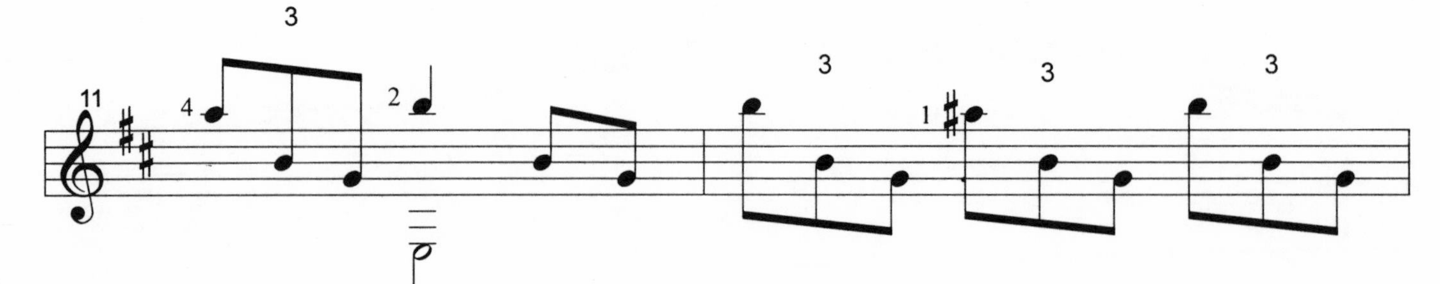

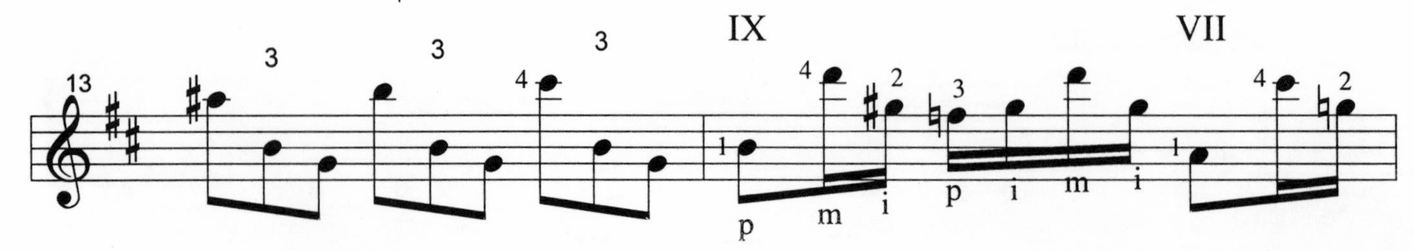

15
CII

17
D
A
G

19
D7

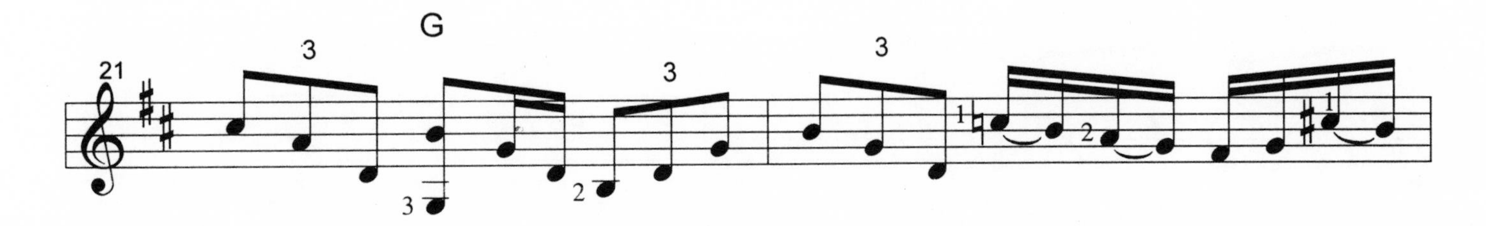
21
G

23

25
7
p m i p i m a

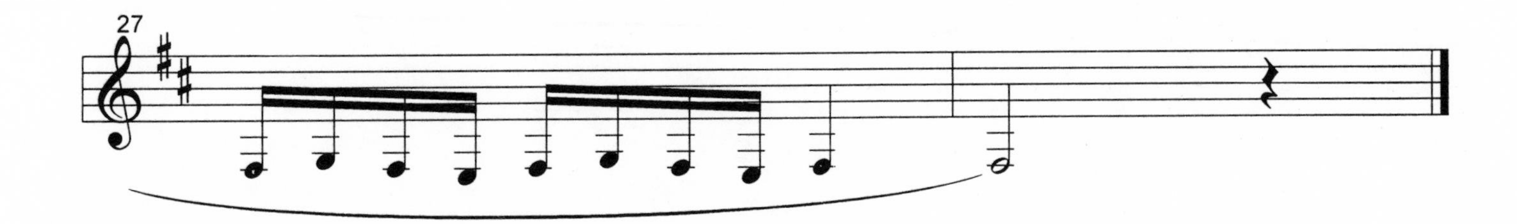
27

## Falseta 7

Juan Serrano

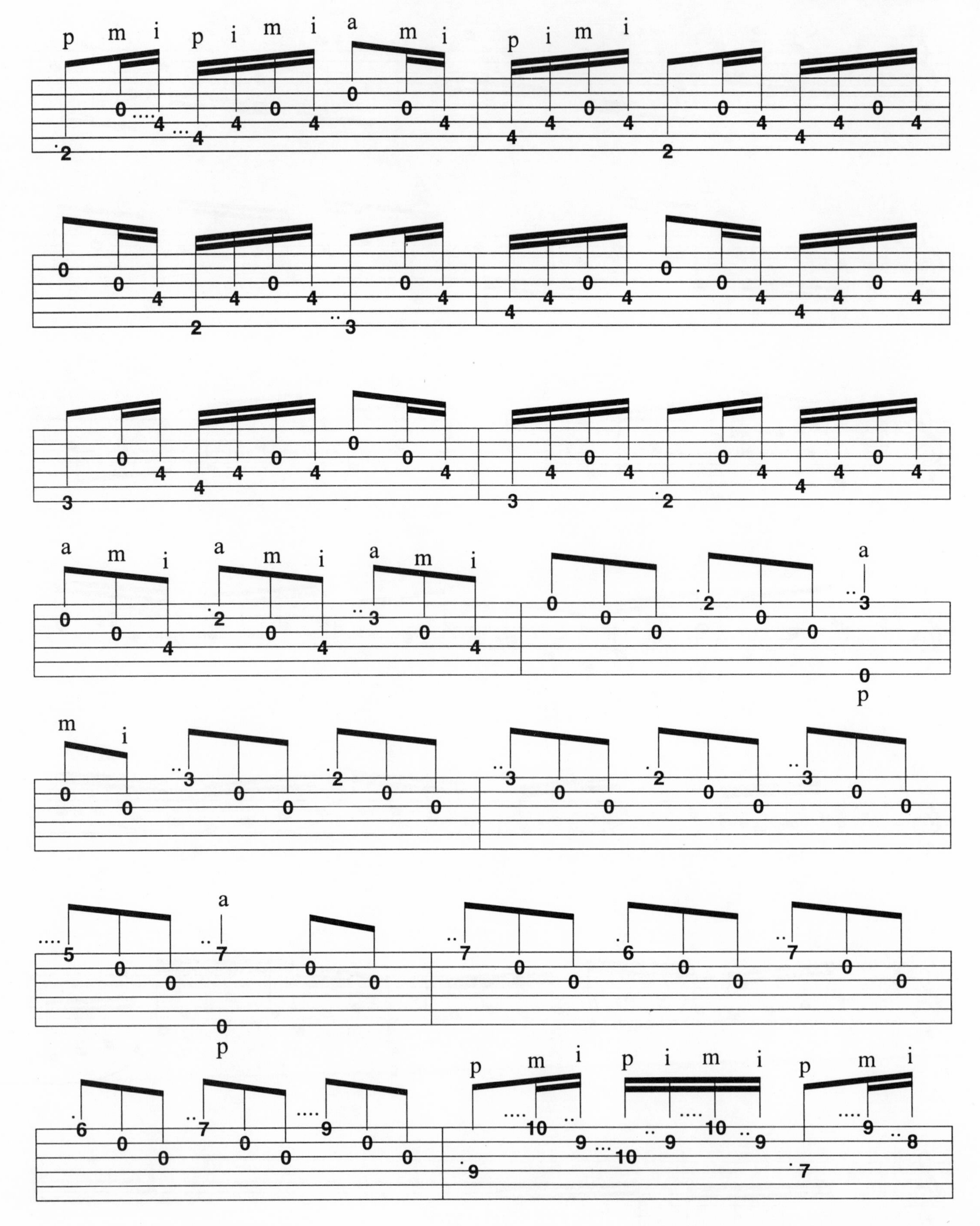

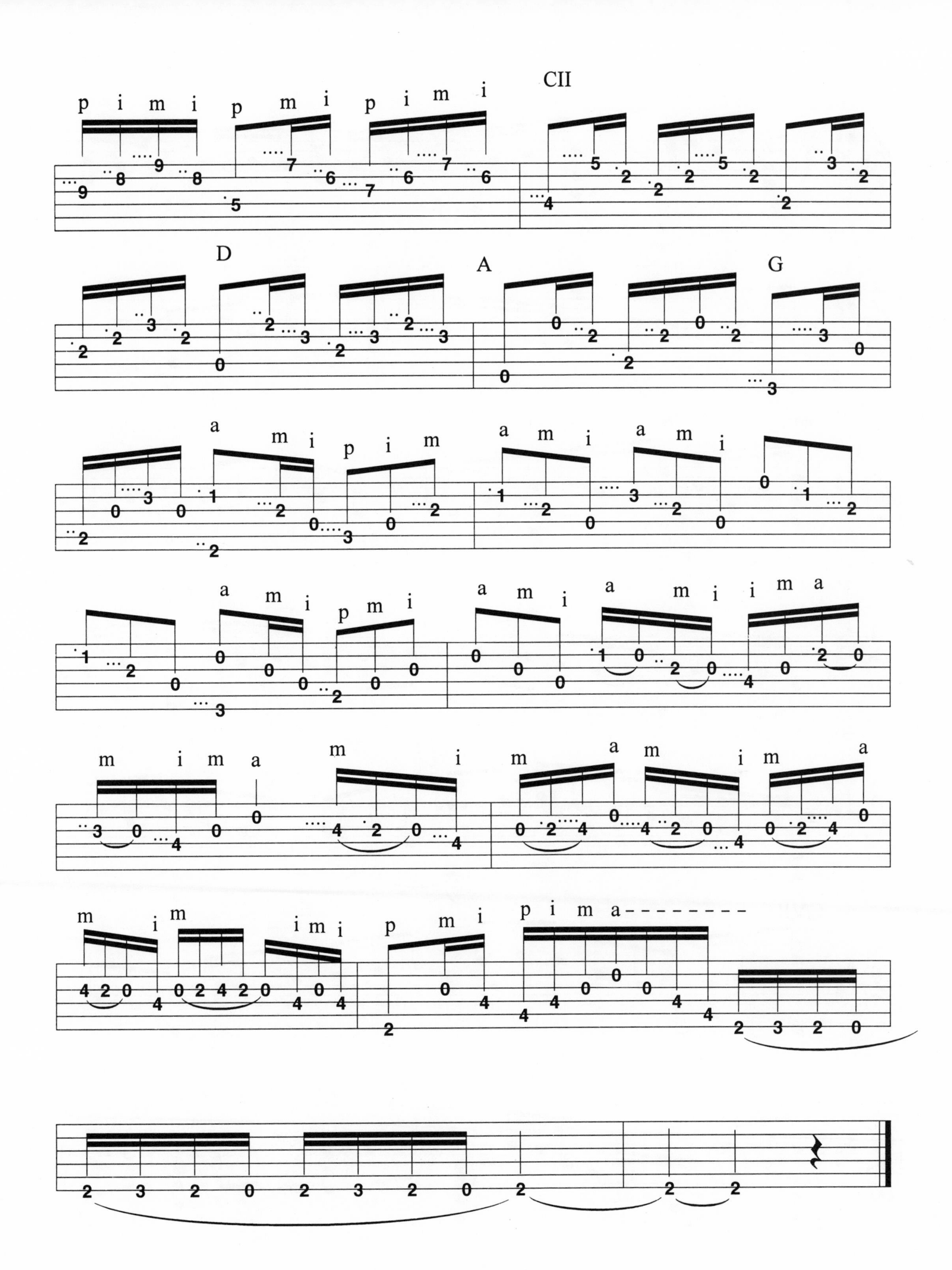
p i m i p m i p i m i
CII
D
A
G
a m i p i m
a m i a m i
a m i p m i
a m i a m i i m a
m i m a m i
m a m i m a
m i m i m i p m i
p i m a

Falseta 8

Juan Serrano

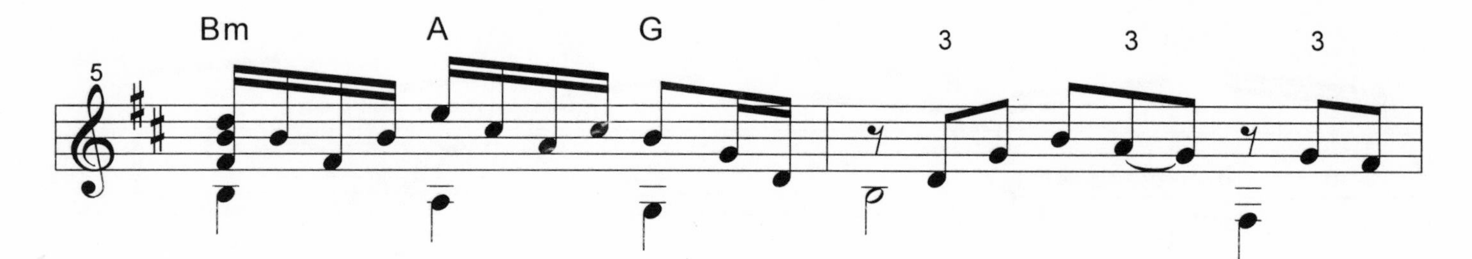

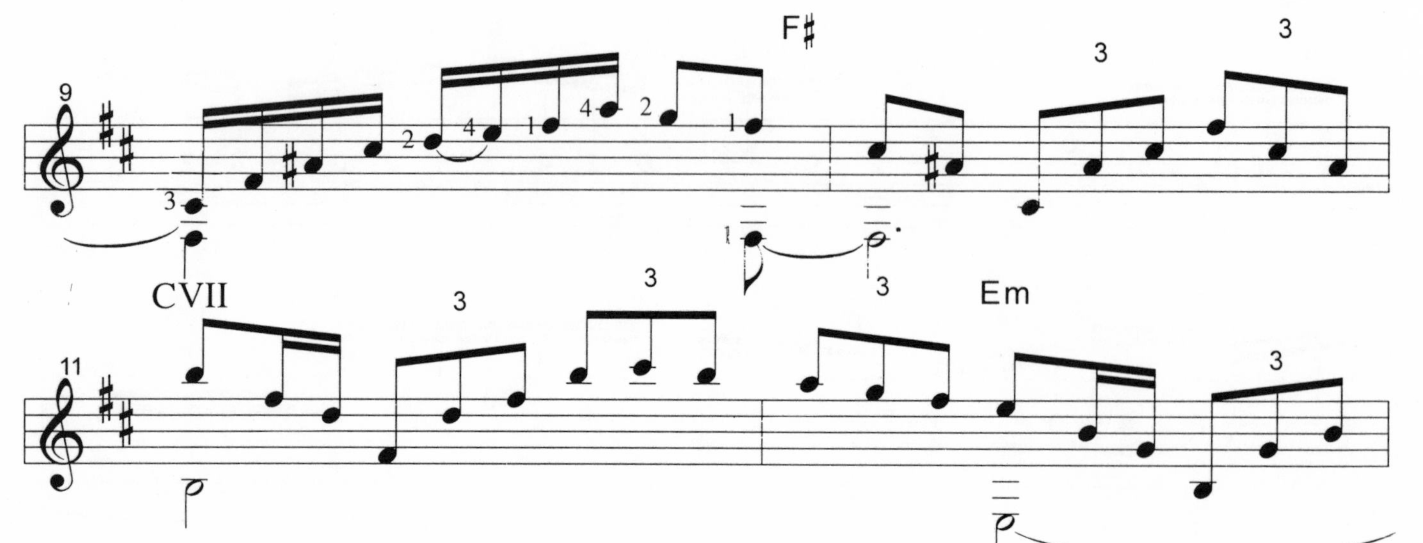


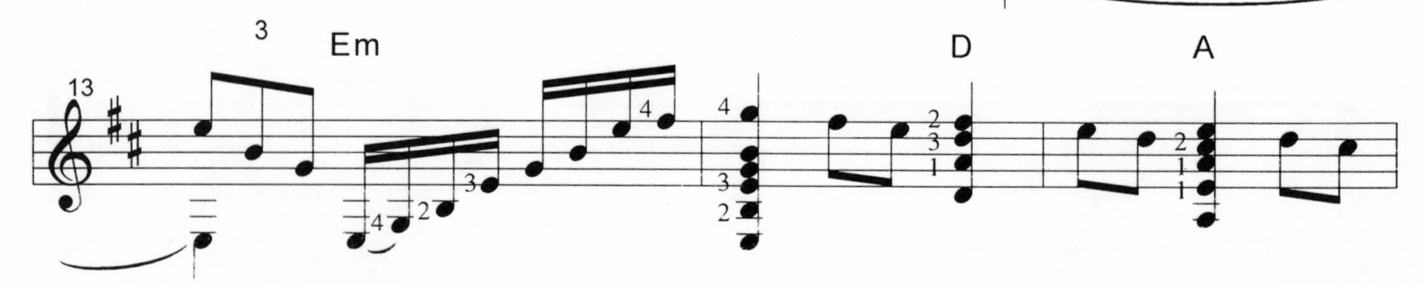

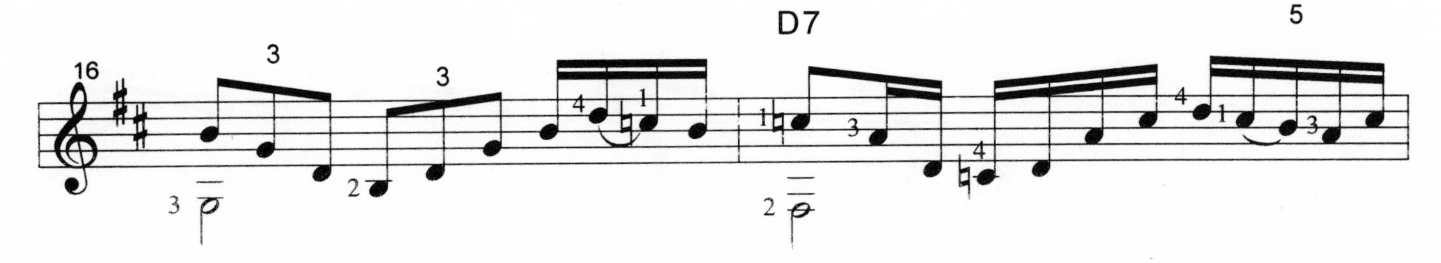
16
D7
5

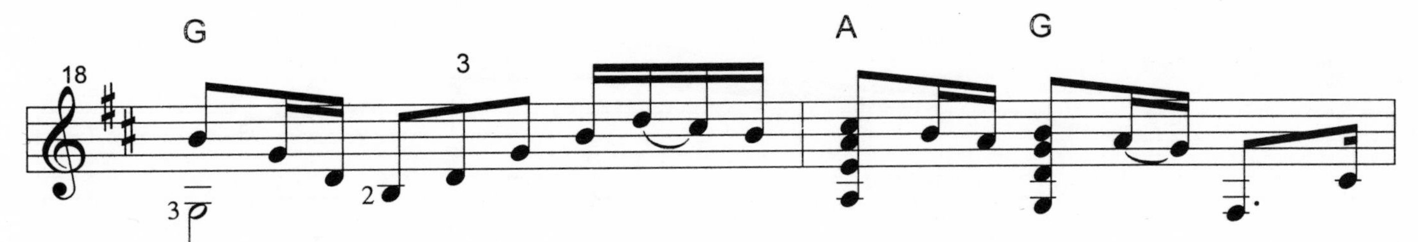
18
G
A
G

20
7
m i p i m a
p

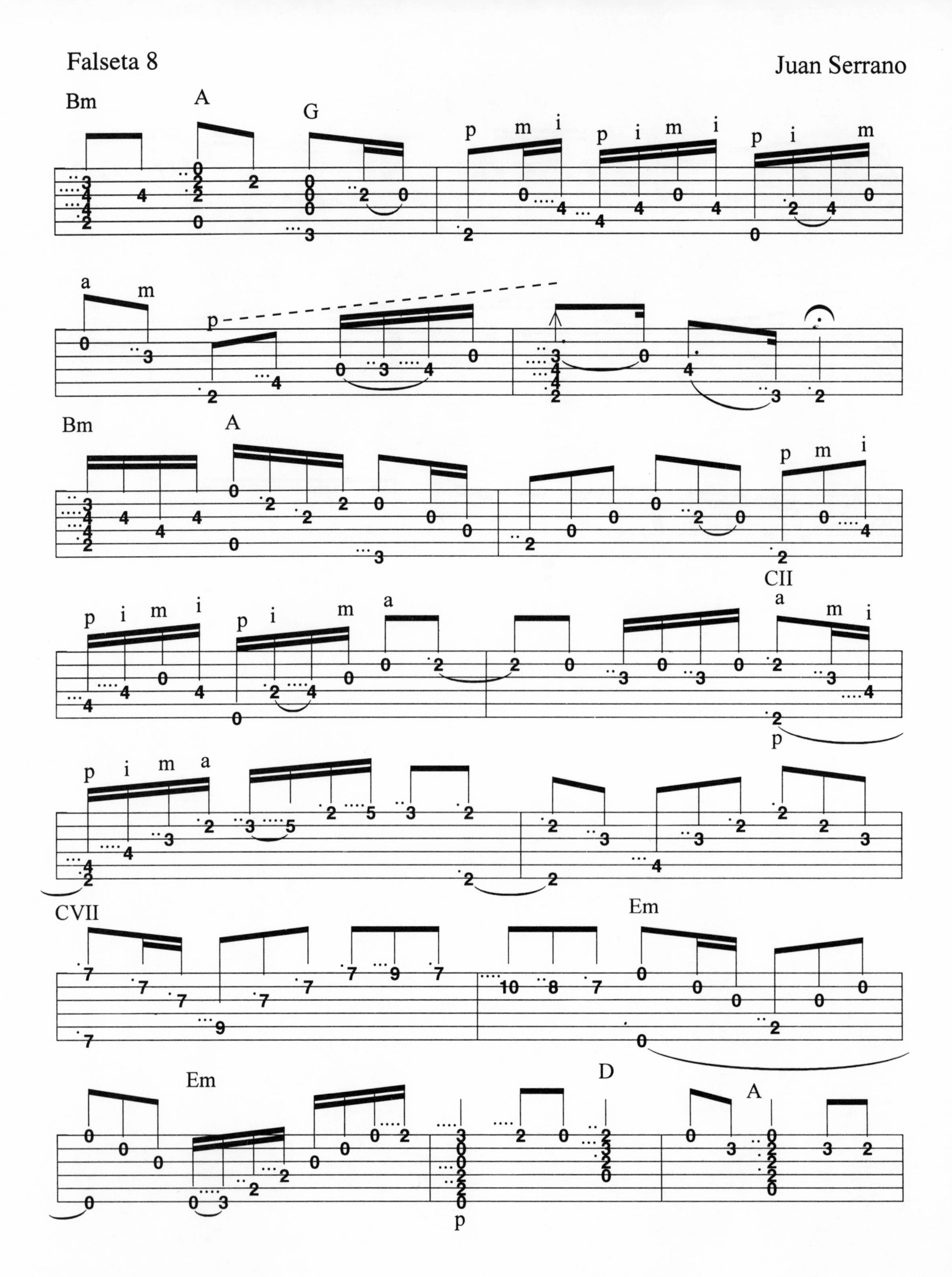
Falseta 8
Juan Serrano
Bm
A
G
Bm
A
CII
CVII
Em
Em
D
A

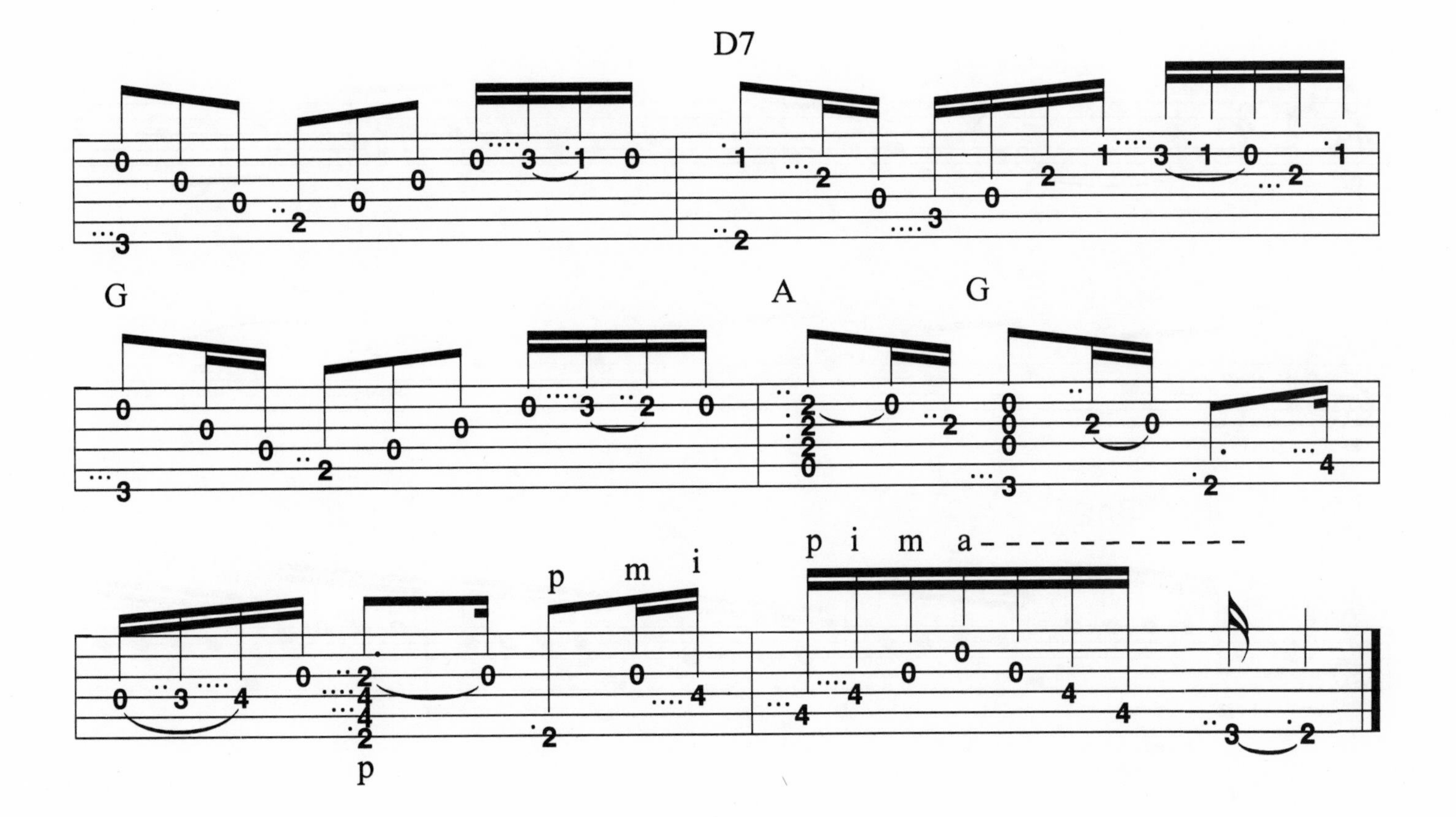
D7
G
A
G
p m i
p i m a
p

Falseta 9

Juan Serrano

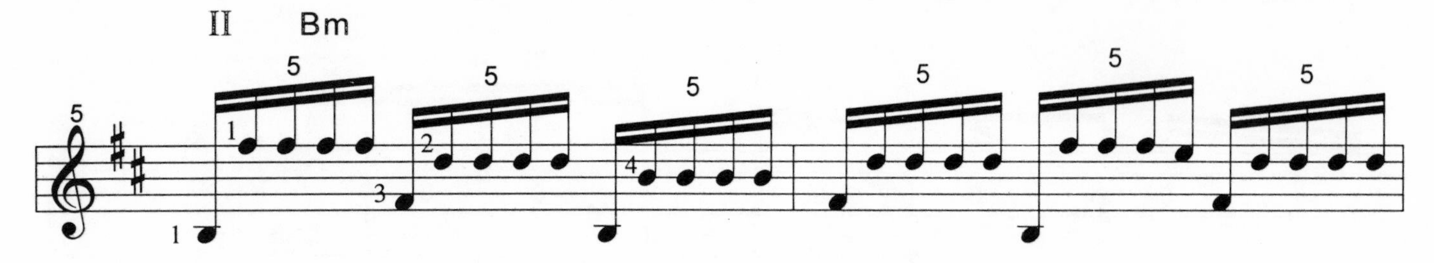


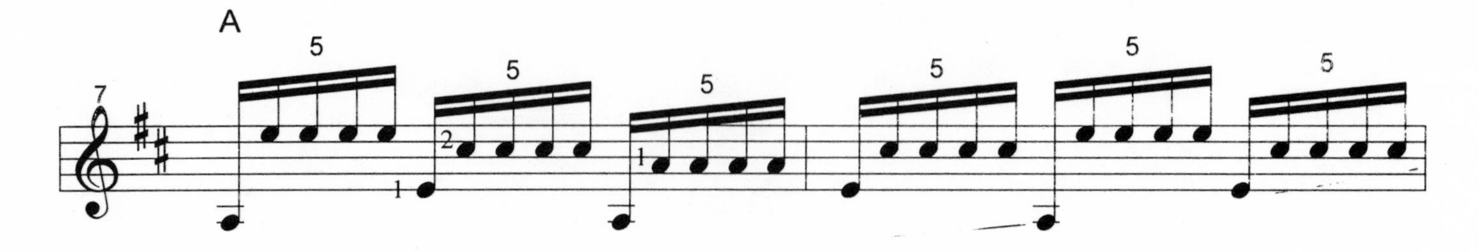


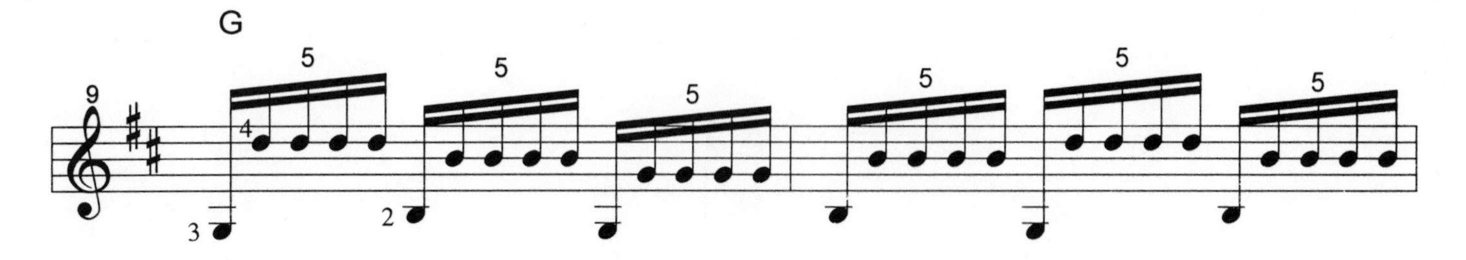


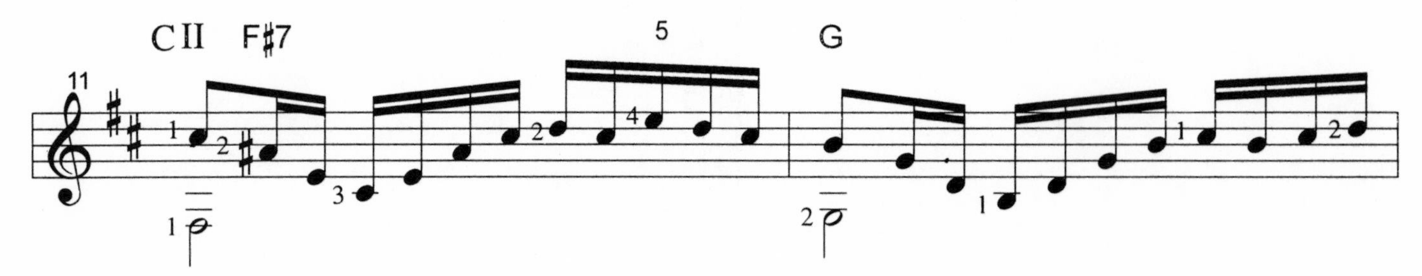

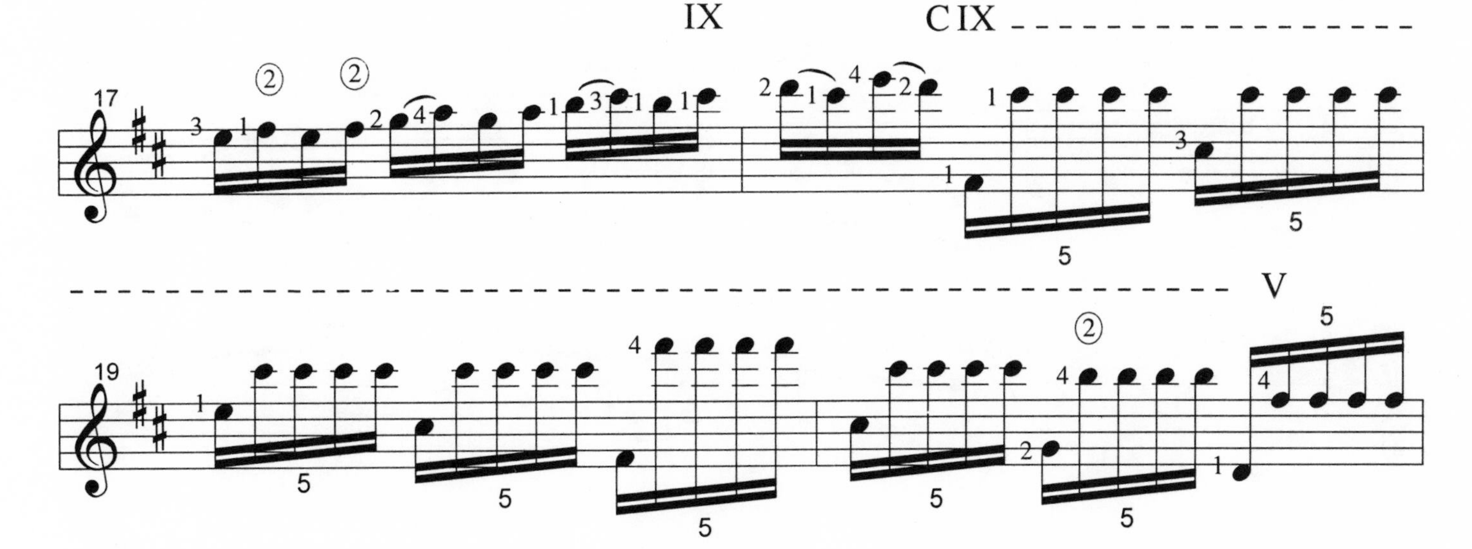


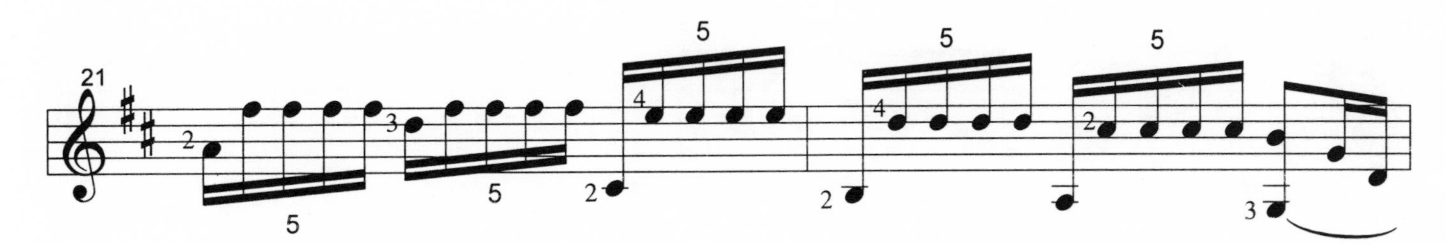

27

IV

29
VII
IV

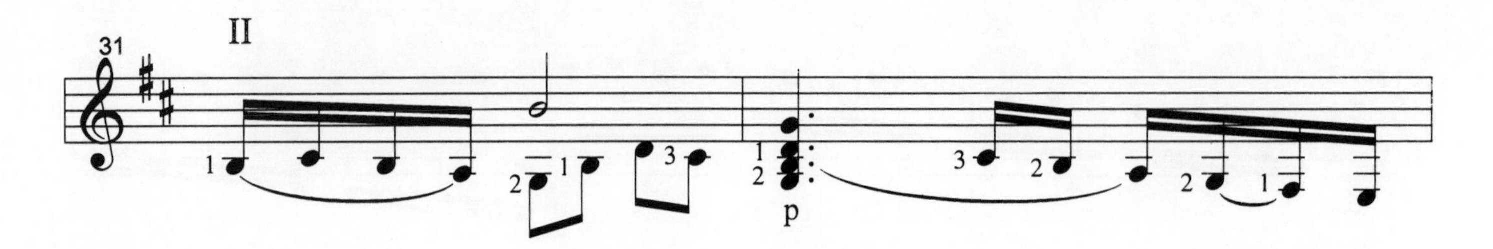
31
II
p

33

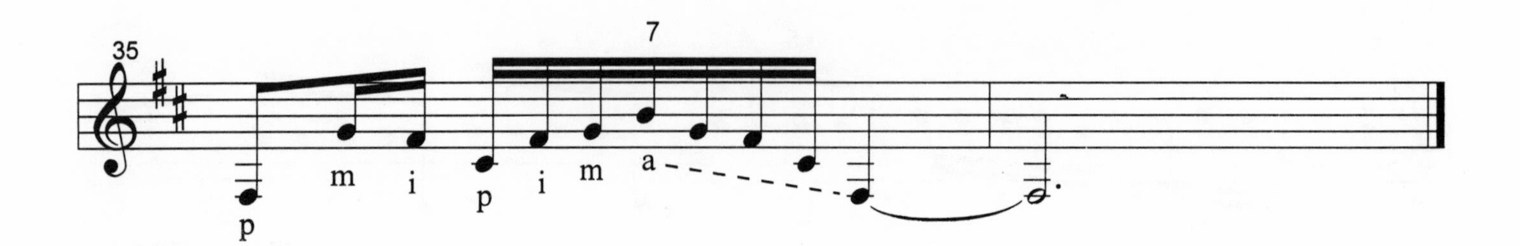
35
p m i p i m a

Falseta 9

Juan Serrano

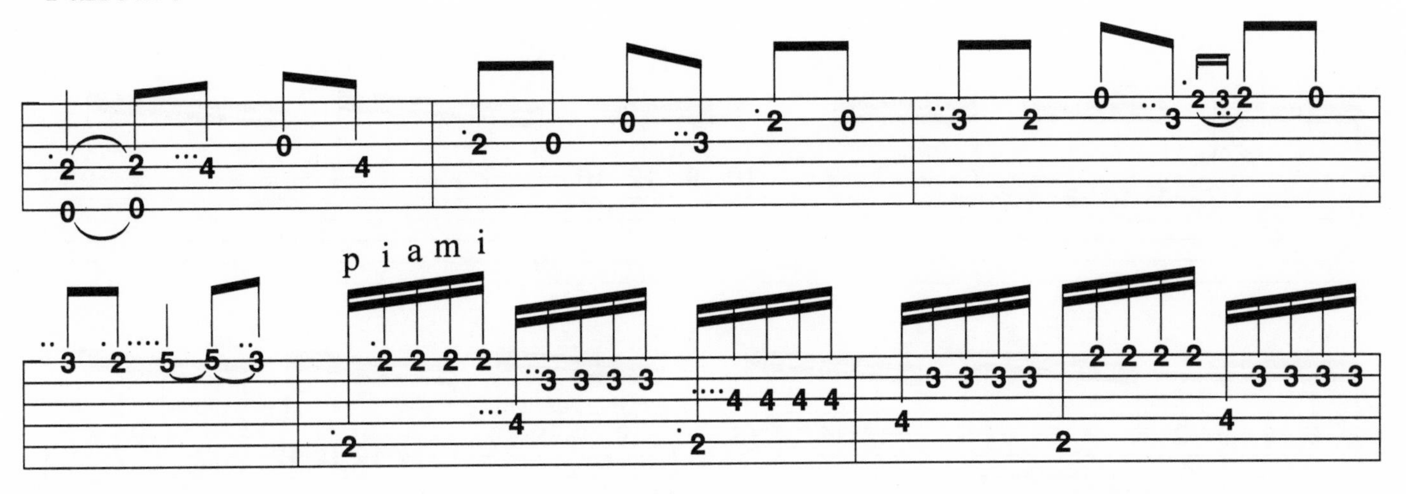


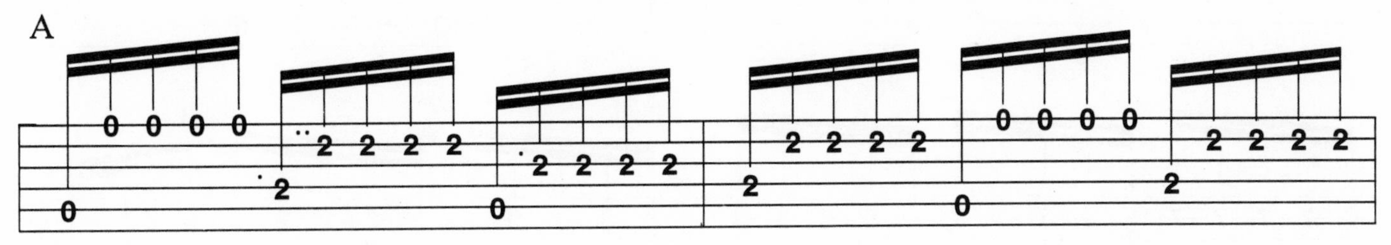


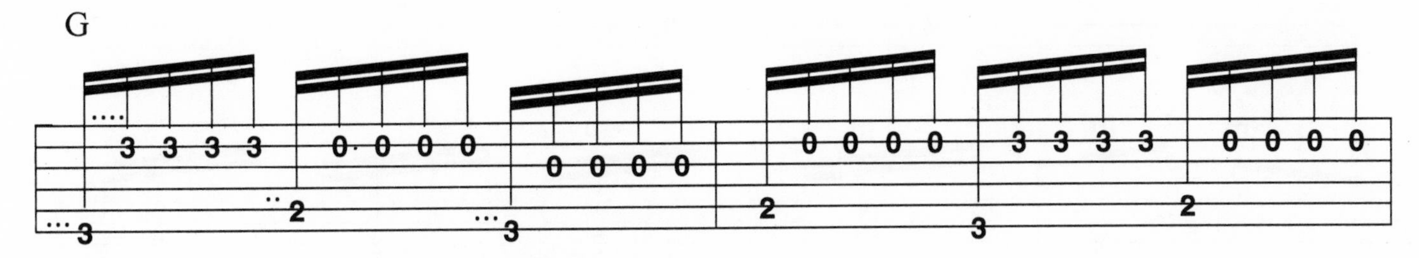


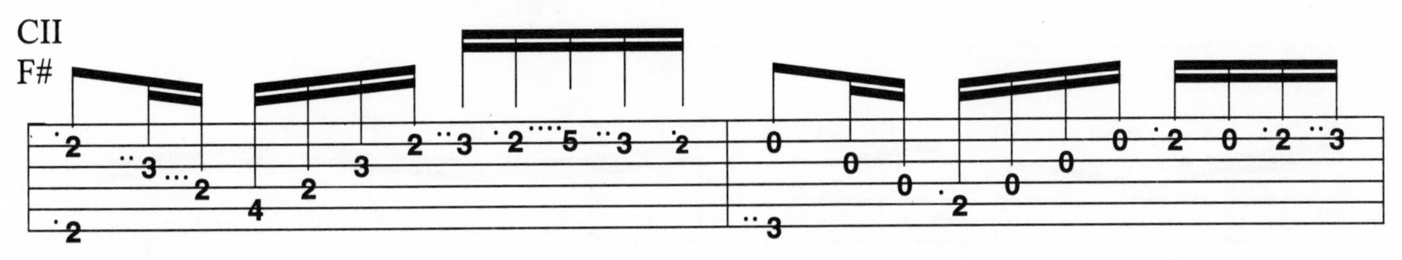


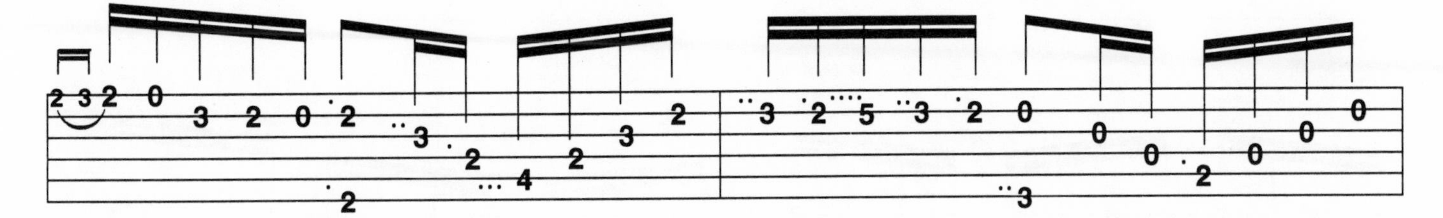

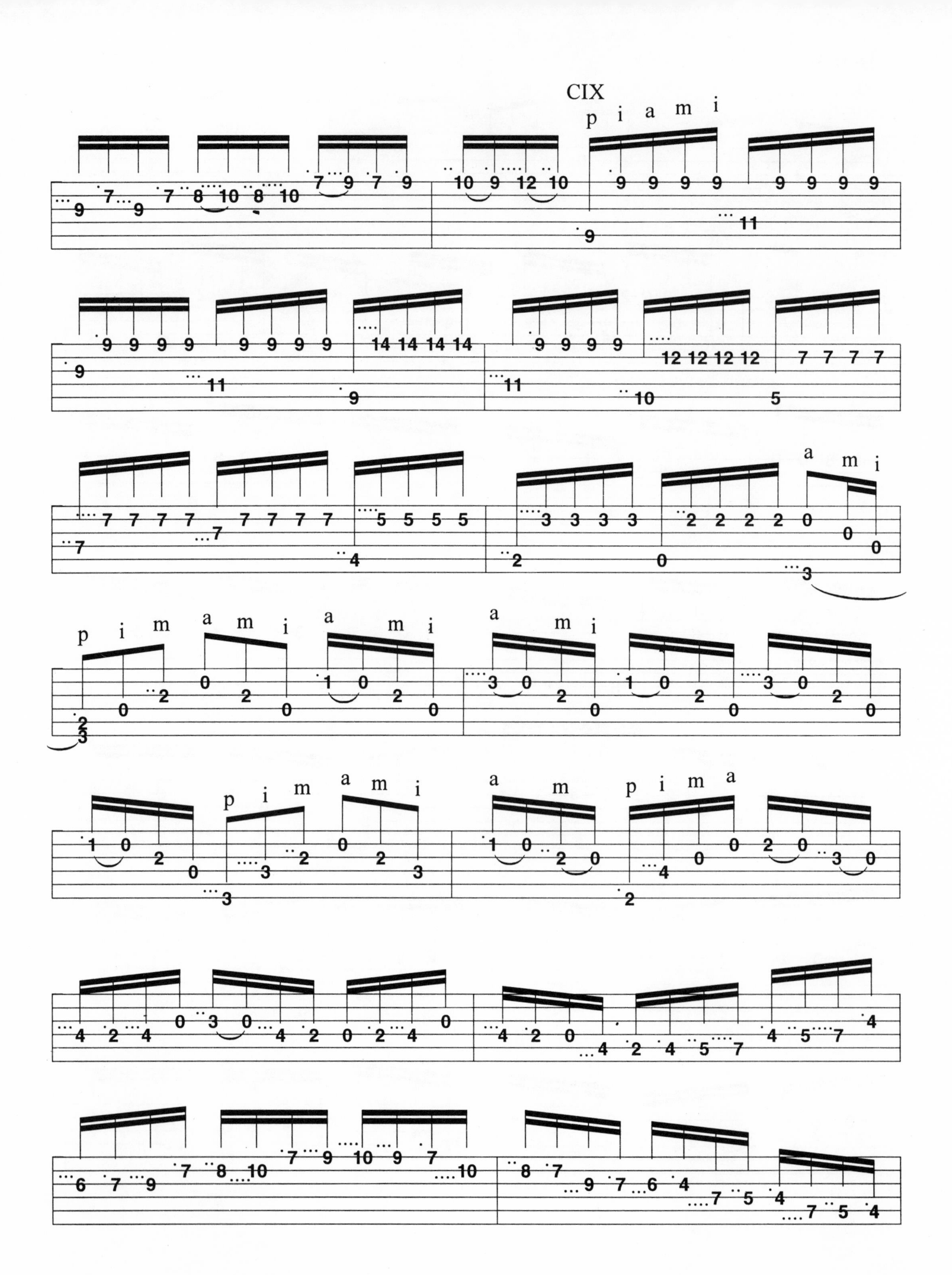
CIX
p i a m i
a m i
p i m a m i a m i
a m i
p i m a m i
a m p i m a

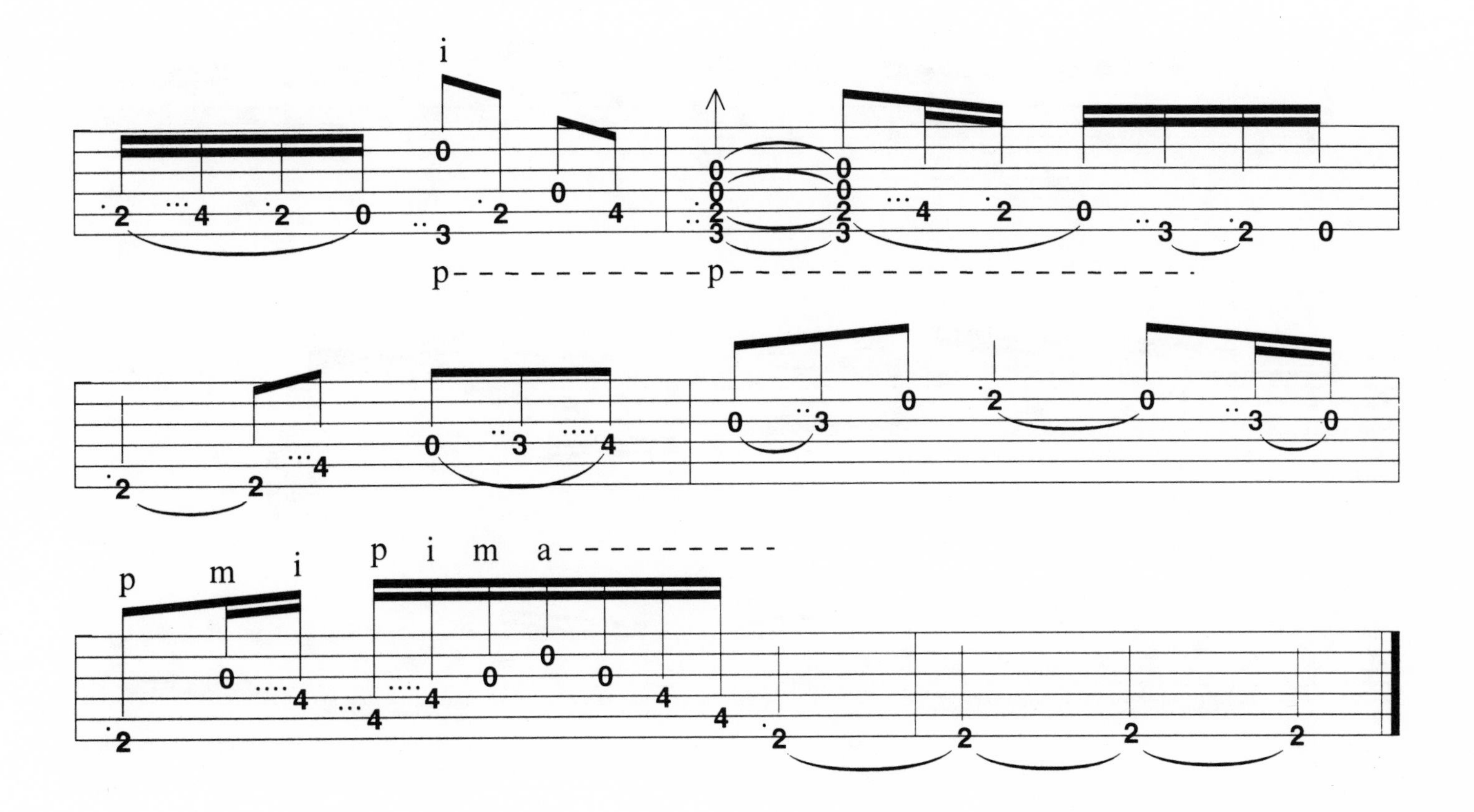
i
p p
p m i
p i m a

Falseta 10

Juan Serrano

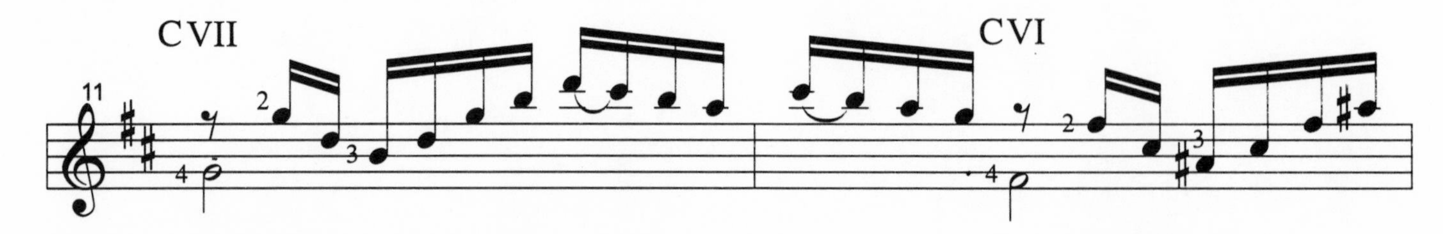


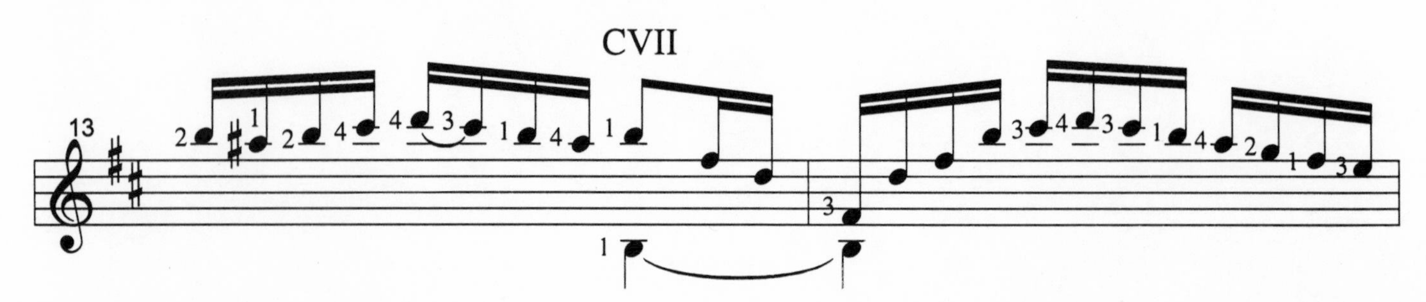

CVII
A

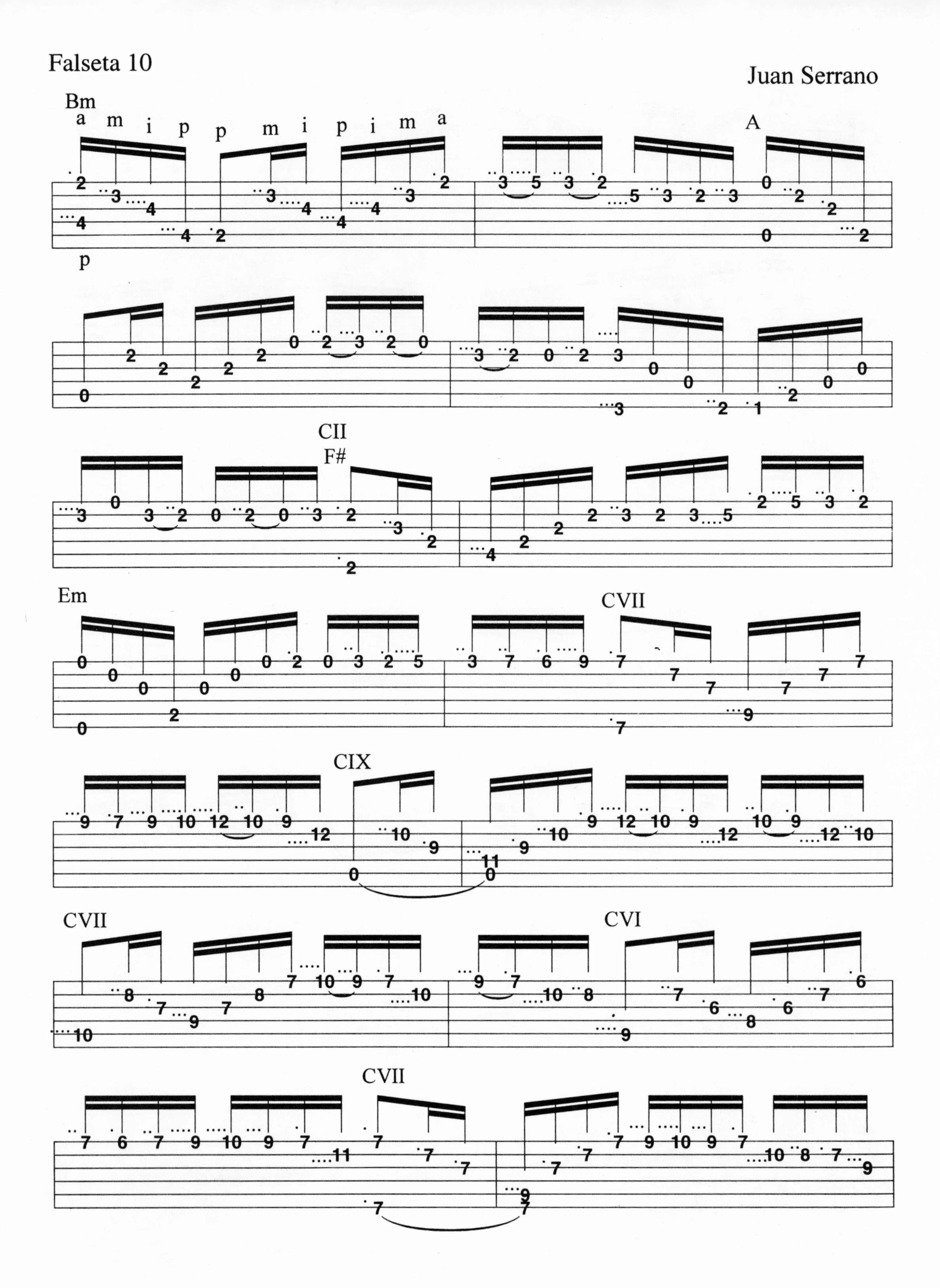
Falseta 10
Juan Serrano
Bm
a m i p p m i p i m a
A
p
CII
F#
Em
CVII
CIX
CVII
CVI
CVII

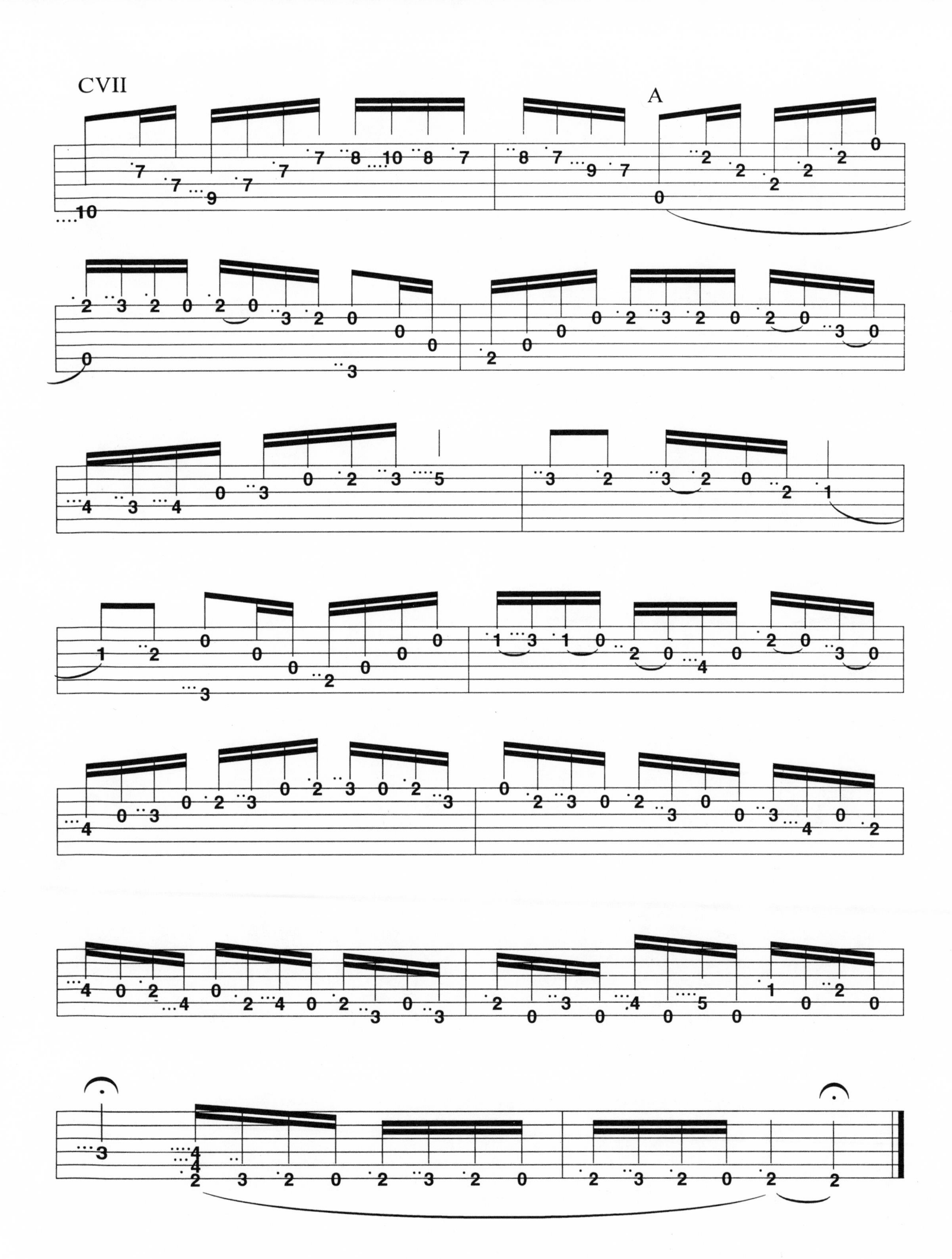
CVII
A